Football Outsiders Almanac 2011

THE ESSENTIAL GUIDE TO THE 2011 NFL AND COLLEGE FOOTBALL SEASONS

Edited by Aaron Schatz

With Dr. Benjamin Alamar, Bill Barnwell, Bill Connelly, Doug Farrar, Brian Fremeau, David Gardner, Tom Gower, Ned Macey, Sean McCormick, Rivers McCown, Brian McIntyre, Ben Muth, Mike Tanier, Danny Tuccitto, Vince Verhei, Robert Weintraub

Copyright 2011 Football Outsiders, Inc.

ISBN-10: 1466246138

ISBN-13: 978-1466246133

Contents

NFL Team Chapters

Player Comments

College Football

Further Research

Introduction

So, how was the lockout for you?

This is Football Outsiders' seventh preseason annual, and the one that went through the strangest process by far. When we were writing *Pro Football Prospectus* and working with standard publishers, the entire book needed to be finished by June 1. The last two years, self-publishing as *Football Outsiders Almanac*, the book was generally finished by July 1. This year, we didn't even know if we would have a full season until July, and writing the book bled into August, right up until (and past) the first preseason game.

We made a decision early on that in order to get the most accurate projections for the 2011 season — especially with a number of teams having uncertainty at the quarterback position — we needed to wait for the results of free agency. That meant waiting for the end of the lockout before we finished the book. We wrote most of *Football Outsiders Almanac 2011* unsure of what the final team projections would be. We've tried to go through and make sure that every comment is updated to account for the results of free agency through August 8, but there's a good chance a few pre-lockout comments snuck through despite our efforts.

The late arrival of free agency is only one reason why the lockout complicated our 2011 projections. The forecasts in this book are based on the idea that year-to-year trends in the past can help predict the future. But that assumes that the year-to-year transition process is the same each season. This season, it isn't. This was the first season where the draft preceded free agency rather than following it. There were no offseason minicamps or organized team activities. Coaches were not allowed to contact players, except for one day in April after a court placed an injunction on the lockout and before a higher court placed a stay on that injunction.

As a result, we have to ask ourselves what is the best way to get the most accurate forecast of the 2011 season. Doing nothing to change our projection systems would be as subjective as making adjustments to our projection systems. We don't have any statistical evidence that the lockout will affect teams in any way, but we also don't have any statistical evidence that the lockout *won't* affect teams in any way.

In the end, we've decided to adjust our projections based on the most commonly accepted theories of the likely effects of the lockout. Teams with new coordinators received a penalty to their projections on the appropriate side of the ball, unless the new coordinators were using the same offense or defense as their predecessors. (For example, in Oakland, Al Saunders has replaced Hue Jackson as offensive coordinator, but Jackson is now head coach. Since the Raiders are still using Jackson's offense, their offensive projection was not penalized.)

Complicating things further, the 2011 offseason was also a period of transition for Football Outsiders itself. Managing editor Bill Barnwell left FO in April, joining Bill Simmons' new Grantland website. He did leave behind a few research essays for this year's book, and wrote parts of the NFC East chapters (what he could write before the draft and lockout, at least). Chapters he was originally supposed to write were taken over by two of our newer writers, Brian McIntyre and Ben Muth. We then hired two new full-time writer/editors, Rivers McCown and Danny Tuccitto, in July, and they've contributed to the book in places. So this year's book probably has the most cooks stirring the pot, as we balanced staff changes with our attempt to get as much done during the lockout as possible — and then worked like crazy once the lockout was over.

Despite the difficulties in producing this year's annual, we think the result brings you the Football Outsiders analysis you've come to know and love. We're still devoted to analyzing the 2011 season by looking at more than just last year's win totals and a few big-name offseason acquisitions. We look deeper — at which statistics help indicate that a team was really better or worse than its record, at how much depth each team has, at what we can anticipate as far as injuries this season, and at numerous other issues.

If this is your first *Football Outsiders Almanac*, you've probably been told that Football Outsiders are "those football stats guys." That's true, but that's not all we're about. As we remind people each year, Football Outsiders is not founded on the idea that statistics are all-encompassing or can tell us everything about football. Everybody who writes about football uses both statistics (whether they be basic yardage totals or more advanced stats like ours) and scouting (whether scouting reports by professionals or just their own eyes). The same goes for us, except that the statistics portion of our analysis is far more accurate than what you normally see from football coverage. Those numbers are based on two ideas:

1) Conventional football statistics are heavily dependent on context. If you want to see which teams are good and which are bad, which strategies work and which do not, you first need to filter out that context. Down and distance, field position, the current score, time left on the clock, the quality of the opponent — all of these elements influence the objective of the play and/or its outcome. Yet, the official NFL stats add together all yardage gained by a specific team or player without considering the impact of that particular yardage on wins and losses.

A close football game can turn on a single bounce of the ball. In a season of only 16 games, those effects can have a huge impact on a team's win-loss record, thus obscuring the team's true talent level. If we can filter out these bits of luck and random chance, we can figure out which teams are really more likely to play better for the rest of the season, or even in the following season.

2) On any one play, the majority of the important action is not tracked by the conventional NFL play-by-play. That's why we started the Football Outsiders game charting project in 2005. A cadre of football-obsessed volunteers watches every single game and adds new detail to our record of each play. We know how many pass rushers teams send on each pass, how often teams go three-wide or use two tight ends, how often teams use a play-fake or a zone blitz, and which defensive backs are in coverage, even when they don't get a tackle in the standard play-by-play.

As with past books, we start off with "Pregame Show" (reviewing the most important research we've done in past books) and "Statistical Toolbox" (explaining all our stats). Once again, we preserve the ridiculousness of the NFL for posterity with another version of "The Year in Quotes" and introduce you to some of the more promising (and lesser-known) young bench players with our fourth annual list of Top 25 Prospects chosen in the third round or later.

Each NFL team gets a full chapter covering what happened in 2010 and our projections for the upcoming season. Are there reasons to believe that the team was actually better or worse than its record last year? What did the team do in the offseason, and what does that mean for the team's chances to win in 2011? Each chapter also includes all kinds of advanced statistics covering 2010 performance and strategic tendencies, plus detailed commentary on each of the major units of the team: Offensive line, defensive front seven, defensive secondary, special teams, and coaching staff.

"Skill players" (by which we mean "players who get counted in fantasy football") get their own section in the back of the book. We list the major players at each position alphabetically, along with commentary and a 2011 KUBIAK projection that will help you win your fantasy football league. We also have the most accurate projections anywhere for two fantasy football positions that people wrongly consider impossible to predict: kickers and team defense.

Next comes our preview of the college football season. We preview every team from the six BCS conferences as well as the top independents and mid-majors. Just like with our NFL coverage, the goal of our college previews is to focus as much as possible on "why" and how," not just "which team is better." We're not just here to rank the Football Bowl Subdivision teams from 1 to 120. We break things down to offense and defense, pass and run, and clutch situations compared to all plays.

In the back of the book, you will find a number of extra essays with some recent research, including analysis of home-field advantage and the value of pass pressure.

We hope our book helps you raise your level of football expertise, win arguments with your friends, and win your fantasy football league. Usually, we end by saying that we hope you enjoy reading our book as much as we enjoy writing it every year. This year, we'll end by saying that we hope you enjoy reading our book as much as we enjoyed the announcement that the lockout was over. Hallelujah!

Aaron Schatz
Framingham, MA
August 15, 2011

P.S. Don't forget to visit FootballOutsiders.com every day for fresh coverage of the NFL and college football, plus the most intelligent football discussion threads on the Internet.

Pregame Show

In the eight years since we launched FootballOutsiders.com, we've done a lot of primary research on the National Football League, and we reference that research in many of the articles and comments in *Football Outsiders Almanac 2011*. New readers may come across an offhand comment in a team chapter about, for example, the idea that fumble recovery is not a skill, and wonder what in the heck we are talking about. We can't repeat all our research in every new edition of *Football Outsiders Almanac*, so we start each year with a basic look at some of the most important precepts that have emerged from Football Outsiders research. You will see these issues come up again and again throughout the book.

You can also find this introduction online at http://www.footballoutsiders.com/info/FO-basics, along with links to the original research in the cases in which that research appeared online instead of (or as well as) in print.

Our various methods for projecting success by college prospects are not listed below, but are referenced at times during the book. Those methods are detailed in an essay on page 502.

You run when you win, not win when you run.

If we could only share one piece of anti-conventional wisdom with you before you read the rest of our book, this would be it. The first article ever written for Football Outsiders was devoted to debunking the myth of "establishing the run." There is no correlation whatsoever between giving your running backs a lot of carries early in the game and winning the game. Just running the ball is not going to help a team score; it has to run successfully.

There are two reasons why nearly every beat writer and television analyst still repeats the tired old school mantra that "establishing the run" is the secret to winning football games. The first problem is confusing cause and effect. There are exceptions, usually when the opponent is strong in every area except run defense, like last year's New Orleans Saints. However, in general, winning teams have a lot of carries because their running backs are running out the clock at the end of wins, not because they are running wild early in games.

The second problem is history. Most of the current crop of NFL analysts came of age or actually played the game during the 1970s. They believe that the run-heavy game of that decade is how football is meant to be, and today's pass-first game is an aberration. As we addressed in an essay in last year's book on the history of NFL stats, it was actually the game of the 1970s that was the aberration. The seventies were far more slanted towards the run than any era since the arrival of Paul Brown, Otto Graham, and the Cleveland Browns in 1946. Optimal strategies from 1974 are not optimal strategies for 2010.

A sister statement to "you have to establish the run" is "team X is 5-1 when running back John Doe runs for at least 100 yards." Unless John Doe is ripping off six-yard gains Jamaal Charles-style, the team isn't winning because of his 100-yard games. He's putting up 100-yard games because his team is winning.

A great defense against the run is nothing without a good pass defense.

This is a corollary to the absurdity of "establish the run." With rare exceptions, teams win or lose with the passing game more than the running game — and by stopping the passing game more than the running game. Ron Jaworski puts it best: "The pass gives you the lead, and the run solidifies it." The reason why teams need a strong run defense in the playoffs is not to shut the run down early; it's to keep the other team from icing the clock if they get a lead. You can't mount a comeback if you can't stop the run.

Note that "good pass defense" may mean "good pass rush" rather than "good defensive backs."

Running on third-and-short is more likely to convert than passing on third-and-short.

On average, passing will always gain more yardage than running, with one very important exception: when a team is just one or two yards away from a new set of downs or the goal line. On third-and-1, a run will convert for a new set of downs 36 percent more often than a pass. Expand that to all third or fourth downs with 1 or 2 yards to go, and the run is successful 40 percent more often. With these percentages, the possibility of a long gain with a pass is not worth the tradeoff of an incomplete that kills a drive.

This is one reason why teams have to be able to both run and pass. The offense also has to keep some semblance of balance so they can use their play-action fakes, and so the defense doesn't just run their nickel and dime packages all game. Balance also means that teams do need to pass occasionally in short-yardage situations; they just need to do it less than they do now. Teams pass roughly 60 percent of the time on third-and-2 even though runs in that situation convert 20 percent more often than passes. They pass 68 percent of the time on fourth-and-2 even though runs in that situation convert twice as often as passes.

Standard team rankings based on total yardage are inherently flawed.

When you open your newspaper on Sunday morning, you'll see that the little agate-type previews of each game list team rankings by total yardage. That is still how the NFL "officially" ranks teams, but these rankings rarely match up with common sense. That is because total team yardage may be the most context-dependent number in football.

It starts with the basic concept that rate stats are generally more valuable than cumulative stats. Yards per carry says more about a running back's quality than total yardage, completion percentage says more than just a quarterback's total number of completions. The same thing is true for teams; in fact, it is even more important because of the way football strategy influences the number of runs and passes in the game plan. Poor teams will give up fewer passing yards and more rushing yards because opponents will stop passing once they have a late-game lead and will run out the clock instead. For winning teams, the opposite is true. Did Detroit really have a better passing game than Pittsburgh did last year? Or did the Lions have more passing yards because they threw the ball 150 more times than the Steelers did?

Total yardage rankings are also skewed because some teams play at a faster pace than other teams. Last year, Tampa Bay (5,362) had roughly the same number of yards as the Washington Redskins (5,392). However, the Bucs were the superior offense and much more efficient; they gained those yards on only 163 drives while the Redskins needed 200 drives.

A team will score more when playing a bad defense, and will give up more points when playing a good offense.

This sounds absurdly basic, but when people consider team and player stats without looking at strength of schedule, they are ignoring this. In 2004, Carson Palmer and Byron Leftwich had very similar numbers, but Palmer faced a much tougher schedule than Leftwich did. Palmer was better that year, and better in the long run. Remember when LaDainian Tomlinson had a big 133-yard game against Buffalo in Week 4, and many people thought he had fully bounced back from his poor 2009 season? Well, Buffalo ranked 31st in run defense DVOA. Meanwhile, the top team in rushing DVOA, Pittsburgh, didn't give up a 100-yard runner all year. When Peyton Hillis could only gain 54 yards on the Steelers in two games, it wasn't a strong sign that something was wrong with Hillis.

If their overall yards per carry are equal, a running back who consistently gains yardage on every play is more valuable than a boom-and-bust running back who is frequently stuffed at the line but occasionally breaks a long highlight-worthy run.

Our brethren at Baseball Prospectus believe that the most precious commodity in baseball is outs. Teams only get 27 of them per game, and you can't afford to give one up for very little return. So imagine if there was a new rule in baseball that gave a team a way to earn another three outs in the middle of the inning. That would be pretty useful, right?

That's the way football works. You may start a drive 80 yards away from scoring, but as long as you can earn 10 yards in four chances, you get another four chances. Long gains have plenty of value, but if those long gains are mixed with a lot of short gains, you are going to put the quarterback in a lot of difficult third-and-long situations. That means more punts and more giving the ball back to the other team rather than moving the chains and giving the offense four more plays to work with.

The running back who gains consistent yardage is also going to do a lot more for you late in the game, when the goal of running the ball is not just to gain yardage but to eat clock time. If you are an Arizona fan watching your team with a late lead, you don't want to see three straight Tim Hightower stuffs at the line followed by a punt. You want to see a game-icing first down.

A common historical misconception is that our preference for consistent running backs means that "Football Outsiders believes that Barry Sanders was overrated." Sanders wasn't just any boom-and-bust running back, though; he was the greatest boom-and-bust runner of all time, with bigger booms and fewer busts. Our play-by-play database currently goes back to 1992, but Sanders ranked second in DYAR three times (1994, 1996, and 1997).

Rushing is more dependent on the offensive line than people realize, but pass protection is more dependent on the quarterback himself than people realize.

Some readers complain that this idea contradicts the previous one. Aren't those consistent running backs just the product of good offensive lines? The truth is somewhere in between. There are certainly good running backs who suffer because their offensive lines cannot create consistent holes, but most boom-and-bust running backs contribute to their own problems by hesitating behind the line whenever the hole is unclear, looking for the home run instead of charging forward for the four-yard gain that keeps the offense moving.

As for pass protection, some quarterbacks have better instincts for the rush than others, and are thus better at getting out of trouble by moving around in the pocket or throwing the ball away. Others will hesitate, hold onto the ball too long, and lose yardage over and over.

Note that "moving around in the pocket" does not necessarily mean "scrambling." In fact, a scrambling quarterback will often take more sacks than a pocket quarterback, because while he's running around trying to make something happen, a defensive lineman will catch up with him.

Shotgun formations are generally more efficient than formations with the quarterback under center.

Over the past three seasons, offenses have averaged 5.9 yards per play from Shotgun, but just 5.2 yards per play with the quarterback under center. This wide split exists even if you analyze the data to try to weed out biases like teams using Shotgun more often on third-and-long, or against prevent defenses in the fourth quarter. Shotgun offense is more efficient if you only look at the first half, on every down, and even if you only look at running back carries rather than passes and scrambles.

Clearly, NFL teams have figured the importance of the Shotgun out for themselves. Over the past five seasons, the average team has gone from using Shotgun 19 percent of the time to 38 percent of the time, not even counting the Wildcat and other college-style option plays that have become popular in recent years. Before 2007, no team had ever used Shotgun on more than half its offensive plays. In the past three seasons, eight different teams have used Shotgun more than half the time. It is likely that if teams continue to increase their usage of the Shotgun, defenses will adapt and the benefit of the formation will become less pronounced.

A running back with 370 or more carries during the regular season will usually suffer either a major injury or a loss of effectiveness the following year, unless he is named Eric Dickerson.

Terrell Davis, Jamal Anderson, and Edgerrin James all blew out their knees. Larry Johnson broke his foot. Earl Campbell and Eddie George went from legendary powerhouses to plodding, replacement-level players. Shaun Alexander broke his foot *and* became a plodding, replacement-level player. This is what happens when a running back is overworked to the point of having at least 370 carries during the regular season.

The "Curse of 370" was expanded in *Pro Football Prospectus 2005*, and now includes seasons with 390 or more carries in the regular season and postseason combined. Research also shows that receptions don't cause a problem, only workload on the ground.

Plenty of running backs get injured without hitting 370 carries in a season, but there is a clear difference. On average, running backs with 300 to 369 carries and no postseason appearance will see their total rushing yardage decline by 15 percent the following year and their yards per carry decline by two percent. The average running back with 370 or more regular-season carries, or 390 including the postseason, will see their rushing yardage decline by 35 percent, and their yards per carry decline by eight percent.

Wide receivers must be judged on both complete and incomplete passes.

We don't yet know enough to precisely parse the blame for incomplete passes, but we know that wide receiver catch rates are almost as consistent from year to year as quarterback completion percentages. Since 2001, Hines Ward has never had caught fewer than 59 percent of intended passes, whether from Kordell Stewart, Tommy Maddox, or Ben Roethlisberger. Plaxico Burress, playing with the same quarterbacks as well as with Eli Manning, never caught more than 58 percent of intended passes, and in three different years had a catch rate below 50 percent. However, it is also important to look at catch rate in the context of the types of routes each receiver runs. Last year we expanded on this idea with a new plus-minus metric, which is explained in the introduction to the chapter on wide receivers and tight ends.

The total quality of an NFL team is three parts offense, three parts defense, and one part special teams.

There are three units on a football team, but they are not of equal importance. Our DVOA ratings provide good evidence for this. The special teams ratings are turned into DVOA by comparing how often field position on special teams leads to scoring compared to field position and first downs on offense. After figuring out these numbers, the top ratings for special teams are roughly one-third as high as the top ratings for offense or defense.

Offense is more consistent from year to year than defense, and offensive performance is easier to project than defensive performance. Special teams is less consistent than either.

Nobody in the NFL understands this concept better than Indianapolis Colts general manager Bill Polian. Both the Super Bowl champion Colts and the four-time AFC champion Buffalo Bills of the early 1990s were built around the idea that if you put together an offense that can dominate the league year after year, eventually you will luck into a year where good health and a few smart decisions will give you a defense good enough to win a championship. (As the Colts learned in 2006, you don't even need a year, just four weeks.) Even the New England Patriots, who are led by a defense-first head coach in Bill Belichick, have been more consistent on offense than on defense since they began their run of success in 2001.

Field-goal percentage is almost entirely random from season to season, while kickoff distance is one of the most consistent statistics in football.

This theory, which originally appeared in the *New York Times* in October 2006, is one of our most controversial, but it is hard to argue against the evidence.

Measuring every kicker from 1999 to 2006 who had at least ten field-goal attempts in each of two consecutive years, the year-to-year correlation coefficient for field-goal percentage was an insignificant .05. Mike Vanderjagt didn't miss a single field goal in 2003, but his percentage was a below-average 74 percent the year before and 80 percent the year after. Adam Vinatieri, supposedly the best kicker in the game, has never has never had two straight seasons with accuracy better than last year's NFL average of 85 percent.

On the other hand, the year-to-year correlation coefficient for kickoff distance, over the same period as our measurement of field-goal percentage and with the same minimum of ten kicks per year, is .61. The same players consistently lead the league in kickoff distance, particularly Rhys Lloyd, Olindo Mare, and Stephen Gostkowski.

Teams with more offensive penalties generally lose more games, but there is no correlation between defensive penalties and losses.

Specific defensive penalties of course lose games; we've all sworn at the television when the cornerback on our favorite team gets flagged for a 50-yard pass interference penalty. Yet overall, there is no correlation between losses and the total of defensive penalties or even the total yardage on defensive penalties. One reason is that defensive penalties often represent *good* play, not bad. Cornerbacks who play tight coverage may be just on the edge of a penalty on most plays, only occasionally earning a flag. Defensive ends who get a good jump on rushing the passer will gladly trade an encroachment penalty or two for ten snaps where they get off the blocks a split-second before the linemen trying to block them.

In addition, offensive penalties have a higher correlation from year to year than defensive penalties. The penalty that correlates highest with losses is the false start, and the penalty that teams will have called most consistently from year to year is the false start.

Recovery of a fumble, despite being the product of hard work, is almost entirely random.

Stripping the ball is a skill. Holding onto the ball is a skill. Pouncing on the ball as it is bouncing all over the place is not a skill. There is no correlation whatsoever between the percentage of fumbles recovered by a team in one year and the percentage they recover in the next year. The odds of recovery are based solely on the type of play involved, not the teams or any of their players.

Fans like to insist that specific coaches can teach their teams to recover more fumbles by swarming to the ball. Chicago's Lovie Smith, in particular, is supposed to have this ability. However, in Smith's first three seasons as head coach of the Bears, their rate of fumble recovery on defense went from a league-best 76 percent in 2004 to a league-worst 33 percent in 2005, then back to 67 percent in 2006.

Fumble recovery is equally erratic on offense. In 2009, the Oakland Raiders fumbled 22 times on offense, and recovered only eight of those fumbles. Last year, the Raiders fumbled 23 times on offense, and recovered 15.

Fumble recovery is a major reason why the general public overestimates or underestimates certain teams. Fumbles are huge, turning-point plays that dramatically impact wins and losses in the past, while fumble recovery percentage says absolutely nothing about a team's chances of winning games in the future. With this in mind, Football Outsiders stats treat all fumbles as equal, penalizing them based on the likelihood of each type of fumble (run, pass, sack, etc.) being recovered by the defense.

Other plays that qualify as "non-predictive events" include blocked kicks and touchdowns during turnover returns. These plays are not "lucky," per se, but they have no value whatsoever for predicting future performance.

Field position is fluid.

As discussed in the Statistical Toolbox, every yard line on the field has a value based on how likely a team is to score from that location on the field as opposed to from a yard further back.. The change in value from one yard to the next is the same whether the team has the ball or not. The goal of a defense is not just to prevent scoring, but to hold the opposition so that the offense can get the ball back in the best possible field position. A bad offense will score as many points as a good offense if it starts each drive five yards closer to the goal line.

A corollary to this precept: The most underrated aspect of an NFL team's performance is the field position gained or lost on kickoffs and punts. This is part of why players like Devin Hester and Josh Cribbs can have such an impact on the game, even when they aren't taking a kickoff or punt all the way back for a touchdown.

The red zone is the most important place on the field to play well, but performance in the red zone from year to year is much less consistent than overall performance.

Although play in the red zone has a disproportionately high importance to the outcome of games relative to plays on the rest of the field, NFL teams do not exhibit a level of performance in the red zone that is consistently better or worse than their performance elsewhere, year after year. The simplest explanation why is a small(er) sample size and the inherent variance of football, with contributing factors like injuries and changes in personnel.

Defenses which are strong on first and second down, but weak on third down, will tend to improve the following year. Defenses which are weak on first and second down, but strong on third down, will tend to decline the following year. This trend also applied to offenses through 2005, but may or may not still apply today.

We discovered this when creating our first team projection system in 2004. It said that the lowly San Diego Chargers would have of the best offenses in the league, which seemed a little ridiculous. But looking closer, our projection system treated the previous year's performance on different downs as different variables, and the 2003 Chargers were actually good on first and second down, but terrible on third.

Teams get fewer opportunities on third down, so third-down performance is more volatile — but it's also is a bigger part of a team's overall performance than first or second down, because the result is usually either very good (four more downs) or very bad (losing the ball to the other team with a punt). Over time, a team will play as well in those situations as it does in other situations, which will bring the overall offense or defense in line with the offense and defense on first and second down.

This trend is even stronger between seasons. Struggles on third down are a pretty obvious problem, and teams will generally target their off-season moves at improving their third-down performance ... which often leads to an improvement in third-down performance.

However, we have discovered something surprising over the past four years: The third-down rebound effect seems to have disappeared on offense, as we explained in the Philadelphia chapter of last year's book. We don't know yet if this change is temporary or permanent, and there is no such change on defense.

Injuries regress to the mean on the seasonal level, and teams that avoid injuries in a given season tend to win more games.

There are no doubt teams with streaks of good or bad health over multiple years. However, teams who were especially healthy or especially unhealthy, as measured by our Adjusted Games Lost (AGL) metric, almost always head towards league average in the subsequent season. Furthermore, injury — or the absence thereof — has a huge correlation with wins, and a significant impact on a team's success. In 2010, four of the six least-injured teams in the league made the playoffs, including surprise division champions Chicago and Kansas City. Teams with a high number of injuries — which last year included Miami, Carolina, and the Super Bowl champion (but wild card) Packers — are a good bet to improve the following season.

By and large, a team built on depth is better than a team built on stars and scrubs.

Connected to the previous statement, because teams need to go into the season expecting that they will suffer an average number of injuries no matter how healthy they were the previous year. The Redskins went into 2006 with a Super Bowl-quality starting lineup, and finished 5-11 because they had no depth. You cannot concentrate your salaries on a handful of star players because there is no such thing as avoiding injuries in the NFL. The game is too fast and the players too strong to build a team based around the idea that "if we can avoid all injuries this year, we'll win."

Running backs usually decline after age 28, tight ends after age 29, wide receivers after age 30, and quarterbacks after age 32.

This research was originally done by Doug Drinen (editor of pro-football-reference.com) in 2000. In recent years, a few players have had huge seasons above these general age limits (most notably Tony Gonzalez), but the peak ages Drinen found a few years ago still apply to the majority of players.

As for "non-skill players," research we did in 2007 for *ESPN The Magazine* suggested that defensive ends and defensive backs generally begin to decline after age 29, linebackers and offensive linemen after age 30, and defensive tackles after age 31. However, because we still have so few statistics to use to study linemen and defensive players, this research should not be considered definitive.

Championship teams are generally defined by their ability to dominate inferior opponents, not their ability to win close games.

Football games are often decided by just one or two plays — a missed field goal, a bouncing fumble, the subjective spot of an official on fourth-and-1. One missed assignment by a cornerback or one slightly askew pass that bounces off a receiver's hands and into those of a defensive back five yards away and the game could be over. In a blowout, however, one lucky bounce isn't going to change things. Championship teams beat their good opponents convincingly and destroy the cupcakes on the schedule.

Aaron Schatz

Statistical Toolbox

After eight years of Football Outsiders, some of our readers are as comfortable with DVOA and ALY as they are with touchdowns and tackles. Yet to most fans, including our newer readers, it still looks like a lot of alphabet soup. That's what this chapter is for. The next few pages define and explain all of all the unique NFL statistics you'll find in this book: how we calculate them, what the numbers mean, and what they tell us about why teams win or lose football games. We'll go through the information in each of the tables that appear in each team chapter, pointing out whether those stats come from advanced mathematical manipulation of the standard play-by-play or simple counting of what see on television with the Football Outsiders game charting project. This chapter covers NFL statistics only. College metrics such as POE and F/+ are explained in the introduction to the college football section on page 417.

We've done our best to present these numbers in a way that makes them easy to understand. This explanation is long, so feel free to read some of it, flip around the rest of the book, and then come back. It will still be here.

Defense-Adjusted Value Over Average (DVOA)

One running back runs for three yards. Another running back runs for three yards. Which is the better run?

This sounds like a stupid question, but it isn't. In fact, this question is at the heart of nearly all of the analysis in this book.

Several factors can differentiate one three-yard run from another. What is the down and distance? Is it third-and-2, or second-and-15? Where on the field is the ball? Does the player get only three yards because he hits the goal line and scores? Is the player's team up by two touchdowns in the fourth quarter and thus running out the clock, or down by two touchdowns and thus facing a defense that is playing purely against the pass? Is the running back playing against the porous defense of the Bills, or the stalwart defense of the Steelers?

Conventional NFL statistics value plays based solely on their net yardage. The NFL determines the best players by adding up all their yards no matter what situations they came in or how many plays it took to get them. Now, why would they do that? Football has one objective — to get to the end zone — and two ways to achieve that, by gaining yards and achieving first downs. These two goals need to be balanced to determine a player's value or a team's performance. All the yards in the world won't help a team win if they all come in six-yard chunks on third-and-10.

The popularity of fantasy football only exacerbates the problem. Fans have gotten used to judging players based on how much they help fantasy teams win and lose, not how much they help *real* teams win and lose. Typical fantasy scoring further skews things by counting the yard between the one and the goal line as 61 times more important than all the other yards on the field (each yard worth 0.1 points, a touchdown worth 6). Let's say Larry Fitzgerald catches a pass on third-and-15 and goes 50 yards but gets tackled two yards from the goal line, and then Tim Hightower takes the ball on first-and-goal from the two-yard line and plunges in for the score. Has Tim Hightower done something special? Not really. When an offense gets the ball on first-and-goal at the two-yard line, they are going to score a touchdown five out of six times. Hightower is getting credit for the work done by the passing game.

Doing a better job of distributing credit for scoring points and winning games is the goal of **DVOA,** or Defense-adjusted Value Over Average. DVOA breaks down every single play of the NFL season, assigning each play a value based on both total yards and yards towards a first down, based on work done by Pete Palmer, Bob Carroll, and John Thorn in their seminal book, *The Hidden Game of Football.* On first down, a play is considered a success if it gains 45 percent of needed yards; on second down, a play needs to gain 60 percent of needed yards; on third or fourth down, only gaining a new first down is considered success.

We then expand upon that basic idea with a more complicated system of "success points," improved over the past four years with a lot of mathematics and a bit of trial and error. A successful play is worth one point, an unsuccessful play zero points with fractional points in between (for example, eight yards on third-and-10 is worth 0.54 "success points"). Extra points are awarded for big plays, gradually increasing to three points for 10 yards (assuming those yards result in a first down), four points for 20 yards, and five points for 40 yards or more. Losing three or more yards is -1 point. Interceptions average -6 points, with an adjustment for the length of the pass and the location of the interception (since an interception tipped at the line is more likely to produce a long return than an interception on a 40-yard pass). A fumble is worth anywhere from -1.7 to -4.0 points depending on how often a fumble in that situation is lost to the defense — no matter who actually recovers the fumble. Red zone plays are worth 25 percent more for teams (and 10 percent more for players), and there is a bonus given for a touchdown that acknowledges that the goal line is significantly more difficult to cross than the previous 99 yards (although this bonus is nowhere near as large as the one used in fantasy football).

(Our system is a bit more complex than the one in *Hidden Game* thanks to our subsequent research, which added larger penalty for turnovers, the fractional points, and a slightly higher baseline for success on first down. The reason why all fumbles are counted, no matter whether they are recovered by the offense or defense, is explained in the essay "Pregame Show.")

Every single play run in the NFL gets a "success value" based on this system, and then that number gets compared to the average success values of plays in similar situations for all players, adjusted for a number of variables. These include down and distance, field location, time remaining in game, and the team's lead or deficit in the game score. Teams are always compared to the overall offensive average, as the team made its own choice whether to pass or rush. When it comes to individual players, however, rushing plays are compared to other rushing plays, passing plays to other passing plays, tight ends to tight ends, wideouts to wideouts, and so on.

Going back to our example of the three-yard rush, if Player A gains three yards under a set of circumstances in which the average NFL running back gains only one yard, then Player A has a certain amount of value above others at his position. Likewise, if Player B gains three yards on a play on which, under similar circumstances, an average NFL back gains four yards, that Player B has negative value relative to others at his position. Once we make all our adjustments, we can evaluate the difference between this player's rate of success and the expected success rate of an average running back in the same situation (or between the opposing defense and the average defense in the same situation, etc.). Add up every play by a certain team or player, divide by the total of the various baselines for success in all those situations, and you get VOA, or Value Over Average.

Of course, the biggest variable in football is the fact that each team plays a different schedule against teams of disparate quality. By adjusting each play based on the opposing defense's average success in stopping that type of play over the course of a season, we get DVOA, or Defense-adjusted Value Over Average. Rushing and passing plays are adjusted based on down and location on the field; passing plays are also adjusted based on how the defense performs against passes to running backs, tight ends, or wide receivers. Defenses are adjusted based on the average success of the *offenses* they are facing. (Yes, technically the defensive stats are actually "offense-adjusted." If it seems weird, think of the "D" in "DVOA" as standing for "opponent-Dependent" or something.)

The biggest advantage of DVOA is the ability to break teams and players down to find strengths and weaknesses in a variety of situations. In the aggregate, DVOA may not be quite as accurate as some of the other, similar "power ratings" formulas based on comparing drives rather than individual plays, but, unlike those other ratings, DVOA can be separated not only by player, but also by down, or by week, or by distance needed for a first down. This can give us a better idea of not just which team is better, but why, and what a team has to do in order to improve itself in the future. You will find DVOA used in this book in a lot of different ways — because it takes every single play into account, it can be used to measure a player or a team's performance in any situation. All Pittsburgh third downs can be compared to how an average team does on third down. Cam Newton and Jimmy Clausen can each be compared to how an average quarterback performs in the red zone, or with a lead, or in the second half of the game.

Since it compares each play only to plays with similar circumstances, it gives a more accurate picture of how much better a team really is compared to the league as a whole. The list of top DVOA offenses on third down, for example, is more accurate than the conventional NFL conversion statistic because it takes into account that converting third-and-long is more difficult than converting third-and-short, and that a turnover is worse than an incomplete pass because it eliminates the opportunity to move the other team back with a punt on fourth down.

One of the hardest parts of understanding a new statistic is interpreting its scale, or what numbers represent good performance or bad performance. We've made that easy with DVOA. In all cases, 0% represents league-average. A positive DVOA represents a situation that favors the offense, while a negative DVOA represents a situation that favors the defense. This is why the best offenses have positive DVOA ratings (last year, New England led the league at +46.1%) and the best defenses have negative DVOA ratings (with Pittsburgh number one at -18.5%). For teams, in most years, the best and worst ratings tend to be around +/-30%; for players, they tend to be around +/- 45%. Because league average is determined across multiple years, no single year will average exactly 0%. This gives DVOA the added benefit of being able to show us how the scoring environment has fluctuated from year to year. Last year's total league DVOA on offense was 3.7%, the fifth straight year above 0%. (Sometime this fall, we will be switching to baselines that gradually change from year to year to reflect changes in the overall offensive environment of the game.)

Team DVOA totals combine offense and defense by subtracting the latter from the former because the better defenses will have negative DVOA ratings. (Special teams performance is also added, as described later in this essay.) Certain plays are counted in DVOA for offense and not for defense, leading to separate baselines and league-wide averages on each side of the ball. Some other important notes about DVOA:

• Only four penalties are included in DVOA, and two of them are included for offense only: false starts and delay of game. The other two, intentional grounding and defensive pass interference, count for both sides.

• Aborted snaps and incomplete backwards lateral passes are only penalized on offense, not rewarded on defense.

• Adjustments for playing from behind or with a lead in the fourth quarter are different for offense and defense, as are adjustments for the final two minutes of the first half when the offense is not near field-goal range.

• Offense gets a slight penalty and defense gets a slight bonus for games indoors.

How well does DVOA work? Using correlation coefficients, we can show that only actual points scored are better than DVOA at indicating how many games a team has won (Table 1) and DVOA is a does a better job of predicting wins in the coming season than

Table 1: Correlation of Various Stats to Wins, 2000-2010

Stat	Offense	Defense	Total
Points Scored/Allowed	.743	-.692	.917
DVOA	.685	-.510	.852
Yards Gained/Allowed	.560	-.469	.699
Yards Gained/Allowed per Play	.541	-.398	.729

Table 2. Correlation of Various Stats to Wins Following Year, 2000-2010

Stat	Correlation
DVOA	.357
Point Differential	.312
Yards per Play Differential	.285
Yardage Differential	.285
Wins	.281

either wins or points scored in the previous season (Table 2).

(Correlation coefficient is a statistical tool that measures how two variables are related by using a number between 1 and -1. The closer to -1 or 1, the stronger the relationship, but the closer to 0, the weaker the relationship.)

Defense-Adjusted Yards Above Replacement (DYAR)

After using DVOA for a few months, we came across a strange phenomenon: Well-regarded players, particularly those known for their durability, had DVOA ratings that came out around average. The reason is that DVOA, by virtue of being a percentage or rate statistic, doesn't take into account the cumulative value of having a player producing at a league-average level over the course of an above-average number of plays. By definition, an average level of performance is better than that provided by half of the league and the ability to maintain that level of performance while carrying a heavy work load is very valuable indeed. In addition, a player who is involved in a high number of plays can draw the defense's attention away from other parts of the offense, and, if that player is a running back, he can take time off the clock with repeated runs.

Let's say you have a running back who carries the

ball 300 times in a season. What would happen if you were to remove this player from his team's offense? What would happen to those 300 plays? Those plays don't disappear with the player, though some might be lost to the defense because of the associated loss of first downs. Rather those plays would have to be distributed among the remaining players in the offense, with the bulk of them being given to a replacement running back. This is where we arrive at the concept of replacement level, borrowed from our partners at Baseball Prospectus. When a player is removed from an offense, he is usually not replaced by a player of similar ability. Nearly every starting player in the NFL is a starter because he is better than the alternative. Those 300 plays will typically be given to a significantly worse player, someone who is the backup because he doesn't have as much experience and/or talent. A player's true value can then be measured by the level of performance he provides above that replacement level baseline, totaled over all of his run or pass attempts.

Of course, the *real* replacement player is different for each team in the NFL. Last year, the backup running back in Cincinnati (Bernard Scott) had a much higher DVOA than the first-string back (Cedric Benson). Chris Ivory started the year as the fourth-string running back for the Giants and ended the year with a 12.9% DVOA for Green Bay. On other teams, the drop from the starter to the backup can be even greater than the general drop to replacement level. Two years ago, we saw an extreme example when the Colts rested Peyton Manning and backup Curtis Painter had a horrific -79.0% DVOA in parts of two games. The choice to start an inferior player or to employ a sub-replacement level backup, however, falls to the team, not the starter being evaluated. Thus we generalize replacement level for the league as a whole as the ultimate goal is to evaluate players independent of the quality of their teammates.

Our estimates of replacement level are computed differently for each position. For quarterbacks, we analyzed situations where two or more quarterbacks had played meaningful snaps for a team in the same season, then compared the overall DVOA of the original starters to the overall DVOA of the replacements. We did not include situations where the backup was actually a top prospect waiting his turn on the bench, since a first-round pick is by no means a "replacement-level" player.

At other positions, there is no easy way to separate players into "starters" and "replacements," since unlike at quarterback, being the starter doesn't make you the only guy who gets in the game. Instead, we used a simpler method, ranking players at each position in each season by attempts. The players who made up the final 10 percent of passes or runs were split out as "replacement players" and then compared to the players making up the other 90 percent of plays at that position. This took care of the fact that not every non-starter at running back or wide receiver is a freely available talent. (Think of Jonathan Stewart or Robert Meachem, for example.)

As noted earlier, the challenge of any new stat is to present it on a scale that's meaningful to those attempting to use it. Saying that DeAngelo Williams' runs were worth 371.3 success value points over replacement in 2009 has very little value without a context to tell us if 371.3 is good total or a bad one. Therefore, we translate these success values into a number called "Defense-adjusted Yards Above Replacement, or DYAR. For example, Arian Foster was second among all running backs with 377 rushing DYAR.

Problems with DVOA and DYAR

Football is a game in which nearly every action requires the work of two or more teammates — in fact, usually 11 teammates all working in unison. Unfortunately, when it comes to individual player ratings, we are still far from the point at which we can determine the value of a player independent from the performance of his teammates. That means that when we say, "In 2010, Matt Forte had a DVOA of 0.4%," what we are really saying is "In 2010, Matt Forte, playing in Mike Martz's offensive system with the Chicago offensive line blocking for him and Jay Cutler selling the fake when necessary, had a DVOA of 0.4%."

DVOA is limited by what's included in the official NFL play-by-play or tracked by the Football Outsiders game charting project (introduced below). Because we need to have the entire play-by-play of a season in order to compute DVOA and DYAR, these metrics are not yet ready to compare players of today to players throughout the league's history. As of this writing, we have processed 19 seasons, 1992 through 2010, and we add seasons at a rate of roughly two per year (the most recent season, plus one season back into history.)

Special Teams

The problem with a system based on measuring both yardage and yardage towards a first down is what to do with plays that don't have the possibility of a first down. Special teams are an important part of football and we needed a way to add that performance to the team DVOA rankings. Our special teams metric includes five separate measurements: field goals and extra points, net punting, punt returns, net kickoffs, and kick returns.

The foundation of most of these special teams ratings is the concept that each yard line has a different value based on the likelihood of scoring from that position on the field. In *Hidden Game*, the authors suggested that the each additional yard for the offense had equal value, with a team's own goal line being worth -2 points, the 50-yard line 2 points, and the opposing goal line 6 points. (-2 points is not only the value of a safety, but also reflects the fact that when a team is backed up in its own territory, it is likely that its drive will stall, forcing a punt that will give the ball to the other team in good field position. Thus, the negative point value reflects the fact that the defense is more likely to score next.) Our studies have updated this concept to reflect the actual likelihood that the offense or defense will have the next score from a given position on the field based on actual results from the past few seasons. The line that represents the value of field position is not straight, but curved, with the value of each yard increasing as teams approach either goal line.

Our special teams ratings compare each kick or punt to league average based on the point value of the position of the kick, catch, and return. We've determined a league average for how far a kick goes based on the line of scrimmage for each kick (almost always the 30-yard line for kickoffs, variable for punts) and a league average for how far a return goes based on both the yard line where the ball is caught and the distance that it traveled in the air.

The kicking or punting team is rated based on net points compared to average, taking into account both the kick and the return if there is one. Because the average return is always positive, punts that are not returnable (touchbacks, out of bounds, fair catches, and punts downed by the coverage unit) will rate higher than punts of the same distance which are returnable. (This is also true of touchbacks on kickoffs.) There are also separate individual ratings for kickers and punters that are based on distance and whether the kick is returnable, assuming an average return in order to judge the kicker separate from the coverage.

For the return team, the rating is based on how many points the return is worth compared to average, based on the location of the catch and the distance the ball traveled in the air. Return teams are not judged on the distance of kicks, nor are they judged on kicks that cannot be returned. As explained below, blocked kicks are so rare as to be statistically insignificant as predictors for future performance and are thus ignored. For the kicking team they simply count as missed field goals, for the defense they are gathered with their opponents' other missed field goals in Hidden value (also explained below).

Field goal kicking is measured differently. Measuring kickers by field goal percentage is a bit absurd, as it assumes that all field goals are of equal difficulty. In our metric, each field goal is compared to the average number of points scored on all field goal attempts from that distance over the past decade, with adjustments for rule changes such as the introduction of the special-teams-use-only "k-ball" in 1999. The value of a field goal increases as distance from the goal-line increases. Kickoffs, punts, and field goals are then adjusted based on weather and altitude. It will surprise no one to learn that it is easier to kick the ball in Denver or a dome than it is to kick the ball in Buffalo in December. Because we do not yet have enough data to tailor our adjustments specifically to each stadium, each one is assigned to one of four categories: Cold, Warm, Dome, and Denver. There is also an additional adjustment dropping the value of field goals in Florida (because the warm temperatures allow the ball to carry better) and raising the value of punts in San Francisco (because of those infamous winds).

Once we've totaled how many points above or below average can be attributed to special teams, we translate those points into DVOA so the ratings can be added to offense and defense to get total team DVOA.

There are three aspects of special teams that have an impact on wins and losses, but don't show up in the standard special teams rating because a team has little or no influence on them. The first is the length of kickoffs by the opposing team, with an asterisk. Obviously, there are no defenders standing on the 35-yard line, ready to block a kickoff after the whistle blows. However, over the past few years, some teams have deliberately kicked short in order to avoid certain top return men, such as Devin Hester and Josh Cribbs. The special teams formula now includes adjustments to give teams extra credit for field position on kick returns if kickers are deliberately trying to avoid a return.

The other two items that special teams have little control over are field goals against your team, and punt distance against your team. Research shows no indication that teams can influence the accuracy or strength of field-goal kickers and punters, except for blocks. As mentioned above, although blocked field goals and punts are definitely skillful plays, they are so rare that they have no correlation to how well teams have played in the past or will play in the future, thus they are included here as if they were any other missed field goal or botched punt, giving the defense no additional credit for their efforts. The value of these three elements is listed separately as "Hidden" value.

Special teams ratings also do not include two-point conversions or onside kick attempts, both of which, like blocks, are so infrequent as to be statistically insignificant in judging future performance.

Pythagorean Projection

The Pythagorean projection is an approximation of each team's wins based solely on their points scored and allowed. This basic concept was introduced by baseball analyst Bill James, who discovered that the record of a baseball team could be very closely approximated by taking the square of team runs scored and dividing it by the sum of the squares of team runs scored and allowed. Statistician Daryl Morey, now general manager of the Houston Rockets, later extended this theorem to professional football, refining the exponent to 2.37 rather than 2.

Until recently, Pythagorean projections did a remarkable job of predicting Super Bowl champions. From 1988 through 2004, 11 of 16 Super Bowls were won by the team that led the NFL in Pythagorean wins, while only seven were won by the team with the most actual victories. Super Bowl champions that led the league in Pythagorean wins but not actual wins include the 2004 Patriots, 2000 Ravens, 1999 Rams, and 1997 Broncos.

From 2005 through 2008, as readers know, the results of the postseason did not quite look like the results of the regular season. The 2006 Colts set a mark for the fewest Pythagorean wins of any Super Bowl champion (9.6), a mark then shattered by the Giants the following season (8.6). The 2008 Arizona Cardinals had the fewest Pythagorean wins of any conference champion in history (8.0), That year was the first since 1995 where neither conference champion led its conference in Pythagorean wins during the regular season. In 2009, Super Bowl teams Indianapolis and New Orleans were among nine teams that were packed together with between 10.8 and 11.8 Pythagorean wins.

Last year, Pythagorean wins re-asserted themselves. Green Bay and Pittsburgh, the two teams that met in the Super Bowl, were tied for second with 12.1 Pythagorean wins, narrowly behind New England at 12.3. For the Packers in particular, who lost six games by four points or less, Pythagorean wins were a more accurate portrayal of the team's postseason changes than their actual 10-6 record.

The Pythagorean projection is also still a valuable predictor of year-to-year improvement. Teams that win a minimum of one full game more than their Pythagorean projection tend to regress the following year; teams that win a minimum of one full game less than their Pythagorean projection tend to improve the following year, particularly if they were at or above .500 despite their underachieving. For example, the 2008 New Orleans Saints went 8-8 despite 9.5 Pythagorean wins, hinting at the improvement that came with the next year's championship season. Two teams qualify for this trend in 2011: the Super Bowl champion Packers and the San Diego Chargers.

Adjusted Line Yards

One of the most difficult goals of statistical analysis in football is isolating the degree to which each of the 22 men on the field is responsible for the result of a given play. Nowhere is this as significant as the running game, in which one player runs while up to nine other players — including wideouts, tight ends, and a fullback — block in different directions. None of the statistics we use for measuring rushing — yards, touchdowns, yards per carry — differentiate between the contribution of the running back and the contribution of the offensive line. Neither do our advanced metrics DVOA and DYAR.

We do, however, have enough play-by-play data amassed that we can try to separate the effect that the running back has on a particular play from the effects of the offensive line (and other offensive blockers) and the opposing defense. A team might have two running backs in its stable: RB A, who averages 3.0 yards per carry, and RB B, who averages 3.5 yards per carry. Who is the better back? Imagine that RB A doesn't just average 3.0 yards per carry, but gets exactly 3 yards on every single carry, while RB B has a highly variable yardage output: sometimes 5 yards, sometimes -2 yards, sometimes 20 yards. The difference in variability between the runners can be exploited not only to determine the difference between the runners, but the effect the offensive line has on every running play.

At some point in every long running play, the running back passes all of his offensive line blocks as well as additional blocking backs or receivers. From there on, the rest of the play is dependent on the runner's own speed and elusiveness and the speed and tackling ability of the opposing defense. If Frank Gore breaks through the line for 50 yards, avoiding tacklers all the way to the goal line, his offensive line has done a great job — but they aren't responsible for the majority of the yards gained. The trick is figuring out exactly how much they *are* responsible for.

For each running back carry, we calculated the probability that the back involved would run for the specific yardage on that play based on that back's average yardage per carry and the variability of their yardage from play to play. We also calculated the probability that the offense would get the yardage based on the team's rushing average and variability using all backs *other* than the one involved in the given play, and the probability that the defense would give up the specific amount of yardage based on its average rushing yards allowed per carry and variability. For example, based on his rushing average and variability, the probability in 2004 that Tiki Barber would have a positive carry was 80 percent while the probability that Giants would have a positive carry without Barber running was only 73 percent.

A regression analysis breaks the value for rushing yardage into the following categories: losses, 0-to-4 yards, 5-to-10 yards, and 11-plus yards. In general, the offensive line is 20 percent more responsible for lost yardage than it is for positive gains up to four yards, but 50 percent less responsible for additional yardage gained between five and ten yards, and not at all responsible for additional yardage past ten yards.

By applying those percentages to every running back carry, we were able to create *Adjusted Line Yards,* a statistic that measured offensive line performance. (We don't include carries by receivers, which are usually based on deception rather than straight blocking, or carries by quarterbacks, which are almost always busted passing plays unless they involve Vince Young.) Those numbers are then adjusted based on down, distance, situation, opponent and whether or not a team is in the shotgun. (Because defenses are generally playing pass when the quarterback is in shotgun, the average running back carry from shotgun last year gained 4.87 yards, compared to just 4.10 yards on other carries.) The adjusted numbers are then normalized so that the league average for Adjusted Line Yards per carry is the same as the league average for RB yards per carry (in 2010, 4.18 yards).

The NFL distinguishes between runs made to seven different locations on the line: left/right end, left/right tackle, left/right guard, and middle. Further research showed no statistically significant difference between how well a team performed on runs listed as having gone up the middle or past a guard, so we separated runs into just five different directions (left/right end, left/right tackle, and middle). Note that there may not be a statistically significant difference between right tackle and middle/guard either, but pending further research (and for the sake of symmetry) we still list runs behind the right tackle separately. These splits allow us to evaluate subsections of a team's offensive line, but not necessarily individual linesmen, as we can't account for blocking assignments or guards who pull towards the opposite side of the line after the snap.

Success Rate

Success rate is a statistic for running backs that measures how consistently they achieve the yardage necessary for a play to be deemed successful. Some running backs will mix a few long runs with a lot of failed runs of one or two yards, while others with similar yards-per-carry averages will consistently gain five yards on first down, or as many yards as necessary on third down. This statistic helps us differentiate between the two.

Since Success Rate compares rush attempts to other rush attempts, without consideration of passing, the standard for success on first down is slightly lower than those described above for DVOA. In addition, the standard for success changes slightly in the fourth quarter when running backs are used to run out the clock. A team with the lead is satisfied with a shorter run as long as it stays in bounds. Conversely, for a team down by a couple of touchdowns in the fourth quarter, four yards on first down isn't going to be a big help.

The formula for Success Rate is as follows:

• A successful play must gain 40 percent of needed yards on first down, 60 percent of needed yards on second down, and 100 percent of needed yards on third or fourth down.

• If the offense is behind by more than a touchdown in the fourth quarter, the benchmarks switch to 50 percent, 65 percent, and 100 percent.

• If the offense is ahead by any amount in the fourth quarter, the benchmarks switch to 30 percent, 50 percent, and 100 percent.

The league-average Success Rate in 2010 was 45.9 percent. Success Rate is not adjusted based on defenses faced, and is not calculated for quarterbacks and wide receivers who occasionally carry the ball.

Similarity Scores

Similarity scores were first introduced by Bill James to compare baseball players to other baseball players from the past. It was only natural that the idea would spread to other sports as statistical analysis spread to other sports. NBA analyst John Hollinger has created his own version to compare basketball players, and we have created our own version to compare football players.

Similarity scores have a lot of uses, and we aren't the only football analysts who use them. Doug Drinen of the website Footballguys.com has his own system that is specific to comparing fantasy football performances. The major goal of our similarity scores is to compare career progressions to try to determine when players have a higher chance of a breakout, a decline, or — due to age or usage — an injury (much like Baseball Prospectus's PECOTA player projection system). Therefore we not only compare numbers such as attempts, yards, and touchdowns, but also age and experience. We are often looking not for players who had similar seasons, but for players who had similar two- or three-year spans in their careers.

Similarity scores have some important weaknesses. The database for player comparison begins in 1978, the year the 16-game season began and passing rules were liberalized (a reasonable starting point to measure the "modern" NFL), thus the method only compares standard statistics such as yards and attempts, which are of course subject to all kinds of biases from strength of schedule to quality of receiver corps. For

our comparisons, we project full-season statistics for the strike years of 1982 and 1987, although we cannot correct for players who crossed the 1987 picket line to play more than 12 games.

In addition to our similarity scores for skill players, we also have a similarity score system for defensive players based on FO's advanced statistics going back to 1997.

If you are interested in the specific computations behind our similarity scores system, we have listed the standards for each skill position online at http://www. footballoutsiders.com/stats/similarity. (The defensive system is not yet listed.) In addition, as part of our online premium package, all player pages for current players — both offensive and defensive — list the top ten similar players over one-, two-, and three-year spans.

KUBIAK Projection System

Most "skill position" players whom we expect to play a role this season receive a projection of their standard 2011 NFL statistics using the KUBIAK projection system. KUBIAK takes into account a number of different factors including expected role, performance over the past two seasons, age, height, weight, historical comparables, and projected team performance on offense and defense. When we named our system KUBIAK, it was a play on the PECOTA system used by our partners at Baseball Prospectus — if they were going to name their system after a long-time '80s backup, we would name our system after a long-time '80s backup. Little did we know that Gary Kubiak would finally get a head coaching job the very next season. After some debate, we decided to keep the name, although discussing projections for Houston players can be a bit awkward.

To clear up a common misconception among our readers, KUBIAK projects individual player performances only, not teams.

2011 Win Projection System

In this book, each of the 32 NFL teams receives a **2011 Mean Projection** at the beginning of its chapter. These projections stem from three equations that forecast 2011 DVOA for offense, defense, and special teams based on a number of different factors including the previous two years of DVOA in various situations, improvement in the second half of 2010, recent draft history, coaching experience, injury history, specific coaching styles, and the combined tenure of the offensive line.

These three equations produce precise numbers representing the most likely outcome, but also produce a range of possibilities, used to determine the probability of each possible offensive, defensive, and special teams DVOA for each team. This is particularly important when projecting football teams, because with only 16 games in a season, a team's performance may vary wildly from its actual talent level due to a couple of random bounces of the ball or badly timed injuries. In addition, the economic structure of the NFL allows teams to make sudden jumps or drops in overall ability more often than in other sports.

As noted in the Introduction to this year's book, the 2011 projections include additional manual adjustments based on the most commonly accepted theories of the likely effects of the lockout. Teams with new coordinators received a penalty to their projections on the appropriate side of the ball, unless the new coordinators were using the same offense or defense as their predecessors. (For example, in Oakland, Al Saunders has replaced Hue Jackson as offensive coordinator, but Jackson is now head coach. Since the Raiders are still using Jackson's offense, their offensive projection was not penalized.)

The next step is a simulation that runs the 2011 NFL season 10,000 times. For each simulated season, we determine each team's DVOA for the season using values and frequencies based on the projection equations described above. We then plug those season-long DVOA ratings into the same equation we use during the season to determine each team's likely remaining wins for our Playoff Odds Report. The simulation takes each season game-by-game, determining the home or road team's chance of winning each game based on the DVOA ratings of each team as well as home-field advantage, warm-weather or dome-stadium teams playing in the cold after November 1, and several other variables that can affect the outcome of each game. Then a random number between 0 and 100 determines whether the home or road team has won that game. Further tweaks adjust the simulation further to produce a more realistic number of 16-, 15-, 1- and 0-win seasons, as these are historically very low probability.

The resulting possible win totals are then separated into five categories:

- On the Clock (0 to 3 wins)
- Loserville (4 to 6 wins)
- Mediocrity (7 to 8 wins)
- Playoff Contender (9 to 10 wins)
- Super Bowl Contender (11-plus wins)

The percentage given for each category is dependent not only on how good we project the team to be in 2011, but the level of variation possible in that projection, and the expected performance of the teams on the schedule. Each variable has a different impact on the variability of the projection. For example, offenses that were better through the air in 2010 have more variation in their 2011 projections than offenses that were better on the ground. Defensive improvement in the second half of last season leads to less variation, while a rookie kicker or punter leads to more variation. This year, because of our manual adjustments to account for the lockout, teams with new coordinators will have more variation in their projections than those who are carrying over the same coaching staffs as in 2010.

In response to reader requests, we also list the mean projection for each team. We do not expect any teams to win the exact number of games in their mean projection, however — particularly since no team can win 0.8 of a game.

Football Outsiders Game Charting Project

Each of the formulas listed above relies primarily on the play-by-play data published by the NFL. When we began to analyze the NFL, that was all that we had to work with. Just as a television broadcast has a color commentator who gives more detail to the facts related by the play-by-play announcer, so too we need some color commentary to provide contextual information that breathes life into these plain lines of numbers and text. The Football Outsiders Game Charting Project is our attempt to provide color for the simple play-by-play.

Providing color to 512 hours of football is a daunting task. To put it into perspective, there were more than 54,000 lines of play-by-play information in the 2009 NFL season and our goal is to add several layers of detail to nearly all of them. We recruited more than 50 volunteers to collectively chart each week's NFL games. Unfortunately, we do not have access to the coaches' film the NFL provides to the 32 teams. That tape includes sideline and end zone perspectives for each play, and shows all 22 players at all times. Only

NFL teams and NFL Films are allowed to have access to the film, and the only place it is ever shown to the public is on NFL Network or ESPN's *NFL Matchup*. Anyone who has watched *Matchup* knows the benefit of watching coaches' film. It is easy to see the type of coverage being run and the cause-and-effect of certain actions taken on the field; the end zone perspective enables the identification of individual linemen.

Without access to coaches' film, we had to chart games using regular broadcast footage. Broadcast footage is not as definitive, but it served our purposes. In the end, we have data on nearly every play from the past six NFL seasons. A handful of plays are missing due to technical difficulties — for example, many games were charted using Direct TV Short Cuts, which would occasionally skip a play to fit the 30-minute window.

Through trial-and-error, we have narrowed our focus to charting things both traceable and definitive. We are limited by the camera angles on standard television broadcasts and the time constraints of our volunteers. Charting a game, and rewinding to make sure mistakes are minimized, can take two to three hours. More than a couple of these per week can be hazardous to one's marriage. Our goal was to provide comprehensive information while understanding that our charters were doing this on a volunteer basis.

We want to emphasize that all data from the charting project is unofficial. (For this reason, we will usually mention the charting project when using this data in comments later in the book.) Other sources for football statistics may keep their own measurements of yards after catch or how teams perform against the blitz. Our data will not necessarily match theirs. However, any other group that is publicly tracking this data is also working off the same television broadcast footage, and thus will run into the same issues of difficulty. No one outside of the league can get official game film from the NFL.

In addition, Football Outsiders has built the game charting project so that we are only tracking events, not rating players. It is not possible to grade player performance on a play without knowledge of the proper assignment or the coach's play call.

The Football Outsiders game charting project tracks the following information:

FORMATION: For each play, charters recorded the number of running backs, wide receivers, and tight ends. The formation was recorded in the moment prior to the snap. Therefore, it does not include any pre-snap motion. Formations have become more fluid in recent years, so these numbers should not be considered gospel. It can be hard to tell where to draw the distinction between an H-back and an offset fullback, or between a flex tight end and a slot receiver. We ask game charters to mark tight ends in the slot as tight ends, because defensive coordinators think of these players as flexed tight ends and assign coverage accordingly. Tight ends are only marked as wide receivers when they actually line up wide, outside the numbers.

RUSHERS AND BLOCKERS: "Blitz" is a rather ubiquitous word in football, and a standard definition is difficult to nail down. Rather than asking charters to determine when a team was blitzing, we asked them to record the number of blockers and rushers on passing plays. Counting rushers was easy, but counting blockers proved to be an art as much as a science. Offenses base their blocking schemes on how many rushers they expect. A running back or tight end's assignment may depend on how many pass-rushers cross the line at the snap. Therefore, an offensive player was deemed to be a blocker if he engaged in an actual block, or there was some hesitation before running a route. A running back that immediately heads out into the flat is not a blocker, but one that waits to verify that the blocking scheme is working and then goes out to the flat would, in fact, be considered a blocker.

We also ask charters to mark down when a defense used a "zone blitz." This was originally defined as any play where at least one down lineman dropped into pass coverage while at least one linebacker or defensive back rushed the passer. In 2009, we expanded the definition of zone blitz to also include plays where a 3-4 defense dropped both outside linebackers into coverage while an inside linebacker or defensive back rushed the passer.

QUARTERBACK ACTION: In passing situations, the charters recorded the movement of the quarterback. This consisted of three items:

• Marking plays which began with a play-action fake, including a fake end-around or a flea flicker.

• Marking when the quarterback left the pocket. Charters marked rollouts and bootlegs. (A rollout has the quarterback moving behind his blockers, while a bootleg has the quarterback moving one way and his blockers the other, usually in connection with a play-action fake.) Charters also marked when a quarterback run past the line of scrimmage was a sneak, a draw, or a scramble. We asked the charters to differentiate between designed runs and plays on which the quarterback originally intended to pass, although this is often a judgment call.

• Marking a defender with a "hurry" if he clearly caused the quarterback to rush his motion or leave the pocket after originally setting up in the pocket to throw. This year, we asked charters to think of hurries from the defensive perspective more than the offensive, so if the quarterback stood tall and delivered the pass with defenders in his face, this counted as a hurry. However, defenders are coming towards the quarterback from behind and he does not see them, that is not a hurry. Charters were allowed to list two names if necessary, and could also attribute a hurry to Overall Pressure or list a play as a Coverage Scramble when the quarterback wasn't under pressure but ran because there were no open receivers.

PASS DETAILS: We divided all pass yardage into two numbers: distance in the air and yards after catch. You will see much of this information throughout the team chapters and in each of the individual player tables. Distance in the air was based on the distance from the line of scrimmage to the place where the receiver either caught or was supposed to catch the pass. We did not count how far the quarterback was behind the line or horizontal yardage if the quarterback threw across the field. All touchdowns were counted to the goal line, so that distance in the air added to yards after catch always equals the official yardage total kept by the league. Charters also marked screen passes and tried to differentiate between passes to running backs that were standard pass routes, swing passes, or dumpoffs.

DEFENDERS: The NFL play-by-play lists tackles and, occasionally, tipped balls, but it does not definitively list the defender on the play. Charters were asked to determine which defender was primarily responsible for covering either the receiver at the time of the throw or the location to which the pass was thrown, regardless of whether the pass was complete or not.

Every defense in the league plays zone coverage at times, some more than others, which leaves us with the question of how to handle plays without a clear man assigned to that receiver. We gave charters three alternatives:

• We asked charters to mark passes that found the holes in zone coverage as Hole in Zone, rather than straining to assign that pass to an individual defender. We asked the charter to also note the player who appeared to be responsible for that zone, and these defenders are assigned half credit for those passes. Some holes were so large that no defender could be listed along with the Hole in Zone designation.

• Charters were free to list two defenders instead of one. This could be used for actual double coverage, or for zone coverage in which the receiver was right between two close defenders rather than sitting in a gaping hole. When two defenders are listed, ratings assign each with half credit.

• Screen passes and dumpoffs are marked as Uncovered unless a defender (normally a linebacker) is obviously shadowing that specific receiver on the other side of the line of scrimmage.

Since we began the charting project four years ago, nothing has changed our analysis more than this information on pass coverage. However, we want to be upfront: It was often the most difficult information to chart. Broadcast camera angles often do not show the setup of the secondary, making it impossible to identify before the play if there is man coverage. On passes longer than a few yards, the camera won't show the receiver until the pass is in the air. The sideline view of network cameras makes seeing the specific numbers on some jerseys difficult. (At this point, we would like to give a big shout out to all the defensive backs with dreadlocks that come out of their helmets, making them easier to identify.) Zone coverage makes things even twice as difficult. That being said, reviewing tape kept mistakes to a minimum and, if two cornerbacks might have been confused for one other once or twice, such mistakes tend to cancel out.

INCOMPLETE PASSES: Quarterbacks are evaluated based on their ability to complete passes. However, not all incompletes should have the same weight. Throwing a ball away to avoid a sack is actually a valuable incomplete, and a receiver dropping an otherwise quality pass is hardly a reflection on the quarterback. Therefore, our charters marked the reason for every incomplete pass. Possible entries included Overthrown, Underthrown, Thrown Away, Tipped/Batted at Line, Hit in Motion (indicating the quarterback was hit as his arm was coming forward to make a pass), Defensed, Dropped, and a few others. Defensed was listed when the pass was incomplete as the direct result of actions by the defender. That action can include balls tipped or batted in coverage or hard hits that jar a ball loose. We also ask charters to track dropped interceptions by defenders.

(Note: Our count of passes defensed will be different from the unofficial totals kept by the league, as explained below in the section on Defensive Secondary tables.)

ADDITIONAL DETAILS: Charters marked each quarterback sack with one of the following terms: Blown Block, Coverage Sack, QB Fault, or Blitz/Overall Pressure. Blown Blocks were listed with the name of a specific offensive player who allowed the defender to come through. Coverage Sack denotes when the quarterback has plenty of time to throw but cannot find an open receiver. QB Fault represents "self sacks" listed without a defender, such as when the quarterback drops back, only to find the ball slip out of his hands with no pass-rusher touching him.

All draw plays were marked, whether by halfbacks or quarterbacks.

"Broken tackles" are tracked on all runs or pass plays. We define a "broken tackle" as one of two events: Either the ballcarrier escapes from the grasp of the defender, or the defender is in good position for a tackle but the ballcarrier jukes him out of his shoes. If the ballcarrier sped by a slow defender who dived and missed, that did not count as a broken tackle. If the defender couldn't bring the ballcarrier down but slowed him and still had his hand on him when another player made a tackle, that did not count as a broken tackle. It was possible to mark multiple broken tackles on the same play (particularly if Marshawn Lynch was involved). Occasionally, the same defender would get a broken tackle, then recover, run upfield, and get a tackle on the same play, but we went through after the season to make sure no charter marked a broken tackle for contact that the league determined was an actual tackle.

Beginning in 2010, we tracked which defensive players drew the most offensive holding calls. Brian Orakpo and Cameron Wake tied for the league lead with nine apiece.

An additional column called Extra Comment allowed the charters to add any description they wanted to the play. These comments might be good blitz pickup by a running back, a missed tackle, a great hit, a description of a pass route, an angry tirade about the poor camera angles of network broadcasts, or a number of other possibilities.

Finally, we asked the game charters to mark when a mistake was made in the official play-by-play. The most common mistake was for an official scorer not to mark a quarterback hit, since that has only been tracked in the official play-by-play for two seasons. Other mistakes included incorrect names on tackles, penalties, or intended receivers, as well as missing direction on runs or passes, or the absence of the "scramble" designation when a quarterback ran on a play that began as a pass. Thanks to the diligence of our volunteer game charters and a friendly contact at the league office, the NFL corrected more than 300 mistakes in the official play-by-play based on the data collected by our game charters.

ACKNOWLEDGEMENTS: None of this would have been possible without the time spent by all the volunteer game charters. There are some specific acknowledgements at the end of the book, but we want to give a general thank you here to everyone who has helped collect data over the last few seasons. Without your unpaid time, the task of gathering all this information would have been too time-consuming to yield anything useful. If you are interested in participating in next year's charting project, please e-mail your contact information to info@footballoutsiders.com with the subject "Game Charting Project." Please make sure to mention where you live, what team you follow, and whether or not you have the Sunday Ticket package.

How to Read the Team Summary Box

Here is a rundown of all the tables and stats that appear in the 32 team chapters. Each team chapter begins with a box in the upper-right hand corner that gives a summary of our statistics for that team, as follows:

2010 Record gives each team's actual win-loss record. **Pythagorean Wins** gives the approximate number of wins expected last year based on this team's raw totals of points scored and allowed, along with their NFL rank. **DVOA** gives the team's total DVOA rating, with rank. **Offense, Defense,** and **Special Teams** list the team's DVOA rating in each category, along with NFL rank. Remember that good offenses and special teams have positive DVOA numbers, while a negative DVOA means better defense, so the lowest defensive DVOA is ranked number one (Pittsburgh Steelers).

Variance measures a team's consistency over the 2010 season. Teams are ranked from most consistent (Baltimore, first) to least consistent (Oakland, 32nd).

2011 Mean Projection gives the average number of wins for this team based on the 2011 Win Projection System described earlier in this chapter. The next few lines give the team's chances of finishing in the five different win categories.

Projected Average Opponent gives the team's strength of schedule for 2011 based not on last year's record but on the median projected DVOA for each opponent. A positive schedule is harder, a negative schedule easier. Teams are ranked from the hardest projected schedule (Kansas City, first) to the easiest (San Francisco, 32nd). This strength of schedule projection does not take into account which games are home and which are away, or the timing of the bye week.

You'll also find a table with the team's 2011 schedule placed within each chapter, along with a graph showing each team's week-to-week performance by single-game DVOA. The second, dotted line on the graph represents a five-week moving average of each team's performance, in order to show a longer-term view of when they were improving and declining. After the essays come statistical tables and comments related to that team and its specific units.

Weekly Performance

The first table gives a quick look at the team's week-to-week performance in 2010. (Table 3) This includes the playoffs for those teams that made the postseason, with the four weeks of playoffs numbered 18 (wild card) through 21 (Super Bowl). All other tables in the team chapters represent regular-season performance only unless otherwise noted.

Looking at the first week for the San Francisco 49ers in Week 1, the first five columns are fairly obvious: the 49ers lost at Seattle, 31-6. **YDF** and **YDA** are net yards on offense and net yards against the defense. These numbers do not include penalty yardage or special teams yardage. **TO** represents the turnover margin. Unlike other parts of the book in which we consider all fumbles as equal, this only represents actual turnovers: fumbles lost and interceptions. So, for example, the 49ers had one more turnover than Seattle when they won in Week 1, then forced five more turnovers than Seattle when they won the rematch in Week 14.

Finally, you'll see DVOA ratings for this game: To-

Table 3: 2010 49ers Stats by Week

Wk	vs.	W-L	PF	PA	YDF	YDA	TO	Total	Off	Def	ST
1	@SEA	L	6	31	263	242	-1	-102%	-78%	17%	-7%
2	NO	L	22	25	417	287	-4	28%	28%	-6%	-6%
3	@KC	L	10	31	251	457	0	-73%	-31%	39%	-4%
4	@ATL	L	14	16	262	357	-1	13%	-18%	-33%	-1%
5	PHI	L	24	27	364	352	-4	6%	0%	-3%	4%
6	OAK	W	17	9	349	179	2	87%	22%	-60%	5%
7	@CAR	L	20	23	282	379	2	-8%	-1%	11%	5%
8	DEN	W	24	16	339	398	2	15%	13%	2%	5%
9	BYE										
10	STL	W	23	20	421	332	0	11%	25%	17%	3%
11	TB	L	0	21	189	299	-2	-68%	-59%	11%	2%
12	@ARI	W	27	6	386	203	1	4%	14%	0%	-10%
13	@GB	L	16	34	269	410	-1	-29%	-7%	21%	0%
14	SEA	W	40	21	336	361	5	0%	6%	-15%	-22%
15	@SD	L	7	34	192	374	-1	-45%	-13%	29%	-2%
16	@STL	L	17	25	331	335	-1	-59%	-48%	18%	7%
17	ARI	W	38	7	362	279	2	54%	28%	-29%	-3%

tal **DVOA** first, then offense (**Off**), defense (**Def**), and special teams (**ST**). Note that these are DVOA ratings, adjusted for opponent, so the 49ers are listed with a higher DVOA for their close loss to the playoff-bound Falcons in Week 4 than they are for their win over the last-place Cardinals in Week 12.

Trends and Splits

Next to the week-to-week performance is a table giving DVOA for different portions of a team's performance, on both offense and defense. Each split is listed with the team's rank among the 32 NFL teams. These numbers represent regular season performance only.

Total DVOA gives total offensive, and defensive DVOA in all situations. **Unadjusted VOA** represents the breakdown of play-by-play considering situation but not opponent. A team whose offensive DVOA is higher than its offensive VOA played a harder-than-average schedule of opposing defenses; a team with a lower defensive DVOA than defensive VOA player a harder-than-average schedule of opposing offenses.

Weighted Trend lowers the importance of earlier games to give a better idea of how the team was playing at the end of the regular season. The final four weeks of the season are full strength; moving backwards through the season, each week is given less and less weight until the first three weeks of the season, which are not included at all. **Variance** is the same as noted above, with a higher percentage representing less consistency. This is true for both offense and defense: San Diego, for example, had the league's *most* consistent offense (3.6% variance) but one of the league's *least* consistent defenses (10.2% variance, which ranked 30th).

Passing and **Rushing** are fairly self-explanatory. Note that rushing includes all rushes, not just those by running backs, including quarterback scrambles that may have began as pass plays.

The next three lines split out DVOA on **First Down, Second Down,** and **Third Down**. Third Down here includes fourth downs on which a team runs a regular offensive play instead of punting or attempting a field goal. **First Half** and **Second Half** represent the first two quarters and last two quarters (plus overtime), not the first eight and last eight games of the regular season. Next comes DVOA in the **Red Zone**, which is any offensive play starting from the defense's 20-yard line through the goal line. The final split is **Late and Close**, which includes any play in the second half or overtime when the teams are within eight points of each other in either direction. (Eight points, of course, is the biggest deficit that can be made up with a single score, a touchdown and two-point conversion.)

Five-Year Performance

This table gives each team's performance over the past five seasons. (Table 4) It includes win-loss record, Pythagorean Wins, **Estimated Wins**, points scored and allowed, and turnover margin. Estimated wins are based on a formula that estimates how many games a team would have been expected to win based on 2010 performance in specific situations, normalized to eliminate luck (fumble recoveries, opponents' missed field goals, etc.) and assuming average schedule strength. The formula emphasizes consistency and overall DVOA as well as DVOA in the most important specific situations: red zone defense, first quarter offense, and performance in the second half when the score is close. The next columns of this table give

total DVOA along with DVOA for offense, defense, and special teams, and the rank for each among that season's 32 NFL teams.

The final four columns give the Adjusted Games Lost for starters on both offense and defense. (Our total for starters here includes players who take over as starters due to another injury, such as Shaun Hill or Melvin Bullitt last year, as well as important situational players who may not necessarily start, such as Reggie Bush when he was in New Orleans.) Adjusted Games Lost was introduced in *Pro Football Prospectus 2008*; it gives a weighted estimate of the probability that players would miss games based on how they are listed on the injury report. Unlike a count of "starter games missed," this accounts for the fact that a player listed as questionable who does in fact play is not playing at 100 percent capability. Teams are ranked from the fewest injuries (2010: Atlanta on offense, Kansas City on defense) to the most (2010: St. Louis on offense, Cleveland on defense).

Individual Offensive Statistics

Each team chapter contains a table giving passing and receiving numbers for any player who either threw five passes or was thrown five passes, along with rushing numbers for any players who carried the ball at least three times. These numbers also appear in the player comments at the end of the book (except for wide receiver rushing attempts). By putting them together in the team chapters we hope we make it easier to compare the performances of different players on the same team.

This year, because of the lockout and the last-minute nature of player movement, we were unable to list the 2010 stats of players added to the team in the offseason. We were also unable to mark players who are no longer on the team. Rookies are also not included.

Table 4: Green Bay Packers' Five-Year Performance

Year	W-L	Pyth	Est W	PF	PA	TO	Total	Rk	Off	Rk	Def	Rk	ST	Rk	Off AGL	Rk	Def AGL	Rk
2006	8-8	6.2	7.7	301	366	0	-2.4%	18	-4.1%	19	-5.6%	11	-3.9%	29	22.8	22	10.3	13
2007	13-3	11.5	11.1	435	291	+4	19.9%	6	16.8%	5	-0.6%	16	2.5%	8	7.6	2	17.1	12
2008	6-10	8.9	8.9	419	380	+7	10.6%	11	12.3%	12	1.4%	12	-0.3%	20	12.5	6	37.2	26
2009	11-5	11.8	11.0	461	297	+24	30.4%	2	22.5%	5	-14.0%	2	-6.1%	32	22.4	15	25.3	16
2010	10-6	12.1	10.9	388	240	10	23.4%	3	14.7%	7	-10.8%	2	-2.1%	26	40.4	28	45.9	29

Table 5: Seattle Seahawks' Passing

Player	DYAR	DVOA	Plays	NtYds	Avg	YAC	C%	TD	Int
M.Hasselbeck	32	-10.1%	475	2858	6.0	4.8	60.3%	12	7
C.Whitehurst	-95	-26.0%	106	501	4.7	4.4	58.0%	2	0

All players are listed with DYAR and DVOA. Passing statistics then list total pass plays (**Plays**), net yardage (**NtYds**), and net yards per pass (**Avg**). These numbers include not just passes (and the positive yardage from them) but aborted snaps and sacks (and the negative yardage from them). Then comes average yards after catch (**YAC**) as determined by the game charting project. This average is based on charted receptions, not total pass attempts. The final three numbers are completion percentage (**C%**), passing touchdowns (**TD**), and interceptions (**Int**).

It is important to note that the tables in the team chapters contain Football Outsiders stats, while the tables in the player comments later in the book contain official NFL totals, at least when it comes to standard numbers like receptions and yardage. This results in a number of differences between the two:

• Team chapter tables list yardage from Defensive Pass Interference; in the player comments, Defensive Pass Interference is reflected in DVOA and DYAR but not listed in yardage.

• Team chapter tables listed aborted snaps as passes, not runs, although aborted handoffs are still listed as runs. Net yardage for quarterbacks in the team chapter tables includes the lost yardage from aborted snaps, sacks, and intentional grounding penalties.

• Football Outsiders stats omit kneeldowns from run totals and clock-stopping spikes from pass totals.

• In the Football Outsiders stats, we have changed a number of lateral passes to count as passes rather than runs, under the theory that a pass play is still a pass play, even if the receiver is standing five inches behind the quarterback. This results in some small differences in totals. For example, Kyle Orton and Eddie Royal

Table 6: Miami Dolphins' Rushing

Player	DYAR	DVOA	Plays	Yds	Avg	TD	Fum	Suc
R.Brown	36	-4.2%	200	735	3.7	5	3	43%
R.Williams	36	-2.8%	159	673	4.2	2	4	53%
L.Polite	34	14.0%	26	62	2.4	1	0	65%
C.Henne	-51	-60.3%	22	73	3.3	0	2	-
T.Thigpen	3	-6.5%	12	66	5.5	0	1	-
P.Cobbs	-15	-108.0%	4	0	0.0	0	0	0%

are each listed with an additional 18 yards due to a Week 14 wide receiver screen pass that was scored by the league as a lateral and thus a running play.

Rushing statistics start with DYAR and DVOA, then list rushing plays and net yards along with average yards per carry and rushing touchdowns. The final two columns are fumbles (**Fum**) — both those lost to the defense and those recovered by the offense — and Success Rate (**Suc**), explained earlier in this chapter. Fumbles listed in the rushing table include all quarterback fumbles on sacks and aborted snaps, as well as running back fumbles on receptions, but not wide receiver fumbles.

Receiving statistics start with DYAR and DVOA and then list the number of passes thrown to this receiver (**Plays**), the number of passes caught (**Catch**) and the total receiving yards (**Yds**). Yards per catch (**Y/C**) includes total yardage per reception, based on standard play-by-play, while yards after catch (**YAC**) is based on information from our game charting project. Finally we list total receiving touchdowns, and catch percentage (**C%**), which is the percentage of passes intended for this receiver which were caught. Wide receivers, tight ends, and running backs are separated on the table by horizontal lines.

Table 7: New York Jets' Receiving

Player	DYAR	DVOA	Plays	Ctch	Yds	Y/C	YAC	TD	C%
B.Edwards	125	2.4%	101	53	904	17.1	5.4	7	52%
S.Holmes	128	4.3%	96	52	746	14.3	4.2	6	54%
J.Cotchery	-70	-23.1%	86	41	433	10.6	2.7	2	48%
B.Smith	-13	-37.7%	7	4	44	11.0	2.5	0	57%
D.Keller	38	-1.6%	100	55	687	12.5	3.9	5	55%
L.Tomlinson	-2	-14.2%	79	52	366	7.0	6.7	0	66%
S.Greene	27	4.4%	24	16	120	7.5	5.4	0	67%

Strategic Tendencies

The Strategic Tendencies table presents a mix of information garnered from both the standard play by play and the Football Outsiders game charting project. It gives you an idea of what kind of plays teams run in what situations and with what personnel. Each category is given a league-wide **Rank** from most often (1) to least often (32) except as noted below. The sample table shown here lists the NFL average in each category for 2010.

The first column of strategic tendencies lists how often teams ran in different situations. These ratios

Table 8: NFL Average Strategic Tendencies, 2010

Run/Pass		Rank	Offense		Rank	Defense		Rank	Other		Rank
Runs, all plays	40%	16	3+ WR	51%	16	Rush 3	8.5%	16	2+ RB, Pct Runs	58%	16
Runs, first half	40%	16	4+ WR	8%	16	Rush 4	58.4%	16	1 RB/2 TE, Pct Runs	48%	16
Runs, first down	50%	16	2+ TE	29%	16	Rush 5	24.0%	16	1 RB/3+ WR, Pct Runs	23%	16
Runs, second-long	34%	16	Single back	59%	16	Rush 6+	9.2%	16	CB1 on WR1	40%	16
Runs, power sit.	59%	16	Play action	18%	16	Zone Blitz	5.8%	16	Go for it on 4th	1.00	16
Runs, behind 2H	27%	16	Max protect	12%	16	Sacks by LB	35.2%	16	Offensive Pace	30.8	16
Pass, ahead 2H	44%	16	Outside pocket	12%	16	Sacks by DB	10.2%	16	Defensive Pace	30.8	16

are based on the type of play, not the actual result, so quarterback scrambles count as "passes" while quarterback sneaks and draws count as "runs."

The first three entries are self-evident: **Runs** on **all plays**, in the **first half**, and on **first down. Runs, second-and-long** is the percentage of runs on second down with seven or more yards to go, giving you an idea of how teams follow up a failed first down. **Runs, power situations** is the percentage of runs on third or fourth down with 1 or 2 yards to go, or at the goal line with 1 or 2 yards to go. **Runs, behind 2H** tells you how often teams ran when they were behind in the second half, generally a passing situation. **Pass, ahead 2H** tells you how often teams passed when they had the lead in the second half, generally a running situation.

In each case, you can determine the percentage of plays that were passes by subtracting the run percentage from 100 (the reverse being true for "Pass, ahead 2H," of course).

The second column gives information about offensive formations and strategy, as tracked by our game charters.

3+ WR/4+ WR: Plays with three or more receivers, and plays with four or more wide receivers. This may include a player normally identified at another position lining up as a wide receiver.

2+ TE: Plays with multiple tight ends, including "H-backs." As noted earlier, this year we asked charters to mark tight ends as wide receivers only if they lined up wide of the numbers; therefore, there will be a higher percentage of two-tight end sets listed than in years past, particularly for teams like Indianapolis that like to use tight ends in the slot.

Single back: Plays with only one running back, no matter the mixture of tight ends and wide receivers.

Play action: The percentage of pass plays (including quarterback scrambles) which began with a play-action fake to the running back. This percentage does not include fake end-arounds unless there was also a fake handoff. It does include flea-flickers.

Max protect: The percentage of this team's passing plays (including quarterback scrambles) on which blockers outnumber pass rushers by at least two, with a minimum of seven blockers.

Outside pocket: The percentage of this team's passing plays in which the quarterback was listed as leaving the pocket on a rollout, bootleg, or unplanned scramble, no matter whether the play ended with a pass attempt, sack, or scramble for positive yardage.

The third column shows strategies used by the **Defense.**

Rush 3/Rush 4/Rush 5/Rush 6+: The percentage of pass plays (including quarterback scrambles) on which our game charters recorded this team rushing the passer with three or fewer defenders, four defenders, five defenders, and six or more defenders. These percentages do not include goal-line plays on the one- or two-yard line.

Zone blitz: The percentage of pass plays where this defense ran a zone blitz.

Sacks by LB/Sacks by DB: The percentage of this team's sacks that came from linebackers and defensive backs. To figure out the percentage of sacks from defensive linemen, simply subtract the sum of these numbers from 100 percent.

The fourth column has data on run strategies that doesn't fit in the first column, and other assorted statistics.

2+ RB, Pct Runs: When this offense came out with two or three running backs, how often did they run the ball, as opposed to passing? Two running backs usually means a fullback and a halfback, but not necessarily. The percentage of runs does not include quarterback scrambles.

1 RB/2 TE, Pct Runs: The percentage of running plays when this offense came out with two tight ends and only one running back.

1 RB/3+ WR, Pct Runs: The percentage of running plays when this offense came out with three or four wide receivers and only one running back.

CB1 on WR1: The percentage of passes targeting

the team's number one cornerback that were thrown with the offense's number one receiver as the intended target. Obviously, both of these designations are subjective, but this gives a good idea of how often a defensive coordinator assigned his top corner to shadow a specific receiver. In some cases, different cornerbacks were used for different weeks depending on injuries.

One of the most important lessons from game charting is that each team's best cornerback does not necessarily match up against the opponent's best receiver. Most cornerbacks play a particular side of the field and in fact cover a wider range of receivers than we assumed before we saw the charting data.

Go for it on fourth: This is the aggressiveness index (AI) introduced by Jim Armstrong in *Pro Football Prospectus 2006*, which measures how often a team goes for a first down in various fourth-down situations compared to the league average. A coach over 1.00 is more aggressive, and one below 1.00 is less aggressive. Coaches are ranked from most aggressive to least aggressive. This year's Aggressive Index has been slightly improved to take into account trends of the last five years and to adjust for fourth-down situations at the end of a half.

Offensive Pace: Situation-neutral pace represents the seconds of game clock per offensive play, with the following restrictions: no drives are included if they start in the fourth quarter or final five minutes of the first half, and drives are only included if the score is within six points or less. Teams are ranked from quickest pace (Indianapolis, 28.4 seconds) to slowest pace (Pittsburgh, 33.3 seconds).

Defensive Pace: Situation-neutral pace based on seconds of game clock per defensive play. This is a representation of how a defense was approached by its opponents, not the strategy of the defense itself (an issue discussed in the Indianapolis chapter of *PFP 2006*).

Teams are ranked from quickest pace (St. Louis, 29.4 seconds) to slowest pace (Houston, 32.1 seconds).

Following each strategic tendencies table, you'll find a series of comments highlighting interesting data from that team's charting numbers. This includes DVOA ratings split for things like different formations, draw plays, or play-action passing. Please note that all DVOA ratings given in these comments are standard DVOA with no adjustments for the specific situation being analyzed, and the average DVOA for a specific situation will not necessarily be 0%. For example, the average offensive DVOA on play-action passes in 2009 was 29.9%, while the average offensive DVOA when the quarterback was hurried (but not sacked) was -11.5%.

How to Read the Offensive Line Tables

The offensive line tables list the last three years of Adjusted Line Yards and other statistics for each team (Table 9).

The first column gives standard yards per carry by each team's running backs (**Yds**). The next two columns give Adjusted Line Yards (**ALY**) followed by rank among the 32 teams.

Power gives the percentage of runs in "power situations" that achieved a first down or touchdown. Those situations include any third or fourth down with one or two yards to go, and any runs in goal-to-go situations from the two-yard line or closer. Unlike the other rushing numbers on the Offensive Line table, Power includes quarterbacks.

Second Level (**2nd Lev**) Yards and **Open Field** Yards represent yardage where the running back has the most power over the amount of the gain. Second

Table 9: Pittsburgh Steelers' Offensive Line

Year	Yards	ALY	Rank	Power	Rank	Stuff	Rank	2nd Lev	Rank	Open Field	Rank
2008	3.79	3.96	24	64%	19	22%	30	1.07	23	0.57	27
2009	4.32	4.13	14	72%	5	18%	15	1.18	15	0.87	13
2010	3.93	3.87	19	64%	12	21%	24	1.04	23	0.73	15

Year	LE	Rank	LT	Rank	Mid	Rank	RT	Rank	RE	Rank	Sacks	ASR	Rank	F-Start	Cont.
2008	4.84	9	4.69	8	3.91	24	3.15	32	4.05	16	50	9.2%	29	20	39
2009	4.58	14	4.30	11	4.08	17	3.72	25	4.70	8	50	8.5%	28	12	37
2010	4.85	6	2.89	30	3.91	19	4.08	17	5.02	5	43	8.6%	29	14	31

Level Yards represent the number of yards per carry that come five to ten yards past the line of scrimmage. Open Field Yards represent the number of yards per carry that come 11 or more yards past the line of scrimmage. A team with a low ranking in Adjusted Line Yards but a high ranking in Open Field Yards is heavily dependent on its running back breaking long runs to make the running game work, and therefore tends to have a less consistent running attack. Second Level Yards fall somewhere in between.

Stuff gives the percentage of runs that are stuffed for zero or negative gain. Since being stuffed is bad, teams are ranked from stuffed least often (1) to most often (32).

The next two columns give Adjusted Sack Rate (**ASR**) and its rank among the 32 teams. Some teams allow a lot of sacks because they throw a lot of passes; Adjusted Sack Rate accounts for this by dividing sacks and intentional grounding by total pass plays. It is also adjusted for situation (sacks are much more common on third down, particularly third-and-long) and opponent, all of which makes it a better measurement than raw sacks totals. Remember that quarterbacks share responsibility for sacks, and two different quarterbacks behind the same line can have very different Adjusted Sack Rates. Particularly if one is named Rob Johnson.

False gives the number of false starts, which is the offensive penalty which best correlates to both wins and wins the following season. This total includes false starts by players other than offensive linemen, but it does not include false starts on special teams. False starts in 2009 ranged from eight (Atlanta) to 29 (Oakland), with the NFL average at 18.7. Finally, Continuity Score (**Cont.**) tells you how much continuity each offensive line had from game-to-game in that season. It was introduced in the Cleveland chapter of *Pro Football Prospectus 2007*. Continuity score starts with 48 and then subtracts:

• The number of players over five who started at least one game on the offensive line;

• The number of times the team started at least one different lineman compared to the game before; and

• The difference between 16 and that team's longest streak where the same line started consecutive games.

The perfect Continuity Score is 48, achieved last year by two teams, Atlanta and New Orleans. The lowest Continuity Score belonged to Philadelphia and Seattle at 21. The NFL average was 32.5.

The second part of the Offensive Line table gives Adjusted Line Yards in each of the five directions with rank among the 32 teams. Note that the league average is higher on the left than the right. Specifically in 2010, the league average was 4.19 on left end runs (**LE**), 4.12 on left tackle runs (**LT**), 4.05 on runs up the middle (**MID**), 4.05 on right tackle runs (**RT**), and 3.96 on right end runs (**RE**).

How to Read the Defensive Front Seven Tables

Defensive players make plays. Plays aren't just tackles — interceptions and pass deflections change the course of the game, and so does the act of forcing a fumble or beating the offensive players to a fumbled ball. While some plays stop a team on third down and force a punt, others merely stop a receiver after he's caught a 30-yard pass. We still cannot measure each player's opportunities to make a tackle. We can measure a linebacker's opportunities in pass coverage, however, thanks to the Football Outsiders game charting project.

DEFENSIVE LINEMEN: Defensive linemen are listed in the team chapters if they made at least 15 plays during the 2010 season. Players are listed with the following numbers:

Age: The player's age, listed simply as the difference between birth year and 2011. Players born in January and December of the same year will have the same listed age.

Position (**Pos**): The player's position on the line.

Plays (**Plays**): The total defensive plays including tackles, pass deflections, interceptions, fumbles forced, and fumble recoveries. This number comes from the official NFL gamebooks and therefore does not include plays on which the player is listed by the Football Outsiders game charting project as in coverage, but does not appear in the standard play-by-play. Special teams tackles are also not included.

Percentage of Team Plays (**TmPct**): The percentage of total team plays involving this defender. The sum of the percentages of team plays for all defenders on a given team will exceed 100 percent, primarily due to shared tackles. This number is adjusted based on games played, so an injured player may be fifth on his

Table 10: Atlanta Falcons' Defensive Line

Defensive Line	Age	Pos	Plays	TmPct	Rk	Stop	Dfts	BTkl	St%	Rk	AvYd	Rk	Sack	Hit	Hur	Runs	St%	Yds	Pass	St%	Yds
						Overall							Pass Rush			vs. Run			vs. Pass		
John Abraham	33	DE	45	6.1%	29	37	25	2	76%	25	1.7	34	13	5	23.5	21	76%	4.1	24	88%	-0.5
Corey Peters	23	DT	33	4.2%	42	23	5	1	74%	52	3.2	62	1	0	3.5	27	74%	2.6	6	50%	5.8
Kroy Biermann	26	DE	30	3.8%	65	23	8	0	79%	47	1.4	29	3	7	20.5	19	79%	1.9	11	73%	0.5
Jonathan Babineaux	30	DT	29	4.0%	47	21	14	4	75%	46	1.7	28	4	3	10.5	16	75%	1.6	13	69%	1.7
Chauncey Davis	28	DE	26	3.3%	73	15	7	0	61%	77	3.5	77	1	1	5	18	61%	2.9	8	50%	4.9
Jamaal Anderson	25	DE	23	2.9%	--	19	7	0	83%	--	0.4	--	2	2	11.5	18	83%	0.9	5	80%	-1.4
James Anderson	25	DE	23	2.9%	--	19	7	0	83%	--	0.4	--	2	2	11.5	18	83%	0.9	5	80%	-1.4
Vance Walker	24	DT	16	2.0%	--	14	4	1	85%	--	1.4	--	0	0	2	13	85%	1.8	3	100%	-0.7

team in plays but third in **TmPct**.

Stops (**Stop**): The total number of plays which prevent a "success" by the offense (45 percent of needed yards on first down, 60 percent on second down, 100 percent on third or fourth down).

Defeats (**Dfts**): The total number of plays which stop the offense from gaining first down yardage on third or fourth down, stop the offense behind the line of scrimmage, or result in a fumble (regardless of which team recovers) or interception.

Broken Tackles (**BTkl**): The number of broken tackles recorded by our game charters.

Stop Rate (**St%**): The percentage of all Plays that are Stops.

Average Yards (**AvYd**): The average number of yards gained by the offense when this player is credited with making the play. Note that passes defensed count as zero yards.

Sack: Standard NFL sack totals.

Hit: To qualify as a quarterback hit, the defender must knock the quarterback to the ground in the act of throwing or after the pass is thrown. We have listed hits on all plays, including those cancelled by penalties. (After all, many of the hardest hits come on plays cancelled because the hit itself draws a roughing the passer penalty.) Beacause official scorers are not entirely consistent, hits are adjusted slightly based on the home team of each game.

Hurries (**Hur**): The number of quarterback hurries recorded by the Football Outsiders game charting project. This includes both hurries on standard plays and hurries that force an offensive holding penalty that cancels the play and costs the offense yardage.

Finally, we split our stats for defensive linemen into **Run** plays and **Pass** plays. The latter category includes sacks, tackles after completions, and pass deflections.

Defensive linemen are ranked by percentage of team plays, Stop Rate, and average yards. The lowest number of average yards earns the top rank (negative numbers indicate the average play ended behind the line of scrimmage). Except for pass-rush specialists, most linemen do not have enough pass plays to make separate rankings of pass and run statistics viable. Defensive ends are ranked if they made 24 or more plays during 2010. There are 80 defensive ends who qualify. Defensive tackles are ranked if they made 20 or more plays during 2009, with 67 players ranked.

LINEBACKERS: Linebackers are listed in team chapters if they made at least 20 plays during the season. Most of the stats for linebackers are the same as those for defensive linemen. The listings of both total plays and percentage of team plays are based on standard play-by-play. Average yards on the left side of the table is also based on standard play-by-play, and gives us a good indication of which linebackers play closer to the line of scrimmage, and which players drop into coverage.

Linebackers are ranked in percentage of team plays, and also in Stop Rate and average yards for running plays specifically. Linebackers are ranked in these standard stats if they have a minimum of 48 plays or 10 games started. Outside, inside (3-4), and middle (4-3) linebackers are all ranked together, with 109 players ranked in total.

The final five columns in the linebacker stats come from the Football Outsiders game charting project.

Targets (**Tgts**): The number of pass players on which our game charters listed this player in coverage.

Success Rate (**Suc%**): The percentage plays of targeting this player on which the offense did not have a successful play. This means not only incomplete passes and interceptions, but also short completions which do not meet our baselines for success (45 percent of needed yards on first down, 60 percent on second down, 100 percent on third or fourth down). This year, unlike in our two previous books, Success Rate is adjusted for the quality of the receiver covered.

Adjusted Yards per Pass (**AdjYd**): The average

Table 11: Jacksonville Jaguars' Linebackers

Linebackers	Age	Pos	Plays	TmPct	Overall Rk	Stop	Dfts	BTkl	AvYd	Pass Rush Sack	Hit	Hur	vs. Run Runs	St%	Rk	Yds	Rk	vs. Pass Tgts	Suc%	Rk	AdjYd	Rk
Daryl Smith	29	OLB	100	13.4%	32	66	35	4	3.9	4	6	12	54	69%	54	2.9	45	35	52%	50	8.3	76
Kirk Morrison	29	MLB	90	12.1%	41	59	19	3	3.6	0	2	3	70	73%	32	2.5	26	21	54%	42	6.4	45
Justin Durant	26	OLB	57	12.2%	40	32	10	4	6.1	0	0	0	27	85%	3	2.2	15	27	41%	71	8.8	78
Russell Allen	25	MLB	35	4.7%	--	22	5	3	3.9	0	0	0	26	77%	--	2.7	--	10	13%	--	13.0	--

number of yards gained on plays on which this defender was the listed target, adjusted for the quality of the receiver covered.

These stats are explained in more detail below, in the section on secondary tables. Plays listed with two defenders or as "Hole in Zone" with this defender as the closest player count only for half credit in computing both Success Rate and Average Yards per Pass. Seventy-nine linebackers are ranked in the charting stats, with a minimum of 16 charted passes. As a result of the different thresholds, some linebackers are ranked in standard stats but not charting stats, or vice versa.

FURTHER DETAILS: Just as we did in the offensive tables, players who are no longer on the team are marked with asterisks, and players who were on other teams last year are in italics. Other than the game charting statistics for linebackers, defensive front seven player statistics are not adjusted for opponent.

Numbers for defensive linemen and linebackers unfortunately do not reflect all of the opportunities a player had to make a play, but they do show us which players were most active on the field. A large number of plays could mean a strong defensive performance, or it could mean that the linebacker in question plays behind a poor part of the line. In general, defensive numbers should be taken as information that tells us what happened on the field in 2010, but not as a strict, unassailable judgment of which players are better than others — particularly when the difference between two players is small (for example, players ranked 20th and 30th) instead of large (players ranked 20th and 70th).

After the individual statistics for linemen and linebackers, the Defensive Front Seven section contains a table that looks exactly like the table in the Offensive Line section. The difference is that the numbers here are for all opposing running backs against this team's defensive front. As we're on the opposite side of the ball, teams are now ranked in the opposite order, so the number one defensive front seven is the one that allows the fewest Adjusted Line Yards, the lowest percentage in Power situations, and has the highest Adjusted Sack

Rate. Directions for Adjusted Line Yards are given from the offense's perspective, so runs left end and left tackle are aimed at the right defensive end and (assuming the tight end is on the other side) weakside linebacker.

How to Read the Secondary Tables

The first few columns in the secondary tables are based on standard play-by-play, not game charting. **Age**, Total Plays, Percentage of Team Plays, Stops, and Defeats are computed the same way they are for other defensive players, so that the secondary can be compared to the defensive line and linebackers. That means that Total Plays here includes passes defensed, sacks, tackles after receptions, tipped passes, and interceptions, but not pass plays on which this player was in coverage but was not given a tackle or passed defense by the NFL's official scorer.

The middle four columns address each defensive back's role in stopping the run. Average Yardage and Stop Rate for running plays is computed in the same manner as for defensive linemen and linebackers.

The third section of statistics represents data from the game charting project:

Targets (**Tgts**): The number of pass plays on which our game charters listed this player in coverage. This number gives full credit to all passes, including those on which two defenders are listed and those listed as "Hole in Zone" with this player as the closest zone defender (both of those count as half credit in the other stats below). We do not count pass plays on which this player was in coverage, but the incomplete was listed as Thrown Away, Tipped at Line, or Hit in Motion.

Target Percentage (**Tgt%**): The number of plays on which this player was targeted divided by the total number of charted passes against his defense, not including plays listed as Uncovered. Like Percentage of Team Plays, this metric is adjusted based on number of games played.

Table 12: Washington Redskins' Secondary

Secondary	Age	Pos	Plays	TmPct	Rk	Stop	Dfts	BTkl	Runs	St%	Rk	Yds	Rk	Tgts	Tgt%	Rk	Dist	Suc%	Rk	APaYd	Rk	PD	Int
				Overall						vs. Run							vs. Pass						
DeAngelo Hall	28	CB	111	12.8%	4	51	28	6	25	44%	40	9.4	72	85	16.5%	28	10.6	41%	81	10.0	81	9	6
LaRon Landry	27	FS	93	19.0%	1	35	14	6	37	49%	19	5.5	20	34	11.6%	1	12.8	52%	49	10.1	68	9	1
Reed Doughty	29	SS	83	10.2%	39	29	5	3	40	45%	28	7.2	50	26	5.4%	48	13.2	63%	15	8.3	46	1	0
Kareem Moore	27	FS	67	10.3%	37	17	8	7	37	24%	78	8.9	66	22	5.6%	45	15.7	60%	24	7.5	37	5	1
Phillip Buchanon	31	CB	66	7.6%	57	33	11	4	14	50%	25	9.5	73	69	13.3%	62	11.6	55%	23	6.4	23	16	2
Carlos Rogers	30	CB	66	10.1%	28	32	11	5	11	45%	38	6.0	31	60	15.6%	39	9.0	51%	48	8.2	62	12	2
Kevin Barnes	25	CB	21	3.9%	--	11	5	1	10	50%	--	8.4	--	10	3.0%	--	12.2	74%	--	3.4	--	5	1

Year	Pass D Rank	vs. #1 WR	Rk	vs. #2 WR	Rk	vs. Other WR	Rk	vs. TE	Rk	vs. RB	Rk
2008	15	-11.2%	8	-4.7%	11	-3.9%	16	-5.2%	12	17.1%	28
2009	20	3.7%	15	10.6%	26	-2.5%	12	0.8%	14	17.1%	25
2010	27	-5.6%	13	12.7%	24	21.7%	29	-9.7%	6	5.8%	17

Distance (**Dist**): The average distance in the air beyond the line of scrimmage of all passes targeted at this defender. It does not include yards after catch, and is useful for seeing which defenders were covering receivers deeper or shorter.

Success Rate (**Suc%**): The percentage of plays targeting this player on which the offense did not have a successful play. This means not only incomplete passes and interceptions, but also short completions that do not meet our baselines for success (45 percent of needed yards on first down, 60 percent on second down, 100 percent on third or fourth down). Defensive pass interference is counted as a failure for the defensive player, similar to a completion of equal yardage (and a new first down).

Average Yards per Pass (**PaYd**): The average number of yards gained on plays on which this defender was the listed target.

Passes Defensed (**PD**): This is our count of passes defensed, and will differ from the total found in NFL gamebooks. Our count includes:

• All passes listed by our charters as Defensed.

• All interceptions, or tipped passes leading to interceptions.

• All passes defensed listed in the NFL gamebooks for games which remain uncharted.

• Any pass on which the defender is given a pass defensed by the official scorer, and the game charter listed a reason for incomplete which can be hard to differentiate from a pass defensed, including: Dropped, Miscommunication, Alligator Arms, and Catch Out of Bounds.

Our count of passes defensed does not include passes marked as defensed in the official gamebooks but listed by our charters as Overthrown, Underthrown, or Thrown Away. It also does not include passes tipped in the act of rushing the passer.

Interceptions (**Int**): Standard NFL interception total.

Cornerbacks need 40 charted passes or eight games started to be ranked in the defensive stats, with 89 cornerbacks ranked in total. Safeties need 16 charted passes or eight games started to be ranked in the defensive stats, with 81 safeties ranked in total. Strong and free safeties are ranked together.

Just like the front seven, the secondary has a table of team statistics following the individual numbers. This table gives DVOA figured against different types of receivers. Each offense's wide receivers have had one receiver designated as number one, and another as number two. (Occasionally this is difficult, due to injury or an amorphous wide receiver corps like last year's Rams, but it's usually pretty obvious.) The other receivers form a third category, with tight ends and running backs as fourth and fifth categories. The defense is then judged on the performance of each receiver based on the standard DVOA method, with each rating adjusted based on strength of schedule. (Opponents with Roddy White and Larry Fitzgerald as top receivers, for example, are tougher than an opponent with Michael Crabtree as its number one receiver.)

Pass D Rank is the total ranking of the pass defense, as seen before in the Trends and Splits table, and combines all five categories plus sacks and passes with no intended target.

The defensive secondary table should be used to analyze the defense as a whole rather than individual players. The ratings against types of receivers are generally based on defensive schemes, not specific cornerbacks, and the ratings against tight ends and running backs are in large part due to the performance of linebackers.

Table 14: Oakland Raiders' Special Teams

Year	DVOA	Rank	FG/XP	Rank	Net Kick	Rank	Kick Ret	Rank	Net Punt	Rank	Punt Ret	Rank	Hidden	Rank
2008	5.8%	2	1.9	14	-0.8	18	3.6	13	13.9	4	15.2	1	16.2	3
2009	0.0%	17	15.0	1	-6.3	27	-16.3	32	18.2	1	-10.4	31	2.7	9
2010	1.5%	13	3.5	10	0.8	16	5.0	10	9.9	4	-10.2	31	16.2	1

How to Read the Special Teams Tables

The special teams tables list the last three years of kick, punt, and return numbers for each team.

The first two columns list total special teams DVOA and rank among the 32 teams. The next two columns list the value in actual points of field goals and extra points (**FG/XP**) when compared to how a league average kicker would do from the same distances, adjusted for weather and altitude, and rank among the 32 teams. Next, we list the estimated value in actual points of field position over or under the league average based on net punting (**Net Punt**), and rank that value among the 32 teams. That is followed by the estimated point values of field position for punt returns (**Punt Ret**), net kickoffs (**Net Kick**), and kick returns (**Kick Ret**) and their respective ranks.

The final two columns represent the value of "**Hidden**" special teams, plays which throughout the past decade have usually been based on the performance of opponents without this team being able to control the outcome. We combine the opposing team's value on field goals, kickoff distance, and punt distance, adjusted for weather and altitude, and then switch the sign to represent that good special teams by the opponent will cost the listed team points, and bad special teams will effectively hand them points. We have to give the qualifier of "usually" because, as explained above, certain returners such as Josh Cribbs will affect opposing special teams strategy. Nonetheless, the "hidden" value is still "hidden" for most teams, and they are ranked from the most hidden value gained (Oakland, 16.2 points) to the most value lost (Denver, -17.6 points). The best and worst individual values for kickers, punters, and returners are listed in the statistical appendix at the end of the book.

Administrative Minutia

Receiving statistics include all passes intended for the receiver in question, including those that are incomplete or intercepted. The word "passes" refers to both complete and incomplete pass attempts. When rating receivers, interceptions are treated as incomplete passes with no penalty.

For the computation of DVOA and DYAR, passing statistics include sacks as well as fumbles on aborted snaps. We do not include kneeldown plays or spikes for the purpose of stopping the clock. Some interceptions which we have determined to be "Hail Mary" plays that end the first half or game are counted as regular incomplete passes, not turnovers.

All mentions of yards after catch, hurries, hits, blitzes, and screens come from the Football Outsiders game charting project and may be different from totals compiled by other sources.

Unless we say otherwise, when we refer to third-down performance in this book we are referring to a combination of third down and the handful of rushing and passing plays that take place on fourth down (primarily fourth-and-1).

Aaron Schatz

The Year In Quotes

Be a jerk to them jerks, yeah that'll make 'em hurt

"He needs to stop crying about blood tests and HGH. He needs to try to get a deal done, that's what he needs to do. He's been on this crusade about HGH, but he needs to be on a crusade about getting these owners together and trying to work out a deal. To me, he's a joke, because every time I look, he's talking about performance enhancements instead of talking about trying to figure out a way to make sure football is played in August."

— *Ravens wide receiver Derrick Mason telling us how he really feels about NFL commissioner Roger Goodell during the NFL lockout.*

I'm a little teapot, blowing off steam. You put me on the heat, I don't whistle, I scream

"They talk about walk softly and carry a big stick. I love that. I agree with that 100 percent. But I guess I feel more like Babe Ruth. I'm going to walk softly, I'm going to carry that big stick, and then I'm going to point, and then I'm going to hit it over the fence."

— *Jets coach Rex Ryan regurgitating his insistence that the Jets would win the Super Bowl. The ball stayed in the park.*

He wears his pride on his sleeve like a bracelet

"I got a high pain tolerance, my pain tolerance is outrageous."

— *Alabama wide receiver Julio Jones' secret to running a 4.39 40-yard dash despite a stress fracture in his foot at the NFL Scouting Combine.*

There are as many opinions as there are experts

"Yeah I watch it and all. Mel Kiper and all, he messed me over, he lied to me said I was Top 20, had me go out and spend X amount of dollars and then owe the bank stuff. So I don't know the guys; they're guessing just like we guess; I can guess who the Dolphins are going to take too. But I look at it a little bit and hear the experts — I guess they call them to hear what they got to say."

— *Dolphins linebacker Channing Crowder when asked whether he pays close attention to all the hype and lead up to the NFL Draft each year.*

SpaceBook would be an appealing name for something

"No, I don't do Twitter or MyFace or any of that stuff."

— *Patriots coach Bill Belichick when asked if he follows Bengals receiver Chad Ochocinco on Twitter.*

He's on a diet, but his pocket's eating cheesecake

"One thing they can do is feed us. Do I look under nourished?"

— *Patriots coach Bill Belichick when asked about skipping a breakfast with the media.*

Jesus wore boxer briefs

"People may say it's underwear, but everyone wears underwear — it's not like I'm doing something risqué. I wouldn't do anything that goes against what I stand for. The whole campaign is very classy."

— *Broncos quarterback Tim Tebow on his advertising campaign with Jockey.*

Well the situation certainly helped the Packers

"It depends if something's good on. Maybe I can DVR Jersey Shore or something and catch up on that. I've been working a little bit this week, man. Hopefully I can catch up there as we get close to game time."

— *Steelers coach Mike Tomlin, explaining how Snookie helps calm his nerves before a big game.*

The Packers hate rolling papers

"We knocked the Eagles and the Falcons and the Bears off. Now we 'bout to cut Troy Polamalu's hair off."

— *Rapper and Packers fan Lil' Wayne in his Packers-themed response to Wiz Khalifa's "Black and Yellow," which has become an anthem for Steelers fans.*

What kind of pipe do you own exactly?

"I went from a zero-star prospect to a two-time All-American. Put that in your pipe and smoke it."

— *Northwestern football coach Pat Fitzgerald's thoughts on how analysts view the players in his recruiting class.*

Charles Woodson is in touch with real America

"Well I voted for [Obama], you know, so why is he not a Green Bay fan? So that was really the thinking behind it. I jumped on his bandwagon a couple of years ago and voted for him. So for him to only go to the Super Bowl because Chicago is there I thought is not fair to me. I'm a voter, I'm a taxpayer, so I want him to root for the Packers as well."

— *Packers cornerback Charles Woodson explaining his pep talk prior to the NFC Championship Game. President Obama had said he would attend the Super Bowl if his hometown Chicago Bears made it.*

Don't you have to be a girl to wear a tampon? Oh wait, I get it

"As I mentioned last week and on Saturday's show, the factor that was going to come down to that game was the X-factor, the Cutler factor, and man, I just never thought that his tampon would fall out on national TV."

— *Former Packers offensive lineman Greg Koch's hygienic thoughts on Bears quarterback Jay Cutler exiting the NFC Championship Game early with a knee injury.*

Maybe the Jets aren't in the media enough

"For all you nonbelievers. Disrespect us. Talk crap about the defense like we ain't the third best defense in the league. All we hear is about [the Patriots'] defense. They can't stop a nose bleed! Twenty-fifth in the league, and we the one that gets disrespected."

— *Jets linebacker Bart Scott on why the Jets played with so much anger while beating the Patriots 28-21 in the divisional round of the AFC Playoffs.*

This was a deceivingly quick press conference

"[We're] really moving forward and we're going out there being good little foot soldiers. We are making sure we are going out there doing everything coach [Belichick] asks us to do: making plays and doing everything necessary to get ready for the game."

— *Patriots wide receiver Wes Welker answering a question about the higher intensity of playoff practices. This was one of eleven different times Welker referred to feet during the press conference in light of Jets coach Rex Ryan's controversial foot fetish video.*

Worst analogy for life ever?

"I hate [taking on blitzers]. Serious. It's like life. You do stuff you don't like to do 'cause you have to do it. If you're, 'Yeah, I want to block a linebacker,' something has to be slightly wrong with you. You have to have that 'want' in order to do it well.

"But if that was a test question — 'Joe, would you want to do it, yes or no?' — I'm going to pick 'no' every time. But it's a 'want to' when you get out there because you know you have to."

— *Colts running back Joseph Addai explaining that he doesn't enjoy picking up blitzers after he was asked about the Jets' affinity for blitzing.*

Someone's been listening to Kanye's new album

"From the bottom of my heart and everybody's, we have a 10-6 season, a 10-win season in the NFL, OK? [The critics] can kiss my ass, OK? They can line up and kiss my ass. It's not an easy thing to do."

— *Giants coach Tom Coughlin during his postgame speech to his team following a win in Washington, which gave the Giants ten wins for the season, but no playoff berth.*

ゴライオン!!!

"I've played with a lot of quarterbacks in my career. If you put all of them together and form a Voltron, they might be as good as he is."

— *Patriots running back Fred Taylor after shrugging when asked if anything new could be said about teammate Tom Brady. Comparing Brady to a super robot from a Japanese science-fiction cartoon would qualify as something new.*

I'm an Xbox, not just an Atari

"No, I want to say, 'F--k you.' And I mean that in the

most professional way."

— *Broncos wide receiver Brandon Lloyd's response when asked if he wanted to say "told you so" to his three previous teams after earning his first Pro Bowl selection.*

Coughlin must have been yelling at Matt Dodge for not pushing the reset button really quickly without anyone noticing

"They dialed up the right things at the right time. It's kind of like Tecmo Bowl when you press the same button as your opponent and everything breaks down. They had the right blitzes dialed up against the right runs, and they got lucky."

— *Giants running back Brandon Jacobs on how the Eagles stopped the Giants' running attack in the final minutes of the collapse.*

Panthers fans certainly got one in Cam Newton

"Don't tell my mom. She's going to want more Christmas presents."

— *Panthers cornerback R.J. Sanford, after being promoted from the practice squad to the 53-man roster.*

Things got awkward after the game when Washington showed Pete Carroll the bruise on his buttocks

"Next time, I'm just gonna pull a Forrest Gump and run clean through the stadium."

— *Seahawks returner Leon Washington, who was headed for a long punt-return touchdown and put his finger in the air at the 40, only to get tripped up just shy of the goal line by pesky Panthers punter Jason Baker.*

That's also what Scar said leading up to the murder of Mufasa

"The other day he had like 'Hakuna Matata' or some [expletive] from 'The Lion King' playing, which I don't think nobody wants to hear. He needs to bump some Lil Wayne on there."

— *Oregon running back and Heisman finalist LaMichael James criticizing coach Chip Kelly's musical selection during team practices.*

Gene Chizik is going to use this as bulletin board material somehow

"I always get bothered when I hear other coaches say: 'We're here 24/7. We really grind.' I mean, c'mon. We choose to do this. We sit in air-conditioned rooms. We watch film. We enjoy watching film and coming up with game plans. Someone who has to grind it out is a guy who's a laborer, or a guy in the military."

— *Oregon coach Chip Kelly on the perceived intensity of being a head coach of a football team.*

It's gotten so bad that he's starting to sign his name as 'Jeff Sunday'

"Is that when it was? Good gracious. I can't really remember, but I get hit in the head a lot."

— *Colts center Jeff Saturday when told that the last time the Colts faced a must-win regular season game was in 2000. The Colts defeated the Titans to improve their record to 7-6.*

Oppressed so hard he wasn't in shape, let my people go

"I guess in this world we don't have a lot of people with, like, backbones. Just because somebody pay you money don't mean they'll make you do whatever they want or whatever. I mean, does that mean everything is for sale? I mean, I'm not for sale. Yeah, I signed the contract and got paid a lot of money, but ... that don't mean I'm for sale or a slave or whatever."

— *Washington defensive tackle Albert Haynesworth on the intricacies of the signee/signer relationship.*

After all this talk about numbers, Albert's headed to In-N-Out Burger for a 4x4

"He wasn't happy this year with the 3-4. He wasn't happy last year with the 4-3. What else do you want to do? Want to run a 2-5?"

— *Redskins defensive coordinator Jim Haslett showing his frustration with the actions of defensive tackle Albert Haynesworth who was suspended by the team.*

They say depth perception is one of the first things to go

"Did I expect to run for the first down? I hadn't expected to run for a first down in quite a while. ... It was

10 yards, really? It felt like 50."

— *Vikings quarterback Brett Favre after his team's 17-13 win over the Redskins. His 10-yard scramble on third-and-8 late in the fourth quarter helped seal the victory.*

What's that? Ah — bowl game? Don't talk about — bowl game? You kidding me? Bowl game?

"The bowl game thing, and I told [the players], you know everyone wants to bring up the bowl game, and it's not that I don't want to talk about the bowl game. It's like maybe that's what they were thinking about last week is the bowl game. I don't want to think about the bowl game. They're grown men you don't think I don't think they don't think about the bowl game?"

— *University of Illinois coach Ron Zook, when asked about the 5-5 Fighting Illini's chance at gaining bowl eligibility after his team blew a late lead in a 38-34 loss to the University of Minnesota.*

Channing Crowder: Uneducated pimp

"Le'Ron McClain spit in my face. That's some real ho s—, so if you talk to him tell him he's a ho. If he ever comes to Miami, he's got to see me."

"Then they said something about they let Karlos Dansby get away with a facemask the play before. Who the f— cares? A guy just spit in my face! I don't give a damn about Karlos pulling somebody's facemask. Like they didn't see Chad Henne get hit twice when he slid. Yeah, a little Stevie Wonder and Anne Frank."

— *Dolphins linebacker Channing Crowder expressing his frustration at Ravens fullback Le'Ron McClain for allegedly spitting on him.*

"Who was that? Is that the blind girl? Helen Keller ... I don't know who the f— Anne Frank is. I'm mad right now. F— it. I'm not as swift as I usually am."

— *Crowder, when asked what he meant by the Anne Frank reference*

Mmm... Fertilizer

"I have a little tradition that humbles me as a man, that lets me know that I'm a part of the field and part of the game. You should have seen some games before this. I can tell you one thing: The grass in Tiger Stadium tastes best."

— *LSU coach Les Miles after CBS cameras caught him eating some blades of grass during his LSU Tigers' victory over Alabama on Saturday.*

Apparently he's more of a seafood person

"We had the whole buffet set up, and we had a nice spread — chicken, ribs, round of beef with a carving station, the whole deal. [Moss], he comes in, and I'm helping one of the guys and didn't look up, and all of a sudden I heard, 'What the [expletive] is this? I wouldn't feed this [expletive expletive] to my [expletive] dog!' And he's screaming it at the top of his lungs."

— *Tinucci's co-owner Gus Tinucci on ex-Vikings wide receiver Randy Moss' reaction when he saw the buffet spread Tinucci's had set up for Vikings players October 29 after practice.*

I just choked on the pizza rolls I was eating in my mom's basement

"Stats are for losers, so you keep looking at stats and we'll keep looking at wins. I mean, you are what your record says you are in this league, and right now we're tied for the fewest losses [in the NFC], so that makes us the best team."

— *Buccaneers coach Raheem Morris defending his claim that Tampa Bay was the best team in the NFC despite a reporter pointing out to him that the Buccaneers ranked 23rd in the league in total offense and 22nd in the league in total defense.*

Freddie Mitchell disproves this theorem

"I like the comment, 'diva receivers.' That means you're very successful. I look at all the divas, whether it's Beyonce or Mariah Carey, those women are very successful. So, someone calls me a 'diva,' that means I'm successful. So, I'll take that and run with it."

— *Dolphins wide receiver Brandon Marshall's thoughts on being labeled a diva in anticipation of the Dolphins matchup with the Bengals and their two divas at wide receiver, Chad Ochocinco and Terrell Owens.*

For the money he's making, Porter should be comparing himself to the Angus Deluxe Burger

"It's like McDonald's. You know what the Big Mac tastes like every time. It's the same with me. You know what you're going to get from me every time."

— *Cardinals linebacker Joey Porter on why people shouldn't fret over his lack of sacks early in the season.*

Sounds like the formula for DVOA

"You're not going in and saying, 'When I take this 20-yard drop, the receiver runs this 15-yard dig, I've got to calculate my steps so I don't hit them in the head, so three by the square root of 25 and OK, this hit is going to hit him in the stomach. No, you can't do that. You have to try and be careful, and that's tough."

— *Cardinals safety Kerry Rhodes commenting on the difficulty for defenders of avoiding helmet-to-helmet hits.*

Next thing you know Justin Beiber will be sporting a Terrell Suggs jersey

"He was trying to tell me how to bag a Hollywood actress. He said, 'If you want to get a Hollywood actress, take my seminar on Saturday.' He was going over the Dow and the economy and politics. He doesn't really talk football that much."

— *Ravens linebacker Terrell Suggs' recollection of what was said in a heated shouting match between he and Patriots quarterback Tom Brady after Brady complained about a non-call.*

It's like choosing between Pat's and Geno's

"This is a beautiful thing. When you're sitting here as a chubby head coach in the National Football League, and you have two good quarterbacks, you're a happy guy. That's a positive thing."

— *Eagles coach Andy Reid on whether the play of quarterback Kevin Kolb would make it difficult to go back to Michael Vick as the starter.*

Back then, Marshawn just wasn't jacked and pumped enough

"Straight up, I couldn't stand him. He was one of the only coaches you would see running up and down the field like he was playing in the game. Running up, jumping and high-fiving with his players. They over there dogging us and you just sit there watching them have all this fun like, 'Man, what is he doing? Run me to that sideline so I can hit him one time.'"

— *Seahawks running back Marshawn Lynch on his*

new coach Pete Carroll, back when Lynch's Cal Bears would take on Carroll's USC Trojans.

In this analogy I'm sure Detroit wasn't the one picking up the check

"[It's] like a blind date — she's not pretty but the personality was fine. Like any ugly dates with great personalities, it was fine, took her out, had some food, but you dumped her. So, we're gonna dump this one off and work on the next date. Try to get a cute one."

— *Packers linebacker Nick Barnett on the Packers unsightly 28-26 win over the Lions.*

That's essentially what Chris Bosh did

"I actually called down to Miami and talked to D-Wade and LeBron to see if they needed any help down there."

— *Jets fullback Tony Richardson on what he did after learning he was cut by the Jets. Richardson was back with the team 48 hours later.*

You know that John Madden doesn't actually do the ratings, right?

"They got me terrible on Madden, man. I wanna tell Madden that too. You know what's crazy? When I had my little shoulder problem [in 2008], I was 93, 94 speed on Madden. After my shoulder, I came back at about 88. What's my shoulder got to do with my feet? I know I ain't that slow. Madden trippin' on my speed, you know I'm not an 88. He got Fred [Taylor] and them faster than me. I know they ain't faster than me."

— *ex-Patriots running back Laurence Maroney on his speed rating in* Madden NFL 11.

A Macadamia nut might have worked better

"We bring the sweet portion to the game. So if you bring one lone chocolate chip, and place it in a single sugar cookie, how much would that chocolate chip stand out? Get my drift?"

— *Rams wide receiver Mardy Gilyard explaining why his nickname for fellow wide receiver Danny Amendola is White Chocolate while the rest of the receiving corps are sugar cookies.*

And at running back, John Wayne Gacy

"We were going to do the same thing without him coming back or not. But do I believe it? I don't even know if I care enough to believe it or not to be honest. It's his career; he's got to do what he's got to do. But it doesn't change nothing for us. We're going to have the same goal whether it's Tarvaris (Jackson), Jeffrey Dahmer or Norman Bates quarterbacking. We're still trying to do the same thing."

— *Packers linebacker Nick Barnett on whether he believed media reports of Brett Favre's "retirement."*

Michael Irvin is the man your man could smell like

"I remember when I was inducted into the Hall of Fame and they gave me my Hall of Fame yellow blazer. I wore it for two straight days. Finally my wife was in bed and said she wanted to make love but that I had to take the coat off. I refused and kept the blazer on because I wanted to perform like a Hall of Famer on the field and off."

— *Hall of Famer Michael Irvin recalling when he was inducted into the Hall of Fame.*

Political quote of the year

"We've become a nation of wusses. The Chinese are kicking our butt in everything. If this was in China, do you think the Chinese would have called off the game? People would have been marching down to the stadium, they would have walked and they would have been doing calculus on the way down."

— *Pennsylvania Gov. Ed Rendell, after the NFL postponed a Sunday night's Philadelphia Eagles-Minnesota Vikings game to a Tuesday because of snow. The Eagles went on to lose 24-14.*

Religious quote of the year

"I PRAISE YOU 24/7!!!!!! AND THIS HOW YOU DO ME!!!!! YOU EXPECT ME TO LEARN FROM THIS??? HOW???!!! ILL NEVER FORGET THIS!! EVER!!! THX THO ..."

— *Bills receiver Steve Johnson questioning His Holiness on his Twitter account following Buffalo's 19-16 loss. Johnson dropped the would-be game winning touchdown pass in overtime.*

Quote of the year

"They're probably four or five games away from being a 9-7 or a 10-6 team easily."

— *Bills linebacker Shawne Merriman's bright diagnosis of the 4-12 Buffalo Bills.*

Arizona Cardinals

2010 Record: 5-11

Pythagorean Wins: 4.4 (30th)

DVOA: -36.3% (32nd)

Offense: -31.4% (31st)

Defense: 8.2% (25th)

Special Teams: 3.3% (9th)

Variance: 23.5% (27th)

2011 Mean Projection: 6.4 wins

On the Clock (0-3): 7%

Loserville (4-6): 46%

Mediocrity (7-8): 33%

Playoff Contender (9-10): 13%

Super Bowl Contender (11+): 2%

Projected Average Opponent: -3.0% (28th)

2010: Arizona learns that quarterback is, in fact, a very important position.

2011: Here, Kevin Kolb, take the keys. You can drive the car now.

There is an old cliché that says "when you have two quarterbacks, you have none." The Arizona Cardinals learned last year that this aphorism applies best when you have three quarterbacks and their names are Max Hall, John Skelton, and Derek Anderson.

The mess at quarterback was the main reason why the Arizona Cardinals backslid after the most successful two-year run since the team's move to the desert in 1988. In the preseason, Ken Whisenhunt and his offensive staff gave up on the idea of Matt Leinart as heir apparent to Kurt Warner and went with Derek Anderson instead. Derek Anderson played pretty much how you would expect Derek Anderson to play, and the Cardinals spent the second half of the year shuffling Skelton, Hall, and even UFL refugee Richard Bartel in and out of the lineup

With such an obvious hole at the quarterback position, the Cardinals spent the lockout getting linked to every potentially available passer in the league. Eventually it became clear that Kevin Kolb was the Cardinals' first choice. Once the lockout was lifted, Arizona sent Philadelphia Dominique Rodgers-Cromartie and a second-round pick in exchange for Kolb. The general consensus around the league was that this was fair compensation for a starting-quality quarterback. The $63 million extension that came afterwards, however, raised some eyebrows.

Kevin Kolb was handed the starting job in Philadelphia last season after just two career starts. He really struggled in his first start against Green Bay before leaving with a concussion and being replaced by Mike Vick. Vick never looked back and won the starting quarterback job, and a ton of fantasy leagues, with brilliant play. Kolb saw some action while Vick was injured, looking great in a win against Atlanta but uninspiring in a loss to Tennessee. Overall, Kolb's numbers for 2010 featured as many interceptions as touchdowns. That had a lot of people puzzled by the Cardinals' urgency to lock Kolb in long term. But if you look closer, the difference between Vick and Kolb was far smaller than you might expect.

A look at Kolb's traditional statistics makes that hard to believe, but there's a mitigating factor. Kolb played in Week 17 against the Cowboys, but he wasn't joined by LeSean McCoy, DeSean Jackson, Jeremy Maclin, or left tackle Jason Peters. Peters was replaced by undrafted free agent Austin Howard, whose first NFL start was marked by a matchup against DeMarcus Ware. In other news, Ware came from behind to win the sack title in Week 17. Furthermore, while Kolb threw three interceptions in the game, two of them were on Hail Mary passes. Another two of Kolb's interceptions earlier in the year also came on Hail Mary passes, a total of four for the season. Vick didn't throw an interception on a Hail Mary all year.

If we remove that Week 17 game from the data set,

2011 Cardinals Schedule

Week	Opp.	Week	Opp.	Week	Opp.
1	CAR	7	PIT	13	DAL
2	at WAS	8	at BAL	14	SF
3	at SEA	9	STL	15	CLE
4	NYG	10	at PHI	16	at CIN
5	at MIN	11	at SF	17	SEA
6	BYE	12	at STL		

Table 1: Vick vs. Kolb (without Week 17)

QB	Off. DVOA	Team Pass DVOA	Team Rush DVOA
Michael Vick	28.9%	30.8%	40.9%
Kevin Kolb	16.9%	26.3%	10.1%

the passing DVOA posted by Kolb and Vick amounts to a wash (Table 1). Instead, the reason why the Eagles offense was more productive with Vick under center was because of Vick's impact on the running game, which is discussed further in the Philadelphia chapter.

There are a variety of reasons why Kolb's performance was undervalued in 2010, even beyond the Hail Mary interceptions. He played a tougher schedule than Vick, who had five games against teams ranked in the bottom seven in pass defense. And while Vick was unquestionably the superior runner, he was sacked on 7.7 percent of his dropbacks, while Kolb's sack rate was at 5.9 percent.

The one other hidden factor aiding Vick's performance was the presence of DeSean Jackson, arguably the Eagles' best receiver. Jackson missed nearly two full games with Kolb under center, thanks to a concussion suffered during Kolb's start against the Falcons. If we split out each receiver's performance under both Vick and Kolb, it's clear to see that the biggest difference between the passing performance of the two quarterbacks is the play and presence of Jackson (Table 2). There's still a risk in paying big money for a quarterback who has yet to start an entire season. But when you look at Kolb's 2010 in that context, it makes much more sense for Cardinals to want to lock him down for the near future.

If Kolb is going to earn that contract, he's going to have to establish an immediate connection to the team's best player and emotional leader, Larry Fitzgerald. Fitzgerald struggled to find a rhythm with any of his quarterbacks last season and had a down year as a result. He had his fewest number of catches and touchdowns since an in injury-riddled 2006, despite having almost 20 more targets than he's had in any of the previous three years. The Cardinals have to hope that it was the loss of a capable starting quarterback that resulted in Fitz's decline, and not the loss of a viable No. 2 receiver like Anquan Boldin.

The Cardinals had hoped Steve Breaston could transition from highly effective slot receiver to a dynamic threat on the outside, opposite of Fitzgerald. He had a reasonable year given the mess at quarterback, but the Cardinals decided not to get into a free-agent bidding war for his services, and he's now gone to Kansas City. That leaves the Cardinals with a bunch of unproven options. The two favorites to take the job are Early Doucet and Andre Roberts. Doucet's career has been a mixture of injuries and disappointments. The LSU product has missed 22 games in the last three seasons, and had offseason hip surgery this year. Andre Roberts was a guy who coaches raved about all last season, but he showed very little in game situations. Roberts also has a skill set that projects better in the slot: He's a small, quick possession receiver with average downfield speed. Another option is newly-acquired Chansi Stuckey, who led the Browns in receptions last year but was still non-tendered. Whoever the Cardinals go with will see a lot of single coverage opposite Fitzgerald.

Quarterback wasn't the only offensive position to get a major overhaul. Both the tight end and running back positions will see change in 2011. Since Ken

Table 2: Where Kolb's Eyes Don't Go

Receiver	Michael Vick at QB				Kevin Kolb at QB			
	Targets	DVOA	Yds/Tgt	Catch Rate	Targets	DVOA	Yds/Tgt	Catch Rate
DeSean Jackson	82	7.8%	12.0	51%	14	-35.4%	5.1	36%
Jeremy Maclin	82	20.1%	8.5	61%	35	9.0%	9.3	62%
Jason Avant	52	6.2%	7.5	65%	18	26.4%	9.0	89%
Brent Celek	52	-3.5%	7.4	58%	28	-21.7%	4.6	43%
LeSean McCoy	61	17.0%	6.3	85%	29	26.3%	6.6	90%

Whisenhunt has arrived in Arizona the tight ends have been described using words like "mediocre," "nondescript," and "wait, you mean the Cardinals have tight ends on the roster?" That changes with the arrival of local boy-made-good Todd Heap, who has both name recognition as an Arizona State legend and a proven track record of being a useful receiver. His 599 receiving yards in just 13 games last season was triple the total of all three Cardinals tight ends combined. Arizona is hoping that the presence of Heap can take some pressure off of both Kolb and Larry Fitzgerald as well. Last year the Cardinals only used a tight end on 64 percent of their offensive plays, by far the lowest rate in the league. The addition of Heap, along with blocking specialist Jeff King and third-round pick Rob Housler, figures to change that.

The Cardinals drafted Virginia Tech running back Ryan Williams in the second round of this year's draft and created a bit of a logjam in the backfield. To deal with it, they shipped their leading rusher of the past three years, Tim Hightower, to Washington. Williams will team with former first-rounder Beanie Wells to provide Arizona with a highly-drafted one-two punch — but it won't necessarily be a highly-efficient one-two punch. Wells was brutal last year by any measurement. He averaged less than 3.5 yards a carry. He only caught five passes. He had one more touchdown than he had fumbles. And on top of all that, he was generally poor in pass protection. With Hightower no longer in front of him, and just a rookie and a situational back (LaRod Stephens-Howling) behind him, Wells will get plenty of opportunity this season. In fact it is safe to say that 2011 will be the make-or-break season of Beanie Wells' career in Arizona.

The Cardinals' biggest offseason moves were on offense, but they made some quietly savvy moves on the defensive side as well. A decline on defense, from 11th in DVOA in 2009 to 25th in 2010, was a quiet contributor to last year's collapse. The first thing the Cardinals did to rectify the situation was draft LSU's Patrick Peterson fifth overall. Peterson was considered by many to be the best overall player to come out of the college ranks this season. He'll be expected to come in and start immediately in place of the departing Rodgers-Cromartie. The good news for Peterson is that Cardinals brought in Ray Horton to be the new defensive coordinator. Horton was the defensive backs coach for the Steelers and had a lot of success turning corners with nowhere near Peterson's pedigree into very good pros.

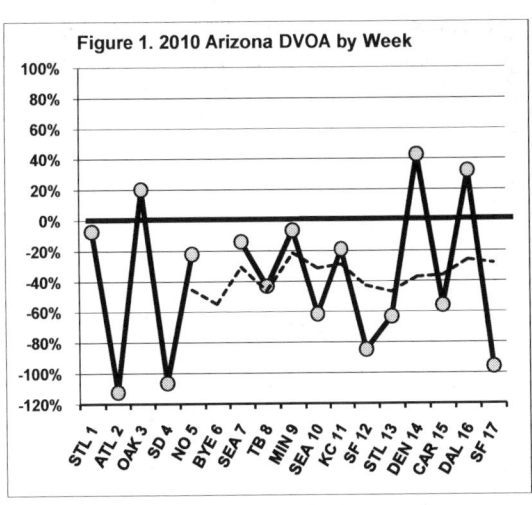

Figure 1. 2010 Arizona DVOA by Week

Arizona's linebacker corps was probably the weakest unit on the defense last year. Arizona struggled to stop the run (30th in DVOA), and the linebackers were a big part of that. Enter Stewart Bradley, a run-stuffing Mike linebacker from the Philadelphia Eagles. Bradley isn't an athletic marvel, especially after a 2009 knee injury, but he is a physical presence between the tackles. The other problem Arizona had was the lack of a pass rush from its outside linebackers. The hope is that fourth-round pick Sam Acho can spell Joey Porter and allow the Cardinals to use the veteran pass-rusher similar to the way Atlanta uses John Abraham — meaning Porter won't play as many snaps, but he will be fresher and in better situations when he is on the field.

It's clear that the Cardinals think they can win the NFC West this season. The team is certainly built to win now. Other teams in the division (most notably Seattle) seem to be getting younger while Arizona is keeping its core group and trying to build around it. Most key players are either in their prime (Darnell Dockett, Larry Fitzgerald, Lyle Sendlein, and Kevin Kolb), or a little past it (Adrian Wilson, Joey Porter, Kerry Rhodes, Paris Lenon). One clear sign that Arizona thinks it can win now is the fact that they decided to keep their offensive line largely intact. With the exception of a retiring Alan Faneca, the Cardinals kept a below average line that has experience playing together, rather than trying to rebuild the line with younger parts. The NFC West is a weak division once again this year, and the Cardinals are certainly trying to take advantage of that.

Ben Muth

2010 Cardinals Stats by Week

Wk	vs.	W-L	PF	PA	YDF	YDA	TO	Total	Off	Def	ST
1	@STL	W	17	13	378	325	0	-7%	-10%	-11%	-8%
2	@ATL	L	7	41	267	444	-2	-112%	-49%	49%	-14%
3	OAK	W	24	23	227	364	-2	20%	-2%	-10%	12%
4	@SD	L	10	41	134	419	-2	-106%	-59%	46%	-2%
5	NO	W	30	20	194	358	3	-22%	-64%	-27%	15%
6	BYE										
7	@SEA	L	10	22	227	302	-4	-14%	-33%	-17%	1%
8	TB	L	35	38	396	407	-2	-43%	-27%	21%	5%
9	@MIN	L	24	27	225	507	2	-7%	-12%	21%	26%
10	SEA	L	18	36	327	490	-1	-62%	-38%	23%	-1%
11	@KC	L	13	31	382	352	0	-19%	7%	28%	2%
12	SF	L	6	27	203	386	-1	-85%	-46%	34%	-5%
13	STL	L	6	19	224	288	-1	-63%	-57%	-2%	-8%
14	DEN	W	43	13	357	288	5	43%	-7%	-42%	8%
15	@CAR	L	12	19	218	303	-1	-56%	-43%	14%	1%
16	DAL	W	27	26	271	382	3	32%	4%	-10%	18%
17	@SF	L	7	38	279	362	-2	-96%	-66%	37%	7%

Trends and Splits

	Offense	Rank	Defense	Rank
Total DVOA	-31.4%	31	8.2%	25
Unadjusted VOA	-26.2%	31	4.3%	21
Weighted Trend	-31.2%	32	8.0%	24
Variance	6.3%	10	7.4%	22
Average Opponent	5.2%	9	-3.6%	5
Passing	-41.5%	32	11.1%	22
Rushing	-4.8%	22	5.3%	30
First Down	-20.3%	31	6.1%	19
Second Down	-32.5%	31	11.1%	24
Third Down	-50.9%	32	8.2%	22
First Half	-23.8%	32	7.6%	21
Second Half	-39.9%	31	8.8%	23
Red Zone	-58.9%	31	-20.9%	6
Late and Close	-33.3%	31	4.7%	25

Five-Year Performance

Year	W-L	Pyth	Est W	PF	PA	TO	Total	Rk	Off	Rk	Def	Rk	ST	Rk	Off AGL	Rk	Def AGL	Rk
2006	5-11	6.0	6.2	314	399	+3	-19.5%	28	-8.8%	25	5.7%	24	-5.0%	32	5.8	4	14.2	17
2007	8-8	8.1	6.3	404	399	-7	-11.6%	23	-2.7%	19	5.2%	20	-3.8%	26	26.0	25	37.2	28
2008	9-7	8.0	7.4	427	426	0	-3.2%	21	9.9%	15	9.4%	23	-3.7%	28	23.5	14	14.3	8
2009	10-6	9.3	10.1	381	325	-7	11.4%	13	10.1%	13	0.3%	11	1.6%	10	13.6	10	10.5	3
2010	5-11	4.4	3.7	289	434	-5	-36.3%	32	-31.4%	31	8.2%	25	3.3%	9	26.8	17	11.4	8

Strategic Tendencies

Run/Pass		Rank	Offense		Rank	Defense		Rank	Other		Rank
Runs, all plays	33%	32	3+ WR	60%	6	Rush 3	4.0%	24	2+ RB, Pct Runs	51%	26
Runs, first half	37%	26	4+ WR	31%	1	Rush 4	56.6%	20	1 RB/2 TE, Pct Runs	63%	1
Runs, first down	47%	22	2+ TE	21%	27	Rush 5	29.9%	6	1 RB/3+ WR, Pct Runs	15%	28
Runs, second-long	28%	27	Single back	60%	13	Rush 6+	9.5%	15	CB1 on WR1	47%	6
Runs, power sit.	44%	31	Play action	15%	27	Zone Blitz	3.1%	23	Go for it on 4th	0.81	21
Runs, behind 2H	21%	30	Max protect	8%	25	Sacks by LB	48.5%	14	Offensive Pace	30.2	12
Pass, ahead 2H	47%	8	Outside pocket	10%	25	Sacks by DB	12.1%	11	Defensive Pace	30.2	4

The Cardinals went without a tight end on 36 percent of offensive plays. No other offense was above 25 percent. This was actually a lower percentage than in 2009, when the Cardinals went without a tight end on 41 percent of plays. However, the Cardinals offense was even worse without a tight end (-33.2% DVOA) than it was with a tight end (-26.2% DVOA). ☞ The Cardinals were twice as likely to throw to Steve Breaston on third down compared to first or second down. ☞ With two backs in the game, the Cardinals passed half the time, much more often than they did in 2009. ☞ The Cardinals were dead last with 3.7 average yards after the catch. ☞ For the second straight year, the Cardinals had the league's lowest DVOA on running back screen passes (-109.0%). Arizona gained only 2.4 yards per pass on these plays, 3.5 yards below the NFL average. ☞ Arizona opponents threw only 12 percent of passes to the "short middle" area, the lowest rate in the league.

Passing

Player	DYAR	DVOA	Plays	NtYds	Avg	YAC	C%	TD	Int
D.Anderson	-150	-18.1%	356	1973	5.5	4.0	51.8%	7	10
J.Skelton	-295	-46.9%	135	568	4.2	3.3	48.0%	2	2
M.Hall	-512	-99.1%	92	277	3.0	3.7	50.0%	1	6
R.Bartel	-91	-49.7%	30	138	4.6	2.4	57.1%	0	1

Rushing

Player	DYAR	DVOA	Plays	Yds	Avg	TD	Fum	Suc
T.Hightower	46	-1.0%	153	747	4.9	5	4	42%
C.Wells	-25	-13.8%	116	397	3.4	2	1	45%
L.Stephens-Howling	19	9.0%	24	118	4.9	1	0	54%
J.Skelton	11	18.4%	7	49	7.0	0	0	–
J.Wright	12	31.9%	6	28	4.7	0	0	50%
D.Anderson	1	-9.4%	5	25	5.0	0	1	–

Receiving

Player	DYAR	DVOA	Plays	Ctch	Yds	Y/C	YAC	TD	C%
L.Fitzgerald	-3	-12.9%	172	90	1137	12.6	2.4	6	52%
S.Breaston	78	-0.7%	87	47	718	15.3	3.4	1	54%
E.Doucet	-122	-40.0%	59	26	291	11.2	3.1	1	44%
A.Roberts	-102	-39.7%	49	24	307	12.8	5.8	2	49%
S.Williams	-26	-26.1%	23	9	101	11.2	4.2	0	39%
M.Komar	-44	-38.3%	22	12	117	9.8	2.8	0	55%
B.Patrick	-7	-13.6%	18	15	123	8.2	3.5	0	83%
S.Spach	-55	-57.0%	17	7	40	5.7	2.9	0	41%
J.Dray	-12	-27.9%	9	3	47	15.7	6.7	0	33%
T.Hightower	-105	-57.9%	42	21	136	6.5	6.5	0	50%
L.Stephens-Howling	18	0.2%	22	15	106	7.1	5.7	0	68%
J.Wright	-30	-46.5%	16	8	42	5.3	4.9	0	50%
C.Wells	25	35.7%	8	5	74	14.8	5.4	0	63%
R.Maui'a	-5	-27.1%	6	2	20	10.0	9.5	0	33%

Offensive Line

Year	Yards	ALY	Rank	Power	Rank	Stuff	Rank	2nd Lev	Rank	Open Field	Rank
2008	3.60	3.68	30	58%	29	20%	26	1.04	24	0.55	29
2009	4.27	4.09	16	56%	28	23%	30	1.36	2	0.81	14
2010	4.31	3.84	21	74%	5	21%	22	1.20	11	1.00	7

Year	LE	Rank	LT	Rank	Mid	Rank	RT	Rank	RE	Rank	Sacks	ASR	Rank	F-Start	Cont.
2008	4.14	19	3.67	26	3.28	31	4.22	16	4.22	10	28	4.4%	8	16	48
2009	5.47	2	3.81	22	3.94	24	4.27	9	3.72	24	26	5.2%	7	17	39
2010	5.18	2	2.84	31	3.68	25	4.41	7	3.84	19	50	8.4%	27	14	39

The Cardinals made a bunch of big moves on the offensive line in the 2010 offseason. They signed Alan Faneca, moved Levi Brown to left tackle (which opened up the right tackle slot for Brandon Keith), and benched perennially out-of-shape Deuce Lutui. None of these moves worked. Reggie Wells wasn't good enough in the preseason, and Lutui ended up winning his job back anyway. Faneca continued the decline that started in New York and retired in the offseason. Keith was in over his head from the start, a fact that was abundantly clear in a Week 4 matchup against the San Diego Chargers and Shaun Phillips, and benched in favor of the more effective Jeremy Bridges in the middle of the season. Brown's shift to left side was a total disaster, and he had 12.5 blown blocks leading to sacks or holding penalties: second in the league, one of only two players with more than ten.

Despite the problems on last year's line, the Cardinals will go to war with most of the same soldiers in 2011. Lutui was ready to leave in free agency but was too heavy to pass a physical for the Bengals (the team that drafted Andre Smith and his DD man boobs sixth overall). So, Lutui had to return to the Cardinals. Opposite of Lutui, Russ Grimm will turn to free-agent signing Daryn Colledge (ex-Packers) at left guard. Bringing in Colledge along with the re-signing of Lyle Sendlein bolsters the interior line, which was already strong last year in short-yardage situations The outside of the offensive line remains a point of weakness.

Defensive Front Seven

Defensive Line	Age	Pos	Plays	TmPct	Overall Rk	Stop	Dfts	BTkl	St%	Rk	AvYd	Rk	Pass Rush Sack	Hit	Hur	vs. Run Runs	St%	Yds	vs. Pass Pass	St%	Yds
Calais Campbell	25	DE	62	7.4%	16	50	19	4	78%	30	1.2	26	6	2	8	51	78%	2.0	11	91%	-2.4
Darnell Dockett	30	DE	52	6.2%	27	41	16	3	80%	38	2.2	46	5	10	17	40	80%	1.9	12	75%	3.0
Dan Williams	24	DT	40	4.8%	31	30	4	0	74%	38	2.3	41	0	0	0	35	74%	2.2	5	80%	2.4
Alan Branch	27	DE	35	3.9%	62	31	10	0	90%	5	1.4	31	2	6	5.5	30	90%	1.7	5	80%	-0.6
Bryan Robinson	37	DT	20	2.2%	68	14	2	0	72%	50	2.6	55	0	0	0	18	72%	2.1	2	50%	7.0

Linebackers	Age	Pos	Plays	TmPct	Overall Rk	Stop	Dfts	BTkl	AvYd	Pass Rush Sack	Hit	Hur	vs. Run Runs	St%	Rk	Yds	Rk	vs. Pass Tgts	Suc%	Rk	AdjYd	Rk
Paris Lenon	34	ILB	131	14.7%	20	85	25	14	4.4	2	1	4	86	66%	63	3.7	72	39	62%	18	7.4	63
Daryl Washington	23	ILB	77	8.6%	70	44	14	4	5.3	1	1	3	51	59%	86	5.3	108	24	74%	2	2.1	1
Joey Porter	34	OLB	49	6.3%	100	36	15	5	3.7	5	9	14.5	33	73%	33	3.6	69	9	68%	--	3.2	--
Clark Haggans	34	OLB	48	6.6%	95	32	7	5	3.4	5	1	11	31	74%	24	3.9	88	8	59%	--	2.7	--
Gerald Hayes	31	ILB	34	10.2%	--	19	4	5	5.8	0	0	0.5	25	68%	--	3.3	--	9	19%	--	13.4	--

Year	Yards	ALY	Rank	Power	Rank	Stuff	Rank	2nd Lev	Rank	Open Field	Rank
2008	3.94	4.16	16	70%	24	17%	22	1.09	13	0.52	7
2009	4.72	3.95	11	61%	10	23%	8	1.26	27	1.31	32
2010	4.60	4.28	23	63%	17	20%	15	1.32	29	1.01	28

Year	LE	Rank	LT	Rank	Mid	Rank	RT	Rank	RE	Rank	Sacks	ASR	Rank
2008	4.91	27	4.02	12	4.61	29	2.76	1	4.15	20	31	5.4%	23
2009	4.29	17	4.41	22	3.91	14	3.27	3	4.09	18	43	7.1%	10
2010	4.84	26	4.52	24	3.98	18	4.49	22	4.67	28	33	6.0%	19

Arizona's defensive ends were a rare bright spot in an otherwise bleak season. Darnell Dockett has proven himself as an impact player on the defensive line, and probably the best defensive player on the team. While he only had five sacks, he added 10 hits and 17 hurries to that total. Dockett's value isn't based solely on his own numbers either. His ability to tie up blockers and command double-teams make things easier for his teammates. Opposing offensive lines' tendency to slide towards Dockett helped Calais Campbell lead the Redbirds in sacks in 2010.

Dan Williams was seen as a steal when he fell to the 26th pick in the 2010 draft. Williams struggled early in the year, especially against the double-teams that are common for a nose tackle. But as the season went along, Williams improved dramatically in the run game, rarely giving any ground against drive blocks. He'll never be an every-down player due to his lack of pass rushing ability, but he certainly showed enough promise as the year went along to warrant a secure spot in this year's starting lineup.

The linebackers are simply old. Daryl Washington was the only contributor under the age of 30. Joey Porter is the most recognizable name of the group, but is showing the signs of age. His sack numbers have gone down each of the last two years. Ken Whisenhunt has talked about limiting his snaps this season in hopes that it was fatigue and not age that dulled the quick twitch muscles in Porter's body. Fourth-round draft pick Sam Acho (Texas) may be called upon to give Porter a breather. It should be interesting to see where Porter's rest comes — on first and second downs, or third downs. Paris Lenon is another 34-year-old linebacker, but has a skill set that has aged far better. Never an ace in pass coverage, Lenon's ability to make plays between the tackles in the running game has remained. Lenon and newly-signed Stewart Bradley, brought over from the Eagles, should combine to form a nice run stopping duo in the middle of the Cardinals 3-4 defense.

Defensive Secondary

Secondary	Age	Pos	Plays	TmPct	Rk	Stop	Dfts	BTkl	Runs	St%	Rk	Yds	Rk	Tgts	Tgt%	Rk	Dist	Suc%	Rk	APaYd	Rk	PD	Int
			Overall						vs. Run					vs. Pass									
Kerry Rhodes	29	FS	101	11.3%	22	32	15	11	50	26%	74	11.0	77	25	5.1%	59	11.7	62%	18	5.7	11	7	0
Greg Toler	26	CB	96	12.3%	7	38	11	8	32	59%	17	5.8	28	89	20.9%	6	13.9	45%	75	7.9	57	8	0
Adrian Wilson	32	SS	96	10.8%	27	53	17	16	52	62%	5	4.2	5	43	8.8%	8	10.7	50%	52	9.0	58	5	0
D. Rodgers-Cromartie	25	CB	61	6.8%	70	25	8	10	7	29%	77	13.7	88	90	18.6%	13	12.1	49%	55	8.3	63	17	3
Mike Adams	26	CB	52	5.8%	80	27	13	3	15	40%	50	9.4	71	54	11.1%	77	8.3	56%	21	7.8	53	7	2
Rashad Johnson	25	FS	38	4.3%	79	10	8	4	11	27%	71	7.2	48	15	3.0%	--	12.0	53%	--	6.6	--	5	1

Year	Pass D Rank	vs. #1 WR	Rk	vs. #2 WR	Rk	vs. Other WR	Rk	vs. TE	Rk	vs. RB	Rk
2008	23	19.8%	27	-0.8%	15	16.7%	27	14.6%	22	1.6%	13
2009	12	19.7%	25	-26.4%	2	-14.1%	9	-3.2%	11	0.5%	17
2010	22	25.0%	28	10.3%	21	-9.3%	12	-6.4%	7	-6.9%	8

The backend of the secondary is home to two of the biggest names on the team, Adrian Wilson and Kerry Rhodes. The problem is their names seem to be bigger than their games at this point in their careers. Wilson in particular had a down year; his high-volume tackling numbers hide the fact that he simply isn't nearly as active or menacing as he has been in the past — particularly against the pass, where he had just six passes defensed and two picks. He has been used like a linebacker more and more as his career has progressed, and is in danger of falling into Roy Williams-with-the-Cowboys territory. The problem is that while Wilson continues to take risks to try and make game-changing plays, he is making those plays less often. He was second in the league in missed tackles by our count, behind only Michael Griffin of Tennessee. Rhodes had a better record than Wilson against the pass, but also had trouble with missed tackles.

The Cardinals have to hope that Patrick Peterson can help replace Dominique Rodgers-Cromartie immediately. Known as a lockdown cover corner in college, Peterson also drew raves for his ability to use his hands at the line of scrimmage to jam receivers. If Peterson makes the kind of impact that is expected, it may take the pressure off of the rest of the secondary, and allow them to take fewer chances. The Cardinals haven't really had an elite corner since Aeneas Williams in the late '90s. Richard Marshall, a free-agent addition from Carolina, will start opposite Peterson. He had an extremely poor Adjusted Success Rate of 41 percent last year but was much better in 2009.

Special Teams

Year	DVOA	Rank	FG/XP	Rank	Net Kick	Rank	Kick Ret	Rank	Net Punt	Rank	Punt Ret	Rank	Hidden	Rank
2008	-3.7%	28	2.1	13	-9.1	29	-1.8	19	-6.5	25	-6.5	28	4.0	8
2009	1.6%	10	4.6	8	-0.6	18	0.2	11	10.7	4	-5.2	24	3.1	8
2010	3.3%	9	9.1	2	7.3	8	13.8	4	0.7	17	-11.5	32	9.0	3

The Cardinals were good on special teams last year largely thanks to two standout players. Jay Feely had a strong year on both kickoffs and field goals. His standout game came against the Broncos in Week 14, as he went five-for-five on field goals and even added a rushing touchdown for the best fantasy football day a kicker had all year. The other standout was LaRod Stephens-Howling at kick returner. He led the league in return yards despite missing three games, and managed to find the end zone twice. Andre Roberts was poor on punt returns, but that job will now go to first-round pick Peterson, who was well-regarded as a punt returner at LSU. Ben Graham returns as punter.

Coaching Staff

The Cardinals defensive staff saw a major change this offseason when Bill Davis was fired and Ray Horton was brought in. The Dick LeBeau protégé comes over to Arizona after spending three years as the Steelers secondary coach. Horton plans to keep the 3-4 scheme that Davis ran intact. The hope in Arizona seems to be that he can revitalize Adrian Wilson's career, and turn him back into a Troy Polamalu-type playmaker. The offensive staff will remain the exact same as it was in 2010. Ken Whisenhunt will still call the plays with heavy input from Russ Grimm on the ground game. Chris Miller will return to coach the quarterbacks after an offseason flirtation with the University of Southern Oregon. The offensive staff has been successful when they have had the right quarterback under center. The question for Arizona is whether Kevin Kolb is the right quarterback.

Atlanta Falcons

2010 Record: 13-3	**2011 Mean Projection:** 9.7 wins
Pythagorean Wins: 11.2 (4th)	**On the Clock (0-3):** 0%
DVOA: 14.9% (8th)	**Loserville (4-6):** 8%
Offense: 10.8% (10th)	**Mediocrity (7-8):** 21%
Defense: 1.2% (12th)	**Playoff Contender (9-10):** 35%
Special Teams: 5.4% (2nd)	**Super Bowl Contender (11+):** 36%
Variance: 5.2% (2nd)	**Projected Average Opponent:** -1.6% (24th)

2010: Four months of fantasy football implodes in a sixty-minute playoff nightmare.

2011: Leaner, faster, and in the title hunt again.

The defining moment of the Atlanta Falcons' 2010 regular season was All-Pro wide receiver Roddy White running down and stripping San Francisco's Nate Clements. The Niners corner had just picked off Matt Ryan with 90 seconds to play, seemingly icing a 14-13 victory. But White's non-stop hustle gave the Falcons new life, and Atlanta drove to a winning field goal with two seconds left. It was a play emblematic of a 13-3 season and a number one seed in the NFC.

Unfortunately, the defining moment of the 2010 postseason, and thus the one that sticks in the minds of fans, is Green Bay's Tramon Williams jumping a quick out and returning it for a pick-six as time expired in the first half of the Packers-Falcons divisional playoff game. This time, neither White nor any of his teammates were able to catch up to (never mind strip) Williams. It was the play that effectively ended the competitive portion of what wound up a humiliating 48-21 beatdown by the eventual Super Bowl champs.

Since 1990, the 2008 Carolina Panthers are the only other team with a first-round bye to be defeated by 20 points or more in the Divisional round. That was the infamous Jake Delhomme six-turnover game, making Carolina's 33-13 loss to Arizona almost purely a self-inflicted wound. By contrast, Green Bay comprehensively whacked Atlanta despite the fact the Falcons played relatively well for most of the first half (they were only down by seven when Williams sucked the air from the Georgia Dome).

Atlanta started that evening as favorites, but few were shocked that they lost to a red-hot Packers team led by Aaron Rodgers. Getting buried by four touchdowns at home, however, was cause to rethink not only the entire season, but the very nature of the ball club and its fundamental underpinnings. Suddenly, the conservative, run-heavy offense seemed obsolete in the pass-first, -second and -third modern NFL. Meanwhile, the defense was far too slow and lacking in playmakers to realistically stop guided missile systems like Rodgers and the Packers offense.

That may seem like an overreaction to a single bad night of football, especially when the Packers went on to hoist the Lombardi Trophy. Yet the phrase "we need more explosive players" was uttered more often than "hot enough for ya?" at Falcons HQ in Flowery Branch this offseason. The team did indeed have a crying need on both sides of the ball for guys who could make a difference on the perimeter and in the open field, as the Pack exposed for all to see. The Falcons were seemingly playing Kezar Stadium football despite hosting home games indoors on a fast track.

As is GM Thomas Dimitroff's wont, he went and did something about it. Dimitroff built the Falcons through savvy drafting, but sensing that the time for patience was past, he exploded the draft and Todd McShay's mind by dealing five picks — including next year's

2011 Falcons Schedule

Week	Opp.	Week	Opp.	Week	Opp.
1	at CHI	7	at DET	13	at HOU
2	PHI	8	BYE	14	at CAR
3	at TB	9	at IND	15	JAC (Thu.)
4	at SEA	10	NO	16	at NO (Mon.)
5	GB	11	TEN	17	TB
6	CAR	12	MIN		

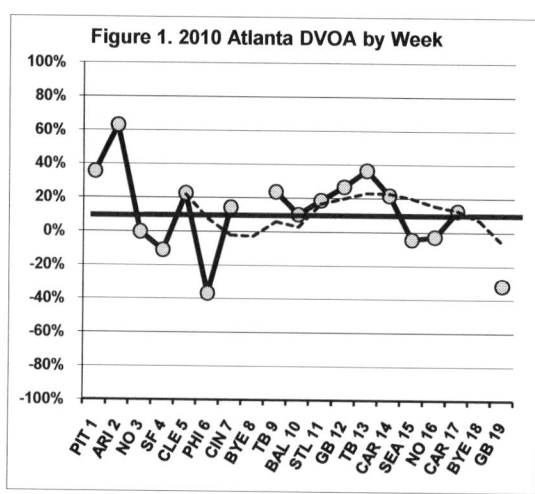

Figure 1. 2010 Atlanta DVOA by Week

first-round choice — to Cleveland in order to move up to the sixth spot and select Julio Jones, the coveted wideout from Alabama. It was a daring move for any team. By Falcons standards, it was Knievelesque.

Securing the ultra-athletic Jones was just the first move to increase the team's escape velocity. Oregon scatback Jacquizz Rodgers was selected in the fifth round. He will replace the oft-injured Jerious Norwood as the elusive element in the backfield. Ray Edwards, who had 16.5 sacks as part of the Vikings' elite front four over the last two seasons, was signed as a free agent. He will be asked to provide much-needed pass rush opposite the 33-year-old John Abraham. Meanwhile, the roster was trimmed of fat (Michael Jenkins, Jamaal Anderson) and the hope is that promising burners with lingering injury issues (Harry Douglas, William Moore, Sean Weatherspoon) will kick the Falcons out of the prelims and into the final heat of the NFL sprints.

While not coming out and saying so, the Falcons have apparently realized their ground-oriented offense paced by Michael Turner can only get them so far. The running attack fell off a cliff in the second half of last season (Table 1). After pounding away in their usual manner through eight games behind Turner and backup Jason Snelling, the Falcons had the league's worst rushing DVOA in the final eight games. The running backs' Success Rate dropped to a pitiful 41.4 percent. Falcons backs were stuffed on 21.2 percent of carries in the second half of the season. And there were but four runs of 20-plus yards in that stretch, one of which was a scramble by quarterback Matt Ryan.

In other words, by the time Green Bay came to At-

lanta in mid-January, the Falcons were positively awful at the one thing they were supposed to do best. Worse, there wasn't the expected compensation in the passing attack to punish defenses for stacking the box against Turner. White was the lone receiver capable of hurting defenses, and he attracted double coverage. Jenkins, Douglas, and tight end Tony Gonzalez were unable to consistently make plays that tilted the field. The three combined for fifteen 20-plus-yard receptions, as many as White had by himself.

Expecting a rookie to come in and change that imbalance by himself is asking a lot, but Jones certainly has the potential to make an immediate impact. His college career didn't have the wow factor that marked A.J. Green's time elsewhere in the SEC, but it was impressive enough, and his combine workout was insane. He has the speed to separate from defenders, the strength to hold position in routes, and the height (6-foot-3) to catch balls over them. At 220 pounds, his frame has room to add an additional 10 to 15 pounds of muscle under a professional strength regimen as well. An outstanding blocker who helped Mark Ingram and Trent Richardson run wild, Jones will likely bolster the running game as well.

On the other hand, there are concerns stemming from his college days. Jones was inconsistent in relation to his outsized talent, as anyone who watched the Crimson Tide regularly these last few years can attest. Jones caught only 17 of the 52 Alabama touchdown passes thrown during his time in Tuscaloosa, a primary reason his Playmaker Score is so much lower than those of this year's other wide receiver prospects. Jones also was lacking in yards per catch and yards per game. 'Bama's run-heavy offense is partly to blame,

Table 1. Atlanta's Rushing Offense, 2010

Weeks	Yd/At	Run DVOA	Rk	Success Rate	Rk
Weeks 1-8	4.37	3.4%	12	50.9%	8
Weeks 9-17	3.58	-17.5%	32	41.4%	29
Overall	3.99	-6.4%	26	46.3%	16

of course, as is the SEC itself, with its preponderance of high-level defensive linemen wreaking havoc on passing game plans. Jones' numbers went up when Nick Saban himself ordered his offensive coaches to get Jones the ball more often last season.

Whatever happens during his rookie season, Jones will get the benefit of the doubt from Atlanta fans (in part due to his SEC roots), despite the huge price the team paid to get him. Matt Ryan, on the other hand, gets cut far too little slack despite 33 wins in three years at the helm. Local talk radio would have you believe that the problem is that Ryan's shoulders aren't broad enough; he's simply too skinny to be a top-flight quarterback. One Atlanta host actually made this comment: "Matt's helmet just doesn't look right on top of that body."

Even by the standards of the country's collective "Fatso and the Coach" sports talk shows, that's a particularly idiotic notion. Ryan also wasn't helped when Michael Vick, who is still beloved by many Atlanta fans in spite of everything, started partying like it was 2002 for the Eagles. It should go without saying, however, that Falcons fans disinclined to ride with Ryan need to have their collective heads examined.

While Peregrine Nation unburdened its issues upon their puny passer, the erosion of the rush defense went completely unnoticed by these same critics. We already mentioned the running game collapsing in the second half — if anything, the run defense was even worse after the first two months. Atlanta's run defense ranked third in the NFL after eight games, but 31st from Weeks 9-to-17. It was an implosion as mysterious as it was epic. There was no significant injury, no radical position change, no obvious schedule strengthening to explain the fade, which was the second-largest in DVOA since 1992. If anything, the schedule got easier, at least in terms of rushing offenses faced. Certainly the poor play wasn't a result of defensive coordinator Brian Van Gorder losing his fiery passion. His invective could often be heard above the Georgia Dome din.

The good news is that second-half slides in run defense don't generally have much carryover to the next season (Table 2). Atlanta had the league's second-best run defense DVOA in 2009, so those last eight games are more likely a hiccup than a sustained gaseous emission. Certainly, if 2009 first-round draft choice Peria Jerry could stay healthy, he might give the front four the run-stuffing power he was selected to provide.

The general consensus in Georgia is that the defense remains far more vulnerable to the pass than to the run, thanks to the lack of pass rush and mediocrity of Dunta

Table 2. Biggest Second Half Rush Defense Collapses and Following Season Rush Defense DVOA, 1992-2010

Year	Team	Wks 1-9	Wks 10-17	Total	Dif.	Next Year
2008	MIA	-18.7%	19.9%	-0.6%	38.6%	5.0%
2010	ATL	-22.7%	15.2%	-4.1%	37.9%	--
2010	KC	-15.2%	21.5%	2.5%	36.7%	--
1999	NO	-13.2%	22.5%	2.7%	35.7%	2.9%
1999	PIT	-25.7%	7.7%	-8.5%	33.4%	-18.3%
1997	SD	-30.0%	1.0%	-13.0%	31.8%	-37.3%
2006	KC	-15.7%	14.3%	-0.8%	29.9%	-1.1%
1998	ARI	-13.3%	16.6%	1.4%	29.9%	2.1%
2009	DEN	-18.2%	11.6%	-1.5%	29.8%	5.2%
2001	BAL	-33.9%	-4.2%	-20.6	29.7%	-5.1%

Robinson in 2010. Brent Grimes was a pleasant surprise a year ago, but the Falcons don't exactly have an Eagles-style collection of corners. They do now have someone to worry the quarterback from the right side of the front four, however. Edwards should team with Abraham and Kroy Biermann to at least up the team's Adjusted Sack Rate from 23rd in the league.

Even without a difference-making pass rush, Atlanta managed to win most of its tight games in 2010, taking seven of nine games that were decided by a touchdown or less. Week after week, the Falcons made decisive plays in winning time. There was the aforementioned White strip of Clements to save the 49ers game. Biermann turned an exceptional pass deflection/diving interception/touchdown return trifecta to ice the game against the Browns the following week. And the Falcons stole a pair of games from Tampa Bay, thanks to a goal-line stand featuring a dramatic stop of LeGarrette Blount by Thomas DeCoud in early November, followed a month later by two late touchdowns, one on a long kickoff return, that effectively bounced the Bucs from the postseason.

Luck played a role as well. Atlanta bested New Orleans in the Superdome when Saints kicker Garrett Hartley botched a gimme field-goal attempt in overtime. White clearly pushed down his defender before catching a Ryan pass and scampering to the end zone in a dramatic win over Baltimore on national television. No call. Green Bay's Matt Wilhelm pulled down Eric Weems by his facemask during a final minute kick return to set up a game-winning field goal. (Indeed, the Falcons did beat the Packers last season, just not when it mattered most.) While the Falcons were good enough to take advantage of what fortune offered, just about everything broke Atlanta's way.

If those two paragraphs read like something you'd normally find in a post-championship recap under the headline "A Dream Season," that's the reason for relative disquiet in Atlanta. Such fortune isn't sustainable. The Falcons should have won 11.2 games under the Pythagorean Theorem last season, and used up a few seasons worth of magical moments in winning the top seed in the NFC. All it got them was a Rocky Marciano-level punch in the stomach come playoff time. Even with the improvements provided by Jones and Edwards, Atlanta isn't likely to reach 13 wins again, especially in the tough NFC South. Dates with the Packers, Bears, Eagles, Colts, and Texans also dot the schedule.

But even nagging doubts that the team overpaid for Jones, or that Turner is due to break down, or that the pass defense is chum for the league's rifle-armed mako sharks are overshadowed by the knowledge that the long-term health of the franchise is secure so long as Dimitroff and head coach Mike Smith are running the show.

Discipline and smarts have been Falcons trademarks since the duo took over the reins in 2008. That is reflected in a little-remarked upon key to the team's success in 2010: avoiding penalties. Atlanta was the least penalized team in the NFL by a wide margin. Only 71 flags were thrown at the feet of Falcons players, 14 fewer than the second-last penalized club, Indianapolis, and 43 and 44 fewer than division rivals New Orleans and Tampa Bay, respectively. Unlike missed field goals and causing interceptors to fumble the ball back to the offense, playing clean, crisp football does tend to carry over from season to season.

That's just one reason why the Falcons should be back in the postseason mix in 2011, regardless of how many of their hoped-upon explosive players turn out to be damp squibs. And if they manage to avoid a lava-hot quarterback in the playoffs, perhaps the team and its fans can accentuate the positive next summer.

Robert Weintraub

2010 Falcons Stats by Week

Wk	vs.	W-L	PF	PA	YDF	YDA	TO	Total	Off	Def	ST
1	@PIT	L	9	15	295	354	0	35%	18%	-14%	3%
2	ARI	W	41	7	444	267	2	63%	43%	-13%	7%
3	@NO	W	27	24	417	398	2	0%	21%	9%	-13%
4	SF	W	16	14	357	262	1	-11%	-22%	-12%	-1%
5	@CLE	W	20	10	338	269	2	23%	7%	-20%	-4%
6	@PHI	L	17	31	293	474	-1	-37%	-4%	19%	-13%
7	CIN	W	39	32	452	469	-1	14%	39%	38%	13%
8	BYE										
9	TB	W	27	21	365	278	2	24%	18%	-24%	-19%
10	BAL	W	26	21	362	320	2	10%	23%	26%	14%
11	@STL	W	34	17	391	304	1	19%	26%	22%	15%
12	GB	W	20	17	294	418	1	27%	11%	-3%	12%
13	@TB	W	28	24	290	325	-1	36%	3%	-12%	21%
14	@CAR	W	31	10	327	288	1	22%	25%	8%	5%
15	@SEA	W	34	18	266	234	2	-4%	-27%	-4%	19%
16	NO	L	14	17	215	368	0	-3%	-15%	-15%	-3%
17	CAR	W	31	10	352	291	1	13%	-6%	15%	34%
18	BYE										
19	GB	L	21	48	194	442	-3	-32%	-12%	42%	22%

Trends and Splits

	Offense	Rank	Defense	Rank
Total DVOA	10.8%	10	1.2%	12
Unadjusted VOA	10.0%	11	-0.6%	10
Weighted Trend	7.7%	13	4.2%	17
Variance	4.2%	3	3.5%	3
Average Opponent	1.0%	23	-1.4%	7
Passing	30.1%	8	5.0%	10
Rushing	-6.4%	26	-4.1%	13
First Down	-3.6%	23	3.0%	12
Second Down	8.9%	10	8.8%	22
Third Down	38.6%	3	-13.5%	4
First Half	12.5%	11	3.7%	19
Second Half	8.8%	10	-0.8%	12
Red Zone	6.8%	10	13.5%	26
Late and Close	8.4%	10	-15.9%	5

Five-Year Performance

Year	W-L	Pyth	Est W	PF	PA	TO	Total	Rk	Off	Rk	Def	Rk	ST	Rk	Off AGL	Rk	Def AGL	Rk
2006	7-9	6.9	7.4	292	328	+6	-6.9%	20	0.0%	16	3.1%	18	-3.8%	28	13.0	13	22.5	22
2007	4-12	8.1	6.3	259	414	+4	-26.5%	28	-15.5%	27	11.0%	28	0.0%	14	26.4	27	20.4	17
2008	11-5	9.7	8.7	391	325	-3	5.6%	16	12.9%	10	10.6%	25	3.3%	7	15.5	11	13.3	7
2009	9-7	9.0	8.6	363	325	+3	1.8%	18	8.9%	14	6.1%	20	-1.0%	22	15.9	12	21.8	14
2010	13-3	11.2	10.4	414	288	+14	14.9%	8	10.8%	10	1.2%	12	5.4%	2	5.2	1	10.9	6

Strategic Tendencies

Run/Pass		Rank	Offense		Rank	Defense		Rank	Other		Rank
Runs, all plays	42%	9	3+ WR	42%	28	Rush 3	13.2%	6	2+ RB, Pct Runs	60%	13
Runs, first half	40%	19	4+ WR	6%	13	Rush 4	56.9%	19	1 RB/2 TE, Pct Runs	50%	12
Runs, first down	54%	10	2+ TE	40%	2	Rush 5	21.9%	19	1 RB/3+ WR, Pct Runs	21%	19
Runs, second-long	34%	15	Single back	48%	30	Rush 6+	7.9%	20	CB1 on WR1	39%	20
Runs, power sit.	63%	12	Play action	16%	23	Zone Blitz	13.4%	1	Go for it on 4th	0.99	9
Runs, behind 2H	32%	5	Max protect	11%	17	Sacks by LB	12.9%	26	Offensive Pace	30.4	14
Pass, ahead 2H	47%	10	Outside pocket	17%	4	Sacks by DB	3.2%	27	Defensive Pace	31.7	29

Even though the Falcons zone-blitzed more than any other team, the percentage of their sacks coming from linebackers and defensive backs went down compared to 2009. In general, the Falcons zone-blitzed by dropping the weakside defensive end (most commonly John Abraham) into coverage while blitzing one player from the strong side and one player up the middle. But sometimes they even dropped defensive tackle Jonathan Babineaux into coverage. The Falcons allowed 5.6 yards per pass when zone-blitzing, 6.4 yards otherwise. ☞ Atlanta had the best defense in the league on third-and-short, but ranked 29th against third-and-long (7-plus yards to go). ☞ In the red zone, Atlanta was much better against the run (-12.3% DVOA, 10th) than against the pass (36.3% DVOA, 27th). ☞ The Falcons' defense ranked 26th in DVOA when defending a lead of more than a touchdown. The rest of the time, they ranked fifth in DVOA. ☞ Atlanta threw a league-high 41 percent of passes to the "short right" area.

Passing

Player	DYAR	DVOA	Plays	NtYds	Avg	YAC	C%	TD	Int
M.Ryan	1348	23.9%	605	3729	6.2	3.8	62.8%	28	9
C.Redman	-11	-37.7%	6	20	3.3	3.8	66.7%	0	0

Rushing

Player	DYAR	DVOA	Plays	Yds	Avg	TD	Fum	Suc
M.Turner	102	-1.4%	334	1371	4.1	12	2	46%
J.Snelling	15	-4.5%	87	325	3.7	2	1	44%
M.Ryan	1	-11.2%	29	141	4.9	0	1	-
O.Mughelli	9	2.2%	13	36	2.8	0	0	77%
G.Johnson	-8	-28.5%	10	36	3.6	0	0	20%

Receiving

Player	DYAR	DVOA	Plays	Ctch	Yds	Y/C	YAC	TD	C%
R.White	294	8.3%	180	116	1392	12.0	3.2	10	64%
M.Jenkins	108	5.8%	73	41	505	12.3	2.0	2	56%
H.Douglas	-59	-26.7%	53	22	294	13.4	5.6	1	42%
B.Finneran	23	-4.3%	31	19	166	8.7	2.4	3	61%
E.Weems	36	58.7%	6	6	61	10.2	3.7	0	100%
T.Gonzalez	72	2.2%	109	70	656	9.4	2.7	6	64%
J.Peelle	20	10.5%	15	10	96	9.6	5.3	1	67%
M.Palmer	-1	-9.8%	8	5	29	5.8	3.2	1	63%
J.Snelling	60	9.0%	51	44	303	6.9	5.8	3	86%
M.Turner	-11	-24.4%	20	12	85	7.1	7.4	0	60%
O.Mughelli	27	17.2%	18	13	126	9.7	8.6	1	72%

Offensive Line

Year	Yards	ALY	Rank	Power	Rank	Stuff	Rank	2nd Lev	Rank	Open Field	Rank
2008	4.62	4.23	9	70%	11	20%	24	1.31	4	1.04	7
2009	4.36	4.26	10	63%	17	18%	12	1.12	17	0.89	10
2010	3.97	4.19	8	68%	9	19%	15	1.03	28	0.71	16

Year	LE	Rank	LT	Rank	Mid	Rank	RT	Rank	RE	Rank	Sacks	ASR	Rank	F-Start	Cont.
2008	3.92	22	4.82	6	4.06	20	4.23	15	4.38	7	17	3.6%	5	18	38
2009	5.18	5	3.85	21	4.12	15	3.96	19	4.62	10	27	4.6%	6	15	34
2010	4.38	15	4.19	17	4.12	12	4.30	11	4.10	13	22	4.1%	3	8	48

This unit is a big reason why the Falcons have put aside decades of inconsistency and futility to emerge as an NFC power. The unit of Sam Baker, Justin Blalock, Todd McClure, Harvey Dahl, and Tyson Clabo has excellent chemistry, and remained healthy all season. For the third straight season, the line was top ten in both of our key stats for running and pass blocking. They were disciplined, too — only 19 penalties were called on Atlanta's big uglies all season, in keeping with the team's allergy to yellow hankies. Yet only Clabo received Pro Bowl honors, and then just as an alternate. It was as a whole that the group was among the league's best.

Unfortunately for the Falcons, Blalock, Dahl, and Clabo were all free agents, and keeping the line intact just wasn't financially feasible. Dahl was allowed to walk to St. Louis, but the team minimized the damage by re-upping both Clabo and Blalock. Contrary to conventional wisdom, the Falcons ran up the middle only 43 percent of the time, below the league average. That's no knock on McClure, who is smart and incredibly durable, not missing a start in a decade. Dahl will be replaced by either Mike Johnson or (Bloody Bloody) Andrew Jackson.

The weak link on the line is actually the highest drafted of the bunch, left tackle Sam Baker. Atlanta moved up to grab him in its memorable 2008 draft, but Baker has been only decent thus far. He had nine blown blocks, which would have led the league were it not for historically inept campaigns by Anthony Davis and Levi Brown. To put Baker's whiffs in context, the Falcons as a team only had 14 blown blocks. He remains a reliable run blocker, and the team runs it left more than right, despite Clabo's emergence as a road grader on the right side.

Defensive Front Seven

Defensive Line	Age	Pos	Plays	TmPct	Overall Rk	Stop	Dfts	BTkl	St%	Rk	AvYd	Rk	Pass Rush Sack	Hit	Hur	vs. Run Runs	St%	Yds	vs. Pass Pass	St%	Yds
John Abraham	33	DE	45	6.1%	29	37	25	2	76%	26	1.7	35	13	5	23.5	21	76%	4.1	24	88%	-0.5
Corey Peters	23	DT	33	4.2%	41	23	5	1	74%	51	3.2	61	1	0	3.5	27	74%	2.6	6	50%	5.8
Kroy Biermann	26	DE	30	3.8%	66	23	8	0	79%	48	1.4	30	3	7	20.5	19	79%	1.9	11	73%	0.5
Jonathan Babineaux	30	DT	29	4.0%	46	21	14	4	75%	45	1.7	27	4	3	10.5	16	75%	1.6	13	69%	1.7
Chauncey Davis	28	DE	26	3.3%	74	15	7	0	61%	78	3.5	78	1	1	5	18	61%	2.9	8	50%	4.9
Jamaal Anderson	25	DE	23	2.9%	--	19	7	0	83%	--	0.4	--	2	2	11.5	18	83%	0.9	5	80%	-1.4
Vance Walker	24	DT	16	2.0%	--	14	4	1	85%	--	1.4	--	0	0	2	13	85%	1.8	3	100%	-0.7

Linebackers	Age	Pos	Plays	TmPct	Overall Rk	Stop	Dfts	BTkl	AvYd	Pass Rush Sack	Hit	Hur	vs. Run Runs	St%	Rk	Yds	Rk	vs. Pass Tgts	Suc%	Rk	AdjYd	Rk
Curtis Lofton	25	MLB	120	15.3%	15	60	22	10	5.3	2	1	1	70	61%	81	3.5	65	31	49%	53	7.5	65
Stephen Nicholas	28	OLB	75	9.6%	63	45	12	3	4.8	0	1	2	38	66%	69	3.0	50	32	59%	25	5.2	21
Mike Peterson	35	OLB	62	7.9%	83	47	11	4	3.2	1	0	0	40	75%	20	3.1	55	19	51%	52	7.6	66
Sean Weatherspoon	24	OLB	43	8.0%	--	19	7	6	6.3	1	1	3	12	67%	--	3.1	--	17	22%	79	7.9	72

Year	Yards	ALY	Rank	Power	Rank	Stuff	Rank	2nd Lev	Rank	Open Field	Rank
2008	4.74	4.20	19	58%	5	20%	9	1.38	30	1.02	27
2009	3.86	3.96	12	69%	24	21%	10	1.11	13	0.52	6
2010	4.28	3.83	13	64%	19	22%	5	1.19	22	0.92	22

Year	LE	Rank	LT	Rank	Mid	Rank	RT	Rank	RE	Rank	Sacks	ASR	Rank
2008	4.44	23	5.25	31	3.86	8	4.19	18	3.98	17	34	6.9%	10
2009	4.51	19	4.18	18	3.80	12	4.15	15	3.68	10	28	5.6%	26
2010	4.31	19	3.40	7	3.58	4	3.83	11	4.69	29	31	5.8%	23

At 33, John Abraham continues to be one of the better pass rush threats of his generation, and a rather unheralded one at that. Abraham's 102.5 career sacks rank only behind Jason Taylor among active players. He didn't get much help from the other side last year, which is why Ray Edwards was signed away from the Vikings. Edwards profited handsomely by playing opposite Jared Allen and next to the Williams Wall, but he came at about half the price Charles Johnson cost the Panthers. The numbers suggest Kroy Biermann, yet another 2008 draftee, will break through in 2011 — with 20.5 pressures, his sack total is likely to rise from the three he managed a year ago, though his snaps will surely drop with Edwards around. Biermann is tireless and has active hands, though he can be overpowered by larger linemen. Jamaal Anderson actually showed signs of life after three seasons of bustdom, mainly by moving inside on passing downs, but was released anyway.

Three-technique tackle Jonathan Babineaux fell off some from his dominant 2009, but he is still an elite player. Third-round rookie Corey Peters was thought to be a "reach pick" by many draftniks, but he did a good job filling the breach left by 2009 top pick Peria Jerry's recurring injury issues. If Jerry can stay on the field and reach anywhere near his potential, the Falcons will have an outstanding tackle rotation.

Linebacker Sean Weatherspoon is another first-rounder hampered by knee problems. 2010's talkative top choice missed five games and seldom got to unleash his top-end speed. Curtis Lofton is a rock in the middle, but doesn't drop particularly well, and can't race past interior linemen on blitzes. Mike Peterson was powerful against the run while flipping between the strong and weak sides, but at 35 can no longer keep pace in space. Stephen Nicholas is a special teams ace, and with a hefty new contract will be expected to step up and start on the strong side as 34-year-old Mike Peterson gets long in the tooth. Georgia's Akeem Dent drives up Highway 316 as a surprise choice in the third round. If he can approach Peters' achievements from a similar draft status, the Falcons will rejoice.

Defensive Secondary

Secondary	Age	Pos	Plays	Overall TmPct	Rk	Stop	Dfts	BTkl	vs. Run Runs	St%	Rk	Yds	Rk	vs. Pass Tgts	Tgt%	Rk	Dist	Suc%	Rk	APaYd	Rk	PD	Int
Brent Grimes	28	CB	104	13.3%	3	41	23	8	23	30%	74	9.3	70	112	22.3%	2	13.0	60%	11	4.9	3	17	5
Thomas DeCoud	26	FS	79	10.1%	44	25	6	9	40	28%	70	10.2	75	26	5.1%	55	10.5	70%	9	7.1	29	4	1
William Moore	26	SS	78	10.0%	46	27	16	11	37	35%	52	6.3	33	36	7.1%	24	10.5	53%	42	6.5	20	7	5
Dunta Robinson	29	CB	62	8.5%	46	23	9	3	8	50%	25	5.3	23	78	16.6%	27	13.3	48%	64	7.3	45	9	1
Brian Williams	32	CB	33	4.2%	--	15	9	6	12	42%	--	4.5	--	19	3.8%	--	8.4	61%	--	6.4	--	2	0
Chris Owens	25	CB	32	4.1%	--	8	2	4	6	33%	--	5.3	--	36	7.1%	--	9.6	27%	--	7.7	--	4	1
Erik Coleman	29	SS	18	3.1%	--	9	1	3	9	89%	--	3.3	--	4	0.9%	--	16.4	30%	--	23.8	--	0	0

Year	Pass D Rank	vs. #1 WR	Rk	vs. #2 WR	Rk	vs. Other WR	Rk	vs. TE	Rk	vs. RB	Rk
2008	18	3.0%	15	5.1%	20	-28.1%	7	25.1%	28	20.6%	29
2009	27	28.2%	31	-1.2%	16	20.5%	30	1.6%	15	24.5%	28
2010	10	7.4%	22	-11.3%	6	-6.9%	13	2.1%	13	3.1%	16

Brent Grimes was among the league's top success stories last season. Grimes had four picks as a nickel defender down the stretch in 2009. He built on that performance when elevated to the starting lineup, turning in 17 passes defensed with five interceptions. Opponents, assuming the diminutive Grimes got lost en route to his Pee-Wee game, went after him all season — only Terrell Thomas of the Giants was targeted more often. Grimes stood up to the pressure with aplomb. "Grime Time" will always struggle with taller receivers, as proven when James Jones went over his head repeatedly in the Wild Card game. But he was the Falcons' best defensive back in 2010.

Dunta Robinson, paid big free agent money to be a top corner, had a mediocre season, though his 48 percent Success Rate was actually a considerable improvement from his godawful 2009. Robinson's speed and swivel are long gone. His lone asset at this point is size, which showed up in his solid run defense. Another midget, Chris Owens, and aging Brian Williams are the other corners, so the Birds need Robinson to show some life. Perhaps Arthur Blank can go down to his Home Depot warehouse and build another corner out of spare parts.

William Moore and Thomas DeCoud give the Falcons a young safety combo with plenty of potential, though neither was outstanding in 2010. The two missed their share of tackles (20 between them), and Moore blitzed frequently without actually getting to the quarterback (eight pressures, zero sacks). Moore was arrested for a panoply of traffic violations in April. With the safety depth nonexistent (veteran Erik Coleman, due $3 million, was cut after the season), he needs to keep his nose clean in 2011.

Special Teams

Year	DVOA	Rank	FG/XP	Rank	Net Kick	Rank	Kick Ret	Rank	Net Punt	Rank	Punt Ret	Rank	Hidden	Rank
2008	3.3%	7	5.2	6	9.2	4	1.8	15	4.8	12	-1.6	19	6.3	5
2009	-1.0%	22	-14.8	32	15.1	1	-0.4	13	-9.6	31	3.9	12	7.3	5
2010	5.4%	2	4.2	8	13.6	2	8.7	8	0.0	19	5.1	7	-9.8	28

Atlanta's special teams were superb across the board in 2010 — only the Bears and the wondrous Devin Hester topped them in overall DVOA. The one ranking in which they were near the bottom was in Hidden value, though the key play of Atlanta's regular season was the Saints' Garrett Hartley missing an easy field-goal attempt in a Week 3 overtime win. Irony can be pretty ironic sometimes.

Eric Weems exploded as a returner after a pedestrian 2009, placing near the top of the league in both disciplines. His kickoff return touchdown against Tampa Bay in December was the key play in an unlikely comeback victory, while the kick he took to the paint in the wild-card game against the Pack was one of the day's few bright spots for Atlanta. He also returned a punt for a score, and led the team in tackles as a gunner on both coverage units, a testament to his versatility.

Michael Koenen turned in another average year punting, but made up for it by booming his kickoffs, including 23 touchbacks, good for fifth in the league. Despite the new touchback rules, the Bucs thought Koenen's leg worth $6.5 million in guaranteed money, and so rookie Matt Bosher from Miami will handle the punting and kickoff jobs in 2011. Bosher will benefit from an outstanding kick coverage unit that helped earn the Falcons more net kickoff points than even Baltimore and touchback machine Billy Cundiff. In the early going, the coverage struggled without Nicholas and Biermann, who led the team in special teams tackles in 2009 but were taken off kickoff duty as their defensive snaps increased. After Michael Spurlock and LeRod Stephens-Howling both took kickoffs back to the house (the latter negated by a dubious holding penalty), Nicholas and Biermann found themselves sprinting, headlong, downfield once again.

Field-goal kicker Matt Bryant, usually unreliable from distance, missed only three kicks all season (9-of-11 from 40-plus yards), made three game-winners, and was fourth in the league in points.

Coaching Staff

Quarterback coaches, like their tutees, tend to get more credit or blame than they deserve. But few can argue that Bill Musgrave played a minor role in Matt Ryan's instant and sustained success. Musgrave is off to run the Vikings offense. In his place comes Bob Bratkowski, who Bengals fans were ready to run out of town several seasons before he was finally canned as offensive coordinator in January. Brat is the son of NFL quarterback Zeke Bratkowski, and certainly had his moments in Cincy when Carson Palmer was a young up-and-coming star, like Ryan is now. Bratkowski also gives Atlanta some insurance should Mike Mularkey depart for a head coaching gig at some point, which he almost did this offseason (the Titans ended up choosing the similarly alliterative Mike Munchak). Defensive coordinator Brian Van Gorder sensed his front four didn't have the pass rushing ability they needed, so he called up an inordinate number of zone blitzes. That number could drop with Edwards in town.

Baltimore Ravens

2010 Record: 12-4	**2011 Mean Projection:** 9.4 wins
Pythagorean Wins: 10.6 (6th)	**On the Clock (0-3):** 1%
DVOA: 22.5% (4th)	**Loserville (4-6):** 12%
Offense: 9.5% (12th)	**Mediocrity (7-8):** 22%
Defense: -7.9% (4th)	**Playoff Contender (9-10):** 32%
Special Teams: 5.1% (4th)	**Super Bowl Contender (11+):** 33%
Variance: 5.1% (1st)	**Projected Average Opponent:** 0.8% (12th)

2010: You come at the king, you best not miss.

2011: Second to Pittsburgh again. What else is new?

It's hard to watch big brother always do just a little bit better than you.

For a long time, the Ravens have lived in the shadow of the Pittsburgh Steelers, but for the last three years it's been particularly bad. For three years, the Ravens have finished second in the AFC North behind the Steelers, with a similar team built on similar principles. In two of those years, the Ravens were directly ushered out of the playoffs by their archrivals.

Last year was supposed to be different, at least according to our projections at Football Outsiders. Baltimore was the No. 1 team in DVOA for 2009, despite going just 9-7. The 2009 Ravens were much like the 2010 Packers: a team that dominated in some games, and came close when they lost. Our numbers looked at the team, with numerous players in their prime and a quarterback who hadn't yet hit his, and forecast another year on top of our ratings … and possibly a Super Bowl championship.

It didn't work out that way. The Ravens actually had their best record since 2006, but based on play-by-play analysis (DVOA) they weren't quite as good as 2008 or 2009. And the surprise was which part of the game let the Ravens down. Their defense declined slightly, but was still ranked fourth in the NFL. The pass offense improved slightly, as did the special teams. No, what let the Ravens down was their vaunted running game, which fell from 4.7 yards per carry and 16.8%

DVOA (third in the NFL in 2009) to 3.9 yards per carry and 0.8% DVOA (13th).

The running game let down Baltimore both during the regular season and in the playoffs, when it proved to be an easily resistible force taking on the immovable object that was Pittsburgh's No.1-ranked run defense. Ray Rice and Willis McGahee combined for just 36 yards on 16 carries. Thirteen of those carries went for two yards or fewer, although the Ravens did convert their only third-down run.

Who was more responsible for the decline of Baltimore's running game in 2010: Rice, or his blockers? The conventional wisdom is that the offensive line couldn't make holes for Rice, but our stats suggest that Rice may have been an issue as well. The Ravens declined in Adjusted Line Yards, but still ranked ninth in the league. However, they dropped from third in Open Field Yards per carry to 27th. That's mostly the running back, not the blocking. Rice was slowed down by a knee injury in the first half of the season, but he wasn't playing any better in the second half; he averaged 3.99 yards per carry before Baltimore's bye week, and 3.96 yards per carry afterwards. Game charting recorded him with just 22 broken tackles, after he had 57 the year before.

The decline on the offensive line was partially related to injury and personnel shuffling, which had three of the five starting linemen playing new positions. The

2011 Ravens Schedule

Week	Opp.	Week	Opp.	Week	Opp.
1	PIT	7	at JAC (Mon.)	13	at CLE
2	at TEN	8	ARI	14	IND
3	at STL	9	at PIT	15	at SD
4	NYJ	10	at SEA	16	CLE
5	BYE	11	CIN	17	at CIN
6	HOU	12	SF (Thu.)		

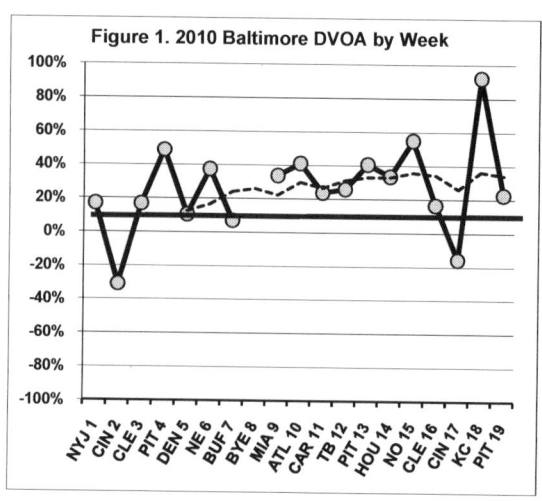

Figure 1. 2010 Baltimore DVOA by Week

Ravens expected to switch Michael Oher to left tackle and Jared Gaither to right tackle, but they didn't expect to lose Gaither altogether due to a back injury. That created a cascade effect. At tackle, they went from the gigantic Gaither (6-foot-9, 340 pounds) to the (relatively) smaller Marshal Yanda (6-foot-3, 315). At right guard, that meant a drop from the physical Yanda to the athletic but less powerful Chris Chester.

The Ravens hope changes on the offensive line will help improve things in 2011. Chester is gone in free agency, as is Gaither, but Yanda will be able to return to right guard. The new right tackle is rookie Jah Reid, a third-round pick out of Florida known in particular for his run blocking. He's a consistent knee-bender with long arms. The Ravens signed Vonta Leach, generally considered the best blocking fullback in the league, away from the Houston Texans. The Ravens will also shuffle the coaches. They replaced offensive line coach John Matsko with his assistant, Andy Moeller, and hired new offensive line assistant Todd Washington.

The Ravens are likely to show a renewed commitment to the running game this year — not in games, per se, but in practice. One theory about the decline of the running game last year is that the Ravens spent so much time concentrating on passing plays in camp, working in new receivers like Anquan Boldin and T.J. Houshmandzadeh, that they didn't give the running backs and the line enough practice time. Looking at preseason numbers suggests that the Ravens weren't worried about their need to practice running plays. In 2009, the Ravens had 65 passing plays and 36 running plays when the first-team offense was in the game. In 2010, they had 73 passing plays and only 21 running plays with the first-team offense. They ran whole drives with nothing but passes, because that's what they wanted to work on.

Improving the running game isn't just important because the Ravens need it to keep the chains moving, or because strong runs on first down lead to advanta-

geous second-and-short situations. It's also important because no team uses play-action as much as the Ravens. Baltimore ran play-action on 31 percent of pass plays last year. That's the highest rate for a team since we started charting in 2005.

Despite all this talk about the running game, we shouldn't overstate the importance of the problem. The Ravens running game declined to average last year, not terrible. And the running game is still generally not as important in the modern NFL as the passing game, and the passing game in Baltimore seems to be doing well.

There's a lot of worry in Baltimore about whether quarterback Joe Flacco is ready to "take the next step," but the signs are certainly strong. Yes, Flacco needs to throw the ball away and take fewer sacks, but he has improved his yards per attempt, touchdown rate, and interception rate each year since he arrived in the NFL. By our similarity scores, the most similar quarterback to Joe Flacco over the years 2008-10 is Tom Brady between 2001 and 2003 — right before he blossomed from a winning quarterback whose stats didn't quite match his reputation, to a winning quarterback whose stats even surpassed his reputation. The list of similar quarterbacks also includes Brett Favre 1992-94 and Jim Kelly 1986-88.

Flacco will be throwing to a number of new receivers this year, but they may be receivers who better fit his skill set. Last year, the Ravens essentially had three possession receivers in their thirties: Anquan Boldin, Derrick Mason, and T.J. Houshmandzadeh. But Flacco is best throwing the ball deep. Without a speed threat, these veteran receivers had to run deeper routes than in past years. In 2009, 15 percent of passes to Boldin went 16 or more yards in the air. In 2010, that went up to 29 percent. For Houshmandzadeh, the same percentage went from 21 percent to 33 percent.

And here's what's strange: It worked. Not quite on the standard longer passes. Take out passes thrown away on purpose, and the Ravens averaged 9.8 yards on Deep passes (16 to 25 yards in the air). That's below the NFL average of 11.2. But they were great when Flacco threw the long bomb. The Ravens threw 40 passes longer than 25 yards, and gained an average of 16.9 yards on these plays, compared to the NFL average of 13.4 yards.

After the new CBA agreement, the Ravens found themselves over the new salary cap, and were forced to make cuts. Two of the players on the chopping block were Mason and tight end Todd Heap. The team hoped to bring them back on lower salaries, but they decided to sign with the Jets and Cardinals, respectively. The Ravens already knew they weren't bringing back Houshmandzadeh. The new receivers who will replace these veterans are generally players known for running deeper routes. Rookie Torrey Smith is a burner with straight-line speed. Tight ends Ed Dickson and Dennis Pitta, who will replace Heap, are even more receiving-oriented than Heap was; Pitta in particular is a Dallas Clark clone. Right before we went to press, the Ravens dealt a fourth-round pick to Buffalo for veteran Lee Evans. Twenty-three percent of passes to Evans last year went longer than 25 yards in the air, and 47 percent went longer than 15 yards.

Deep threats not only are a better complement to Flacco's skills, they also may help solve Baltimore's struggles against the Steelers. One reason why the Ravens are 2-6 against the Steelers over the last three seasons is a dearth of explosive plays (Table 1). The two Baltimore wins have two things in common: They are the only two games where Baltimore had more explosive plays than Pittsburgh, and not coincidentally, they are the only two games where Ben Roethlisberger did not play for the Steelers. The gap between the teams would be even larger if we weren't considering gains off Defensive Pass Interference, of which there are four for Baltimore and only one for Pittsburgh[1].

The salary cap constraints that will change the Ravens receiving corps also did their part to change the Ravens defense. The Ravens had to cut nose tackle Kelly Gregg, who was still playing at a high level, and were unable to re-sign safety Dawan Landry. These

Table 1. Explosions in the Sky : Pass Plays of 20-plus Yards in Ravens-Steelers Games Since 2008

Game	Result	Steelers (Passes/Yds)	Ravens (Passes/Yds)
Week 4, 2008	PIT 23-20 (OT)	4/136	2/61
Week 15, 2008	PIT 13-9	3/75	1/24
Playoffs, 2008	PIT 23-14	5/183	3/62
Week 12, 2009	BAL 20-17 (OT)	3/75	5/162
Week 16, 2009	PIT 23-20	5/140	2/57
Week 4, 2010	BAL 17-14	2/54	3/90
Week 13, 2010	PIT 13-10	4/100	2/128
Playoffs, 2010	PIT 31-24	3/115	2/54
Totals		29/878	20/638

Note: Includes Defensive Pass Interference

changes do help the Ravens defense to get younger, however. Before the lockout, we projected the Ravens' defensive starting lineup with an average age of 30.6. Now that average age is 27.8. The 35-year-old Gregg will be replaced by 2010 second-round pick Terrence Cody (23) and Landry (29) will be replaced by Tom Zbikowski (26). In addition, it looks like 2010 fifth-round pick Arthur Jones will start ahead of 31-year-old veteran Cory Redding. Highly regarded going into his senior year, Jones fell in the draft due to injury concerns — he tore both a pectoral muscle and knee ligaments in 2009 — but he appears to be fully healthy now.

The youth movement on defense hasn't yet hit the team's biggest stars. Two of the team's three best players on that side of the ball are still Ray Lewis, now 36, and Ed Reed, 33. The players surveyed for NFL Network's "Top 100 of 2011" show chose them as the fourth- and fifth-best players in the NFL, respectively.

Lewis seems a little overrated by his peers, and he's probably not the best linebacker in the league at this point, but he might be underrated by fans outside of Baltimore. For a defender to play at this level at Lewis' age is exceedingly rare. By official NFL stats, Lewis had 139 tackles last season (including assists). Lewis and London Fletcher were the first players since 1996 to have at least 110 tackles at age 35 or older. Only four linebackers in the NFL were involved in a higher rate of team tackles than Lewis, and he had good all-around stats against both the run and pass.

While Lewis is the older of the two veterans, Reed

---

[1] Thanks to Chad Reuter of NFLDraftScout.com, who pointed these numbers out to us.

is the one whose future is more questionable. He has missed 10 games over the last two seasons because of various hip, groin, and neck injuries. He's constantly affected by a nerve impingement in his neck and shoulder that had him considering retirement before the 2010 season. At this point, he's decided to play on, delaying surgery until after his career.

Reed is generally considered the best free safety in the league. He had eight interceptions last year in only ten games, and came out very well in our advanced game charting pass coverage stats. So it's surprising to note that the Ravens emphatically haven't been any worse without Reed on the field (Table 2). Contrast this with the situation in Pittsburgh, where the Steelers have been dramatically worse without Troy Polamalu on the field over the last two seasons. Even stranger, since Reed is a free safety who primarily plays deep centerfield against the pass, the Ravens have been worse against the run but better against the pass without Reed in the lineup.

The Ravens certainly would disagree with the numbers here. They want Reed in the lineup and all those big plays he brings. But they could use one of those big plays in one of the big games against their rivals. Reed has missed two of the eight games against Pittsburgh over the last three years, and in the six games he has played, he doesn't have an interception or a forced fumble.

It seems silly to criticize Reed for not having a turnover in a six-game sample when he's played so well overall, but that goes to the heart of Baltimore's problem. They've built a strong team that plays well overall, but they can't seem to get past the Steelers. After three strong years, this franchise won't consider another wild card and playoff loss as a successful season. The road to an AFC North division title goes through Pittsburgh, and the road to the Super Bowl probably does as well.

Aaron Schatz

Table 2. Baltimore Defense with and without Ed Reed, 2009-2010

	DVOA	Yd/Play	TO/Game	DVOA vs. Run	Yds vs. Run	DVOA vs. Pass	Yds vs. Pass
without Reed	-14.7%	4.80	1.60	-11.7%	3.98	-17.1%	5.39
with Reed	-7.6%	5.24	1.82	-16.2%	3.63	-1.4%	6.33

2010 Ravens Stats by Week

Wk	vs.	W-L	PF	PA	YDF	YDA	TO	Total	Off	Def	ST
1	@NYJ	W	10	9	282	176	-2	17%	-22%	-45%	-6%
2	@CIN	L	10	15	259	253	-4	-31%	-48%	-22%	-5%
3	CLE	W	24	17	365	304	0	17%	48%	35%	4%
4	@PIT	W	17	14	320	210	-1	49%	37%	-12%	0%
5	DEN	W	31	17	415	346	1	10%	34%	34%	11%
6	@NE	L	20	23	377	394	2	37%	7%	-29%	1%
7	BUF	W	37	34	364	514	2	7%	20%	29%	16%
8	BYE										
9	MIA	W	26	10	402	289	3	34%	34%	-7%	-7%
10	@ATL	L	21	26	320	362	-2	41%	38%	0%	3%
11	@CAR	W	37	13	378	270	0	24%	-6%	-19%	11%
12	TB	W	17	10	349	263	-1	26%	7%	-15%	4%
13	PIT	L	10	13	269	288	0	41%	5%	-33%	2%
14	@HOU	W	34	28	253	489	2	33%	-16%	-15%	34%
15	NO	W	30	24	356	269	1	55%	23%	-17%	15%
16	@CLE	W	20	10	258	280	3	17%	11%	-7%	-1%
17	CIN	W	13	7	199	395	3	-16%	-28%	-7%	5%
18	@KC	W	30	7	390	161	2	92%	15%	-78%	0%
19	@PIT	L	24	31	126	263	3	23%	-10%	-25%	8%

Trends and Splits

	Offense	Rank	Defense	Rank
Total DVOA	9.5%	12	-7.9%	4
Unadjusted VOA	8.9%	14	-2.1%	9
Weighted Trend	9.5%	12	-10.4%	3
Variance	7.4%	14	5.3%	8
Average Opponent	2.1%	19	7.6%	25
Passing	31.8%	7	-3.2%	6
Rushing	0.8%	13	-14.6%	5
First Down	5.5%	18	3.5%	15
Second Down	18.5%	6	-20.4%	4
Third Down	2.1%	17	-9.5%	7
First Half	13.1%	8	-8.1%	3
Second Half	5.7%	16	-7.7%	8
Red Zone	-5.4%	23	-19.6%	7
Late and Close	8.4%	11	-18.1%	3

Five-Year Performance

Year	W-L	Pyth	Est W	PF	PA	TO	Total	Rk	Off	Rk	Def	Rk	ST	Rk	Off AGL	Rk	Def AGL	Rk
2006	13-3	12.7	11.8	353	201	+17	28.8%	2	1.7%	15	-23.6%	1	3.5%	4	27.1	26	9.7	12
2007	5-11	5.0	6.9	275	384	-17	-3.9%	18	-12.7%	25	-8.7%	5	0.1%	13	26.2	26	32.4	26
2008	11-5	11.9	11.7	385	244	+13	29.1%	3	4.3%	19	-24.5%	2	0.3%	16	23.4	13	53.9	31
2009	9-7	11.6	11.8	391	261	+10	30.5%	1	16.7%	8	-11.8%	4	2.0%	8	8.4	5	22.2	15
2010	12-4	10.6	11.4	357	270	+7	22.5%	4	9.5%	12	-7.9%	4	5.1%	4	23.8	15	27.1	19

Strategic Tendencies

Run/Pass		Rank	Offense		Rank	Defense		Rank	Other		Rank
Runs, all plays	45%	4	3+ WR	45%	20	Rush 3	17.3%	4	2+ RB, Pct Runs	57%	18
Runs, first half	42%	10	4+ WR	5%	20	Rush 4	49.8%	28	1 RB/2 TE, Pct Runs	50%	12
Runs, first down	57%	3	2+ TE	21%	28	Rush 5	24.5%	12	1 RB/3+ WR, Pct Runs	29%	8
Runs, second-long	38%	6	Single back	47%	31	Rush 6+	8.3%	18	CB1 on WR1	34%	23
Runs, power sit.	69%	4	Play action	31%	1	Zone Blitz	8.3%	8	Go for it on 4th	0.86	20
Runs, behind 2H	25%	22	Max protect	24%	2	Sacks by LB	61.1%	7	Offensive Pace	30.0	9
Pass, ahead 2H	44%	17	Outside pocket	12%	17	Sacks by DB	3.7%	26	Defensive Pace	31.5	28

Baltimore ran play-action on 31 percent of pass plays last year. That's the highest rate for a team since we started charting in 2005 ... Yet once again, Baltimore wasn't any better using play-action compared to regular passes. The NFL average was 7.5 yards per pass with play-action, 6.1 yards per pass otherwise. Baltimore had 6.5 yards per pass both with and without play-action. ☞ Baltimore ranked fourth in offensive DVOA in the first quarter, but only 16th for the rest of the game. ☞ Baltimore's offensive DVOA was sixth in the league when losing or tied, 20th in the league when winning. ☞ The Ravens were at the bottom of the league with only 16 dropped passes. ☞ Baltimore allowed only 5.1 yards per play when big-blitzing with six or more pass rushers, compared to 6.1 yards per play the rest of the time. ☞ Ed Reed led the league with eight passes defensed when another player was listed as the main player in coverage. Lofa Tatupu of Seattle was second with six. Jon McGraw of Kansas City was third with four.

Passing

Player	DYAR	DVOA	Plays	NtYds	Avg	YAC	C%	TD	Int
J.Flacco	906	15.6%	540	3585	6.6	4.9	62.6%	25	9

Rushing

Player	DYAR	DVOA	Plays	Yds	Avg	TD	Fum	Suc
R.Rice	115	0.8%	307	1220	4.0	5	0	46%
W.McGahee	6	-7.1%	100	382	3.8	5	2	49%
L.McClain	19	1.1%	28	85	3.0	0	0	75%
J.Flacco	-23	-26.9%	25	93	3.7	1	2	-
D.Stallworth	8	-10.2%	5	45	9.0	0	1	-

Receiving

Player	DYAR	DVOA	Plays	Ctch	Yds	Y/C	YAC	TD	C%
A.Boldin	152	4.8%	109	64	837	13.1	3.5	7	59%
D.Mason	216	13.5%	100	61	802	13.1	2.1	7	61%
T.Houshmandzadeh	89	6.7%	57	30	399	13.3	2.6	3	53%
T.Heap	134	25.9%	64	40	599	15.0	5.6	5	63%
E.Dickson	-24	-24.5%	23	11	152	13.8	6.5	1	48%
R.Rice	120	14.4%	83	63	556	8.8	8.4	1	76%
L.McClain	11	-6.9%	26	21	134	6.4	6.9	0	81%
W.McGahee	-27	-42.5%	17	14	55	3.9	6.7	1	82%

Offensive Line

Year	Yards	ALY	Rank	Power	Rank	Stuff	Rank	2nd Lev	Rank	Open Field	Rank
2008	3.99	4.17	11	76%	3	16%	8	0.97	31	0.64	22
2009	5.00	4.45	4	68%	8	16%	7	1.29	6	1.27	3
2010	3.88	4.19	9	55%	24	15%	6	0.97	29	0.46	27

Year	LE	Rank	LT	Rank	Mid	Rank	RT	Rank	RE	Rank	Sacks	ASR	Rank	F-Start	Cont.
2008	4.75	12	4.00	18	4.27	11	3.93	24	4.00	19	33	6.8%	20	23	27
2009	4.22	17	4.15	15	4.46	5	3.98	18	5.79	1	37	6.6%	19	17	29
2010	4.63	10	4.11	18	3.99	15	5.04	2	5.24	4	40	7.9%	25	25	38

The Ravens went into free agency with three offensive linemen to deal with, and only one will be back. However, it's the one they want: Marshal Yanda, who is a devastating run blocker and versatile enough to play both guard and tackle. He played at tackle last year because of injuries to the now-departed Jared Gaither, but will return to right guard this year and replace Chris Chester (who signed with Washington). Fitting in at right tackle is third-round pick Jah Reid, a huge (6-foot-7, 326 pounds) road-grader out of Florida. He's tough and has long arms, although he can be susceptible to spin moves. Oniel Cousins could play if Reid isn't ready for the NFL by Week 1. Michael Oher and Ben Grubbs are fully established on the left side now. While it's surprising to see the Ravens do so much better running right as opposed to running left, the left side is where the better pass blocking is. We marked Oher down with only 2.5 blown blocks leading to sacks, a ridiculously low number for a left tackle. There are questions at center, where 35-year-old veteran Matt Birk had to have arthroscopic surgery in early August. Former Washington center Casey Rabach failed his physical, which leaves longtime practice-squadder Bryan Mattison — a converted defensive tackle with only two NFL games under his belt — as the first-string center until Birk returns.

Defensive Front Seven

Defensive Line	Age	Pos	Plays	TmPct	Overall Rk	Stop	Dfts	BTkl	St%	Rk	AvYd	Rk	Pass Rush Sack	Hit	Hur	vs. Run Runs	St%	Yds	vs. Pass Pass	St%	Yds
Haloti Ngata	27	DE	67	8.5%	6	56	16	5	86%	18	1.4	33	5.5	8	18	50	86%	1.8	17	76%	0.4
Cory Redding	31	DE	46	6.2%	26	33	10	2	65%	63	1.5	34	3	4	13.5	37	65%	2.3	9	100%	-1.9
Kelly Gregg	35	DT	37	4.7%	33	25	3	1	69%	54	2.7	57	0	1	6	36	69%	2.5	1	0%	9.0

Linebackers	Age	Pos	Plays	TmPct	Overall Rk	Stop	Dfts	BTkl	AvYd	Pass Rush Sack	Hit	Hur	vs. Run Runs	St%	Rk	Yds	Rk	vs. Pass Tgts	Suc%	Rk	AdjYd	Rk
Ray Lewis	36	ILB	142	18.0%	5	79	23	9	5.3	2	2	7.5	80	71%	40	3.8	83	40	58%	29	6.3	44
Jarret Johnson	30	OLB	73	9.3%	65	47	10	2	3.3	1.5	4	14	54	69%	54	2.9	39	20	72%	3	3.7	7
Jameel McClain	26	ILB	70	8.9%	67	35	3	6	4.2	1	0	1	42	57%	91	3.7	77	25	46%	68	6.6	50
Terrell Suggs	29	OLB	69	8.8%	69	58	24	2	0.5	11	12	38	48	85%	2	1.6	1	9	52%	--	6.8	--
Dannell Ellerbe	26	ILB	29	5.4%	--	15	8	1	7.4	1	0	3	15	67%	--	6.1	--	13	42%	--	6.1	--
Tavares Gooden	27	ILB	17	3.5%	--	9	4	3	7.1	0	1	4.5	6	67%	--	4.2	--	19	57%	30	7.1	61

Year	Yards	ALY	Rank	Power	Rank	Stuff	Rank	2nd Lev	Rank	Open Field	Rank
2008	3.32	3.17	1	64%	14	24%	4	0.86	1	0.62	13
2009	3.40	3.42	1	62%	11	20%	11	0.86	1	0.48	4
2010	3.84	3.81	12	67%	24	19%	17	1.04	8	0.56	10

Year	LE	Rank	LT	Rank	Mid	Rank	RT	Rank	RE	Rank	Sacks	ASR	Rank
2008	3.31	6	3.55	7	3.10	1	3.00	3	3.12	9	34	6.2%	16
2009	3.07	6	3.19	4	3.80	13	2.80	1	3.07	3	32	5.8%	23
2010	2.36	2	4.21	19	3.67	7	4.75	28	4.84	31	27	5.5%	27

The front seven is still the greatest strength of the Ravens, but it has been surprisingly poor at rushing the passer. The Ravens essentially had a two-man pass rush last year: outside linebacker Terrell Suggs and defensive end Haloti Ngata. Together they had 17 sacks; no other Ravens defender had more than three. Together they had 20 quarterback hits; no other Ravens defender had more than four. The biggest absence in the pass rush was the outside linebacker opposite Suggs, Jarret Johnson. Johnson was very good dropping into pass coverage, but he didn't really bring pressure on the quarterback from the outside. The Ravens claim he was struggling with injuries all season, but he only appeared on the injury report four times, with back spasms. The Ravens didn't grab a linebacker in the draft, hoping that 2010 second-rounder Sergio Kindle can overcome his off-field problems (a December DUI arrest, a broken skull injury that cost him his entire rookie season) and actually make an impact on the field.

Up the middle, Ray Lewis is still the veteran leader of the Ravens defense. Although he's a special player, the Ravens do need to start worrying about Lewis' eventual decline. Both Dannell Ellerbe and Tarvares Gooden got a shot at the starting job next to Lewis and both lost out to undrafted third-year player Jameel McClain. In many ways, McClain's poor advanced stats are related to his role in the Ravens defense: Lewis is the instinctual player who charges into the breach, while McClain hangs back to cover tight ends and clean up mistakes, usually lined up 1 or 2 yards behind Lewis at the snap. Ellerbe replaces McClain in nickel situations.

Terrence Cody made only 13 tackles as a rookie, and struggles with his weight kept him off the field. But the Ravens are counting on their 2010 second-round pick for significant improvement in 2011; in fact, he's going to replace the released Kelly Gregg in the Ravens' starting lineup. Veteran Cory Redding is in the final year of his contract and may lose some of his snaps to a couple of young players, Arthur Jones and Paul Kruger.

Defensive Secondary

Secondary	Age	Pos	Plays	TmPct	Rk	Stop	Dfts	BTkl	Runs	St%	Rk	Yds	Rk	Tgts	Tgt%	Rk	Dist	Suc%	Rk	APaYd	Rk	PD	Int
				Overall						vs. Run						vs. Pass							
Dawan Landry	29	SS	112	14.2%	4	48	14	6	63	48%	21	6.1	32	40	7.7%	20	12.1	58%	28	6.6	21	4	0
Chris Carr	28	CB	68	8.6%	41	27	11	2	12	67%	5	7.0	48	81	15.5%	41	9.9	55%	26	5.4	6	6	2
Lardarius Webb	26	CB	63	8.5%	44	23	10	6	12	58%	18	4.8	18	70	14.3%	56	15.2	55%	31	6.7	28	10	2
Ed Reed	33	FS	53	10.8%	26	20	12	3	11	18%	82	11.2	78	23	7.1%	26	15.3	73%	4	5.3	9	16	8
Josh Wilson	26	CB	50	7.3%	66	23	12	2	3	67%	5	5.7	25	58	12.6%	71	13.7	58%	16	8.0	58	15	3
Fabian Washington	28	CB	39	5.7%	81	13	4	5	7	29%	77	5.7	27	44	9.5%	84	11.1	40%	86	10.6	85	4	0
Tom Zbikowski	26	FS	17	4.3%	--	3	1	3	11	27%	--	15.3	--	6	2.1%	--	16.4	34%	--	12.6	--	0	0
Haruki Nakamura	25	FS	16	2.0%	--	6	2	3	4	50%	--	7.8	--	12	2.2%	--	7.3	46%	--	8.1	--	1	0

Year	Pass D Rank	vs. #1 WR	Rk	vs. #2 WR	Rk	vs. Other WR	Rk	vs. TE	Rk	vs. RB	Rk
2008	2	-15.2%	5	-26.4%	4	-14.9%	11	-33.0%	1	-7.5%	6
2009	8	-19.9%	8	-5.7%	13	7.1%	20	-26.4%	1	-19.3%	3
2010	6	-12.1%	8	5.2%	17	-29.6%	2	-14.0%	2	0.5%	12

The Ravens may start three new defensive backs in 2011. Ed Reed, of course, isn't going anywhere. Dawan Landry left for Jacksonville and will be replaced in the starting lineup by part-time boxer Tom Zbikowski. Bernard Pollard, signed away from Houston, will also get some snaps when the Ravens really need a safety who can stop the run. The second starter to leave was cornerback Josh Wilson, who signed with Washington. As for the third of those three defensive backs being replaced, Chris Carr did re-sign with the Ravens, but his starting spot is not secure even though he started all 16 games last year. Lardarius Webb would like to move up from slot cornerback to starter. He actually was second on the team in targets last year, ahead of Wilson, and had very good game charting numbers. Domonique Foxworth would like to return to starting, but he's having a very slow recovery from the torn ACL that cost him the 2010 season. He was 19th in Adjusted Success Rate in 2009 (56 percent), although he was a less impressive 60th in Adjusted Yards per Pass (8.3). The third candidate to start is Jimmy Smith, the 27th overall pick out of Colorado. Smith is tall, fluid, and athletic, although he'll need to learn to avoid double moves and giving up big plays due to overaggressiveness. There are also questions about

Smith's character both on and off the field. Some teams are concerned about Smith's dedication to football after he made the decision to skip the Senior Bowl. Teams are equally concerned about his three positive drug tests and his arrest for third-degree assault while at Colorado. If Smith can set his personal ship right, the Ravens may have a steal here. Or, they may have Pacman Jones Part II.

Special Teams

Year	DVOA	Rank	FG/XP	Rank	Net Kick	Rank	Kick Ret	Rank	Net Punt	Rank	Punt Ret	Rank	Hidden	Rank
2008	0.3%	16	-2.1	22	-6.8	25	-7.4	27	20.9	1	-2.8	23	-15.7	30
2009	2.0%	8	-4.7	24	9.8	6	9.8	4	-2.2	23	-0.6	16	-1.7	16
2010	5.1%	4	4.3	7	13.5	3	0.8	15	17.4	1	-5.7	26	-16.1	31

Before last year, Bill Cundiff was a run-of-the-mill kicker who had bounced around NFL rosters. Last year, he suddenly put up Herculean numbers, blasting the ball into the end zone on kickoff after kickoff. Cundiff was the first kicker to have a touchback percentage higher than 50 percent since the kickoff line was moved to the 30 in 1994. (Now that the line has returned to the 35, perhaps we should say "only kicker.") Cundiff attributed the improvement to a combination of technique (trying to strike higher on the ball, to get more distance and less hang time) and improved confidence. More likely, Cundiff's season was a fluke, but with the change in kickoff rules, he won't need another Herculean effort to hit a bunch of touchbacks in 2011. As long as he can hold onto some of last year's improved kickoff distance, he'll be one of the better kickers in the league.

Less surprising than Cundiff's performance was that of Sam Koch, who rebounded from an off-year in 2009 and was once again one of the league's top punters. The Ravens got much better results on kick returns at midseason when they replaced Jalen Parmele with David Reed; Reed ended up leading the league (minimum 20 returns) with 29.3 yards per return. On punt returns, Lardarius Webb (-0.5 points on 21 returns) and Tom Zbikowski (-2.2 points on 16 returns) are nothing special.

Coaching Staff

The big change on the Ravens staff this season is the departure of defensive coordinator Greg Mattison, who returned to the college ranks with the University of Michigan so he could be closer to family. (Well, some of his family; he left behind son Bryan, now the backup center.) It's an uncommon move, although one that happened twice this offseason (Mattison and Charlie Weis). The Ravens immediately promoted defensive backs coach Chuck Pagano to replace Mattison. This is Pagano's first NFL coordinator gig, but he's well regarded both with his players and around the league, and he was also a candidate for the Oakland Raiders coordinator job this offseason. He'll be running the same aggressive style of defense that Mattison continued from his predecessor Rex Ryan. Teryl Austin, who was defensive coordinator for the University of Florida, will replace Mattison coaching the secondary. On the offensive side of the ball, there were some questions about Cam Cameron's future after the Ravens offense struggled in the playoff game against Pittsburgh, but in the end the only change is that Cameron will allegedly be giving Joe Flacco more room to audible in 2011.

Buffalo Bills

2010 Record: 4-12	**2011 Mean Projection:** 7.1 wins
Pythagorean Wins: 4.4 (31st)	**On the Clock (0-3):** 11%
DVOA: -20.6% (28th)	**Loserville (4-6):** 32%
Offense: -10.4% (26th)	**Mediocrity (7-8):** 26%
Defense: 10.1% (28th)	**Playoff Contender (9-10):** 19%
Special Teams: -0.1% (17th)	**Super Bowl Contender (11+):** 12%
Variance: 20.5% (21st)	**Projected Average Opponent:** 3.1% (5th)

2010: Insanity is doing the same thing over and over again and expecting different results.

2011: Insanity is doing the same thing over and over again and expecting different results.

Every Bills season is very much like every other, and every Bills preview is the same.

The Bills have been stuck in a rut since we started writing these books seven years ago, and composing a Bills "season outlook" chapter, whether for *Football Outsiders Almanac* or any other publication, has become an exercise in rote predictability. Every year, we hit the same marks. We discuss the merits of the new quarterback, dissecting his modest success from the previous year and expressing measured skepticism about his often dubious credentials as a long-term solution. We do something similar for the running back, always a recent first-round pick, usually concluding that he is likely to max out as a committee back, not a superstar. We note the flow of talented young free agents out of Buffalo and the trickle of troubled second-chance veterans in. We talk about economic depression in upstate New York and the prospects of relocation. We search for polite ways to say that nothing will change until Ralph Wilson earns a reward greater than any Super Bowl trophy, and feel ghoulish and self-ashamed if we express that depressing fact too directly. Almost guiltily, we applaud whatever truly great players are still on the roster — Kyle Williams, hooray! — or give the scouting department undue praise for simple accomplishments, like not squandering a draft pick or successfully developing a few young players. We don't

want to sound like we are bashing the Bills, because we feel kind of sorry for them.

So we are now on familiar ground. We have gone from J.P. Losman to Trent Edwards to Ryan Fitzpatrick, and from Willis McGahee to Marshawn Lynch to C.J. Spiller. We have seen a roster's worth of too-expensive-to-keep youngsters leave and a motley dribble of Terrell Owens/Shawne Merriman types arrive seeking image rehabilitation and a steady paycheck. We've seen draft after unproductive draft, with the Bills squandering early picks either on running backs (an outmoded draft strategy the team clings to) or defensive linemen who don't work out (Aaron Maybin, John McCargo). We've gone from Mike Mularkey to Dick Jauron to Chan Gailey in an increasingly desperate coach recycling program, but the paradigm hasn't changed because there isn't one. The Toronto experiment brought optimism (and something new to write about) for a few years, but it turns out that Toronto football fans have little interest in watching a bad team for ridiculous prices. And Wilson, bless his soul, is now approaching the age of 93, still sound of mind and as sound as possible of body, a man who built a football franchise by himself and has earned the right to keep it in the stadium that bears his name as long as it remains (barely) economically viable.

So really, you have read this all before. And if we quit now, we will have an extra 1,200 words or so for

2011 Bills Schedule

Week	Opp.	Week	Opp.	Week	Opp.
1	at KC	7	BYE	13	TEN
2	OAK	8	WAS (Tor.)	14	at SD
3	NE	9	NYJ	15	MIA
4	at CIN	10	at DAL	16	DEN
5	PHI	11	at MIA	17	at NE
6	at NYG	12	at NYJ		

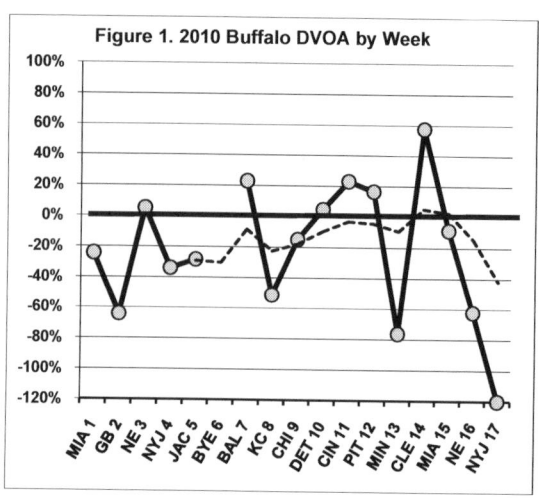

Figure 1. 2010 Buffalo DVOA by Week

the Jets or Patriots, which are much more interesting teams in regions where we sell many more books. What do you say, Aaron? No? Very well.

The arrivals of Chan Gailey and defensive coordinator George Edwards brought major strategic changes to the Bills in 2010. Gailey's offense grew from something predictable and straightforward in his late-'90s stint with the Cowboys into a gadget-heavy amalgam of Pistol formations, spread principles, and other flourishes. Edwards planned to switch the Bills from a vanilla Cover-2 defense into a blitzing 3-4. The plan, if it can be called that, was for all of the strategic window dressing to hide the relative lack of talent on the roster. But the scant talent that was available was not well-suited to the new schemes. The one offensive position at which the Bills were deep was running back, where two first-round picks (Lynch and Spiller) were expected to battle good soldier Fred Jackson for playing time. Gailey's pass-heavy schemes meant fewer opportunities for the team's high-profile runners. On defense, veterans like Chris Kelsey, Kawika Mitchell, Marcus Stroud, and Akin Ayodele had to adjust to new roles, sometimes on the fly.

On offense, the strategic changes worked, eventually and for a while. It took Gailey all of training camp and the first two weeks of the season to reach the conclusion all of us knew he would eventually make: that the mobile Fitzpatrick was a better fit for his rollouts-and-shotgun-heavy offense than Trent Edwards. Once Gailey demoted and dismissed Edwards (and traded Lynch), he was able to serve up some of the famous chicken salad he makes from chicken scratch personnel. Gailey dialed up empty backfields a league-leading 15.1 percent of the time, used four or five wide receivers on 25 percent of offensive snaps, and mixed in Wildcat plays, bootlegs, wide receiver screens, and just about every other gadget play ever invented to keep defenses on their toes. Perennial prospect Steve Johnson blossomed at wide receiver, Fitzpatrick dis-

tributed the ball and kept plays alive with his legs, and from Weeks 3 through 7 the Bills scored 104 points in four games, all of them losses.

The Bills kept losing because Edwards' defense was a disaster. The Bills didn't intercept a single pass in their first four games, picked David Garrard off once, then embarked on another three-game stretch without an interception. They allowed more than 200 rushing yards four times in one five-week stretch. There were obvious coverage mix-ups and blown gap responsibilities. Edwards made desperate changes on the fly, and by midseason the Bills were a 4-3 team with 3-4 wrinkles. Just as Edwards quelled the emergency on defense, Gailey's offense began to fade due to injuries and opponents' familiarity. For a while, though, everything clicked just enough for the Bills to win four games in a six-week span: a wild comeback against the Bengals, and tight wins against the Lions, Browns, and Dolphins.

In the standings, 2010 was the worst Bills season since 2001, but it yielded some curious optimism. While the team's four wins were close calls against bad opponents, they were clumped near the end of the season, creating a feeling that the team was "headed in the right direction." Gailey wasn't accomplishing much, but at least he was doing *something*: shuffling the roster, giving new players a chance, tinkering with strategies. Unlike Dick Jauron, who appeared to coach on autopilot, Gailey always looked busy, and his loopy tactics made the Bills fun to watch. Squint and use a lot of wishful thinking, and the Bills start to look like a low-budget version of the Saints: mad scientist coach, brainy little quarterback, lots of skill position talent, a defense that can be dangerous if it figures things out.

The reality is more distressing. Ryan Fitzpatrick is no Drew Brees. He's more of a Jay Fiedler: a late-blooming Ivy League touch passer with good legs and spotty accuracy beyond 15 yards or so. Fiedler led some defense-oriented teams assembled by Jimmy Johnson to 10- and 11-win seasons. Fitzpatrick is expected to be the triggerman for a pass-happy team assembled on a tight budget. The Bills are so enthusiastic about Fitzpatrick that they didn't bother drafting a quarterback of the future, which is just as well, because the team burns through quarterbacks of the future like dollar store batteries. Tyler Thigpen, who knows Chan Gailey's system from Kansas City, signed on in July as Fitzpatrick disaster insurance.

Skill position talent is indeed the Bills' strength. Johnson received some premature coronation as the NFL's next great receiver, but he's very good: a big target who makes plays in traffic, can use his size to separate defenders from the ball, and can glide past defenders on deep routes. Lee Evans can still get deep. David Nelson has the potential to be a Muhsin Muhammad type over the middle. Roscoe Parrish has frequent brain cramps but was flourishing in Gailey's system (which creates lots of space for jitterbugs in the slot) before getting hurt. Newcomer Brad Smith is a perfect fit in Gailey's scheme as a runner/receiver/Wildcat source of confusion. C.J. Spiller couldn't convert his speed into production as a rookie, but he proved that he can break long runs if he beats defenders in his first two steps. Fred Jackson is tough and persistent, and backup receivers Donald Jones and Naaman Roosevelt were impressive in limited action. The Bills will produce some 24- to 31-point performances against weaker defenses; better opponents like the Jets and Patriots will beat up their offensive line (still a work in progress, to put it kindly), choke out the short routes, and dare Fitzpatrick to burn them deep.

On defense, first-round pick Marcell Dareus joins Williams to give the Bills two-thirds of a solid 3-4 line. Dareus may have been the best player in the draft class: an end/tackle hybrid with an extraordinary size-agility mix who will disrupt a lot of plays when aligned over the offensive tackle. Merriman, rescued from A.J. Smith's doghouse at the end of last season, is reportedly healthy and eager to prove himself. At 27, he's hardly washed up. Dave Wannstedt's arrival as assistant head coach/linebackers coach puts George Edwards on notice and provides either a stabilizing or subversive presence on the defensive staff, depending on your pessimism level. Wannstedt, it should be noted, is excellent Bills head coaching material: He has outstanding references but little track record of real success, and he would gladly accept the job if offered so he can pump up his IRAs.

The influx of fresh talent partially offsets the annual departures of young free agents. Donte Whitner and Paul Posluszny skipped town as soon as the free agent market opened. Neither was a great player, but both were highly-drafted prospects (Whitner was the eighth overall pick in 2006, Poz a high second-rounder in 2007) who left Buffalo without looking back the moment their contracts expired. Such departures are the rule, not the exception, in Buffalo, which is why the team is always drafting not to get stronger, but to catch up. Third-round pick Kelvin Sheppard should step in for Poz, and fourth-round pick Da'Norris Searcy will pick up some of the slack left by Whitner, but a 4-12 team cannot afford to make this many treadmill selections.

That puts us back where we started: throwing cold water on the quarterback situation, cataloging the progression of young free agents out of Buffalo, seeking and polishing small nuggets of good news so the Bills preview isn't a total downer. (Did we mention how well Kyle Williams played last year?) Bills discussions always return to this familiar territory. A .500 season is certainly possible, a playoff appearance is extremely unlikely, and any suggestion that the Bills are taking the right steps toward a better future is squelched by the fact that their quarterback is a 28-year-old journeyman and any middle-tier stars the team develops fly out of Buffalo on the first plane that leaves after their contracts expire. So we end by noting that things will be different for the Los Angeles Bills in a few years, then realize that most Bills previews end with this once-clever observation, and finally sigh in resignation and disappointment, a sound with which Bills fans are very, very familiar.

Mike Tanier

2010 Bills Stats by Week

Wk	vs.	W-L	PF	PA	YDF	YDA	TO	Total	Off	Def	ST
1	MIA	L	10	15	166	296	0	-24%	-25%	6%	6%
2	@GB	L	7	34	186	346	-2	-64%	-31%	31%	-2%
3	@NE	L	30	38	374	445	-1	5%	18%	28%	16%
4	NYJ	L	14	38	223	444	-2	-34%	9%	39%	-5%
5	JAC	L	26	36	306	381	3	-28%	-6%	18%	-4%
6	BYE										
7	@BAL	L	34	37	514	364	-2	23%	40%	34%	17%
8	@KC	L	10	13	328	414	-1	-51%	-35%	17%	1%
9	CHI	L	19	22	340	283	-2	-15%	13%	26%	-2%
10	DET	W	14	12	288	390	0	5%	-12%	-18%	-1%
11	@CIN	W	49	31	449	361	1	23%	25%	-9%	-11%
12	PIT	L	16	19	329	426	-1	16%	15%	8%	9%
13	@MIN	L	14	38	239	387	-1	-76%	-62%	2%	-13%
14	CLE	W	13	6	323	187	2	58%	3%	-57%	-3%
15	@MIA	W	17	14	282	326	1	-9%	3%	11%	-1%
16	NE	L	3	34	369	348	-7	-62%	-57%	-4%	-8%
17	@NYJ	L	7	38	162	388	-5	-121%	-101%	21%	1%

Trends and Splits

	Offense	Rank	Defense	Rank
Total DVOA	-10.4%	26	10.1%	28
Unadjusted VOA	-12.8%	27	15.7%	29
Weighted Trend	-13.2%	30	3.0%	15
Variance	14.0%	30	5.7%	9
Average Opponent	-0.7%	29	9.6%	30
Passing	-5.0%	26	14.8%	25
Rushing	-4.7%	21	6.4%	31
First Down	-9.0%	28	7.1%	21
Second Down	-13.4%	27	21.1%	32
Third Down	-8.7%	22	-1.4%	15
First Half	-8.3%	26	18.0%	31
Second Half	-12.2%	25	1.5%	15
Red Zone	-18.2%	25	24.8%	30
Late and Close	-6.0%	25	-1.0%	18

Five-Year Performance

Year	W-L	Pyth	Est W	PF	PA	TO	Total	Rk	Off	Rk	Def	Rk	ST	Rk	Off AGL	Rk	Def AGL	Rk
2006	7-9	7.7	7.9	300	311	-11	-2.7%	19	-6.7%	22	1.9%	15	5.9%	2	13.4	14	7.3	7
2007	7-9	4.9	8.3	252	354	+9	-5.8%	19	-8.9%	22	1.0%	18	4.2%	6	22.6	18	43.6	30
2008	7-9	7.8	6.9	336	342	-8	-8.4%	24	-5.3%	24	9.3%	22	6.1%	1	13.3	8	34.9	25
2009	6-10	5.8	6.9	258	326	+3	-9.3%	24	-17.1%	29	-6.5%	8	1.2%	12	60.7	32	62.1	32
2010	4-12	4.4	5.6	283	425	-17	-20.6%	28	-10.4%	26	10.1%	28	-0.1%	17	10.4	5	31.2	22

Strategic Tendencies

Run/Pass		Rank	Offense		Rank	Defense		Rank	Other		Rank
Runs, all plays	38%	22	3+ WR	71%	2	Rush 3	10.3%	11	2+ RB, Pct Runs	60%	11
Runs, first half	41%	13	4+ WR	25%	2	Rush 4	64.4%	8	1 RB/2 TE, Pct Runs	58%	4
Runs, first down	52%	12	2+ TE	13%	31	Rush 5	21.3%	23	1 RB/3+ WR, Pct Runs	31%	4
Runs, second-long	28%	26	Single back	55%	20	Rush 6+	4.1%	28	CB1 on WR1	43%	14
Runs, power sit.	52%	22	Play action	10%	31	Zone Blitz	2.9%	25	Go for it on 4th	0.89	18
Runs, behind 2H	29%	13	Max protect	12%	12	Sacks by LB	35.2%	15	Offensive Pace	31.1	21
Pass, ahead 2H	40%	23	Outside pocket	11%	22	Sacks by DB	18.5%	4	Defensive Pace	31.0	23

Chan Gailey dramatically changed the use of formations in the Buffalo offense. The Bills went from the team that ran the most two-tight end sets to 31st, and their frequency using three or more wideouts shot up from 44 percent to 71 percent. ☜ Buffalo used an empty backfield on a league-leading 15 percent of plays. Although the league-wide DVOA was 16.6% on these plays, Buffalo's DVOA was just -3.7%. ☜ Despite Steve Johnson's high-profile drop in an aborted comeback against Pittsburgh, holding onto the ball is actually the strength of Buffalo's receivers. They dropped only 21 passes (tied for second) after dropping only 19 the year before. ☜ Buffalo averaged a league-low 2.8 yards per carry on draw plays. ☜ Buffalo's offense led the league in passes that were incomplete because the quarterback was hit while in his throwing motion. ☜ The Bills gained a league-low 619 yards on opponent penalties.

Passing

Player	DYAR	DVOA	Plays	NtYds	Avg	YAC	C%	TD	Int
R.Fitzpatrick	415	2.9%	468	2876	6.1	4.8	58.1%	23	15
T.Edwards	-278	-50.4%	115	483	4.2	4.5	55.0%	2	5
B.Brohm	-182	-125.0%	26	101	3.9	3.9	43.5%	0	3

Rushing

Player	DYAR	DVOA	Plays	Yds	Avg	TD	Fum	Suc
F.Jackson	81	0.2%	222	929	4.2	5	4	47%
C.Spiller	-6	-10.5%	74	288	3.9	0	2	43%
R.Fitzpatrick	19	-2.2%	36	271	7.5	0	2	-
T.Edwards	13	5.3%	14	58	4.1	0	0	-
Q.Ganther	-5	-22.7%	9	18	2.0	0	0	33%
C.McIntyre	8	16.4%	4	5	1.3	1	0	75%

Receiving

Player	DYAR	DVOA	Plays	Ctch	Yds	Y/C	YAC	TD	C%
S.Johnson	236	8.7%	142	82	1073	13.1	4.8	10	58%
L.Evans	-26	-16.6%	84	37	578	15.6	3.2	4	44%
R.Parrish	42	-2.4%	52	33	415	12.6	4.0	2	63%
D.Nelson	95	15.2%	47	31	353	11.4	2.5	3	66%
D.Jones	-76	-35.4%	41	18	213	11.8	4.8	1	44%
N.Roosevelt	18	0.6%	17	9	139	15.4	3.7	0	53%
J.Stupar	5	-0.9%	13	12	111	9.3	7.1	0	92%
D.Martin	0	-7.3%	8	7	43	6.1	2.1	1	88%
F.Jackson	-57	-32.9%	54	31	215	6.9	7.8	2	57%
C.Spiller	39	12.5%	30	24	157	6.5	6.6	1	80%
C.McIntyre	-24	-67.0%	8	4	32	8.0	7.0	0	50%

Offensive Line

Year	Yards	ALY	Rank	Power	Rank	Stuff	Rank	2nd Lev	Rank	Open Field	Rank
2008	4.21	4.13	14	62%	24	18%	16	1.16	10	0.68	20
2009	4.29	4.19	12	50%	31	16%	5	1.15	16	0.63	21
2010	4.05	3.85	20	65%	11	20%	21	1.10	19	0.66	19

Year	LE	Rank	LT	Rank	Mid	Rank	RT	Rank	RE	Rank	Sacks	ASR	Rank	F-Start	Cont.
2008	5.67	2	4.16	15	3.77	25	4.68	2	4.22	9	38	8.1%	25	15	30
2009	3.27	26	4.21	13	4.39	7	3.22	30	4.78	7	46	9.9%	32	32	21
2010	3.57	22	5.25	1	3.85	20	3.11	30	3.65	23	34	6.5%	17	20	26

The Bills' offensive line graded out rather well once you factor in all of the injuries, flunked tryouts, and experimentation at various positions. Chan Gailey was more willing than most coaches to rotate players on the offensive line, so there were several games in which Eric Wood rotated with Kraig Urbik at right guard or Mansfield Wrotto traded series with Erik Pears at right tackle. At times, sorting out who was who on game tape of the Bills' line caused eyestrain, but some trends revealed themselves. 1) Urbik was pretty terrible, and Corey Rinehart wasn't much better when he eventually won the right guard spot. 2) Wood can be run over by bull rushers, but he looked much better when he moved to center to replace injured Geoff Hangartner. Wood will probably move to center, his college position, permanently. 3) Pears, a late-season rescue from the Broncos' sinking ship, is a better option than Wrotto, and will probably win the right tackle job in camp.

Left tackle Demetrius Bell has slowly developed into a solid option at left tackle. A seventh-round pick in 2008, Bell earned the starting job at left tackle in 2009 but was mistake- and penalty-prone (four blown blocks and 10 flags in nine games) before suffering a knee injury. Bell cut down on the mistakes last year, and he frequently draws comparisons to Jason Peters, which means he will be overrated before you know it. Left guard Andy Levitre played through injuries and got through the 2010 season without drawing attention to himself, which is all the Bills can ask for from a young lineman.

Defensive Front Seven

Defensive Line	Age	Pos	Plays	TmPct	Rk	Stop	Dfts	BTkl	St%	Rk	AvYd	Rk	Pass Rush Sack	Hit	Hur	vs. Run Runs	St%	Yds	vs. Pass Pass	St%	Yds
Kyle Williams	28	DT	77	8.6%	2	61	21	4	77%	28	1.4	19	5.5	8	10.5	65	77%	2.1	12	92%	-2.4
Dwan Edwards	30	DE	59	9.5%	2	39	8	2	65%	72	3.4	77	1	4	4	51	65%	3.5	8	75%	2.5
Spencer Johnson	30	DT	58	7.4%	17	41	10	1	68%	66	2.3	56	2	0	5.5	53	68%	2.8	5	100%	-2.8
Marcus Stroud	33	DE	51	6.1%	30	37	10	2	70%	60	2.5	62	3.5	0	6.5	44	70%	3.1	7	86%	-1.7

Linebackers	Age	Pos	Plays	TmPct	Rk	Stop	Dfts	BTkl	AvYd	Pass Rush Sack	Hit	Hur	vs. Run Runs	St%	Rk	Yds	Rk	vs. Pass Tgts	Suc%	Rk	AdjYd	Rk
Paul Posluszny	27	ILB	155	19.7%	2	73	21	3	5.1	2	2	5.5	107	50%	106	4.0	91	38	46%	66	6.5	49
Akin Ayodele	32	ILB	105	12.5%	39	54	10	6	4.4	0	0	0	85	51%	103	4.1	93	18	71%	5	3.7	6
Chris Kelsay	32	OLB	74	8.2%	79	50	12	8	3.1	4	6	18	57	68%	56	3.1	56	10	54%	--	6.5	--
Reggie Torbor	30	OLB	44	7.8%	--	24	3	2	4.1	0	0	1.5	29	66%	--	3.1	--	9	66%	--	2.8	--
Andra Davis	33	ILB	41	12.2%	--	19	6	3	4.6	0	0	0	33	52%	--	3.8	--	3	1%	--	13.7	--
Arthur Moats	22	OLB	24	2.8%	--	15	4	2	3.3	2.5	4	10.5	16	63%	--	4.9	--	5	18%	--	12.1	--
Keith Ellison	27	ILB	16	3.6%	--	9	1	1	5.9	0	0	0	9	67%	--	4.0	--	6	65%	--	6.3	--

Year	Yards	ALY	Rank	Power	Rank	Stuff	Rank	2nd Lev	Rank	Open Field	Rank
2008	4.09	3.81	8	65%	15	20%	8	1.06	11	0.84	22
2009	4.78	4.26	21	75%	30	18%	18	1.25	25	1.13	29
2010	4.73	4.88	32	65%	21	12%	32	1.32	31	0.71	13

Year	LE	Rank	LT	Rank	Mid	Rank	RT	Rank	RE	Rank	Sacks	ASR	Rank
2008	4.15	18	4.40	19	3.74	6	3.48	6	3.05	8	24	4.7%	28
2009	3.54	9	3.84	11	4.26	23	4.90	29	5.16	27	34	7.1%	9
2010	4.86	27	4.96	29	4.86	32	4.30	18	6.15	32	27	5.7%	24

With Marcell Dareus on the defensive line, Kyle Williams will no longer have to be the Lone Ranger against the run. The Bills plan to use Dareus as a 3-4 end on rushing downs, then move him to tackle on passing downs. Williams, presumably, will remain on the field on passing downs — think of a Packers-style front — with Dwan Edwards or Spencer Johnson leaving the field on third-and-long. Edwards is expected to start at the other end position, with Johnson relegated to wave duty.

Shawne Merriman injured his Achilles during his first workout after signing with the Bills in November, but after signing a two-year contract extension in January, he's a major part of the team's plans. Merriman is a natural 3-4 pass rusher, unlike Chris Kelsey, who was much more effective when the team scaled back its 3-4 looks and let him rush from a three-point stance. A Merriman-Kelsey pass rush, with Williams and Dareus eating up the middle, should provide plenty of pass rush with minimal creativity. That's a good thing for the Bills: The more exotic their defense got last year, the more likely it was to make some critical mistake.

Nick Barnett, like the departed Paul Posluszny, is an effective defender in space, but he can get wired to blockers and pushed around. Poz looked out of place as a 3-4 inside linebacker last year; Barnett has experience in both the 3-4 and the 4-3, which is perfect for the Bills. Third-round pick Kelvin Sheppard (LSU) is a big, stout gap-filler with limited range. Sheppard is a tough guy who is at his best when attacking the line of scrimmage; if Poz departs, he'll be the "Mike" in the Bills' system, with Akin Ayodele sliding over to the rangy "Will" inside position. Arthur Moats manned the "Joker" outside position at the end of last season and gives the Bills another pass rushing option if they move Kelsey to the line in some packages.

Defensive Secondary

Secondary	Age	Pos	Plays	TmPct	Overall Rk	Stop	Dfts	BTkl	Runs	vs. Run St%	Rk	Yds	Rk	Tgts	vs. Pass Tgt%	Rk	Dist	Suc%	Rk	APaYd	Rk	PD	Int
Donte Whitner	26	SS	145	16.1%	2	43	15	4	94	29%	65	8.3	58	33	7.3%	22	12.7	53%	43	8.6	50	4	1
Jairus Byrd	25	FS	90	10.0%	45	23	8	3	50	38%	45	6.9	46	22	4.9%	63	12.1	47%	63	7.0	26	2	1
Drayton Florence	31	CB	73	8.1%	49	32	13	8	21	43%	42	6.0	35	73	16.2%	33	11.2	46%	72	7.2	41	16	3
Leodis McKelvin	26	CB	69	7.7%	55	28	14	9	22	32%	72	9.3	69	70	15.6%	38	14.7	54%	32	8.6	67	12	2
Bryan Scott	30	SS	35	4.2%	81	22	14	4	10	80%	1	2.7	1	25	5.8%	39	9.3	45%	66	7.0	28	3	0
Reggie Corner	28	CB	27	3.0%	--	9	6	4	6	17%	--	7.8	--	36	7.9%	--	8.7	55%	--	5.9	--	4	0
George Wilson	30	FS	21	2.3%	--	14	3	3	13	62%	--	4.2	--	5	1.1%	--	20.4	80%	--	2.6	--	3	2
Terrence McGee	31	CB	18	3.6%	--	5	2	0	6	17%	--	10.5	--	16	6.2%	--	10.6	72%	--	5.1	--	1	0

Year	Pass D Rank	vs. #1 WR	Rk	vs. #2 WR	Rk	vs. Other WR	Rk	vs. TE	Rk	vs. RB	Rk
2008	24	29.1%	30	-8.9%	10	-16.8%	9	-2.1%	13	16.0%	26
2009	3	-30.0%	4	-8.3%	10	-33.4%	1	-8.7%	8	-12.1%	8
2010	25	32.3%	31	9.9%	20	-43.5%	1	13.2%	23	-8.7%	7

Terrence McGee missed seven games last year with a nerve problem in his knee. His absence set off a chain reaction: Drayton Florence, who re-signed with the team (a rarity for a Bills cornerback) was Peter-Principled into taking on number-one receivers more frequently, while Leodis McKelvin moved from a nickel role into a starting job. Florence held his own, but McKelvin was in over his head, allowing nine pass plays of 25 or more yards. McGee also missed five games in 2009, so the Bills drafted Aaron Williams out of Texas at the start of the second round. At six feet tall and 205 pounds, Williams is bigger than the typical Bills cornerback (McGee and Florence are under 5-foot-10, and the Bills have preferred small, feisty corners since the days of Nate Clements) and should provide a matchup option against Braylon Edwards/Brandon Marshall types.

Jairus Byrd followed up his Pro Bowl appearance as a rookie with a miserable sophomore campaign. He didn't intercept a pass until Week 17, and he spent much of the year arriving late in deep support or misplaying angles when chasing ballcarriers in the open field. Byrd is a classic free safety who usually plays deep center-field, so his interception totals are going to be flaky: A few dumb passes over the middle will make him look like a superstar. He's not as good as we thought he was in 2009, but he must get better than he was in 2010: "Playing deep" is no excuse for recording just four Pass Stops in 16 games.

Strong safety Donte Whitner left as a free agent, signing with the Bengals. Wait, the Niners: he agreed to terms with the Bengals, then heard about better terms in San Francisco. Anyway, he's gone. Bryan Scott saw a lot of playing time as a safety/linebacker hybrid in the nickel package and could replace Whitner. Fourth-round pick Da'Norris Searcy (North Carolina) is a similar player, a 220-pound in-the-box thumper who is fast enough to chase most tight ends.

Special Teams

Year	DVOA	Rank	FG/XP	Rank	Net Kick	Rank	Kick Ret	Rank	Net Punt	Rank	Punt Ret	Rank	Hidden	Rank
2008	6.1%	1	-3.6	25	6.4	9	17.3	1	7.3	8	8.8	3	0.9	11
2009	1.2%	12	3.7	10	4.7	12	-1.4	14	5.9	8	-5.8	25	1.3	12
2010	-0.1%	17	-0.5	18	3.4	10	-4.5	21	-0.4	21	1.6	14	0.2	14

C.J. Spiller returned a kickoff 95 yards and two punts 33 and 34 yards, but in between the few highlights there were long stretches of fair catches and 18-yard kickoff returns straight into the nearest pile. Spiller's speed makes him a natural choice on kickoffs, but he may not have the initial quickness to excel on punts, though he is less susceptible to epic brain cramps than one-time return specialist Roscoe Parrish. Brad Smith is also an excellent return man and will compete with Spiller for the role.

Ryan Lindell missed the first extra point of his career last year — the Bears blocked it — and also had a 53-yard field goal taken away against the Chiefs when Todd Haley "iced" him with a sudden timeout midway through the fourth quarter. Lindell endured a mini-slump after the Chiefs game but rebounded late in the year. Punter Brian Moorman had an uncharacteristic off year but should rebound in 2011.

Coaching Staff

Defensive coordinator George Edwards and assistant head coach/linebackers coach Dave Wannstedt coached together on the Dolphins and Cowboys staffs. Like Chan Gailey, they are part of the Jimmy Johnson family tree, but they branched in very different directions. Wannstedt isn't much of a 3-4 guy, making him an odd choice for his assigned role: Inside linebacker is a very different job in the 3-4 and 4-3 defenses. (It's essentially two jobs in most 3-4 schemes, with one player shooting gaps while the other flows to the play.) Wannstedt's real job, of course, is to provide a ready alternative if Edwards' system flops the way it did in 2010. There are also several holdovers from the Dick Jauron staff among the defensive coaches, including outside linebackers coach Bob Sanders and secondary coach George Catavolos. The ingredients are in place for confusion and politicking.

Quarterbacks coach George Cortez has an impressive, if random resume. He worked with Jeff Garcia in the CFL, then moved to Cal, where he was Aaron Rodgers' quarterbacks coach (and Kyle Boller's, though no one mentions that anymore). From there, it was back to Calgary, which is well outside the box, and therefore right in line with Chan Gailey's brainwaves. Cortez did a fine job preparing Ryan Fitzpatrick, though he also did a pretty terrible job preparing Trent Edwards, which goes to show how an assistant coach's reputation is built by stringing together successes and burying failures. At least Cortez's CFL experience prepared him for the wide-open lunacy of Gailey's offense.

Carolina Panthers

2010 Record: 2-14

Pythagorean Wins: 2.4 (32nd)

DVOA: -35.0% (31st)

Offense: -31.9% (32nd)

Defense: 1.8% (16th)

Special Teams: -1.3% (20th)

Variance: 9.4% (6th)

2011 Mean Projection: 6.2 wins

On the Clock (0-3): 11%

Loserville (4-6): 45%

Mediocrity (7-8): 29%

Playoff Contender (9-10): 13%

Super Bowl Contender (11+): 2%

Projected Average Opponent: -1.8% (25th)

2010: Secretly reasonable defense hidden by total offensive implosion.

2011: Cam Newton is … THE ENTERTAINER!

Despite the lack of success that the Panthers enjoyed from their 2009 idea, *The 2008 Carolina Panthers but One Year Older*, general manager Marty Hurney and owner Jerry Richardson decided to greenlight *The 2008 Carolina Panthers without Julius Peppers and Jake Delhomme* for the 2010 season. Unlike in the real movies, many Panthers were harmed during the recording of this 2-14 disaster, and the ensuing chaos led to the overthrow of long-time coach John Fox. Certainly the Panthers have made their mistakes in the last couple of offseasons. They locked themselves into Delhomme's services with an extension after his meltdown against the Cardinals in the 2009 playoffs, despite mountains of factual evidence that this was a bad idea. Their inability to find a consistent set of hands next to Steve Smith since Muhsin Muhammad retired, despite spending multiple high-round picks on receivers, was baffling. Nevertheless, very few fans saw this kind of season coming. *Football Outsiders Almanac 2010* projected the Panthers to win just about the same number of games they did in 2009: 8.2.

Instead, behind a rash of injuries to key contributors, the Panthers offense reverted to an embryonic stage, replete with second-round quarterback Jimmy Clausen assuming the fetal position. After a promising sophomore season that saw him emerge as one of the best young run blockers in the NFL, right tackle Jeff Otah's knee kept him out for the entire year, forcing the Panthers to move guard Geoff Schwartz outside. DeAngelo Williams sprained his foot and didn't play after Week 7's win against the 49ers, and backup Jonathan Stewart also missed time with a concussion, forcing the Panthers to start Mike Goodson for a few games in the middle of the season. Mauler Travelle Wharton went down with turf toe after Week 10, making the Panthers offensive line even thinner.

Worst of all, star wide receiver Smith played through the season with a quadriceps injury and a high ankle sprain. Describing himself later as "playing on one leg," he posted by far the worst numbers of his career, notching just 554 receiving yards in 14 starts and finishing with an astonishing -153 DYAR, good for dead last in the NFL among wideouts. With Smith effectively gone, so was the Panthers' passing attack. FO's KUBIAK system wasn't a fan of incumbent quarterback Matt Moore, who finished 2009 with four straight solid starts, but it didn't expect this horrendous showing. Moore was concussed in Week 1, benched for Clausen in Week 2, was back in the lineup after Week 5, and led the Panthers to one of their two wins of the season with a 308-yard effort against the 49ers in Week 7. In between injuries and benchings, Moore managed -270 DYAR in just six games before Sedrick Ellis decided to save Fox the effort of playing quarterback musical chairs by tearing Moore's labrum for

2011 Panthers Schedule

Week	Opp.	Week	Opp.	Week	Opp.
1	at ARI	7	WAS	13	at TB
2	GB	8	MIN	14	ATL
3	JAC	9	BYE	15	at HOU
4	at CHI	10	TEN	16	TB
5	NO	11	at DET	17	at NO
6	at ATL	12	at IND		

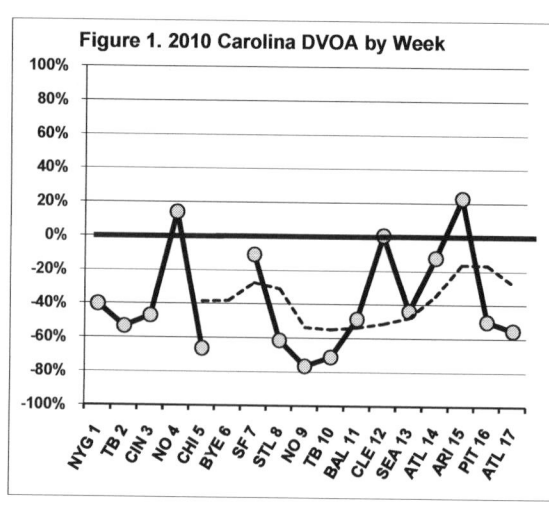

Figure 1. 2010 Carolina DVOA by Week

him in Week 9. Then the job fell to Clausen, thought to be the Panthers quarterback of the future. It's hard to imagine that there would be a worse situation to be in than quarterbacking Carolina last season, but Clausen brought back memories of David Carr beatings past by taking 33 sacks in just 339 dropbacks. When he actually did get his throws off, he was very small in the pocket, meaning a lot of them were batted right back at him. A low release point and poor mechanics contributed to a rookie season that was right in line with his star receiver's: -609 DYAR, also last in the NFL.

Casting calls for the role of After Quarterback ("Ahh! Much Better!") in this season's reprisal landed the Panthers a big-budget entertainer to match their offseason spending: Cam Newton. It's hard to find anyone who thought Newton was the best player in the draft, but apparently need overcame pure talent in Hurney's eyes. Given their foibles with drafting wide receivers, it's hard to believe they passed on A.J. Green, but the referendum on Clausen's franchise signal-caller potential was quite clear. Some in the media brought up comparisons to JaMarcus Russell, based on the evidence that Russell was the last SEC quarterback taken with the first overall pick. The better college comparison for Newton is Vince Young: value as a runner, a track record of winning, questions about the ability to read coverages coming out of college, and concerns about his maturity.

Like Young, Newton is in a position to be eased into the offense. With the unit on their way to full health, and the Panthers dishing out $21 million in guaranteed money to keep Williams in the fold, Carolina will likely have a powerful running game again. New offensive coordinator Rob Chudzinski, who came over from San Diego, would be wise to learn from Mike Heimerdinger's recent experiments with the Titans. When your franchise quarterback's second or third read in college was "run," keeping progressions

simple is always a plus. Mixing in some option plays and concepts for Newton to help open up more passing lanes would be enormous for his weak receiving group. "Chud" said in an interview with the Panthers' official website that he wanted an "attacking style offense," mentioning that big plays were the way down the ball field. The Panthers can likely have success on the ground this year, but if Chud wants big plays, look for him to spend his off-days watching tape of Phillip Rivers sticking deep outs whilst openly weeping.

New head coach Ron Rivera and Chudzinski will have their work cut out for them as they try to reshape this team's passing game. For one thing, the 2008 vintage of Steve Smith likely won't be walking through that door. Smith spent most of the offseason trying to cannily force his way out of Charlotte and into the arms of a nice contending franchise. Might he suggest the Ravens on the T.J. Houshmandzadeh Fellowship? The real problem is that Smith's star receiver days are likely over. His two closest three-year comps in FO's similarity scores, Brian Blades and Jake Reed, were possession receivers or non-factors over the rest of their careers. Even if Smith does have a bounce-back year in him, it likely won't be enough to get the Panthers receiving game to the middle ground it needs to be at for them to contend. He finally wised up a week into free agency and decided that the grass was greener in Carolina, probably because the Panthers didn't ask him take a pay cut.

Behind Smith, the Panthers wide receiver corps is young and unproven. 2010 sixth-rounder David Gettis showed flashes of effectiveness last year, 2010 third-rounder Brandon LaFell proved that he could run pretty fast (catching balls was a different matter), and fellow 2010 third-rounder Armanti Edwards was the best quarterback on the roster last season, so at least he has that going for him. That and making Rich Eisen cower due to repressed painful memories. Carolina did manage to finagle tight end Greg Olsen from Chicago for a third-round pick during a momentary break in handing out big contracts to their own defenders. Though that was probably a bit too much to pay for the infamous Seventh Floor crew member, G-Reg will supply Newton with a decent red zone target and some inconsistent hands.

A funny thing happened to the pass defense that was supposed to fall off a cliff after Peppers fled for Chicago: It didn't. A pair of first-year starters took the reins and delivered excellent performances to keep the unit humming, forcing Richardson and Hurney to spend Michael Bay money to keep the core intact. 2007 third-rounder Charles Johnson, freed from Peppers' shadow, stepped in at defensive end and put together a strong season, notching 11.5 sacks, 22 defeats, and 30.5 hurries. When the new CBA made fourth-year players unrestricted free agents, the Panthers were so concerned with losing Johnson that they handed him a big new contract with $32 million in guaranteed money. Not to be outdone, 2006 third-rounder James Anderson earned the starting spot on the strong side and had an extremely impressive season with 30 Defeats of his own, putting him in the same company as players like DeMarcus Ware, Cameron Wake, and James Harrison. Carolina rewarded him with a five-year contract worth a maximum of $22 million, then gave All-Pro linebacker Jon Beason $25 million guaranteed just in case he was feeling envious.

To the point that the Carolina defense declined, it was mostly in the running game. The Panthers have been patching their defensive tackles since the defections of Kris Jenkins and Ma'ake Kemoeatu, and it's helped lead them to a pair of disappointing finishes in run stopping DVOA the last two seasons. A second straight torn ACL to linebacker Thomas Davis was also unhelpful, though Dan Connor, a former FO honorable mention prospect, played well before fracturing his hip bone in Week 8. Carolina again showed questionable judgement in re-signing Davis to a five-year deal, but at least they learned last season that they have a capable backup plan in Connor.

New defensive coordinator Sean McDermott, fresh off being scapegoated by the Eagles for only holding the Super Bowl champion Packers to 21 points in the playoffs, picked up some new pieces at defensive tackle early in the draft. Sione Fua, acquired with the compensation pick the Panthers got for Peppers, was brought in from Stanford to man the nose. Fellow third-rounder Terrell McClain out of South Florida will play across from Fua as the penetrating off tackle. The Panthers supplemented those selections by bringing in veteran Ron Edwards from Kansas City. Edwards has compiled a decent run-stuffing resume, and should play over one of the two early on. No matter who earns the first chance to start, it should be an improvement over the skeleton crew that manned the position last year.

Despite all the cash the Panthers have thrown around this offseason, not a lot has changed with the basic structural model. Drawing the NFC North on the schedule won't help too much, but a good running game and a good defense will likely help the Panthers grind out a few more wins now than they were able to last season — provided that the passing game regresses to being merely bad. Don't look for *The Panthers Return to the Playoffs* any time soon, as we hear that's a 2013 joint and they're still trying to bring on Justin Blackmon to co-star, but *The Panthers Are Merely Bad* could be coming to a stadium near you this year.

Rivers McCown

2010 Panthers Stats by Week

Wk	vs.	W-L	PF	PA	YDF	YDA	TO	Total	Off	Def	ST
1	@NYG	L	18	31	237	376	-1	-40%	-56%	-9%	6%
2	TB	L	7	20	278	273	-3	-53%	-50%	-6%	-9%
3	CIN	L	7	20	267	305	-2	-47%	-52%	-9%	-5%
4	@NO	L	14	16	251	383	1	14%	13%	1%	2%
5	CHI	L	6	23	147	247	1	-66%	-98%	-44%	-12%
6	BYE										
7	SF	W	23	20	379	282	-2	-11%	-9%	8%	6%
8	@STL	L	10	20	201	246	-4	-61%	-54%	10%	2%
9	NO	L	3	34	195	408	-1	-77%	-60%	10%	-6%
10	@TB	L	16	31	300	421	1	-71%	-11%	73%	14%
11	BAL	L	13	37	270	378	0	-49%	-57%	-7%	1%
12	@CLE	L	23	24	326	379	2	1%	-4%	-4%	1%
13	@SEA	L	14	31	283	371	1	-44%	-15%	22%	-7%
14	ATL	L	10	31	288	327	-1	-12%	-13%	6%	7%
15	ARI	W	19	12	303	218	1	23%	-5%	-23%	5%
16	@PIT	L	3	27	119	408	0	-50%	-28%	19%	-3%
17	@ATL	L	10	31	291	352	-1	-55%	-33%	-1%	-23%

Trends and Splits

	Offense	Rank	Defense	Rank
Total DVOA	-31.9%	32	1.8%	16
Unadjusted VOA	-34.9%	32	2.4%	17
Weighted Trend	-24.1%	31	7.3%	22
Variance	8.5%	19	6.1%	13
Average Opponent	0.5%	25	1.6%	10
Passing	-35.9%	31	3.1%	8
Rushing	-17.0%	32	0.6%	21
First Down	-36.3%	32	6.1%	20
Second Down	-35.4%	32	-1.8%	10
Third Down	-19.3%	25	-1.0%	16
First Half	-22.3%	31	10.1%	23
Second Half	-40.2%	32	-8.5%	6
Red Zone	-57.7%	30	-13.9%	11
Late and Close	-36.4%	32	-1.9%	17

Five-Year Performance

Year	W-L	Pyth	Est W	PF	PA	TO	Total	Rk	Off	Rk	Def	Rk	ST	Rk	Off AGL	Rk	Def AGL	Rk
2006	8-8	6.9	7.9	270	305	-5	5.8%	14	-1.4%	17	-10.0%	4	-2.8%	24	26.8	25	23.6	23
2007	7-9	8.1	6.3	267	347	+1	-20.1%	26	-14.0%	26	1.2%	19	-4.9%	30	20.4	15	5.4	3
2008	12-4	10.1	10.1	414	329	+6	19.0%	6	18.0%	5	1.5%	13	2.5%	10	14.4	9	5.6	4
2009	8-8	8.2	8.9	315	308	+6	9.4%	14	1.5%	20	-10.9%	5	-2.9%	29	28.9	20	39.8	25
2010	2-14	2.4	3.8	196	408	-8	-35.0%	31	-31.9%	32	1.8%	16	-1.3%	20	39.8	27	35.2	24

Strategic Tendencies

Run/Pass		Rank	Offense		Rank	Defense		Rank	Other		Rank
Runs, all plays	42%	11	3+ WR	38%	31	Rush 3	12.2%	8	2+ RB, Pct Runs	64%	7
Runs, first half	50%	1	4+ WR	7%	11	Rush 4	56.1%	21	1 RB/2 TE, Pct Runs	47%	22
Runs, first down	54%	9	2+ TE	37%	5	Rush 5	20.5%	24	1 RB/3+ WR, Pct Runs	11%	32
Runs, second-long	46%	2	Single back	55%	22	Rush 6+	11.2%	9	CB1 on WR1	33%	24
Runs, power sit.	58%	18	Play action	21%	9	Zone Blitz	7.2%	10	Go for it on 4th	1.37	3
Runs, behind 2H	31%	6	Max protect	12%	11	Sacks by LB	22.6%	18	Offensive Pace	30.8	18
Pass, ahead 2H	39%	24	Outside pocket	12%	16	Sacks by DB	3.2%	27	Defensive Pace	30.5	6

The Panthers had the league's worst DVOA on RB runs from single-back sets (-25.3%) and the biggest difference between runs with one back (3.7 ypc) and runs with two backs (4.7 ypc). It was the second straight year that the Panthers ran much better with multiple backs in the game. ☞ Carolina ran more often on second-and-long than any team except for Kansas City — but they were terrible at it, gaining 4.05 yards per carry with -39.1% DVOA. This was a huge drop from previous seasons; the Panthers averaged 5.52 yards per carry running on second-and-long in 2009. ☞ Carolina's offense was second in the league in the number of passes thrown away due to pressure. ☞ Carolina's defense was last in the league, causing only five incomplete passes by tipping a pass or batting it down at the line of scrimmage.

Passing

Player	DYAR	DVOA	Plays	NtYds	Avg	YAC	C%	TD	Int
J.Clausen	-609	-41.1%	339	1345	4.0	5.2	53.0%	3	9
M.Moore	-270	-37.5%	158	810	5.1	4.5	55.6%	5	9
B.St Pierre	-89	-69.6%	31	150	4.8	8.1	46.4%	1	2
T.Pike	-25	-40.1%	13	37	2.8	3.8	50.0%	0	0

Rushing

Player	DYAR	DVOA	Plays	Yds	Avg	TD	Fum	Suc
J.Stewart	-21	-11.7%	178	769	4.3	2	4	36%
M.Goodson	-25	-14.9%	103	437	4.2	3	4	38%
D.Williams	-24	-16.2%	87	369	4.2	1	1	30%
J.Clausen	-42	-74.8%	16	43	2.7	0	2	-
T.Sutton	9	9.3%	13	71	5.5	0	0	31%
T.Fiammetta	1	-6.5%	7	22	3.1	0	0	57%
M.Moore	1	-8.8%	5	25	5.0	0	0	-

Receiving

Player	DYAR	DVOA	Plays	Ctch	Yds	Y/C	YAC	TD	C%
S.Smith	-153	-32.7%	99	46	554	12.0	4.7	2	46%
B.LaFell	-41	-19.4%	77	38	468	12.3	3.5	1	49%
D.Gettis	62	-0.8%	67	37	508	13.7	4.2	3	55%
D.Clowney	6	-7.4%	16	7	124	17.7	5.6	0	44%
D.Rosario	-79	-28.6%	58	32	264	8.3	4.3	0	55%
J.King	-23	-17.6%	31	19	121	6.4	1.8	2	61%
G.Barnidge	-48	-85.3%	9	0	0	0.0	0.0	0	0%
M.Goodson	25	-5.6%	57	40	310	7.8	8.8	0	70%
J.Stewart	30	25.0%	14	8	103	12.9	8.4	1	57%
D.Williams	9	-2.3%	13	11	61	5.5	6.3	0	85%
T.Sutton	17	11.0%	12	12	70	5.8	6.1	0	100%
T.Fiammetta	-2	-17.0%	10	5	34	6.8	4.2	0	50%

Offensive Line

Year	Yards	ALY	Rank	Power	Rank	Stuff	Rank	2nd Lev	Rank	Open Field	Rank
2008	5.01	4.27	8	79%	1	19%	18	1.31	3	1.33	2
2009	4.93	4.03	17	67%	11	22%	27	1.40	1	1.31	2
2010	4.29	3.74	27	62%	14	21%	23	1.22	9	0.99	9

Year	LE	Rank	LT	Rank	Mid	Rank	RT	Rank	RE	Rank	Sacks	ASR	Rank	F-Start	Cont.
2008	4.14	20	4.08	17	4.26	12	4.60	4	4.20	11	20	5.0%	9	32	25
2009	4.05	21	4.83	6	3.98	22	3.66	27	3.54	26	33	6.5%	17	16	38
2010	2.52	32	3.59	27	3.97	17	3.67	25	4.59	8	50	9.9%	31	22	36

Two-fifths of this line is set and solid with Jordan Gross at left tackle and Ryan Kalil at center. Outside of those two spots, Carolina's line underachieved in both run and pass blocking. The line dropped from 17th to 27th in Line Yards, and from 17th to 31st in Sack Rate, and the difference between line yards and running back yards (not to mention the talents of running backs DeAngelo Williams and Jonathan Stewart) tell the story. That line also finished in the top 10 in both false start and offensive holding penalties.

Knee and shoulder injuries cost right tackle Jeff Otah his entire 2010 season, and that was a major hit to a line designed to block more with power than pure agility. Garry Williams replaced Otah on the right side, but both he and right guard Geoff Schwartz were among the NFL's top 20 in blown blocks leading to sacks. Schwartz also tried his hand at right tackle from time to time, and he had to sub at left guard as Mackenzy Bernadeau struggled.

Ideally, the Gross/Otah/Kalil combo would be strong enough in 2011 for fill-in guards to find their places, with a running game still defined by the twosome of DeAngelo Williams and Jonathan Stewart, and Cam Newton running a lot of option looks sooner than later. The Panthers don't have the personnel to run a lot of zone slide or advanced pulling/trapping stuff; you'll see more man slide and basic pulling from the Panthers when they're not just going man-on-man and trying to win the physical battles.

Defensive Front Seven

Defensive Line	Age	Pos	Plays	TmPct	Overall								Pass Rush			vs. Run			vs. Pass		
					Rk	Stop	Dfts	BTkl	St%	Rk	AvYd	Rk	Sack	Hit	Hur	Runs	St%	Yds	Pass	St%	Yds
Charles Johnson	25	DE	62	7.2%	19	51	22	5	86%	25	1.0	24	11.5	13	30.5	42	86%	1.9	20	75%	-0.9
Derek Landri	28	DT	44	5.1%	23	34	16	1	75%	31	1.1	14	3	2	5	40	75%	1.5	4	100%	-3.5
Nick Hayden	25	DT	32	4.3%	40	19	6	1	54%	62	2.5	51	1	2	2.5	28	54%	3.5	4	100%	-5.0
Greg Hardy	23	DE	26	3.2%	77	19	8	1	65%	59	3.2	76	3	7	9	26	65%	5.0	6	100%	-2.7
Everette Brown	24	DE	25	3.6%	70	21	11	1	79%	16	-0.1	7	3.5	4	10.5	19	79%	2.2	6	100%	-7.3
Ed Johnson	28	DT	24	3.7%	51	19	5	1	77%	29	1.8	33	0	3	0	22	77%	2.0	2	100%	0.0
Tyler Brayton	32	DE	23	2.9%	--	19	8	1	84%	--	2.0	--	0	4	10.5	19	84%	1.9	4	75%	2.5

Linebackers	Age	Pos	Plays	TmPct	Overall					Pass Rush			vs. Run					vs. Pass				
					Rk	Stop	Dfts	BTkl	AvYd	Sack	Hit	Hur	Runs	St%	Rk	Yds	Rk	Tgts	Suc%	Rk	AdjYd	Rk
James Anderson	28	OLB	130	15.2%	17	83	30	7	3.5	4	4	5.5	83	66%	64	2.8	34	36	54%	41	5.6	29
Jon Beason	26	OLB	129	15.0%	19	68	24	6	4.8	0.5	1	3	83	59%	85	3.5	66	49	55%	38	6.9	55
Dan Connor	26	MLB	48	11.2%	48	31	13	2	2.9	1	3	3	39	69%	51	2.1	11	7	62%	--	5.3	--
Nic Harris	25	MLB	31	3.9%	--	18	6	4	5.4	1.5	0	1.5	21	71%	--	3.6	--	7	50%	--	13.1	--
Jason Williams	35	OLB	17	3.5%	--	8	4	1	4.4	0	1	1	11	45%	--	3.6	--	5	59%	--	5.0	--

Year	Yards	ALY	Rank	Power	Rank	Stuff	Rank	2nd Lev	Rank	Open Field	Rank
2008	4.53	4.33	24	68%	20	16%	26	1.26	25	0.86	23
2009	4.42	4.40	27	63%	14	17%	22	1.27	28	0.71	13
2010	4.02	3.77	10	62%	14	22%	6	1.15	18	0.87	20

Year	LE	Rank	LT	Rank	Mid	Rank	RT	Rank	RE	Rank	Sacks	ASR	Rank
2008	4.75	24	4.46	22	4.65	31	2.93	2	3.91	15	37	7.4%	5
2009	4.99	27	4.23	19	4.26	22	4.93	31	3.96	16	31	6.9%	13
2010	4.35	20	3.87	12	3.84	12	3.01	1	3.50	7	31	6.2%	18

The Panthers had an 8-8 defense on a 2-14 team, and the better unit started up front with one of the NFL's most underrated players in Charles Johnson. Not only did Johnson finish in the NFL's top 15 in sacks, hits, and hurries, he did so replacing a legend in the departed Julius Peppers, and without a complementary defender to take some of the blocking heat, as evidenced by the numbers above. Johnson wasn't just a speed rusher — when the Panthers ran three-man fronts with delayed blitzes, he also showed the ability to bull-rush and stunt his way out of blocking. In a better defense and on a better team, he'd be a name more people would already know. The Panthers knew enough to re-sign Johnson to a six-year contract with more than $30 million guaranteed; losing an edge-rushing cornerstone for the second straight year would have been too much of a burden.

Beyond Johnson, however, the Panthers didn't feature anyone of note in their fronts — just a group of rotation guys and role-players who made plays when needed. Tyler Brayton may have been the most frustrating member of the line; $3 million for zero sacks isn't a good ROI no matter how many hurries are on the stat sheet. Second-year end Everette Brown was starting to develop as a pass-rusher, standing out in a rotational role before missing the last three games of the season with a fractured wrist.

Carolina's tackle group has been assembled with spit and baling wire over the last few seasons, and while some may have wanted Marcell Dareus to solve that problem with the first overall pick, the Panthers actually got excellent value with two third-rounders — South Florida's Terrell McClain and Sione Fua of Stanford. McClain replaced the injured Stephen Paea at the Senior Bowl and showed what a few knew about his potential as a disruptive three-tech tackle, and Fua is a true hole-plugger with experience in one- and two-gap roles.

Thomas Davis, the man who was supposed to start at weakside linebacker, never made it to the field after tearing his right ACL for the second time in two years. The Panthers re-signed Davis to a five-year contract, but the real story was what happened in his absence. Jon Beason replaced Davis until ostensible middle linebacker Dan Connor was placed on IR himself in November, leaving Beason back in the middle and Nic Harris as the final replacement on that side. While all that was happening, James Anderson was absolutely blowing stuff up on the strong side, building himself a spot next to Charles Johnson on that list of the league's most unknown defensive stars. Week after week, Anderson put on a clinic in precision linebacker play — he's as good as any in the league at sifting through trash and putting a bead on a ballcarrier with minimal wasted movement. Anderson ended up fifth in the league in Stops and sixth in Defeats. In their free agency re-signing cash-grab, the Panthers also gave Anderson a new five-year deal.

Defensive Secondary

Secondary	Age	Pos	Plays	TmPct	Rk	Stop	Dfts	BTkl	Runs	St%	Rk	Yds	Rk	Tgts	Tgt%	Rk	Dist	Suc%	Rk	APaYd	Rk	PD	Int
											vs. Run							vs. Pass					
Richard Marshall	27	CB	95	11.1%	17	35	18	11	25	48%	34	7.6	54	84	18.1%	16	9.4	41%	83	7.7	51	4	3
Charles Godfrey	26	SS	91	10.6%	33	35	11	9	43	35%	53	8.4	59	35	7.4%	21	15.4	66%	11	7.9	41	2	5
Sherrod Martin	27	FS	85	10.6%	34	37	8	10	41	54%	13	5.9	26	21	4.7%	66	9.2	77%	2	2.9	1	4	1
Captain Munnerlyn	23	CB	57	6.6%	72	21	15	3	9	22%	83	6.4	40	63	13.5%	59	12.5	56%	22	6.7	30	12	3
Chris Gamble	28	CB	43	7.3%	63	17	4	4	12	58%	18	4.0	10	43	13.5%	60	13.0	39%	87	8.4	64	7	0

Year	Pass D Rank	vs. #1 WR	Rk	vs. #2 WR	Rk	vs. Other WR	Rk	vs. TE	Rk	vs. RB	Rk
2008	8	-5.1%	10	-0.2%	16	-2.5%	17	-13.0%	8	-13.7%	4
2009	2	-27.9%	7	-21.4%	5	-27.8%	5	13.8%	22	-18.1%	5
2010	8	-8.4%	10	-27.4%	1	8.6%	24	35.1%	32	-17.5%	3

When your team finishes eighth overall in pass defense DVOA *and* has a historically inept offense, you don't expect the coaching staff to be building doghouses in the secondary. And yet, that's where the doghouses were in John Fox's final year. With the lockout restrictions on team-player contact, Carolina's new coaching staff will have far less time to assess where the problems really lie.

Chris Gamble was the primary doghouse tenant. Signed to an enormous contract in November of 2008, Gamble spent 2009 combining tremendous athleticism with a boom-and-bust style that had him living up to his name. This year, he made the biggest news in Week 12, when he was benched against the Cleveland Browns for missing a team meeting. Once Gamble and John Fox finally made amends, Gamble started missing time due to a balky ankle. Captain Munnerlyn played well in his place, and is now set to start opposite Gamble because of the departure of Richard Marshall. Marshall has been doing the contract dance with the team over the last few years, especially since he moved from nickel to starting cornerback in 2009. The Panthers tagged him with a restricted tender before the lockout, but wound up letting him go when the labor war was over (maybe it was all that extra time to watch tape), and Marshall went off to the Cardinals. Safeties Charles Godfrey and Sherrod Martin are good young players, but Godfrey dealt with his own injuries last year, and Martin had best learn a different way of tackling — he's found himself on Ray Anderson's short list, and the $40,000 fine he picked up for a helmet-to-helmet hit against the Browns amounted to about one-tenth of his base salary.

Special Teams

Year	DVOA	Rank	FG/XP	Rank	Net Kick	Rank	Kick Ret	Rank	Net Punt	Rank	Punt Ret	Rank	Hidden	Rank
2008	2.5%	10	6.6	4	17.3	1	-2.4	20	-10.5	29	4.0	5	-1.0	13
2009	-2.9%	29	-1.1	20	-3.0	23	-6.3	25	-5.4	27	-1.5	19	2.6	10
2010	-1.3%	20	6.4	6	6.3	9	-9.5	28	-9.0	28	-1.7	18	-5.3	21

Well, at least the Panthers' special teams were not responsible for their demise — and unusually for a franchise with middling draft results over the past few seasons, Carolina had enough depth to fill out coverage teams of reasonable quality. Panthers opponents started their average drive with only 66.8 yards to go for a touchdown — second-worst in the NFL, behind only Buffalo — but that starting drive location was much more about Carolina's three-and-out offense than it was trouble on special teams.

Nobody should be happier about the new rookie wage scale than kicker Olindo Mare; the former Seahawks specialist signed a four-year, $12 million deal with the Panthers with some of that leftover Cam Newton money. It's a ridiculous contract for a kicker, but if you're going to give a ridiculous contract to a kicker, you might as well go with one we know can consistently boom kickoffs. With Mare kicking from the 35-yard line, the Panthers' kickoff coverage unit may not get a lot of work. Punter Jason Baker finished 25th in gross yards-per-punt average and 25th in net average — based on stats both traditional and sabermetric, there's room for improvement in both punting and punt coverage. Captain Munnerlyn provided league-average value as a returner, though Mike Goodson didn't quite measure up. Between his subpar return value and issues with blown blocks and fumbles, Goodson might find his opportunities decreasing until he can find some consistency.

Coaching Staff

Poor Ron Rivera. The longtime defensive coordinator waited years to get his shot at a head coach position, had a few near-misses in various coaching searches, and finally landed his optimal job with last year's worst team, a questionable general manager, and a lockout that prevents Rivera and his staff from interacting with the players. When Rivera finally does get on the field, his defense should be a point of emphasis, especially if a few key free agents can be retained. Both Rivera and new defensive coordinator Sean McDermott are disciples of the late, great Jim Johnson, so expect some outside-the-box blitzes and pressure concepts.

New offensie coordinator Rob Chudzinski has spent a lot of time as a tight ends coach, following Rivera from San Diego after having performed that task for the Chargers. Perhaps best known for running the 2007 Cleveland Browns offense that featured Derek Anderson's one miracle year and the debut of Joe Thomas, Chudzinski has his work cut out for him teaching a first overall pick who will need a crash course in NFL Playbook 101. He'll have the help of quarterbacks coach David Shula, who comes over from Jacksonville just as the expiration date hits on David Garrard.

Chicago Bears

2010 Record: 11-5	**2011 Mean Projection:** 8.9 wins
Pythagorean Wins: 9.5 (9th)	**On the Clock (0-3):** 1%
DVOA: 2.0% (16th)	**Loserville (4-6):** 14%
Offense: -12.0% (28th)	**Mediocrity (7-8):** 28%
Defense: -7.7% (6th)	**Playoff Contender (9-10):** 34%
Special Teams: 6.3% (1st)	**Super Bowl Contender (11+):** 24%
Variance: 25.4% (30th)	**Projected Average Opponent:** -1.4% (21st)

2010: The NFC Championship Game was a great spectator sport. Just ask Jay Cutler.

2011: A team built for .500 shocks everyone by going .500.

When the Bears win, they do it with great defense and just enough offense to get the job done.

That's how they did it in 1985, that's how they did it in 2006, and that's how they did it when George Halas was head coach, Bill George was at middle linebacker, and guys like Billy Wade were at quarterback.

The Bears would like to believe that they used that same formula for success last year. They didn't. The 2010 Bears did not have a great defense and just enough offense. They had a pretty good defense and a terrible offense. They won with special teams, an advantageous schedule, a few close wins, and some dubious officiating. They were an 8.2-win team according to our Adjusted Wins metric, and that's with their excellent special teams factored in. They had the kind of offense that wins five or six games, even with the defense picking up a fair share of slack.

Yes, this is another example of that least popular of Football Outsiders subgenres, the "Why Playoff Team X wasn't that Good" essay. Let's blast through the laundry list as quickly as possible before the angry e-mails arrive. Last year, the Bears beat the Panthers with Jimmy Clausen at quarterback, the Dolphins with Tyler Thigpen, the Lions with Drew Stanton, and the Vikings with Joe Webb. Their first win against the Lions was a direct result of the first-ever application of the Calvin Johnson Rule. They even caught a break in playoff tiebreakers. In a world where Matt Dodge obeys Tom Coughlin and kicks away from DeSean Jackson, the Bears are a third- or fourth-seeded playoff team, so they do not get to host the pluckily overmatched Seahawks after a bye week and waltz into the NFC Championship game.

The Bears also won one game as a direct result of their special teams play: They beat the Packers on a Devin Hester touchdown and a blocked Mason Crosby field goal. (The Bears also benefitted from 152 yards of Packers penalties, two of which erased Jay Cutler interceptions, in that game). Special teams also played a huge part in several other games. For example, a blocked extra point changed the entire complexion of the 22-19 win over the Bills, and long Devin Hester returns set up two touchdowns against the Jets. The Bears' special teams prowess should not be written off as a fluke, especially since they have excelled on special teams for years and possess such a unique weapon in Hester. But the huge role played by the special teams underscores just how weak the Bears were on offense. The offense benefitted from the best field position in the NFL: The average Bears drive started beyond the 33-yard line. The defense, meanwhile, looked better statistically because of the parade of third-string quarterbacks they faced, something DVOA does not adjust for.

The Bears did improve as the year progressed. The team that beat the Eagles and Jets late in the season

2011 Bears Schedule

Week	Opp.	Week	Opp.	Week	Opp.
1	ATL	7	vs. TB (U.K.)	13	KC
2	at NO	8	BYE	14	at DEN
3	GB	9	at PHI (Mon.)	15	SEA
4	CAR	10	DET	16	at GB (Sun.)
5	at DET (Mon.)	11	SD	17	at MIN
6	MIN	12	at OAK		

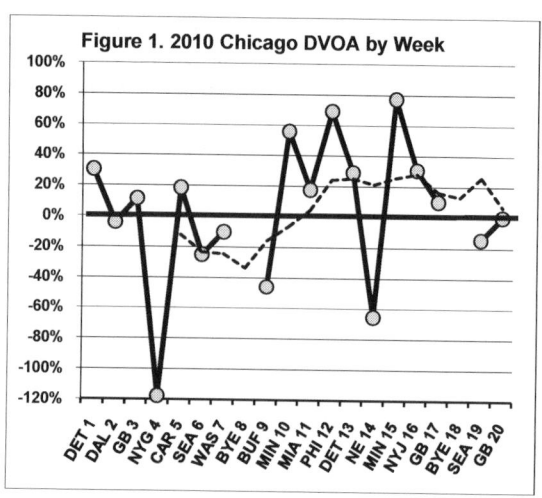

Figure 1. 2010 Chicago DVOA by Week

was better than the team that allowed ten sacks in a 17-3 loss to the Giants early in the year and bumbled through narrow wins against the Panthers and Bills. It was not a transition from mediocrity to greatness, though; more a slow climb to respectability. The offense in particular got undue credit for very modest improvements. The Bears cut down on their sack totals as the season went on (Cutler might have been killed, otherwise) and became a little more willing and able to run the ball. But the Bears executed just 936 offensive plays, the fourth lowest total in the NFL, and finished 30th in total yards. They spent the second half of the season in offensive tortoise mode, hoping that a dozen Cutler completions, a few Matt Forte runs, and a lightning strike by Hester would provide enough offense to win games. It was a shockingly effective strategy. It's hard to imagine how a team can gain 322 offensive yards, complete 13 passes, and convert just three third downs, yet still score 38 points against the Jets defense. But it happened, in part because four Bears scoring drives started in Jets territory.

In short, the Bears caught a break or two last season, and were a team that needed significant improvements in the offseason. They did not make them, which is why they are much more likely to slide onto the Wild Card bubble than seriously compete for the Super Bowl.

The offensive line, which stabilized (a better adjective than "improved," in this case) as the season progressed, is once again in flux. Chris Spencer replaces longtime starter Olin Kreutz in the middle, while first-round pick Gabe Carimi takes over at right tackle. With Carimi on the right side, J'Marcus Webb moved from right to left tackle at the start of training camp, replacing Frank Omiyale. Talent-wise, the moves are an upgrade. Kreutz was a Hall of Fame-caliber center at his peak, but his play slipped badly last year; the days when he could control a nose tackle without the help of one of his guards were long gone. Spencer is younger (29) and is powerful enough to do

many of the things Kreutz did late in his prime years. Carimi looks like he was molded out of titanium, and he should thrive at right tackle, where he will match up against bigger left defensive ends (smaller speed rushers can get under his pads). Omiyale was an all-purpose lineman who took over at left tackle as an emergency stopgap; Webb was roughed up early but grew into his role on the right side and has potential.

Most of the Bears' line problems last year stemmed from a lack of continuity, which is why all of the new personnel and position-flipping is such a cause for concern. Given a whole offseason, training camp, and preseason to work with, offensive coordinator Mike Martz and line coach Mike Tice were still playing mix-and-match on the offensive line when the 2010 season started. They must now work in two new starters and also move a third player to a new position during a truncated camp. The configuration we just described was how the Bears lined up in early August. By the time you read this, Carimi or Omiyale may be back at left tackle, or the Mikes may have come up with some new configuration.

(Sure enough, the Mikes starting juggling while this chapter was in editing. Robert Garza was at center by August 9th, with the dreadful Lance Louis getting yet another look at guard. So our point has been made for us.)

The Bears also shook up their offensive skill positions, trading tight end Greg Olsen while acquiring former Cowboys headcase Roy Williams. Olsen caught just 41 passes but was a major part of the team's attempt to achieve offensive balance last year. Olsen played all over the formation, from receiver to blocking back, and helped the Bears as a point-of-attack run blocker, pass protector, and possession receiver. Williams started his season in Dallas feuding publically with Dez Bryant about rookie pranking practices and ended it shuttling back and forth from the bench, catching one or two passes per game. Olsen-for-Williams represents the swap of a valuable multi-position player for a second-fiddle diva. It also suggests that Martz may once again try to relive the Greatest Show on Turf, which did not work out so well in Detroit or San Francisco.

For the Bears defense, no news is good news. The stalwarts are still in place and effective: Brian Urlacher, Lance Briggs, Charles Tillman. They are all a year older but not quite "old" yet, though Urlacher is now susceptible to the embarrassing open-field juke. Julius Peppers, with 34 Stops on running plays, had a bigger impact than his 7.5 sacks would suggest, and Israel Idonije emerged as a fine complementary pass rusher. The only major free agent loss was safety Danieal Manning. There is no reason to expect a sudden decline just yet, though since everyone mentioned in this paragraph is more than 30 years old, it's going to happen eventually. Any statistical dropoff in 2011 will come from the fact that the Bears are more likely to face Donovan McNabb than Joe Webb on any given Sunday this fall.

Special teams remain a top priority for the Bears. Punter Adam Podlesh signed a five-year, $10-million contract to replace Brad Maynard, and the team quickly re-signed Corey Graham, Nick Roach, and Brian Iwuh to anchor their coverage and blocking units, acquiring Sam Hurd (14 special teams tackles) from the Cowboys for even more depth. Hester is unlikely to return three punts for touchdowns again this year, but teams will still kick away from him, and the Bears' investment in gunners and blockers shows that their special teams excellence is not just a one-man show. Now that opponents kick from the 35-yard line, touchbacks will be easier to come by, which will erode the Bears' field position advantage. But Hester is more dangerous on punts than kickoffs, and the team's ability to cover punts (they allowed just 7.8 yards per return last year) should hold steady.

So the defense will be pretty good, the special teams great, and the offense may be more Martz-like, for better or for worse. Have we mentioned the quarterback? Far too much was made of Jay Cutler's decision to sit out the second half of the NFC championship game: None of us know how injured he really was, and he shouldn't have to hobble around in an unnecessary cast to convince us that he was too hurt to play.

Cutler's problem is not his toughness or personality, but that he has not developed. He still throws off his back foot and into coverage, consistently and alarmingly. Those who claim that he improved late in the season overlook his performances against the Patriots (12-of-26, 152 yards, no touchdowns, two interceptions) and in the second meeting with the Packers (21-of-39-168-0-2). Cutler has now thrown 2,207 regular season passes, putting him way past the prospect stage. What you see is what you get with him, and what you get is a mistake-prone passer who will throw dozens of passes downfield per game if Martz decides to get his groove back. Cutler is capable of having an excellent season if everything around him is humming, but everything around him won't hum this year. Expect him to once again alternate three-touchdown performances with turnover spectacles.

There is a good chance that the Bears end up with a Wild Card berth, despite their shortcomings. If that happens, it will be a 9-7, one-and-done affair — and then the organization will have some tough decisions to make. Lovie Smith received a two-year contract extension in February, but general manager Jerry Angelo is only signed through the 2011 season. The Bears will have had a string of 7-9 or 9-7 finishes dating back to 2007, with 2010 sticking out as a fate-assisted anomaly. The defense will be a year older, and Angelo's signature acquisition (Cutler) will have proven once again that he's a mistake-prone middle-tier passer for whom the team paid too much. Angelo's Super Bowl success is receding into history and the Bears might be due for a paradigm shift, even if Lovie sticks around to provide continuity and a firm foundation in the Cover-2 defense.

Some fresh ideas wouldn't hurt. Winning with field position was a great strategy in Halas' day, but it is time for the Bears to try something new.

Mike Tanier

2010 Bears Stats by Week

Wk	vs.	W-L	PF	PA	YDF	YDA	TO	Total	Off	Def	ST
1	DET	W	19	14	463	168	-1	30%	-15%	-43%	3%
2	@DAL	W	27	20	308	410	3	-4%	22%	9%	-17%
3	GB	W	20	17	276	379	1	11%	13%	17%	15%
4	@NYG	L	3	17	110	372	0	-118%	-107%	7%	-4%
5	@CAR	W	23	6	247	147	-1	18%	-59%	-57%	21%
6	SEA	L	20	23	307	353	0	-25%	-15%	37%	27%
7	WAS	L	14	17	322	308	-3	-10%	-60%	-46%	4%
8	BYE										
9	@BUF	W	22	19	283	340	2	-46%	-15%	22%	-10%
10	MIN	W	27	13	360	240	2	56%	2%	-43%	11%
11	@MIA	W	16	0	268	187	0	18%	-6%	-18%	5%
12	PHI	W	31	26	349	398	1	69%	57%	-11%	1%
13	@DET	W	24	20	311	302	-1	29%	30%	3%	2%
14	NE	L	7	36	185	475	-4	-66%	-64%	-1%	-2%
15	@MIN	W	40	14	293	273	4	77%	7%	-38%	33%
16	NYJ	W	38	34	322	393	1	31%	33%	15%	13%
17	@GB	L	3	10	227	284	0	10%	-22%	-27%	5%
18	BYE										
19	SEA	W	35	24	437	276	-1	-14%	10%	23%	2%
20	GB	L	14	21	301	356	-1	16%	-11%	-11%	16%

Trends and Splits

	Offense	Rank	Defense	Rank
Total DVOA	-12.0%	28	-7.7%	6
Unadjusted VOA	-13.6%	28	-7.1%	5
Weighted Trend	-5.3%	25	-8.6%	4
Variance	18.2%	31	8.1%	25
Average Opponent	1.7%	21	2.2%	12
Passing	-7.0%	28	-5.2%	5
Rushing	-3.8%	19	-11.4%	7
First Down	-4.7%	25	3.2%	14
Second Down	-3.1%	21	-20.8%	3
Third Down	-41.9%	30	-9.5%	8
First Half	-9.7%	27	-1.1%	13
Second Half	-14.3%	26	-14.4%	2
Red Zone	-27.2%	28	-21.0%	5
Late and Close	-14.0%	27	-12.0%	8

Five-Year Performance

Year	W-L	Pyth	Est W	PF	PA	TO	Total	Rk	Off	Rk	Def	Rk	ST	Rk	Off AGL	Rk	Def AGL	Rk
2006	13-3	12.4	10.8	427	255	+8	23.2%	6	-4.0%	18	-19.7%	2	7.6%	1	19.7	20	36.0	30
2007	7-9	7.6	7.5	334	348	-1	-5.8%	20	-21.3%	30	-6.0%	8	9.5%	1	18.4	10	50.3	31
2008	9-7	8.7	9.2	375	350	+5	6.2%	15	-4.8%	23	-6.8%	7	4.2%	5	14.4	10	19.3	15
2009	7-9	6.7	5.7	327	375	-6	-19.8%	25	-16.8%	28	7.1%	22	4.1%	3	8.2	4	42.7	26
2010	11-5	9.5	8.2	334	286	+4	2.0%	16	-12.0%	28	-7.7%	6	6.3%	1	6.8	3	5.5	2

Strategic Tendencies

Run/Pass		Rank	Offense		Rank	Defense		Rank	Other		Rank
Runs, all plays	40%	15	3+ WR	59%	8	Rush 3	1.1%	31	2+ RB, Pct Runs	54%	24
Runs, first half	36%	27	4+ WR	10%	8	Rush 4	72.8%	3	1 RB/2 TE, Pct Runs	50%	12
Runs, first down	50%	15	2+ TE	27%	19	Rush 5	16.3%	30	1 RB/3+ WR, Pct Runs	30%	6
Runs, second-long	32%	19	Single back	61%	12	Rush 6+	9.9%	14	CB1 on WR1	45%	9
Runs, power sit.	51%	25	Play action	15%	26	Zone Blitz	4.7%	18	Go for it on 4th	0.73	26
Runs, behind 2H	28%	18	Max protect	19%	4	Sacks by LB	23.5%	17	Offensive Pace	32.4	27
Pass, ahead 2H	45%	16	Outside pocket	13%	13	Sacks by DB	2.9%	30	Defensive Pace	31.5	27

Chicago's defense ranked 13th in DVOA in the first half of games, but second after halftime. This was the second straight year that the Bears defense improved significantly in the second half. ☞ Chicago blitzed on third down less often than any defense in the league, sending five or more pass rushers only 22 percent of the time. The Bears were one of the few teams that actually blitzed more often on first and second down (28 percent) than they did on third down. ☞ The Chicago defense benefited from a league-leading 46 dropped passes by opponents. ☞ Lovie Smith was back to his usually conservative self on fourth down (28th) after his shocking number-one ranking in Aggressiveness Index in 2009. ☞ Chicago used shotgun on a league-low 10 percent of plays. In case you were wondering how the NFL has changed in the last few years, that would have ranked 17th in 2004. Ironically, the Bears themselves faced shotgun more often than any other defense, 46 percent of plays.

Passing

Player	DYAR	DVOA	Plays	NtYds	Avg	YAC	C%	TD	Int
J.Cutler	292	-1.5%	491	3070	6.3	5.5	60.4%	23	16
T.Collins	-280	-159.0%	29	53	1.8	4.3	37.0%	0	5
C.Hanie	9	15.5%	9	40	4.4	2.4	71.4%	0	0

Rushing

Player	DYAR	DVOA	Plays	Yds	Avg	TD	Fum	Suc
M.Forte	87	0.4%	236	1060	4.5	6	0	41%
C.Taylor	-107	-31.2%	112	267	2.4	3	0	36%
J.Cutler	72	35.3%	32	251	7.8	1	1	-
D.Hester	17	9.5%	7	30	4.3	0	0	-
G.Wolfe	-13	-117.7%	4	8	2.0	0	0	0%

Receiving

Player	DYAR	DVOA	Plays	Ctch	Yds	Y/C	YAC	TD	C%
J.Knox	207	14.7%	100	51	964	18.9	4.7	5	51%
D.Hester	55	-3.2%	73	40	475	11.9	5.5	4	55%
E.Bennett	118	9.2%	70	46	564	12.3	4.5	3	66%
D.Aromashodu	-31	-29.2%	24	10	149	14.9	5.1	0	42%
R.Davis	34	20.3%	13	9	84	9.3	2.9	1	69%
G.Olsen	-36	-15.0%	70	41	404	9.9	3.8	5	59%
B.Manumaleuna	13	16.7%	7	5	43	8.6	4.8	1	71%
M.Forte	105	14.0%	70	51	551	10.8	8.6	3	73%
C.Taylor	30	8.1%	26	20	139	7.0	5.9	0	77%

Offensive Line

Year	Yards	ALY	Rank	Power	Rank	Stuff	Rank	2nd Lev	Rank	Open Field	Rank
2008	3.89	3.94	25	63%	20	18%	15	0.99	30	0.67	21
2009	4.04	4.01	19	58%	25	19%	16	0.95	30	0.81	15
2010	3.79	3.64	29	44%	32	25%	30	1.06	22	0.80	13

Year	LE	Rank	LT	Rank	Mid	Rank	RT	Rank	RE	Rank	Sacks	ASR	Rank	F-Start	Cont.
2008	2.78	28	4.08	16	4.17	15	3.92	25	3.78	22	29	5.3%	11	22	48
2009	4.93	10	3.77	23	4.05	20	3.38	29	3.91	20	35	5.9%	13	26	33
2010	5.45	1	3.76	22	3.50	30	2.57	32	3.95	17	56	10.4%	32	23	34

Ironically, the Bears best lineman in 2010 has probably lost his job. Frank Omiyale moved from right to left tackle early in the season when Chris Williams had an awful preseason, pulled a hamstring, and finally earned a demotion to guard. Omiyale committed seven false starts but held his own against some good pass rushers, putting out the fire on the blind side. Early in camp, Omiyale has been working with the second team, with first-round pick Gabe Carimi at right tackle and J'Marcus Webb at left tackle. Webb blew 7.5 blocks and committed 10 penalties last year, looking particularly lost against the Dolphins in Week 11. He did show signs of life at season's end, but the Bears may spend another season juggling offensive linemen if he bombs on the left side.

Chris Spencer signed a two-year contract with the Bears and replaces Olin Kreutz at center. Kreutz committed five holding penalties and had trouble with the big young defensive tackles of the NFC North, so Spencer is a modest upgrade. Roberto Garza is also getting old and coming off a poor season; likely challengers for him at right guard include Lance Louis, the original 2010 left guard who was benched after the Giants' 10-sack jamboree in Week 4. Despite this, he still has the size-ability-age profile to improve.

Defensive Front Seven

Defensive Line	Age	Pos	Plays	TmPct	Rk	Stop	Dfts	BTkl	St%	Rk	AvYd	Rk	Sack	Hit	Hur	Runs	St%	Yds	Pass	St%	Yds
						Overall							Pass Rush			vs. Run			vs. Pass		
Julius Peppers	31	DE	61	7.7%	12	53	23	5	81%	7	0.9	21	8	15	30.5	42	81%	2.2	19	100%	-1.9
Israel Idonije	31	DE	47	5.9%	31	41	18	1	81%	6	-0.3	6	8	9	16	32	81%	1.8	15	100%	-4.5
Anthony Adams	31	DT	34	4.3%	39	29	8	1	82%	13	1.4	21	2	4	6	28	82%	1.8	6	100%	-0.5
Matt Toeaina	29	DT	25	3.1%	60	19	6	1	79%	35	2.1	37	2	2	7	19	79%	2.6	6	67%	0.7

Linebackers	Age	Pos	Overall							Pass Rush			vs. Run					vs. Pass				
			Plays	TmPct	Rk	Stop	Dfts	BTkl	AvYd	Sack	Hit	Hur	Runs	St%	Rk	Yds	Rk	Tgts	Suc%	Rk	AdjYd	Rk
Brian Urlacher	33	MLB	135	17.0%	9	76	27	6	4.7	4	0	4.5	63	67%	62	2.8	35	53	56%	34	5.3	23
Lance Briggs	31	OLB	96	12.9%	38	59	28	11	4.4	2	0	2.5	39	85%	6	2.0	6	37	56%	35	5.2	19
Pisa Tinoisamoa	30	OLB	39	6.5%	96	24	8	2	3.7	1	1	5.5	19	74%	28	2.3	16	20	46%	67	5.8	35
Brian Iwuh	27	OLB	16	2.0%	--	9	5	1	4.2	1	0	0	9	67%	--	2.1	--	1	-12%	--	13.1	--

Year	Yards	ALY	Rank	Power	Rank	Stuff	Rank	2nd Lev	Rank	Open Field	Rank
2008	3.64	3.28	2	64%	11	28%	1	1.03	8	0.84	21
2009	4.31	4.17	19	64%	15	23%	6	1.28	29	0.82	18
2010	3.95	3.54	2	72%	31	25%	1	1.16	20	0.80	18

Year	LE	Rank	LT	Rank	Mid	Rank	RT	Rank	RE	Rank	Sacks	ASR	Rank
2008	2.13	1	3.08	4	3.62	3	4.08	17	2.43	1	28	5.0%	27
2009	5.08	28	4.72	26	3.64	8	4.43	25	3.90	14	35	5.9%	21
2010	3.82	10	4.45	22	3.28	1	3.48	9	3.65	11	34	6.0%	20

The Bears defensive philosophy hasn't changed much during the Lovie Smith era. Brian Urlacher and Lance Briggs still threaten the A-gap, then drop into zone coverage, just as they did back in 2005. Urlacher bounced back from the injury that erased his 2009 season with one of the best years of his career. Both Briggs and Urlacher are over 30, and they sometimes have senior moments, like when Urlacher got juked by the barely-nifty James Starks in the NFC Championship Game. But both linebackers are still ideal system fits who can start a play over center and end it in perfect position to defend a short pass over the middle.

Occasionally, Urlacher and/or Briggs blitz up the middle, but Smith was more blitz-averse in 2010 than in past years: The Bears rushed four defenders 56 percent of the time in 2009 but slid that average up to 73 percent last season. Julius Peppers' presence gave Lovie the option of blitzing less frequently. Six of Peppers' eight sacks came in one four-week stretch from Week 11 to Week 14, and he was not as dominant as he was in his prime: some ordinary blockers fought him to a stalemate. But Peppers played stout run defense and drew extra pass protectors at times, creating opportunities for others. Israel Idonije's sack total was padded by a 2.5-sack game against the Panthers: At one point, a befuddled Jimmy Clausen ran right into Idonije's arms while escaping Peppers. Idonije does what complementary pass rushers are supposed to: He generates "hustle" sacks, forces some bad throws, and cleans up after screen passes.

The Bears released defensive tackle Tommie Harris in February. Harris was a three-time Pro Bowl selection who was hampered by knee and ankle injuries in recent years; he was a healthy scratch for several games in 2010. Second-round pick Stephen Paea could provide some of the interior punch Harris used to provide. Paea forced nine fumbles in his college career and is a perfect fit as a three-tech in Lovie's system. There are few new faces on the front seven, though the Bears did sign Vernon Gholston for some reason.

Defensive Secondary

Secondary	Age	Pos	Overall						vs. Run					vs. Pass								
			Plays	TmPct	Rk	Stop	Dfts	BTkl	Runs	St%	Rk	Yds	Rk	Tgts	Tgt%	Rk	Dist	Suc%	Rk	APaYd	Rk	PD	Int
Charles Tillman	30	CB	96	12.1%	10	35	18	5	17	53%	22	7.9	58	88	17.6%	19	11.1	41%	82	8.5	65	9	5
Danieal Manning	29	FS	79	9.9%	47	32	9	3	39	38%	43	9.8	72	28	5.5%	47	15.6	57%	31	6.5	19	7	1
Chris Harris	29	SS	76	9.6%	52	19	11	9	28	25%	76	7.6	53	28	5.5%	46	11.9	62%	19	5.9	12	6	5
Tim Jennings	28	CB	61	7.7%	56	24	8	4	16	38%	61	5.3	24	64	12.9%	69	11.7	58%	18	6.4	22	4	1
D.J. Moore	24	CB	49	6.2%	--	28	23	3	14	64%	--	3.6	--	34	6.7%	--	8.1	55%	--	7.0	--	7	4
Zach Bowman	27	CB	28	4.3%	--	8	5	0	5	80%	--	8.8	--	28	6.9%	--	10.7	36%	--	9.4	--	0	0
Major Wright	23	FS	19	3.5%	--	0	0	0	6	0%	--	11.0	--	5	1.5%	--	22.0	85%	--	3.3	--	0	0

Year	Pass D Rank	vs. #1 WR	Rk	vs. #2 WR	Rk	vs. Other WR	Rk	vs. TE	Rk	vs. RB	Rk
2008	11	-2.1%	12	-14.4%	9	-2.1%	19	-25.8%	3	11.4%	24
2009	24	13.8%	20	5.4%	22	-0.2%	16	-5.9%	10	13.2%	22
2010	5	-1.8%	15	16.6%	28	-22.1%	6	-0.9%	11	-17.6%	2

Three of Charles Tillman's five interceptions last year came against Tyler Thigpen, Matt Moore, and Joe Webb. Tillman remains an adequate Cover-2 cornerback, but he doesn't match up well with quicker receivers. Despite his 6-foot-1 frame, Tillman had trouble with big receivers like Seattle's Mike Williams last year. Tim Jennings cut his Cover-2 teeth as a sometime-starter in Indianapolis for three seasons. Jennings is small and doesn't jam well on the line, so better receivers can run away from him by releasing inside on slants.

Major Wright and third-round rookie Chris Conte are the favorites to replace strong safety Danieal Manning, who is now in Houston. Wright got high marks from coaches for his talent and effort but only played in dime situations. Conte is a developmental project who only played one year at safety at Cal; he intercepted just two passes in his college career but is considered a fine size-speed-effort prospect. Both Wright and Conte have reputations as tough open-field tacklers and would likely be asked to roll into the box for run support while veteran Chris Harris plays center field.

Special Teams

Year	DVOA	Rank	FG/XP	Rank	Net Kick	Rank	Kick Ret	Rank	Net Punt	Rank	Punt Ret	Rank	Hidden	Rank
2008	4.2%	5	4.2	10	-3.4	23	16.2	2	15.7	3	-8.3	29	19.6	2
2009	4.1%	3	4.8	7	-1.6	19	14.2	3	1.8	15	5.1	8	9.0	3
2010	6.3%	1	0.6	16	-4.0	24	14.6	3	-0.2	20	26.0	1	4.7	6

Specialists Corey Graham, Garrett Wolfe, Brian Iwuh, and Rashied Davis combined for 49 special teams tackles. They helped hold opponents to just 7.8 yards per punt return and were part of the blocking convey that sprung Devin Hester for three punt return touchdowns. All four were free agents in the offseason, but the team made re-signings a post-lockout priority, retaining Graham (22 special teams tackles) and Iwuh while losing Davis to the Lions. (Wolfe was still a free agent at press time). Newcomer Sam Hurd is also an experienced special-teamer.

New punter Adam Podlesh, formerly of the Jaguars, is younger and has a bigger leg than the departed Brad Maynard. The Bears prefer to alternate their kickoff returners; with Davis and Danieal Manning gone, Hurd or Johnny Knox will share the role with Hester. Robbie Gould is a very average kicker.

Coaching Staff

Mike Martz the Coach was in danger of becoming Mike Martz the Caricature before last year: an obstinate, pass-happy mad genius too in love with his doomed contraption of an offense to hold down a steady job. Martz reclaimed a little dignity last year. The Bears' official 414-carry rushing total is misleading, as it includes 72 carries in the fourth quarter with the Bears winning and 42 Jay Cutler scrambles/kneels. Takes those out, though, and Martz still called almost 19 runs per game when he had the option of passing, which is practically Chuck Knox-like by his standards. Martz didn't give up on Matt Forte after three carries or bench Greg Olsen in favor of an extra receiver. When his offensive line started falling apart, as his lines often do, Martz took prudent steps to increase the pass protection. Most tellingly of all, Martz didn't clash with Lovie Smith the way he did with defensive-minded head coaches in Detroit and San Francisco. Instead of putting up impressive passing numbers in a losing effort, Martz's offense put up mediocre numbers in a winning effort. It wasn't a great coaching effort — there was no excuse for breaking camp with an offensive line that mixed up — but at least it was a coaching effort, not another attempt to recreate the 2001 Rams without the personnel.

Cincinnati Bengals

2010 Record: 4-12

Pythagorean Wins: 6.1 (25th)

DVOA: -2.7% (19th)

Offense: 5.1% (17th)

Defense: 4.8% (19th)

Special Teams: -3.0% (28th)

Variance: 12.1% (10th)

2011 Mean Projection: 6.6 wins

On the Clock (0-3): 9%

Loserville (4-6): 40%

Mediocrity (7-8): 30%

Playoff Contender (9-10): 16%

Super Bowl Contender (11+): 4%

Projected Average Opponent: -1.1% (19th)

2010: Beat on the Brat, Beat on the Brat, Beat on Bob Bratkowski with a baseball bat, oh yeah.

2011: The Cincinnati West Coast offense returns to Cincinnati.

The 2009 Cincinnati Bengals were one of the NFL's big surprises. The offense leaned on a highly efficient ground game, while the defense improved significantly in its second year under coordinator Mike Zimmer. Coming off a 4-11-1 season, they turned things around with a 10-6 playoff season that included a first-place finish in the AFC North.

The 2010 Cincinnati Bengals were one of the NFL's big disappointments. Offensive coordinator Bob Bratkowski went away from the ground-oriented 1970s style attack that had worked in 2009, and quarterback Carson Palmer struggled for most of the year. The defense, except at cornerback, was unremarkable. The 10-6 playoff team once again dissolved into a mess and finished 4-12.

That's basically how conventional wisdom sees the Cincinnati Bengals, but that's not how the FO statistics see the Cincinnati Bengals. Would you believe that the 2009 AFC North champion Bengals and the rotten 2010 Bengals were essentially the same team?

Based on total DVOA rating, they were. The 2009 Bengals, despite their winning record, finished 19th overall with a total DVOA of 1.2%. The 2010 Bengals had a slightly lower total DVOA of -2.7%, which ranked them … 19th overall. Their offensive DVOA actually went up by two percentage points, and their defensive DVOA went down by just four percentage points.

What was the real difference between the 2009 and 2010 Bengals? Close wins and schedule strength. The 2009 Bengals were 6-3 in games decided by a touchdown or less. The 2010 Bengals were 2-7. The 2009 Bengals had an average schedule. The 2010 Bengals had the second-hardest schedule in the league according to average DVOA of opponent.

Was Bob Bratkowski's offensive scheme responsible for the Bengals' poor record in 2010? Some fans criticized Bratkowski's play-calling as too predictable. Other fans criticized him for not being conservative *enough*; for example, his decision to pass on third-and-13 against Tampa Bay, leading by a touchdown with just 2:28 left in the game. Fans criticized his schemes for being too complex, and they criticized him for not tailoring the offense to the talents of his best players.

He also didn't get along with his players, publicly feuding with both Carson Palmer and Cedric Benson. Benson complained to the press that Bratkowski had gotten away from the power-running attack that worked in 2009. Apparently Benson didn't notice that the Bengals' offense was mediocre in 2009 and that the trend throughout the NFL favors dynamic offenses rather than conservative ones.

Cedric Benson (and Bengals fans) may not agree, but Bratkowski had a reason to move away from the run-first attack: The run simply wasn't working as well as it did the year before. To be honest, the running game in 2009 wasn't that great to start with. It

2011 Bengals Schedule

Week	Opp.	Week	Opp.	Week	Opp.
1	at CLE	7	BYE	13	at PIT
2	at DEN	8	at SEA	14	HOU
3	SF	9	at TEN	15	at STL
4	BUF	10	PIT	16	ARI
5	at JAC	11	at BAL	17	BAL
6	IND	12	CLE		

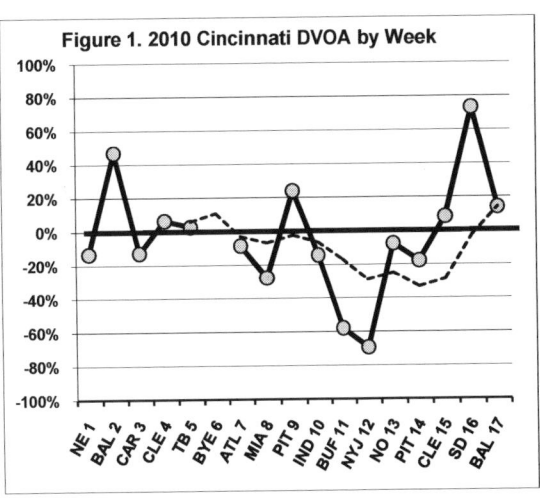

Figure 1. 2010 Cincinnati DVOA by Week

was built on volume (505 carries, fourth in the NFL) rather than efficiency. The Bengals had a run offense DVOA of 1.1%, 14th in the NFL that season. They were just 21st with 4.07 average yards per carry.

In 2010, things got worse. The Bengals dropped to 29th in DVOA, at -9.7%, and finished dead last in the league with 3.56 yards per carry. Benson was a bit off all year, a data point against the "big contract year" theory, and the right side of the offensive line in particular had problems getting push against the tough defenses on Cincinnati's schedule.

Unfortunately, improvements to the Cincinnati passing game were just enough to offset the decline in the ground game, and not enough to really uplift the team overall. The Carson Palmer of 2005 was gone, killed by the elbow injury Palmer suffered in 2008. Palmer was very consistent all year, but consistently average: For most of the year, his single-game DVOA ratings hovered between -30% and +30%, with no particularly awful games. Palmer ended the season hot, but in reality what we're talking about are two good games and one spectacular one, the Week 16 upset of the Chargers where he inexplicably went 16-of-21 for 269 yards and four touchdowns against one of the league's top pass defenses.

Bengals fans are probably not soothed by all this evidence that their team wasn't really as bad as their 4-12 record. "Hey, we're really mediocre! Huzzah!" In reality, it works out well that things went in this order. A 10-6 season often convinces the front office that your team is one player away from becoming a Super Bowl contender. (Antonio Bryant! Terrell Owens!) A 4-12 season convinces the front office that it's time to rip things apart and start over. And that's what the Bengals did with their offense this season.

Gone is Palmer, who demanded a trade, was refused by general manager Mike Brown, and then called Brown's bluff by retiring. Gone are Terrell Owens and Chad Ochocinco, one in free agency and the other in trade. And gone is Bob Bratkowski, who had been in

Cincinnati longer than even head coach Marvin Lewis.

To rebuild their offense, the Bengals brought in Jay Gruden, brother of Jon. Gruden has been a head coach in the Arena league and UFL, but hasn't been in the NFL since he served as a part-time assistant with Tampa Bay. Gruden's game is the West Coast offense he picked up from his brother, a member of the Mike Holmgren coaching tree. Gruden claims he'll still build the offense around Benson first and foremost, but the Bengals won't be play-faking so they can chuck it deep. There will be more short passes designed to get yards after the catch. The Bengals finished just 27th with 4.5 average yards after catch last year; they'll rank a lot higher in 2011.

The Bengals then put together what amounts to a Football Outsiders dream draft. In the first round, they chose wide receiver A.J. Green out of Georgia, who led all receiving prospects in our Playmaker Score metric. In the second round, they took quarterback Andy Dalton from TCU, the top quarterback prospect according to our Lewin Career Forecast metric. In the third round, they took defensive end Dontay Moch of Nevada, tapped as the top sleeper candidate in the draft by our SackSEER metric. They missed hitting for the cycle when they let Denver sign Auburn's Mario Fannin (he of the record Speed Score) as an undrafted free agent.

Nobody questions the talent of Green or Moch, but Dalton is another story. He was one of a number of controversial quarterback prospects in this year's draft, who split not only scouts from statisticians but scouts from other scouts.

Statistically, it's tough to find a collegiate record better than Dalton's. He was a four-year starter at TCU. He completed 61.7 percent of his passes, including 66.1

percent in his senior year with 27 touchdowns and just six interceptions. He did all this against lesser competition to be sure, but even with opponent adjustments, TCU ranked 17th in our Pass Offense S&P+ college stats last season, and 14th in overall offense. Scouting-wise, he has good touch on his passes and the intelligence to properly adjust plays at the line and hit his hot read. He also has all the intangibles — he's tough, spirited, and practically drenched in mythological "winner sauce" with a 36-3 record over the last three years.

On the other hand, Dalton faces the same problems as a lot of other passers coming from collegiate spread offenses. He's used to taking a short drop from shotgun and then hitting a pass out of multiple clearing routes designed to split less-talented college defenses. He'll need work reading more complex NFL schemes. He often rolled right at TCU to cut the field in half and limit his reads. There are also major questions about his arm strength; he can't make the stick throws of 15 to 25 yards and tends to over-arc longer passes. When things got windy during Senior Bowl week, his passes really hung in the air — not the best attribute for a guy who has to play in the AFC North.

The good news is that Dalton's strengths fit the most important skills that a passer needs to run the classic West Coast offense where yardage is more about hitting the right guy and letting him run with the ball, and less about airing it out and getting yardage purely through the air. Worried about Dalton's arm strength? His new offensive coordinator Gruden told Bengals. com, "it's so overrated, it's stupid." The one thing he's missing, the ability to fully recognize complex NFL schemes, will come with more experience. And he'll get that experience right away. Dalton is the unquestioned Bengals starter from Week 1. He's the horse that Lewis and Gruden have bet all their money on.

Most of the successful rookie quarterbacks in recent years played for teams that were built on a running-and-defense blueprint. Gruden will likely help Dalton along by going back to a run/pass split more in line with what the Bengals did in 2009. Cedric Benson gets his wish, and re-signed with Cincinnati after free agency. But what about the defense part of that blueprint?

The Bengals defense is rebuilding as well, but it's been a far more gradual process rather than the shock to the system the offense got this offseason. The Bengals defense is mostly a mix of players in their primes and young players on the rise, with very few veterans in their 30s. This won't be immediately obvious looking at their starting lineup on Opening Day, but a couple of the most important players are still playing situational roles and waiting for the Bengals to decide they are ready to start.

Most discussion of the youth on the Bengals defense starts at linebacker, with 25-year-old Keith Rivers and 24-year-old Ray Maualuga. The Bengals have jettisoned the aged Dhani Jones and will move Maualuga to the middle linebacker position this year, and they're looking for a big leap forward from him. The third starting linebacker is 27-year-old Manny Lawson, signed away from San Francisco in free agency. (Rivers had wrist surgery this offseason and will likely start the season on PUP, with former Raider Thomas Howard starting in his place on the weak side.)

On the defensive line, the Bengals have a solid rotation of mostly 20-somethings. Gene Atkins in particular had a very strong rookie year, and he should be a starter soon, even if 30-year-old Tank Johnson is currently ahead of him on the depth chart. The defensive end position is also undergoing some transition. Carlos Dunlap had a phenomenal year as a pass-rush specialist, with 9.5 sacks even though he essentially didn't start playing until Week 7. The Bengals won't be able to keep him out of the starting lineup much longer. At right end, Michael Johnson is still only 24 years old. The Bengals are finally letting him settle in at defensive end after moving him back and forth between the line and linebacker the last two years.

The problem with most of these front seven players is that they are still developing, rather than developed. The Bengals don't really have holes, but they have younger players who still have weak spots in their games (Maualuga must take a leadership role, Dunlap must become more of an all-around player, etc.). As for the secondary, that showed another problem with developing young players. Not only do you need to wait for them to develop, but once they develop, you need to keep them. The Bengals were unable to do that when the new CBA made four-year veteran cornerback Johnathan Joseph a free agent. Nate Clements never lived up to his big-money contract in San Francisco; he's both a downgrade and the only place in the defensive lineup where the Bengals actually got older rather than younger this offseason. With Leon Hall playing at a high level, you can expect opposing quarterbacks to pick on Clements and nickelback Morgan Trent.

But Clements is the only addition this offseason who really didn't fit into the team's overall design for going young. This franchise is trying to establish a clear identity: on offense, Bill Walsh revisited, and on defense, an aggressive scheme built around a constantly fresh defensive line and frequent big blitzes. There no guarantee the front office won't screw it up, as they have so many times, but right now the Bengals do seem to have a legitimate plan for the future. Bengals fans are just going to have to suffer a bit while they wait for the future to arrive.

Aaron Schatz

2010 Bengals Stats by Week

Wk	vs.	W-L	PF	PA	YDF	YDA	TO	Total	Off	Def	ST
1	@NE	L	24	38	428	376	-2	-13%	20%	14%	-20%
2	BAL	W	15	10	253	259	4	47%	-21%	-55%	12%
3	@CAR	W	20	7	305	267	2	-13%	-12%	12%	11%
4	@CLE	L	20	23	413	295	-1	6%	25%	2%	-16%
5	TB	L	21	24	358	391	-1	3%	-13%	-7%	9%
6	BYE										
7	@ATL	L	32	39	469	452	1	-9%	35%	33%	-10%
8	MIA	L	14	22	262	354	1	-28%	-4%	20%	-4%
9	PIT	L	21	27	272	314	0	24%	29%	-16%	-21%
10	@IND	L	17	23	341	256	-5	-14%	-33%	-11%	8%
11	BUF	L	31	49	361	449	-1	-58%	-12%	42%	-5%
12	@NYJ	L	10	26	163	319	-2	-69%	-31%	6%	-32%
13	NO	L	30	34	311	436	1	-8%	19%	42%	16%
14	@PIT	L	7	23	190	354	-3	-18%	-18%	4%	4%
15	CLE	W	19	17	397	278	0	8%	39%	40%	9%
16	SD	W	34	20	371	313	1	73%	58%	-21%	-5%
17	@BAL	L	7	13	395	199	-3	14%	-1%	-22%	-7%

Trends and Splits

	Offense	Rank	Defense	Rank
Total DVOA	5.1%	17	4.8%	19
Unadjusted VOA	0.6%	20	9.3%	24
Weighted Trend	6.6%	17	9.0%	25
Variance	7.4%	15	7.3%	21
Average Opponent	-1.9%	32	8.4%	28
Passing	26.2%	11	6.9%	14
Rushing	-9.7%	29	2.2%	25
First Down	9.5%	12	4.2%	17
Second Down	-0.4%	17	13.9%	27
Third Down	5.0%	14	-9.2%	10
First Half	4.5%	18	-5.8%	7
Second Half	5.7%	17	16.5%	28
Red Zone	-1.1%	18	8.5%	23
Late and Close	-11.3%	26	16.6%	30

Five-Year Performance

Year	W-L	Pyth	Est W	PF	PA	TO	Total	Rk	Off	Rk	Def	Rk	ST	Rk	Off AGL	Rk	Def AGL	Rk
2006	8-8	9.1	8.6	373	331	+7	7.4%	11	15.1%	5	9.0%	26	1.3%	12	26.8	24	24.3	24
2007	7-9	7.9	8.5	380	385	+5	2.2%	14	12.7%	7	9.8%	27	-0.7%	20	20.8	16	24.4	21
2008	4-11-1	3.2	5.2	204	364	-2	-19.3%	26	-13.4%	28	3.8%	16	-2.1%	26	59.8	31	48.3	30
2009	10-6	8.4	8.4	305	291	0	1.2%	19	2.9%	19	0.8%	13	-0.9%	21	34.1	24	36.5	24
2010	4-12	6.1	7.2	322	395	-8	-2.7%	19	5.1%	17	4.8%	19	-3.0%	28	14.9	7	47.5	30

Strategic Tendencies

Run/Pass		Rank	Offense		Rank	Defense		Rank	Other		Rank
Runs, all plays	39%	20	3+ WR	63%	3	Rush 3	4.8%	22	2+ RB, Pct Runs	54%	23
Runs, first half	42%	11	4+ WR	6%	12	Rush 4	63.0%	9	1 RB/2 TE, Pct Runs	50%	12
Runs, first down	45%	26	2+ TE	23%	22	Rush 5	20.3%	25	1 RB/3+ WR, Pct Runs	25%	11
Runs, second-long	38%	7	Single back	64%	8	Rush 6+	11.8%	6	CB1 on WR1	41%	16
Runs, power sit.	54%	21	Play action	13%	30	Zone Blitz	4.7%	17	Go for it on 4th	1.04	8
Runs, behind 2H	28%	16	Max protect	10%	21	Sacks by LB	13.0%	25	Offensive Pace	31.0	20
Pass, ahead 2H	43%	18	Outside pocket	7%	30	Sacks by DB	14.8%	6	Defensive Pace	30.7	16

After leading the league in using six offensive linemen in 2009, the Bengals only ranked fifth in 2010. ☞ Cincinnati's low rate of play-action fakes (13 percent of passes) seems like an odd choice given their offensive identity as a run-first team. It looks like even more of an odd choice when you see that the Bengals had a DVOA rating 61.6% higher when they were using play-action. Only Minnesota had a larger gap between performance with play-action and performance without play-action. ☞ Cincinnati allowed a league-low 2.0 yards per pass on running back screens. ☞ Cincinnati ranked seventh in defensive DVOA in the first half, and 28th after halftime.

Passing

Player	DYAR	DVOA	Plays	NtYds	Avg	YAC	C%	TD	Int
C.Palmer	1009	13.8%	622	3892	6.3	4.5	62.1%	26	20

Rushing

Player	DYAR	DVOA	Plays	Yds	Avg	TD	Fum	Suc
C.Benson	-61	-13.1%	321	1121	3.5	7	7	45%
B.Scott	70	17.7%	61	299	4.9	1	0	54%
C.Palmer	-18	-28.2%	17	61	3.6	0	1	--
B.Leonard	15	23.3%	9	61	6.8	0	0	56%

Receiving

Player	DYAR	DVOA	Plays	Ctch	Yds	Y/C	YAC	TD	C%
T.Owens	140	-0.2%	139	72	983	13.7	4.0	9	52%
C.Ochocinco	120	-0.5%	126	67	831	12.4	2.8	4	53%
J.Shipley	156	14.1%	74	52	600	11.5	4.0	3	70%
A.Caldwell	91	16.9%	37	25	345	13.8	4.2	0	68%
J.Simpson	109	44.1%	25	20	277	13.9	3.9	3	80%
J.Gresham	-33	-13.0%	83	52	471	9.1	7.0	4	63%
R.Kelly	-36	-50.2%	13	10	42	4.2	2.9	0	77%
C.Benson	22	-3.2%	37	28	178	6.4	6.4	1	76%
B.Leonard	41	12.4%	26	20	137	6.9	4.8	1	77%
B.Scott	9	-1.9%	13	11	60	5.5	7.0	0	85%

Offensive Line

Year	Yards	ALY	Rank	Power	Rank	Stuff	Rank	2nd Lev	Rank	Open Field	Rank
2008	3.22	3.31	32	56%	30	24%	32	0.90	32	0.37	31
2009	4.14	3.97	24	79%	1	19%	17	1.20	12	0.74	16
2010	3.76	4.04	18	51%	28	23%	27	1.15	15	0.38	31

Year	LE	Rank	LT	Rank	Mid	Rank	RT	Rank	RE	Rank	Sacks	ASR	Rank	F-Start	Cont.
2008	1.45	32	3.28	29	3.66	28	3.23	30	3.35	25	51	8.6%	27	14	37
2009	3.79	23	4.45	9	4.26	10	3.82	24	2.78	28	29	5.6%	10	24	27
2010	4.02	20	4.95	3	3.75	24	3.99	21	2.78	31	28	5.1%	7	21	29

Andrew Whitworth had a great year and was even the leading Pro Bowl vote-getter among offensive tackles, but the general impression among Cincinnati fans was that the rest of the line took a step backwards in 2010. Yet the Bengals improved in both Adjusted Sack Rate and Adjusted Line Yards, and they ranked sixth by allowing a hurry on just 16.3 percent of all pass plays. The line's biggest problem was run-blocking up the gut. Cincinnati's ALY up the middle dropped while the success rate in power situations fell through the floor. Center Kyle Cook also led the team with six blown blocks that led to sacks, and left guard Nate Livings also gave up a good amount of pressure in pass protection. Right guard Bobbie Williams had a solid season but is 35 and in the final year of his contract. His heir apparent is fourth-round pick Clint Boling out of Georgia, who has strong technique but average talent. At right tackle, the Bengals continue to wait for 2009 sixth overall pick Andre "Godot" Smith to stay healthy. Smith finally made it into the starting lineup full-time in Week 7, then broke his foot three weeks later. He has managed only five starts in two seasons. When Smith can't play, the right tackle spot goes to the hulking (6-foot-9) Dennis Roland, who is a good run blocker but inconsistent in pass protection.

Defensive Front Seven

Defensive Line	Age	Pos	Plays	TmPct	Rk	Stop	Dfts	BTkl	St%	Rk	AvYd	Rk	Sack	Hit	Hur	Runs	St%	Yds	Pass	St%	Yds
Domata Peko	27	DT	43	5.6%	17	37	7	0	84%	12	1.7	31	0.5	4	6.5	37	84%	2.5	6	100%	-2.8
Michael Johnson	24	DE	38	5.0%	44	30	10	0	77%	37	2.9	70	2.5	4	11.5	26	77%	2.3	12	83%	4.3
Robert Geathers	28	DE	35	4.6%	53	25	3	1	71%	63	2.2	49	0.5	5	12.5	28	71%	2.2	7	71%	2.1
Pat Sims	26	DT	32	4.8%	32	29	9	2	89%	3	0.8	11	2.5	5	3.5	27	89%	1.8	5	100%	-4.2
Carlos Dunlap	22	DE	27	4.7%	49	22	15	1	71%	27	-0.9	3	9	3	4	7	71%	3.6	20	85%	-2.5
Frosty Rucker	28	DE	18	4.2%	--	13	2	0	69%	--	2.6	--	1	5	7	13	69%	2.8	5	80%	1.8
Geno Atkins	23	DT	17	2.2%	--	15	9	1	75%	--	-0.5	--	3.5	9	17.5	8	75%	2.3	9	100%	-2.9

The header for the Defensive Line table spans: Overall | Pass Rush | vs. Run | vs. Pass

Linebackers	Age	Pos	Plays	TmPct	Rk	Stop	Dfts	BTkl	AvYd	Sack	Hit	Hur	Runs	St%	Rk	Yds	Rk	Tgts	Suc%	Rk	AdjYd	Rk
				Overall						Pass Rush			vs. Run					vs. Pass				
Dhani Jones	33	MLB	126	16.5%	12	69	16	10	5.3	1	2	0	71	66%	65	3.3	61	36	46%	63	6.9	54
Keith Rivers	25	OLB	75	10.5%	54	44	11	12	4.3	1	1	3	56	64%	75	3.8	82	16	47%	62	6.1	41
Rey Maualuga	24	OLB	75	9.8%	61	42	9	4	4.7	1	1	2	53	66%	67	3.5	68	19	54%	40	5.7	33
Brandon Johnson	28	OLB	36	4.7%	--	27	14	2	4.6	0.5	2	2	16	56%	--	4.8	--	23	64%	13	6.5	47

Year	Yards	ALY	Rank	Power	Rank	Stuff	Rank	2nd Lev	Rank	Open Field	Rank
2008	3.85	4.16	15	64%	12	18%	14	1.09	14	0.50	6
2009	3.88	4.35	25	74%	29	16%	27	1.15	18	0.30	1
2010	4.53	4.19	19	73%	32	18%	22	1.17	21	1.05	30

Year	LE	Rank	LT	Rank	Mid	Rank	RT	Rank	RE	Rank	Sacks	ASR	Rank
2008	5.09	30	3.95	10	4.49	26	3.96	14	2.54	2	17	3.6%	31
2009	4.95	26	3.60	6	4.57	27	4.51	26	3.20	4	34	5.4%	28
2010	3.72	8	3.89	13	4.32	23	4.70	26	3.52	9	27	5.3%	30

At first glance, the Bengals' run defense collapsed last season, but the Bengals' defensive line was no different than it was in 2009: below-average against the run, and extremely poor in short-yardage situations. The problem was that the linebackers got pushed around and some of the defensive backs forgot how to tackle running backs entirely.

Dhani Jones spent more time in pass coverage than either Keith Rivers or Ray Maualuga, but he's not particularly good at it. This was the third straight season Jones ranked 55th or lower among linebackers in Success Rate against the pass. Jones was allowed to leave in free agency, and the Bengals will move Ray Maualuga into the middle linebacker spot. To replace him on the strong side, the Bengals signed former 49ers linebacker Manny Lawson. Lawson never quite seemed to meet San Francisco's hopes as a pass-rushing 3-4 linebacker, but he may be a better fit in Cincinnati. He has the speed to stay with tight ends and he plays the run well. If he doesn't work out, or if Rivers is slow to recover from offseason wrist surgery, the Bengals also signed ex-Raider Thomas Howard and brought back veteran Brandon Johnson. Third-round pick Dontay Moch will play in pass-rushing situations.

The defensive line is in transition, but the youngsters did a good job of establishing themselves last year. Geno Atkins started only one game in 2010, but he'll slide in next to veteran Domata Peko, with Tank Johnson and Pat Sims also playing roles in the rotation. Robert Geathers will start at left end, but Carlos Dunlap will come in to wreak havoc on passing downs. Dunlap and Atkins both show why you need to analyze all kinds of pass pressure. Dunlap had 9.5 sacks last year, but three hits and four hurries. Geno Atkins had only three sacks but nine hits and 17.5 hurries.

Defensive Secondary

Secondary	Age	Pos	Plays	TmPct	Rk	Stop	Dfts	BTkl	Runs	St%	Rk	Yds	Rk	Tgts	Tgt%	Rk	Dist	Suc%	Rk	APaYd	Rk	PD	Int
				Overall					vs. Run					vs. Pass									
Roy Williams	31	SS	60	10.5%	36	22	8	7	38	37%	49	5.9	28	4	1.2%	81	19.4	23%	80	17.8	80	1	1
Chinedum Ndukwe	26	FS	58	10.1%	43	27	9	3	28	50%	17	6.0	30	20	5.9%	38	8.0	58%	26	7.0	27	3	1
Reggie Nelson	28	FS	55	7.2%	69	16	7	0	23	26%	73	8.1	57	15	3.4%	74	16.0	54%	41	8.8	54	5	2
Leon Hall	27	CB	50	6.5%	73	24	14	4	14	36%	65	13.1	86	66	14.9%	50	14.6	58%	17	8.8	69	10	4
Johnathan Joseph	27	CB	50	8.7%	39	24	12	6	8	50%	25	6.0	31	59	17.8%	18	11.2	52%	43	7.3	43	6	3
Chris Crocker	31	FS	46	10.7%	28	20	8	3	26	38%	43	7.7	54	25	10.0%	3	16.7	58%	27	7.9	39	5	0
Jonathan Wade	27	CB	45	7.8%	52	13	7	1	7	43%	42	7.9	57	42	11.6%	75	15.1	35%	89	10.4	84	4	0
Morgan Trent	26	CB	26	6.8%	--	13	4	0	4	75%	--	5.5	--	32	14.2%	--	10.2	57%	--	5.7	--	3	1
Adam Jones	28	CB	17	7.1%	--	7	5	1	4	0%	--	15.5	--	16	11.6%	--	14.3	56%	--	9.6	--	3	1
Rico Murray	24	CB	15	7.8%	--	5	2	0	0	0%	--	0.0	--	13	11.7%	--	13.9	49%	--	9.7	--	4	0

Year	Pass D Rank	vs. #1 WR	Rk	vs. #2 WR	Rk	vs. Other WR	Rk	vs. TE	Rk	vs. RB	Rk
2008	21	18.8%	26	20.7%	25	4.2%	23	-28.6%	2	4.2%	17
2009	10	-29.8%	5	-21.5%	4	22.9%	31	-25.7%	2	22.2%	27
2010	14	0.5%	17	-1.7%	14	-5.6%	14	2.8%	14	-25.0%	1

Who's better: Leon Hall or Johnathan Joseph? That question won't matter as much anymore now that Joseph has departed in free agency, gone to the greener (and more humid) fields of Houston. The good news for Bengals fans is that our game charting stats suggest Hall might be better. He had better charting stats in 2009. In 2010, he had a better Success Rate than Joseph but was easier to beat deep. Either way, it's pretty clear that both are better than the cornerback who will now replace Joseph in the lineup, Nate Clements. Perhaps Clements will be able to turn his hips easier now that his wallet is no longer weighed down by that $80 million contract the 49ers gave him back in 2007. He came a little cheaper this time: $10.5 million over two years, $6 million guaranteed.

Roy Williams has left town, and taken with him his eternal inability to cover receivers. The Bengals thought they had free agent Donte Whitner, then got left at the Twitter altar when Whitner decided to go to San Francisco after tweeting that he was headed to Cincinnati. That leaves Reggie Nelson as the starting strong safety; he played reasonably well after coming over from Jacksonville in trade last year. Chris Crocker does an admirable job at free safety, and the Bengals will also have Gibril Wilson back after he blew out his ACL in last year's training camp.

Special Teams

Year	DVOA	Rank	FG/XP	Rank	Net Kick	Rank	Kick Ret	Rank	Net Punt	Rank	Punt Ret	Rank	Hidden	Rank
2008	-2.1%	26	2.2	12	-1.3	19	-1.2	18	-8.8	28	-3.3	24	2.7	10
2009	-0.9%	21	-5.0	25	-3.8	24	-4.2	18	-3.3	25	11.0	4	4.2	6
2010	-3.0%	28	-7.4	31	-11.2	29	-3.5	19	8.7	6	-4.3	24	-3.8	18

Kickers are fungible, we always say, and it should be easy to find a reasonable replacement on the waiver wire. Unless you are Cincinnati, apparently. When Mike Nugent tore his ACL, the Bengals got awful performances from waiver-wire kickers Aaron Pettrey and Clint Stitser. Nugent should be back this season. Kevin Huber was nothing special at punter, but the Bengals got a very strong performance from their punt coverage team. Returns were slightly below average — Bernard Scott on kickoffs, Quan Cosby on punts — but there likely won't be any change in those jobs this year.

Coaching Staff

Mike Brown seems to hire assistant coaches completely separately from head coaches. Bob Bratkowski had been here ten years, pre-dating Marvin Lewis, and Jay Gruden inherits most of Bratkowski's assistants to teach an entirely new offense. Paul Alexander has been offensive line coach for 17 years, and Jim Anderson has been running backs coach for 28 years. Ken Zampese, who has been in town since 2003, remains quarterback coach. It may seem strange to have a Zampese coaching a West Coast offense quarterback, but Ernie's son is a good example of how coaching trees are never quite as simple as you might think. He worked for Andy Reid and Ray Rhodes in the late '90s, then spent three years with Mike Martz before coming to the Bengals, giving him experience with both Walsh-influenced and Coryell-influenced coaches.

Cleveland Browns

2010 Record: 5-11

Pythagorean Wins: 6.1 (24th)

DVOA: -3.1% (20th)

Offense: -1.4% (22nd)

Defense: 4.1% (17th)

Special Teams: 2.3% (10th)

Variance: 19.0% (17th)

2011 Mean Projection: 8.5 wins

On the Clock (0-3): 0%

Loserville (4-6): 14%

Mediocrity (7-8): 35%

Playoff Contender (9-10): 37%

Super Bowl Contender (11+): 14%

Projected Average Opponent: -3.6% (31st)

2010: Square Mangini peg, round Holmgren hole.

2011: They could follow in the footsteps of last year's Buccaneers ... with the same disappointing ending.

Theatre fans know that Broadway shows do not simply premiere in their final, complete form. First they go through a preview phase. The writer and director get to see how the show looks on stage, and how an audience reacts. They can tweak the parts, move around scenes, and take out or adjust songs that aren't working. Over the last year, for example, *Spider-Man: Turn off the Dark* has famously suffered through the longest preview period ever: 182 different performances. Eventually, the producers felt the musical couldn't work with the current creative team. They brought in new consultants and fired the director. After a month off, the show re-opened with the same cast but significant structural changes.

Before the 2010 season, the Cleveland Browns essentially hired a new executive producer to remake their entire franchise. Last year was essentially the preview run for *Mike Holmgren Presents: The New Cleveland Browns*. Overall, it wasn't quite as bad as *Spider-Man: Turn off the Dark,* although there were about the same number of injuries. Colt McCoy got surprisingly good reviews in the lead role. But after the season, just like the folks who run *Spider-Man,* Holmgren felt he needed to change the creative team and bring in a director whose vision for the show was more in line with the vision of The Big Show.

It made sense for Holmgren to keep head coach Eric Mangini on when he arrived before the 2010 season.

It's hard to fire a coach who ends the season with four straight wins, which is how the Browns ended 2009. In addition, Holmgren was just beginning to analyze his roster to determine which players would fit what he wanted to do, and some continuity was useful.

But Holmgren and Mangini were an odd fit in a number of ways. Holmgren, of course, is a leading acolyte of Bill Walsh and progenitor of the West Coast offense. Mangini's offensive coordinator, Brian Daboll, coached with the Patriots for seven years and prefers a scheme more influenced by Air Coryell and Ernie Zampese. Holmgren's teams in Seattle and Green Bay always ran 4-3 defensive schemes. Mangini runs multiple fronts, but the base is a 3-4. Holmgren's style has always been to put your best players on the field and run your best plays, to beat your opponent doing what you do best. Mangini comes more from the Bill Belichick school of analyzing opposing weaknesses, installing different plays and using different groups of players each week in order to attack those weaknesses.

After the Browns lost their last four games in a row, the departure of Mangini was a fait accompli. To replace him, Holmgren picked some fruit off the expansive Mike Holmgren coaching tree. There are many connections between Holmgren and his new head coach Pat Shurmur. Before two years as offensive coordinator in St. Louis, Shurmur had been quarterbacks coach in Philadelphia under former

2011 Browns Schedule

Week	Opp.	Week	Opp.	Week	Opp.
1	CIN	7	SEA	13	BAL
2	at IND	8	at SF	14	at PIT (Thu.)
3	MIA	9	at HOU	15	at ARI
4	TEN	10	STL	16	at BAL
5	BYE	11	JAC	17	PIT
6	at OAK	12	at CIN		

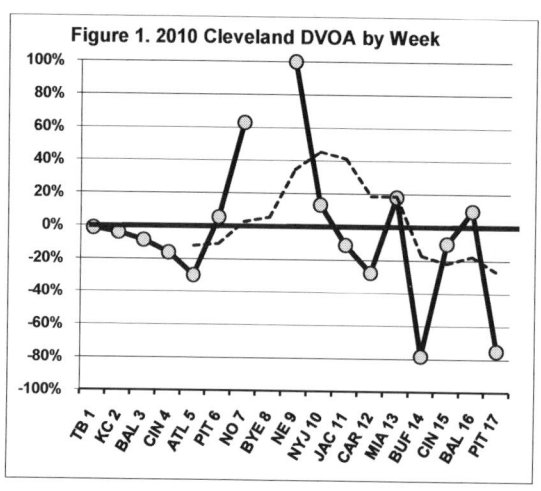

Figure 1. 2010 Cleveland DVOA by Week

Holmgren employee Andy Reid. Sherman's late uncle, Fritz, was Holmgren's defensive coordinator in Green Bay when the Packers won the Super Bowl in 1996. And Holmgren, Shurmur, and general manager Tom Heckert are all represented by the same agent, Bob LaMonte. (The Holmgren coaching tree basically grows in a pot in LaMonte's office, as his clients also include Steve Spagnuolo, Marty Mornhinweg, and both Gruden brothers.)

Shurmur will install a prototypical Holmgren offense, with routes generally designed to maximize yards after the catch. There will be long, methodical drives down the field, and fewer attempts at a quick strike deep. Shurmur uses short passes to receivers, like screens and smoke routes, more often than Daboll did. The offensive talent on the Cleveland roster already fits the new offense, starting with quarterback Colt McCoy. The knock on McCoy coming out of college was that he was accurate on short passes but didn't have the arm strength to make all the downfield throws. His ability to read defenses, find open receivers, and hit them quickly will fit perfectly with a West Coast scheme. He's already gotten quite a vote of confidence from his head coach, who told reporters after being hired, "I really am a Colt McCoy guy." Terry Pluto of the *Cleveland Plain-Dealer* reported that the Rams had McCoy as their No. 2 quarterback prospect in the 2010 draft, behind Sam Bradford. Wide receivers Mohamed Massaquoi and Brian Robiskie are route-runners with good hands rather than burners, and the Browns used their second-round pick to draft an even more talented receiver made from the same mold, Greg Little.

However, there are places where Shurmur's offense, at least in St. Louis, differed from the classic Holmgren structure. For example, there is an assumption that Cleveland will use the running backs often in the passing game. That's a classic staple of the West Coast offense, and Peyton Hillis as well as his backups are strong receivers. But last year, St. Louis had an excellent receiving running back in Steven Jackson, yet the Rams passed to running backs just 14 percent of the time, 30th in the NFL. Shurmur also used his tight ends as blockers more than receivers, although that might have had more to do with the talent he was stuck with in St. Louis. With strong receiving tight ends like Benjamin Watson and Evan Moore, he's likely to give the tight end position its usual central place in the West Coast scheme.

To coach the defense, Shurmur brought on board former Bills and Lions head coach Dick Jauron. Jauron never was a success as a head coach but he's considered one of the finer 4-3 coordinators of the last two decades. The linemen in his system tend to play a "two-gap" style, keeping the blockers off the linebackers. Compared to, say, the classic Tampa-2 scheme, this isn't as much of a change from the 3-4 the Browns ran before. However, Rob Ryan's exotic personnel packages and blitzes are gone. Jauron is much more conservative when it comes to sending pressure. Last year, we tracked the Browns sending the standard four pass rushers on only 33.5 percent of pass plays, which was dead last in the league. Compare that to Dick Jauron's last full season in Buffalo, 2008, when the team rushed four 66.5 percent of the time.

Given how much the Browns changed their coaching staff and schemes this offseason, it is remarkable how few free agents they signed specifically to fit those schemes. In fact, they signed so few we can list them all here: free safety Usama Young, punter Richmond McGee, third-down back Brandon Jackson, and dime back Dimitri Patterson. Instead, the Browns will populate their new schemes with a combination of draft picks and players that Holmgren acquired last off-season. Scott Fujita and Chris Gocong, for example, were both linebackers in 4-3 schemes before arriving in Cleveland. Perhaps Holmgren and general manager Tom Heckert, when they signed these players, were already looking for players who could fit not only in Mangini's defense but also in a future 4-3.

Certainly, the midseason trade for veteran defensive end Jayme Mitchell was a hint that the Browns intended to return to a 4-3 scheme. Mitchell is too small to play 3-4 end and not well-rounded enough to be a 3-4 outside linebacker. He didn't even take the field for Cleveland last year, but is expected to start this year. The rest of the defensive line is going young, with 25-year-old nose tackle Ahtyba Rubin and two rookies: first-round pick Phil Taylor and second-round pick Jabaal Sheard. The Browns don't have a defensive lineman over age 29 on the roster.

Like all teams with new coordinators installing new schemes, the Browns are likely to suffer through larger-than-usual growing pains thanks to the lockout-shortened offseason. Nonetheless, there are plenty of encouraging signs that the Browns will improve — not just in the long run, but right now in 2011. First and foremost, the 2010 club was far better than its 5-11 record indicates. They were 3-7 in games decided by a touchdown or less. Our Estimated Wins metric projects that, with average luck and an average schedule, the Browns would have finished 7-8-1. The Browns ranked 20th in DVOA, ahead of two 8-8 teams and the entire NFC West.

That division conveniently shows up on the Browns schedule this year, along with the declining AFC South. As a result, we have the Browns going from the fourth-hardest schedule in the league in 2010 to what we project as the second-easiest schedule in 2011. The Browns somehow ended up with all four Pittsburgh and Baltimore games stuck in December, but they are going to enter that month with a winning record. The average projected DVOA of their first 11 opponents is a miserable -9.0%.

The Browns are also likely to be healthier in 2011 after finishing dead last in Adjusted Games Lost in 2010. The Browns don't have a good track record for avoiding injury. They've ranked 24th or worse in AGL in seven of the last nine seasons. But even if the Cleveland Browns' mean for expected injuries is higher than the NFL norm, the team is still likely to regress towards it. All four of the original starting linebackers from last year's squad spent time on the injury report, including D'Qwell Jackson missing the entire season with a torn pectoral. The defensive line struggled with nagging injuries, with linemen listed on the injury report as "Questionable" 31 times. Special-teams star and Wildcat operator Josh Cribbs dealt with foot and ankle injuries as well as a midseason concussion courtesy of James Harrison.

Certainly the new kickoffs from the 35-yard line diminish the value of a healthy Cribbs, but not by much. Cribbs isn't just a kick returner; he's the best all-around special teams player in the league. A healthy Cribbs also improves the Browns on punt returns as well as kick and punt coverage. If the offense and defense play at the same level as 2010, and the special teams return to being a top-five unit, that combined with the easy schedule is enough to make the Browns a surprising presence in the AFC playoff hunt.

So forget about the disappointing preview run of *Mike Holmgren Presents: The New Cleveland Browns*. The Big Show's big show may turn out a lot better now that he has a director and a script more to his liking. Just remember that they're opening in a crowded AFC North theatre district, where they'll have to compete with two long-time hits and a circus.

Aaron Schatz

2010 Browns Stats by Week

Wk	vs.	W-L	PF	PA	YDF	YDA	TO	Total	Off	Def	ST
1	@TB	L	14	17	340	288	-1	-1%	-17%	-25%	-10%
2	KC	L	14	16	299	312	0	-4%	-24%	-23%	-3%
3	@BAL	L	17	24	304	365	0	-9%	32%	46%	5%
4	CIN	W	23	20	295	413	1	-16%	1%	25%	8%
5	ATL	L	10	20	269	338	-2	-30%	-32%	-7%	-5%
6	@PIT	L	10	28	327	378	-2	5%	30%	33%	9%
7	@NO	W	30	17	210	394	4	63%	13%	-29%	20%
8	BYE										
9	NE	W	34	14	404	283	2	101%	48%	-40%	13%
10	NYJ	L	20	26	303	456	-1	13%	28%	18%	4%
11	@JAC	L	20	24	283	371	5	-11%	-25%	-22%	-8%
12	CAR	W	24	23	379	326	-2	-28%	-6%	21%	-1%
13	@MIA	W	13	10	252	281	3	18%	1%	-21%	-4%
14	@BUF	L	6	13	187	323	-2	-78%	-69%	14%	5%
15	@CIN	L	17	19	278	397	0	-10%	37%	42%	-5%
16	BAL	L	10	20	280	258	-3	10%	5%	3%	8%
17	PIT	L	9	41	225	418	-3	-75%	-42%	36%	2%

Trends and Splits

	Offense	Rank	Defense	Rank
Total DVOA	-1.4%	22	4.1%	17
Unadjusted VOA	-2.7%	23	5.8%	23
Weighted Trend	-1.6%	21	7.1%	21
Variance	10.3%	26	8.1%	26
Average Opponent	-0.2%	27	7.9%	27
Passing	5.4%	22	7.3%	16
Rushing	-0.8%	15	1.0%	22
First Down	5.5%	17	3.0%	13
Second Down	-2.2%	18	4.1%	17
Third Down	-13.2%	24	5.9%	19
First Half	7.2%	16	5.1%	20
Second Half	-11.5%	24	3.1%	16
Red Zone	0.4%	16	-14.1%	10
Late and Close	-33.3%	30	2.9%	22

Five-Year Performance

Year	W-L	Pyth	Est W	PF	PA	TO	Total	Rk	Off	Rk	Def	Rk	ST	Rk	Off AGL	Rk	Def AGL	Rk
2006	4-12	4.4	4.8	238	356	-15	-16.1%	26	-15.5%	29	3.2%	19	2.6%	8	27.8	27	55.0	32
2007	10-6	8.5	8.9	402	382	-2	8.5%	12	8.5%	10	6.8%	21	6.9%	2	12.6	5	30.5	25
2008	4-12	4.4	6.1	232	350	+5	-19.3%	27	-16.4%	29	7.2%	17	4.3%	4	43.3	26	31.3	23
2009	5-11	4.3	5.3	245	375	-12	-23.3%	26	-13.0%	24	18.7%	30	8.4%	1	37.4	25	43.3	27
2010	5-11	6.1	7.5	271	332	-1	-3.1%	20	-1.4%	22	4.1%	17	2.3%	10	42.7	31	52.0	32

Strategic Tendencies

Run/Pass		Rank	Offense		Rank	Defense		Rank	Other		Rank
Runs, all plays	41%	14	3+ WR	42%	29	Rush 3	19.5%	1	2+ RB, Pct Runs	68%	3
Runs, first half	42%	8	4+ WR	2%	30	Rush 4	33.5%	32	1 RB/2 TE, Pct Runs	46%	23
Runs, first down	48%	19	2+ TE	35%	7	Rush 5	36.7%	1	1 RB/3+ WR, Pct Runs	13%	29
Runs, second-long	38%	8	Single back	61%	11	Rush 6+	10.3%	11	CB1 on WR1	32%	25
Runs, power sit.	80%	1	Play action	20%	12	Zone Blitz	5.8%	14	Go for it on 4th	0.69	31
Runs, behind 2H	28%	15	Max protect	10%	20	Sacks by LB	60.3%	8	Offensive Pace	31.4	22
Pass, ahead 2H	38%	26	Outside pocket	16%	8	Sacks by DB	13.8%	9	Defensive Pace	30.6	14

It will be interesting to see how Pat Shurmur uses tight ends in the Cleveland offense. St. Louis went without a tight end on 16.8 percent of plays, one of the higher figures in the league. But Cleveland went without a tight end on a league-low 1.2 percent of plays — and half the time when the Browns did use a tight end, it was because they were running a gimmick play like the Flash package or the Emory and Henry. ☞ The Browns had the NFL's biggest difference between DVOA running from one-back sets (-21.7%, ahead of only Carolina) and running from two-back sets (4.5%, seventh). These numbers do not include Josh Cribbs in the Flash formation. ☞ Cleveland ranked fifth in offensive DVOA in the first quarter, but only 23rd for the rest of the game. ☞ The Cleveland defense benefited from a league-low 16 dropped passes by opponents.

Passing

Player	DYAR	DVOA	Plays	NtYds	Avg	YAC	C%	TD	Int
C.McCoy	236	3.8%	246	1503	6.1	5.5	61.3%	6	9
J.Delhomme	-256	-37.0%	156	825	5.3	4.1	63.5%	2	7
S.Wallace	198	18.2%	108	675	6.3	5.3	63.4%	4	2

Rushing

Player	DYAR	DVOA	Plays	Yds	Avg	TD	Fum	Suc
P.Hillis	152	5.0%	270	1178	4.4	11	8	53%
M.Bell	-68	-44.0%	47	101	2.1	0	1	28%
C.McCoy	66	49.9%	21	141	6.7	1	0	-
J.Cribbs	-20	-31.0%	20	67	3.4	0	1	50%
J.Davis	-6	-17.0%	19	60	3.2	0	0	26%
T.Clayton	-1	-11.0%	7	17	2.4	0	0	57%
L.Vickers	-1	-10.9%	5	11	2.2	0	0	40%
S.Wallace	-18	-97.6%	4	-5	-1.3	0	1	-
J.Delhomme	-27	-92.4%	4	3	0.8	0	1	-

Receiving

Player	DYAR	DVOA	Plays	Ctch	Yds	Y/C	YAC	TD	C%
M.Massaquoi	-8	-14.0%	73	36	488	13.6	3.9	2	49%
C.Stuckey	-70	-26.5%	64	41	362	8.8	5.2	0	64%
B.Robiskie	3	-11.8%	49	29	310	10.7	2.0	3	59%
J.Cribbs	37	-0.3%	39	23	292	12.7	6.0	1	59%
B.Watson	125	11.3%	103	69	762	11.0	3.9	3	67%
E.Moore	83	41.4%	26	16	323	20.2	5.6	1	62%
R.Royal	-21	-30.7%	12	5	56	11.2	3.0	1	42%
P.Hillis	138	18.9%	77	61	477	7.8	7.2	2	79%
M.Bell	1	-12.2%	10	7	66	9.4	7.6	0	70%
L.Vickers	-24	-57.9%	9	4	15	3.8	3.3	0	44%

Offensive Line

Year	Yards	ALY	Rank	Power	Rank	Stuff	Rank	2nd Lev	Rank	Open Field	Rank
2008	3.94	4.08	19	59%	27	14%	5	1.02	27	0.59	26
2009	3.93	4.01	21	65%	14	18%	13	1.10	22	0.50	30
2010	3.95	4.04	17	74%	4	14%	4	0.93	30	0.55	24

Year	LE	Rank	LT	Rank	Mid	Rank	RT	Rank	RE	Rank	Sacks	ASR	Rank	F-Start	Cont.
2008	4.20	17	3.68	24	4.02	22	4.53	7	4.58	6	24	4.4%	7	22	30
2009	5.21	4	3.73	26	3.97	23	4.09	17	2.69	30	30	6.1%	15	17	28
2010	3.34	29	4.56	8	3.84	21	4.74	5	4.00	15	36	7.6%	23	12	31

In many ways, the offensive line stats for Cleveland tell a bigger story about the type of runner Peyton Hillis is. The opposite of a boom-and-bust back, Hillis gets steady gains without many long highlight runs. The Browns are well-anchored by Pro Bowl left tackle Joe Thomas, and both left guard Eric Steinbach and center Alex Mack are solid. The right side, however, has some question marks. You can mostly ignore the Adjusted Line Yards stats which show run-blocking improvement on the right side of the line; the Browns rarely run to the right, with only 14 percent of last year's runs going right tackle or right end. And the real issue is pass-blocking, as game charters blamed the right side of the line for most of the pass pressure felt by Cleveland quarterbacks last season. The Browns gave tackle Tony Pashos a nice free agent contract, but he couldn't even earn the right tackle job out of camp and once he got it, he only lasted three weeks before a season-ending ankle injury. The Browns have penciled in Pashos to start at right tackle this year, but it's hard to trust in the health of a player who has only 11 games in the past two seasons. John St. Clair, who started most of last year, became a free agent; so did Floyd Womack, who started most of the year at right guard. He'll be replaced by 2010 third-rounder Shawn Lauvao, who has the strength Browns coaches prize in their linemen but isn't particularly athletic. Another starting possibility is versatile fifth-round draft pick Jason Pinkston out of Pittsburgh, who could play either guard or tackle. He's a strong drive-blocker but struggles against speed-rushers and stunts.

Defensive Front Seven

Defensive Line	Age	Pos	Plays	TmPct	Rk	Stop	Dfts	BTkl	Overall St%	Rk	AvYd	Rk	Pass Rush Sack	Hit	Hur	vs. Run Runs	St%	Yds	vs. Pass Pass	St%	Yds
Ahtyba Rubin	25	DT	84	9.8%	1	45	8	3	51%	64	3.8	66	2	2	5	75	51%	4.1	9	78%	0.8
Kenyon Coleman	32	DE	68	7.9%	11	50	5	2	73%	57	3.1	74	2.5	2	8.5	62	73%	3.2	6	83%	1.8
Brian Schaefering	28	DE	31	3.6%	69	17	2	0	57%	79	3.2	75	0	2	3	30	57%	3.0	1	0%	9.0
Robaire Smith	34	DE	25	9.3%	3	16	1	1	64%	76	3.0	73	0	0	2	25	64%	3.0	0	0%	0.0
Derreck Robinson	29	DE	24	3.2%	78	17	1	0	70%	65	2.7	68	0.5	1	2.5	23	70%	3.0	1	100%	-4.0
Shaun Rogers	32	DT	17	2.1%	--	15	6	1	85%	--	0.9	--	2.5	10	14	13	85%	2.7	4	100%	-5.0

Linebackers	Age	Pos	Plays	TmPct	Rk	Stop	Dfts	BTkl	Overall AvYd	Pass Rush Sack	Hit	Hur	vs. Run Runs	St%	Rk	Yds	Rk	vs. Pass Tgts	Suc%	Rk	AdjYd	Rk
Matt Roth	29	OLB	88	10.3%	58	58	14	5	2.5	3.5	7	24.5	71	66%	65	2.4	21	10	53%	--	4.1	--
Chris Gocong	28	ILB	77	9.0%	66	52	13	8	3.5	2	2	8.5	61	67%	60	3.0	52	15	59%	--	4.8	--
Eric Barton	34	ILB	67	7.8%	84	38	9	2	4.7	0	1	4.5	48	73%	31	3.4	63	13	34%	--	6.1	--
Scott Fujita	32	OLB	52	10.8%	52	38	12	1	2.8	3.5	2	5	32	75%	20	2.9	44	17	66%	10	3.1	3
David Bowens	34	OLB	46	5.7%	--	26	10	3	4.5	0.5	2	12	29	55%	--	4.8	--	10	34%	--	6.8	--
Marcus Benard	26	OLB	28	3.5%	--	19	14	1	2.5	7	10	9.5	13	62%	--	5.0	--	3	33%	--	12.1	--
Jason Trusnik	27	ILB	16	1.9%	--	11	1	0	4.1	1	1	3.5	13	69%	--	3.7	--	2	106%	--	8.0	--

Year	Yards	ALY	Rank	Power	Rank	Stuff	Rank	2nd Lev	Rank	Open Field	Rank
2008	4.68	4.71	32	58%	4	14%	30	1.18	20	0.91	24
2009	4.50	4.61	30	67%	18	13%	31	1.11	14	0.77	16
2010	4.18	4.68	31	68%	28	14%	31	1.00	4	0.44	4

Year	LE	Rank	LT	Rank	Mid	Rank	RT	Rank	RE	Rank	Sacks	ASR	Rank
2008	5.44	31	4.72	27	4.62	30	4.54	26	4.83	27	18	4.5%	30
2009	4.86	24	4.10	15	4.73	31	4.24	17	5.75	32	41	7.0%	11
2010	4.84	25	4.99	30	4.63	30	4.47	21	4.43	26	29	5.9%	21

Browns fans, and the Browns front office, felt that Ahtyba Rubin had a breakout year in 2010. No defensive tackle was involved in a higher percentage of his team's defensive Plays. However, our advanced stats suggest Rubin was maybe getting pushed around a little bit. His 51 percent Stop Rate against the run was the lowest in the league for a defensive tackle with more than 30 Plays. Rubin might be better suited for his new position; in the new 4-3, he'll move over into the three-technique spot and be more responsible for pass rushing while 338-pound rookie Phil Taylor clogs up the middle as the one-technique tackle. Taylor has to watch his weight to make sure he's not clogging things up too much — he was nearly 400 pounds for the 2009 season after he transferred from Penn State to Baylor.

There are some question marks at defensive end. The Browns used a high second-round pick on Jabaal Sheard. Scouts love Sheard, but our SackSEER projection system does not; Sheard had a poor 31.5-inch vertical jump at the combine and struggled with agility drills during his Pro Day. He also didn't have a great track record at Pitt, with just 19.5 sacks in four full years of playing time. It's a bit surprising that the Browns didn't find a veteran during free agency who could play opposite Sheard. Instead, it looks like they're going with Jayme Mitchell, who came over from Minnesota in a midseason trade and has played just six games with one sack in the last three years.

D'Qwell Jackson hasn't played since October 2009, due to two separate pectoral tears (one on each side). He's back, healthy, and will take the middle linebacker spot. Chris Gocong had a very successful season transferring to an inside position last year; now he'll move back outside, where he played with Philadelphia. Veteran Scott Fujita mans the strongside spot, where our game charting stats have always suggested he's an underrated pass defender.

Defensive Secondary

Secondary	Age	Pos	Plays	TmPct	Rk	Stop	Dfts	BTkl	Runs	St%	Rk	Yds	Rk	Tgts	Tgt%	Rk	Dist	Suc%	Rk	APaYd	Rk	PD	Int
				Overall						vs. Run					vs. Pass								
T.J. Ward	25	SS	115	13.4%	10	43	13	5	60	42%	34	5.1	11	40	9.0%	7	14.4	61%	22	7.1	30	8	2
Abram Elam	30	FS	87	10.2%	41	27	12	3	41	32%	61	9.5	71	28	6.2%	32	11.5	70%	8	6.0	14	8	2
Joe Haden	22	CB	74	8.6%	40	33	16	4	14	29%	77	6.3	37	67	14.9%	48	14.0	60%	14	6.0	13	16	6
Sheldon Brown	32	CB	73	8.5%	45	30	9	9	22	64%	10	3.4	5	67	14.9%	49	13.6	46%	70	9.1	71	10	2
Eric Wright	26	CB	51	7.3%	62	22	12	3	13	62%	14	3.7	8	55	15.2%	43	12.4	45%	74	10.1	83	9	1
Mike Adams	30	FS	40	5.0%	77	17	11	3	6	33%	55	4.8	9	36	8.6%	9	8.1	48%	60	7.2	31	5	2

Year	Pass D Rank	vs. #1 WR	Rk	vs. #2 WR	Rk	vs. Other WR	Rk	vs. TE	Rk	vs. RB	Rk
2008	17	-1.0%	14	49.5%	32	-30.8%	5	-10.2%	10	-4.1%	9
2009	28	18.3%	23	-20.1%	7	14.5%	28	47.1%	32	34.1%	31
2010	16	12.1%	25	6.7%	18	5.3%	21	-0.8%	12	1.4%	14

The Browns finally drafted the right cornerback, as Joe Haden was everything that Eric Wright was supposed to be back in 2007. Based on our game charting numbers, Haden, not Devon McCourty, was actually last year's top rookie cornerback. Wright was demoted to nickel and dime duties, then he signed with Detroit after the lockout. The other starter opposite Haden will be veteran Sheldon Brown, although Cleveland might want to figure out what caused his performance to take a massive nosedive in 2010. Brown finished 70th in Success Rate in Cleveland after five straight years of above-average Success Rate in Philadelphia. In fact, Brown was No. 1 in the stat in 2008, and 11th in 2009. The drop isn't related to the shoulder injury Brown suffered against the Jets in Week 10, either; Brown's charting stats actually got slightly better after midseason. Most likely, Brown is not really *this* bad, but he's clearly on the downside of his career at age 32. (Although, curiously, Brown had a career-high Stop Rate against the run the same year his pass stats divebombed.) The Browns also added former Eagles cornerback Dimitri Patterson, who was terrible last year when pressed into starting duty: 77th with 9.5 adjusted yards per pass, plus 12 penalties.

Haden, of course, wasn't the only quality defensive back added in the 2010 draft. T.J. Ward had an excellent rookie year, playing strong against both the run and the pass. Usama Young, picked up in free agency from the Saints, will battle with veteran Mike Adams to replace Abram Elam at free safety. Both players are former cornerbacks, which is certainly useful in coverage, and both can play nickelback if needed. Fifth-round pick Buster Skrine out of Tennessee-Chattanooga is built to play slot receivers: he's extremely fast and athletic, but also extremely small (5-foot-9, 185 pounds) and undisciplined.

Special Teams

Year	DVOA	Rank	FG/XP	Rank	Net Kick	Rank	Kick Ret	Rank	Net Punt	Rank	Punt Ret	Rank	Hidden	Rank
2008	4.3%	4	1.8	15	-3.0	21	8.2	5	17.5	2	0.6	13	8.0	4
2009	8.4%	1	4.8	6	10.3	4	21.0	1	2.1	14	11.2	3	7.5	4
2010	2.3%	10	-1.1	21	12.5	4	-7.3	24	11.8	3	-2.1	19	2.2	10

Pre-lockout confusion led to some strange franchise tags this season, but perhaps the strangest was the one Cleveland put on kicker Phil Dawson. Dawson is about as run-of-the-mill as kickers get. His field goal rates bounce up and down unpredictably, while his kickoffs are reliably mediocre. The Browns have been near the top of our ratings for kickoff value the last couple years, but the positive value is entirely kick coverage. Assuming average returns, Dawson's kickoffs were worth -0.7 estimated points of field position last year and -2.1 points the year before.

Joshua Cribbs had a down year on returns, even before the foot injury that slowed him down for the last month and half of the season. His returns were worth a combined 31.7 points of estimated field position in 2009, then plummeted to -6.0 points in 2010 — with no touchdowns. It's reasonable to assume performance somewhere between those two numbers in 2011. One thing Cribbs will need to fix is the case of butterfingers that infected him in 2010; he fumbled three returns and muffed another two punts, although the Browns managed to recover all five balls. Punter Reggie Hodges tore his Achilles at the start of camp and will be replaced by Richmond McGee, who's been bumming around Chicago's preseason camps and practice squad the last couple seasons.

Coaching Staff

A few of the coaches were kept on from the previous administration, including offensive line coach George Warhop and running backs coach Gary Brown. Hard to argue with the success their charges had in 2010. Mark Whipple takes over as quarterbacks coach, and will try to mold Colt McCoy the same way he helped mold Ben Roethlisberger as Pittsburgh quarterbacks coach from 2004 through 2006. Of course, McCoy and Roethlisberger have very different skill sets. Dick Jauron has a couple of former coordinators on his defensive staff. Last year's Arizona coordinator, Billy Davis, coaches linebackers. Longtime Holmgren coaching tree associate Ray Rhodes is "senior assistant/defense." Strength and conditioning coach Kent Johnson served the same role for Holmgren's Green Bay and Seattle teams.

Dallas Cowboys

2010 Record: 6-10	**2011 Mean Projection:** 7.7 wins
Pythagorean Wins: 7.0 (19th)	**On the Clock (0-3):** 5%
DVOA: -10.3% (24th)	**Loserville (4-6):** 27%
Offense: -0.9% (21st)	**Mediocrity (7-8):** 29%
Defense: 9.9% (27th)	**Playoff Contender (9-10):** 24%
Special Teams: 0.5% (15th)	**Super Bowl Contender (11+):** 14%
Variance: 22.3% (23rd)	**Projected Average Opponent:** 0.7% (13th)

2010: Cowboys can't get the breaks all year… except the break in Tony Romo's collarbone.

2011: A rebound in fortune will return them to relevance, but the defense still may keep them from the playoffs.

The 2010 season for the Dallas Cowboys, as you undoubtedly already know, did not exactly go to plan. Jerry Jones's dream of winning a Super Bowl in his glorious new cathedral for Texas football was snuffed out before Halloween. For the first time in several seasons, America's Team even failed to hit its famously pessimistic projection in our annual, as the team finished the year looking up at *FOA 2010's* expectation of 7.5 wins.

But why did Dallas fail to launch? The Cowboys returned virtually the same lineup that went 11-5 in 2009 and 33-15 overall under Wade Phillips. While Tony Romo's broken collarbone is the easy answer, at the time Romo went down, the Cowboys were losing a game that would have left them at 1-5. Was it really just Romo's injury that brought down the Cowboys?

Not really; in fact, while injury projections by FO over the past few years have suggested that the Cowboys would suffer more injuries before each of the past several seasons, the 2010 Cowboys weren't a team that was particularly beset by missed games. By our count, the Cowboys had six starters miss a total of 28 games. That was the fifth-lowest total in the league, and of the four teams whose starters missed fewer games, only one (San Francisco) failed to make the playoffs.

The problem here is in accounting; namely, not all injuries are created equal. Obviously, an injury to a Pro Bowl quarterback matters more than an injury to a starting fullback, but our AGL system counted them as injuries to starting players, regardless of the impact. In 2008, when Romo went down with a fractured pinkie and missed three games, the statistical difference between him and backup Brad Johnson was the biggest that we've seen during the DVOA Era. The Cowboys missed the playoffs in 2008 almost entirely because of the injury to Romo. That was not the case in 2010.

With this in mind, we've developed new (proprietary) injury metrics for our projection system that model the impact of injuries at different positions as they have throughout the past decade. As a result, our projection system has the best injury information it's ever had. And as you might suspect, quarterback injuries are by far the most impactful injuries a team can deal with. Absent any inside information about Romo's breakability, we have to assume that the Dallas starter will be back for a full, healthy slate in 2011, which should improve things for the Cowboys next year. But it still doesn't explain why the Cowboys were so bad when he was in the lineup.

FOA 2010 surmised that the increase in injuries would be joined with a serious decline by the Dallas offensive line, and it was right on both fronts. Although left tackle Doug Free immediately went from question mark to valuable contributor, the rest of the

2011 Cowboys Schedule

Week	Opp.	Week	Opp.	Week	Opp.
1	at NYJ	7	STL	13	at ARI
2	at SF	8	at PHI	14	NYG
3	WAS (Mon.)	9	SEA	15	at TB (Sat.)
4	DET	10	BUF	16	PHI
5	BYE	11	at WAS	17	at NYG
6	at NE	12	MIA (Thu.)		

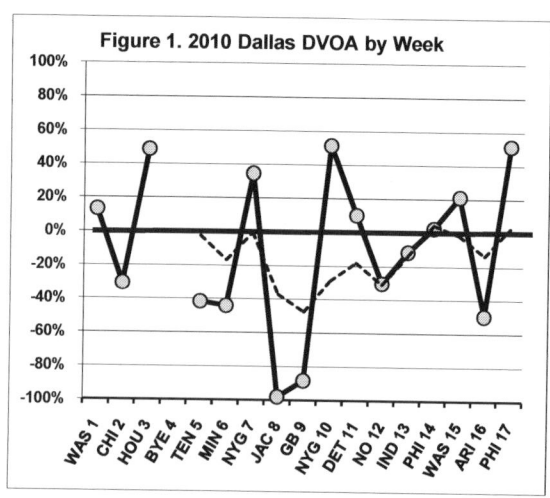

Figure 1. 2010 Dallas DVOA by Week

line had an uneven year. Left guard Kyle Kosier struggled with knee and leg injuries and was never healthy, as was the case with right tackle Marc Colombo. Right guard Leonard Davis, coming off of three straight Pro Bowl selections, was so slow in pass protection that the team benched him in a game. Of the four holdovers from 2009, only center Andre Gurode had a passable year, although the Pro Bowl nod bestowed on him was kind at best.

But the offensive line's collapse was not enough to bring the Cowboys down singlehandedly. Even after the Giants game in Week 7 that saw the end of Romo's season, the 1-5 Cowboys ranked ninth in the league in offensive DVOA. Instead, the Cowboys were 24th in defensive DVOA through six games, and by the end of the year, their now 27th-ranked defense had one very clear flaw: the secondary.

During the Wade Phillips era, the Cowboys had stayed within a relatively consistent range at each aspect of the game short one. Their rushing offense had made a small improvement from 10th (2007) to fourth (2009). During Romo's two healthy seasons, they were in the top five in passing DVOA. The rushing defense stayed slightly above average, never falling lower than 14th or rising higher than 11th. But the pass defense had been in a steady decline. The unit that ranked eighth during Phillips' debut season as the head coach had dropped to 11th in 2008 and 15th in 2009.

Arresting the decline seemed simple enough. The Cowboys' Adjusted Sack Rate had fallen from first in the league in 2008 to a disappointing 12th in 2009, as DeMarcus Ware's sack rate fell from "historic" to merely "excellent." Ware's return to the rarified air of 2008 would solve the problem, as would an expected improvement by fellow outside linebacker Anthony Spencer. With the presence of newly-christened shutdown corner Mike Jenkins and a healthy year from Terence Newman behind them, it seemed reasonable

to believe that the Cowboys could aim for the top ten in pass defense in 2010.

It certainly did not turn out that way. While the pass rush improved, the difference ended up being ever so slight: The Cowboys moved up to 12th in Adjusted Sack Rate, an improvement of one spot. Their actual ASR declined from 7.0 percent to 6.9 percent, as an excellent season by Ware was met with disappointing sack totals by the likes of Spencer (five sacks) and Jay Ratliff (3.5). While the Phillips 3-4 hasn't been designed to get pass pressure from its defensive ends since the days of Patrick Kerney in Atlanta, Dallas defensive ends produced a total of just three sacks all season. Former Chargers lineman Igor Olshansky played in all 16 games and started 14 of them; he produced 4.5 quarterback hurries, three quarterback hits, and no sacks. That's absurd; a starting defensive end should have the opposing offensive lineman fall down and create free hurries for him five or six times a year. Only two defensive ends that started 14 games or more had fewer hurries recorded than the Ukranian one.

Scarily, the pass rush was the successful part of the pass defense. While the Cowboys had question marks at safety, a set of cornerbacks that were occasionally dominant in 2009 absolutely collapsed in 2010. For Newman, the cause was yet another injury. During that same Giants game that ended Romo's season, Newman suffered a debilitating rib injury that, truthfully, should have forced him to sit out a few games. A combination of toughness and modern medicine was able to keep Newman in the starting lineup, but he was a shell of his normal self. Before the injury, Newman had allowed 7.1 yards per attempt with a 58 percent Success Rate over his 26 targets. Afterwards, those figures reached for the sky. He hit an even 10 yards per attempt, and his Success Rate collapsed to 37 percent. An ankle injury only exacerbated his troubles. It beggars belief that Newman was playing through such pain for a going-nowhere team.

Even more disconcerting was the play of Jenkins. At least Newman had an excuse. After putting up elite numbers in his second season, Jenkins was arguably the worst regular cornerback in the NFL last season. He allowed 10.6 adjusted yards per attempt and produced a 40 percent Success Rate, and when he wasn't giving up big plays, he was committing penalties. His six defensive pass interference penalties placed him among the league leaders in a category better left alone. He tied for the team lead with eight missed tackles. He said the art in Cowboys Stadium was tacky at best. He forgot to install that new temporary seating before the Super Bowl. His expert consulting job during the lockout is making sure that *Madden NFL 12* gets the back of every wide receiver's helmet right. You get the idea. We know that cornerback charting stats can be wildly inconsistent from year-to-year, but a swing like Jenkins' from 2009 to 2010 is just about unprecedented, and in this case the numbers are clearly backed up by what we all saw on the field. All we can say about his 2011 performance is that it's all but sure to fit somewhere between those two extremes. Jenkins has proven that he's quite capable of both brilliance and slapstick, and it's impossible to say which version will show up in 2011.

There was one other factor, though, that had a huge impact on the Cowboys' win-loss record: luck in close games. The Cowboys were 3-8 in games decided by a touchdown or less, including an incredible 0-6 start to the season in such games. A virtually identical roster went 11-8 in those games from 2007-09, and history suggests that the Cowboys should regress towards a .500 record in such games in 2010.

Now, this is a bit of research that requires some explanation. When we suggested at midseason that the Cowboys had been unlucky to go 0-5 in close games and that their record would improve in such games during the second half, it nearly sent Mike Golic into a murderous frenzy on his radio show. That they went 3-3 in those games during the second half is easily chalked up to the calming balm of Jason Garrett or Jon Kitna's leadership or one of a dozen other factors, not the usurious mathematical concept of "regression towards the mean." But there's little doubt that our old

friend regression had a lot to do with what happened.

The reality is that wins aren't always a great proxy for team performance, because they're not created equal. Consider the first of these losses, the 13-7 defeat by the Redskins in Week 1. It's easy to point to the stupid checkdown the Cowboys threw at the end of the first half that resulted in a fumble return for a touchdown. Afterwards, though, remember that the Cowboys were in a position to win the game on the final play. Down six points with 13 yards to go for a touchdown, Romo hit Miles Austin for what looked to be a game-winning score, only for the play to be taken off the board by a game-ending holding penalty on backup tackle Alex Barron. Of course, the holding penalty was the right call, but there are plenty of game-deciding plays that see holding go uncalled. That same exact performance from top-to-bottom would have earned the Cowboys a win with a more conservative set of officials on the final play. When the difference between winning and losing is the referee's call on one play, giving a team a 1 or a 0 for their performance isn't the best measure of how they're playing.

That's an extreme example of how thin the line can be between winning and losing a close game, but the preponderance of historical evidence is on the side of close games being mostly luck. As an example, we know that from 2000 through 2010, the previous year's win total explained about 7.9 percent of each team's subsequent win total. That's a really low figure, but it blows away the predicative value of how teams play in close games from year-to-year. Over the same timeframe, a team's winning percentage in games decided by a touchdown or less explained 0.6 percent of their winning percentage in the following season. That's just about useless.

Take 2009, for example. The team with the best record in games decided by a touchdown was Indianapolis, which went 7-0. Last year, they were 5-4. The top five teams in close games in 2009 (the Colts, Chargers, Vikings, Raiders, and Panthers) went 24-5 that year. In 2010, those teams were 14-18 in those same games. Meanwhile, the bottom five teams went from 8-27 to 18-20, and the team ranked 27th — Chicago — went from 2-5 to 7-3.

The same is true of other years, too. If we split the teams from 1983 to 2009 into five groups of equal size based on winning percentage in close games and then compare it to their winning percentage in those games the next season, we get virtually identical results that hint at nothing of their past performance (Table 1).

Table 1: Historical Close Game Predicative Value, 1983-2009

Win Pct, Year 1	Win Pct, Year 2
0 to .333	.475
.334 to .444	.505
.445 to .571	.518
.572 to .667	.516
.668 to 1.000	.518

So the offense is likely to be better, and the team's overall luck is likely to be better. The defense is what pulls our mean projection down to 8-8. The Cowboys hope that Rob Ryan can design blitzes that bring more pass pressure, but like every other team with a new coordinator, the Cowboys are starting

the 2011 season behind. An improving defense will have to fight upstream against the third-down rebound trend, as the Cowboys ranked 27th in defensive DVOA last year but 11th on third downs. And without any idea of what went wrong with Jenkins last year, and with Terence Newman unlikely to get healthier at the age of 33, it's hard to expect significant improvement in the secondary. Newman will already miss the preseason, and there's little depth behind Orlando Scandrick if Newman misses significant time. It's not as bad as blowing the chance to play the Super Bowl in their own stadium, but the Cowboys aren't likely to be playing a Super Bowl in Jim Irsay's new stadium either.

Bill Barnwell

2010 Cowboys Stats by Week

Wk	vs.	W-L	PF	PA	YDF	YDA	TO	Total	Off	Def	ST
1	@WAS	L	7	13	380	250	-1	13%	21%	-3%	-11%
2	CHI	L	20	27	410	308	-3	-31%	6%	49%	12%
3	@HOU	W	27	13	385	340	3	49%	28%	-16%	5%
4	BYE										
5	TEN	L	27	34	511	321	-3	-42%	10%	35%	-17%
6	@MIN	L	21	24	314	188	-1	-44%	-6%	16%	-22%
7	NYG	L	35	41	254	497	3	34%	15%	12%	31%
8	JAC	L	17	35	415	387	-3	-98%	-59%	42%	3%
9	@GB	L	7	45	205	415	-4	-88%	-51%	28%	-9%
10	@NYG	W	33	20	427	480	2	51%	63%	3%	-8%
11	DET	W	35	19	265	338	1	10%	-11%	10%	31%
12	NO	L	27	30	457	414	-1	-30%	-8%	32%	9%
13	@IND	W	38	35	368	405	4	-12%	3%	-1%	-15%
14	PHI	L	27	30	349	429	0	3%	-3%	-9%	-3%
15	WAS	W	33	30	434	341	3	21%	17%	5%	9%
16	@ARI	L	26	27	382	271	-3	-50%	-18%	34%	3%
17	@PHI	W	14	13	272	244	3	52%	0%	-62%	-10%

Trends and Splits

	Offense	Rank	Defense	Rank
Total DVOA	-0.9%	21	9.9%	27
Unadjusted VOA	1.1%	19	11.6%	27
Weighted Trend	-4.3%	24	7.1%	20
Variance	8.3%	18	7.5%	23
Average Opponent	2.9%	15	4.5%	21
Passing	10.6%	19	21.5%	28
Rushing	-1.2%	16	-5.5%	11
First Down	-1.3%	22	22.6%	30
Second Down	-14.2%	28	5.1%	18
Third Down	20.1%	10	-8.5%	11
First Half	-6.9%	23	12.0%	26
Second Half	5.4%	18	8.0%	22
Red Zone	2.7%	13	20.6%	29
Late and Close	0.4%	20	-2.4%	16

Five-Year Performance

Year	W-L	Pyth	Est W	PF	PA	TO	Total	Rk	Off	Rk	Def	Rk	ST	Rk	Off AGL	Rk	Def AGL	Rk
2006	9-7	9.8	8.6	425	350	+1	13.6%	9	13.0%	6	-0.9%	14	-0.2%	20	1.3	1	7.5	8
2007	13-3	11.0	10.8	455	325	+5	22.9%	4	17.4%	4	-5.8%	11	-0.4%	18	19.6	14	26.2	22
2008	9-7	7.9	8.3	362	365	-11	4.4%	19	6.7%	17	-0.6%	9	-2.8%	27	24.2	17	29.1	19
2009	11-5	11.3	11.2	361	250	+2	25.5%	5	24.9%	3	0.4%	12	1.0%	14	14.5	11	7.7	2
2010	6-10	7.0	6.8	394	436	0	-10.3%	24	-0.9%	21	9.9%	27	0.5%	15	20.7	12	11.1	7

Strategic Tendencies

Run/Pass		Rank	Offense		Rank	Defense		Rank	Other		Rank
Runs, all plays	37%	23	3+ WR	46%	17	Rush 3	10.0%	13	2+ RB, Pct Runs	60%	15
Runs, first half	38%	22	4+ WR	3%	27	Rush 4	55.9%	23	1 RB/2 TE, Pct Runs	35%	30
Runs, first down	42%	29	2+ TE	34%	10	Rush 5	23.9%	14	1 RB/3+ WR, Pct Runs	16%	27
Runs, second-long	31%	22	Single back	51%	27	Rush 6+	10.2%	12	CB1 on WR1	62%	1
Runs, power sit.	59%	17	Play action	16%	22	Zone Blitz	3.7%	22	Go for it on 4th	1.14	5
Runs, behind 2H	28%	17	Max protect	13%	8	Sacks by LB	67.1%	3	Offensive Pace	32.5	29
Pass, ahead 2H	47%	9	Outside pocket	12%	18	Sacks by DB	14.3%	8	Defensive Pace	30.5	8

For a window into this year's Dallas defense, look at Rob Ryan's defense last year in Cleveland. The Browns sent the standard four pass rushers just one-third of the time, last in the NFL. They led the league in pass plays where they sent three (19.5 percent) or five (36.7 percent). ☞ Ryan's defense also blitzed (five or more pass rushers) more often than any other defense on first or second down, 49 percent of passes. But Ryan actually blitzed *less* often on third downs, just 42 percent of passes. ☞ Jason Garrett was much more aggressive on fourth down than Wade Phillips. ☞ The Cowboys didn't use the draw as much as they did the previous two years, but still ranked second with 45 draws. They were slightly above-average on the play, 5.3 yards per carry and 14.7% DVOA.

Passing

Player	DYAR	DVOA	Plays	NtYds	Avg	YAC	C%	TD	Int
J.Kitna	368	5.6%	339	2264	6.7	6.5	66.0%	16	12
T.Romo	434	20.6%	221	1570	7.1	5.3	69.8%	11	7
S.McGee	-10	-14.5%	48	208	4.3	5.5	52.4%	2	0

Rushing

Player	DYAR	DVOA	Plays	Yds	Avg	TD	Fum	Suc
F.Jones	124	8.2%	184	790	4.3	1	1	50%
M.Barber	-21	-12.5%	113	374	3.3	4	0	48%
T.Choice	12	-4.9%	66	243	3.7	3	0	42%
J.Kitna	-6	-16.7%	23	149	6.5	1	2	-
S.McGee	22	33.8%	11	75	6.8	0	0	-
M.Austin	49	77.0%	7	93	13.3	1	0	-
C.Gronkowski	10	30.8%	5	17	3.4	0	0	80%
T.Romo	21	86.4%	4	40	10.0	0	0	-

Receiving

Player	DYAR	DVOA	Plays	Ctch	Yds	Y/C	YAC	TD	C%
M.Austin	236	12.2%	119	69	1047	15.2	6.2	7	58%
D.Bryant	105	5.8%	73	45	561	12.5	4.3	6	62%
R.Williams	77	3.2%	64	37	542	14.6	5.6	5	58%
S.Hurd	5	-10.0%	23	14	120	8.6	4.8	0	61%
K.Ogletree	-1	-14.3%	6	3	34	11.3	2.0	0	50%
J.Witten	215	18.9%	128	94	1002	10.7	4.2	9	73%
M.Bennett	-53	-24.8%	47	33	262	7.9	5.5	0	70%
F.Jones	138	35.4%	53	49	460	9.4	11.6	1	92%
T.Choice	-6	-19.3%	22	17	114	6.7	7.2	0	77%
M.Barber	-27	-48.1%	15	11	49	4.5	6.9	0	73%
C.Gronkowski	-2	-16.2%	14	7	35	5.0	4.3	1	50%

Offensive Line

Year	Yards	ALY	Rank	Power	Rank	Stuff	Rank	2nd Lev	Rank	Open Field	Rank
2008	4.48	4.10	15	68%	15	18%	17	1.25	7	1.00	8
2009	5.00	4.48	3	58%	26	17%	10	1.36	3	1.15	5
2010	3.87	4.14	12	54%	26	18%	13	1.10	20	0.49	26

Year	LE	Rank	LT	Rank	Mid	Rank	RT	Rank	RE	Rank	Sacks	ASR	Rank	F-Start	Cont.
2008	5.12	4	3.65	27	4.12	17	4.60	3	3.03	29	31	5.8%	13	24	31
2009	5.21	3	5.03	4	4.19	13	4.16	15	4.87	4	34	6.2%	16	25	39
2010	4.52	12	3.46	29	4.17	11	4.33	9	3.99	16	31	5.8%	11	27	34

A big reason Football Outsiders was relatively tepid about the Cowboys last year was concern about the age of the offensive line. Well, the Cowboys offensive line regressed in just about every conceivable way in 2010 (ALY, Power Situations, and Stuff Rate). The Cowboys certainly made an effort to right the ship in the offseason. They re-signed their youngest starter Doug Free to a big contract. Free will start at tackle again this year, but which side of the line he will play is still in question. The Cowboys spent the ninth overall pick on Tyron Smith, and Jerry Jones has made it clear Smith will compete for a starting job from day one. Typically teams don't draft tackles that high, with that kind of athleticism, unless they plan to play them on the quarterback's blind side, where they are most valuable. But due to the fact that Smith played right tackle at USC and is just 20 years old, he may start his career on the right side. With the release of Marc Colombo the Cowboys have effectively removed the safety net from under Smith, and with no veteran presence behind him the rookie will have to perform immediately. No matter where Free and Smith line up, the Cowboys will have two well-paid offensive tackles for the foreseeable future.

The interior O-line starts with returning starters and veterans Kyle Kosier and Andre Gurode. Gurode is a perennial Pro Bowler and the Cowboys' best offensive lineman. Kosier is effective when he's healthy, but has struggled to stay healthy the last couple of years. The right guard spot is wide open after the release of the statue that Leonard Davis had become. Montrae Holland replaced Davis mid-game a couple of times last season, as well as starting in place of an injured Kosier. He is the favorite going into camp, and the only players challenging him are fourth-rounder David Arkin of Missouri State and 2010 UFA Phil Costa. The Cowboys are paying Free, Smith, and Gurode a lot of money, leaving very little money for depth. If any of the Cowboys starters get injured it could be a long year for Tony Romo.

Defensive Front Seven

Defensive Line	Age	Pos	Plays	TmPct	Rk	Stop	Dfts	BTkl	St%	Rk	AvYd	Rk	Sack	Hit	Hur	Runs	St%	Yds	Pass	St%	Yds
						Overall								Pass Rush			vs. Run			vs. Pass	
Igor Olshansky	29	DE	40	5.2%	42	32	1	0	83%	34	2.9	69	0	4	4.5	35	83%	2.5	5	60%	5.4
Jay Ratliff	30	DT	32	4.1%	42	20	7	0	56%	60	3.3	62	3.5	4	18.5	25	56%	3.8	7	86%	1.4
Stephen Bowen	27	DE	23	3.0%	--	19	7	0	79%	--	0.4	--	1.5	6	10	19	79%	1.2	4	100%	-3.5
Marcus Spears	28	DE	19	4.9%	--	11	4	0	65%	--	3.2	--	0	1	1	17	65%	2.2	2	0%	11.0
Josh Brent	23	DT	16	2.1%	--	12	0	0	75%	--	2.6	--	0	0	0	16	75%	2.6	0	0%	0.0

Linebackers	Age	Pos	Plays	TmPct	Rk	Stop	Dfts	BTkl	AvYd	Sack	Hit	Hur	Runs	St%	Rk	Yds	Rk	Tgts	Suc%	Rk	AdjYd	Rk
						Overall				Pass Rush			vs. Run					vs. Pass				
Bradie James	30	ILB	120	15.5%	13	74	17	4	4.9	0	2	4	78	71%	45	3.7	78	37	47%	59	7.6	67
Keith Brooking	36	ILB	103	13.3%	34	53	15	2	5.8	1	3	4	60	62%	80	3.7	73	39	66%	9	4.7	11
DeMarcus Ware	29	OLB	66	8.5%	74	57	31	2	0.3	15.5	8	39	35	91%	1	1.9	4	6	82%	--	3.9	--
Anthony Spencer	27	OLB	65	8.4%	75	57	13	7	2.5	5	5	14	48	77%	16	3.2	59	12	59%	--	3.3	--
Sean Lee	25	ILB	24	3.5%	--	20	7	1	2.3	0	0	0	16	81%	--	2.5	--	7	56%	--	6.1	--
Victor Butler	24	OLB	16	2.2%	--	11	3	0	5.1	2	1	2	7	71%	--	7.1	--	1	-8%	--	2.8	--

Year	Yards	ALY	Rank	Power	Rank	Stuff	Rank	2nd Lev	Rank	Open Field	Rank
2008	4.41	4.19	18	74%	26	17%	20	1.08	12	1.00	26
2009	4.02	3.99	13	67%	19	17%	23	1.05	5	0.69	12
2010	4.40	4.27	22	70%	29	14%	29	1.10	14	0.87	19

Year	LE	Rank	LT	Rank	Mid	Rank	RT	Rank	RE	Rank	Sacks	ASR	Rank
2008	2.86	3	4.04	14	4.21	18	4.66	28	4.96	28	59	9.9%	1
2009	2.91	4	3.80	10	4.05	17	4.33	22	4.23	22	43	7.0%	12
2010	4.72	23	3.39	6	4.39	24	4.16	16	4.79	30	35	6.9%	11

The biggest question for the Cowboys up front was whether new defensive coordinator Rob Ryan would move three-time Pro Bowler Jay Ratliff from nose tackle to defensive end. That answer came early in camp when Ratliff was listed as the nose tackle, though Ryan plans to maximize Ratliff's versatility by moving him around on defense. Ratliff struggled against the run last year, but while his sack numbers declined for a second straight season, Ratliff did produce 18.5 hurries in 2010. (He had just six hurries in 2009.) Moving Ratliff around will give 6-foot-2, 325-pound nose tackle Josh Brent, a 2010 Supplemental Draft choice, a chance to see additional playing time, particularly on early downs. Defensive ends Marcus Spears and Igor Olshansky were solid against the run, but offer little in terms of pass rush. Spears opened the 2010 season with a knee injury, and then a calf injury landed him on injured reserve. When his replacement in the starting lineup last season, Stephen Bowen, received a five-year, $27.5 million contract from the Washington Redskins, Spears was re-signed to a five-year, $19.2 million contract. Depth behind Olshansky and Spears was addressed with the re-signing of Jason Hatcher and the addition of Kenyon Coleman, a former Cowboy who spent the last two seasons playing for Ryan with the Cleveland Browns.

DeMarcus Ware continues to be one of the most dominant defensive players of the era, picking up his second quarterback sack title in three years with a 15.5-sack performance in 2010 and improving his performance against the run. Last year's charting data also placed Ware second among defensive players in hurries with 39, behind only St. Louis Rams defensive end Chris Long (42.5). Ryan's creative blitz packages should benefit Ware, who has often had to fight through double-teams to get to opposing quarterbacks. Fellow outside line-backer Anthony Spencer continued to play well against the run, but could not build on his impressive pass-rushing performance from late in the 2009 season. Spencer produced five quarterback sacks, one fewer than in 2009, but two of those sacks came against the Philadelphia Eagles' jayvee squad. 2011 is an important year for Spencer, who is entering the final year of his rookie contract. 2009 fourth-round picks Victor Butler and Brandon Williams primarily contribute on special teams, though Ryan may give Butler increased opportunities to rush the quarterback.

Veteran inside linebackers Bradie James (knee) and Keith Brooking (foot) made frequent appearances on the Cowboys injury reports. Both missed or were limited in practices, but neither missed a start and they finished one-two on the team in tackles, with James recording a career-high 118. Both will return, though only James is assured of a starting role. Dallas traded up in the second-round in 2010 to select Penn State linebacker Sean Lee, who was expected to play in nickel packages. Quadriceps and hamstring injuries limited his playing time early, but two interceptions in an overtime win over the Indianapolis Colts earned Lee NFC Defensive Player of the Week honors and showed why the Cowboys held him in such high regard. If healthy, and capable of overcoming a lost offseason with no OTAs or mini-camps, Lee has a chance to push Brooking for the starting job. This year, Dallas used a second-round pick on North Carolina linebacker Bruce Carter, who is projected to move inside in Ryan's system. Carter is coming off a torn ACL and his NFL career may begin on the PUP list.

Defensive Secondary

Secondary	Age	Pos	Plays	TmPct	Rk	Stop	Dfts	BTkl	Runs	St%	Rk	Yds	Rk	Tgts	Tgt%	Rk	Dist	Suc%	Rk	APaYd	Rk	PD	Int
				Overall					vs. Run					vs. Pass									
Terence Newman	33	CB	86	11.1%	16	21	8	5	16	6%	87	10.1	81	85	17.9%	17	13.2	45%	73	9.7	80	6	5
Gerald Sensabaugh	28	SS	79	10.2%	40	41	14	8	31	55%	12	5.9	25	37	7.8%	17	12.1	67%	10	6.2	16	12	5
Mike Jenkins	26	CB	64	8.2%	48	21	4	8	16	38%	61	13.3	87	82	17.2%	22	15.5	40%	85	10.6	86	9	1
Orlando Scandrick	24	CB	54	7.0%	69	30	19	6	5	60%	15	1.6	1	62	12.9%	68	9.8	54%	35	6.7	29	7	1
Alan Ball	26	FS	49	6.3%	72	9	5	6	16	19%	81	12.6	82	22	4.5%	68	14.8	42%	71	11.3	73	3	2

Year	Pass D Rank	vs. #1 WR	Rk	vs. #2 WR	Rk	vs. Other WR	Rk	vs. TE	Rk	vs. RB	Rk
2008	10	4.4%	16	24.7%	26	-11.5%	12	19.5%	25	4.0%	15
2009	15	-10.3%	10	-8.7%	9	13.0%	26	22.1%	27	16.1%	24
2010	28	44.1%	32	15.5%	26	2.9%	20	-11.9%	4	-11.2%	6

One year removed from Pro Bowl appearances, cornerbacks Terence Newman and Mike Jenkins both struggled in 2010. Jenkins' collapse from a fine 2009 is a complete mystery, apparently unrelated to injury. His season reached a low point when he declined to attempt to make a touchdown-saving tackle on wide receiver James Jones in the Cowboys' Week 9 45-7 loss to the Green Bay Packers on national television. Former NFL head coach Jim Mora, who coached defensive backs throughout the league, called Jenkins out on the NFL Network, referring to the lack of effort on that play as "high treason" and suggesting that interim head coach Jason Garrett should remove Jenkins from the team's locker room. Mora had a point, but Pro Bowl cornerbacks don't grow on trees and Jenkins certainly possesses the talent to play at that level. Newman played through a painful rib injury last season, but his performance has been steadily declining as he ventures further into his 30. Newman turns 33 in September and is due $8 million in base salary for 2011, yet he was not one of the players the Cowboys targeted for restructures when the league year opened. Newman is expected to miss all of training camp, and perhaps the season opener against the New York Jets, with a groin injury. Newman's injury creates an opportunity for third-year cornerback Orlando Scandrick to show that he's capable of handling a starting job at this level. If Scrandrick does start in the base defense, he'll likely move inside in nickel situations. Defensive backs accounted for more than 13 percent of the Browns' quarterback sacks under Ryan between 2009 and 2010, and Scandrick (4.5 career quarterback sacks, 2.5 in 2010) has been effective blitzing from the slot.

Starting strong safety Gerald Sensabaugh was the secondary's top performer, tying for the team lead with five interceptions, four of which came in the final six weeks of the season. Dallas re-signed Sensabaugh and brought in Abram Elam, another former Cowboy who started 31 games for Ryan the last two seasons in Cleveland. Elam's signing allows Alan Ball, who looked out of place as a free safety, to move back to his natural cornerback position in 2011. The Cowboys are high on second-year safety Barry Church, a standout player on special teams who could start at strong safety at some point down the line.

Special Teams

Year	DVOA	Rank	FG/XP	Rank	Net Kick	Rank	Kick Ret	Rank	Net Punt	Rank	Punt Ret	Rank	Hidden	Rank
2008	-2.8%	27	7.9	2	-7.1	27	-1.1	17	-7.4	27	-8.9	30	-8.5	25
2009	1.0%	14	-10.7	29	10.7	3	-5.9	23	1.2	19	10.7	5	-4.4	22
2010	0.5%	15	-5.5	29	1.2	15	-14.6	31	6.3	10	15.3	2	-14.6	30

After he led the NFL in touchbacks as a rookie kickoff specialist, the Cowboys wanted David Buehler to show that he could handle both kickoff and field goal duties in 2010. An impressive showing in the preseason, where Buehler converted on 10-of-11 field goal attempts and pumped 12 of his 19 kickoffs for touchbacks, validated the decision to not have him compete with another kicker during camp. Once the regular season began, Buehler remained solid on kickoffs, ranking fourth with 22 touchbacks, but converted on just 75 percent of his field goal attempts. Buehler also missed a pair of extra points, clanging one attempt off the left upright in the fourth quarter of a one-point loss to Arizona in Week 16. That missed kick allowed the Cardinals to win the game with a field goal on the ensuing drive, and veteran kicker Kris Brown was signed to a two-year contract the following week. Brown does not possess as strong a leg on kickoffs as Buehler, but is a veteran kicker whose lack of leg strength is likely mitigated by the NFL moving kickoffs back to the 35-yard line. If Buehler struggles again in 2011, the Cowboys won't hesitate to give Brown a call.

Three Cowboys rookies — Dez Bryant, Akwasi Owusu-Ansah, and Bryan McCann — made their mark in the return game last year. Bryant fearlessly handled punt return duties, not once signaling for a fair catch and bringing two of his 15 returns back for touchdowns. Bryant's 10.9 estimated points of field position ranked him second behind Chicago's Devin Hester among NFL punt returners. Bryant is moving into a starting role in the offense, but head coach Jason Garrett won't hesitate to put Bryant back there when he needs a big play on special teams. Owusu-Ansah, McCann, and sixth-round wide receiver Dwayne Harris (23.5-yard career average and three kickoff returns for touchdowns at East Carolina; 11.7-yard punt return average last season) will compete for roles in the return game during the preseason.

Punter Mat McBriar picked up Pro Bowl and All-Pro honors for the second time in his career, although by Football Outsiders' measures, he himself accounted for only 3.6 estimated points of field position in gross value (tenth in the league).

Coaching Staff

Jerry Jones removed the interim tag on Jason Garrett shortly after the season, signing him to a four-year contract and disclosing that Garrett, not Jones, would have final say on coaching hires and 53-man roster approval. Paul Pasqualoni, who took over as defensive coordinator when Wade Phillips was fired at midseason, returned to the college ranks, accepting the head coaching position at the University of Connecticut. Garrett hired Rob Ryan to coordinate the defense, with Ryan bringing linebackers coach Matt Eberflus with him from Cleveland. Coming off a season where the Cowboys defense gave up the most points in franchise history, the hiring of Ryan to coordinate a talented but underachieving defense was perhaps the team's most important addition of the offseason. Like his father, Buddy, and more famous twin Rex, Ryan devises creative, complex schemes around his personnel. As a result, his defenses often employ unconventional personnel groupings and formations to confuse and attack opposing offenses. Garrett also hired defensive line coach Brian Baker away from the University of North Carolina and raided the Patriots for strength and conditioning coach Mike Woicik. Two important veterans stay from last year's staff: Hudson Houck (offensive line) and Dave Campo (secondary).

Denver Broncos

2010 Record: 4-12

Pythagorean Wins: 5.2 (29th)

DVOA: -15.5% (26th)

Offense: 6.3% (15th)

Defense: 19.6% (30th)

Special Teams: -2.2% (27th)

Variance: 20.7% (22nd)

2011 Mean Projection: 5.6 wins

On the Clock (0-3): 22%

Loserville (4-6): 43%

Mediocrity (7-8): 20%

Playoff Contender (9-10): 9%

Super Bowl Contender (11+): 5%

Projected Average Opponent: 1.8% (8th)

2010: Josh McDaniels' chickens come home to roost.

2011: Things can't get worse, but they probably won't get much better.

In Miami, there's Nick Saban. In New York, there's Rich Kotite. In Atlanta, there's Bobby Petrino. In D.C., there's Steve Spurrier. And now, we can officially add Denver's Josh McDaniels to the list of former NFL head coaches who took over a mediocre team, turned it into a horrible team, and left a gutted roster in their wake. Indeed, in order to fully understand what happened to the Broncos in 2010, and describe the state of the franchise in 2011, you have to consider the totality of personnel failures during the McDaniels era.

Heading into 2009, anyone who watched Mike Shanahan's 2008 team could have told you that their 31st-ranked defense was the problem. Indeed, we did just that in *Football Outsiders Almanac 2009*, pinpointing the root cause as a lack of young talent. We even went so far as to note that Denver's projected starting secondary in 2009 was the oldest to take the field since the turn of the 21st century. Instead of making an attempt to get younger, however, McDaniels decided to simply import Mike Nolan and his hybrid 3-4 from San Francisco.

Initially, the strategy seemed to work: the 2009 defense finished seventh in defense DVOA. The writing was still on the wall, though, which we again pointed out in last season's *Football Outsiders Almanac 2010*. Specifically, they had an unrepeatable amount of good injury fortune in 2009 (i.e., the second-lowest defense

AGL since 2003); the last eight weeks of 2009 revealed them to be an incredibly bad run-stopping unit; and they still lacked young, impact talent aside from sack champion Elvis Dumervil.

The logical thing to do at that point would have been to get younger, get some quality depth, do *something*, right? Nope, that's not what the Broncos did. Instead, the defense again entered last season as one of the oldest in the league, and McDaniels inexplicably allowed Nolan to make a rare-for-the-NFL lateral career move, joining Miami as defensive coordinator. Lo and behold, the bottom ended up falling out. The injury bug finally hit, and it hit especially hard, ending the season of their best defensive player before it even began.

So, to bring this story to the present day, when you look at the Broncos' DVOA splits from last season, it's pretty apparent that much of their overall decline as a team from 2009 (12th to 26th) was attributable to a collapse in defensive efficiency (seventh to 30th). It's also apparent that much of that defensive collapse can be blamed on a rash of injuries that began during the preseason. However, chalking up Denver's 4-12 season to a simple case of bad luck lets McDaniels off the hook too easily. The defense was a ticking time bomb when he got the job, and he let the clock tick for two years. In 2010, the bomb went off, and McDaniels' job understandably lay amongst the rubble.

With it understood that McDaniels' apathy towards

2011 Broncos Schedule

Week	Opp.	Week	Opp.	Week	Opp.
1	OAK (Mon.)	7	at MIA	13	at MIN
2	CIN	8	DET	14	CHI
3	at TEN	9	at OAK	15	NE
4	at GB	10	at KC	16	at BUF
5	SD	11	NYJ (Thu.)	17	KC
6	BYE	12	at SD		

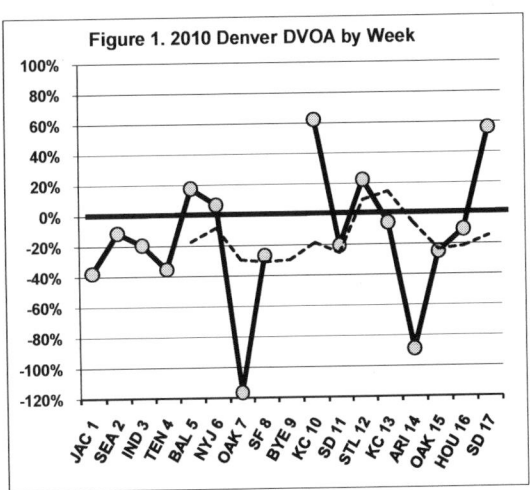

Figure 1. 2010 Denver DVOA by Week

defense played a large role in the team's downfall, it nevertheless can't be understated how much of a toll that injuries took on Denver's defense last season. To put their wild year-to-year swings in the context of recent NFL history, consider this. In the past five NFL seasons, only one defense's injury fortunes turned more unfavorably than last year's Broncos: the 2008 Detroit Lions, whose Defense AGL was nearly 56 games worse than it had been in 2007. As you'll recall, that team won exactly zero games — seven fewer than the previous season — thanks at least in part to a 12.4% rise in their defensive DVOA.

What made things even worse for Denver's defense last season was that the injury bug predominately took bites out of their pass rush and secondary. As we're all well aware, the NFL is becoming more and more of a passing league, so having starters at these positions either playing injured or missing games altogether puts a team's pass defense at a considerable disadvantage.

That disadvantage is even more pronounced when a team is forced on short notice to replace the pass-rushing production of the reigning NFL sack leader, which is exactly what happened to Denver when outside linebacker Elvis Dumervil suffered a season-ending torn pectoral muscle in training camp. It can't be understated how rare a predicament this was for an NFL team of recent vintage. From 1992 to 2009, 13 of the 18 sack leaders gave the same team at least 14 games of pass rushing production the following season. Unfortunately for the Broncos in 2010, Dumervil

is the only one of the remaining five who was lost for the entire subsequent season due to injury (Table 1).

The novelty of Denver's predicament means that apples-to-apples comparisons don't readily exist. However, the 1997 Panthers and 2008 Chiefs found themselves in analogous situations, albeit for reasons unrelated to injury. Specifically, Carolina and Kansas City had to replace the entirety of a reigning sack leader's production after losing Kevin Greene and Jared Allen, respectively. And as was the case with the 2010 Broncos, the sack, pass defense DVOA, and win results weren't pretty. We're talking about a sample that's way too small for bold declarations, but nevertheless, the history here seems instructive: Having an elite pass rusher disappear from your starting lineup is not an easy obstacle to overcome.

The 2010 Broncos also had to endure chronic leg injuries to cornerback Champ Bailey and free safety Brian Dawkins, both of whom were coming off of Pro Bowl seasons in 2009. Add Dumervil to these players along with cornerback Andre' Goodman, whose thigh injury in Week 3 led to sporadic playing time after starting all 16 games opposite Bailey in 2009, and what you have is a situation where Denver suffered season-long injuries to their four most important start-

Table 1. Teams Losing Previous Season's Sack Leader, 1992-2010

Year	Player	Team	Next Yr Games	Reason	Team Sacks Change	Pass Def DVOA Change	Win Change
2009	Elvis Dumervil	DEN	0	Injured Pectoral	-16	+49.0%	-4
2007	Jared Allen	KC	0	Traded to MIN	-27	+28.6%	-2
1996	Kevin Greene	CAR	0	Signed with SF	-25	+21.4%	-5
2003	Michael Strahan	NYG	8	Injured Pectoral	-5	-0.4%	+2
1995	Bryce Paup	BUF	11	Injured Groin	-1	-6.4%	0

ers in pass defense. In that context, it's easy to understand how that unit can go from a sixth-best DVOA of -12.7% one season to a second-worst DVOA of 36.3% the next. Of course, it would have helped if McDaniels hadn't traded away developing young cornerback Alphonso Smith for a song named tight end Dan Gronkowski before the season, but we digress. (Incidentally, Smith ended up leading the Lions in interceptions last season.)

The ultimate irony of McDaniels' inability to replace his most important defensive player is that his hiring in 2009 was due in no small part to the job he did when forced to replace New England's most important *offensive* player after a season-ending injury. Furthermore, his early ascension to football wunderkind in Denver was due in no small part to the seamless transition he orchestrated after trading (arguably) Denver's most important offensive player.

In 2008, Jay Cutler was the fifth-ranked quarterback according to DYAR. McDaniels decided to trade Cutler to Chicago for Kyle Orton, a quarterback who had spent his entire career to that point having difficulties winning the starting job from such legendary passers as Rex Grossman and Brian Griese. After never having been ranked higher than 21st in DYAR prior to playing in McDaniels' system, Orton finished both 2009 and 2010 with the 12th-best DYAR among quarterbacks. Similarly, one year later, McDaniels' "replaced" Brandon Marshall, who ranked 24th among wide receivers according to DYAR, with previously unproductive journeyman Brandon Lloyd. Upon entering McDaniels' offensive system, all Lloyd did in 2010 was have the second-best DYAR season by a wide receiver.

Overall though, despite his clear expertise in offensive football, McDaniels' shortcomings in the personnel and defense departments ended up doing more harm to the franchise than those offensive exploits did good. As an illustration of this, we went back and tracked every trade McDaniels made during his tenure. Table 2 shows the players he acquired in comparison to the players he traded away, as well as the players ultimately selected with the draft picks he traded (except for an as-of-yet unnamed 2012 draft pick traded for Peyton Hillis).

If that list isn't an indictment of McDaniels as a personnel chief, we don't know what is. Among the 15 players he traded away, 14 are either projected starters for their current teams or figure to be significant contributors as backups. The only player that can't be

Table 2. Josh McDaniels' Trade Record in Denver

Traded Away		Received in Return	
Position	Player Traded or Selected with Traded Pick	Position	Player Traded or Selected with Traded Pick
WR	Dez Bryant	LB	Robert Ayers
QB	Jay Cutler	WR	Eric Decker
LB	Andra Davis	OT	Orlando Franklin
TE	Ed Dickson	TE	Dan Gronkowski
DE	Brandon Graham	OG	Seth Olsen
TE	Aaron Hernandez	QB	Kyle Orton
RB	Peyton Hillis	QB	Brady Quinn
LB	Sergio Kindle	LB	Robert Quinn
WR	Johnny Knox	QB	Tim Tebow
OT	DeMarcus Love	WR	Demaryius Thomas
WR	Brandon Marshall		
TE	Dennis Pitta		
CB	Alphonso Smith		
WR	Mike Wallace		
OT	Kraig Urbik		

considered "one that got away" as of yet is DeMarcus Love, a sixth-round rookie for Minnesota.

Thankfully for Broncos fans, the team revamped the coaching and personnel duties this offseason by replacing McDaniels with John Fox as head coach, promoting Brian Xanders from figurehead general manager to actual general manager, and hiring franchise legend John Elway as executive vice president of football operations.

Obviously, given what we've said here, the primary task for the new powers that be was to improve the defense in general, and make it younger in the specific. An important first step in this direction was selecting Texas A&M's standout linebacker Von Miller with the second overall pick in the draft. According to our SackSEER projections, Miller was by far the best pass-rushing prospect in this year's class, a full 10 sacks ahead of the next-highest five-year projection. Whether or not Miller fulfills that potential, of course, depends on whether or not Fox is able to successfully implement his 4-3 scheme. It's debatable whether or not Miller's pass-rushing abilities fit well with the SAM linebacker position in which he's projected to start, and whether or not a healthy Dumervil — listed at just south of 250 pounds — has the physique suited for weakside defensive end. At the very least, however, with Miller and Dumervil in the fold, the Broncos are deeper when it comes to pass-rushing production.

The same can be said of Denver's defensive backfield. The drafting of safeties Rahim Moore and Quinton Carter and the departure of the mediocre Renaldo Hill helps make Denver younger. On the outside, Goodman will be in the third year of a five-year contract he signed in 2009, and Bailey was re-signed in February for $43 million over four years. Although it would be a cruel joke if either were hampered by a chronic injury once again in 2011, the valuable experience gained by Perrish Cox during his nine starts in place of Bailey and Goodman in 2010 bodes well for the Broncos' ability to withstand any of Lady Luck's shenanigans.

Although improvement on defense is definitely the top priority, one final question worth considering heading into this season is how well Denver's offense will be able to make the switch from McDaniels to Mike McCoy as its chief architect. Although it's easy to assume that McCoy's ties to Fox in Carolina dictate that he'll be implementing a Panthers-esque run-oriented offense, the truth of the matter is that McCoy and McDaniels come from the same Coryell digit-system school of offensive thought, and McCoy was Fox's passing game coordinator; Jeff Davidson was his running game coordinator. In other words, even though McCoy recently admitted, "We all know John wants to run the ball. We will run the football," we don't anticipate a Denver offense that sets football back 40 years.

To find evidence of this, one need not look any further than the moves Denver *didn't* make this offseason. After a brief free-agency flirtation with Fox favorite DeAngelo Williams as a potential replacement for starter Knowshon Moreno, the team instead opted to sign Willis McGahee to serve only as a short-yardage back. Similarly, despite shopping Orton as unceremoniously as any NFL quarterback since Cutler (and not alienating the quarterback in the process), the Broncos decided to stick with Orton as their starter rather than handing the offense over to Tim Tebow.

So how well will the Broncos transition from the Josh McDaniels Era to the John Elway as Management Era? Obviously, our projection suggests we're not very optimistic, at least for this season. The defense has finally gotten a bit younger, but we're not sure how well its best players fit the 4-3. The offense may be more balanced, but seriously, can we honestly expect them to be more efficient under McCoy than a legitimate offensive guru like McDaniels? Regardless of our reservations, though, considering the scorched earth left roster behind by McDaniels and the extent to which Denver's defense was decimated by injuries last season, things can't get much worse.

Danny Tuccitto

2010 Broncos Stats by Week

Wk	vs.	W-L	PF	PA	YDF	YDA	TO	Total	Off	Def	ST
1	@JAC	L	17	24	363	299	-2	-38%	-5%	29%	-4%
2	SEA	W	31	14	369	339	4	-11%	9%	11%	-10%
3	IND	L	13	27	519	365	-2	-19%	-1%	21%	3%
4	@TEN	W	26	20	327	288	1	-35%	-6%	19%	-10%
5	@BAL	L	17	31	346	415	-1	18%	52%	32%	-2%
6	NYJ	L	20	24	346	319	1	7%	14%	2%	-6%
7	OAK	L	14	59	240	508	-3	-116%	-55%	56%	-6%
8	@SF	L	16	24	398	339	-2	-27%	4%	20%	-11%
9	BYE										
10	KC	W	49	29	452	484	1	62%	69%	9%	2%
11	@SD	L	14	35	235	400	0	-20%	3%	24%	0%
12	STL	L	33	36	449	431	-2	22%	61%	31%	-7%
13	@KC	L	6	10	247	359	0	-6%	-10%	5%	9%
14	@ARI	L	13	43	288	357	-5	-89%	-54%	34%	-1%
15	@OAK	L	23	39	235	502	2	-25%	-7%	15%	-2%
16	HOU	W	24	23	431	401	0	-10%	0%	11%	0%
17	SD	L	28	33	337	447	-1	56%	35%	-14%	7%

Trends and Splits

	Offense	Rank	Defense	Rank
Total DVOA	6.3%	15	19.6%	30
Unadjusted VOA	6.8%	16	20.5%	30
Weighted Trend	7.5%	14	17.6%	30
Variance	12.1%	29	2.6%	1
Average Opponent	4.0%	12	2.6%	13
Passing	30.1%	9	36.3%	31
Rushing	-13.2%	30	5.2%	29
First Down	6.7%	16	16.0%	29
Second Down	22.6%	4	17.7%	31
Third Down	-21.4%	26	30.5%	31
First Half	2.2%	21	10.5%	25
Second Half	10.4%	7	29.8%	32
Red Zone	-5.3%	22	8.4%	22
Late and Close	-16.7%	28	14.0%	28

Five-Year Performance

Year	W-L	Pyth	Est W	PF	PA	TO	Total	Rk	Off	Rk	Def	Rk	ST	Rk	Off AGL	Rk	Def AGL	Rk
2006	9-7	8.4	7.0	319	305	0	-0.4%	15	-4.1%	20	-3.0%	12	0.7%	15	6.1	5	21.7	21
2007	7-9	5.7	7.3	320	409	+1	-1.1%	17	10.3%	8	7.0%	23	-4.4%	28	44.3	31	23.4	20
2008	8-8	6.2	7.0	370	448	-17	-6.5%	22	24.0%	2	24.7%	31	-5.8%	31	45.3	28	30.1	22
2009	8-8	8.1	9.4	326	324	+7	11.9%	12	4.7%	18	-7.3%	7	-0.1%	18	16.5	13	3.3	1
2010	4-12	5.2	6.1	344	471	-9	-15.5%	26	6.3%	15	19.6%	30	-2.2%	27	11.0	6	40.8	28

Strategic Tendencies

Run/Pass		Rank	Offense		Rank	Defense		Rank	Other		Rank
Runs, all plays	36%	26	3+ WR	59%	7	Rush 3	11.5%	9	2+ RB, Pct Runs	42%	32
Runs, first half	40%	18	4+ WR	6%	15	Rush 4	40.9%	30	1 RB/2 TE, Pct Runs	54%	9
Runs, first down	46%	23	2+ TE	30%	15	Rush 5	31.4%	4	1 RB/3+ WR, Pct Runs	24%	14
Runs, second-long	22%	31	Single back	69%	5	Rush 6+	16.2%	3	CB1 on WR1	61%	2
Runs, power sit.	65%	9	Play action	25%	3	Zone Blitz	4.9%	16	Go for it on 4th	0.97	10
Runs, behind 2H	25%	21	Max protect	14%	7	Sacks by LB	70.8%	1	Offensive Pace	28.8	2
Pass, ahead 2H	46%	15	Outside pocket	15%	10	Sacks by DB	12.5%	10	Defensive Pace	30.8	18

Denver led the NFL with 12.4 average Yards after Catch on passes behind the line of scrimmage, but was dead last with just 2.9 average YAC on passes past the line of scrimmage. The Broncos ranked second in the number of wide receiver screens run, and third in the number of running back screens. They also gained a league-leading 10.2 average yards on running back screens. ⊜ Denver's defense allowed a league-high 6.0 average yards after the catch. ⊜ Denver had the league's most consistent defense (consistently poor, unfortunately) but ranked 29th in consistency on offense. ⊜ Department of Bad Defensive Strategy: The Broncos big-blitzed more often than any team except New Orleans and St. Louis, and allowed 8.4 yards per play, more than any other team except Washington. Overall, the more pass rushers they sent, the more yards per play the Broncos allowed. ⊜ The more opponents spread the field, the better the Denver defense played. The Broncos ranked 30th in defensive DVOA against formations with fewer than two wideouts, 10th against formations with two wideouts, fourth against formations with three wideouts, and second against formations with four or more wideouts.

Passing

Player	DYAR	DVOA	Plays	NtYds	Avg	YAC	C%	TD	Int
K.Orton	869	14.4%	541	3610	6.7	5.1	59.3%	20	9
T.Tebow	168	19.9%	89	660	7.4	6.2	51.3%	5	3

Rushing

Player	DYAR	DVOA	Plays	Yds	Avg	TD	Fum	Suc
K.Moreno	31	-4.4%	183	777	4.2	5	4	43%
C.Buckhalter	-56	-32.4%	59	147	2.5	2	1	25%
L.Ball	-23	-23.2%	41	158	3.9	0	1	34%
T.Tebow	73	24.2%	38	231	6.1	6	0	-
L.Maroney	-85	-62.2%	36	74	2.1	0	1	28%
K.Orton	16	6.5%	16	104	6.5	0	2	-
E.Royal	0	-37.7%	5	45	9.0	0	1	-

Receiving

Player	DYAR	DVOA	Plays	Ctch	Yds	Y/C	YAC	TD	C%
B.Lloyd	414	20.0%	152	77	1448	18.8	2.4	11	51%
J.Gaffney	109	-0.2%	112	65	875	13.5	3.2	2	58%
E.Royal	-43	-17.9%	106	60	645	10.8	6.6	3	57%
D.Thomas	23	-4.9%	39	22	283	12.9	6.2	2	56%
E.Decker	33	53.3%	8	6	106	17.7	4.0	1	75%
D.Graham	-133	-60.7%	37	18	153	8.5	2.7	0	49%
D.Gronkowski	-14	-23.7%	13	8	65	8.1	3.8	0	62%
K.Moreno	131	35.9%	48	37	372	10.1	9.8	3	77%
C.Buckhalter	71	24.5%	38	28	240	8.6	8.5	2	74%
L.Maroney	14	24.6%	7	4	50	12.5	12.8	0	57%
L.Ball	-2	-20.6%	6	3	16	5.3	8.3	0	50%

Offensive Line

Year	Yards	ALY	Rank	Power	Rank	Stuff	Rank	2nd Lev	Rank	Open Field	Rank
2008	4.96	4.78	1	70%	10	14%	3	1.49	2	0.84	11
2009	4.27	4.30	6	58%	27	21%	22	1.29	5	0.61	24
2010	3.62	3.60	30	52%	27	23%	25	1.12	16	0.45	28

Year	LE	Rank	LT	Rank	Mid	Rank	RT	Rank	RE	Rank	Sacks	ASR	Rank	F-Start	Cont.
2008	5.84	1	4.89	5	4.51	5	4.31	12	5.19	2	12	3.3%	4	11	48
2009	4.96	8	3.47	29	4.41	6	3.38	28	5.05	2	34	5.9%	12	19	26
2010	3.51	24	3.75	24	3.78	23	3.30	28	3.40	24	40	6.4%	16	17	32

The Broncos got a major scare when left tackle Ryan Clady tore the patellar tendon in his left knee in an April 2010 pickup basketball game. A full tear might have kept Clady out for a full season — according to the FO injury database, former Atlanta Falcons center Robbie Tobeck was the only player to return from such an injury in less than six months — but something was different about Clady's injury, or about Clady himself, because he started all 16 games in 2010. He struggled early on, giving up a sack and a quarterback pressure to rookie Tyson Alualu in Denver's season opener against the Jaguars, but he eventually put it back together and started to resemble the Clady who had been one of the best overall tackles in the league since his rookie season of 2008. Clady gave up 5.5 blown blocks leading to sacks in 2010, the same number he allowed in 2009, and he racked up just one more penalty in 2010 (eight) than in 2009. Factor in the blocking scheme change Clady had to adjust to under Josh McDaniels over the last two years, and his career looks even more impressive to date.

Center J.D. Walton obviously filled a need, because the Baylor rookie started every game in his rookie campaign and missed just a handful of snaps. He was the sixth offensive lineman to start his first game for the Broncos since 1970 (Clady was the most recent before him), and Walton allowed just one sack all year. He impressed from his first game, proving able to drive-block, kick to the second level, drop back fairly seamlessly into pass protection, and flare out to catch the occasional rogue pass rusher. He ran into the occasional rookie mistake, but thrown into the fire as he was, that was to be expected. Right guard Chris Kuper, the recipient of a six-year, $28.12 million contract with $13 million guaranteed in June, has just 4.5 total blown blocks leading to sacks in the last three seasons.

The rest of the line was patchwork at best. Russ Hochstein alternated between right and left guard but was playing on borrowed time on a line that a new administration will build back up. Rookie Zane Beadles was a bit of an overdraft in the second round — most scouting services had him projected at least a round lower — but he held the starting job at right tackle for the first six weeks until Josh McDaniels gave him an public endorsement at the position. Of course, Beadles then finished the season with seven straight starts at left guard, where he might be the best fit in future.

Second-round pick Orlando Franklin from Miami played guard and left tackle for the Hurricanes, but he may project best as a right tackle; he's not nimble enough against elite speed rushers and plays too tall (which you'd expect for a 6-foot-6 player) to impress with NFL-level inline power. The question for Franklin and the Broncos will be which quarterback they start in 2011; Franklin may develop into a star on the right side, but asking him to protect Tim Tebow's blind side might be a bit much at the start. In any case, Franklin is the projected replacement for free agent Ryan Harris, who John Elway tried to trade before the deadline, and who will now battle Winston Justice for the starting right tackle spot in Philadelphia.

Defensive Front Seven

Defensive Line	Age	Pos	Plays	TmPct	Rk	Stop	Dfts	BTkl	Overall St%	Rk	AvYd	Rk	Pass Rush Sack	Hit	Hur	vs. Run Runs	St%	Yds	vs. Pass Pass	St%	Yds
Jamal Williams	35	DT	47	5.6%	15	42	3	0	89%	7	2.6	55	0	0	0	46	89%	2.6	1	100%	0.0
Kevin Vickerson	28	DE	45	5.7%	33	34	4	2	71%	55	2.2	50	2	0	2.5	38	71%	2.5	7	100%	0.6
Justin Bannan	32	DE	39	4.7%	52	28	12	3	67%	62	2.3	55	1	10	8	30	67%	2.6	9	89%	1.0
Marcus Thomas	26	DT	34	4.1%	43	29	7	0	84%	13	2.3	42	1	4	5.5	31	84%	2.4	3	100%	1.0
Ronald Fields	30	DT	22	2.6%	66	16	0	0	73%	43	2.5	52	0	2	4.5	22	73%	2.5	0	0%	0.0
Ryan McBean	27	DE	18	2.2%	--	11	2	1	56%	--	3.0	--	0	1	7	16	56%	3.6	2	100%	-2.0

Linebackers	Age	Pos	Plays	TmPct	Rk	Stop	Dfts	BTkl	Overall AvYd	Sack	Hit	Pass Rush Hur	Runs	St%	vs. Run Rk	Yds	Rk	Tgts	vs. Pass Suc%	Rk	AdjYd	Rk
D.J. Williams	29	ILB	127	15.2%	16	70	28	4	4.9	5.5	3	4	73	52%	102	4.2	94	39	65%	12	5.6	27
Mario Haggan	31	ILB	89	10.6%	53	63	18	5	3.0	5	9	15.5	72	71%	43	3.0	49	14	51%	--	10.2	--
Jason Hunter	28	OLB	61	7.3%	88	43	16	2	2.0	3	2	11	53	70%	49	2.6	27	3	68%	--	3.4	--
Robert Ayers	26	OLB	39	6.8%	92	28	9	2	2.7	1.5	9	12.5	31	74%	24	2.8	38	6	63%	--	3.8	--
Joe Mays	26	ILB	32	5.1%	--	23	5	2	2.6	0	1	0	23	70%	--	2.1	--	11	66%	--	6.7	--
Wesley Woodyard	25	ILB	21	3.7%	--	9	2	4	7.9	1	1	1	15	47%	--	3.7	--	6	25%	--	11.6	--

Year	Yards	ALY	Rank	Power	Rank	Stuff	Rank	2nd Lev	Rank	Open Field	Rank
2008	5.12	4.27	22	63%	10	17%	16	1.36	29	1.43	31
2009	4.54	4.13	17	67%	20	18%	21	1.26	26	1.00	24
2010	4.52	4.40	29	57%	9	15%	27	1.11	16	0.99	26

Year	LE	Rank	LT	Rank	Mid	Rank	RT	Rank	RE	Rank	Sacks	ASR	Rank
2008	3.82	11	4.48	23	4.41	25	4.52	25	3.78	14	26	5.8%	19
2009	4.52	20	5.02	30	3.93	15	4.58	27	3.49	6	39	7.4%	7
2010	5.22	31	4.48	23	4.24	22	4.49	23	4.42	23	23	4.6%	32

Eric Mangini and Herm Edwards, you have company. Add Josh McDaniels' name to the list of recent head coaches who can partly blame their firings on the superimposition of a 3-4 scheme on 4-3 personnel. You can also give McDaniels extra points for letting MIke Nolan go in January of 2010, losing nearly all of the on-field and statistical benefits of the Nolan-engineered defensive turnaround of 2009. Replacement Don "Wink" Martindale didn't have the personnel to maintain that level, the defense plummeted in total DVOA, and Dennis Allen became Denver's seventh defensive coordinator in the last decade when John Fox was hired and it was announced that the Broncos would move back to a base 4-3.

The problems started upfront, where Kevin Vickerson, Jamal Williams, and Justin Bannan are each rotational-quality players. There wasn't a true star on that line. Bannan and Williams were both cut after the season, and the Broncos brought in some new players including Ty Warren (ex-Patriots, trying to come back from a torn hip labrum) and Brodrick Bunkley (ex-Eagles).

Dumervil, who missed all of the 2010 season with a torn pectoral muscle, will return to defensive end after playing outside linebacker in 2009. Robert Ayers is expected to fill the other end role, and it's hoped that switching him back to the end position he played at Tennessee will turn his disappointing pro career around. Dumervil and Ayers will get plenty of help from second overall pick Von Miller, who is projected to play strong-side linebacker. Given Miller's specific (and near-demonic) pass-rush ability, and Fox's acknowledged need to play some hybrid fronts as the Broncos back out of McDaniels' mistakes, you can expect to see Miller at the line as often as not. Miller showed some ability to drop back in coverage at the Senior Bowl, but that's hardly his primary skill.

Inside linebackers D.J. Williams and Mario Haggan saw more than enough action behind that porous defensive front; something they were used to from the previous season. Williams especially has been soaking up tackles. He'll move to the weak side in the new defense, with Haggan and Joe Mays competing for starting spots with third-round pick Nate Irving from North Carolina State. Irving missed the entire 2009 season after a horrible car accident, but came back for a strong 2010. He's a good fit in a Fox-run defense that demands speed from each linebacker.

Defensive Secondary

Secondary	Age	Pos	Plays	TmPct	Rk	Stop	Dfts	BTkl	Runs	St%	Rk	Yds	Rk	Tgts	Tgt%	Rk	Dist	Suc%	Rk	APaYd	Rk	PD	Int
				Overall						vs. Run							vs. Pass						
Brian Dawkins	38	FS	71	12.4%	15	24	7	3	36	39%	40	8.7	63	29	9.6%	5	12.3	46%	64	11.7	75	5	1
Perrish Cox	24	CB	67	8.5%	43	25	8	6	15	33%	67	7.2	52	83	20.2%	8	14.5	50%	53	9.3	74	14	1
Renaldo Hill	33	SS	66	7.9%	63	17	7	3	34	24%	79	11.3	79	22	5.0%	60	13.4	49%	57	8.2	45	3	2
Champ Bailey	33	CB	57	7.3%	64	29	14	3	9	67%	5	8.6	62	66	16.0%	35	14.7	52%	42	7.9	56	13	2
Nate Jones	29	CB	54	6.5%	74	15	5	2	19	21%	84	9.2	67	44	9.9%	83	9.0	51%	47	6.6	27	3	0
Andre' Goodman	33	CB	25	6.0%	76	12	4	1	4	50%	25	7.5	53	38	17.4%	21	14.5	57%	19	9.6	79	6	0
Darcel McBath	26	FS	16	4.4%	--	4	0	1	7	43%	--	8.0	--	9	4.7%	--	17.3	66%	--	9.4	--	1	0
David Bruton	24	SS	15	1.8%	--	7	2	2	12	50%	--	4.5	--	3	0.7%	--	5.3	63%	--	2.1	--	0	0

Year	Pass D Rank	vs. #1 WR	Rk	vs. #2 WR	Rk	vs. Other WR	Rk	vs. TE	Rk	vs. RB	Rk
2008	31	16.1%	24	25.2%	27	23.8%	30	31.9%	31	11.3%	23
2009	6	-5.6%	11	-25.7%	3	-31.7%	2	21.2%	25	-11.7%	9
2010	31	7.1%	21	16.1%	27	28.9%	32	13.5%	24	8.8%	21

Denver learned some sad news last year: No matter how much age and experience you have in the secondary, yelling "get off my lawn" isn't going to stop opposing receivers. The original starting lineup for Denver's 2010 secondary averaged 33.3 years of age per player, the oldest intended secondary since 2000. And even when 24-year-old Perrish Cox played most of the season in place of the oft-injured 33-year-old André Goodman, that only brought the average down to 31.0 — still fourth-lowest in that same time frame.

Table 3: Highest Average Age, Starting Secondaries, 2000-2010

Year	Team	Age	Year	Team	Age
2009	DEN	32.3	2003	NO	30.8
2003	DET	32.3	2009	GB	30.5
2000	CAR	31.3	2004	DET	30.5
2010	DEN	31.0	2002	NE	30.5

The secondary is in flux as the new management tries to get younger, but one piece isn't going to change: Champ Bailey. The Broncos spent a lot on security with a four-year, $43 million extension that guarantees the longtime lockdown corner at least $15 million. There's a $7 million roster bonus due in March of 2012, so 2011 will be a big deal for Bailey in a lot of ways. It's thought that Bailey could spend the first two years of that extension at cornerback, and move to safety through the end of his career. One aspect of his play in 2010 suggested that Bailey would have success if he needed to transition to the safety position. Bailey was especially good at the physical aspect of pass coverage in 2010, which is one reason his YAC numbers were so good. Bailey did a good job all season fighting off blocks and tackling receivers around him, whether the coverage was his or not. Goodman will likely hold off Cox and return to the starting spot opposite Bailey, with Nate Jones also seeing action as nickelback.

As old as the Denver cornerbacks were last year, the Denver safeties were even older. (Brian Dawkins is so far off the age curve at this point, we keep expecting him to come around the other side and turn into a 15-year-old high school player.) So UCLA second-rounder Rahim Moore was a blue-ribbon pick for a team needing better deep coverage. Moore is less a pure safety and more the new wave of center fielder who brings a lot of nickel cornerback traits to the field. He can play the slot and is less of a hitter than you'd expect from at his position. Oklahoma's Quinton Carter, taken in the fourth round, is more of a headhunter but also has the coverage ability needed to play the deeper zone looks Fox prefers.

Special Teams

Year	DVOA	Rank	FG/XP	Rank	Net Kick	Rank	Kick Ret	Rank	Net Punt	Rank	Punt Ret	Rank	Hidden	Rank
2008	-5.8%	31	-12.2	32	-8.9	28	-7.3	26	-5.8	24	0.2	14	-7.6	24
2009	-0.1%	18	-1.1	19	9.8	5	-4.2	19	-9.6	30	4.2	10	-5.2	24
2010	-2.2%	27	2.4	11	-4.5	26	2.9	14	-13.0	29	-0.6	16	-17.6	32

Punter Britton Colquitt (the lesser of the AFC West's two Fightin' Colquitts) had the seventh-lowest gross punt value among qualifying punters. Denver's punt coverage was also below average, so it didn't help that so many of Colquitt's punts were returned. 50 punts came back (second-most in the NFL) out of 86 total. Kicker Matt Prater, who was replaced by Stephen Hauschka after a trip to injured reserve, nailed 16 of his 18 attempted field goals last season, missing only twice from 40 or more yards out. He had an above-average year on kickoffs (even with altitude adjustments), but again, Denver's return coverage didn't quite match up.

The Broncos' new coaching staff seems interested in reversing the previous administration's plan to reduce Eddie Royal's return role; the new Denver offense isn't likely to feature as many multi-receiver sets. Improved special teams is one of the best ways to provide quick improvements to a team coming off serious roster churnage. When he did return punts in 2010, Royal provided 3.7 points of field position value. There were just six returns by other players, but they were so bad that they dragged Denver's net punt return value into the negative. Kick returns last year were split between Eric Decker and Demaryius Thomas, but are more likely to go to Decker this season.

Coaching Staff

You may remember that way back when, Fox took over a 1-15 disaster in Carolina and turned things around enough to put the team in the Super Bowl two years later. Now he's taking over another team in serious need of redemption after Josh McDaniels stripped the roster nearly to the bone. Fox seems to be in step with John Elway and Brian Xanders, though we'll have to wait to get the most accurate look at who's driving this particular plane. Fox will bring a sense of fundamentals to a team very often lacking in them through McDaniels' tenure, and he'll get a free pass to a point as long as he can bring a sense of order to a franchise with such spiky performance in recent years.

Offensive coordinator Mike McCoy combines Fox's old and new worlds; he spent seven years coaching quarterbacks and running passing games for Fox in Carolina before becoming McDaniels' off-stage keyboard player for two seasons in Denver. Defensive coordinator Dennis Allen says that he prefers an aggressive, attacking defense with speed as a priority and multiple fronts and configurations, which jibes well with the notion that the Broncos will have to be schematically diverse to take advantage of their hybrid personnel.

Detroit Lions

2010 Record: 6-10

Pythagorean Wins: 7.8 (17th)

DVOA: -1.4% (18th)

Offense: 3.0% (19th)

Defense: 6.6% (22nd)

Special Teams: 2.2% (11th)

Variance: 9.3% (5th)

2011 Mean Projection: 8.2 wins

On the Clock (0-3): 2%

Loserville (4-6): 21%

Mediocrity (7-8): 32%

Playoff Contender (9-10): 30%

Super Bowl Contender (11+): 15%

Projected Average Opponent: -1.6% (23rd)

2010: My Name is Suh. How do you do?

2011: In year 12 of the four-year plan, the Lions are getting close.

The Lions may not be a very good team, but at least they are very good at *something*. That's a vast improvement over their status during the interminable Millen Era.

Under Matt Millen, the Lions were both awful and directionless. From year to year, it was hard to figure out exactly what they were trying to do, except "get better" in the vaguest sense. Were they building the passing offense? The run defense? Every transaction, draft, or coaching change provided a different, highly speculative answer. Sure, the Lions drafted a wide receiver almost every year, but there was no sense that the team was trying to create some run 'n' shoot passing attack … until Mike Martz arrived as offensive coordinator, after Charles Rogers was gone and when Mike Williams was already flunking out of town. Trades and free agent signings had a haphazard, grab-a-guy quality, with a veteran like Earl Holmes or R.W. McQuarters showing up in the starting lineup for a year or two, then vanishing. There was probably a plan, or multiple plans — all of those first round picks on offense were supposed to amount to something — but nothing came of them. When the Lions briefly built an effective unit, it was quickly dissembled: Dick Jauron's defense finished 19th in DVOA in 2005, but the gains evaporated as soon as Rod Marinelli took over.

It has been a long time, then, since we've been able to write things like "The Lions plan to build around Unit X" with a straight face. But finally, we can do it: The Lions plan to build around their excellent defensive front four. It was one of the best in the NFL in 2010. With the addition of rookie Nick Fairley, it has the potential to be one of the best defensive lines of the next decade.

Last year, the Lions drafted Ndamukong Suh and signed Kyle Vanden Bosch and Corey Williams to join Cliff Avril on a completely revamped defensive front. The acquisitions were part of a concerted effort by Jim Schwartz to not just get better on defense, but bigger as well. At the 2011 Scouting Combine, Schwartz made it clear that size is a priority for him on defense; Schwartz's philosophy is at odds with prevailing NFL wisdom, which prides speed above all else. The new linemen definitely made the Lions bigger, and each player had a clearly defined role: Williams as the 315-pound gap-plugger; Suh as the three-technique penetrator; Vanden Bosch as the relentless outside pursuer; Avril as the shy, big-brotherly type (and quick complementary rusher with multiple moves).

The unit looked good on paper but much better on the field. The Lions recorded four sacks in the season opener against the Bears, then five more against Michael Vick and the Eagles, with Suh running Vick down from behind at one point. Williams intercepted a Brett Favre screen pass in Week 3. The Lions con-

2011 Lions Schedule

Week	Opp.	Week	Opp.	Week	Opp.
1	at TB	7	ATL	13	at NO
2	KC	8	at DEN	14	MIN
3	at MIN	9	BYE	15	at OAK
4	at DAL	10	at CHI	16	SD
5	CHI (Mon.)	11	CAR	17	at GB
6	SF	12	GB (Thu.)		

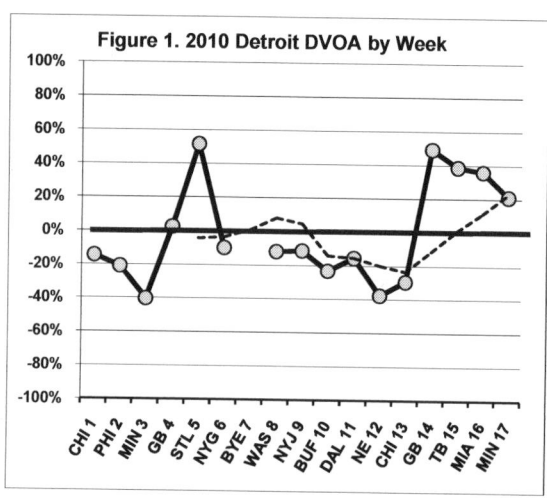

Figure 1. 2010 Detroit DVOA by Week

tributed to the beginning of the end of the Donovan McNabb era by recording seven sacks against the Redskins, with Vanden Bosch and Suh welcoming Rex Grossman into the lineup with a sack (Vanden Bosch) and fumble-return touchdown (Suh). Vanden Bosch suffered a season-ending injury in Week 11, but the Lions replaced him with Sammy Hagar — Turk McBride and Lawrence Jackson, actually — and didn't miss a beat, recording 16 sacks in the final five games. It was a fine 43-sack haul, accomplished with almost no blitzing: the Lions rushed just four defenders 76 percent of the time, the highest percentage in the league.

All of that pass pressure didn't amount to many wins for most of the season. Injuries forced the Lions to juggle quarterbacks throughout the year, and the team had an uncanny knack for losing close games on weird calls (the "Calvin Johnson rule") and improbable opponent rallies (the Jets game). The front four's success also didn't translate to much success on run defense. The Lions ranked 26th in the league in Second Level Yards and 23rd in Open Field Yards, meaning they were in big trouble when running backs made it past the front four. The Lions secondary was also weak, particularly at free safety, so quarterbacks who had time to throw often found wide-open receivers. Still, the front four was something for the Lions to hang their hat on, and a four-game season ending winning streak offered hope that the team got all of the fluky losses out of its system for a while.

With Fairley in the lineup, the Lions pass rush can graduate from "impressive" to "terrifying." Fairley and Marcell Dareus were the two best defensive tackles in the draft and two of the four or five best players overall, but Fairley slipped to the 12th pick because of some worrisome character issues. He committed several violent, flagrant fouls in college, including a series of late hits against University of Georgia quarterback Aaron Murray that looked more at home in the

original *The Longest Yard* movie than in contemporary game film. Fairley also reportedly missed some meetings with teams during the scouting process, supporting suspicions that he has motivational issues. Fairley may have some growing up to do, but he's in an ideal situation. He will play next to Suh, the reigning Defensive Rookie of the Year, and on the same line as Vanden Bosch, who is considered one of the hardest workers in the NFL. Williams is still available to play a 25-snap role. Fairley will stay fresh so he can use his quickness to shoot gaps, and he may never see a double-team.

Fairley won't be expected to provide a dozen sacks. He will be expected to commit fewer than a dozen penalties. Suh committed 11 penalties last year, five for some form of roughness or another, and he was clearly a marked man after a few early-season instances of over-enthusiasm. In one game, he was flagged for grabbing a running back's hair (a legal move, according to the rulebook). Late in the year, he drew a roughness foul on Jay Cutler for a forceful shove on the shoulders that wouldn't merit an argument in a two-hand touch game. Suh is so strong that everything he does looks violent; pair him with a guy who thought the whistle was a suggestion for much of his college career, and the Lions (who were second in the league with 157 fouls last year) may be buried under a pile of flags. Schwartz will trade a few roughness penalties for a 55-sack season, but the situation bears watching: The Lions may lead the league in big defensive plays that turn into opponent first downs in 2011.

Having used their first-round pick on Fairley, the Lions spent two second-round picks on an offense that lacked a true No. 1 running back or No. 2 receiver last year. Boise State's Titus Young is a burner and boundary receiver who can stretch defenses, attracting safeties away from Calvin Johnson. Mikel LeShoure is an old-fashioned, durable power runner. Young and LeShoure will take pressure off Travis Best and Nate Burleson, who were miscast last year. Best is a change-up back who was given too many early-season touches last year; Burleson, a screens-and-hitches slot receiver forced into a starting role. Factor in the Brandon Pettigrew-Tony Scheffler one-two punch at tight end, and the Lions now have solid depth and diversity behind Megatron.

Just who will use these diverse weapons remains a mystery. The Lions have three viable quarterback options, which is not at all preferable to having one good one. Matthew Stafford keeps rehabbing his shoulder, reentering the lineup, playing well, then injuring his shoulder. Stafford looked so good against the Redskins and Jets that it's hard to rule him out, but the Lions may always need a Plan B if Stafford is the Plan A. Shaun Hill started and finished the year at quarterback. While Stafford is best suited for firing fastballs to Megatron and Young, Hill is a pesky ball distributor who can move the chains by floating passes to Best, Pettigrew, and Burleson. Former second-round pick Drew Stanton is the stone the builders keep rejecting. He battled through an awful era of Michigan State football, blew out his knee before he could even take a preseason snap in his rookie season, got stuck behind Daunte Culpepper and Dan Orlovsky on the depth chart of an 0-16 team, and was left for dead as a prospect when he threw six interceptions in 51 attempts in 2009. Yet there he was late in the 2010 season, beating the Buccaneers and Packers and playing well in a losing effort against the Bears. Stanton has a better arm than Hill and runs better than Hill or Stafford. A quarterback with Stafford's talent, Hill's touch, and Stanton's survival ability would be a Hall of Famer; the Lions, unfortunately, lack a DNA recombinator.

Uncertainty at quarterback is one of the reasons we cannot project a playoff appearance for the Lions. Issues in the secondary are another. The Lions ranked 26th in the league at defending No. 1 receivers, 25th at stopping non-starting wideouts, and 29th at stopping tight ends. They ranked second at stopping No. 2 receivers, but there are only so many footballs to go around. Chris Houston is an acceptable cornerback, though at 178 pounds he will always have matchup problems. He will probably be joined by Eric Wright, a free agent acquisition coming off an injury-marred

year with the Browns. Alphonso Smith, who looked good at the start of the season but started biting on double moves and getting burned deep before dislocating a shoulder late in the year, moves to the nickel. Free agent Erik Coleman fills a major need at free safety, but there are a lot of question marks here: Wright got burned so often last year (see the first Ravens game) that Browns fans sent him death threats, and Smith was almost as bad before his injury. Depth is also an issue, especially for a team facing the Packers and Bears twice per season.

The Lions pass rush will protect the secondary to a degree, of course, but you can only smear one unit's excellence so far across the rest of the roster. The questions in the secondary and dearth of experienced skill-position talent demonstrate just how bad the Lions were for so long. In the wake of the 0-16 meteor of 2008, Schwartz and GM Martin Mayhew have had to build from scratch, acquiring not just all of the front-tier talent but the role players and backups as well. Any position that they haven't turned their attention to in the last two-and-a-half years is still a jumble, and some of the positions they have worked on (like quarterback) still need work. It's like purchasing an empty house: Not only must you acquire beds and televisions, but bathmats, kitchen sponges, power strips, and a thousand other things you never think about until the moment you realize you do not have them. Mayhew, Schwartz, and the staff are still building a culture in which fourth-round picks can be developed into stars and seventh-round picks into useful subs. This may be the year that the acquisition-development pipeline clicks together. Until it does, the Lions will continue to import Wright and Coleman types to fill needs most teams can fill from within.

The best thing that can be said about the Lions is that they are still growing, building, and improving. A four-game winning streak like last year's would probably have sent Millen into a tizzy. He might have felt he was "one player away" and done something loopy like trade up in the draft or declare Stanton as his starter for the future. Schwartz and Mayhew opted to strengthen their strength, address some other needs, and take a measured approach toward improvement. For an entire decade, a 6-10 or 7-9 season has been a high-water mark from which the Lions receded. Now, it really looks like a stepping stone toward something better.

Mike Tanier

2010 Lions Stats by Week

Wk	vs.	W-L	PF	PA	YDF	YDA	TO	Total	Off	Def	ST
1	@CHI	L	14	19	168	463	1	-14%	-23%	-4%	4%
2	PHI	L	32	35	444	410	-2	-21%	3%	29%	5%
3	@MIN	L	10	24	295	368	0	-40%	-22%	11%	-8%
4	@GB	L	26	28	431	261	1	2%	8%	18%	12%
5	STL	W	44	6	322	341	3	51%	11%	-14%	26%
6	@NYG	L	20	28	366	334	-2	-10%	3%	22%	9%
7	BYE										
8	WAS	W	37	25	304	275	0	-12%	-20%	-19%	-11%
9	NYJ	L	20	23	306	437	2	-11%	0%	12%	0%
10	@BUF	L	12	14	390	288	0	-23%	-24%	-3%	-2%
11	@DAL	L	19	35	338	265	-1	-15%	8%	1%	-23%
12	NE	L	24	45	406	447	-2	-38%	12%	49%	-1%
13	CHI	L	20	24	302	311	1	-30%	14%	53%	9%
14	GB	W	7	3	286	258	1	49%	1%	-51%	-3%
15	@TB	W	23	20	433	403	0	39%	57%	18%	-1%
16	@MIA	W	34	27	275	425	3	36%	32%	10%	14%
17	MIN	W	20	13	357	211	-1	21%	3%	-15%	4%

Trends and Splits

	Offense	Rank	Defense	Rank
Total DVOA	3.0%	19	6.6%	22
Unadjusted VOA	-0.5%	22	5.0%	22
Weighted Trend	7.2%	15	6.3%	18
Variance	4.4%	4	6.7%	17
Average Opponent	-0.3%	28	3.0%	14
Passing	17.8%	17	9.9%	19
Rushing	-5.0%	23	2.8%	27
First Down	-4.0%	24	-0.5%	8
Second Down	-6.3%	22	9.0%	23
Third Down	27.6%	7	17.4%	26
First Half	9.8%	13	9.2%	22
Second Half	-4.3%	22	4.1%	19
Red Zone	21.6%	6	7.2%	20
Late and Close	-3.5%	23	5.6%	26

Five-Year Performance

Year	W-L	Pyth	Est W	PF	PA	TO	Total	Rk	Off	Rk	Def	Rk	ST	Rk	Off AGL	Rk	Def AGL	Rk
2006	3-13	5.6	5.6	305	398	-9	-22.1%	31	-13.4%	28	11.4%	28	2.7%	6	12.5	10	14.9	19
2007	7-9	5.7	6.3	346	444	-1	-29.2%	30	-9.5%	24	16.7%	32	-3.0%	23	24.5	23	4.7	2
2008	0-16	2.8	2.3	268	517	-9	-48.4%	32	-20.6%	30	29.2%	32	1.4%	14	44.3	27	60.7	32
2009	2-14	2.9	2.3	262	494	-18	-50.7%	32	-25.2%	31	21.2%	32	-4.3%	31	20.4	14	55.1	31
2010	6-10	7.8	7.8	362	369	+4	-1.4%	18	3.0%	19	6.6%	22	2.2%	11	26.6	16	24.4	17

Strategic Tendencies

Run/Pass		Rank	Offense		Rank	Defense		Rank	Other		Rank
Runs, all plays	36%	27	3+ WR	58%	10	Rush 3	3.4%	25	2+ RB, Pct Runs	52%	25
Runs, first half	39%	21	4+ WR	3%	26	Rush 4	76.9%	1	1 RB/2 TE, Pct Runs	48%	20
Runs, first down	52%	14	2+ TE	31%	14	Rush 5	13.2%	32	1 RB/3+ WR, Pct Runs	27%	9
Runs, second-long	27%	28	Single back	75%	2	Rush 6+	6.5%	22	CB1 on WR1	40%	18
Runs, power sit.	49%	28	Play action	10%	32	Zone Blitz	3.9%	21	Go for it on 4th	0.71	28
Runs, behind 2H	23%	25	Max protect	4%	32	Sacks by LB	4.7%	31	Offensive Pace	29.6	4
Pass, ahead 2H	51%	7	Outside pocket	11%	19	Sacks by DB	4.7%	25	Defensive Pace	32.1	31

The Lions went shotgun on 64 percent of snaps last year, the highest rate in the league. In fact, it was the highest rate in our records, which means it is probably the highest rate ever. (The previous record belonged to the 2008 Chiefs at 63 percent.) The Lions were also a lot better in shotgun:

Table 1: Shotgun in Detroit

DVOA Shotgun	Rank	Yds Shotgun	Rank	DVOA Not Shotgun	Rank	Yds Not Shotgun	Rank
14.0%	15	5.7	18	-13.9%	27	4.2	31

Note that the Lions' usage of shotgun wasn't particularly higher or lower in the three games Matt Stafford started. ☞ Detroit was the only team that game charters did not record using a 6OL set in 2010. ☞ The Lions ran up the middle or behind guards on only 33 percent of runs, the lowest figure in the league. ☞ The Lions were second in the NFL with 159 penalty flags (including declined and offsetting). ☞ Detroit rarely blitzes, except on third down.

The Lions only sent five or more pass rushers 14 percent of the time on first or second down, but they sent five or more pass rushers 34 percent of the time on third down. ☞ Detroit faced more draw plays than any defense except for Houston and Tennessee, and allowed a league-worst 7.3 yards per carry and 55.8% DVOA on these plays. Detroit also faced more running back screen passes than any other defense, but were roughly league-average against these plays.

Passing

Player	DYAR	DVOA	Plays	NtYds	Avg	YAC	C%	TD	Int
S.Hill	650	12.8%	432	2583	6.0	5.5	62.3%	16	12
D.Stanton	229	19.4%	123	722	5.9	6.1	59.5%	4	3
M.Stafford	130	9.0%	101	531	5.3	5.3	59.4%	6	1

Rushing

Player	DYAR	DVOA	Plays	Yds	Avg	TD	Fum	Suc
J.Best	-62	-18.0%	171	557	3.3	4	1	37%
M.Morris	52	4.7%	90	336	3.7	5	1	46%
K.Smith	-22	-25.9%	35	131	3.7	0	1	29%
J.Felton	-7	-15.5%	22	76	3.5	0	1	41%
S.Hill	4	-8.5%	20	124	6.2	0	1	-
A.Brown	2	-5.6%	17	58	3.4	0	0	47%
S.Logan	49	30.4%	15	95	6.3	0	0	-
D.Stanton	28	21.1%	15	116	7.7	1	0	-
N.Burleson	43	71.6%	7	81	11.6	0	0	-
M.Stafford	-3	-27.1%	4	6	1.5	1	1	-

Receiving

Player	DYAR	DVOA	Plays	Ctch	Yds	Y/C	YAC	TD	C%
C.Johnson	258	11.2%	138	78	1122	14.4	3.9	12	57%
N.Burleson	58	-4.3%	86	55	625	11.4	5.5	6	64%
B.Johnson	-109	-41.0%	49	18	210	11.7	3.5	0	37%
B.Pettigrew	74	3.2%	111	71	722	10.2	4.9	4	64%
T.Scheffler	-35	-14.9%	72	45	378	8.4	3.3	1	63%
J.Best	52	-2.0%	80	58	487	8.4	10.2	2	73%
M.Morris	43	11.2%	31	25	170	6.8	6.2	0	81%
K.Smith	50	39.0%	16	11	123	11.2	9.5	0	69%
J.Felton	-2	-16.5%	15	8	54	6.8	7.8	0	53%
A.Brown	-13	-28.9%	13	8	45	5.6	3.1	0	62%

Offensive Line

Year	Yards	ALY	Rank	Power	Rank	Stuff	Rank	2nd Lev	Rank	Open Field	Rank
2008	3.81	3.47	31	71%	9	24%	31	1.15	12	0.72	15
2009	3.72	3.64	29	59%	22	22%	26	1.07	23	0.56	27
2010	3.46	3.35	32	56%	21	23%	28	1.04	26	0.43	30

Year	LE	Rank	LT	Rank	Mid	Rank	RT	Rank	RE	Rank	Sacks	ASR	Rank	F-Start	Cont.
2008	2.14	31	3.84	22	2.83	32	4.24	13	4.65	4	52	9.7%	32	22	21
2009	5.18	6	3.56	28	3.28	31	4.71	3	2.13	32	43	7.0%	21	24	25
2010	4.66	9	3.75	23	3.54	29	2.77	31	1.52	32	27	4.3%	4	22	42

The Lions ranked dead last in the league in Adjusted Line Yards but finished fourth in Adjusted Sack Rate. When Shaun Hill or Drew Stanton were under center, the Lions built their passing game around screens and short timing routes, which made things easier for the offensive line. Still, this oft-maligned unit did a solid job in pass protection, even if it could not open things up in the running game.

Jeff Backus has been the Lions' starting left tackle for ten seasons, which qualifies as both a career and a divine punishment. Backus has never missed a start, and he has grown into his role, enjoying his best season last year. Backus doesn't blow many blocks, and when he is beaten, it's rarely because of a technical error; Jared Allen or someone just gets the drop on him. Backus has committed just nine penalties in the last two seasons, and he does a fine job blocking for screens. Lions fans generally have a low opinion of Backus; when someone has hung around through a miserable decade of failure, people just start to assume that he is part of the problem.

Like Backus, center Dominic Raiola has been around forever — Raiola, Backus and Jason Hanson are the only players on the current roster who played in the team's last Monday Night Football game in 2001 — and has become an undeserved criticism magnet. Raiola has missed just four starts in 10 years, but like Backus, he will not be around forever. The Lions have no obvious heir apparent on the roster, and they did not address the interior line in the draft.

Right tackle Gosder Cherilus looked like a typical Lions first-round bust in his first two seasons, but he came on strong in the first half of 2009. Cherilus will still miss some assignments but can overwhelm defenders when blocking on the move. Corey Hilliard replaced the injured Cherilus for the final four games of the season and also played well. Neither is a likely eventual replacement for the aging Backus, so the team may give a long training camp look to Jason Fox, a 2010 undrafted rookie who was a four-year starter at the U.

Defensive Front Seven

Defensive Line	Age	Pos	Plays	TmPct	Rk	Stop	Dfts	BTkl	St%	Rk	AvYd	Rk	Sack	Hit	Hur	Runs	St%	Yds	Pass	St%	Yds
									Overall				**Pass Rush**			**vs. Run**			**vs. Pass**		
Ndamukong Suh	24	DT	69	8.6%	3	57	29	2	84%	20	1.8	34	10	7	18	43	84%	2.4	26	81%	0.8
Kyle Vanden Bosch	33	DE	47	8.5%	7	31	16	3	67%	73	2.2	46	4	11	23.5	33	67%	2.8	14	64%	0.6
Corey Williams	31	DT	38	4.7%	32	32	11	1	82%	17	1.2	16	2	5	12.5	28	82%	1.5	10	90%	0.1
Cliff Avril	25	DE	37	5.6%	35	28	17	5	62%	53	0.7	19	8.5	4	33.5	21	62%	3.8	16	94%	-3.4
Lawrence Jackson	26	DE	35	6.3%	23	23	13	1	54%	75	1.8	37	6	2	12.5	24	54%	4.5	11	91%	-4.2
Turk McBride	26	DE	32	4.2%	58	25	11	2	75%	42	1.4	31	5	5	14.5	24	75%	3.0	8	88%	-3.4
Sammie Lee Hill	25	DT	30	4.0%	45	23	10	1	77%	33	1.7	28	2.5	3	5.5	26	77%	2.2	4	75%	-1.5

Linebackers	Age	Pos	Plays	TmPct	Rk	Stop	Dfts	BTkl	AvYd	Sack	Hit	Hur	Runs	St%	Rk	Yds	Rk	Tgts	Suc%	Rk	AdjYd	Rk
									Overall	**Pass Rush**			**vs. Run**					**vs. Pass**				
Julian Peterson	33	OLB	87	11.5%	44	44	13	9	6.1	1	1	1	43	58%	89	5.0	106	32	47%	61	7.8	70
DeAndre Levy	24	MLB	76	13.7%	30	40	9	10	6.9	0	3	3.5	38	74%	28	3.7	76	28	52%	49	7.1	62
Ashlee Palmer	25	OLB	43	5.3%	--	23	7	1	4.6	1	0	0	30	63%	--	3.5	--	5	45%	--	4.2	--
Landon Johnson	30	OLB	40	6.6%	--	17	6	1	6.7	0	0	3	25	48%	--	4.8	--	14	37%	--	9.0	--
Bobby Carpenter	28	OLB	29	3.8%	--	15	2	2	5.7	0	0	0	13	85%	--	3.1	--	10	44%	--	7.7	--
Zack Follett	24	OLB	17	6.7%	--	10	2	2	4.5	0	0	0	11	73%	--	1.7	--	9	31%	--	10.1	--

Year	Yards	ALY	Rank	Power	Rank	Stuff	Rank	2nd Lev	Rank	Open Field	Rank
2008	5.38	4.57	29	72%	25	19%	12	1.55	32	1.49	32
2009	4.66	4.14	18	63%	12	21%	9	1.22	22	1.27	31
2010	4.44	4.07	17	56%	7	20%	13	1.25	26	0.93	23

Year	LE	Rank	LT	Rank	Mid	Rank	RT	Rank	RE	Rank	Sacks	ASR	Rank
2008	4.09	15	5.07	30	5.01	32	3.86	12	4.34	23	30	6.9%	11
2009	1.59	1	4.50	24	4.52	26	3.98	14	5.37	30	26	4.4%	30
2010	3.68	7	3.40	8	4.46	28	4.28	17	3.52	8	44	7.7%	6

Assuming Nick Fairley returns from his start-of-camp foot injury and doesn't drive his helmet into Josh Freeman's knee during warm-ups in the season opener, Jim Schwartz will be able to get very creative with his fronts and personnel groupings. Corey Williams is an effective run-plugger who will be even better when limited to a 20-snap role; he could line up beside Fairley on running downs, with Ndamukong Suh moving outside to give Cliff Avril a rest. Ends Turk McBride and Lawrence Jackson filled in very well for the injured Kyle Vanden Bosch last year; Jackson could join Avril, Vanden Bosch, and Suh on a "speed line," while McBride could play early downs to keep the other ends fresh. Imagine Suh and Fairley lined up in the B-gaps on third-and-long, with Vanden Bosch and Avril attacking from the same side (and DeAndre Levy threatening, then dropping into zone). Are you feeling it? It's one of the deepest, most talented lines the NFL has seen in years.

The Lions linebackers, meanwhile, are nothing special. Julian Peterson, who was used as an edge rusher at times last year, was released before the lockout. Levy over-pursues plays and gets flat-footed in coverage, though he hustles and still has room to grow. Bobby Carpenter replaced the injured Peterson in Week 17 and earned spot opportunities in other games. Carpenter was shockingly decent; the former Cowboys super-bust handled the point of attack well against the run. Fifth-round pick Doug Hogue (Syracuse) is a classic Cover-2 weakside linebacker who has the potential to be more effective in coverage than Levy or Ashlee Palmer. The Lions won't be looking for pass rush from their linebackers very often; they just need consistent tacklers who don't make mistakes.

Defensive Secondary

Secondary	Age	Pos	Overall						vs. Run					vs. Pass									
			Plays	TmPct	Rk	Stop	Dfts	BTkl	Runs	St%	Rk	Yds	Rk	Tgts	Tgt%	Rk	Dist	Suc%	Rk	APaYd	Rk	PD	Int
Louis Delmas	24	FS	85	11.2%	24	27	11	6	43	28%	69	6.3	36	25	6.0%	35	12.5	49%	56	6.8	23	0	0
Chris Houston	27	CB	66	8.7%	38	24	11	3	12	42%	47	9.6	74	71	16.9%	25	13.3	50%	52	6.3	19	8	1
Amari Spievey	23	SS	49	6.5%	71	14	5	7	24	38%	48	6.9	45	13	3.1%	76	21.6	49%	54	11.2	72	3	2
Alphonso Smith	26	CB	47	7.8%	54	19	9	10	12	33%	67	5.7	25	49	14.5%	54	14.0	45%	76	10.6	87	9	5
C.C. Brown	28	SS	44	5.8%	74	18	6	9	25	44%	30	5.4	19	21	4.9%	62	13.7	59%	25	8.6	49	4	0
Nathan Vasher	30	CB	22	3.1%	--	9	4	5	5	20%	--	4.8	-	31	8.0%	--	12.9	57%	--	8.0	--	3	1

Year	Pass D Rank	vs. #1 WR	Rk	vs. #2 WR	Rk	vs. Other WR	Rk	vs. TE	Rk	vs. RB	Rk
2008	32	41.3%	32	43.8%	31	22.3%	28	38.2%	32	-3.1%	10
2009	32	18.2%	22	34.2%	32	11.5%	24	34.2%	30	24.6%	29
2010	19	15.4%	26	-23.4%	2	10.8%	25	23.6%	29	6.9%	20

Alphonso Smith was part of the great Broncos Talent Diaspora of 2009-10. The Broncos traded their 2010 first-round pick to move up in the second round and select Smith in 2009, then watched the overmatched rookie wash out as a nickel corner. Darth McDaniels lost patience with Smith at the end of camp in 2010, trading him for one of the Gronkowski brothers (and not the good one). Smith worked his way into the Lions lineup and intercepted five passes by Week 9, but he missed a lot of tackles and gave up some very easy deep passes: Donald Driver, Braylon Edwards, and Deion Branch made him look silly. Smith is still figuring things out, but he has potential to be a solid starter. News flash: Josh McDaniels gave up on a player too quickly.

Opposite Smith, Chris Houston has developed into a solid starter at cornerback, and Nathan Vasher provided veteran Cover-2 wisdom and adequacy when Smith was injured late in the year. Newcomer Eric Wright had a frustrating 2010 season in Cleveland and is no lock to unseat Smith. Free safety Louis Delmas is a fly-around guy who is more effective close to the line of scrimmage. Erik Coleman, acquired as a free agent before the lockout, quells an emergency at the other safety position, where veteran C.C. Brown and rookie Amari Spievey mastered the art of the cleanup tackle after the 20-yard reception last season. Depth is an issue, and the Lions did not address their secondary in the draft.

Special Teams

Year	DVOA	Rank	FG/XP	Rank	Net Kick	Rank	Kick Ret	Rank	Net Punt	Rank	Punt Ret	Rank	Hidden	Rank
2008	1.4%	14	10.7	1	7.7	6	-13.2	32	7.2	9	-4.4	27	-5.4	20
2009	-4.3%	31	-3.6	23	-9.0	31	-8.0	28	-2.4	24	-2.4	21	-4.4	21
2010	2.2%	11	6.4	5	-1.4	18	10.9	7	-6.8	26	3.7	10	-13.3	29

Jason Hanson had arthroscopic surgery before 2010 training camp, then hit the shelf with tendinitis after eight games. Hanson was 3-of-4 on 50-plus-yard field goals before getting hurt, and he arrived in Lions camp ready to compete with Dave Rayner, who signed a one-year contract after the lockout. Rayner has kicked for six teams in five years. He made some important kicks down the stretch, including an overtime game-winner against the Buccaneers and a 47-yarder in the fourth quarter that tied the Dolphins game.

The Lions acquired Stefan Logan in the final days of the 2010 preseason, at about the same time they traded for cornerback Alphonso Smith and defensive end Lawrence Jackson. The Steelers waived Logan because he didn't make enough of a contribution on offense, so the Lions picked him up and immediately solidified the kick and punt return positions. Logan calls for more fair catches than he should but is consistent about ripping off 10- to 15-yard punt returns. On kickoffs, he slips through arm tackles and is fearless about lowering his head (or leaping) at the end of runs.

Coaching Staff

Jim Schwartz's staff did an excellent job integrating all of the players the Lions acquired in early September into their system. Defensive coordinator Gunther Cunningham and secondary coach Tim Walton took Alphonso Smith from the bottom of the Broncos depth chart to the field in three weeks, and by season's end the Lions were getting major contributions from Nathan Vasher, Lawrence Jackson, and Bobby Carpenter, players who were not in the team's plans when camp started in July. Special teams coach Danny Crossman didn't have a full-time return man to work with until September 4 and had to replace an 18-year veteran kicker on the fly. Scott Linehan and his offensive staff created game-plans for Drew Stanton that protected him without being gimmicky. The Lions could have rolled over and played dead when they reached mid-December with a 2-10 record and a third-string quarterback at the helm. It's a credit to the staff that they didn't.

Green Bay Packers

2010 Record: 10-6	**2011 Mean Projection:** 9.4 wins
Pythagorean Wins: 12.1 (2nd)	**On the Clock (0-3):** 0%
DVOA: 23.4% (3rd)	**Loserville (4-6):** 8%
Offense: 14.7% (7th)	**Mediocrity (7-8):** 24%
Defense: -10.8% (2nd)	**Playoff Contender (9-10):** 38%
Special Teams: -2.1% (26th)	**Super Bowl Contender (11+):** 29%
Variance: 14.8% (15th)	**Projected Average Opponent:** -2.6% (27th)

2010: Recycled talent puts the Green in Green Bay.

2011: The undrafted rookie who helps the Packers win a playoff game this year was probably not mentioned in this chapter.

When we evaluate general managers, we typically focus on their flashy moves: their first-round picks, free-agent acquisitions, major trades, and quarterback decisions. These are the most important personal maneuvers, as well as their most interesting, so it makes sense to weight them heavily when judging a GM's performance.

But GMs have other responsibilities that are almost as important but far less sexy: filling out the seventh round of the draft board, signing rookie free agents, evaluating and adjusting the bottom of the roster, scouting the rosters and practice squads of other teams, scanning the waiver wire, and meshing the opinions of scouts and the needs of coaches with the realities of a limited budget and talent pool. These jobs are often overlooked, and good or bad performances in these areas are usually misattributed to coaches, scouts, or fate. But a general manager great at the grunt work can win championships, while a GM who is bad at it will get fired by the Browns after sending obscene e-mails to angry fans.

Ted Thompson proved himself to be a fourth-degree black belt in front office drudgery last year. As a drafter, he's a solid "B" student, and he doesn't spend enough money on the free agent market to earn a grade. But when it comes to turning roster compost into rich topsoil, Thompson has become the guru of the mountaintop.

Let's look back at where some of the key players on the Packers active roster in the Super Bowl came from:

James Starks, running back: a rookie sixth-round pick turned starter. Starks was in the lineup because Ryan Grant, a former rookie free agent acquired from the Giants practice squad, was out for the year.

John Kuhn, fullback: a former rookie free agent acquired from the Steelers practice squad.

Andrew Quarless, tight end: a rookie fifth-round pick in the lineup because Jermichael Finley was injured.

Sam Shields, cornerback: an undrafted rookie free agent. Shields was technically the nickelback, but the Packers used 2-4-5 personnel groupings so frequently that Shields was essentially a starter.

Frank Zombo, outside linebacker: an undrafted rookie free agent.

C.J. Wilson, defensive end: a rookie seventh-round pick.

Howard Green, defensive tackle: a former sixth-round pick claimed off waivers from the Jets in October.

We can go on. Erik Walden, injured for the Super Bowl, had three regular season sacks; the Packers signed Walden in October after he spent the previous seasons on the Chiefs and Dolphins practice squads. Tramon Williams, now one of the league's best cornerbacks, started his career as an undrafted rookie acquired off the Texans practice squad in 2006. Desmond Bishop was a former sixth-round pick who

2011 Packers Schedule

Week	Opp.	Week	Opp.	Week	Opp.
1	NO (Thu.)	7	at MIN	13	at NYG
2	at CAR	8	BYE	14	OAK
3	at CHI	9	at SD	15	at KC
4	DEN	10	MIN (Mon.)	16	CHI (Sun.)
5	at ATL	11	TB	17	DET
6	STL	12	at DET (Thu.)		

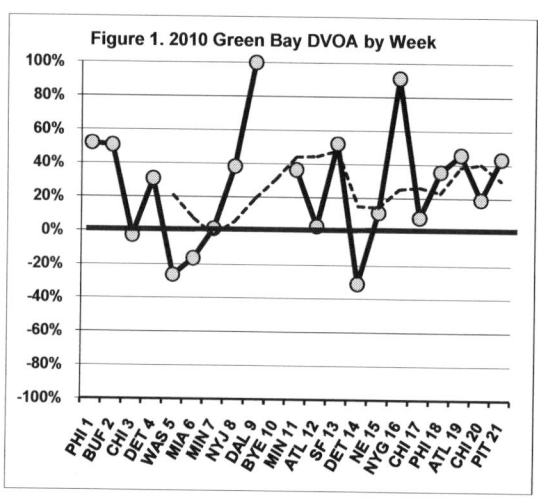

Figure 1. 2010 Green Bay DVOA by Week

started most of the year at inside linebacker after hanging around on special teams for several seasons. Jarrett Bush was a former undrafted rookie who spent several seasons covering kicks and playing in dime packages before Super Bowl XLV.

It's a remarkable collection of nearly free talent, players of a type you might expect to see on the roster of a six-win rebuilding team, not surrounding the Lombardi Trophy. Thompson turned this collection of castoffs into his masterpiece. The Packers' two picks in the Super Bowl are a great example. Green — who had one sack in his six-year career before joining the Packers — slammed into Ben Roethlisberger in the end zone, setting up an interception-return touchdown by Nick Collins. Roethlisberger's second interception came at the hands of Bush.

Lots of people noticed that the Packers roster was filled with unknowns and emergency injury replacements during their Super Bowl run, so Thompson was immediately hailed as the NFL's latest talent appraisal genius. He is both more and less than that. He's a detail-oriented film junkie, even by the high standards set by NFL personnel gurus, but he doesn't have a Midas touch in the draft. His high-round selections since 2006 included A.J. Hawk (a decent player selected far too high), Brandon Jackson, Justin Harrell, and Brian Brohm. Clay Matthews, Aaron Rodgers, and B.J. Raji were also among his selections, of course, so it's best to think of Thompson as a home-run hitter with a somewhat high strikeout total in the early parts of the draft. Few of the spare cog players listed at the start of the chapter are destined to be stars, and a few of them filled in for high picks who didn't cut it: Starks would be unnecessary if Jackson were a better player. Hailing every Thompson acquisition as an act of genius is granting him a halo effect after a Super Bowl season.

What Thompson does best is identify needs and doggedly fill them with the type of players his coaches want. That last bit is crucial: He doesn't find generic players in most cases, but precise system fits. Pass rushers like Zombo and Walden were not overlooked because other teams do not know how to find good players. They were overlooked because they are pass-rushing 3-4 outside linebackers with less-than-elite tools and limited usefulness in coverage. Most teams don't have a lot of use for those players, but Dom Capers' defense has a big role for a pass-rushing bookend such as Matthews. Zombo and Walden filled the role for bargain prices, combining for seven hustle sacks as quarterbacks ran away from Matthews. Fullbacks have been going slowly extinct for 25 years, but the Packers needed blocker/receivers for Mike McCarthy's full-house backfield and other power formations. Enter Kuhn and Korey Hall, another cheap acquisition. McCarthy and Capers have niche needs, and Thompson fills those niches.

What Thompson does best is not technically scouting; it's *management*. It requires foresight, communication skills, prioritization ability, and determination, in addition to old-fashioned personnel evaluation skills. There are not many executives as gifted in all phases of management as Thompson, and some that are never get the opportunity Thompson has had: the good fortune to work in a stable organization with a unified vision; smart coaches; a franchise quarterback under center; and no meddlesome owner on the speaker phone. Of course, Thompson crafted his opportunity as surely as he crafted the Packers roster. The unified vision is his, the coaches were his hires, the organization was in a salary cap quagmire when he came aboard, and the quarterback got a chance to develop thanks to one daring, unpopular roster move that will be remembered by history long after all the

Zombos and Kuhns are forgotten. Those who downplay Thompson's successes need only look at the Vikings to see what the 2010 Packers could have looked like under less decisive leadership.

Thompson's efforts have created a Packers team that is both coming off a championship season and likely to improve over the next few years. It's a scary combination. No contender in the league accomplished more by standing still during the lockout than the Packers. They are likely to see more wins simply by virtue of being a 10-6 team that still underperformed its DVOA rating and Pythagorean record. Green Bay will also get a huge boost from the return to health of players like Finley and Grant. The emergences of players like Starks and Bishop allowed the Packers to play hardball with many of their own free agents. With Starks joining Grant in the backfield, the team could part ways with Jackson without risking a running back emergency. Bishop's play, and Hawk's willingness to accept a restructured contract, made Nick Barnett and his sometimes contentious habits expendable. A few of the teams offseason losses will hurt, like the departure of Cullen Jenkins and a deep dig into the linebacker corps that saw Brady Poppinga and Brandon Chillar depart with Barnett. But the Packers are brimming with stars like Raji, Matthews, and Finley who are just entering their prime, not to mention players like Rodgers, Williams, and Greg Jennings who are squarely in theirs. The Packers have a large nucleus of core players who are still getting better.

With his top-tier players under contract and depth at nearly every position, Thompson could draft for the short-term future. Derrick Sherrod is the heir apparent to Chad Clifton, one of the few truly "old" players on the roster, at left tackle. Randall Cobb will eventually fill the shoes of Donald Driver, another old guy, but his biggest duty in 2011 will be to return kicks and punts so Charles Woodson isn't pressed into hazardous duty. Fourth-round pick Davon House is a long shot to grow into a cornerback of Woodson's caliber, but he's a big, hard-hitting corner who could adequately fill a Woodson-like role as a slot pass rusher. Later picks were spent on more parts for the Packers machine: another Zombo/Walden- type at outside linebacker (Ricky Elmore), more Kuhn-type blocking back/ special teamers (D.J. Williams, Ryan Taylor) and so on.

Thanks to Thompson's willingness to sift through rookie free agents and his ability to roll boxcars in the first round now and then, the Packers are an incredibly healthy franchise. They will remain high-level contenders for the foreseeable future. Other teams will try to copy their success, but some things are not easily copied. Sure, we are likely to see more teams imitate McCarthy by going to an empty backfield 11 percent of the time (the second highest percentage in the league, behind the Bills), sprinkling in heavy jumbo formations, and boldly using quarterback draws and T-formation runs as red zone tactics. We will also see defenses adopting more 2-4-5 looks and turning veteran cornerbacks into Woodson-esque pass rushers from the slot. What cannot be easily imitated is the synergy between coaches, scouts, and management that turns undrafted rookies or off-the-street acquisitions into championship-caliber plug 'n' play starters. A team that adopts a Capers-like defense as if buying the hottest new smartphone may discover that its coaches aren't clear about what to ask for, scouts aren't certain what to look for, and the general manager lacks the vision and patience to get everyone on the same page. By the time the details are sorted out, the owner has changed the paradigm and issued ultimatums, and long-range planning is out the window as everyone focuses on saving his job.

The only way to imitate the Packers is to find and cultivate executives of Thompson's ability. Teams have always understood the importance of managerial grunt work; Thompson's success was an eye-opener for media types who scream "A.J. Hawk is overpaid!" but not insiders who know the value of practice-squad scrounging. But just because we know something's important doesn't mean we do it. We know oil changes are important, but we skip them. Companies around the world talk about the importance of providing staff development and keeping equipment state-of-the-art, then slash education and infrastructure budgets at the first hint of fiscal trouble. NFL teams are no different, which is why the general manager who stresses building through the draft at his welcome interview can usually be found shoveling money at free agents a year or two later. Thompson practices what he preaches, and it allowed him to build not just a contender, but a potential dynasty.

Mike Tanier

2010 Packers Stats by Week

Wk	vs.	W-L	PF	PA	YDF	YDA	TO	Total	Off	Def	ST
1	@PHI	W	27	20	299	320	-1	52%	29%	-7%	16%
2	BUF	W	34	7	346	186	2	51%	28%	-24%	-1%
3	@CHI	L	17	20	379	276	-1	-3%	31%	8%	-26%
4	DET	W	28	26	261	431	-1	31%	36%	-7%	-12%
5	@WAS	L	13	16	427	373	-1	-26%	-12%	11%	-3%
6	MIA	L	20	23	359	381	0	-16%	0%	9%	-7%
7	MIN	W	28	24	379	402	1	1%	17%	10%	-6%
8	@NYJ	W	9	0	237	360	3	38%	-8%	-46%	0%
9	DAL	W	45	7	415	205	4	100%	40%	-54%	5%
10	BYE										
11	@MIN	W	31	3	374	300	2	36%	32%	-3%	1%
12	@ATL	L	17	20	418	294	-1	3%	4%	-4%	-4%
13	SF	W	34	16	410	269	1	52%	39%	-17%	-3%
14	@DET	L	3	7	258	286	-1	-31%	-42%	-7%	4%
15	@NE	L	27	31	369	249	-2	11%	0%	-16%	-4%
16	NYG	W	45	17	515	386	5	91%	64%	-27%	1%
17	CHI	W	10	3	284	227	0	8%	-19%	-23%	4%
18	@PHI	W	21	16	309	352	-1	36%	23%	-11%	1%
19	@ATL	W	48	21	442	194	3	46%	41%	-32%	-28%
20	@CHI	W	21	14	356	301	1	5%	9%	-11%	-14%
21	PIT	W	31	25	338	387	3	43%	40%	-7%	-4%

Trends and Splits

	Offense	Rank	Defense	Rank
Total DVOA	14.7%	7	-10.8%	2
Unadjusted VOA	14.5%	7	-11.1%	3
Weighted Trend	12.1%	10	-13.5%	2
Variance	7.5%	16	3.7%	4
Average Opponent	1.2%	22	2.0%	11
Passing	32.9%	6	-17.8%	1
Rushing	1.8%	11	-1.9%	16
First Down	17.8%	5	-8.8%	3
Second Down	12.5%	8	-12.1%	6
Third Down	12.1%	12	-12.6%	5
First Half	19.8%	4	-7.7%	4
Second Half	9.6%	9	-13.9%	3
Red Zone	-0.9%	17	-19.6%	8
Late and Close	4.3%	15	-16.6%	4

Five-Year Performance

Year	W-L	Pyth	Est W	PF	PA	TO	Total	Rk	Off	Rk	Def	Rk	ST	Rk	Off AGL	Rk	Def AGL	Rk
2006	8-8	6.2	7.7	301	366	0	-2.4%	18	-4.1%	19	-5.6%	11	-3.9%	29	22.8	22	10.3	13
2007	13-3	11.5	11.1	435	291	+4	19.9%	6	16.8%	5	-0.6%	16	2.5%	8	7.6	2	17.1	12
2008	6-10	8.9	8.9	419	380	+7	10.6%	11	12.3%	12	1.4%	12	-0.3%	20	12.5	6	37.2	26
2009	11-5	11.8	11.0	461	297	+24	30.4%	2	22.5%	5	-14.0%	2	-6.1%	32	22.4	15	25.3	16
2010	10-6	12.1	10.9	388	240	+10	23.4%	3	14.7%	7	-10.8%	2	-2.1%	26	40.4	28	45.9	29

Strategic Tendencies

Run/Pass		Rank	Offense		Rank	Defense		Rank	Other		Rank
Runs, all plays	36%	25	3+ WR	60%	5	Rush 3	17.4%	3	2+ RB, Pct Runs	61%	10
Runs, first half	32%	31	4+ WR	19%	3	Rush 4	51.8%	27	1 RB/2 TE, Pct Runs	49%	17
Runs, first down	46%	24	2+ TE	20%	29	Rush 5	27.7%	8	1 RB/3+ WR, Pct Runs	18%	25
Runs, second-long	30%	25	Single back	49%	29	Rush 6+	3.2%	30	CB1 on WR1	47%	8
Runs, power sit.	47%	30	Play action	17%	20	Zone Blitz	6.6%	13	Go for it on 4th	0.90	16
Runs, behind 2H	29%	14	Max protect	11%	16	Sacks by LB	54.3%	11	Offensive Pace	31.5	23
Pass, ahead 2H	53%	4	Outside pocket	17%	3	Sacks by DB	6.5%	23	Defensive Pace	31.4	25

The Packers used an empty backfield on 11 percent of plays, making them one of only two teams that went empty more than 10 percent of the time (Buffalo was the other). ☞ James Jones, not Greg Jennings, was Green Bay's most common target on third down — nearly 25 percent of throws. Jennings was actually third, behind Jones and Donald Driver. On first down, Jennings had twice as many targets as any other receiver. ☞ The Packers offense ranked 24th in DVOA on third-and-short, but fifth on all other third downs. ☞ Only two defenses sent a big blitz of six or more less often than the Packers, but the Packers allowed a league-low 3.8 yards per play on those few blitzes. ☞ The Packers defense was second in the league in DVOA on passes marked "deep left," but 30th in DVOA on passes marked "deep right." This isn't particularly an issue of Tramon Williams vs. Charles Woodson; a lot of those deep-left pass breakups are Sam Shields, and the passes marked "deep right" were covered by a variety of defensive backs.

Passing

Player	DYAR	DVOA	Plays	NtYds	Avg	YAC	C%	TD	Int
A.Rodgers	1514	33.6%	508	3736	7.4	5.7	66.2%	28	10
M.Flynn	7	-9.6%	75	396	5.3	6.0	60.6%	3	2

Rushing

Player	DYAR	DVOA	Plays	Yds	Avg	TD	Fum	Suc
B.Jackson	-9	-9.9%	190	703	3.7	3	1	43%
J.Kuhn	43	1.3%	84	279	3.3	4	1	60%
A.Rodgers	101	25.2%	51	368	7.2	4	1	-
D.Nance	-31	-28.6%	36	95	2.6	0	0	44%
J.Starks	17	6.6%	29	101	3.5	0	0	48%
R.Grant	11	23.5%	8	45	5.6	0	0	38%
M.Flynn	-8	-35.2%	7	28	4.0	0	0	-

Receiving

Player	DYAR	DVOA	Plays	Ctch	Yds	Y/C	YAC	TD	C%
G.Jennings	330	19.6%	125	76	1265	16.6	5.3	12	61%
J.Jones	59	-4.0%	87	50	687	13.7	5.8	5	57%
D.Driver	27	-8.7%	84	51	565	11.1	3.5	4	61%
J.Nelson	115	9.8%	64	45	582	12.9	5.6	2	70%
B.Swain	4	-6.6%	9	6	72	12.0	9.8	0	67%
A.Quarless	12	-2.1%	33	21	238	11.3	5.3	1	64%
J.Finley	109	57.8%	26	21	301	14.3	4.6	1	81%
D.Lee	17	11.7%	12	11	73	6.6	4.6	3	92%
T.Crabtree	-4	-14.5%	7	4	61	15.3	8.8	0	57%
B.Jackson	156	42.0%	50	43	342	8.0	8.4	1	86%
J.Kuhn	50	33.4%	18	15	97	6.5	7.3	2	83%

Offensive Line

Year	Yards	ALY	Rank	Power	Rank	Stuff	Rank	2nd Lev	Rank	Open Field	Rank
2008	4.25	4.09	18	74%	7	20%	23	1.14	17	0.88	10
2009	4.17	4.28	9	73%	3	15%	2	1.04	26	0.73	17
2010	3.52	3.82	23	55%	25	18%	12	0.88	31	0.44	29

Year	LE	Rank	LT	Rank	Mid	Rank	RT	Rank	RE	Rank	Sacks	ASR	Rank	F-Start	Cont.
2008	4.97	7	4.30	12	4.25	13	3.57	28	3.18	28	34	6.0%	14	16	30
2009	2.83	30	3.76	24	4.71	1	4.26	11	4.83	5	51	8.6%	30	19	29
2010	2.54	31	3.97	21	4.34	8	4.07	18	3.10	27	38	7.2%	21	20	42

Ted Thompson targeted Derek Sherrod as the offensive tackle he wanted in the draft and was happy when Sherrod slipped to the bottom of the first round. Sherrod doesn't have the freakish size and athletic potential of Gabe Carimi, but he was arguably the most NFL-ready tackle in the draft, and he did not allow a sack in his final two seasons at Mississippi State. Chad Clifton is still on the roster, and Clifton may bring Sherrod along the way Mark Tauscher eased Bryan Bulaga along at right tackle last year: Clifton can start the first few games of the season, then give way as soon as his 35-year-old body starts getting dinged up. The team released Tauscher, who was mulling retirement as we went to press.

The departures of interior linemen Daryn Colledge (Cardinals) and Jason Spitz (Jaguars) created a void at guard. The team is high on Marshall Newhouse, a three-year starter at TCU whom they stashed on the practice squad last year. Newhouse had great 2010 Combine workouts but didn't pass the Under Armour test; after a year in the weight room, he will get a chance to replace Colledge. T.J. Lang, who subbed for a banged-up Clifton in the NFC Championship game without causing a disaster, will also get a look at guard, as will another 2010 undrafted free agent, Nick McDonald out of Grand Valley State. Scott Wells is a quietly dependable center who rarely makes a mistake in a scheme that calls for about 30 shotgun snaps per game.

Defensive Front Seven

Defensive Line	Age	Pos	Plays	TmPct	Rk	Stop	Dfts	BTkl	St%	Rk	AvYd	Rk	Sack	Hit	Hur	Runs	St%	Yds	Pass	St%	Yds
B.J. Raji	25	DT	41	5.2%	22	35	14	2	80%	12	0.1	3	6.5	2	6.5	30	80%	1.9	11	100%	-4.9
Ryan Pickett	32	DE	33	4.8%	49	28	4	2	87%	12	2.9	72	1	1	1	30	87%	3.0	3	67%	2.7
C.J. Wilson	24	DE	18	2.4%	--	11	1	0	59%	--	3.0	--	1	3	4	17	59%	3.2	1	100%	-1.0
Cullen Jenkins	30	DE	18	3.3%	--	16	10	0	100%	--	-1.3	--	7	5	15	7	100%	0.4	11	82%	-2.5

Linebackers	Age	Pos	Plays	TmPct	Rk	Stop	Dfts	BTkl	AvYd	Sack	Hit	Hur	Runs	St%	Rk	Yds	Rk	Tgts	Suc%	Rk	AdjYd	Rk
				Overall						**Pass Rush**			**vs. Run**					**vs. Pass**				
A.J. Hawk	27	ILB	119	15.1%	18	60	18	5	5.2	0.5	3	5	67	46%	108	4.6	102	35	60%	23	5.0	16
Desmond Bishop	27	ILB	106	14.3%	24	55	16	5	5.3	3	3	3	66	50%	104	4.2	97	23	69%	7	3.6	5
Clay Matthews	25	OLB	63	8.5%	73	49	27	0	1.0	13.5	12	20.5	38	68%	56	3.4	64	8	88%	--	1.9	--
Frank Zombo	24	OLB	36	5.6%	--	25	9	4	3.2	4	3	5.5	23	74%	--	3.8	--	6	37%	--	4.4	--
Nick Barnett	30	ILB	25	12.7%	--	14	3	1	4.6	0	1	2.5	12	67%	--	3.1	--	12	56%	--	4.8	--
Brad Jones	25	OLB	25	8.5%	--	10	3	3	6.1	0	1	2	17	41%	--	3.6	--	2	-2%	--	15.3	--
Erik Walden	26	OLB	20	4.5%	--	9	4	0	4.6	2	0	1.5	10	40%	--	4.9	--	4	78%	--	4.4	--
Brandon Chillar	29	ILB	16	4.1%	--	7	5	2	6.1	1	0	0	5	40%	--	4.4	--	16	49%	54	6.2	42

Year	Yards	ALY	Rank	Power	Rank	Stuff	Rank	2nd Lev	Rank	Open Field	Rank
2008	4.56	4.46	27	74%	27	13%	32	1.15	18	0.94	25
2009	3.59	3.62	3	68%	21	26%	1	1.03	3	0.50	5
2010	4.02	4.26	21	46%	2	18%	21	1.11	15	0.44	5

Year	LE	Rank	LT	Rank	Mid	Rank	RT	Rank	RE	Rank	Sacks	ASR	Rank
2008	4.83	25	3.37	6	4.41	23	5.10	30	4.59	25	27	5.6%	21
2009	3.80	12	4.02	13	3.47	3	3.78	10	3.54	7	37	6.0%	19
2010	4.58	21	4.82	28	4.03	21	4.60	25	4.00	16	47	8.1%	4

Clay Matthews' greatest strength is his ability to get off blocks. Other pass rushers are about as quick off the snap, and there are many players as relentless at pursuit, but no other defender disengages from a left tackle as quickly and efficiently as Matthews. His presence is an X-Factor that allows the Packers not only to scheme creatively to make best use of their personnel, but to make sacrifices at other positions. The Packers can afford to be a little thin on the defensive line and use complementary talents at the other linebacker positions because Matthews causes so much disruption on his side of the field.

The Packers use their 2-4-5 formation so often that defensive line depth may not be a major problem for them. Still, the loss of Cullen Jenkins to the Eagles takes away some of their versatility on the defensive line. B.J. Raji is a force at nose tackle, and Ryan Pickett is an effective gap-plugger, but Jenkins gave the Packers a traditional defensive end with both size and pass-rush ability when they opted for a more conventional defensive front. Mike Neal, the team's second-round pick last year, has a Jenkins-like skill set but is coming off a rotator cuff injury and played in just three games last year. 2010 seventh-round pick C.J. Wilson played well at season's end but is strictly a gap-plugger, while Super Bowl hero Howard Green (the guy who flattened Ben Roethlisberger in the end zone to set up a pick-six) fits best as a run-stopping specialist. There are plenty of 250-pound high-effort linebackers like Frank Zombo and Erik Walden hanging around who can play with their hands in the dirt in a pinch (to say nothing of Mr. Matthews), but the Packers will be in trouble if opponents get into position to run out leads.

Nick Barnett helped create a silly pre-Super Bowl controversy when he got into a verbal battle with Aaron Rodgers over who belonged in the team photograph, then made many soothing noises in the offseason. Those soothing noises went for naught, and he is now in Buffalo. The Packers restructured A.J. Hawk's contract in March, filling their quota for highly-ordinary big-name middle linebackers, so Barnett will not be missed much. Hawk spent the offseason rehabbing a wrist injury and complaining that player-organized workouts were "a disaster." That's the kind of talk that gets you kicked out of the team photo, A.J.

Defensive Secondary

Secondary	Age	Pos	Plays	TmPct	Rk	Stop	Dfts	BTkl	Runs	St%	Rk	Yds	Rk	Tgts	Tgt%	Rk	Dist	Suc%	Rk	APaYd	Rk	PD	Int
										vs. Run							**vs. Pass**						
Charles Woodson	35	CB	105	13.3%	2	63	24	5	43	70%	3	4.0	12	69	14.1%	57	10.9	55%	25	7.7	52	8	2
Nick Collins	28	FS	75	9.5%	53	24	14	5	31	26%	75	8.6	62	26	5.3%	51	15.9	56%	33	10.7	71	10	4
Tramon Williams	28	CB	75	9.5%	29	36	15	5	17	47%	35	6.8	46	84	17.0%	23	14.4	65%	4	5.7	9	20	6
Charlie Peprah	28	SS	63	9.1%	55	29	12	3	31	39%	42	6.6	40	31	7.1%	23	15.4	61%	20	8.9	56	5	2
Sam Shields	24	CB	34	4.9%	84	14	8	3	11	27%	80	8.1	60	48	11.1%	79	14.0	54%	36	6.9	33	8	2
Morgan Burnett	22	SS	15	7.6%	--	6	2	2	8	63%	--	4.0	--	7	5.3%	--	15.3	47%	--	8.4	--	1	1

Year	Pass D Rank	vs. #1 WR	Rk	vs. #2 WR	Rk	vs. Other WR	Rk	vs. TE	Rk	vs. RB	Rk
2008	7	-23.2%	1	13.8%	23	-47.9%	3	-12.6%	9	1.5%	12
2009	4	-29.2%	6	-5.0%	15	-17.1%	8	-21.7%	3	-12.4%	7
2010	1	-23.5%	3	-18.5%	5	-24.6%	4	12.8%	22	-15.7%	5

Tramon Williams evolved from Admiral Armbar, the most feared illegal contact specialist in the Rebel Alliance, into an All-Pro cornerback. Williams is similar to former Packers cornerback Al Harris in many ways: He is always going to draw a few interference penalties (though he committed just one in the 2010 regular season), but that's the nature of his bump-and-run style, and the trade-off is worth it. Sam Shields was just your run-of-the-mill undrafted Packers rookie who came from nowhere to fill an important role on the team, intercepting two passes in the NFC Championship game. Shields has great ball skills and is growing into a role as a man defender. Officially, Shields is the nickel corner, but he plays on the outside when Charles Woodson plays the slot in the 2-4-5 formation, which is all the time. Fourth-round pick Davon House (New Mexico State) is a big bump-and-run guy with a lot to learn; he may fill Williams' old role as the guy who draws multiple fouls on Monday Night Football. Free safety Nick Collins has made three straight Pro Bowls. He plays a deep centerfield and gets a lot of interceptions, although he also drops some (six in the last two seasons). There's a job battle at strong safety between Morgan Burnett, the original 2010 starter, and Charlie Peprah, who took over when Burnett blew out his knee early in the season.

Special Teams

Year	DVOA	Rank	FG/XP	Rank	Net Kick	Rank	Kick Ret	Rank	Net Punt	Rank	Punt Ret	Rank	Hidden	Rank
2008	-0.3%	20	-1.1	20	-1.6	20	-6.6	23	5.1	11	2.6	6	-1.4	16
2009	-6.1%	32	-6.1	26	-8.3	30	-3.4	16	-16.2	32	-2.1	20	-2.8	18
2010	-2.1%	26	-0.1	17	-7.0	27	-6.1	23	3.5	15	-2.4	20	-5.7	22

Mason Crosby entered the 2010 season on the hot seat after making just 11 of 22 field goals from beyond 30 yards in 2009. Crosby was more consistent on field goals in 2010, but he was weak on kickoffs, recording just four touchbacks. Crosby signed a five-year contract after the lockout; now that he will kick off from the 35-yard line, touchbacks will be easier to come by.

Second-round pick Randall Cobb fills a major need in the return game. Cobb is a Josh Cribbs-like all-purpose talent who returned kicks and punts for Kentucky, played running back and receiver, threw some option passes, and even held for field goals. The Packers cycled players like Tramon Williams, Jordy Nelson, and Sam Shields through the return duties, even using Charles Woodson as a kickoff returner in the playoffs. Cobb should take away the need to use starters or important role players in the return game.

Long snapper Brett Goode is one of Aaron Rodgers' best friends. They are in a band together and were seen double-dating during Rodgers' Jessica Szohr phase before the Super Bowl. (Oh, but to have a Jessica Szohr phase). So when you see *People Magazine* photos with Rodgers, new arm candy Destiny Wilson, and a goofy balding guy with a fuzzy goatee, the unidentified third guy is probably Goode.

Coaching Staff

Mike McCarthy has been able to keep most of his staff together for several seasons. Offensive coordinator Joe Philbin has ridden shotgun with McCarthy since 2007. Winston Moss earned the "assistant head coach" title in 2007 and survived the defensive changeover when Dom Capers arrived and added Kevin Greene and others to his staff in 2009. The Cowboys hired wide receivers coach Jimmy Robinson away in February, but McCarthy simply slid Edgar Bennett over from running backs and promoted Jerry Fontenot from assistant offensive line coach.

Other teams will soon come knocking for many of these assistants. Bennett, a punishing running back in his playing days, also has some front office experience and is building a head coach/general manager resume. Moss would have at least gotten defensive coordinator interviews in a more typical offseason. Philbin spent several years coaching the great offensive lines at Iowa before joining McCarthy's staff and will make an attractive option as a college or pro head coach. Retirement always looms for Capers. Everything broke just right for the Packers to retain this staff: Their Wild Card regular season didn't attract much attention from teams in need of coaches, their trip to the Super Bowl limited interview options, and the lockout discouraged some needy teams from making major changes. After 2011, we will probably start hearing about a Mike McCarthy coaching "family."

Houston Texans

The Houston Texans had an excellent offense in 2010. They ranked second in DVOA, behind only the juggernaut New England Patriots. They were very good both throwing the ball, ranking fourth, and running the ball, where they ranked third. Despite that excellence, the Texans only went 6-10 and lost eight of their last ten games. What happened?

What happened was very obvious: The Texans' defense was very, very bad. In particular, the secondary was among the worst in recent memory. The Texans' DVOA against the pass was 37.0%, worst in the NFL, but even that dismal figure probably overstates how good the pass defense was. The Texans had only two games where the pass defense put up an above-average DVOA: Week 12 at home against the Titans, where rookie sixth-round pick Rusty Smith made his first (and possibly only) career start, and Week 17 at home against the Jaguars, who played without both David Garrard and Maurice Jones-Drew. Without those two games, the Texans' pass defense DVOA falls to 50.5%, which would be the worst pass defense in DVOA history by more than ten percentage points.

With that sort of ineptitude, change was inevitable, even for an organization as static as the Texans. The excellent offensive performance helped head coach Gary Kubiak retain his job, and his lack of connection to the defense helped GM Rick Smith keep his, but out went hapless defensive coordinator Frank Bush and his 4-3

scheme and in came shiny new defensive coordinator Wade Phillips and his primarily one-gap 3-4 scheme.

The Phillips hire brings with it a lot of excitement, particularly in Houston. Wade's father, Bum, was the most beloved head coach in Oilers history, and in some ways Bum's firing in 1980 was the event that kick-started the Oilers' eventual move out of Houston a decade and a half later. Of greater relevance, Wade Phillips defenses have an impressive record of first-year improvement. The Texans are his fifth new team in the DVOA era (dating back to 1992). For each of the previous four teams, in Wade's first year with the team, the defense as a whole has improved, and the pass defense in particular has improved by at least 15 percentage points (Table 1).

What did these teams have in common, other than the arrival of Phillips — and are these elements pres-

Table 1. Defenses Before, After Wade Phillips

Team	Year	Total DVOA	Rk	Pass DVOA	Rk	Run DVOA	Rk
BUF	1994	1.9%	19	17.5%	24	-15.6%	10
	1995	-6.8%	10	-4.1%	10	-10.1%	10
ATL	2001	9.3%	27	17.4%	27	-0.6%	24
	2002	-3.0%	12	-7.0%	8	1.3%	21
SD	2003	11.0%	30	22.1%	30	0.1%	18
	2004	-3.9%	12	-1.3%	13	-7.7%	11
DAL	2006	-0.9%	14	9.7%	24	-12.3%	7
	2007	-5.8%	11	-5.5%	8	-6.3%	13

2011 Texans Schedule

Week		Opp.	Week		Opp.	Week		Opp.
1		IND	7		at TEN	13		ATL
2		at MIA	8		JAC	14		at CIN
3		at NO	9		CLE	15		CAR
4		PIT	10		at TB	16		at IND (Thu.)
5		OAK	11		BYE	17		TEN
6		at BAL	12		at JAC			

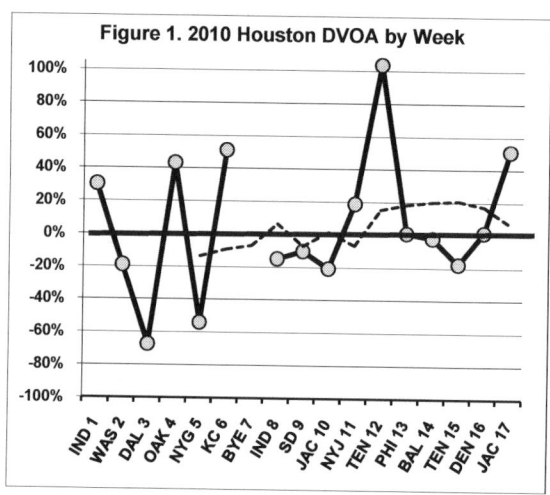

Figure 1. 2010 Houston DVOA by Week

ent in the 2011 Houston Texans? Phillips' presence improves the pass rush results (Atlanta, Buffalo, and Dallas), unless it doesn't (San Diego). Phillips seems to be fine with new, younger corners, except that in Atlanta he started holdover 30-somethings Ray Buchanan and Ashley Ambrose. The closest thing to a commonality seems to be an addition of talented defenders; not true in Atlanta, but San Diego and Dallas drafted first-round rookies who contributed in the defensive front seven, while Buffalo added impact outside linebacker Bryce Paup in free agency. Most below average defenses, though, make personnel additions. You don't need Wade Phillips in the organization to use a high draft pick on a defensive player.

On the other hand, it helps to have someone who knows how to identify a *valuable* defensive player with your high draft pick. The Texans have added defensive players in the draft before, and a good number of them never lived up to their draft position. Neither Kubiak nor Smith has any background on the defensive side of the ball, and the Texans have struggled on defense with both personnel additions and player development. Phillips' personnel acumen may be his most important contribution to the Texans, and the team wasted no time in starting a defensive makeover. The Texans used their first three picks in this year's draft on defensive players, selecting defensive end J.J. Watt in the first round and outside linebacker Brooks Reed in the second round, then trading back up later in the second round to draft cornerback Brandon Harris.

Reed's selection, and indirectly Watt's, helped answer one of the obvious questions confronting the Texans: how was a team that couldn't field more than two competent linebackers in 2010 going to play a formation that normally had four linebackers on the field? Watt will play one of the two defensive end positions along with Antonio Smith, who did well in Arizona's three-man fronts and played (and will play) defensive tackle in nickel packages. With Smith and

Watt playing end, defensive end Mario Williams will become the league's biggest outside linebacker in perhaps Phillips' most controversial decision to date.

Williams seemed like an excellent fit for one of those defensive end spots. It was an obvious match, and he was endorsed for such a role by no less than Bruce Smith, who had four straight seasons of double-digit sacks from his defensive end spot while playing for Phillips. But that weakside outside linebacker position is the marquee pass rush spot in Phillips' defense, and it's where DeMarcus Ware plays. Williams has the phenomenal athleticism you'd expect from a first-overall pick, and has experience dropping back from Frank Bush's ill-conceived zone blitz schemes, although he is more than 30 pounds heavier than Ware. In fact, there does not seem to be any NFL outside linebacker in history as big as Williams. Williams has enough talent to make the move work, but success isn't guaranteed.

Starting opposite Williams, and also likely to kick down to defensive end in nickel packages, will be some combination of Reed and third-year player Connor Barwin, a fellow college defensive end conversion project who missed virtually all of 2010 with an ankle injury. The Texans must hope Reed and Barwin provide a credible pass rush threat and are viable options in coverage, or Williams may once again pressure the passer over and over, only to see him find an open receiver to avoid a sack.

The middle of the Texans' defense is made up of holdovers. Heretofore unimpressive and relatively unpromising defensive tackles Shaun Cody and Earl Mitchell man the nose tackle position. Phillips' version of the 3-4 does not require a massive nose tackle, and relatively svelte (at least for a 3-4 nose tackle) Jay Ratliff manned the position quite well in Dallas. Still, neither Cody nor Mitchell has ever demonstrated Ratliff's quickness, and Phillips in past stops has benefited from the services of plus-size nose tackles Ted Washington and Jamal Williams. It's not necessarily a major liability, but also won't be a position of strength to build around. Luckily for the Texans, their two competent NFL linebackers will be filling the holes between Cody and Mitchell. While neither DeMeco Ryans nor Brian Cushing reached their 2009 level of play in 2010, both at least have played linebacker very successfully in the NFL before.

After sorting out the front seven while the lockout was still going on, the Texans still had to solve their secondary woes, which is where the real problems were. The defense was awful overall, but the rush defense was only slightly below average in 2010, and the pass rush was average even with all the pressures that didn't result in a sack. It was the secondary's struggles in coverage that Phillips had to address, particularly at safety, and there the Texans focused their dollars. They added cornerback Jonathan Joseph from the Bengals and safety Danieal Manning from the Bears. Joseph was generally regarded as the second-best corner on the market, after only Nnamdi Asomugha, though his 2010 charting statistics were only average. Manning was a particularly important addition as well, as Phillips has had at least one experienced veteran at safety to rely on in each of his previous defensive rebuildings.

Despite these additions in the secondary, the Texans defense still faces a steep climb to respectability. Phillips' average improvement in pass defense the first year is 21.2%. To put that in perspective, if the Texans' average performance improved by that amount, they'd have a pass defense every bit as good as that of the 2010 Indianapolis Colts, who ranked 26th in the league. Is that sort of performance realistic? How quickly can very bad defenses improve?

There were 23 teams with a pass defense of 30.0% or worse between 1992 and 2009, ranging from the 1994 Buccaneers to the Jaguars, Seahawks, Rams, and Lions in 2009. Only once did a team with a pass defense that bad actually get worse: the 2008 Lions actually declined and put up the worst pass defense in DVOA history in 2009 with 40.1%. Every other team in the sample improved, by an average of 21.6%, and four teams improved enough that they had a negative pass defense DVOA the next year.

While none of Phillips' prior teams had a pass defense bad enough to qualify for this sample, all of them were bad, and improved by an average of 21.2%,

virtually the same amount by which very bad teams improved. As noted in the Pregame Show, our research has taught us that defenses tend to be less consistent year-to-year than offenses. Bad defenses tend to improve from one year to the next unless they're well and truly untalented like those Lions. What looked like tremendous defensive acumen on the part of Wade Phillips instead now looks much more like tremendous career acumen. His first-year defensive improvement may be a selection effect as much as the result of any particular skill on his part. With the personnel moves the Texans have made and the free agents in the secondary, a better pass defense performance is virtually inevitable in 2011, no matter who the defensive coordinator is.

Will that defensive improvement be enough to get the Texans into the playoffs in 2011? That question depends more on whether the offense can sustain its outstanding 2011 play. The Texans have had a good offense since Matt Schaub arrived, but they went to new heights in 2010 thanks to improvement in the run game. That run game improvement was the result of particularly good blocking by the offensive line, but also by the skills of Arian Foster, who emerged from injury and occasional ball security issues to lead the league in rushing. Foster was particularly effective the first half of the year, covering up some struggles by the passing game, then the passing game improved while the running game performance's sagged a little.

While the mix varied, the Texans' offense was very effective all year and in all situations, ranking in the NFL's top ten in all field zones and on first, second, and third downs. Assuming continued health by Matt Schaub, Andre Johnson, and Arian Foster, the Texans' offense should once again be among the league's best. The questions then will be just how good can the offense remain, and just how big will the defensive improvement be? If the Texans get positive answers to both those questions, they will exceed 2009's 9-7 mark for the best in franchise history and seize the top position in what we see as a down AFC South. Alternatively, the offense won't be quite as good, the defense will improve some but not enough, and the Texans will make it ten years without a postseason appearance. If that happens, then it may be goodbye, Gary Kubiak and Rick Smith, and Phillips once again stumbles into a head coaching position by benefit of being in the right place at the right time. No pressure, gentlemen.

Tom Gower

2010 Texans Stats by Week

Wk	vs.	W-L	PF	PA	YDF	YDA	TO	Total	Off	Def	ST
1	IND	W	34	24	355	463	0	30%	43%	26%	13%
2	@WAS	W	30	27	526	421	-1	-19%	36%	43%	-12%
3	DAL	L	13	27	340	385	-3	-67%	-17%	47%	-4%
4	@OAK	W	31	24	441	363	3	43%	62%	15%	-4%
5	NYG	L	10	34	195	414	0	-54%	-31%	23%	-1%
6	KC	W	35	31	421	417	0	51%	86%	36%	1%
7	BYE										
8	@IND	L	17	30	291	366	-2	-15%	-9%	6%	0%
9	SD	L	23	29	392	367	1	-10%	28%	44%	5%
10	@JAC	L	24	31	395	491	-1	-21%	32%	58%	5%
11	@NYJ	L	27	30	343	401	1	19%	33%	7%	-7%
12	TEN	W	20	0	346	162	3	104%	26%	-79%	-2%
13	@PHI	L	24	34	431	416	-1	1%	40%	34%	-5%
14	BAL	L	28	34	489	253	-2	-2%	16%	-10%	-28%
15	@TEN	L	17	31	323	359	0	-18%	0%	14%	-3%
16	@DEN	L	23	24	401	431	0	2%	12%	27%	17%
17	JAC	W	34	17	497	322	2	51%	60%	10%	1%

Trends and Splits

	Offense	Rank	Defense	Rank
Total DVOA	26.1%	2	21.0%	31
Unadjusted VOA	27.2%	2	23.1%	32
Weighted Trend	27.2%	2	16.1%	29
Variance	9.3%	22	10.0%	29
Average Opponent	4.3%	11	7.2%	24
Passing	34.4%	4	37.0%	32
Rushing	22.3%	3	2.2%	24
First Down	18.2%	4	23.4%	32
Second Down	38.0%	2	14.3%	28
Third Down	23.8%	8	27.5%	30
First Half	10.0%	12	19.7%	32
Second Half	40.1%	2	22.5%	30
Red Zone	29.4%	3	17.3%	27
Late and Close	32.3%	3	35.8%	32

Five-Year Performance

Year	W-L	Pyth	Est W	PF	PA	TO	Total	Rk	Off	Rk	Def	Rk	ST	Rk	Off AGL	Rk	Def AGL	Rk
2006	6-10	5.1	5.8	267	366	-3	-21.6%	30	-5.5%	21	14.0%	31	-2.1%	23	3.4	3	8.8	10
2007	8-8	7.9	7.7	379	384	-13	-6.3%	21	2.0%	15	14.2%	30	5.9%	3	24.2	20	26.4	23
2008	8-8	7.3	6.7	366	394	-10	-6.8%	23	11.0%	14	17.9%	29	0.1%	17	20.3	12	22.7	17
2009	9-7	9.4	9.6	388	333	-1	9.4%	15	13.2%	11	6.0%	19	2.1%	7	39.9	28	17.5	7
2010	6-10	7.1	8.2	390	427	0	3.7%	13	26.1%	2	21.0%	31	-1.5%	23	31.0	20	24.2	16

Strategic Tendencies

Run/Pass		Rank	Offense		Rank	Defense		Rank	Other		Rank
Runs, all plays	39%	16	3+ WR	43%	23	Rush 3	2.9%	27	2+ RB, Pct Runs	64%	5
Runs, first half	42%	12	4+ WR	4%	25	Rush 4	59.9%	14	1 RB/2 TE, Pct Runs	33%	31
Runs, first down	44%	27	2+ TE	30%	17	Rush 5	27.8%	7	1 RB/3+ WR, Pct Runs	22%	17
Runs, second-long	31%	23	Single back	55%	21	Rush 6+	9.4%	16	CB1 on WR1	39%	21
Runs, power sit.	70%	3	Play action	25%	2	Zone Blitz	3.0%	24	Go for it on 4th	1.09	7
Runs, behind 2H	25%	20	Max protect	6%	29	Sacks by LB	11.7%	28	Offensive Pace	30.4	15
Pass, ahead 2H	35%	30	Outside pocket	14%	12	Sacks by DB	11.7%	13	Defensive Pace	32.1	32

The Texans had the league's best rushing DVOA from one-back sets, and also the league's best rushing DVOA from two-back sets. New England was second in both categories. Yet the Patriots had a higher rushing DVOA than the Texans did overall because the Patriots ran much more often from one-back sets (79 percent of runs) while the Texans ran much more often from two-back sets (65 percent), and rushing numbers league-wide are better from single-back sets. ☜ Matt Schaub led the league with 38 passes marked "thrown away" by our game charters. ☜ Houston was second in the league with 42 dropped passes, and first in rate of drops per pass. ☜ Houston was dead last in the league with only 33 penalty flags on offense. ☜ Houston faced more draw plays than any defense other than Tennessee, more than twice as many as the NFL average. They allowed a poor 6.0 yards per carry on these plays. ☜ When you play Houston, you need to defend the middle of the field. Houston led the league in passes marked as "short middle" (28 percent) as well as "deep middle" (8.3 percent). ☜ For the second straight year, the Texans pass defense was much better when they sent more pass rushers: 8.1 yards per play with three or four rushers, 7.1 yards per play with five, and 5.4 yards per play with six or more. ☜ Houston hurried the quarterback on a league-leading 27.2 percent of passes, but still allowed 22.8% DVOA on those passes (not counting sacks).

Passing

Player	DYAR	DVOA	Plays	NtYds	Avg	YAC	C%	TD	Int
M.Schaub	1173	18.2%	614	4257	6.9	5.5	64.3%	24	12

Rushing

Player	DYAR	DVOA	Plays	Yds	Avg	TD	Fum	Suc
A.Foster	377	18.0%	325	1617	5.0	16	3	52%
D.Ward	112	39.1%	51	312	6.1	4	1	57%
S.Slaton	15	10.0%	19	93	4.9	0	0	47%
M.Schaub	14	6.9%	11	36	3.3	0	0	-

Receiving

Player	DYAR	DVOA	Plays	Ctch	Yds	Y/C	YAC	TD	C%
A.Johnson	284	13.2%	139	87	1215	14.0	4.1	8	63%
K.Walter	183	14.0%	80	51	621	12.2	2.6	5	64%
J.Jones	51	-4.4%	78	51	562	11.0	4.5	3	65%
D.Anderson	2	-11.6%	18	11	117	10.6	4.8	0	61%
O.Daniels	39	1.2%	68	38	471	12.4	6.6	2	56%
J.Dreessen	120	28.6%	54	36	518	14.4	5.1	4	67%
J.Casey	-3	-10.3%	14	8	98	12.3	7.6	0	57%
A.Foster	197	25.6%	86	68	603	8.9	8.8	2	79%
V.Leach	8	-6.0%	15	8	91	11.4	8.6	0	53%
D.Ward	4	-6.4%	11	7	61	8.7	9.3	0	64%

Offensive Line

Year	Yards	ALY	Rank	Power	Rank	Stuff	Rank	2nd Lev	Rank	Open Field	Rank
2008	4.43	4.19	10	70%	13	18%	14	1.14	14	1.07	5
2009	3.73	4.10	15	60%	21	22%	25	1.12	18	0.41	31
2010	5.12	4.52	4	66%	10	16%	9	1.42	1	1.32	2

Year	LE	Rank	LT	Rank	Mid	Rank	RT	Rank	RE	Rank	Sacks	ASR	Rank	F-Start	Cont.
2008	4.66	13	2.96	31	4.48	6	4.05	19	4.17	13	32	6.1%	16	23	48
2009	3.62	25	3.56	27	4.24	11	4.16	14	4.63	9	26	5.2%	8	16	32
2010	4.19	19	4.55	9	4.89	1	4.32	10	4.21	12	32	5.9%	12	12	31

The Texans offensive line had probably the best season in franchise history in 2010. The pass protection was slightly down from 2009, but was not a major problem, and the running game made tremendous improvements across the board. That was partly the work of Arian Foster, of course, but it was also partly due to big improvements in guard play. Free-agent acquisition Wade Smith stepped into the starting lineup at left guard, started all 16 games, and was reliable both as a pass and run blocker. The other guard spot was split between Mike Brisiel and Antoine Caldwell. Brisiel has been injury-plagued for most of his career and also ended 2010 on injured reserve, but before that had been very good. Caldwell began the year in a rotation, but had slipped behind Brisiel in the pecking order. He's a better run blocker than pass blocker. Center Chris Myers isn't the league's strongest player, but did an excellent job of getting to the second level. None of Smith, Caldwell, or Myers had a single false start penalty all year.

The tackles are both known quantities. Duane Brown isn't a star. He can be exploited by the league's better defensive ends, and isn't a mauler in the run game. Texans fans got a taste of what the alternative could be, though, when he was suspended four games for violating the league's substance abuse policy, and backup Rashad Butler impersonated a turnstile and false-started as often as Alex Barron. Eric Winston had another good year at right tackle. He's not an ideal pass-blocker, and led the Texans in both penalties (ten) and blown blocks leading to sacks (seven), but is a good fit for the Texans' zone-blocking scheme and would be difficult to upgrade. Overall, the Texans' offensive line is a good example of a group that is greater than the sum of its parts. An injury at tackle, where the depth chart is thin, would be a problem.

Defensive Front Seven

Defensive Line	Age	Pos	Plays	TmPct	Overall Rk	Stop	Dfts	BTkl	St%	Rk	AvYd	Rk	Pass Rush Sack	Hit	Hur	vs. Run Runs	St%	Yds	vs. Pass Pass	St%	Yds
Amobi Okoye	24	DT	44	5.6%	17	28	13	3	64%	58	2.4	49	3	10	20	39	64%	3.1	5	60%	-2.6
Antonio Smith	30	DE	38	4.8%	48	33	12	3	87%	8	0.5	14	4	20	36.5	30	87%	1.4	8	88%	-3.0
Shaun Cody	28	DT	38	4.8%	29	29	6	1	82%	34	2.4	50	0	2	6	33	82%	2.1	5	40%	4.6
Mario Williams	26	DE	30	4.7%	51	26	15	2	77%	9	-1.6	1	9	9	34	13	77%	1.3	17	94%	-3.9
Mark Anderson	28	DE	29	3.9%	64	21	9	2	62%	61	2.2	54	3.5	5	16.5	21	62%	4.0	8	100%	-2.5
Earl Mitchell	24	DT	28	3.8%	49	15	4	0	54%	64	3.1	60	1	0	3	24	54%	3.2	4	50%	3.0
Damione Lewis	33	DT	18	3.7%	--	15	2	1	86%	--	2.8	--	1	0	1	14	86%	3.5	4	75%	0.3
Tim Jamison	25	DE	15	3.0%	--	9	4	0	62%	--	3.3	--	1	3	9	13	62%	3.6	2	50%	1.5

Linebackers	Age	Pos	Plays	TmPct	Overall Rk	Stop	Dfts	BTkl	AvYd	Pass Rush Sack	Hit	Hur	vs. Run Runs	St%	Rk	Yds	Rk	vs. Pass Tgts	Suc%	Rk	AdjYd	Rk
Zach Diles	26	OLB	81	11.0%	51	29	9	7	5.7	0	3	3	40	48%	107	4.2	95	38	27%	78	7.9	71
Brian Cushing	24	OLB	79	13.4%	33	51	18	6	3.9	1.5	9	19.5	54	70%	46	2.8	33	27	53%	43	5.3	22
DeMeco Ryans	27	MLB	56	18.9%	3	28	8	3	5.3	1	1	2	28	71%	37	2.8	37	13	61%	--	4.4	--
Kevin Bentley	32	MLB	52	8.1%	81	30	10	4	5.1	0	2	5	30	63%	77	2.9	40	13	43%	--	7.7	--
Darryl Sharpton	23	MLB	21	3.5%	--	11	4	3	3.8	1	0	3	19	53%	--	3.7	--	3	74%	--	6.7	--
Xavier Adibi	27	OLB	18	3.3%	--	10	4	1	5.8	0	0	0	9	78%	--	1.8	--	10	48%	--	10.0	--

Year	Yards	ALY	Rank	Power	Rank	Stuff	Rank	2nd Lev	Rank	Open Field	Rank
2008	4.46	4.64	30	76%	29	14%	29	1.31	28	0.59	12
2009	4.28	3.65	5	59%	8	23%	7	1.07	7	1.11	28
2010	4.14	4.28	24	62%	15	19%	19	1.32	30	0.53	9

Year	LE	Rank	LT	Rank	Mid	Rank	RT	Rank	RE	Rank	Sacks	ASR	Rank
2008	5.01	28	5.44	32	4.41	24	4.65	27	4.64	26	25	5.4%	24
2009	3.18	7	3.10	2	3.79	11	3.62	7	4.04	17	30	6.0%	20
2010	3.99	14	4.63	26	4.42	25	3.99	15	4.05	19	30	6.3%	17

Mario Williams can't do it all by himself, though he certainly tries. He missed the final three games with a sports hernia, but still had 9.5 sacks, to give him 30.5 over the last three seasons, and 34 hits, seventh best in the league. He had another good year against the run as well, with most of his plays made close to the line of scrimmage, not downfield. He's now the largest outside linebacker in history, but that's very much a pass rush-focused position, and the Wade Phillips 3-4 is practically a 5-2. With a full season and better secondary coverage in 2011, double-digit sacks are a near certainty. The second-best defensive lineman was Antonio Smith. He doesn't quite have Mario's closing speed and ended up a bridesmaid on too many passing plays. Better coverage should help him get home as often as well, but Smith has never had more than 5.5 sacks, even in Arizona.

It would be easy to point at DeMeco Ryans' season-ending injury in Week 6 and see that as the turning point for the Texans' defensive struggles last year. Ryans was having a typically good season, and the players who played in his stead, particularly Kevin Bentley, were poor, but the Texans had their four best defensive games by DVOA without Ryans in the lineup. What exacerbated the defensive problems was that Ryans and Brian Cushing spent hardly any time on the field together. Cushing missed the first four games with a suspension for PED use, and never had quite the same impact he did as Defensive Rookie of the Year after that. He had fewer than half as many Defeats, and 30 fewer Stops. Without Ryans in the lineup, his tendency to play aggressively to the point of recklessness too often left the defense out of shape. Later in the season, he sometimes compensated for this by playing less aggressively, which too often let the opposing offense be productive.

Defensive Secondary

Secondary	Age	Pos	Plays	TmPct	Rk	Stop	Dfts	BTkl	Runs	St%	Rk	Yds	Rk	Tgts	Tgt%	Rk	Dist	Suc%	Rk	APaYd	Rk	PD	Int
									Overall						**vs. Run**					**vs. Pass**			
Bernard Pollard	27	SS	117	15.8%	3	50	17	13	65	52%	14	4.7	8	29	6.5%	31	11.6	41%	72	8.3	47	4	0
Glover Quin	25	CB	99	12.5%	5	36	12	11	27	41%	49	5.0	21	91	19.0%	12	10.0	49%	60	7.4	47	9	3
Kareem Jackson	23	CB	80	10.1%	27	26	9	7	18	44%	39	7.7	55	74	15.5%	40	14.6	47%	68	11.5	89	10	2
Jason Allen	28	CB	67	9.1%	34	27	12	3	18	39%	56	9.2	68	58	13.4%	61	15.5	52%	44	10.1	82	12	6
Eugene Wilson	31	FS	59	8.5%	61	13	4	8	28	29%	66	8.8	65	11	2.5%	79	18.0	82%	1	8.6	51	1	0
Troy Nolan	25	FS	40	5.1%	75	14	8	4	22	32%	59	8.7	64	12	2.5%	79	17.7	71%	5	5.9	13	4	3
Brice McCain	25	CB	24	4.1%	--	7	5	6	3	0%	--	11.0	--	35	9.6%	--	11.9	39%	--	9.7	--	3	0

Year	Pass D Rank	vs. #1 WR	Rk	vs. #2 WR	Rk	vs. Other WR	Rk	vs. TE	Rk	vs. RB	Rk
2008	26	13.1%	22	-0.8%	14	32.0%	32	4.3%	18	16.0%	27
2009	18	13.4%	19	5.7%	23	-1.8%	13	24.7%	29	-36.3%	1
2010	32	16.0%	27	28.1%	29	0.9%	19	26.3%	30	33.8%	32

What we saw from the Houston Texans secondary in 2010 that was good:

- Bernard Pollard was heavily involved in the defense, and put up some pretty good numbers against the run.
- Cornerback Glover Quin had a solid season and was better than his mediocre Success Rate on passing plays suggests.
- Cornerback Jason Allen was an upgrade on Kareem Jackson after being plucked from the waiver wire mid-season.

What we saw that was bad:

- Everything else.

Everything else starts with the play of 2010 first-round draft pick Jackson at cornerback. After playing for Nick Saban at Alabama, he was supposed to be ready to start as a rookie. The Texans did start him, and he was not as pro-ready as they expected. Teams targeted him early and often, and found success regularly and for big yardage. The Texans eventually adjusted, having him play less aggressively, but that only resulted in teams easily completing passes in front of Jackson. For the year, Jackson allowed 11.5 Adjusted Yards per Pass, worst of any corner in the league who played regularly. The Texans tried sitting Jackson and playing Brice McCain, but he was even worse. Allen's acquisition let the Texans avoid further traumatizing, even if Allen's upgrade was over Jackson was not very significant.

Competent safety play would have certainly helped Jackson, McCain, and Allen. Pollard was as bad in coverage as he was good against the run, constantly getting lost in man coverage and flailing as a zone defender. The Texans didn't even bother to tender him. Free safety Eugene Wilson's No. 1 ranking in Success Rate may be the single most misleading indicator you'll find in *Football Outsiders Almanac 2011*. As that number suggests, he was relatively competent when the Texans put him in mostly undemanding man coverage assignments, but failed at the free safety's task of assisting his cornerbacks in their coverage assignments. Note that Wilson is only listed as being in coverage on 11 passes, which 1) is the smallest sample size of any ranked safety and 2) points out that Wilson was often so far away from the play that our game charters didn't bother marking him down as being part of "double coverage," even on deep passes.

The Texans recognized their need for defensive backs and added two starters in free agency. Cornerback Jonathan Joseph's arrival will let cornerback Glover Quin move to free safety, as has been rumored since he was drafted, while the Texans added natural safety Danieal Manning from the Bears. There may be an adjustment period here, as the Bears always struggled to find Manning's best mix of responsibilities and Quin hasn't played safety in the NFL, but both should be big upgrades over what the Texans had last year. Now the Texans just have to find a reliable No. 2 cornerback out of Jackson, Allen, and second-round University of Miami rookie Brandon Harris, and they could have an above-average pass defense for the first time in the history of the franchise.

Special Teams

Year	DVOA	Rank	FG/XP	Rank	Net Kick	Rank	Kick Ret	Rank	Net Punt	Rank	Punt Ret	Rank	Hidden	Rank
2008	0.1%	17	0.6	17	6.8	8	-6.6	24	-6.6	26	6.3	4	-12.7	28
2009	2.1%	7	-12.1	31	5.5	11	4.7	10	10.3	5	4.0	11	-13.8	30
2010	-1.5%	23	9.2	1	1.6	13	-10.0	30	-4.5	25	-4.9	25	2.2	11

Neil Rackers made Texans fans grateful by hitting 27 of 30 field goals, helping them bury their memories of Kris Brown after winning a training camp competition for the kicking job. With no games in Denver in 2011, he probably won't make 54- and 57-yard field goals in the same game again, and at 35 it wouldn't be a surprise to see his kickoff distance decline from a little above-average to a little below-average like it was in 2009. But until he starts missing game-winning field goals, he's not Kris Brown, and he's better than the punter. In 2010, that was 42-year-old Matt Turk. The Texans let Turk depart in free agency, and instead brought in 37-year-old Brad Maynard, who was one of the few punters worse than Turk in 2010. He'll battle undrafted rookie free agent Brett Hartmann for the job.

In 2010, Jacoby Jones demonstrated the patience of an elite punt returner — except usually when an elite punt returner is patient, that patience helps him find lanes. Too often for Jones, it resulted in him getting tackled without ever bothering to run forward. Jones was also below average on kickoffs, though he was better than primary returner Steve Slaton. Slaton was neither explosive nor elusive, and ranked last in the league in our measure of kick return value (-8.8 estimated points of field position on 39 returns). Free agent acquisition Danieal Manning is the new favorite to return kicks, but it's probably too early to count out 2010 sixth-round pick Trindon Holliday, an excellent return man at LSU who spent his entire rookie year on injured reserve.

Coaching Staff

Head coach Gary Kubiak was under fire after the Texans' fifth straight non-playoff season under his tutelage, but owner Bob McNair elected to stay the course. With a ready-made replacement now on staff in Wade Phillips, any offensive backsliding or general underperformance likely results in a change at the top. Phillips brought with him two new position coaches for the defense. Vance Joseph faces the toughest challenge as the new secondary coach. Reggie Herring follows Phillips over from the Cowboys and will have to instruct the linebackers in the intricacies of Houston's new 3-4 scheme.

Offensive coordinator Rick Dennison is currently basking in the reflected glory of the improved running game in his first season as a coordinator. As a former offensive line coach for the Broncos, credit for that probably flows more to him than the Texans offensive line coach John Benton, who's been in place as long as Kubiak.

Indianapolis Colts

2010 Record: 10-6

Pythagorean Wins: 9.1 (13th)

DVOA: 3.0% (15th)

Offense: 16.6% (6th)

Defense: 8.2% (24th)

Special Teams: -5.4% (31st)

Variance: 7.4% (3rd)

2011 Mean Projection: 7.8 wins

On the Clock (0-3): 5%

Loserville (4-6): 27%

Mediocrity (7-8): 27%

Playoff Contender (9-10): 25%

Super Bowl Contender (11+): 15%

Projected Average Opponent: 1.5% (10th)

2010: Division title masks serious team-wide decline.

2011: Colts are at a crossroads for the first time in a decade.

The Colts' 2010 season ended like so many in recent years. The Colts were bounced from the playoffs in a close loss. Remarkably, the Colts have lost their first playoff game by less than a touchdown six times in the past 12 seasons. Last year, it was a one-point loss to the Jets on a last-minute field goal. While one more early-playoff defeat is disappointing enough, the truth is even worse. The Colts have regressed, and their apparent playoff struggles are the least of their concerns. The Colts' system of building their team has broken down, and they need to rethink their approach to adding talent.

The Colts have been on an amazing run of consistency, thanks largely to their franchise quarterback Peyton Manning. Since Manning's second year, 1999, the Colts have made the playoffs every year except for 2001, with two AFC titles and a Super Bowl championship. The presence of Manning and the dependable winning from week to week leads people to view the Colts as steady throughout that time. In reality, the Colts had an amazing run from 2003 to 2009 that stands above Manning's earlier teams. It now appears that run is over, and the Colts are merely an average team, fighting decline and hoping for new stars to support the still-great Manning.

The foundation of the Colts' run was built on an absurd string of successful first-round draft picks. From 1996 through 2002, seven of the Colts' eight first-round picks made multiple Pro Bowls. In 2003, they added Dallas Clark, another Pro Bowler. This run of players included both early and late first-round picks. For instance, Manning went first overall (ahead of Ryan Leaf), while Reggie Wayne went 30th (ahead of Quincy Morgan). Combined with a few key late-round or undrafted free agents such as Jeff Saturday, Robert Mathis, and Gary Brackett, this core gave the Colts as many elite-level talents as any team in the league.

These elite talents combined with role players acquired almost exclusively through the draft or as rookie free agents to form a team of almost exclusively homegrown players. Since 2003, the Colts' only major free agent signings were defensive tackle Corey Simon in 2005 and kicker Adam Vinatieri in 2006. Team architect Bill Polian has instead focused on drafting and developing players, believing that a young player who knows the system will always be better prepared than a player from outside the Colts' system.

This approach has led to a stunningly successful run. Unfortunately, the strategy becomes woefully inadequate if the serendipitous string of draft excellence ends, which it most definitely has. Over the past five drafts, the Colts have picked a total of two players who made the Pro Bowl: running back Joseph Addai and safety Antoine Bethea. Neither player is among

2011 Colts Schedule

Week	Opp.	Week	Opp.	Week	Opp.
1	at HOU	7	at NO	13	at NE
2	CLE	8	at TEN	14	at BAL
3	PIT	9	ATL	15	TEN
4	at TB (Mon.)	10	JAC	16	HOU (Thu.)
5	KC	11	BYE	17	at JAC
6	at CIN	12	CAR		

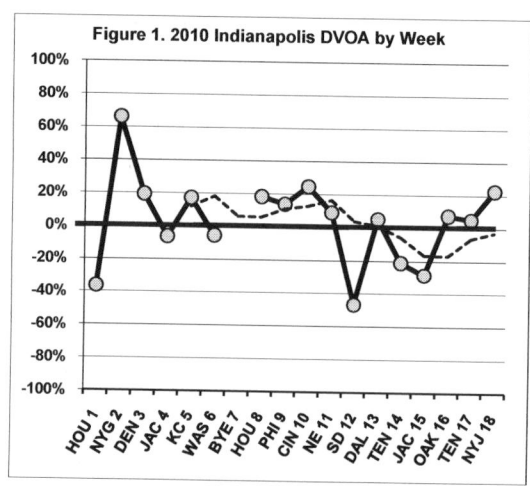

Figure 1. 2010 Indianapolis DVOA by Week

the very best at his position.

As the talents accumulated in the late 1990s have retired or declined in ability, the Colts have simply been unable to replace the production. Of those great first-round picks from 1996 through 2002, only Manning and Wayne are still on the team. The result is a severe decline on both offense and defense. The offense, which ranked in the top three in DVOA from 2003 through 2007, has now ranked sixth for three consecutive years. Defensively, the team has backslid from second in 2007 to 10th in 2008 to 16th in 2009 to 24th last season.

While the problems are team-wide, on a practical basis, the Colts' biggest hole is the offensive line. The Colts throughout the Manning era have not had a bevy of bruising offensive linemen. But the last several years have seen competent system players replaced by second-rate players who are clearly struggling. Saturday, the anchor, has been slowed by Father Time and has slipped to merely average. Right tackle Ryan Diem, who has played well at times, struggled with injuries last year and was a major problem. Meanwhile, the rest of the line was a ramshackle of mediocrity. Charlie Johnson, a former sixth-round pick who should be used as a decent guard, instead served as one of the team's more reliable linemen at left tackle.

The offensive line difficulties highlight the failure of the Colts' recent drafts. The core of the Colts line from 1999 through 2006 was left tackle Tarik Glenn and Saturday. After Glenn's surprising retirement following the 2006 season, the Colts traded their 2008 first-round pick to move up in the 2007 second round and draft Tony Ugoh. Despite flashing early signs of promise, Ugoh failed to develop, was released, and did not play in the NFL last season. In 2008, the Colts used their first pick (59th overall) on Mike Pollak, an interior lineman who has not earned a consistent starting position.

Without a stout offensive line, the Colts' once-

powerful offense sputtered. The run game was inconsistent, leading Manning to throw a career-high 679 passes. Manning's ability to get rid of the ball kept his sacks down as always. But the team had to move to a much shorter passing attack than in previous years, lacking the time to develop plays down the field and needing to compensate for the lack of a running game. As a result, Manning set a career low in yards per completion and had his lowest yards per attempt since his rookie season.

The team does understand the problems along the offensive line and went to the draft to solve them, spending their two first-round picks on tackles Anthony Castonzo and Ben Ijalana (who will likely play guard this year). The Colts accurately determined the area of need, but they went back to the draft, where they have struggled to find offensive linemen for the past few years. The team lost the serviceable Johnson to free agency, leaving them extremely thin along the offensive line and highly reliant on their two draft picks.

Defensively, the Colts are counting on better health being the elixir for the unit that posted its second-worst DVOA since 2001. Of course, the seriousness of injuries is all in the eye of the beholder. Injuries ravaged the Colts' secondary, but their defensive line remained healthy. Freeney and Mathis, the Colts' two most indispensable players besides Manning, did not miss a single game. Young defensive tackles Fili Moala and Daniel Muir also stayed healthy. The Colts will be in even more trouble if injuries hit their defensive line instead of their secondary.

Even if healthy, the Colts are unlikely to have an above-average defense. Freeney, Mathis, and Brackett are all 30 or older, and the team has not developed a young star with the possible exception of Bethea. The Colts are thin at cornerback after cutting Kelvin Hayden, and must hope that Justin Tryon or Jacob Lacey can emerge as a legitimate starter opposite Jerraud Powers.

That the Colts are taking a step back is only natural because their recent run was remarkable and impossible to sustain. From 2003 through 2009, the Colts had a DVOA higher than 15% every single season. In the DVOA era (since 1992), only one team has matched that level of success over seven consecutive seasons: the 1992-98 San Francisco 49ers. (Table 1). Nobody else has done it more than five consecutive seasons.

Compared to those 49ers, the Colts have a couple of points in their favor. Peyton Manning's style of play means he's less likely than other quarterbacks to have a major injury like the one that Steve Young had in 1999. In addition, the ever-escalating salary cap means the Colts can avoid facing some of the tough personnel decisions that the 49ers confronted in the late 1990s. Still, the Colts need to appreciate that their run of success was extremely rare, and while it involved great planning, coaching, and execution, it also included a fair sprinkling of good fortune.

The team cannot be afraid to change its approach. Drafting and player development were central to the run of success, but the elite core of talent is gone. The team can no longer afford to fill its depth chart with late-round picks and rookie free agents and count on them to "step up" when someone else is injured. The Colts were unable to "step up" on the offensive line or in the secondary last year. The margin is just too thin when the team has few remaining dominant players at the other positions.

In some ways, arguing for the Colts to adopt a new approach after one mediocre season (where they won 10 games and came within one play of winning a playoff game) is contrary to the Football Outsiders approach. However, the fundamental flaws with the current roster are simply impossible to overlook. The team has a handful of aging stars and some serviceable young players. The mix is insufficient to create an elite-level team.

The Colts appear to understand that their usual course of business is insufficient. Rather than eschewing the free agent market as usual, the Colts made a trio of interesting signings. They added three former first-round selections: defensive linemen Jamaal Anderson and Tommie Harris as well as linebacker Er-

Table 1. Teams with 15% or Higher DVOA for Four or More Straight Seasons

Team	Streak	Era
Indianapolis Colts	7	2003-09
San Francisco 49ers	7	1992-98
Dallas Cowboys	5	1992-96
Philadelphia Eagles	5	2000-04
San Diego Chargers	5	2004-08
Green Bay Packers	5	1994-98
Pittsburgh Steelers	4	1994-97
Oakland Raiders	4	1999-02
Kansas City Chiefs	4	2002-05
Pittsburgh Steelers	4	2007-10

nie Sims. All three are low-risk, high-upside signings who bring talent to the Colts that they rarely acquire from the outside.

The signings, however, highlight an important issue the Colts have had in adjusting to the post-Tony Dungy era: They cannot determine how committed they are to the Tampa-2 defense. The Colts ran a defense as vanilla as imaginable during the Dungy era, emphasizing execution over deception. Head coach Jim Caldwell signaled an intent to change by letting Dungy's defensive coordinator Ron Meeks go and hiring Larry Coyer. Coyer has spent two years playing Tampa-2 as a base but tweaking with increased blitzes, new formations, and, in Coyer's mind at least, more deception.

By adding three talented players, the Colts could start moving away from the Tampa-2. Sims and Harris are actually well-suited for the Tampa-2, though, and the thought is Anderson may play some defensive tackle, which would be consistent with an undersized, Tampa-2 style line. Perhaps this is a concerted effort to commit to the Tampa-2. The Colts' roster is still filled with players best suited for the Tampa-2. The two best are Dwight Freeney and Robert Mathis, undersized defensive ends who rush the passer and almost demand that the team stick with its traditional scheme.

Yet Coyer seems to want to continue developing his own defensive identity. The problem is not the Tampa-2 scheme itself; the problem is that the team feels compelled to run it, rather than developing an approach that the current coaching staff feels most comfortable running. The new additions in some way only further cloud this conundrum, and how Coyer incorporates the new pieces will be crucial for returning the defense to the respectability it maintained throughout the Dungy era.

While the free agent signings are fascinating in the sense that they indicate a willingness to think outside the box, three low-salary free agents hardly shift the balance of power in the AFC. What's important about these moves is that they show the Colts are willing to begin altering their approach to talent acquisition. A more aggressive approach is essential because Manning only has so many high-quality seasons left in him. No matter how many good things the Colts have done as an organization since Polian arrived, everything was made possible by the development of Manning into arguably the greatest quarterback of all time. But, with a crumbling supporting cast around him, the Colts are in danger of having to rebuild while Manning slowly declines.

In that sense, the Colts in some ways mirror the Dolphins during Dan Marino's final seasons. The team was good enough to compete for the playoffs but was never close to being a Super Bowl contender. During Marino's last five years, the Dolphins ranked between 13th and 16th in DVOA four times. The Colts as currently constructed are headed for a similar end to Manning's career.

By entering the free agent market on a limited basis, the Colts avoided spending huge money on past-their-prime players. The three additions are all in their mid- to late twenties. Even if none of the three emerge as stars, or even starters, it provides depth for when the Colts' undersized defense inevitably suffers injuries. The minor foray into free agency is still insufficient, as the team would have been well-served to add a veteran nickelback, a reserve safety, and some offensive line depth. Nonetheless, if any of the three are successful, it could help the Colts appreciate that sometimes you can find useful young players outside your organization, and it is possible to add free agents without adding a bunch of guys in their mid-thirties.

You may be surprised by our relatively lowly projection for the 2011 Indianapolis Colts. We know that the idea of a Manning-led team having a losing record may seem absurd to some. We also know that we have a history of under-projecting the Colts. We're certainly not saying that the Colts have no shot at another division title; we don't believe the AFC South is particularly strong this year, and Manning, as long as his neck is healthy, is still one of the top quarterbacks in the game. The Colts should remain competitive for their tenth consecutive playoff berth.

Yet the basic problems still apply, even if the Colts go 10-6 and win another division title. A team that has prospered with a clear plan and mode of operation has now followed that plan into decline. A new direction is needed for the Colts. That does not necessarily require new leadership, new coaches, or a radically changed scheme. But the Colts need to come to terms with the fact that their remarkable run of excellence is over. They need to start thinking creatively not about how to get back what they had, but rather how to get the best players around Manning for the end of his career. The method that successfully did that throughout the past decade is not necessarily the best method for going forward.

Ned Macey

2010 Colts Stats by Week

Wk	vs.	W-L	PF	PA	YDF	YDA	TO	Total	Off	Def	ST
1	@HOU	L	24	34	463	355	0	-36%	12%	35%	-14%
2	NYG	W	38	14	410	257	2	66%	45%	-19%	3%
3	@DEN	W	27	13	365	519	2	19%	15%	-8%	-3%
4	@JAC	L	28	31	406	337	-2	-6%	38%	42%	-3%
5	KC	W	19	9	341	261	0	17%	0%	-14%	4%
6	@WAS	W	27	24	469	335	-1	-5%	32%	14%	-23%
7	BYE										
8	HOU	W	30	17	366	291	2	18%	-5%	-25%	-1%
9	@PHI	L	24	26	338	402	-2	14%	28%	11%	-4%
10	CIN	W	23	17	256	341	5	25%	-8%	-30%	3%
11	@NE	L	28	31	467	346	-3	9%	37%	22%	-6%
12	SD	L	14	36	303	301	-5	-47%	-24%	10%	-13%
13	DAL	L	35	38	405	368	-4	5%	7%	3%	1%
14	@TEN	W	30	28	399	365	2	-21%	25%	49%	3%
15	JAC	W	34	24	376	356	2	-28%	8%	16%	-21%
16	@OAK	W	31	26	370	290	-2	8%	32%	9%	-16%
17	TEN	W	23	20	358	341	0	5%	22%	16%	-1%
18	NYJ	L	16	17	312	353	1	23%	19%	-3%	1%

Trends and Splits

	Offense	Rank	Defense	Rank
Total DVOA	16.6%	6	8.2%	24
Unadjusted VOA	19.5%	5	11.7%	28
Weighted Trend	14.7%	7	9.4%	26
Variance	3.7%	2	5.2%	7
Average Opponent	7.4%	3	10.7%	31
Passing	33.4%	5	15.6%	26
Rushing	1.9%	10	0.1%	18
First Down	8.5%	13	9.0%	24
Second Down	29.4%	3	13.8%	26
Third Down	9.4%	13	-2.4%	14
First Half	21.5%	2	-1.6%	11
Second Half	10.7%	6	16.7%	29
Red Zone	46.5%	2	-4.2%	15
Late and Close	7.7%	12	-9.0%	12

Five-Year Performance

Year	W-L	Pyth	Est W	PF	PA	TO	Total	Rk	Off	Rk	Def	Rk	ST	Rk	Off AGL	Rk	Def AGL	Rk
2006	12-4	9.6	10.6	427	360	+7	17.3%	7	29.0%	1	8.8%	25	-2.9%	25	18.5	18	31.3	29
2007	13-3	12.5	12.4	450	262	+18	30.7%	2	24.3%	2	-12.3%	2	-5.9%	32	19.3	12	51.0	32
2008	12-4	10.2	10.5	377	298	+9	15.3%	8	17.2%	6	0.1%	10	-1.8%	24	31.8	21	39.6	27
2009	14-2	10.8	11.0	416	307	+2	17.9%	8	20.3%	6	1.7%	15	-0.7%	20	30.1	21	51.9	30
2010	10-6	9.1	8.8	435	388	-4	3.0%	15	16.6%	6	8.2%	24	-5.4%	31	42.5	30	48.1	31

Strategic Tendencies

Run/Pass		Rank	Offense		Rank	Defense		Rank	Other		Rank
Runs, all plays	35%	28	3+ WR	79%	1	Rush 3	6.1%	19	2+ RB, Pct Runs	55%	22
Runs, first half	34%	29	4+ WR	7%	9	Rush 4	76.7%	2	1 RB/2 TE, Pct Runs	58%	3
Runs, first down	45%	25	2+ TE	22%	26	Rush 5	14.3%	31	1 RB/3+ WR, Pct Runs	30%	7
Runs, second-long	20%	32	Single back	94%	1	Rush 6+	2.8%	31	CB1 on WR1	43%	13
Runs, power sit.	52%	24	Play action	17%	18	Zone Blitz	1.9%	31	Go for it on 4th	0.94	13
Runs, behind 2H	20%	32	Max protect	5%	31	Sacks by LB	12.1%	27	Offensive Pace	28.4	1
Pass, ahead 2H	53%	3	Outside pocket	3%	32	Sacks by DB	1.7%	32	Defensive Pace	31.0	22

The Colts were 31st in the NFL with 85 penalties, including declined and offsetting, but they had 25 special teams penalties worth a league-leading 227 yards. ☞ Peyton Manning avoids sacks because he knows to throw the ball away under pressure, right? Actually, wrong. Indianapolis had only six passes marked as "thrown away" by our charters. Manning is not only good enough to get rid of the ball, he's good enough to get rid of it with a pass that at least has a chance of being completed. (For those of you who are Brady-Manning obsessed, we point out that the Patriots were 30th with only ten passes marked "thrown away.") ☞ Manning's numbers were hurt because Colts receivers dropped a league-high 48 passes according to our game charters. ☞ The Colts ran more draw plays than any other team, and though they had a league-average DVOA on draws, that was still much better than their overall performance running the ball. The Colts also led the league with 44 wide receiver screens; their 6.0 yards per pass were close to the league average but they had a nice 50.0% DVOA since they tended to use these plays in second-and-medium or second-and-short situations. ☞ The Colts were in shotgun on 58 percent of snaps; only Detroit used shotgun more often. ☞ Only five percent of Colts runs came with two backs; every other NFL team was above 20 percent.

Passing

Player	DYAR	DVOA	Plays	NtYds	Avg	YAC	C%	TD	Int
P.Manning	1679	25.0%	704	4747	6.7	4.2	66.3%	33	16

Rushing

Player	DYAR	DVOA	Plays	Yds	Avg	TD	Fum	Suc
D.Brown	22	-4.8%	129	497	3.9	2	0	44%
J.Addai	92	9.6%	116	495	4.3	4	2	54%
J.James	27	4.3%	46	112	2.4	6	0	48%
M.Hart	14	-1.6%	43	185	4.3	1	0	47%
D.Rhodes	10	-2.4%	37	172	4.6	0	1	51%

Receiving

Player	DYAR	DVOA	Plays	Ctch	Yds	Y/C	YAC	TD	C%
R.Wayne	180	0.3%	175	111	1355	12.2	3.7	6	63%
P.Garcon	55	-7.0%	119	67	784	11.7	3.7	6	56%
A.Collie	231	28.4%	71	58	649	11.2	4.9	8	82%
B.White	90	7.0%	57	36	355	9.9	1.8	5	63%
B.James	-21	-36.0%	11	6	40	6.7	2.3	0	55%
A.Gonzalez	-10	-28.3%	9	5	67	13.4	3.2	0	56%
J.Tamme	124	12.6%	93	67	631	9.4	4.6	4	72%
D.Clark	48	6.0%	53	37	347	9.4	3.7	3	70%
B.Eldridge	-14	-30.9%	9	5	39	7.8	4.4	0	56%
G.Robinson	-16	-36.3%	7	3	12	4.0	1.7	1	43%
D.Brown	67	28.5%	28	20	205	10.3	9.0	0	71%
J.Addai	15	-2.9%	26	19	124	6.5	5.2	0	73%
J.James	-12	-31.4%	11	9	63	7.0	8.8	0	82%
M.Hart	5	1.1%	6	6	25	4.2	4.0	0	100%

Offensive Line

Year	Yards	ALY	Rank	Power	Rank	Stuff	Rank	2nd Lev	Rank	Open Field	Rank
2008	3.60	4.00	23	62%	21	21%	27	1.14	18	0.31	32
2009	3.80	3.92	26	66%	12	22%	29	1.11	21	0.51	29
2010	3.91	3.82	22	56%	22	20%	20	1.04	24	0.64	21

Year	LE	Rank	LT	Rank	Mid	Rank	RT	Rank	RE	Rank	Sacks	ASR	Rank	F-Start	Cont.
2008	4.84	10	3.94	19	4.09	18	4.23	14	2.67	31	14	2.8%	1	19	29
2009	2.63	31	3.97	20	4.39	8	3.92	21	3.91	21	13	3.1%	1	16	26
2010	3.96	21	4.53	12	3.63	26	3.29	29	4.35	11	16	2.8%	1	20	29

After the 2009 season, Bill Polian blamed the offensive line for the team's Super Bowl loss to the Saints; then he did nothing to upgrade the personnel. Polian's criticism was overstated but prescient, as the offensive line did hold back the 2010 offense. In particular, the team struggled at guard, never finding the right combination. At right guard, undrafted rookie Jeff Linkenbach ended up as the starter, while Kyle DeVan took over for Jamey Richard at left guard midseason. Mike Pollak was seemingly demoted and reinserted into the line-up at both guard spots a dozen times. None of these players are starting-caliber on a supposed top offense. More troubling, long-time star center Jeff Saturday started to show his age and simply cannot get the necessary push on running plays. Saturday is 36 years old, Peyton Manning's security blanket and the longest-tenured Colt besides No. 18. Any further decline, however, will force the team to make a very difficult decision about his future.

In this year's draft, the Colts finally tried to address the offensive line issues, spending their first- and second-round draft picks on offensive tackles. First-rounder Anthony Castonzo (Boston College) should step in at left tackle, replacing Charlie Johnson, who left in free agency. In the second round, the Colts added Ben Ijalana from Villanova. He projects as the long-term answer at right tackle, but the Colts probably won't want to go with two rookie tackles. That means one more year with Rian Diem, leaving Ijalana in reserve or possibly playing right guard. Diem had a terrible season last year, leading the team with ten penalties and six blown blocks that led to sacks. Still, 32 isn't as old for an offensive lineman as it is for a skill player, so a rebound is possible. The lockout could slow the development of the rookies, meaning Linkenbach could start the year at left tackle, which is surely not ideal for protecting the franchise.

Defensive Front Seven

Defensive Line	Age	Pos	Plays	TmPct	Rk	Stop	Dfts	BTkl	St%	Rk	AvYd	Rk	Sack	Hit	Hur	Runs	St%	Yds	Pass	St%	Yds
						Overall							Pass Rush			vs. Run			vs. Pass		
Robert Mathis	30	DE	61	7.4%	15	42	22	2	66%	68	1.8	40	11	7	23.5	41	66%	2.6	20	75%	0.2
Daniel Muir	28	DT	38	5.3%	18	20	4	3	54%	66	3.4	63	0	2	6.5	37	54%	3.3	1	0%	8.0
Eric Foster	26	DT	33	4.0%	44	27	10	1	80%	23	0.9	13	3.5	0	7	25	80%	1.6	8	88%	-1.3
Keyunta Dawson	26	DE	28	3.4%	72	13	4	1	43%	80	4.4	80	0	5	2	23	43%	3.7	5	60%	7.4
Dwight Freeney	31	DE	27	3.3%	75	22	15	1	64%	28	-1.1	2	10	10	33.5	11	64%	3.1	16	94%	-4.0
Fili Moala	26	DT	27	3.3%	56	17	4	1	64%	59	2.6	56	0	3	4	25	64%	2.4	2	50%	4.5
Antonio Johnson	27	DT	26	3.6%	53	15	2	4	59%	63	3.5	64	0.5	2	1	22	59%	2.8	4	50%	7.0

Linebackers	Age	Pos	Plays	TmPct	Rk	Stop	Dfts	BTkl	AvYd	Sack	Hit	Hur	Runs	St%	Rk	Yds	Rk	Tgts	Suc%	Rk	AdjYd	Rk
						Overall				Pass Rush			vs. Run					vs. Pass				
Pat Angerer	24	OLB	77	9.4%	64	33	7	3	5.2	1	0	0	42	55%	97	4.6	101	23	32%	77	7.7	69
Gary Brackett	31	MLB	74	12.0%	42	42	15	9	4.5	0.5	2	1	47	66%	68	2.5	23	17	59%	26	5.0	18
Tyjuan Hagler	30	OLB	57	8.6%	72	26	10	2	6.9	1	0	0	18	56%	95	7.6	109	15	43%	--	4.9	--
Philip Wheeler	27	OLB	49	6.0%	102	27	3	4	4.1	0	0	1.5	32	72%	35	2.1	8	14	28%	--	8.5	--
Kavell Conner	24	OLB	47	7.6%	--	26	4	1	4.3	0	0	0	31	77%	--	2.6	--	7	34%	--	8.2	--
Clint Session	27	OLB	39	15.2%	--	18	6	2	5.0	1	0	2	21	48%	--	4.7	--	17	36%	72	6.0	39

Year	Yards	ALY	Rank	Power	Rank	Stuff	Rank	2nd Lev	Rank	Open Field	Rank
2008	4.26	4.25	21	78%	30	16%	23	1.13	17	0.76	16
2009	4.47	4.53	29	57%	6	15%	29	1.21	20	0.63	11
2010	4.58	4.40	28	57%	8	17%	24	1.28	27	0.89	21

Year	LE	Rank	LT	Rank	Mid	Rank	RT	Rank	RE	Rank	Sacks	ASR	Rank
2008	3.81	10	4.04	13	4.51	27	4.20	19	3.54	13	30	5.5%	22
2009	4.64	21	4.90	29	4.23	21	4.68	28	5.58	31	34	6.3%	16
2010	4.14	16	3.83	11	4.48	29	5.10	32	4.30	20	30	5.6%	25

The Colts' mediocre season obscured the fact that they had arguably the best defensive line of the Peyton Manning era. Bookends Dwight Freeney and Robert Mathis remained healthy all season, a rarity in recent years, and combined for 21 sacks. A deep defensive tackle rotation remained active, excelled in short-yardage situations, and brought a variety of looks. Defensive tackle Fili Moala went from potential bust to solid starter in one year and anchors the unit. Antonio Johnson should return to the starting lineup and is solid if unspectacular. The team let Daniel Muir, too often pushed around in the running game, leave as a free agent. In his stead, they have imported Tommie Harris, the once-great Bears' tackle. Harris has struggled with injuries and was simply ineffective last year but returns to a pure one-gap system this season. The Colts also added Jamaal Anderson, who will play defensive end on running downs and slide inside on passing downs. The one disappointment was the lack of development of first-round pick Jerry Hughes. Hughes did a Vernon Gholston impersonation as a rookie, but it's never a good idea to write off pass rushers after just one season. Still, as another undersized defensive end, he only will see significant playing time if Freeney or Mathis are hurt.

The solid play of the defensive line was often obscured by abysmal performance from the linebackers. The Colts were hampered by injuries to Clint Session and Gary Brackett. Brackett returns at full strength, but Session signed a big deal with Jacksonville, leaving the Colts thin at linebacker. Rookie Pat Angerer was over his head as a fill-in for both, specializing in jumping on piles and being dragged three yards after contact. Still, Angerer has physical tools and could take a big step forward this season as a starter. At weakside linebacker, the Colts want to go with 2010 seventh-round pick Kavell Conner, the latest in a long line of undersized Colts' linebackers. Conner was respectable as an injury fill-in last season but will be pushed by free agent acquisition Ernie Sims.

Defensive Secondary

Secondary	Age	Pos	Plays	TmPct	Rk	Stop	Dfts	BTkl	Runs	St%	Rk	Yds	Rk	Tgts	Tgt%	Rk	Dist	Suc%	Rk	APaYd	Rk	PD	Int
Antoine Bethea	27	FS	110	13.4%	11	33	11	3	69	38%	47	7.0	47	24	5.4%	49	18.8	52%	48	9.1	59	5	1
Kelvin Hayden	28	CB	69	12.2%	8	32	14	6	26	46%	36	4.7	16	50	16.1%	34	11.1	47%	66	9.2	73	8	2
Jacob Lacey	24	CB	63	10.2%	26	25	10	6	15	40%	50	11.1	84	46	13.6%	58	10.0	39%	88	9.6	78	4	1
Jerraud Powers	24	CB	62	12.1%	9	27	15	6	20	40%	50	5.8	30	60	21.5%	5	10.8	54%	34	5.9	12	9	2
Aaron Francisco	28	SS	59	9.6%	51	13	5	9	28	32%	58	6.6	39	11	3.1%	75	16.4	40%	74	9.7	63	5	2
Justin Tryon	27	CB	42	6.8%	71	18	11	6	8	75%	2	2.1	3	44	13.1%	65	10.0	55%	29	6.1	16	7	0

Year	Pass D Rank	vs. #1 WR	Rk	vs. #2 WR	Rk	vs. Other WR	Rk	vs. TE	Rk	vs. RB	Rk
2008	14	21.6%	28	-15.8%	8	-10.7%	13	1.6%	14	8.4%	20
2009	11	-0.9%	14	4.1%	20	-1.0%	15	-0.5%	13	-6.2%	12
2010	26	-9.0%	9	-6.0%	10	-2.9%	17	28.8%	31	18.8%	28

The Colts knew Bob Sanders would get hurt and were well-prepared with Melvin Bullitt ready to replace him. But when Bullitt went down, they suddenly were stuck starting ex-Arizona backup Aaron Francisco, who should be making a living on special teams. Bullitt missed the season with a shoulder injury, but he should return and form a nice tandem with Antoine Bethea, who is now so often discussed as underrated that he is bordering on being overrated. Bethea, however, is the steadying influence on the defense and arguably the defense's most important player outside the Pro Bowl defensive ends.

At corner, the Colts let Kelvin Hayden leave in free agency, leaving only Jerraud Powers as an above-average corner. Powers missed six games a year ago and went on IR after Week 13 with a broken arm. His return solidifies one starting spot. On the other side, Justin Tryon should push the more-established Jacob Lacey. The team would be better served with Tryon emerging, allowing them to shift Lacey inside. Lacey, a year removed from starting in the Super Bowl as a rookie, struggled last season as a starter and limited the Colts' ability to play more creative defenses. For depth, one interesting name is Kevin Thomas, a third-round pick out of USC a year ago who went down with a knee injury in minicamp and never played.

Special Teams

Year	DVOA	Rank	FG/XP	Rank	Net Kick	Rank	Kick Ret	Rank	Net Punt	Rank	Punt Ret	Rank	Hidden	Rank
2008	-1.8%	24	-2.9	24	2.4	14	-9.0	29	9.0	7	-10.2	32	-4.7	19
2009	-0.7%	20	-2.1	21	1.5	14	-1.6	15	3.9	12	-5.8	26	-12.3	29
2010	-5.4%	31	6.9	4	-3.4	23	-17.6	32	-8.1	27	-9.5	30	-4.2	19

Jim Caldwell's most-applauded move as a rookie coach in 2009 was to fire Tony Dungy's long-time special teams' coach and seemingly emphasize the long-neglected unit. The unit under Ray Rychelski finished a respectable 20th in DVOA, the best since 2003. Apparently, however, that was just a sign of the unpredictable nature of special teams because the Colts' were back to their anemic ways last season, ranking 31st in DVOA, ahead of only the historically awful Chargers.

Adam Vinatieri returns for another season. The leg is not as strong as it used to be, but when healthy, he continues to hit a high percentage of kicks. Vinatieri was the team's only bright spot on special teams last season. The biggest black mark was simply woeful kickoff returns; the team averaged fewer than 20 yards per return. Their kickoff and punt coverage was barely better. The Colts will be the biggest beneficiary of the return to kickoffs from the 35, as they will happily start on the 20-yard line on offense and, with punter Pat McAfee kicking off, should be able to force a decent number of touchbacks.

Coaching Staff

The honeymoon is over for Jim Caldwell, who may be coaching for his job this season. The Colts' 10-6 record was their worst since 2002, and the team often looked listless throughout the season. Of course, Caldwell had serious injuries to deal with all over the field, and his offensive playmakers are simply not as explosive as they were in the peak of the Colts' recent run. The offense finally loses Tom Moore as its guru this year, with nominal offensive coordinator Clyde Christensen actually assuming those duties. The team is also down long-time offensive line coach Howard Mudd. Following last year's disappointing performance by the Colts' blockers, Pete Metzelaars, who held the title but not the responsibility last season, needs to strengthen the unit.

Defensively, the team continues its uneasy transition from the Tony Dungy era. Dungy and his defensive coordinator, Ron Meeks, played a pure Tampa-2 defense with almost no blitzing. New coordinator Larry Coyer has spent two years hinting at wanting to move away from the Tampa-2 and has incorporated more aggressive rush packages. Unfortunately, despite increasing the number of looks the defense shows, the results are not better. Last year's unit was worse than all but one under Dungy (interestingly, the Colts' Super Bowl season). It was by far the team's worst pass defense since adopting the Tampa-2. The problem is that the team continues to acquire players for Dungy's system, but Coyer is coaching as if the players are more versatile then they are.

Jacksonville Jaguars

2010 Record: 8-8	**2011 Mean Projection:** 7.6 wins
Pythagorean Wins: 6.4 (22nd)	**On the Clock (0-3):** 8%
DVOA: -9.5% (22nd)	**Loserville (4-6):** 28%
Offense: 7.7% (14th)	**Mediocrity (7-8):** 26%
Defense: 21.2% (32nd)	**Playoff Contender (9-10):** 22%
Special Teams: 4.1% (7th)	**Super Bowl Contender (11+):** 16%
Variance: 19.5% (19th)	**Projected Average Opponent:** 2.4% (7th)

2010: Upset bid unraveled by ugly defense.

2011: Hot Run Time Machine

Going into Week 15, the Jaguars had a chance to clinch the AFC South by beating Indianapolis at Lucas Oil Stadium. The majority of the division has been suffering at the hands of Peyton Manning since it was formed in 2002, but perhaps no team moreso than the Jaguars. Despite winning just two of the first five meetings in Indiana under head coach Jack Del Rio, the Jags have always been a tough out for the Colts at home. Over the last five years, they'd kept every game in Indianapolis within a touchdown. In fact, with opponent adjustments, Jacksonville had notched a better DVOA than Indianapolis each of the last three times the two had met in Indy.

Jacksonville again trotted out Maurice Jones-Drew and their impressive running attack to pound away at the Colts and their undersized front seven, but with Jones-Drew's knee hurting, the Jags watched as their running attack was shut down by Gary Brackett and company. After averaging 167.4 yards on the ground in those last five games in Indy, Jacksonville could rack up only 67 this time around. They looked on in horror as Donald Brown shredded their running defense en route to a comfortable 34-24 Colts win that not only kept the Jags from clinching, but also reinstated Indianapolis with all the tiebreaker advantages in what figured to be a tight division crown race.

It was later revealed that Jones-Drew was suffering through a painful bone-on-bone meniscus injury rather than the vague "sore knee," and he skipped the last few games of the season. Garrard slammed his hand into the helmet of a Colts defender in that Week 15 loss, injuring a finger on his throwing hand. A pair of costly interceptions mixed with other inaccurate throws cost the Jags a must-win game against the Redskins before surgery on the finger ended Garrard's season. Left in the hands of Trent Edwards, the Jaguars face-planted in Week 17 against the Texans and the Colts were division champions once again.

Looking at what actually happened on the field, it's clear that the Jaguars were more than a bit lucky to find themselves in the position they did in Week 15. Jacksonville finished with a pedestrian -9.5% DVOA rating, good for 22nd in the NFL, and had just 6.4 Pythagorean wins. The real root of that problem was on display against Indianapolis: a defense that has quietly turned into one of the laughingstocks of the NFL.

The Jaguars had a top 10 DVOA defense in each of Del Rio's first four seasons. They slipped to 15th in 2007, and for the last three seasons they've finished in the bottom eight, cratering to dead last in 2010. The run defense had been just fine up until last year, but the Jaguars have been looking for a real pass-rusher to keep up with divisional foes like Mario Williams and Dwight Freeney ever since Tony Brackens was released in 2004. The last Jaguar to notch 10 sacks in a season was Bobby McCray in 2006. Last year's

2011 Jaguars Schedule

Week	Opp.	Week	Opp.	Week	Opp.
1	TEN	7	BAL (Mon.)	13	SD (Mon.)
2	at NYJ	8	at HOU	14	TB
3	at CAR	9	BYE	15	at ATL (Thu.)
4	NO	10	at IND	16	at TEN
5	CIN	11	at CLE	17	IND
6	at PIT	12	HOU		

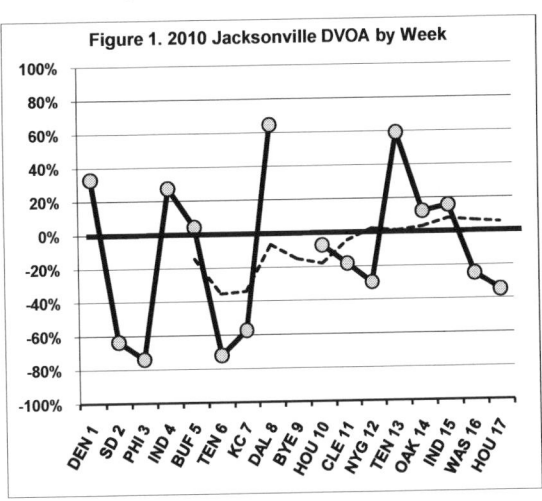

Figure 1. 2010 Jacksonville DVOA by Week

leader, Jeremy Mincey, had just five. The secondary has gone from Pro Bowler Rashean Mathis and supporting veterans to a slower Rashean Mathis and youngsters that were handed their jobs on necessity rather than performance.

How did it get this bad though? As you might imagine, there are multiple layers to a collapse this dramatic.

The first problem the Jaguars faced was that the 2006 defensive core was pretty old to begin with. NFL teams that don't have a star quarterback generally don't have very long windows to compete, and 2006 was one of the last years that the Jaguars defense was able to play at their peak talent. John Henderson and Marcus Stroud formed a veritable brick wall in the middle of the Jacksonville defensive line, but they were the two youngest contributing players on that line aside from McCray, and at 28 and 29 respectively coming into the 2007 season, they were nearing the end of their prime. Stroud had also become rather injury-prone, and was dealt to Buffalo for a pair of draft picks after 2007.

Daryl Smith, one of the few Jaguars from that team who is still around and productive today, led a weak linebacker corps. Mike Peterson was a great player in the few seasons leading up to 2006, but missed a lot of time that season and had just turned 30. Clint Ingram and Nick Greisen were just journeymen, and Ingram never showed enough to be granted a starting job in 2007, let alone the next three.

In the secondary, every position had nowhere to go but down after 2006. While Mathis was going to be a solid player even if he wasn't quite playing at a Pro Bowl level, Brian Williams was always a short-term solution on the other side of the field. Donovan Darius, one of the more successful Jaguars in the team's history, had become noticeably slower as he aged. Deon Grant was an impending free agent, and one who seemed likely to leave. Gerald Sensabaugh looked like he could pick up the pieces at one safety

spot, but that still left the Jags with a pair of holes in the starting 11 and no real nickelback of note.

The Jaguars focused on their defense in the draft over the last four years, adding only three offensive players in the first three rounds, and just one of them at wide receiver even though it had been a gaping wound for the team since the days of Jimmy Smith. Despite eight picks in the top three rounds spent on defense, the only three players they drafted in those four years who are firmly entrenched as NFL starters are Justin Durant, Terrence Knighton, and Tyson Alualu.

They've paid the price for back-to-back awful drafts in 2007 and 2008. Supposed Grant replacement Reggie Nelson has been a complete and utter bust after a decent first year, and the Jaguars sent a ransom of draft picks (a first, a second, two thirds, a fourth, a fifth, and a seventh) to move up twice in 2007 for Derrick Harvey and Quentin Groves. Those trades looked questionable at the time, but with Harvey and Groves combining for just 10.5 career sacks at this point, they've been a complete fiasco. Losing all those draft picks forced the Jaguars to either push their recent picks into the lineup before they were ready to be there or acquire speed bump stopgaps in their stead, and a lot of last year's problems could be directly traced to those two deals.

Speaking of stopgaps, the Jaguars have also made some pretty disastrous free agent signings over that period of time. Sure, they were hurt a bit recently by the restricted movement of younger players after the Collective Bargaining Agreement expired, but that doesn't excuse signings like Drayton Florence. Florence managed to start just eight games for Jacksonville in the 2008 season before wearing out his welcome, and he was benched after just four games. He collected $13 million in guaranteed money for that effort. After noticing that Harvey and Groves weren't very good at actually, you know, rushing the passer, the Jags spent big to bring in Green Bay's Aaron Kampman last year. Kampman looked good when he did play, but tore his ACL for the second straight season. The Jags appear to be counting on the 31-year-old to anchor their pass rush again this year: It would be surprising if that ended well, or without him spending some more time on the IR or PUP lists.

In today's NFL, where the passing game has become more important than the running game, the Jaguars have been built on the '70s smashmouth side of the ball. Knighton, Alualu, and Smith have generally done a good job at putting the kibosh on opposing backs. Over the last three years, the Jaguars' run defense has finished in the top 10 by DVOA twice. This has been purely a passing game problem, and while they had free agent dollars to throw at possible solutions, they spent mostly on stopping the run again to prevent another loss like the one in Week 15 last season. The Jaguars brought in four free agents of note on the defensive side of the ball: Buffalo linebacker Paul Posluszny, Indianapolis linebacker Clint Session, Baltimore safety Dawan Landry, and New York Jets nickelback Drew Coleman. Landry and Coleman will be upgrades in the secondary, but while they were both solid against the pass last year, neither of them have long track records of success in coverage.

Coleman will compete with Derek Cox for the job across from Mathis. Cox could still blossom and become a starting cornerback for Jacksonville, but he's been firmly in the bottom half of the league by both Success Rate and Yards per Pass each of the last two years. David Jones was named to our Keep Chopping Wood team despite starting just six games last season, an incredible feat of concentrated sadness. Courtney Greene and Don Carey played exactly how you'd expect a pair of late-round picks with zero starting experience to play. Rookie fifth-round defensive end Austen Lane started nine games after Kampman was hurt and accumulated zero sacks, and only unproven defensive ends are behind role player Mincey after Harvey was mercifully released. Short of Alualu becoming the next Warren Sapp while Landry and Coleman repeat their best years, there's very little reason to expect the Jaguars pass defense to improve significantly this year.

Assuming Jones-Drew stays healthy, the Jaguars running game again figures to be their main strength. In the short-term, our good friend and injury expert Will Carroll doesn't think his knee injury will be a problem, though it could cut some years off the end of his career. Blaine Gabbert's selection marked the beginning of a transitional phase in Jacksonville. Rather than continuing to throw first-round picks at areas of need, as they'd done for most of the mid-aughts, the Jaguars will now attempt to develop a successor to David Garrard. Gabbert is looking at an adjustment period as he moves from the Missouri spread offense to Dirk Koetter's power-based attack. Our Lewin 2.0 system doesn't project great things for Gabbert, but it does suggest that he can be a competent NFL passer, perhaps one that will wind up better than Garrard.

After Mike Sims-Walker's defection to St. Louis, the receivers are led by Pro Bowl tight end Marcedes Lewis, who has shed his bust label by becoming much more of a threat in the short passing game. Mike Thomas gives them another sure-handed, wiry receiver who can catch short balls, and Zach Miller is a competent second receiving tight end. After those three, their receiving depth is more strung out than the cast of *Celebrity Rehab*. The plan is to go into training camp with Jason Hill as their second starting wideout, despite the fact that he is 26 and has yet to have a season with 350 receiving yards. Rookie fourth-rounder Cecil Shorts will compete with Jarett Dillard and Tiquan Underwood for the slot receiver job, in a competition that should be followed closely by approximately four fantasy owners.

The Jaguars continue to be a team with a primary focus on stopping the run, slamming the ball down their opponent's throats, and grinding out close wins. They're modeled after the classic Pittsburgh Steelers. Meanwhile, the real Pittsburgh Steelers have updated their game for the 21st century. They understand the value of sacks, hurries, and otherwise disrupting the quarterback. They understand that in the modern NFL, you need more than one or two quality receivers. Gabbert is a good start, but until the Jaguars really commit to shoring up their passing game on both sides of the ball, they can expect another year of plodding mediocrity as Steelers-lite. That might be enough to compete in what we expect to be a weak AFC South this year, but the ceiling is an unfulfilling playoff thumping against a team built more along the lines of the actual Steelers.

Rivers McCown

2010 Jaguars Stats by Week

Wk	vs.	W-L	PF	PA	YDF	YDA	TO	Total	Off	Def	ST
1	DEN	W	24	17	299	363	2	33%	24%	7%	15%
2	@SD	L	13	38	350	477	-3	-64%	-36%	31%	4%
3	PHI	L	3	28	191	373	-1	-74%	-46%	27%	-2%
4	IND	W	31	28	337	406	2	27%	45%	32%	15%
5	@BUF	W	36	26	381	306	-3	4%	20%	34%	18%
6	TEN	L	3	30	249	324	-4	-72%	-33%	35%	-4%
7	@KC	L	20	42	300	426	-3	-57%	-17%	48%	8%
8	@DAL	W	35	17	387	415	3	65%	39%	-21%	5%
9	BYE										
10	HOU	W	31	24	491	395	1	-7%	47%	43%	-11%
11	CLE	W	24	20	371	283	-5	-18%	-19%	0%	0%
12	@NYG	L	20	24	328	361	-2	-30%	8%	42%	4%
13	@TEN	W	17	6	377	220	2	59%	53%	-21%	-14%
14	OAK	W	38	31	385	476	1	12%	39%	47%	20%
15	@IND	L	24	34	356	376	-2	16%	5%	14%	25%
16	WAS	L	17	20	336	251	-1	-25%	-28%	-16%	-12%
17	@HOU	L	17	34	322	497	-2	-35%	10%	43%	-2%

Trends and Splits

	Offense	Rank	Defense	Rank
Total DVOA	7.7%	14	21.2%	32
Unadjusted VOA	8.9%	13	21.6%	31
Weighted Trend	12.2%	9	19.8%	31
Variance	10.9%	28	6.0%	11
Average Opponent	6.1%	5	7.8%	26
Passing	7.3%	21	36.2%	30
Rushing	14.0%	4	4.2%	28
First Down	16.7%	7	23.3%	31
Second Down	3.2%	13	15.0%	29
Third Down	-2.4%	18	26.1%	29
First Half	17.6%	6	17.5%	30
Second Half	-2.2%	21	25.1%	31
Red Zone	22.2%	5	17.7%	28
Late and Close	0.9%	18	25.1%	31

Five-Year Performance

Year	W-L	Pyth	Est W	PF	PA	TO	Total	Rk	Off	Rk	Def	Rk	ST	Rk	Off AGL	Rk	Def AGL	Rk
2006	8-8	10.8	9.6	371	274	+1	23.7%	5	7.4%	10	-16.5%	3	-0.2%	19	12.3	8	40.3	31
2007	11-5	10.7	11.4	411	304	+9	23.7%	3	21.9%	3	-1.8%	15	0.0%	15	16.8	9	34.3	27
2008	5-11	6.2	8.9	302	367	-7	1.9%	20	12.6%	11	10.2%	24	-0.5%	21	48.8	29	15.4	11
2009	7-9	5.5	7.3	290	380	+2	-8.5%	23	7.0%	17	14.1%	28	-1.3%	25	4.5	2	43.5	28
2010	8-8	6.4	6.7	353	419	-15	-9.5%	22	7.7%	14	21.2%	32	4.1%	7	19.7	9	17.8	11

Strategic Tendencies

Run/Pass		Rank	Offense		Rank	Defense		Rank	Other		Rank
Runs, all plays	46%	3	3+ WR	46%	19	Rush 3	5.3%	21	2+ RB, Pct Runs	71%	2
Runs, first half	50%	2	4+ WR	2%	28	Rush 4	59.4%	15	1 RB/2 TE, Pct Runs	36%	29
Runs, first down	55%	8	2+ TE	24%	21	Rush 5	23.7%	16	1 RB/3+ WR, Pct Runs	21%	21
Runs, second-long	34%	16	Single back	50%	28	Rush 6+	11.6%	8	CB1 on WR1	31%	27
Runs, power sit.	77%	2	Play action	17%	19	Zone Blitz	8.4%	7	Go for it on 4th	0.86	19
Runs, behind 2H	31%	7	Max protect	7%	27	Sacks by LB	15.4%	22	Offensive Pace	32.1	26
Pass, ahead 2H	34%	31	Outside pocket	13%	15	Sacks by DB	7.7%	19	Defensive Pace	31.4	26

Although they didn't have a great offense, the Jaguars rarely went out with a whimper. Jacksonville only went three-and-out on 10.5 percent of drives in 2010. That's the lowest rate since for any team since 1998, passing the 2001 Rams who were at 10.8 percent. ☞ The Jaguars tweaked their run-pass ratio significantly in 2010, keeping the ball on the ground much more than in 2009. The two biggest changes: They went from 38 percent runs in the first half of games to 50 percent, and they went from 58 percent runs with two backs in the game to 71 percent. ☞ For the second straight year, the Jaguars were the league's most effective offense running the ball on second-and-long, with 36.5% DVOA and 6.44 yards per carry. ☞ Jacksonville went empty backfield on a league-low four plays, and even on those plays, Maurice Jones-Drew was in the game lined up at wide receiver. ☞ Once again, David Garrard led the league with 55 quarterback hits (not counting sacks). He was first in 2009 and second in 2008. ☞ Jacksonville sent six pass rushers twice as often as they did the year before, and sent only three pass rushers half as often. ☞ Jacksonville was 27th in defensive DVOA against the run out of formations with three or more wide receivers — after ranking first in 2009.

Passing

Player	DYAR	DVOA	Plays	NtYds	Avg	YAC	C%	TD	Int
D.Garrard	385	4.8%	401	2547	6.4	5.0	64.8%	23	15
T.Bouman	52	10.4%	37	271	7.3	6.7	52.9%	2	2
L.McCown	50	31.8%	19	120	6.3	5.3	57.9%	0	0

Rushing

Player	DYAR	DVOA	Plays	Yds	Avg	TD	Fum	Suc
M.Jones-Drew	238	9.4%	300	1324	4.4	5	3	51%
R.Jennings	137	29.3%	84	459	5.5	4	0	52%
D.Garrard	79	12.4%	54	279	5.2	5	4	-
D.Karim	4	-5.6%	35	160	4.6	0	1	51%
M.Thomas	57	53.8%	12	114	9.5	0	0	-

Receiving

Player	DYAR	DVOA	Plays	Ctch	Yds	Y/C	YAC	TD	C%
M.Thomas	185	11.2%	102	67	828	12.4	4.5	4	66%
M.Sims-Walker	154	11.5%	79	42	550	13.1	2.9	7	53%
T.Underwood	-18	-23.1%	22	8	111	13.9	2.4	0	36%
J.Hill	56	22.2%	21	11	248	22.5	3.8	1	52%
K.Osgood	-29	-36.2%	16	6	60	10.0	3.3	1	38%
M.Lewis	124	13.0%	88	58	700	12.1	4.5	10	66%
Z.Miller	44	19.1%	26	20	216	10.8	4.9	1	77%
Z.Potter	-15	-35.1%	8	3	24	8.0	4.7	0	38%
M.Jones-Drew	98	29.4%	44	34	317	9.3	9.5	2	77%
R.Jennings	40	9.9%	34	26	222	8.5	8.3	0	76%
G.Jones	3	-9.3%	11	11	47	4.3	3.8	0	100%
D.Karim	-25	-71.0%	7	3	10	3.3	3.7	0	43%

Offensive Line

Year	Yards	ALY	Rank	Power	Rank	Stuff	Rank	2nd Lev	Rank	Open Field	Rank
2008	4.06	4.09	17	76%	6	18%	13	1.14	16	0.68	18
2009	4.55	4.24	11	68%	10	17%	11	1.12	19	1.07	6
2010	4.62	4.63	2	63%	13	13%	3	1.35	2	0.70	18

Year	LE	Rank	LT	Rank	Mid	Rank	RT	Rank	RE	Rank	Sacks	ASR	Rank	F-Start	Cont.
2008	3.64	24	4.22	14	4.03	21	4.59	5	4.61	5	42	7.9%	24	14	32
2009	5.66	1	4.49	8	4.06	19	3.92	20	4.44	11	44	8.5%	29	14	34
2010	4.70	8	4.75	5	4.63	3	4.26	13	4.78	6	38	7.7%	24	13	30

The Jaguars like to run the ball, and last season they had an offensive line to run behind. Left tackle Eugene Monroe, their 2009 first-round pick, has become an excellent run blocker, although he is too inconsistent in pass protection and simply cannot be relied on to protect without help. On the right side, 2009 second-round pick Eben Britton flashed the potential to be a force, as well as a mean streak, but he lost the second half of the season due to a torn labrum in his shoulder. The Jaguars haven't finished higher than 24th in Adjusted Sack Rate since 2007, and if their tackles continue to show little improvement, it could put offensive line coach Andy Heck's job in jeopardy.

The line was anchored by veteran center Brad Meester and the surprising return to form of Vince Manuwai at guard. Manuwai had been replaced when the Jaguars traded for veteran Justin Smiley in the offseason, but the Jaguars decided that they needed Manuwai's run blocking and put him back in the starting lineup for good as of Week 8. Jacksonville averaged 4.15 ALY per carry before Manuwai took over, 4.99 ALY after. Surprisingly, the Jaguars chose not to bring Manuwai back in free agency, instead signing Jason Spitz away from the Green Bay Packers. At right guard, Uche Nwaneri has entered his prime and developed into a solid contributor, a nice rise for the former fifth-rounder that resulted in a long-term extension last September. The Jaguars used a third-round pick on Will Rackley, the first Lehigh player drafted in 16 years, as a developmental project.

Defensive Front Seven

Defensive Line	Age	Pos	Plays	TmPct	Rk	Stop	Dfts	BTkl	St%	Rk	AvYd	Rk	Sack	Hit	Hur	Runs	St%	Yds	Pass	St%	Yds
													Overall				Pass Rush		vs. Run		vs. Pass
Tyson Alualu	24	DT	39	5.2%	19	29	12	0	73%	41	1.3	17	3.5	5	6.5	33	73%	2.1	6	83%	-3.5
Terrance Knighton	25	DT	37	5.0%	26	33	13	2	92%	8	0.1	2	4	4	9	25	92%	0.9	12	83%	-1.6
Jeremy Mincey	28	DE	34	4.9%	46	27	12	4	72%	35	0.2	11	5	3	8.5	25	72%	1.6	9	100%	-3.4
Aaron Kampman	32	DE	27	7.2%	18	21	10	1	81%	45	0.6	15	3.5	12	7.5	16	81%	1.0	11	73%	0.0
Austen Lane	24	DE	20	3.9%	--	11	2	0	55%	--	2.7	--	0	2	2	20	55%	2.7	0	0%	0.0

Linebackers	Age	Pos	Plays	TmPct	Rk	Stop	Dfts	BTkl	AvYd	Sack	Hit	Hur	Runs	St%	Rk	Yds	Rk	Tgts	Suc%	Rk	AdjYd	Rk
Daryl Smith	29	OLB	100	13.4%	32	66	35	4	3.9	4	6	12	54	69%	54	2.9	45	35	52%	50	8.3	76
Kirk Morrison	29	MLB	90	12.1%	41	59	19	3	3.6	0	2	3	70	73%	32	2.5	26	21	54%	42	6.4	45
Justin Durant	26	OLB	57	12.2%	40	32	10	4	6.1	0	0	0	27	85%	3	2.2	15	27	41%	71	8.8	78
Russell Allen	25	MLB	35	4.7%	--	22	5	3	3.9	0	0	0	26	77%	--	2.7	--	10	13%	--	13.0	--

Year	Yards	ALY	Rank	Power	Rank	Stuff	Rank	2nd Lev	Rank	Open Field	Rank
2008	4.03	3.98	10	57%	3	23%	6	1.20	23	0.74	15
2009	4.23	4.07	15	71%	26	17%	24	1.10	10	0.79	17
2010	4.76	3.89	15	68%	26	23%	3	1.22	24	1.43	32

Year	LE	Rank	LT	Rank	Mid	Rank	RT	Rank	RE	Rank	Sacks	ASR	Rank
2008	4.09	14	4.67	26	4.06	11	3.85	11	3.25	12	29	6.3%	14
2009	3.75	11	4.55	25	4.03	16	4.92	30	3.48	5	14	3.8%	31
2010	3.11	3	4.37	20	3.81	11	5.04	31	4.33	22	26	5.8%	22

The Jaguars finished 28th in defensive DVOA against the run, but that was not the fault of their defensive tackles. First-round pick Tyson Alualu made an impact as the under tackle, making some all-rookie teams over Gerald McCoy. Alualu is still developing, particularly as a pass-rusher, but he solidified the defensive line and provides plenty of promise for the future. Paired next to him is Terrence "Pot Roast" Knighton, who finished eighth among defensive linemen in Stop Rate and second in yards per play. The home cooking during the lockout might have been a bit too much for Knighton, as he missed time early in camp because he was out of shape.

Aaron Kampman did what many 30-year-old free agents do coming off of a devastating injury — he got injured again, tearing his right ACL rather than his left this time. When healthy, he did provide some of the pass rush he showed in Green Bay, but the Jaguars are taking quite a risk relying on him to be their main pass rusher this season. With the release of Derrick Harvey, 2010 fifth-rounder Austen Lane is expected to join the starting lineup. Lest you think that he will be any sort of panacea for the pass rush, he accrued no sacks and just two hurries in nine starts following Kampman's injury.

With Kirk Morrison and Justin Durant hitting free agency, the Jaguars were extremely proactive in inking Paul Posluszny and Clint Session immediately after the lockout. Neither of them has traditionally graded out very well in our metrics, but they both also come from much-maligned run defenses; that lack of help could hide their true value. $26.5 million is a lot of guaranteed money to pay to two guys who are primarily run stoppers, particularly since Session missed most of last year after dislocating his elbow. However, scouts have always loved Posluszny, who is an excellent tackler (only three missed tackles with 103 solo tackles), and Session was regarded highly by Greg Cosell.

Strongside linebacker Daryl Smith generally comes out average in our advanced metrics, but he does make big plays at important times, and he led the league with 35 Defeats. Most players build their Defeats total with turnovers and sacks, but Smith had an uncanny ability to make key stops on third down. In Week 8, he stopped Marion Barber from the one-yard line on two straight plays. In Week 13, he had two tackles where he stopped Chris Johnson one-yard short of a conversion. He also had nine different plays where he tackled receivers short of the sticks on third down.

Defensive Secondary

Secondary	Age	Pos	Plays	TmPct	Rk	Stop	Dfts	BTkl	Runs	St%	Rk	Yds	Rk	Tgts	Tgt%	Rk	Dist	Suc%	Rk	APaYd	Rk	PD	Int
										vs. Run						**vs. Pass**							
Courtney Greene	25	SS	80	12.3%	16	26	6	5	47	43%	33	6.3	34	22	5.6%	43	10.5	52%	47	10.3	70	4	1
Rashean Mathis	31	CB	63	8.5%	47	16	5	1	19	21%	84	9.9	79	67	14.9%	47	14.1	42%	80	10.8	88	7	1
Derek Cox	25	CB	56	9.3%	32	20	9	4	12	42%	47	6.7	43	67	18.2%	14	12.9	53%	40	7.8	54	9	4
Don Carey	24	FS	52	7.4%	66	12	6	8	24	33%	55	10.3	76	18	4.2%	71	9.7	32%	78	9.9	65	1	1
Sean Considine	29	SS	47	7.2%	68	22	10	8	19	47%	24	8.5	61	19	4.8%	64	12.4	54%	39	10.1	69	2	1
William Middleton	25	CB	41	5.5%	82	10	8	3	14	36%	65	8.6	63	40	8.8%	87	8.3	42%	79	6.4	21	1	1
David Jones	26	CB	33	4.4%	--	9	4	2	7	43%	--	5.4	--	31	6.8%	--	14.2	43%	--	12.0	--	4	1
Anthony Smith	28	FS	21	6.4%	--	6	2	1	9	56%	--	8.1	--	8	3.7%	--	7.5	32%	--	6.6	--	1	1
Gerald Alexander	27	FS	19	20.4%	--	11	6	3	9	56%	--	5.2	--	10	16.9%	--	12.3	56%	--	6.8	--	3	0

Year	Pass D Rank	vs. #1 WR	Rk	vs. #2 WR	Rk	vs. Other WR	Rk	vs. TE	Rk	vs. RB	Rk
2008	30	9.1%	21	2.6%	18	23.3%	29	26.6%	30	34.3%	32
2009	31	20.1%	27	29.2%	31	13.5%	27	11.2%	19	10.8%	21
2010	30	28.8%	29	8.7%	19	26.3%	30	9.3%	17	5.8%	18

Rashean Mathis has been a good player for a long time, but the brief period where he was considered an elite cornerback was a serious overreaction to flashy playmaking. Now Mathis is on the wrong side of 30, and he is quickly moving from overrated to an actual liability, particularly on deep balls. Mathis' instincts are good, but his recovery speed is not there when he guesses wrong. The Jags spent a small bit of cash to bring in Jets nickelback Drew Coleman, who may find himself in the starting lineup more than he expects if Derek Cox continues to be benched like he was early last season. Cox was burned early and often in Week 1, but his benching put David Jones on the field, which was a terrible mistake. Jones didn't have enough targets for our cornerback rankings, but he was bad enough in his six weeks as the starter to win the coveted "Jason David award" for allowing more yards per pass than plays marked Hole in Zone. Jones likely finds himself as the dime back going forward, which fits his talent level better and will leave the Jags singing Coleman's praises when they play Houston and Indianapolis.

Safety was the team's weakest position in 2010. The Jaguars relied heavily on Courtney Greene and Don Carey, two players with no experience and a tendency to be wildly out of position. Greene steadied himself as the year went on but continues to struggle in coverage. Carey, a converted cornerback, took over for Sean Considine, who was last seen struggling to cover people in Philadelphia. (Note: the move to Florida did not improve his coverage skills.) The Jaguars addressed the Carey issue by bringing in Dawan Landry from Baltimore. Landry had an excellent season in 2010 and should be counted on to solidify free safety, but he's historically been better against the run than the pass in our metrics. Fourth-rounder Chris Prosinski out of Wyoming will probably push for playing time at strong safety this season, so long as Greene continues to show poor range.

Special Teams

Year	DVOA	Rank	FG/XP	Rank	Net Kick	Rank	Kick Ret	Rank	Net Punt	Rank	Punt Ret	Rank	Hidden	Rank
2008	-0.5%	21	-7.2	29	14.1	2	-7.7	28	-1.4	20	-0.6	16	-9.8	27
2009	-1.3%	25	-8.2	27	0.4	17	-5.6	22	6.0	7	-0.5	15	-8.4	27
2010	4.1%	7	1.9	13	12.2	5	-1.8	16	8.6	7	3.0	13	-1.8	17

Last offseason, the Jaguars signed all-everything special teams player Kassim Osgood. Osgood persevered despite having to escape a gunman, the ex-boyfriend of the cheerleader he was with, by jumping out of a second-story window. Add one happy, not-dead Osgood, and you get strong coverage teams, particularly on kickoffs. Josh Scobee has only been a little bit above average on kickoffs the last couple years, so that coverage really helped. Punter Adam Podlesh improved significantly over the performance of his first two seasons and provided excellent hang time, but he's now off to Chicago to replace Brad Maynard. The ageless Matt Turk will compete with Durant Brooks for the punter job this season. Turk was one of the worst punters in the NFL last season, but Brooks hasn't punted in the NFL since 2008. No matter who wins the job, the Jaguars will probably lose value on their punts this year.

Mike Thomas, on top of being an excellent receiver, is a very good punt return man who eschews fair catches and still manages to average 10 yards per return. Kickoff returns weren't quite as good. Deji Karim and Tiquan Underwood shared the role and neither really distinguished himself as a solid option. Fourth-round pick Cecil Shorts, a speedy but undersized receiver out of Mount Union, looks like the favorite to return kicks this year, so long as he doesn't win the third receiver job.

Coaching Staff

In eight years as the Jaguars' head coach, Jack Del Rio is two games over .500 and has made the playoffs just twice. In a normal scenario, the safe assumption would be that Del Rio would be on the hot seat, but that assumption would also have seemed safe last year, when Del Rio saved his job even though the team collapsed down the stretch to finish 8-8. After eight years, Del Rio is what he is: an aggressive game coach who is fickle with his players. He changes line-ups too quickly and hasn't developed much young talent. The team is inconsistent both on a game-to-game basis and on a year-to-year basis. He oversaw four top ten DVOA defenses in his first four years but had the league's worst defense last year. Del Rio might not be the problem with the Jaguars, but he is not the solution either.

After the departure of long-time defensive coordinator Mike Smith in 2008, the Jaguars turned to Gregg Williams to run the show, but he only lasted one year before joining New Orleans to oversee a Super Bowl-winning defense. Mel Tucker took over in 2009 and played around with moving to a 3-4 defense before finally relenting and playing to the strengths of his unit. After another horrendous year in 2010, Tucker's job is clearly on the line, and he'll have to integrate all his new pieces seamlessly despite little experience coaching the 4-3. The uncertainty spawning from the lockout may have stopped the Jaguars from investing in a new defensive coordinator (and head coach) this offseason, despite plenty of evidence suggesting a change was justified, and that could hurt the team this year.

Offensive coordinator Dirk Koetter was a somewhat bizarre selection in 2007, having never coached in the NFL before, but he's regarded highly enough that he was interviewed for the Broncos head coaching gig. He has overseen a consistently above-average offense that is efficient passing the ball and dominant at times running the ball. Koetter has gotten the most out of David Garrard and will now be tasked with transitioning Blaine Gabbert away from the spread.

Kansas City Chiefs

2010 Record: 10-6

Pythagorean Wins: 9.1 (12th)

DVOA: -0.1% (17th)

Offense: 7.8% (13th)

Defense: 6.1% (21st)

Special Teams: -1.8% (24th)

Variance: 22.5% (24th)

2011 Mean Projection: 6.3 wins

On the Clock (0-3): 21%

Loserville (4-6): 34%

Mediocrity (7-8): 21%

Playoff Contender (9-10): 13%

Super Bowl Contender (11+): 11%

Projected Average Opponent: 5.5% (1st)

2010: Charlie Weis + easy schedule = penthouse.

2011: Todd Haley + hard schedule = outhouse.

Overall, 2010 ended up being a pretty accurate year for *Football Outsiders Almanac*, but if we were to single out one team for which we could pat ourselves on the back, and say, "Nailed it," that team was the Kansas City Chiefs. Based on a variety of factors, we surmised that the Chiefs would come out of nowhere to win the AFC West after finishing 4-12 in 2009. Some of these same factors are also reasons for why we have them finishing back out of the playoffs this year, so it's useful to review them.

The first factor was strength of schedule. Because we use current-year DVOA projections rather than previous-year win totals, we're able to obtain a more accurate estimate of each team's schedule strength than what you see in other media. Case in point: We projected Kansas City to face the easiest schedule in 2010, and they ended up facing the fifth-easiest. Playing 10 games against two of the worst divisions in the NFL, along with a home game against the Bills and a road game against the pre-Colt McCoy Browns, helped the Chiefs' cause considerably in 2010.

The opposite is likely to be true this season, however, as this year's projections suggest Kansas City can expect to face the league's toughest schedule. Gone are the 49ers and Cardinals of the world, having been replaced by the Packers and Bears. Goodbye Bills and Browns, hello Patriots and Steelers. Worst of all, they play these four juggernauts in a brutal five-game stretch between Week 11 and Week 15, with the fifth team being the New York Jets. Needless to say, those aren't the kinds of opponents conducive to a successful playoff run.

The second factor we mentioned that would likely propel Kansas City to the playoffs was an elite running game. After having the highest DYAR of any running back during the second half of 2009, we predicted big things for Jamaal Charles heading into 2010. He didn't disappoint, once again leading the DYAR rankings, except this time for the entire season. Statistically speaking, then, Charles has literally been the most valuable running back in the league for a year and a half.

What's more, however, is that Charles' 6.38 yards per carry last season was the best single-year mark — by nearly a quarter-yard — from any qualifying running back (i.e., 100 or more carries) since the passing game expanded in the late 1970s. If we limit the minimum to 200 carries, Charles is only the second back

2011 Chiefs Schedule

Week	Opp.	Week	Opp.	Week	Opp.
1	BUF	7	at OAK	13	at CHI
2	at DET	8	SD (Mon.)	14	at NYJ
3	at SD	9	MIA	15	GB
4	MIN	10	DEN	16	OAK
5	at IND	11	at NE (Mon.)	17	at DEN
6	BYE	12	PIT		

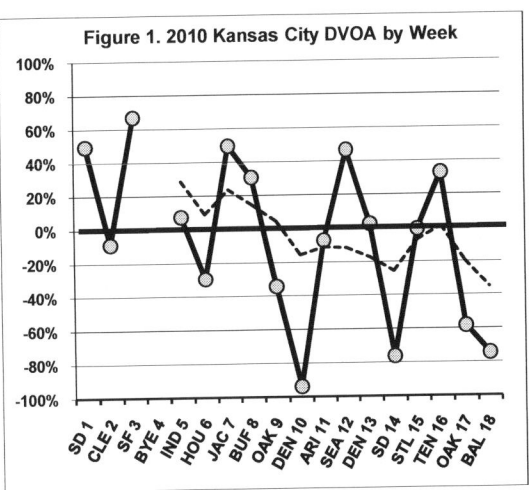

Figure 1. 2010 Kansas City DVOA by Week

since 1978 to surpass 5.7 yards per carry. (Table 1)

Obviously, judging from that group of names, Charles has been breathing some rarified air so far in his career. So then why should things be any different in 2011? The short answer is, well, just look at that list. Even Barry Sanders only broke the 6.0 barrier once in his Hall of Fame career, and only one running back has topped 5.5 yards per carry in two straight seasons. Basically, the likelihood of Charles repeating the feat is something like zero percent.

A longer answer has to do with the internecine battle that ended with former offensive coordinator Charlie Weis choosing a career demotion over spending another minute in the same room as Todd Haley's ego. Here are the facts. In 2009, Haley, then serving as his own offensive coordinator, looked at an offensive roster with one good receiver (Dwayne Bowe), a superstar running back in the making (Charles), and a quarterback (Matt Cassel) whose lone season as a starter was under passing magician Josh McDaniels. From this, he concluded that the best course of action would be to start an already-washed-up Larry Johnson at running back, and build an offense in the mold

Table 1. Best Yards per Carry Averages, 1978-2010 (min. 200 carries)

Player	Team	Year	Carries	Yards	YPC	YPC Next Year
Jamaal Charles	KC	2010	230	1,467	6.38	—
Barry Sanders	DET	1997	335	2,053	6.13	4.35
Barry Sanders	DET	1994	331	1,883	5.69	4.78
Adrian Peterson	MIN	2007	238	1,341	5.63	4.85
James Brooks	CIN	1989	221	1,239	5.61	5.15
Chris Johnson	TEN	2009	358	2,006	5.60	4.32
Eric Dickerson	LARM	1984	379	2,105	5.55	4.23
DeAngelo Williams	CAR	2008	273	1,515	5.55	5.17
Clinton Portis	DEN	2002	273	1,508	5.52	5.49
Clinton Portis	DEN	2003	290	1,591	5.49	3.83

of the 2008 Cardinals. The team frequently lined up in four-wide-receiver sets (10th-most in the league), passed the ball on more than 60 percent of all plays, and ended up with the 25th-ranked offensive DVOA in 2009.

Enter Weis in 2010. With Haley handing over control of the offense (for the most part, at least), gone were the days of fitting square pegs into round holes. Instead, the Chiefs offensive tendencies better reflected what some would call "logic." Last season, with Charles now getting the bulk of the carries, they were the only team in the NFL to run on at least half of their plays. They lined up in two-tight-end formations almost 40 percent of the time (third), they ran out of a three-wide set more than any other team, and they used a ninth-ranked running game to set up the pass (sixth in play-action frequency). When all was said and done last season, the Chiefs finished with the league's third-largest improvement in offensive DVOA (22.0 percentage points better than in 2009).

Mysteriously, Haley assessed this situation as unacceptable, decided to force Weis out, and — just for kicks, we presume — stripped him of his play-calling duties in the Chiefs' blowout playoff loss. Is that performance a harbinger of things to come? Will Kansas City's offense revert back to its illogical, inefficient 2009 form? We think it's pretty likely, especially after the team signed a Cardinals wide receiver in free agency (Steve Breaston), and used their first-round pick to select a wide receiver (Pittsburgh's Jonathan Baldwin). Not to mention that Haley's search for a figurehead offensive coordinator resulted in a promotion from within: Bill Muir, who's been the team's offensive line coach since 2009, and has never called offensive plays in his 33-year NFL coaching career.

The third factor we cited pointing to a likely Kansas City playoff berth last season was its perennial standing among the league's healthiest teams. 2010 was no different. According to our Adjusted Games Lost (AGL) metric, the Chiefs ended up being the team least affected by injury last season, with only 11 games missed by their 22 starters combined. Obviously, a lot more goes into team health than the identity of the head athletic trainer, but it should be noted that Kansas City's David Price has the second-best AGL track record among the current 32 head trainers. In his five years filling that role, Kansas City has ranked in the top 10 of AGL four times.

Nevertheless, even if we were to interpret these stats as some kind of team-wide injury-avoidance skill — which we can't as yet — it's still unlikely from a statistical perspective that they'll repeat as AGL champions in 2011. In other words, it's possible — maybe even probable — that they enjoy another season of above-average health, but even above-average health is not as advantageous as best-in-the-league health. Therefore, the likelihood of an increased injury impact is another reason for our pessimism about Kansas City this season.

Protagonist number four in the story of the Chiefs' 2010 season was general manager Scott Pioli, who successfully improved the roster at its weakest spots: center and strong safety. The team brought in Casey Wiegmann to replace Rudy Niswanger, and that move — along with the signing of right guard Ryan Lilja — ended up solidifying the interior of Kansas City's offensive line. Better still, the Chiefs transformed the unit into one of the best in the NFL according to a variety of stats. They improved from 30th to fifth in overall Adjusted Line Yards, from 30th to 13th in ALY on up-the-middle runs, and from 22nd to fifth in preventing ball carriers from being stopped for zero or negative yardage.

Heading into 2011, however, the offensive line once again becomes a bit of a concern. Offensive line continuity is something we look at as part of the science behind our team projections, and the Chiefs appear to be have four of their five starters returning this year. Unfortunately, the one change involved releasing one of the better linemen, two-time All Pro left guard Brian Waters. He's not the player he once was, but he was still an anchor on the line. In addition, with the aforementioned return of Haley's square-peg offense, added pressure will be placed on the tackles, which

are the weakest spots along the line. At press time, the projected starters are Branden Albert on the left side, and Barry Richardson on the right. The pair was poor in pass protection last season, allowing a total of 13 sacks to opposing rushers.

At strong safety, the Chiefs made the unusual choice of drafting one near the top of the first round, but that player, Eric Berry, ended up making the Pro Bowl — for whatever that's worth nowadays. There's no denying Berry's talent, which was on display for a national audience during last year's playoff loss. (He definitely outperformed his head coach on that day.) However, his rookie season was a perfect example of why we need better performance measures for defensive players. Do we believe his awesome standard stats (92 tackles and four interceptions), his mediocre-at-best advanced stats (38th amongst qualifying safeties in adjusted yards per pass, 69th in Adjusted Success Rate against the pass), or ignore both and go with what our eyes see?

It's a problem we're not going to solve here, but our sneaking suspicion is that the Chiefs' secondary benefits more than most from the quarterback pressure created by outside linebacker Tamba Hali, who led the team with 14.5 sacks. Joining Hali this season will be 2011 third-round pick Justin Houston, who our SackSEER system projected as the second-best pass-rushing prospect available.

Sticking with the defense for a moment, Pioli worked on improving another weakness this offseason: stopping the run, where the unit ranked 26th in DVOA last season. With a defensive ALY on up-the-middle runs that ranked 27th, much of the overall inefficiency in run defense could be attributed to nose tackle Ron Edwards, who we also identified last year as the line's weakest link after a dead-last ALY ranking for Kansas City in 2009. This offseason, Pioli allowed Edwards to leave in free agency and signed former Ravens nose tackle Kelly Gregg to replace him. Gregg might be old, but he's still able to do the one thing a coach asks from a 3-4 nose tackle: Occupy blockers. Last season, Baltimore ranked seventh in defensive ALY on up-the-middle runs, which suggests a potential improvement over Edwards.

Putting all the puzzle pieces together, we anticipate a down year for Kansas City based on (a) having a much tougher schedule, (b) trying once again to shoehorn prolific running talent into an ill-fitting passing offense, (c) the unlikelihood of another year atop our AGL rankings, and (d) the likely improvement of the San Diego Chargers. (You can read about that in San

Diego's chapter.) With that said, however, we do have one caveat, which we'll of course bring up in *Football Outsiders Almanac 2012* if this year's projection turns out to be as inaccurate as a Brodie Croyle pass.

When we crunch the numbers and run our 10,000 season simulations, the Football Outsiders supercomputer spits out two basic types of results. One is each team's mean projection, which we present at the beginning of each chapter. The other thing we get from the supercomputer is the standard deviation associated with each team's mean projection. We also present this at the beginning of the chapter, albeit translated into the form of a probability associated with a given range of win totals.

This year, Kansas City ended up with the largest standard deviation of the 32 projections (Table 2), meaning that our model is more uncertain about the fate of the 2011 Chiefs than it is about any other team. What's more, three of the top eight standard deviations belong to AFC West teams, in large part because of their difficult out-of-division schedules. I suppose

Table 2. Standard Deviation in FOA 2011 Win Projections

Highest		Lowest	
Team	StDev	Team	StDev
KC	3.76	SF	1.85
OAK	3.62	PIT	1.87
MIA	3.42	CLE	1.87
NYJ	3.38	MIN	1.94
NE	3.18	ARI	1.98
TEN	3.06	GB	2.04
BUF	3.06	NO	2.10
DEN	3.03	CAR	2.20
JAC	2.92	ATL	2.22
NYG	2.81	DET	2.22

that could be some consolation to Chiefs fans, if only we weren't projecting San Diego to win the AFC West by five games.

Danny Tuccitto

2010 Chiefs Stats by Week

Wk	vs.	W-L	PF	PA	YDF	YDA	TO	Total	Off	Def	ST
1	SD	W	21	14	197	389	1	49%	10%	-14%	25%
2	@CLE	W	16	14	312	299	0	-9%	-18%	-14%	-5%
3	SF	W	31	10	457	251	0	67%	43%	-23%	0%
4	BYE										
5	@IND	L	9	19	261	341	0	7%	-9%	-11%	5%
6	@HOU	L	31	35	417	421	0	-30%	27%	53%	-4%
7	JAC	W	42	20	426	300	3	49%	43%	-9%	-3%
8	BUF	W	13	10	414	328	1	31%	22%	-15%	-6%
9	@OAK	L	20	23	304	321	1	-34%	-19%	-9%	-25%
10	@DEN	L	29	49	484	452	-1	-94%	-23%	63%	-8%
11	ARI	W	31	13	352	382	0	-7%	34%	50%	10%
12	@SEA	W	42	24	503	288	2	47%	61%	-11%	-25%
13	DEN	W	10	6	359	247	0	3%	-11%	-9%	5%
14	@SD	L	0	31	67	426	2	-76%	-43%	29%	-4%
15	@STL	W	27	13	383	224	1	-1%	1%	3%	2%
16	TEN	W	34	14	458	270	0	33%	21%	-12%	-1%
17	OAK	L	10	31	201	344	-1	-58%	-43%	19%	3%
18	BAL	L	7	30	161	390	-3	74%	-61%	13%	-1%

Trends and Splits

	Offense	Rank	Defense	Rank
Total DVOA	7.8%	13	6.1%	21
Unadjusted VOA	12.5%	8	3.4%	19
Weighted Trend	6.6%	16	14.1%	28
Variance	9.9%	23	7.9%	24
Average Opponent	7.5%	2	0.8%	8
Passing	21.6%	15	8.8%	18
Rushing	5.5%	9	2.5%	26
First Down	13.8%	8	3.7%	16
Second Down	3.1%	14	3.3%	16
Third Down	3.9%	16	14.9%	23
First Half	9.1%	14	1.9%	18
Second Half	6.3%	13	10.2%	25
Red Zone	5.3%	12	39.3%	31
Late and Close	9.3%	8	-0.5%	19

Five-Year Performance

Year	W-L	Pyth	Est W	PF	PA	TO	Total	Rk	Off	Rk	Def	Rk	ST	Rk	Off AGL	Rk	Def AGL	Rk
2006	9-7	8.5	8.4	331	315	+4	6.1%	13	7.3%	11	2.3%	16	1.2%	13	21.5	21	3.6	1
2007	4-12	4.5	5.1	226	335	-11	-18.9%	25	-18.2%	29	-2.5%	13	-3.3%	24	22.8	19	4.2	1
2008	2-14	4.4	4.5	291	440	+5	-27.8%	30	-4.6%	22	17.5%	28	-5.7%	30	30.4	20	16.9	13
2009	4-12	4.7	4.6	294	424	+1	-27.6%	28	-14.2%	25	11.9%	26	-1.5%	26	13.0	9	15.3	6
2010	10-6	9.1	8.0	366	326	+9	-0.1%	17	7.8%	13	6.1%	21	-1.8%	24	5.8	2	4.2	1

Strategic Tendencies

Run/Pass		Rank	Offense		Rank	Defense		Rank	Other		Rank
Runs, all plays	50%	1	3+ WR	38%	30	Rush 3	17.2%	5	2+ RB, Pct Runs	64%	6
Runs, first half	47%	3	4+ WR	4%	22	Rush 4	55.7%	24	1 RB/2 TE, Pct Runs	56%	8
Runs, first down	58%	2	2+ TE	38%	3	Rush 5	21.7%	21	1 RB/3+ WR, Pct Runs	34%	1
Runs, second-long	48%	1	Single back	59%	17	Rush 6+	5.4%	25	CB1 on WR1	22%	32
Runs, power sit.	55%	20	Play action	22%	6	Zone Blitz	2.7%	27	Go for it on 4th	1.52	2
Runs, behind 2H	35%	2	Max protect	17%	5	Sacks by LB	52.6%	12	Offensive Pace	30.6	16
Pass, ahead 2H	37%	28	Outside pocket	13%	14	Sacks by DB	11.8%	12	Defensive Pace	30.7	15

The Chiefs ran more than any other NFL team on second-and-long, but were surprisingly mediocre in that situation. Once again, it had to do with splitting the running back role between Jamaal Charles and Thomas Jones. Charles had 50 carries on second-and-long for 33.5% DVOA and 6.5 yards per carry. Jones had 43 carries on second-and-long, almost as many, but -31.5% DVOA and 3.5 yards per carry. ☜ K.C. led the league by running on 24 percent of plays with three or more wide receivers in the formation. ☜ Chiefs opponents ran up the middle or behind guards on a league-high 63 percent of runs. ☜ The Chiefs had trouble stopping short passes, ranking 29th (37.1% DVOA) against passes at or behind the line of scrimmage. ☜ The Chiefs were only called offside on defense twice, with no Encroachment or Neutral Zone Infraction penalties.

Passing

Player	DYAR	DVOA	Plays	NtYds	Avg	YAC	C%	TD	Int
M.Cassel	795	15.2%	476	2958	6.2	5.7	59.3%	27	7
B.Croyle	-127	-117.9%	23	9	0.4	1.8	42.1%	0	1
T.Palko	-6	-21.3%	8	25	3.1	3.3	66.7%	0	0

Rushing

Player	DYAR	DVOA	Plays	Yds	Avg	TD	Fum	Suc
T.Jones	-94	-17.5%	246	903	3.7	6	3	43%
J.Charles	389	33.9%	231	1466	6.3	5	3	56%
M.Cassel	0	-12.0%	23	134	5.8	0	0	-
J.Battle	5	-4.1%	20	50	2.5	1	0	45%
D.McCluster	-6	-45.5%	17	67	3.9	0	1	-
T.Castille	-19	-82.9%	5	3	0.6	0	0	20%

Receiving

Player	DYAR	DVOA	Plays	Ctch	Yds	Y/C	YAC	TD	C%
D.Bowe	255	11.9%	133	72	1162	16.1	5.1	15	54%
C.Chambers	-30	-21.4%	43	22	213	9.7	1.7	1	51%
D.McCluster	-21	-19.7%	39	21	209	10.0	7.9	1	54%
T.Copper	-16	-19.7%	28	18	157	8.7	3.4	0	64%
V.Tucker	-21	-27.6%	19	6	114	19.0	3.7	1	32%
T.Moeaki	98	13.9%	72	47	557	11.9	4.0	3	65%
L.Pope	-20	-21.4%	19	10	76	7.6	3.4	2	53%
J.Charles	150	31.3%	64	45	471	10.5	9.3	3	70%
T.Jones	29	13.1%	20	14	122	8.7	8.2	0	70%
T.Castille	-15	-33.1%	12	10	43	4.3	4.9	0	83%

Offensive Line

Year	Yards	ALY	Rank	Power	Rank	Stuff	Rank	2nd Lev	Rank	Open Field	Rank
2008	4.46	3.73	28	58%	28	22%	29	1.16	11	1.09	4
2009	4.39	3.63	30	63%	18	21%	20	1.26	9	1.00	7
2010	4.82	4.44	5	57%	20	15%	5	1.35	3	1.00	8

Year	LE	Rank	LT	Rank	Mid	Rank	RT	Rank	RE	Rank	Sacks	ASR	Rank	F-Start	Cont.
2008	4.23	16	4.29	13	3.55	30	3.18	31	4.17	14	37	7.0%	21	13	29
2009	4.30	16	5.66	1	3.33	30	2.14	32	4.24	15	46	7.8%	25	22	27
2010	4.97	5	4.74	6	4.11	13	4.00	20	5.31	3	32	6.8%	18	17	32

The 2010 Chiefs led the league in rushing according to traditional metrics; they also ranked highly in most of our numbers. Pass-blocking was a strength as well — the Chiefs dropped from 26 blown blocks leading to sacks in 2009 to just 14 last season. Kansas City's line developed a lethal chemistry with Jamaal Charles last season — the line would run zone slide concepts in perfect sync, and Charles would use his ridiculous speed to find a gap, hit the seam and get upfield in a major hurry. That's why, as much as Charles' own numbers were somewhere in the stratosphere, the Chiefs' line wasn't just along for the ride. That said, there are issues all along the line that may not be easy to fix.

Left tackle Branden Albert improved to a degree in 2010, but he's still not far enough past the disappointing player Todd Haley was talking about moving to right tackle or guard before the season. He started last season strong before going though elbow, knee, and groin injuries, and Haley hasn't exactly been effusive with praise. In April, just before a draft in which the Chiefs didn't take a single player at his position, Haley told the press that Albert would continue to be the starter at left tackle "as long as he was the best one." It's doubtful that Joe Thomas, Ryan Clady, and Jake Long have to deal with such uncertainty.

Barry Richardson didn't get anyone killed in brief replacement jags for Albert on the left side, but he was best-known for the tantrum he threw following his benching in a December game against the Broncos. Playing right tackle, Richardson lost it when the coaches pulled him from the field. Haley was unperturbed by the outburst, telling the media after that fact that "at least we have a lot of guys who really care." Like Albert, Richardson can best be described as an athletic project — he has the basics of run and pass protection down, but defenders will slide off and get by him too easily. As is the case with many zone-heavy lines, the scheme covers a multitude of individual sins.

Brian Waters and Casey Weigmann have been the stalwarts at left guard and center, respectively, but two youngsters are looking to take their places. Waters made his fifth Pro Bowl, but Haley also intimated that his run-blocking was a concern at times. The Chiefs' coaching staff is reportedly very high on 2010 third-round pick Jon Asamoah, and he'll get his shot after the Chiefs released Waters in late July. In the second round this year, Kansas City took Florida State guard Rodney Hudson, who dominated at his collegiate position at the Senior Bowl, but may have a frame better suited to center.

Defensive Front Seven

Defensive Line	Age	Pos	Plays	TmPct	Rk	Stop	Dfts	BTkl	St%	Rk	AvYd	Rk	Pass Rush Sack	Hit	Hur	vs. Run Runs	St%	Yds	vs. Pass Pass	St%	Yds
Glenn Dorsey	26	DE	68	8.6%	5	55	12	2	81%	30	2.6	65	2.5	5	8	59	81%	2.7	9	78%	1.7
Shaun Smith	30	DE	54	6.8%	20	42	5	1	76%	45	2.5	63	1	1	0.5	51	76%	2.6	3	100%	0.7
Tyson Jackson	25	DE	31	5.2%	40	21	2	0	71%	71	2.9	70	1	1	1	28	71%	2.7	3	33%	5.0
Ron Edwards	32	DT	27	3.4%	55	20	3	0	70%	42	1.5	24	2	1	0.5	23	70%	2.3	4	100%	-3.0
Wallace Gilberry	27	DE	23	2.9%	--	20	16	1	91%	--	-0.3	--	7	7	10.5	11	91%	1.8	12	83%	-2.2

Linebackers	Age	Pos	Plays	TmPct	Rk	Stop	Dfts	BTkl	AvYd	Pass Rush Sack	Hit	Hur	vs. Run Runs	St%	Rk	Yds	Rk	vs. Pass Tgts	Suc%	Rk	AdjYd	Rk
Derrick Johnson	29	ILB	136	17.1%	8	73	24	8	5.0	1	0	3	72	58%	88	3.6	71	44	56%	33	4.9	14
Jovan Belcher	24	ILB	82	10.3%	56	41	7	5	5.1	1	1	6	64	53%	100	4.6	103	18	41%	70	7.4	64
Tamba Hali	28	OLB	54	6.8%	91	42	22	2	0.6	14.5	12	36.5	27	78%	15	2.6	28	2	76%	--	4.3	--
Mike Vrabel	36	OLB	49	6.2%	101	28	3	5	5.2	0	6	6.5	26	69%	51	3.0	53	19	46%	64	6.9	58
Andy Studebaker	26	OLB	16	2.0%	--	10	5	2	3.7	2.5	2	3	7	57%	--	5.3	--	5	101%	--	3.0	--

Year	Yards	ALY	Rank	Power	Rank	Stuff	Rank	2nd Lev	Rank	Open Field	Rank
2008	5.16	4.46	26	81%	32	14%	31	1.26	26	1.35	30
2009	4.93	4.70	32	64%	17	13%	32	1.21	21	1.08	26
2010	4.34	4.29	25	66%	22	14%	28	1.12	17	0.67	12

Year	LE	Rank	LT	Rank	Mid	Rank	RT	Rank	RE	Rank	Sacks	ASR	Rank
2008	5.05	29	4.26	17	4.37	21	4.86	29	3.94	16	10	2.9%	32
2009	5.42	32	5.24	31	4.63	28	4.27	19	4.13	19	22	3.5%	32
2010	4.60	22	4.09	17	4.42	27	4.42	20	2.82	2	39	6.5%	12

Tamba Hali played through the 2010 season with tears in both shoulders and a muscle pull in one foot. Somehow, he also managed to top most of his single-season stats from previous years in one of the great recent pass-rushing seasons. Hali had one season before 2010 in which he enjoyed the benefits of another sack artist on the other side of the line — his rookie campaign of 2007, when he teamed with Jared Allen for 23 total sacks. In 2008 and 2009, he became known as one of the NFL's primary "heroes without help" — those unfortunate players whose quarterback takedowns and hurries tower over those of their teammates. But last year, things turned around, to a point; Hali and end Wallace Gilberry combined for 21.5 sacks (Gilberry got three of those sacks in one game against the Rams in Week 15), and all of a sudden, Hali wasn't the only one harassing the quarterback anymore. The Chiefs gave Hali the franchise tag, but that was just a precursor to a well-deserved five-year, $60 million deal with more than $30 million guaranteed. Gilberry, primarily a nickel rotation player, signed a second-round tender. Second-round pick Justin Houston from Georgia should be a great fit for Kansas City's hybrid fronts — he's played entire collegiate seasons as both a 4-3 end and 3-4 pass-rushing linebacker. Andy Studebaker will likely be the interim option opposite Hali until Houston gets up to speed. Derrick Johnson finally pushed through early disappointments to become the player the team wanted him to be from a tackling perspective. Now, if he could just catch the ball; Johnson tied for the league lead with five interceptions, although it could be a one-year fluke (he had zero in 2009). The undrafted Jovan Belcher moved up from special teams to starter last year, And he'll compete with ex-Chargers free agent Brandon Siler for the inside job next to Johnson.

Elsewhere in that front seven, you'll find two linemen still looking to justify very high draft picks in recent years. Tyson Jackson (third overall in 2009) hurt his knee in the 2010 season opener, missed four games, and had so little playing time upon his return that he didn't rack up his first NFL sack until his 25th game. Veteran Shaun Smith was the stalwart at the left defensive end position instead, but he signed with Tennessee after the lockout. Glenn Dorsey (fifth overall in 2008) did show improvement last season. Dorsey beat more blocks at the right end position (often, obviously, against blockers worried about Hali's pressure efforts on that same side) and proved more agile in short spaces against the run than many may have thought. The Chiefs will need an upgrade at nose tackle; Ron Edwards was serviceable, but this defense's primary liability, now that the pass rush issues have been solved, is its performance against the run up the middle.

Defensive Secondary

Secondary	Age	Pos	Plays	TmPct	Rk	Stop	Dfts	BTkl	Runs	St%	Rk	Yds	Rk	Tgts	Tgt%	Rk	Dist	Suc%	Rk	APaYd	Rk	PD	Int
						Overall					vs. Run						vs. Pass					
Eric Berry	23	SS	95	12.0%	19	38	16	10	44	45%	27	5.8	24	41	8.0%	13	12.2	44%	69	7.5	38	5	4
Brandon Carr	25	CB	82	10.3%	24	34	15	6	16	31%	73	8.0	59	105	20.5%	7	16.0	59%	15	7.4	48	24	1
Brandon Flowers	25	CB	79	10.6%	21	32	6	1	21	38%	60	4.7	14	95	19.7%	10	14.3	56%	20	6.2	17	13	2
Javier Arenas	24	CB	47	5.9%	79	14	12	3	3	0%	88	10.0	80	52	10.2%	82	8.1	42%	78	5.3	5	8	0
Jon McGraw	32	FS	44	7.4%	67	21	13	2	18	39%	40	9.0	67	12	3.0%	77	16.7	55%	34	8.1	44	5	2
Kendrick Lewis	23	FS	35	5.9%	73	10	4	8	13	23%	80	11.8	80	20	5.2%	52	19.4	55%	36	8.1	43	6	3
Donald Washington	25	SS	17	2.9%	--	5	2	2	7	43%	--	7.0	--	5	1.2%	--	9.4	44%	--	8.4	--	0	0

Year	Pass D Rank	vs. #1 WR	Rk	vs. #2 WR	Rk	vs. Other WR	Rk	vs. TE	Rk	vs. RB	Rk
2008	28	7.7%	19	-3.3%	12	-53.0%	1	15.7%	23	22.5%	30
2009	19	-18.0%	9	26.3%	30	-17.5%	7	-1.1%	12	5.4%	18
2010	18	-12.4%	7	11.2%	22	-3.3%	16	11.3%	20	16.1%	26

The Chiefs started their secondary makeover with the Dueling Brandons — Carr and Flowers — at cornerback, and finally filled the safety spots in last season. Fifth overall pick Eric Berry was as advertised, bringing every bit of his versatile skill set from Tennessee to the pros. The only Chiefs defender to be on the field for every single play in 2010, Berry also participated in about half of Kansas City's special teams plays, which is something the coaching staff will reconsider in 2011 — toward the end of the season, even the hyper-competitive Berry admitted that he was "just through."

Berry and fellow 2010 rookie Earl Thomas (of the Seahawks) are two of the new generation of safeties tasked with applying cornerback coverage skills with safety tackling talents, and while Thomas has a way to go in the latter department, Berry can do it all, just as he did in college. But while Berry is well-known, the Chiefs also had a rookie safety flying under the radar: fifth-round pick Kendrick Lewis. The Mississippi free safety got a few injuries out of the way early on, and then filled in as the final fourth in what is now one of the best young defensive backfields in the NFL.

Carr and Flowers were the known commodities, and Flowers is still the star. He can cover as much ground as any cornerback in the league, but what makes him a truly well-rounded player is his ability to come up and stop the run with ridiculous closing speed from off-coverage. Carr doesn't make as many splash plays, but he's generally more consistent. More than anything else during the Haley/Pioli regime, the development of this secondary is the primary indicator that things are on the right track.

Special Teams

Year	DVOA	Rank	FG/XP	Rank	Net Kick	Rank	Kick Ret	Rank	Net Punt	Rank	Punt Ret	Rank	Hidden	Rank
2008	-5.7%	30	-8.4	30	-15.9	32	-6.8	25	0.7	19	-3.4	25	-15.7	31
2009	-1.5%	26	3.9	9	-3.9	25	-7.1	26	4.8	10	-6.7	27	3.9	7
2010	-1.8%	24	-2.8	28	-2.3	21	-9.1	27	-1.5	23	5.3	6	-1.3	15

Punter Dustin Colquitt is the more effective of the Fightin' Colquitts, beating out brother Britton of the Broncos, but the concern should be that his net value in 2010 (-1.1 points) was a major comedown from 2009's net value of +9.6 points. Colquitt's punts inside the opposing 20-yard line dropped from 41 in 2009 to 33 last year, and his number of downed punts plummeted from 22 to six. Kicker Ryan Succop transcended a 66 percent field goal rate in his senior season and "Mister Irrelevant" status to win the kicker's job. He connected on 76 percent of his attempts in his first NFL season, with the misses coming outside of 40 yards for the most part. Kickoffs were slightly below average. The return duo of Javier Arenas and Dexter McCluster wasn't as effective as desired; Jamaal Charles was the only Chiefs player with a positive net value on punt or kick returns, and as the team looks to be finally giving Charles the carries he deserves, someone's going to have to make it work in his absence.

Coaching Staff

Kansas City's head coach may look like an extra in *Talladega Nights*, and his sideline demeanor wouldn't give it away, but Todd Haley is a traditionalist with deep roots in the Bill Parcells camp. Haley's father Dick ran personnel for Parcells during his swing with the Jets, and Haley himself served on the Tuna's staff in Dallas. The Cardinals offensive coordinator you saw calling all those pseudo-spread sets in Arizona's Super Bowl year was adjusting to personnel; the real Haley is the one who will stick to his guns (even to his own detriment) and sit Jamaal Charles in key situations because Charles hasn't displayed enough traditional versatility in his mind. That headstrong nature may be Haley's Achilles' heel.

Haley prizes versatility, and doesn't mind using square pegs from a personnel standpoint, but his ideal offense would have more smashmouth that you might expect. He is also the team's de facto offensive coordinator, with Maurice Carthon helping out with the run game and Jim Zorn now on board to work with Matt Cassel. Carthon also worked with Haley in Arizona and Dallas.

Defensive coordinator Romeo Crennel did an excellent job of bringing the Patriots' defensive principles to Kansas City. Few teams ran their hybrid and nickel fronts more effectively. But the star among the assistants has to be offensive line coach Bill Muir, who got an inconsistent group rolling (literally and figuratively) in the same direction to great effect. The 33-year coaching veteran has guided offensive lines with seven different NFL teams, and has roots going back to the World Football League. He was named offensive coordinator when Charlie Weis took his talents to North Florida, but he'll work in concert with Haley more than anything. It's a similar relationship to the one Muir had with Jon Gruden in Tampa Bay.

Miami Dolphins

2010 Record: 7-9	**2011 Mean Projection:** 8.3 wins
Pythagorean Wins: 6.2 (23rd)	**On the Clock (0-3):** 5%
DVOA: 3.4% (14th)	**Loserville (4-6):** 23%
Offense: 4.7% (18th)	**Mediocrity (7-8):** 23%
Defense: -1.9% (10th)	**Playoff Contender (9-10):** 24%
Special Teams: -3.1% (29th)	**Super Bowl Contender (11+):** 24%
Variance: 13.6% (11th)	**Projected Average Opponent:** 5.5% (2nd)

2010: Seven home losses in eight tries leaves owner, fans pining for a retro Miami experience.

2011: Sparano and Ireland get one last chance; Crockett and Tubbs on deck.

When Stephen Ross bought the Miami Dolphins in 2009, things were sober, serious, and professional over at 347 Don Shula Drive. Bill Parcells was the head of football operations, and the new owner was appropriately deferential, insisting that he would be a hands-off guy who left the football people to run the show. That meant that Parcells proteges Jeff Ireland and Tony Sparano would be free to continue running the personnel department and coaching the team as they saw fit, a recipe which had just delivered the Dolphins their first division title since 2001. Two seasons later, a few things have changed around South Florida. Parcells is gone, and the Dolphins are coming off consecutive disappointing 7-9 seasons. Dolphin Stadium is called Sun Life Stadium. The team now boasts a slew of celebrity minority owners, including Gloria Estefan, Marc Anthony, Jennifer Lopez, Fergie of the Black Eyed Peas, and the Williams sisters, Venus and Serena. And Stephen Ross has gone rogue.

Ross kicked off the offseason by conducting an energetic and high-profile coaching search, with the catch being that there was no head coaching vacancy. Instead, Tony Sparano was left to twist with one year left on his contract as Ross chased after flashy names, first former Super Bowl winners Jon Gruden and Bill Cowher and then Stanford coach and rising star Jim Harbaugh. Ross flew out to the West Coast to meet with Harbaugh, a media conference was scheduled in Miami, and rumors flew that the Dolphins were prepared to offer a contract averaging between $7 million and $8 million per year. Instead, Harbaugh accepted the open position in San Francisco, and on the same day that the 49ers were introducing their new coach to the local media, Ross and Jeff Ireland were down in Miami announcing that Sparano would receive a two-year extension after all.

Ross placed the blame for any embarrassment caused by his phantom coaching search on his inexperience with the hiring process, a dubious defense for a multimillionaire CEO. Any self-reflection Ross might have had about the wisdom of butting in on the football operations side of the business didn't last long, however. After his attempt to lure in Harbaugh collapsed, Ross took to the airwaves to promote his new vision for a new and improved team, one that would keep the home crowd happy. "I've told Tony that, to me, I want an aggressive, creative (offense), not playing just to keep it close," Ross said in an interview on WINZ 940 AM. "A little bit more unpredictable, and opening it up. That's what I think South Florida wants, and that's what this climate demands. We have the weather in August, September and October. Our players are training in that weather; let's take advantage of it. Let's go with a hurry-up offense, let's wear them down. We've never done that. This isn't the

2011 Dolphins Schedule

Week	Opp.	Week	Opp.	Week	Opp.
1	NE (Mon.)	7	DEN	13	OAK
2	HOU	8	at NYG	14	PHI
3	at CLE	9	at KC	15	at BUF
4	at SD	10	WAS	16	at NE
5	BYE	11	BUF	17	NYJ
6	at NYJ (Mon.)	12	at DAL (Thu.)		

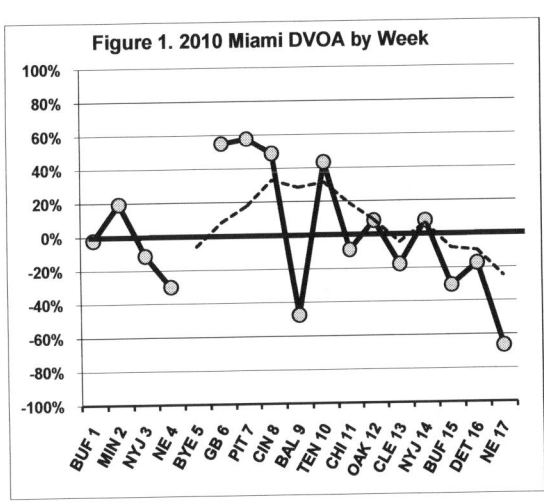

Figure 1. 2010 Miami DVOA by Week

North, where you want to just take it four yards and a cloud of dust. I think I look for a different brand. Seeing the Dolphins, how fans want to see them, how we win, we're going downfield, the days of Dan Marino, the days we all want to go back to."

So Ross isn't familiar with the Larry Csonka/Mercury Morris/Jim Kiick years. But he is all too familiar with what happened last year, when the Dolphins managed only a single win at home and lost to perennial dregs like Detroit, Buffalo, and Cleveland. No owner likes to see his fan base unhappy, and Ross was treated to a fourth-quarter exodus of downtrodden fans in aqua and orange past his owner's box with depressing regularity. But rather than clean house and begin another painful rebuilding process, Ross is demanding a miracle makeover. That means that the pressure is on Ireland and Sparano to construct a team that is not only better in the win/loss column, but that wins with style. It's a daunting task.

The word that best describes the 2010 Miami offense is "plodding." With the Wildcat no longer confounding defenses, Ronnie Brown and Ricky Williams were unable to find much daylight, and neither showed the speed or explosiveness to turn a routine play into a big gain. The Dolphins were dead last in the league in Open Field Yards and in Second Level Yards, and despite their different usage patterns, Brown and Williams ended up with nearly identical rushing DYAR and DVOA. The need for an upgrade at running back was glaringly obvious, which is why most mock drafts had Miami spending their first-round pick on Heisman Trophy winner Mark Ingram. Instead, Ireland stayed conservative, selecting Florida guard/center prospect Mike Pouncey. Pouncey, whose brother Maurkice made the Pro Bowl as a rookie with Pittsburgh, was the consensus best interior lineman available, but interior linemen are tough to sell to an owner with visions of Marino-to-Clayton.

The Dolphins got their back in the second round, trading up to nab Kansas State's Daniel Thomas. Thomas doesn't have instant name recognition, but he's a big, powerful back with good instincts, he can catch the ball out of the backfield, and he has experience taking direct snaps, which is obviously a plus for any team looking to run the Wildcat. The scouting reports on Thomas suggest that he can excel at picking up yards in chunks when working between the tackles or making cutback runs, but that he lacks the pure explosiveness to get to the edge consistently or to break away from NFL defenders. In fact, Thomas resembles nothing so much as a young Ronnie Brown, which is to say that his skill set fits the old Tony Sparano offense much better than the new and improved version that is supposed to arrive in September.

If there wasn't much flash to Miami's draft, they made up for it when they traded cornerback Jonathon Amaya to New Orleans for Reggie Bush. Bush has the kind of star power that Ross is craving, and there is no question that his presence on the field provides something for defensive coordinators to chew on. Bush is the only back on the roster who can create mismatches in the passing game by simply by splitting out wide or by lining up in the backfield and using pre-snap motion, and he usually has his way with linebackers when he runs option routes against man coverage. Provided Miami is willing to be creative with their personnel groupings and their playcalling, Bush can make a mark ... as a receiver. For his career, Bush has more receiving than rushing yards, and he has posted a positive receiving DVOA three times, something he has only done once as a rusher. Bush does not run well between the tackles, and he seems to have problems seeing the play develop when asked to follow a fullback through the hole. Under Dan Henning, the Dolphins had a lot of power runs off-tackle that they used as staples, and while new offensive coordinator Brian Daboll mixes in a healthy dose of trick plays, he also leans on many of those same power runs. Bush can't run any of them. His best chance to contribute as a true running back is probably in the Wildcat set, where he can quickly get to the perimeter by running jet sweeps and reverses. Bush has no shortage of naysayers — as Pat Yasinskas, ESPN's NFC South blogger noted, the Saints won more games, scored more points and generated more yardage over the last few years when Bush was out of the lineup, and New Orleans seemed perfectly happy to jettison Bush and replace him with Darren Sproles. But the Saints have plenty of offensive weapons, whereas the Dolphins have decidedly few. Bush wanted to get around 15 touches a game with his new team, and considering the dearth of options, Tony Sparano is likely to oblige.

Upgrading the backfield is all well and good, but when Ross was demanding a more aggressive, creative offense, he wasn't talking about swapping out one pair of running backs for another. That brings us to the passing game, which any Miami fan will tell you was dreadful last season ... only it wasn't. Miami's pass DVOA was 20.8%, which was 16th in the league, sandwiched between Kansas City and Detroit. In fact, the Dolphins were moderately better throwing the ball than they had been in 2009, and embattled quarterback Chad Henne saw his yards per pass, his completion percentage and his touchdowns all tick up. Henne's DVOA was virtually unchanged from 2009, and he posted the 17th-best DYAR for the second year in a row.

So why is it that Henne has gone from being a young up-and-comer to a guy who needs to be replaced in the space of a single season, despite playing at essentially the same level? There are several reasons. The first is the fact that the trade for Brandon Marshall was supposed to spark major improvement in the passing game and it didn't. Marshall was targeted 146 times, but he didn't top 100 receptions for the first time since his rookie year, and he only hauled in three touchdowns. Marshall was supposed to lift Miami's red zone offense, but his DVOA inside the 20 was a paltry -23.2%, and he caught only 43 percent of his intended red zone targets. It often seemed like Henne was locking in on Marshall rather

than going through his reads, and he rarely hit his big receiver in stride, limiting Marshall's opportunities to run after the catch. Far from being appreciative, Marshall spent the second half of the season flexing his diva bona fides, getting into frequent jawing matches with Henne on the sidelines, and pointing to backup Tyler Thigpen after Henne threw an interception in Detroit. After the season, Marshall did an interview with Michael Irvin where he openly admitted he preferred playing with Thigpen, saying, "I think Tyler gets it a little more." (In this case, "it" means throwing it to Marshall every time he sees single coverage, regardless of the called play.)

The bigger issue was Henne's propensity for throwing interceptions. Henne threw 19 interceptions, a high number under any circumstances, but particularly when running such a conservative offense. It's not as if Mike Martz was the offensive coordinator and Henne was slinging 18-yard dig routes every time he dropped back; Henne averaged 6.7 yards per attempt, putting him in the bottom quarter of the league. If your quarterback isn't going to push the ball down the field, then the least he can do is avoid turnovers. On the surface it's a fair criticism of Henne, but it doesn't take the role luck can play in these things. As we point out in the introduction to our section on quarterbacks on page 262, Henne had the worst luck imaginable when it came to throwing interceptions last year. He had only one dropped interception, which is to say that he almost never got away with a mistake throw. Henne had an above-average DVOA despite all these picks; remember, DVOA is based on play-by-play, not game charting, so it doesn't know the difference between a "dropped interception" and any other incomplete pass.

All things considered, the best course of action would be to quietly ignore last season, install Henne as the undisputed starter, and let him continue to develop. But quarterback instability is like a genie, and once you open up the bottle, it's hard to close it back up. Henne was benched during the regular season, and the Dolphins spent a fair amount of time in the offseason kicking the tires on potential replacements — first by taking a long, hard look at Arkansas quarterback Ryan Mallett, and then by playing footsie with Denver for the rights to Kyle Orton, who would have come with the Brandon Marshall seal of approval. Instead, the Dolphins ended up settling for Matt Moore, who was last seen losing his job to Jimmy Clausen. There really shouldn't be anything resembling an open competition, but Henne's hold on the starting job might have been weakened to the point where he can't afford a sluggish training camp.

While the owner and the fans might be pining for the days of Dan Marino, the Dolphins probably have a better chance of replicating the days of Jimmy Johnson, as a series of strong drafts and astute free agent acquisitions have improved the talent base significantly. There is excellent depth along the line, a legitimate pass rushing star in Cameron Wake, a do-everything linebacker in Karlos Dansby, and a pair of developing young corners in Vontae Davis and Sean Smith.

There are problem spots at safety, and it would be nice to get some pressure from someone other than Wake, but all in all, there are enough pieces for defensive coordinator Mike Nolan to work with. The question is, can the offense hold up its end of the bargain? If it does, then the Dolphins will remain competitive in the rugged AFC East. If it does not, then it's probable that Stephen Ross will get rid of the Parcells infrastructure and go in search of a high profile coach who will improve the franchise's visibility.

Sean McCormick

2010 Dolphins Stats by Week

Wk	vs.	W-L	PF	PA	YDF	YDA	TO	Total	Off	Def	ST
1	@BUF	W	15	10	296	166	0	-2%	0%	-10%	-12%
2	@MIN	W	14	10	226	364	2	19%	-7%	-21%	6%
3	NYJ	L	23	31	436	402	-1	-11%	43%	44%	-11%
4	NE	L	14	41	400	265	-4	-30%	-4%	-1%	-27%
5	BYE										
6	@GB	W	23	20	381	359	0	55%	24%	-14%	17%
7	PIT	L	22	23	313	348	0	58%	35%	-20%	3%
8	@CIN	W	22	14	354	262	-1	49%	21%	-9%	18%
9	@BAL	L	10	26	289	402	-3	-47%	-14%	30%	-4%
10	TEN	W	29	17	404	259	2	43%	43%	2%	3%
11	CHI	L	0	16	187	268	0	-9%	-13%	-1%	3%
12	@OAK	W	33	17	471	263	2	8%	9%	-9%	-9%
13	CLE	L	10	13	281	252	-3	-18%	-23%	1%	6%
14	@NYJ	W	10	6	131	280	-1	8%	-50%	-49%	9%
15	BUF	L	14	17	326	282	-1	-30%	3%	12%	-21%
16	DET	L	27	34	425	275	-3	-17%	4%	14%	-8%
17	@NE	L	7	38	250	502	-1	-66%	-29%	11%	-27%

Trends and Splits

	Offense	Rank	Defense	Rank
Total DVOA	4.7%	18	-1.9%	10
Unadjusted VOA	2.1%	17	0.2%	12
Weighted Trend	1.2%	19	-3.2%	8
Variance	6.8%	12	4.6%	5
Average Opponent	-1.1%	30	6.4%	22
Passing	20.8%	16	12.1%	23
Rushing	-4.1%	20	-16.6%	4
First Down	7.5%	14	2.1%	10
Second Down	1.5%	15	-8.3%	8
Third Down	4.4%	15	0.9%	17
First Half	3.4%	19	-3.8%	9
Second Half	6.0%	15	-0.1%	13
Red Zone	22.7%	4	-22.9%	4
Late and Close	8.8%	9	-12.3%	7

Five-Year Performance

Year	W-L	Pyth	Est W	PF	PA	TO	Total	Rk	Off	Rk	Def	Rk	ST	Rk	Off AGL	Rk	Def AGL	Rk
2006	6-10	7.2	7.2	260	283	+2	-0.8%	16	-9.4%	26	-9.3%	6	-0.7%	21	39.8	32	8.4	9
2007	1-15	3.8	4.2	267	437	-7	-22.2%	27	-5.3%	21	14.7%	31	-2.2%	22	24.4	22	37.8	29
2008	11-5	8.8	9.3	345	317	+17	8.8%	14	16.6%	7	3.0%	15	-4.8%	29	24.1	16	1.6	1
2009	7-9	7.2	8.7	360	390	-8	4.9%	16	7.5%	16	4.3%	18	1.8%	9	26.9	18	21.2	13
2010	7-9	6.2	8.9	273	333	-12	3.4%	14	4.7%	18	-1.9%	10	-3.1%	29	27.1	19	24.0	15

Strategic Tendencies

Run/Pass		Rank	Offense		Rank	Defense		Rank	Other		Rank
Runs, all plays	39%	18	3+ WR	49%	15	Rush 3	5.5%	20	2+ RB, Pct Runs	51%	27
Runs, first half	41%	15	4+ WR	7%	10	Rush 4	61.9%	11	1 RB/2 TE, Pct Runs	23%	32
Runs, first down	48%	20	2+ TE	23%	23	Rush 5	26.5%	11	1 RB/3+ WR, Pct Runs	20%	24
Runs, second-long	31%	21	Single back	37%	32	Rush 6+	6.1%	24	CB1 on WR1	45%	10
Runs, power sit.	60%	16	Play action	20%	10	Zone Blitz	5.5%	15	Go for it on 4th	0.63	32
Runs, behind 2H	21%	28	Max protect	27%	1	Sacks by LB	62.8%	5	Offensive Pace	30.1	11
Pass, ahead 2H	41%	21	Outside pocket	11%	23	Sacks by DB	10.3%	16	Defensive Pace	30.7	17

Miami's conservative offense included a league-leading 27 percent of plays with fewer than two wide receivers. The Dolphins also ranked fifth in DVOA on such plays. ☞ More conservative offense: Only 22 percent of Miami's running plays came from single-back sets, the lowest figure in the league, and Miami was one of only two teams (along with Chicago) to go shotgun less than 20 percent of the time. ☞ Continuing the theme, the Dolphins offense was also more conservative when it came to the Wildcat. They ran the formation roughly half as often as they did in 2009, and without much success: -8.3% DVOA and only 3.3 yards per play. ☞ Miami led the league in using max protect blocking for the third straight season. ☞ The Miami pass rush was second in the NFL with 10.8 Adjusted Sack Rate on third down, but just 28th with 5.0 percent ASR on first or second down. ☞ Miami's defense was tied for second with 19 passes tipped away or batted down at the line. ☞ Although it wasn't quite as bad as in 2009, Miami was once again poor on yards after catch on both sides of the ball: 4.3 yards (28th) on offense and 5.7 yards (26th) on defense.

Passing

Player	DYAR	DVOA	Plays	NtYds	Avg	YAC	C%	TD	Int
C.Henne	621	7.6%	526	3186	6.1	4.3	61.8%	15	18
T.Thigpen	76	6.5%	71	417	5.9	3.9	53.2%	2	2

Rushing

Player	DYAR	DVOA	Plays	Yds	Avg	TD	Fum	Suc
R.Brown	36	-4.2%	200	735	3.7	5	3	43%
R.Williams	36	-2.8%	159	673	4.2	2	4	53%
L.Polite	34	14.0%	26	62	2.4	1	0	65%
C.Henne	-51	-60.3%	22	73	3.3	0	2	-
T.Thigpen	3	-6.5%	12	66	5.5	0	1	-
P.Cobbs	-15	-108.0%	4	0	0.0	0	0	0%

Receiving

Player	DYAR	DVOA	Plays	Ctch	Yds	Y/C	YAC	TD	C%
B.Marshall	127	-1.8%	146	86	1014	11.8	2.8	3	59%
D.Bess	111	-0.9%	126	80	817	10.2	3.9	5	63%
B.Hartline	113	6.2%	73	43	615	14.3	4.9	1	59%
M.Moore	-13	-22.0%	19	6	128	21.3	12.0	1	32%
R.Wallace	4	-6.3%	10	6	62	10.3	2.7	0	60%
A.Fasano	144	29.1%	60	39	528	13.5	5.1	4	65%
R.Brown	45	5.1%	42	33	242	7.3	6.2	0	79%
R.Williams	10	-7.9%	30	19	141	7.4	5.8	1	63%
P.Cobbs	16	2.2%	19	8	91	11.4	3.4	2	42%
L.Polite	-11	-25.2%	17	12	61	5.1	3.8	0	71%

Offensive Line

Year	Yards	ALY	Rank	Power	Rank	Stuff	Rank	2nd Lev	Rank	Open Field	Rank
2008	4.28	4.16	12	76%	5	16%	9	1.03	25	0.62	25
2009	4.44	4.51	1	79%	2	14%	1	1.00	28	0.63	22
2010	3.78	4.07	16	83%	1	16%	7	0.86	32	0.38	32

Year	LE	Rank	LT	Rank	Mid	Rank	RT	Rank	RE	Rank	Sacks	ASR	Rank	F-Start	Cont.
2008	4.16	18	3.89	21	3.98	23	4.39	8	4.78	3	26	5.7%	12	22	39
2009	4.99	7	3.46	30	4.59	3	4.36	8	4.12	19	34	6.5%	18	18	35
2010	3.46	25	4.53	10	4.01	14	4.14	15	4.61	7	38	6.3%	15	18	24

The offensive line took a lot of heat during the season for its poor play, but at least some of that was unwarranted. The Dolphins had the best blocking in the league in power situations, and they were good at keeping defenders from dropping runners in the backfield. The problem was that there were simply no big plays at all, but how much of that can be attributed to the blocking and how much to the plodding duo of Ronnie Brown and Ricky Williams?

Whatever the problem was, it wasn't Jake Long, who played through injuries on his way to a third straight Pro Bowl selection. Long had surgery in the offseason to repair his separated left shoulder, but it didn't stop him from organizing the team's workouts during the lockout. Long was arguably the best offensive linemen in football in the first half of the season, and he has dispelled the concerns about his athleticism that prompted some draft observers to project him as a right tackle. The Dolphins brought in former Cowboy Marc Colombo to anchor the right side. Colombo was a five-year starter in Dallas who played for Tony Sparano, but he is a declining and increasingly injury-prone player. He's missed eight games the last two years. Ray Willis is a Seattle castoff who couldn't crack one of the five worst lines in football. He'll compete for a reserve role with Lyndon Murtha, who started four games at right tackle last year.

While the tackles are set, the interior line is in flux. The Dolphins were sufficiently scarred from one year of Joe Berger at center, so they used the 15th pick in the draft on Mike Pouncey, who is best known as the younger brother (and former Florida teammate) of Steelers rookie sensation Maurkice Pouncey. Most draft experts considered Maurkice the better prospect, so fans expecting Mike to play up to his brother's standard might be disappointed, but after last season, the team will simply be happy with someone who doesn't get pushed around at the point of attack. Richie Incognito only committed three penalties while starting 14 games at left guard and two at center; more importantly, he had none of the meltdowns or off-the-field episodes that have plagued him throughout his career. Incognito was rewarded with a new contract in March that could keep him in Miami for another three seasons. Vernon Carey is kicking inside to guard to bump out John Jerry. Carey put together a streak of 88 consecutive starts before a knee injury landed him on injured reserve in December, but he came to camp heavy and there are concerns about how he will hold up. Our game charters pegged Carey for an uncharacteristically high number of blown blocks last year, but with the poor performance all along the right side of the line, it's hard to know how much of that was due to larger breakdowns in the blocking scheme. Regardess, he should be an improvement over Jerry, who struggled equally against the run and the pass. Despite standing 6-foot-5 and weighing 328 pounds, Jerry rarely showed much strength, in part because of an undisclosed illness he suffered early in the season, and in part because of some poor work habits.

Defensive Front Seven

Defensive Line	Age	Pos	Plays	TmPct	Overall Rk	Stop	Dfts	BTkl	St%	Rk	AvYd	Rk	Pass Rush Sack	Hit	Hur	vs. Run Runs	St%	Yds	vs. Pass Pass	St%	Yds
Randy Starks	28	DE	32	4.1%	60	29	6	0	92%	2	2.2	47	3	3	13	25	92%	2.6	7	86%	0.6
Kendall Langford	25	DE	50	6.4%	22	37	13	1	71%	55	2.3	57	3	4	9	41	71%	2.7	9	89%	0.4
Paul Soliai	28	DT	41	5.2%	21	36	10	1	86%	9	0.7	9	2	1	4	36	86%	1.1	5	100%	-2.2
Tony McDaniel	26	DE	40	5.4%	35	33	9	2	77%	23	2.4	58	2.5	1	8.5	31	77%	3.0	9	100%	0.1

Linebackers	Age	Pos	Plays	TmPct	Overall Rk	Stop	Dfts	BTkl	AvYd	Pass Rush Sack	Hit	Hur	vs. Run Runs	St%	Rk	Yds	Rk	vs. Pass Tgts	Suc%	Rk	AdjYd	Rk
Channing Crowder	28	ILB	41	7.6%	87	30	2	4	3.2	1	0	3	30	80%	10	3.0	47	11	63%	--	3.5	--
Cameron Wake	29	OLB	61	7.8%	85	48	32	2	0.9	14	15	38	34	76%	17	2.4	20	4	50%	--	9.0	--
Koa Misi	24	OLB	42	5.3%	105	25	12	3	3.8	4.5	5	14	24	63%	78	3.0	46	11	78%	--	3.3	--
Quentin Moses	28	OLB	16	2.2%	--	12	4	0	3.1	1	3	5	13	77%	--	3.6	--	6	49%	--	9.5	--
Karlos Dansby	30	ILB	99	14.4%	23	59	18	6	5.1	3	2	5	59	71%	41	3.8	86	36	53%	44	6.7	52
Tim Dobbins	29	ILB	44	5.6%	--	30	10	4	3.1	1	1	4	31	71%	--	2.6	--	10	28%	--	10.9	--

Year	Yards	ALY	Rank	Power	Rank	Stuff	Rank	2nd Lev	Rank	Open Field	Rank
2008	4.06	4.12	14	69%	21	19%	13	1.22	24	0.49	5
2009	4.12	4.33	24	74%	28	17%	25	1.23	24	0.47	3
2010	3.56	3.76	9	61%	12	23%	4	1.03	5	0.41	2

Year	LE	Rank	LT	Rank	Mid	Rank	RT	Rank	RE	Rank	Sacks	ASR	Rank
2008	3.64	9	3.80	8	4.29	19	4.29	22	3.13	11	40	6.5%	13
2009	3.25	8	4.74	28	4.09	18	5.17	32	4.17	21	44	9.1%	1
2010	3.86	11	3.43	10	3.98	19	3.04	2	4.32	21	39	7.1%	9

Planet Theory alert: Nowhere is Bill Parcells' imprint more visible than on the defensive line, which is brimming with young, big and mobile players. Kendall Langford is 6-foot-6 and 295 pounds, which are prototype numbers for a 3-4 defensive end. Langford only tallied two sacks, but that's not his job; he is there to tie up blockers and let the linebackers clean up. As good as the Hampton product was, our numbers suggest that

Randy Starks was the MVP of the line. Starks was supposed to be the nose tackle, but an early injury to rookie Jared Odrick forced Starks to return to his old right end spot, where he posted the second best Stop Rate in the league. Even so, Starks may be rewarded with a trip to the bench, because Odrick looked like a player in his limited action, and because Paul Soliai locked up the nose tackle spot with a performance that got him a $12 million raise, courtesy of the franchise tag. Philip Merling and Tony McDaniel also factor into the rotation, which means that Miami can withstand injury at any of the front-line positions without suffering a serious dropoff in talent. It's an enviable position to be in.

One of the most astute signings of the last few years was Jeff Ireland's decision to uppluck two-time CFL Most Outstanding Defensive Player Cameron Wake from up north and sign him to a four-year, $4.9 million deal. Last year Wake rewarded that investment with 14 sacks while coming off the weakside, erasing the bad memories of both the Joey Porter experiment and the release of Jason Taylor. There was nothing flukey about Wake's performance, either. In addition to the sacks, our game charters credited Wake with another 39 hurries; only St. Louis' Chris Long had more. On the strong side, Koa Misi only tallied 4.5 sacks, a number he'll have to improve on if Wake isn't going to see a steady succession of double- and triple-teams every week. While Misi wasn't able to transform his athleticism into production as a rookie, he did a good job of setting the edge in the run game, and coaches think he is ready to take the next step. If not, there is old reliable Jason Taylor, who is back after a year-long stint with the hated Jets. Taylor is no longer a full-time player, but he got to the quarterback more times than Misi despite playing many fewer snaps.

The interior duo of Kevin Burnett and Karlos Dansby is very solid. The team lured Burnett away from San Diego with a four-year, $21 million contract, and he should have no problem replacing Channing Crowder. The Miami scheme will allow Burnett to play going forward, while asking Karlos Dansby to be a jack-of-all trades, blitzing one down and dropping into coverage the next. Dansby made 95 tackles despite missing two games, and he should eclipse the century mark next season if he stays healthy.

Defensive Secondary

Secondary	Age	Pos	Plays	TmPct	Rk	Stop	Dfts	BTkl	Runs	St%	Rk	Yds	Rk	Tgts	Tgt%	Rk	Dist	Suc%	Rk	APaYd	Rk	PD	Int
										Overall						vs. Run					vs. Pass		
Yeremiah Bell	33	SS	106	13.5%	9	37	18	7	58	40%	38	5.4	16	36	8.0%	14	13.6	48%	58	6.9	24	3	0
Benny Sapp	30	CB	47	6.0%	77	24	13	3	13	69%	4	3.6	7	54	12.0%	73	9.1	55%	30	7.0	37	9	2
Vontae Davis	23	CB	63	8.0%	50	28	8	9	20	40%	50	6.3	38	66	14.8%	51	10.7	46%	71	8.2	61	11	1
Sean Smith	24	CB	59	8.0%	51	27	9	5	18	39%	56	6.7	45	49	11.7%	74	11.5	62%	10	6.9	35	10	1
Chris Clemons	26	FS	64	8.7%	60	23	13	8	25	28%	68	7.9	55	25	5.9%	36	19.6	55%	35	11.6	74	5	1
Reshad Jones	23	SS	16	2.5%	--	7	3	0	6	50%	--	5.8	--	7	1.8%	--	17.0	55%	--	6.0	--	2	1

Year	Pass D Rank	vs. #1 WR	Rk	vs. #2 WR	Rk	vs. Other WR	Rk	vs. TE	Rk	vs. RB	Rk
2008	12	-7.2%	9	36.7%	30	-22.2%	8	-14.2%	7	-24.8%	2
2009	13	15.2%	21	2.7%	19	-1.5%	14	16.9%	24	-2.8%	15
2010	23	11.2%	24	-7.2%	8	11.2%	26	20.6%	28	9.0%	22

Much of the Miami essay in *Football Outsiders Almanac 2010* was devoted to forecasting the futures of Vontae Davis and Sean Smith. A quick glance at their conventional stats would suggest that the two were virtually interchangeable, but Smith gave up on average 1.3 fewer yards per pass play and had a much better Success Rate. The knock on Smith is that he too often fails to haul in passes that he gets his hands on, and it's hard to argue the point when he has only made one interception in two seasons and tied for the NFL lead with five dropped picks last year. Davis was no better in that department, failing to generate the big plays he made as a rookie, but in his case it seems more like an aberration than a trend. Benny Sapp and the 33-year-old veteran Will Allen will compete for the nickelback job, with the loser likely to be released. The winner shouldn't get too comfortable, because the coaching staff envisions second-year man Nolan Carroll as the long-term solution. Strong safety Yeremiah Bell is very much an in-the-box defender at this stage of his career, and his usage stats reflect as much. Bell was involved in more running plays than any Dolphins defender not named Karlos Dansby, and made more than twice as many run stops as fellow safety Chris Clemons. Clemons has the requisite athleticism to cover the deep middle or get to the sidelines, but he is more effective in zone coverage than man, he doesn't consistently provide help over the top, and his tackling is problematic. 2010 fifth-round pick Reshad Jones finished the Tennessee game with a flurry, sandwiching a near-interception, a sack and a game-sealing interception into a five-minute stretch, and he could challenge Clemons for the starting spot. Seventh-rounder Jimmy Wilson (Montana) impressed in camp and should at the very least be a solid special teams contributor.

Special Teams

Year	DVOA	Rank	FG/XP	Rank	Net Kick	Rank	Kick Ret	Rank	Net Punt	Rank	Punt Ret	Rank	Hidden	Rank
2008	-4.8%	29	0.1	18	-9.2	30	-3.4	21	-13.7	30	-2.1	22	-3.1	18
2009	1.8%	9	7.0	5	-2.7	22	4.8	9	4.8	11	-3.4	22	-6.5	25
2010	-3.1%	29	-2.0	24	-7.7	28	-3.6	20	-4.1	24	-1.0	17	-9.5	25

Throughout the season, Miami's special teams were both bad and unlucky. The Dolphins ranked 25th in the league in hidden yardage, which measures how teams were affected by elements outside of their control like opposing field goal percentage and opposing kickoff and punt distances. But often Miami was their own worst enemy, most spectacularly during a historically inept second half against the Patriots. After allowing a kickoff return for a touchdown on the opening kick of the third quarter, the Dolphins gave up a blocked punt later in the quarter, and then a blocked Dan Carpenter field goal attempt was returned for yet another touchdown in the fourth quarter. The meltdown was so embarrassing that special teams coach Jon Bonamego was fired the next day and replaced by Darren Rizzi. Still, not everything was bad. Carpenter hit 30 field goals out of a whopping 41 attempts, and all 11 misses were from 40-plus yards out. He continues to be very reliable in close, and so long as the offense continues to sputter in the red zone, Carpenter will get plenty of opportunities. Brandon Fields had two punts blocked, and his 46.2-yard gross punting average was shaved down to a net of 39.8 because of indifferent coverage. Nate Carroll and Patrick Cobb will share kickoff duties, while Davone Bess will once again handle punts. The Miami return men aren't standouts, either positively or negatively.

Coaching Staff

It seems that Tony Sparano has more to worry about these days than being confused with James Gandolfini. In addition to owner Steve Ross' very public flirtation with Jim Harbaugh, Sparano also had to contend with multiple players and ex-players publicly complaining about his habit of micromanaging. Now Sparano is under pressure to win games, and to do so with a more exciting brand of offense. To that end, Sparano shook up his staff, letting longtime offensive coordinator Dan Henning go and replacing him with Brian Daboll. Daboll is considered a bright young mind, but he's a curious hire considering that his offense in Cleveland would hardly be described as high-flying. In fact, one of Daboll's attributes is that he has experience running the Wildcat, and he will be expected to breathe some life into the formation. Daboll made a star of Peyton Hillis, and his offense is predicated on a heavy dose of play-action, so it sounds like a cosmetic change rather than a philosophical one. Sparano also did some minor rearranging of the deck chairs, shifting Karl Dorrall from receivers coach to quarterbacks coach, moving Steve Bush from quality control to receivers, bringing in Ike Hilliard as the new receivers coach, and hiring his son Tony Sparano, Jr., as the new offensive quality control coach.

The Dolphins' defensive DVOA climbed from 18th to 10th in Mike Nolan's first year as defensive coordinator, in large part due to a massive improvement in run defense. Nolan largely played it straight up, relying on putting players in the right place rather than attempting to dazzle offenses with an array of blitz packages and personnel groupings. Nolan's primary task now is to improve the coverage on the back end through a combination of personnel tweaks and the continued development of Vontae Davis and Sean Smith. With another strong season, Nolan could resurrect his image and once again draw interest as a head coach candidate.

Minnesota Vikings

2010 Record: 6-10	**2011 Mean Projection:** 8.5 wins
Pythagorean Wins: 6.0 (26th)	**On the Clock (0-3):** 0%
DVOA: -13.8% (25th)	**Loserville (4-6):** 15%
Offense: -11.8% (27th)	**Mediocrity (7-8):** 34%
Defense: 0.9% (11th)	**Playoff Contender (9-10):** 36%
Special Teams: -1.2% (19th)	**Super Bowl Contender (11+):** 15%
Variance: 13.8% (12th)	**Projected Average Opponent:** -3.2% (29th)

2010: I've been waiting all week for Tuesday Night Football.

2011: The battle of personnel attrition vs. statistical regression.

If Christopher Guest, the comic genius behind *This is Spinal Tap* and *A Mighty Wind*, decided to produce a football movie, he could use the 2010 Vikings season as its plot.

Guest's stable of improv comics each has a role. Guest portrays Brad Childress, bald, officious, and in denial about his fate. Michael McKean plays Brett Favre, self-absorbed and living forever in the past. Fred Willard's clueless glad-hander persona is a dead ringer for Zygi Wilf. It's not even a stretch to see Eugene Levy, at his Bobby Bittman-zaniest, slipping into the role of Randy Moss. The Moss "self interview" is no different from one of Nigel Tufnel's Spinal Tap rants. The collapsing Metrodome roof is something out of "Stonehenge." Ryan Longwell's trip to Hattiesburg to grill steaks and talk Favre out of retirement is as nutty as anything in *Best in Show* or *Waiting for Guffman*. Parker Posey plays Deanna Favre, Catherine O'Hara the plucky caterer who incurs Moss' wrath for serving "garbage."

We could fill an entire chapter with 2010 Vikings jokes and still have room left over at the end for their Tuesday Night Football appearance. But there is no point. Favre is gone. Moss is gone. Childress is gone. The Metrodome will soon be gone, or renovated, or at least patched up and avalanche-proofed. Just as Guest's comedy troupe creates memorable characters and situations, then moves on, so too the Vikings offered a one-year satire of the football world, then moved on to a new project.

Unfortunately, the nature of that new project isn't clear. On the stadium front, the Vikings are torn between a massive long-term building project — a billion-dollar stadium in nearby Arden Hills — or a series of cheaper, more convenient short-term patch jobs. They face the same dilemma on their roster. In both cases, they have no choice but to address long-term solutions while girding themselves for business as near-usual for at least another year. No Arden Hills stadium is going to sprout like a bamboo shoot by September, and the Vikings are in no position to launch the full-scale roster overhaul they so desperately need.

The Vikings, you recall, played in the NFC Championship Game in 2009. They are a veteran team, not far removed from Super Bowl contention, which is why the Favre return and Moss trade weren't foolish moves in isolation. As a pattern, they were a disaster, and the Vikings now have the roster of a team that chased a championship at all costs and fell on its face. There are on-the-decline veterans manning many key positions and very few prospects on the roster. The organization is trying to sell stadium deals, so a salary purge is ill-advised, and head coach Leslie Frazier, a holdover from Childress staff, was a pre-lockout plan of least resistance and probably knows it. So the Vikings must go through the "win now" motions while

2011 Vikings Schedule

Week	Opp.	Week	Opp.	Week	Opp.
1	at SD	7	GB	13	DEN
2	TB	8	at CAR	14	at DET
3	DET	9	BYE	15	NO
4	at KC	10	at GB (Mon.)	16	at WAS
5	ARI	11	OAK	17	CHI
6	at CHI	12	at ATL		

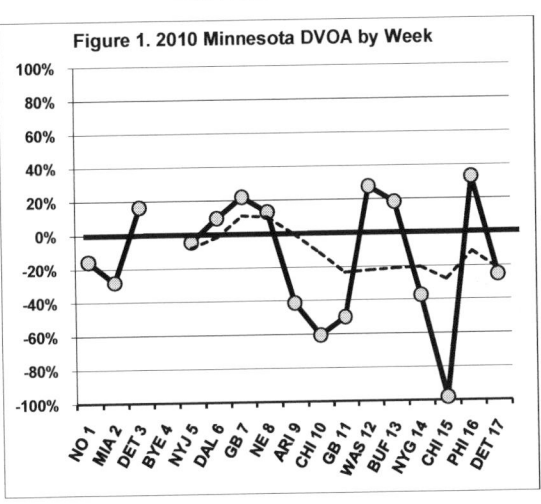

Figure 1. 2010 Minnesota DVOA by Week

grooming a new quarterback and waiting for a bunch of 30-ish veterans to play out their contracts.

Even the new quarterback is a consolation prize. The Vikings got caught at the end of a quarterback run early in the first round. The Jaguars jumped ahead of them to select Blaine Gabbert, a move they may not have anticipated (though they should have entertained the possibility that the Redskins, who held that pick, might take a quarterback). The Titans had already selected Jake Locker, leaving the Vikings to take Florida State's Christian Ponder. Scouts were somewhat divided on Ponder; Russ Lande ranked him as the third-best quarterback, Nolan Nawrocki the sixth, but no one considered him worthy of the 12th pick in the draft.

Ponder, though overdrafted, does have starter potential. He can play through injuries, and certainly has a lot of experience at it, having suffered shoulder and elbow injuries, a ruptured bursa sack, and a concussion in his college career. He appears to have a weak arm and lousy mechanics, but it is possible that his elbow injury may have been such a problem that it drained his arm strength and fouled up his delivery. He's a great leader, a good runner, and a tough guy, but you have to stack up a lot of intangibles to ignore the questionable arm and long injury history.

Knowing Ponder was a long-term project, the Vikings acquired Donovan McNabb during the Shanahan Doghouse Rummage Sale after the lockout. According to DVOA, McNabb was a league-average quarterback, a fading star who could still throw deep but has lost a lot of athleticism and was never the most precise passer. According to the Shanahan family, McNabb was responsible for the Black Death. Frazier knows McNabb from their Philly days, and it's a testimony to how seriously other coaches take Mike Shanahan's allegations that the Vikings think their allegedly lazy insubordinate is an ideal mentor.

McNabb brings the promise of stability, if not excellence, at quarterback. He should mesh well with new coordinator Bill Musgrave, who arrives from Atlanta looking to install a Falcons-style offense: lots of extra pass protection and old-fashioned power running. Adrian Peterson will be the focal point of the attack. The offensive line may well be better off without Bryant McKinnie, a Pro Bowler by reputation only who was released at the start of training camp because of weight issues. McNabb can still handle what Musgrave needs him to do: hand off 25 times per game, then play-fake, drop seven steps behind seven-man protection, and heave a bomb. The system has built-in training wheels for when Ponder takes the reins. The Vikings don't need an A+ quarterback to win some games this year, and they won't get one, at least not in 2011.

Offensively, the Vikings can point to Ponder and Musgrave as evidence that they are moving forward. Defensively, the team is stuck in 2007. The famed Williams Wall, which has been slowly cracking since 2006 (when it allowed just 985 rushing yards and an amazing 2.8 yards per carry) is about to come tumbling down. Ray Edwards departed for Atlanta after spending the lockout pursuing his boxing career. Pat Williams is a 39-year-old free agent. If you thought the Star Caps scandal disappeared during the Clinton administration, think again: In the spring, judges ordered that Kevin and Pat Williams were both eligible for suspension, which could impact Kevin Williams' status for the start of the season. Jared Allen is still around, but the dropoff from Williams Wall to Allen and the Irregulars could be Beatles-to-Wings steep.

Age is an issue across the defense. Kevin Williams is 31. E.J. Henderson is 30. Antoine Winfield is 33.

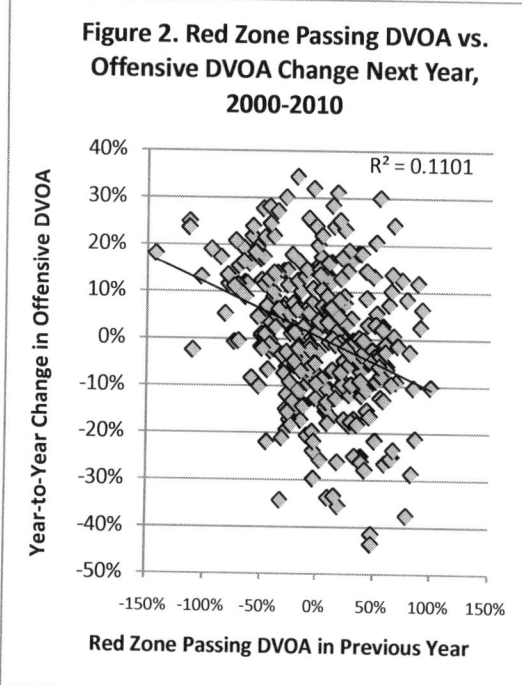

Figure 2. Red Zone Passing DVOA vs. Offensive DVOA Change Next Year, 2000-2010

$R^2 = 0.1101$

Year-to-Year Change in Offensive DVOA

Red Zone Passing DVOA in Previous Year

their overall total offensive DVOA improve the following year by an average of 12.6%.

On defense, the Vikings are likely to improve due to the "third-down rebound effect." Their defense ranked fifth on first downs last year, 12th on second downs, and 24th on third downs. The offense also might improve due to the third-down effect, although as we noted in last year's Philadelphia chapter, the third-down effect hasn't been as prevalent on offense over the last few seasons.

Even if the Vikings slip into the Wild Card picture, the long-term prognosis is pessimistic. Ponder is not a five-star prospect, and few other future building blocks are in place. To envision the Vikings making a quick turnaround, you must anoint Ponder the answer, think very highly of players like Abdullah, assume Peterson and Allen won't fade quickly in the next two years (and that Percy Harvin finds a way to stay healthy), and anticipate fertile drafts in 2012 and 2013. You must also have a high opinion of Frazier and Musgrave, who appear to be steady hands but not miracle workers, and you must believe the front office that brought you the Favre-Moss "Smell the Glove" experience can make smart personnel decisions on the fly. Barring all of that, we have to assume that the Vikings will be out of serious contention for a while, that Frazier won't be around when they do return to the Super Bowl picture, and that the team will look very different by the time they move into their new suburban dream house.

It is all very grim, despite the chance that the Vikings ride McNabb, Peterson, Allen, and a last-place schedule to a 9-7 season. What did you expect after last season? The roof collapsed. The quarterback fluttered in at the last minute and was carted off in the fetal position. A kickoff returner played quarterback for the last two games. A former superstar returned to the fold as a jabbering lunatic. These are not spackle-and-tape problems, and the Vikings weren't ready for most of them, even if they should have been. This year's team at least won't make fans wince. They can watch Ponder grow, enjoy Purple Jesus while he lasts, and debate the merits of paying hundreds of million dollars to fund a rent-free stadium while watching the Vikings in a reinflated bubble. At least the rest of the football world won't be laughing at their team.

The youngsters who were pressed into service last year didn't accomplish much: Asher Allen and Chris Cook got hurt, and Hussain Abdullah was ordinary at strong safety. Allen and Chad Greenway are the only defensive players who are healthy and in their prime. There are a few prospects, but no up-and-coming "core" of defenders.

The Vikings roster, then, is in a holding pattern: The veterans are past their collective prime, and it has been too many years since the team has invested seriously in the future. Thus you may be surprised to see that we are predicting a bit of a rebound for the Vikings. A .500 season in 2011 is very possible, for a variety of reasons with are more related to regression towards the mean than to personnel improvement.

For one thing, Minnesota's futility passing near the goal line is unsustainable. The Vikings were very good at running in the red zone last year (27.5% DVOA, sixth in the NFL), but they had a red-zone passing DVOA of -83.2%, the ninth worst figure since 2000. Red-zone rushing is more consistent than red-zone passing, and teams that struggle passing in the red zone generally improve on offense the following year (Figure 2). This is particularly true at the extreme. Teams with red-zone passing below -70% DVOA see

Mike Tanier

2010 Vikings Stats by Week

Wk	vs.	W-L	PF	PA	YDF	YDA	TO	Total	Off	Def	ST
1	@NO	L	9	14	253	308	-1	-16%	0%	14%	-1%
2	MIA	L	10	14	364	226	-2	-28%	-33%	-9%	-5%
3	DET	W	24	10	368	295	0	16%	-11%	-23%	4%
4	BYE										
5	@NYJ	L	20	29	336	328	-3	-5%	-11%	-11%	-5%
6	DAL	W	24	21	188	314	1	10%	-8%	-3%	15%
7	@GB	L	24	28	402	379	-1	22%	17%	-1%	4%
8	@NE	L	18	28	410	362	-1	13%	21%	16%	8%
9	ARI	W	27	24	507	225	-2	-41%	5%	21%	-25%
10	@CHI	L	13	27	240	360	-2	-61%	-32%	15%	-14%
11	GB	L	3	31	300	374	-2	-50%	-22%	28%	0%
12	@WAS	W	17	13	299	216	1	28%	16%	-17%	-6%
13	BUF	W	38	14	387	239	1	18%	-23%	-32%	9%
14	NYG	L	3	21	164	395	1	-37%	-57%	1%	21%
15	CHI	L	14	40	273	293	-4	-98%	-58%	5%	-35%
16	@PHI	W	24	14	337	331	2	33%	29%	1%	5%
17	@DET	L	13	20	211	357	1	-25%	-26%	4%	5%

Trends and Splits

	Offense	Rank	Defense	Rank
Total DVOA	-11.8%	27	0.9%	11
Unadjusted VOA	-16.2%	29	-0.2%	11
Weighted Trend	-12.9%	28	3.1%	16
Variance	6.8%	13	2.7%	2
Average Opponent	0.0%	26	3.7%	17
Passing	-16.4%	30	9.9%	20
Rushing	7.8%	8	-10.0%	8
First Down	11.7%	9	-5.4%	5
Second Down	-18.3%	30	-1.1%	12
Third Down	-45.7%	31	15.2%	24
First Half	-8.3%	25	10.4%	24
Second Half	-15.3%	27	-9.0%	5
Red Zone	-28.4%	29	-1.8%	16
Late and Close	-5.8%	24	-9.6%	10

Five-Year Performance

Year	W-L	Pyth	Est W	PF	PA	TO	Total	Rk	Off	Rk	Def	Rk	ST	Rk	Off AGL	Rk	Def AGL	Rk
2006	6-10	6.6	7.9	282	327	+4	-10.9%	23	-17.3%	31	-10.0%	5	-3.6%	27	18.0	17	10.6	14
2007	8-8	9.5	8.9	365	311	+1	2.0%	15	0.1%	16	0.3%	17	2.1%	9	11.9	4	7.6	4
2008	10-6	9.2	8.3	379	333	-6	4.9%	18	-5.8%	25	-17.2%	4	-6.5%	32	10.0	4	24.0	18
2009	12-4	11.6	10.2	470	312	+6	18.4%	7	16.1%	9	1.8%	17	4.1%	4	9.4	7	13.1	4
2010	6-10	6.0	6.7	281	348	-11	-13.8%	25	-11.8%	27	0.9%	11	-1.2%	19	35.7	25	19.7	14

Strategic Tendencies

Run/Pass		Rank	Offense		Rank	Defense		Rank	Other		Rank
Runs, all plays	41%	13	3+ WR	52%	13	Rush 3	1.0%	32	2+ RB, Pct Runs	60%	14
Runs, first half	47%	5	4+ WR	6%	16	Rush 4	69.1%	5	1 RB/2 TE, Pct Runs	57%	5
Runs, first down	50%	16	2+ TE	34%	9	Rush 5	23.3%	17	1 RB/3+ WR, Pct Runs	22%	16
Runs, second-long	35%	14	Single back	69%	6	Rush 6+	6.6%	21	CB1 on WR1	29%	28
Runs, power sit.	61%	15	Play action	19%	14	Zone Blitz	9.5%	6	Go for it on 4th	0.79	22
Runs, behind 2H	26%	19	Max protect	12%	9	Sacks by LB	8.1%	30	Offensive Pace	32.7	30
Pass, ahead 2H	41%	22	Outside pocket	14%	11	Sacks by DB	11.3%	15	Defensive Pace	30.6	12

The Vikings averaged 5.2 yards rushing from one-back sets, but just 3.1 yards rushing from two-back sets. Only Indianapolis (which rarely uses two backs) had a larger difference. ➾ Minnesota had 41.4% passing DVOA when using play-action (7.7 yards per pass) but -21.9% DVOA without play-action (5.5 yards per pass). That was the highest gap in the NFL. ➾ Interestingly, the Vikings had the highest DVOA gap between play-action passes and other passes on *defense* as well. Against standard passes, the Vikings gave up 5.7 yards per pass with 1.3% DVOA. Against play-action passes, the Vikings gave up 8.2 yards per pass with 57.8% DVOA.

Passing

Player	DYAR	DVOA	Plays	NtYds	Avg	YAC	C%	TD	Int
B.Favre	-134	-16.6%	389	2442	6.3	5.7	61.1%	11	19
J.Webb	-49	-19.0%	98	477	4.9	4.2	60.7%	0	3
T.Jackson	-84	-31.0%	66	294	4.5	3.4	58.6%	3	4

Rushing

Player	DYAR	DVOA	Plays	Yds	Avg	TD	Fum	Suc
A.Peterson	229	10.6%	284	1295	4.6	12	2	45%
T.Gerhart	19	-2.8%	81	322	4.0	1	1	42%
P.Harvin	94	63.5%	18	107	5.9	1	0	-
J.Webb	56	53.5%	18	124	6.9	2	0	-
A.Young	-28	-67.4%	13	29	2.2	0	0	31%
T.Jackson	19	79.9%	5	63	12.6	0	0	-
B.Favre	-12	-62.8%	5	16	3.2	0	1	-

Receiving

Player	DYAR	DVOA	Plays	Ctch	Yds	Y/C	YAC	TD	C%
P.Harvin	153	5.2%	109	71	871	12.3	6.0	5	65%
R.Moss	72	2.0%	63	28	393	14.0	2.3	5	44%
B.Berrian	-65	-26.8%	54	28	252	9.0	2.8	0	52%
S.Rice	37	-1.5%	42	17	280	16.5	2.5	2	40%
G.Lewis	-40	-26.9%	37	17	197	11.6	4.2	0	46%
G.Camarillo	35	1.5%	33	20	240	12.0	4.4	1	61%
V.Shiancoe	6	-6.1%	79	47	530	11.3	3.7	2	59%
J.Kleinsasser	19	8.1%	20	17	148	8.7	4.6	0	85%
A.Peterson	93	20.0%	50	36	341	9.5	9.2	1	72%
T.Gerhart	-20	-26.4%	29	21	168	8.0	8.3	0	72%
N.Tahi	29	47.7%	6	6	39	6.5	6.0	1	100%
L.Booker	3	-5.0%	6	5	34	6.8	6.2	0	83%

Offensive Line

Year	Yards	ALY	Rank	Power	Rank	Stuff	Rank	2nd Lev	Rank	Open Field	Rank
2008	4.63	4.14	13	73%	8	19%	21	1.25	8	1.13	3
2009	4.18	4.01	20	59%	23	24%	32	1.18	14	0.94	8
2010	4.33	4.15	11	70%	6	19%	18	1.25	8	0.82	12

Year	LE	Rank	LT	Rank	Mid	Rank	RT	Rank	RE	Rank	Sacks	ASR	Rank	F-Start	Cont.
2008	4.27	15	4.70	7	4.06	19	3.59	27	4.34	8	43	8.9%	28	16	32
2009	3.83	22	4.59	7	4.10	16	3.67	26	3.82	22	34	6.0%	14	23	32
2010	4.50	13	4.56	7	4.22	10	3.72	22	3.73	21	36	6.8%	20	27	30

The Vikings have spent a lot of free agent money and high draft picks building an incredibly ordinary offensive line in recent years. Based on the reputations and pedigrees of some of the players, this should be a dominating unit, but Adrian Peterson spent a lot of the 2010 season fighting for three-yard gains, and Vikings coaches used Visanthe Shiancoe and others as pass protectors far more often than recommended.

Right tackle Phil Loadholt (14 total penalties) is a graduate of the Alex Barron School of Snap Count Anticipation. Loadholt committed seven false starts, usually when trying to beat a speed rusher off the line. Shiancoe, who spent a lot of time helping Loadholt block on the right side, pitched in seven false starts and three holds. H-back Jim Kleinsasser, who also provided extra support on the right side, added three more holds. In short, blocking on the right side was a recurring problem. Loadholt is great at straight-ahead run blocking but can be beaten to the edge when he doesn't jump offside or hold, and he spends screens and reverses jogging around looking for defenders to stand still so he can block them.

Bryant McKinnie, who reportedly spent the lockout flirting with the 400-pound mark, got released at the start of camp. He was another example of a "name" lineman playing well below reputation. Free agent Charlie Johnson will replace McKinnie. Johnson is a typical Colts lineman: smaller and quicker than the average blocker, and harder to evaluate because of Peyton Manning's ability to make his line look good.

Steve Hutchinson will turn 34 during the season and is just a good-not-great player at a non-critical position. Center John Sullivan and right guard Anthony Herrera are both Just Another Guys; Sullivan is back from the injuries that slowed him last year, while Herrera missed the start of camp while recovering from a November knee injury. The offensive line was less of a crisis area than other units, so the Vikings didn't make major upgrades in the draft. Sixth-round pick DeMarcus Love will get a look as a swing guard. Sixth-round pick Brandon Fusco started 44 games at center for Slippery Rock and could be groomed as Sullivan's eventual replacement.

Defensive Front Seven

Defensive Line	Age	Pos	Plays	TmPct	Overall								Pass Rush			vs. Run			vs. Pass		
					Rk	Stop	Dfts	BTkl	St%	Rk	AvYd	Rk	Sack	Hit	Hur	Runs	St%	Yds	Pass	St%	Yds
Jared Allen	29	DE	65	8.3%	8	51	23	0	74%	40	1.0	24	11	15	28.5	39	74%	2.1	26	85%	-0.6
Ray Edwards	26	DE	39	5.7%	33	33	13	2	78%	12	0.0	8	8	9	27.5	23	78%	2.0	16	94%	-2.9
Pat Williams	39	DT	30	3.9%	48	25	4	0	85%	19	1.3	19	0	1	3	27	85%	1.0	3	67%	3.3
Kevin Williams	31	DT	48	6.2%	12	37	17	2	76%	33	1.7	32	1	8	22	33	76%	1.5	15	80%	2.1
Brian Robison	28	DE	15	1.9%	--	10	4	1	64%	--	3.1	--	2	3	2	11	64%	3.5	4	75%	2.0
Letroy Guion	24	DT	16	2.2%	--	13	5	0	75%	--	1.5	--	2	3	4.5	12	75%	3.0	4	100%	-3.0

Linebackers	Age	Pos	Plays	TmPct	Overall					Pass Rush			vs. Run					vs. Pass				
					Rk	Stop	Dfts	BTkl	AvYd	Sack	Hit	Hur	Runs	St%	Rk	Yds	Rk	Tgts	Suc%	Rk	AdjYd	Rk
Chad Greenway	28	OLB	143	18.4%	4	79	28	5	5.0	1.5	4	7	77	71%	37	2.9	43	38	53%	46	5.8	34
E.J. Henderson	31	MLB	109	14.0%	26	64	18	5	4.2	1	2	5	81	65%	71	2.7	30	22	49%	55	5.9	36
Ben Leber	33	OLB	49	6.3%	99	25	10	5	5.3	0	2	8	29	41%	109	5.1	107	17	71%	4	4.8	13

Year	Yards	ALY	Rank	Power	Rank	Stuff	Rank	2nd Lev	Rank	Open Field	Rank
2008	3.46	3.50	4	55%	2	24%	5	1.03	7	0.54	9
2009	3.86	3.67	7	44%	2	25%	3	1.20	19	0.59	8
2010	3.80	3.64	6	66%	23	22%	8	1.05	9	0.71	14

Year	LE	Rank	LT	Rank	Mid	Rank	RT	Rank	RE	Rank	Sacks	ASR	Rank
2008	3.56	8	3.95	11	3.62	4	3.45	5	2.58	3	45	9.0%	2
2009	4.91	25	3.70	8	3.56	5	3.63	8	2.73	2	48	7.8%	4
2010	3.54	5	4.56	25	3.86	13	3.29	6	2.26	1	31	5.6%	26

The Vikings defensive line is in a state of flux because of age, legal problems, free agency, and the lure of the sweet science. Pat Williams is a 39-year-old free agent coming off an injury who is not expected back; Williams was still weighing his options in the weeks after the lockout. Newcomer Remi Ayodele was part of a Saints line that was terrible against the run in 2009 but much better in 2010. Ayodele's Run Stop Rate improved from 65 percent to 81 percent last year. He could never replace Pat Williams 2007, but he is as good as Pat Williams 2010. Kevin Williams remains one of the best all-around tackles in the league, disrupting plays in the backfield and doing a great job on screens and reverses, but he may be suspended this season in the StarCaps scandal that broke so long ago that Carl Eller and Alan Page were originally involved.

Ray Edwards left for Atlanta, leaving Jared Allen as the only sure thing on a once impenetrable line. Fourth-round rookie Christian Ballard (Iowa) is quick but undersized and technically raw; on the plus side, he has shown no interest in boxing (Edwards' off-field hobby) or dehydration tablets.

The Vikings franchised linebacker Chad Greenway before the lockout. Greenway is a consistent all-purpose defender who rarely leaves the field. He drew a lot of tough coverage assignments, picking up the likes of Jason Witten, Brett Celek, and Brandon Pettigrew, which make his Pass Stops and Defeats more impressive in context. Two of E.J. Henderson's three interceptions came on tipped passes. Henderson attacks the line of scrimmage well and is adequate in middle zone coverage, but he has gotten a lot of help over the years from playing behind the Williams Wall.

Ben Leber signed with St. Louis. Possible replacements include Jasper Brinkley, a big defender who looked good at the start of camp, and Erin Henderson, who may be E.J.'s sister.

Defensive Secondary

Secondary	Age	Pos	Plays	TmPct	Overall Rk Stop		Dfts	BTkl	Runs	St%	vs. Run Rk	Yds	Rk	Tgts	Tgt%	vs. Pass Rk	Dist	Suc%	Rk	APaYd	Rk	PD	Int
Husain Abdullah	26	FS	78	10.7%	29	26	6	4	41	37%	50	6.8	43	30	7.1%	25	12.3	47%	62	8.9	57	7	3
Madieu Williams	30	FS	76	11.1%	25	18	6	6	42	31%	64	9.9	73	27	6.9%	29	19.6	40%	73	13.2	78	2	1
Chris Cook	24	CB	22	7.5%	--	3	2	2	5	0%	--	11.0	--	25	14.7%	--	10.6	31%	--	12.2	--	2	0
Antoine Winfield	34	CB	96	12.3%	6	48	21	4	21	62%	12	3.5	6	58	12.9%	67	9.1	64%	7	4.5	2	4	0
Frank Walker	30	CB	23	4.3%	--	10	4	4	6	67%	--	4.5	--	23	7.5%	--	17.7	65%	--	6.1	--	5	1
Asher Allen	23	CB	60	8.8%	37	21	9	3	10	30%	76	8.9	65	62	15.8%	37	12.5	48%	63	9.3	75	6	2
Lito Sheppard	30	CB	21	3.3%	--	12	5	0	3	67%	--	4.0	--	31	8.6%	--	11.5	45%	--	8.5	--	4	0

Year	Pass D Rank	vs. #1 WR	Rk	vs. #2 WR	Rk	vs. Other WR	Rk	vs. TE	Rk	vs. RB	Rk
2008	5	-13.8%	7	-33.5%	2	-1.5%	20	18.0%	24	9.0%	22
2009	22	19.2%	24	-7.5%	11	19.7%	29	16.6%	23	6.7%	20
2010	20	-1.2%	16	14.5%	25	14.0%	27	-6.0%	8	-16.7%	4

While he is still a very good defender, Antoine Winfield typifies the problems that the Vikings face as they move forward. Winfield graded out very well in our charting stats, still throws his body around against the run, and can be effective off the blitz. At the same time, he cost the team a lot of money and is now 34 years old. He is a holdover from the team's attempt to win the Super Bowl two years ago, and while he is still playing at a high level, he will soon need to be replaced by a player who may not even be on the roster right now. Instead of trying out young cornerbacks at the end of last season, the Vikings rounded out their bench with veterans like Frank Walker and Lito Sheppard.

Cornerback Cedric Griffin suffered his second major knee injury in 10 months last October. Griffin tore his left ACL in the 2009 NFC Championship, battled back into the lineup by Week 3, then tore his right ACL against the Jets. Griffin was rehabbing diligently on his own in the offseason, but his future is uncertain. Chris Cook, a second-round pick last year, only played five games and missed most of the season with injuries to both knees. Cook also suffered a broken leg and some sprained ankles in college, so injuries may be a chronic problem. Cook was accused of gun charges in an offseason argument with a neighbor but later cleared. The incident started when Cook rode his bicycle around the street to be "a nosy neighbor" (his words) during an arrest next door to his mother's house, the neighbor accused Cook of calling the police and called him a "snitch," and things somehow got more ridiculous from there. Cook may need to ride his bicycle around the secondary to patch all of the holes in the Vikings defense this year.

Safety Madieu Williams left via free agency. The team re-signed Husain Abdullah and backup Eric Frampton, but safety will be another position of concern unless Frampton comes al ... no, that joke is beneath us.

Special Teams

Year	DVOA	Rank	FG/XP	Rank	Net Kick	Rank	Kick Ret	Rank	Net Punt	Rank	Punt Ret	Rank	Hidden	Rank
2008	-6.5%	32	-0.5	19	-4.9	24	-4.4	22	-24.6	32	-3.8	26	5.2	7
2009	4.1%	4	7.7	4	-6.3	28	18.7	2	0.5	21	3.7	13	1.4	11
2010	-1.2%	19	2.0	12	-15.7	31	4.3	11	6.2	11	-3.7	22	1.8	12

If Football Outsiders readers or writers were football players, we would be like Chris Kluwe. We would love our jobs and do our very best, then retreat into a world of Warcraft, comic books, Syfy original movies, and other geeky pleasures in our free time. In NFL circles, Kluwe is an oddball, and if he played a position other than punter or kicker, his "eccentricities" would be used to explain his failure the first time he slumped or had a bad game. As it stands, Kluwe is still probably two shanked punts away from hearing that playing Guitar Hero or reading *Preacher* distracts him from his job. It's a parochial word, but luckily Kluwe has thick skin, and a high armor class.

Ryan Longwell made most of his headlines last year as a Favre Retrieval Unit; try not to hold it against him. On the field, he's the classic veteran dome kicker, deadly from inside 40 yards but rarely called upon to kick from distance. Unfortunately, Longwell's kickoffs were poor last year, and the kick coverage was even worse; Minnesota opponents got a league-leading 9.5 estimated points worth of field position on kick returns. The Vikings re-signed Longwell last year but rescinded his Mississippi barbecue privileges. Greg Camarillo lacks Percy Harvin's big-play ability as a punt returner, but he takes what the coverage unit offers and gets up after tackles without clutching his head or limping. Harvin is electrifying on kickoff returns but takes too many hits. Everyone from Lorenzo Booker to Joe Webb got chances to return kicks last year, and the Vikings may reserve Harvin for critical situations.

Coaching Staff

New offensive coordinator Bill Musgrave is expected to use a lot of two-tight end sets to emphasize the running game and provide pass protection for Christian Ponder. This will not be a major change for the Vikings, who used six or more pass protectors about as often as Musgrave's Falcons last year (56 percent to 57 percent) and often employed Visanthe Shiancoe and Jim Kleinsasser in two-tight end sets. The main difference is that Brad Childress used max protect out of necessity, because of injuries to the receiving corps, some deficiencies on the offensive line, and a quarterback older than Enoch. Musgrave will use them by design.

Mike Singletary's get-tough sermonizing should be much more effective now that he is the linebackers coach under a defense-minded head coach. Singletary gets to be more of a drill sergeant and less of a general; long-range tactics just weren't his bag.

New England Patriots

2010 Record: 14-2	**2011 Mean Projection:** 11.5 wins
Pythagorean Wins: 12.3 (1st)	**On the Clock (0-3):** 0%
DVOA: 45.4% (1st)	**Loserville (4-6):** 5%
Offense: 46.1% (1st)	**Mediocrity (7-8):** 9%
Defense: 4.7% (18th)	**Playoff Contender (9-10):** 18%
Special Teams: 4.0% (8th)	**Super Bowl Contender (11+):** 68%
Variance: 19.2% (18th)	**Projected Average Opponent:** 4.9% (4th)

2010: One journey ends, another begins.

2011: Why is a 14-win team getting its chemistry lessons from *Breaking Bad*?

It is the dawning of the Third Age of Belichick in New England.

The First Age began in 2001, when Bill Belichick rounded up a bunch of bargain-bin free agents, replaced his injured franchise quarterback with an unheralded second-year player from Michigan, and inexplicably landed in the Super Bowl. Even people who grumble about The Tuck Rule forget what a trip-and-fall-into-success story those 2001 Patriots were, with veteran castoffs like Anthony Pleasant and Roman Phifer playing major roles on defense and Antowain Smith rushing for 1,100 yards while Tom Brady threw passes to guys like Marc Edwards and Charles Johnson.

The Patriots were a much better team when they returned to the Super Bowl by 2003, but the First Age philosophy was still in place. They won with Belichick's defensive wizardry, Tom Brady's emerging brilliance, and a conservative, committee-minded approach on offense. Belichick and Scott Pioli still grabbed low-priced late-career free agents like Tyrone Poole and Larry Centers to plug temporary holes. The Patriots drafts were fertile, but there was no watershed year when the Patriots suddenly acquired overwhelming talent. They won with their scheme, particularly their defensive scheme, in those early years.

The First Age ended in the AFC Championship Game after the 2006 season, when Reche Caldwell dropped two passes, one of which practically tried to bury itself in his jersey. Caldwell was the Patriots' leading receiver that season, and despite the team's continued success, their reliance on plug-ins on both sides of the ball was yielding diminishing returns. So the team acquired Wes Welker and Randy Moss, entering the attack-kill-destroy Second Age. The Patriots became passing game extremists; the defense embarked on a massive youth movement and became the supporting player. Belichick evolved from defensive mastermind to evil genius, a title some people took a little too literally.

We all know what happened in the Second Age: 19-and-no, Spygate, Brady's injury, year after year of 100-catch seasons by Welker, and a mini-era in which we forgot all about the days when Corey Dillon ran off tackle and Troy Brown caught eight-yard slants and played defense in the dime package. The Second Age ended when the Ravens rushed for 234 yards against the Patriots in a 2009 Wild Card victory. The Patriots had once again achieved diminishing returns, this time from their flash-bang offense and a defense increasingly built to hold opponents under 27 points instead of stopping them. They were too vulnerable to the Ravens' primitive tactics, too dependent on ten eight-yard passes to Welker (and Julian Edelman, when Welker was hurt) to gain 80 yards.

It was time for the Third Age to begin, for the Patriots to abandon the empty backfields and jettison Moss, to rediscover ball control, and to get back to their roots.

2011 Patriots Schedule

Week	Opp.	Week	Opp.	Week	Opp.
1	at MIA (Mon.)	7	BYE	13	IND
2	SD	8	at PIT	14	at WAS
3	at BUF	9	NYG	15	at DEN
4	at OAK	10	at NYJ	16	MIA
5	NYJ	11	KC (Mon.)	17	BUF
6	DAL	12	at PHI		

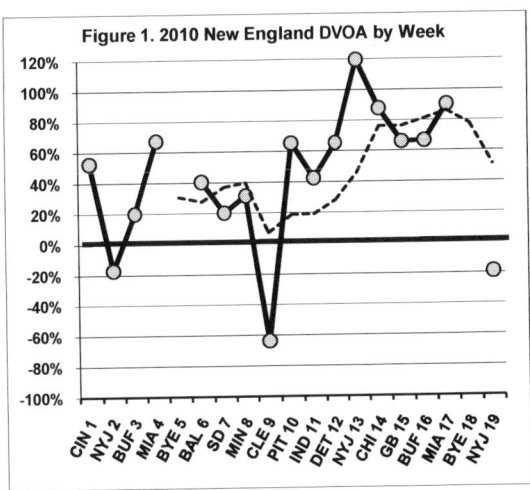

Figure 1. 2010 New England DVOA by Week

The changeover was sudden, but not unplanned: The 2010 draft was heavy in tight ends, so the Patriots were clearly up to something. Randy Moss hung around into the season, the target of a couple of ejaculatory bombs per game, then was sent away. Moss was targeted for seven passes with an air length of 30 or more yards in the Patriots' first three games. With Moss gone, the Patriots attempted just 15 passes of 30-plus yards in 13 games. The Patriots used a two-back backfield just 21 times in their first three games, many of them short-yardage or goal-line situations. From Week 10 on, they averaged 12.4 two-back sets per game. (Two-tight end sets were common all year). Plenty of other stats can illustrate just how quickly the Patriots offense changed, but this one sums it up nicely: The Patriots used zero- or one-receiver personnel groupings 15 percent of the time (much more than league average), and finished fourth in the league in DVOA in those sets. They finished first in the league in DVOA from two-wide receiver sets. These Patriots could still run 'n' gun when they wanted to (they finished first in DVOA in four-plus receiver sets, too), but they no longer wanted to. The conservative committee approach was back, merged with the spread approach in a way that made both styles more efficient. The Patriots were odds-on favorites to reach the Super Bowl until the Jets both outsmarted and outslugged them in the playoffs.

It's hard to predict how this Third Age will play out. The trade acquisitions of Chad Ochocinco and Albert Haynesworth defy easy categorization, as do the players themselves. On the one hand, the arrivals of Ocho and the Wumpus hearken back to the Randy Moss signing: Belichick has purchased top talent at rock-bottom prices. It's also a reflection of First Age philosophy: the acquisition of older veterans to fill niches. For all of the attention they draw, Ochocinco and Haynesworth are players on the downside who are expected to be role players, not superstars: Ochocinco adding back a little bit of the red-zone threat

that departed with Moss, Haynesworth providing 20 to 30 snaps per game in the line rotation. They are the kind of benefit-of-the-doubt gambles a coach with three Super Bowl rings would make.

Belichick and his staff can light temporary fires under distracted veterans, and Haynesworth could provide a huge boost, even in a limited role. The Patriots defense has been in slow freefall since 2007, and it took another step backward last season, even as it added talent. Rookie cornerback Devin McCourty led all cornerbacks in interceptions; we all know that meant he was regularly picked on, but McCourty got better as the season progressed and will be a fixture in the secondary. Linebackers Brandon Spikes and Jermaine Cunningham played well against the run, adding to a young core that includes Jerod Mayo, Patrick Chung, Brandon Meriweather, and Gary Guyton. The nucleus of a fine defense is in place, but some veteran buttressing was needed. If Haynesworth cannot provide it, he could slip quietly to the bottom of the depth chart, costing the Patriots nothing but a mid-round draft pick.

The Third Age may not be a golden era on defense, but it is a time of aggressive, clever personnel strategies. The 2006-08 Second Age drafts were not very productive, yielding Mayo and Meriweather but plenty of whiffs like Laurence Maroney, Chad Jackson and Terrence Wheatley. The Patriots did very little pick acquisition in those years: The Welker and Moss acquisitions left them short on picks in 2007, and of course they lost a first-round pick in 2008 because of Spygate.

In 2009, Belichick the former Defensive Guru and Evil Genius began to think like Belichick the Economist, and the Patriots started sliding all over the draft board and hoarding second-round picks. The 2009, 2010, and 2011 drafts found the Patriots acting as draft-day pawnbrokers. In each of the last three years, the Patriots left the draft with a high draft choice for the following year. In 2009 and 2010, they acquired future second-round picks for their third-round picks. In 2011, they acquired the Saints' 2012 first-round pick in exchange for one of their own while sliding down into the middle of the second round. The Patriots have selected 11 players in the first two rounds of the last three drafts, and they are still stocked with an extra pick entering 2012. None of these picks were high first-rounders, but Belichick the Economist knows that a) high first-round picks are expensive and bring excessive risk and b) there's little real talent drop-off between the end of the first round (where the Patriots typically draft) and the middle of the second, so there's no good reason to hang up the phone on another team that really, really wants his pick. With so many extra second- and third-round picks piled up, the Patriots can afford to risk a few later picks on aging Pro Bowl-caliber head cases.

Like the changes in offensive strategy, the change of draft philosophy happened so quickly that few people noticed. We forget that this is not how the Patriots always did business. Remember that the team relied heavily on veteran free agents and wait-their-turn draft choices during their Super Bowl runs of the First Age. They were sellers of draft picks in the Second Age, not just for Moss and Welker, but for Duane Starks and to move up to select the likes of Bethel Johnson. As fascinating as the Patriots' post-lockout trades were, this is still a team poised to build through the draft, this year and beyond.

The Third Age, then, is best thought of as a brilliantly-devised plan to keep the Patriots competitive as long as possible during the end of Brady's peak, and as a parachute plan for Brady's eventual decline/retirement/divine assumption. The return to a share-the-wealth approach limits their need for Moss-caliber talents on offense and lets them get the most from tight ends and situational backs, the types of players available in bulk in middle rounds. Brady's presence makes an offense built around guys like Aaron Hernandez and Danny Woodhead not only viable, but dangerous. Defensively, the Patriots surround Mayo and the linemen with waves of middle-tier role players and reclamation projects for Belichick to mix and match. It's not a great unit, but it is cheap and sustainable. The Third Age philosophy allows the Patriots to stay young while cranking out 14-win seasons. It will extend the Patriots' run as contenders long past the period when teams like the 1970s Steelers and 1990s Cowboys faded badly. There will be no end-of-an-era drop-off, just more double-digit winning seasons, extending until Brady cannot lift his arm anymore and Ryan Mallett takes over, or even beyond.

Whether those double-digit seasons blossom into more Super Bowls is an unsettled matter. The last two early exits from the playoffs were not pretty. Both the Ravens and Jets losses echoed the 2007 Super Bowl loss in many ways. The Patriots were beaten up physically in all three games, losing in the trenches. More critically, they were out-schemed at times: they had no answer for a strong opposing pass rush, and they displayed the same weakness against straight-ahead running tactics that Mike Shanahan's Broncos used to exploit.

The emergence of a two tight-end offense gives the Patriots a natural counter-strategy against the blitz, but a defense built from middle-round picks and role players will always be susceptible to the power tactics that playoff opponents like the Jets, Steelers, and Ravens prefer. Belichick must also prove that he won't try to outsmart the universe every time the opportunity arises: The playoff fake punt against the Jets, like the fourth-and-3 gamble against the Colts two years ago, showed that Belichick can be too clever for his own good at the worst times. (Patrick Chung actually audibled into that fake, but few coaches would authorize a second-year player to call a fake punt in a playoff game.) The Ocho-Haynesworth moves and some of the Patriots' Third Age draft-dealing could become part of the same illness: a compulsion to outsmart the system at every turn.

Such criticisms amount to picking at the fringes. The Patriots are a young team led by a Hall of Fame quarterback and coach. They have the capacity to get better at nearly every position except quarterback, which is a terrifying thing to say about a 14-win team. In January, they will be where they always are, duking it out with the usual competition, but while some of the AFC contenders are ready to enter their decline (the Colts, for example), the Patriots are just entering a new phase in their development. And when this Third Age runs its course, they may just reinvent themselves again. It has worked for a full decade, and there's no reason to think it cannot continue.

Mike Tanier

2010 Patriots Stats by Week

Wk	vs.	W-L	PF	PA	YDF	YDA	TO	Total	Off	Def	ST
1	CIN	W	38	24	376	428	2	52%	52%	16%	17%
2	@NYJ	L	14	28	291	336	-3	-17%	18%	33%	-2%
3	BUF	W	38	30	445	374	1	20%	64%	26%	-18%
4	@MIA	W	41	14	265	400	4	67%	43%	-5%	20%
5	BYE										
6	BAL	W	23	20	394	377	-2	40%	23%	3%	20%
7	@SD	W	23	20	179	363	4	20%	3%	-13%	4%
8	MIN	W	28	18	362	410	1	31%	61%	25%	-5%
9	@CLE	L	14	34	283	404	-2	-64%	-2%	51%	-10%
10	@PIT	W	39	26	453	425	1	65%	93%	24%	-4%
11	IND	W	31	28	346	467	3	42%	55%	19%	6%
12	@DET	W	45	24	447	406	2	65%	80%	9%	-5%
13	NYJ	W	45	3	405	301	3	120%	90%	-27%	3%
14	@CHI	W	36	7	475	185	4	88%	52%	-40%	-4%
15	GB	W	31	27	249	369	2	66%	45%	-13%	8%
16	@BUF	W	34	3	348	369	7	67%	20%	-34%	13%
17	MIA	W	38	7	502	250	1	90%	49%	-16%	25%
18	BYE										
19	NYJ	L	21	28	372	314	-1	-19%	7%	35%	9%

Trends and Splits

	Offense	Rank	Defense	Rank
Total DVOA	46.1%	1	4.7%	18
Unadjusted VOA	41.3%	1	3.7%	20
Weighted Trend	49.1%	1	-1.6%	11
Variance	8.1%	17	6.8%	18
Average Opponent	-1.6%	31	3.8%	18
Passing	72.5%	1	7.0%	15
Rushing	27.1%	2	1.4%	23
First Down	32.0%	2	-0.5%	7
Second Down	39.0%	1	0.2%	14
Third Down	88.4%	1	20.7%	27
First Half	46.2%	1	-1.0%	14
Second Half	45.9%	1	10.2%	24
Red Zone	47.3%	1	-9.7%	13
Late and Close	53.5%	1	-3.6%	14

Five-Year Performance

Year	W-L	Pyth	Est W	PF	PA	TO	Total	Rk	Off	Rk	Def	Rk	ST	Rk	Off AGL	Rk	Def AGL	Rk
2006	12-4	12.2	11.0	385	237	+8	27.1%	4	15.1%	4	-9.3%	7	2.6%	7	12.8	12	27.3	26
2007	16-0	13.8	14.2	589	274	+16	53.1%	1	45.2%	1	-5.0%	12	3.0%	7	14.5	7	16.4	10
2008	11-5	10.6	9.6	410	309	+1	11.7%	9	16.5%	8	8.4%	21	3.6%	6	38.6	25	39.9	28
2009	10-6	11.6	11.3	427	285	+6	29.1%	3	29.6%	1	1.7%	16	1.2%	13	27.1	19	19.1	10
2010	14-2	12.3	14.1	518	313	+28	45.4%	1	46.1%	1	4.7%	18	4.0%	8	32.9	23	39.5	27

Strategic Tendencies

Run/Pass		Rank	Offense		Rank	Defense		Rank	Other		Rank
Runs, all plays	44%	7	3+ WR	46%	18	Rush 3	19.4%	2	2+ RB, Pct Runs	57%	19
Runs, first half	39%	20	4+ WR	6%	14	Rush 4	52.9%	25	1 RB/2 TE, Pct Runs	59%	2
Runs, first down	55%	6	2+ TE	57%	1	Rush 5	21.3%	22	1 RB/3+ WR, Pct Runs	33%	2
Runs, second-long	32%	20	Single back	73%	3	Rush 6+	6.5%	23	CB1 on WR1	22%	30
Runs, power sit.	66%	6	Play action	23%	5	Zone Blitz	2.1%	29	Go for it on 4th	1.74	1
Runs, behind 2H	32%	4	Max protect	11%	14	Sacks by LB	56.9%	9	Offensive Pace	29.2	3
Pass, ahead 2H	46%	13	Outside pocket	4%	31	Sacks by DB	2.8%	31	Defensive Pace	31.0	21

The Patriots went with two tight ends on 57 percent of snaps last year. No other offense was above 40 percent. In 2009, before drafting Aaron Hernandez and Rob Gronkowski, the Patriots used tight ends on 34 percent of plays. 😑 After three straight years of going shotgun at least 50 percent of the time, the 2010 Patriots only used shotgun on 40 percent of snaps. 😑 The Patriots' rushing success doesn't just come from spreading out opposing defenses. The Patriots had the league's second-best DVOA running from one-back sets, but also the league's second-best DVOA running from two-back sets. In both categories, they were behind only the Texans. 😑 Although they used to be known as a screen team, the Patriots ran just a dozen screen passes to running backs last season, 30th in the NFL. 😑 As great as the Patriots offense was, it still went three-and-out on 21.5 percent of drives, only 13th in the NFL. 😑 The Patriots allowed a league-high 46.8% DVOA on passes thrown at or behind the line of scrimmage. They were actually better than average against passes thrown beyond the line of scrimmage (30.8% DVOA fifth best in the NFL). Their defense struggled because they couldn't stop short passes and they couldn't pressure the quarterback.

Passing

Player	DYAR	DVOA	Plays	NtYds	Avg	YAC	C%	TD	Int
T.Brady	2137	53.3%	525	3830	7.3	5.8	66.0%	36	3
B.Hoyer	34	22.5%	15	122	8.1	5.9	46.7%	1	1

Rushing

Player	DYAR	DVOA	Plays	Yds	Avg	TD	Fum	Suc
B.Green-Ellis	354	26.4%	229	1008	4.4	13	0	57%
D.Woodhead	185	41.3%	97	547	5.6	5	1	57%
F.Taylor	-8	-13.1%	43	155	3.6	0	0	47%
S.Morris	7	-1.6%	20	56	2.8	0	0	50%
T.Brady	-5	-16.2%	16	43	2.7	1	0	-
K.Faulk	19	66.1%	8	45	5.6	0	0	50%
B.Tate	45	129.0%	5	62	12.4	0	0	-

Receiving

Player	DYAR	DVOA	Plays	Ctch	Yds	Y/C	YAC	TD	C%
W.Welker	166	4.2%	124	86	843	9.8	4.7	7	69%
D.Branch	246	20.5%	92	61	818	13.4	4.5	6	66%
B.Tate	41	-0.3%	46	24	432	18.0	5.8	3	52%
J.Edelman	-16	-28.3%	14	7	86	12.3	14.1	0	50%
A.Hernandez	160	30.9%	64	45	563	12.5	6.5	6	70%
R.Gronkowski	249	53.3%	59	42	546	13.0	4.4	10	71%
A.Crumpler	10	5.9%	10	6	52	8.7	5.8	2	60%
D.Woodhead	156	56.3%	44	34	379	11.1	9.2	1	77%
B.Green-Ellis	31	17.9%	16	12	85	7.1	4.1	0	75%
S.Morris	10	-0.6%	12	7	77	11.0	9.7	0	58%
K.Faulk	20	22.5%	10	6	62	10.3	5.7	0	60%

Offensive Line

Year	Yards	ALY	Rank	Power	Rank	Stuff	Rank	2nd Lev	Rank	Open Field	Rank
2008	4.60	4.62	3	70%	12	14%	1	1.30	5	0.72	14
2009	4.29	4.39	5	68%	9	15%	3	1.22	11	0.59	26
2010	4.54	4.82	1	68%	8	12%	2	1.30	6	0.56	22

Year	LE	Rank	LT	Rank	Mid	Rank	RT	Rank	RE	Rank	Sacks	ASR	Rank	F-Start	Cont.
2008	4.04	21	5.11	3	4.79	2	3.95	23	2.52	32	48	8.5%	26	10	35
2009	4.96	9	4.21	12	4.55	4	3.84	23	3.63	25	18	3.6%	2	15	29
2010	5.04	4	4.08	19	4.82	2	5.25	1	5.35	2	25	4.9%	6	13	34

First-round pick Nate Solder resembles right tackle Sebastian Vollmer physically, and the Patriots hope he can make the same quick transition from raw prospect to solid starter. Solder is long and angular at 6-foot-8 and 315 pounds, and shorter defenders often ripped under him when he failed to get into proper position at the University of Colorado. But his pure strength, wingspan, and overall athleticism made him a first-round value. Matt Light re-signed with the team, though he started camp on the PUP list. Light will probably start the season at left tackle if he is healthy, but Solder is the starter of the future.

Marcus Cannon occupies the other side of the body-type spectrum from Solder. Cannon, a fifth-round pick, weighs 358 pounds but is relatively nimble. He rarely took a three-point stance in TCU's spread offense, and his limitations at left tackle were protected by an offense full of quick throws and sprint-outs, but he blocked well on the move and could be a bulldozer in the running game. Cannon was seen as a likely second-round pick before a diagnosis of non-Hodgkin's lymphoma knocked him down draft boards, but there are indications he may already be ready to play by the start of the season. Like Solder, he is a fascinating athletic specimen, and Cannon may end up at guard if he proves he can keep his weight under four bucks.

The Patriots franchised guard Logan Mankins, who joined Vincent Jackson during the lockout as players who hoped for their own settlement. But let's forget all of that. Mankins, Dan Koppen, and Dan Connelly will hold down the middle of the line for one more season. After that, Koppen and probably Mankins will be free agents, so the franchise's ability to overhaul the roster on the fly will again be tested.

Defensive Front Seven

Defensive Line	Age	Pos	Plays	TmPct	Overall Rk	Stop	Dfts	BTkl	St%	Rk	AvYd	Rk	Pass Rush Sack	Hit	Hur	vs. Run Runs	St%	Yds	vs. Pass Pass	St%	Yds
Ron Brace	25	DT	22	3.2%	60	16	2	0	73%	44	2.2	39	0	0	2	22	73%	2.2	0	0%	0.0
Vince Wilfork	30	DT	58	6.9%	10	40	11	0	69%	53	2.2	40	2	2	10	49	69%	2.4	9	67%	1.3
Mike Wright	29	DE	15	2.9%	--	10	8	2	43%	--	-0.4	--	5.5	3	10	7	43%	2.7	8	88%	-3.1
Gerard Warren	33	DE	28	3.3%	72	19	8	0	59%	69	1.4	28	3.5	1	4	22	59%	2.5	6	100%	-2.8

Linebackers	Age	Pos	Plays	TmPct	Overall Rk	Stop	Dfts	BTkl	AvYd	Pass Rush Sack	Hit	Hur	vs. Run Runs	St%	Rk	Yds	vs. Pass Rk	Tgts	Suc%	Rk	AdjYd	Rk
Jerod Mayo	25	ILB	178	21.1%	1	85	16	1	6.0	2	3	3	99	57%	93	4.5	99	48	56%	32	5.9	37
Gary Guyton	26	ILB	67	8.0%	82	38	10	4	5.0	3	2	4	29	69%	53	3.8	81	30	46%	65	5.7	32
Tully Banta-Cain	31	OLB	45	5.7%	--	30	11	0	2.8	5	7	24.5	34	68%	--	3.4	--	6	15%	--	5.1	--
Brandon Spikes	24	ILB	61	9.7%	62	41	7	1	3.9	0	0	1	46	74%	27	3.1	57	10	57%	--	3.4	--
Rob Ninkovich	27	OLB	56	6.7%	94	38	13	2	3.2	4	4	11.5	34	71%	44	3.0	48	17	70%	6	3.0	2
Jermaine Cunningham	23	OLB	36	4.6%	109	26	9	2	2.1	1	4	17	31	74%	24	2.2	14	4	28%	--	6.5	--
Dane Fletcher	25	ILB	15	2.2%	--	10	4	1	4.1	2	3	4.5	5	40%	--	5.0	--	9	83%	--	5.9	--
Eric Moore	30	OLB	15	7.1%	--	11	6	0	1.3	2	1	2	9	67%	--	3.0	--	0	0%	0	0.0	0

Year	Yards	ALY	Rank	Power	Rank	Stuff	Rank	2nd Lev	Rank	Open Field	Rank
2008	4.08	4.11	13	67%	18	17%	19	0.96	5	0.65	14
2009	4.57	4.39	26	56%	5	16%	28	1.22	23	0.75	15
2010	4.10	4.25	20	71%	30	14%	30	1.06	11	0.52	8

Year	LE	Rank	LT	Rank	Mid	Rank	RT	Rank	RE	Rank	Sacks	ASR	Rank
2008	4.32	20	2.88	2	4.19	15	4.31	23	4.43	24	31	6.0%	18
2009	4.30	18	3.11	3	4.72	30	3.81	11	5.20	28	31	6.2%	18
2010	4.03	15	5.62	32	3.98	17	4.40	19	3.83	14	36	6.3%	15

The Patriots defensive line will look completely different this year. Albert Haynesworth will get a lot of attention, both from opposing blockers and television cameras. Haynesworth was well-behaved and dominating in short bursts early in camp. Fellow newcomer Shaun Ellis is still an effective run defender and comes with much less baggage.

Ron Brace and Brandon Deaderick are also in the mix along the defensive line. Brace looked solid before suffering a head injury that limited his effectiveness late last season. Deaderick is quick off the line, but he can be blown backward at times, and he was suspended in the playoffs after missing several team meetings during the regular season. Vince Wilfork is the one constant; he can line up anywhere on the line, and he may not have to play as many snaps now that the team has more veteran depth.

Jerod Mayo led the NFL with 178 total plays and 72 pass tackles. He was the only defender in the NFL to register more than 20 percent of his team's total tackles, and our game charters counted only one broken tackle from him all season. Mayo's Stop and Defeat rates are not impressive, but he takes on more difficult zone coverage assignments than most linebackers and makes a lot of clean-up tackles after other defenders make mistakes. Seventeen of his pass tackles and passes defensed came against wide receivers, including Anquan Boldin, Brandon Marshall, Reggie Wayne, and Pierre Garcon, a sign of how often Mayo was asked to do more than just shadow the running back on a flat route. Tedy Bruschi handled similar assignments in his heyday, and Mayo has stepped completely into Bruschi's role on and off the field, organizing the team's offseason workouts and standing in for Bruschi at the retired linebacker's youth clinic.

Brandon Spikes was effective as an early-down run stuffer before missing the final four games of the regular season with a drug suspension. Only three of Spikes' 61 Plays occurred on third down (one of them on third-and-2), which shows how much Bill Belichick trusted him on passing downs. Gary Guyton handled passing-down duties well; he is adequate in coverage and times his blitz well, but Spikes is due for an increased role if he becomes more reliable on and off the field. At outside linebacker, Rob Ninkovich made a name for himself with a two-interception game against the Dolphins on Monday Night Football. He also had two sacks and a fumble recovery in the rematch against Miami, making him the biggest Dolphin killer since tuna casserole. Ninkovich has great open-field speed and instincts and will generate a few hustle sacks. Andre Carter still has some quickness of the edge and should thrive in a reduced role. Jermaine Cunningham is a big, hard-to-block load who must stay healthy and become more creative and quicker as a pass rusher. The team would like to ease veteran Eric Moore into a minimal role.

Defensive Secondary

Secondary	Age	Pos	Plays	TmPct	Rk	Stop	Dfts	BTkl	Runs	St%	Rk	Yds	Rk	Tgts	Tgt%	Rk	Dist	Suc%	Rk	APaYd	Rk	PD	Int
						Overall					vs. Run					vs. Pass							
Brandon Meriweather	27	SS	74	8.8%	59	16	4	4	26	27%	72	9.0	69	27	4.7%	65	14.5	48%	61	10.0	67	5	3
Kyle Arrington	25	CB	64	7.6%	58	15	6	4	13	23%	82	6.6	42	73	13.0%	66	12.1	49%	58	9.1	72	7	1
Jonathan Wilhite	27	CB	22	4.6%	–	11	6	2	4	25%	–	8.8	–	19	5.8%	–	8.4	55%	–	5.8	–	2	0
James Sanders	28	FS	62	7.9%	64	16	7	7	24	25%	76	7.2	49	35	6.5%	30	10.2	48%	59	7.5	35	7	3
Darius Butler	25	CB	29	3.7%	88	13	7	3	4	50%	25	5.8	28	49	9.2%	85	11.7	47%	69	7.2	39	8	0
Devin McCourty	24	CB	89	10.6%	22	43	19	3	19	53%	23	6.8	47	92	16.3%	31	13.3	53%	41	7.1	38	13	0
Patrick Chung	24	SS	97	13.2%	12	37	16	5	47	45%	29	5.4	18	51	10.4%	2	9.3	45%	65	7.2	32	6	0

Year	Pass D Rank	vs. #1 WR	Rk	vs. #2 WR	Rk	vs. Other WR	Rk	vs. TE	Rk	vs. RB	Rk
2008	27	6.1%	17	30.6%	28	-2.2%	18	2.2%	15	4.1%	16
2009	16	20.1%	26	-14.0%	8	-6.8%	10	12.2%	21	20.1%	26
2010	15	7.9%	23	-5.9%	11	-23.3%	5	11.9%	21	23.0%	30

Other than rookie Devin McCourty, there were few bright spots in the defensive backfield last season. Brandon Meriweather went from the Pro Bowl to the bench to the police blotter. Meriweather earned two brief benchings during the season, one for freelancing too often during the preseason and one for a dumb helmet-to-helmet hit on Todd Heap. In March, he was accused of shooting two men in his Florida hometown. Police confirmed that Meriweather was present at the shooting, but Meriweather's lawyer expressed confidence that his client would not be charged.

When he did play, Meriweather spent too much time flatfooted at deep safety, though that had much to do with the players in front of him. Darius Butler lost his starting job after a double pass interference meltdown in the fourth quarter of the Week 2 loss to the Jets. Replacement Kyle Arrington was just as bad as Butler but less likely to wig out. Butler has Asante Samuel's skill set (smooth coverage ability, good hands, tackling force of a moist sponge) and had a reasonable 2009 rookie season before coming unglued last year. Arrington's positive qualities were hard to find on tape or in the stats, although it was fun when Bill Belichick experimented with a formation that had Arrington rushing the passer as a defensive end. Second-round pick Ras-I Dowling (Virginia Tech) may beat out both of them for a starting job. At 6-foot-2, Dowling has the size to match up with Braylon Edwards/Brandon Marshall types, one of many things Butler and Arrington lack. Leigh Bodden, who missed all of last season with a torn rotator cuff, may also be in the mix; Bill Belichick likes finding roles for older cornerbacks, though the strategy sometimes backfires (see Starks, Duane).

Strong safety Patrick Chung joined McCourty, Bodden, and other NFL players to serve as interns for a day at *Maxim* Magazine in June. Among other staged-for-the-cameras events, Chung had a water pistol fight with a foxy blonde, Bodden primped a model's hair, McCourty argued with his twin brother over a book of girlie photos, and Kyle Arrington got beat for a 50-yard touchdown by one of the Pretty Little Liars. It's important to note that only the last of those four items was a joke; the others really happened. The photo shoot was just as useful as everything else players did during the lockout, and probably a hell of a lot more fun.

Special Teams

Year	DVOA	Rank	FG/XP	Rank	Net Kick	Rank	Kick Ret	Rank	Net Punt	Rank	Punt Ret	Rank	Hidden	Rank
2008	3.6%	6	7.5	3	-0.2	17	9.6	3	3.0	16	1.5	9	3.0	9
2009	1.2%	13	0.5	18	7.7	8	-5.2	21	-6.0	28	10.1	6	-8.1	26
2010	4.0%	8	1.2	15	-4.1	25	11.4	6	7.3	9	7.7	3	7.6	4

Brandon Tate and Julian Edelman excelled in the return game last year. Tate returned two kickoffs for touchdowns early in the season. Edelman came to the rescue on punt returns when Kevin Faulk got hurt, replacing the too-valuable Wes Welker and producing runbacks of 94, 42, 34, and 28 yards while rarely calling for a fair catch. Guard Dan Connelly produced the most exciting return of the year, of course, but there are no plans to get him more touches on special teams.

Kicker Stephen Gostkowski told reporters in June that he was fully recovered from the quad injury that sidelined him last season. With Gostkowski at full strength, Shayne Graham, who kicked well in relief, will hit the free agent market. Second-year punter Zoltan Mesko is a fine overall athlete who was extremely consistent as a rookie.

Coaching Staff

The Patriots have a coordinator again. For two years, Bill Belichick withheld the coordinator title on offense and defense because whoever he chose was snatched by another team a year later, then promptly became autocratic, obnoxious, and ineffective. The same thing could happen to Bill O'Brien, the quarterbacks coach and play-caller since Josh McDaniels left. O'Brien helped the Patriots transition from a spread-based offense to a two-tight end attack with minimal confusion last year, meaning that he is both flexible and versed in a variety of systems. Another season like 2010, and O'Brien (who is 41 years old) will be a hot head coaching commodity.

Belichick still acts as his own defensive coordinator, but Mike Patricia is being groomed as a future signal caller. Patricia moves from linebackers to safeties coach this season. Special teams coordinator Scott O'Brien is a lifer who coached with Belichick in Cleveland. He is no threat to leave for a head coaching vacancy, which is why he has retained his "coordinator" title.

New Orleans Saints

2010 Record: 11-5	**2011 Mean Projection:** 9.5 wins
Pythagorean Wins: 9.2 (11th)	**On the Clock (0-3):** 0%
DVOA: 10.7% (10th)	**Loserville (4-6):** 8%
Offense: 9.5% (11th)	**Mediocrity (7-8):** 23%
Defense: -2.6% (9th)	**Playoff Contender (9-10):** 37%
Special Teams: -1.3% (21st)	**Super Bowl Contender (11+):** 32%
Variance: 11.2% (8th)	**Projected Average Opponent:** -2.3% (26th)

2010: Broken backfield and lack of takeaways part of post-title letdown.

2011: Expect a deeper playoff run, so long as Marshawn Lynch isn't anywhere in the vicinity.

The 2010 Saints were typical of recent defending Super Bowl champs. They reached the postseason only to go one-and-done, getting whipped as 10.5-point favorites by the Seattle Laughingstocks, who were being used as Exhibit A for a revamped playoff system right up until kickoff. New Orleans roared out to a 10-0 lead, then were outscored 41-26 thanks to a shambolic display of covering and tackling. Safety Roman Harper is still searching for the pants he was repeatedly faked out of, the entire defensive backfield is still looking for Brandon Stokley, and Matt Hasselbeck is still laughing at the lack of pressure the Saints brought. By the time Marshawn Lynch was done Tecmo-Bowling through the hapless Saints defense, the warm feelings from the win in Miami Gardens and Drew Brees' Sportsman of the Year Award and all the book and endorsement deals had dissipated into the cool Pacific breeze.

It was the first time in NFL history a defending Super Bowl champion had blown a 10-point lead in the postseason. Otherwise, the letdown was par for the course for Super Bowl winners. No champ since 2000 has made it past the Divisional round the following season except for the 2004 Patriots, who repeated. Aside from the boys from Foxboro, defending champs have won exactly one playoff game in that span, a wildcard win by the 2001 Ravens. Four Lombardi lifters missed the postseason altogether the following year.

So in that light, the Saints 2010 season was rather typical of the species. Discounting them in any way as a 2011 Super Bowl contender based on the Northwest Nightmare is silly.

New Orleans was held back from a serious run at another title by injury — specifically, injury at the running back position. The full unit went down hard. The backs missed a total of 42.1 Adjusted Games Lost, the second largest figure since we've been tracking the numbers (Table 1). Only the 2002 Colts had more. Edgerrin James struggled with hamstring and ankle injuries for that team, while backup Dominic Rhodes and fourth-stringer Syrone Stith were out for all or much of the season. They still made the playoffs, because Peyton Manning was not hurt, but then they suffered an even worse playoff defeat than the Saints did in Seattle, getting blasted 41-0 by the Jets. (Imagine

Table 1. Most Adjusted Games Lost by Running Backs 2000-2010

Year	Team	AGL	Year	Team	AGL
2002	IND	42.3	2000	CIN	36.3
2010	NO	42.1	2000	GB	32.2
2008	DEN	41.6	2006	KC	30.7
2005	GB	38.6	2010	IND	29.6
2007	CIN	38	2000	DEN	29.1

Includes all running backs, not just starters.

2011 Saints Schedule

Week	Opp.	Week	Opp.	Week	Opp.
1	at GB (Thu.)	7	IND	13	DET
2	CHI	8	at STL	14	at TEN
3	HOU	9	TB	15	at MIN
4	at JAC	10	at ATL	16	ATL (Mon.)
5	at CAR	11	BYE	17	CAR
6	at TB	12	NYG (Mon.)		

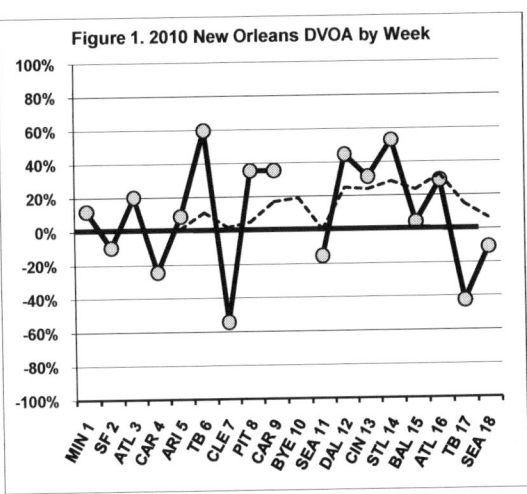

Figure 1. 2010 New Orleans DVOA by Week

if Rex Ryan was on the sidelines to crow about that one.) The next year, the 2003 Colts were 12-4 and in the AFC Championship game, so the Saints have history on their side.

Pierre Thomas, who was such a big part of the Super Bowl run, skipped OTAs in pursuit of a fat contract. He went down in September with a nasty ankle injury and missed ten games. Reggie Bush, who used his Super Bowl ring's shine to blind detractors who continued to call him a bust, hurt a knee and missed eight games and parts of two others. Lynell Hamilton, pegged to replace Mike Bell as the designated goal-line blaster, tore an ACL in preseason and never played a snap.

The carnage appeared to have a classic NFL silver lining (see: Bledsoe/Brady 2001) when undrafted rookie Chris Ivory heard the call "Next Man Up!" and answered with some powerful running. He broke 27 tackles in a dozen games, leading to fans comparing Ivory to Deuce McAllister over post-game meals at Galatoire's and Johnny's Po-Boys. Pete Carroll called him a "freakin' stud" after Ivory punished the Seahawks for 99 yards and a touchdown in the teams' first encounter in November. But then Ivory went down too. According to NOLA.com, Ladell Betts, of all people, wound up leading the running backs in snaps with 258. It should go without saying by this point that Betts also wound up on injured reserve, with a neck injury.

The Saints had to play the wild-card game with their fifth starting running back, Julius Jones. Jones ran for a couple of short touchdowns before, incredibly, he too was injured in the game, suffering a concussion when he was plastered by Lofa Tatupu. Bush, who was back for the game but at less than full strength, suffered another leg injury and went out in the third quarter. DeShawn Wynn, signed on the Monday before the game, was pressed into action. By all rights, he should have trotted on to the field accompanied by

Adagio for Strings (that's the music from *Platoon*, folks — next year a copy of *Classical Music for Dummies* will come with every *FOA 2012* purchase).

Like the 2002 Colts, the 2010 Saints were able to stay afloat despite the storm in the backfield thanks to the anchor behind center. Drew Brees was forced to sling it more times, 658, than he has ever had to in his career — more times, in fact, than anyone in league history except Drew Bledsoe in 1994 and Peyton Manning last season. (By the way, if you thought the ball was in the air more this past season than most, you're right. There were 17,269 pass attempts in 2010, more than any other year except 2002.) His completion percentage remained high, a testimony to Brees' accuracy and ability to adjust routes based on what he sees at the line of scrimmage. His cumulative numbers also were solid.

But, unsurprisingly, all those tosses lowered Brees' overall effectiveness. His DVOA plummeted from 41.0% (third overall in the NFL) to 19.3% (12th). He threw a career-high 22 interceptions, and his yards per attempt fell off by a yard and a half. Brees is commonly lumped in with Manning and Brady atop the quarterback pyramid, a stature only enhanced by his named inclusion with the Terrific Twosome atop the lawsuit filed by the players against the owners this offseason. But in 2010, his efficiency numbers placed him closer to the Matt Schaubs and Joe Flaccos of the league.

Fortunately, Brees has a complement of receivers that only got scarier with the emergence of rookie tight end Jimmy Graham. His tremendous athleticism encouraged the team to part company with oft-injured Jeremy Shockey, and gives Payton another mismatch with which to bedevil defenses. The Colston/

Meacham/Moore/Henderson quartet is tough enough to handle, and NFC South opponents continue to fail to improve enough in the secondary to keep pace.

The presumed return to health of at least a couple of the running backs, plus the drafting of Alabama standout Mark Ingram, should help return balance to the Saints offense — which in turn should help return Brees' DVOA to its accustomed place in the league's gated community. Some consistency at running back will surely allow head coach Sean Payton to return to more varied and unpredictable personnel groupings, a strength that was severely handicapped in 2010. Again according to NOLA.com, the Saints used its "Posse" formation, three wide receivers and a single back, on 41 percent of their plays, up from 33 percent in 2009. The Saints used three or more receivers on well over half their snaps, and the four-plus-receiver sets leapt nine percent The standard two-wides, two-backs set, which the team ran a quarter of the time in 2009, was used only 18 percent of the time. Fullback Heath Evans was forced to watch much of the action from the sideline despite being the rare back that was actually healthy. He only got in for 312 of the team's 1,067 plays.

The health pendulum should surely swing back to the mean, although Ivory missed the beginning of camp while recovering from his foot injury. Meanwhile, much has been placed on Ingram's powerful shoulders. He won the 2009 Heisman, but arguably wasn't even the best runner in his own backfield last year (Trent Richardson, wow). Ingram certainly seems to fit the Saints perfectly. But Ryan Mathews was a perfect fit in San Diego, as was Knowshon Moreno in Denver, and Donald Brown in Indy, and on and on. After last year, New Orleans would probably be ecstatic if Ingram manages to simply dress for all 16 games.

Ingram's selection caused Bush to tweet out a farewell message to Saints fans. The long goodbye became official when the Saints dealt the polarizing playmaker to Miami. The new perimeter threat out of the backfield is Darren Sproles, rejoining former Chargers teammate Brees (he's also the cousin of Saints special teamer Courtney Roby). Sproles is two years older than Bush, but has been far healthier, save for an ankle injury that cost him all of 2006. Ironically, that season was the only one Bush has made it through unscathed. Sproles is likely to provide the same breakaway threat Bush did, and according to DVOA has been far superior as a receiver.

The Saints scored 126 fewer points in 2010 than the year before, and a large reason for that was the drop-off in short fields created by turnovers. The team's average starting position of drives fell from sixth in the league to 26th. Brees & Co.'s Drive Success Rate remained stable, not to mention excellent, so that missing field position was critical. The hallmark of the 2009 Saints was a defense that blitzed from all angles and forced turnovers by the bushel, masking the fact that the personnel was either average or infirm (especially in the secondary). The Saints had 39 takeaways in 2009, and eight more in the postseason, including a couple of famous picks off a pair of future first-ballot Cantonites.

There was little chance that the Saints secondary was going to remain a turnover machine at that level in consecutive seasons. That didn't mean the team changed its approach any. Before the season, New Orleans defenders were confident they would be chest-bumping even more while running off the field with new-found treasure. "Even though 39 was a great number, we can do better," said defensive tackle Sedrick Ellis. Middle linebacker Jonathan Vilma thought 40 or more turnovers was "very realistic." "If there is a way to practice harder at getting turnovers," he boasted, "we've been doing that, emphasizing it more."

Practice, in this case, didn't get the Saints to Carnegie Hall. After picking off 26 passes in 2009, the Saints managed a mere nine last year, dead last in the league. And New Orleans recovered only 13 of the 27 fumbles it forced. They were 14th in the NFL in stopping drives with turnovers, down from third. The strategy didn't change — New Orleans ranked first both seasons in "big blitzing" (six or more rushers) and near the bottom in zone blitzes. If anything, the defense was healthier last season. But the performance in pass rush and coverage of secondary receivers was lacking.

Thanks in large part to 2009, and the fact that Payton gave up some of his salary to procure his services, defensive coordinator Gregg Williams has a rep around the NFL as a "turnover whisperer" — a coach whose defenses rip the ball away with a ferocity other coaches can't impart, or something like that. His career history suggests otherwise (Table 2). The 2009 Saints were only Williams' second defense to finish in the top five in turnovers. Even if given a pass for the Buffalo years, when head coach Williams' mind was presumably focused on a larger canvas, his teams have hardly been turnover machines, even when the

Table 2. Turnovers Forced by Gregg Williams Defenses, 1997-2010

Year	Team	TO	Rank	Year	Team	TO	Rank
1997	TEN	32	T-6	2004	WAS	26	22
1998	TEN	19	T-28	2005	WAS	28	T-18
1999	TEN	40	4	2006	WAS	12	32
2000	TEN	30	T-14	2007	WAS	24	25
2001	BUF	19	30	2008	JAC	17	31
2002	BUF	19	32	2009	NO	39	2
2003	BUF	18	32	2010	NO	25	T-20

randomness of fumble recovery is factored in.

That said, the turnover number is likely to rise in 2011, as regression theory and Williams' history suggests. His takeaway number has dropped off by double-digits two other times. In his first year with Tennessee, 1997 (when the team was so new to the Volunteer State it was still called the Oilers, and played home games in Memphis), the unit had 32 takeaways. In 1998, that figure fell to 19. In 1999, now in Nashville and officially Titanic, a major rebound — up to 40 turnovers, the most ever forced by a Williams defense. The 2006 Redskins dropped from 28 to 12, then were back to normal in 2007, with 24 takeaways.

Other defensive shortcomings were addressed despite the lockout. Highly ranked end Cameron Jordan was drafted in the first round; pass-rushing outside linebacker Martez Wilson was added in the third; and another end, Greg Romeus, who has strong potential but had an injury-riddled career at Pitt, was selected in the seventh. Aging but immense run-stuffing tackle Shaun Rogers was signed before the owners shut the doors, and after the lockout he was joined by the younger and just as run-stuffing former 49ers nose tackle Aubrayo Franklin. Corner Fabian Washington and defensive tackle Turk McBride were signed from Baltimore and Detroit, respectively, to add depth. In its neck-and-neck race with Atlanta for division supremacy, and with Tampa coming up fast on the outside, the Saints need to be able to stop teams more reliably. Counting on turnovers, as last season showed, is a fool's errand.

So long as Brees and Payton are in command, the Saints will be contenders. These are the glory days in franchise history, and should be appreciated as such. Brees is 32, and Payton has two years left on his contract, while seemingly dreaming of a Texas-sized homecoming. The time for Who Dat Nation to roar is now, which is why the Seattle defeat was more crushing than it would be for other franchises with richer legacies and more stable futures. Coach/quarterback combos as potent as this one don't come around very often. It would be a shame to see the duo derailed by factors beyond their control, like fluky injury vectors, in 2011 and beyond.

Robert Weintraub

2010 Saints Stats by Week

Wk	vs.	W-L	PF	PA	YDF	YDA	TO	Total	Off	Def	ST
1	MIN	W	14	9	308	253	1	12%	21%	1%	-8%
2	@SF	W	25	22	287	417	4	-10%	14%	31%	8%
3	ATL	L	24	27	398	417	-2	20%	18%	7%	9%
4	CAR	W	16	14	383	251	-1	-24%	8%	31%	-1%
5	@ARI	L	20	30	358	194	-3	9%	-31%	-50%	-11%
6	@TB	W	31	6	475	277	0	60%	36%	-29%	-6%
7	CLE	L	17	30	394	210	-4	-54%	-21%	20%	-13%
8	PIT	W	20	10	318	279	0	35%	5%	-26%	5%
9	@CAR	W	34	3	408	195	1	35%	13%	-17%	6%
10	BYE										
11	SEA	W	34	19	494	424	0	-15%	31%	31%	-15%
12	@DAL	W	30	27	414	457	1	45%	36%	-2%	6%
13	@CIN	W	34	30	436	311	-1	31%	53%	12%	-10%
14	STL	W	31	13	345	327	0	53%	20%	-36%	-3%
15	@BAL	L	24	30	269	356	-1	4%	13%	13%	5%
16	@ATL	W	17	14	368	215	0	29%	-7%	-25%	11%
17	TB	L	13	23	305	317	-1	-43%	-36%	3%	-4%
18	@SEA	L	36	41	474	415	0	-11%	23.0%	40.0%	7.0%

Trends and Splits

	Offense	Rank	Defense	Rank
Total DVOA	9.5%	11	-2.6%	9
Unadjusted VOA	10.4%	9	-5.1%	7
Weighted Trend	10.2%	11	-4.7%	6
Variance	6.0%	9	6.6%	16
Average Opponent	2.7%	16	-4.3%	3
Passing	24.4%	13	3.7%	9
Rushing	-5.9%	25	-9.2%	9
First Down	1.2%	20	8.8%	23
Second Down	11.3%	9	-21.4%	2
Third Down	22.8%	9	6.3%	20
First Half	12.6%	10	-5.6%	8
Second Half	6.4%	12	0.7%	14
Red Zone	-11.1%	24	-33.9%	2
Late and Close	2.9%	17	-0.4%	20

Five-Year Performance

Year	W-L	Pyth	Est W	PF	PA	TO	Total	Rk	Off	Rk	Def	Rk	ST	Rk	Off AGL	Rk	Def AGL	Rk
2006	10-6	10.3	9.1	413	322	-4	6.6%	12	10.5%	8	4.6%	22	0.7%	14	30.6	29	14.6	18
2007	7-9	7.8	7.6	379	388	-7	-9.0%	22	7.9%	11	13.3%	29	-3.6%	25	21.4	17	13.7	8
2008	8-8	9.5	9.5	463	393	-4	9.9%	13	21.1%	4	10.7%	26	-0.6%	22	24.0	15	33.4	24
2009	13-3	11.6	11.6	510	341	+11	23.5%	6	27.8%	2	1.5%	14	-2.7%	28	45.6	30	32.9	21
2010	11-5	9.2	9.7	384	307	-6	10.7%	10	9.5%	11	-2.6%	9	-1.3%	21	19.8	10	25.2	18

Strategic Tendencies

Run/Pass		Rank	Offense		Rank	Defense		Rank	Other		Rank
Runs, all plays	34%	29	3+ WR	53%	12	Rush 3	10.1%	12	2+ RB, Pct Runs	56%	20
Runs, first half	31%	32	4+ WR	16%	4	Rush 4	41.0%	29	1 RB/2 TE, Pct Runs	38%	28
Runs, first down	40%	31	2+ TE	29%	18	Rush 5	23.8%	15	1 RB/3+ WR, Pct Runs	20%	22
Runs, second-long	30%	24	Single back	53%	23	Rush 6+	25.2%	1	CB1 on WR1	42%	15
Runs, power sit.	65%	8	Play action	20%	11	Zone Blitz	1.8%	32	Go for it on 4th	1.14	6
Runs, behind 2H	31%	11	Max protect	11%	15	Sacks by LB	18.2%	20	Offensive Pace	30.6	17
Pass, ahead 2H	56%	1	Outside pocket	8%	28	Sacks by DB	19.7%	3	Defensive Pace	30.9	20

No discussion of strategic tendencies in New Orleans is complete without a discussion of the wide variety of offensive formation looks that Sean Payton uses to confuse opponents. Empty sets, power sets, spread sets, standard sets... New Orleans runs them all. New Orleans ranked fourth in frequency of empty backfields, 9.6 percent of plays, with 8.6 yards per play (first in the NFL) and 77.0% DVOA (second behind New England). The Saints also ranked third in usage of six-OL sets, behind the Raiders and Giants, but gained only 3.8 yards per play from these sets — even though they weren't just using six linemen in short yardage. In fact, the Saints passed the ball with six linemen 44 percent of the time. ☞ The Saints really, really love to blitz, far more than any other team. Overall, they sent five or more on 49 percent of pass plays, which led the league. They sent five or more pass rushers 65 percent of the time on third down; the Jets were the only other defense over 50 percent. They also ran a big blitz of six or more 50 percent more often than the next-highest team, St. Louis. The Saints allowed 5.5 yards per pass with a big blitz, 6.3 yards per pass otherwise. ☞ The Saints ranked first in defensive DVOA in the first quarter, then 12th the rest of the game.

Passing

Player	DYAR	DVOA	Plays	NtYds	Avg	YAC	C%	TD	Int
D.Brees	1360	19.3%	684	4479	6.5	4.6	68.5%	33	21

Rushing

Player	DYAR	DVOA	Plays	Yds	Avg	TD	Fum	Suc
C.Ivory	133	12.9%	137	717	5.2	5	4	59%
P.Thomas	34	0.7%	82	269	3.3	2	0	50%
J.Jones	-19	-16.2%	60	223	3.7	0	1	38%
L.Betts	-5	-10.6%	45	148	3.3	2	1	51%
R.Bush	-4	-11.1%	36	150	4.2	0	0	42%
R.Meachem	5	-15.4%	4	14	3.5	0	0	-
D.Brees	-5	-35.1%	4	9	2.3	0	0	-

Receiving

Player	DYAR	DVOA	Plays	Ctch	Yds	Y/C	YAC	TD	C%
M.Colston	220	8.6%	132	84	1023	12.2	3.2	7	64%
L.Moore	205	14.6%	94	66	763	11.6	4.4	8	70%
R.Meachem	187	22.7%	66	44	638	14.5	3.0	5	67%
D.Henderson	33	-5.3%	59	34	464	13.6	3.8	1	58%
A.Arrington	28	28.0%	9	7	79	11.3	3.6	0	78%
J.Shockey	65	8.7%	59	41	408	10.0	3.0	3	69%
D.Thomas	-35	-18.3%	46	30	219	7.3	4.4	2	65%
J.Graham	98	24.8%	43	31	356	11.5	4.5	5	72%
R.Bush	29	-1.5%	42	34	208	6.1	5.9	1	81%
L.Betts	-11	-20.4%	31	23	141	6.1	7.3	0	74%
P.Thomas	56	17.1%	30	30	201	6.7	8.7	0	100%
J.Jones	-42	-51.1%	22	17	59	3.5	6.6	0	77%
H.Evans	7	-5.5%	11	7	41	5.9	5.4	1	64%

Offensive Line

Year	Yards	ALY	Rank	Power	Rank	Stuff	Rank	2nd Lev	Rank	Open Field	Rank
2008	4.17	4.37	6	64%	18	15%	7	1.15	13	0.63	24
2009	4.62	4.48	2	69%	7	18%	14	1.27	8	0.93	9
2010	4.23	4.42	6	68%	7	19%	17	1.21	10	0.71	17

Year	LE	Rank	LT	Rank	Mid	Rank	RT	Rank	RE	Rank	Sacks	ASR	Rank	F-Start	Cont.
2008	4.53	14	5.17	2	4.45	8	4.31	11	3.20	27	13	2.9%	2	20	28
2009	3.67	24	4.18	14	4.65	2	4.63	4	4.87	3	21	4.2%	4	14	34
2010	4.75	7	4.53	11	4.59	4	3.71	23	4.02	14	26	4.7%	5	14	48

If any team proved our seminal tenet that building the line is critical, it was the 2010 Saints. Despite the Ulysses-length injury list to its running backs, New Orleans had a productive season on the ground. Sure, Arian Foster had more yards than the entire Saints backfield corps, but only five teams bested the Saints in Adjusted Line Yards. The front five was similarly efficient at keeping Drew Brees upright. The line might not have won John Madden's Most Valuable Protectors Award (and its ridiculous 102-pound trophy), as it did in 2009, but it was inarguably the most valuable unit on the team.

The strength of the line is at guard, where Pro Bowlers Jahri Evans and Carl Nicks mash enemy linemen. Evans signed a contract before the season making him the richest guard in the NFL, and mostly earned it, except in one critical area: penalty flags. Evans was called for 12 penalties, including nine holds (one was declined), and quick, slashing tackles like Geno Atkins gave him trouble. Nicks only had five penalties, and often outplayed his better-compensated teammate (he blew half as many blocks as Evans, for example). New Orleans ran it more efficiently up the middle better than anywhere else, and better than all but three other teams. Center Jonathan Goodwin gets his share of the credit as well, though he was unable to repeat his Pro Bowl trip from 2009, likely because the Saints were no longer the feel-good story of the NFL. Goodwin turned down the Saints to sign with San Francisco after the lockout, and the Saints signed former Bears center Olin Kreutz as his replacement. 2010 fifth-rounder Matt Tennant (Boston College) was the likely starter before the Kreutz signing and is still waiting in the wings.

On the subject of ostensible free agents, left tackle Jermon Bushrod settled down after a rocky 2009 to earn himself a new contract with the Saints, albeit only for two seasons. Jonathan Stinchcomb had sports hernia surgery last summer, and this offseason went under the knife to reattach the quadricep to his left knee. If Stinchcomb cannot regain his pre-injury form, promising second-year man Charles Brown is set to take over. If Brown develops, he should flip over to the left side, where he is probably better suited, and let Bushrod play right tackle — one reason the Saints didn't lock up Bushrod with left tackle money.

Defensive Front Seven

Defensive Line	Age	Pos	Plays	TmPct	Rk	Stop	Dfts	BTkl	St%	Rk	AvYd	Rk	Sack	Hit	Hur	Runs	St%	Yds	Pass	St%	Yds
							Overall						Pass Rush			vs. Run			vs. Pass		
Sedrick Ellis	26	DT	44	5.7%	14	29	11	1	64%	55	2.3	45	6	4	7	33	64%	3.5	11	73%	-1.4
Will Smith	30	DE	43	5.9%	32	36	14	2	83%	17	0.6	18	5.5	5	19	29	83%	1.4	14	86%	-1.0
Alex Brown	32	DE	41	5.3%	39	31	13	1	71%	54	2.2	49	2	5	17.5	35	71%	2.9	6	100%	-2.2
Remi Ayodele	28	DT	38	4.9%	27	31	7	2	81%	26	2.3	41	1	2	8	36	81%	2.5	2	100%	-1.5
Anthony Hargrove	28	DT	25	3.7%	52	16	6	0	68%	57	3.0	59	1	5	4.5	22	68%	2.1	3	33%	9.3
Jeff Charleston	28	DE	24	3.1%	79	20	7	1	79%	19	0.4	13	3	1	1.5	19	79%	2.0	5	100%	-5.6
Jimmy Wilkerson	30	DE	16	2.1%	--	12	2	0	71%	--	2.5	--	2	0	9	14	71%	3.6	2	100%	-5.5

Linebackers	Age	Pos	Plays	TmPct	Rk	Stop	Dfts	BTkl	AvYd	Pass Rush			vs. Run					vs. Pass				
										Sack	Hit	Hur	Runs	St%	Rk	Yds	Rk	Tgts	Suc%	Rk	AdjYd	Rk
Jonathan Vilma	29	MLB	107	13.8%	28	70	24	5	3.4	4	6	5	75	69%	50	3.1	54	32	62%	16	5.5	26
Scott Shanle	32	OLB	76	11.2%	49	30	7	11	6.6	0	3	6.5	33	55%	98	4.0	90	31	33%	76	6.7	51
Danny Clark	34	OLB	57	8.4%	76	36	6	4	3.3	0	2	3.5	41	76%	18	2.3	17	11	65%	--	4.4	--
Jo-Lonn Dunbar	26	OLB	40	6.3%	--	26	9	2	3.6	1	0	0	28	71%	--	2.7	--	6	40%	--	4.2	--
Marvin Mitchell	27	MLB	31	4.0%	--	16	14	1	4.9	1	1	2.5	14	57%	--	1.3	--	16	61%	21	5.2	20

Year	Yards	ALY	Rank	Power	Rank	Stuff	Rank	2nd Lev	Rank	Open Field	Rank
2008	4.15	4.21	20	80%	31	17%	15	1.19	21	0.58	11
2009	4.51	4.28	22	69%	23	19%	17	1.10	11	0.89	20
2010	4.01	4.00	16	40%	1	21%	12	1.06	12	0.79	17

Year	LE	Rank	LT	Rank	Mid	Rank	RT	Rank	RE	Rank	Sacks	ASR	Rank
2008	4.43	22	4.26	18	4.18	14	4.28	21	4.01	18	28	5.1%	25
2009	5.19	29	5.42	32	4.11	19	4.20	16	2.67	1	36	6.3%	17
2010	2.23	1	4.19	18	3.87	14	4.77	29	4.45	27	33	6.3%	16

Sedrick Ellis was drafted to sponge up blockers and bounce from three-technique tackle to the nose when the Saints play coverage formations. Rushing the passer wasn't in his performance envelope, yet there he was last year, leading the Saints with six sacks. True, he didn't chase down the most elusive scramblers — Brett Favre, Carson Palmer, Matt Ryan, and Joe Flacco accounted for two-thirds of his prey, while his sacks of Jimmy Clausen and Matt Moore probably shouldn't even count, given the Panthers' offensive line. But the unexpected heat from the inside helped offset a poor outside rush, despite blitzers coming from as far away as Metairie. Ellis unveiled a lively sack dance as well. Look for it on a coming episode of *Treme*.

Most press reportage this spring posited that the lockout prevented any free agents from signing. That's true, but overlooks the fact that the Saints snuck space-eating tackle Shaun Rogers into the fold before the labor strife hit. The crucial numbers for Rogers are 85 percent and 32. The latter is Rogers' age, and in conjunction with his injury history that makes him an unreliable entity. But his Run Stop Rate, the first figure, hits a Saints weakness square on target. The Saints further solidified the tackle position after the season by grabbing 31-year-old Aubrayo Franklin from the 49ers on a one-year deal. According to our defensive similarity scores, Franklin's nearest match over the past three seasons is the late Norman Hand, who steadied the Saints line at the turn of the century. Run stuffers are in for New Orleans; Anthony Hargrove, Remi Ayodele, and their poor Run Stop Rates are out.

Will Smith remains an effective end, but on the other side Alex Brown got around the quarterback 22.5 times (hits plus hurries) while only bringing him down twice. That's the fewest sacks of any end in the league with twenty or more pressures, and the only tackle to have a worse ratio was Kevin Williams of Minnesota (30 pressures, one sack). Simple spatial relations suggest Brown should find his way into at least a couple more sacks in 2011, but he may not get the chance if Cameron Jordan, the Saints' top pick, eats up his playing time. Jordan could help on all downs; he was among the top run-stopping ends in college last season.

The linebackers, despite all the blitzes, contributed a mere six sacks total, and only two from 'backers not named Jonathan Vilma. The man in the middle remained formidable, but the outside guys need help. Scott Shanle is supposed to be the cover specialist, but his Success Rate against the pass was brutal, as tight ends burned the Saints all year (27th in the league). He'll be replaced by Jonathan Casillas, who lost the season to Lisfranc foot surgery but is beloved by Gregg Williams for his speed and decision-making. On the strong side, Danny Clark was a good tackler in 2010, but at 34 figures to be the odd man out with third-round draftee Martez Wilson (Illinois) battling Jo-Lonn Dunbar for the starting gig.

Defensive Secondary

Secondary	Age	Pos	Plays	TmPct	Rk	Stop	Dfts	BTkl	Runs	St%	Rk	Yds	Rk	Tgts	Tgt%	Rk	Dist	Suc%	Rk	APaYd	Rk	PD	Int
				Overall						**vs. Run**					**vs. Pass**								
Roman Harper	29	SS	100	13.7%	7	52	17	5	57	56%	8	4.4	7	32	7.8%	16	9.7	65%	12	4.0	2	4	1
Michael Jenkins	24	FS	74	10.1%	42	32	17	10	23	35%	54	12.3	81	41	10.0%	4	12.3	71%	6	4.1	3	11	2
Jabari Greer	29	CB	73	10.7%	19	30	15	9	9	33%	67	4.9	20	62	16.4%	29	12.5	49%	59	8.6	66	11	2
Tracy Porter	25	CB	66	11.3%	15	26	15	7	19	37%	64	7.1	50	55	16.9%	26	11.8	48%	62	7.3	44	6	1
Patrick Robinson	24	CB	27	5.0%	--	9	3	1	8	38%	--	7.9	--	24	7.9%	--	11.9	59%	--	4.4	--	2	0
Leigh Torrence	29	CB	22	3.5%	--	7	3	3	5	20%	--	10.6	--	21	5.9%	--	10.2	54%	--	8.5	--	3	1
Darren Sharper	36	SS	18	4.6%	--	3	1	4	9	22%	--	9.7	--	7	3.2%	--	15.5	32%	--	12.0	--	1	0
Usama Young	26	FS	18	3.4%	--	6	4	4	4	50%	--	3.0	--	6	1.9%	--	9.2	28%	--	5.5	--	2	0

Year	Pass D Rank	vs. #1 WR	Rk	vs. #2 WR	Rk	vs. Other WR	Rk	vs. TE	Rk	vs. RB	Rk
2008	22	23.5%	29	-30.7%	3	-0.7%	21	7.4%	20	7.5%	19
2009	9	-34.9%	2	9.2%	25	9.7%	21	-17.8%	5	6.5%	19
2010	9	2.3%	18	1.8%	16	-14.7%	7	19.4%	27	14.3%	24

In a development approximately as surprising as October having 31 days, safety Darren Sharper fell off dramatically. Playing centerfield like Willie Mays in his prime, Sharper led the NFL with nine interceptions in 2009. But his surgically repaired knee let him down in 2010, as the 35-year-old missed half the season. When he was on the field, Sharper was ineffective, necessitating Malcolm Jenkins' full time move to free safety, a position he is better suited for than corner. Strong safety Roman "The Neck" Harper (so-nicknamed for his bulging trapezius muscles) remained a punishing force against the run. He was incinerated in the wild-card game by the slick play action and hot reads of Matt Hasselbeck, accentuating Harper's rep as a poor pass defender, but the numbers actually show Harper had a good season when the ball was in the air, too.

One minute Tracy Porter was making the defining play in franchise history, his Super Bowl pick-six to clinch the 2009 title. Little more than a year later, Porter may have to relinquish his No. 22 jersey to hot draftee Mark Ingram. So much for the Ring of Honor. Porter and fellow corner Jabari Greer managed only three picks between them in 2010, while missing six games combined to injury, a problem that figures to be perennial given their small frames. Both are swift and comfortable in man coverage, if reliant on the pass rush to help. The corners didn't shut down enemy top receivers as well as they did in 2009, but it was tight ends and running backs that torched the Saints, not guys covered by the corners. Rookie third corner Patrick Robinson was raw but looks comfortable in the blitz-heavy scheme, and he's faster than either starter. The defensive backfield was also unlucky — only the Browns had a lower percentage of passes dropped against them than did New Orleans (only 19 drops, 3.9 percent of passes).

Special Teams

Year	DVOA	Rank	FG/XP	Rank	Net Kick	Rank	Kick Ret	Rank	Net Punt	Rank	Punt Ret	Rank	Hidden	Rank
2008	-0.6%	22	-5.3	28	-7.0	26	1.3	16	-3.8	22	11.4	2	-2.7	17
2009	-2.7%	28	-9.2	28	1.2	16	7.3	7	-7.7	29	-7.8	30	1.3	13
2010	-1.3%	21	-6.1	30	1.4	14	-3.3	17	4.1	14	-3.9	23	-9.6	27

In a September showdown with division rival Atlanta, Garrett Hartley managed to badly miss a chip shot 29-yard field-goal attempt in overtime. The Falcons went on to win, a result that wound up costing New Orleans the division title. Sean Payton was incensed, and brought in John Carney to kick, a message to the 23-year-old hero of the 2009 title run about as subtle as a cosh to the temple. Unsurprisingly, the ancient Carney missed a 29-yarder of his own a couple of weeks later, and Payton was glad he hadn't released Hartley in a fit of pique. Given his job back, the Oklahoma grad missed only two more the rest of the season, one fewer than he missed in the first three games of 2010. The redemption resembled 2009, when Hartley rebounded from a bad overtime miss against the Bucs to drill every big kick in the postseason.

Hartley's travails were indicative of the Saints special teams overall, a unit that continues to underperform. Courtney Roby, a kickoff return revelation in 2009, fell off in effectiveness, though the Bengals didn't get the message — they squib-kicked rather than let Roby return it on them in their December matchup, providing Heath Evans with three of his four returns on the season. The Reggie Bush/Lance Moore combo struck little fear on punt returns; Bush was below-average on punt returns for the second straight season. The coverage units seemed to miss Troy Evans, the special teams captain in 2009, who was cut in late August. At least Thomas Morestead was a solid punter, although with a mere 57 boots he was hardly at risk of overuse. The Saints were unusual in that the team only decided who would kick off, Morstead or Hartley, as kickoff itself approached each Sunday. Morestead's kicks were worth 2.9 points of estimated field position over average, Hartley's -1.8 points under average.

Despite the overall mediocrity, the Saints actually moved up seven spots in the overall special teams rankings — but they fell considerably in the "Hidden" rankings, pointing out the amount of good fortune it takes in every phase of the game to make a Super Bowl run.

Coaching Staff

Sean Payton brought in on himself: every distracting question, every blind gossip item on Pro Football Talk, every ounce of speculation from the pigskin media industrial complex. By moving his family mid-contract out of his supposedly beloved New Orleans (as elucidated in his recent memoir) and over to Dallas, Payton has used a power cable to spark rumors that he will eventually coaching or general-managing the Cowboys to life. Surely, it isn't a requirement that Payton's family remain in Louisiana for him to be an effective coach, but given that the Saints kiboshed the idea of Payton living in Dallas back when they hired him in 2006 (Payton wrote that Saints GM Mickey Loomis "wasn't keen on that at all" in *Home Team*), it makes one wonder why things are different now. Two years remain on Payton's contract. Should he intend to honor them both, he will need to reach out and mend fences in the community that he did so much to unite over the last few years.

Why Jerry Jones or any other owner should wish to employ Payton is obvious. He is among the league leaders in creativity, both in offensive scheming and play-calling. No team in the league threw it when leading in the second half as much as the Saints, and that's the Sean Payton ethos in one tidy stat. Other stats indicated a drop-off, however — New Orleans lost 30 yards and eight points per game off its 2009 numbers, and nine spots in DVOA. Perhaps Payton senses he has pushed this attack to its red line, and is setting up his next challenge. He is only 47, after all, and is a coaching descendant of the franchise-hopping Bill Parcells. If you squint hard, you can already make out the extreme closeups of Payton on the giant HDTV in Cowboys Stadium on the horizon. What that will mean for the Saints franchise is anyone's guess.

Defensive coordinator Gregg Williams doesn't possess enough curse words in his famously blue vocabulary to sum up the Saints' defensive effort in the playoff game in Seattle. Best to forget it and move on. Williams remains big blitz-giddy — the Saints sent seven defenders after the quarterback 37 times, easily the most in the league — and zone-blitz averse. How Williams conjures a better pass rush off the edge will be closely watched in 2011. Joe Vitt, the linebackers coach at the center of last year's Vanishing Vicodin controversy, has survived with his job, but if the unit's play doesn't improve, he may not for much longer.

New York Giants

2010 Record: 10-6

Pythagorean Wins: 10.1 (7th)

DVOA: 14.6% (9th)

Offense: 11.5% (8th)

Defense: -8.0% (3rd)

Special Teams: -4.9% (30th)

Variance: 22.9% (25th)

2011 Mean Projection: 8.2 wins

On the Clock (0-3): 5%

Loserville (4-6): 23%

Mediocrity (7-8): 26%

Playoff Contender (9-10): 26%

Super Bowl Contender (11+): 21%

Projected Average Opponent: 1.8% (9th)

2010: The masterfade … I coulda played along.

2011: Finish or famine.

More than perhaps any team in football, this current edition of the New York Giants would have been incredibly ill-equipped for the possibility of an 18-game schedule. 2010 was only the most recent example of a disturbing trend that's developed under Tom Coughlin's watch in New York: The Giants have established themselves as a team that collapses in the second half of the season.

The numbers are remarkable. During Coughlin's seven seasons as Giants head coach, the team has gone 41-15 during their first eight games of the season, only to finish 24-32 over the second half. Not once have they put up a second-half record that surpasses their record in the first-half. And only once did the team have an obvious excuse for doing so: In 2004, when Coughlin benched Kurt Warner at midseason and replaced him with the comedy stylings of rookie Eli Manning. That year, the Giants started 5-3 and finished 1-7, but developing Manning for the future is at least an understandable and defensible goal.

Even if we just take a look at the past five years under Coughlin, the figures are remarkable. Since 2006, the Giants have been 30-10 during the first half and just 18-22 during the second half, a difference of 12 wins. To put it into a seasonal context: the Giants start the season as a 12-win team and finish it playing like a seven-win squad. The last time a team besides the Giants had such a consistently dramatic split between their performance in the first and second halves of the season was the 1996-2000 Steelers. The 2000 Steelers finished up a five-year stretch that saw them go 27-13 during the first half of their season and finish up 16-24, an 11-win difference.

While win-loss record isn't always the best measure of team performance, this isn't some mirage that gets revealed by DVOA. Over the past five years, the Giants have put up an 22.3% DVOA during the first half and a 0.5% DVOA during the second half, a decline of 21.8%.

So, we know that the Giants have fallen mightily during the second half of their seasons. But why? In looking over the numbers, we've identified two things that also shift drastically with the Giants' performance over the two halves:

Their schedule has gotten significantly more difficult during the second half. It's not surprising that the Giants would face a difficult schedule in the consistently competitive NFC East, but those difficult divisional games have mostly happened during the second half of seasons. 18 of the Giants' 30 games against their NFC East opponents over the past five years have taken place during their final eight games of each year.

Because of this, it turns out that most of their cupcake games against the weaker sisters of lesser divisions take place during the first half of the campaign. Consider 2009, when the Giants got off to a 5-0 start before finishing 3-5. Outside of a two-point

2011 Giants Schedule

Week	Opp.	Week	Opp.	Week	Opp.
1	at WAS	7	BYE	13	GB
2	STL (Mon.)	8	MIA	14	at DAL
3	at PHI	9	at NE	15	WAS
4	at ARI	10	at SF	16	at NYJ
5	SEA	11	PHI	17	DAL
6	BUF	12	at NO (Mon.)		

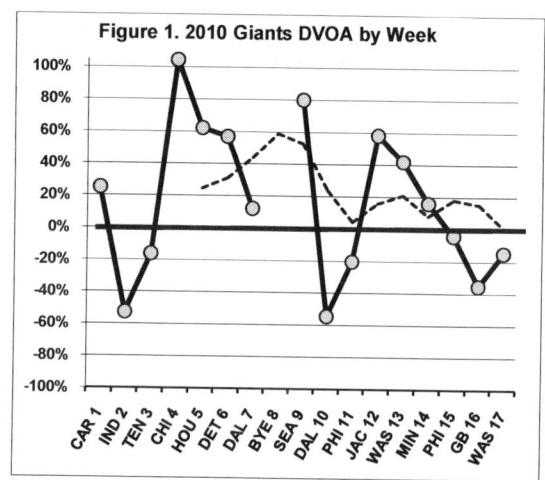

Figure 1. 2010 Giants DVOA by Week

win against the 11-5 Cowboys, the Giants picked up four wins over teams that would finish the season a combined 14-48. That included a game against the Redskins, but the Giants also got to face the Chiefs, Raiders, and Buccaneers. That streak ended when the eventual Super Bowl champion Saints stomped the Giants by 21 points.

Over the entire five-year stretch, the Giants' first-half opponents have had an average winning percentage of .444, just about the equivalent to that of a 7-9 team. During the second half of their schedule, their average opponent's winning percentage is at .566; that's the equivalent of a 9-7 team. They've played 26 games over the timeframe against teams that won ten games or better, and 15 of them came in the second half. They have also played 26 games against teams that won six games or less, and 20 of those games came in the first half.

That scenario seems likely to play out again in 2011. The Giants play only three teams projected to finish higher than them in the first eight weeks: Philadelphia, Miami, and New England. In addition to that, they draw three NFC West teams, Washington, and Buffalo. Given that Miami's public profile is not anywhere near what FO is forecasting for them, it's not hard for Giants fans to imagine a nice cushy record going into the second half of the season. However, in those last eight weeks, they play Philadelphia again,

Table 1: Giants Change in DVOA Rank after Week 9, 2006-10

Year	Offense	Rush	Pass	Defense	Rush	Pass
2006	-9	-6	-9	-22	+1	-22
2007	-9	-12	-6	+3	+1	+1
2008	-3	-5	+3	-8	+7	-19
2009	+5	-9	+6	-20	-7	-19
2010	-7	-11	-2	-14	-20	-9
Average	-4.6	-8.6	-1.6	-12.2	-3.6	-13.6

Dallas twice, Green Bay, New Orleans, and the Jets. Once again, the familiar split of four NFC East games in the last eight compared to two in the first eight pops out. If the Giants want back into the playoffs, they're going to have to stop the broken record.

DVOA adjusts for the quality of a team's opposition, though, so there's more in play here than merely the schedule. Both the offense and defense decline in the second half, but the offense declines only by an average of only 8.9% DVOA over the past five years, whereas the defense declines by 17.5% DVOA. If we look at how the team's performance changed from half-to-half in each of the offensive and defensive categories, one key decline stands out (Table 1).

The collapse of the Giants' pass defense has driven a decline in their performance in four of the past five seasons, and they've fallen an average of 14 spots in pass defense DVOA from one half to the other. And while a decline of nine spots in 2010 doesn't necessarily seem all that bad after back-to-back declines of 19 spots, consider that this year's fall was from first to tenth.

In 2009, it was pretty simple to figure out why the pass defense declined: Everybody in the secondary got hurt. In 2010, though, the Giants' four starters in the secondary combined to miss just one game. In fact, the only player on defense to suffer a long-term injury was reserve pass rusher Mathias Kiwanuka, who chipped in with four sacks during his three healthy games.

When we think about the Giants pass defense, of course, we associate it with a fierce pass rush that creates turnovers and forces quarterbacks into bad situations and mistakes. That didn't change in 2010: The Giants finished seventh in Adjusted Sack Rate and, thanks to a league-record 10 forced fumbles by resurgent defensive end Osi Umenyiora, only the Patriots created more turnovers per drive than the Giants.

On the other hand, we also know that the decline in pass defense during the second half was joined by a decline in the pass rush, as the Giants' sack rate fell from 8.7 percent to 7.0 percent. Over a full season, those respective sack rates would have ranked second and tenth, almost perfectly mirroring the overall decline in performance. Although one decline is far from enough to prove that a trend exists, it raises an interesting question: Do teams that rely heavily on their pass rush to produce quality pass defense generally wilt in the second half? Anecdotally, it could make sense, as those defensive legs begin to tire and the inexperienced offensive lines that teams pick on improve their communication and close up their gaps.

Unfortunately for the camp of simple explanations, the evidence doesn't fit the narrative. Going back through the 2000 season, we looked at each team's pass defense over the first and second halves of their respective seasons and identified 50 pairs of defenses for the study. Each pair had a remarkably similar first-half defensive DVOA, with an average difference of 0.1%. They also had dramatically different sack rates. The average difference in sack rate within each pair was 4.1 percent, with a difference of 22 spots in the sack rate rankings.

The hope in doing this was to identify teams that have roughly similar pass defenses through dramatically different methods, with one team in the pair deriving a significant amount of its pass defense's performance from the pass rush, while the other one did not. If our theory was correct, the teams that rely heavily on a pass rush would decline in the second half far more frequently and significantly than those teams that rely on coverage. Instead, the results were just about down the middle, as 26 of the 50 teams within the pairs with the superior pass rush suffered the greater decline.

In doing this, though, we discovered a fascinating tidbit about how pass rushes work. Remember that in separating these teams, we were trying to identify great pass rushes and awful pass rushes by using their sack rate in the first half of the season. Naturally, we would expect the teams with great sack rates to maintain a relatively high sack rate over the second half of the season. Instead, incredibly, the teams with the awful sack rates in the first half of the season actually put up a higher sack rate than their brethren with a previously-elite pass rush over the second half of the

season (Table 2). If we look at every team since 2000, the correlation between first half sack rate and second half sack rate is just 0.10; that means that exactly one percent of a team's second half sack rate is explained by their figure in the first half.

Table 2: The Case of the Disappearing Sack Rate

Team Type	1H Sack Rate	Rank	2H Sack Rate	Rank
Strong Sack Rates in Games 1-8	8.4%	5.5	6.2%	17.6
Weak Sack Rates in Games 1-8	4.3%	27.7	6.3%	16.4

It's a tricky quandary to figure out. Maybe teams see those high sack rates on film and devote more of their efforts to pass protection. Maybe it's just the nature of a smaller sample size, as each team faces an average of about 283 dropbacks during the first half of the season. Although these "strong pass rush" teams have twice the average number of sacks that the "weak pass rush" teams do, it's only a difference of 12 sacks. Maybe it's regression towards the mean exhibiting itself yet again. Or, well, maybe what we are seeing is tired legs from the elite pass rushers that are causing those impressive first-half sack rates, and once they slow down, their previously-untested secondaries can't hold up.

The Giants don't project to be much different than they were last season. A tougher overall schedule (tied for seventh-hardest in the NFL) will take its toll on New York's playoff chances. Their offensive projection dips a bit mainly because of the loss of offensive line continuity. The releases of long-time center Shaun O'Hara and guard Rich Seubert have shaken up a line that had been in place since the 2007 season. David Diehl kicks inside to replace Seubert, 2009 second-rounder William Beatty will take over at left tackle, and the Giants signed 49ers lineman David Baas to take O'Hara's snaps at center. They were probably necessary moves considering the lack of youth on the New York offensive line, but they will hurt in the short term.

The Giants have maintained a good core and don't appear to have any glaring weaknesses, but they'll have to overcome a few separate obstacles — some familiar, some due to a lack of familiarity — to claim the playoff spot they just missed out on last year.

Bill Barnwell

2010 Giants Stats by Week

Wk	vs.	W-L	PF	PA	YDF	YDA	TO	Total	Off	Def	ST
1	CAR	W	31	18	376	237	1	25%	0%	-45%	-20%
2	@IND	L	14	38	257	410	-2	-53%	-25%	33%	5%
3	TEN	L	10	29	471	271	-3	-16%	22%	24%	-14%
4	CHI	W	17	3	372	110	0	104%	24%	-92%	-12%
5	@HOU	W	34	10	414	195	0	62%	4%	-54%	4%
6	DET	W	28	20	334	366	2	57%	37%	-24%	-4%
7	@DAL	W	41	35	497	254	-3	12%	22%	-4%	-13%
8	BYE										
9	@SEA	W	41	7	487	162	2	80%	42%	-39%	-1%
10	DAL	L	20	33	480	427	-2	-55%	1%	54%	-2%
11	@PHI	L	17	27	208	392	-3	-20%	-33%	-13%	-1%
12	JAC	W	24	20	361	328	2	58%	42%	-9%	8%
13	WAS	W	31	7	358	338	5	42%	26%	-14%	2%
14	@MIN	W	21	3	395	164	-1	16%	0%	-33%	-17%
15	PHI	L	31	38	364	418	1	-4%	19%	16%	-7%
16	@GB	L	17	45	386	515	-5	-35%	-3%	34%	1%
17	@WAS	W	17	14	325	385	3	-15%	-8%	-5%	-11%

Trends and Splits

	Offense	Rank	Defense	Rank
Total DVOA	11.5%	8	-8.0%	3
Unadjusted VOA	10.3%	10	-12.5%	2
Weighted Trend	12.2%	8	-3.3%	7
Variance	5.0%	5	14.1%	31
Average Opponent	5.8%	7	1.4%	9
Passing	23.2%	14	-12.1%	3
Rushing	8.3%	7	-2.6%	15
First Down	36.3%	1	-3.2%	6
Second Down	-2.5%	19	-2.0%	9
Third Down	-23.2%	27	-26.5%	1
First Half	16.6%	7	-6.3%	5
Second Half	6.1%	14	-9.9%	4
Red Zone	10.8%	8	-12.6%	12
Late and Close	34.7%	2	-18.2%	2

Five-Year Performance

Year	W-L	Pyth	Est W	PF	PA	TO	Total	Rk	Off	Rk	Def	Rk	ST	Rk	Off AGL	Rk	Def AGL	Rk
2006	8-8	7.8	9.0	355	362	0	14.3%	8	12.8%	7	-1.1%	13	0.4%	16	16.4	16	31.0	28
2007	10-6	8.6	8.0	373	351	-9	1.1%	16	-0.3%	18	-2.1%	14	-0.7%	19	13.8	6	14.5	9
2008	12-4	11.3	11.4	427	294	+9	27.0%	4	23.7%	3	-1.5%	8	1.8%	11	6.2	1	29.6	20
2009	8-8	7.4	8.1	402	427	-7	3.9%	17	11.9%	12	6.4%	21	-1.6%	27	8.5	6	47.2	29
2010	10-6	10.1	10.3	394	347	-3	14.6%	9	11.5%	8	-8.0%	3	-4.9%	30	39.7	26	18.4	13

Strategic Tendencies

Run/Pass		Rank	Offense		Rank	Defense		Rank	Other		Rank
Runs, all plays	44%	8	3+ WR	44%	22	Rush 3	2.8%	28	2+ RB, Pct Runs	66%	4
Runs, first half	41%	14	4+ WR	4%	23	Rush 4	61.4%	13	1 RB/2 TE, Pct Runs	53%	10
Runs, first down	53%	11	2+ TE	23%	24	Rush 5	24.2%	13	1 RB/3+ WR, Pct Runs	21%	20
Runs, second-long	44%	3	Single back	57%	18	Rush 6+	11.7%	7	CB1 on WR1	44%	11
Runs, power sit.	62%	14	Play action	16%	24	Zone Blitz	2.8%	26	Go for it on 4th	0.92	15
Runs, behind 2H	33%	3	Max protect	11%	13	Sacks by LB	4.4%	32	Offensive Pace	32.4	28
Pass, ahead 2H	46%	14	Outside pocket	7%	29	Sacks by DB	7.8%	18	Defensive Pace	30.6	10

Eli Manning took only three sacks on third down last year. In fact, because of adjustments for opponent and situation, the Giants actually had a *negative* Adjusted Sack Rate on third downs. ☞ The Giants were sixth in the league in frequency of draw plays, and fourth in efficiency on draw plays. ☞ The Giants ranked second behind Oakland in usage of six-OL sets, primarily during the weeks when tight end Kevin Boss was injured. ☞ The Giants went max protect more than twice as often as they did in 2009. ☞ The Giants' offense improved gradually the more wide receivers they had in the formation: 26th with fewer than two wideouts, 15th with two or three wideouts, and third with four or more wideouts. ☞ The Giants defense led the league with 23 passes batted down or tipped away at the line of scrimmage. They also led the league with 74 quarterback hits. ☞ Even though they blitzed at roughly the same rate as 2009, the Giants went from having 34.8 percent of sacks from non-linemen to having only 12.2 percent of sacks from non-linemen. ☞ The Giants defense was 22nd with 5.8 percent Adjusted Sack Rate on first and second down, but led the league with 12.1 percent ASR on third downs.

Passing

Player	DYAR	DVOA	Plays	NtYds	Avg	YAC	C%	TD	Int
E.Manning	792	11.0%	564	4036	7.2	4.8	63.4%	31	24

Rushing

Player	DYAR	DVOA	Plays	Yds	Avg	TD	Fum	Suc
A.Bradshaw	121	2.5%	275	1243	4.5	8	7	46%
B.Jacobs	172	18.1%	148	824	5.6	9	3	54%
D.Ware	11	3.8%	20	73	3.7	0	0	65%
E.Manning	35	51.0%	12	87	7.3	0	1	–

Receiving

Player	DYAR	DVOA	Plays	Ctch	Yds	Y/C	YAC	TD	C%
H.Nicks	276	14.6%	128	79	1052	13.3	3.7	11	62%
M.Manningham	187	12.4%	92	60	944	15.7	5.8	9	65%
S.Smith	88	1.9%	75	48	529	11.0	2.2	3	64%
D.Hagan	-17	-17.6%	43	25	231	9.2	1.3	1	58%
R.Barden	3	-6.5%	7	5	64	12.8	2.0	0	71%
K.Boss	11	-5.0%	70	35	531	15.2	7.0	5	50%
T.Beckum	21	9.9%	18	13	116	8.9	3.1	2	72%
B.Pascoe	11	6.5%	13	9	72	8.0	6.0	0	69%
A.Bradshaw	71	10.6%	59	48	316	6.6	7.9	0	81%
B.Jacobs	-1	-15.8%	13	7	59	8.4	5.0	0	54%
D.Ware	21	34.1%	9	7	67	9.6	8.7	0	78%

Offensive Line

Year	Yards	ALY	Rank	Power	Rank	Stuff	Rank	2nd Lev	Rank	Open Field	Rank
2008	5.28	4.62	4	62%	23	17%	10	1.49	1	1.35	1
2009	4.18	4.14	13	60%	20	20%	18	1.23	10	0.68	19
2010	4.83	4.22	7	59%	18	19%	16	1.31	4	1.25	3

Year	LE	Rank	LT	Rank	Mid	Rank	RT	Rank	RE	Rank	Sacks	ASR	Rank	F-Start	Cont.
2008	5.02	5	5.18	1	4.85	1	4.04	20	3.72	24	28	5.0%	10	12	48
2009	4.11	19	4.04	18	4.04	21	4.56	6	4.19	18	32	5.3%	9	11	32
2010	3.44	26	4.31	15	4.48	6	4.39	8	3.89	18	16	3.3%	2	16	23

Although the Giants' offensive line was in a bit of transition last year, it was still one of just four units to finish in the top 10 in both Adjusted Line Yards and Adjusted Sack Rate. That didn't stop the Giants from shaking things up to begin training camp. Things are stable on the right side, where Kareem McKenzie and perennial Pro Bowler Chris Snee started all 16 games at guard and tackle respectively, and look to do the same in 2011. Both are known as very good run blockers, a big reason why the Giants are so successful running up the middle and off right tackle. The other three positions are in flux. Veterans Shaun O'Hara and Rich Seubert were cut. The Giants signed free agent David Baas away from San Francisco to replace O'Hara, and David Diehl will be moved back inside to left guard after a couple of years at left tackle. Diehl wasn't an elite left tackle, but he is consistent and durable, missing just three games in the past five years. The move inside fits his current skill set far better and opens the door for 2009 second-rounder William Beatty to move into the big-money left tackle position. Beatty is unproven, but the Giants' coaching staff clearly likes the improvement they've seen over the past couple of seasons. New York will have to hope Beatty plays more like Doug Free than Brandyn Dombrowski, two players who got similar votes of confidence from their organizations last year but produced very different results. One thing the Giants do have is a lot of depth on the offensive line, with Adam Koets and Stacy Andrews as capable and experienced backups who can play multiple positions.

Defensive Front Seven

Defensive Line	Age	Pos	Plays	TmPct	Rk	Stop	Dfts	BTkl	Overall St%	Rk	AvYd	Rk	Pass Rush Sack	Hit	Hur	vs. Run Runs	St%	Yds	vs. Pass Pass	St%	Yds
Justin Tuck	28	DE	79	10.3%	1	70	33	3	85%	4	0.3	12	11.5	14	21	54	85%	2.0	25	96%	-3.6
Barry Cofield	27	DT	56	7.3%	9	42	11	0	68%	37	1.7	32	4	4	9	41	68%	2.9	15	93%	-1.5
Osi Umenyiora	31	DE	48	6.3%	24	41	21	1	83%	11	0.0	8	11.5	18	18.5	30	83%	1.9	18	89%	-3.2
Chris Canty	29	DT	40	5.2%	21	33	8	1	81%	21	1.5	25	1.5	2	7.5	32	81%	2.0	8	88%	-0.6
Jason Pierre-Paul	22	DE	25	3.3%	76	19	10	1	73%	50	0.6	16	4.5	5	9.5	11	73%	2.5	14	79%	-0.9
Rocky Bernard	32	DT	22	3.3%	57	18	5	0	80%	23	1.5	23	2	0	1.5	15	80%	1.8	7	86%	0.7

Linebackers	Age	Pos	Plays	TmPct	Rk	Stop	Dfts	BTkl	Overall AvYd	Pass Rush Sack	Hit	Hur	vs. Run Runs	St%	Rk	Yds	Rk	vs. Pass Tgts	Suc%	Rk	AdjYd	Rk
Michael Boley	29	OLB	80	10.4%	55	42	9	1	6.5	1	8	9.5	46	59%	87	4.5	100	37	56%	31	6.9	57
Jonathan Goff	26	MLB	76	9.9%	59	50	12	2	3.7	1	2	1	53	75%	19	2.0	7	18	59%	27	4.6	9
Keith Bulluck	34	OLB	33	5.3%	--	23	3	2	3.6	0	0	0	25	72%	--	3.2	--	5	76%	--	-0.1	--

Year	Yards	ALY	Rank	Power	Rank	Stuff	Rank	2nd Lev	Rank	Open Field	Rank
2008	3.71	3.33	3	58%	6	24%	3	0.89	3	0.79	19
2009	4.16	3.63	4	73%	27	25%	2	1.09	9	1.09	27
2010	3.96	3.78	11	65%	20	19%	20	1.03	6	0.75	15

Year	LE	Rank	LT	Rank	Mid	Rank	RT	Rank	RE	Rank	Sacks	ASR	Rank
2008	3.15	4	3.32	5	3.27	2	3.97	15	3.12	10	42	7.2%	7
2009	5.39	31	3.65	7	3.32	1	3.00	2	3.88	13	33	6.7%	15
2010	3.64	6	3.97	15	3.91	16	3.35	7	3.78	13	46	7.6%	7

The Giants pass rush regained its ferocity in 2010, ranking seventh in Adjusted Sack Rate and leaving a trail of injured quarterbacks in its wake. Starting defensive ends Justin Tuck and Osi Umenyiora posted 11.5 quarterback sacks each, with Tuck earning Pro Bowl and first-team All-Pro honors and Umenyiora named second-team All-Pro following the season. Umenyiora's future with the club had been uncertain due to a contract dispute. In a sworn affidavit attached to the Brady v. NFL antitrust case, Umenyiora alleged that the front office had promised to re-work his contract or trade him to a team that would. When the lockout was lifted, Umenyiora and his agent were briefly allowed to pursue a trade before that permission was rescinded amid complaints from Unemyiora's camp that the Giants' asking price (a first-round pick) was too high. Umenyiora then missed practice time with a sore knee before being cleared by a specialist. The two sides are still trying to work out a contract. Defensive end/linebacker Mathias Kiwanuka was off to a great start (four sacks in three games) in 2010 before suffering a season-ending neck injury. Medically cleared to return to the football field, Kiwanuka is expected to start at strongside linebacker and could move to defensive end in nickel situations. 2010 first-round pick Jason Pierre-Paul was used both as an edge rusher and an inside pass-rusher on nickel downs after Kiwanuka's injury, and is sure to have an increased role in 2011. The raw Pierre-Paul posted 4.5 sacks in the second half of the season, matching his five-year SackSEER projection from *FOA 2010*. Whoops.

Chris Canty improved in year two of his six-year, $42 million contract, starting all 16 games and playing solid against the run while providing some pass rush. The Giants will need a stronger season from Canty due to the free agent departure of Barry Cofield, who signed a six-year, $36 million contract with the Washington Redskins. The Giants had prepared for Cofield's exit, using second-round picks in 2010 and 2011 on Linval Joseph and Marvin Austin. The 6-foot-5, 328-pound Joseph rarely saw the field as a rookie, but has impressive strength, is more athletic than his size belies, and could earn a starting role this summer. Austin had first-round talent, but fell in the draft due to character concerns after he was suspended by the NCAA for his senior season at North Carolina for accepting improper benefits. With no OTAs or mini-camps this offseason, Austin will have to knock the rust off during the preseason, but he is too talented to not see significant playing time this year. Rocky Bernard was released for salary cap purposes, but was re-signed along with Gabe Watson to provide veteran depth inside.

Prior to last year's training camp, the Giants signed veteran Keith Bulluck to play middle linebacker. That plan was derailed by the struggles of 2009 second-round pick Clint Sintim on the strong side, prompting Perry Fewell to kick Bulluck outside, with Jonathan Goff starting in the middle and Michael Boley manning the weak side. Goff played well for a first-year starter, and he and Boley remained on the field on nickel downs. Life as a two-down player was unfamiliar for Bulluck, who only started eight games as the Giants further altered their back seven by frequently starting three safeties in a 4-2-5 nickel package. Bulluck is gone for 2011, and Goff and Boley will be joined in the starting lineup by Kiwanuka, with Sintim, who is recovering from a torn ACL, relegated to special teams duties. The Giants are working to develop a number of young linebackers, including 2010 draft picks Phillip Dillard and Adrian Tracy and 2011 additions Greg Jones and Jacquian Williams.

Defensive Secondary

Secondary	Age	Pos	Plays	TmPct	Rk	Stop	Dfts	BTkl	Runs	St%	Rk	Yds	Rk	Tgts	Tgt%	Rk	Dist	Suc%	Rk	APaYd	Rk	PD	Int
Terrell Thomas	26	CB	122	15.9%	1	52	26	10	35	43%	42	9.7	76	112	23.0%	1	11.4	50%	54	7.0	36	13	5
Antrel Rolle	29	FS	91	11.8%	20	41	14	7	50	50%	17	5.1	15	26	5.4%	50	11.7	50%	51	14.7	79	1	1
Kenny Phillips	25	SS	82	10.7%	30	30	9	5	41	44%	31	6.8	41	25	5.2%	54	12.0	49%	53	7.5	36	3	1
Deon Grant	32	SS	68	8.9%	58	37	24	9	17	71%	3	3.6	3	41	8.4%	10	8.8	51%	50	6.4	18	9	3
Corey Webster	29	CB	64	8.9%	36	21	7	3	13	38%	59	8.9	66	69	15.1%	45	13.1	55%	28	7.6	50	11	4
Aaron Ross	29	CB	39	5.4%	--	18	10	4	8	63%	--	7.5	-	35	7.6%	--	7.9	45%	--	8.8	--	2	0

Year	Pass D Rank	vs. #1 WR	Rk	vs. #2 WR	Rk	vs. Other WR	Rk	vs. TE	Rk	vs. RB	Rk
2008	9	-16.1%	3	6.4%	21	-15.8%	10	8.9%	21	30.3%	31
2009	17	24.6%	30	-0.6%	18	1.9%	17	7.9%	18	-4.2%	14
2010	3	-25.4%	2	-10.1%	7	26.8%	31	-13.0%	3	-0.9%	11

Entering 2010, conventional wisdom said that the Giants secondary had the makings of being a good unit, if only certain parts could stay healthy. As it turned out, health wasn't an issue for this group in 2010. Strong safety Kenny Phillips returned from microfracture surgery on his left knee to start all 16 games, and nickel corner Aaron Ross missed just one game, as did left cornerback Corey Webster. Webster and right cornerback Terrell Thomas enter 2011 having started 60 of the 64 games over the last two seasons. Webster remains a solid cornerback, but his Adjusted Success Rate has dropped and his yards allowed per pass have steadily risen since becoming a nearly $9 million-per-year player. Thomas is an ascending player entering his contract year. The 26-year-old ranked among the league leaders with 26 Defeats. Webster and Thomas are projected to start again in 2011 and hope to cut down on the number of big plays in the passing game. Both corners allowed more than seven yards per pass, with the Giants allowing ten plays of more than 40 yards. The Giants received an unexpected gift in the form of University of Nebraska cornerback Prince Amukamara, who fell into the Giants' lap with the 19th pick in the 2011 draft. Amukamara has perennial Pro Bowl potential and will challenge Ross for the nickel corner duties before ultimately replacing Webster or Thomas in the starting lineup. However, Amukamara's career has gotten off to a rather rocky start. The last of the 254 players chosen in the 2010 entry draft to sign a contract, he suffered a break to the fifth metatarsal in his left foot during his second practice and will miss the first month or two of the regular season.

Safety Antrel Rolle is a true ball-hawk in the deep secondary, but his interception total dropped as he was used closer to the line of scrimmage last season. Rolle would adapt to his new role, leading all NFL defensive backs with 12.5 quarterback hurries (up from five in 2010). The Giants frequently employed a three-safety/ two-linebacker setup (the "Big Nickel"), with Deon Grant credited with eight starts. Grant was not re-signed, meaning 2011 sixth-round safety Tyler Sash out of Iowa has the inside track for the No. 3 safety role.

Special Teams

Year	DVOA	Rank	FG/XP	Rank	Net Kick	Rank	Kick Ret	Rank	Net Punt	Rank	Punt Ret	Rank	Hidden	Rank
2008	1.8%	11	3.7	11	-11.3	31	4.4	9	11.7	5	2.0	8	0.4	12
2009	-1.6%	27	-3.0	22	1.2	15	-10.3	30	-4.8	26	7.4	7	-3.7	19
2010	-4.9%	30	-0.7	19	3.4	11	-7.9	25	-15.6	30	-8.2	29	1.5	13

Injuries and age forced master directional punter Jeff Feagles into retirement following the 2009 season. Rookie Matt Dodge struggled in his first season as Feagles' replacement, with each low line-drive kick prompting speculation that a veteran would replace him. Dodge's season hit a low point against the Philadelphia Eagles in Week 15 when the seventh-round pick failed to kick the ball out of bounds at his coach's request. Eagles punt returner DeSean Jackson returned the punt 65 yards for a game-winning touchdown as time expired, sending the Giants on a two-game losing streak that would end their playoff hopes. The Giants brought in veteran Steve Weatherford (ex-Jets) to compete with Dodge for the punter job. Weatherford was worth nearly 15 points of field position for the Jets last season, second-most among NFL punters. Dodge was second from the bottom with negative-15.6 points of field position. We think we know who is going to win this battle.

Kicker Lawrence Tynes struggled early, missing three of his first six field-goal attempts before connecting on 16-of-17 to finish the season. Never prone to placing his kickoffs into the opponents' end zone, Tynes again ranked towards the bottom of the league in touchbacks with six. Moving kickoffs up five yards should help Tynes improve upon those numbers. After losing Domenik Hixon to a torn ACL during an offseason workout, the Giants acquired return specialist Darius Reynaud from the Minnesota Vikings in the Sage Rosenfels trade in early September. Reynaud was ineffective in both duties and spent much of the second half of the season on the gameday inactive list, with running back Danny Ware returning kicks and Aaron Ross and Will Blackmon returning punts. Ross and Ware are expected to handle the return duties in 2011, though Reynaud, 2011 third-round pick Jerrel Jernigan, and second-year receiver Victor Cruz may also get opportunities during the preseason.

Coaching Staff

Despite being in the midst of yet another late-season swoon, and ugly back-to-back losses to the Philadelphia Eagles and Green Bay Packers in Weeks 15 and 16, Tom Coughlin was informed by co-owner John Mara prior to the team's Week 17 game against the Washington Redskins that he would return for the 2011 season. "The players play hard for him," Mara said after the 17-14 win over Washington. "He's very organized. He's everything you want in a coach. I'm obviously disappointed we didn't make the playoffs. Everybody in this locker room is disappointed. But that doesn't mean you blow this whole thing up." 2011 was scheduled to be is the final year of Coughlin's four-year, $21 million contract, but the front office extended his deal through the 2012 season.

The only staff change this offseason was Assistant Special Teams Coach Thomas McGaughey leaving for LSU, though defensive coordinator Perry Fewell was allowed to interview for several head coaching vacancies. Fewell was a new hire for the 2010 season, quickly winning over a veteran defense that had struggled under Bill Sheridan, and needs to be taken seriously as a head coaching candidate. Any team that just uses him to mark off its "Rooney Rule" checkbox is doing itself a disservice.

New York Jets

2010 Record: 11-5	**2011 Mean Projection:** 9.3 wins
Pythagorean Wins: 9.8 (8th)	**On the Clock (0-3):** 3%
DVOA: 18.3% (6th)	**Loserville (4-6):** 17%
Offense: 5.6% (16th)	**Mediocrity (7-8):** 19%
Defense: -7.8% (5th)	**Playoff Contender (9-10):** 25%
Special Teams: 4.9% (5th)	**Super Bowl Contender (11+):** 36%
Variance: 24.0% (28th)	**Projected Average Opponent:** 5.4% (3rd)

2010: Jets return to AFC Championship game despite some problems on pass defense.

2011: Once again, there's a big red-white-and-blue roadblock between the Jets and a division title.

In his preview to Super Bowl XL, *Slate* columnist Josh Levin coined the term "cryptodynasty" to refer to teams that were perpetually championship contenders but who never got around to actually winning championships. Citing everyone from the Ewing-era Knicks to the mid-'90s Cleveland Indians to the Stockton-and-Malone Jazz, Levin argued that there were some teams whose destiny was to be a stepping stone for the true champions of the sport. As it turns out, cryptodynasties have been a regular staple of the NFL landscape for as long as the league has been around. Since the merger in 1970, no fewer than 11 teams have lost consecutive conference championships.

The 49ers kicked things off in the NFC by losing in 1970 and 1971, then the Cowboys dropped a pair of NFC title games the following two seasons. The Rams went winless in NFC Championship games for three straight seasons between 1975 and 1977, and the Cowboys pulled off the same trick by losing each NFC championship game between 1980 and 1982. Steve Young's 49ers lost two heavyweight matches to Dallas in 1992 and 1993 before finally exacting retribution in 1994, and the McNabb/Reid Eagles lost championship games in 2001, 2002, and 2003 before Terrell Owens helped them break through to the Super Bowl in 2004.

In the AFC, Oakland played the bridesmaids from 1973-75, losing first to Don Shula's Dolphins and then twice to Chuck Noll's Steelers. The Houston Oilers lost a pair of lopsided championship games to those same Steelers in 1978-79. The Chargers were next up, dropping title tilts in a shootout against Oakland in 1980 and then in a second Ice Bowl against Cincinnati in 1981. The Browns lost two iconic games against John Elway's Broncos, giving up The Drive in Cleveland in 1986, and then coughing up The Fumble in Denver the following season. And now the Jets have joined the list after dropping championship games in Indianapolis and Pittsburgh.

As the only team to make it to two straight conference championships as a sixth seed, the Jets are something of an outlier cryptodynasty. Their closest parallel would probably be the 1978-79 Houston Oilers teams, a good but not exceptional group built around defense and the superlative play of Earl Campbell. The Oilers had the bad fortune to play in the same division as the mighty Steelers, and so they inevitably entered the playoffs via the wild card route. The Jets have the bad fortune to play in the same division as the New England Patriots, who are capable of tossing off 14-2 seasons when they are supposed to be rebuilding. If the Jets want to get over the hump and reach the Super Bowl, they would be well served to win the AFC East and earn a bye, because the odds of their winning three road playoff games in the rugged AFC are remote.

2011 Jets Schedule

Week	Opp.	Week	Opp.	Week	Opp.
1	DAL	7	SD	13	at WAS
2	JAC	8	BYE	14	KC
3	at OAK	9	at BUF	15	at PHI
4	at BAL	10	NE	16	NYG
5	at NE	11	at DEN (Thu.)	17	at MIA
6	MIA (Mon.)	12	BUF		

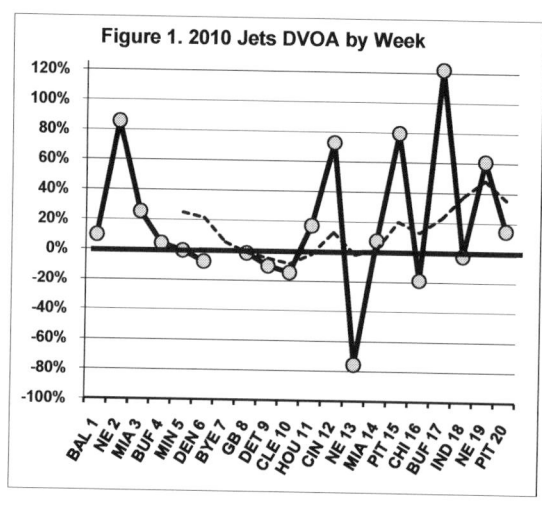

Figure 1. 2010 Jets DVOA by Week

The first step is to fix whatever was ailing the defense last year. The 2009 Jets sported the best defense in football by a healthy margin, with a DVOA of -23.4%, and a pass defense that ranked among the best of the DVOA era thanks to a combination of Ryan's relentless blitzing and an otherworldly performance from cornerback Darrelle Revis. Last year's defense was still good, but no longer dominant, and the primary culprit was a pass defense that was suddenly downright erratic. As we noted in last year's Jets chapter, it's quite common for historically great pass defenses to soften up the following season. On average, the top 12 pass defenses recorded by DVOA between 1993-2010 declined by 22.5 percentage points worth of DVOA in the subsequent season, and not a single one of them was able to maintain their level of play. That said, there are drop-offs and there are drop-offs, and the slide in the Jets' pass defense DVOA from -34.6% to 1.5% marks the largest decline experienced by any of the top 12, beating out both the 2004-05 Buffalo Bills and the 2008-09 Pittsburgh Steelers.

It would be tempting to lay the blame for the team's struggles in 2010 on Darrelle Revis, who conducted a prolonged and bitter holdout that kept him out of training camp and preseason. It's hard to keep in football shape when you can't do any football-related training, and sure enough, Revis pulled his hamstring while trying to cover Randy Moss in a Week 2 game against the Patriots. Revis missed two games, and struggled in his return, getting burned for a 34-yard touchdown by Percy Harvin. But the narrative doesn't hold up very well, as Revis Island quickly returned to form. Revis' 71 percent Success Rate was the second best number in the league behind only Asante Samuel, and he only surrendered an average of 5.7 yards per pass attempt. Moreover, Antonio Cromartie stepped into the breach admirably, smothering Moss in the second half against New England, and holding down the fort against opposing number-one receivers while Revis recovered

from his injury. Cromartie couldn't be everywhere, however, and anyone who watched rookie Kyle Wilson flail around helplessly after being forced into the starting lineup would be unsurprised that the Jets posted a positive (i.e., worse than average) pass defense DVOA in four consecutive weeks after Revis' injury. Things were bad enough that the team demoted their first-round pick in favor of journeyman Drew Coleman — first as an injury replacement for Revis, and then as the regular nickelback. Wilson certainly isn't the first highly-drafted rookie to get a rough initiation to the league, and his natural maturation could help make this one of the strongest secondaries in football. If Wilson doesn't develop, however, the cornerback depth will continue to be a sore spot,

While a lack of depth certainly didn't help matters, the real problem appears to have been schematic. According to ESPN's Stats & Info blog, in 2009 the Jets blitzed defensive backs on 85 of 168 third-down pass attempts. With Revis erasing the primary read and linebackers or safeties bracketing second options, quarterbacks panicked under the pressure, completing only 37.7 percent of their passes for barely four yards an attempt. New York's pass defense DVOA on third downs led the league at an eye-boggling -54.3%, more than twice as good as second-ranked Baltimore. But last year offenses adjusted their blocking schemes to buy additional time, and quarterbacks who had been getting sacked or hit as they threw suddenly had the time to find and exploit single coverage. The results were devastating. New York's third-down defense wasn't average, or even bad — it was actually *the worst in the NFL* — and the longer the offense had to go, the more incompetent the defenders became.

The biggest problem wasn't conversions as much as it was big plays; the Jets allowed 22 plays of 20-plus yards on third down, three more than any other team. Things got so bad that Rex Ryan had to dial down his pressure packages and play something akin to a bend-but-don't-break defense in the playoffs.

A true pass rushing threat would allow Ryan to get heat on the quarterback without having to rely on sending extra bodies, but the spectacular flameout of Vernon Gholston, along with the failure to acquire any edge rushing talent in this year's draft, means that the burden will once again fall on the coaching staff. Considering the sustained success Ryan and defensive coordinator Mike Pettine have had in both Baltimore and New York, it seems likely that they will come up with some adjustments of their own. They'll also get some help from good old regression to the mean, as the third-down performance figures to fall more in line with the first- and second-down performance. The heights of 2009 are probably out of reach, but the Jets don't have to be great on third downs to field the best defense in football.

The bigger issue is the need for continued improvement on offense, where the Jets are loaded with talent along the line and at the skill positions, but are still in the process of taking the training wheels off third-year quarterback Mark Sanchez. The Sanchize was given more to do in his second season, throwing the ball 507 times for 3,291 yards and attempting more than 30 passes in ten of his 16 starts. Sanchez built a reputation for late-game heroics, driving the Jets down the field at the end of regulation for game-winning scores in three consecutive weeks against Detroit, Cleveland, and Houston. The game-winning drive against Houston was perhaps Sanchez's finest moment, as he took the Jets 72 yards in only 39 seconds with no time-outs, threading a 42-yard bomb to Braylon Edwards between the corner and the oncoming safety, and then finishing off the drive with a perfect fade to Santonio Holmes in the corner of the end zone. For the second consecutive year, Sanchez upped his game in the post-season, where through six games he now has a higher completion percentage, more yards per attempt, and a higher touchdown-to-interception ratio than in regular action. If you just tuned into the postseason and watched Sanchez confidently go toe-to-toe with Tom Brady or Ben Roethlisberger, you might be forgiven for thinking that the young USC product has arrived.

Despite the positive signs, there are reasons to temper the optimism surrounding Sanchez. In many ways, his numbers were fairly static. His yards per attempt and completion percentage were nearly identical to his rookie season. Sanchez threw a few more touchdowns as a sophomore, but his big accomplishment was protecting the ball better, as he trimmed his interception rate from 5.5 percent to 2.6 percent. Avoiding interceptions is a huge part of being a successful quarterback, but there is also an element of luck to it, and our game charters think that Sanchez was very lucky indeed. No quarterback in the league came close to throwing as many dropped interceptions as Sanchez, who had 15 throws that hit unwary defenders in the hands. If those defenders hold onto a few more errant passes next year, fans may start grumbling that the young quarterback is regressing, when in fact the law of averages is simply catching up with him. (This is addressed further in the quarterbacks section on page 262.)

If Sanchez is going to develop, he is going to have to do it with a largely new group of receivers. The lone holdover is Santonio Holmes, who the Jets locked up with a 5-year, $50 million contract. Holmes is fast, but what makes him dangerous is his ability to run precise routes, his body control on sideline passes, and his explosiveness after the catch. Holmes was one of the premiere talents available in free agency and the Jets were wise to retain him, but the cost rippled down through the depth chart, as the team had to make a number of cost-cutting moves in the wake of the Holmes contract. The most interesting move is the addition of Plaxico Burress, who spurned the Steelers and Giants to sign with the Jets. The team envisions Burress as a bigger, stronger version of Braylon Edwards, who was the primary deep threat the last two seasons. There are obviously many reasons to wonder if the 34-year-old receiver will be able to recapture his skills after two years away from football, but at the very least, Burress provides a big target who can shield defenders with his body and create mismatches in the red zone. After releasing Jerricho Cotchery, who would have cost nearly $4 million against the cap, general manager Mike Tannenbaum signed 37-year-old Derrick Mason for the veteran minimum. The consensus is that Mason is fading badly, but his advanced metrics tell a different story — Mason was 16th in DYAR and 14th in DVOA last season, and was easily the most effective of the Ravens receivers. From a long-term perspective, trading Cotchery for Mason doesn't make a lot of sense, but as a one year stopgap, you could do a whole lot worse. And tight end Dustin Keller is a matchup problem who can be split out wide or line up along the line of scrimmage, and who is frequently Sanchez's first target on play-action or rollout plays. This is a good group of receivers, and their skills mesh well together.

The passing attack will only take off, however, if offensive coordinator Brian Schottenheimer allows it to. The Jets were again among the most run-happy teams in football in 2010, running on 47 percent of all offensive snaps; only Kansas City ran more frequently. Schottenheimer called for a run on first down 63 percent of the time, and no coordinator was more willing to stick with the run while behind in the second half. How much of that was out of a desire to protect a young quarterback and how much out of a more general philosophical orientation towards the ground game remains to be seen. The Jets run the ball well, and with a full stable of running backs that includes LaDainian Tomlinson, Shonn Greene, Joe McKnight and rookie Bilal Powell, Schottenheimer is going to be tempted to continue hammering defenses with off tackle runs, which would be more excusable if he didn't have so much receiving talent to waste. With Brad Smith off to Buffalo, the Seminole package

(New York's version of the Wildcat) will have a new triggerman, most likely rookie Jeremy Kerley, though it is possible Tomlinson will get a look in the role.

The overall talent level in New York remains high, and the coaching staff has no lack of confidence or ability. It's likely that the Jets will return to the playoffs for a third straight season, but the question is how many games will they have to play once they get there, and will they be at home or on the road? While the 28-21 Divisional round victory against the Patriots should give Rex Ryan's crew confidence that they can play with their division rivals, the reality is that New England was not only the stronger team last year, but also the younger one. The Patriots may not go 14-2 again, but with their bevy of developing young players, their tremendous coaching staff, and their future Hall of Fame quarterback, New England remains the favorite to win the AFC East and to claim a first-round bye in the playoffs. If the NFL's resident crypotdynasty is going to break through and reach the Super Bowl, they will likely have to do it via the wild card route. Again.

Sean McCormick

2010 Jets Stats by Week

Wk	vs.	W-L	PF	PA	YDF	YDA	TO	Total	Off	Def	ST
1	BAL	L	9	10	176	282	2	10%	-37%	-39%	7%
2	NE	W	28	14	336	291	3	86%	47%	-38%	2%
3	@MIA	W	31	23	402	436	1	25%	48%	30%	8%
4	@BUF	W	38	14	444	223	2	4%	35%	25%	-6%
5	MIN	W	29	20	328	336	3	0%	-5%	13%	18%
6	@DEN	W	24	20	319	346	-1	-8%	-5%	12%	9%
7	BYE										
8	GB	L	0	9	360	237	-3	-2%	-34%	-30%	2%
9	@DET	W	23	20	437	306	-2	-10%	-10%	-2%	-2%
10	@CLE	W	26	20	456	303	1	-14%	17%	15%	-16%
11	HOU	W	30	27	401	343	-1	17%	2%	1%	15%
12	CIN	W	26	10	319	163	2	73%	11%	-46%	16%
13	@NE	L	3	45	301	405	-3	-76%	-39%	30%	-7%
14	MIA	L	6	10	280	131	1	8%	-48%	-49%	7%
15	@PIT	W	22	17	276	377	0	80%	49%	2%	33%
16	@CHI	L	34	38	393	322	-1	-19%	34%	42%	-11%
17	BUF	W	38	7	388	162	5	122%	13%	-100%	9%
18	@IND	W	17	16	353	312	-1	-2%	-4%	0%	1%
19	@NE	W	28	21	314	372	1	61%	32%	-44%	-16%
20	@PIT	L	19	24	289	287	1	12%	13%	-2%	-2%

Trends and Splits

	Offense	Rank	Defense	Rank
Total DVOA	5.6%	16	-7.8%	5
Unadjusted VOA	8.6%	15	-5.9%	6
Weighted Trend	1.0%	20	-8.5%	5
Variance	10.5%	27	14.6%	32
Average Opponent	2.4%	18	8.6%	29
Passing	10.3%	20	1.5%	7
Rushing	9.6%	5	-19.5%	2
First Down	9.7%	11	-7.7%	4
Second Down	-2.6%	20	-33.4%	1
Third Down	12.2%	11	32.1%	32
First Half	6.3%	17	-10.6%	2
Second Half	5.0%	19	-4.8%	10
Red Zone	-2.7%	20	3.9%	19
Late and Close	13.5%	5	-3.2%	15

Five-Year Performance

Year	W-L	Pyth	Est W	PF	PA	TO	Total	Rk	Off	Rk	Def	Rk	ST	Rk	Off AGL	Rk	Def AGL	Rk
2006	10-6	8.7	7.7	316	295	0	-1.2%	17	6.2%	12	10.6%	27	3.2%	5	7.6	7	4.2	2
2007	4-12	5.4	5.0	268	355	-4	-16.7%	24	-9.0%	23	9.1%	26	1.4%	10	19.6	13	18.5	14
2008	9-7	9.2	9.0	405	356	-1	5.4%	17	5.1%	18	2.5%	14	2.8%	8	7.3	2	10.5	5
2009	9-7	11.4	9.4	342	236	+1	16.9%	9	-9.0%	22	-23.4%	1	2.5%	6	4.1	1	21.0	12
2010	11-5	9.8	9.8	367	304	+9	18.3%	6	5.6%	16	-7.8%	5	4.9%	5	8.9	4	33.0	23

Strategic Tendencies

Run/Pass		Rank	Offense		Rank	Defense		Rank	Other		Rank
Runs, all plays	47%	2	3+ WR	43%	27	Rush 3	12.9%	7	2+ RB, Pct Runs	60%	12
Runs, first half	47%	4	4+ WR	4%	24	Rush 4	40.8%	31	1 RB/2 TE, Pct Runs	56%	7
Runs, first down	63%	1	2+ TE	32%	13	Rush 5	33.0%	3	1 RB/3+ WR, Pct Runs	24%	13
Runs, second-long	38%	9	Single back	51%	26	Rush 6+	13.4%	5	CB1 on WR1	38%	22
Runs, power sit.	66%	5	Play action	18%	17	Zone Blitz	10.4%	4	Go for it on 4th	0.69	30
Runs, behind 2H	38%	1	Max protect	11%	18	Sacks by LB	48.8%	13	Offensive Pace	30.1	10
Pass, ahead 2H	42%	20	Outside pocket	15%	9	Sacks by DB	26.8%	1	Defensive Pace	30.3	5

The Jets were second in the NFL with 9.8 percent Adjusted Sack Rate on first and second down. However, they were dead last with just 1.0 percent ASR on third down. Only six of their 40 sacks came on third down. It's a big reason why they went from the best third-down defense in the league in 2009 to the worst in 2010. ⊜ The Jets only benefited from 91 penalties on their opponents (including declined and offsetting), the lowest total in the league. In fact, apparently, the league generally assigned their less-strict officials to AFC East games, because Buffalo, Miami, New England, and the Jets ranked 26th, 28th, 31st, and 32nd in opponent penalties. ⊜ The Jets ran fewer draw plays than any other offense. ⊜ The Jets averaged 5.7 yards per play when Brad Smith came in the game for the "Seminole" option package, which was roughly once every 25 plays. ⊜ The Jets kill runs from a spread set, with a league-best -32.8% DVOA against runs with three or more wideouts on the field. ⊜ Jets opponents only threw to running backs on a league-low 14 percent of passes. However, the Jets allowed an average of 10.9 yards after the catch on passes at or before the line of scrimmage, the highest figure in the league.

Passing

Player	DYAR	DVOA	Plays	NtYds	Avg	YAC	C%	TD	Int
M.Sanchez	438	1.6%	537	3233	6.0	4.7	55.5%	17	13
M.Brunell	7	-3.8%	14	110	7.9	3.3	53.8%	2	1

Rushing

Player	DYAR	DVOA	Plays	Yds	Avg	TD	Fum	Suc
L.Tomlinson	110	3.6%	220	908	4.1	6	3	44%
S.Greene	124	7.8%	185	767	4.1	2	2	55%
J.McKnight	34	13.2%	39	189	4.8	0	0	59%
B.Smith	77	45.5%	38	299	7.9	1	1	53%
M.Sanchez	27	8.4%	21	115	5.5	3	2	-
J.Conner	17	46.4%	8	44	5.5	1	0	50%
T.Richardson	7	16.6%	5	13	2.6	0	0	80%

Receiving

Player	DYAR	DVOA	Plays	Ctch	Yds	Y/C	YAC	TD	C%
B.Edwards	125	2.4%	101	53	904	17.1	5.4	7	52%
S.Holmes	128	4.3%	96	52	746	14.3	4.2	6	54%
J.Cotchery	-70	-23.1%	86	41	433	10.6	2.7	2	48%
B.Smith	-13	-37.7%	7	4	44	11.0	2.5	0	57%
D.Keller	38	-1.6%	100	55	687	12.5	3.9	5	55%
L.Tomlinson	-2	-14.2%	79	52	366	7.0	6.7	0	66%
S.Greene	27	4.4%	24	16	120	7.5	5.4	0	67%

Offensive Line

Year	Yards	ALY	Rank	Power	Rank	Stuff	Rank	2nd Lev	Rank	Open Field	Rank
2008	4.81	4.72	2	61%	25	14%	4	1.26	6	0.98	9
2009	4.48	4.28	8	70%	6	15%	4	1.11	20	0.87	12
2010	4.48	4.56	3	76%	2	12%	1	1.15	14	0.56	23

Year	LE	Rank	LT	Rank	Mid	Rank	RT	Rank	RE	Rank	Sacks	ASR	Rank	F-Start	Cont.
2008	5.16	3	2.83	32	4.75	3	4.96	1	5.30	1	30	6.5%	19	20	48
2009	3.05	29	4.06	17	4.21	12	5.06	1	3.75	23	30	7.7%	23	21	48
2010	5.04	3	4.06	20	4.52	5	4.90	4	4.37	10	28	5.4%	8	19	43

The Jets have put together one of the best and most consistent lines in football, in large part because they have been able to keep their starters healthy. From 2008-09, the Jets were the only team in football to have the same five offensive linemen start every game. They broke the streak of their own accord when they released an aging and overpriced Alan Faneca and replaced him with Matt Slauson, a former sixth-round pick who played for offensive line coach Bill Callahan at Nebraska. Slauson rewarded the team by starting every game and providing solid if not spectacular left guard play. Now the Jets are going to try to keep the line smoothly functioning while swapping out the only player to miss time last year, right tackle Damien Woody, who retired after becoming a cap casualty in April. For now, the job will go to Wayne Hunter, who is considered to be one of the better swing tackles in the league, but who didn't play up to his reputation in 2010. Hunter gave up two sacks and multiple pressures to Cameron Wake in a December loss to the Dolphins, when the offense scored just six points.

The rest of the line looks as formidable as ever. D'Brickashaw Ferguson and Nick Mangold came into the league together in 2006, and they have combined for 160 starts and five Pro Bowls while anchoring the two most important positions on the line. At 295 pounds, Ferguson is one of the lighter left tackles in the league, and he can sometimes struggle with power rushers who get under his pads and drive him back. That said, he has the athleticism and the wingspan to keep speed rushers off Mark Sanchez, which is why the Jets were willing to lock him up for six years and $60 million at the start of the 2010 season. Mangold is the best center in the game, a player who combines natural ability with superb technique. (That he wasn't considered in the casting for *Thor* is a criminal oversight.) Brandon Moore is solidly entrenched as the right guard. The odd man out is Vladimir Ducasse, the 6-foot-5, 330-pound behemoth from UMass whom the Jets selected in the second round last year. Ducasse fell on his face as a rookie, playing himself out of the left guard competition in training camp, and appeared in only two games all year. He is exactly the kind of player who would be hurt by the lockout, as he badly needed to participate in OTAs and receive additional coaching. Ducasse will be groomed to play tackle, but will be pressed into service at guard if a starter goes down.

Defensive Front Seven

Defensive Line	Age	Pos	Plays	TmPct	Rk	Stop	Dfts	BTkl	St%	Rk	AvYd	Rk	Sack	Hit	Hur	Runs	St%	Yds	Pass	St%	Yds
Sione Pouha	32	DT	62	8.5%	5	44	4	0	70%	47	2.3	44	2	0	3	56	70%	2.7	6	83%	-1.5
Mike Devito	27	DE	60	8.2%	10	49	14	0	82%	27	2.2	53	0	3	7	57	82%	2.1	3	67%	4.0
Shaun Ellis	34	DE	37	5.4%	37	34	12	2	90%	1	0.9	23	5	5	15.5	30	90%	2.1	7	100%	-4.3

Linebackers	Age	Pos	Plays	TmPct	Rk	Stop	Dfts	BTkl	AvYd	Sack	Hit	Hur	Runs	St%	Rk	Yds	Rk	Tgts	Suc%	Rk	AdjYd	Rk
David Harris	27	ILB	103	14.1%	25	63	17	6	4.0	3	4	8	76	67%	61	3.7	74	30	48%	57	7.6	68
Bart Scott	31	ILB	83	11.3%	46	54	12	2	2.8	1	9	15.5	64	70%	47	2.5	25	21	36%	73	7.1	60
Calvin Pace	31	OLB	54	9.8%	60	40	15	1	2.3	5.5	4	10.5	36	81%	9	2.1	13	7	42%	--	8.3	--
Jason Taylor	37	OLB	41	5.6%	--	33	14	2	1.3	4.5	2	14	29	76%	--	1.9	--	3	33%	--	13.6	--
Bryan Thomas	32	OLB	39	5.3%	106	34	12	1	1.0	6	0	12	27	85%	3	1.7	2	11	80%	--	2.1	--

Year	Yards	ALY	Rank	Power	Rank	Stuff	Rank	2nd Lev	Rank	Open Field	Rank
2008	3.66	3.94	9	68%	19	16%	24	0.88	2	0.47	4
2009	3.77	3.55	2	58%	7	23%	5	1.04	4	0.62	10
2010	3.47	3.64	5	67%	25	19%	16	0.88	3	0.42	3

Year	LE	Rank	LT	Rank	Mid	Rank	RT	Rank	RE	Rank	Sacks	ASR	Rank
2008	4.11	16	4.42	21	3.92	9	4.22	20	2.83	5	41	6.8%	12
2009	2.92	5	4.17	17	3.35	2	3.40	4	4.41	24	32	6.9%	14
2010	5.19	30	3.43	9	3.70	8	3.06	3	3.27	5	40	7.0%	10

This unit was in need of some fresh blood and they got it, courtesy of the draft. Temple's Muhammed Wilkerson has experience playing as a five-technique defensive end in a true 3-4, and at 6-foot-4 and 315 pounds he has the kind of girth that Rex Ryan prefers from his front defenders. The Jets' first-round pick is also scheme versatile, and could provide reps at nose tackle or at defensive tackle when the team goes to a four-down linemen look. Third-rounder Kenrick Ellis (Hampton) brings both a true nose tackle frame and another 346 pounds to add to the rotation, but he also totes a veritable baggage cart with him. He was kicked off the team in South Carolina for multiple team violations, and he has a felony assault case pending. Should Ellis skate on the charges, he will be the primary backup to Sione Pouha, a former rotation player who has distinguished himself the last two seasons stepping in for an injured Kris Jenkins. Mike DeVito has quietly nailed down one of the defensive end spots, which leaves open the one Shaun Ellis capably filled for the last 11 seasons before leaving for New England this August. Wilkerson will get every opportunity to take over for Ellis, but a dark horse candidate is fourth-year veteran Ropati Pitoitua; the coaching staff is high on him, but he missed all of last season with a torn Achilles injury after a fantastic training camp.

All four starting linebackers are guaranteed to be back thanks to the decision to commit to David Harris with a four-year, $36 million new contract. Harris is not an elite athlete, but he is young, productive, and respected by his teammates, who voted him team MVP. Lining up next to Harris is Bart Scott, who is flexible enough to handle coverage, blitzing, and trash talking responsibilities simultaneously. Scott is frequently asked to crash the A gap on blitzes, and according to our game charters he did it very well, leading the team with 15.5 quarterback pressures. More than any other player, Scott has changed the attitude and demeanor of the defense, which is precisely why Rex Ryan brought him over from Baltimore. Calvin Pace and Bryan Thomas are similar players. Both came into the league as highly athletic 4-3 defensive ends who were supposed to terrorize quarterbacks, and now both have settled in as jack-of-all-trades outside linebackers in the 3-4. Jamaal Westerman has been lingering at the bottom of the roster as a developmental project, but it may be now or never for the Rutgers product to step up, as the team is desperate to find someone who can provide pressure off the edge on third downs.

Defensive Secondary

Secondary	Age	Pos	Plays	TmPct	Rk	Stop	Dfts	BTkl	Runs	St%	Rk	Yds	Rk	Tgts	Tgt%	Rk	Dist	Suc%	Rk	APaYd	Rk	PD	Int
Brodney Pool	27	FS	61	8.9%	56	33	11	3	30	60%	6	5.5	21	22	4.6%	67	9.5	77%	3	4.7	5	10	1
Antonio Cromartie	27	CB	59	8.6%	42	25	11	6	12	25%	81	9.7	75	103	21.5%	4	17.2	65%	5	6.5	26	15	3
Jim Leonhard	29	SS	59	11.7%	21	15	7	4	22	41%	35	8.5	60	20	5.7%	42	14.9	34%	77	8.9	55	3	1
Eric Smith	28	FS	46	7.7%	65	16	4	3	16	69%	4	5.0	10	24	5.8%	41	12.2	36%	76	8.5	48	2	0
Darrelle Revis	26	CB	42	7.1%	68	18	4	4	15	33%	67	8.4	61	55	13.2%	64	16.1	71%	2	5.7	11	10	7
Drew Coleman	29	CB	36	4.9%	85	19	13	5	6	50%	25	9.8	77	53	10.3%	81	10.0	51%	49	7.5	49	3	3
Dwight Lowery	25	CB	25	3.9%	--	12	10	6	0	0%	--	0.0	--	34	7.5%	--	11.4	55%	--	9.4	--	8	3
Kyle Wilson	24	CB	24	3.3%	89	9	2	2	2	100%	1	2.0	2	41	8.0%	88	14.4	53%	38	6.3	18	6	0

Year	Pass D Rank	vs. #1 WR	Rk	vs. #2 WR	Rk	vs. Other WR	Rk	vs. TE	Rk	vs. RB	Rk
2008	16	-5.1%	11	-1.6%	13	7.9%	25	25.2%	29	8.7%	21
2009	1	-39.6%	1	-20.4%	6	-29.9%	3	-21.3%	4	-20.9%	2
2010	7	-7.5%	12	12.2%	23	-9.6%	11	-3.4%	9	-6.0%	9

Forget the holdout and the jokes about the holdout on *Hard Knocks*. Forget the poor start, punctuated by a nagging hamstring injury he suffered in Week 2. By the end of the season, Darrelle Revis had re-established himself as the best cornerback in football, and possibly the league's best defender. Revis didn't log a single interception, but once he was healthy, he erased opposing receivers from the stat sheet. Antonio Cromartie filled in as the team's top cornerback when Revis was hurt, and he performed credibly. Cromartie is at his best when matched up against tall, long-striding vertical receivers who he can run down the field with; he frustrated Randy Moss in both their meetings. Unfortunately, Cromartie struggled with penalties, particularly in the season opener against Baltimore when he was flagged four times. After striking out on Nnamdi Asomugha, the Jets were quick to resign Cromartie because Kyle Wilson looked like a deer in the headlights for much of his rookie season, struggling to maintain situational awareness with the ball in the air. In one series in Miami, the Dolphins sent Davone Bess on consecutive corner routes out of the slot, and in each case Wilson ruined tight coverage by failing to turn and track the ball, giving up identical 17-yard gains. Rookie corners often struggle, and Wilson should be an improved player in 2011, but it would be risky to pencil him in as a starter. Jim Leonhard is fully recovered from a broken tibia suffered during an early December practice, and he should have no problem reclaiming his starting spot. Leonhard is another Baltimore import, a locker room leader who is effective but not a standout. Eric Smith was named the other starter, but that was before the team re-signed Brodney Pool; the two figure to battle it out in training camp, but it may not matter who wins, as both will log significant snaps.

Special Teams

Year	DVOA	Rank	FG/XP	Rank	Net Kick	Rank	Kick Ret	Rank	Net Punt	Rank	Punt Ret	Rank	Hidden	Rank
2008	2.8%	8	-3.7	26	7.4	7	9.0	4	1.9	17	2.1	7	-6.6	21
2009	2.5%	6	2.8	12	-2.3	20	7.6	6	1.7	16	5.0	9	-0.4	15
2010	4.9%	5	-2.2	25	-0.1	17	19.4	1	14.8	2	-3.2	21	5.9	5

Mike Westhoff has been able to consistently replace top kick returners without any dropoff in production, and he may have to do it again this year now that Brad Smith is moving on. Antonio Cromartie has elite return ability, as he demonstrated with a 47-yard kickoff return in the playoffs against Indianapolis that set the Jets up for the winning field goal. If the team doesn't want to risk Cromartie, they could turn to second-year man Kyle Wilson or rookie Jeremmy Kerley, both of whom flashed as returners in college. Joe McKnight is expected to step in for Jim Leonhard and add some explosiveness as a punt returner. Kicker Nick Folk was inconsistent enough that the Jets felt compelled to check into free agent alternatives late in the season. Despite having a strong leg, Folk struggled from distance, connecting on only 5-of-11 field goal attempts of more than 40 yards. He also remains among the league's worst on kickoffs, so his roster spot is far from assured. Punter Steve Weatherford excelled at pinning offenses deep, tying a league record with 42 punts inside the opposition's 20-yard line. He had something of a meltdown in the playoffs, however, which may explain why the Jets opted not to tender him. Indications are that the team would like him back, but they won't get into a bidding war for his services.

Coaching Staff

In between starring on *Hard Knocks*, writing a book, becoming an iconic figure on Kissing Suzy Kolber, and appearing on just about every media platform known to man, Rex Ryan has done what every Jets coach before him has failed to do: Make the Giants an afterthought in New York. Part of it has been sheer braggadocio, but there is more to Ryan than a predilection for Super Bowl predictions. Ryan takes an inclusive approach to coaching, which he explained to NPR host Steve Inskeep in a radio interview. "With our defense we'll actually have the entire defense in a meeting and we'll teach the entire defense to everybody. Everybody is in the same room, and there's accountability because you all know each other's jobs. You teach the whole defense to everybody and it may sound complicated, but it's not." Defensive coordinator Mike Pettine is a former Philadelphia high school coach whose North Penn team was once the subject of an ESPN documentary. Brian Schottenheimer's name cropped up as a potential head coaching candidate a few years ago, but his star seems to have dimmed somewhat. Schottenheimer has received a lot of heat for his play-calling, particularly in the AFC Championship loss in Pittsburgh, where he called for two passes in a four-play goal-line sequence in the fourth quarter that came up empty. To Schottenheimer's credit, he has put together a scheme that highlights the strengths of Mark Sanchez, with a healthy dose of rollouts, waggles, and quick slants. Offensive line coach Bill Callahan continues to do a tremendous job keeping his line healthy and playing at a high level.

Oakland Raiders

2010 Record: 8-8	2011 Mean Projection: 5.0 wins
Pythagorean Wins: 8.9 (14th)	On the Clock (0-3): 31%
DVOA: -4.2% (21st)	Loserville (4-6): 41%
Offense: -4.3% (23rd)	Mediocrity (7-8): 16%
Defense: 1.5% (15th)	Playoff Contender (9-10): 8%
Special Teams: 1.5% (13th)	Super Bowl Contender (11+): 3%
Variance: 34.0% (32nd)	Projected Average Opponent: 2.9% (6th)

2010: After nearly a decade of sliding back, the Raiders find another atypical way to succeed.

2011: What, you expected consistency?

As much as the story of the Oakland Raiders' last 15 years is about the franchise's increasing floundering under the always-mercurial watch of "Weird Al" Davis, the underlying success tales revolve around two firebrands who re-established a winning (or, at least, non-losing) culture by doing things their own way, warts and all. After Davis hired Jon Gruden in time for the 1998 season, Gruden went away from the vertical passing system Davis always preferred, opting instead for the West Coast offense principles he learned from Mike Holmgren in Green Bay. The result? Four years in, Gruden had reformed the Raiders from the 4-12 mess he inherited to an absolute playoff contender that missed the 2001 AFC Championship by a Tuck Rule. He did it with an abrasive personality, an absolute belief in his own abilities, and a system he knew could work if he had the players to make it go.

When offensive line coach Tom Cable replaced Lane Kiffin four games into the 2008 season, he inherited a team that had sunk to the lowest possible depths, with Davis' infamous overhead projector evisceration of Kiffin and ridiculous defense of Ja-Marcus Russell as the backdrop. But just as Gruden had, Cable attacked the job, literally and figuratively. And like Gruden, he saw the source of success as an atypical approach for the Raiders — a run-heavy, two-back system with a serious emphasis on toughness (not the clichés of toughness, but the consis-

tency that actual toughness creates). All of a sudden, the team we called "a farce first and a football team second" in last year's *Football Outsiders Almanac* had become a serious team again.

In 2010, things kicked in for the Raiders in a way they hadn't since the early part of the decade, and that began with another play against type: an excellent draft. In prior years, the franchise's obsession with raw speed and other overstuffed attributes at the expense of football acumen had led them down the primrose path. But whatever had to coalesce for the front office to get it back together — the stars aligned, Cable was more involved, Davis took a three-day nap — it happened in the 2010 draft.

First-round linebacker Rolando McClain from Alabama led all qualifying rookie inside linebackers (at least 50 plays) in Stop Rate against the pass, and developed through the year against the run. Second-round defensive lineman Lamarr Houston from Texas paired with Matt Shaughnessy to form an estimable end duo, and slipped inside to three-tech defensive tackle when Richard Seymour was hurt. In the third round, small-school gem Jared Veldheer from Hillsdale proved that you could go from playing left tackle against Ferris State to doing the same against the San Diego Chargers at above replacement value ... especially if the guy you're replacing is Mario Henderson. Former tackle Bruce Campbell might find his way

2011 Raiders Schedule

Week	Opp.	Week	Opp.	Week	Opp.
1	at DEN (Mon.)	7	KC	13	at MIA
2	at BUF	8	BYE	14	at GB
3	NYJ	9	DEN	15	DET
4	NE	10	at SD (Thu.)	16	at KC
5	at HOU	11	at MIN	17	SD
6	CLE	12	CHI		

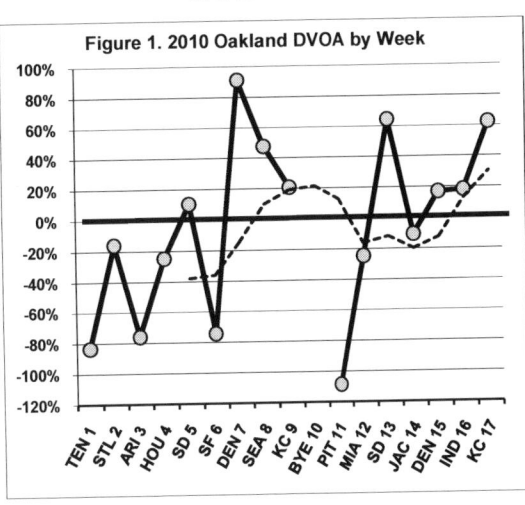

Figure 1. 2010 Oakland DVOA by Week

at guard in the NFL, but the important thing to note about Campbell is that the Raiders got him in the fourth round — he's the king of unfinished, hyper-athletic reach who would have been snapped up by Oakland on the first day in previous years. Fifth-round receiver Jacoby Ford, by all accounts, could be the game's next great deep threat, and he returned three kicks for touchdowns in his rookie year.

It was a huge upgrade from the legendary "reach draft" of 2009, the one that gave the NFL mega-bust Darrius Heyward-Bey, three-round overdraft Mike Mitchell, and the legendary Stryker Sulak.

Top that with the fact that former Raiders disappointments finally played to their potential (or even above their heads) in 2010. Cornerback Stanford Routt, selected early in the 2005 draft because of his 40 time, had bounced around from starter to nickel sets to the bench in previous seasons. Last year, he came up big as the one guy who could handle the burden of all those targets opposite Nnamdi Asomugha. Running back Darren McFadden finally justified his high pick by going from 49th to 14th in both rushing DVOA and DYAR.

And that run game was at the root of the Raiders' relatively successful season, especially after Veldheer replaced Henderson. While large rushing totals are often the result of blowout wins and not the other way around, the per-game totals against the Denver Broncos in Week 7 (328 yards; 40.7% rushing DVOA); Seattle in Week 8 (239 yards; 6.7% DVOA); the Chargers in Week 13 (251 yards; 50.7% DVOA); Denver again in Week 15 (264 yards, 25.0% DVOA); and Kansas City in Week 17 (209 yards; 24.8% DVOA) proved that no matter the mechanism or motivation, the Raiders had put together a ground game that allowed them to dictate schematic terms in the face of some very iffy quarterback play from Jason Campbell and Bruce Gradkowski.

So, the Raiders were finally on the way up, and thing

were looking relatively bright from a coaching and personnel perspective. If you've followed this team's story at all over the last decade, and were waiting for the other shoe to drop, it was about to happen. Davis decided not to pick up Cable's option after the 2010 season for a number of reasons; the most public was Cable's history of alleged assault and seeming inability to act as a professional at times.

There was the incident in August of 2009, in which defensive assistant Randy Hanson accused Cable of breaking his jaw in a confrontation following a coaches' meeting. Charges were eventually dropped against Cable, but that brought up other issues — he eventually admitted to slapping his first wife two decades ago but denied attacking a former girlfriend more recently. When Davis explained his decision not to being Cable back in January, things got predictably more bizarre.

"As far as his ability goes, you have to look at the years, the four years where he was the play-caller, or the three years, and see where we ended up every year in the past offense," Davis said. "We were either 32nd, 33rd, 34th. I just don't think he can be a head coach calling plays. I don't think he's an offensive coordinator."

"He is a zone blocking purist, and I'm not a zone blocking purist, and we switched this year already. We got it started into gap, we got it into power, and we got it into zone, and that's where Hue believes. He did it at Baltimore, and that intrigued me."

(Note: We were unable to find any instance in which the Raiders ranked 33rd or 34th in the league in any of our advanced metrics.)

The "Hue" in question was offensive coordinator Hue Jackson, who was named to replace Cable as head coach in mid-January. Primarily a quarterback guru known for his work with Joe Flacco in Baltimore, Jackson did bring one connection to the successful Raiders past: his work with Gruden when the two men coached for the University of the Pacific in 1989.

"Jon Gruden raised me as a coach," Jackson told Yahoo Sports' Mike Silver in late July. "You've got to understand, a lot of my belief system stems from him. A lot of my quirkiness, my energy and my understanding of Xs and Os come because I shared an office with a guy with so much passion, who showed me how to put that passion toward something I love."

Gruden's response to Silver: "I'll tell you what a good job Hue and I did — UOP dropped football [in 1995]."

Fun in the abstract, but reality tells a different tale. Not only was Jackson swimming upstream as a first-time head coach with a capricious owner, but the Cable dismissal was a very unpopular move with the players. That showed up on the roster when left guard Robert Gallery and tight end Zach Miller signed lucrative deals with the Seattle Seahawks, where Cable was now the offensive line coach. Both losses will be huge hits — Gallery hasn't lived up to his second-overall selection in 2004, but he credits Cable with resuscitating his career after Cable first coached him in 2006 and moved him from tackle to guard. And Miller, for all the talk about Oakland's deep receivers and "thrilling" vertical schemes, has been the team's primary passing target in each of the last three seasons.

Defensive coordinator John Marshall, credited with much of the defense's turnaround, will be replaced by Chuck Bresnahan, who served that same function for the Raiders in the Gruden glory years. Bresnahan's last job was with the UFL's Florida Tuskers, which leads one to wonder whether Davis is trying to re-create the Gruden-era "greatness of the Raiduhs" without the primary factor in that equation … namely, Gruden or anyone else with that same sense of authority and connection to the players. This will also be the first

year in almost a decade in which the Raiders will draw up coverages without Nnamdi Asomugha taking away half of the field — another challenge for Bresnahan. New secondary coach Rod Woodson could be a factor, or he could be yet another old Raiders player hired on retainer to fill a coaching spot better left to a more qualified person. Because of the lockout, there are too many unanswered questions.

Justifying the Raiders' NFL-lowest win projection isn't a stretch. They've lost their best and most consistent offensive and defensive players, and while there may be adequate replacements, finding replacements for the replacements will be an issue. The offensive line has very little experience (only Seattle's has less in 2011). Jackson and Bresnahan have been a part of Raiders' staffs before, but Jackson is making the first-time transition from coordinator to coach, and Bresnahan has been out of the system for more than a decade. So, while the Raiders will be running offensive and defensive schemes with which they are familiar, there still may be lockout-related issues because of the lack of preparation time this offseason.

The 2011 draft, which saw an unfortunate return to form, doesn't project to help much. The Raiders went back to their old classics, engaging in moves based on name familiarity (second-round pick Stefen Wisniewski is the nephew of current Oakland offensive line coach and former Raiders great tackle Steve Wisniewski), and cornerbacks with more speed than NFL style (Demarcus Van Dyke and Chimdi Chekwa). Fourth-round running Taiwan Jones from Eastern Washington has a chance to make a Jamaal Charles-style impact over time, but that's dependent on whether Al wants to go zone or power these days.

Like it or not, the revolution has ceded power to the ruler in Oakland. And as it's been for many years, the team will be worse for it.

Doug Farrar

2010 Raiders Stats by Week

Wk	vs.	W-L	PF	PA	YDF	YDA	TO	Total	Off	Def	ST
1	@TEN	L	13	38	286	345	-1	-84%	-46%	31%	-7%
2	STL	W	16	14	404	210	-1	-16%	-19%	-3%	0%
3	@ARI	L	23	24	364	227	2	-76%	-35%	22%	-19%
4	HOU	L	24	31	363	441	-3	-25%	1%	33%	6%
5	SD	W	35	27	279	506	3	10%	6%	4%	9%
6	@SF	L	9	17	179	349	-2	-74%	-55%	19%	0%
7	@DEN	W	59	14	508	240	3	91%	40%	-46%	5%
8	SEA	W	33	3	545	164	1	48%	14%	-48%	-15%
9	KC	W	23	20	321	304	-1	21%	-15%	-22%	14%
10	BYE										
11	@PIT	L	3	35	182	431	-2	-109%	-60%	40%	-9%
12	MIA	L	17	33	263	471	-2	-25%	-20%	10%	5%
13	@SD	W	28	13	368	286	1	64%	45%	-17%	3%
14	@JAC	L	31	38	476	385	-1	-11%	33%	27%	-17%
15	DEN	W	39	23	502	235	-2	17%	2%	-1%	13%
16	IND	L	26	31	290	370	2	18%	0%	19%	37%
17	@KC	W	31	10	344	201	1	62%	12%	-53%	-2%

Trends and Splits

	Offense	Rank	Defense	Rank
Total DVOA	-4.3%	23	1.5%	15
Unadjusted VOA	1.2%	18	1.6%	16
Weighted Trend	3.8%	18	-2.8%	10
Variance	10.3%	24	9.1%	27
Average Opponent	6.0%	6	4.4%	20
Passing	-0.4%	24	7.7%	17
Rushing	8.6%	6	-4.5%	12
First Down	0.2%	21	10.2%	25
Second Down	-9.6%	24	-13.0%	5
Third Down	-5.1%	20	6.6%	21
First Half	-16.0%	30	-3.6%	10
Second Half	7.0%	11	7.1%	21
Red Zone	-3.1%	21	7.9%	21
Late and Close	3.1%	16	14.4%	29

Five-Year Performance

Year	W-L	Pyth	Est W	PF	PA	TO	Total	Rk	Off	Rk	Def	Rk	ST	Rk	Off AGL	Rk	Def AGL	Rk
2006	2-14	2.7	3.9	168	332	-23	-31.4%	32	-36.5%	32	-8.1%	8	-3.0%	26	25.3	23	4.5	3
2007	4-12	4.9	4.1	283	398	-11	-28.8%	29	-17.4%	28	6.8%	22	-4.6%	29	25.1	24	18.2	13
2008	5-11	4.6	5.0	263	388	+1	-23.3%	29	-21.3%	31	7.8%	19	5.8%	2	35.8	23	18.4	14
2009	5-11	2.8	4.4	197	379	-13	-32.9%	30	-22.3%	30	10.6%	24	0.0%	17	32.4	23	18.9	8
2010	8-8	8.9	6.9	410	371	-2	-4.2%	21	-4.3%	23	1.5%	15	1.5%	13	15.1	8	15.4	10

Strategic Tendencies

Run/Pass		Rank	Offense		Rank	Defense		Rank	Other		Rank
Runs, all plays	44%	6	3+ WR	43%	26	Rush 3	3.0%	26	2+ RB, Pct Runs	62%	9
Runs, first half	45%	6	4+ WR	1%	31	Rush 4	68.7%	6	1 RB/2 TE, Pct Runs	43%	25
Runs, first down	56%	5	2+ TE	11%	32	Rush 5	17.1%	29	1 RB/3+ WR, Pct Runs	22%	18
Runs, second-long	40%	4	Single back	52%	24	Rush 6+	11.2%	10	CB1 on WR1	56%	3
Runs, power sit.	63%	10	Play action	22%	7	Zone Blitz	2.1%	30	Go for it on 4th	0.93	14
Runs, behind 2H	29%	12	Max protect	21%	3	Sacks by LB	20.7%	19	Offensive Pace	31.0	19
Pass, ahead 2H	39%	25	Outside pocket	16%	6	Sacks by DB	17.4%	5	Defensive Pace	29.9	3

Penalties are about more than just the teams involved; some crews just give out more flags than others. And apparently, those crews worked Oakland games last year. It isn't surprising to see that Oakland led the league with 165 penalty flags and 1,276 penalty yards. But it might be surprising to see that Oakland opponents were flagged 135 times, third in the NFL, for a league-leading 1,171 penalty yards. ⏚ Oakland led the league in usage of six-OL sets last year, using a sixth lineman — usually Khalif Barnes — roughly once every eight plays. It was a smart strategy, as the Raiders also led the league with 6.2 yards per play from six-OL sets. It also helps explain why the Raiders went with two tight ends less than any other team in the league: Why use two tight ends when you have a sixth lineman? ⏚ Oakland threw passes to running backs 27 percent of the time on third down, easily the highest rate in the league. ⏚ Oakland was 30th in offensive DVOA before halftime, but 11th after halftime.

Passing

Player	DYAR	DVOA	Plays	NtYds	Avg	YAC	C%	TD	Int
J.Campbell	181	-2.9%	364	2304	6.3	6.7	59.6%	13	8
B.Gradkowski	-33	-14.2%	169	1025	6.1	6.3	53.2%	5	7

Rushing

Player	DYAR	DVOA	Plays	Yds	Avg	TD	Fum	Suc
D.McFadden	112	4.6%	223	1150	5.2	7	3	42%
M.Bush	101	6.5%	157	631	4.0	8	0	45%
J.Campbell	25	2.8%	35	233	6.7	1	1	-
M.Reece	-2	-9.9%	30	124	4.1	1	1	57%
J.Ford	112	236.9%	10	155	15.5	2	0	-
R.Cartwright	-17	-62.4%	9	22	2.4	0	0	22%
B.Gradkowski	2	-6.7%	9	46	5.1	0	0	-
K.Boller	-24	-112.6%	5	21	4.2	0	1	-
D.Heyward-Bey	8	-1.1%	4	48	12.0	0	1	-

Receiving

Player	DYAR	DVOA	Plays	Ctch	Yds	Y/C	YAC	TD	C%
L.Murphy	23	-8.9%	78	41	609	14.9	5.1	2	53%
D.Heyward-Bey	-82	-28.6%	64	26	366	14.1	3.9	1	41%
J.Ford	39	-2.9%	54	25	470	18.8	4.1	2	46%
J.Higgins	-85	-47.4%	30	10	103	10.3	2.2	0	33%
C.Schilens	12	3.9%	9	5	40	8.0	2.6	1	56%
Z.Miller	81	6.2%	92	60	685	11.4	4.6	5	65%
B.Myers	-13	-19.5%	16	12	80	6.7	3.2	0	75%
D.McFadden	172	40.8%	61	47	507	10.8	11.0	3	77%
M.Reece	85	22.3%	43	25	333	13.3	12.2	3	58%
M.Bush	96	57.9%	25	19	218	11.5	11.4	0	76%

Offensive Line

Year	Yards	ALY	Rank	Power	Rank	Stuff	Rank	2nd Lev	Rank	Open Field	Rank
2008	4.15	3.93	26	62%	22	19%	19	1.14	15	0.71	16
2009	4.02	3.97	23	72%	4	16%	6	1.03	27	0.63	20
2010	4.60	4.11	15	61%	15	16%	8	1.10	18	1.15	6

Year	LE	Rank	LT	Rank	Mid	Rank	RT	Rank	RE	Rank	Sacks	ASR	Rank	F-Start	Cont.
2008	5.00	6	4.55	9	3.55	29	4.36	9	2.97	30	39	9.4%	30	30	29
2009	4.81	11	3.74	25	3.72	26	4.12	16	4.27	14	49	9.5%	31	21	25
2010	4.41	14	4.92	4	3.98	16	4.03	19	3.71	22	44	8.3%	26	29	33

Last year, this was a patchwork unit with middling results that failed to reflect the attention the coaching staff paid to it. Things could get even worse in 2011 unless the personnel is there for the switch from Tom Cable's power zone blocking to a more standard pulling/trapping scheme espoused by Bob Wylie, who "helped" Josh McDaniels make that same change in Denver. The Raiders morphed from past to future at the left tackle position in 2010, starting the season with veteran Mario Henderson and switching to rookie Jared Veldheer in Game 7 against the Broncos in late October. Henderson, who gave up the third-most blown blocks leading to sacks in 2009, may have been even worse in 2010, and Veldheer was an easy choice to replace him there despite the fact that he was coming to the NFL from Division II Hillsdale College. The Raiders had rushed for more than 100 yards in every game with Henderson at left tackle, but they blew up in the first two with Veldheer, amassing 328 yards on the ground on 51 attempts against Denver and 239 on 39 attempts versus the Seattle Seahawks the next week.

Veldheer is a potentially dynamic blocker at the line and the second level, but he fit the team very well in another sense — the Raiders have finished in the top five in total penalties every season since 2004, and led the league the last two years. Veldheer tied with three other players for the league lead in penalties with 15, and 11 of those were called from his first start in Week 7 and onward. One thing that Veldheer won't have in 2011 is veteran guard Robert Gallery to his immediate right — Gallery has enjoyed a bit of a professional reformation since Tom Cable moved him inside in 2007, and he followed Cable to Seattle. The Raiders tried to recover from that loss by signing veteran pulling/trapping guard Justin Smiley, but Smiley chose to retire.

So, it's unknown how the Raiders will fill Gallery's shoes, but the center position appears locked up no matter what. Samson Satele may have been the team's most consistent lineman in 2010, but new former Raiders legend Steve Wisniewski, now past of Oakland's coaching staff, certainly wasn't unhappy with the second-round selection of nephew Stefen Wisniewski in the second round. The younger Wisniewski projects better as a center at the NFL level — he doesn't play with enough consistent power to avoid getting washed out at the guard position.

Right guard Cooper Carlisle, the only Raiders offensive lineman to play the same position all 16 games last season, was generally underwhelming. Some in the front office (read: Al Davis) are convinced that the 6-foot-7 Bruce Campbell can be a starting guard in the NFL, but most teams (especially power teams) generally want their guards a bit shorter to gain advantage in the leverage battle. Gallery was an exception to that rule, but the Raiders are dropping him in part because he doesn't fit that blocking paradigm. There was some thought that Satele might make a good guard when he was in Miami, but that's about as certain as things get right now. Third-round pick Joseph Barksdale of LSU could compete at right tackle or either guard spot.

Defensive Front Seven

Defensive Line	Age	Pos	Plays	TmPct	Rk	Stop	Dfts	BTkl	St%	Rk	AvYd	Rk	Sack	Hit	Hur	Runs	St%	Yds	Pass	St%	Yds
							Overall							**Pass Rush**		**vs. Run**			**vs. Pass**		
Tommy Kelly	31	DT	59	7.8%	7	44	15	2	73%	40	1.4	20	7	7	10	44	73%	2.2	15	80%	-1.0
Matt Shaughnessy	25	DE	57	7.6%	13	49	19	2	83%	10	0.9	20	7	2	15	47	83%	1.9	10	100%	-3.9
Richard Seymour	32	DT	50	8.2%	6	41	16	4	78%	22	0.6	7	5.5	9	7.5	41	78%	1.8	9	100%	-4.4
Lamarr Houston	24	DE	39	5.2%	41	35	12	6	91%	3	0.6	17	5	10	16	33	91%	1.3	6	83%	-3.0
John Henderson	32	DT	33	7.8%	8	30	4	0	90%	2	1.7	28	0	2	3	30	90%	1.8	3	100%	0.0
Trevor Scott	27	DE	22	4.7%	–	18	4	0	82%	–	1.7	–	1.5	4	13	17	82%	2.2	5	80%	0.0
Desmond Bryant	26	DT	21	3.0%	61	19	5	1	88%	4	0.9	12	2.5	1	6	17	88%	2.0	4	100%	-3.8

Linebackers	Age	Pos	Plays	TmPct	Rk	Stop	Dfts	BTkl	AvYd	Sack	Hit	Hur	Runs	St%	Rk	Yds	Rk	Tgts	Suc%	Rk	AdjYd	Rk
							Overall			**Pass Rush**			**vs. Run**				**vs. Pass**					
Rolando McClain	22	MLB	91	12.9%	37	64	22	4	3.7	0.5	2	1	60	73%	30	2.9	42	42	59%	24	6.9	56
Kamerion Wimbley	28	OLB	58	7.7%	86	31	15	4	4.4	9	2	9	28	61%	82	3.9	87	23	46%	69	8.1	74
Quentin Groves	27	OLB	41	5.8%	103	29	8	4	2.6	0	1	2	32	75%	20	1.9	3	11	60%	–	5.1	–

Year	Yards	ALY	Rank	Power	Rank	Stuff	Rank	2nd Lev	Rank	Open Field	Rank
2008	4.65	4.48	28	75%	28	15%	27	1.26	27	0.80	20
2009	4.79	4.07	16	68%	22	19%	15	1.31	30	1.27	30
2010	4.38	3.63	4	62%	13	24%	2	1.09	13	1.17	31

Year	LE	Rank	LT	Rank	Mid	Rank	RT	Rank	RE	Rank	Sacks	ASR	Rank
2008	3.83	12	4.09	15	4.38	22	5.23	32	5.38	30	32	7.3%	6
2009	4.25	16	3.44	5	4.18	20	4.39	23	3.56	8	37	7.5%	6
2010	3.13	4	3.27	4	3.80	10	3.41	8	4.05	18	47	9.5%	1

There's a wealth of talent on Oakland's front four, and that talent aligned in 2010. The Raiders didn't have a first-round pick in 2010; Richard Seymour was their first-round pick by dint of a September 2009 trade. And when he was healthy, Seymour proved the wisdom of the deal with a series of dominant performances in the middle of the season. Hamstring injuries got in the way at the start and end of the season, but he still had a worthy Pro Bowl campaign, and the front office didn't hesitate to reward Seymour with a two-year, $30 million contract in February. It's a wise move, because Seymour still commands a great deal of attention from enemy blockers, and he was quite conversant with Oakland's mixed fronts. However, those teams that focused too much on Seymour were forced to understand that fellow tackle Tommy Kelly was Seymour's ideal bookend. Able to alternate with Seymour at the one- and three-technique spots, Kelly was a load to handle all on his own.

And with all that said about Seymour and Kelly, the elite talent going forward could come from the end positions. Second-year right end Matt Shaughnessy, originally one of the top three names in the Raiders' infamous "reach draft" of 2009, put it all together and won a starting spot after Greg Ellis was released and when Trevor Scott had to move to weakside linebacker following injuries to Thomas Howard and Quentin Groves. Shaughnessy has flashed ability from the start, putting up four sacks in his rookie campaign, but he hit a different level in the 2010 season. Not only was he able to harass quarterbacks on a near-constant basis, he was also one of four qualifying Oakland linemen to finish in the top 10 in the NFL in Stop Rate against the run. Rookie end Lamarr Houston was even more of a pleasant surprise, playing well at left end and at three-technique tackle when Seymour was hurt.

As we predicted in last year's *Almanac*, the Raiders turned over their entire starting linebacker corps in 2010, starting with first-round pick Rolando McClain in the middle. McClain had a rocky first pro season, struggling with foot injuries and refusing to talk with the media until a long streak of Raiders home blackouts was snapped. He came on a bit toward the end, and more will be expected of him in 2011, especially with the talent on the line in front of him.

Groves (Jacksonville) and Kamerion Wimbley (Cleveland) were each acquired via trade from original teams that expected more from their former high draft picks. Wimbley alternated between strongside linebacker and nickel pass rusher — another hidden asset in the Raiders' creative use of fronts — and ended his 2010 season with the most sacks since his rookie year. Groves was less impressive on the weak side; he just hasn't shown NFL starter potential to this point in his career at any position.

Defensive Secondary

Secondary	Age	Pos	Plays	TmPct	Rk	Stop	Dfts	BTkl	Runs	St%	Rk	Yds	Rk	Tgts	Tgt%	Rk	Dist	Suc%	Rk	APaYd	Rk	PD	Int
								Overall			**vs. Run**					**vs. Pass**							
Tyvon Branch	25	SS	103	13.7%	8	43	22	7	61	48%	23	6.0	29	35	8.0%	15	13.7	43%	70	9.5	62	1	1
Michael Huff	28	FS	90	12.0%	18	34	21	5	45	31%	63	9.0	68	31	6.9%	28	15.9	56%	32	12.1	77	3	3
Stanford Routt	28	CB	68	9.0%	35	24	8	4	23	30%	74	7.7	56	96	21.9%	3	15.4	65%	6	6.8	32	13	2
Mike Mitchell	24	SS	52	6.9%	70	25	16	3	21	48%	21	4.2	6	31	6.9%	27	7.2	63%	13	7.0	25	4	1
Chris Johnson	32	CB	25	4.4%	86	10	6	2	3	0%	88	11.0	83	44	13.2%	63	13.1	67%	3	6.7	31	10	2
Nnamdi Asomugha	30	CB	25	3.8%	87	12	6	7	6	50%	25	4.0	10	31	7.9%	89	15.4	62%	9	6.5	25	5	0
Stevie Brown	24	SS	15	2.1%	--	3	1	1	6	17%	--	9.0	--	2	0.5%	--	16.5	83%	--	7.0	--	1	0

Year	Pass D Rank	vs. #1 WR	Rk	vs. #2 WR	Rk	vs. Other WR	Rk	vs. TE	Rk	vs. RB	Rk
2008	13	-19.6%	2	31.0%	29	-0.4%	22	-16.6%	5	3.8%	14
2009	26	28.3%	32	22.3%	28	4.5%	19	1.6%	16	-4.6%	13
2010	17	5.0%	20	-3.6%	13	-4.9%	15	14.4%	25	1.0%	13

More than any other possible personnel hole, the challenge of replacing Nnamdi Asomugha will be a titanic one for the Raiders. Taken for granted through the Raiders' worst years, the man who's been the best cornerback in football over the last half-decade found a loophole in his contract, and exercised it all the way to Philadelphia. The bull's eye now falls on Stanford Routt, but as you can tell by our target numbers, that's nothing new for the Houston alum, who signed a three-year, $31.5 million dollar contract in February. That was a reward for a breakout season which came after many years of struggles; Routt was one of the game's best cornerbacks last year by stats both traditional and sabermetric. Everyone thought the Raiders were nuts when they assigned a first- and third-round tender to Routt prior to the 2010 season, but the subsequent $3.3 million tender turned out to be a bargain.

With Asomugha gone, the targets should be more evenly split among the starting cornerbacks, and Chris Johnson looks most likely to take the job opposite Routt. Originally known as the guy who replaced DeAngelo Hall and made everyone thank God for the end of one of Oakland's most disastrous personnel experiments, Johnson was the primary target of opposing offenses in 2009. So, both men know what it's like to get the ball thrown in their direction all the time; the question now is how they'll do without the obvious legend at the pole position. Both players can play tight man and trail speed receivers down the sideline; the latter is Johnson's specialty. At safety, Tyvon Branch is a good box player known for giving up big plays in coverage, and the Raiders have to hope to get more consistency out of Michael Huff now that he signed a four-year, $32 million contract to stay in town.

Special Teams

Year	DVOA	Rank	FG/XP	Rank	Net Kick	Rank	Kick Ret	Rank	Net Punt	Rank	Punt Ret	Rank	Hidden	Rank
2008	5.8%	2	1.9	14	-0.8	18	3.6	13	13.9	4	15.2	1	16.2	3
2009	0.0%	17	15.0	1	-6.3	27	-16.3	32	18.2	1	-10.4	31	2.7	9
2010	1.5%	13	3.5	10	0.8	16	5.0	10	9.9	4	-10.2	31	16.2	1

Punter Shane Lechler didn't quite amass the same net punting value he did in 2009, but only the Dallas Cowboys had a better net punting average than the Raiders, and that had as much to do with an improvement in Oakland's coverage teams. Punt returns were still a problem — neither Johnnie Lee Higgins nor Nick Miller did much in that department, but between explosive kick returner Jacoby Ford (who took three kickoffs back for touchdowns in 2010, a franchise record) and rookie running back Taiwan Jones (one of the fastest players in the nation), there are other options.

As for Sebastian Janikowski, he set a personal mark with 33 field goals, which — of course — is always a bit of a mixed bag, because you're leaving a lot of touchdowns on the field. He also missed eight field goals, including seven from 40 yards and out, after blowing just three in 2009. Kickoffs were slightly better than in 2009, and only the Baltimore Ravens had a higher percentage of touchbacks than Oakland's 31.2 percent, and the Raiders allowed a middle-of-the-pack 23.1 yards per opponent kick return, down from 25.7 the season before.

Coaching Staff

Hue Jackson is the latest in a long line of former position coaches with no NFL head coaching experience that the Raiders organization will most likely mold (read: push around) in whatever image is the order of the day. Jackson is a quarterback guru with a record of success, which is good news for whatever quarterback the Raiders decide to trot out there in 2011. And the Oakland offense did improve with his help in 2010. However, between personnel issues and the lack of a dominant voice on the field, the Raiders look to be in regression mode once again. Bringing Wisniewski on board to work with the offensive line, as well as Hall-of-Fame defensive back Rod Woodson to help with the secondary, extends a long tradition of former Raiders greats on the sideline, and not always with the best results.

New offensive coordinator Al Saunders will bring his three-digit system and 700-page playbook to town. Of course, Saunders coached Jason Campbell with the Redskins in 2006 and 2007, Campbell's first two seasons, and we'll just have to see if Saunders is comfortable with using more than two percent of his playbook this time.

Returning defensive coordinator Chuck Bresnahan held that same position for the Raiders from 2000-03. Serving as the defensive coordinator for the UFL's Florida Tuskers in 2010 meant that Bresnahan was very happy to return to the NFL. So happy, in fact, that he didn't even mind a provision during the lockout which forced all Raiders staffers to get on the phone and sell season tickets to avoid pay cuts. "I've got to sell millionaires in a room every day to run and crash heads," he told *USA Today*. "So this is easy. Most of the people I've encountered have been understanding. I think the public looks at us as caught in the middle. The hardest thing is looking someone in the eye during this economy. But on the other hand, people really want football."

Sounds like the perfect attitude for an Al Davis coach.

Philadelphia Eagles

2010 Record: 10-6	**2011 Mean Projection:** 11.7 wins
Pythagorean Wins: 9.4 (10th)	**On the Clock (0-3):** 0%
DVOA: 21.8% (5th)	**Loserville (4-6):** 2%
Offense: 21.2% (3rd)	**Mediocrity (7-8):** 6%
Defense: 1.4% (14th)	**Playoff Contender (9-10):** 20%
Special Teams: 2.0% (12th)	**Super Bowl Contender (11+):** 72%
Variance: 9.5% (7th)	**Projected Average Opponent:** 0.1% (16th)

2010: Is it a comeback if you are better than you were the first time?

2011: Super Bowl or bust.

Rip Van Eagles Fan, who fell asleep just after the Eagles lost to the Cardinals in the 2008 NFC Championship game, would not recognize his favorite team if he woke up on August 1st of 2011.

Rip fell asleep on a team that had been doing the same thing for eight years. Andy Reid wound the key in Donovan McNabb's back, sent him onto the field to win 9 to 13 games, then grunted through the press conference after each playoff loss. The offensive philosophy was predictable: McNabb bombs, usually to second-rate receivers, with Brian Westbrook making the absolute most of limited opportunities on draws and screens. The free agent philosophy was also predictable: slow and steady, prudent and a little disappointing, with few splashy moves but lots of roster attrition. The only exception was the 2004 offseason, when the Eagles acquired Jevon Kearse and Terrell Owens. That ended with a Super Bowl appearance and a driveway sit-up session the team never wants to repeat.

Rip Van Eagles fan drifted off knowing that McNabb would eventually be replaced; if Rip was a typical Eagles fan, he was pining for it. But the heir apparent was Kevin Kolb. Two-and-a-half years ago, there was no indication that Eagles football would look or feel different at any time in the foreseeable future. Even with Kolb and a few youngsters like DeSean Jackson rising up, the Eagles would still pass too often, spend too little on the open market, be a man or two short on defense, and come up infuriatingly short in the postseason, always and forever.

So let's shake Rip out of his slumber. Michael Vick is not just the Eagles quarterback, but one of the league's biggest stars. Vince Young is now his backup. Kolb, after one of history's briefest tenures as an uncontested starter (10 pass attempts), is now in Arizona. Despite the presence of Vick and an exciting young corps of skill position talent, the Eagles' strongest unit may be the defense. And that defense is not a jerry-rigged contraption built from draft picks and middle-shelf free agents, but a star-studded squad built around what could be the strongest cornerback corps in NFL history: incumbent Asante Samuel (four Pro Bowls), trade acquisition Dominique Rodgers-Cromartie (one Pro Bowl), and eye-opening free agent signee Nnamdi Asomugha (two-time first-team All-Pro). For good measure, they added Jason Babin, the bookend pass rusher to Trent Cole that the team tried and failed to acquire through the draft several times. For extra good measure, they brought in Cullen Jenkins, a 3-4 end who should be a gap-penetrating tackle in the 4-3.

Not all of this is quite as new and shocking as it seems. Reid still relies on a bomb-heavy offense. Vick now has the skill set of the younger McNabb: bombs, improvisations, and a suddenly cardboard personality after years of being far too interesting

2011 Eagles Schedule

Week	Opp.	Week	Opp.	Week	Opp.
1	at STL	7	BYE	13	at SEA (Thu.)
2	at ATL	8	DAL	14	at MIA
3	NYG	9	CHI (Mon.)	15	NYJ
4	SF	10	ARI	16	at DAL
5	at BUF	11	at NYG	17	at WAS
6	at WAS	12	NE		

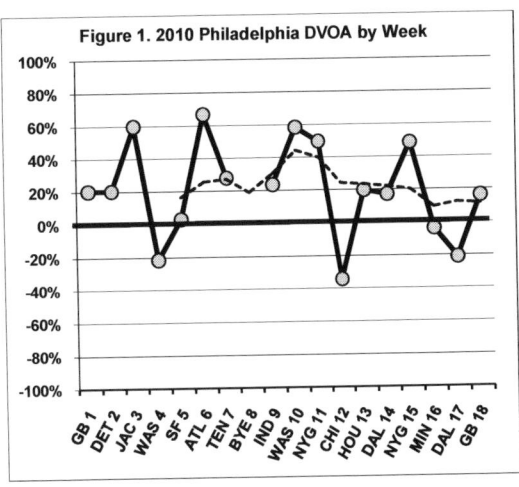

Figure 1. 2010 Philadelphia DVOA by Week

for his own good. The Eagles have had other great cornerback tandems in recent history, including Troy Vincent and Bobby Taylor as well as Lito Sheppard and Sheldon Brown.

It's the boldness of the recent moves that would make Rip sit straight up in his bed. The Eagles were come-from-nowhere bidders for Vick in 2009 and Asomugha in late July. (Baseball's Phillies did something equally shocking when they came from nowhere to acquire pitcher Cliff Lee.) The Vick signing was a huge gamble for a coach and organization that preferred the nickel slots, and the team made a similar wager by signing the troubled Young after trading the dependably blah Kolb. And as fine as Vincent-Taylor and Sheppard-Brown were, they have nothing on the current trio of defensive backs, who turned the team's biggest 2010 weakness into the league's strongest unit in three whirlwind days.

It's hard to quantify just how good the Eagles cornerbacks can be using our charting stats, because there just aren't enough stats. No matter what we measure on the field, teams must throw in a cornerback's direction before we can assess his performance. So for cornerbacks, absence of evidence can be evidence of excellence. Our rankings for Success Rate or Yards per Pass Attempt have a "minimum eight games started" baseline specifically to include Asomugha; otherwise, he wouldn't have enough pass targets to be listed. Samuel finished first in both figures, allowing a staggeringly low 3.2 yards per pass. (Think of throwing to Samuel's receiver as nearly equivalent to running up the middle with the fullback, and you get an idea of how effectively he shut his side of the field down.) Entire offensive game plans have been built in around avoiding Samuel or Asomugha. Now, teams will have no choice. They may turn to the less reliable Rodgers-Cromartie as Plan C: he ranked 50th in Success Rate and 62nd in Yards per Attempt. But DRC is exactly the kind of talented, mistake-prone defender who ex-

cels in the slot: He can gamble and guess against No. 3 receivers, providing a few pick-six plays to offset the occasional mistake. With Cole and Babin rushing from either side, and Jenkins coming up the middle, quarterbacks may not be able to find their third receivers anyway.

The Eagles would not have embarked on such a go-for-broke defensive overhaul in late July if not for Vick, who took over for the injured/ineffective Kolb in Week 1 last year and looked more like the Vick of video game fantasy than the Vick of old. In a system that relies on timing and accuracy, Vick bested his previous career-high completion percentage by more than six points. He recorded a career-low in interception rate and a career high in yards per attempt. He ranked eighth in DVOA last year, after never finishing higher than 17th back in the Era of Bad Newz.

Vick opened up the offense in a way that the mechanical Kolb and aging, rickety McNabb couldn't. LeSean McCoy was a totally different animal when Vick was under center. When McCoy was in the backfield behind Kevin Kolb, he posted a respectable 1.9% rushing DVOA, while averaging 3.8 yards per carry. When Vick was under center, though, McCoy had a rushing DVOA of 26.5%, and he averaged a full 5.9 yards per carry. McCoy had five runs of 40 yards or more in 2010, and Vick was at quarterback for each of them. Vick was the quarterback on 25 of 28 McCoy runs for ten yards or more. Vick made the Eagles both a better rushing and a better passing team, even if you take his scrambling yardage out of the equation.

Vick and DeSean Jackson became one of the league's most frightening big-play tandems, but Jackson was the team's biggest lingering question when we finally went to press about eight seconds before you downloaded this book. While Jackson's ability to stretch defenses is vital to the Eagles' scheme, it's important to note that his Catch Rate through his first three seasons is just 51 percent. Home-run threats often have low Catch Rates, but Jackson also has a low Plus-Minus rate, meaning that he catches fewer passes than a typical receiver would catch given passes of a similar length. Keep in mind that the guys throwing Jackson the ball were pretty darn good over the last three years, so those low rates are not the result of quarterback ineptitude.

Jackson's low Catch Rate and Plus-Minus Rate provide some insight into why the Eagles played hardball with his contract renegotiation demands. A look back at recent players with a similar target totals and Catch Rates through their first three years reveals a mixed bag of players, most of whom did not take the next step into superstardom. Plaxico Burress had a 50.6 percent Catch Rate in years 1-to-3 with the Steelers, and a 48.7 percent Catch Rate in his subsequent season. Chris Chambers regressed, going from a 51.3 percent Catch Rate in his early years with the Dolphins to a 46.0 percent figure as his role expanded. And Braylon Edwards went from a 51.3 percent Catch Rate to 45.8 percent. All three players changed teams due to managerial frustration of one kind or another. Other similar players, like Peter Warrick (50.9 percent to 63.0 percent), Rod Gardner (49.3 percent to 46.8 percent) and Darnay Scott (47.4 percent to 56.2 percent) saw their Catch Rates ebb and flow as their roles slowly shrunk. Factor in Jackson's injury history, and there's a good reason why the Eagles are leery of overpaying him.

Assuming Jackson returns to the fold and keeps opposing safeties so deep that they can shop at the King of Prussia Mall in Cover-2, the Eagles have become a team of several overwhelming strengths and very few minor weaknesses. The offensive line is unsettled, with right tackle Winston Justice on the PUP list at the start of camp, but Vick keeps opponents from teeing off with blitzes. Some unusual early injuries, like

Mike Patterson's sudden collapse and Jeremy Maclin's mystery ailment (still unknown at press time), opened holes in the Eagles lineup at the beginning of camp. (The Eagles promptly insulated themselves at wide receiver by grabbing former Giants receiver Steve Smith.) A pedestrian linebacker corps may make the Eagles easy to run straight at, just as they were in the playoff loss to the Packers. But running off tackle will only get opponents so far when the Eagles offense is producing 28 points per game and Asante's Corner Kings are turning every pass into a leap of faith. The Eagles really have become like baseball's Phillies: Delaware Valley fans can fret about the Phillies' lack of a sixth starting pitcher or eighth baseman, and they can worry about whether Casey Matthews is the answer at middle linebacker or if Jason Peters can go two quarters without a false start. But beyond the compulsive hand-wringing, these teams are stacked for deep playoff runs, and the only apparent question is when those runs will end.

For all of the change, this year may well end in a way Rip Van Eagles Fan would find familiar: a postseason loss. Vince Young called the Eagles a "Dream Team" at the very start of camp, and the comparison to LeBron James' Miami Heat underlines just what the Eagles have gotten themselves into. The Asomugha, Jenkins, and DRC additions made them prohibitive favorites to win the conference, the team with the national target on its back. It also revealed a sense of urgency in South Philly. The Eagles didn't squander their future at all during their defensive upgrade; DRC even arrived with an extra second-round pick in his travel bag. But the team stopped acting like they could go 11-5 forever and started acting like a team that wants to win a Super Bowl, this year, or else.

In other words, Andy Reid may finally be feeling the heat. His Eagles have an excellent chance to win the Super Bowl this year. If they don't, a slumbering Eagles fan who wakes up in 2012 may find that absolutely nothing is familiar.

Mike Tanier and Bill Barnwell

2010 Eagles Stats by Week

Wk	vs.	W-L	PF	PA	YDF	YDA	TO	Total	Off	Def	ST
1	GB	L	20	27	320	299	1	20%	29%	6%	-3%
2	@DET	W	35	32	410	444	2	20%	30%	7%	-2%
3	@JAC	W	28	3	373	191	1	60%	33%	-28%	-1%
4	WAS	L	12	17	353	293	-1	-22%	2%	22%	-2%
5	@SF	W	27	24	352	364	4	3%	17%	5%	-9%
6	ATL	W	31	17	474	293	1	67%	52%	-24%	-9%
7	@TEN	L	19	37	326	328	-1	28%	10%	-11%	7%
8	BYE										
9	IND	W	26	24	402	338	2	24%	23%	4%	4%
10	@WAS	W	59	28	592	375	3	58%	68%	9%	0%
11	NYG	W	27	17	392	208	3	50%	10%	-45%	-5%
12	@CHI	L	26	31	398	349	-1	-34%	15%	59%	10%
13	HOU	W	34	24	416	431	1	20%	30%	22%	11%
14	@DAL	W	30	27	429	349	0	17%	1%	0%	16%
15	@NYG	W	38	31	418	364	-1	49%	47%	4%	5%
16	MIN	L	14	24	331	337	-2	-4%	20%	20%	-4%
17	DAL	L	13	14	244	272	-3	-21%	-46%	-10%	15%
18	GB	L	16	21	352	309	1	16%	19%	5%	2%

Trends and Splits

	Offense	Rank	Defense	Rank
Total DVOA	21.2%	3	1.4%	14
Unadjusted VOA	22.0%	4	0.6%	13
Weighted Trend	19.9%	5	2.8%	14
Variance	6.5%	11	5.7%	10
Average Opponent	3.7%	13	3.3%	16
Passing	24.4%	12	5.8%	11
Rushing	27.8%	1	-3.8%	14
First Down	17.7%	6	4.2%	18
Second Down	18.6%	5	8.0%	20
Third Down	32.4%	5	-15.1%	3
First Half	18.0%	5	-1.5%	12
Second Half	24.8%	4	4.2%	20
Red Zone	1.7%	15	63.6%	32
Late and Close	12.9%	6	-9.3%	11

Five-Year Performance

Year	W-L	Pyth	Est W	PF	PA	TO	Total	Rk	Off	Rk	Def	Rk	ST	Rk	Off AGL	Rk	Def AGL	Rk
2006	10-6	9.8	11.6	398	328	+5	27.2%	3	22.0%	3	-7.1%	9	-1.9%	22	13.6	15	21.3	20
2007	8-8	9.1	9.6	336	300	-8	13.7%	10	13.1%	6	-5.9%	9	-5.4%	31	15.4	8	23.2	19
2008	9-6-1	11.3	11.7	416	289	+3	33.5%	1	11.7%	13	-20.3%	3	1.6%	13	35.5	22	3.5	2
2009	11-5	10.2	10.9	429	337	+15	28.4%	4	13.5%	10	-10.7%	6	4.3%	2	37.4	26	31.5	20
2010	10-6	9.4	10.8	439	377	+9	21.8%	5	21.2%	3	1.4%	14	2.0%	12	41.4	29	28.7	21

Strategic Tendencies

Run/Pass		Rank	Offense		Rank	Defense		Rank	Other		Rank
Runs, all plays	34%	30	3+ WR	63%	4	Rush 3	4.0%	23	2+ RB, Pct Runs	44%	31
Runs, first half	33%	30	4+ WR	12%	6	Rush 4	58.3%	17	1 RB/2 TE, Pct Runs	43%	27
Runs, first down	39%	32	2+ TE	16%	30	Rush 5	22.7%	18	1 RB/3+ WR, Pct Runs	31%	3
Runs, second-long	33%	17	Single back	59%	15	Rush 6+	15.1%	4	CB1 on WR1	40%	19
Runs, power sit.	63%	11	Play action	20%	13	Zone Blitz	12.8%	2	Go for it on 4th	0.75	24
Runs, behind 2H	20%	31	Max protect	10%	22	Sacks by LB	10.3%	29	Offensive Pace	29.9	7
Pass, ahead 2H	52%	5	Outside pocket	22%	1	Sacks by DB	10.3%	16	Defensive Pace	31.3	24

The Eagles ran a league-high 47 running back screens last year, gaining 7.0 yards per pass with 48.9% DVOA. ⬥ The Eagles allowed 4.3 yards per play when zone blitzing, compared to 6.6 yards per play otherwise. They showed a similar trend in 2008, although last year their defense was roughly the same zone blitzing vs. not zone blitzing. ⬥ In addition, the Eagles allowed just 4.1 yards per play when sending six or more pass rushers, compared to 5.5 yards per play when sending five and 7.2 yards per play when sending four or fewer. ⬥ The Eagles had the best defense in the league against third-and-long, but ranked 28th against third-and-short. ⬥ Philadelphia led the league by causing 13 incompletes by hitting a quarterback during his throwing motion. They were also tied for second with 19 passes tipped away or batted down at the line. ⬥ Eagles opponents threw to tight ends on a league-high 26 percent of passes. ⬥ Philadelphia led the NFL with 29 penalties on special teams, including four during conversion attempts.

Passing

Player	DYAR	DVOA	Plays	NtYds	Avg	YAC	C%	TD	Int
M.Vick	835	20.6%	406	2864	7.1	5.7	63.1%	21	6
K.Kolb	97	-3.3%	201	1069	5.3	5.0	61.6%	8	3

Rushing

Player	DYAR	DVOA	Plays	Yds	Avg	TD	Fum	Suc
L.McCoy	224	17.8%	207	1080	5.2	7	1	49%
M.Vick	195	29.7%	90	681	7.6	9	3	-
J.Harrison	-35	-21.1%	71	330	4.6	1	2	35%
E.Buckley	-16	-26.1%	21	67	3.2	0	0	33%
D.Jackson	72	49.5%	16	104	6.5	1	0	-
K.Kolb	-6	-23.6%	11	65	5.9	0	1	-
C.Hall	12	-19.9%	9	29	3.2	0	0	-

Receiving

Player	DYAR	DVOA	Plays	Ctch	Yds	Y/C	YAC	TD	C%
J.Maclin	251	15.5%	115	70	964	13.8	3.7	10	61%
D.Jackson	109	2.3%	96	47	1056	22.5	7.2	6	49%
J.Avant	113	6.6%	75	51	574	11.3	3.1	1	68%
R.Cooper	4	-9.4%	18	7	116	16.6	2.6	2	39%
C.Hall	-17	-24.5%	18	11	115	10.5	1.9	1	61%
B.Celek	-9	-8.9%	79	42	511	12.2	5.7	4	53%
C.Harbor	-13	-19.9%	15	9	72	8.0	2.6	1	60%
L.McCoy	179	20.0%	90	78	577	7.4	8.9	2	87%
O.Schmitt	47	19.1%	24	19	136	7.2	4.7	1	79%
J.Harrison	24	22.9%	13	12	85	7.1	6.7	0	92%

Offensive Line

Year	Yards	ALY	Rank	Power	Rank	Stuff	Rank	2nd Lev	Rank	Open Field	Rank
2008	4.05	4.06	21	55%	31	19%	22	1.11	22	0.68	19
2009	4.25	4.30	7	63%	19	16%	8	1.05	25	0.61	25
2010	4.96	4.17	10	76%	3	17%	10	1.25	7	1.35	1

Year	LE	Rank	LT	Rank	Mid	Rank	RT	Rank	RE	Rank	Sacks	ASR	Rank	F-Start	Cont.
2008	3.44	25	3.10	30	4.45	7	4.36	10	3.76	23	23	4.2%	6	13	30
2009	4.36	15	5.17	3	4.07	18	4.26	10	4.22	16	40	6.6%	20	23	31
2010	4.56	11	4.46	13	4.28	9	3.57	27	3.82	20	49	8.4%	28	16	21

Blocking for Michael Vick is the most unique assignment any offensive line has in the entire NFL. His speed and quickness leads to great escapabilty and allows plays to be kept alive. But because of his willingness to take off and move around in the pocket his linemen never know where he is going to be, which makes pass blocking difficult. Vick ended up outside the pocket on 22 percent of plays, first in the NFL. Not only that, but the Eagles run the ball just 34 percent of the time, which is 30th in the NFL.

Last year's problems were mainly on the interior. Winston Justice and Pro Bowl left tackle Jason Peters (the better of the pair) gave up more pressures overall, but Philadelphia's interior linemen gave up a higher percentage of pressures than the league average for interior linemen. Unfortunately, with Justice starting the year on the PUP list, right tackle is also now a question mark. He's likely to be replaced by ex-Bronco Ryan Harris. To fix the interior problem, the Eagles took Baylor's Danny Watkins in the first round. The former Canadian firefighter has played just four years of organized football, but showed enough talent and technique to turn in one of the best performances of the Senior Bowl. Watkins is already 27, so he will be expected to contribute immediately.

The biggest addition to the Eagles' offensive line, though, is probably Howard Mudd. The blocking guru is coming out of retirement to take the charge of the O-line just a year after he left the same job with the Colts, a position he had held since 1998. In his first season with the Colts he helped cut down the sack total from 62 to 22. If he brings around a similar change in Philadelphia, the Eagles' line has a chance to be really good. Many Eagles linemen spent the offseason trying to shed weight in preparation for Mudd's schematic changes.

Defensive Front Seven

Defensive Line	Age	Pos	Plays	TmPct	Rk	Stop	Dfts	BTkl	St%	Rk	AvYd	Rk	Sack	Hit	Hur	Runs	St%	Yds	Pass	St%	Yds
						Overall							Pass Rush			vs. Run			vs. Pass		
Trent Cole	29	DE	66	9.0%	4	52	26	4	77%	40	1.1	26	10	12	26.5	48	77%	1.9	18	83%	-1.1
Mike Patterson	28	DT	37	5.1%	25	28	4	1	74%	36	2.3	43	2	0	2	35	74%	2.8	2	100%	-7.5
Antonio Dixon	26	DT	32	4.4%	36	28	9	2	89%	10	0.8	9	2	0	2	27	89%	1.1	5	80%	-1.0
Darryl Tapp	27	DE	30	4.4%	55	22	16	1	67%	58	1.8	37	3	5	13	15	67%	2.7	15	80%	0.9
Juqua Parker	33	DE	24	3.8%	67	20	13	4	80%	19	-0.8	4	6	4	13	15	80%	1.5	9	89%	-4.7
Brodrick Bunkley	28	DT	20	2.9%	63	17	5	1	83%	15	1.2	15	0	0	3.5	18	83%	1.2	2	100%	0.5
Trevor Laws	26	DT	20	2.7%	64	17	10	0	80%	15	0.1	4	4	4	6.5	10	80%	1.8	10	90%	-1.6

Linebackers	Age	Pos	Plays	TmPct	Rk	Stop	Dfts	BTkl	AvYd	Sack	Hit	Hur	Runs	St%	Rk	Yds	Rk	Tgts	Suc%	Rk	AdjYd	Rk
						Overall				Pass Rush			vs. Run					vs. Pass				
Stewart Bradley	28	MLB	65	11.1%	50	35	9	7	4.9	1	1	3	40	55%	96	3.7	79	28	48%	56	10.1	79
Ernie Sims	27	OLB	60	8.2%	80	41	13	7	5.6	2	2	6	35	74%	23	2.5	22	34	53%	45	8.0	73
Moise Fokou	26	OLB	37	4.8%	108	24	5	3	4.7	1	1	3	22	68%	58	3.7	75	9	64%	--	6.9	--
Jamar Chaney	25	MLB	35	5.1%	--	21	10	0	5.5	0	0	0	22	68%	--	3.6	--	3	57%	--	3.0	--
Omar Gaither	27	MLB	27	4.0%	--	13	3	3	6.1	0	0	0	17	71%	--	3.6	--	11	0%	--	13.7	--
Akeem Jordan	26	OLB	16	2.1%	--	10	2	2	3.1	0	1	2	12	67%	--	1.8	--	3	32%	--	7.2	--

Year	Yards	ALY	Rank	Power	Rank	Stuff	Rank	2nd Lev	Rank	Open Field	Rank
2008	3.60	3.70	6	61%	9	22%	7	0.99	6	0.55	10
2009	4.03	3.69	9	59%	9	24%	4	1.07	6	0.83	19
2010	4.03	3.71	8	63%	16	22%	9	1.20	23	0.76	16

Year	LE	Rank	LT	Rank	Mid	Rank	RT	Rank	RE	Rank	Sacks	ASR	Rank
2008	3.24	5	3.04	3	4.21	16	4.31	24	3.02	7	48	8.4%	4
2009	2.70	3	4.39	21	3.57	6	3.89	12	4.14	20	44	7.1%	8
2010	4.19	17	3.04	2	3.36	2	4.55	24	3.69	12	39	7.7%	5

Philadelphia's Adjusted Sack Rate improved in 2010, thanks largely to the efforts of Trent Cole, who in addition to playing well against the run, had a team-high 10 sacks (and 26.5 hurries, according to our charters). However, the Eagles pass rush declined in the second half of the year; they had just 15 sacks, and their ASR dropped from 8.6 percent to 6.7 percent. The Eagles did not address the defensive line in the 2011 NFL Draft, leaving the improvement to the capable hands of new defensive line coach Jim Washburn, who in Tennessee would refer to sacks as "$acks" and keep a running tally of contract values that his players had signed to motivate his unit. Washburn brings his "Wide Nine" alignment to Philadelphia, with both ends lining up in the "9" technique, outside the tight ends, in order to maximize the speed of players like Cole, Juqua Parker, Darryl Tapp, and free-agent addition Jason Babin. A former first-round pick of the Houston Texans, Babin has bounced around the league, including a stop in Philadelphia in 2009, before posting 12.5 sacks and going to the Pro Bowl with the Tennessee Titans (and Washburn) in 2010. Babin finished right behind Cole with 25.5 quarterback hurries last season. 2010 first-round pick Brandon Graham remains a big part of the team's long-term plans, but is recovering from a torn ACL and may spend the first six weeks of the season on the physically unable to perform list.

Washburn is also changing the Eagles' approach at defensive tackle, a position he refers to as "guard killers" who will be tasked with beating the guards or driving them into the opposing backfield. The attacking style suits Trevor Laws and Antonio Dixon, but not former first-round pick and starter Brodrick Bunkley, a solid run-stopper who was traded to the Denver Broncos (after a failed trade to the Cleveland Browns). Mike Patterson possesses the athleticism to succeed in the new system, but his playing future is in question following a seizure during training camp and a diagnosis of arteriovenous malformation (an abnormal tangle of blood vessels in the brain). The Eagles were active in the free agent defensive tackle market, signing Green Bay's Cullen Jenkins (15 quarterback hurries in 2010) to a five-year, $27.5 million contract and bringing in unheralded and undersized tackles Anthony Hargrove (ex-Saints) and Derek Landri (ex-Panthers). While Cole, Parker, Jenkins, and Dixon or Laws will start, the Eagles will actively rotate their defensive linemen during games. With the exception of Cole, new personnel will be on the field every four to six plays.

A former linebacker during his days at Texas A&I-Kingsville, defensive coordinator Juan Castillo is overhauling the position in his first season on the job. Middle linebacker Stewart Bradley and weakside linebacker Ernie Sims are gone, leaving Moise Fokou the only returning starter along this unit, and he's moving to the weak side. 2010 seventh-round pick Jamar Chaney took over for an injured Bradley at middle linebacker late last season and is penciled in at strongside linebacker next to 2011 fourth-round pick Casey Matthews, who opened camp and the preseason as Castillo's middle linebacker. "Penciled in" is the operative term here. Matthews is an average athlete with above-average football I.Q. and instincts, which he used to make big plays during his days at the University of Oregon. The Pac-10 (now Pac-12) is not the NFC East, so Matthews will have to demonstrate that he's able to shed blocks, drop into coverage, blitz effectively, and be an on-field leader of a high-priced, veteran defense to open the regular season in that role. If he's not, the slightly more experienced Chaney could end up back in the middle. Veteran Akeem Jordan adds depth behind Chaney, while 2010 fourth-round pick Keenan Clayton backs up Fokou and could see time in nickel packages.

Defensive Secondary

Secondary	Age	Pos	Plays	TmPct	Rk	Stop	Dfts	BTkl	Runs	St%	Rk	Yds	Rk	Tgts	Tgt%	Rk	Dist	Suc%	Rk	APaYd	Rk	PD	Int
										vs. Run						**vs. Pass**							
Quintin Mikell	31	SS	103	14.1%	6	53	18	12	51	55%	11	5.4	17	41	9.0%	6	13.1	61%	21	5.3	8	12	3
Nate Allen	24	FS	56	8.9%	57	20	11	6	24	33%	55	10.0	74	24	6.1%	33	18.1	44%	68	11.7	76	5	3
Dimitri Patterson	29	CB	55	7.1%	67	25	12	5	7	43%	42	4.7	17	62	12.9%	70	14.2	47%	67	9.5	77	10	4
Asante Samuel	30	CB	40	7.5%	61	27	11	7	6	50%	25	7.2	51	38	11.6%	76	15.5	76%	1	3.4	1	14	7
Joselio Hanson	30	CB	38	5.2%	83	20	7	2	6	50%	25	8.7	64	48	10.6%	80	9.6	63%	8	5.0	4	9	1
Kurt Coleman	23	SS	28	3.8%	--	6	4	1	12	25%	--	8.1	--	6	1.3%	--	16.5	49%	--	9.2	--	2	1
Ellis Hobbs	28	CB	20	5.1%	--	9	2	2	5	40%	--	9.8	--	36	14.9%	--	14.9	52%	--	8.7	--	3	1
Trevard Lindley	25	CB	20	3.7%	--	5	4	3	5	0%	--	11.0	--	23	6.8%	--	8.2	52%	--	8.0	--	2	1

Year	Pass D Rank	vs. #1 WR	Rk	vs. #2 WR	Rk	vs. Other WR	Rk	vs. TE	Rk	vs. RB	Rk
2008	3	-1.4%	13	-26.2%	5	-51.1%	2	6.9%	19	7.4%	18
2009	5	-30.0%	3	9.0%	24	-29.8%	4	-9.1%	7	-1.9%	16
2010	11	-8.0%	11	-19.3%	4	-12.6%	9	10.9%	19	27.7%	31

Welcome to a wealth of riches. Asante Samuel is coming off a superb season where he ranked first in Adjusted Success Rate (by five percentage points over second-ranked Darrelle Revis) and yards allowed per pass (by a full yard over second-ranked Antoine Winfield). Dominique Rodgers-Cromartie is coming off a down year, but did rank third in Adjusted Success Rate in 2009. Nnamdi Asomugha is an eager participant in run support and takes away one side of the field (the offense's left, which should translate to more targets at Samuel). We list him with 31 targets last year; no other cornerback with at least 12 games started had fewer than 54. Castillo plans to move all three cornerbacks around, but Asomugha is the most physical of the three and may end up seeing more time in the slot in nickel packages. The Eagles have impressive depth behind the "Big Three" with Joselio Hanson, Trevard Lindley, and 2011 third-round pick Curtis Marsh (Utah State).

2010 second-round pick Nate Allen earned the starting free safety job as a rookie and was having a pretty solid campaign before tearing the patellar tendon in his right knee in mid-December. Allen is expected to make a full recovery and open the preseason as the starting strong safety, replacing departed free agent Quintin Mikell. Fellow second-year player Kurt Coleman starts at free safety, but will eventually face a challenge from 2011 second-round pick Jaiquawn Jarrett, who has a reputation of being a heavy-hitter in the secondary.

Special Teams

Year	DVOA	Rank	FG/XP	Rank	Net Kick	Rank	Kick Ret	Rank	Net Punt	Rank	Punt Ret	Rank	Hidden	Rank
2008	1.6%	13	-1.8	21	3.5	13	4.3	10	3.4	15	0.1	15	-12.7	29
2009	4.3%	2	3.6	11	9.1	7	-7.5	27	3.8	13	16.3	1	-10.9	28
2010	2.0%	12	3.7	9	8.2	7	-9.9	29	8.6	8	1.1	15	-5.1	20

The Eagles will turn over both their specialist jobs to rookies in 2011. They used the second of the team's two fourth-round picks on Nebraska kicker Alex Henery, the NCAA's all-time leader in field-goal accuracy (89.5 percent), and allowed David Akers to walk in free agency. Sav Rocca is also gone, and the Eagles signed undrafted rookie Chas Henry from the University of Florida. Henry averaged 45.1 yards per punt and won the Ray Guy Award last season. DeSean Jackson is an unquestioned home run hitter in the punt return game, but his slight build, concussion history, and importance to the offense may limit his exposure in this facet of the game going forward. Second-year cornerback Jorrick Calvin, a sixth-round pick of the Arizona Cardinals who was acquired in August, was average on punt returns and below average on kick returns (-5.4 points worth of value) With the depth the Eagles have at cornerback, Calvin will have to stand out in the return game to a roster spot. The Eagles brought in free-agent wide receiver Johnnie Lee Higgins, who was worth a league-high 15.2 points of field position on punt returns in 2008, but has been below average the last two seasons, Wide receivers Sinorice Moss and Chad Hall and perhaps rookie cornerback Curtis Marsh could factor into the return game as well.

Coaching Staff

After the playoff loss to the Packers, head coach Andy Reid insisted that defensive coordinator Sean McDermott's job was safe. Less than a week later, Reid fired him, saying that the shadow of the late Jim Johnson "was too large in a place like Philly." After a two-week search, the Eagles named longtime offensive line coach Juan Castillo to be defensive coordinator. Castillo played linebacker in college and coached on the defensive side of the ball at the college and high school level before moving to the offensive side of the ball in 1990. Prior to his promotion, Castillo had been drawing interest from the Cleveland Browns (i.e., Eagles West), and he plans to bring a simpler approach than McDermott had defensively. Legendary offensive line coach Howard Mudd was hired to replace Castillo, and Reid's staff added the highly-regarded Jim Washburn away from the Tennessee Titans to replace Rory Segrest as coach of a defensive line that underperformed in the second half of 2010.

Pittsburgh Steelers

2010 Record: 12-4

Pythagorean Wins: 12.1 (3rd)

DVOA: 36.8% (2nd)

Offense: 17.9% (5th)

Defense: -18.5% (1st)

Special Teams: 0.4% (16th)

Variance: 14.0% (13th)

2011 Mean Projection: 13.0 wins

On the Clock (0-3): 0%

Loserville (4-6): 0%

Mediocrity (7-8): 1%

Playoff Contender (9-10): 7%

Super Bowl Contender (11+): 92%

Projected Average Opponent: -3.2% (30th)

2010: Ho hum. Another Super Bowl.

2011: Aged defense should be able to gut out another strong year.

In retrospect, it's remarkable how many national writers did not expect the Pittsburgh Steelers to have a good season in 2010. We picked them to be the second best team in the AFC, and Peter King famously (and correctly) predicted a Green Bay-Pittsburgh Super Bowl. But only six of 17 ESPN.com analysts picked Pittsburgh to make the playoffs. For FOXSports.com it was just one of six. Conventional wisdom overstated just how important the four-game suspension of Ben Roethlisberger would be, and understated just how important the return of Troy Polamalu would be.

The Steelers went 3-1 during Roethlisberger's suspension, the only loss being a last-minute comeback by division rival Baltimore. During that four-game stretch, they gave up a total of 50 points. Clearly, the defense was back to greatness. Once Roethlisberger came back, the offense was pretty good as well. The Steelers' season was marked by a tendency to beat up on the teams they were supposed to beat up on. They slaughtered the Raiders, blew out the Panthers, and stomped the Browns twice. Against other good teams, they played a lot of close games. They won some, and they lost some. They won the two that came in the AFC playoffs, but lost the one that decided the NFL championship.

On offense, the 2010 Steelers are emblematic of their era in the same way the 1970s Super Bowl champion Steelers were emblematic of theirs. The Steelers are no longer a running-and-defense team. They're a passing-and-defense team. The Steelers ran on 40 percent of plays in the first half last year, around the league average. They spread the ball out with three or more wide receivers more than half the time. And they aren't spreading the ball out so they can run it — in fact, the Steelers averaged a league-low 3.25 yards per carry on runs from three-wide sets. No, they're spreading it out and throwing it, ranking third in pass offense DVOA.

On defense, the Steelers were the Steelers, once again leading the NFL in defensive DVOA. The Steelers allowed 3.0 yards per carry, only the third team since 2000 to reach that mark. And they completely shut down the run on first down, allowing just 2.7 yards per carry. They forced opponents into second- and third-and-long, then confused opposing quarterbacks with Dick LeBeau's blitz scheme. It was a return to glory, paced in part by the return of Polamalu, who was healthy enough to stay on the field for most of the season (although not healthy enough to play at full strength in the postseason).

Pittsburgh's defense was so good last year that you may not have noticed just how old they are. In fact, the Pittsburgh defense is probably one of the oldest in league history. The planned lineup going into 2010 averaged 30.5 years of age, although the actual lineup for the season ended up averaging 29.5 years because Ziggy Hood replaced an injured Aaron Smith.

Put Smith back into the lineup instead of Hood, and the average age of Pittsburgh's projected defensive starting lineup for 2011 is 31.5. If those remain the starters for the entire season, the Steelers will be the oldest defense of the century by more than a year. Only Lawrence Timmons and LaMarr Woodley are under the age of 30. Even if Hood starts over Smith at defensive end, the average age is still 30.5, which would be the oldest defense since 2000.

Now, being old on defense isn't a bad thing. Eleven of the 12 oldest defenses since 2000 had defensive DVOA below 0% (Table 1). There's virtually no correlation between average age and defensive DVOA — and the tiny correlation that exists trends towards older defenses being slightly better (Figure 2).

On the other hand, there's a reason why we don't have a lot of defenses in our database with an average age over 30. Yes, the oldest defenses tend to be good defenses, but once they hit an average age of 30, they also tend to start replacing players. To give a few examples:

• The 2001 Panthers replaced six out of 11 starters. They lost Eugene Robinson (38) to retirement and Reggie White (40) to re-retirement. First-round pick Dan Morgan and second-round pick Kris Jenkins were among the new starters. The average age of the starters dropped to 25.9.

• The 2007 Dolphins cut Kevin Carter (34) and lost Zach Thomas (34) and Yeremiah Bell (29) to injury. All three were replaced by younger players, and the average age of the starters dropped to 28.8.

• The 2004 Patriots drafted Vince Wilfork to replace 36-year-old Ted Washington and put 2003 first-rounder Ty Warren into the starting lineup. They also lost their 30-something cornerbacks to injury during the season and ended up starting Asante Samuel (23) and Randall Gay (22) in the Super Bowl. The average age of the starters dropped to 28.1.

• The 2002 Ravens replaced safeties Rod Woodson (37) and Corey Harris (33) with two rookies, Ed Reed and Will Demps. Tony Siragusa retired, and they let 35-year-old Rob Burnett leave in free agency, replacing him with rookie Anthony Weaver. The average age of the starters dropped to 25.4.

The Steelers may be approaching a year much like these, where they will need to replace numerous pieces of their defense at once. The good news for Steelers fans is that perhaps no team does a better job of drafting young defensive players and grooming them in part-time roles until they know the system and are ready to step in. Neither Woodley nor Hood was a regular starter until his second season. Timmons wasn't a regular starter until his third season.

The steady stream of young defenders continues with two of last year's draft picks. Former Virginia Tech standout Jason Worilds spent his rookie year learning and is now waiting in the wings in case Harrison falters. The Steelers are high on last year's fifth-round pick Stevenson Sylvester, and are grooming him to take over for James Farrior. Pittsburgh also spent this year's first-round pick on Ohio State's Cameron Hayward, and he and Hood should be the starting

Table 1: Oldest Defenses by Mean Age of Most Common Starting Lineup, 2000-10

Year	Team	Age	DVOA
2000	CAR	30.4	-0.5%
2006	MIA	30.1	-9.3%
2003	NE	30.0	-21.8%
2002	NE	29.9	-0.7%
2004	MIA	29.8	-10.6%
2009	PIT	29.7	-2.1%
2010	DEN	29.6	19.6%
2001	BAL	29.6	-16.8%
2009	DEN	29.5	-7.3%
2008	PIT	29.5	-26.9%
2010	PIT	29.5	-18.5%
2005	MIA	29.5	-8.4%

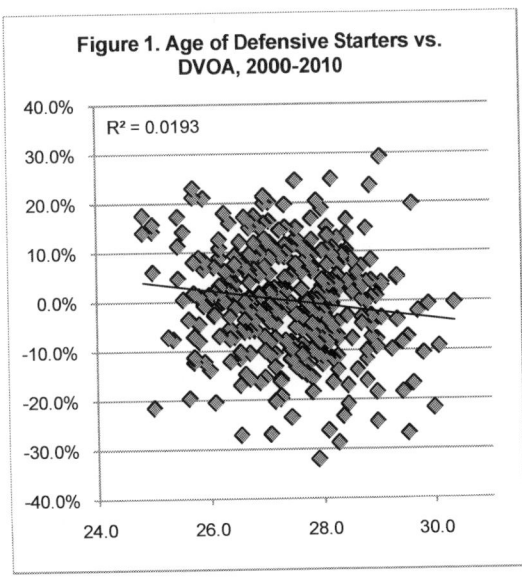

Figure 1. Age of Defensive Starters vs. DVOA, 2000-2010

$R^2 = 0.0193$

2011 Steelers Schedule

Week	Opp.	Week	Opp.	Week	Opp.
1	at BAL	7	at ARI	13	CIN
2	SEA	8	NE	14	CLE (Thu.)
3	at IND	9	BAL	15	at SF (Mon.)
4	at HOU	10	at CIN	16	STL
5	TEN	11	BYE	17	at CLE
6	JAC	12	at KC		

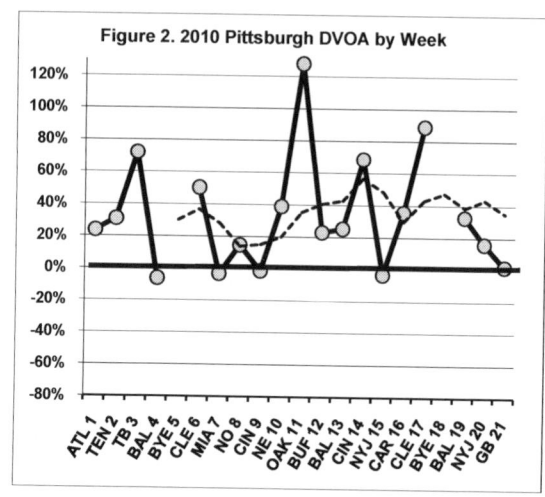

Figure 2. 2010 Pittsburgh DVOA by Week

defensive ends by 2012.

Not that the Steelers are perfect when it comes to finding young defenders; 2008 third-rounder Bruce Davis and 2010 fourth-rounder Thaddeus Gibson were both cut within a year. And there are two positions in particular where there aren't clear talents waiting in the wings. The first is nose tackle, where Casey Hampton is 34 and backup Chris Hoke is 35. The other is cornerback, and that's a hole that nearly opened up this offseason. William Gay had excellent stats in 2008 and 2010 as a nickelback, but his poor stats as a starter in 2009 show that he's the type of player whose weaknesses are easily exposed in a larger role. Keenan Lewis was a third-round pick back in 2009, but he's only played 13 games since being drafted — almost entirely on special teams. The Steelers passed over the top cornerbacks in the draft, players like Aaron Williams and Ras-I Dowling who might be able to start from day one. They did address depth at the position by drafting Curtis Brown from Texas in the third round and Cortez Allen from the Citadel in the fourth round. However, even first-round rookie cornerbacks usually struggle to adjust to the NFL. It's hard to imagine that Brown or Allen would be able to serve as a regular starter. That's why the Steelers had to bring back veteran cornerback Ike Taylor, who agreed to a new four-year contract on the first day of 2011 free agency.

The Pittsburgh offense is much younger than the defense. In fact, most of its players are just entering their primes. Roethlisberger is 29, Rashard Mendenhall is still only 24, and Mike Wallace is 25. Veteran tackle Flozell Adams and slot receiver Antwaan Randle El were cut, leaving 35-year-old Hines Ward behind as the only older player on the Steelers offense. Ward may still be nimble enough to win *Dancing with the Stars,* but he did start to slip a bit as a receiver last year, and he will miss most of this year's training

camp recovering from offseason thumb surgery.

Ward was one of a number of Steelers who made headlines this offseason, not only for his appearance on *Dancing with the Stars* but also for drinking his way into a DUI address in July. Rashard Mendenhall made the news with controversial tweets after the Navy SEALs killed bin Laden. However, the worst event from a team perspective was James Harrison criticizing teammates Mendenhall and Roethlisberger in an interview in *Men's Journal.* Some members of the media used this opportunity to pen ridiculous "are the Steelers the new Bengals?" columns, but we can safely expect Mike Tomlin to settle differences and make sure the team is focused on proper goals. Harrison went to the media with the expected apologies, and Harrison and Roethlisberger were palling around on camera within the first few days of training camp.

Now that they're all friends again, the Steelers can get back to business: winning the seventh Super Bowl championship that they missed out on in February. The NFL schedule makers have already put the Steelers a step ahead on the road to home-field advantage in the AFC. This year's opponents include the weakened AFC South and the always cupcake-alicious NFC West. Their rivals in Baltimore have to take on the rebounding Chargers while the Steelers get the likely-to-decline Chiefs. Strong offense, strong defense, and an easy schedule: It all adds up to another long Pittsburgh march through the playoffs and perhaps a trip to the NFL's first Pennsylvania Bowl.

Aaron Schatz

2010 Steelers Stats by Week

Wk	vs.	W-L	PF	PA	YDF	YDA	TO	Total	Off	Def	ST
1	ATL	W	15	9	354	295	0	24%	0%	-23%	0%
2	@TEN	W	19	11	127	238	6	31%	-58%	-73%	16%
3	@TB	W	38	13	387	303	0	72%	37%	-28%	8%
4	BAL	L	14	17	210	320	1	-6%	5%	0%	-11%
5	BYE										
6	CLE	W	28	10	378	327	2	50%	48%	2%	4%
7	@MIA	W	23	22	348	313	0	-3%	2%	4%	-1%
8	@NO	L	10	20	279	318	0	15%	-5%	-24%	-4%
9	@CIN	W	27	21	314	272	0	-1%	-6%	-6%	-1%
10	NE	L	26	39	425	453	-1	39%	63%	21%	-3%
11	OAK	W	35	3	431	182	2	128%	57%	-59%	12%
12	@BUF	W	19	16	426	329	1	23%	15%	1%	9%
13	@BAL	W	13	10	288	269	0	25%	-5%	-25%	5%
14	CIN	W	23	7	354	190	3	69%	23%	-45%	0%
15	NYJ	L	17	22	377	276	0	-3%	35%	13%	-25%
16	CAR	W	27	3	408	119	0	36%	18%	-22%	-4%
17	@CLE	W	41	9	418	225	3	89%	46%	-43%	1%
18	BYE										
19	BAL	W	31	24	263	126	1	33%	2%	-44%	-13%
20	NYJ	W	24	19	287	289	-1	15%	12%	-4%	-1%
21	GB	L	25	31	387	338	-3	2%	14%	13%	1%

Trends and Splits

	Offense	Rank	Defense	Rank
Total DVOA	17.9%	5	-18.5%	1
Unadjusted VOA	17.4%	6	-16.7%	1
Weighted Trend	25.4%	3	-14.9%	1
Variance	9.3%	21	7.0%	19
Average Opponent	0.7%	24	4.2%	19
Passing	45.8%	3	-13.0%	2
Rushing	0.1%	14	-27.7%	1
First Down	11.1%	10	-34.7%	1
Second Down	15.5%	7	2.7%	15
Third Down	35.6%	4	-21.3%	2
First Half	21.4%	3	-21.9%	1
Second Half	13.8%	5	-15.6%	1
Red Zone	2.1%	14	-38.7%	1
Late and Close	11.3%	7	-12.7%	6

Five-Year Performance

Year	W-L	Pyth	Est W	PF	PA	TO	Total	Rk	Off	Rk	Def	Rk	ST	Rk	Off AGL	Rk	Def AGL	Rk
2006	8-8	9.1	8.5	353	315	-8	10.9%	10	8.1%	9	-7.0%	10	-4.1%	30	12.6	11	14.0	16
2007	10-6	11.4	9.3	393	269	+3	20.0%	5	9.6%	9	-11.8%	3	-1.4%	21	9.1	3	19.7	16
2008	12-4	11.8	11.4	347	223	+4	29.6%	2	3.7%	21	-26.9%	1	-1.1%	23	37.6	24	16.5	12
2009	9-7	9.2	10.4	368	324	-3	16.1%	10	17.9%	7	-2.1%	9	-3.9%	30	23.9	16	29.2	17
2010	12-4	12.1	12.2	375	232	+17	36.8%	2	17.9%	5	-18.5%	1	0.4%	16	32.0	22	17.9	12

Strategic Tendencies

Run/Pass		Rank	Offense		Rank	Defense		Rank	Other		Rank
Runs, all plays	45%	5	3+ WR	54%	11	Rush 3	9.2%	14	2+ RB, Pct Runs	78%	1
Runs, first half	40%	17	4+ WR	13%	5	Rush 4	52.5%	26	1 RB/2 TE, Pct Runs	57%	6
Runs, first down	57%	4	2+ TE	37%	4	Rush 5	34.0%	2	1 RB/3+ WR, Pct Runs	27%	10
Runs, second-long	37%	10	Single back	69%	4	Rush 6+	4.3%	27	CB1 on WR1	55%	4
Runs, power sit.	66%	7	Play action	13%	29	Zone Blitz	8.1%	9	Go for it on 4th	0.89	17
Runs, behind 2H	31%	10	Max protect	7%	28	Sacks by LB	67.7%	2	Offensive Pace	33.3	32
Pass, ahead 2H	42%	19	Outside pocket	11%	24	Sacks by DB	14.6%	7	Defensive Pace	30.6	13

Once again, Ben Roethlisberger was much more likely to take a sack trying to make something happen on third or fourth down, rather than on first or second down. Pittsburgh's Adjusted Sack Rate on third or fourth down (12.9 percent) was nearly double what it was on first or second down (6.5 percent). ☞ The Steelers tied Oakland for the lead with 26 offensive holding flags (not counting special teams plays). ☞ Pittsburgh allowed a league-low average of 3.8 yards after the catch, including a miniscule 2.8 yards after catch on passes past the line of scrimmage. ☞ Pittsburgh opponents only ran seven draw plays last year (the NFL average was 25) and gained just three yards per carry on those plays. ☞ Surprisingly, the Steelers allowed more yardage when our game charters marked them running a zone blitz: 7.9 yards on zone blitzes, 5.4 yards otherwise. However, this does not seem to be schematic, as the 2009 Steelers allowed fewer yards when zone blitzing than they did otherwise.

Passing

Player	DYAR	DVOA	Plays	NtYds	Avg	YAC	C%	TD	Int
B.Roethlisberger	1238	38.2%	417	3061	7.3	5.5	63.3%	17	5
C.Batch	-20	-17.2%	55	338	6.1	4.1	61.2%	3	3
D.Dixon	-63	-37.8%	38	216	5.7	4.5	68.8%	0	1
B.Leftwich	3	-5.6%	9	35	3.9	3.6	71.4%	0	0

Rushing

Player	DYAR	DVOA	Plays	Yds	Avg	TD	Fum	Suc
R.Mendenhall	77	-2.8%	324	1279	3.9	13	2	44%
I.Redman	20	-1.3%	53	241	4.5	0	2	58%
M.Moore	-36	-37.2%	33	99	3.0	0	0	21%
B.Roethlisberger	69	39.8%	22	184	8.4	2	1	-
J.Dwyer	-12	-42.2%	9	28	3.1	0	0	33%
M.Wallace	26	81.0%	5	39	7.8	0	0	-
D.Dixon	-1	-17.3%	4	32	8.0	0	0	-

Receiving

Player	DYAR	DVOA	Plays	Ctch	Yds	Y/C	YAC	TD	C%
M.Wallace	457	48.8%	98	60	1257	21.0	6.0	10	61%
H.Ward	157	9.1%	95	61	759	12.4	3.9	5	64%
E.Sanders	67	5.2%	50	28	376	13.4	2.5	2	56%
A.Randle El	21	-5.8%	39	22	254	11.5	2.3	0	56%
A.Brown	57	26.2%	19	16	167	10.4	6.9	0	84%
H.Miller	36	1.0%	67	42	512	12.2	5.4	2	63%
M.Spaeth	-17	-21.5%	18	9	80	8.9	4.2	1	50%
D.Johnson	0	-6.3%	6	4	46	11.5	7.5	0	67%
R.Mendenhall	23	-2.3%	34	23	167	7.3	7.6	0	68%
M.Moore	53	17.0%	31	26	205	7.9	7.6	0	84%
I.Redman	55	101.4%	10	9	72	8.0	9.0	2	90%

Offensive Line

Year	Yards	ALY	Rank	Power	Rank	Stuff	Rank	2nd Lev	Rank	Open Field	Rank
2008	3.79	3.96	24	64%	19	22%	30	1.07	23	0.57	27
2009	4.32	4.13	14	72%	5	18%	15	1.18	15	0.87	13
2010	3.93	3.87	19	64%	12	21%	24	1.04	23	0.73	15

Year	LE	Rank	LT	Rank	Mid	Rank	RT	Rank	RE	Rank	Sacks	ASR	Rank	F-Start	Cont.
2008	4.84	9	4.69	8	3.91	24	3.15	32	4.05	16	50	9.2%	29	20	39
2009	4.58	14	4.30	11	4.08	17	3.72	25	4.70	8	50	8.5%	28	12	37
2010	4.85	6	2.89	30	3.91	19	4.08	17	5.02	5	43	8.6%	29	14	31

It's nice to come off a Super Bowl appearance knowing you have at least one unit that will undoubtedly be better next year. The Steelers led all of football last year with 30.0 Adjusted Games Lost from their offensive line, and now they get right tackle Willie Colon back from the Achilles tear that cost him the entire year. Colon has been a bit overrated in recent years, but he's still a huge step up from over-the-hill veteran Flozell Adams, who was cut. However, the Steelers will still have problems on the left side, because the new salary cap forced them to cut left tackle Max Starks. Jonathan Scott is now penciled in as the starter, and he was a clear weakness when he had to take over for an injured Starks halfway through last season. He struggles in particular with quick pass rushers off the edge. Sitting behind Scott and Colon is second-round pick Marcus Gilbert. The Florida product shined at the Outback Bowl but was extremely inconsistent throughout his college career. The Steelers need to figure out a way to set his motor to "always on."

The interior line was much better than the exterior. Center Maurkice Pouncey went straight from college to the Pro Bowl, showcasing good pass blocking technique and tremendous athletic ability that lets him get to the second level, lock onto linebackers, and knock them out of running lanes. Both left guard Chris Kemoeatu and right guard Ramon Foster are better drive blockers than they are pull blockers; Kemoeatu was also a better pass blocker than Foster, a second-year undrafted free agent in his first year as a starter. Don't be surprised to see Foster lose his job to Doug Legursky, who did an excellent job replacing an injured Pouncey in the Super Bowl and can play either guard or center. Sixth-rounder Keith Williams (Nebraska) is a mauler who needs work on pass-blocking technique.

Defensive Front Seven

Defensive Line	Age	Pos	Plays	TmPct	Rk	Stop	Dfts	BTkl	St%	Rk	AvYd	Rk	Sack	Hit	Hur	Runs	St%	Yds	Pass	St%	Yds
													Pass Rush			vs. Run			vs. Pass		
Brett Keisel	33	DE	40	7.4%	14	28	7	3	67%	67	2.1	45	3	0	3	27	67%	2.9	13	77%	0.6
Casey Hampton	34	DT	20	2.7%	65	14	1	0	72%	49	1.9	36	1	2	3	18	72%	2.2	2	50%	-1.5
Ziggy Hood	24	DE	20	2.6%	--	14	5	0	60%	--	1.1	--	3	5	0	15	60%	2.7	5	100%	-3.8
Nick Eason	31	DE	17	2.2%	--	13	4	1	77%	--	1.8	--	1.5	0	4	13	77%	2.6	4	75%	-0.8

Linebackers	Age	Pos	Plays	TmPct	Rk	Stop	Dfts	BTkl	AvYd	Sack	Hit	Hur	Runs	St%	Rk	Yds	Rk	Tgts	Suc%	Rk	AdjYd	Rk
									Overall	Pass Rush			vs. Run					vs. Pass				
Lawrence Timmons	25	ILB	141	18.0%	6	93	29	9	3.5	3	4	16.5	82	78%	14	2.5	24	59	55%	39	4.7	12
James Farrior	36	ILB	113	14.5%	22	76	21	7	3.7	6	2	17	64	80%	12	2.1	8	23	47%	60	5.4	24
James Harrison	33	OLB	103	13.2%	35	76	31	2	2.4	10.5	16	31	59	85%	5	2.0	5	19	63%	15	5.5	25
LaMarr Woodley	27	OLB	55	7.0%	90	43	20	3	0.5	10.0	10	33	28	71%	37	2.1	10	23	63%	14	4.6	10
Larry Foote	31	ILB	22	2.8%	--	7	4	2	5.2	1.5	0	5.5	8	25%	--	5.4	--	13	45%	--	4.8	--

Year	Yards	ALY	Rank	Power	Rank	Stuff	Rank	2nd Lev	Rank	Open Field	Rank
2008	3.41	3.81	7	53%	1	17%	18	0.95	4	0.30	1
2009	3.55	3.66	6	82%	32	18%	19	1.00	2	0.37	2
2010	3.07	3.46	1	59%	10	21%	10	0.85	2	0.17	1

Year	LE	Rank	LT	Rank	Mid	Rank	RT	Rank	RE	Rank	Sacks	ASR	Rank
2008	4.35	21	4.83	29	3.64	5	3.95	13	2.87	6	51	8.7%	3
2009	2.67	2	3.76	9	3.66	9	3.58	6	4.33	23	47	8.2%	2
2010	3.89	13	2.98	1	3.47	3	3.82	10	2.99	3	48	8.3%	3

Lawrence Timmons blossomed into a Pro Bowl-level star, strong in the pass rush, in coverage, and against the run. According to FO similarity scores, the most similar single season to Timmons' 2010 was Ray Lewis for the 2000 Super Bowl champion Ravens. Nice company. LaMarr Woodley had his third straight season with double-digit sacks, and the Steelers' decision to put the franchise tag on him proved to be a good one when the new CBA allowed four-year veterans to become free agents. James Farrior and James Harrison continue to play at a high level, even into their mid-30s. Harrison in particular is much stronger against the run than people might realize. Rookie outside linebackers Jason Worilds (second round) and Stevenson Sylvester (fifth) had your typical Pittsburgh Steelers redshirt rookie seasons, learning the system and barely seeing the field except on special teams.

The front line is in transition, but both the old and new players are high quality. Aaron Smith's torn triceps made room for Ziggy Hood in the starting lineup, and Hood finished the season strong. Smith was still rehabbing the injury this spring, so Hood may be the starter again in 2011. At the other position, the Steelers drafted Ohio State's Cameron Hayward to serve as the heir apparent to 33-year-old veteran Brett Keisel. Heyward is a prototypical 5-technique end with instincts and smarts to match his physical skills, but Keisel is far from done. Although Keisel's advanced stats (run tackles, hits and hurries) dropped a little bit last year, he actually made his first-ever Pro Bowl, albeit as an injury replacement. Casey Hampton remains in the middle and still sucks up lots of blockers. There's a lot of talent here if Dick LeBeau feels like experimenting with some four-man fronts.

Defensive Secondary

Secondary	Age	Pos	Plays	TmPct	Rk	Stop	Dfts	BTkl	Runs	St%	Rk	Yds	Rk	Tgts	Tgt%	Rk	Dist	Suc%	Rk	APaYd	Rk	PD	Int
				Overall						vs. Run							vs. Pass						
Ryan Clark	32	FS	97	12.4%	14	34	5	4	44	52%	15	5.1	14	34	6.0%	34	12.4	49%	55	8.7	52	6	2
Bryant McFadden	30	CB	91	11.6%	12	39	14	3	15	60%	15	3.3	4	108	19.1%	11	10.8	49%	57	7.4	46	8	2
Troy Polamalu	30	SS	73	10.7%	32	34	19	7	24	58%	7	4.1	4	38	7.7%	19	9.3	45%	67	5.4	10	11	7
Ike Taylor	31	CB	71	9.1%	33	26	13	4	12	33%	67	6.7	43	85	15.1%	44	12.4	52%	45	7.2	42	12	2
William Gay	26	CB	50	6.4%	75	25	16	4	10	40%	50	7.0	48	51	9.1%	86	9.0	53%	39	6.1	14	8	0
Ryan Mundy	26	SS	22	2.8%	--	13	4	1	13	54%	--	4.9	-	9	1.5%	--	10.9	71%	--	2.3	--	3	0

Year	Pass D Rank	vs. #1 WR	Rk	vs. #2 WR	Rk	vs. Other WR	Rk	vs. TE	Rk	vs. RB	Rk
2008	1	-14.4%	6	2.9%	19	-40.4%	4	-14.6%	6	-26.6%	1
2009	14	8.3%	18	-6.0%	12	-3.5%	11	21.7%	26	-6.3%	11
2010	2	-18.5%	4	-23.3%	3	0.2%	18	-9.7%	5	2.0%	15

Troy Polamalu may have won Defensive Player of the Year, but the Steelers need to start worrying about his health going forward. He was bothered all year by a calf strain; then an Achilles injury cost him two games in December and had him playing at half-speed in the playoffs. The year before, he missed most of the year with knee injuries. Polamalu is now 30, and his style of play doesn't exactly avoid contact. The Steelers are simply not the same team without Polamalu in the lineup. Last year, their league-leading defense was close to average (-2.6% DVOA) in Weeks 15 and 16. The year before, the difference was stunning: -28.2% DVOA with Polamalu, 9.5% DVOA without him. Ryan Clark at free safety is the kind of good player you need to fill out a lineup around stars like Polamalu and Harrison. It was interesting to see that Clark accumulated more tackles, specifically more run tackles, than Polamalu. On most defenses, the strong safety makes many more run tackles than the free safety.

The Steelers have a definite pattern in how they use their cornerbacks: Ike Taylor tends to play tight coverage at the line, while Bryant McFadden gives his guy more space. On that snap, this will either break into man coverage or a Cover-3 that has McFadden and the two safeties in the deep zones while Taylor and a linebacker or two are short. Our charting stats had the two surprisingly close, although Taylor had a better Adjusted Auccess Rate and generally covered longer passes when he was in man coverage. William Gay returns as the nickel. Behind the veterans are two rookie draft picks. Third-rounder Curtis Brown (Texas) has good ball skills, fast feet, and can change direction quickly, but can sometimes be caught looking in the backfield and losing contact with his receiver. Fourth-rounder Cortez Allen is a strong athlete with size and strength, but is extremely raw, coming from FCS school The Citadel.

Special Teams

Year	DVOA	Rank	FG/XP	Rank	Net Kick	Rank	Kick Ret	Rank	Net Punt	Rank	Punt Ret	Rank	Hidden	Rank
2008	-1.1%	23	0.9	16	8.1	5	-10.3	30	4.4	13	-9.4	31	-7.3	22
2009	-3.9%	30	2.3	14	-34.7	32	5.0	8	5.7	9	-1.3	18	-4.5	23
2010	0.4%	16	-1.9	23	-2.1	20	3.8	13	8.7	5	-6.3	28	-6.3	23

We wrote in last year's *Football Outsiders Almanac* that the Steelers could go a long way towards turning their record around simply by fielding a league-average kick coverage team. And so they did. With the debacle of 2009 in the rearview mirror, the Steelers special teams returned to their usual status of "average, but slightly better when punter Daniel Sepulveda is healthy." The Steelers got better kicking once they replaced Jeff Reed with Shaun Suisham at midseason, but that's really just a function of small sample size. In reality, Reed and Suisham are both part of the amorphous population of functional kickers who bounce from team to team being unremarkable. Suisham re-signed, so he'll get to continue being unremarkable in black and yellow. Antonio Brown will likely handle both kickoff and punt return duties.

Coaching Staff

Ken Whisenhunt wanted to hire away one of his old Pittsburgh officemates to be Arizona's new defensive co-ordinator this offseason, and he effectively let the Steelers pick which one. The Steelers denied the Cardinals permission to speak to linebackers coach Keith Butler, Dick LeBeau's heir apparent, and so the Cardinals hired away secondary coach Ray Horton instead. He's been replaced by longtime Steelers Pro Bowl defensive back Carnell Lake. Otherwise, the Steelers' coaching staff remains fairly stable for 2011, not a surprise from the team that has historically enjoyed the most stable coaching situation in the NFL. It won't surprise you that LeBeau, entering his eighth season, has the longest tenure of any current offensive or defensive coordinator. But it may surprise you to learn that offensive coordinator Bruce Arians, entering his fifth year, is now tied for fourth behind LeBeau along with Brian Schottenheimer and Marty Mornhinweg (six years each).

St. Louis Rams

2010 Record: 7-9

Pythagorean Wins: 6.8 (21st)

DVOA: -20.8% (29th)

Offense: -15.2% (30th)

Defense: 6.0% (20th)

Special Teams: 0.5% (14th)

Variance: 11.6% (9th)

2011 Mean Projection: 5.5 wins

On the Clock (0-3): 19%

Loserville (4-6): 49%

Mediocrity (7-8): 23%

Playoff Contender (9-10): 8%

Super Bowl Contender (11+): 1%

Projected Average Opponent: -1.3% (20th)

2010: Sam Bradford is the real deal, but the Rams can't save the world from the horror of a 7-9 playoff team.

2011: Can the offense sort through all the new skill players and learn a new system quickly enough to avoid a step backwards?

As the 2010 St. Louis Rams boarded their return flight from Seattle on January 2, they had to look back at the previous four months and ask themselves "What if?" What if they held onto those fourth-quarter leads against the Arizona Cardinals in Week 1, the Tampa Bay Buccaneers in Week 6, and San Francisco 49ers in Week 10? Win any one of those three games, and the Rams enter the last week 8-7, NFC West champions preparing to host their first playoff game since January 10, 2004. Instead, the Rams entered the regular season finale with a 7-8 record, one game better than the Seattle Seahawks. But since both teams had identical 3-2 records within the NFC West, all Seattle needed to do to win the worst division in the league was get Charlie Whitehurst ready for his second NFL start and get its run defense — which had allowed an average of 152.3 yards over the previous six weeks — primed to face Steven Jackson.

Defensively, the Rams limited the Seahawks to 16 points and 4-of-15 on third downs, but Whitehurst hit journeyman receiver Ruvell Martin for a 61-yard reception on the second play of the game, after Martin got behind strong safety Craig Dahl. That set up what was ultimately the game-winning touchdown pass from Whitehurst to Mike Williams. The Rams never seemed to fully recover from that first series of the game. The defense did not generate much pressure on the untested Whitehurst, and the few times they did, Whitehurst was able to get out of trouble. Seattle racked up 141 yards on the ground (30 from Whitehurst), controlling the clock and keeping the Rams' two most dangerous weapons — Sam Bradford and Steven Jackson — on the sidelines. When Bradford and Co. were on the field, they struggled, posting a season-low -65.1% DVOA. Jackson, usually a workhorse, was rendered invisible with 11 carries for the game, and just four in the second half of a one-score game. Seattle's defense loaded up the box to take Jackson out of the game and put their rookie safety Earl Thomas on Bradford's security blanket, slot receiver Danny Amendola, daring offensive coordinator Pat Shurmur to let his rookie throw downfield. The Rams had a season-low 184 yards of total offense, settled for two Josh Brown field goals, and limped home with the 14th pick in the 2011 NFL Draft as their consolation prize.

The positives from 2010 certainly outweigh the negatives. As painful as it may have been for Rams fans to endure that six-win stretch from 2007-09, that woefulness, particularly the one-win 2009 campaign, enabled the club to get a franchise quarterback (Bradford) and left tackle (Rodger Saffold) with the first and 33rd overall picks in the 2010 draft. Bradford, Saffold, and 2009 first-round offensive tackle Jason Smith provide the foundation for general manager Billy Devaney to build upon. After passing on adding a quarterback with top-five picks in 2008 (Matt Ryan) and 2009 (Mark Sanchez), Marc Bulger's declining health and production (three straight seasons of negative DYAR and DVOA)

2011 Rams Schedule

Week	Opp.	Week	Opp.	Week	Opp.
1	PHI	7	at DAL	13	at SF
2	at NYG (Mon.)	8	NO	14	at SEA (Mon.)
3	BAL	9	at ARI	15	CIN
4	WAS	10	at CLE	16	at PIT
5	BYE	11	SEA	17	SF
6	at GB	12	ARI		

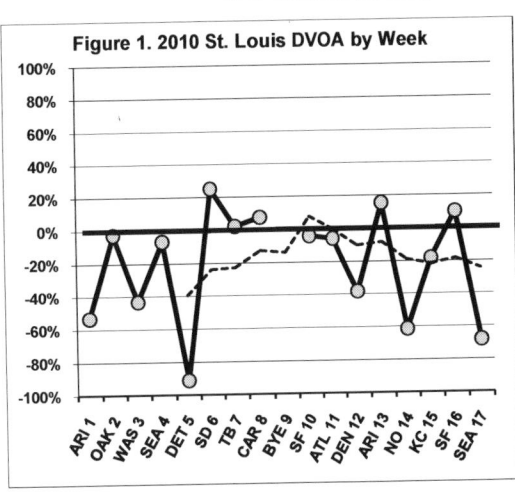

Figure 1. 2010 St. Louis DVOA by Week

and increasing age and salary was a situation the Rams could no longer afford to ignore. The Rams needed a quarterback and Bradford, the 2008 Heisman Trophy winner, was one of two consensus first-round quarterbacks in the 2010 draft, and the only one worth taking as highly as first overall. Bradford has all the physical and mental tools a team could want in a franchise quarterback, but he was coming off surgery on his throwing shoulder, which raised questions about his durability.

With $50 million in guaranteed money on the line, the Rams were not going to just throw Bradford to the wolves. Spagnuolo publicly stated that journeyman A.J. Feeley had a better command of the offense and was ahead of Bradford on the depth chart. When Bradford played lights-out in the final two preseason games — 21-of-28 for 257 yards and three touchdowns against New England and Baltimore — the job was his. Despite the lack of a true No. 1 wide receiver on the roster, and injuries forcing the Rams to constantly shuffle personnel at the wide receiver and tight end position, Bradford managed to complete 60 percent of his passes for just over 3,500 yards, and break Peyton Manning's records for completions and attempts by a rookie. Shurmur and the staff were careful with Bradford, supplementing their short-to-medium passing attack with frequent use of max protection and taking advantage of Bradford's mobility by moving him out of the pocket. As a result, Bradford was sacked just 34 times (the team's lowest total since 1999, the first of the "Greatest Show on Turf" years) and was able to take every one of the team's snaps from center, answering the durability question many draft analysts had on him.

Bradford has a way to go before reaching the Kurt Warner level, but he's very close to the Joe Flacco/Matt Ryan/Josh Freeman level, if he isn't there already. Taking that next step will involve working with a new offensive coordinator, though, as Shurmur left to become head coach of the Cleveland Browns. Though most Rams fans and observers were not saddened by the departure of Shurmur and his conservative game plans and play-calling, Bradford understandably had mixed emotions about the departure of Shurmur, as well as the retirement of longtime quarterbacks coach Dick Curl. "Yeah. I definitely will be starting over, which to a certain extent is kind of frustrating," Bradford said of the coaching changes. "Just the fact that a part of me wishes that our system would've remained the same. It would've made it a lot easier for me." Bradford must have quickly realized that the statistics from his Heisman Trophy-winning season of 2008 — 67.9% completion percentage, 4,720 passing yards, 50 touchdowns, eight interceptions — were nearly identical to the numbers New England Patriots quarterback Tom Brady put up — 68.9% completion percentage, 4,806 yards, 50 touchdowns, eight interceptions — in 2007 with McDaniels coordinating the offense and calling the plays. "If you look at what Josh has done with some of his offenses in the past, what his quarterbacks have been able to do, I'm extremely excited for this opportunity. I can't wait to get into the (playbook) with him and just learn about what we're going to do next year."

The Rams will also help Bradford develop by improving the personnel around him. Running back Steven Jackson and oft-injured rookies Danario Alexander and Michael Hoomanawanui were Bradford's only receiving targets with positive DYAR and DVOA last season. The Rams traded for Mark Clayton right before the start of the season and he became Bradford's preferred target. Perhaps that can be attributed to some sort of Oklahoma Sooners telepathy, but it was more likely a function of a guy (Clayton) who was a No. 4 receiver in Baltimore being the best option on the Rams roster. In a bizarro offseason where the draft occurred before free agency, the Rams got a head start on addressing the skill-position players by using three of their first four picks on receiving targets for Bradford. Wisconsin tight end/H-back Lance Kendricks arrived in the second round, and provides the Rams with an athletic, Aaron Hernandez-type whom McDaniels will move around in the offense. Kendricks is just as likely to line up outside the numbers as he is to line up as a traditional, in-line tight end. In the next round, the Rams grabbed Boise State wide receiver Austin Pettis, a smart, big-bodied (6-foot-3, 209-pound), sure-handed receiver who won't run by NFL cornerbacks, but will run precise routes and find the holes in a zone. Hawaii receiver Greg Salas, who predominantly worked out of the spread, was added in the fourth. When free agency opened up, the Rams were expected to target a legitimate No. 1 receiver for Bradford. Instead, they signed wide receiver Mike Sims-Walker, a bigger (6-foot-2, 209-pound) target who has 14 touchdowns the last two seasons — but also a player the Jacksonville Jaguars, who are thin at the receiver position, had zero interest in retaining. Jackson got some company in the backfield with the signings of Jerious Norwood and Cadillac Williams, instantly improving the depth at a position that had become far too dependent on one single (very good) player.

While the new additions will increase competition in training camp and the preseason, particularly at the wide receiver position, their immediate impact could be dampened by only having 38 days to implement McDaniels' complex system. A lengthy lockout meant that Bradford and McDaniels were not able to get into the playbook with one another at all during the offseason. The Rams were able to get a copy of McDaniels' playbook into the quarterback's hands. Along with some offseason film study sessions with McDaniels' mentor, University of Florida offensive coordinator Charlie Weis, that helped Bradford serve as de facto offensive coordinator during the player-run workouts at Lindenwood University and in Arizona. As bright as the 23-year-old Bradford is, it's questionable how much of a head start he and his receivers actually got during those workouts with a Cliff Notes version of the playbook and no coordinator or position coaches to provide guidance and corrections. The "work in progress" nature of a very young offense (at 28, Jackson is the oldest of the skill-position players expected to be significant contributors in 2011) is the complete opposite of what's going on with the Rams defense.

The Rams' defense improved from 31st to 20th in defensive DVOA in year two of the Spagnuolo Era, and has the potential to be even better in 2011. If Bradford, Saffold, and Smith are the building blocks on the offensive side of the ball, defensive end Chris Long and middle linebacker James Laurinaitis are the foundation of the defense. Both are young, Pro Bowl-caliber defenders in need of better talent around them. The Rams added another significant piece to the puzzle with the 14th overall pick in North Carolina defensive end Robert Quinn, who possesses the double-digit sack potential that makes front offices in San Francisco and Seattle glad they've recently invested a lot of draft capital in the offensive tackle position. At least four new starters were added to the defense in free agency, three of whom are over 30. Two of the "thirtysomething" additions — 32-year-old defensive tackle Justin Bannan and 31-year-old safety Quintin Mikell — received multi-year deals. Conventional wisdom in the NFL suggests that if you're going to go young on one side of the ball, do it on defense, the thinking being that the speed and energy of a younger player can compensate for his lack of experience. Of course, it's not feasible for a team to go completely young on defense (even the Tampa Bay Buccaneers, the youngest team in the league, have some older veterans like Ronde Barber and Sean Jones), and the players the Rams brought in are certainly upgrades over what they had last season. With the Rams committing early-round draft picks to get younger weapons for Bradford and McDaniels, adding veteran pieces around Laurinaitis and Long in free agency makes some sense in the short term. Teams implementing new systems on one or both sides of the ball are those most likely to be negatively affected by the lockout. St. Louis' offense is unlikely to be a finely-tuned machine when they host the Philadelphia Eagles on September 11, but the older free agents can be easily assimilated into the defense — particularly Mikell, who played for Spagnuolo in Philadelphia and should pick up the system quickly — to get them through a brutal schedule at the start of the regular season.

Though the Rams open with three of four games at the Edward Jones Dome, their first three opponents — Philadelphia, the New York Giants, and Baltimore Ravens — had a combined record of 32-16 in 2010. The Rams also have back-to-back road games against the defending champion Green Bay Packers and the Dallas Cowboys and face the New Orleans Saints in the first seven weeks of the season. On the bright side, if the Rams can manage to stay afloat during the first half of the season, six of their final nine games are within the NFC West, a division that once again may be won by a team with a losing record.

Brian McIntyre

2010 Rams Stats by Week

Wk	vs.	W-L	PF	PA	YDF	YDA	TO	Total	Off	Def	ST
1	ARI	L	13	17	325	378	0	-53%	-31%	28%	6%
2	@OAK	L	14	16	210	404	1	-3%	-7%	-13%	-10%
3	WAS	W	30	16	365	349	0	-43%	-8%	30%	-6%
4	SEA	W	20	3	349	257	1	-7%	-26%	-21%	-2%
5	@DET	L	6	44	341	322	-3	-91%	-38%	31%	-23%
6	SD	W	20	17	300	287	1	25%	5%	-12%	8%
7	@TB	L	17	18	285	313	-1	2%	-3%	-9%	-4%
8	CAR	W	20	10	246	201	4	8%	-9%	-21%	-4%
9	BYE										
10	@SF	L	20	23	332	421	0	-4%	8%	28%	16%
11	ATL	L	17	34	304	391	-1	-6%	13%	19%	0%
12	@DEN	W	36	33	431	449	2	-38%	12%	48%	-2%
13	@ARI	W	19	6	288	224	1	15%	-19%	-17%	18%
14	@NO	L	13	31	327	345	0	-61%	-54%	10%	3%
15	KC	L	13	27	224	383	-1	-18%	-24%	2%	8%
16	SF	W	25	17	335	331	1	10%	3%	-12%	-6%
17	@SEA	L	6	16	184	333	0	-68%	-65%	10%	7%

Trends and Splits

	Offense	Rank	Defense	Rank
Total DVOA	-15.2%	30	6.0%	20
Unadjusted VOA	-11.7%	26	2.4%	18
Weighted Trend	-13.2%	29	6.8%	19
Variance	5.4%	7	4.9%	6
Average Opponent	5.8%	8	-5.1%	1
Passing	-6.6%	27	10.2%	21
Rushing	-14.0%	31	0.5%	20
First Down	-14.5%	29	11.7%	27
Second Down	-9.3%	23	8.3%	21
Third Down	-25.8%	28	-9.4%	9
First Half	-9.8%	29	1.3%	17
Second Half	-21.2%	30	10.8%	26
Red Zone	-63.0%	32	11.7%	24
Late and Close	-3.4%	21	9.6%	27

Five-Year Performance

Year	W-L	Pyth	Est W	PF	PA	TO	Total	Rk	Off	Rk	Def	Rk	ST	Rk	Off AGL	Rk	Def AGL	Rk
2006	8-8	7.6	7.4	367	381	+14	-13.8%	25	3.3%	14	12.7%	30	-4.4%	31	3.3	2	5.0	4
2007	3-13	3.7	3.7	263	438	-10	-34.9%	32	-22.0%	31	9.1%	25	-3.9%	27	52.4	32	27.4	24
2008	2-14	2.6	2.0	232	465	-5	-47.5%	31	-24.0%	32	23.4%	30	-0.2%	18	50.3	30	29.9	21
2009	1-15	1.6	2.5	175	436	-13	-45.1%	31	-26.4%	32	20.3%	31	1.6%	11	38.4	27	36.3	23
2010	7-9	6.8	5.7	289	328	+5	-20.8%	29	-15.2%	30	6.0%	20	0.5%	14	47.1	32	9.7	4

Strategic Tendencies

Run/Pass	Rank	Offense	Rank	Defense	Rank	Other	Rank
Runs, all plays	39%	21	3+ WR	59%	9	Rush 3	2.2%	29	2+ RB, Pct Runs	50%	28
Runs, first half	38%	24	4+ WR	10%	7	Rush 4	58.7%	16	1 RB/2 TE, Pct Runs	46%	24
Runs, first down	49%	18	2+ TE	22%	25	Rush 5	21.9%	20	1 RB/3+ WR, Pct Runs	30%	5
Runs, second-long	36%	12	Single back	64%	9	Rush 6+	17.1%	2	CB1 on WR1	43%	12
Runs, power sit.	50%	27	Play action	24%	4	Zone Blitz	10.8%	3	Go for it on 4th	0.95	12
Runs, behind 2H	23%	26	Max protect	12%	10	Sacks by LB	17.4%	21	Offensive Pace	29.7	6
Pass, ahead 2H	47%	11	Outside pocket	16%	7	Sacks by DB	11.6%	14	Defensive Pace	29.4	1

Sam Bradford led the league with 21 passes tipped away or batted down at the line. He also led the league with 13 passes that were incomplete because he was hit during his throwing motion. (As a team, St. Louis was second in both categories.) ☞ The Rams threw to Danny Amendola on third down more than twice as often as they threw to any other one receiver. ☞ The Rams used play-action fakes 50 percent more often than they did in 2009. They ranked fourth in the league at 24.3 percent of pass plays… just behind Josh McDaniels' Denver offense at 24.5 percent. The Rams ranked 18th in DVOA on plays with play-action, but 29th in plays without it. ☞ It wasn't quite as bad as previous years, but once again the Rams defense seriously struggled to stop play-action passing. The Rams had a reasonable 4.9% defensive DVOA on pass plays without a play-fake, but a terrible 41.1% DVOA on pass plays with a fake. ☞ The Rams drew a league-leading 148 penalty flags by opponents (including declined and offsetting), nine more than second-place Tennessee.

Passing

Player	DYAR	DVOA	Plays	NtYds	Avg	YAC	C%	TD	Int
S.Bradford	72	-9.3%	626	3299	5.3	5.3	60.4%	18	13

Rushing

Player	DYAR	DVOA	Plays	Yds	Avg	TD	Fum	Suc
S.Jackson	-48	-12.1%	330	1241	3.8	6	1	40%
K.Darby	3	-6.6%	34	107	3.1	2	0	38%
K.Toston	-23	-35.1%	19	54	2.8	0	0	32%
S.Bradford	5	-6.0%	17	72	4.2	1	0	-
D.Amendola	47	81.4%	7	81	11.6	0	0	-
M.Karney	-2	-13.2%	6	12	2.0	0	0	67%

Receiving

Player	DYAR	DVOA	Plays	Ctch	Yds	Y/C	YAC	TD	C%
D.Amendola	-70	-19.8%	123	85	689	8.1	4.3	3	69%
B.Gibson	20	-9.9%	91	53	620	11.7	4.2	2	58%
L.Robinson	-141	-36.6%	75	34	344	10.1	3.1	2	45%
M.Clayton	3	-11.9%	42	23	306	13.3	4.2	2	55%
D.Alexander	43	1.0%	37	20	306	15.3	5.7	1	54%
M.Gilyard	-38	-44.6%	16	6	63	10.5	2.3	0	38%
D.Fells	19	-2.5%	65	41	391	9.5	6.5	2	63%
B.Bajema	-4	-10.0%	24	14	153	10.9	5.8	2	58%
M.Hoomanawanui	13	1.1%	22	13	146	11.2	7.9	3	59%
S.Jackson	45	-1.2%	61	46	374	8.1	8.1	0	75%
K.Darby	5	-4.0%	13	10	61	6.1	7.7	1	77%

Offensive Line

Year	Yards	ALY	Rank	Power	Rank	Stuff	Rank	2nd Lev	Rank	Open Field	Rank
2008	4.08	4.08	20	78%	2	15%	6	1.02	28	0.69	17
2009	3.54	4.01	18	46%	32	17%	9	0.95	31	0.40	32
2010	4.18	4.12	14	61%	16	19%	19	1.11	17	0.78	14

Year	LE	Rank	LT	Rank	Mid	Rank	RT	Rank	RE	Rank	Sacks	ASR	Rank	F-Start	Cont.
2008	3.18	26	3.81	23	4.34	10	4.17	17	4.18	12	25	6.1%	17	16	33
2009	3.20	27	4.35	10	3.85	25	4.79	2	4.42	12	26	4.5%	5	16	33
2010	4.21	18	3.73	26	4.34	7	4.27	12	3.23	26	38	6.8%	19	11	28

Second-rounder Rodger Saffold was originally projected to play right tackle opposite 2009 second-overall pick Jason Smith, but he proved to be much further along in his pass blocking than originally thought and earned the left tackle spot during training camp while Smith was recovering from a toe injury incurred during OTAs. That alignment carried into the regular season, with Saffold starting all 16 games protecting Sam Bradford's blind side. Though not nearly as bad as his predecessor Alex Barron, who led the league with 14 penalties in 2009, Saffold was penalized eight times as a rookie, including a team-high six false starts. Smith, meanwhile, recovered from an injury-plagued rookie season to start 15 games at right tackle. While he had some rough moments, most notably a team-high six blown blocks and eight penalties, Smith is a solid run blocker who showed improvement in pass protection before struggling, along with the rest of the offensive line, down the stretch.

The Rams' three interior linemen — left guard Jacob Bell, center Jason Brown, and right guard Adam Goldberg — also started all 16 games last season. This unprecedented continuity did not translate into greatly improved performance, as the Rams' Adjusted Line Yards slightly decreased while their ranking slightly increased. Rams general manager Billy Devaney has invested $73.5 million in free agent contracts on Bell and Brown and two early picks on Smith and Saffold — and with a running back like Steven Jackson, the Rams should rank significantly higher than 31st in rushing DVOA. Devaney again turned to free agency to improve the offensive line, signing free agent guard Harvey Dahl to a four-year contract. Dahl was the right guard for an Atlanta Falcons offensive line that has ranked in the top 10 in Adjusted Line Yards and Adjusted Sack Rate the past three seasons, and he brings a toughness and tenacity that the interior line has been lacking. Brown hasn't been the Pro Bowl player the Rams envisioned when they made him the highest-paid center in league history in 2009, but he makes few mistakes (three penalties and one blown block in 2010) and provides solid leadership. Bell is very good in pass protection, but is undersized and not a pile-moving road-grader in the running game. Goldberg and Renardo Foster are back in reserve roles.

Defensive Front Seven

Defensive Line	Age	Pos	Plays	TmPct	Rk	Stop	Dfts	BTkl	St%	Rk	AvYd	Rk	Sack	Hit	Hur	Runs	St%	Yds	Pass	St%	Yds
						Overall							Pass Rush			vs. Run			vs. Pass		
James Hall	34	DE	54	6.8%	21	41	16	1	74%	51	2.5	63	10.5	5	18	31	74%	2.8	23	78%	2.1
Fred Robbins	34	DT	35	4.4%	38	34	17	2	95%	1	-0.6	1	6	7	14.5	19	95%	0.1	16	100%	-1.5
Chris Long	26	DE	30	3.8%	68	25	10	6	71%	19	-0.6	5	8	16	42.5	17	71%	2.2	13	100%	-4.4
Gary Gibson	29	DT	19	2.4%	--	13	1	1	73%	--	2.7	--	0	2	6	15	73%	2.6	4	50%	3.0
George Selvie	24	DE	19	2.4%	--	12	7	1	57%	--	4.2	--	1.5	3	4	14	57%	4.4	5	80%	3.8
Darell Scott	25	DT	18	4.0%	--	9	1	0	58%	--	7.9	--	0	0	0	12	58%	3.2	6	33%	17.5
C.J. Ah You	29	DE	17	2.1%	--	15	9	0	100%	--	1.1	--	4	6	9	7	100%	0.6	10	80%	1.4
Jermelle Cudjo	25	DT	15	3.0%	--	13	3	0	83%	--	1.1	--	0.5	0	1	12	83%	2.2	3	100%	-3.0

Linebackers	Age	Pos	Plays	TmPct	Rk	Stop	Dfts	BTkl	AvYd	Sack	Hit	Hur	Runs	St%	Rk	Yds	Rk	Tgts	Suc%	Rk	AdjYd	Rk
						Overall				Pass Rush			vs. Run					vs. Pass				
James Laurinaitis	25	MLB	117	14.6%	21	77	23	6	4.5	3.5	4	6	74	72%	36	3.3	62	40	62%	17	5.0	17
Na'il Diggs	33	OLB	38	6.3%	98	23	6	6	4.1	0	1	2	30	60%	83	2.9	40	8	58%	--	7.5	--
Bryan Kehl	27	OLB	28	3.7%	--	14	2	1	6.2	0	1	4.5	14	64%	--	3.9	--	9	45%	--	5.7	--
David Vobora	25	OLB	26	3.7%	--	15	5	3	4.2	2	0	2.5	15	80%	--	3.9	--	6	-4%	--	5.9	--
Chris Chamberlain	26	OLB	21	3.8%	--	14	4	3	4.2	0	0	0	10	80%	--	1.7	--	6	36%	--	6.8	--
Larry Grant	26	OLB	17	2.1%	--	8	4	4	3.4	2	1	0	13	38%	--	4.2	--	7	46%	--	12.1	--

Year	Yards	ALY	Rank	Power	Rank	Stuff	Rank	2nd Lev	Rank	Open Field	Rank
2008	5.23	4.65	31	66%	17	17%	21	1.54	31	1.24	29
2009	4.36	4.31	23	63%	13	18%	20	1.15	17	0.90	21
2010	4.56	4.07	18	55%	6	21%	11	1.31	28	1.05	29

Year	LE	Rank	LT	Rank	Mid	Rank	RT	Rank	RE	Rank	Sacks	ASR	Rank
2008	5.74	32	3.89	9	4.37	20	5.20	31	5.28	29	30	6.2%	15
2009	4.71	23	4.33	20	4.29	24	4.40	24	3.92	15	25	5.4%	27
2010	5.65	32	3.25	3	3.87	15	3.97	14	3.97	15	43	7.1%	8

Pass rushers can sometimes take a year or two to develop. Chris Long, the second overall pick of the 2008 NFL Draft, is an example of that. Long had a breakout season in 2010, posting a career-high 8.5 quarterback sacks with a league-high 42.5 quarterback hurries. Long's tenacity coming off the edge certainly had a positive impact on veteran James Hall, who tallied 10.5 quarterback sacks in 2010, his highest total since 2004. Hall turned 34 in February, one reason the Rams used their first-round pick on University of North Carolina defensive end Richard Quinn. Quinn had 13 quarterback sacks his first two seasons in Chapel Hill before he was suspended for the 2010 season for his involvement in an agent scandal. That suspension, coupled with a brain tumor that ended his high school career, likely dropped Quinn out of the top five picks of the draft. (The loss of eligible games also limited his SackSEER projection to 15.5 sacks over his first five seasons.) Quinn's prolonged absence from the gridiron may result in a reduced role this season, coming off the bench to rush the quarterback on obvious passing downs. Veteran C.J. Ah You (four sacks) and 2010 late-round picks George Selvie and Eugene Sims received snaps in situational pass-rusher roles, opportunities that figure to be scarce with the arrival of Quinn.

In addition to the solid seasons by Long and Hall, another factor in the Rams' increase from 27th to eighth in Adjusted Sack Rate was the addition of veteran defensive tackle Fred Robbins. After a disappointing final season with the New York Giants, Robbins was outstanding as a penetrating three-technique tackle, posting ten tackles for a loss and notching a career-high six quarterback sacks with 14.5 quarterback hurries. Journeyman Gary Gibson started all 16 games as a predominantly two-down nose tackle next to Robbins, a spot the Rams upgraded with the signing of Justin Bannan to a three-year, $8.25 million contract. St. Louis had been interested in Bannan a year earlier, but lost out to the Denver Broncos' five-year, $22 million contract offer. Bannan is not a flashy player, but he is another quick, penetrating tackle who can be a disruptive presence in opposing backfields. The Rams also brought back Gibson and signed ex-Colt Daniel Muir, a 28-year-old alleged run-stopper who is, in the grand Indianapolis tradition, easily pushed around on running plays.

Second-year middle linebacker James Laurinaitis appeared more comfortable in his role as on-field leader and quarterback of Spagnuolo's defense. Laurinaitis continues to be a productive tackler, and took another step towards being a perennial Pro Bowler by showing improvement both rushing the quarterback and when dropping into coverage. Stabilizing the supporting cast around Laurinaitis may allow Laurinaitis to take that leap. Strongside linebacker Na'il Diggs was solid against the run before landing on injured reserve with a torn pectoral muscle, and Larry Grant, David Vobora, Chris Chamberlain, and Bryan Kehl comprised a revolving door on the weak side. The Rams took steps they hope will solidify the outside linebacker spots. Free agents Zac Diles and Ben Leber were brought in to flank Laurinatis. Both have played on the weak side during their careers, but Leber has the versatility to play the strong side. Leber (who ranked fourth in adjusted success rate and 13th in yards allowed per pass) and Laurinatis (who ranked 17th in both categories) are likely to be paired in nickel defense. Adding Diles and Leber, as well as Brady Poppinga, led to the release of Vobora and could mean the end of Diggs' stay in St. Louis.

Defensive Secondary

Secondary	Age	Pos	Overall Plays	TmPct	Rk	Stop	Dfts	BTkl	vs. Run Runs	St%	Rk	Yds	Rk	vs. Pass Tgts	Tgt%	Rk	Dist	Suc%	Rk	APaYd	Rk	PD	Int
Craig Dahl	26	SS	91	12.1%	17	34	14	5	38	47%	24	7.3	51	37	7.7%	18	14.4	53%	44	9.3	60	3	2
O.J. Atogwe	30	FS	82	10.3%	38	28	16	7	44	32%	59	8.0	56	30	5.9%	37	15.8	57%	29	7.3	34	3	3
Bradley Fletcher	25	CB	82	10.3%	25	27	12	1	31	39%	58	6.2	36	75	14.6%	53	15.1	49%	56	6.9	34	8	4
Ronald Bartell	29	CB	71	9.5%	30	28	9	6	12	58%	18	12.3	85	83	17.4%	20	13.3	60%	12	5.6	8	12	0
Kevin Dockery	27	CB	25	5.0%	--	12	9	4	3	67%	--	1.3	--	27	8.3%	--	9.8	57%	--	9.8	--	4	1
James Butler	29	SS	23	3.3%	--	8	5	2	8	13%	--	11.9	--	11	2.5%	--	17.0	47%	--	7.4	--	3	2
Jerome Murphy	24	CB	23	3.3%	--	8	5	3	2	0%	--	10.0	--	22	4.9%	--	9.3	46%	--	6.1	--	3	1
Justin King	24	CB	20	5.0%	--	13	9	0	5	80%	--	2.6	--	21	8.0%	--	9.9	67%	--	6.5	--	1	0
Darian Stewart	23	FS	15	2.3%	--	9	5	3	4	75%	--	4.3	--	11	2.7%	--	11.7	57%	--	8.5	--	2	0

Year	Pass D Rank	vs. #1 WR	Rk	vs. #2 WR	Rk	vs. Other WR	Rk	vs. TE	Rk	vs. RB	Rk
2008	25	7.2%	18	7.3%	22	25.5%	31	2.8%	16	-0.8%	11
2009	29	21.0%	29	22.7%	29	12.5%	25	22.8%	28	-15.3%	6
2010	21	-17.0%	5	28.6%	30	7.7%	23	10.0%	18	16.9%	27

The team's most experienced corner, Ron Bartell starts on the left side and usually draws the opponents' top receiver. As a result, Bartell is among the most-targeted cornerbacks in the league, having been thrown at 80-plus times in each of the last two seasons. Despite the many opportunities, Bartell hasn't recorded an interception since December 21, 2008, a dry spell that currently stands at 31 regular-season games. 2009 third-round pick Bradley Fletcher bounced back from knee surgery to lead the Rams with four interceptions and 11 passes defensed, establishing himself as the starting right cornerback opposite Bartell. The Rams would like to see similar improvement from 2010 third-round corner Jerome Murphy, who has the size, speed, and skills in press coverage that should have him vying for a starting job. Unfortunately, Murphy suffered a broken ankle in the early days of training camp and will miss time into the regular season.

The Rams were a bit disappointed with O.J. Atogwe's 2010 season, and terminated his contract before an $8 million roster bonus came due on February 21. They acted quickly to replace Atogwe in free agency, signing Quintin Mikell to a four-year, $27 million contract. Mikell spent the previous eight seasons with the Philadelphia Eagles, including a rookie season (2003) where Steve Spagnuolo was his position coach. The Rams are banking on Mikell being the elite, game-changing safety they felt Atogwe wasn't in 2010. Craig Dahl replaced James Butler as the other starting safety. Dahl is familiar with Spagnuolo's defense, having followed him from New York to St. Louis in 2009, and ranked second on the defense in tackles, but struggled in pass coverage. Safeties in Spagnuolo's defense are interchangeable; the bigger Dahl spent more time in the box last year, but Mikell was also more of a box safety during his years with Philadelphia. Butler restructured his contract to stay with the team, and be the third safety while the Rams develop 2011 draft picks Jermale Hines (Ohio State) and Jonathan Nelson (Oklahoma).

Special Teams

Year	DVOA	Rank	FG/XP	Rank	Net Kick	Rank	Kick Ret	Rank	Net Punt	Rank	Punt Ret	Rank	Hidden	Rank
2008	-0.2%	18	5.1	7	2.3	15	-10.9	31	4.2	14	-1.8	20	-16.6	32
2009	1.6%	11	1.5	16	-2.3	21	-6.0	24	15.0	2	1.3	14	-2.7	17
2010	0.5%	14	-2.3	27	2.4	12	-8.8	26	5.6	12	6.0	5	-9.6	26

Veteran kicker Josh Brown overcame a few early season miscues to finish 33-of-39 on field-goal attempts in 2010, including 10-of-13 from beyond 40 yards. Brown does not possess a booming leg on kickoffs, averaging just seven touchbacks per season since arriving in St. Louis in 2008. Donnie Jones continued to be one of the NFL's busiest punters, called upon a career-high 94 times in 2010. Despite battling a calf injury on his kicking leg for much of the season, and for the first time in his career having one of his punts returned for a touchdown, Jones ranked third in net punting average and second in FO's measure of gross punt value.

The short-area quickness and elusiveness that make Danny Amendola an effective slot receiver also make him an effective punt returner, ranking in the top ten the last two seasons in value over average. Amendola is not a home-run hitter in the mold of a Devin Hester, and is below average as a kick returner. The Rams thought 2010 fourth-round pick Mardy Gilyard could be the game-breaking kick returner the franchise had lacked in recent seasons, but he was below average in his 16 returns, lost a fumble, and was replaced with Amendola at midseason. Gilyard will be given every opportunity to display his return skills again during training camp and the preseason, and with the logjam at receiver, that may be his only path to a roster spot. If Gilyard doesn't make the roster, Amendola may be back as punt returner, with No. 3 running back Jerious Norwood or seventh-round cornerback Mikail Baker returning kicks.

Coaching Staff

Steve Spagnuolo's second season as an NFL head coach nearly resulted in the team's first playoff appearance since 2004, which would have been quite an accomplishment for a franchise that had won just six games over the previous three seasons. A former defensive coordinator, Spagnuolo plays an active role in the devising the defensive game plan, but play-calling duties are left to coordinator Ken Flajole. An improved defense had a great deal to do with the Rams being in position to make the postseason. Pat Shurmur's offense also improved, but with a rookie quarterback and two young tackles, his play-calling was often criticized for being too conservative. That changed in the regular-season finale, when Shurmur called just 15 running plays in the team's 16-6 loss to the Seahawks.

Shurmur has moved on, accepting the head coaching position with the Cleveland Browns. Fans in St. Louis might not be sad to see the conservative play-calling go, but Shurmur and longtime quarterbacks coach Dick Curl deserve a lot of credit for getting first overall pick Sam Bradford ready to start as a rookie. In addition to Shurmur moving to the Browns, Curl announced his retirement in January. Replacing Shurmur and Curl is former Denver Broncos head coach Josh McDaniels, who successfully handled the same dual role with the New England Patriots from 2006-08. McDaniels may have been a disaster in a head coach/personnel executive role with the Broncos, but he has a solid track record as a quarterbacks coach, offensive coordinator, and play-caller. McDaniels promises to bring a balanced but aggressive approach to the offense.

San Diego Chargers

2010 Record: 9-7	**2011 Mean Projection:** 10.6 wins
Pythagorean Wins: 10.9 (5th)	**On the Clock (0-3):** 0%
DVOA: 17.1% (7th)	**Loserville (4-6):** 6%
Offense: 19.3% (4th)	**Mediocrity (7-8):** 14%
Defense: -6.4% (7th)	**Playoff Contender (9-10):** 28%
Special Teams: -8.6% (32nd)	**Super Bowl Contender (11+):** 52%
Variance: 23.2% (26th)	**Projected Average Opponent:** 0.7% (14th)

2010: A.J. Smith's hubris finally gets the better of him.

2011: Has Smith finally thrown money at the right problems?

No matter how talented and valuable you may be as a football executive, it's always possible to believe your own press clippings, take your "genius" more seriously than you should, and throw your career down the stairs before you realize what's happened. If San Diego Chargers general manager/executive vice-president A.J. Smith doesn't know the story of Joe Thomas, he should learn it quickly.

Thomas was a football executive who helped assemble the Minnesota Vikings of the 1960s and the Miami Dolphins of the early 1970s. He had a brilliant eye for talent until he developed an arrogant belief in the idea that any move he made would work based simply on the fact that he made it. He demolished the Baltimore Colts in the mid-1970s and took the San Francisco 49ers to perhaps the lowest point in franchise history, and he managed to anger just about everyone he encountered along the way.

Primarily, Thomas' problem was that his later moves were more about forwarding the notion of his own genius, and this was never more evident than in 1972, when he benched and then traded the aging Johnny Unitas. Not a bad football move on its face — Unitas was done — but it was Thomas' reaction to fan anger that set his modus operandi apart. "I told my wife to be ready for an explosion," Thomas told *Sports Illustrated* in December of 1975. "There were signs all over town, letters, editorials, phone calls, the whole

bit. Listen, someone had to be the bad guy. I had a long-term contract, so I didn't have to worry about the flak."

Over the next few years, Thomas fired coach after coach, put together some really horrible drafts (10 schlubs for every Bert Jones or Lydell Mitchell), and ran the Colts into the ground. Hired by new 49ers owner Eddie DeBartolo in 1977 on Al Davis' recommendation, Thomas insisted that all historical team memorabilia be removed from the team's facility, kept firing coaches, traded a first-round pick for a version of O.J. Simpson that was even closer to the end than the Unitas he had dumped five years before, and declared himself the target of an assassination attempt. Thomas eventually left the game more well-known for his tremendous ego and late-career blundering than anything else.

A.J. Smith has been in charge of San Diego's personnel since 2003, when he replaced the late John Butler. He started out hot, with a series of great drafts that stocked the Chargers' roster with the kind of talent that would keep the team competing for years. His 2004 draft was the crown jewel. Smith got seven players of starting caliber: Philip Rivers, Igor Olshansky, Nate Kaeding, Nick Hardwick, Shaun Phillips, Dave Ball, and Michael Turner. 2005 brought Shawne Merriman, Luis Castillo, Vincent Jackson, and Darren Sproles. 2006 brought Anto-

2011 Chargers Schedule

Week	Opp.	Week	Opp.	Week	Opp.
1	MIN	7	at NYJ	13	at JAC (Mon.)
2	at NE	8	at KC (Mon.)	14	BUF
3	KC	9	GB	15	BAL
4	MIA	10	OAK (Thu.)	16	at DET
5	at DEN	11	at CHI	17	at OAK
6	BYE	12	DEN		

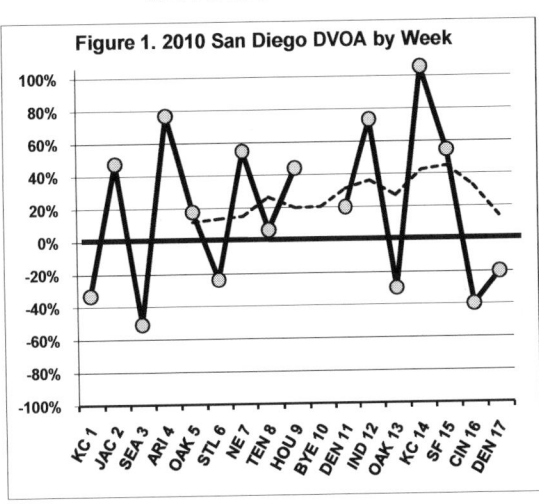

Figure 1. 2010 San Diego DVOA by Week

nio Cromartie and Marcus McNeill, but as the years went on, Smith started trading up for players with questionable value for the draft picks given. Safety Eric Weddle should be a Pro Bowler, and Ryan Mathews may be a great player in time, but the lack of draft depth has come home to roost.

At the 2008 scouting combine, New York Giants general manager Jerry Reese said that the second day of the draft is where personnel executives make their money, and that's where Smith has failed in recent years. Phillips, Turner, and Sproles were great examples of later-round picks that showed Smith's undeniable eye for football talent, but recent drafts have shown just as convincingly that talent evaluation can be a complete and total crapshoot in the wrong hands.

More worrisome than Smith's recent strikeouts in later rounds is the fact that even the early rounds of San Diego's recent drafts haven't shown much success. 2008 has brought only cornerback Antoine Cason (first round) and fullback Jacob Hester (third round) as players of note, and neither player has put up starting-level performances on a consistent basis. 2009 saw Larry English drafted as the supposed successor to Shawne Merriman as the team's elite pass rusher, but English has done very little to date, and the rest of San Diego's picks have been unimpressive for their selection spots. In 2010, Smith traded up to draft Mathews and third-round linebacker Donald Butler. Unfortunately, Butler missed his rookie season with a torn Achilles, and Mathews disappointed behind an offensive line that was short-staffed for reasons we'll delve into shortly.

"You don't want to force the issue," Smith told the Chargers' official website in March of 2010. "If there's somebody there that you need as a starter or somebody there that you think is significantly better than someone else that you've had for a few years, that's where you get better as a football team. You make the move."

But Smith's impetuous nature (despite his recent insistence that he makes no hasty decisions when it comes to personnel) has negatively affected the team in other ways — specifically, his determination to remove key personnel from his roster over needless escalations of contract disputes. Two such disputes helped lead to the Chargers' first season without a playoff berth since 2005.

The first was Smith's battle with Vincent Jackson, one of the NFL's top receivers in 2008 and 2009. Jackson didn't help his case by drawing a three-game suspension for violations of the NFL's personal conduct policy, but Smith exacerbated the issue by cutting Jackson's tender amount from $3.2 million to $583,000 and placing him on the Roster Exempt list. Jackson didn't sign his tender until late October. The Chargers actually finished second in passing DVOA through the first half of the season, but that had to do with an outlier — Antonio Gates was having one of the all-time tight end seasons. San Diego's best qualifying wide receiver in DYAR was Malcom Floyd, and he ranked 33rd.

Second, there was the matter of left tackle Marcus McNeill. Smith bumped McNeill's restricted free agent tender down to the lowest possible amount, placed him on the Roster Exempt list, and prepared to wait him out just like he was waiting out Jackson. Two things sped the process — McNeill signed his $444,000 tender in September, and quarterback Philip Rivers was just about killed by the constant pressure from Seahawks defensive end Chris Clemons in a 27-20 loss in Week 3. Swing tackle-turned-left tackle Brandyn Dombrowski was put in an impossible situation; asked to go up against some of the league's best edge rushers, he proved to be overmatched more often than not.

The Seahawks loss also exposed the Chargers' most obvious on-field problem: a special teams unit that was the worst in our metrics in a decade. Seattle's Leon Washington returned two kicks for touchdowns and almost broke free for a third score. Punter Mike Scifres had two straight punts blocked in a loss to the Raiders, and the Chargers had the worst coverage units in the NFL. That's an issue of depth to a large degree — having the second-level talent to maintain excellent coverage units is key — and that goes back to Smith's recent draft impetuousness. He may be getting the players he wants, but the draft picks he's burning in the process could be used to provide the depth he needs.

In the last few months, Smith seems to have come around to the fact that he can't field a team of extras and hope to be competitive. McNeill was eventually signed to a five-year deal worth more than $48 million, and Jackson signed a new one-year, $11.933 million tender after affixing his name to the Brady v. NFL antitrust lawsuit and reportedly threatening to delay the resolution of the lockout until he got what he deserved.

The one move that showed that Smith could reward the talent on his team without driving everyone nuts in the process was the five-year, $50 million contract given to Weddle. Those who don't watch All-22 film and don't understand the importance of a safety who can freelance in center field and crash down in run support may have thought the deal to be too rich, but Weddle has been San Diego's best defensive player over the last two seasons, and retaining him was a major step towards re-establishing the Chargers as a team led by a personnel voice and not a guy at a desk looking to enforce his will on his players.

Nonetheless, the 2011 draft still brought its own share of surprises. First-round defensive lineman Corey Liuget from Illinois is a natural fit in the team's hybrid fronts, but Smith confounded just about everyone by selecting Michigan linebacker Jonas Mouton in the second round, despite the fact that most every public scouting service had a fifth- to sixth-round grade on a player with limited range and ability to diagnose what's in front of him. "I'm told I can't find one person who thought the linebacker we took in the second round ... wasn't a fifth- or sixth-round guy,"

Smith told Nick Canepa of the *San Diego Union Tribune*. "Well, I've found one guy. Me. He's a second-rounder here." The more things change...

Smith's hubris aside, we do have the Chargers bouncing back from a disappointing year and winning their division. All positive projections must begin with Philip Rivers, who has to be mentioned in the MVP conversation because of the patchwork nature of his receiving corps. For the second straight season, San Diego's run game didn't measure up, and as a result, Rivers took every snap with a bull's-eye on his back. Factor in Jackson's absence then and presence now, Gates' recovery from the foot injury that caused him to miss the final four games of the 2010 season, and the fact that McNeill will be manning the left tackle spot, and Rivers has to be a hot pick to bring home an MVP award in 2011 — and maybe more.

For the offense to really move forward, Mathews will have to rebound. He spent a great deal of the 2010 season dealing with various injuries, and though he's believed to be the team's primary running back going forward, he's had trouble with conditioning tests through training camp. There are other concerns that could keep the Chargers from mounting a serious Super Bowl campaign — run-stopping, the pass rush, and offensive line depth — but things at least appear to be moving in a sensible direction for the first time in a number of years.

One other capricious Smith move — the firing of Marty Schottenheimer after a 14-2 record in 2006 — leaves questions about Norv Turner's standing. Norv's developed as a head coach to a degree, and the problems of 2010 couldn't really be considered his fault, but if the Chargers don't make the rebound everyone expects, it's always possible that the next head to roll could be his. One thing's for sure: If that move is made, A.J. Smith will do it with absolute certainty, and he won't give a damn what anyone else thinks. The long-term wisdom of that outlook remains to be seen.

Joe Thomas never learned his lesson, by the way. Summarily dismissed by the 49ers in 1978, he was replaced by some guy named Bill Walsh. That's another lesson for A.J. Smith and other "my way or the highway" executives: Somewhere, someone is building a better highway.

Doug Farrar

2010 Chargers Stats by Week

Wk	vs.	W-L	PF	PA	YDF	YDA	TO	Total	Off	Def	ST
1	@KC	L	14	21	389	197	-1	-33%	-9%	-9%	-33%
2	JAC	W	38	13	477	350	3	47%	24%	-30%	-7%
3	@SEA	L	20	27	518	271	-3	-51%	-1%	5%	-45%
4	ARI	W	41	10	419	134	2	77%	44%	-37%	-5%
5	@OAK	L	27	35	506	279	-3	18%	36%	-5%	-23%
6	@STL	L	17	20	287	300	-1	-24%	5%	15%	-13%
7	NE	L	20	23	363	179	-4	55%	7%	-54%	-7%
8	TEN	W	33	25	456	370	-1	7%	45%	29%	-10%
9	@HOU	W	29	23	367	392	-1	44%	48%	-6%	-10%
10	BYE										
11	DEN	W	35	14	400	235	0	20%	19%	-10%	-9%
12	@IND	W	36	14	301	303	5	74%	21%	-42%	11%
13	OAK	L	13	28	286	368	-1	-30%	18%	40%	-8%
14	KC	W	31	0	426	67	-2	106%	31%	-65%	10%
15	SF	W	34	7	374	192	1	55%	35%	-18%	2%
16	@CIN	L	20	34	313	371	-1	-40%	3%	44%	2%
17	@DEN	W	33	28	447	337	1	-20%	-8%	12%	0%

Trends and Splits

	Offense	Rank	Defense	Rank
Total DVOA	19.3%	4	-6.4%	7
Unadjusted VOA	23.1%	3	-7.8%	4
Weighted Trend	20.5%	4	-2.8%	9
Variance	3.6%	1	10.2%	30
Average Opponent	8.8%	1	3.3%	15
Passing	48.7%	2	-6.2%	4
Rushing	-2.2%	18	-6.6%	10
First Down	23.4%	3	0.7%	9
Second Down	8.0%	11	-10.9%	7
Third Down	29.7%	6	-11.6%	6
First Half	8.5%	15	-6.1%	6
Second Half	30.7%	3	-6.7%	9
Red Zone	11.9%	7	13.4%	25
Late and Close	15.5%	4	-11.2%	9

Five-Year Performance

Year	W-L	Pyth	Est W	PF	PA	TO	Total	Rk	Off	Rk	Def	Rk	ST	Rk	Off AGL	Rk	Def AGL	Rk
2006	14-2	12.1	12.0	492	303	+13	29.1%	1	27.0%	2	2.4%	17	4.4%	3	7.3	6	28.1	27
2007	11-5	11.3	9.6	412	284	+24	18.4%	7	5.8%	14	-8.2%	6	4.3%	5	24.4	21	12.9	7
2008	8-8	10.2	10.6	439	347	+4	17.5%	7	24.1%	1	8.3%	20	1.7%	12	12.4	5	22.2	16
2009	13-3	11.1	10.1	454	320	+8	13.6%	11	22.9%	4	9.6%	23	0.3%	16	26.6	17	29.5	18
2010	9-7	10.9	9.6	441	322	-6	17.1%	7	19.3%	4	-6.4%	7	-8.6%	32	26.8	18	12.7	9

Strategic Tendencies

Run/Pass		Rank	Offense		Rank	Defense		Rank	Other		Rank
Runs, all plays	41%	12	3+ WR	34%	32	Rush 3	8.0%	16	2+ RB, Pct Runs	58%	16
Runs, first half	41%	16	4+ WR	5%	21	Rush 4	62.7%	10	1 RB/2 TE, Pct Runs	49%	18
Runs, first down	52%	13	2+ TE	35%	8	Rush 5	26.8%	10	1 RB/3+ WR, Pct Runs	13%	31
Runs, second-long	32%	18	Single back	52%	25	Rush 6+	2.6%	32	CB1 on WR1	22%	31
Runs, power sit.	63%	12	Play action	17%	21	Zone Blitz	2.6%	28	Go for it on 4th	0.74	25
Runs, behind 2H	23%	23	Max protect	9%	24	Sacks by LB	63.8%	4	Offensive Pace	32.0	25
Pass, ahead 2H	37%	29	Outside pocket	9%	27	Sacks by DB	3.2%	29	Defensive Pace	29.5	2

Even though injuries frequently left them using wide receivers pulled off the street, the Chargers still got successively better on offense the more wide receivers they put into the game. San Diego was 29th in DVOA with fewer than two wideouts, but third in DVOA with two wideouts and tops in DVOA with three or more wideouts. ☞ San Diego threw passes to running backs 38 percent of the time on first down, easily the highest rate in the league. ☞ San Diego was 15th in offensive DVOA before halftime, but third after halftime. ☞ Based on week-to-week variance of DVOA, San Diego had the league's most consistent offense, but ranked 30th in consistency on defense. ☞ San Diego's pass rush dramatically improved in terms of sacks last year, but it still didn't improve in terms of hits and hurries. Once again, as in past years, the Chargers were dead last in hurries, hurrying quarterbacks on just 13.2 percent of pass plays. And once again they were dead last in hits, with only 15. Every other team had at least twice that many.

Passing

Player	DYAR	DVOA	Plays	NtYds	Avg	YAC	C%	TD	Int
P.Rivers	1652	34.0%	584	4480	7.7	6.3	66.4%	30	13

Receiving

Player	DYAR	DVOA	Plays	Ctch	Yds	Y/C	YAC	TD	C%
M.Floyd	128	9.1%	77	37	717	19.4	3.0	6	48%
L.Naanee	21	-6.8%	46	23	371	16.1	4.6	1	50%
P.Crayton	172	41.1%	42	28	514	18.4	7.6	1	67%
C.Davis	-3	-13.8%	39	21	259	12.3	4.2	1	54%
V.Jackson	96	38.7%	23	14	248	17.7	3.4	3	61%
S.Ajirotutu	91	39.6%	23	13	262	20.2	5.4	2	57%
K.Washington	96	80.0%	14	13	173	13.3	7.1	1	93%
A.Gates	371	79.5%	65	50	782	15.6	6.2	10	77%
R.McMichael	69	31.2%	27	20	221	11.1	4.2	2	74%
D.Sproles	166	26.9%	75	59	520	8.8	8.2	2	79%
M.Tolbert	84	37.2%	30	26	229	8.8	8.1	0	87%
J.Hester	53	20.2%	26	22	145	6.6	7.1	1	85%
R.Mathews	-8	-19.4%	26	22	145	6.6	8.2	0	85%
K.Wilson	-9	-33.1%	9	6	75	12.5	10.0	0	67%

Rushing

Player	DYAR	DVOA	Plays	Yds	Avg	TD	Fum	Suc
M.Tolbert	53	-1.9%	181	725	4.0	11	5	51%
R.Mathews	64	1.9%	158	678	4.3	7	4	46%
D.Sproles	-16	-17.4%	50	270	5.4	0	1	34%
J.Hester	-14	-18.7%	26	60	2.3	0	0	50%
P.Rivers	9	-0.5%	14	67	4.8	0	0	-

Offensive Line

Year	Yards	ALY	Rank	Power	Rank	Stuff	Rank	2nd Lev	Rank	Open Field	Rank
2008	4.08	4.08	20	78%	2	15%	6	1.02	28	0.69	17
2009	3.54	4.01	18	46%	32	17%	9	0.95	31	0.40	32
2010	4.18	4.12	14	61%	16	19%	19	1.11	17	0.78	14

Year	LE	Rank	LT	Rank	Mid	Rank	RT	Rank	RE	Rank	Sacks	ASR	Rank	F-Start	Cont.
2008	3.18	26	3.81	23	4.34	10	4.17	17	4.18	12	25	6.1%	17	16	33
2009	3.20	27	4.35	10	3.85	25	4.79	2	4.42	12	26	4.5%	5	16	33
2010	4.21	18	3.73	26	4.34	7	4.27	12	3.23	26	38	6.8%	19	11	28

San Diego's offensive line was one personification of the lethal combination of team talent attrition and bad feelings between management and labor that has been a growing issue for A.J. Smith and his players over the last few years. Left tackle Marcus McNeill held out after refusing to sign his original restricted free agent tender, which prompted Smith to lower the original tender offer from $3.168 million to $444,000. McNeill held out through the first five regular-season games before the Chargers finally signed him to a six-year, $48.98 million contract extension through 2015.

Replacing McNeill in those first five games was second-year man Brandyn Dombrowski, an undrafted lineman from San Diego State who was playing for the first time on the left side at the NFL level. It showed right away, as Dombrowski struggled as expected — especially in a Week 3 loss to the Seattle Seahawks, when he proved unable to stop Chris Clemons at any time through the game. When McNeill came back, it took a while for everyone to get on the same page, and quarterback Philip Rivers was under siege in a Week 6 loss to the St. Louis Rams, who sacked him seven times. Especially considering the fact that no team ran fewer three-plus-receiver sets than the Chargers, that line (with and without McNeill) proved disconcertingly unable to pick up blitzes, and this may be a function of the lack of continuity.

Left guard Kris Dielman, long considered one of the best at his position, played decently enough to make a return trip to the Pro Bowl (his fourth straight). Though the game tape doesn't always jibe with Dielman's reputation as it once did, he was a much-needed bastion of consistency. Center Nick Hardwick manned the middle for all 16 games after missing a full quarter of his possible starts in previous seasons, and 13 games in 2009. The Chargers ran the ball best up the middle, and Hardwick was the primary reason.

Things are a bit filmier on the right side — the team alternated between Louis Vasquez and Tyronne Greene at right guard, and Jeromey Clary played all 16 games at right tackle, but the Vasquez-Greene combo wasn't overwhelming. Despite the fact that Clary seemed overmatched against speed rushers a bit too often, the Chargers signed him to a new four-year, $20 million contract after the lockout was over. Clary has always had a problem with blown blocks leading to sacks, going from 8.0 in 2008 to 4.5 in 2009 to 5.0 in 2010, and leading the team in that troublesome stat in each of the last three seasons. If there's an upside to the Clary re-signing, it's that Dombrowski can develop as a swing tackle, as opposed to being planted in impossible situations by the holdouts of others. Sixth-round guard Steve Schilling from Michigan might sneak his way into that unstable right guard rotation.

Defensive Front Seven

Defensive Line	Age	Pos	Plays	TmPct	Rk	Stop	Dfts	BTkl	St%	Rk	AvYd	Rk	Sack	Hit	Hur	Runs	St%	Yds	Pass	St%	Yds
							Overall						Pass Rush			vs. Run			vs. Pass		
Antonio Garay	32	DT	48	6.5%	11	43	13	0	90%	6	0.9	11	6	0	3	41	90%	1.7	7	86%	-4.0
Jacques Cesaire	31	DE	31	4.2%	59	25	8	1	85%	31	2.4	61	1.5	2	2	26	85%	1.5	5	60%	7.0
Luis Castillo	28	DE	26	3.5%	71	20	9	1	74%	47	2.0	44	2.5	0	6	23	74%	2.7	3	100%	-2.7
Ogemdi Nwagbuo	26	DT	19	2.7%	--	11	3	1	59%	--	2.5	--	0.5	0	0	17	59%	2.6	2	50%	1.0

Linebackers	Age	Pos	Plays	TmPct	Rk	Stop	Dfts	BTkl	AvYd	Sack	Hit	Hur	Runs	St%	Rk	Yds	Rk	Tgts	Suc%	Rk	AdjYd	Rk
							Overall			Pass Rush			vs. Run					vs. Pass				
Kevin Burnett	29	ILB	101	13.6%	31	63	27	9	4.5	6	1	5	48	65%	73	3.0	51	38	65%	11	5.6	28
Shaun Phillips	30	OLB	62	8.4%	78	50	24	2	1.5	11	1	13	35	80%	10	2.7	31	9	53%	--	6.0	--
Stephen Cooper	32	ILB	49	8.8%	68	31	10	5	4.9	1	0	2	20	70%	48	3.8	85	31	58%	28	5.0	15
Antwan Applewhite	26	OLB	48	6.5%	97	30	12	4	4.0	3	3	6	29	66%	70	3.1	58	9	66%	--	4.4	--
Brandon Siler	26	ILB	37	6.6%	--	23	9	2	3.3	1	2	1	30	63%	--	3.0	--	7	91%	--	1.2	--
Antwan Barnes	27	OLB	15	2.5%	--	11	7	1	-1.1	4	2	0	9	67%	--	1.3	--	1	6%	--	8.7	--

Year	Yards	ALY	Rank	Power	Rank	Stuff	Rank	2nd Lev	Rank	Open Field	Rank
2008	4.13	4.45	25	61%	8	15%	28	1.15	19	0.44	3
2009	4.50	4.65	31	54%	4	17%	26	1.36	32	0.55	7
2010	3.74	3.86	14	50%	3	20%	14	1.06	10	0.46	6

Year	LE	Rank	LT	Rank	Mid	Rank	RT	Rank	RE	Rank	Sacks	ASR	Rank
2008	4.86	26	4.75	28	4.11	12	3.65	7	5.95	32	28	5.6%	20
2009	4.68	22	4.74	27	4.67	29	3.43	5	5.31	29	35	5.8%	22
2010	4.28	18	4.73	27	3.65	6	3.96	13	3.41	6	47	9.0%	2

And speaking of talent attrition … in the last few seasons, the Chargers' front seven has morphed from one of the league's best to a group that frequently looks outsized and outmatched. However, there were positive signs in 2010. Nose tackle Antonio Garay came out of nowhere to win a preseason battle for the position that was manned by Jamal Williams for so long, and the 31-year-old put up the first 5.5 sacks of his NFL career. The Chargers improved against runs up the middle and were stalwart against runs in short-yardage situations.

Rookie tackle Cam Thomas, who Garay beat out for the inside job, picked up two sacks in rotation. Luis Castillo and Jacques Cesaire maintained their starting end jobs through the season, each starting all 16 games, but the average level of play exhibited by the two veterans was frustrating for an easily frustrated front office, and the Chargers selected potentially dominant Illinois defensive end Corey Liuget with the 18th overall pick. Liuget should take Cesaire's spot right away.

Linebacker Shaun Phillips has quietly become one of the better quarterback disruptors in the league, but the lack of a pass rush outside of Phillips has to be an ongoing concern. 2009 first-round pick Larry English has yet to develop, held back by chronic injuries. Inside linebacker Kevin Burnett, who was second on the team with six sacks, is gone to Miami in free agency. Outside linebacker Antwan Applewhite, who played opposite Phillips, signed with San Francisco.

There will be a new combination at inside linebacker, joining experience with youth. Veteran Takeo Spikes was brought in by new defensive coordinator Greg Manusky to play the same role he played for Manusky in San Francisco:

inside run-stopper and defensive leader. Two younger players will get time next to Spikes. A.J. Smith took Michigan State's Jonas Mouton in the second round, despite the fact that nearly all draftniks had a third-day (not third-round) grade on the player. Smith predictably responded to concerns about Mouton's value by insisting that as long as Mouton had a second-round grade in his draft room, that was all that mattered. The pick and the reaction were typical of Smith's brio in such matters, but given his recent track record with alleged "sleepers," Smith may have some explaining to do if Mouton can't transcend his liabilities from college. He's a good straight-on tackler, but he tends to break down when asked to change direction in space. The Chargers should also have the services of 2010 third-round pick Donald Butler, who missed his entire rookie season with a torn Achilles tendon. Butler could very well be more talented than Mouton, despite his lower-pick status — it's a good indicator of Smith's recently inconsistent talent valuations.

Defensive Secondary

Secondary	Age	Pos	Plays	TmPct	Overall Rk	Stop	Dfts	BTkl	Runs	vs. Run St%	Rk	Yds	Rk	Tgts	vs. Pass Tgt%	Rk	Dist	Suc%	Rk	APaYd	Rk	PD	Int
Eric Weddle	26	FS	105	14.2%	5	39	13	4	53	40%	39	5.6	22	26	5.6%	44	17.7	70%	7	5.1	7	8	2
Antoine Cason	25	CB	84	11.3%	14	42	16	6	23	52%	24	6.3	39	92	20.0%	9	14.6	55%	27	6.1	15	13	4
Paul Oliver	27	SS	61	8.2%	62	19	8	7	30	40%	37	5.1	12	23	4.9%	61	13.2	55%	37	6.3	17	4	1
Quentin Jammer	32	CB	56	7.5%	59	24	9	7	11	64%	10	3.7	9	75	16.4%	30	14.9	50%	50	8.9	70	10	2
Steve Gregory	28	SS	44	10.5%	35	17	8	6	20	55%	10	5.1	12	13	5.1%	58	15.0	52%	45	7.2	33	2	2
Dante Hughes	26	CB	19	3.4%	--	9	3	0	6	50%	--	6.5	--	17	4.8%	--	4.5	56%	--	4.0	--	1	0
Donald Strickland	31	CB	19	2.6%	--	10	4	2	4	50%	--	3.5	--	21	4.6%	--	9.5	59%	--	5.5	--	2	0

Year	Pass D Rank	vs. #1 WR	Rk	vs. #2 WR	Rk	vs. Other WR	Rk	vs. TE	Rk	vs. RB	Rk
2008	20	17.0%	25	-22.8%	6	-6.8%	14	21.1%	27	-10.5%	5
2009	21	-2.4%	12	4.5%	21	3.6%	18	-7.8%	9	36.4%	32
2010	4	-35.5%	1	-4.5%	12	-26.9%	3	18.1%	26	15.4%	25

For the second straight season, free safety Eric Weddle was the Chargers' best defender. Not only is he solid in coverage, but he has a real knack for coming down and wiping out screen passes and outside run plays — particularly after other Chargers defenders have missed tackles. Weddle shows great discipline when ending a play in space; he's rarely juked or forced out of place by misdirection, which is why the Chargers can trust him as the last line of defense. Receivers running directional routes past the Chargers' linebackers could find themselves playing the role of defender if they were in the wrong place. Weddle isn't physical enough for some, but that's nitpicking when you consider his overall value to the team. He still didn't make the Pro Bowl, which makes you wonder what the poor guy has to do. For the second straight year, New England's Brandon Meriweather made the cut, and for the second straight season, Weddle was by far the better player — after all, Weddle wasn't benched twice in 2010, and Meriweather was! A.J. Smith thought more of Weddle than the Pro Bowl voters, and gave him a new five-year, $50 million deal that only offends people who don't watch Weddle on the field.

With Antonio Cromartie taking his feast-or-famine talents to New York, the pressure was on fourth-year cornerback Antoine Cason to step up, just a year after he was pushed out of the nickel corner role due to poor performance. Cason wasn't perfect in his first starting season, but he was much improved over that disastrous 2009. There was some talk about moving the 31-year-old Quentin Jammer to safety in 2011, but he's still playing well enough to keep his position as the team's top cornerback. The idea, of course, is for Cason to take that title this season. This offseason the Chargers also took a one-year, incentive-laden flyer on safety Bob Sanders, who started a total of nine games in his last three seasons with the Colts. If Sanders can somehow reconcile his small stature and kamikaze style, the Chargers could have a huge steal on their hands. As long as it's a low-risk move and the front office isn't expecting multiple starts out of Sanders, there isn't any harm in the signing. Strong safety and former cornerback Steve Gregory was undone by a four-game PED suspension four games into the season; he'll be a free agent after 2011.

Special Teams

Year	DVOA	Rank	FG/XP	Rank	Net Kick	Rank	Kick Ret	Rank	Net Punt	Rank	Punt Ret	Rank	Hidden	Rank
2008	1.7%	12	-2.4	23	-3.3	22	6.7	7	10.1	6	-1.1	18	-1.4	15
2009	0.3%	16	7.7	3	-6.1	26	-0.3	12	1.4	18	-0.7	17	10.0	2
2010	-8.6%	32	1.5	14	-17.7	32	-3.5	18	-34.3	32	3.2	12	-7.8	24

In a word, ugh. The 2010 Chargers put up the worst total Special Teams DVOA since the Buffalo Bills' epic -12.9% DVOA in 2000. The main culprits, at least in the public eye, were special teams coach Steve Crosby (who was fired) and formerly bulletproof punter Mike Scifres, who suffered five of the nine blocked punts in the league last season. However, it wasn't entirely his fault — the worst day of Scifres' career came against the Oakland Raiders on October 10, when two straight punts were blocked, and the Chargers' God-awful blocking allowed Raiders to shoot straight up the middle. San Diego went through four different long-snappers due to injury, which didn't help. In addition, the Chargers' punt return coverage teams were also the NFL's worst. Nate Kaeding didn't have a great year either. He was reasonable on field goals, missing just two kicks below 50 yards, but extremely poor on kickoff distance. This was the third straight year Kaeding was one of the league's four worst kickers in gross kickoff value, and the problem was compounded by coverage teams that were as bad on kickoffs as they were on punts.

The Chargers' return teams were no great shakes, either — Darren Sproles fell off in return productivity for the third straight season, and though Antoine Cason was one of the league's more effective punt returners, Sproles got more reps. The good news for San Diego is that special teams are the most inconsistent unit on any football team, and the Chargers can't possibly be this bad again in 2011.

Coaching Staff

The 2010 Chargers looked a lot like previous editions under Norv Turner — an early-season swoon buttressed by a late winning streak, a mad dash to late relevance, and a dynamic passing attack holding it all together. The differences between the playoff Chargers of 2009 and last year's disappointment included A.J. Smith's willingness to play chicken with some of his most talented players, draft disappointments coming home to roost, and proof positive that epically horrible special teams performances can negate serious defensive improvements.

The man responsible for those defensive improvements, Ron Rivera, is now charged with turning the Carolina Panthers around. He has been replaced in San Diego by Greg Manusky, who previously installed similar improvements on the defense in San Francisco. Of course, the real challenge is laid at the feet of new special teams coach Rich Bisaccia. Most of the Chargers' other 2010 coaches are still with the team, giving the franchise that advantage over staffs with more changes in the wake of the lockout.

San Francisco 49ers

2010 Record: 6-10

Pythagorean Wins: 6.8 (20th)

DVOA: -10.0% (23rd)

Offense: -7.3% (24th)

Defense: 1.4% (13th)

Special Teams: -1.4% (22nd)

Variance: 24.5% (29th)

2011 Mean Projection: 7.5 wins

On the Clock (0-3): 1%

Loserville (4-6): 28%

Mediocrity (7-8): 41%

Playoff Contender (9-10): 25%

Super Bowl Contender (11+): 5%

Projected Average Opponent: -3.7% (32nd)

2010: Mike Singletary loses his locker room.

2011: In the NFC West, the mediocre can become champions.

Alex Smith started 10 games for San Francisco last season, and Troy Smith started six. Yet it was a journeyman quarterback, a passer whose season consisted entirely of one lousy game, who ironically defined the 49ers' 2010 campaign.

Late in a loss to the Eagles that would drop the 49ers to 0-5, Alex Smith trotted off the field following another three-and-out. The crowd made their feelings known loud and clear as a nation watched on Sunday night: "We want Carr! We want Carr!"

Carr? David Carr? The guy who played his way out of three cities in four seasons? The guy with the career record of 23-56 and a passer rating of 75.2? You want *that* David Carr?

In defense of the fans, they didn't really want Carr; they just wanted someone who was not Alex Smith. In the five frustrating years since the 49ers had made Smith the draft's first overall selection, the fans had seen enough of their so-called franchise quarterback. They had seen enough fumbles, enough interceptions, enough dumpoffs on third down. They saw a team with an explosive running back, a uniquely gifted tight end, and a sturdy defense, and thought they could win a weak division if they could just get average quarterback play.

The thing is, though, after stinking up the Bay Area for his entire career, Smith finally *was* average in 2010. The 49ers' eighth straight non-playoff season had as much to do with an overmatched coaching staff, gaping holes at key positions on both sides of the ball, and other quarterbacks as it did with Smith.

The whole thing was a mess, and it cost head coach Mike Singletary his job when all was said and done. In steps new coach Jim Harbaugh, who lasted 15 seasons as an NFL quarterback himself before turning the Stanford Cardinal into a top-ten college program. Though the lockout prohibited Harbaugh from making sweeping changes to his new team, he did immediately make one decision that Singletary never could, stating front and center that Alex Smith is his guy.

"I've been studying Alex Smith and watching him," Harbaugh said on Sports 1140 AM in Sacramento, "and I believe that Alex Smith can be a winning quarterback in the National Football League."

"Hey, here comes Alex/Yes it's true, your darkest nightmare, horror show."
— *Die Toten Hosen, "Return of Alex," 1994*

Fed up 49ers fans may see Smith in their nightmares, but in 2010, he was nobody's horror show. On the other hand, he wasn't particularly good, either. He was merely average. Ridiculously average. A grayish, flavorless, puddle of mediocrity. His raw numbers, especially, look like they were lifted directly from the bottom line of a league-wide stats table. His passer

2011 49ers Schedule

Week	Opp.	Week	Opp.	Week	Opp.
1	SEA	7	BYE	13	STL
2	DAL	8	CLE	14	at ARI
3	at CIN	9	at WAS	15	PIT (Mon.)
4	at PHI	10	NYG	16	at SEA
5	TB	11	ARI	17	at STL
6	at DET	12	at BAL (Thu.)		

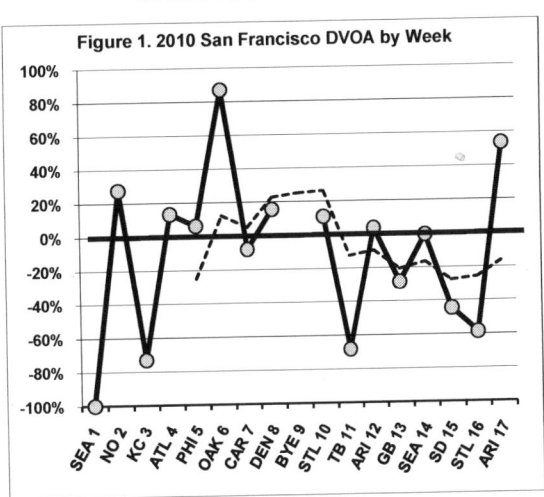

Figure 1. 2010 San Francisco DVOA by Week

rating was virtually equal to the league average, and breaking the rating down to its four component parts shows that Smith did everything at C level (Table 1).

Table 1. Alex Smith, C Student

2010 Stat	Smith	NFL Avg.
Comp Pct	59.6%	60.8%
Yd/Att	6.9	7.0
TD Rate	4.1%	4.3%
INT Rate	2.9%	3.0%
Passer Rating	82.1	82.2

Now those are just his raw numbers, and if you've read this far you know how we feel about raw numbers. Smith was 33rd in passing DVOA, a number that accounts for the NFC West defenses Smith faced, his sack rate, and his affection for third-down dumpoffs that pad his raw stats but don't help his team win games.

Even there, though, Smith's total DVOA doesn't tell his entire story. Smith started the year with a disaster of a game, averaging only 5.0 yards per attempt and throwing two interceptions against Seattle in Week 1. It was a game you will not find defended here nor anywhere else, a minus-171 DYAR game in which Smith and his receivers appeared to be playing different sports.

Smith played well the next week in a close loss to the Saints, then struggled in a Week 3 loss to Kansas City. Offensive coordinator Jimmy Raye was fired after that game, but it didn't matter much — in a Week 4 loss to Atlanta, the 49ers scored only 14 points, half of them on a blocked punt.

Next came Week 5, the Eagles, and We Want Carr. By the end of the game all anyone remembered was the 49ers' 0-5 record and the cries for a change at quarterback. Nobody seemed to notice that after fans demanded he be benched, Smith talked Singletary

into leaving him in the game. He then completed 11 of his next 12 passes, leading San Francisco on a pair of touchdown drives and nearly pulling out a win before he was hit during a pass attempt and lofted a game-ending interception.

That seemed to be a watershed moment for Smith, who was quietly efficient from that point on. Through Week 5, Smith had thrown six touchdowns and nine interceptions, and ranked 30th out of 39 qualifying quarterbacks with a DVOA of -17.6%. From Week 6 onward, he threw eight touchdowns with only one interception, and his DVOA of 10.1% ranked 19th out of 44. He was consistent, too, with a DVOA of 12.4% or higher in all but one of his games over the second half of the season. His late success, though, was masked by that 0-5 record and the ensuing quarterback controversy — the random, chaotic quarterback controversy.

"Alexander the Great/He died of fever in Babylon"
— *Iron Maiden, "Alexander the Great," 1986*

According to the Greek historian Plutarch of Chaeronea, when Alexander the Great arrived at Troy in 334 B.C., he mourned his fallen ancestors by running naked around their graves. We have no evidence that Mike Singletary used nude footraces through cemeteries to determine his starting quarterbacks, but it couldn't have been any less logical than what actually unfolded.

The fans who so desperately chanted Carr's name in Week 5 finally got him in Week 7 when Smith injured his shoulder against Carolina. Carr took the field with a tie score against a winless team and proceeded to complete just five of 13 passes for 67 yards and a key interception, costing San Francisco the game. It was Carr's final game of the season, and quite possibly his career.

With nowhere else to turn, Singletary, like Alexander the Great, arrived at Troy — Troy Smith, the former Heisman Trophy winner who had languished on Baltimore's bench for years. In his first start since 2007, Smith scorched the Broncos in London, going 12-for-19 for 196 yards and a 64.7% DVOA. Following the bye week, Smith ripped the Rams, going 17-of-28 for 356 yards and a 55.7% DVOA in an overtime win.

The 49ers had won two in a row behind Smith, but there were cracks in the armor. The Rams had sacked Smith five times, exploiting his tendency to hold the ball and look for big plays downfield. Given the opportunity to study game tape, opponents realized that if you just took away the deep ball, Smith had nothing else. After that Rams game, Smith completed fewer than half his passes, with a DVOA of -46.5%, and not a single game above replacement level.

Over the last part of the season, the two Smiths moved in and out of the starting lineup basically at random. Following his good games against the Broncos and Rams, Troy stunk up the joint against the Bucs, Cards, and Packers. In Week 14 he was benched for Alex, whose second tenure as a starter lasted all of two games. Troy started again in Week 16, but was benched again for Alex *in that same game* after a sideline shouting match with Singletary. With the fall of Troy complete, Alex finished the season as he began, as the 49ers' starting quarterback.

The erratic performance at quarterback was not the only problem plaguing San Francisco. There was plenty of blame to go around for the 49ers' struggles, starting with an offensive line that couldn't provide decent pass protection. The 49ers overall passing numbers were pretty ugly, but they were especially dreadful in non-blitz situations. Against four or fewer pass rushers, the 49ers were 31st in Success Rate and 29th in sack rate. Opponents didn't need elaborate schemes or tactics to put 49ers passers on the ground. They could just count on their rushers to beat San Francisco's blockers one-on-one, and it usually worked.

On the other side of the ball, San Francisco's reputation as an intimidating defense was only partly accurate. They were every bit as effective against the run as you've heard, but opponents had little trouble moving the ball through the air. And the deeper the pass, the more trouble the 49ers had defending it. The San Francisco defense had a success rate of just 42 percent on passes 20 or more yards past the line of scrimmage. No other defense was below 50 percent.

Free agency brought massive changes to the defensive side of the ball. Not all of those changes were negative (Carlos Rogers should be both better and cheaper than Nate Clements, for example), but the defense could see as many as six new starters, which is an awful lot of turnover to overcome in one year.

Meanwhile, the 49ers did little in the draft or free agency to boost their offensive line, hoping instead that Davis and Iupati will improve. If they can't, it'll be up to Alex Smith and his receivers to build chemistry together if the team is going to improve this season. So it's unfortunate that the team's best wideout has shown little interest in playing with his quarterback.

"I am human and I need to be loved/Just like everybody else does"
— *The Smiths, "How Soon Is Now?," 1984*

Even though he was technically a free agent, Alex Smith took a leadership role in organizing informal offensive player workouts during the lockout. A few linemen attended, but the exercise was primarily for quarterbacks and receivers to run routes and establish timing and chemistry. Conspicuous by his absence: Michael Crabtree, the 49ers' first-round draft choice in 2009 who was coming off a disappointing sophomore season. A reporter from the *San Jose Mercury News* asked Smith where Crabtree was. "Great question," Smith said. "Asking the wrong guy, honestly."

Crabtree finally arrived, weeks after his teammates. His first move: publicly questioning Smith's status as the team's leader. When asked if catching passes from Smith would build chemistry, Crabtree responded with a question of his own: "Who's the quarterback?" He was then told that Smith was almost certain to start in 2011, but he sounded unconvinced. "He's the quarterback? I'm just asking," he said, adding, "I wish I could tell you who is going to be the quarterback. I don't know. I don't know. Whoever the quarterback is, I'm 100 percent down with it and I'm ready to go. That's it."

Crabtree proceeded to work out for one day, then took several days off, claiming his feet were sore from working in new cleats.

For his part, Smith tried to mend fences with Crabtree, saying he was "disgusted" with himself for his choice of words, that it "looked like a jab," and that he had apologized to Crabtree. As for Crabtree's doubt that Smith would be the starter, Smith reminded everyone that he was a free agent and not technically on the roster. "So for (Crabtree) to be confused as to the quarterback situation isn't the strangest thing in the world in my opinion."

Later, Smith said his perceived feud with Crabtree was "something that has been totally off-base," and that "Things have come out in the paper that I think we both wish we could take back. I know I feel that way."

The controversy lasted long enough that in mid-July, as the lockout was winding down, Niners general manager Trent Baalke was still talking about it. "It's like any relationship, right?" he told Tim Kawakami of the *San Jose Mercury News*. "When you're growing up with your family, your friends, there's going to be disagreements. There's going to be arguments. There's going to be fights. Those things happen, especially in a competitive environment, which these guys are in.

"So when these guys have a little spat here or there or have a little disagreement, that's part of it. They're grown men, they'll figure it out."

Perhaps this was all blown out of proportion by a news-starved media that had nothing better to do during the lockout. But if nothing else, it showed a remarkable lack of communication between a quarterback and receiver, particularly when those players have showed a lack of on-field chemistry to go with it.

Smith's relationship with his star receiver may be contentious, but at least he knows he'll have a better relationship with his head coach. From the moment he took office, Jim Harbaugh made it clear that he had faith in Smith and that he wanted him back with the team. Even after the 49ers drafted Colin Kaepernick in the second round, Harbaugh couldn't stop gushing about Smith. "The plan for Alex is unchanged," Harbaugh said after Kaepernick was drafted. "Alex has the ability and the license to be the starting quarterback."

That's all well and good for 2011, but afterwards? The 49ers didn't draft Kaepernick to sit on the bench, and at some point he'll have to see the field. In a somewhat similar situation, Drew Brees couldn't hold off Philip Rivers in San Diego, and Alex Smith is no Drew Brees.

So this is what fate has dealt Alex Smith: A one-year tryout in 2011 to try and reach the playoffs. Success means a starting job somewhere else in 2012. Failure likely means a new occupation. Time to put that Utah economics degree to work.

Meanwhile, the 49ers find themselves with a new coach, a lame duck quarterback, a star receiver who doesn't play well with others, and a makeshift defense with new faces across the roster. They would contend for last place in most divisions. In the NFC West, they have as good a shot as anyone.

Vince Verhei

2010 49ers Stats by Week

Wk	vs.	W-L	PF	PA	YDF	YDA	TO	Total	Off	Def	ST
1	@SEA	L	6	31	263	242	-1	-102%	-78%	17%	-7%
2	NO	L	22	25	417	287	-4	28%	28%	-6%	-6%
3	@KC	L	10	31	251	457	0	-73%	-31%	39%	-4%
4	@ATL	L	14	16	262	357	-1	13%	-18%	-33%	-1%
5	PHI	L	24	27	364	352	-4	6%	0%	-3%	4%
6	OAK	W	17	9	349	179	2	87%	22%	-60%	5%
7	@CAR	L	20	23	282	379	2	-8%	-1%	11%	5%
8	DEN	W	24	16	339	398	2	15%	13%	2%	5%
9	BYE										
10	STL	W	23	20	421	332	0	11%	25%	17%	3%
11	TB	L	0	21	189	299	-2	-68%	-59%	11%	2%
12	@ARI	W	27	6	386	203	1	4%	14%	0%	-10%
13	@GB	L	16	34	269	410	-1	-29%	-7%	21%	0%
14	SEA	W	40	21	336	361	5	0%	6%	-15%	-22%
15	@SD	L	7	34	192	374	-1	-45%	-13%	29%	-2%
16	@STL	L	17	25	331	335	-1	-59%	-48%	18%	7%
17	ARI	W	38	7	362	279	2	54%	28%	-29%	-3%

Trends and Splits

	Offense	Rank	Defense	Rank
Total DVOA	-7.3%	24	1.4%	13
Unadjusted VOA	-4.6%	24	-2.4%	8
Weighted Trend	-2.0%	23	1.6%	12
Variance	10.3%	25	6.5%	15
Average Opponent	4.8%	10	-3.6%	6
Passing	-0.7%	25	14.2%	24
Rushing	-1.8%	17	-13.8%	6
First Down	-5.8%	27	2.3%	11
Second Down	-10.2%	26	-0.9%	13
Third Down	-5.8%	21	3.2%	18
First Half	-8.1%	24	-0.7%	15
Second Half	-6.4%	23	3.3%	18
Red Zone	5.3%	11	-14.8%	9
Late and Close	0.8%	19	2.7%	21

Five-Year Performance

Year	W-L	Pyth	Est W	PF	PA	TO	Total	Rk	Off	Rk	Def	Rk	ST	Rk	Off AGL	Rk	Def AGL	Rk
2006	7-9	5.1	6.2	298	412	-5	-19.3%	27	-7.5%	23	11.8%	29	0.0%	18	19.4	19	6.2	5
2007	5-11	3.7	4.0	219	364	-12	-34.2%	31	-31.3%	32	7.4%	24	4.5%	4	31.8	28	19.5	15
2008	7-9	6.9	6.9	339	381	-17	-13.9%	25	-11.3%	27	7.3%	18	4.6%	3	24.9	18	5.4	3
2009	8-8	9.5	7.8	280	390	-8	1.0%	20	-10.2%	23	-11.8%	3	-0.6%	19	9.5	8	34.1	22
2010	6-10	6.8	7.1	305	346	-1	-10.0%	23	-7.3%	24	1.4%	13	-1.4%	22	20.7	11	6.8	3

Strategic Tendencies

Run/Pass		Rank	Offense		Rank	Defense		Rank	Other		Rank
Runs, all plays	39%	19	3+ WR	43%	25	Rush 3	8.7%	15	2+ RB, Pct Runs	58%	17
Runs, first half	42%	9	4+ WR	6%	17	Rush 4	66.4%	7	1 RB/2 TE, Pct Runs	43%	26
Runs, first down	47%	21	2+ TE	36%	6	Rush 5	19.7%	26	1 RB/3+ WR, Pct Runs	23%	15
Runs, second-long	36%	13	Single back	56%	19	Rush 6+	5.1%	26	CB1 on WR1	31%	26
Runs, power sit.	48%	29	Play action	19%	15	Zone Blitz	7.1%	11	Go for it on 4th	0.76	23
Runs, behind 2H	22%	27	Max protect	7%	26	Sacks by LB	62.5%	6	Offensive Pace	31.8	24
Pass, ahead 2H	37%	27	Outside pocket	17%	5	Sacks by DB	6.9%	21	Defensive Pace	32.0	30

Jim Harbaugh should have some good players for installing a YAC-friendly West Coast system, because the 49ers already led the league with 6.7 average yards after catch last season. They had 5.8 average yards after catch on passes past the line of scrimmage, where only two other offenses were above 5.0. ☞ Harbaugh may also have a quarterback who can find the hot read. Surprisingly, Alex Smith excels against big blitzes. Last year he gained 11.2 yards per play on the big blitz of six or more defenders, compared to 5.7 yards per play otherwise. The year before, he gained 7.7 yards per play against the big blitz, and 5.5 yards per play otherwise. ☞ San Francisco threw a league-low 10 percent of passes to the "short middle" area of the field (NFL average was 18 percent). That's bound to change in Harbaugh's offense. ☞ San Francisco allowed 5.1 yards per play on zone blitzes, compared to 6.5 yards per play on other pass plays. ☞ San Francisco opponents threw to running backs on a league-high 25 percent of passes.

Passing

Player	DYAR	DVOA	Plays	NtYds	Avg	YAC	C%	TD	Int
A.Smith	134	-5.4%	367	2243	6.1	6.1	61.1%	14	10
T.Smith	-18	-12.8%	168	1130	6.7	7.9	51.4%	5	4
D.Carr	-26	-51.1%	13	62	4.8	9.2	41.7%	0	1

Rushing

Player	DYAR	DVOA	Plays	Yds	Avg	TD	Fum	Suc
F.Gore	-2	-8.9%	203	853	4.2	3	3	48%
B.Westbrook	75	17.3%	76	337	4.4	4	0	45%
A.Dixon	-18	-14.4%	70	237	3.4	2	0	46%
T.Smith	9	-1.9%	18	123	6.8	1	2	-
A.Smith	5	-0.4%	11	66	6.0	0	0	-

Receiving

Player	DYAR	DVOA	Plays	Ctch	Yds	Y/C	YAC	TD	C%
M.Crabtree	120	2.8%	100	55	741	13.5	5.3	6	55%
J.Morgan	59	-3.2%	80	44	698	15.9	6.8	2	55%
T.Ginn	-61	-35.9%	35	12	163	13.6	1.8	1	34%
D.Zeigler	-7	-19.4%	15	9	98	10.9	1.6	0	60%
V.Davis	207	27.5%	93	56	914	16.3	7.5	7	60%
D.Walker	24	0.3%	46	30	336	11.2	5.8	0	65%
N.Byham	-9	-28.7%	6	5	27	5.4	5.2	0	83%
F.Gore	57	0.4%	72	46	452	9.8	10.0	2	64%
B.Westbrook	22	2.6%	25	17	153	9.0	9.0	1	68%
M.Norris	-19	-44.5%	9	4	20	5.0	3.5	0	44%

Offensive Line

Year	Yards	ALY	Rank	Power	Rank	Stuff	Rank	2nd Lev	Rank	Open Field	Rank
2008	3.96	4.30	7	52%	32	17%	11	1.01	29	0.51	30
2009	4.24	3.51	32	63%	16	23%	31	0.92	32	1.25	4
2010	4.05	4.14	13	56%	23	17%	11	1.04	25	0.65	20

Year	LE	Rank	LT	Rank	Mid	Rank	RT	Rank	RE	Rank	Sacks	ASR	Rank	F-Start	Cont.
2008	4.90	8	3.94	20	4.54	4	3.55	29	3.88	21	55	9.4%	31	24	26
2009	4.58	13	2.63	32	3.51	29	3.22	31	4.22	17	40	8.1%	26	16	31
2010	4.31	16	5.10	2	3.92	18	4.96	3	3.04	30	44	8.9%	30	20	33

In 2009, few teams in the NFL could sport a unit as shoddy as the 49ers' offensive line. San Francisco aggressively addressed the situation in the draft, trading up two picks in the first round to select Rutgers' Anthony Davis, then grabbing Idaho guard Mike Iupati later in the round. The rookies started from day one: Davis at right tackle, Iupati at left guard. Former left guard David Baas slid over to center, and along with holdovers Joe Staley at left tackle and right guard Chilo Rachal, the line took a giant step forward towards adequate run blocking in 2010.

Unfortunately, the same can't be said for pass protection. Both Davis and Staley played like they had lead in their shoes, struggling to keep up with smaller, speedier rushers. When 49ers played Kansas City, the Chiefs matched Tamba Hali up against whichever tackle didn't have tight end help, and he ate their lunches, getting sacks against both men. Davis also looked unprepared for NFL schemes, as stunts and blitzes sometimes left him completely mystified. He had 13 blown blocks that led to sacks or offensive holding calls, the highest total in the five years we've been charting that stat. Staley, meanwhile, had been San Francisco's best lineman before tearing ligaments in his knee in 2009. In 2010, he managed nine games of sub-average performance before breaking his leg against St. Louis, costing him the final seven games of the season. When Staley was injured in 2009, the dropoff between him and Barry Sims was obvious. When Sims took over for Staley in 2010, nobody really noticed. After two injury-ravaged seasons, it's doubtful that Staley will ever be a dominant player in the future.

In defense of the line, the 49ers fielded two quarterbacks with terrible pocket presence, and both Troy and Alex Smith bear some responsibility for that 30th-ranked Adjusted Sack Rate. There's a lot of room for improvement here, but these players should have time to grow together. Baas left for the Giants in free agency, but the other four remaining starters are all under 30. The 49ers signed 10-year veteran Jonathan Goodwin from the Saints to take Baas' spot. Goodwin hasn't missed a start in two years. Also, another full year of continuity and experience for Davis and Iupati can only help matters. The struggles of Davis are not a sign of a draft bust. They are a sign of the fact that rookie tackles often struggle.

Defensive Front Seven

Defensive Line	Age	Pos	Plays	TmPct	Rk	Stop	Dfts	BTkl	St%	Rk	AvYd	Rk	Sack	Hit	Hur	Runs	St%	Yds	Pass	St%	Yds
Justin Smith	32	DE	71	8.3%	9	54	20	0	76%	49	1.8	36	8.5	9	20	55	76%	2.2	16	75%	0.3
Aubrayo Franklin	31	DT	40	4.7%	34	36	4	1	89%	5	1.8	35	0	0	0	38	89%	1.9	2	100%	0.5
Isaac Sopoaga	30	DE	26	3.0%	80	22	6	2	89%	13	1.9	42	1.5	1	3	19	89%	1.4	7	71%	3.3
Ray McDonald	27	DE	21	2.5%	--	17	8	2	78%	--	1.5	--	0	0	14	18	78%	1.5	3	100%	1.3
Demetric Evans	32	DE	16	1.9%	--	13	4	0	77%	--	2.1	--	0	1	2	13	77%	2.7	3	100%	-0.3

Linebackers	Age	Pos	Plays	TmPct	Rk	Stop	Dfts	BTkl	AvYd	Sack	Hit	Hur	Runs	St%	Rk	Yds	Rk	Tgts	Suc%	Rk	AdjYd	Rk
									Overall		Pass Rush			vs. Run						vs. Pass		
Patrick Willis	26	ILB	132	16.5%	11	70	24	5	4.7	6	2	9.5	69	57%	94	4.7	104	33	52%	48	4.4	8
Takeo Spikes	35	ILB	117	13.7%	29	72	13	2	4.2	0	2	5.5	73	73%	34	2.7	32	36	52%	47	5.7	30
Manny Lawson	27	OLB	57	6.7%	93	34	12	2	3.3	2.5	9	15.5	31	71%	42	2.7	29	13	64%	--	4.2	--
Parys Haralson	27	OLB	42	5.3%	107	30	11	2	2.3	4	5	12.5	29	83%	7	2.3	19	10	42%	--	6.0	--
Travis LaBoy	30	OLB	30	4.0%	--	17	7	3	2.1	5	6	11	18	50%	--	3.5	--	3	-7%	--	16.9	--
Ahmad Brooks	27	OLB	28	3.5%	--	21	12	2	1.5	5	5	12.5	15	80%	--	1.1	--	8	47%	--	3.8	--
NaVorro Bowman	23	ILB	26	3.0%	--	17	6	4	5.1	0	0	1	11	82%	--	3.3	--	10	25%	--	8.2	--

Year	Yards	ALY	Rank	Power	Rank	Stuff	Rank	2nd Lev	Rank	Open Field	Rank
2008	3.89	4.03	12	70%	22	17%	17	1.09	15	0.53	8
2009	3.73	3.68	8	64%	16	20%	14	1.08	8	0.59	9
2010	3.36	3.56	3	61%	11	19%	18	0.78	1	0.48	7

Year	LE	Rank	LT	Rank	Mid	Rank	RT	Rank	RE	Rank	Sacks	ASR	Rank
2008	3.36	7	4.63	25	3.96	10	4.03	16	4.26	21	30	5.0%	26
2009	4.15	13	3.09	1	3.72	10	3.66	9	3.56	9	44	7.8%	3
2010	3.80	9	3.98	16	3.63	5	3.18	4	3.23	4	36	6.4%	14

The 49ers rotated their outside linebackers so heavily that both backups (Travis LaBoy and Ahmad Brooks) finished with more sacks than either starter (Manny Lawson and Parys Haralson). Expect that to change this season with the arrival of Aldon Smith, the seventh overall pick in the draft. A defensive end with the Missouri Tigers, the 263-pound Smith fits as an outside linebacker in the 49ers' 3-4 defense. At the same time, he has the versatility to put a hand in the dirt as a pure pass rushing end in nickel situations, or in any unusual fronts defensive coordinator Vic Fangio can dream of. Haralson will battle Brooks for the other starting spot, with Lawson and LaBoy having left in free agency.

On the inside, Patrick Willis had something of an off year — meaning, he was a an A- player instead of an A+. Though he still excelled in pass defense — both rushing the passer and in coverage (he's the biggest reason San Francisco had the league's best defense against tight ends) — his role against the run was that of a cleanup man, with most of his tackles coming farther downfield than you'd expect. Instead, Takeo Spikes was the run-stuffer, finishing tenth in the league in successful run tackles. However you want to slice it, the duo deserve a great deal of credit for San Francisco's terrific run defense — you don't lead the league in SLY allowed without elite linebacker play. Spikes signed with the Chargers in free agency. His place will be taken by 2010 third-rounder NaVorro Bowman.

Justin Smith enjoyed his best season since arriving in San Francisco in 2008, but he's been quietly effective through the years and puts up big numbers for a 3-4 end. Hopefully he and Aldon Smith can enjoy success as bookend pass rushers, if only because it would probably lead to a great nickname. The 49ers kept nose tackle Aubrayo Franklin around with the franchise tag in 2010, but didn't put up much of a fight for him in 2011, and he signed with New Orleans. The 49ers will slide defensive end Isaac Sopoaga over to the nose tackle, and promote Ray McDonald into Sopoaga's spot at end. A third-round draftee in 2007, McDonald started nine games in 2008, but otherwise has been strictly a bench player for San Francisco.

Defensive Secondary

Secondary	Age	Pos	Plays	TmPct	Rk	Stop	Dfts	BTkl	Runs	St%	Rk	Yds	Rk	Tgts	Tgt%	Rk	Dist	Suc%	Rk	APaYd	Rk	PD	Int
								Overall			vs. Run						vs. Pass						
Nate Clements	32	CB	91	10.7%	20	43	25	6	30	43%	41	4.8	19	71	14.9%	46	11.8	50%	51	7.9	55	6	3
Dashon Goldson	27	FS	83	9.7%	48	24	11	8	37	38%	46	6.3	35	28	5.8%	40	14.9	52%	46	8.7	53	3	1
Shawntae Spencer	29	CB	51	6.0%	78	22	8	11	3	67%	5	6.0	31	69	14.6%	52	11.0	41%	84	8.2	60	9	3
Reggie Smith	25	SS	36	4.2%	80	11	5	6	9	56%	9	5.8	23	20	4.2%	70	10.8	54%	38	4.3	4	4	1
Taylor Mays	23	SS	33	3.9%	82	11	1	1	15	47%	26	7.5	52	14	2.9%	78	23.6	21%	81	18.4	81	1	0
Tarell Brown	26	CB	29	3.6%	--	8	5	1	3	0%	--	7.3	--	33	7.5%	--	9.4	34%	--	7.3	--	4	1

Year	Pass D Rank	vs. #1 WR	Rk	vs. #2 WR	Rk	vs. Other WR	Rk	vs. TE	Rk	vs. RB	Rk
2008	19	8.1%	20	0.8%	17	8.2%	26	3.3%	17	-4.4%	8
2009	7	5.9%	17	-33.2%	1	-18.9%	6	-13.3%	6	15.5%	23
2010	24	31.3%	30	33.3%	31	6.1%	22	-16.9%	1	-2.9%	10

The pre-lockout, pre-free agency draft of this section said that all four starters could be gone by 2012. Turns out the 49ers changed faster than we expected, releasing cornerback Nate Clements, sending a mass e-mail to every team in the league saying that Taylor Mays was available for trade, and waiting until the very last minute (August 8) to re-sign safety Dashon Goldson.

So what's left? Shawntae Spencer will return at one cornerback. He's due more than $3 million in each of the next two years, but he didn't play like a $6 million man last year. The other corner will be Carlos Rogers, who in six years with the Redskins was basically average in coverage, with little big-play ability (only eight interceptions in his career). Third-round cornerback Chris Culliver figures to see a lot of playing time. He clashed with coaches at South Carolina, but he has man-to-man coverage skills and has also played safety. Last year's nickelback Tarell Brown actually started briefly ahead of Clements in 2009, but quickly played his way back to the bench.

Safety Donte Whitner comes over from Buffalo, where he was one of the NFL's premiere cleanup men (second among safeties in percentage of team's plays, but 62nd in Stop Rate). The other safety will either be Goldson or Reggie Smith, who started seven games last year only because Mays was such a disaster. Smith's contract expires at the end of the season, so he'll be playing to stay in the league this year. The 49ers also signed former Vikings starter Madieu Williams for depth.

And then there's Mays. He started six games in his rookie season, but soon found himself back on the sideline when opponents realized he was hopeless against play-fakes. His fate was sealed against Denver in London, when he gave up 96 yards to Brandon Lloyd on a pair of play-action passes, and he was also badly fooled on a flea-flicker that resulted in an easy 38-yard touchdown to Jabar Gaffney that was called back for a chop block. At press time, he had not been traded and was still practicing with the 49ers, but it's hard to see that relationship lasting long.

Special Teams

Year	DVOA	Rank	FG/XP	Rank	Net Kick	Rank	Kick Ret	Rank	Net Punt	Rank	Punt Ret	Rank	Hidden	Rank
2008	4.6%	3	4.4	8	9.6	3	6.0	8	5.6	10	1.4	10	-1.0	14
2009	-0.6%	19	1.9	15	2.6	13	-3.6	17	12.8	3	-17.5	32	-16.2	31
2010	-1.4%	22	-1.3	22	-11.8	30	-5.0	22	4.9	13	5.1	8	-1.6	16

Joe Nedney's midseason knee strain may have signaled the end of his career — he's now a 38-year-old kicker with an injury history (he also missed two games in 2009), which is just the kind of player teams love to replace. In his place the 49ers tried Shane Andrus, who missed two field goals in his only game, and then former Steeler Jeff Reed, who hit 9-of-10 field goals but was a disaster on kickoffs. Between short kicks and long returns, Reed's kickoffs cost the Niners 14 points in field position in just half a season. Only Nate Kaeding in San Diego and Ryan Longwell in Minnesota were worst when it came to net kickoff value, and it took them 16 games each to inch ahead of Reed. The 49ers will replace Reed with former Eagle David Akers, who has consistently ranked in the top ten in kickoff value. His field-goal kicking has been a little more adventurous in recent seasons.

Going by gross punt value, Andy Lee was still among the top five players at his position, but his coverage teams let him down on more than one occasion. Ted Ginn, Jr., was also a top-five punt returner, but was well below average returning kickoffs. He's only 26 years old and has four total career kick return touchdowns, so he must be considered a dangerous weapon, if not a particularly reliable one.

Coaching Staff

It may seem like a rapid rise up the coaching ranks for Jim Harbaugh, but he actually brings 17 years coaching experience to San Francisco. His Stanford teams favored a power-running attack — the Cardinal only passed the ball about 40 percent of the time under Harbaugh, despite the presence of the nation's best quarterback in Andrew Luck. Harbaugh's offense also featured a healthy dose of tight ends (three of them caught at least 16 balls last season), so his scheme and philosophy should mesh well with the 49ers' existing talent. And of course, Harbaugh deserves some credit for Luck's development. Whether he can have similar success with Alex Smith and Colin Kaepernick remains to be seen. New defensive coordinator Vic Fangio was with Harbaugh at Stanford in 2010, but also has 11 years experience as an NFL coordinator with the Panthers, Colts, and Texans. He has experience running both the 3-4 and the 4-3, and has used a healthy dose of blitzes in the past. Running Fangio's 4-3 in 2000, Colts linebackers and defensive backs totaled 14 sacks, a number that seems impossible given the Colts' defensive strategies since he left town.

Seattle Seahawks

2010 Record: 7-9

Pythagorean Wins: 5.5 (28th)

DVOA: -24.0% (30th)

Offense: -14.3% (29th)

Defense: 15.0% (29th)

Special Teams: 5.3% (3rd)

Variance: 28.9% (31st)

2011 Mean Projection: 5.4 wins

On the Clock (0-3): 21%

Loserville (4-6): 47%

Mediocrity (7-8): 22%

Playoff Contender (9-10): 9%

Super Bowl Contender (11+): 2%

Projected Average Opponent: -0.6% (18th)

2010: Transitional squad stumbles into history as the worst playoff team ever.

2011: Strangers on the line, exchanging glances… strangers on the line, in three-point stances…

Take one team that won a playoff game last January. Add two highly drafted players on the offensive line, plus another lineman returning from injury and a fourth blocker gained in free agency. Speaking of free agency, let's throw in clear upgrades at wide receiver and tight end. After all those additions, make one key subtraction, cutting loose a washed-up quarterback. Make all those moves, and what do you get?

If our projections are correct, you get the worst offense in the NFL.

This is not fantasy football, where a bunch of players score and perform independently of each other. It's not baseball, where nine hitters take turns trying to get hits one at a time. In the NFL, chemistry and continuity aren't just soundbites for coaches' press conferences, they're critical elements to winning games. And in the weirdest, shortest offseason in recent history, the Seahawks have a brand new collection of players who are just barely getting to know each other. The list of fresh faces on offense runs all the way from offensive coordinator (Darrell Bevell) to quarterback (Tarvaris Jackson) to wide receiver (Sidney Rice) to tight end (Zach Miller) and finally to the offensive line.

Ah yes, the offensive line. Partly due to bad luck, partly by design, the Seahawks have put together a line in which *no two starters have ever played a meaningful snap together.*

The Seahawks brought in three starters on the line,

and they'll be joining two very inexperienced players. Left tackle Russell Okung has played only one season in Seattle, while center Max Unger has played only two. Due to various injuries, though, they've never actually played together. Between them they've started only 27 games for the Seahawks. Seattle will be just the eleventh team since 1999 (not counting expansion teams) to field an offensive line with fewer than five combined seasons of tenure with that team (Table 1).

Not surprisingly, offenses that overhaul their offen-

Table 1: Rebuilding the Wall: Most Inexperienced Offensive Lines, 1999-2011

Year	Team	Tenure with Team, Seasons	DVOA Prev Yr.	DVOA That Year	Change
1999	PHI	3	-26.8%	-28.7%	-1.9%
2000	CLE	3	-17.3%	-30.0%	-12.7%
2001	CAR	4	-19.5%	-29.6%	-10.1%
2001	NE	4	-5.6%	0.6%	6.2%
2003	HOU	3	-41.4%	-16.4%	25.0%
2004	MIA	3	-6.6%	-28.5%	-21.9%
2004	SD	2	2.2%	18.2%	16.0%
2007	CLE	2	-15.5%	8.5%	24.0%
2009	BUF	4	-5.3%	-17.1%	-11.8%
2009	CLE	4	-16.4%	-13.0%	3.4%
2011	SEA	3	-14.3%	?	?

Expansion teams not included.

2011 Seahawks Schedule

Week	Opp.	Week	Opp.	Week	Opp.
1	at SF	7	at CLE	13	PHI (Thu.)
2	at PIT	8	CIN	14	STL (Mon.)
3	ARI	9	at DAL	15	at CHI
4	ATL	10	BAL	16	SF
5	at NYG	11	at STL	17	at ARI
6	BYE	12	WAS		

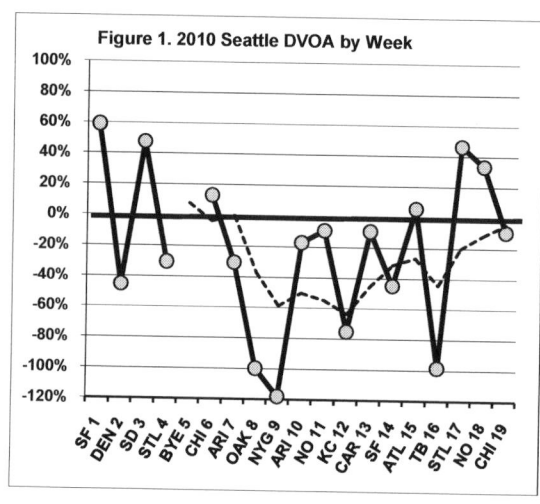

Figure 1. 2010 Seattle DVOA by Week

sive lines like this are almost always coming off bad seasons. Only one, the 2004 Chargers, was coming off a year with a positive offensive DVOA. Despite those lowly beginnings, though, improvement was far from guaranteed after this kind of reset. Only half of the teams got better, while the others actually regressed following their overhaul. The average change was virtually negligible, an increase of just 1.6% in DVOA.

Why was it necessary for the Seahawks to hit the reset button? For that answer we must go back to the spring of 2006. The Seahawks were coming off a loss in the Super Bowl, a game that turned on a controversial holding call that, in hindsight, bode poorly for the fate of Seattle's offensive line. Following the season, then-Seahawks general manager Tim Ruskell chose to use the franchise tag on running back Shaun Alexander, allowing the Minnesota Vikings to steal guard Steve Hutchinson away. It wasn't just one bad personnel move; it was an indication of the importance (or lack thereof) that Ruskell placed on the offensive line. This philosophy was evidenced in the next four years of drafting, which saw Ruskell repeatedly select defensive players (who repeatedly disappointed, but that's a subject for another essay) or trade picks away:

2006: The Seahawks spend their first-round draft pick on cornerback Kelly Jennings and their second-rounder on defensive end Darryl Tapp, passing on successful NFL linemen like Marcus McNeil, Deuce Lutui, Jeremy Trueblood, and Daryn Colledge.

2007: Seattle has no first-round pick, having traded it away the season before for Deion Branch, a blatant (and feeble) attempt to sacrifice long-term depth for short-term success. In the second round they pick another cornerback, Josh Wilson. They miss a chance to take someone like Joe Staley, Justin Blalock, Ryan Kalil, or Samson Satele.

2008: Seahawks spend their first-round pick on defensive end Lawrence Jackson and a second-round pick on tight end John Carlson. In Ruskell's defense,

this was a very shallow draft for offensive linemen. The best blocker they missed out on is probably Carl Nicks, a three-year starter at guard for the New Orleans Saints.

2009: Seattle takes linebacker Aaron Curry with the draft's fourth overall selection, passing on players like Eugene Monroe, Andre Smith, and Alex Mack. In the second round, Ruskell finally selects Max Unger, a center/guard prospect out of Oregon.

Ruskell showed his versatility by ignoring the offensive line in free agency as well. In the four years following the Super Bowl, the contributions of veteran free agent linemen for Seattle consisted entirely of ten starts in 2008 by Mike Wahle, who promptly retired.

As Ruskell fiddled, Rome burned. Long-time Seahawks linemen like Walter Jones, Robbie Tobeck and Chris Gray got older and older, but the Seahawks made no moves to prepare for their inevitable departure.

Ruskell was finally given the boot at the end of the 2009 season. New coach Pete Carroll and team CEO Tod Leiweke grabbed tackle Russell Okung with the sixth overall selection of the 2010 draft, finding a replacement for Walter Jones at least two years too late. They filled out the rest of the line with rejects from other teams, as a whopping six veteran linemen in their first year on the team started at least five games.

The result of all this: A dominant offensive line that led Seattle to the Super Bowl immediately sunk to the bottom of the league and pretty much stayed there (Table 2).

This is why the Seahawks were unable to invest major resources in a new quarterback this offseason, even as Matt Hasselbeck's play continued to deteriorate. Spending a high draft pick on a quarterback

Table 2: Offensive, Indeed: Seattle Offensive Line Stats, Year By Year

Year	ALY	Rk	Power%	Rk	Stuff%	Rk	ASR	Rk
2005	4.43	6	81.1%	1	21.3%	25	5.9%	12
2006	3.75	30	70.0%	10	20.0%	26	8.8%	26
2007	3.69	29	52.4%	27	25.5%	31	7.1%	19
2008	3.82	27	75.8%	4	19.6%	25	7.0%	22
2009	3.91	27	55.6%	29	20.9%	21	7.0%	22
2010	3.66	29	47.7%	29	26.9%	32	6.2%	14

would have made no sense, since that quarterback would have soon been killed playing behind this offensive line. Trading for Kevin Kolb or Carson Palmer would have been even worse, since it would have cost the team multiple draft picks, sabotaging the line even further.

Instead, new general manager John Schneider took what he had and went to work, finding three new starters in the draft and free agency. He selected Alabama tackle James Carpenter in the first round of the draft and Wisconsin guard John Moffitt in the third. (The Seahawks gave up their second-round pick in a trade with Detroit that netted them an extra selection later.) Offensive line coach Tom Cable publicly referred to "free agent anonymous" as a projected starter during the draft. Coincidentally, Robert Gallery, who played for Cable in Oakland, would quickly sign with Seattle after the lockout ended.

And quarterback? Schneider refused to take any kind of chance. Making a long-term commitment to Matt Hasselbeck was out of the question. By all accounts, Hasselbeck is a great person and teammate who led the franchise to its apex, and as such he remained one of the most popular athletes in the city despite a complete dropoff in on-field performance. Since the Super Bowl, Hasselbeck has posted a cumulative DVOA of -9.0%. That's not the worst rate in the league in that timeframe, but it's close (Table 3).

Table 3: Bottom of the Barrel: Worst Passers by DVOA, 2006-10

Rk	Name	DVOA	Passes
27	Matt Hasselbeck	-9.0%	2,239
28	Derek Anderson	-9.3%	1,517
29	Ryan Fitzpatrick	-9.5%	1,126
30	Trent Edwards	-13.1%	1,004
31	Alex Smith	-17.8%	1,448

Minimum 1,000 passes.

(The names at the top of the list, by the way, are exactly who you'd expect: Tom Brady, Peyton Manning, Philip Rivers, Drew Brees, and Tony Romo.)

Hasselbeck wanted a multi-year deal and got one in Tennessee, so good for him. His departure left only one quarterback on the Seattle roster: Charlie Whitehurst, whose acquisition in a trade with San Diego makes no more sense now than it did when it was made a year ago. Schneider added Tarvaris Jackson in free agency, because he was young, cheap, freely available, and (most importantly) familiar with Darrell Bevell's offense after his time in Minnesota. Carroll immediately tabbed Jackson as the starter due solely to his knowledge of the offense, but suggested that Whitehurst could win the job by the end of the season. We'll see about that one.

Jackson started for one year in Minnesota, and teammates and coaches were so impressed with his performance that they spent two seasons making multiple visits to Mississippi to get someone else to throw a football. Was he really that hopeless, though? Jackson's first season as a starter was similar to Hasselbeck's, of all people, and that guy turned out OK (Table 4).

The similarities aren't just numerical. After their debuts, both Hasselbeck and Jackon were replaced by quarterbacks with Super Bowl rings. Hasselbeck was benched for Trent Dilfer, who (being Trent Dilfer and all) quickly played his way back to second string, giving Hasselbeck a chance to reclaim the throne. Jackson, meanwhile, sat behind Brett Favre, and has barely played since.

Is Jackson's statistical resemblance to Hasselbeck merely coincidence? Probably. While Hasselbeck was the hand-picked project of quarterback guru Mike Holmgren, Jackson was rejected by a Minnesota team desperate for a quarterback, and might not have had a job offer outside of Seattle.

In the NFL, it's hard to find talent at quarterback, but much easier to find it at other positions. So while the Seahawks found a passer on the cheap, they made it rain across the rest of the roster. They added Gallery, Rice, and Miller on offense. On defense, they were able to re-sign Brandon Mebane, one of the top defensive tackles in free agency, while also adding Alan Branch and Jimmy Wilkerson. That's 600 pounds of insurance in case of injuries like those that ruined the defensive line in 2010. The Seahawks were 29th in DVOA a year ago, but a variety of stat trends project them to be better in 2011. Eight projected starters on defense are younger than 30, and safety Earl Thomas

Table 4: MattVaris HasselJacks: Comparing Hasselbeck's and Jackson's First Starting Seasons

Player	Year	Age	Team	Games	Cmp	Att	Cmp%	Yds	Y/A	TD	Int	Rate	Sacks	DVOA
Hasselbeck	2001	26	SEA	13	176	321	54.8%	2,023	6.3	7	8	70.9	38	-21.1%
Jackson	2007	24	MIN	12	171	294	58.2%	1,911	6.5	9	12	70.8	19	-5.8%

could be on the verge of superstardom.

With improved defense and the NFC West still being the NFC West, the offense will only need to be slightly better than we expect to win a second consecutive division crown. And if doesn't work out? Then Seattle can turn to the draft for Andrew Luck or Matt Barkley or whoever. This is not to say that Seattle is deliber- ately tanking this year — you don't sign Pro Bowl tight ends to $34 million contracts when you're trying to lose games — but the goal for 2011 is to determine whether they need to go get a passer in 2012.

And if they do, now they'll be able to protect him.

Vince Verhei

2010 Seahawks Stats by Week

Wk	vs.	W-L	PF	PA	YDF	YDA	TO	Total	Off	Def	ST
1	SF	W	31	6	242	263	1	59%	5%	-46%	9%
2	@DEN	L	14	31	339	369	-4	-45%	-36%	19%	9%
3	SD	W	27	20	271	518	3	48%	2%	2%	47%
4	@STL	L	3	20	257	349	-1	-31%	-37%	-3%	4%
5	BYE										
6	@CHI	W	23	20	353	307	0	13%	38%	9%	-16%
7	ARI	W	22	10	302	227	4	1%	-35%	3%	7%
8	@OAK	L	3	33	164	545	-1	-100%	-64%	37%	2%
9	NYG	L	7	41	162	487	-2	-118%	-67%	51%	0%
10	@ARI	W	36	18	490	327	1	-17%	7%	27%	3%
11	@NO	L	19	34	424	494	0	-9%	19%	34%	6%
12	KC	L	24	42	288	503	-2	-75%	-16%	57%	-2%
13	CAR	W	31	14	371	283	-1	-9%	10%	26%	6%
14	@SF	L	21	40	361	336	-5	-45%	-44%	19%	18%
15	ATL	L	18	34	234	266	-2	6%	-25%	-33%	-3%
16	@TB	L	15	38	174	439	0	-98%	-35%	55%	-8%
17	STL	W	16	6	333	184	0	46%	5%	-34%	7%
18	NO	W	41	36	415	474	0	33%	50%	27%	10%
19	@CHI	L	24	35	276	437	1	-9%	12%	25%	3%

Trends and Splits

	Offense	Rank	Defense	Rank
Total DVOA	-14.3%	29	15.0%	29
Unadjusted VOA	-17.6%	30	10.8%	26
Weighted Trend	-12.8%	27	21.4%	32
Variance	9.3%	20	9.9%	28
Average Opponent	2.7%	17	-4.9%	2
Passing	-8.4%	29	27.0%	29
Rushing	-9.2%	28	-0.1%	17
First Down	-16.7%	30	12.1%	28
Second Down	-15.2%	29	12.2%	25
Third Down	-9.0%	23	24.4%	28
First Half	-9.8%	28	17.5%	29
Second Half	-19.0%	29	12.0%	27
Red Zone	-24.5%	27	-6.3%	14
Late and Close	-3.5%	22	-18.8%	1

Five-Year Performance

Year	W-L	Pyth	Est W	PF	PA	TO	Total	Rk	Off	Rk	Def	Rk	ST	Rk	Off AGL	Rk	Def AGL	Rk
2006	9-7	7.8	6.3	335	341	-8	-12.9%	24	-10.0%	27	5.5%	23	2.6%	9	31.1	30	6.7	6
2007	10-6	10.7	9.1	393	291	+10	14.2%	9	7.4%	12	-5.9%	10	0.9%	11	18.9	11	21.9	18
2008	4-12	5.4	5.6	294	392	-7	-21.9%	28	-9.7%	26	14.9%	27	2.6%	9	66.3	32	12.7	6
2009	5-11	5.0	3.7	330	281	+9	-30.8%	29	-16.7%	27	14.9%	29	0.9%	15	44.3	29	30.9	19
2010	7-9	5.5	6.2	310	407	-9	-24.0%	30	-14.3%	29	15.0%	29	5.3%	3	34.3	24	27.2	20

Strategic Tendencies

Run/Pass		Rank	Offense		Rank	Defense		Rank	Other		Rank
Runs, all plays	37%	24	3+ WR	51%	14	Rush 3	7.8%	18	2+ RB, Pct Runs	48%	29
Runs, first half	35%	28	4+ WR	5%	18	Rush 4	56.0%	22	1 RB/2 TE, Pct Runs	49%	19
Runs, first down	41%	30	2+ TE	34%	11	Rush 5	27.3%	9	1 RB/3+ WR, Pct Runs	24%	12
Runs, second-long	26%	30	Single back	64%	7	Rush 6+	8.9%	17	CB1 on WR1	47%	6
Runs, power sit.	52%	23	Play action	15%	28	Zone Blitz	4.5%	19	Go for it on 4th	1.32	4
Runs, behind 2H	31%	8	Max protect	16%	6	Sacks by LB	15.3%	23	Offensive Pace	29.7	5
Pass, ahead 2H	52%	6	Outside pocket	11%	20	Sacks by DB	20.8%	2	Defensive Pace	30.5	7

Seattle last year fumbled only 11 times on offense — but they only recovered two of those. ☞ In 2009, the Seahawks ran more running back screen passes than any other offense, even though they were extremely poor on these plays (-40.0% DVOA). Offensive coordinator Jeremy Bates clearly learned something from the film, because last year the Seahawks ran the *fewest* number of running back screen passes in the league. ☞ The defense, by the way, gave up a league-leading 10.2 yards per pass on running back screens. ☞ Seattle opponents threw a league-high 28 percent of passes to their number one receiver.

Passing

Player	DYAR	DVOA	Plays	NtYds	Avg	YAC	C%	TD	Int
M.Hasselbeck	32	-10.1%	475	2858	6.0	4.8	60.3%	12	17
C.Whitehurst	-95	-26.0%	106	501	4.7	4.4	58.0%	2	3

Receiving

Player	DYAR	DVOA	Plays	Ctch	Yds	Y/C	YAC	TD	C%
M.Williams	50	-6.7%	110	65	751	11.6	3.3	2	59%
D.Butler	-46	-20.7%	70	36	385	10.7	3.2	4	51%
B.Obomanu	110	15.8%	49	30	494	16.5	5.6	4	61%
B.Stokley	91	16.5%	43	31	354	11.4	2.9	0	72%
G.Tate	-42	-26.5%	40	22	230	10.5	5.3	0	55%
R.Martin	59	68.9%	9	7	158	22.6	7.3	1	78%
J.Carlson	-94	-31.2%	58	31	318	10.3	4.1	1	53%
C.Baker	-8	-12.9%	19	9	116	12.9	5.2	1	47%
C.Morrah	-11	-16.6%	18	9	117	13.0	7.1	0	50%
J.Forsett	34	-0.2%	51	33	252	7.6	7.0	0	65%
M.Lynch	9	-7.6%	26	22	154	7.0	6.9	0	85%
L.Washington	20	13.6%	13	9	79	8.8	7.6	0	69%
M.Robinson	-27	-50.9%	13	8	37	4.6	5.5	0	62%

Rushing

Player	DYAR	DVOA	Plays	Yds	Avg	TD	Fum	Suc
M.Lynch	-53	-14.7%	201	737	3.7	6	2	44%
J.Forsett	12	-6.2%	118	523	4.4	2	0	38%
L.Washington	12	1.0%	27	100	3.7	1	0	44%
M.Robinson	27	21.3%	13	77	5.9	0	0	77%
M.Hasselbeck	43	36.0%	13	70	5.4	3	0	-
C.Whitehurst	14	10.4%	12	50	4.2	1	0	-

Offensive Line

Year	Yards	ALY	Rank	Power	Rank	Stuff	Rank	2nd Lev	Rank	Open Field	Rank
2008	4.13	3.82	27	76%	4	20%	25	1.12	20	0.84	12
2009	4.15	3.91	27	56%	29	21%	21	1.19	13	0.72	18
2010	3.90	3.67	28	48%	29	26%	32	1.06	21	0.84	11

Year	LE	Rank	LT	Rank	Mid	Rank	RT	Rank	RE	Rank	Sacks	ASR	Rank	F-Start	Cont.
2008	2.88	27	4.37	10	3.70	27	3.96	22	4.15	15	36	7.0%	22	24	29
2009	1.26	32	4.11	16	4.16	14	4.22	13	4.27	13	41	7.0%	22	19	30
2010	3.00	30	3.48	28	3.60	28	4.24	14	3.06	29	35	6.2%	14	21	21

You can take those rows of numbers labeled "2010," 964 offensive snaps' worth of play-by-play data, and throw them right in the trash. They tell us almost nothing about what's going to happen for the Seahawks' offensive line in 2011. Seattle's projected starters — Russell Okung, Robert Gallery, Max Unger, John Moffitt, and James Carpenter — contributed a total of 11 starts for Seattle last year, 10 of them by Okung, the rookie first-rounder out of Oklahoma State. Okung was in and out of the lineup all year with sprains to both ankles. When he did play, he was very reliable, with no holding calls all year, and only three false starts. He did struggle late in the year, surrendering two sacks and four hurries in back-to-back games against San Francisco and Atlanta. Max Unger, a 2009 second-rounder, started 16 games at guard as a rookie, but his sophomore season lasted just one game as he injured his toe in the opener against San Francisco. He'll take over at center for Chris Spencer, who will not be missed. They'll be joined by Robert Gallery, formerly of the Oakland Raiders, who has quietly become an effective guard after busting out at tackle.

A pair of rookies takes over on the right side of the line. First-rounder James Carpenter out of Alabama will play tackle this year, though like Gallery, he could move in to a guard position later in his career. The Seahawks were criticized for passing on Gabe Carimi and Derek Sherrod for Carpenter, but they felt he was the best run blocker in the draft, and scouting expert Russ Lande said before the draft that Carpenter has the physical skills to become "a very good starting left tackle" if he can improve his pass-blocking technique. Third-round pick John Moffitt will take over at guard; he played all three interior line positions at Wisconsin.

Defensive Front Seven

Defensive Line	Age	Pos	Plays	TmPct	Overall Rk	Stop	Dfts	BTkl	St%	Rk	AvYd	Rk	Pass Rush Sack	Hit	Hur	vs. Run Runs	St%	Yds	vs. Pass Pass	St%	Yds
Chris Clemons	30	DE	52	6.2%	25	43	21	2	83%	23	0.9	22	11	7	27	32	78%	3.5	20	90%	-3.3
Colin Cole	31	DT	49	8.5%	4	40	5	2	81%	25	2.3	47	1	0	1	42	81%	2.4	7	86%	1.7
Raheem Brock	33	DE	34	4.1%	60	27	16	1	72%	35	2.6	66	8	10	18.5	18	72%	4.4	16	88%	0.6
Brandon Mebane	26	DT	32	5.1%	24	24	9	2	75%	37	1.4	22	1	0	10.5	28	75%	1.6	4	75%	0.3
Junior Siavii	33	DT	32	4.4%	37	25	3	0	79%	30	2.4	48	0	3	3	28	79%	2.2	4	75%	4.0
Red Bryant	27	DE	17	4.7%	--	16	4	0	94%	--	0.9	--	1	3	4	16	94%	1.4	1	100%	-7.0

Linebackers	Age	Pos	Plays	TmPct	Overall Rk	Stop	Dfts	BTkl	AvYd	Pass Rush Sack	Hit	Hur	vs. Run Runs	St%	Rk	Yds	Rk	vs. Pass Tgts	Suc%	Rk	AdjYd	Rk
David Hawthorne	26	OLB	108	12.9%	36	56	5	11	5.2	0	1	3	76	57%	92	4.4	98	27	61%	20	7.0	59
Lofa Tatupu	29	MLB	95	11.4%	45	58	21	12	4.6	1	1	2	57	65%	72	3.5	67	42	52%	51	6.8	53
Aaron Curry	25	OLB	72	8.6%	71	43	15	5	3.5	3.5	5	12	45	64%	74	3.2	60	23	33%	75	5.7	31
Will Herring	28	OLB	28	3.6%	--	18	9	2	8.3	1	0	2	9	100%	--	2.0	--	14	61%	--	8.1	--

Year	Yards	ALY	Rank	Power	Rank	Stuff	Rank	2nd Lev	Rank	Open Field	Rank
2008	4.18	4.17	17	70%	23	19%	10	1.04	10	0.76	17
2009	4.24	3.93	10	50%	3	20%	13	1.11	15	0.99	23
2010	4.34	4.29	26	68%	27	16%	26	1.04	7	0.93	24

Year	LE	Rank	LT	Rank	Mid	Rank	RT	Rank	RE	Rank	Sacks	ASR	Rank
2008	4.14	17	4.41	20	4.21	17	3.84	10	4.15	19	35	6.0%	17
2009	4.16	14	3.88	12	3.48	4	4.28	20	4.72	26	28	5.3%	29
2010	4.98	28	3.95	14	4.42	26	3.83	12	4.42	25	36	5.3%	28

The four-man combination of Red Bryant, Colin Cole, Brandon Mebane, and Chris Clemons was nearly dominant when healthy, but they only played four games together. Mebane missed four games in the middle of the season with a calf injury, and by the time he came back, Bryant was done for the year with a torn MCL, and Cole was on the shelf with a severe ankle sprain, though he would return at the end of the year. The result was a wildly erratic season for Seattle's run defense:

Table 5: Seahawks Rush Defense, 2010 (RBs only)

Weeks	Healthy Starters	DVOA	Rush Avg.	RB Suc%	Stuff Rate	Rk	ASR	Rk
1-4	Bryant, Clemons, Cole, Mebane	-33.7%	2.83	38%	23%	25	5.9%	12
5-8	Bryant, Clemons, Cole	16.3%	5.45	36%	19%	26	8.8%	26
9-13	Clemons, Mebane	27.3%	4.62	59%	15%	31	7.1%	19
14-17	Clemons, Cole, Mebane	-21.6%	4.69	33%	24%	25	7.0%	22

To protect themselves from similar chaos in 2011, the Seahawks were aggressive in free agency, re-signing Mebane and adding a pair of defensive tackles, Alan Branch from the Cardinals and Jimmy Wilkerson from the Saints. Colin Cole is recovering from ankle surgery, so Mebane will slide over to nose tackle, with Branch starting at three-technique. It's not clear when Cole will return, but if he does, Branch can also play five-technique, adding depth behind Bryant at left end.

Lofa Tatupu was asked to take a paycut. He asked for his release instead. The Seahawks were fine with this, as Tatupu has been mediocre at best for several seasons. His spot in the middle will be taken by David Hawthorne, who has a penchant for racking up tons of tackles (38 in a three-game stretch against New Orleans, Kansas City, and Carolina) that don't really help his team win games. Pete Carroll and company got very creative with Aaron Curry, playing him at strongside linebacker on standard downs, then moving him to defensive tackle (sometimes even nose tackle) on third-and-long situations. But he still has a long way to fill the hopes Seattle had for him when they drafted him fourth overall in 2009. The other outside linebacker will be none other than Leroy Hill. After multiple incidents of arrest, suspension, and injury, Hill was harder to find than D.B. Cooper in 2010, but he's hoping to return to Seattle headlines just like Cooper did this year. He played in only one game last season, tearing his Achilles' tendon in Week 2 against Denver. In his last healthy season, 2008, he was top six among linebackers in both Yards per Play and Stop Rate against the run.

Defensive Secondary

Secondary	Age	Pos	Plays	TmPct	Rk	Stop	Dfts	BTkl	Runs	St%	Rk	Yds	Rk	Tgts	Tgt%	Rk	Dist	Suc%	Rk	APaYd	Rk	PD	Int
Lawyer Milloy	38	SS	89	10.7%	31	38	10	8	52	52%	16	5.9	27	22	4.4%	69	9.7	63%	16	7.9	42	1	0
Marcus Trufant	31	CB	88	10.6%	23	24	10	7	19	42%	46	9.9	78	92	18.2%	15	13.0	43%	77	8.7	68	7	1
Earl Thomas	22	FS	78	9.4%	54	23	11	9	32	31%	62	9.3	70	42	8.2%	12	10.3	62%	17	6.2	15	7	5
Kelly Jennings	29	CB	53	7.3%	65	21	9	1	9	56%	21	10.4	82	67	15.2%	42	12.7	48%	61	7.2	40	13	1
Jordan Babineaux	29	SS	42	5.0%	76	25	19	3	7	71%	2	3.6	2	26	5.2%	53	8.2	61%	23	6.7	22	4	2
Walter Thurmond	24	CB	40	5.5%	--	12	4	4	9	22%	--	5.7	--	37	8.3%	--	12.9	53%	--	8.2	--	7	0
Roy Lewis	26	CB	22	3.0%	--	11	11	4	2	50%	--	5.0	--	26	5.9%	--	11.5	58%	--	5.5	--	4	0

Year	Pass D Rank	vs. #1 WR	Rk	vs. #2 WR	Rk	vs. Other WR	Rk	vs. TE	Rk	vs. RB	Rk
2008	29	40.2%	31	15.0%	24	-5.4%	15	20.2%	26	14.3%	25
2009	30	20.7%	28	16.2%	27	23.0%	32	11.5%	20	31.0%	30
2010	29	-3.0%	14	33.8%	32	20.9%	28	-2.8%	10	19.4%	29

Marcus Trufant has ranked 55th or worse in both Success Rate and Yards per Pass in four of the last five seasons and is grossly overpaid at this point, but the Seahawks had tons of cap room and weren't interested in getting in a bidding war for any of the free agent corners, so Trufant will get one more season in Seattle as kind of a farewell tour. He has two more years left on his contract, but it would be stunning to see him on the roster in 2012. The diminutive Kelly Jennings (generously listed at 5-foot-11 and 180 pounds) is as run-aversive a cornerback as you'll ever see, with 344 targets and only 25 run tackles in his five-year career, but Seattle liked him enough to re-sign him in free agency. Walter Thurmond and Kennard Cox will battle for the nickelback spot, and to see who might take over for Trufant next year.

The Seahawks drafted Earl Thomas 14th overall out of Texas. He played as advertised, an undersized centerfielder with absurd athletic potential and a tendency to play out of control. If he can cut down on the big plays he allows and maintain the big plays he makes, he's a Pro Bowler. With Lawyer Milloy not re-signed (and likely retiring) and Jordan Babineaux moving on to Tennessee in free agency, Kam Chancellor steps into the starting spot at strong safety. A fifth-round selection in 2010, Chancellor has the size (6-foot-3, 232 pounds) to play in the box, but also has the speed to cover deep. Seattle coaches have high hopes for Chancellor. If he's all that they expect, he'll combine with Thomas to give Seattle maybe the best young safety duo in the game.

Special Teams

Year	DVOA	Rank	FG/XP	Rank	Net Kick	Rank	Kick Ret	Rank	Net Punt	Rank	Punt Ret	Rank	Hidden	Rank
2008	2.6%	9	4.4	9	5.8	10	4.0	11	0.7	18	0.6	12	-9.7	26
2009	0.9%	15	2.4	13	11.8	2	-4.4	20	-0.8	22	-3.9	23	-4.2	20
2010	5.3%	3	-2.3	26	11.6	6	18.3	2	-1.0	22	4.4	9	11.1	2

Leon Washington had three touchdowns on kickoff returns last season, giving him seven in his career, more than anyone in NFL history except Josh Cribbs. As such, the NFL's new rules for kickoffs should hurt Seattle as much as any other team. Washington hasn't been anything special as a punt returner in his career, but he did have an 84-yarder last season. Olindo Mare's big leg was second in the NFL in kickoff value, and the Seahawks were quite good in covering kicks as well, but he signed with the Panthers in free agency. The Seahawks signed two kickers to fight for his spot: Jeff Reed (who was horrible on kickoffs last season in limited action in San Francisco) and Brandon Coutu (a 2008 draft pick in Seattle who has yet to play in a regular-season game). This looks like a recipe for disaster, but thankfully the Seahawks offense won't be scoring much anyway, so this weakness won't be exposed. It's kind of cunning, when you think about it. Punter Jon Ryan returns for his sixth year in the league, his fourth in Seattle. His punting average last year was by far the worst of his career, but he pinned 27 punts inside the 20 with just one touchback. Seattle's punt coverage was mediocre.

Coaching Staff

Two surprising facts about Pete Carroll: Among active NFL coaches, only Tom Coughlin is older, and only Bill Belichick and Mike Shanahan earn more money. Those three coaches have a combined 31 playoff wins and six Super Bowl championships. Carroll has two playoff victories and has yet to reach a conference championship game. For now, though, one division title (however tainted) and a postseason upset have bought him credibility with Seattle players and fans. New offensive coordinator Darrell Bevell comes over from Minnesota. His offense there was similar to the ones Seahawks fans have seen in recent years, with West Coast passing principles out of single-back formations with multiple tight ends and wide receivers. Wide receivers coach Kippy Brown has more than 30 years experience in the NCAA, NFL, and XFL (if you hate the Seahawks uniforms, you should have seen what the Memphis Maniax used to wear), and deserves a lot of credit for turning around the careers of Ben Obomanu and Mike Williams. Former Oakland Raiders head coach Tom Cable will run Seattle's offensive line. He's had success as a line coach for the Raiders, Falcons, and UCLA Bruins.

Tampa Bay Buccaneers

2010 Record: 10-6

Pythagorean Wins: 8.7 (15th)

DVOA: 4.1% (12th)

Offense: 11.5% (9th)

Defense: 6.9% (23rd)

Special Teams: -0.4% (18th)

Variance: 14.5% (14th)

2011 Mean Projection: 7.5 wins

On the Clock (0-3): 4%

Loserville (4-6): 30%

Mediocrity (7-8): 34%

Playoff Contender (9-10): 24%

Super Bowl Contender (11+): 9%

Projected Average Opponent: -1.4% (22nd)

2010: Less money, more problems.

2011: Should we start with the "New Bengals" jokes now, or wait until later?

In a general sense, the Moneyball ethos is about finding undervalued talent. More specifically, it's about finding undervalued talent based on specific guidelines, optimized for your coaches and personnel. Taking shots on good football players that other teams won't touch due to off-field issues may be one way to go, but as the Cincinnati Bengals have proven over the last decade, that approach will tend to net a team a series of completely unpredictable seasons.

The Tampa Bay Buccaneers, 2010's youngest team, benefitted from character risks at key positions in their offense, and put up the franchise's best record since 2005. Receiver Mike Williams, an undeniable first-round raw talent, was taken in the third round out of Syracuse because he basically quit on his team halfway through the 2009 season after missing the 2008 season due to an academic suspension. Williams nonetheless came to the NFL with a preternatural understanding of route concepts, and absolutely blew it up in the Bucs' passing offense, becoming the first rookie receiver to post double-digit touchdowns since Randy Moss.

Oregon running back LeGarrette Blount wasn't even drafted; the concern about his proclivity for off-field distractions and the wrong kind of on-field violence had scouts and personnel men looking the other way. Blount became infamous for decking Boise State defensive end Byron Hout after Oregon's 19-8 loss in the 2009 season opener for both teams, but he's had issues before, primarily revolving around his inability to stay at a consistent weight and make meetings on time. Originally suspended for the rest of the season by Oregon head coach Chip Kelly, he came back for the final month of the season when he was a) able to impress his coaches that he understood what he did wrong; and b) too much of a factor to miss as the Ducks went on a bowl run. Originally signed and then cast aside by the Tennessee Titans, Blount was picked up by the Bucs, got more and more carries as the season went on, and finished 2010 as the NFL's leader among rookie backs in rushing yards (1,007) and rushing touchdowns (six).

Combined with quarterback Josh Freeman — considered a 2009 draft afterthought with Matthew Stafford and Mark Sanchez off the board — the Bucs' trio of youngsters proved difficult to stop. The former Kansas State standout obliterated concerns that he wouldn't be able to grasp pro-style offenses, became the offense's leader, and put up the ninth-best touchdown-to-interception ratio (25-to-6) in NFL history. While some would contend that such a low pick percentage (1.3 percent) is unrepeatable, a number of quarterbacks would beg to differ, starting with Donovan McNabb. From 2002 through 2008, McNabb had an interception rate over 2.0 percent just twice, and he threw more than 300 passes in each of those seasons.

2011 Buccaneers Schedule

Week	Opp.	Week	Opp.	Week	Opp.
1	DET	7	vs. CHI (U.K.)	13	CAR
2	at MIN	8	BYE	14	at JAC
3	ATL	9	at NO	15	DAL (Sat.)
4	IND (Mon.)	10	HOU	16	at CAR
5	at SF	11	at GB	17	at ATL
6	NO	12	at TEN		

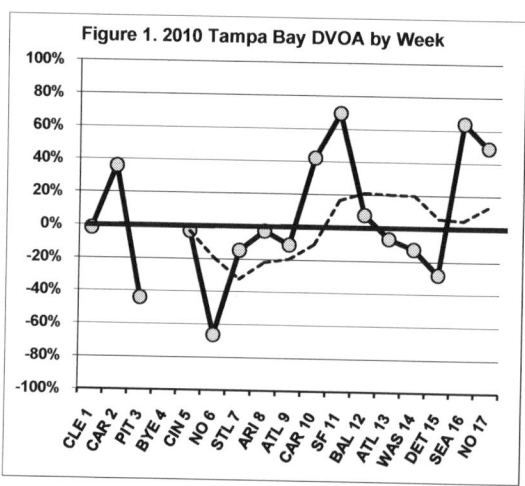

Figure 1. 2010 Tampa Bay DVOA by Week

Like McNabb, Freeman is a big, mobile quarterback who sometimes struggles with consistent completion percentage, but the arrow is definitely trending up.

Freeman didn't present any character concerns, but he proved to be the exception during the lockout, which was when the Bucs' proclivity for taking flyers on guys with iffy pasts came back to bite them in a big way. Cornerback Aqib Talib was charged with aggravated assault with a deadly weapon. Defensive end Alex Magee was busted for expired car tabs and possession of marijuana. Assistant coach Jayson Kaiser got a DUI. And on and on. The weirdest and most disturbing charge against a Buccaneers employee didn't even happen to one of the players. Luxury Suite Sales Manager Brian Weiss was arrested and charged in June with being part of an Internet sex scheme designed to lure underage girls. Short of trading for Kenny Britt, there weren't many ways in which the Buccaneers' organization could have become more familiar with the police.

All that offseason "fun" led to the obvious question: Who's driving this plane? Head coach Raheem Morris is an excellent defensive mind and one of the youngest coaches in the league. General Manager Mark Dominik is impressing from a personnel standpoint with his first opportunity to buy the groceries. Malcolm Glazer has helped to breathe new life into the franchise since he bought it in 1995, but the Glazer family's debt-laden ownership of the Manchester United soccer franchise has raised questions about the team's stability.

The Bucs went into the post-lockout landscape more than $50 million under the new $120 million salary cap, and while youth will dictate that to a certain degree, there's also the question of where the excess money is going. Starting in 2012, new cash-to-cap commitments will require each team to spend at least 89 percent of each year's salary cap on player costs. More profligate owners like Jerry Jones and Dan Snyder were beyond

tired of investing (however wisely) in their teams at a different level than the Glazers and other lower-staked owners in a revenue-sharing economy. According to London's *Daily Mirror*, the Glazers are spending more than $73 million in annual interest on an $818 million debt from buying Manchester United. And if you're spending about as much on players for your American football team as you are in interest for the debt on your English football team, it doesn't take a financial whiz to figure out that something's wrong.

With the coaching staff and front office seemingly unable to put a cap on undisciplined behavior, and the ownership unable to put major stakes into free agency, young draft-acquired talent must produce to win. That puts even more pressure on Dominik and his staff to hit the bull's-eye with every draft pick. While they had every reason to believe that they did so in 2010, things didn't quite go as expected — and that's where the defense comes in.

Just one year after they took defensive tackles (Gerald McCoy, Brian Price) with their first- and second-round picks, the Bucs went back to the well in 2011 and selected defensive ends (Iowa's Adrian Clayborn and Clemson's Da'Quan Bowers) with their first two picks. The need was substantial, both because of an insufficient pass rush and because of the defense's worrisome inability to stand up to power-based offenses (See: Falcons, Atlanta). Tampa Bay's Adjusted Sack Rate wasn't just the second-worst in the NFL last season; it was also the franchise's worst in the history of our advanced metrics. The Bucs also ranked dead last in DVOA against the run last year, their second straight poor year after eight straight years as an above-average run defense.

The Bucs hope for better results out of their two new top draftees than they got out of last year's duo. McCoy, selected one pick after Ndamukong Suh, looked a bit better on tape than he did on the stat sheets early on — he didn't record a sack until Week 11, but he was the primary target of opposing offensive linemen and faced more double teams than any other Bucs lineman from day one. Just as he was learning how split those blocks and make things happen, McCoy tore his left biceps and missed the last month of the season. McCoy has great potential, but those hoping for Suh-level dominance had best re-calibrate their expectations.

Price, who was supposed to be the inside fireplug complement to McCoy's athleticism, had a very frustrating season that ended soon after it began. He showed signs of life in early games, but fell prey to hip and pelvis injuries that may put his career in jeopardy, depending on who you're asking.

Despite the weakness of the defensive line, the Bucs put up double-digit wins in an absolutely brutal division and still didn't make the playoffs. They had to stay home and watch the 7-9 Seahawks eke out a thriller against the Saints with the knowledge that they had beaten the daylights out of those same Seahawks just a few weeks before. Many Bucs fans are expecting the team to take the proverbial next step to greatness in 2011, but our numbers predict some regression. The continued quality of the NFC South is one of the reasons our projections aren't as rosy, as is the seeming inevitability that Freeman can't possibly have the same type of season he did last year. Factor in a defense still trying to find its way despite considerable investment, and the cracks could start showing. In the long run, Tampa Bay is still a young team on the rise; now the challenge is to manage the personalities while continuing to maintain that pipeline of young talent.

One thing the Bucs did after the lockout was to re-sign their own. They started with a seven-year, $53 million deal for right guard Davin Joseph, one of the best in the game. Then came a two-year, $10 million deal for blown block-master Jeremy Trueblood. Linebacker Quincy Black was also re-upped, and though those deals pushed the Bucs to or near the cash-to-cap compliant figure required of them by the end of the league year, there will be room to extend the contracts of other key difference-makers — specifically Freeman, who looks to be the league's next great young quarterback. Talib, the best player in the secondary, won't likely see a trial on his assault charge until early next year, and though he may be in line for NFL suspension, there's no way Tampa Bay was going to release him. There are teams with no interest in troubled players with great talent, and that again is where the Bucs find their bargains — by being first in line to scout outside the box when character questions are posed.

The Buccaneers are in a strong position going forward, because they've combined youth and depth in ways that most teams are unable or unwilling to do. The aforementioned recent Bengals teams are the obvious comparison — talent all over the place, discipline issues, two 800-pound gorillas above them in their division (the Bucs have the Atlanta Falcons and New Orleans Saints, where the Bengals had the Pittsburgh Steelers and Baltimore Ravens), a coach who may or may not be running the asylum, and an ownership group that could do a better job of representing the franchise from a financial perspective. The primary difference between the two organizations is that there's no Mike Brown-style buffoon in Tampa Bay, no owner without qualifications demanding to be involved in personnel decisions.

But at some point, the Buccaneers are likely to have to square up in this deal with the proverbial devil. As other teams have discovered, the more you rely on players of questionable character, the more you're opening yourself up to the vagaries of the actions inevitably drawn from such personal problems. The question is, how much is too much?

Doug Farrar

2010 Buccaneers Stats by Week

Wk	vs.	W-L	PF	PA	YDF	YDA	TO	Total	Off	Def	ST
1	CLE	W	17	14	288	340	1	-2%	-17%	-8%	7%
2	@CAR	W	20	7	273	278	3	36%	9%	-20%	7%
3	PIT	L	13	38	303	387	0	-44%	-7%	34%	-3%
4	BYE										
5	@CIN	W	24	21	391	358	1	-3%	1%	-1%	-5%
6	NO	L	6	31	277	475	0	-66%	-13%	40%	-14%
7	STL	W	18	17	313	285	1	-15%	0%	22%	7%
8	@ARI	W	38	35	407	396	2	-3%	20%	11%	-12%
9	@ATL	L	21	27	278	365	-2	-11%	-12%	22%	23%
10	CAR	W	31	16	421	300	-1	42%	71%	19%	-10%
11	@SF	W	21	0	299	189	2	70%	32%	-47%	-10%
12	@BAL	L	10	17	263	349	1	8%	6%	5%	7%
13	ATL	L	24	28	325	290	1	-7%	10%	-2%	-18%
14	@WAS	W	17	16	365	399	-1	-13%	10%	27%	3%
15	DET	L	20	23	403	433	0	-28%	23%	53%	2%
16	SEA	W	38	15	439	174	0	64%	52%	-15%	-3%
17	@NO	W	23	13	317	305	1	49%	11%	-28%	10%

Trends and Splits

	Offense	Rank	Defense	Rank
Total DVOA	11.5%	9	6.9%	23
Unadjusted VOA	9.8%	12	1.3%	15
Weighted Trend	18.1%	6	7.7%	23
Variance	5.6%	8	7.1%	20
Average Opponent	1.9%	20	-4.0%	4
Passing	29.8%	10	6.7%	13
Rushing	1.5%	12	7.2%	32
First Down	4.1%	19	8.7%	22
Second Down	0.8%	16	-1.7%	11
Third Down	40.3%	2	15.8%	25
First Half	13.0%	9	17.2%	28
Second Half	10.1%	8	-4.7%	11
Red Zone	8.4%	9	0.0%	18
Late and Close	5.7%	13	-6.4%	13

Five-Year Performance

Year	W-L	Pyth	Est W	PF	PA	TO	Total	Rk	Off	Rk	Def	Rk	ST	Rk	Off AGL	Rk	Def AGL	Rk
2006	4-12	3.6	5.1	211	353	-12	-20.0%	29	-15.6%	30	4.6%	21	0.1%	17	30.0	28	26.6	25
2007	9-7	10.0	10.1	334	270	+15	17.1%	8	6.1%	13	-10.8%	4	0.2%	12	42.0	30	12.6	6
2008	9-7	9.0	9.0	361	323	+4	11.1%	10	4.0%	20	-7.3%	6	-0.3%	19	27.6	19	15.2	10
2009	3-13	3.8	5.1	244	400	-5	-23.8%	27	-15.7%	26	11.3%	25	3.2%	5	32.3	22	18.9	9
2010	10-6	8.7	8.6	341	318	+9	4.1%	12	11.5%	9	6.9%	23	-0.4%	18	22.9	14	37.9	25

Strategic Tendencies

Run/Pass		Rank	Offense		Rank	Defense		Rank	Other		Rank
Runs, all plays	39%	17	3+ WR	43%	24	Rush 3	11.1%	10	2+ RB, Pct Runs	63%	8
Runs, first half	38%	23	4+ WR	2%	29	Rush 4	61.4%	12	1 RB/2 TE, Pct Runs	50%	12
Runs, first down	49%	17	2+ TE	27%	20	Rush 5	19.5%	27	1 RB/3+ WR, Pct Runs	13%	30
Runs, second-long	39%	17	Single back	60%	14	Rush 6+	8.0%	19	CB1 on WR1	25%	29
Runs, power sit.	56%	19	Play action	19%	16	Zone Blitz	10.4%	5	Go for it on 4th	0.72	27
Runs, behind 2H	31%	9	Max protect	9%	23	Sacks by LB	32.7%	16	Offensive Pace	32.9	31
Pass, ahead 2H	46%	12	Outside pocket	18%	2	Sacks by DB	7.7%	19	Defensive Pace	30.6	11

Tampa Bay Defensive end Tim Crowder led all linemen with nine pass targets in game charting. Trent Cole of Philadelphia was second with seven. ☞ Josh Freeman was big-blitzed on 14 percent of passes, the highest rate in the league. It didn't really work — he was just as good against the big blitz as he was against standard pass rushes. ☞ No team used play-action as often on second down as it did on first down, but Tampa Bay came closest, using a play-fake on 21 percent of first-down passes and 20 percent of second-down passes. ☞ When opponents ran the ball out of spread sets with three or more wide receivers, Tampa Bay allowed a 31.9% DVOA (worst in the NFL) and 5.45 yards per carry (30th). ☞ Tampa Bay ranked 28th in defensive DVOA before halftime, but 11th after halftime.

Passing

Player	DYAR	DVOA	Plays	NtYds	Avg	YAC	C%	TD	Int
J.Freeman	1031	20.5%	510	3375	6.6	5.2	61.6%	25	6
J.Johnson	28	17.4%	18	103	5.7	3.6	87.5%	0	0

Rushing

Player	DYAR	DVOA	Plays	Yds	Avg	TD	Fum	Suc
L.Blount	98	4.0%	201	1007	5.0	6	3	45%
C.Williams	-68	-22.2%	125	437	3.5	2	1	36%
J.Freeman	95	19.2%	56	373	6.7	0	2	-
E.Graham	-10	-18.9%	20	99	5.0	1	1	45%
A.Benn	15	0.1%	6	35	5.8	0	0	-
K.Huggins	-3	-32.7%	4	11	2.8	0	0	50%
J.Johnson	25	152.3%	4	39	9.8	0	0	-

Receiving

Player	DYAR	DVOA	Plays	Ctch	Yds	Y/C	YAC	TD	C%
M.Williams	65	-6.3%	128	64	964	15.1	4.9	11	50%
S.Stroughter	11	-9.1%	39	25	248	9.9	4.0	0	64%
A.Benn	113	23.7%	38	25	395	15.8	6.4	2	66%
M.Spurlock	25	-2.9%	33	17	250	14.7	1.9	2	52%
P.Parker	-16	-30.8%	10	5	49	9.8	8.4	0	50%
M.Stovall	19	12.1%	9	7	81	11.6	8.0	1	78%
D.Briscoe	40	57.0%	7	6	93	15.5	5.5	1	86%
K.Winslow	135	14.8%	97	66	733	11.1	3.5	5	68%
J.Gilmore	47	30.9%	18	13	160	12.3	7.5	1	72%
R.Purvis	4	3.9%	6	5	38	7.6	5.2	0	83%
C.Williams	72	6.3%	64	46	355	7.7	6.9	1	72%
E.Graham	36	18.4%	19	16	130	8.1	7.3	1	84%
L.Blount	-33	-93.0%	7	5	14	2.8	3.8	0	71%

Offensive Line

Year	Yards	ALY	Rank	Power	Rank	Stuff	Rank	2nd Lev	Rank	Open Field	Rank
2008	4.09	4.04	22	65%	17	17%	12	1.02	26	0.75	13
2009	3.80	3.58	31	65%	13	21%	23	1.06	24	0.62	23
2010	4.43	3.78	25	60%	17	23%	26	1.18	13	1.21	5

Year	LE	Rank	LT	Rank	Mid	Rank	RT	Rank	RE	Rank	Sacks	ASR	Rank	F-Start	Cont.
2008	2.16	30	3.54	28	4.35	9	3.92	26	3.90	20	32	6.3%	18	17	35
2009	4.18	18	4.87	5	3.17	32	4.26	12	2.43	31	33	5.7%	11	22	40
2010	3.41	28	4.25	16	3.81	22	3.57	26	3.40	25	30	6.1%	13	16	24

The Bucs rose up a bit from a next-to-worst ALY ranking in 2009, but that was more about the pure power of running back LeGarrette Blount — check out the RB Yards and Open Field Yards improvements to see the proof. Tampa Bay's offensive line was a group that had to adjust to frequent injuries, but a couple of newer players popped up and impressed. What is needed for the team to take the proverbial next step is a more consistent set of performances from the rock star on the line, left tackle Donald Penn. Penn agreed to a six-year, $43 million contract in July of 2010, giving the very young Bucs offense a reasonable linchpin at a crucial position. Penn is not an elite tackle — he is powerful at the point of attack and can fend off pass rushers with his upper-body strength, but he can be beaten from side to side and his kick-step is average at best. That can work in an offensive system that has the quarterback rolling right a lot of the time — indeed, though Penn was debited with just three blown blocks leading to sacks, he was flat-out clowned too often by quicker speed ends on plays that went away from the left side by choice or by force.

Versatility is a crucial attribute for any offensive lineman, but Jeremy Zuttah might need a map by now. After starring at tackle at Rutgers before the Bucs picked him in the third round of the 2008 draft, Zuttah moved inside to left guard early in his pro career, subbed in at right guard from time to time, and started seven games at center in 2010 when Jeff Faine's leg and triceps injuries proved overwhelming. He doesn't have Faine's power, but Zuttah proved to be a decent blocker inline and in zone slides, with the ability to get upfield in a hurry. The Bucs have said that they want the 30-year-old Faine back, but he's due $4.6 million in 2011, and for a team that prefers youth on the cheap for the most part, the message could be mixed. Because the Bucs had so much room under the salary cap when the lockout ended, they can take their time in either restructuring Faine's contract or going in a different direction.

Right tackle Jeremy Trueblood led the league with 10 blown blocks in 2009, and he wound up losing his job to second-year undrafted free agent James Lee when he returned from a knee injury in 2010. Somehow, Tampa

Bay's front office decided that it would be a good idea to re-sign him to a two-year, $10 million deal. The Bucs had an important decision to make with right guard Davin Joseph, who was among the best in the game at his position not too long ago, but whose effectiveness had dimmed even before a foot injury that put him on injured reserve in November. The Bucs showed their faith in Joseph's ability to rebound by signing him to a seven-year, $52.5 million contract with $19 million guaranteed just as soon as they could.

Defensive Front Seven

Defensive Line	Age	Pos	Plays	TmPct	Overall Rk	Stop	Dfts	BTkl	St%	Rk	AvYd	Rk	Pass Rush Sack	Hit	Hur	vs. Run Runs	St%	Yds	vs. Pass Pass	St%	Yds
Roy Miller	24	DT	47	6.0%	13	34	5	1	74%	46	2.5	53	1.5	0	5	43	74%	2.8	4	50%	0.0
Stylez White	32	DE	36	4.6%	53	29	15	3	80%	33	1.8	41	4.5	10	20	25	80%	3.6	11	82%	-2.3
Tim Crowder	26	DE	34	4.3%	57	21	7	3	62%	77	3.6	79	3	2	10.5	21	62%	4.4	13	62%	2.3
Gerald McCoy	23	DT	31	4.9%	28	25	10	1	77%	27	0.3	5	3	8	16.5	22	77%	1.4	9	89%	-2.3
Kyle Moore	25	DE	18	5.3%	--	11	0	1	63%	--	3.7	--	0	1	6.5	16	63%	3.2	2	50%	7.5
Al Woods	24	DT	17	3.9%	--	13	1	0	73%	--	2.4	--	0.5	0	1	15	73%	2.9	2	100%	-2.0
Michael Bennett	26	DT	16	2.5%	--	13	4	1	91%	--	2.2	--	1	1	6.5	11	91%	1.0	5	60%	4.8

Linebackers	Age	Pos	Plays	TmPct	Overall Rk	Stop	Dfts	BTkl	AvYd	Pass Rush Sack	Hit	Hur	vs. Run Runs	St%	Rk	Yds	Rk	vs. Pass Tgts	Suc%	Rk	AdjYd	Rk
Barrett Ruud	28	MLB	121	15.5%	14	65	20	8	5.7	1.5	1	4.5	82	62%	79	4.8	105	24	47%	58	6.3	43
Geno Hayes	24	OLB	88	11.2%	47	61	29	8	3.6	4	2	5.5	44	82%	8	2.1	12	28	55%	37	6.0	38
Quincy Black	27	OLB	62	11.5%	43	37	12	2	5.0	2	1	1	32	59%	84	4.1	92	19	62%	19	8.2	75
Adam Hayward	27	OLB	20	2.6%	--	11	2	0	4.4	1	1	3	13	54%	--	3.4	--	6	82%	--	1.6	--
Dekoda Watson	23	OLB	19	2.6%	--	7	4	0	8.1	0	1	0	10	40%	--	7.6	--	3	72%	--	6.7	--

Year	Yards	ALY	Rank	Power	Rank	Stuff	Rank	2nd Lev	Rank	Open Field	Rank
2008	4.52	4.03	11	66%	16	16%	25	1.11	16	1.05	28
2009	4.86	4.44	28	80%	31	14%	30	1.31	31	1.06	25
2010	4.92	4.56	30	55%	5	17%	23	1.49	32	1.01	27

Year	LE	Rank	LT	Rank	Mid	Rank	RT	Rank	RE	Rank	Sacks	ASR	Rank
2008	3.83	13	4.56	24	4.15	13	3.83	9	2.73	4	29	7.1%	8
2009	3.71	10	4.14	16	4.76	32	4.26	18	3.76	12	28	5.8%	24
2010	4.83	24	4.40	21	4.67	31	4.71	27	4.04	17	26	4.8%	31

A dearth of talent at a key position forced the Bucs to take defensive ends (Iowa's Adrian Clayborn and Clemson's Da'Quan Bowers) in the first and second rounds of April's draft. Stylez G. White was half-decent when it came to quarterback hits and hurries, but his inability to get home to the quarterback on a regular basis put him on the bench late in the season. Ryan Sims, who started the season as White's early bookend, was eventually released. Late in the season, Tampa Bay's edge rush was commandeered by guys like Michael Bennett and Tim Crowder, leaving fans to wonder just how much that lack of quarterback disruption kept the resurgent Bucs out of the playoffs. The front office helped answer that question by informing line coach Todd Wash that he should seek alternate employment.

Clayborn and Bowers are talented players, but both come to the NFL with question marks. Clayborn is dynamic off the edge in fits and starts, and he's very fast for his size, but he can get washed out by inferior blockers at times and there are concerns about his ability to transition to a league with better week-to-week blockers. He may be a better NFL fit as a 3-4 end. Bowers is a good pass-rusher and one of the best run-stopping ends to come out of college in recent memory, but he plummeted in the draft due to issues with a balky knee and postseason surgery that left him unable to do much in pre-draft workouts.

A return to health would help Gerald McCoy and Brian Price live up to their lofty draft status. Roy Miller and Al Woods held things down decently after things fell apart for the rookies. Right now, Tampa Bay's front four is full of "what if?" — one of the league's best should everything go right, but that's a lot to hope for at this point. There's a lot of talent that could be spending too much time on the trainer's table.

Middle linebackers in straight 4-3 defenses are tackle magnets under the worst circumstances, so we generally advise against making too much of their tackle totals. However, Barrett Ruud did impress by becoming the second player in Bucs history to lead the team in tackles four years in a row. The other guy? Derrick Brooks. That said, the Bucs were looking to get younger in the middle, and the free agent moved on to Tennessee. Geno Hayes was the guided missile on the weak side in many plays in which Ruud was otherwise occupied; his more physical style makes him an ideal inside linebacker in nickel sets, and he specialized in crashing down on run plays after backing into coverage. The front office found its Ruud replacement with the third-round selection of Washington's Mason Foster, a Ruud-style player to a degree — smart and versatile, but not physically intimidating. Quincy Black filled out an outstanding starting threesome, and was rewarded with a five-year deal to stay in Tampa Bay.

Defensive Secondary

| | | | | | | | | | | vs. Run | | | | | vs. Pass | | | | | | | | |
Secondary	Age	Pos	Plays	TmPct	Rk	Stop	Dfts	BTkl	Runs	St%	Rk	Yds	Rk	Tgts	Tgt%	Rk	Dist	Suc%	Rk	APaYd	Rk	PD	Int
Ronde Barber	36	CB	94	12.0%	11	49	22	14	42	62%	12	4.7	14	54	12.5%	72	8.8	52%	46	5.7	10	11	3
Sean Jones	29	SS	76	9.7%	49	28	9	8	51	43%	32	6.8	44	16	3.7%	72	11.3	54%	40	4.9	6	1	1
E.J. Biggers	24	CB	61	7.8%	53	23	10	5	12	17%	86	15.4	89	68	15.9%	36	13.0	60%	13	5.4	7	9	1
Cody Grimm	24	FS	52	9.7%	50	21	4	4	33	48%	20	6.6	37	10	3.4%	73	14.3	38%	75	9.8	64	1	1
Aqib Talib	25	CB	51	9.5%	31	20	9	3	10	40%	50	4.4	13	50	17.0%	24	13.0	55%	24	8.1	59	11	6
Corey Lynch	26	FS	25	3.2%	--	4	2	4	15	13%	--	9.5	--	2	0.5%	--	21.5	80%	--	6.4	--	1	1
Sabby Piscitelli	28	FS	16	2.0%	--	4	2	0	9	22%	--	7.1	--	3	0.6%	--	7.0	64%	--	-0.2	--	1	1

Year	Pass D Rank	vs. #1 WR	Rk	vs. #2 WR	Rk	vs. Other WR	Rk	vs. TE	Rk	vs. RB	Rk
2008	6	15.5%	23	-49.7%	1	6.1%	24	-18.7%	4	-24.2%	3
2009	23	4.2%	16	-5.1%	14	11.0%	23	7.0%	17	-9.7%	10
2010	13	-14.2%	6	0.7%	15	-12.0%	10	3.9%	16	12.3%	23

If anyone wondered whether Raheem Morris was going to lose his DB-coaching acumen when he switched to a larger role, the Bucs' above-average pass defense should have put those questions to rest. The Bucs' pass defense DVOA improved despite several personnel hits, a moribund pass rush, and a rookie position coach in Jimmy Lake. Tampa Bay lost safety Tanard Jackson to a suspension just two games into the season after Jackson violated the league's substance abuse policy. As Jackson was involved in more defensive plays than any other Bucs defensive back in 2009, that was a problem. And Aqib Talib ranked second in the league with six picks when he was lost for the season with more than a month left due to a hip injury.

Another issue was the late-August benching and eventual release of Sabby Piscitelli, though those two gambits may have been cases of addition by subtraction. Piscitelli, the 2009 NFL leader in missed tackles per our numbers, claimed to be very surprised by the move. He was the only one. Rookie Cody Grimm did a very solid job after early struggles, but he too saw an early end to his season courtesy of the injury bug. And speaking of all those injuries, Ronde Barber should be marketing the secret to his durability to his teammates — at age 35, Barber was one of just eight Bucs players to start all 16 games throughout the 2010 season. His coverage was average and he ranked tied for fourth in the league with 14 broken tackles, so the writing is on the wall there.

Special Teams

Year	DVOA	Rank	FG/XP	Rank	Net Kick	Rank	Kick Ret	Rank	Net Punt	Rank	Punt Ret	Rank	Hidden	Rank
2008	-0.3%	19	-4.8	27	4.5	12	2.9	14	-5.4	23	1.4	11	5.5	6
2009	3.2%	5	-11.2	30	6.8	9	9.6	5	1.6	17	11.8	2	13.1	1
2010	-0.4%	18	-0.7	20	-3.1	22	3.9	12	3.3	16	-5.9	27	3.1	8

Apparently up for a major challenge, special teams coach Rich Bisaccia left the Bucs after nine seasons to try and coach up the San Diego Chargers' Three Stooges version of the return game. Kick returner Micheal Spurlock, forever famous for becoming the first Bucs player to return a punt or kick for a touchdown in franchise history after a 30-year drought, came back from an indifferent 2009 to re-establish himself as one of the more dangerous at his position. Punt returns were an afterthought without Clifton Smith, and this showed up in Tampa Bay's serious decline in return value.

Kicker Connor Barth, who survived a round robin in-season audition process in 2009, hit 23 of 28 field goals in his first full season with the Bucs, missing only from 40 yards and out. He did not win any lead foot awards in his kickoffs, averaging 61.7 yards per boot and producing just one touchback in 78 kickoffs. Punter Robert Malone finished the season among the lowest in gross punting average (41.5 — just three qualifying punters were worse), punts inside the opponent's 20-yard line (17), and fair catches caused (12). Tampa Bay's punt value was almost entirely the product of its coverage units, which is a solid indicator that the super-subs are buying into the program.

Coaching Staff

As an assistant coach living on one of the more distant branches of the Dungy coaching tree, Raheem Morris was long thought to be a great coach-in-waiting. He's proven his worth by getting the NFL's youngest roster to believe in a rebuilding program that nearly resulted in a playoff berth for the Bucs in 2010. Morris has generally had his hands full with players whose off-field issues can cause roster problems, but he seems to do a good job of controlling what he can.

The most interesting dynamic between the Bucs' coaching staff and players could be with new line coach Keith Millard and a front four full of elite talent … if injuries can be kept at bay. Millard was one of the best inside pass disruptors in NFL history, then spent some time coaching in Denver and Oakland. In the past few years, he has built up a training center for draft prospects, where he worked with current Bucs defensive tackle Brian Price and helped Oakland's Lamarr Houston become one of the NFL's pleasant rookie surprises in 2010.

Tennessee Titans

2010 Record: 6-10	**2011 Mean Projection:** 5.0 wins
Pythagorean Wins: 8.5 (16th)	**On the Clock (0-3):** 29%
DVOA: 7.7% (11th)	**Loserville (4-6):** 44%
Offense: -0.8% (20th)	**Mediocrity (7-8):** 18%
Defense: -4.0% (8th)	**Playoff Contender (9-10):** 8%
Special Teams: 4.5% (6th)	**Super Bowl Contender (11+):** 2%
Variance: 20.4% (20th)	**Projected Average Opponent:** 1.2% (11th)

2010: The last stand of the Fisher King.

2011: The first qualification for a job with the Titans? A past job with the Titans.

When the Tennessee Titans open the 2011 regular season September 11 at Jacksonville, for the first time in 263 regular season games, Jeff Fisher won't be directing the team as its head coach. In NFL history, only Don Shula, Tom Landry, Curly Lambeau, Chuck Noll, and Steve Owen spent more consecutive games prowling the sidelines as the head coach of a single team. But all things must pass, and a second consecutive tumultuous season, one that ended with a 1-8 finish following a 5-2 start, resulted in the Titans and Fisher agreeing to part ways.

Fisher's departure did not come immediately after the end of the season, however. At first, it seemed he might make it to a 17th full season after owner Bud Adams and the rest of the powers that be decided that, if the choice came down to Fisher or quarterback Vince Young, Fisher would be the one to stay. The evaluation of Fisher's performance and tenure continued past the decision to part ways with Young, however, and the Titans eventually decided to make the change.

Fisher's departure doesn't mean the Titans will be lacking in continuity at the head coach position, though, as his replacement has actually spent even more time on the Titans' sideline. The Titans ended up promoting from within, hiring offensive line coach Mike Munchak as head coach. With the promotion, Munchak will be entering his 30th consecutive season receiving a paycheck from the team. He joined the then-Houston Oilers in 1982 after being selected eighth overall in the NFL draft and spent a dozen seasons at offensive guard, three as an offensive assistant, and then 14 as offensive line coach before being ascending to the top on-field job.

Munchak's path to the head coaching position is an unusual one. The typical path to becoming a head coach is to move from position coach to coordinator, and only then to head coach, having first proven your ability to handle a broader scope of responsibility. Munchak, however, has never had to manage more than the small group of offensive linemen. How have coaches fared with that level of inexperience?

The answer, unsurprisingly, is that coaches don't normally get hired with that level of inexperience. Even relative neophytes like Tony Sparano, Lane Kiffin, and Raheem Morris had experience as a head coach or coordinator, albeit only at the college level. (Sparano was head coach at the University of New Haven and offensive coordinator at Boston University, Kiffin was offensive coordinator at USC, and Morris was defensive coordinator at Kansas State.) Munchak is only the eighth coach in the DVOA era (dating back to 1992) to become a head coach without serving as a head coach or offensive or defensive coordinator either in college or the NFL (Table 1).

History shows us that even those inexperienced head

2011 Titans Schedule

Week	Opp.	Week	Opp.	Week	Opp.
1	at JAC	7	HOU	13	at BUF
2	BAL	8	IND	14	NO
3	DEN	9	CIN	15	at IND
4	at CLE	10	at CAR	16	JAC
5	at PIT	11	at ATL	17	at HOU
6	BYE	12	TB		

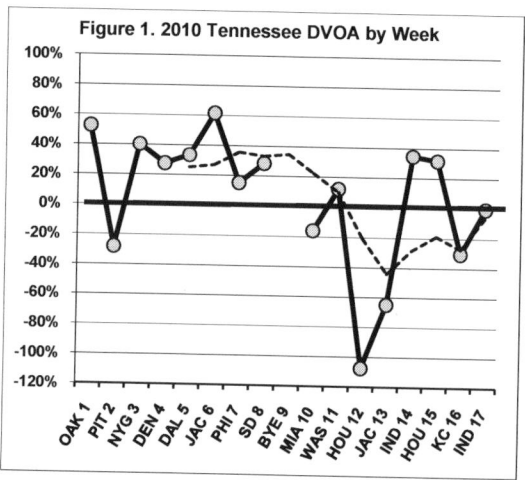

Figure 1. 2010 Tennessee DVOA by Week

coaches have had a certain level of success in their first year, with the team's DVOA improving in their first year at the helm even if only by a small amount. That's not very surprising, however, as teams that make coaching changes are generally bad teams that will improve the next year regardless of a coaching change.

The history of these coaches is mixed. Andy Reid is of course still the head coach of the Philadelphia Eagles, who have been one of the league's winningest teams in his tenure. Herm Edwards had a run with the Jets and then with the Chiefs, and made the playoffs several times. John Harbaugh has made the playoffs all three seasons with the Ravens. On the other hand, Mike Tice, Rod Marinelli, Jim Zorn, and Mike Singletary were all notoriously overmatched as head coaches, and the latter three all had some notoriously dysfunctional experiences. Of the seven, Mike Tice is the only one who shares Mike Munchak's offensive line background. Like Munchak, Tice was hired by an owner who had an oft-deserved reputation for cheapness (Vikings then-owner Red McCombs), and his unfamiliarity with the broader aspects of coaching proved to be his undoing.

That inexperience may show up in a number of areas, especially with a coach, like Munchak, who seemingly had not been seriously preparing to be a

Table 1. Coaches with no Coordinator Experience, 1992-2010

Coach	Team	Year Before	DVOA	Year After	DVOA
Andy Reid	PHI	1998	-35.1%	1999	-10.0%
Herm Edwards	NYJ	2000	11.0%	2001	13.0%
Mike Tice	MIN	2001*	-26.1%	2002	-18.5%
Rod Marinelli	DET	2005	-22.5%	2006	-22.1%
John Harbaugh	BAL	2007	-3.9%	2008	29.1%
Jim Zorn	WAS	2007	6.2%	2008	10.4%
Mike Singletary	SF	2008*	-13.9%	2009	1.0%

* Took over as interim head coach

head coach. Munchak admitted his unfamiliarity after the first day of training camp:

"I didn't know half these things went on during practice. During seven-on-seven I was lost. I had never been down for seven-on-seven. I stayed with drills I haven't been around much. It was fun watching the coaches coach a little bit, watching their techniques and seeing their interaction with the players and getting to watch the different positions and seeing how guys are working and their work ethic."

While it is commendable for an organization's leader to learn new things and enjoy his job, it's slightly disconcerting to think of an NFL head coach who had never watched one of the most basic passing-game drills before.

Another typical problem area for inexperienced head coaches is in-game decision-making. This was a notorious problem area for Edwards, for whom the Jets eventually hired a clock-management assistant, and still is probably Andy Reid's biggest weakness as a head coach. The only coach on the list who hasn't had major problems on game day is John Harbaugh. Harbaugh, however, had a key advantage that none of the other coaches on the list really had: He went to an established team with an excellent GM and strong infrastructure in place. Harbaugh's success was less the result of John Harbaugh going in and instituting a new culture. It was a matter of him adjusting to Ozzie Newsome and the Ravens' organizational philosophy, and adjusting to the team as much as it adjusted to him.

Munchak, alas, is not stepping into nearly as favorable a scenario, as the Titans are undergoing scheme changes on both offense and defense. Out with Young went quarterback Kerry Collins (retired) and offensive coordinator Mike Heimerdinger. In came quarterbacks Matt Hasselbeck (from Seattle, in free agency) and Jake Locker (from the University of Washington, in the first round of the draft) and offensive coordinator Chris Palmer (from the new-defunct Hartford Colonials of the UFL).

In addition to his all-important previous experience with the franchise, as wide receivers coach in the Warren Moon era, Palmer will implement something closer to the traditional West Coast offense with quick timing routes. This represents a major philosophy change from Heimerdinger's more vertical passing game, and also change in the quarterback's skill set. Even when Young was at his most successful in the second half of 2009 and the first half of 2010, he struggled with both timing and accuracy on shorter routes. Hasselbeck has extensive experience in a similar offense from his time with Mike Holmgren in Seattle, and if he can stay healthy should bridge the gap until Locker is ready to take over.

For Munchak to defy the odds against inexperienced head coaches, Locker needs to develop into a very good NFL quarterback. Locker was a bit of a surprise choice as the second quarterback off the board. His biggest problem is the one that tends to be the hardest for college quarterbacks to solve, namely poor accuracy. It is very difficult to find any recent quarterbacks with a career 53.9 percent completion rate who had more than the most modest NFL success. No, Locker's Washington teams were not particularly talented, especially at wideout. Neither were Jay Cutler's Vanderbilt teams, or Matt Ryan's Boston College teams, and both quarterbacks had higher completion rates. Locker's accuracy will have to improve substantially for him to be even an average-quality NFL starter. That is more likely to be an issue for the future, however, as the lost offseason likely means Locker will see no or limited work in 2011.

Over on defense, out went defensive coordinator Chuck Cecil. Following him out the door, though voluntarily, was defensive line coach Jim Washburn. Washburn's departure signified a changing of the guard in the Titans' defensive scheme. Since Jim Schwartz's hire as defensive coordinator following the 2000 season, the Titans had played primarily an aggressive attacking one-gap style with their front seven and on pass plays sent four rushers with an occasional defensive back off the slot. Cecil had been slightly more creative, running more zone and line-backer blitzes, but had not made fundamental changes. New defensive coordinator Jerry Gray, however, will install a different scheme. (And yes, of course Gray has a history with the franchise: cornerback 1992, quality control coach 1997-98, and defensive backs coach 1999-2000.)

Gray, who spent several years coaching with former Titans defensive coordinator Gregg Williams, has shown some of the changes he wants to make. The Schwartz/Cecil scheme also essentially played two weakside linebackers, while Gray has formally announced he plans to play a true strongside linebacker and the Titans drafted Akeem Ayers in the second-round to fill that role. The third-round pick also betrayed Gray's influence as the Titans drafted defensive tackle Jurrell Casey, who projects as more of a standard nose tackle than the Schwartz/Cecil scheme typically showcased. That Casey represents a new trend in defensive line thinking was reinforced by the free agency acquisition of nose tackle Shaun Smith from the Chiefs and their 3-4 scheme, and by the move of Jason Jones from defensive tackle to defensive end.

The bigger question for both coordinators is whether the 2011 Titans will look more like the team that went 1-15 at the beginning of 2009 and the end of 2010, or the team that went 13-4 at the end of 2009 and the beginning of 2010. The transitions on both offense and defense will take time.

On offense, the Titans' success came on passes thrown downfield. In fact, they ranked first in the league in both the frequency and success rate of passes thrown 21 to 30 yards downfield. The downside is that their receiving corps does not tend to be very explosive with the ball in their hands, finishing 31st in the league with 3.8 average yards after the catch. Kenny Britt was the only receiver who saw significant action and was quick as well as fast, and also the only one who could avoid tacklers. But Britt once again found legal trouble in the offseason that may result in him involuntarily missing games, and the hamstring troubles that caused him to miss time in 2010 also kept him out of training camp early in 2011. The Titans will need younger players such as wideout Damian Williams and tight end Jared Cook to play bigger roles in the offense and turn Hasselbeck's seven-yard passes into 17-yard gains.

On defense, Gray has not yet revealed how he intends to pressure the opposing quarterback. During the defense-driven 5-2 start in 2010, Washburn's defensive line was particularly adept at rushing the passer, and the secondary benefited. In the second half of the year, when the pass rush dropped off, the secondary struggled. With the secondary returning essentially intact, the defensive backs are likely to struggle again unless the Titans can get pressure. Whether it is linebacker Ayers, new defensive end Jones, or 2010 first-round defensive end pick Derrick Morgan, who missed most of last season with a knee injury, the Titans need to find someone who can reliably rush the passer.

Normally when a team finishes 11th in DVOA despite a 6-10 record, you're going to see Football Outsiders projecting a much better record the following year. But with all the changes in personnel, coaching, and scheme, the 2011 Titans are a very different team. Unless and until the offense and the defense can show that the new schemes will work with the available talent, the Titans will be hard-pressed to exceed last year's 6-10 mark.

Tom Gower

2010 Titans Stats by Week

Wk	vs.	W-L	PF	PA	YDF	YDA	TO	Total	Off	Def	ST
1	OAK	W	38	13	345	286	1	53%	23%	-21%	9%
2	PIT	L	11	19	238	127	-6	-28%	-71%	-61%	-18%
3	@NYG	W	29	10	271	471	3	40%	25%	-3%	12%
4	DEN	L	20	26	288	327	-1	28%	2%	-23%	2%
5	@DAL	W	34	27	321	511	3	33%	27%	6%	12%
6	@JAC	W	30	3	324	249	4	62%	15%	-38%	9%
7	PHI	W	37	19	328	326	1	15%	-12%	-19%	8%
8	@SD	L	25	33	370	456	1	28%	39%	17%	6%
9	BYE										
10	@MIA	L	17	29	259	404	-2	-16%	1%	23%	6%
11	WAS	L	16	19	373	465	-1	12%	9%	18%	21%
12	@HOU	L	0	20	162	346	-3	-108%	-120%	-8%	4%
13	JAC	L	6	17	220	377	-2	-65%	-41%	27%	3%
14	IND	L	28	30	365	399	-2	35%	53%	11%	-7%
15	HOU	W	31	17	359	323	0	32%	1%	-28%	2%
16	@KC	L	14	34	270	458	0	-30%	-26%	5%	1%
17	@IND	L	20	23	341	358	0	0%	5%	10%	5%

Trends and Splits

	Offense	Rank	Defense	Rank
Total DVOA	-0.8%	20	-4.0%	8
Unadjusted VOA	0.4%	21	0.7%	14
Weighted Trend	-2.0%	22	2.1%	13
Variance	18.7%	32	6.1%	12
Average Opponent	7.1%	4	11.0%	32
Passing	15.5%	18	6.4%	12
Rushing	-6.5%	27	-17.3%	3
First Down	7.4%	15	-12.8%	2
Second Down	-9.9%	25	5.7%	19
Third Down	-2.4%	19	-2.5%	13
First Half	-0.4%	22	0.2%	16
Second Half	-1.3%	20	-8.2%	7
Red Zone	-1.5%	19	-27.7%	3
Late and Close	5.5%	14	4.7%	24

Five-Year Performance

Year	W-L	Pyth	Est W	PF	PA	TO	Total	Rk	Off	Rk	Def	Rk	ST	Rk	Off AGL	Rk	Def AGL	Rk
2006	8-8	6.0	6.8	324	400	+2	-9.6%	22	-8.2%	24	3.9%	20	2.5%	10	34.2	31	9.0	11
2007	10-6	8.1	9.2	301	297	0	9.5%	11	-3.4%	20	-13.3%	1	-0.4%	17	4.7	1	10.3	5
2008	13-3	12.1	11.6	375	234	+14	26.9%	5	9.0%	16	-16.6%	5	1.3%	15	9.0	3	14.4	9
2009	8-8	6.8	7.5	354	402	-4	-6.4%	22	7.6%	15	12.7%	27	-1.3%	24	7.4	3	14.9	5
2010	6-10	8.5	8.8	356	339	-4	7.7%	11	-0.8%	20	-4.0%	8	4.5%	6	21.0	13	10.6	5

Strategic Tendencies

Run/Pass		Rank	Offense		Rank	Defense		Rank	Other		Rank
Runs, all plays	42%	10	3+ WR	45%	21	Rush 3	1.2%	30	2+ RB, Pct Runs	56%	21
Runs, first half	44%	7	4+ WR	1%	32	Rush 4	69.6%	4	1 RB/2 TE, Pct Runs	52%	11
Runs, first down	55%	7	2+ TE	33%	12	Rush 5	19.4%	28	1 RB/3+ WR, Pct Runs	20%	23
Runs, second-long	37%	11	Single back	62%	10	Rush 6+	9.9%	13	CB1 on WR1	50%	5
Runs, power sit.	51%	26	Play action	15%	25	Zone Blitz	4.3%	20	Go for it on 4th	0.96	11
Runs, behind 2H	23%	24	Max protect	11%	19	Sacks by LB	13.8%	24	Offensive Pace	29.9	8
Pass, ahead 2H	33%	32	Outside pocket	9%	26	Sacks by DB	5.0%	24	Defensive Pace	30.5	9

As you might expect, when your best player is your running back, your offense isn't going to go empty very often. The Titans went empty just six times all year, and four of those came in one game, Week 14 against Indianapolis. ☞ The Titans had the third-best offensive DVOA in the league on third-and-short, but ranked 15th on third-and-medium (4 to 6 yards to go) and 30th on third-and-long (7-plus yards to go). ☞ Tennessee faced more draw plays than any defense in the NFL, although the Titans' DVOA against draws was actually close to the NFL average. The Titans also faced more wide receiver screens than any other defense, and they weren't very good against these plays — allowing 6.9 yards per pass with 59.9% DVOA. ☞ Tennessee led the league with 38 penalties for the various offsides penalties (Defensive Offside, Encroachment, and Neutral Zone Infraction). The Titans had nine more of these flags than any other team.

Passing

Player	DYAR	DVOA	Plays	NtYds	Avg	YAC	C%	TD	Int
K.Collins	266	3.0%	293	1766	6.0	3.4	58.2%	14	8
V.Young	423	26.8%	176	1300	7.4	4.4	59.6%	10	2
R.Smith	-178	-90.6%	42	220	5.2	4.2	50.0%	0	4

Rushing

Player	DYAR	DVOA	Plays	Yds	Avg	TD	Fum	Suc
C.Johnson	18	-7.2%	316	1365	4.3	11	2	39%
J.Ringer	25	5.1%	51	239	4.7	2	0	37%
V.Young	8	-0.6%	16	132	8.3	0	2	-
K.Collins	-23	-99.2%	4	0	0.0	0	1	-

Receiving

Player	DYAR	DVOA	Plays	Ctch	Yds	Y/C	YAC	TD	C%
N.Washington	74	-3.0%	94	42	687	16.4	2.7	6	45%
K.Britt	252	28.5%	73	42	775	18.5	2.9	9	58%
J.Gage	0	-12.5%	43	20	266	13.3	2.5	1	47%
D.Williams	17	-4.5%	28	16	219	13.7	2.5	0	57%
L.Hawkins	35	55.7%	6	5	61	12.2	1.0	0	83%
B.Scaife	-13	-11.0%	52	36	316	8.8	2.9	4	69%
J.Cook	82	23.6%	45	29	361	12.4	4.7	1	64%
C.Stevens	-14	-16.0%	23	11	122	11.1	6.2	2	48%
C.Johnson	-43	-27.9%	57	44	245	5.6	5.6	1	77%
A.Hall	15	-0.4%	20	15	100	6.7	7.1	0	75%
J.Ringer	15	20.7%	8	7	44	6.3	3.7	0	88%

Offensive Line

Year	Yards	ALY	Rank	Power	Rank	Stuff	Rank	2nd Lev	Rank	Open Field	Rank
2008	4.45	4.10	16	61%	26	22%	28	1.21	9	1.07	6
2009	5.29	4.01	22	64%	15	21%	24	1.28	7	1.77	1
2010	4.36	3.47	31	46%	31	26%	31	1.20	12	1.25	4

Year	LE	Rank	LT	Rank	Mid	Rank	RT	Rank	RE	Rank	Sacks	ASR	Rank	F-Start	Cont.
2008	3.86	23	4.35	11	4.14	16	4.04	21	4.01	18	12	3.2%	3	16	45
2009	4.11	20	3.45	31	3.71	27	4.44	7	4.81	6	15	3.7%	3	18	35
2010	4.25	17	2.82	32	3.14	32	4.60	6	3.06	28	27	5.6%	9	22	34

No matter who was the quarterback, the Titans kept him protected. They allowed a league-low 24 quarterback hits to go with finishing ninth in Adjusted Sack Rate. However, Tennessee's run blocking seriously regressed in 2010, suffering from both personnel and schematic issues that will have to be resolved for the Titans' offense to be more successful. Chris Johnson's greatest success in 2009 came when running to the outside, particularly to the right side. In 2010, opposing defenses paid particular attention to not letting Johnson reach the edge. When Johnson tried to reach the edge anyway, he too often found no room to run or a defender already in place. The obvious alternative would be to run between the tackles, but here Johnson's patience and desire for long plays sometimes hurt the Titans as he too often passed on potential two-yard gains in search of ten-yard gains only to find himself tackled for no gain.

Johnson's style exacerbated the issues caused by mediocre play in the middle of the Titans' offensive line. Right guard Jake Scott had remained a good run blocker even though his pass protection slipped in 2009, but in 2010 he struggled mightily in both phases of the game and also had nine false starts. Like the other Titans' linemen, his game is less pure power than opening up angles on zone runs. At center, Eugene Amano moved over from left guard to replace the retired Kevin Mawae. He was an upgrade over Mawae, but that upgrade was only from poor to below average. His combination play with new left guard Leroy Harris was particularly disappointing, as both of them struggled mightily at reaching the second level and sustaining blocks. Fernando Velasco struggled at times as an injury fill-in for Harris and Amano.

The previous mainstays of the offensive line were left tackle Michael Roos and right tackle David Stewart, but both had mediocre years in 2010. Roos in particular had some lapses in pass protection that were shocking given the mostly consistent smooth play he'd demonstrated since moving to left tackle in 2006. Stewart, as he has most years except for 2009, struggled at times with speed rushers, and the Titans' results running to the right side failed to match his reputation at a mauler.

Defensive Front Seven

Defensive Line	Age	Pos	Plays	TmPct	Rk	Stop	Dfts	BTkl	St%	Rk	AvYd	Rk	Sack	Hit	Hur	Runs	St%	Yds	Pass	St%	Yds
						Overall							Pass Rush			vs. Run			vs. Pass		
Jason Babin	31	DE	58	6.2%	28	48	24	1	78%	22	0.2	10	12.5	15	25.5	36	78%	1.6	22	91%	-2.0
Jacob Ford	28	DE	41	5.0%	44	27	9	0	70%	74	2.4	60	3	5	12	33	70%	2.2	8	50%	3.0
Jason Jones	25	DT	41	4.7%	35	34	18	0	81%	19	0.6	6	3.5	3	13	27	81%	0.4	14	86%	0.8
Dave Ball	30	DE	33	5.1%	43	25	13	1	61%	52	1.3	28	7	6	10	18	61%	4.2	15	93%	-2.2
William Hayes	26	DE	32	3.9%	65	25	7	1	79%	42	1.8	39	1.5	7	6	28	79%	2.1	4	75%	0.0
Jovan Haye	29	DT	31	3.8%	50	22	4	1	69%	47	2.3	46	0	1	2.5	29	69%	2.5	2	100%	-0.5
Tony Brown	31	DT	23	3.6%	54	15	7	0	69%	56	1.7	26	3.5	1	7	13	69%	2.0	10	60%	1.2
Sen'Derrick Marks	24	DT	23	3.3%	58	14	5	3	59%	61	4.3	67	0	7	2	17	59%	5.0	6	67%	2.5
Marques Douglas	34	DT	19	5.4%	--	15	3	1	82%	--	2.2	--	0	1	1	17	82%	1.6	2	50%	6.5

Linebackers	Age	Pos	Plays	TmPct	Rk	Stop	Dfts	BTkl	AvYd	Sack	Hit	Hur	Runs	St%	Rk	Yds	Rk	Tgts	Suc%	Rk	AdjYd	Rk
						Overall				Pass Rush			vs. Run					vs. Pass				
Stephen Tulloch	26	MLB	164	17.4%	7	101	25	13	4.1	1	4	3	98	67%	59	2.8	36	77	60%	22	6.0	40
Will Witherspoon	31	OLB	97	10.3%	57	58	26	15	4.9	3	4	4	48	79%	13	3.6	70	51	55%	36	6.4	46
Gerald McRath	25	OLB	59	8.4%	77	26	7	2	5.3	1.5	1	3	34	50%	104	3.9	89	15	39%	--	8.1	--

Year	Yards	ALY	Rank	Power	Rank	Stuff	Rank	2nd Lev	Rank	Open Field	Rank
2008	3.81	3.62	5	64%	13	25%	2	1.03	9	0.79	18
2009	4.49	4.22	20	71%	25	19%	16	1.13	16	0.91	22
2010	3.88	3.71	7	64%	18	22%	7	1.16	19	0.59	11

Year	LE	Rank	LT	Rank	Mid	Rank	RT	Rank	RE	Rank	Sacks	ASR	Rank
2008	2.52	2	2.69	1	3.85	7	3.32	4	5.39	31	44	7.1%	9
2009	5.20	30	4.09	14	4.33	25	3.90	13	3.68	11	32	5.7%	25
2010	5.19	29	3.32	5	3.75	9	3.23	5	3.53	10	40	6.5%	13

The Titans defensively had a tale of two half-seasons in 2010. In the first half of the season, the Titans' defensive line terrorized opposing passers (9.5 percent Adjusted Sack Rate through Week 6). In the second half of the season, opposing passers stayed upright more often and picked apart the Titans' pass defense (4.6 percent ASR from Week 7 on). Combined with defensive line coach Jim Washburn's offseason departure, that second-half swoon may have spelled the end for the era of the Titans playing an attack-oriented style with their defensive line.

The biggest beneficiary of that style in 2010 was the Titans' most consistent defensive lineman, Jason Babin, but he left in free agency to re-join Washburn in Philadelphia. None of the Titans' other defensive ends stood out as particularly fine. Dave Ball had a surprisingly productive year as a pass rusher, but sometimes found himself out of position in run plays. William Hayes was mediocre as a pass rusher, but fair as a run defender. Jacob Ford was Hayes's mirror image, though he failed to get to the quarterback as often as he did in 2008 or 2009. With the philosophy change, Ford likely finds himself relegated to obvious pass-rushing situations. Fifth-round pick Karl Klug (Iowa) could add more size to the defensive end rotation, but the biggest impact would come from a full recovery by 2010 first-round selection Derrick Morgan, who was lost for the season in Week 4.

Tony Brown was supposed to be the team's mainstay at defensive tackle after signing a three-year extension, but was in and out of the lineup with a knee injury, and he struggled to be as productive as a pass rusher when he was in the lineup. Realizing he'd never again be fully healthy, the Titans released him in July. Jason Jones played in a career-high 15 games and flashed dominance at times, including getting Cowboys right guard Leonard Davis benched after abusing him with quickness for two sacks, but was inconsistent and could be overwhelmed at the point of attack, and will be moved to defensive end. Jovan Haye once again was unproductive against the run and the pass, and has failed to justify the free agent contract he signed in 2009. Defensive coordinator Jerry Gray decided Haye should add back the 25 pounds he lost before 2010, but it may not be enough to preserve his roster spot. 2009 second-round pick Sen'Derrick Marks has also struggled to fulfill expectations. After trading away Kevin Vickerson on draft day 2010, the Titans played the year without a true 4-3 nose tackle, then added USC's Jurrell Casey in the third round and Shaun Smith in free agency this year to rectify that absence.

Will Witherspoon was the best and most reliable of the Titans' linebackers, adding some much-needed professionalism and discipline to the group. While he had more sacks than any Titans linebacker in several years, he was not a great pass rusher. His most notable flaws were poor tackling and lack of either great speed or agility. Middle linebacker Stephen Tulloch made a lot of tackles, and his pass coverage stats were better than his reputation, but he signed with Detroit in the offseason. Gerald McRath had a deeply disappointing sophomore campaign after an up-and-down rookie season. He still made too many mistakes due to inexperience and over-aggressiveness and was quickly yanked when the Titans tried to play him in nickel instead of Witherspoon in an attempt to get more speed and athleticism on the field. The depth behind the top three was virtually nonexistent, so the Titans had to add to the position in the draft and free agency. They drafted Akeem Ayers in the second round and will install him as the starter at strongside linebacker as part of the scheme change. Then they signed middle linebacker Barrett Ruud (ex-Tampa Bay) to a one-year deal. He may not be quite as good a run-stopper as Tulloch, but is an upgrade in pass coverage and should be able to direct the defense. Fourth-round selection Colin McCarthy (Miami) likely is the middle linebacker of the future. Witherspoon and McRath will fight it out for the starting spot opposite Ayers, but the role is likely McRath's in the future. Undersized 2010 third-round selection Rennie Curran may find himself odd man out in the new scheme after failing to get on the field as a rookie.

Defensive Secondary

Secondary	Age	Pos	Plays	TmPct	Rk	Stop	Dfts	BTkl	Runs	St%	Rk	Yds	Rk	Tgts	Tgt%	Rk	Dist	Suc%	Rk	APaYd	Rk	PD	Int
Michael Griffin	26	SS	119	12.7%	13	44	18	17	52	40%	36	6.6	38	46	8.3%	11	12.3	63%	14	7.9	40	8	4
Cortland Finnegan	27	CB	107	11.4%	13	34	16	9	27	37%	63	6.0	31	90	16.3%	32	13.1	48%	65	9.4	76	9	2
Chris Hope	31	FS	106	11.3%	23	29	14	7	59	36%	51	6.8	42	28	5.1%	56	15.4	57%	30	9.5	61	3	1
Alterraun Verner	23	CB	104	11.1%	18	45	14	9	24	46%	37	6.5	41	80	14.4%	55	7.9	54%	37	6.5	24	9	3
Jason McCourty	24	CB	53	7.5%	60	24	13	1	12	67%	5	5.0	21	46	11.1%	78	10.7	54%	33	6.3	20	8	2
Vincent Fuller	29	FS	32	4.5%	78	9	6	2	7	29%	66	6.0	31	21	5.1%	57	7.4	24%	79	9.9	66	2	1

Year	Pass D Rank	vs. #1 WR	Rk	vs. #2 WR	Rk	vs. Other WR	Rk	vs. TE	Rk	vs. RB	Rk
2008	4	-15.5%	4	-16.0%	7	-30.2%	6	-8.8%	11	-7.4%	7
2009	25	-1.6%	13	-0.7%	17	10.6%	22	37.8%	31	-18.1%	4
2010	12	4.4%	19	-6.1%	9	-14.3%	8	3.2%	15	6.0%	19

When the defensive line got pressure in 2010, the Titans' secondary was very good in coverage. When the defensive line didn't get pressure, the Titans' secondary was exploited. Unlike in 2009, when Nick Harper was an obvious major liability, there was no individual culprit you could single out as being the one most responsible. Rather, it was a team effort.

Cornerback Cortland Finnegan looked stellar in 2009 compared to the play around him, but 2010 demonstrated that while still a competent lead cornerback he was not an elite one. The pass rush problems are partly to blame for the drop in his charting metrics; for example, Finnegan allowed 8.8 adjusted yards per pass in Weeks

1 to 6, then 9.6 adjusted yards per pass after Week 7 when the pass pressure was cut in half. Still, Finnegan can, and last year did, get beat by opposing wide receivers, though only rarely was it by someone other than the opposing team's best wideout. He also got less safety help than did the other corner, rookie fourth-round pick Alterraun Verner. Verner started the year on the bench, but quickly supplanted first Vinny Fuller as the nickelback and then Jason McCourty as a starter. He had an above-average rookie year, but struggled more as the year went on both against the run and the pass. Verner seems better suited for a zone scheme that lets him attack the receiver and doesn't expose his lack of top-level speed and athleticism. Jason McCourty began the year as a starter, but got hurt and missed Weeks 4 to 7 and lost his starting position to Verner, though he still played in nickel packages with Verner moving to slot. Not quite as athletic as his twin Devin (of Patriots fame), he's limited to playing the outside but had a better year than his benching would suggest. Depth beyond the top three is virtually nil, and took a hit when Ryan Mouton tore his ACL in training camp.

The Titans' stated preference for several years has been to have two interchangeable safeties who play right and left and may on any given play be either the free safety or the strong safety if the call dictates that distinction. Between the two, Michael Griffin is more athletic, younger, and faster than Chris Hope. If you'd have to choose one of them to play free safety or as the deep safety in a single-high scheme, you'd expect Griffin to be the choice, especially because he was AFC Defensive Player of the Month for October and made his second Pro Bowl. That's not how it played out in 2010, however. The Titans for most of the year abandoned the idea of interchangeable safeties and played Hope at free safety and Griffin at strong safety, with Hope the single-high safety in any one-deep look. The reason was Griffin's unreliability in a deep safety role, demonstrated time and again in 2009 and again in 2010, even in two-deep looks. Hope is not an ideal fit at deep safety, as age has degraded his range and he sometimes bites too strongly on play action, but like Will Witherspoon he provides much-needed discipline and professionalism. Nevertheless, the Titans are expected to again try Griffin at free safety and Hope at strong safety in 2011. That is, if Hope makes the roster, as his $6.5 million salary this year may prove too rich for his play. Free-agent addition Jordan Babineaux is the primary backup at both safety positions.

Special Teams

Year	DVOA	Rank	FG/XP	Rank	Net Kick	Rank	Kick Ret	Rank	Net Punt	Rank	Punt Ret	Rank	Hidden	Rank
2008	1.3%	15	6.6	5	1.4	16	3.7	12	-2.4	21	-1.8	21	20.4	1
2009	-1.3%	24	11.9	2	-6.7	29	-11.8	31	6.1	6	-7.1	28	-0.2	14
2010	4.5%	6	9.0	3	-2.0	19	11.9	5	0.2	18	7.3	4	2.5	9

Rob Bironas may be the rare exception to the Football Outsiders tenet that every field-goal kicker is inconsistent. The Titans have ranked in the top five in our FG/XP ratings each of the last four seasons. His weakness in 2009 was kickoff distance, which declined by three yards from 2008, but he recovered most of that loss in 2010 and the number of touchbacks went up. Thanks in part to linebackers Tim Shaw and Patrick Bailey, added off the waiver wire before the season, kickoff coverage also improved. The strong leg punter Brett Kern showcased in 2009 was less evident in 2010, as he ranked 28th in the league in our Gross Punt Pts+ figure, but overall the Titans got value out of the punting game because the coverage there was excellent.

The Titans may have drafted wideout Marc Mariani in the seventh round in 2010 because he had the good fortune to play with Jeff Fisher's son Brandon at Montana, but he more than ably filled both the punt and kickoff return duties in 2010, finishing fourth in value in our measures for both. Mariani lacks the explosiveness and elusiveness that characterizes the elite returners, but did an excellent job of finding good holes and taking the yards that were available. He may not rank among the league's best again in 2011, but should still do a good job.

Coaching Staff

Mike Munchak is the first new coach in the history of Nashville's major-league franchises, since Jeff Fisher came with the team from Houston and the NHL Predators still employ their initial head coach, Barry Trotz. Given that the Titans are a team in transition, 2011 will be a good year for him to make the mistakes characteristic of rookie head coaches, and indeed all coaches taking on a new role. Offensive coordinator Chris Palmer was plucked from the UFL ranks; he was replaced as head coach of the Hartford Colonials by former Oilers head coach Jerry Glanville. Palmer's experience as a head coach should help him serve as a sounding board for Munchak, and his experience with the expansion Browns and Texans should help him endure a likely season of losing. Bruce Matthews steps into Munchak's shoes as offensive line coach. Defensive coordinator Jerry Gray was taken from the college ranks, where he was defensive coordinator at Texas after spending several years as the Redskins' secondary coach. His previous coordinator stint in Buffalo under Gregg Williams ended in 2005. Tracy Rocker has a difficult task replacing Jim Washburn as defensive line coach.

Washington Redskins

2010 Record: 6-10

Pythagorean Wins: 5.9 (27th)

DVOA: -18.6% (27th)

Offense: -7.5% (25th)

Defense: 9.2% (26th)

Special Teams: -1.9% (25th)

Variance: 9.1% (4th)

2011 Mean Projection: 5.6 wins

On the Clock (0-3): 21%

Loserville (4-6): 43%

Mediocrity (7-8): 22%

Playoff Contender (9-10): 11%

Super Bowl Contender (11+): 3%

Projected Average Opponent: 0.7% (15th)

2010: Snyderio ad absurdum.

2011: Mike Shanahan hitches his wagon to John Beck. No, seriously.

Of all the Dan Snyder seasons Redskins fans have had to endure in the last decade, 2010 was by far the Dan Snyderest. It was the Platonic ideal of Snyderity, a masterpiece of NFL delusion, the *Guernica* of managerial miscommunication, the *Rubber Soul* of misplaced energy and ambition. Last year was a Redskins season like any other, only more so: a loud, expensive, muddled catastrophe, one which would set a typical franchise back three years but only kept the Redskins splaying mud in the rut they've called home since 2002.

Every time Snyder embarks on one of his splashy paradigm shifts, those of us who cover the sport with an analytical slant briefly hold our breath. Blind squirrels trip and fall over acorns, and bumbling owners sometimes throw their millions at just the right combination of players and coaches to achieve brief success. "I told you so" seasons are inevitable — the Redskins had one in 2005 — and careful analysts don't want to be caught the one time an owner like Snyder rolls boxcars. While the best way to assemble a team is to draft well, use free agency sparingly, hire a smart and stable coaching staff, and be patient, there's no reason to think that grabbing a Super Bowl coach and a former All-Pro quarterback won't occasionally yield short-term success.

So when our DVOA projections spat out a 10-win season for the Redskins in the spring of 2010, we didn't panic or check the software for viruses. The Redskins went 4-12 in 2009, but Estimated Wins considered them a 7.9-win team sabotaged by bad luck and bad coaching. Surely the additions of Mike Shanahan and Donovan McNabb were worth a few wins. Our statistical optimism did not extend past 2010 — the Redskins had once again dealt away useful future draft picks for veterans, didn't bother acquiring a quarterback of the future, and were busily signing geezers like Joey Galloway and Vonnie Holliday when *FOA 2010* went to press. We expected a 2005-style one-year blip for the Redskins, writing the most pessimistic preview we possibly could for a team that we projected to make the playoffs.

Early in the season, the projection appeared dead on. The Redskins were 5-3, with nearly every game either a close win or a close loss, when they entered the last two minutes of a wild game against the Lions trailing 31-25. Rex Grossman inexplicably took the field in place of McNabb with 1:45 to play, and being Rex Grossman, he promptly fumbled while getting sacked, giving the Lions the game-clinching touchdown. The bye week ensued, and while Redskins coaches issued various grievances against McNabb through "sources" (lack of knowledge of the offense, poor conditioning, ring around the collar) the front office finished the job it started when trading for McNabb: The suddenly-beleaguered starter received a five-year

2011 Redskins Schedule

Week	Opp.	Week	Opp.	Week	Opp.
1	NYG	7	at CAR	13	NYJ
2	ARI	8	at BUF (Tor.)	14	NE
3	at DAL (Mon.)	9	SF	15	at NYG
4	at STL	10	at MIA	16	MIN
5	BYE	11	DAL	17	at PHI
6	PHI	12	at SEA		

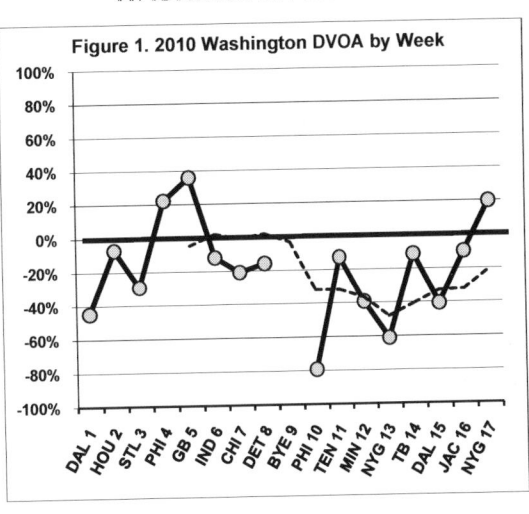

Figure 1. 2010 Washington DVOA by Week

contract extension that included nearly $40 million in guaranteed money.

And with that, common sense died, irony rolled over in its grave, and Snyder single-handedly redefined self-parody. McNabb returned to the lineup for a handful of games while reports of his toxic relationship with offensive coordinator Kyle Shanahan flew out of the Beltway. After McNabb failed to execute a game-winning drive against the Buccaneers — he led the Redskins to a touchdown, but the extra point was blocked, probably due to his bad attitude — McNabb hit the bench in favor of Grossman. Grossman threw four touchdowns in his first start against the Cowboys, and the McNabb era appeared to be over, except that the team still owed him a garden shed full of money, and both sides kept mouthing through gritted teeth that they planned to come back and do it all over again in 2011.

Meanwhile, Albert Haynesworth refused to get in shape, demanded trades, rarely played and took obvious dives when he did play. But Haynesworth had become like a landfill: huge, revolting, and seemingly impossible to get rid of. The fact that his drama ran in the background of the McNabb saga showed just how transcendent the Redskins' dysfunction had become.

This is all ancient history, of course, but it informs the state of the Redskins, a team that those who do not learn from the mistakes of history are doomed to someday own. As soon as the lockout lifted, the Redskins parted ways with McNabb and Haynesworth. In the fine Snyder tradition, the team which bought at exorbitant prices sold at a song: Trading McNabb to the Vikings netted just two sixth-round picks, one of them conditional, while the Patriots acquired Haynesworth for a fifth-round pick. It was a sad case of two former Pro Bowl performers getting sold for scrap, and it didn't have to be that way.

McNabb, certainly, would have fetched more on the open market if the Shanahans had not worked so hard to drive his value down. Even the most inveterate McNabb apologist must admit that the quarterback was partly to blame for his clash with the Shanahans. McNabb probably arrived set in his ways and used to some kid-gloves treatment from Eagles coaches. He likely tuned out his 31-year-old coach's-son coordinator and his 30-year-old position coach at times, which is unprofessional. That said, McNabb had the ultimate "company man" reputation in Philly and has made a career of being exactly the opposite of the Haynesworth-like renegade. Had the Redskins kept a lid on some of their grievances, they certainly could have shopped McNabb more aggressively on the post-lockout "mentor quarterback" market.

The Redskins were still making accusations against McNabb when anyone with a whiff of marketing acumen would have at least shut their mouths. In May, the Redskins floated a story that the real reason for the McNabb benching was that the quarterback refused to wear a wristband cheat sheet. This new development only added layers of questions, the first of which was why anyone felt the need to create new developments seven months later. Brian Mitchell, a former Redskins return man and McNabb teammate, brushed off the wristband story as business as usual for the Redskins. "This reminds me of how I was released by the Redskins," Mitchell said on a radio show. "Every three months they changed the reason why they did it." Those radio quotes are taken from the *Washington City Paper*, which happens to be in the midst of a libel suit by Snyder, who can't keep his coaches in line or control his spending needs but has plenty of time to bully the alt press.

With McNabb gone, the Shanahans are committed to

John Beck as their starting quarterback of the present/future. Beck, who will turn 30 before the season starts and hasn't taken a snap under fire since his days with the 2007 Dolphins, only qualifies as a "prospect" in the Redskins' fractured altiverse. Mike Shanahan kept insisting that Beck was the Redskins starter long into the lockout, as news filtered from the Redskins organization that members of the front office were "dismayed" by his stubbornness. It's never a good sign when your company's public face is one of dismay during a time in which you aren't even technically doing business. Grossman is still around to challenge Beck, which somehow makes things even worse.

Getting rid of McNabb and Haynesworth at least allowed the Redskins to start moving forward, but their troubles run far deeper than a few frustrated veterans. Thanks to all of the Galloway/Willie Parker malarkey at the bottom of last year's training camp depth chart, there is almost no young talent in the pipeline at wide receiver or running back except for the slew of new draft picks, most of whom played for Nebraska last season. Much of the veteran core from 2008-09 is back this year: London Fletcher at middle linebacker, DeAngelo Hall at cornerback. Fading speedster Santana Moss re-signed as the top receiver, though the team did release aging veterans Philip Daniels and Ma'ake Kemoeatu on the defensive line. For the most part, this is the same veteran core that won 10 games in two years and isn't getting younger or better, minus the established starting quarterback. From a roster development or rebuilding standpoint, 2010 was a shameful waste of time, money, and energy.

Worst of all, the season left few reasons for optimism that the Shanahan reign will be any different than the Steve Spurrier era or Joe Gibbs Part Deux.

Even if we assign near-total guilt to McNabb for the quarterback fiasco and assume the Haynesworth situation was an unwinnable war, many of the Shanahans' other decisions appear shortsighted and autocratic. The team hinted that third-year receiver Malcolm Kelly was dogging a minor injury in 2010 training camp. When it became clear that Kelly actually had a significant hamstring tear, the Redskins stashed him on injured reserve, but Mike Shanahan bristled when reporters suggested that he downplayed the severity of Kelly's injury. Fellow 2008 draft pick Devin Thomas was caught sleeping through a team meeting; Brandon Banks snapped a picture of his slumbering teammate (and, probably not coincidentally, his top rival for the kick return job) and tweeted the photo. Mike Shanahan buried Thomas on the depth chart, then released him after Week 4. Redskins Park sounded like a hell of a place to work, with injured players limping gamely about to avoid criticism while teammates posted incriminating evidence on the Internet to move up the depth chart, all while Haynesworth and McNabb thumbed their noses at everyone.

The Redskins allegedly had a general manager through all of this. Bruce Allen, who replaced yesman Vinny Cerrato after the 2009 season, was supposed to cut spending, facilitate long-term planning, and prevent the types of miscommunication that result in writing $40 million checks to hated employees. Allen was nearly invisible in 2010 — there was never an indication that any of the team's major initiatives were his idea — and when the *Washington Post* reported in May that the Redskins were "chomping at the bit" to spend some cash as soon as the lockout ended, it didn't sound like there was any voice of reason among the power structure to mention that the team's last two splurges also happen to be the team's biggest problems. True to form, the Redskins made one of the first major moves of free agency, signing defensive tackle Barry Cofield to a six-year deal. The team then added Stephen Bowen, giving the former Cowboys rotation lineman $12.5 million in guaranteed money. Both are solid players who are now significantly overpaid.

Allen did apparently have a hand in the draft. The Redskins opted out of a first-round quarterback run, trading down so the Jaguars could select Blaine Gabbert, and picking up high-effort pass rusher Ryan Kerrigan and a slew of extra picks. Kerrigan is a fine building block for the front seven, and several of the extra picks, including receiver Leonard Hankerson and running back Roy Helu, will compete immediately for starting jobs. The Cofield signing, the arrival of Kerrigan, and the influx of young offensive players would be more impressive if, like, John Beck wasn't at the top of the freakin' depth chart, and if the Redskins didn't pass up Gabbert and others in an attempt to saturation-draft the skill positions. Assuming Allen exercises most of his control in college scouting, you can almost see him working from a completely different script from Snyder and the Shanahans: He comes home with fresh fruits and vegetables, the Shanahans fry up burgers, and Snyder orders out.

The disconnect from reality is clearly evident in the Redskins' 2011 frighteningly Orwellian slogan: "The Future is Now." As usual, the Redskins are not in rebuilding mode; they are poised for immediate gratification. They've reached the point where not even the team's most ardent fans believe that anymore, the point at which most fans would greet a massive salary purge and painful youth movement with a standing ovation. The Redskins don't know what they need anymore, and they don't even know what their fans want. There's no more need to acknowledge the Redskins if they sign another big name, no reason to fear

that they will win 11 games and Snyder will crow about his acumen in hiring the Shanahans and signing every free agent with a heartbeat. We are long past "I told you so;" Snyder's management is a plague, and all of the money in the world won't help the Redskins as long as he's making decisions.

Mike Tanier

2010 Redskins Stats by Week

Wk	vs.	W-L	PF	PA	YDF	YDA	TO	Total	Off	Def	ST
1	DAL	W	13	7	250	380	1	-45%	-15%	28%	-2%
2	HOU	L	27	30	421	526	1	-7%	12%	18%	-1%
3	@STL	L	16	30	349	365	0	-29%	-4%	16%	-10%
4	@PHI	W	17	12	293	353	1	22%	14%	-5%	3%
5	GB	W	16	13	373	427	1	36%	18%	-18%	0%
6	IND	L	24	27	335	469	1	-12%	7%	30%	11%
7	@CHI	W	17	14	308	322	3	-21%	-39%	-34%	-16%
8	@DET	L	25	37	275	304	0	-16%	-38%	-12%	10%
9	BYE										
10	PHI	L	28	59	375	592	-3	-79%	-32%	63%	15%
11	@TEN	W	19	16	465	373	1	-13%	25%	14%	-24%
12	MIN	L	13	17	216	299	-1	-39%	-28%	21%	10%
13	@NYG	L	7	31	338	358	-5	-61%	-25%	25%	-11%
14	TB	L	16	17	399	365	1	-11%	5%	-1%	-17%
15	@DAL	L	30	33	341	434	-3	-41%	-7%	26%	-7%
16	@JAC	W	20	17	251	336	1	-10%	-41%	-26%	6%
17	NYG	L	14	17	385	325	-3	20%	5%	-14%	1%

Trends and Splits

	Offense	Rank	Defense	Rank
Total DVOA	-7.5%	25	9.2%	26
Unadjusted VOA	-6.5%	25	10.5%	25
Weighted Trend	-11.3%	26	9.9%	27
Variance	5.0%	6	6.4%	14
Average Opponent	3.4%	14	6.5%	23
Passing	2.5%	23	16.6%	27
Rushing	-5.5%	24	0.1%	19
First Down	-4.8%	26	11.6%	26
Second Down	7.5%	12	16.5%	30
Third Down	-37.6%	29	-7.6%	12
First Half	3.4%	20	15.1%	27
Second Half	-17.5%	28	3.1%	17
Red Zone	-20.6%	26	-0.9%	17
Late and Close	-22.4%	29	2.9%	23

Five-Year Performance

Year	W-L	Pyth	Est W	PF	PA	TO	Total	Rk	Off	Rk	Def	Rk	ST	Rk	Off AGL	Rk	Def AGL	Rk
2006	5-11	6.1	6.8	307	376	-5	-8.3%	21	4.9%	13	14.9%	32	1.7%	11	12.4	9	10.6	15
2007	9-7	8.7	8.3	334	310	-5	6.2%	13	-0.2%	17	-6.7%	7	-0.3%	16	36.6	29	16.8	11
2008	8-8	7.0	8.9	265	296	0	10.4%	12	13.1%	9	0.8%	11	-2.0%	25	12.6	7	42.5	29
2009	4-12	5.8	7.3	266	336	-11	-5.9%	21	-4.7%	21	-0.1%	10	-1.3%	23	55.0	31	20.2	11
2010	6-10	5.9	5.9	302	377	-4	-18.6%	27	-7.5%	25	9.2%	26	-1.9%	25	31.6	21	38.3	26

Strategic Tendencies

Run/Pass		Rank	Offense		Rank	Defense		Rank	Other		Rank
Runs, all plays	33%	31	3+ WR	47%	16	Rush 3	7.8%	17	2+ RB, Pct Runs	46%	30
Runs, first half	37%	25	4+ WR	5%	19	Rush 4	57.3%	18	1 RB/2 TE, Pct Runs	47%	21
Runs, first down	43%	28	2+ TE	30%	16	Rush 5	31.0%	5	1 RB/3+ WR, Pct Runs	17%	26
Runs, second-long	27%	29	Single back	59%	16	Rush 6+	3.8%	29	CB1 on WR1	40%	17
Runs, power sit.	42%	32	Play action	21%	8	Zone Blitz	6.7%	12	Go for it on 4th	0.71	29
Runs, behind 2H	21%	29	Max protect	6%	30	Sacks by LB	56.9%	10	Offensive Pace	30.2	13
Pass, ahead 2H	56%	2	Outside pocket	11%	21	Sacks by DB	6.9%	22	Defensive Pace	30.8	19

Washington's defense got successively worse the more wideouts the opponent put on the field. The Redskins were third in defensive DVOA against formations with fewer than two wideouts, eighth against two wideouts, 19th against three wideouts, and 26th against four or more wideouts. ☜ A big part of the problem was an inability to stop runs from a spread set. When opponents ran the ball out of spread sets with three or more wide receivers, Washington allowed a 21.6% DVOA (31st in the NFL) and 5.78 yards per carry (32nd). ✏ Washington's offense led the league with 23 passes tipped away or batted down at the line. ✏ Both Washington's offense and defense got successively worse the more the Redskins had a lead, and successively better the farther behind they were.

Passing

Player	DYAR	DVOA	Plays	NtYds	Avg	YAC	C%	TD	Int
D.McNabb	354	0.2%	512	3126	6.1	5.8	58.5%	14	13
R.Grossman	-76	-19.1%	142	807	5.7	5.6	56.9%	7	4

Rushing

Player	DYAR	DVOA	Plays	Yds	Avg	TD	Fum	Suc
R.Torain	19	-5.6%	164	742	4.5	4	2	44%
K.Williams	62	14.8%	65	261	4.0	3	0	51%
C.Portis	35	7.3%	54	227	4.2	2	0	48%
D.McNabb	26	13.3%	20	158	7.9	0	1	-
L.Johnson	-13	-89.6%	5	2	0.4	0	0	20%
S.Moss	-16	-105.6%	5	-6	-1.2	0	0	-
D.Young	1	-3.2%	4	19	4.8	0	0	25%
M.Sellers	-13	-56.2%	4	2	0.5	0	0	25%

Receiving

Player	DYAR	DVOA	Plays	Ctch	Yds	Y/C	YAC	TD	C%
S.Moss	117	-2.1%	145	93	1115	12.0	5.1	6	64%
A.Armstrong	133	7.4%	86	44	873	19.8	3.6	3	51%
J.Galloway	-83	-41.9%	37	12	173	14.4	1.5	0	32%
R.Williams	-23	-29.4%	18	8	109	13.6	7.4	0	44%
C.Cooley	0	-7.2%	126	77	849	11.0	4.8	3	61%
F.Davis	97	40.0%	30	21	316	15.0	8.0	3	70%
K.Williams	15	-8.9%	58	39	309	7.9	7.9	2	67%
M.Sellers	6	-11.2%	40	20	224	11.2	7.4	0	50%
R.Torain	39	12.3%	27	18	125	6.9	8.6	2	67%
C.Portis	22	40.8%	9	5	55	11.0	12.8	0	56%

Offensive Line

Year	Yards	ALY	Rank	Power	Rank	Stuff	Rank	2nd Lev	Rank	Open Field	Rank
2008	4.13	4.41	5	69%	14	14%	2	1.11	21	0.56	28
2009	3.73	3.93	25	59%	24	21%	19	1.00	29	0.54	28
2010	4.19	3.81	24	48%	30	25%	29	1.30	5	0.90	10

Year	LE	Rank	LT	Rank	Mid	Rank	RT	Rank	RE	Rank	Sacks	ASR	Rank	F-Start	Cont.
2008	4.77	11	5.04	4	4.18	14	4.07	18	4.02	17	38	6.0%	15	18	29
2009	3.19	28	3.97	19	4.30	9	4.60	5	3.13	27	46	8.5%	27	18	23
2010	3.43	27	4.38	14	3.43	31	4.10	16	4.43	9	46	7.3%	22	22	22

The Redskins brought in two high-profile offensive tackles last year to bolster a unit that had been below average, but Trent Williams and Jammal Brown couldn't keep the 2010 itineration of the Hogs from being in the bottom half in the league in just about every statistical category. Williams came out of the gates strong, with good performances against DeMarcus Ware and Mario Williams. He struggled in the middle of the schedule, partly due to injuries suffered in that Houston game, but rebounded by the end of the year. (It may have looked like he was allowing sacks in December, but it doesn't help when Rex Grossman has a tendency to scramble *toward* the pass rush.) Williams has elite athleticism but will need to get a bit stronger in the running game if he wants to develop to a Pro Bowl level. While Williams provides a sound long-term solution on the left side, Jammal Brown provided a terrible short-term solution on the right. Brown arrived in a trade with the Saints, playing his way back into shape from hernia and labrum surgeries on the Redskins' dime. Despite his poor performance, Brown received a five-year contract from the Redskins in July.

Stephon Heyer earned spot starts when Brown and Williams were hurt, but he is now in Oakland; his versatility and lower price tag would make him a more attractive player to retain than Brown for most franchises, but these are the Redskins. Sean Locklear, formerly of the Seahawks, will replace Heyer as the multi-position depth. Derrick Dockery lasted only two games before getting benched for Kory Lichtensteiger at left guard;

Dockery was released in March, as was center Casey Rabach. Will Montgomery should replace Rabach; he played well at right guard for the final five games of the season after Artis Hicks suffered a groin injury. Former Ravens lineman Chris Chester was signed in free agency and will take over at right guard. Overall, the Mike Shanahan staff has proven a willingness to go with young guys up front; they just need to convince the front office to do the same.

Defensive Front Seven

Defensive Line	Age	Pos	Plays	TmPct	Overall								Pass Rush			vs. Run			vs. Pass		
					Rk	Stop	Dfts	BTkl	St%	Rk	AvYd	Rk	Sack	Hit	Hur	Runs	St%	Yds	Pass	St%	Yds
Adam Carriker	27	DE	38	4.4%	56	32	8	2	85%	15	2.0	43	1.5	1	3	33	85%	1.9	5	80%	2.6
Kedric Golston	28	DE	34	4.8%	47	27	3	1	81%	35	2.2	52	0.5	2	3	31	81%	2.3	3	67%	1.0
Vonnie Holliday	36	DE	32	3.9%	62	25	10	0	75%	42	2.3	57	3	4	9.5	20	75%	3.1	12	83%	1.0
Maake Kemoeatu	32	DT	29	3.8%	48	20	4	2	74%	52	3.0	58	0	1	0	27	74%	2.5	2	0%	9.0
Phillip Daniels	38	DE	21	2.8%	--	16	5	0	75%	--	1.6	--	1.5	2	3	16	75%	1.8	5	80%	1.2
Albert Haynesworth	30	DT	16	3.7%	--	14	9	0	83%	--	-0.1	--	2.5	2	7	12	83%	2.1	4	100%	-6.5

Linebackers	Age	Pos	Plays	TmPct	Overall						Pass Rush			vs. Run					vs. Pass			
					Rk	Stop	Dfts	BTkl	AvYd	Sack	Hit	Hur	Runs	St%	Rk	Yds	Rk	Tgts	Suc%	Rk	AdjYd	Rk
London Fletcher	36	ILB	147	16.9%	10	76	27	8	5.3	2.5	2	3.5	95	58%	90	4.2	96	41	67%	8	6.5	48
Rocky McIntosh	29	ILB	113	13.9%	27	53	12	11	5.2	2	2	4.5	55	53%	101	3.7	80	39	34%	74	8.4	77
Brian Orakpo	25	OLB	58	7.1%	89	42	19	3	2.1	8	10	24.5	36	64%	76	2.3	18	6	66%	--	8.1	--
Lorenzo Alexander	28	OLB	47	5.4%	104	23	7	4	4.6	1.5	1	10.5	28	54%	99	3.8	84	16	76%	1	3.3	4
Andre Carter	32	OLB	44	5.1%	--	27	10	3	3.3	2.5	6	12	24	71%	--	2.7	--	9	25%	--	6.5	--

Year	Yards	ALY	Rank	Power	Rank	Stuff	Rank	2nd Lev	Rank	Open Field	Rank
2008	3.97	4.30	23	61%	7	19%	11	1.20	22	0.43	2
2009	4.11	4.06	14	42%	1	20%	12	1.10	12	0.74	14
2010	4.62	4.37	27	52%	4	17%	25	1.24	25	0.97	25

Year	LE	Rank	LT	Rank	Mid	Rank	RT	Rank	RE	Rank	Sacks	ASR	Rank
2008	4.28	19	4.19	16	4.53	28	3.78	8	4.33	22	24	4.7%	29
2009	4.18	15	4.45	23	3.59	7	4.30	21	4.47	25	40	7.5%	5
2010	3.87	12	5.40	31	3.99	20	4.96	30	4.42	24	29	5.3%	29

No Redskins defender besides Brian Orakpo registered more than 2.5 sacks last year. Ryan Kerrigan will change that. Kerrigan recorded 25.5 sacks and 12 forced fumbles in his final two seasons at Purdue. He's incredibly strong and tenacious (he once won Purdue's Pit Bull Award — write your own Redskins-Eagles joke here), and he'll rack up second-effort sacks while keeping opponents from double-teaming Orakpo whenever they want to.

Barry Cofield and Stephen Bowen add a no-nonsense presence to a defensive line that saw more than its share of nonsense last season. Cofield frequently lined up over the center and guard in the Giants' 4-3 and should adjust to playing the nose. Bowen is an experienced 3-4 end. Adam Carriker, Kedric Gholston, and second-round pick Jarvis Jenkins round out a defensive line that should be stout against the run and won't generate any negative headlines.

London Fletcher is an absolute marvel, an undersized linebacker who constantly reinvents himself (the switch from 4-3 to 3-4 isn't easy) and shows no sign of slowing down at age 36. Consistently stellar tackle totals combined with his small size and advanced age make Fletcher a very unique player. According to our defensive similarity scores, five of the ten spans most similar to Fletcher's last three seasons are other three-year spans from earlier in Fletcher's career. Three of the other five most similar spans belong to Ray Lewis from 2006 to 2010.

Defensive Secondary

Secondary	Age	Pos	Plays	TmPct	Rk	Stop	Dfts	BTkl	Runs	St%	Rk	Yds	Rk	Tgts	Tgt%	Rk	Dist	Suc%	Rk	APaYd	Rk	PD	Int
DeAngelo Hall	28	CB	111	12.8%	4	51	28	6	25	44%	40	9.4	72	85	16.5%	28	10.6	41%	81	10.0	81	9	6
LaRon Landry	27	FS	93	19.0%	1	35	14	6	37	49%	19	5.5	20	34	11.6%	1	12.8	52%	49	10.1	68	9	1
Reed Doughty	29	SS	83	10.2%	39	29	5	3	40	45%	28	7.2	50	26	5.4%	48	13.2	63%	15	8.3	46	1	0
Kareem Moore	27	FS	67	10.3%	37	17	8	7	37	24%	78	8.9	66	22	5.6%	45	15.7	60%	24	7.5	37	5	1
Phillip Buchanon	31	CB	66	7.6%	57	33	11	4	14	50%	25	9.5	73	69	13.3%	62	11.6	55%	23	6.4	23	16	2
Carlos Rogers	30	CB	66	10.1%	28	32	11	5	11	45%	38	6.0	31	60	15.6%	39	9.0	51%	48	8.2	62	12	2
Kevin Barnes	25	CB	21	3.9%	--	11	5	1	10	50%	--	8.4	--	10	3.0%	--	12.2	74%	--	3.4	--	5	1

Year	Pass D Rank	vs. #1 WR	Rk	vs. #2 WR	Rk	vs. Other WR	Rk	vs. TE	Rk	vs. RB	Rk
2008	15	-11.2%	8	-4.7%	11	-3.9%	16	-5.2%	12	17.1%	28
2009	20	3.7%	15	10.6%	26	-2.5%	12	0.8%	14	17.1%	25
2010	27	-5.6%	13	12.7%	24	21.7%	29	-9.7%	6	5.8%	17

DeAngelo Hall had a DeAngelo Hall kind of year. His four-interception game against the Bears was a reminder of why he is sometimes mistaken for a superstar by people other than himself: He can do incredible things with the ball in his hands, and he is great at chasing down wayward passes. He committed just one penalty last year, so his big play-to-headache ratio was better than it has been in past seasons. Still, there were long stretches where he allowed lots of catches in front of him, and by the end of the year he was getting burned deep by luminaries like Arrelious Benn and Jason Hill. Take away the Bears game and a Hall Mary against the Eagles, and he only intercepted one pass all season.

Carlos Rodgers, the man with flow-through hands, is now in San Francisco. The new starter opposite Hall is the diminutive (5-foot-9) Josh Wilson, ex- of the Seahawks and Ravens. Wilson was far more consistent than Hall last year (58 percent Adjusted Success Rate, 16th) but still gave up some deep balls (8.0 Adjusted Yards per Pass, 58th). The team re-signed Phillip Buchanon after a great year as a nickel defender, but Buchanon is now 31 and played for his fifth NFL team in 2010. In the fine Redskins tradition, Buchanon's presence choked out playing time and roster opportunities for younger players. 2009 third-round pick Kevin Barnes barely played last season.

The Redskins signed O.J. Atogwe to a five-year, $26-million contract before the lockout. He will join LaRon Landry at safety. Atogwe is a capable veteran, but he is 30 years old, overpriced and … aw, shucks, he's a Redskins free-agent acquisition, you get the idea. Landry was asked to blitz frequently as the Redskins tried everything they could to apply pass pressure last season, but he recorded just one sack. (He did have 11 hurries, third among defensive backs.) Fifth-round pick DeJon Gomes played free safety at Nebraska (the Redskins' AAA affiliate), and he's a big hitter and run support player who fits best as an in-the-box defender. He could take over Landry's blitz-happy role in nickel situations, allowing Landry to play like a more traditional safety.

Special Teams

Year	DVOA	Rank	FG/XP	Rank	Net Kick	Rank	Kick Ret	Rank	Net Punt	Rank	Punt Ret	Rank	Hidden	Rank
2008	-2.0%	25	-9.4	31	5.7	11	7.7	6	-15.3	31	-0.6	17	-7.4	23
2009	-1.3%	23	1.4	17	5.8	10	-8.0	29	0.8	20	-7.5	29	-16.4	32
2010	-1.9%	25	-16.6	32	17.0	1	6.9	9	-22.1	31	3.4	11	4.3	7

The Redskins have used four different punters in each of the last two seasons; if that's not a sign of dysfunction, then nothing is. Josh Bidwell started the season well but suffered a hip injury. Hunter Smith returned and had some very strong games (his punts kept the Packers pinned deep in Washington's 16-13 Week 5 win), but when Smith whiffed on an extra point snap against the Buccaneers, he was sent back to the recording studio to cut more Connersvine tracks. Enter Sam Paulescu, who also had a cup of coffee as the Redskins punter in 2009; only the Redskins require the punting equivalent of middle relievers. The Redskins signed Sav Rocca after the lockout, but Rocca had a hard time getting a work visa and spent the first week of training camp in his native Australia. Who needs a punter when John Beck is your quarterback?

Return man Brandon Banks is expected back despite a brutal February stabbing; a nightclub patron pulled a knife on Banks for making fun of his wardrobe, and Banks ended up hospitalized for several days. Banks has exceptional quickness and was effective in 2010 despite the fact that he was not fully recovered from a knee injury. The draft brought several other possible return men, including Aldrick Robinson, a tiny burner from SMU with 4.3 speed.

Graham Gano missed five field-goal attempts from inside 40 yards last year and was 0-for-3 beyond 50 yards. He has worked on changing his approach in the offseason. Good idea. At least Gano was average on kickoffs, but the praise for that unit's fine performance should really go to the coverage team, led by Reed Doughty and H.B. Blades. The Redskins allowed only three returns longer than 30 yards, and we estimate that kickoff returns against the Redskins were worth -15.2 points worth of field position compared to average.

Coaching Staff

Jim Haslett's amazing ability to fail in plain sight without being called on it should be bottled and marketed. The team fell from 10th to 26th in defensive DVOA on his watch, and the "attacking" 3-4 defense yielded few sacks and turnovers; only so much can be laid at the feet of one insubordinate problem-child lineman. Haslett's amazing career was recounted in *FOA 2010*. He made the Saints and Rams defenses worse during his tenures, and even the Steelers fell off from "excellent" to "pretty good" under his coaching. The one benefit of loading the roster with 30-year-old veterans is that it's more likely to result in mediocrity than disaster. Under Haslett, a defense full of hired guns almost produced a disaster. No one really noticed, because the Redskins provided so many other distractions.

Quarterbacks

One of the hallmarks of Mark Sanchez's sophomore improvement was an improvement in his turnover rate. As a rookie, Sanchez threw 20 interceptions in just 364 pass attempts. Last year, Sanchez had many more pass attempts, 507, and threw only 13 interceptions. That meant a lot fewer passes were finding the hands of defenders.

Or were they?

Week 4: The Jets have the ball on first-and-10. Sanchez makes a play-fake to Shonn Greene and then launches the ball deep down the right sideline to Braylon Edwards. But Leodis McKelvin is with Edwards step for step, and as the ball hangs up, both players turn back to catch it. McKelvin puts out his arms and cradles the ball in his hands for the pick — until Edwards reaches around his right side and tips the ball out of his hands.

Week 8: It's third-and-1, and the Jets line up in a 3x1 set with Dustin Keller flexed out as the near slot receiver. Keller runs a short little hook pattern, right past the sticks, but inside linebacker Desmond Bishop reads it all the way. He jumps the route, puts up his hands to catch it … and watches the ball bounce off his face mask.

Week 14: On the Jets' first drive, it's third-and-3, and Jerricho Cotchery runs a short little out pattern to get the first down. Miami cornerback Sean Smith recognizes the move, jumps in front of the ball, and it bounces off his hands. Later in the second quarter, Smith will get drop another pass that hits him right in the chest. And in the third quarter, he'll do it again.

All told, the Football Outsiders game charting project marked 15 dropped interceptions for Sanchez in 2010. That's where all the interceptions went; they bounced off opponents' hands and chest and facemasks. If we add together actual picks and dropped interceptions, Sanchez didn't go from 20 to 13 in more pass attempts. He went from 25 to 28 in more pass attempts. If defenders had caught every possible interception in both years, his interception rate would have only dropped slightly.

Interceptions are one of the hardest stats in football to forecast. They often bounce up and down from year to year. Eli Manning led the league in picks with 20 in 2007 and 25 last year. But in the two years between,

he had just 10 and 14. Drew Brees had just 11 picks when the Saints won the Super Bowl in 2009. The next year, he doubled that to 22, a career high.

Could we do a better job of predicting interceptions if we looked at interception possibilities, not just actual picks? The answer is, somewhat, yes.

In December of last year, we proposed a new stat on our website: Adjusted Interceptions. We went farther than simply including both interceptions and dropped interceptions. We removed Hail Mary passes and other interceptions that ended the fourth quarter, plays that don't matter. We also removed picks when a perfectly catchable ball deflected off the receiver's hands or chest and into the arms of a defender. This was part of why Eli Manning had so many interceptions in 2010; he had five picks that were listed in our game charting as being dropped by receivers first.

Manning doesn't lead the league in the resulting stat, Adjusted Interceptions. Carson Palmer and Mark Sanchez do, with 28 apiece. David Garrard leads the league in Adjusted Interception rate rather than Manning or Brett Favre. (See Table 1, next page.)

Adjusted Interceptions can also make some quarterbacks look like they were better in 2010 than most people thought. Chad Henne had 19 interceptions, but only one dropped interception. Jon Kitna had 12 picks, but no dropped picks and four passes tipped into defenders' hands by his receivers. That gives him only eight Adjusted Interceptions, the same number as Tom Brady, who had only four picks (one a Hail Mary) but five dropped picks.

As you might expect, these numbers of Adjusted Interceptions have a better year-to-year correlation than the numbers for standard interceptions. Looking at players with at least 100 pass attempts in two straight years from 2007 through 2010, the year-to-year correlation of interceptions is .20. The year-to-year correlation for Adjusted Interceptions is .40. Surprisingly, the correlations are actually worse for the rate stats: .08 for interception rate, and .33 for Adjusted Interception rate.

We took Adjusted Interceptions into account when putting together this year's KUBIAK projections for quarterbacks, and we'll be tweaking the stat and looking at it more when analyzing quarterbacks in future seasons.

Table 1. Adjusted Interceptions, 2010

Name	Team	INT	HM/End Q4	Drop INT	Tip INT	Adj INT	Net Pass Att (no DPI)	INT Rate	Adj Rate
D.Garrard	JAC	15	0	7	0	22	401	3.7%	5.5%
B.Favre	MIN	19	0	3	1	21	389	4.9%	5.4%
M.Sanchez	NYJ	13	0	15	0	28	537	2.4%	5.2%
J.Cutler	CHI	16	0	8	0	24	491	3.3%	4.9%
C.Palmer	CIN	20	0	9	1	28	622	3.2%	4.5%
D.Anderson	ARI	10	0	6	0	16	356	2.8%	4.5%
R.Fitzpatrick	BUF	15	0	6	0	21	468	3.2%	4.5%
C.McCoy	CLE	9	0	3	1	11	246	3.7%	4.5%
M.Hasselbeck	SEA	17	0	5	1	21	475	3.6%	4.4%
E.Manning	NYG	25	1	5	5	24	564	4.4%	4.3%
D.Brees	NO	22	1	7	2	26	684	3.2%	3.8%
D.McNabb	WAS	15	2	7	1	19	512	2.9%	3.7%
T.Romo	DAL	7	0	2	1	8	221	3.2%	3.6%
J.Campbell	OAK	8	0	6	1	13	364	2.2%	3.6%
P.Manning	IND	17	1	9	0	25	704	2.4%	3.6%
K.Kolb	PHI	7	4	4	0	7	201	3.5%	3.5%
S.Hill	DET	12	0	4	1	15	432	2.8%	3.5%
C.Henne	MIA	19	1	1	1	18	526	3.6%	3.4%
K.Orton	CHI	9	0	8	0	17	541	1.7%	3.1%
K.Collins	TEN	8	0	1	0	9	293	2.7%	3.1%
M.Vick	PHI	6	0	7	1	12	406	1.5%	3.0%
A.Rodgers	GB	11	1	6	1	15	508	2.2%	3.0%
J.Clausen	CAR	9	0	1	0	10	339	2.7%	2.9%
P.Rivers	SD	13	0	4	1	16	584	2.2%	2.7%
M.Cassel	KC	7	0	6	0	13	476	1.5%	2.7%
S.Bradford	STL	15	2	4	0	17	626	2.4%	2.7%
M.Ryan	ATL	9	0	8	1	16	605	1.5%	2.6%
J.Freeman	TB	6	0	8	1	13	510	1.2%	2.5%
A.Smith	SF	10	0	0	1	9	367	2.7%	2.5%
J.Flacco	BAL	10	1	4	0	13	540	1.9%	2.4%
J.Kitna	DAL	12	0	0	4	8	339	3.5%	2.4%
M.Schaub	HOU	12	0	3	3	12	614	2.0%	2.0%
B.Roethlisberger	PIT	5	0	3	0	8	417	1.2%	1.9%
T.Brady	NE	4	1	5	0	8	525	0.8%	1.5%

Minimum 200 pass plays; rates are based on all pass plays, including sacks.

In the rest of this section, we'll introduce the player comment tables and explain how to read them. For quarterbacks, we provide the last three years worth of numbers for the top two quarterbacks on each team's depth chart as of the end of free agency, as well as a variety of other quarterbacks who may prove to be relevant in 2011.

Each quarterback gets a projection from our KUBIAK fantasy football projection system, based on a complicated regression analysis that takes into account numerous variables including projected role,

performance over the past two years, performance on third down vs. all downs, experience of the projected offensive line, historical comparables, collegiate stats, height, age, and strength of schedule.

It is difficult to accurately project statistics for a 162-game baseball season, but it is exponentially more difficult to accurately project statistics for a 16-game football season because of the small size of the data samples involved. With that in mind, we ask that you consider the listed projections not as a prediction of exact numbers, but the mean of a range of possible performances. What's important is not so much the exact number of yards and touchdowns we project, but whether or not we're projecting a given player to improve or decline. Along those same lines, rookie projections will not be as accurate as veteran projections due to lack of data.

Our quarterback projections look a bit different than our projections for the other skill positions. At running back and wide receiver, second-stringers see plenty of action, but, at quarterback, either a player starts or he does not start. We recognize that, when a starting quarterback gets injured in Week 8, you don't want to grab your *Football Outsiders Almanac* to find out if his backup is any good only to find that we've projected that the guy will throw 12 passes this year. Therefore, like we did last year, we have projected all quarterbacks to start all 16 games. If, say, Tom Brady goes down in November, you can look up Brian Hoyer, divide the stats by 16, and get an idea of what we think each player will do in an average week.

We also include a Risk variable for each player, which measures the likelihood of the player hitting his projection. The default rating for each player is Green. As the risk of a player failing to hit his projection rises, he's given a rating of Yellow or, in the worst cases, Red. A few players with the strongest chances of surpassing their projections are given a Blue rating. Most players marked Blue will be backups with low projections, but a handful are starters or situational players who can be considered slightly better breakout candidates.

How to Read the Quarterback Statistics Table

The first line contains biographical data—each player's name, height, weight, college, draft position, birth date, and age. Height and weight are the best data we could find; weight, of course, can fluctuate during the offseason. **Age** is very simple: the number of years be-

tween the player's birth year and 2011, but birthdate is provided if you want to figure out exact age.

Draft position gives draft year and round, with the overall pick number with which the player was taken in parentheses. In the sample table, it says that Aaron Rodgers was chosen in the 2005 NFL Draft in the first round with the 24th overall pick. Undrafted free agents are listed as "FA" with the year they came into the league, even if they were only in training camp or on a practice squad.

To the far right of the first line is the player's **Risk** for fantasy football in 2011.

Next, we give the last three years of player stats. The majority of these statistics are passing numbers, although the final five columns on the right are the quarterback's rushing statistics.

The first few columns after the year and team the player played for are standard numbers: games (**G**), pass attempts (**Att**), pass completions (**Cmp**), completion percentage (**C%**), passing yards (**Yds**), passing touchdowns (**TD**), and interceptions (**INT**). These numbers are official NFL totals and therefore include plays we leave out of our own metrics, such as clock-stopping spikes, and omit plays we include in our metrics, such as sacks and aborted snaps. Note that the games total includes all games the player appeared in, not just games started, which is why a backup quarterback who holds on field goals will often be listed with 16 games played. (Other differences between official stats and Football Outsiders stats are described in the "Statistical Toolbox" introduction at the front of the book.)

The next column is fumbles (**FUM**), which adds together all fumbles by this player, whether turned over to the defense or recovered by the offense (explained in the essay "Pregame Show"). Even though this fumble total is listed among the passing numbers, it includes all fumbles, including those on sacks, aborted snaps, and rushing attempts. By listing fumbles and interceptions next to one another we hope to give a general idea of how many total turnovers the player was responsible for.

Aaron Rodgers   Height: 6-2   Weight: 223   College: California   Draft: 2005/1 (24)   Born: 2-Dec-1983   Age: 28 Risk: Yellow

Year	Team	G	Att	Comp	C%	Yds	TD	INT	FUM	ASR	NY/P	Rk	DVOA	Rk	DYAR	Rk	YAR	Runs	Yds	TD	DVOA	DYAR
2008	GB	16	536	341	63.6%	4038	28	13	9	6.4%	6.8	12	14.8%	14	932	10	966	56	207	4	16.3%	73
2009	GB	16	541	350	64.7%	4434	30	7	8	8.7%	7.1	10	22.7%	9	1294	9	1512	58	316	5	46.0%	136
2010	GB	15	475	312	65.7%	3922	28	11	3	6.9%	7.4	2	33.6%	4	1514	4	1467	64	356	4	25.2%	101
2011	GB		523	338	64.6%	4207	31	14			7.0		23.6%					75	331	4	15.6%	

| 2010: | 53% Short | 28% Mid | 11% Deep | 8% Bomb | YAC: 5.7 (12) | 2009: | 48% Short | 35% Mid | 10% Deep | 7% Bomb | YAC: 5.9 (7) |

Next comes Adjusted Sack Rate (**ASR**). This is the same statistic you'll find in the team chapters, only here it is specific to the individual quarterback. It represents sacks per pass play (total pass plays = pass attempts + sacks) adjusted based on down, distance, and strength of schedule. For reference, the NFL average over the past three seasons is 6.4 percent.

The next two columns are Net Yards per Pass (**NY/P**), a standard stat but a particularly good one, and the player's rank (**Rk**) in Net Yards per Pass for that season. Consider the inclusion of this number our tribute to the godfather of football stats, Bud Goode. It consists of passing yards minus yards lost on sacks, divided by total pass plays.

The five columns remaining in passing stats give our advanced metrics: **DVOA** (Defense-Adjusted Value Over Average), **DYAR** (Defense-Adjusted Yards Above Replacement), and **YAR** (Yards Above Replacement), along with the player's rank in both DVOA and DYAR. These metrics compare each quarterback's passing performance to league-average or replacement-level baselines based on the game situations that quarterback faced. DVOA and DYAR are also adjusted based on the opposing defense. The methods used to compute these numbers are described in detail in the "Statistical Toolbox" introduction at the front of the book. The important distinctions between them are:

• DVOA is a rate statistic, while DYAR is a cumulative statistic. Thus, a higher DVOA means more value per pass play, while a higher DYAR means more aggregate value over the entire season.

• Because DYAR is defense-adjusted and YAR is not, a player whose DYAR is higher than his YAR faced a harder-than-average schedule. A player whose DYAR is lower than his YAR faced an easier-than-average schedule.

To qualify for a ranking in Net Yards per Pass, passing DVOA, and passing DYAR in a given season, a quarterback must have had 100 pass plays in that season. There are 46 quarterbacks ranked for both 2010 and 2009, and 41 quarterbacks ranked for 2008.

The final five columns contain rushing statistics, starting with **Runs**, rushing yards (**Yds**), and rushing touchdowns (**TD**). Once again, these are official NFL totals and include kneeldowns, which means you get to enjoy statistics such as Billy Volek rushing six times for minus-5 yards. The final two columns give **DYAR** and **DVOA** for quarterback rushing, which are calculated separately from passing. Rankings for these statistics, as well as numbers that are not adjusted for defense (YAR and VOA) can be found on our website, FootballOutsiders.com.

The italicized row of statistics for the 2011 season is our 2011 KUBIAK projection, as detailed above. Again, in the interest of producing meaningful statistics, all quarterbacks are projected to start a full 16-game season, regardless of the likelihood of them actually doing so.

The final line represents data from the Football Outsiders game charting project. First, we break down charted passes based on distance: **Short** (5 yards or less), **Mid** (6-15 yards), **Deep** (16-25 yards), and **Bomb** (26 or more yards). These numbers are based on distance in the air only and include both complete and incomplete passes. Passes thrown away or tipped at the line are not included, nor are passes on which the quarterback's arm was hit by a defender while in motion. We also give Yards after Catch (**YAC**) and with the Rank in parentheses for the 46 quarterbacks who qualify.

A number of third- and fourth-string quarterbacks are briefly discussed at the end of the chapter in a section we call "Going Deep."

Top 20 QB by Passing DYAR (Total Value), 2010

Rank	Player	Team	DYAR
1	Tom Brady	NE	2,137
2	Peyton Manning	IND	1,679
3	Philip Rivers	SD	1,652
4	Aaron Rodgers	GB	1,514
5	Drew Brees	NO	1,360
6	Matt Ryan	ATL	1,348
7	Ben Roethlisberger	PIT	1,238
8	Matt Schaub	HOU	1,173
9	Josh Freeman	TB	1,031
10	Carson Palmer	CIN	1,009
11	Joe Flacco	BAL	906
12	Kyle Orton	DEN	869
13	Michael Vick	PHI	835
14	Matt Cassel	KC	795
15	Eli Manning	NYG	792
16	Shaun Hill	DET	650
17	Chad Henne	MIA	621
18	Mark Sanchez	NYJ	438
19	Tony Romo	DAL	434
20	Vince Young	TEN	423

Top 20 QB by Passing DVOA (Value per Pass), 2010

Rank	Player	Team	DVOA
1	Tom Brady	NE	53.3%
2	Ben Roethlisberger	PIT	38.2%
3	Philip Rivers	SD	34.0%
4	Aaron Rodgers	GB	33.6%
5	Vince Young	TEN	26.8%
6	Peyton Manning	IND	25.0%
7	Matt Ryan	ATL	23.9%
8	Michael Vick	PHI	20.6%
9	Tony Romo	DAL	20.6%
10	Josh Freeman	TB	20.5%
11	Drew Stanton	DET	19.4%
12	Drew Brees	NO	19.3%
13	Matt Schaub	HOU	18.2%
14	Seneca Wallace	CLE	18.2%
15	Joe Flacco	BAL	15.6%
16	Matt Cassel	KC	15.2%
17	Kyle Orton	DEN	14.4%
18	Carson Palmer	CIN	13.8%
19	Shaun Hill	DET	12.8%
20	Eli Manning	NYG	11.0%

Derek Anderson
Height: 6-6   Weight: 229   College: Oregon State   Draft: 2005/6 (213)   Born: 15-Jun-1983   Age: 28   Risk: Red

Year	Team	G	Att	Comp	C%	Yds	TD	INT	FUM	ASR	NY/P	Rk	DVOA	Rk	DYAR	Rk	YAR	Runs	Yds	TD	DVOA	DYAR
2008	CLE	10	283	142	50.2%	1615	9	8	8	4.7%	5.1	36	-11.9%	32	-15	33	-140	25	55	0	-41.1%	-29
2009	CLE	8	182	81	44.5%	888	3	10	5	5.5%	4.3	43	-38.9%	44	-340	42	-421	10	8	2	-3.9%	5
2010	ARI	12	327	169	51.7%	2065	7	10	5	7.0%	5.4	37	-18.1%	39	-150	41	-87	5	25	0	-9.4%	1
2011	CAR		425	218	51.3%	2553	11	19			5.2		-22.6%					40	44	1	-40.6%	

2010: 43% Short 35% Mid 17% Deep 5% Bomb   YAC: 4.0 (43)   2009: 64% Short 23% Mid 10% Deep 3% Bomb   YAC: 4.4 (36)

This man is not an NFL starting quarterback. 22.4 percent of Anderson's passes were marked by our game charters as inaccurate, the highest rate for any quarterback with at least 200 passes. (That's a combination of passes marked overthrown, underthrown, thrown ahead, or thrown behind.) 12.1 percent of Anderson's passes were marked by our game charters as defensed, the second highest rate for any quarterback with at least 200 passes. So when Anderson wasn't throwing into coverage, he was missing guys entirely. The Panthers signed him so they would have a veteran to hold a clipboard and mentor Cam Newton, but Anderson may not be the best mentor when it comes to things like "accuracy" and "holding postgame press conferences."

Charlie Batch
Height: 6-2   Weight: 220   College: Eastern Michigan   Draft: 1998/2 (60)   Born: 5-Dec-1974   Age: 37   Risk: Green

Year	Team	G	Att	Comp	C%	Yds	TD	INT	FUM	ASR	NY/P	Rk	DVOA	Rk	DYAR	Rk	YAR	Runs	Yds	TD	DVOA	DYAR
2009	PIT	1	2	1	50.0%	17	0	0	0	3.0%	8.5	--	47.9%	--	7	--	7	0	0	0	--	--
2010	PIT	3	49	29	59.2%	352	3	3	1	8.2%	6.2	--	-17.2%	--	-20	--	-40	7	30	0	34.1%	9
2011	PIT		415	269	64.9%	2990	19	10			6.4		24.8%					48	23	1	-20.5%	

2010: 45% Short 30% Mid 9% Deep 15% Bomb   YAC: 4.1 (--)   2009: 50% Short 0% Mid 50% Deep 0% Bomb   YAC: 2.0 (--)

For the last couple years, Batch's off-field life has been more interesting than his on-field life. He was one of the most active members of the NFLPA during the lockout negotiations. He also declared bankruptcy after blowing his money on a number of bad business ventures, including a bakery and a real estate company. On the field, he's still your basic veteran backup: a replacement-level quarterback who won't make big mental mistakes.

John Beck

Height: 6-2   Weight: 215   College: BYU   Draft: 2007/2 (40)   Born: 21-Aug-1981   Age: 30   Risk: Red

Year	Team	G	Att	Comp	C%	Yds	TD	INT	FUM	ASR	NY/P	Rk	DVOA	Rk	DYAR	Rk	YAR	Runs	Yds	TD	DVOA	DYAR
2007	MIA	5	107	60	56.1%	559	1	3	7	8.7%	4.3	48	-51.7%	50	-303	49	-304	9	12	0	12.0%	10
2011	WAS		499	302	60.6%	3262	15	11			5.4		-4.5%					44	87	0	-45.6%	
2010:	-- Short		-- Mid		-- Deep		-- Bomb				2009:		-- Short		-- Mid		-- Deep		-- Bomb			

What can we expect from a 30-year-old quarterback with so little game experience? Here's a list of quarter-backs over 30 with fewer than 10 career NFL starts who then started at least seven games in a season:

Thirty-something first-time starters

Player	Team	Year	Age	Career GS	GS	Att	Comp	C%	Yds	TD	INT	Yd/At
Dieter Brock*	LARM	1985	34	0	15	365	218	59.7%	2658	16	13	7.28
Bob Gagliano*	DET	1989	31	1	7	232	117	50.4%	1671	6	12	7.20
Jeff Hostetler*	NYG	1991	30	4**	12	285	179	62.8%	2032	5	4	7.13
Stan Gelbaugh	SEA	1992	30	3	8	255	121	47.5%	1307	6	11	5.13
Doug Pederson*	PHI	1999	31	0	9	227	119	52.4%	1276	7	9	5.62
Jim Miller	CHI	2001	30	6	13	395	228	57.7%	2299	13	10	5.82
Alex Van Pelt	BUF	2001	31	3	8	307	178	58.0%	2056	12	11	6.70
Tommy Maddox	PIT	2002	31	4	11	377	234	62.1%	2836	20	16	7.52
Kelly Holcomb*	CLE	2003	30	3	8	302	193	63.9%	1797	10	12	5.95
Damon Huard	KC	2006	33	6	8	244	148	60.7%	1878	11	1	7.70

*Opening Day starter / ** Does not include 3 playoff starts

As you can see, it is very rare for a team to hand the keys to an older starter with so little experience. Most of these players at least had experience starting in other leagues: Dieter Brock in the CFL, Bob Gagliano in the USFL, Tommy Maddox in the XFL, and Kelly Holcomb, Stan Gelbaugh, and Doug Pederson in the WLAF. Jeff Hostetler had playoff starting experience, thanks to Phil Simms' 1990 injury. So most of these players had a lot more experience than Beck, which also means more film and more numbers to judge them on. Obviously, the dream for the Redskins is to have Beck play as well as Damon Huard did in his half-season as the Kansas City starter a few years ago. But except for Hostetler, none of these players really established themselves as long-term NFL starters.

Kyle Boller

Height: 6-3   Weight: 220   College: California   Draft: 2003/1 (19)   Born: 17-Jun-1981   Age: 30   Risk: Red

Year	Team	G	Att	Comp	C%	Yds	TD	INT	FUM	ASR	NY/P	Rk	DVOA	Rk	DYAR	Rk	YAR	Runs	Yds	TD	DVOA	DYAR
2009	STL	7	176	98	55.7%	899	3	6	2	8.6%	4.1	44	-35.7%	42	-306	40	-283	13	76	0	0.8%	8
2010	OAK	5	4	2	50.0%	25	0	1	1	20.4%	3.8	--	-261.0%	--	-75	--	-69	7	18	0	-112.6%	-24
2011	OAK		474	287	60.6%	3287	13	13			6.0		-2.5%					47	138	1	-15.4%	
2010:	72% Short		25% Mid		0% Deep		4% Bomb		YAC: 1.0 (--)		2009:	48% Short		35% Mid		10% Deep		7% Bomb		YAC: 5.9 (7)

After a one-year stopoff as part of St. Louis' pre-Bradford Rotation of Quarterback Suckitude, Boller came to the place that would have seemed to be his ideal home. The Raiders have always loved quarterbacks with howitzer arms, and they're not always cognizant of the need for, well, anything else. That said, Boller barely got on the field and was re-signed to a minimum backup contract. Even if something were to happen to Jason Campbell, it probably wouldn't take Oakland too long to find another option.

Sam Bradford

Height: 6-4   Weight: 236   College: Oklahoma   Draft: 2010/1 (1)   Born: 8-Nov-1987   Age: 24   Risk: Yellow

Year	Team	G	Att	Comp	C%	Yds	TD	INT	FUM	ASR	NY/P	Rk	DVOA	Rk	DYAR	Rk	YAR	Runs	Yds	TD	DVOA	DYAR
2010	STL	16	590	354	60.0%	3512	18	15	7	5.6%	5.3	40	-9.3%	34	72	34	244	27	63	1	-6.0%	5
2011	STL		588	366	62.2%	3877	21	17			5.7		1.4%					37	69	1	-31.5%	

2010:	60% Short	29% Mid	7% Deep	4% Bomb	YAC: 5.3 (21)	2009:	-- Short	-- Mid	-- Deep	-- Bomb

Bradford answered those who questioned his durability by not only starting all 16 games as a rookie, but by being on the field for all of his team's snaps last season. Bradford's mobility and former coordinator Pat Shurmur's conservative approach—Bradford's 5.95 yards per attempt ranked 30th of 31 qualifying quarterbacks—helped kept the rookie on the field, where his performance earned AP NFL Offensive Rookie of the Year honors. Among the areas that Bradford needs to improve upon are his performance inside the red zone (-55.0% DVOA in 95 red-zone pass attempts, second-most in the league) and in the second half of games. Bradford completed 62 percent of his passes with 13 touchdowns and four interceptions before halftime, but had just five touchdowns and was intercepted 11 times in the second. Nine of Bradford's 15 interceptions on the season came on non-Hail Mary throws in the fourth quarter. Improving the personnel around him should help, as will the hiring of Josh McDaniels as offensive coordinator.

Tom Brady

Height: 6-4   Weight: 225   College: Michigan   Draft: 2000/6 (199)   Born: 3-Aug-1977   Age: 34   Risk: Green

Year	Team	G	Att	Comp	C%	Yds	TD	INT	FUM	ASR	NY/P	Rk	DVOA	Rk	DYAR	Rk	YAR	Runs	Yds	TD	DVOA	DYAR
2008	NE	1	11	7	63.6%	76	0	0	0	1.2%	7.1	--	4.3%	--	13	--	23	0	0	0	--	--
2009	NE	16	565	371	65.7%	4398	28	13	4	3.4%	7.4	5	44.2%	2	2170	1	1799	29	44	1	-19.5%	-10
2010	NE	16	492	324	65.9%	3900	36	4	2	5.0%	7.2	3	53.3%	1	2137	1	1987	31	30	1	-16.2%	-5
2011	NE		505	339	67.0%	4033	31	10			7.1		54.2%					16	20	1	-30.8%	

2010:	55% Short	32% Mid	8% Deep	5% Bomb	YAC: 5.8 (9)	2009:	45% Short	39% Mid	9% Deep	6% Bomb	YAC: 5.8 (10)

One of two things have happened to quarterbacks who posted interception percentages as low as Brady's 2010 figure. Either a) his interception percentage regressed back to something close to the mean or b) he lost his job. Damon Huard holds the league record for interception percentage with 0.4 percent (one pick in 244 attempts) in 2006, but he threw 13 interceptions the next year. Steve DeBerg threw four interceptions in 1990 but 14 in 1991. David Garrard followed his three-pick 2007 season with 13 interceptions in 2008. Steve Bartkowski threw five interceptions in 1983 but ten in 11 games in 1984. Neil O'Donnell lasted just one season in Cincy despite his ability to avoid interceptions in non-Super Bowls. Jason Campbell followed a six-interception season with 16 and a ticket out of D.C.; Brian Griese went from four interceptions in 2000 to 19 in 2001.

None of those quarterbacks have much in common with Brady, but Bart Starr does. Starr threw just three interceptions in 251 attempts in 1966, which was downright amazing for that era. The next year, he threw 17 interceptions, the highest total of his career. Phil Simms also had some Brady qualities (at least, more Brady qualities than Damon Huard ever had); he followed his four-pick, 1.2 percent 1990 season with a two-year bench stint. The moral of the story: these low interception percentages are never a sign of a new level of production for the quarterback. They are either a fluke in the data, or in a few cases (Simms, Bartkowski, Starr to a degree), an indicator that a quarterback is compensating for diminishing skills by concentrating on safe passes. Brady's 2010 season contains elements of both; we believe that it was more of the former, but it is time to respect the possibility of the latter.

Drew Brees

Height: 6-0   Weight: 209   College: Purdue   Draft: 2001/2 (32)   Born: 15-Jan-1979   Age: 32   Risk: Yellow

Year	Team	G	Att	Comp	C%	Yds	TD	INT	FUM	ASR	NY/P	Rk	DVOA	Rk	DYAR	Rk	YAR	Runs	Yds	TD	DVOA	DYAR
2008	NO	16	635	413	65.0%	5069	34	17	5	2.5%	7.8	1	33.9%	3	1921	1	1799	22	-1	0	-24.0%	-7
2009	NO	15	514	363	70.6%	4388	34	11	8	4.2%	8.0	2	41.0%	3	1845	4	1884	22	33	2	49.3%	39
2010	NO	16	658	448	68.1%	4620	33	22	6	4.6%	6.5	13	19.3%	12	1360	5	1336	18	-3	0	-35.1%	-5
2011	NO		596	392	65.8%	4390	34	13			6.9		26.8%					26	22	1	-10.4%	

2010:	54% Short	30% Mid	9% Deep	7% Bomb	YAC: 4.6 (34)	2009:	44% Short	38% Mid	10% Deep	8% Bomb	YAC: 5.3 (16)

Brees did considerably better than the other two quarterbacks whose interceptions increased by double digits, Eli Manning and Brett Favre. The desperate straits of the Saints running game played a hand in Brees' decline in stats, and it's not like he fell to the bottom of the league — just out of the top five in many numbers. Brees had only thrown two picks after a month of Sundays, but then came apart in a handful of ugly losses: three interceptions in a loss at Arizona, four in a home loss to the Browns. Throw in two more in the key overtime loss to the Falcons in Week 3, and that's almost half of his giveaways in three poor games. KUBIAK thinks his interceptions will fall, and he may throw the ball fewer times (like 2009) and thus be more effective.

Mark Brunell

Height: 6-1 Weight: 217 College: Washington Draft: 1993/5 (118) Born: 17-Sep-1970 Age: 41 Risk: Red

Year	Team	G	Att	Comp	C%	Yds	TD	INT	FUM	ASR	NY/P	Rk	DVOA	Rk	DYAR	Rk	YAR	Runs	Yds	TD	DVOA	DYAR
2009	NO	4	30	15	50.0%	102	0	1	0	3.6%	3.0	--	-46.2%	--	-67	--	-109	4	-12	0	--	--
2010	NYJ	2	13	7	53.8%	117	2	1	0	7.8%	7.9	--	-3.8%	--	7	--	12	0	0	0	--	--
2011	NYJ		442	247	55.8%	2984	13	19			5.7		-31.6%					39	37	1	-19.4%	

2010:	17% Short	50% Mid	17% Deep	17% Bomb	YAC: 3.3 (--)	2009:	67% Short	26% Mid	7% Deep	0% Bomb	YAC: 5.9 (--)

It can be hard to find a balance between having a backup quarterback who can mentor a young starter and one who can actually step in and be effective if called upon, and Brunell at this point is more mentor than substitute. The legs that carried Jacksonville to playoff victories are long since gone, and Brunell has trouble stepping into his throws, which makes him a scattershot passer. Brunell has completed 60 percent of his passes only once in the last five years, and there is little reason to think he will improve on that at age 41. If Mark Sanchez goes down for any length of time, it's doubtful Brunell will be able to hold down the fort.

Marc Bulger

Height: 6-3 Weight: 215 College: West Virginia Draft: 2000/6 (168) Born: 5-Apr-1977 Age: 34 Risk: N/A

Year	Team	G	Att	Comp	C%	Yds	TD	INT	FUM	ASR	NY/P	Rk	DVOA	Rk	DYAR	Rk	YAR	Runs	Yds	TD	DVOA	DYAR
2008	STL	15	440	251	57.0%	2720	11	13	5	7.9%	5.2	35	-19.8%	36	-259	38	-149	14	41	0	8.8%	8
2009	STL	9	247	140	56.7%	1469	5	6	5	6.1%	5.3	34	-19.1%	32	-134	30	34	8	22	0	-81.3%	-18

2010:	-- Short	-- Mid	-- Deep	-- Bomb		2009:	55% Short	32% Mid	9% Deep	3% Bomb	YAC: 4.8 (29)

Marc Bulger isn't the kind of quarterback who is likely to be remembered by many fans 20 years from now. He was awesome in his half-season replacing an injured Kurt Warner in 2002, finishing second in the league with a 34.6% DVOA. He helped lead the Rams to a 12-4 record in 2003, although they had a lot of luck. (Bulger actually had a negative DVOA that season.) From 2004 through 2006, Bulger was 11th, 10th, and then 11th again in DVOA. That qualifies as good, but non-descript. Rams fans will remember these years and Marc Bulger playing well for their team, and they'll get to explain this to fans who don't remember the difference between Marc Bulger and Mark Brunell.

Jason Campbell

Height: 6-5 Weight: 223 College: Auburn Draft: 2005/1 (25) Born: 31-Dec-1981 Age: 30 Risk: Red

Year	Team	G	Att	Comp	C%	Yds	TD	INT	FUM	ASR	NY/P	Rk	DVOA	Rk	DYAR	Rk	YAR	Runs	Yds	TD	DVOA	DYAR
2008	WAS	16	506	315	62.3%	3245	13	6	6	7.1%	5.5	32	8.3%	18	655	16	582	47	258	1	44.2%	88
2009	WAS	16	507	327	64.5%	3618	20	15	10	8.4%	6.1	18	-1.8%	25	335	20	378	46	236	1	21.0%	61
2010	OAK	13	329	194	59.0%	2387	13	8	9	9.1%	6.1	24	-2.9%	31	181	30	249	47	222	1	2.8%	25
2011	OAK		475	280	58.8%	3402	17	15			6.0		-7.0%					58	236	2	22.8%	

2010:	58% Short	24% Mid	10% Deep	7% Bomb	YAC: 6.7 (2)	2009:	46% Short	39% Mid	10% Deep	5% Bomb	YAC: 6.3 (2)

For the first time in his career, either college or pro, Campbell will go into a season with an offensive coordinator he's worked with before. Of course, the disclaimer is that said coordinator, Al Saunders, worked with Campbell in Washington at the same time Campbell was learning the game and being usurped by Todd Collins. But Campbell has a bit more pull this time; all accounts have him replacing Richard Seymour as the offseason team leader. "He is reaching out to people, taking charge of situations and people are looking to him," receiver Nick

Miller told the *San Francisco Chronicle* of Campbell's efforts. "You can feel it. The whole vibe has changed ... The quarterback is the leader of the team and he's definitely the guy now." It's a contract year for Campbell, and it's probably his last chance to a) cash in; and b) prove that the schematic inconsistency he faced as a result of all those coaching changes was the real reason it took him so long to hit an above-average level. With 2010 offensive coordinator Hue Jackson as his head coach now, Campbell's out of excuses. One major problem: Tight end Zach Miller, the Raiders' leading target in each of the last three seasons and Campbell's security blanket, is now in Seattle. Giving Campbell Kevin Boss in exchange doesn't quite feed the bulldog.

David Carr

Height: 6-3   Weight: 215   College: Fresno State   Draft: 2002/1 (1)   Born: 21-Jul-1979   Age: 32 Risk: Green

Year	Team	G	Att	Comp	C%	Yds	TD	INT	FUM	ASR	NY/P	Rk	DVOA	Rk	DYAR	Rk	YAR	Runs	Yds	TD	DVOA	DYAR
2008	NYG	3	12	9	75.0%	115	2	0	0	7.1%	8.7	--	138.4%	--	128	--	113	8	10	0	25.0%	3
2009	NYG	6	33	21	63.6%	225	1	0	0	5.2%	6.3	--	34.7%	--	92	--	103	9	27	1	71.3%	16
2010	SF	1	13	5	38.5%	67	0	1	0	7.5%	4.8	--	-51.1%	--	-26	--	-30	0	0	0	--	--
2011	NYG		511	308	60.1%	3394	13	18			5.8		8.6%					24	11	2	10.4%	

| 2010: | 33% Short | 17% Mid | 50% Deep | 0% Bomb | YAC: 9.2 (--) | 2009: | 48% Short | 39% Mid | 10% Deep | 3% Bomb | YAC: 5.1 (--) |

In June, Carr told Matt Maiocco of CSNBayArea.com that the starting spot in San Francisco was up for grabs, that the team was "going to roll the balls out and the best player is going to play," and that he was "pretty confident" in his chance of winning a starting job. It's nice to dream. In reality, Carr's only action of the 2010 season came against the Carolina Panthers in Week 7, and he played so poorly that he never saw the field again, even as the team's quarterback depth chart spun through seemingly endless cycles. Carr signed with the Giants, where he will battle Sage Rosenfels and Ryan Perilloux (who was kicked off of LSU for failing a drug test, then transferred to Jacksonville State and spent last season in the UFL) for the No. 2 job behind Eli Manning.

Matt Cassel

Height: 6-5   Weight: 230   College: USC   Draft: 2005/7 (230)   Born: 17-May-1982   Age: 29 Risk: Green

Year	Team	G	Att	Comp	C%	Yds	TD	INT	FUM	ASR	NY/P	Rk	DVOA	Rk	DYAR	Rk	YAR	Runs	Yds	TD	DVOA	DYAR
2008	NE	16	516	327	63.4%	3693	21	11	7	8.7%	6.2	17	6.4%	20	655	17	781	73	270	2	15.8%	82
2009	KC	15	493	271	55.0%	2924	16	16	13	7.9%	5.0	36	-24.3%	37	-450	44	-412	50	189	0	-29.9%	-33
2010	KC	15	450	262	58.2%	3116	27	7	2	6.1%	6.3	18	15.2%	16	795	14	999	33	125	0	-12.0%	0
2011	KC		495	279	56.3%	3247	20	15			5.7		-4.2%					39	78	1	2.9%	

| 2010: | 52% Short | 30% Mid | 13% Deep | 5% Bomb | YAC: 5.7 (13) | 2009: | 57% Short | 31% Mid | 8% Deep | 4% Bomb | YAC: 4.2 (44) |

Cassel is that rare player to succeed after leaving the hothouse effect of the New England offense. He's still gangly in the pocket and takes too many sacks, and he's in an offense where most of the big plays are the products of his running backs or receivers (especially when Dwayne Bowe started going all thermonuclear in the second half of the season). His playoff performance against the Baltimore Ravens brought out the fact that the last time Cassel started a playoff game, he was playing for the Chatsworth High Chancellors. However, you can see the lights going on, and in an offense where Todd Haley's calling the plays unimpeded by those pesky offensive coordinators, there might be a brighter future. One thing Cassel needs to do is to throw better downfield and find more downfield targets consistently — part of the reason he was so susceptible to pressure in the pocket was that his downfield reads seemed to close as soon as they opened, Bowe excepted. The high touchdown-to-interception ratio is a plus, but must be taken in context; he played an easy schedule, and he took a lot of hits after running out of time in exchange for the picks that didn't happen.

Jimmy Clausen

Height: 6-3   Weight: 222   College: Notre Dame   Draft: 2010/2 (48)   Born: 21-Sep-1987   Age: 24 Risk: Green

Year	Team	G	Att	Comp	C%	Yds	TD	INT	FUM	ASR	NY/P	Rk	DVOA	Rk	DYAR	Rk	YAR	Runs	Yds	TD	DVOA	DYAR
2010	CAR	13	299	157	52.5%	1558	3	9	8	10.7%	4.1	45	-41.1%	44	-609	46	-613	23	57	0	-74.8%	-42
2011	CAR		432	261	60.5%	2625	12	13			5.2		-12.7%					61	130	1	-45.5%	

| 2010: | 63% Short | 24% Mid | 8% Deep | 5% Bomb | YAC: 5.2 (25) | 2009: | -- Short | -- Mid | -- Deep | -- Bomb | |

Clausen's legacy, such as it may be, is that he'll probably be the last college quarterback overdrafted because he played in a "pro-style" offense. As the spread offense met the NFL halfway over the last few years, and the definition of "pro-style" changed the Panthers switched gears and took Auburn's run-and-gunner Cam Newton with the first overall pick just a year after picking Clausen. With a limited skill set at best — think of him as a Matt Hasselbeck Lite (or align him with any one of half a dozen less-talented noodle-armed passers) — Clausen's NFL future is questionable. If there was one game that typified the deer-in-the-headlights feel of his rookie season, it was the Week 14 contestagainst the Falcons. That was the final game in a six-game stretch that saw Clausen go without a touchdown pass, and he didn't even throw a pass against Atlanta until the third drive. When Cam Newton was drafted and took a No. 1 jersey over Clausen's No. 2, it reflected the depth chart now, and probably in perpetuity.

Kerry Collins

Height: 6-5 Weight: 248 College: Penn State Draft: 1995/1 (5) Born: 30-Dec-1972 Age: 39 Risk: N/A

Year	Team	G	Att	Comp	C%	Yds	TD	INT	FUM	ASR	NY/P	Rk	DVOA	Rk	DYAR	Rk	YAR	Runs	Yds	TD	DVOA	DYAR
2008	TEN	16	415	242	58.3%	2676	12	7	5	2.2%	6.2	16	15.3%	13	738	15	715	25	49	0	10.4%	11
2009	TEN	7	216	119	55.1%	1225	6	8	3	3.6%	5.3	33	-16.9%	29	-81	28	-76	11	15	1	56.6%	14
2010	TEN	10	278	160	57.6%	1823	14	8	5	5.1%	6.0	31	3.0%	26	266	26	337	10	1	0	-99.2%	-23
2010:	46% Short		29% Mid		15% Deep		10% Bomb			YAC: 3.4 (45)		2009:	55% Short		35% Mid		6% Deep		4% Bomb		YAC: 4.7 (32)	

Back in 1998, Kerry Collins was a first-round draft bust who could barely complete half his passes. He was an alcoholic who referred to teammates with racial slurs and then allegedly quit on the Panthers in midseason. At that point, the idea that Collins would eventually turn into a trustworthy veteran caretaker backup was ridiculous. And yet, that's what happened, thanks to alcohol rehab, years of therapy, and the Giants giving Collins a third chance after he flopped with the Panthers and Saints. By last year, he was clearly nearing the end, as his trademark arm strength failed him on downfield passes. Although he was expected to return to mentor Jake Locker, Collins decided to announce his retirement in July. Collins was never a great quarterback, but since he faced his alcoholism he has spent a dozen years constantly exceeding expectations. That's a much better legacy to have than the one he had built by 1998.

Brodie Croyle

Height: 6-2 Weight: 205 College: Alabama Draft: 2006/3 (85) Born: 6-Feb-1983 Age: 28 Risk: N/A

Year	Team	G	Att	Comp	C%	Yds	TD	INT	FUM	ASR	NY/P	Rk	DVOA	Rk	DYAR	Rk	YAR	Runs	Yds	TD	DVOA	DYAR
2008	KC	2	29	20	69.0%	151	0	0	0	3.2%	4.7	--	-0.1%	--	21	--	19	0	0	0	--	--
2009	KC	3	40	23	57.5%	230	2	0	1	6.6%	4.9	--	20.4%	--	80	--	41	0	0	0	--	--
2010	KC	2	19	8	42.1%	38	0	1	0	14.2%	0.4	--	-117.9%	--	-127	--	-146	0	0	0	--	--
2010:	45% Short		36% Mid		5% Deep		14% Bomb			YAC: 1.8 (--)		2009:	59% Short		32% Mid		5% Deep		3% Bomb		YAC: 5.7 (--)	

Croyle's DVOA was bad overall, but it was epically bad on third down (-232.0%) — with an average of 11.9 yards to go on 10 third-down attempts, he averaged minus-1 yard per play. The efficiency numbers are especially horrible considering that Croyle's primary performance in a 31-0 loss to the Chargers was a series of dumpoffs — he went 7-of-17 for 40 yards. A free agent, his NFL options are very limited.

Jay Cutler

Height: 6-3 Weight: 225 College: Vanderbilt Draft: 2006/1 (11) Born: 29-Apr-1983 Age: 28 Risk: Red

Year	Team	G	Att	Comp	C%	Yds	TD	INT	FUM	ASR	NY/P	Rk	DVOA	Rk	DYAR	Rk	YAR	Runs	Yds	TD	DVOA	DYAR
2008	DEN	16	616	384	62.3%	4526	25	18	3	2.3%	7.2	7	22.0%	7	1380	5	1503	57	200	2	-4.0%	16
2009	CHI	16	555	336	60.5%	3666	27	26	9	6.0%	5.9	23	-17.0%	30	-222	36	-156	40	173	1	15.1%	41
2010	CHI	15	432	261	60.4%	3274	23	16	10	10.5%	6.1	26	-1.5%	30	292	25	266	50	232	1	35.3%	72
2011	CHI		480	291	60.7%	3555	22	18			6.5		-2.0%					49	218	1	20.9%	
2010:	49% Short		34% Mid		11% Deep		6% Bomb			YAC: 5.5 (18)		2009:	54% Short		30% Mid		10% Deep		6% Bomb		YAC: 4.8 (30)	

In the 1989 NFC Championship Game, Rams quarterback Jim Everett dropped to pass against a three-man 49ers rush, couldn't find his primary receiver, and dropped to the turf despite a complete lack of pressure. He had only been sacked once in that game but was knocked down several times, and by the end of the game he had thrown three interceptions in a 30-3 loss that marked the turning point in his young career. Everett was a star on the rise entering the game, having led the NFL in touchdowns two straight years and led the Rams to victories over two excellent defenses (the Bill Parcells Giants and Buddy Ryan Eagles) in the previous two games. From that point on, he became Jittery Jim, or "Chris" Everett for those who perfected their comic timing in middle school. He never reached the playoffs again; in fact, he never again led a team to a winning record.

Cutler had an Everett moment in last year's NFC Championship Game. The similarities between the two quarterbacks are obvious: big arm, big stats, tendency to throw off the back foot, checkered-at-best reputation as a clubhouse personality. Everett had several statistically productive years after his playoff dive, but his public reputation was tarnished, and it was hard to refute the "bad leader" allegations when he was playing out WWE-type skits with talk show hosts. Cutler faces a similar predicament. If he hopes to avoid the Everett path, he must rehabilitate his image off the field, but more importantly, stop making so many boneheaded mistakes on the field.

Andy Dalton   Height: 6-2   Weight: 215   College: TCU   Draft: 2011/2 (35)   Born: 29-Oct-1987   Age: 24 Risk: Yellow

Year	Team	G	Att	Comp	C%	Yds	TD	INT	FUM	ASR	NY/P	Rk	DVOA	Rk	DYAR	Rk	YAR	Runs	Yds	TD	DVOA	DYAR
2011	CIN		494	281	56.9%	3138	16	17			5.3		-6.2%					68	169	2	-5.0%	

The Cincinnati chapter goes into detail on all the scouting questions about Andy Dalton, but there's no questioning his college record. Throughout his career at TCU, Andy Dalton overcame middling physical gifts with mobility and accuracy. In four years under the ginger-haired Dalton, TCU's Passing S&P+ ranking rose from 80th in 2007, to 61st in 2008, to Top 20 in both 2009-10. Turnover-prone early in his career, Dalton threw only 14 interceptions in 639 passes (a 2.2-percent interception rate) his last two seasons as a Horned Frog. He also knew when to tuck and run; he rushed for at least 500 pre-sack rushing yards in each of his last three seasons

Chase Daniel   Height: 6-1   Weight: 225   College: Missouri   Draft: 2009/ (FA)   Born: 7-Oct-1986   Age: 25 Risk: Yellow

Year	Team	G	Att	Comp	C%	Yds	TD	INT	FUM	ASR	NY/P	Rk	DVOA	Rk	DYAR	Rk	YAR	Runs	Yds	TD	DVOA	DYAR
2010	NO	13	3	2	66.7%	16	0	0	1	26.8%	1.5	--	-55.8%	--	-13	--	-14	2	16	0	-109.5%	-16
2011	NO		526	327	62.2%	3689	27	20			6.6		14.3%					73	142	1	40.4%	

2010:	75% Short	25% Mid	0% Deep	0% Bomb	YAC: 5.5 (--)	2009:	-- Short	-- Mid	-- Deep	-- Bomb	YAC: 5.9 (7)

Drew Brees has started 79 of his 80 games in New Orleans (he didn't bother to play the meaningless final game of 2009), so it's not as though his backup is going to get much work. Daniel is mobile and, according to Sean Payton, adept at making the pre-snap reads his offense requires, so he fits the Saints system. Should the catastrophic happen and Brees go down for a significant length of time, that assessment will be put to the test. Note to Saints fans: this is an experiment you can live without.

Jake Delhomme   Height: 6-2   Weight: 215   College: Louisiana-Lafayette   Draft: 1998/ (FA)   Born: 10-Jan-1975   Age: 36 Risk: N/A

Year	Team	G	Att	Comp	C%	Yds	TD	INT	FUM	ASR	NY/P	Rk	DVOA	Rk	DYAR	Rk	YAR	Runs	Yds	TD	DVOA	DYAR
2008	CAR	16	414	246	59.4%	3288	15	12	4	4.7%	7.3	6	18.0%	11	828	13	817	20	21	2	51.5%	20
2009	CAR	11	321	178	55.5%	2015	8	18	6	6.7%	5.4	31	-19.0%	31	-171	33	-290	17	60	0	-13.9%	-1
2010	CLE	5	149	93	62.4%	872	2	7	3	5.2%	5.3	38	-37.0%	42	-256	42	-254	8	-2	0	-92.4%	-27

2010:	57% Short	29% Mid	8% Deep	6% Bomb	YAC: 4.1 (42)	2009:	56% Short	30% Mid	10% Deep	4% Bomb	YAC: 4.8 (31)

The Browns should have never expected a 35-year-old Delhomme to suddenly rebound from his sudden 2009 collapse. He may be in demand as a backup and mentor for the next couple years, but his career numbers don't suggest that he was the world's greatest reader of coverages. Delhomme will live the rest of his life as two datapoints: One, in favor of the idea that you don't need a great quarterback to make it to a Super Bowl. Two, in favor of the idea that a massive meltdown in the postseason (see: five interceptions against Arizona in the 2008 playoffs) suggests that an aging quarterback is about to fall apart completely.

Dennis Dixon
Height: 6-3 Weight: 195 College: Oregon   Draft: 2008/5 (156) Born: 11-Jan-1985 Age: 26 Risk: Yellow

Year	Team	G	Att	Comp	C%	Yds	TD	INT	FUM	ASR	NY/P	Rk	DVOA	Rk	DYAR	Rk	YAR	Runs	Yds	TD	DVOA	DYAR
2009	PIT	1	26	12	46.2%	145	1	1	0	0.2%	5.6	--	-14.7%	--	-5	--	-29	3	27	1	90.6%	23
2010	PIT	2	32	22	68.8%	254	0	1	2	13.5%	5.9	--	-37.8%	--	-63	--	-67	5	32	0	-17.3%	-1
2011	PIT		427	272	63.6%	3016	17	15			6.3		8.9%					63	86	2	-13.1%	

2010: 62% Short 24% Mid 11% Deep 3% Bomb YAC: 4.5 (--)   2009: 61% Short 22% Mid 13% Deep 4% Bomb YAC: 6.7 (--)

With Ben Roethlisberger suspended and Byron Leftwich injured, Dennis Dixon took the field as Pittsburgh's starting quarterback on opening day of the 2010 season. That lasted about a game and a quarter, until Dixon tore the lateral meniscus in his left knee early in the Week 2 game against Tennessee. Going into the season, the word on Dixon was that he would take fewer sacks than Roethlisberger but was less accurate. In his small amount of playing time, the opposite was true: his accuracy was fine but he took too many sacks and fumbled twice.

Trent Edwards
Height: 6-4 Weight: 231 College: Stanford   Draft: 2007/3 (92) Born: 30-Oct-1983 Age: 28 Risk: Red

Year	Team	G	Att	Comp	C%	Yds	TD	INT	FUM	ASR	NY/P	Rk	DVOA	Rk	DYAR	Rk	YAR	Runs	Yds	TD	DVOA	DYAR
2008	BUF	14	374	245	65.5%	2699	11	10	9	6.3%	6.5	14	-0.3%	24	278	24	476	37	117	3	8.0%	28
2009	BUF	8	183	110	60.1%	1169	6	7	1	11.2%	5.0	37	-24.5%	38	-165	32	-139	14	106	0	0.9%	9
2010	2TM	5	101	55	54.5%	521	2	5	0	10.3%	3.8	46	-50.4%	46	-278	44	-272	14	58	0	5.3%	13
2011	OAK		463	270	58.2%	3244	10	12			5.8		-14.3%					56	117	2	-7.6%	

2010: 65% Short 27% Mid 5% Deep 2% Bomb YAC: 4.5 (36)   2009: 53% Short 33% Mid 8% Deep 6% Bomb YAC: 5.4 (14)

When he was a rookie, Edwards was already capable enough to be a reasonable caretaker quarterback, and there were hopes he could develop even further. Instead, he hasn't developed at all. As time goes on, he's shown a difficult time dealing with pressure, with more and more checkdowns and more and more sacks. His good conventional stats in 2008 (especially that 65 percent completion rate) were in large part due to an extremely easy schedule. For some inexplicable reason, deep ball-loving Al Davis signed Captain Checkdown to backup Jason Campbell.

Brett Favre
Height: 6-2 Weight: 225 College: Southern Mississippi   Draft: 1991/2 (33) Born: 10-Oct-1969 Age: 42 Risk: N/A

Year	Team	G	Att	Comp	C%	Yds	TD	INT	FUM	ASR	NY/P	Rk	DVOA	Rk	DYAR	Rk	YAR	Runs	Yds	TD	DVOA	DYAR
2008	NYJ	16	522	343	65.7%	3472	22	22	10	5.9%	6.0	23	-2.2%	26	334	20	559	21	43	1	-71.3%	-42
2009	MIN	16	531	363	68.4%	4202	33	7	2	6.2%	7.1	11	39.0%	4	1808	5	1867	9	7	0	-35.6%	-6
2010	MIN	13	358	217	60.6%	2509	11	19	6	6.3%	6.3	17	-16.6%	38	-134	40	-206	17	8	0	-62.8%	-12

2010: 53% Short 29% Mid 11% Deep 7% Bomb YAC: 5.7 (10)   2009: 47% Short 36% Mid 11% Deep 6% Bomb YAC: 5.2 (19)

The lockout was not even over when we felt the first Favre aftershock. Favre to Philly! The rumor found its way from sports radio to Pro Football Talk to Twitter to the part of our brains that controls sorrow. It was not fair. Couldn't we enjoy the impending return of football in peace, without contemplating yet another manufactured Favre drama? Luckily, the Favre story was nothing more than the ranting of a Philly talk-show host eager to rile up his constituency: Favre was the one man in America the Eagles didn't sign. Another Favre claxon sounded in Miami days later, but even fans willing to chant "We Want Orton" and "We Want Henne" draw the line somewhere. These rumblings will continue for a year or so, and the media will respond involuntarily, like a dog that paces and pants at every distant peal of thunder. In time, we will accept that Favre is gone, long gone, unable to annoy us anymore.

The aftershocks showed us just what Favre has become: the rim shot, the unsubstantiated rumor, the bogeyman who arrives in the night to turn your favorite team sport into a media-adrenalized sideshow. It was part his doing, part ours, and part beyond anyone's control: an avalanche of deafening hype for which no one pebble could be held accountable. Eventually, after a good, long absence, we will miss him, and appreciate him in a way that became impossible over the last few seasons. In five years, when he takes the podium again in Canton, much of the exasperation we feel now will be gone. Unless he spends the next five years coyly encouraging un-retirement rumors. Let's hope he lays low — really, really low — until we have all forgotten the fawning and fretting enough to give him the wholehearted applause he deserves.

A.J. Feeley

Height: 6-3   Weight: 225   College: Oregon   Draft: 2001/5 (155)   Born: 16-May-1977   Age: 34   Risk: Green

Year	Team	G	Att	Comp	C%	Yds	TD	INT	FUM	ASR	NY/P	Rk	DVOA	Rk	DYAR	Rk	YAR	Runs	Yds	TD	DVOA	DYAR
2011	STL		549	357	64.9%	3525	21	20			5.6		-4.0%					32	25	1	-21.9%	

Signed to a two-year, $6 million contract in 2010, Feeley entered training camp as the No. 1 quarterback on the Rams' depth chart. A thumb injury in the second preseason game sidelined Feeley for the remainder of the summer and provided Sam Bradford with enough first-team reps to earn the starting job entering the regular season. Feeley handled the situation like a professional, embracing his role as mentor and sounding board for the first overall pick, but that night in Cleveland would be the last game action Feeley would see in 2010. In fact, Feely has not appeared in a regular season game since Week 13 of the 2007 season when his favorite target appeared to be Seattle Seahawks middle linebacker Lofa Tatupu, who intercepted Feeley three times. Feeley will once again be the Rams' No. 2 quarterback behind Bradford.

Ryan Fitzpatrick

Height: 6-2   Weight: 221   College: Harvard   Draft: 2005/7 (250)   Born: 24-Nov-1982   Age: 29   Risk: Green

Year	Team	G	Att	Comp	C%	Yds	TD	INT	FUM	ASR	NY/P	Rk	DVOA	Rk	DYAR	Rk	YAR	Runs	Yds	TD	DVOA	DYAR
2008	CIN	12	372	221	59.4%	1905	8	9	10	9.4%	4.2	40	-18.0%	35	-185	37	-327	60	304	2	21.7%	88
2009	BUF	10	227	127	55.9%	1422	9	10	3	9.1%	5.3	35	-22.7%	36	-178	34	-243	31	141	1	26.5%	50
2010	BUF	13	441	255	57.8%	3000	23	15	7	5.6%	6.2	22	2.9%	27	415	21	330	40	269	0	-2.2%	19
2011	BUF		497	297	59.8%	3467	18	17			5.9		-4.5%					46	158	2	13.7%	

| 2010: | 47% Short | 33% Mid | 13% Deep | 7% Bomb | YAC: 4.8 (30) | 2009: | 59% Short | 30% Mid | 7% Deep | 4% Bomb | YAC: 4.9 (28) |

Fitzpatrick in his final five games of 2011: 86-of-156 (55.1 percent) for 1,139 yards, five touchdowns, and six interceptions. If that sounds like the stat line of a quarterback of the future, we have some old J.P. Losman statistics to show you. The red flags just keep on coming once you start analyzing Fitzpatrick's numbers or game tape closely. He's the classic example of a veteran backup surprising opponents during a four-to-six game run. Eighteen percent of his career touchdown production came in two 2010 games: the overtime loss to the Ravens, and the wacky comeback when the Bengals led 31-14 at half and decided they were finished for the week. Factor in a three-touchdown performance against the Colts backups in Week 17 of 2009, and you account for 25 percent of his career production. Fitzpatrick has the potential to accumulate impressive "opportunity" stats this year — he has no competition whatsoever for his starting job — so he could be a useful fantasy backup.

Joe Flacco

Height: 6-6   Weight: 236   College: Delaware   Draft: 2008/1 (18)   Born: 16-Jan-1985   Age: 26   Risk: Green

Year	Team	G	Att	Comp	C%	Yds	TD	INT	FUM	ASR	NY/P	Rk	DVOA	Rk	DYAR	Rk	YAR	Runs	Yds	TD	DVOA	DYAR
2008	BAL	16	428	257	60.0%	2971	14	12	11	7.0%	6.0	22	2.4%	22	384	19	282	52	180	0	-9.0%	5
2009	BAL	16	499	315	63.1%	3613	21	12	7	6.8%	6.3	17	12.8%	19	815	14	878	35	56	0	-32.7%	-29
2010	BAL	16	489	306	62.6%	3622	25	10	9	7.9%	6.3	16	15.6%	15	906	11	896	43	84	1	-26.9%	-23
2011	BAL		521	322	61.8%	3749	22	14			6.3		7.1%					43	44	2	2.2%	

| 2010: | 49% Short | 30% Mid | 14% Deep | 7% Bomb | YAC: 4.9 (29) | 2009: | 48% Short | 36% Mid | 11% Deep | 5% Bomb | YAC: 5.3 (18) |

Joe Flacco has a lot in common with his division rival Ben Roethlisberger. Both men are tall and athletic, both men have strong arms, and both men take way too many sacks. J.J. Cooper, formerly of AOL Fanhouse, did a study where he timed every sack during the 2010 season, and he found that Flacco held the ball for three seconds or longer on 25 sacks, five more than any other quarterback. Our game charters tended to agree in their observations, leaving comments like "[Flacco] gets out to the sidelines, then inexplicably decides not to throw it away despite the defender coming right into his face" and "Flacco rolls when no one's open, then just runs out of bounds instead of throwing it away." In particular, Flacco will pump fake in the face of pressure without actually getting rid of the ball, or he'll start to scramble when there's no room to run. Flacco needs fix the internal clock in his brain if he wants to fully establish himself as a top NFL quarterback, and not merely an above-average one.

Matt Flynn

Height: 6-2 Weight: 230 College: Louisiana State　　　Draft: 2008/7 (209) Born: 20-Jun-1985　Age: 26 Risk: Green

Year	Team	G	Att	Comp	C%	Yds	TD	INT	FUM	ASR	NY/P	Rk	DVOA	Rk	DYAR	Rk	YAR	Runs	Yds	TD	DVOA	DYAR
2008	GB	4	5	2	40.0%	6	0	0	1	0.0%	1.2	--	-57.4%	--	-15	--	-25	4	4	0	-47.3%	-3
2009	GB	4	12	7	58.3%	58	0	1	0	6.8%	4.0	--	-45.9%	--	-31	--	-26	5	-5	0	--	--
2010	GB	7	66	40	60.6%	433	3	2	1	9.4%	5.4	--	-9.6%	--	7	--	7	9	26	0	-35.2%	-8
2011	GB		506	312	61.6%	3492	21	13			6.0		9.0%					66	117	1	-14.1%	

2010:	59% Short	25% Mid	10% Deep	7% Bomb	YAC: 6.0 (--)	2009:	54% Short	31% Mid	8% Deep	8% Bomb	YAC: 6.0 (--)

Flynn's 24-of-37, 251-yard and three-touchdown performance in a loss to the Patriots showed that he has a future as an NFL backup; previous stints in 2009 and 2010 were less encouraging. Flynn trade rumors circulated during the lockout, and though they might have just been the chattering dialogue of bored sportsweiters, Flynn might have moved in a typical offseason. If the Packers had a full transaction cycle and minicamp to work with, getting value for Flynn while grabbing a free agent backup would have made sense. Making the same move in late July would have been crazy, so Flynn will play out the final year of his contract in Green Bay, or at least sit on the bench while that final year plays itself out.

Josh Freeman

Height: 6-6 Weight: 248 College: Kansas State　　　Draft: 2009/1 (17) Born: 13-Jan-1988　Age: 23 Risk: Green

Year	Team	G	Att	Comp	C%	Yds	TD	INT	FUM	ASR	NY/P	Rk	DVOA	Rk	DYAR	Rk	YAR	Runs	Yds	TD	DVOA	DYAR
2009	TB	10	290	158	54.5%	1855	10	18	9	6.6%	5.7	27	-26.2%	39	-295	39	-410	30	161	0	33.8%	53
2010	TB	16	474	291	61.4%	3451	25	6	7	6.0%	6.5	14	20.5%	10	1031	9	1046	68	364	0	19.2%	95
2011	TB		500	294	58.9%	3566	22	10			6.3		5.7%					84	346	1	4.8%	

2010:	54% Short	26% Mid	12% Deep	7% Bomb	YAC: 5.2 (24)	2009:	55% Short	30% Mid	10% Deep	5% Bomb	YAC: 4.2 (42)

The first quarterback to be selected in the first round by the Bucs since Trent Dilfer in 1994, Freeman has already far outstripped the "try-hard" Dilfer in sheer athletic effect. But what made Freeman so impressive in his second NFL season is that the light went on in ways both sabermetric and intangible. Freeman's leadership was obvious, his decision-making seemed to outpace itself from week to week, and his nascent ability to lead his team to victory from behind as time ran low brought an element of the Staubach/Elway gunslinger legend to the table. Say what you will about such urban legends; they do hold currency with teammates who need to trust their quarterbacks. The numbers matched up — Freeman's touchdown/interception ratio was the ninth-best in NFL history, and he threw nine touchdowns with no picks in the last month of the season. Per Football Outsiders' similarity scores, the closest comparisons for the 2010 version of Freeman were the 2006 version of Philip Rivers, 2007's Jay Cutler, 2009's Joe Flacco, and 1981's Joe Montana. In each of those comparative cases, elite performance and perception were well on the way, with further breakthroughs to come. Everything seems to be lining up for Freeman — he's firmly in charge of a balanced offense, he's got young talent with potential all around him, and his ability to reset himself in adverse situations against the toughest defenses speaks to a higher ceiling than you find in the average quarterbacks. Matt Stafford and Mark Sanchez were the more glamorous names from the 2009 draft, but there's a growing school of thought that Freeman may be the best of the lot years down the road.

Blaine Gabbert

Height: 6-4   Weight: 234   College: Missouri   Draft: 2011/1 (10)   Born: 15-Oct-1989   Age: 22   Risk: Red

Year	Team	G	Att	Comp	C%	Yds	TD	INT	FUM	ASR	NY/P	Rk	DVOA	Rk	DYAR	Rk	YAR	Runs	Yds	TD	DVOA	DYAR
2011	JAC		448	248	55.3%	3211	14	16			5.8		3.6%					55	160	1	-11.7%	

Blaine Gabbert was born with natural physical gifts and leadership ability. He wasn't, however, born with pocket presence. The cannon-armed righty struggles in the fight-or-flight department, occasionally scrambling into pressure and failing to read when he should step up in the pocket. This could improve, in theory, with repetition. Gabbert completed 61 percent of his passes in two years as Missouri's starting quarterback; his style changed more from all-or-nothing as a sophomore (58 percent completion rate, 8.1 yards per pass) to efficiency-first as a junior (63 percent completion rate, 6.7 yards per pass) as Missouri's run game and defense improved. He adapts well and studies hard. If Jacksonville's offensive staff can help improve his instincts and reactions, he has all the other tools necessary for success.

David Garrard

Height: 6-1   Weight: 244   College: East Carolina   Draft: 2002/4 (108)   Born: 14-Feb-1978   Age: 33   Risk: Yellow

Year	Team	G	Att	Comp	C%	Yds	TD	INT	FUM	ASR	NY/P	Rk	DVOA	Rk	DYAR	Rk	YAR	Runs	Yds	TD	DVOA	DYAR
2008	JAC	16	535	335	62.6%	3620	15	13	7	7.6%	5.9	26	11.0%	15	824	14	734	73	322	2	9.6%	80
2009	JAC	16	516	314	60.9%	3597	15	10	14	8.2%	6.1	19	0.1%	23	399	19	431	77	323	3	4.4%	57
2010	JAC	14	366	236	64.5%	2734	23	15	10	8.6%	6.2	19	4.8%	24	385	22	424	66	279	5	12.4%	79
2011	JAC		463	276	59.7%	3104	19	14			5.6		-1.6%					70	253	4	-1.8%	

2010: 56% Short   26% Mid   12% Deep   6% Bomb   YAC: 5.0 (27)   2009: 50% Short   32% Mid   13% Deep   5% Bomb   YAC: 4.7 (34)

Congratulations on having arguably your best season since 2007's famous fluky interception rate, Mr. Garrard! Hope you enjoy the job competition! The Jaguars seem to (publicly) expect Garrard to remain the starter this year despite the selection of Blaine Gabbert, so expect another competent-yet-inconsistent performance as his career heads on to the Jon Kitna Transitional Quarterback Program. Garrard dramatically improved on his atrocious red zone numbers in 2009 (-49.1% DVOA), posting a 69.2% DVOA there with the help of Marcedes Lewis' emergence. His deep ball, however, continues to be maligned by Jaguars observers.

Bruce Gradkowski

Height: 6-1   Weight: 220   College: Toledo   Draft: 2006/6 (194)   Born: 27-Jan-1983   Age: 28   Risk: Yellow

Year	Team	G	Att	Comp	C%	Yds	TD	INT	FUM	ASR	NY/P	Rk	DVOA	Rk	DYAR	Rk	YAR	Runs	Yds	TD	DVOA	DYAR
2008	CLE	2	21	7	33.3%	26	0	3	0	15.3%	0.3	--	-192.2%	--	-234	--	-269	1	2	0	-34.0%	-1
2009	OAK	7	150	82	54.7%	1007	6	3	5	7.1%	5.9	24	-0.8%	24	107	25	44	18	108	0	7.9%	16
2010	OAK	6	157	83	52.9%	1059	5	7	3	6.3%	5.9	34	-14.2%	37	-33	37	13	12	41	0	-6.7%	2
2011	CIN		474	270	57.0%	3108	17	15			5.5		-7.9%					38	33	1	-34.2%	

2010: 51% Short   29% Mid   14% Deep   5% Bomb   YAC: 6.3 (5)   2009: 55% Short   24% Mid   16% Deep   4% Bomb   YAC: 4.9 (25)

Bruce Gradkowski is the very definition of "just a guy." The Raiders inexplicably benched Jason Campbell in favor of Gradkowski in the middle of their Week 2 game against St. Louis. When Gradkowski managed to lead them to a 16-14 victory, their irrational exuberance led to him starting the next three games. They lost two of them, and won the third only because Gradkowski was himself benched for Campbell. Gradkowski signed with Cincinnati and should hold off Jordan Palmer for the No. 2 job behind Andy Dalton.

Rex Grossman

Height: 6-1   Weight: 222   College: Florida   Draft: 2003/1 (22)   Born: 23-Aug-1980   Age: 31   Risk: Green

Year	Team	G	Att	Comp	C%	Yds	TD	INT	FUM	ASR	NY/P	Rk	DVOA	Rk	DYAR	Rk	YAR	Runs	Yds	TD	DVOA	DYAR
2008	CHI	3	62	32	51.6%	257	2	2	0	3.1%	3.8	--	-27.9%	--	-70	--	-94	3	4	2	24.7%	12
2009	HOU	1	9	3	33.3%	37	0	1	1	3.3%	3.7	--	-87.9%	--	-39	--	-21	3	9	0	-75.5%	-12
2010	WAS	4	133	74	55.6%	884	7	4	4	7.9%	5.8	36	-19.1%	40	-76	38	-43	3	6	0	-31.5%	-2
2011	WAS		518	317	61.2%	3443	17	14			5.6		-1.3%					15	24	0	-39.1%	

2010:	58% Short	25% Mid	14% Deep	3% Bomb	YAC: 5.6 (14)	2009:	67% Short	17% Mid	17% Deep	0% Bomb	YAC: 2.3 (--)

There was a large gap between Grossman's VOA and DVOA. His long-awaited return to the starting lineup saw him get games against the Cowboys and Jaguars, two of the five worst pass defenses in football. And while he faced the third-ranked Giants in his final game of the year, the Giants had ranked as the worst pass defense in football in the three weeks before they played Grossman. And even before the opponent adjustments, Grossman's performance was pretty bad. That the Shanaclan perceived him to be an upgrade on McNabb is a reflection on their ability to account for opponent adjustments or an exercise in denial. Long story short: Rex Grossman still sucks.

Max Hall

Height: 6-1   Weight: 209   College: Brigham Young   Draft: 2010/ (FA)   Born: 1-Oct-1985   Age: 26   Risk: Green

Year	Team	G	Att	Comp	C%	Yds	TD	INT	FUM	ASR	NY/P	Rk	DVOA	Rk	DYAR	Rk	YAR	Runs	Yds	TD	DVOA	DYAR
2010	ARI	6	78	39	50.0%	370	1	6	5	14.9%	3.0	--	-99.1%	--	-512	--	-498	1	-5	0	-214.1%	-10
2011	ARI		485	328	67.8%	3443	17	24			6.1		4.1%					18	35	1	-60.0%	

2010:	62% Short	22% Mid	10% Deep	6% Bomb	YAC: 3.7 (--)	2009:	-- Short	-- Mid	-- Deep	-- Bomb	

Hall certainly had an unusual rookie season. He went from going undrafted out of BYU to drawing Kurt Warner comparisons in the preseason. After winning his first career start against the Saints and getting national praise, he played like an undrafted free agent for a couple games, got hurt, and has been all but forgotten by fans in the offseason. He will have to fight to make the roster again in 2011.

Caleb Hanie

Height: 6-2   Weight: 225   College: Colorado State   Draft: 2008/ (FA)   Born: 11-Sep-1985   Age: 26   Risk: Yellow

Year	Team	G	Att	Comp	C%	Yds	TD	INT	FUM	ASR	NY/P	Rk	DVOA	Rk	DYAR	Rk	YAR	Runs	Yds	TD	DVOA	DYAR
2009	CHI	2	7	3	42.9%	11	0	1	0	0.9%	1.6	--	-146.7%	--	-71	--	-77	0	0	0	--	--
2010	CHI	2	7	5	71.4%	55	0	0	0	20.1%	4.4	--	15.5%	--	9	--	-1	1	-1	0	--	--
2011	CHI		433	256	59.1%	2993	22	17			6.4		4.0%					24	58	1	-5.1%	

2010:	56% Short	22% Mid	11% Deep	11% Bomb	YAC: 2.4 (--)	2009:	100% Short	0% Mid	0% Deep	0% Bomb	YAC: 2.0 (--)

The Bears used their backup quarterbacks the way a bad baseball team uses relief pitchers last year. When Jay Cutler got hurt, Todd Collins came in the game as the crafty old veteran with no stuff. Once Collins made a horrible mess of everything (or in the case of the Panthers game, made an easy win far harder than it had to be) Hanie served as the mop-up man straight from Triple-A whose primary job was to throw strikes and get things over with. Hanie's mop job in the NFC Championship game (13-of-20, 153 yards, one touchdown, two interceptions but some spirited drives) was good enough to prove that he deserved a promotion to No. 2 quarterback.

Matt Hasselbeck

Height: 6-4   Weight: 223   College: Boston College   Draft: 1998/6 (187)   Born: 25-Sep-1975   Age: 36   Risk: Red

Year	Team	G	Att	Comp	C%	Yds	TD	INT	FUM	ASR	NY/P	Rk	DVOA	Rk	DYAR	Rk	YAR	Runs	Yds	TD	DVOA	DYAR
2008	SEA	7	209	109	52.2%	1216	5	10	1	9.0%	4.8	38	-34.2%	39	-334	40	-262	11	69	0	46.2%	28
2009	SEA	14	488	293	60.0%	3029	17	17	11	6.8%	5.4	30	-20.9%	34	-334	41	-156	26	119	0	-9.3%	3
2010	SEA	14	444	266	59.9%	3001	12	17	6	6.4%	6.0	30	-10.1%	35	32	35	82	23	60	3	36.0%	43
2011	TEN		480	261	54.5%	3032	15	18			5.2		-17.8%					30	31	1	12.6%	

2010:	51% Short	30% Mid	12% Deep	7% Bomb	YAC: 4.8 (32)	2009:	55% Short	34% Mid	7% Deep	4% Bomb	YAC: 5.8 (11)

It's kind of amazing how little Hasselbeck's reputation has fallen, given his performance on the field. Hasselbeck has ranked outside the top 30 in DVOA four times in the last five years, and in that fifth year (2007) he was just mediocre, ranking 14th in DVOA. If Hasselbeck has any strengths left, they come in medium-length passes, where his accuracy and decision-making shine. Hasselbeck's DVOA on such throws was 68.2%, well above the average of 42.8%. Anything deeper than 15 yards, however, and his declining arm strength left Hasselbeck woefully inadequate. He also struggled on short routes, which suggests a lack of chemistry and/or timing with his receivers. He's still capable of teasing fans with a good week or two (in back-to-back games against Arizona and New Orleans, he complete 69 percent of his passes for 9.0 yards per attempt with no sacks or interceptions), but then he'll crash down to earth. Hasselbeck was the unquestioned leader of Seattle's informal workouts, but the Seahawks didn't offer him a long-term contract. Tennessee signed him to what is theoretically a three-year deal, but Jake Locker will likely be starting by the beginning of 2012.

Chad Henne

Height: 6-2   Weight: 230   College: Michigan   Draft: 2008/2 (57)   Born: 2-Jul-1985   Age: 26   Risk: Red

Year	Team	G	Att	Comp	C%	Yds	TD	INT	FUM	ASR	NY/P	Rk	DVOA	Rk	DYAR	Rk	YAR	Runs	Yds	TD	DVOA	DYAR
2008	MIA	1	12	7	58.3%	67	0	0	0	0.7%	5.6	--	-2.3%	--	8	--	17	0	0	0	--	--
2009	MIA	14	451	274	60.8%	2878	12	14	4	6.1%	5.7	26	7.9%	21	586	17	424	16	32	0	-5.2%	3
2010	MIA	15	490	301	61.4%	3301	15	19	5	5.7%	6.0	28	7.6%	22	621	17	508	35	52	0	-60.3%	-51
2011	MIA		532	333	62.6%	3623	21	15			6.1		9.8%					52	75	1	-5.9%	

2010:	52% Short	34% Mid	10% Deep	4% Bomb	YAC: 4.3 (40)	2009:	49% Short	39% Mid	9% Deep	3% Bomb	YAC: 4.2 (41)

Henne had a miserable season that started in late August when a report came out that Bill Parcells was very disappointed in Henne's development, continued when he was benched for Chad Pennington in November (only to have Pennington predictably get injured), and finished with him injured and on the sidelines watching Tyler Thigpen run the offense into the ground. In between, Henne threw 19 interceptions and put up several horrendous stat lines, including a 5-of-18, 55-yard "performance" against the Jets and a 6-of-16, 71-yard clunker in New England. About the only thing that went Henne's way was that the team failed in their bid to trade up into the third round and draft Ryan Mallett to replace him. It's possible that the coaches and players have lost confidence in Henne, but if he does return as the starter, there are reasons to think he is poised for a bounce-back year. Henne had exceptionally bad luck with his turnovers last year. According to our game charters, defenders only dropped one potential interception, meaning that almost every time Henne threw the ball in a bad spot, he didn't get away with it. Assuming defenders don't have a cheat code, that's unlikely to happen again. Meanwhile, Henne's yardage, completion percentage and yards per attempt all climbed for the third straight season.

Shaun Hill

Height: 6-5   Weight: 210   College: Maryland   Draft: 2002/ (FA)   Born: 9-Jan-1980   Age: 31   Risk: Green

Year	Team	G	Att	Comp	C%	Yds	TD	INT	FUM	ASR	NY/P	Rk	DVOA	Rk	DYAR	Rk	YAR	Runs	Yds	TD	DVOA	DYAR
2008	SF	9	288	181	62.8%	2046	13	8	8	7.7%	6.2	18	-2.4%	28	180	28	306	24	115	2	24.5%	38
2009	SF	6	155	87	56.1%	943	5	2	3	11.6%	4.8	40	-31.4%	40	-211	35	-69	8	70	0	76.4%	24
2010	DET	11	416	257	61.8%	2686	16	12	2	3.9%	6.0	33	12.8%	19	650	16	537	22	123	0	-8.5%	4
2011	DET		534	301	56.3%	3219	21	18			5.3		-2.3%					50	92	2	-6.6%	

2010:	57% Short	26% Mid	13% Deep	3% Bomb	YAC: 5.5 (16)	2009:	54% Short	33% Mid	10% Deep	4% Bomb	YAC: 5.9 (6)

Hill played through a chronic back condition last year; he had surgery in May, then attended player-organized workouts a week later. Hill also suffered a broken forearm and finger last year, making it easy for him to mentor Stafford while they were hanging around radiology. Hill rarely has a truly bad game: give him the start, and he will complete 60 percent of his passes, throw for about 200 yards, avoid any backup-quarterback turnover meltdowns (he has just one three-interception game in his career), and provide a little value with his feet. He's a good spot starter, but as a 31-year-old trying to stay ahead of "old athlete" health problems, that's all he is.

Brian Hoyer Height: 6-2 Weight: 215 College: Michigan State Draft: 2009/ (FA) Born: 13-Oct-1985 Age: 26 Risk: Blue

Year	Team	G	Att	Comp	C%	Yds	TD	INT	FUM	ASR	NY/P	Rk	DVOA	Rk	DYAR	Rk	YAR	Runs	Yds	TD	DVOA	DYAR
2009	NE	4	27	19	70.4%	142	0	0	0	7.8%	4.3	--	-7.7%	--	6	--	7	10	25	1	11.2%	8
2010	NE	5	15	7	46.7%	122	1	1	0	0.0%	8.1	--	22.5%	--	34	--	33	10	-8	0	-117.2%	-5
2011	NE		509	331	65.1%	3883	23	13			6.5		23.0%					26	6	1	-1.8%	

2010: 33% Short 47% Mid 13% Deep 7% Bomb YAC: 5.9 (--) 2009: 56% Short 37% Mid 7% Deep 0% Bomb YAC: 6.5 (--)

Hoyer was 32-of-57 for 471 yards, three touchdowns, and 1 interception in the 2010 preseason. As usual, we are stuck evaluating a Patriots backup based on preseason efforts, some mop-up work, and the vote of confidence that comes automatically from being a Patriots backup. There are no real red flags on Hoyer's record, and he played well enough against Miami in Week 17 to suggest that he can get the Patriots through a start or two. Ryan Mallett will probably not challenge Hoyer this year, but the stage is set for a 2012 battle that will be far more interesting than the usual nobody-versus-nobody duel to be Brady's backup.

Tarvaris Jackson Height: 6-2 Weight: 226 College: Alabama State Draft: 2006/2 (64) Born: 21-Apr-1983 Age: 28 Risk: Red

Year	Team	G	Att	Comp	C%	Yds	TD	INT	FUM	ASR	NY/P	Rk	DVOA	Rk	DYAR	Rk	YAR	Runs	Yds	TD	DVOA	DYAR
2008	MIN	7	149	88	59.1%	1056	9	2	5	8.8%	6.1	20	10.0%	17	219	25	211	26	139	0	-15.2%	-4
2009	MIN	8	21	14	66.7%	201	1	0	0	0.3%	9.6	--	80.2%	--	111	--	132	17	-10	0	-27.2%	-1
2010	MIN	3	58	34	58.6%	341	3	4	1	8.7%	4.7	--	-31.0%	--	-84	--	-122	7	63	0	79.9%	19
2011	SEA		495	296	59.8%	3680	21	19			6.3		-4.3%					48	91	1	-35.9%	

2010: 57% Short 33% Mid 3% Deep 7% Bomb YAC: 3.4 (--) 2009: 42% Short 32% Mid 11% Deep 16% Bomb YAC: 11.0 (--)

Jackson turned over his No. 7 jersey to Christian Ponder after the draft and bought the first bus ticket out of town ... well, he didn't buy the bus ticket, but the Vikings showed no signs of wanting him back as a "mentor." Jackson squandered his final chance to prove doubters wrong when Favre was injured last season: he threw three interceptions against the Bills, looked lost against the Giants (four sacks and pick) then got injured himself. Jackson has been essentially handed a starting job by the Seahawks. He knows Darrell Bevell's system, though he has only the most rudimentary ability to execute it. Early preseason results were not encouraging, and Jackson will likely be yanked in and out of the lineup with fellow retread Charlie Whitehurst.

Josh Johnson Height: 6-3 Weight: 213 College: San Diego Draft: 2008/5 (160) Born: 15-May-1986 Age: 25 Risk: Green

Year	Team	G	Att	Comp	C%	Yds	TD	INT	FUM	ASR	NY/P	Rk	DVOA	Rk	DYAR	Rk	YAR	Runs	Yds	TD	DVOA	DYAR
2009	TB	5	125	63	50.4%	685	4	8	5	7.5%	4.6	--	-38.6%	43	-227	37	-301	22	148	0	4.4%	15
2010	TB	11	16	14	87.5%	111	0	0	0	10.5%	5.7	--	17.4%	--	28	--	29	4	39	0	152.3%	25
2011	TB		455	229	50.4%	2516	17	18			3.9		-23.4%					88	527	1	-6.4%	

2010: 65% Short 20% Mid 10% Deep 5% Bomb YAC: 3.6 (--) 2009: 57% Short 30% Mid 8% Deep 5% Bomb YAC: 4.4 (37)

Johnson completed all six of his passes against the Steelers in Week 3 after Josh Freeman was injured, and that was most of the action he saw. Johnson was the NCAA leader in career passing efficiency when he left the University of San Diego in 2008, and he really would rather go to a team that gives him an opportunity to fight for a starting job, but that's very unlikely. He could move to San Francisco when he hits free agency after this season, as Jim Harbaugh was Johnson's coach and mentor with the Toreros.

Colin Kaepernick Height: 6-5 Weight: 233 College: Nevada Draft: 2011/2 (36) Born: 3-Nov-1987 Age: 24 Risk: Yellow

Year	Team	G	Att	Comp	C%	Yds	TD	INT	FUM	ASR	NY/P	Rk	DVOA	Rk	DYAR	Rk	YAR	Runs	Yds	TD	DVOA	DYAR
2011	SF		461	231	50.0%	2858	13	18			5.5		2.6%					108	408	4	-20.4%	

A strangely long-legged athlete who developed into an actual quarterback, Colin Kaepernick possesses the best play-fake of any quarterback in the draft and one of the best in the NFL. He got by on his legs early in his career, completing just 54 percent of his passes in each of his first two seasons at Nevada but posting ridiculous numbers on the ground; Kaepernick rushed for 1,257 pre-sack rushing yards and a devastating plus-48.6 Adj. POE. In 2009, however, he began to become a quarterback. He raised his completion percentage to 59 percent while still rushing for 1,148 yards, and as a senior, he exploded: 2,830 passing yards, a 65 percent completion rate, a 2.1 percent interception rate, and another 1,265 rushing yards. If his running ability is hemmed in a bit, it is unclear whether his passer instincts will be where they need to be, but he had too many unique tools for the 49ers to pass up.

Jon Kitna

Height: 6-2   Weight: 220   College: Central Washington   Draft: 1996/ (FA)   Born: 21-Sep-1972   Age: 39 Risk: Green

Year	Team	G	Att	Comp	C%	Yds	TD	INT	FUM	ASR	NY/P	Rk	DVOA	Rk	DYAR	Rk	YAR	Runs	Yds	TD	DVOA	DYAR
2010	DAL	10	318	209	65.7%	2365	16	12	6	6.3%	6.7	10	5.6%	23	368	23	364	31	147	1	-16.7%	-6
2011	DAL		492	309	62.8%	3650	17	14			6.3		11.0%					16	16	1	-22.0%	
2010:	59% Short		27% Mid		9% Deep		5% Bomb			YAC: 6.5 (3)		2009:		-- Short		-- Mid		-- Deep		-- Bomb		

The absurd speculation during the offseason was that Kitna's performance was roughly similar to Tony Romo's. (We'll save you the page turn; Romo had a 20.6% DVOA, which was ninth in the league.) Their passer ratings were within six points of each other, which highlights the problem with passer ratings far more than it identifies the similarities between the two Cowboys quarterbacks. Kitna fumbled six times; Romo didn't fumble once. Kitna's interception rate was worse. His sack rate was nearly twice as high. He played an easier schedule than Romo. There were games where Kitna certainly didn't get help from a drop-happy group of receivers, but he's not on Romo's level.

Kevin Kolb

Height: 6-3   Weight: 218   College: Houston   Draft: 2007/2 (36)   Born: 24-Aug-1984   Age: 27 Risk: Yellow

Year	Team	G	Att	Comp	C%	Yds	TD	INT	FUM	ASR	NY/P	Rk	DVOA	Rk	DYAR	Rk	YAR	Runs	Yds	TD	DVOA	DYAR
2008	PHI	6	34	17	50.0%	144	0	4	0	0.3%	4.2	--	-75.7%	--	-139	--	-175	13	2	0	-67.3%	-9
2009	PHI	5	96	62	64.6%	741	4	3	1	5.2%	7.1	8	16.0%	16	180	23	160	5	-1	1	8.5%	4
2010	PHI	7	189	115	60.8%	1197	7	7	5	7.9%	5.3	39	-3.3%	32	97	33	105	15	65	0	-23.6%	-6
2011	ARI		496	326	65.7%	3786	21	17			6.6		5.8%					35	22	1	-6.2%	
2010:	61% Short		21% Mid		10% Deep		8% Bomb		YAC: 5.0 (28)		2009:	49% Short		37% Mid		7% Deep		7% Bomb		YAC: 5.6 (12)	

As we discussed in the Eagles chapter, Kolb's seasonal line looks a lot worse than it should because of the Week 17 scout team game against the Cowboys. His biggest flaw as a passer remains his total lack of pocket presence, undoubtedly stemming from his shotgun-heavy system at Houston and his lack of experience in the pocket around an NFL-caliber pass rush. Kolb prematurely senses the collapse of the pocket and then doesn't know where to go to avoid the pressure, resulting in a desperate scramble or one of his vaunted checkdowns. There's no guarantee that Kolb will get it even with further experience, but the Cardinals banked hard on it in the offseason by giving up Dominique Rodgers-Cromartie and a second round pick for his services. KUBIAK thinks he can be a solid quarterback right away, but Arizona paid a steep price for the upgrade.

Byron Leftwich

Height: 6-5   Weight: 245   College: Marshall   Draft: 2003/1 (7)   Born: 14-Jan-1980   Age: 31 Risk: Green

Year	Team	G	Att	Comp	C%	Yds	TD	INT	FUM	ASR	NY/P	Rk	DVOA	Rk	DYAR	Rk	YAR	Runs	Yds	TD	DVOA	DYAR
2008	PIT	5	36	21	58.3%	303	2	0	0	7.2%	7.4	--	66.0%	--	175	--	170	4	7	1	662.7%	16
2009	TB	3	107	58	54.2%	594	4	3	2	1.3%	5.5	29	5.0%	22	115	24	13	6	6	0	-10.3%	0
2010	PIT	1	7	5	71.4%	42	0	0	0	22.9%	3.9	--	-5.6%	--	3	--	4	0	0	0		
2011	PIT		446	287	64.3%	3234	21	12			6.5		23.9%					39	11	2	0.5%	
2010:	67% Short		33% Mid		0% Deep		0% Bomb		YAC: 3.6 (--)		2009:	63% Short		25% Mid		8% Deep		4% Bomb		YAC: 3.3 (46)	

Thanks to the Ben Roethlisberger suspension, Byron Leftwich was going to get one more month to showcase himself as the starting quarterback of a playoff-caliber team… until he tore his left MCL in the final preseason game. So much for that. Instead, his only action came from relieving Roethlisberger at the end of a meaningless Week 17 game. He remains a quality backup as long as your offensive line can protect him long enough for him to complete his infamous slow windup.

Matt Leinart

Height: 6-5 Weight: 225 College: USC Draft: 2006/1 (10) Born: 11-May-1983 Age: 28 Risk: Green

Year	Team	G	Att	Comp	C%	Yds	TD	INT	FUM	ASR	NY/P	Rk	DVOA	Rk	DYAR	Rk	YAR	Runs	Yds	TD	DVOA	DYAR
2008	ARI	4	29	15	51.7%	264	1	1	2	6.8%	8.0	--	-23.9%	--	-26	--	-20	4	5	0	63.7%	5
2009	ARI	8	77	51	66.2%	435	0	3	0	3.5%	5.4	--	-10.1%	--	5	--	25	9	-6	0	-71.9%	-3
2011	HOU		498	270	54.2%	3349	17	15			6.0		2.1%					40	54	1	-18.9%	
2010:	-- Short		-- Mid		-- Deep		-- Bomb					2009:	63% Short		23% Mid		13% Deep		1% Bomb		YAC: 3.6 (--)	

Leinart showed enough on the bench as the third quarterback in 2010 that the Texans parted ways with previous backup Dan Orlovsky at the start of training camp. Until he shows he can stand up to an NFL pass rush and consistently make throws that beat man coverage, though, he'll have plenty of doubters. The Texans do have a better offensive line and running game than the Cardinals did, so he should be able to exceed his numbers in Arizona if he's forced into action.

Jake Locker

Height: 6-3 Weight: 231 College: Washington Draft: 2011/1 (8) Born: 15-Jun-1988 Age: 23 Risk: Yellow

Year	Team	G	Att	Comp	C%	Yds	TD	INT	FUM	ASR	NY/P	Rk	DVOA	Rk	DYAR	Rk	YAR	Runs	Yds	TD	DVOA	DYAR
2011	TEN		489	260	53.1%	3315	16	18			5.2		-13.4%					96	447	2	-18.7%	

Locker is a tough athlete was picked twice in the MLB draft but stuck with football. He was named the top NFL prospect in the draft class before his senior season began; this came despite a horrible completion percentage (53 percent) and a career 36-to-26 touchdown-to-interception ratio. A 4-for-20, 70-yard day against Nebraska pretty much ended his hopes of going first overall. He has arm strength and decent mobility, but even in his senior season he was completing only 55 percent of his passes. Recent history suggests a player cannot succeed in the NFL with college efficiency numbers this low, but Locker has won over a lot of believers in his career.

Ryan Mallett

Height: 6-7 Weight: 253 College: Arkansas Draft: 2011/3 (74) Born: 5-Jun-1988 Age: 23 Risk: Yellow

Year	Team	G	Att	Comp	C%	Yds	TD	INT	FUM	ASR	NY/P	Rk	DVOA	Rk	DYAR	Rk	YAR	Runs	Yds	TD	DVOA	DYAR
2011	NE		480	304	63.4%	3578	27	15			5.4		18.4%					17	26	2	5.8%	

Blessed with size and an incredible right arm, Ryan Mallett fell to the third round because of supposed character and maturity concerns. He allegedly was not always the best teammate, but the football comes out of his hand like he's throwing a pea. Arkansas' downfield passing was incredible in 2010; playing against one of the toughest schedules in the country, Mallett completed 65 percent of his passes at almost 15 yards per completion, and he kept his interception rate under three percent. An old-school, never-leaves-the-pocket guy, he could be wonderfully influenced by Tom Brady in New England.

Eli Manning

Height: 6-4 Weight: 218 College: Mississippi Draft: 2004/1 (1) Born: 3-Jan-1981 Age: 31 Risk: Green

Year	Team	G	Att	Comp	C%	Yds	TD	INT	FUM	ASR	NY/P	Rk	DVOA	Rk	DYAR	Rk	YAR	Runs	Yds	TD	DVOA	DYAR
2008	NYG	16	479	289	60.3%	3238	21	10	5	5.6%	6.1	19	19.7%	9	1032	9	942	20	10	1	17.2%	14
2009	NYG	16	509	317	62.3%	4021	27	14	13	5.3%	7.1	9	21.1%	11	1105	10	977	17	65	0	11.5%	12
2010	NYG	16	539	339	62.9%	4002	31	25	6	3.3%	7.0	6	11.0%	20	792	15	858	32	70	0	51.0%	35
2011	NYG		537	331	61.6%	3797	27	14			6.5		14.3%					26	30	0	-19.3%	
2010:	47% Short		32% Mid		14% Deep		6% Bomb		YAC: 4.8 (31)		2009:	49% Short		34% Mid		10% Deep		7% Bomb		YAC: 5.5 (13)	

Without a true healthy fullback for most of the season, the Giants became a team that operated mostly out of three-wideout sets. They lined up three-wide on more than 56 percent of Manning's passes, and he wasn't better for it. In those sets, he completed 59.7 percent of his passes and threw an interception once every 19.3 attempts. When they had two wideouts in the lineup, Manning completed 69.7 percent of his passes and threw interceptions once every 58 passes. Correlation isn't causation, but going three-wide places more defenders into intermediate zones, where all those tipped passes went. His interception rate is sure to decline in 2011, but he's going to take more sacks and throw fewer touchdowns, too.

Peyton Manning   Height: 6-5   Weight: 230   College: Tennessee   Draft: 1998/1 (1)   Born: 24-Mar-1976   Age: 35   Risk: Red

Year	Team	G	Att	Comp	C%	Yds	TD	INT	FUM	ASR	NY/P	Rk	DVOA	Rk	DYAR	Rk	YAR	Runs	Yds	TD	DVOA	DYAR
2008	IND	16	555	371	66.8%	4002	27	12	1	2.8%	6.9	11	36.1%	1	1783	2	1780	20	21	2	-35.2%	-20
2009	IND	16	571	393	68.8%	4500	33	16	2	2.7%	7.6	4	38.2%	5	1936	2	2017	19	-13	0	-132.7%	-21
2010	IND	16	679	450	66.3%	4700	33	17	3	2.8%	6.6	11	25.0%	6	1679	2	1880	18	18	0	80.6%	13
2011	IND		612	392	64.0%	4354	31	14			6.8		24.1%					27	14	0	-30.9%	

2010:	54% Short	27% Mid	12% Deep	8% Bomb	YAC: 4.2 (41)	2009:	45% Short	38% Mid	11% Deep	5% Bomb	YAC: 5.0 (24)

4,700 yards and 33 touchdowns. Carrying a decimated offense practically on his own. It certainly seems like Manning is still Manning, but at age 35, there were troubling signs a year ago. His counting stats were inflated by a career-high 679 passing attempts, and he had the lowest yards per attempt figure since his rookie year. His DVOA was the lowest since 2002, and after six years of ranking first or second in DVOA, he has now ranked fifth in 2009 and sixth last year. Certainly Manning's supporting cast has struggled the past several years due to age, injury, and ineffectiveness, but it is impossible to ignore the fact that the all-time great is on the downside of his career. Manning sometimes has problems when plays break down and his pre-snap first option is covered. In those cases, Manning too often forces balls into bad situations and throws interceptions. None of this means Manning is not still great and as essential to his team as anyone in the game. It is just a simple acknowledgment that he no longer is at the peak of his abilities. Recovery from offseason neck surgery should not linger into the season but is a further reminder that Manning is aging and may no longer be indestructable. Still, the Colts remain committed, giving Manning a new $90 million, five-year contract that should keep him with the Colts into the absolute sunset of his career.

Luke McCown   Height: 6-3   Weight: 208   College: Louisiana Tech   Draft: 2004/4 (106)   Born: 12-Jul-1981   Age: 30   Risk: Green

Year	Team	G	Att	Comp	C%	Yds	TD	INT	FUM	ASR	NY/P	Rk	DVOA	Rk	DYAR	Rk	YAR	Runs	Yds	TD	DVOA	DYAR
2009	JAC	3	3	1	33.3%	2	0	0	0	40.9%	-1.0	--	-141.9%	--	-41	--	-37	0	0	0	--	--
2010	JAC	1	19	11	57.9%	120	0	0	0	0.0%	6.3	--	31.8%	--	50	--	34	1	4	0	-53.2%	-2
2011	JAC		464	288	62.2%	3161	18	12			5.9		1.0%					41	57	0	-9.3%	

2010:	42% Short	32% Mid	16% Deep	11% Bomb	YAC: 5.3 (--)	2009:	100% Short	0% Mid	0% Deep	0% Bomb	YAC: 0.0 (--)

McCown relieved an ineffective David Garrard in Week 2 against the Chargers, and after some empty yardage that led to zero points in the wrong end of a blowout, he promptly blew out his ACL while making a cut. He was re-signed before the lockout, which shows how highly the Jags think of him, but with Blaine Gabbert joining the club, McCown will probably spend most of 2012 as the third quarterback. He'll be 30 before the season starts, and there's little upside left to tap here, so that's probably a role he's better qualified for at this point.

Colt McCoy   Height: 6-1   Weight: 216   College: Texas   Draft: 2010/3 (85)   Born: 5-Sep-1986   Age: 25   Risk: Yellow

Year	Team	G	Att	Comp	C%	Yds	TD	INT	FUM	ASR	NY/P	Rk	DVOA	Rk	DYAR	Rk	YAR	Runs	Yds	TD	DVOA	DYAR
2010	CLE	8	222	135	60.8%	1576	6	9	1	9.3%	6.0	32	3.8%	25	236	27	173	28	136	1	49.9%	66
2011	CLE		483	315	65.1%	3510	22	16			6.2		8.3%					60	265	2	-4.3%	

2010:	56% Short	27% Mid	10% Deep	7% Bomb	YAC: 5.5 (19)	2009:	-- Short	-- Mid	-- Deep	-- Bomb

Well, that went better than expected. McCoy took control of the Browns offense with ease, showing the same poise and accuracy that helped him win an NCAA-record 45 games in college. As an added bonus, he picked up extra value as a scrambler. One criticism of McCoy clearly still applies, however: He doesn't throw the deep ball well enough to be a star NFL quarterback. McCoy completed just 36 percent of his passes over 15 yards; the league average was 40 percent. He threw seven of his nine picks on deep passes; around the league, only 45 percent of picks came on deep passes. Drew Brees had a similar scouting report coming out of Purdue, and he worked hard enough to develop as one of the best deep passers in the league. If he wants to take his game to the next level, McCoy has to follow in those footsteps.

Stephen McGee   Height: 6-3   Weight: 225   College: Texas A&M   Draft: 2009/4 (101)   Born: 27-Sep-1985   Age: 26   Risk: Green

Year	Team	G	Att	Comp	C%	Yds	TD	INT	FUM	ASR	NY/P	Rk	DVOA	Rk	DYAR	Rk	YAR	Runs	Yds	TD	DVOA	DYAR
2010	DAL	2	44	22	50.0%	238	2	0	1	8.1%	4.8	--	-14.5%	--	-10	--	-24	13	74	0	33.8%	22
2011	DAL		534	314	58.8%	3611	17	16			5.6		-2.9%					73	192	1	-18.5%	

2010:	72% Short	25% Mid	0% Deep	4% Bomb	YAC: 5.5 (--)	2009:	-- Short	-- Mid	-- Deep	-- Bomb

The big-armed developmental third quarterback is compulsory on NFL rosters, but they very rarely get a chance to actually suit up. McGee did after injuries to the two quarterbacks ahead of him, and while he looked good as a substitute against the Cardinals, he had a middling Week 17 game against the Philadelphia B-teamers, completing 40 percent of his passes. McGee did show off some scrambling ability, which makes Quincy Carter the easy comp. Fortunately, the Cowboys are smart enough to not give McGee the starting job, too.

Donovan McNabb   Height: 6-5   Weight: 230   College: Tennessee   Draft: 1998/1 (1)   Born: 24-Mar-1976   Age: 35   Risk: Red

Year	Team	G	Att	Comp	C%	Yds	TD	INT	FUM	ASR	NY/P	Rk	DVOA	Rk	DYAR	Rk	YAR	Runs	Yds	TD	DVOA	DYAR
2008	PHI	16	571	345	60.4%	3916	23	11	7	4.5%	6.4	15	15.6%	12	1048	8	1079	39	147	2	-31.3%	-38
2009	PHI	14	443	267	60.3%	3553	22	10	10	7.1%	6.9	12	8.9%	20	619	16	648	37	140	2	43.0%	56
2010	WAS	13	472	275	58.3%	3377	14	15	9	7.1%	6.1	25	0.2%	29	354	24	282	29	151	0	13.3%	26
2011	MIN		506	306	60.5%	3599	18	16			6.4		7.6%					45	27	1	-37.2%	

2010:	56% Short	27% Mid	9% Deep	8% Bomb	YAC: 5.8 (8)	2009:	49% Short	32% Mid	11% Deep	8% Bomb	YAC: 6.1 (3)

Should we have been surprised that McNabb failed to turn things around for the Redskins? Probably not. Quarterbacks can shift context more than players at any other position, but even the best quarterback is going to look a lot worse throwing to Santana Moss and Anthony Armstrong than he does on passes to DeSean Jackson and Jeremy Maclin. McNabb is in the decline phase of his career, but that decline will not be as steep as it appeared to be last season, when the Shanahans blamed him for everything but the national budget crisis. Playing in Minnesota will take McNabb away from the Northeast media crush, and getting away from the spotlight will do him some good. McNabb will have a quiet season while Christian Ponder learns. Quiet will probably sound wonderful to him.

Matt Moore   Height: 6-3   Weight: 202   College: Oregon State   Draft: 2007/ (FA)   Born: 9-Aug-1984   Age: 27   Risk: Green

Year	Team	G	Att	Comp	C%	Yds	TD	INT	FUM	ASR	NY/P	Rk	DVOA	Rk	DYAR	Rk	YAR	Runs	Yds	TD	DVOA	DYAR
2009	CAR	7	138	85	61.6%	1053	8	2	2	5.6%	6.7	15	21.6%	10	304	21	320	12	-3	0	-36.3%	-3
2010	CAR	6	143	79	55.2%	857	5	10	4	7.9%	4.9	42	-37.5%	43	-270	43	-288	5	25	0	-8.8%	1
2011	MIA		464	285	61.3%	3058	15	13			5.7		6.6%					27	14	1	-21.1%	

2010:	55% Short	23% Mid	16% Deep	6% Bomb	YAC: 4.5 (37)	2009:	52% Short	36% Mid	5% Deep	7% Bomb	YAC: 5.0 (21)

Moore was the subject of some media traction as the next undrafted star after a 2009 season in which he finished tenth in passing DVOA, but 2010 was a harsh snap back to reality. Trapped in an offense that would have to rise several levels to be called "disappointing," Moore alternated between balky, too-soon throws and plays that got him debacled on the field because he couldn't get rid of the ball quickly enough. He was placed on injured reserve in early November, but Moore was already leaving the scene after a brutal three-pick game against the Rams. The Miami Dolphins, fresh off their bollixed negotiations with the Denver Broncos over Kyle Orton and contemplating another season of Chad Henne in the pilot's chair, took a two-year contract shot on Moore's raw potential.

Cam Newton

Height: 6-5   Weight: 248   College: Auburn   Draft: 2011/1 (1)   Born: 11-May-1989   Age: 22   Risk: Yellow

Year	Team	G	Att	Comp	C%	Yds	TD	INT	FUM	ASR	NY/P	Rk	DVOA	Rk	DYAR	Rk	YAR	Runs	Yds	TD	DVOA	DYAR
2011	CAR		466	232	49.8%	2945	14	16			4.7		-40.0%					115	575	5	-18.6%	

The savior is here, and he has brought all the Tostitos. Newton isn't as explosive on the ground as Randall Cunningham or Michael Vick, and he doesn't have the development as a pure passer we've seen from Josh Freeman or the young Steve McNair. Vince Young is the closest comparison. Just as Young has been most effective in option misdirection sets with formations that force defenses to key as much on running backs, Auburn with Newton was just about unstoppable when they ran the Pistol formation and similar concepts. (Auburn was first in the nation in Rushing S&P+ last year, sixth in Passing S&P+.) There are two big differences between Newton and most of the other spread/option quarterbacks who have been controversial draftees in recent years. First, Newton's lack of experience means there is a possibility he is nothing more than a flash in the pan. The absence of a track record is the reason our Lewin Career Forecast is so down on him. He's one of only three quarterbacks since 1990 drafted despite only one year as a starter at a four-year school. (The others were Mark Sanchez and 1992 second-round pick Matt Blundin.) Second, Newton comes to the NFL with as good a pure arm as you'll see — he can zip it 50 yards downfield with reasonable accuracy and without extra effort. He's going to struggle under center, and timing patterns are very problematic (he's especially weak on quick outs, for some reason), but the raw tools are there to develop in the right kind of system. Very, very raw tools. He's not scheme-transcendent, but there are things the Panthers can do to make this work in a big way.

Dan Orlovsky

Height: 6-5   Weight: 230   College: Connecticut   Draft: 2005/5 (145)   Born: 18-Aug-1983   Age: 28   Risk: Green

Year	Team	G	Att	Comp	C%	Yds	TD	INT	FUM	ASR	NY/P	Rk	DVOA	Rk	DYAR	Rk	YAR	Runs	Yds	TD	DVOA	DYAR
2008	DET	10	255	143	56.1%	1616	8	8	3	5.5%	5.7	29	0.3%	23	198	26	157	7	29	0	56.1%	13
2011	IND		576	318	55.2%	3826	18	21			6.0		-2.3%					35	58	1	-23.2%	

Orlovsky spent two years in Houston backing up previously injury-prone Matt Schaub, but an inconsistent work ethic, Matt Leinart's sheen, and fifth-round pick T.J. Yates made him expendable. Orlovsky nonetheless credits Gary Kubiak for making him a better quarterback. Is he better enough to beat out Curtis Painter as Peyton Manning's backup?

Kyle Orton

Height: 6-4   Weight: 226   College: Purdue   Draft: 2005/4 (106)   Born: 14-Nov-1982   Age: 29   Risk: Red

Year	Team	G	Att	Comp	C%	Yds	TD	INT	FUM	ASR	NY/P	Rk	DVOA	Rk	DYAR	Rk	YAR	Runs	Yds	TD	DVOA	DYAR
2008	CHI	15	465	272	58.5%	2972	18	12	6	5.9%	5.7	27	-0.9%	25	334	21	323	24	39	3	-15.4%	-3
2009	DEN	16	541	336	62.1%	3802	21	12	4	5.3%	6.4	16	13.3%	17	887	12	920	24	71	0	-18.6%	-6
2010	DEN	13	498	293	58.8%	3653	20	9	3	6.6%	6.5	15	14.4%	17	869	12	911	22	98	0	6.5%	16
2011	DEN		519	297	57.2%	3565	19	13			5.9		-3.9%					49	86	1	-15.1%	

2010:	50% Short	30% Mid	13% Deep	8% Bomb	YAC: 5.1 (26)	2009:	51% Short	34% Mid	10% Deep	5% Bomb	YAC: 5.9 (8)

We know that Orton put up some fairly ridiculous numbers on Josh McDaniels' offenses over the last two seasons. Then again, McDaniels got surprising stats out of a guy in New England (Matt Cassel) who hadn't started a game since about grade school, or so the legend goes. How will he fare in a more conservative system, where his receivers aren't running themselves open in multi-wide sets? After a failed trade with the Miami Dolphins, the Broncos decided to keep Orton, and named him the 2011 starter after further dalliances with the Tim Tebow idea. In truth, Orton is most likely a shorter-term option for a number of reasons: his own limitations, Denver's continued love affair with Tebow and the Broncos' awareness of that fact, and quite possibly the desire of the new front office to plant its own flag at the quarterback position.

Curtis Painter

Height: 6-3 Weight: 225 College: Purdue   Draft: 2009/6 (201) Born: 24-Jun-1985   Age: 26 Risk: Green

Year	Team	G	Att	Comp	C%	Yds	TD	INT	FUM	ASR	NY/P	Rk	DVOA	Rk	DYAR	Rk	YAR	Runs	Yds	TD	DVOA	DYAR
2009	IND	2	28	8	28.6%	83	0	2	2	10.0%	2.2	--	-79.0%	--	-133	--	-192	3	4	0	-139.3%	-18
2011	IND		530	291	54.9%	3534	16	19			4.7		-16.6%					17	26	2	64.6%	
2010:	-- Short		-- Mid		-- Deep		-- Bomb					2009:	72% Short		20% Mid		8% Deep		0% Bomb		YAC: 3.3 (--)	

The Colts were forced to win in Week 17, costing Painter his annual opportunity to demonstrate he is not an NFL-caliber quarterback. As Manning ages, you have to fear that he may be injured at some point, leaving Painter in over his head. He has given no indication he would be a competent NFL starter, and he has to beat out Dan Orlovsky in training camp, which is no sure thing.

Carson Palmer

Height: 6-5 Weight: 230 College: USC   Draft: 2003/1 (1)   Born: 27-Dec-1979   Age: 32 Risk: N/A

Year	Team	G	Att	Comp	C%	Yds	TD	INT	FUM	ASR	NY/P	Rk	DVOA	Rk	DYAR	Rk	YAR	Runs	Yds	TD	DVOA	DYAR
2008	CIN	4	129	75	58.1%	731	3	4	2	7.9%	4.8	39	-5.0%	29	54	30	-56	6	38	0	50.0%	15
2009	CIN	16	466	282	60.5%	3094	21	13	6	4.9%	6.0	21	12.9%	18	739	15	779	39	93	3	19.6%	46
2010	CIN	16	586	362	61.8%	3970	26	20	6	4.8%	6.2	20	13.8%	18	1009	10	855	32	50	0	-28.2%	-18
2010:	48% Short		36% Mid		10% Deep		6% Bomb		YAC: 4.5 (35)			2009:	50% Short		35% Mid		12% Deep		3% Bomb		YAC: 4.6 (35)	

Carson Palmer has never been the same since a partially torn ligament and tendon in his elbow cost him most of the 2008 season. In retrospect, maybe it would have been a better idea to have Tommy John surgery instead of letting the injury try to heal on its own. After 2008, Palmer's arm strength was sapped, and a lot of his confidence went with it. He can no longer get those stick throws into small windows. But that doesn't mean he's not still a good quarterback. He still has good timing, the ability to read a zone and anticipate where the holes are going to be. Those 20 interceptions last year were partly due to a particularly difficult schedule. If Palmer does come back for some team, he will help them. But it's not likely to happen. Maybe Palmer was bluffing when he threatened to retire if the Bengals did not trade him, and Mike Brown called his bluff. Or perhaps Mike Brown was bluffing when he said that if Palmer wanted to play football he had to play for Cincinnati, and Palmer called Brown's bluff. Either way, people who know Palmer report that he's a quiet, thoughtful guy who isn't particularly driven to play football until his arm falls off. Brown is too proud to fold his hand, and Palmer is too comfortable with the money he's already made to fold his hand. Palmer's not coming back.

Chad Pennington

Height: 6-3 Weight: 225 College: Marshall   Draft: 2000/1 (18) Born: 26-Jun-1976   Age: 35 Risk: N/A

Year	Team	G	Att	Comp	C%	Yds	TD	INT	FUM	ASR	NY/P	Rk	DVOA	Rk	DYAR	Rk	YAR	Runs	Yds	TD	DVOA	DYAR
2008	MIA	16	476	321	67.4%	3653	19	7	3	5.0%	7.1	10	25.7%	5	1172	6	1399	30	62	1	36.8%	32
2009	MIA	3	74	51	68.9%	413	1	2	3	8.4%	5.0	--	-4.8%	--	32	--	65	3	7	0	-54.8%	-13
2010	MIA	1	2	1	50.0%	19	0	0	0	1.3%	9.5	--	65.7%	--	10	--	9	0	0	0	--	--
2010:	0% Short		100% Mid		0% Deep		0% Bomb		YAC: 13.0 (--)			2009:	45% Short		46% Mid		9% Deep		0% Bomb		YAC: 3.3 (--)	

In 2010, the two great Chad Pennington truisms staged a climactic battle. In the red corner, it was the Even Year Rule, which meant that Pennington was due to claw to the top of the depth chart, put up a stellar season, and win his third Comeback Player of the Year award. In the blue corner, it was the This is Chad Pennington We're Talking About Rule, which meant that his body was going to break into a million pieces as soon as it hit the turf. Score a 2-1 decision for the blue corner. Pennington did indeed retake the starting job in Week 9.

He even managed to throw two passes before suffering a torn capsule in his shoulder the first time a defender made contact with him. The Chad Pennington We're Talking About Rule went ahead for good in April when the quarterback tore his ACL playing basketball while rehabbing his shoulder. Pennington hasn't officially retired, but he is taking the year off to work for FOX as a broadcaster, where his intelligence, charisma and hard work should pay off... at least until he suffers a tragic season-ending injury stepping out of the elevator.

Christian Ponder

Height: 6-2   Weight: 229   College: Florida St.   Draft: 2011/1 (12)   Born: 25-Feb-1988   Age: 23   Risk: Yellow

Year	Team	G	Att	Comp	C%	Yds	TD	INT	FUM	ASR	NY/P	Rk	DVOA	Rk	DYAR	Rk	YAR	Runs	Yds	TD	DVOA	DYAR
2011	MIN		486	288	59.3%	3457	17	17			6.0		2.6%					75	113	4	-16.5%	

Christian Ponder is something of an amalgamation of all the other rookie quarterbacks. He is athletic, but he's not Cam Newton. He is an intangibles-and-instincts guy, but he's not Andy Dalton. His value comes in the simple fact that he has no on-field weakness. He is a bit small, but not too small to succeed. He improved significantly throughout his first three years (from a 56 percent completion rate and 6.3 yards per pass as a sophomore, to 69 percent and 8.2 as a junior), then fought injuries and declined as a senior. His durability is perhaps his biggest liability; he missed four games in 2009 and parts of quite a few others in 2010. Assuming the Shanahan clan doesn't mail rare viruses to Donovan McNabb as a going-away present, McNabb will probably hold down the starting job in 2011. More than most of the other highly-drafted rookies, Ponder needs a year to get stronger and straighten out his mechanics.

Chris Redman

Height: 6-3   Weight: 223   College: Louisville   Draft: 2000/3 (75)   Born: 7-Jul-1977   Age: 34   Risk: Green

Year	Team	G	Att	Comp	C%	Yds	TD	INT	FUM	ASR	NY/P	Rk	DVOA	Rk	DYAR	Rk	YAR	Runs	Yds	TD	DVOA	DYAR
2009	ATL	5	119	69	58.0%	781	4	3	1	6.4%	6.0	22	19.1%	12	236	22	164	6	4	0	5.1%	2
2010	ATL	2	6	4	66.7%	20	0	0	0	0.6%	3.3	--	-37.7%	--	-11	--	-14	1	-1	0	--	--
2011	ATL		507	298	58.7%	3511	21	13			6.2		-0.2%					77	85	0	-10.5%	

| 2010: | 83% Short | 17% Mid | 0% Deep | 0% Bomb | YAC: 3.8 (--) | 2009: | 46% Short | 41% Mid | 10% Deep | 4% Bomb | YAC: 4.2 (43) |

It was back to the stasis tube for Redman in 2010. After filling in capably if generically for Matt Ryan in 2009, Redman threw but six passes a season ago. Redman is 33, and while the Falcons would be wise to start looking at a younger backup in the near future, Redman looks like the sort who will be cashing NFL paychecks until he's 40.

Philip Rivers

Height: 6-5   Weight: 228   College: North Carolina State   Draft: 2004/1 (4)   Born: 8-Dec-1981   Age: 30   Risk: Green

Year	Team	G	Att	Comp	C%	Yds	TD	INT	FUM	ASR	NY/P	Rk	DVOA	Rk	DYAR	Rk	YAR	Runs	Yds	TD	DVOA	DYAR
2008	SD	16	478	312	65.3%	4009	34	11	8	5.4%	7.7	2	35.6%	2	1522	3	1621	31	84	0	-9.8%	3
2009	SD	16	486	317	65.2%	4254	28	9	6	4.6%	8.0	1	45.9%	1	1915	3	1853	26	50	1	-13.9%	-1
2010	SD	16	541	357	66.0%	4710	30	13	6	6.8%	7.8	3	34.0%	3	1652	3	1853	29	52	0	-0.5%	9
2011	SD		503	327	65.0%	4430	34	12			7.3		44.9%					23	9	1	-41.9%	

| 2010: | 54% Short | 26% Mid | 14% Deep | 6% Bomb | YAC: 6.3 (4) | 2009: | 46% Short | 31% Mid | 16% Deep | 7% Bomb | YAC: 6.0 (5) |

The positive nature of Rivers' season goes far beyond statistical value; the reason he garnered so much traction in the MVP discussion was for what he did with an undermanned offense. At times, his own general manager seemed to be working against him by causing friction and missed time with his left tackle (Marcus McNeill) and primary receiver (Vincent Jackson). When A.J. Smith wasn't proving points off the field and losing points on the field, the Chargers' running game was also falling apart. Everyone who played the Chargers had a bead on Rivers, and between the limited pass protection at times, compromises in receivers, Rivers was rarely playing with a full deck. When replacement left tackle Brandyn Dombrowski had his lunch eaten early on by speed ends, Rivers learned how better to throw on the run. And when that running game did fall apart, Rivers was the point man in an offense where three different backs had a receiving DVOA above 20%. There's no telling just how good he would have been had his front office been working on his behalf, just as there's no doubt (if there had been before) that Rivers is one of the game's elite quarterbacks. He's ranked third in DYAR in each of the last three seasons (behind Brady and Manning in each of the last two, and behind Brees and Manning in 2008, when Brady was hurt), and it's his rare gift to be able to do so no matter the circumstances.

Aaron Rodgers Height: 6-2 Weight: 223 College: California Draft: 2005/1 (24) Born: 2-Dec-1983 Age: 28 Risk: Yellow

Year	Team	G	Att	Comp	C%	Yds	TD	INT	FUM	ASR	NY/P	Rk	DVOA	Rk	DYAR	Rk	YAR	Runs	Yds	TD	DVOA	DYAR
2008	GB	16	536	341	63.6%	4038	28	13	9	6.4%	6.8	12	14.8%	14	932	10	966	56	207	4	16.3%	73
2009	GB	16	541	350	64.7%	4434	30	7	8	8.7%	7.1	10	22.7%	9	1294	9	1512	58	316	5	46.0%	136
2010	GB	15	475	312	65.7%	3922	28	11	3	6.9%	7.4	2	33.6%	4	1514	4	1467	64	356	4	25.2%	101
2011	GB		523	338	64.6%	4207	31	14			7.0		23.6%					75	331	4	15.6%	

| 2010: | 53% Short | 28% Mid | 11% Deep | 8% Bomb | YAC: 5.7 (12) | 2009: | 48% Short | 35% Mid | 10% Deep | 7% Bomb | YAC: 5.9 (7) |

Rodgers was dating model Destiny Newton as we went to press, having broken up with Gossip Girl Jessica Szohr sometime after the Super Bowl. The gossip blogs displayed beach pics of Rodgers and Newton with the same voyeuristic zeal used on Tom Brady and Tony Romo (with their wives/paramours mind you, not each other). Pro Football Talk informed us a week before the Super Bowl that Rodgers disrespects cancer sufferers, based on an interpretation of a 15-second crowd video. We are only three years removed from that carefully-edited footage of Rodgers overthrowing receivers at a Packers scrimmage, a brief clip that served as proof positive that Rodgers would never, ever be able to replace Brett Favre. Joe Theisman is no doubt gearing up to give Rodgers the "heart of a champion" happy ending treatment during telecasts; bloggers have already started bleating that the kid from Chico has sold out and become a jerk. Welcome to the epicenter of the echo chamber, Aaron. Please try to tune it all out and play football exactly the way you have played it for the past two years, because it is awfully fun to watch.

Ben Roethlisberger Height: 6-5 Weight: 240 College: Miami (Ohio) Draft: 2004/1 (11) Born: 2-Mar-1982 Age: 29 Risk: Green

Year	Team	G	Att	Comp	C%	Yds	TD	INT	FUM	ASR	NY/P	Rk	DVOA	Rk	DYAR	Rk	YAR	Runs	Yds	TD	DVOA	DYAR
2008	PIT	16	469	281	59.9%	3301	17	15	14	9.4%	5.9	25	-2.2%	27	288	23	228	34	102	1	-13.6%	-2
2009	PIT	15	506	337	66.6%	4328	28	14	7	9.0%	7.2	7	27.8%	8	1390	8	1459	40	82	2	10.9%	35
2010	PIT	12	389	240	61.7%	3200	17	5	6	8.0%	7.2	4	38.2%	2	1238	7	1187	34	176	2	39.8%	69
2011	PIT		457	303	66.2%	3865	28	12			7.2		37.6%					42	121	3	0.0%	

| 2010: | 48% Short | 31% Mid | 15% Deep | 7% Bomb | YAC: 5.5 (15) | 2009: | 44% Short | 37% Mid | 12% Deep | 7% Bomb | YAC: 5.3 (17) |

We all know how good Ben Roethlisberger is under pressure. Last year, he had a 74.6% DVOA on passes when our game charters listed a hurry, the best figure of any quarterback in the league. A year before, he had the third-highest DVOA on passes with pressure. But it is not impossible to get to Roethlisberger. The trick is that if you want to go after Big Ben, you either go big or you don't go at all and play coverage instead. Over the last three years, Roethlisberger has been one of the worst quarterbacks in the league against big blitzes with six or more pass rushers:

Ben Roethlisberger vs. Big Blitzes, 2008-2010

	Plays	Yd/Pass	DVOA	Sack Rate
3-5 rushers	1319	7.3	42.4%	8.0%
6-8 rushers	196	4.5	1.2%	12.2%

Sure, he could still get outside the pocket and perform some of his magic. But with a big blitz, you're more likely to trap Roethlisberger in the pocket, where he either goes down or makes an ill-advised throw with defenders hanging off him.

Tony Romo   Height: 6-2   Weight: 219   College: Eastern Illinois   Draft: 2003/ (FA)   Born: 21-Apr-1980   Age: 31   Risk: Green

Year	Team	G	Att	Comp	C%	Yds	TD	INT	FUM	ASR	NY/P	Rk	DVOA	Rk	DYAR	Rk	YAR	Runs	Yds	TD	DVOA	DYAR
2008	DAL	13	450	276	61.3%	3448	26	14	10	5.1%	7.1	8	18.5%	10	879	11	732	28	41	0	-12.2%	0
2009	DAL	16	550	347	63.1%	4483	26	9	5	6.2%	7.4	6	32.3%	7	1589	7	1493	35	105	1	59.6%	41
2010	DAL	6	213	148	69.5%	1605	11	7	0	4.5%	7.2	5	20.6%	9	434	19	460	6	38	0	86.4%	21
2011	DAL		548	351	64.1%	4194	26	13			6.8		19.0%					28	29	1	-20.7%	

2010:	49% Short	36% Mid	10% Deep	5% Bomb	YAC: 5.3 (20)	2009:	50% Short	33% Mid	11% Deep	7% Bomb	YAC: 6.4 (1)

Oh, messy life. Romo's second broken bone in three seasons ended his 2010 after six and a half games, and while it's easy to push the "injury-prone" label onto him, these aren't the sort of muscle and ligament injuries that slowed Carson Palmer and stopped Daunte Culpepper. Broken bones heal. Romo's performance before the injury was pretty standard, with the offensive line woes causing him to dump off far more frequently than he otherwise would. (Note the dramatic increase in completion percentage and simultaneous tradeoff in both yards per attempt and sack rate.) Even in the limited sample, though, his interception rate regressed back from his outlier season of 2009 to his career average of three percent. Of his three past seasons, the one that's likeliest to re-occur is 2008. That's still a plenty valuable quarterback, both in real-life and on your fantasy team.

Sage Rosenfels   Height: 6-4   Weight: 222   College: Iowa State   Draft: 2001/4 (109)   Born: 6-Mar-1978   Age: 33   Risk: Green

Year	Team	G	Att	Comp	C%	Yds	TD	INT	FUM	ASR	NY/P	Rk	DVOA	Rk	DYAR	Rk	YAR	Runs	Yds	TD	DVOA	DYAR
2008	HOU	6	174	116	66.7%	1431	6	10	4	5.4%	7.6	3	3.7%	21	183	27	140	11	37	0	-60.6%	-27
2010	NYG	12	0	0	0.0%	0	0	0	--	--	--	--	--	--	--	--	--	3	-3	0	--	--
2011	NYG		508	325	64.0%	3494	14	18			5.9		-3.5%					24	27	0	-9.5%	

There just aren't many snaps to be had behind Eli Manning. In fact, if Rosenfels had avoided a pre-season trade to the Giants, he probably would have seen playing time amidst the Vikings quarterback fiasco. His only value in 2011 is in leagues where folks get points for holds. Those exist, right?

Matt Ryan   Height: 6-4   Weight: 228   College: Boston College   Draft: 2008/1 (3)   Born: 17-May-1985   Age: 26   Risk: Green

Year	Team	G	Att	Comp	C%	Yds	TD	INT	FUM	ASR	NY/P	Rk	DVOA	Rk	DYAR	Rk	YAR	Runs	Yds	TD	DVOA	DYAR
2008	ATL	16	434	265	61.1%	3440	16	11	5	3.5%	7.4	4	30.9%	4	1167	7	1030	55	104	1	-30.0%	-34
2009	ATL	14	451	263	58.3%	2916	22	14	5	4.1%	6.1	20	16.7%	15	828	13	582	30	49	1	10.4%	27
2010	ATL	16	571	357	62.5%	3705	28	9	4	4.1%	6.0	29	23.9%	7	1348	6	1308	46	122	0	-11.2%	1
2011	ATL		562	338	60.2%	4084	26	15			6.7		15.3%					62	61	2	-4.7%	

2010:	50% Short	32% Mid	14% Deep	4% Bomb	YAC: 3.8 (44)	2009:	50% Short	38% Mid	8% Deep	4% Bomb	YAC: 4.4 (38)

A certain segment of Atlanta's population will never embrace Ryan, not even if he wins a Lombardi Trophy for them. He isn't Mike Vick, you see, and that's apparently a negative to these folks. To the reality-based community, however, Ryan is just fine. One of the best quarterbacks in the league, actually. The Falcons were a third-down converting machine in 2010, so it stands to reason that Ryan would save his best work for that down, with 770 DYAR and 48.9% DVOA (only the league MVP up in Foxboro did better). Ryan also made a definitive leap into fantasy stud status with 28 TD passes. Now if he can just get that playoff monkey off his back, perhaps that "Matty Slush" thing would go away.

Mark Sanchez   Height: 6-2   Weight: 227   College: USC   Draft: 2009/1 (5)   Born: 11-Nov-1986   Age: 25   Risk: Green

Year	Team	G	Att	Comp	C%	Yds	TD	INT	FUM	ASR	NY/P	Rk	DVOA	Rk	DYAR	Rk	YAR	Runs	Yds	TD	DVOA	DYAR
2009	NYJ	15	364	196	53.8%	2444	12	20	10	7.3%	5.9	25	-21.9%	35	-266	38	-258	36	106	3	13.4%	42
2010	NYJ	16	507	278	54.8%	3291	17	13	9	5.4%	5.9	35	1.6%	28	438	18	422	30	105	3	8.4%	27
2011	NYJ		509	288	56.5%	3281	21	16			5.5		-13.4%					43	108	3	-14.6%	

2010:	51% Short	30% Mid	11% Deep	8% Bomb	YAC: 4.7 (33)	2009:	56% Short	27% Mid	10% Deep	6% Bomb	YAC: 5.0 (22)

Sanchez has become the latest lightning rod for the argument over whether or not a quarterback should get the credit for team achievement — the "he's a winner" argument, if you will. Proponents will point to Sanchez's two AFC Championship appearances in as many years, as well as the game-winning drives he engineered against Cleveland and Houston, and perhaps his gritty performance that fell short in the second-half against Pittsburgh. His detractors will point to almost everything else, from his poor completion percentage to his middling yards per attempt to his propensity for throwing into coverage, even if he got away with it more often last year. Regardless of which side of the fence you fall, two things are clear. 1) Sanchez is still a very inexperienced player, a guy who only started for one season in college and who still has a lot to learn about going through progressions and making good decisions with the ball. Philip Rivers started more games at N.C. State than Sanchez has started in college and the pros combined. 2) Sanchez improved in his second season, generally playing at a league-average level. Is he as good as his press clippings? Absolutely not. But if Sanchez keeps improving, he might get there in another year or two.

Matt Schaub Height: 6-5 Weight: 235 College: Virginia   Draft: 2004/3 (90) Born: 25-Jun-1981 Age: 30 Risk: Yellow

Year	Team	G	Att	Comp	C%	Yds	TD	INT	FUM	ASR	NY/P	Rk	DVOA	Rk	DYAR	Rk	YAR	Runs	Yds	TD	DVOA	DYAR
2008	HOU	11	380	251	66.1%	3043	15	10	10	6.7%	7.3	5	21.7%	8	863	12	672	31	68	2	4.0%	19
2009	HOU	16	583	396	67.9%	4770	29	15	3	5.3%	7.7	3	33.6%	6	1796	6	1860	48	57	0	-42.9%	-50
2010	HOU	16	574	365	63.6%	4370	24	12	8	5.9%	6.9	9	18.2%	13	1173	8	1168	22	28	0	6.9%	14
2011	HOU		532	333	62.6%	3977	27	12			6.8		28.3%					38	11	1	-14.9%	

2010:	54% Short	31% Mid	11% Deep	4% Bomb	YAC: 5.5 (17)	2009:	43% Short	39% Mid	11% Deep	6% Bomb	YAC: 5.4 (15)

By this point in his career, Schaub is a known quantity who doesn't offer many surprises. He's excellent at play-fakes and uses them to good advantage, including on the bootleg. His arm is normally good enough, but not great and can be a limitation in the vertical passing game. His pocket presence can be less than ideal, especially against pressure up the middle. After a good year operating out of the shotgun in 2009, he regressed in 2010, as his DVOA in shotgun fell from 43.3% to 2.8%. Schaub will be plagued by occasional bouts of spraying his passes, which is one of the reasons the Texans offense was inconsistent even within games. He's had trouble staying healthy in the past, but he started all 16 games for the second straight year and was healthier than he was in 2009. On a team with fewer offensive weapons, and in a different offensive scheme, he might not be more than a marginal starter, but for the Houston Texans he's pretty darn good.

John Skelton Height: 6-6 Weight: 243 College: Fordham   Draft: 2010/5 (155) Born: 17-Mar-1988 Age: 23 Risk: Green

Year	Team	G	Att	Comp	C%	Yds	TD	INT	FUM	ASR	NY/P	Rk	DVOA	Rk	DYAR	Rk	YAR	Runs	Yds	TD	DVOA	DYAR
2010	ARI	5	126	60	47.6%	662	2	2	3	7.8%	4.5	44	-46.9%	45	-295	45	-228	10	49	0	18.4%	11
2011	ARI		507	254	50.1%	3003	13	22			5.0		-16.3%					48	199	1	-6.7%	

2010:	52% Short	25% Mid	15% Deep	8% Bomb	YAC: 3.3 (46)	2009:	-- Short	-- Mid	-- Deep	-- Bomb	

The Cardinals second rookie quarterback to start in 2001 fared better than Max Hall, just like Chris Weinke had a better pro career than Gino Torretta. The 6-foot-6 Skelton is athletic, averaging 4.9 yards a carry on the ground. He will probably stick around for a couple years as Kevin Kolb's backup.

Alex Smith Height: 6-4 Weight: 212 College: Utah   Draft: 2005/1 (1) Born: 7-May-1984 Age: 27 Risk: Green

Year	Team	G	Att	Comp	C%	Yds	TD	INT	FUM	ASR	NY/P	Rk	DVOA	Rk	DYAR	Rk	YAR	Runs	Yds	TD	DVOA	DYAR
2009	SF	11	372	225	60.5%	2350	18	12	3	6.5%	5.7	28	-15.4%	28	-106	29	68	24	51	0	-11.9%	0
2010	SF	11	342	204	59.6%	2370	14	10	4	7.8%	6.2	21	-5.4%	33	134	31	159	18	60	0	-0.4%	5
2011	SF		504	306	60.8%	3363	18	14			5.7		-1.8%					22	27	0	5.2%	

2010:	60% Short	24% Mid	9% Deep	7% Bomb	YAC: 6.1 (6)	2009:	52% Short	33% Mid	8% Deep	6% Bomb	YAC: 4.9 (26)

Last year in this space, we noted that the 49ers had finally figured out that Smith was more comfortable in the shotgun, and that he was likely to use it a lot more often in 2010. Smith did throw 58 percent of his passes out of the shotgun (league average: 55 percent), but he wasn't very effective, with a DVOA of -2.9% (league average: 6.1%). Part of that may be Smith's increasing reliance on short passes. In 2007, only 45 percent of Smith's passes qualified as short (fewer than six yards through the air), a rate that then increased substantially in 2009 and again last season. It's a trend the 49ers will have to reverse in 2011. Short passes are not typically an efficient method of gaining yardage (the league averaged a 44 percent Success Rate on short passes, compared to 55 percent on all other throws), and that's especially true for Smith (38 percent Success Rate on short passes, 57 percent on other throws). That could be a reflection of Smith's environment - if you were taking snaps behind the 49ers' offensive line, you'd be checking down too.

Rusty Smith   Height: 6-5   Weight: 224   College: Florida Atlantic   Draft: 2010/6 (176)   Born: 28-Jan-1987   Age: 24 Risk: Green

Year	Team	G	Att	Comp	C%	Yds	TD	INT	FUM	ASR	NY/P	Rk	DVOA	Rk	DYAR	Rk	YAR	Runs	Yds	TD	DVOA	DYAR
2010	TEN	2	40	20	50.0%	200	0	4	0	2.8%	4.9	--	-90.6%	--	-178	--	-133	0	0	0	--	--
2011	TEN		495	264	53.3%	3311	14	19			5.7		-19.2%					43	135	1	12.3%	

| 2010: | 35% Short | 48% Mid | 10% Deep | 8% Bomb | YAC: 4.2 (--) | 2009: | -- Short | -- Mid | -- Deep | -- Bomb |

Pressed into starting duty when both Kerry Collins and Vince Young were injured, Rusty Smith made the theretofore Worst Pass Defense in DVOA History, the 2010 Texans, look like worldbeaters and showed once again why starting rookie sixth-round picks is a Really, Really Bad Idea. With Matt Hasselbeck and Jake Locker in the fold, Smith has neither a short-term nor a long-term future on the field in Tennessee and will have to look for another team interested in a tall quarterback with spotty accuracy in college who needs a couple years of seasoning.

Troy Smith   Height: 6-0   Weight: 225   College: Ohio State   Draft: 2007/5 (174)   Born: 20-Jul-1984   Age: 27 Risk: N/A

Year	Team	G	Att	Comp	C%	Yds	TD	INT	FUM	ASR	NY/P	Rk	DVOA	Rk	DYAR	Rk	YAR	Runs	Yds	TD	DVOA	DYAR
2008	BAL	5	4	3	75.0%	82	1	0	0	19.4%	16.2	--	184.2%	--	62	--	66	9	24	0	-10.0%	1
2009	BAL	4	9	5	55.6%	24	0	1	0	0.0%	2.7	--	-115.5%	--	-57	--	-49	8	31	1	13.8%	10
2010	SF	6	145	73	50.3%	1176	5	4	6	11.5%	6.6	12	-12.8%	36	-18	36	-26	23	121	1	-1.9%	9

| 2010: | 51% Short | 26% Mid | 15% Deep | 8% Bomb | YAC: 7.9 (1) | 2009: | 48% Short | 35% Mid | 10% Deep | 7% Bomb | YAC: 5.9 (7) |

Smith's starts in Weeks 8 and 10 against Denver and St. Louis were his first in three years, and he led the 49ers to a pair of wins. His big-play style was a radical departure from Alex Smith, and he was completing more than 60 percent of his passes for 19 yards a catch, with 14 20-yard plays and a DVOA of 63.7%. Then opponents figured out that most of the time, Smith was just playing "three flies up," holding the ball forever and chucking it deep downfield. For the rest of the season he completed less than 45 percent of his passes, with only 10 20-yarders and a DVOA of -23.5%. With Alex Smith sticking around and Colin Kaepernick in town, there's no room in San Francisco for Troy, who remained unsigned at press time. If he can't find an NFL roster spot, his highlight ability and Heisman Trophy marquee value would be much appreciated in the UFL.

Matthew Stafford   Height: 6-2   Weight: 225   College: Georgia   Draft: 2009/1 (1)   Born: 7-Feb-1988   Age: 23 Risk: Yellow

Year	Team	G	Att	Comp	C%	Yds	TD	INT	FUM	ASR	NY/P	Rk	DVOA	Rk	DYAR	Rk	YAR	Runs	Yds	TD	DVOA	DYAR
2009	DET	10	377	201	53.3%	2267	13	20	4	6.0%	5.3	32	-31.8%	41	-529	45	-380	20	108	2	27.8%	33
2010	DET	3	96	57	59.4%	535	6	1	2	4.7%	5.0	41	9.0%	21	130	32	118	4	11	1	-27.1%	-3
2011	DET		573	326	56.8%	3639	17	15			5.6		-3.6%					60	141	3	26.9%	

| 2010: | 61% Short | 27% Mid | 5% Deep | 7% Bomb | YAC: 5.3 (23) | 2009: | 57% Short | 31% Mid | 8% Deep | 4% Bomb | YAC: 6.0 (4) |

Stafford announced that he was 100 percent healthy in May; blooming crocuses and an injury-free Stafford are two sure signs that it is not autumn. Stafford has not yet strung together two straight good games. Last year's Redskins-Jets sequence was solid, but it's hard to say a quarterback had a "good" game when he suffers a season-ending injury and his team loses. Nearly half of Stafford's career touchdown production came in two games: last year's four-touchdown effort against the Redskins and the wild five-touchdown 38-37 shootout against the Browns in 2009. Stafford aces the eyeball test when he is in the lineup, but his career lacks traction, so we still don't know what to expect if Stafford manages to string 8-10 consecutive games together. Even if Stafford conquers injuries, there is not much evidence to suggest that he will suddenly blossom into Matt Ryan. Three years into his career, he still has some rookie growing pains to work through.

Drew Stanton

Height: 6-3 Weight: 230 College: Michigan State   Draft: 2007/2 (43)   Born: 7-May-1984   Age: 27 Risk: Green

Year	Team	G	Att	Comp	C%	Yds	TD	INT	FUM	ASR	NY/P	Rk	DVOA	Rk	DYAR	Rk	YAR	Runs	Yds	TD	DVOA	DYAR
2008	DET	3	17	9	52.9%	119	1	0	0	25.5%	3.7	--	-27.6%	--	-21	--	-11	3	20	0	-13.3%	0
2009	DET	3	51	26	51.0%	259	0	6	1	8.3%	4.2	--	-70.4%	--	-228	--	-282	9	33	1	-2.5%	4
2010	DET	6	119	69	58.0%	780	4	3	2	5.4%	6.0	27	19.4%	11	229	28	139	18	113	1	21.1%	28
2011	DET		518	307	59.3%	3589	11	10			6.0		-4.4%					66	79	2	-18.9%	

| 2010: | 59% Short | 30% Mid | 5% Deep | 6% Bomb | YAC: 6.1 (7) | 2009: | 69% Short | 18% Mid | 12% Deep | 2% Bomb | YAC: 5.4 (--) |

The Lions, recognizing that Matthew Stafford and Shaun Hill could bump into one another in a cafeteria line and shatter like Christmas balls, re-signed Stanton after the lockout. Stanton's 2010 season was a rise from the ashes for a player on a downward trajectory; he was awful in 2009, a third stringer on an 0-16 team in 2008, and arrived in Detroit as a down-on-his-luck prospect after a poor senior season for a bad Michigan State team. Stafford and Hill's medical histories suggest that Stanton will play, and if he can repeat the minor success of 2010, he will attract the attention of teams looking to reshuffle their quarterback decks in 2012.

Ricky Stanzi

Height: 6-4 Weight: 221 College: Iowa   Draft: 2011/5 (135)   Born: 3-Sep-1987   Age: 24 Risk: Blue

Year	Team	G	Att	Comp	C%	Yds	TD	INT	FUM	ASR	NY/P	Rk	DVOA	Rk	DYAR	Rk	YAR	Runs	Yds	TD	DVOA	DYAR
2011	KC		442	236	53.4%	2433	11	17			4.5		-30.8%					20	46	0	8.0%	

It's a 2011 quarterback class full of players with significant skill-set deficits, and Stanzi is no exception. Stanzi comes to the NFL with questions about accuracy and consistency. At the 2011 Senior Bowl, he struggled in comparison to other marquee throwers, displaying real issues with route depth. Still, on a team with a lot of pieces in place, he may be able to manage the field, make his reads and avoid mistakes. His upside is lower than a lot of other rookies, but his downside might not be as low either.

Tyrod Taylor

Height: 6-1 Weight: 216 College: Virginia Tech   Draft: 2011/6 (180)   Born: 3-Aug-1989   Age: 22 Risk: Green

Year	Team	G	Att	Comp	C%	Yds	TD	INT	FUM	ASR	NY/P	Rk	DVOA	Rk	DYAR	Rk	YAR	Runs	Yds	TD	DVOA	DYAR
2011	BAL		466	298	63.9%	3366	12	20			6.2		-8.2%					101	549	2	52.3%	

While some saw Taylor as a conversion project, he's currently the Ravens backup due to Marc Bulger's retirement. Taylor owns an intriguing athletic profile and has good touch on his throws, but he's also a bit short for the position and pulls it down to run a bit too quickly at times. His Virginia Tech team ranked 10th in the nation in passing in our college metrics last year.

Tim Tebow

Height: 6-3 Weight: 236 College: Florida   Draft: 2010/1 (25)   Born: 14-Aug-1987   Age: 24 Risk: Green

Year	Team	G	Att	Comp	C%	Yds	TD	INT	FUM	ASR	NY/P	Rk	DVOA	Rk	DYAR	Rk	YAR	Runs	Yds	TD	DVOA	DYAR
2010	DEN	9	82	41	50.0%	654	5	3	1	5.4%	7.3	--	19.9%	--	168	--	177	43	227	6	24.2%	73
2011	DEN		470	266	56.7%	3281	16	19			5.7		8.2%					120	676	7	11.1%	

| 2010: | 49% Short | 27% Mid | 14% Deep | 10% Bomb | YAC: 6.2 (--) | 2009: | -- Short | -- Mid | -- Deep | -- Bomb | |

When Orton was lost for the season with a rib injury, Tebow came in for the last three games of the season as a starter. He provided some rudimentary passing ability, but became the team's must effective rusher on the field. Most of his scores came on simple read-option plays, but that's what he ran so effectively at Florida, and when your second-string quarterback leads your team in rushing touchdowns as Tebow did in 2010, asking how he did it is not part of the package. Small sample sizes abound, but perhaps the most interesting thing about Tebow's rookie numbers is that he was actually more effective when under center (30.8% DVOA, compared to 13.6% DVOA in shotgun). There's something to his potential; it's just hard to figure out where it's going to lead.

Tyler Thigpen

Height: 6-3   Weight: 235   College: Coastal Carolina   Draft: 2007/7 (217)   Born: 14-Apr-1984   Age: 27   Risk: Green

Year	Team	G	Att	Comp	C%	Yds	TD	INT	FUM	ASR	NY/P	Rk	DVOA	Rk	DYAR	Rk	YAR	Runs	Yds	TD	DVOA	DYAR
2008	KC	14	420	230	54.8%	2608	18	12	4	6.2%	5.5	31	-6.2%	30	146	29	219	62	386	3	15.2%	78
2009	2TM	1	8	4	50.0%	83	1	2	0	0.0%	10.4	--	-51.5%	--	-23	--	-28	2	3	0	-39.2%	-1
2010	MIA	5	62	33	53.2%	435	2	2	1	11.9%	5.5	--	6.5%	--	76	--	39	13	73	0	-6.5%	3
2011	BUF		483	310	64.2%	3518	18	20			5.8		-27.5%					47	192	2	8.0%	

| 2010: | 46% Short | 29% Mid | 15% Deep | 10% Bomb | YAC: 3.9 (--) | 2009: | 38% Short | 38% Mid | 0% Deep | 25% Bomb | YAC: 6.3 (--) |

There are only a finite number of good-to-great quarterbacks in the NFL, and once you get past those you're more likely to see an established mediocrity like Jake Delhomme or Kerry Collins under center than a less-experienced backup like Thigpen. Thigpen doesn't help matters by succeeding mainly as a spread quarterback, and thus the obvious fit for him will be Buffalo where he can re-unite with Chan Gailey, his offensive coordinator on the 2009 Chiefs. There isn't a whole lot of upside here, but Thigpen can be a perfectly cromulent quarterback in his preferred system. That's more than you can say for quite a few quarterbacks who were allowed more snaps than him last season.

Michael Vick

Height: 6-0   Weight: 215   College: Virginia Tech   Draft: 2001/1 (1)   Born: 26-Jun-1980   Age: 31   Risk: Yellow

Year	Team	G	Att	Comp	C%	Yds	TD	INT	FUM	ASR	NY/P	Rk	DVOA	Rk	DYAR	Rk	YAR	Runs	Yds	TD	DVOA	DYAR
2009	PHI	12	13	6	46.2%	86	1	0	0	0.9%	6.6	--	-4.7%	--	6	--	13	24	95	2	8.4%	26
2010	PHI	12	372	233	62.6%	3018	21	6	10	8.7%	7.0	7	20.6%	8	835	13	840	100	676	9	29.7%	195
2011	PHI		477	306	64.1%	3763	26	11			6.5		26.5%					125	519	8	18.7%	

| 2010: | 57% Short | 24% Mid | 9% Deep | 10% Bomb | YAC: 5.7 (11) | 2009: | 83% Short | 0% Mid | 0% Deep | 17% Bomb | YAC: 2.2 (--) |

Vick will turn the ball over more in 2011. Whether you consider his past, the Eagles offense's past, or the past of players around the league as a whole, his 1.6 percent interception rate just isn't sustainable. For reference, consider that Peyton Manning's never had an interception rate that low. Vick isn't suddenly going to throw 25 interceptions, but it wouldn't be a surprise to see Vick's interceptions to double over the course of a full season next year. He was also able to recover seven of his ten fumbles. Of course, he will still be a valuable asset as his turnover rate increases, both for his abilities and the impact he has on LeSean McCoy. Vick's long-term contract negotiations will end up being very interesting. Nobody else has a skill set or career path that matches Vick's, so how do you find any references for valuation? As important as Vick's 2010 season was in establishing a new level of ability, his 2011 season and ability to repeat that performance is going to be just as important for his future earning potential.

Billy Volek

Height: 6-2   Weight: 214   College: Fresno State   Draft: 2000/ (FA)   Born: 28-Apr-1976   Age: 35   Risk: Green

Year	Team	G	Att	Comp	C%	Yds	TD	INT	FUM	ASR	NY/P	Rk	DVOA	Rk	DYAR	Rk	YAR	Runs	Yds	TD	DVOA	DYAR
2009	SD	4	31	20	64.5%	231	1	1	0	2.4%	7.2	--	21.7%	--	71	--	83	9	-9	0	--	--
2010	SD	3	1	1	100.0%	8	0	0	0	0.0%	8.0	--	161.3%	--	10	--	11	6	-5	0	--	--
2011	SD		476	292	61.3%	3580	20	10			6.7		24.5%					46	56	0	-22.6%	

| 2010: | 71% Short | 14% Mid | 14% Deep | 0% Bomb | YAC: 7.0 (--) | 2009: | 52% Short | 32% Mid | 10% Deep | 6% Bomb | YAC: 6.3 (--) |

Volek's been a name put on every team's veteran quarterback need list at one time or another, primarily because he's generally done well in limited action. The recent time learning under Norv Turner can't hurt; after all Charlie Whitehurst got $10 million from the Seahawks based on his knowledge and ability, and Whitehurst was decidedly under Volek on the depth chart. However, Whitehurst also popped that longtime "Any quarterback under Norv will be pro-ready" balloon in Seattle, so any hope Rob Johnson/Scott Mitchell dreams Volek may have had are long gone.

Seneca Wallace
Height: 5-11　Weight: 196　College: Iowa State　　　Draft: 2003/4 (110)　Born: 6-Aug-1980　Age: 31　Risk: Red

Year	Team	G	Att	Comp	C%	Yds	TD	INT	FUM	ASR	NY/P	Rk	DVOA	Rk	DYAR	Rk	YAR	Runs	Yds	TD	DVOA	DYAR
2008	SEA	10	242	141	58.3%	1532	11	3	4	5.6%	5.7	28	7.3%	19	295	22	286	16	78	0	1.3%	8
2009	SEA	13	120	78	65.0%	700	3	2	5	7.8%	5.0	39	-11.3%	26	-1	26	-3	13	16	1	-38.7%	-13
2010	CLE	8	101	64	63.4%	694	4	2	1	6.3%	6.2	23	18.2%	14	198	29	160	7	9	0	-97.6%	-18
2011	CLE		431	279	64.8%	2830	18	13			5.5		-1.6%					19	25	0	-10.7%	
2010:	50% Short		32% Mid		12% Deep		7% Bomb			YAC: 5.3 (22)		2009:	54% Short		35% Mid		10% Deep		1% Bomb		YAC: 4.3 (40)	

Now settled into the "elder statesman backup quarterback" portion of his career, Wallace was actually pretty good last year. The Browns were 1-3 in his four starts, but those three losses were all to playoff teams, by an average of less than a touchdown. Cleveland blogs desperate for something to write about during the lockout made a big deal about Wallace's confidence during player-led workouts, where he insisted that he wasn't conceding the starting position to Colt McCoy, but he's not really going to be competing for the starting position. He's a backup who is extra useful because he already understands the Holmgren-influenced offense that Pat Shurmur is bringing in.

Joe Webb
Height: 6-3　Weight: 223　College: UAB　　　Draft: 2010/6 (199)　Born: 14-Nov-1986　Age: 25　Risk: Green

Year	Team	G	Att	Comp	C%	Yds	TD	INT	FUM	ASR	NY/P	Rk	DVOA	Rk	DYAR	Rk	YAR	Runs	Yds	TD	DVOA	DYAR
2010	MIN	5	89	54	60.7%	477	0	3	1	7.7%	4.5	--	-19.0%	--	-49	--	-90	18	120	2	53.5%	56
2011	MIN		470	280	59.6%	3176	16	20			5.7		-8.7%					81	329	3	7.3%	
2010:	61% Short		28% Mid		5% Deep		7% Bomb			YAC: 4.2 (--)		2009:	-- Short		-- Mid		-- Deep		-- Bomb			

We now have a clearer picture of what "slash" receivers like Antwaan Randle El or Josh Cribbs might do if forced to start a couple of games. It's not a terrible picture, really: the DVOA was low, but Webb did no worse than your basic third stringer or 32-year-old McCown/Huard-type grabbed off waivers. He ran the specialized "scrambling guy" offense well enough, tossing lots of screens to Percy Harvin and the backs and rollout passes to his tight ends. He made a few plays with the legs. It wasn't the stuff a starting quarterback career is based on, but if a team's resident Slash guy is no worse than the typical third-stringer, why bother with third-stringers unless they are on a development track? Webb probably would have made a heck of a quarterback in the 1940s.

Charlie Whitehurst
Height: 6-4　Weight: 220　College: Clemson　　　Draft: 2006/3 (81)　Born: 6-Aug-1982　Age: 29　Risk: Red

Year	Team	G	Att	Comp	C%	Yds	TD	INT	FUM	ASR	NY/P	Rk	DVOA	Rk	DYAR	Rk	YAR	Runs	Yds	TD	DVOA	DYAR
2010	SEA	6	99	57	57.6%	507	2	3	1	4.3%	4.8	43	-26.0%	41	-95	39	-120	20	43	1	10.4%	14
2011	SEA		476	267	56.2%	2898	21	15			5.2		-6.4%					47	127	1	-26.6%	
2010:	64% Short		22% Mid		9% Deep		6% Bomb			YAC: 4.4 (38)		2009:	-- Short		-- Mid		-- Deep		-- Bomb			

Whitehurst was largely unknown when the Seahawks traded for him, he was largely unknown when he signed an extension through 2011, and a year later, he's still largely unknown. We know he didn't look very good in what little regular-season time he saw, and wasn't much in the 2010 preseason (51 percent completion rate) either. We know that his biggest play of the year — a 61-yard catch-and-run to Ruvell Martin on the first drive of the Week 17 playoff-clinching win over St. Louis — came as a result of a busted coverage, and that if anything Whitehurst underthrew Martin on the play. We know Whitehurst told reporters that he expected to start this fall, but we also know that the Seahawks signed Tarvaris Jackson instead. And that's about all we know.

Vince Young   Height: 6-5   Weight: 230   College: Texas   Draft: 2006/1 (3)   Born: 18-May-1983   Age: 28   Risk: Green

Year	Team	G	Att	Comp	C%	Yds	TD	INT	FUM	ASR	NY/P	Rk	DVOA	Rk	DYAR	Rk	YAR	Runs	Yds	TD	DVOA	DYAR
2008	TEN	3	36	22	61.1%	219	1	2	2	7.8%	5.2	--	-69.7%	--	-150	--	-121	8	27	0	-17.4%	-1
2009	TEN	12	259	152	58.7%	1879	10	7	8	3.8%	6.9	13	17.7%	14	491	18	461	55	281	2	-1.6%	26
2010	TEN	9	156	93	59.6%	1255	10	3	6	7.0%	7.0	8	26.8%	5	423	20	428	25	125	0	-0.6%	8
2011	PHI		470	302	64.2%	3568	24	12			6.3		10.4%					85	394	2	18.7%	

2010:	49% Short	24% Mid	18% Deep	9% Bomb	YAC: 4.4 (39)	2009:	51% Short	32% Mid	11% Deep	5% Bomb	YAC: 5.0 (20)

In some ways, 2010 was the best year of Vince Young's career. The Titans had found out what Young was best at (deeper passes) and what he wasn't best at (short and intermediate timing routes), and gameplanned accordingly. He did his best work on first down (45.0% DVOA) and under center (48.4% DVOA), particularly when throwing to Kenny Britt. The rest of the story is that the 2009 improvement in pocket presence disappeared, he was benched for poor play in Week 2 against the Steelers after missing meetings in practice, and then suffered a season-ending thumb injury and cursed out Jeff Fisher in the locker room after a game. Young is now skilled enough to be an average or above-quality starter for the right team, and he found the right lake to land in at Andy Reid's Halfway House for Wayward Scramblers. If he plays, it will be in an offense tuned to his improvisational gifts. If he rides the bench for a year and re-enters the market, he will get plenty of "well, it worked for Michael Vick" benefit of the doubt.

Going Deep

Richard Bartel, ARI: Bartel spent most of last year as the backup to Daunte Culpepper with the UFL's Sacramento Mountain Lions. Arizona signed him when they needed a depth quarterback near the end of the year, and he ended up coming in to play most of a game after John Skelton got hurt. He probably won't have a roster spot this year. (2010 stats: 16-for-28, 150 yards, 1 INT, -91 DYAR, -49.7% DVOA)

Rhett Bomar, MIN: Bomar was waived by the Giants at the end of 2010 training camp, re-signed to their practice squad at the start of the season, then acquired by the Vikings when their quarterback situation became unspeakably grim late in the year. He's a decent size-speed-arm prospect who played pretty well in the 2010 preseason, but the Giants preferred signing Sage Rosenfels off the street to giving Bomar the No. 2 job, and the Vikings started a receiver/return man at quarterback instead of him, so the endorsements aren't exactly solid.

Todd Bouman, JAC: Todd Bouman lives in a little cubbyhole at Jacksonville Jaguars headquarters, behind a glass door marked "break in case of emergency." He was signed and then cut by the team in 2007, again in 2008, and then again in 2009. Last year he was signed by the Jaguars three times and cut twice. The team was so desperate for quarterbacks that Bouman actually started a game against Kansas City when both David Garrard and Trent Edwards were out. Now, who's ready for an 18-game season? (2010 stats: 18-for-34, 222 yards, 2 TD, 2 INT, 52 DYAR, 10.4% DVOA)

Brian Brohm, FA: Add Brohm's regular season stats (zero touchdowns, five interceptions) to his career preseason numbers in Green Bay and Buffalo (zero touchdowns, five interceptions) and you get a clear, depressing picture of absolute futility. Brohm looked like a very good prospect at Louisville, but we were watching the latest member of a college quarterback dynasty run a highly structured, pass-happy offense. He was a carefully handled, manufactured prospect who maxed out as a guy who could win in what was essentially a mid-major conference. (2010 stats: 10-for-23, 106 yards, 3 INT, -182 DYAR, -125.0% DVOA)

Levi Brown, BUF: Chan Gailey began talking Brown up in 2010 minicamps, waxing rhapsodic about the former Sun Belt Conference star's arm, grasp of the offense, and intangibles. Brown got just enough preseason face time to throw two interceptions (remember that the Bills were trying to choose between Ryan Fitzpatrick and Trent Edwards, so those game reps were precious), then threw three passes in Week 17, completing all three, one of them to Jets cornerback Dwight Lowery. Brown is the kind of quarterback who looks like an up-and-comer if you have been staring at Brian Brohm and Trent Edwards too long.

Sean Canfield, NO: Unusually for a third-stringer, this 2010 seventh-rounder from Oregon State is an accurate passer without a howitzer for an arm. He wouldn't be on most other rosters, but the Saints value what he brings, which is Brees/Daniel Lite.

Kellen Clemens, WAS: Clemens was considered an under-the-radar talent during the 2006 draft, someone who you could get in the second round who might end up being as good as Vince Young or Matt Leinart. As it turns out, that was a pretty low bar to clear, but Clemens still failed to clear it. After an eight-game audition in 2007, he was shelved as a starter in favor of first Brett Favre and then Mark Sanchez. He's in a much better situation in Washington, where John Beck and Rex Grossman hardly have their spots set in stone on the depth chart, but even so, it's unlikely that Clemens will see the field in 2011.

Todd Collins, FA: Collins milked a three-game 2007 hot streak with the Redskins into over three years of gainful employment. He deserves a cabinet level position - Secretary of Conservation, or Director of Homeland Job Security, or somesuch. (2010 stats: 10-for-27, 68 yards, 5 INT, -280 DYAR, -159.0% DVOA)

Jonathan Crompton, FA: Finally, someone to fill out the Jason Campbell support group! Crompton played for four different offensive coordinators in Tennessee, spent 2010 training camp with the Chargers, then joined the Patriots practice squad in November. The arrival of Ryan Mallett ended his time in New England. Crompton is a natural drop-back passer with lots of college experience, but he was never a top athlete or cannon-armed prospect, and he's never had time to master a system, which can really screw up a young quarterback.

Pat Devlin, MIA: Devlin's post collegiate career: 2-for-7, 22 yards, and an interception in the East-West Shrine game, followed by showing up 30 minutes late for his own Pro Day. That explains the undrafted part. The Delaware product lacks elite arm strength and can have problems picking up pressure. On the bright side, he landed with Miami, so as long as they continue to focus on what Chad Henne can't do, he could see the field at some point.

Nathan Enderle, CHI: Enderle has a great set of tools: compact delivery, great frame, solid athleticism. He hasn't lived up to them yet, but the Bears believed in him enough to draft him in the fifth round, so he'll hang around behind Caleb Hanie and pray that Mike Martz's memory of him is as long as it was with J.T. O'Sullivan.

Charlie Frye, OAK: Frye has now played like hot garbage for three teams since the Browns took him in the third round of the 2005 draft. His appeal to the Raiders, who tend to prefer rocket-armed quarterbacks, was a mystery, but a preseason wrist injury in 2010 may have ended his NFL career.

Mike Kafka, PHI: Much like Kevin Kolb, Kafka's combines above-average accuracy with a below-average arm and a lack of experience in the pocket. Unlike Kolb, though, Kafka just doesn't have much experience whatsoever; he only started one year at Northwestern, and has just 637 pass attempts above the high school level. Marty Mornhinweg said that Kafka picked up the playbook in camp better than any rookie he's ever seen, which can't hurt.

Dan LeFevour, CIN: The Central Michigan product was lousy in the preseason, so Chicago cut him and he signed with the Bengals. Since he owns all the MAC passing records, shouldn't he be with the Steelers?

J.P. Losman, SEA: Losman never took a snap for the Seahawks last season, which is good. A quarterback with 103 sacks in 1,045 career dropbacks, playing behind the 2010 Seattle offensive line, might have resulted in a fatality. Losman's career completion rate is just south of 60 percent. He's spent the past few years walking the fine line between UFL starter and NFL third-stringer. He's fine in either role.

Greg McElroy, NYJ: After scoring a 43 on the Wonderlic and leading Alabama to a National Championship, McElroy was officially qualified for the label of Game Manager. If he could speed up his delivery a little bit, McElroy might become an adequate starter who can nail the short routes but has an inconsistent deep ball. The Jets will see if they can instill that in him while Mark Brunell holds the clipboard for another season.

Keith Null, FA: After doing time as one of several ineffective quarterbacks at the end of what will become known as the Pre-Bradford era in St. Louis, Null landed on the Jaguars' practice squad before the Panthers gave him a shot. He was waived after the lockout, and may not make it past camp body status from now on.

Kevin O'Connell, MIA: Before Ryan Mallett was the Patriots' third-round pick-turned-developmental quarterback prospect, Kevin O'Connell played that role. The Patriots hope things go better with Mallett. O'Connell was the Jets' third-stringer in 2009, then spent 2010 on IR with a torn labrum.

J.T. O'Sullivan, FA: The dream is just about over for Mr. O'SmellingSalts, who parlayed a role as a Mike Martz favorite into a decent season in 2008, did little of note for the Bengals in 2009, and did nothing at all for the Raiders in 2010. He's an injury replacement at this point.

Tyler Palko, KC: The Chiefs are said to be high on Palko as a future project, but they also let Brodie Croyle get debacled against the Chargers instead, and they selected Iowa's Ricky Stanzi in the fifth round. It's safe to say that the backup spot behind Matt Cassel is wide open.

Jordan Palmer, CIN: Palmer will now be backing up rookie Andy Dalton instead of his big brother, but that doesn't mean he's changing his name to Jordan Dalton. Team coaches rave that he's well-prepared for every game, like his brother. Coming out of UTEP, the knock on him was that he tended to stare down his receivers, and in each of the last two preseasons he's thrown three picks in roughly one game's worth of attempts.

Tony Pike, CAR: The Panthers drafted three quarterbacks last year, and now all three have limited future use. Like Armanti Edwards, Pike was occasionally put in to play, but was really more of an afterthought as John Fox looked to do different things with other quarterbacks. The common denominator seemed to be that Fox preferred quarterbacks more comfortable under center — now, Pike's problem is that Cam Newton is in line for the shotgun snaps, and the Panthers may still spend some of 2011 trying to prove that they didn't blow it with the Jimmy Clausen pick. Pike has some potential, but he'd be better off on a team where he wasn't buried under so many iffy quarterback selections. (2010 stats: 6-for-12, 47 yards, -25 DYAR, -40.1% DVOA)

Terrelle Pryor, Unknown: Here we go again with all the same questions about athletic, running quarterbacks. Pryor doesn't have the arm strength of Cam Newton, he has poor touch on his passes, and he throws off his back foot too much. He has been studying with Ken Anderson in an attempt to develop into more of an NFL quarterback. At press time, the NFL was still stringing Pryor along, trying to figure out if they were going to let him into the supplemental draft or not.

Brady Quinn, DEN: Quinn told the *Denver Post* that he felt he didn't get an opportunity last year, but if there's one area in which we'll generally trust Josh McDaniels, it's quarterback evaluation and development. McDaniels had more than enough time to look at what Quinn had to offer, he was on the hook to make Quinn work out after the abysmal Peyton Hillis trade, and Quinn still couldn't get on the field. Cleveland's Mike Holmgren, who knows a few things about quarterbacks himself, didn't seem too heartbroken about making the Hillis deal — he couldn't wait to overpay Jake Delhomme (of all people) instead. Quinn's story seems less about opportunity and far more about harsh reality.

Patrick Ramsey, FA: Ramsey spent time on three rosters last year: Jacksonville, Miami, and Minnesota. When the injuries come, he will inevitably spend time on someone's roster this year. He will not play.

Zac Robinson, DET: The Patriots' seventh-round pick out of Oklahoma State spent time with the Patriots, Seahawks, and Lions last year, bouncing back and forth from practice squad to roster. He has a strong arm, quick feet, and extremely inconsistent mechanics.

Chris Simms, FA: That Chris Simms had an NFL job at all in 2010 was a fluke created by his knowledge of the Titans' playbook and Rusty Smith's level of play. He avoided further legal problems from his 2010 marijuana arrest, but that doesn't make him a serviceable quarterback.

Jim Sorgi, NYG: A torn capsule in his shoulder ended Sorgi's season in August, calling into question for the first time his reliable ability to back up Manning brothers. Fortunately for him, the lockout presented an opportunity: He spent the summer of 2011 fetching coffee for Cooper Manning.

Brian St. Pierre, FA: St. Pierre was a stay-at-home dad who had thrown five passes in his eight NFL seasons until injuries to Jimmy Clausen and Matt Moore had him picking up a starting spot for the Panthers against the Baltimore Ravens. After a two-interception performance in which he put up a DVOA of -69.6%, St. Pierre will most likely trundle back to his Mr. Mom life and the occasional TV spot. Hey, it beats having Terrell Suggs and Haloti Ngata use you to make a wish. (2010 stats: 13-for-28, 173 yards, 1 TD, 2 INT, -89 DYAR, -69.6% DVOA)

John Parker Wilson, ATL: The Alabama grad and 2009 UFA hasn't thrown an NFL pass as yet, but he apparently made strides during the lockout. Early returns from Falcons camp had Wilson gaining ground on incumbent backup Chris Redman. Wilson's younger brother Ross was a featured player on MTV's "Two-a-Days," which followed Hoover High's soon-to-be-disgraced football team. But Wilson should really strive to be like the namesake of his other brother, Peyton.

T.J. Yates, HOU: Yates' North Carolina offense is just about the same offense that Houston runs, so his selection was a solid scheme fit for the Texans. While Yates is a good athlete for a quarterback, and lost a lot with all the suspensions the Tarheels did last season, he still makes a startling number of mental errors. That profile sounds a lot like the quarterback he'll be replacing in Houston: Dan Orlovsky.

Running Backs

In our "Audibles at the Line" column at FO each Monday, we pick on Phil Simms a lot. There's no doubt that Simms was an intelligent field general who understood the game on the field. However, as the top analyst for CBS, Simms' commentary often produces a mix of meaningless compliments, contradictory statements, and oversimplified explanations for the wide variance of things that can happen in a football game.

Even when his theories stand up to the scrutiny of some common sense, it's important to actually test seemingly logical statements to see if they're actually true. Take Simms' commentary during the playoff game between the Kansas City Chiefs and Baltimore Ravens this past season. While the Ravens undoubtedly outplayed the Chiefs, they benefited from two Kansas City fumbles, each of which came from a young player. Early in the second quarter, 24-year-old Jamaal Charles put the ball on the ground in the midst of being engulfed by Terrence Cody. Then in the third quarter, 22-year-old Dexter McCluster was stripped after a reception while trying to make a move on third down. Simms suggested that these players' youth, combined with the pressure of the playoffs, had a lot to do with their fumbles.

On one hand, Simms' theory makes some sense. While Charles's fumble was the product of displacement, McCluster had no hope of getting a first down on third-and-forever and probably should have just gone down. On the other hand, though, it's not as if ball-handling mistakes in the playoffs are exclusive to rookies; only a week later, T.J. Houshmandzadeh would drop a potentially game-extending pass to end the Ravens season. Hall of Fame tight end Jackie Smith famously dropped a crucial pass in the end zone during Super Bowl XIII, and he was 38. Kurt Warner threw an awful interception at the end of the first half of Super Bowl XLIII at age 37. Both Eli Manning and Tom Brady fumbled in the previous Super Bowl. We could go on.

Listing individual anecdotes doesn't prove anything, though. If Simms' point about young players — especially rookies like McCluster — is correct, we should see it in a broader look at history. And if it hasn't been exhibited by players in the past, we can safely throw out Simms' theory as irrelevant.

To try and focus on modern players, we'll limit the study to all seasons since the 1990 campaign. And in order to work with the largest possible sample and variety of touches, we'll look exclusively at running backs.

The simplest way to test Simms' theory is just to look at the fumble rates for backs, split out by their NFL experience level. Table 1 does just that and suggests that Simms' theory is actually *correct*. Rookies (players with an Experience of "1") fumble at the highest rate, and as players gain more experience, they fumble less frequently. On the other hand, it's not a very strong effect. Take Jamaal Charles (three years of experience in 2010) and Thomas Jones (11 years), for example. All things being equal besides their experience level, the difference in their expected fumble rates would amount to about one fumble per season. Is that really enough to justify keeping the ball away from a player with the talent of Charles?

Table 1: RB Fumble Rates by Experience, 1990-2010

Experience	Touches	Fumbles	Rate	per 300 touches
1	38,037	688	1.8%	5.4
2	43,551	754	1.7%	5.2
3	42,914	712	1.7%	5.0
4	39,434	568	1.4%	4.3
5	36,020	485	1.3%	4.0
6	30,654	432	1.4%	4.2
7	23,235	294	1.3%	3.8
8	17,271	213	1.2%	3.7
9	11,714	134	1.1%	3.4
10	8,988	114	1.3%	3.8
11	5,249	68	1.3%	3.9
12	2,915	38	1.3%	3.9
13	1,638	21	1.3%	3.8

There's another factor built into Table 1 that adulterates the numbers towards Simms' theory: Selection bias. Selection bias occurs when the sample of the population involved in a study is biased for a particular reason. Here, we're not accounting for the natural selection that's built into evaluating NFL players. If a rookie fumbles a lot, well, he's not going to stick around in the

NFL for very long unless he's Adrian Peterson.

In addition, it's unfair to exclude somebody like Ryan Grant from the "rookie" pool. Grant spent two years on the practice squad before emerging as a starter in Green Bay in 2007, but Simms' point about inexperienced backs touching the ball in key situations would undoubtedly extend to him. Table 2 accounts for backs like Grant by defining a player's first meaningful season as the year in which he touched the ball 150 times. If we compare those players' first season with significant touches to the rest of their careers, there's virtually no difference in the fumble rates between the two groups. Over a full season of touches, we would be looking at a difference of just about one-half of one fumble between the two groups.

Table 2: The 150-Touch Crowd

Type	Touches	Fumbles	Rate	per 300 touches
First Year w/ 150 Touches	51,409	733	1.4%	4.3
Those Players Afterwards	184,377	2266	1.2%	3.7

The other factor that comes into play in Simms' discussion of rookies — and this is often seen elsewhere when rookies make mistakes — is the idea that rookies can't be trusted in the clutch situations of the playoffs. Although rookies have to go through a series of tests in college and pro ball before even getting to touch the rock in the playoffs, the trials and tribulations of playoff football should force them into cracking.

Unfortunately, Table 3 suggests that any rise in fumbles by rookie running backs is mild at best, the sort of difference that amounts to about a quarter of a fumble more over the course of even a full playoff workload (80 touches).

The problem with these sorts of seemingly reasonable theories is that we don't hear about them when the event doesn't happen. James Starks went 64 touches in the playoffs without a fumble, but nobody mentioned that it was surprising to see Starks get so many touches as a rookie in the playoffs without fum-

Table 3: Playoff Fumble Rates by Experience, 1993-2009

Experience	Touches	Fumbles	Rate
1	1,210	20	1.7%
2	1,089	17	1.6%
3	1,023	27	2.6%
4	1,603	24	1.5%
5	1,380	14	1.0%
6	1,123	7	0.6%
7	865	14	1.6%
8	739	7	0.9%
9	363	4	1.1%
10	370	2	0.5%
11	169	1	0.6%
12	157	3	1.9%
13	85	3	3.5%
Total	10,176	143	1.4%

bling. It's the sort of *ex post facto* logic that gets applied to playoff performances on a regular basis. If a team wins after a bye, it's because they were rested; if they lost, it's because they were rusty. If the winners were old, their victory came through experience; if they were young, they had fresh legs and didn't know that they were supposed to lose.

So, was Simms right? Not really. Inexperienced backs do fumble more frequently than their more experienced brethren, but the difference between the two on a given play or in a game is just about negligible. Teams would be wise to give the ball to their most talented players, regardless of how much pro experience they have.

How to Read the Running Back Statistics Table

In the following section we give the last three years' statistics, as well as a 2011 KUBIAK projection, for every running back who either played a significant role in 2010 or is expected to do so in 2011.

Rashard Mendenhall Height: 5-10 Weight: 225 College: Illinois Draft: 2008/1 (23) Born: 19-Jun-1987 Age: 24 Risk: Yellow

Year	Team	G	Runs	Yds	Yd/R	TD	FUM	DVOA	Rk	DYAR	Rk	YAR	Suc%	Rec	Pass	Yds	C%	Yd/C	TD	DVOA	Rk	DYAR	Rk
2008	PIT	4	19	58	3.1	0	0	-20.8%	—	-8	—	-10	26%	2	3	17	67%	8.5	0	24.7%	—	5	—
2009	PIT	16	242	1108	4.6	7	3	-0.8%	31	80	25	107	46%	25	32	261	78%	10.4	1	55.6%	1	117	5
2010	PIT	16	324	1273	3.9	13	2	-2.8%	26	77	22	81	44%	23	34	167	68%	7.3	0	-2.3%	39	23	39
2011	PIT		327	1374	4.2	12		2.8%						31	38	286	82%	9.2	1	33.5%			

The first line contains biographical data—each player's name, height, weight, college, draft position, birth date, and age. Height and weight are the best data we could find; weight, of course, can fluctuate during the offseason. **Age** is very simple, the number of years between the player's birth year and 2010, but birthdate is provided if you want to figure out exact age.

Draft position gives draft year and round, with the overall pick number with which the player was taken in parentheses. In the sample table, it says that Rashard Mendenhall was chosen in the 2008 NFL Draft in the first round with the 23rd overall pick. Undrafted free agents are listed as "FA" with the year they came into the league, even if they were only in training camp or on a practice squad.

To the far right of the first line is the player's Risk for fantasy football in 2010. As explained in the quarterback section, the standard is for players to be marked Green. Players with higher than normal risk are marked Yellow, and players with the highest risk are marked Red. Players who are most likely to match or surpass our forecast — primarily second- stringers with low projections — are marked Blue.

Next we give the last three years of player stats. The first number is games played (**G**). This is the official NFL total and may include games in which a player appeared on special teams, but did not carry the ball or catch a pass. The next four columns are familiar: **Runs**, rushing yards (**Yds**), yards per rush (**Yd/R**) and rushing touchdowns (**TD**).

The entry for fumbles (**FUM**) includes all fumbles by this running back, no matter whether they were recovered by the offense or defense. Holding onto the ball is an identifiable skill; fumbling it so that your own offense can recover it is not. (For more on this issue, see the essay "Pregame Show" in the front of the book.) This entry combines fumbles on both carries and receptions.

The next five columns give our advanced metrics for rushing: **DVOA** (Defense-Adjusted Value Over Average), **DYAR** (Defense-Adjusted Yards Above Replacement), and **YAR** (Yards Above Replacement), along with the player's rank (**Rk**) in both **DVOA** and **DYAR**. These metrics compare every carry by the running back to a league-average baseline based on the game situations in which that running back carried the ball. DVOA and DYAR are also adjusted based on the opposing defense. The methods used to compute these numbers are described in detail in the "Statistical Toolbox" introduction in the front of the book. The

important distinctions between them are:

• DVOA is a rate statistic, while DYAR is a cumulative statistic. Thus, a higher DVOA means more value per play, while a higher DYAR means more aggregate value over the entire season.

• Because DYAR is defense-adjusted and YAR is not, a player whose DYAR is higher than his YAR faced a harder-than-average schedule. A player whose DYAR is lower than his YAR faced an easier-than-average schedule.

To qualify for ranking in rushing DVOA and DYAR, a running back must have had 100 carries in that season. There are 52 running backs ranked for 2010, 50 backs for 2009, and 49 backs for 2008.

The final rushing statistic is Success Rate (**Suc%**). This number represents running back consistency, measured by successful running plays divided by total running plays. (The definition for success is explained in the "Statistical Toolbox" introduction in the front of the book.) A player with high DVOA and a low Success Rate mixes long runs with plays on which he was stuffed at or behind the line of scrimmage. A player with low DVOA and a high Success Rate generally gets the yards needed, but rarely gets more. The league-average Success Rate in 2010 was 46 percent. Success Rate is not adjusted for the defenses a player faced.

The ten columns to the right of Success Rate give data for each running back as a pass receiver. Receptions (**Rec**) counts passes caught, while Passes (**Pass**) counts total passes thrown to this player, complete or incomplete. The next four columns list receiving yards (**Yds**), Catch Rate (**C%**), yards per catch (**Yd/C**), and receiving touchdowns (**TD**).

Our research has shown that receivers bear some responsibility for incomplete passes, even though only their catches are tracked in official statistics. Catch Rate represents receptions divided by all intended passes for this running back. The average NFL running back caught 73 percent of passes in 2010. Unfortunately, we don't have room to post the best and worst running backs in the plus-minus metric we introduced last year (explained in the Wide Receivers section, p. 337), but you'll find the top 10 and bottom 10 running backs in this metric listed in the statistical appendix.

Finally we have receiving DVOA and DYAR, which are entirely separate from rushing DVOA and DYAR. To qualify for ranking in receiving DVOA and DYAR, a running back must have 25 passes thrown to him in that season. There are 54 running backs ranked for

2010, and 52 backs for both 2008 and 2009. Numbers without opponent adjustment (YAR, and VOA) can be found on our website, FootballOutsiders.com.

The italicized row of statistics for the 2011 season is our 2011 KUBIAK projection based on a complicated regression analysis that takes into account numerous variables including projected role, performance over the past two years, projected team offense and defense, historical comparables, height, age, experience of the offensive line, and strength of schedule.

For rookie running backs, we'll also include statistics from our college football arsenal, notably **POE** (Points Over Expected) and **Highlight Yards**. POE analyzes the output of college football running backs by comparing the expected EqPts value of every carry for a given ballcarrier (based on the quality of the rushing defense against which he's running) to the actual output. A positive POE indicates an above-average runner, with an average runner accruing exactly 0 POE. Highlight Yards are yards gained more than 10 yards past the line of scrimmage on a run, those yards

not included in Adjusted Line Yards. Anything over 2.50 should be considered good. For more details on these stats, see the college football section of the book (p. 417).

It is difficult to accurately project statistics for a 162-game baseball season, but it is exponentially more difficult to accurately project statistics for a 16-game football season. Consider the listed projections not as a prediction of exact numbers, but the mean of a range of possible performances. What's important is less the exact number of yards we project, and more which players are projected to improve or decline. Actual performance will vary from our projection less for veteran starters and more for rookies and third-stringers, for whom we must base our projections on much smaller career statistical samples. Touchdown numbers will vary more than yardage numbers.

Finally, in a section we call "Going Deep," we briefly discuss lower-round rookies, free-agent veterans, and practice-squad players who may play a role during the 2010 season or beyond.

Top 20 RB by Rushing DYAR (Total Value), 2010

Rank	Player	Team	DYAR
1	Jamaal Charles	KC	389
2	Arian Foster	HOU	377
3	BenJarvus Green-Ellis	NE	354
4	Maurice Jones-Drew	JAC	238
5	Adrian Peterson	MIN	229
6	LeSean McCoy	PHI	224
7	Brandon Jacobs	NYG	172
8	Peyton Hillis	CLE	152
9	Chris Ivory	NO	133
10	Felix Jones	DAL	124
11	Shonn Greene	NYJ	124
12	Ahmad Bradshaw	NYG	121
13	Ray Rice	BAL	115
14	Darren McFadden	OAK	112
15	LaDainian Tomlinson	NYJ	110
16	Michael Turner	ATL	102
17	Michael Bush	OAK	101
18	LaGarrette Blount	TB	98
19	Joseph Addai	IND	92
20	Matt Forte	CHI	87

Top 20 RB by Rushing DVOA (Value per Rush), 2010

Rank	Player	Team	DVOA
1	Jamaal Charles	KC	33.9%
2	BenJarvus Green-Ellis	NE	26.4%
3	Brandon Jacobs	NYG	18.1%
4	Arian Foster	HOU	18.0%
5	LeSean McCoy	PHI	17.8%
6	Chris Ivory	NO	12.9%
7	Adrian Peterson	MIN	10.6%
8	Joseph Addai	IND	9.6%
9	Maurice Jones-Drew	JAC	9.4%
10	Felix Jones	DAL	8.2%
11	Shonn Greene	NYJ	7.8%
12	Michael Bush	OAK	6.5%
13	Peyton Hillis	CLE	5.0%
14	Darren McFadden	OAK	4.6%
15	LaGarrette Blount	TB	4.0%
16	LaDainian Tomlinson	NYJ	3.6%
17	Ahmad Bradshaw	NYG	2.5%
18	Ryan Mathews	SD	1.9%
19	Ray Rice	BAL	0.8%
20	Matt Forte	CHI	0.4%

Top 10 RB by Receiving DYAR (Total Value), 2010

Rank	Player	Team	DYAR
1	Arian Foster	HOU	197
2	LeSean McCoy	PHI	179
3	Darren McFadden	OAK	172
4	Darren Sproles	SD	166
5	Danny Woodhead	NE	156
6	Brandon Jackson	GB	156
7	Jamaal Charles	KC	150
8	Peyton Hillis	CLE	138
9	Felix Jones	DAL	138
10	Knowshon Moreno	DEN	131

Top 10 RB by Receiving DVOA (Value per Pass), 2010

Rank	Player	Team	DVOA
1	Michael Bush	OAK	57.9%
2	Danny Woodhead	NE	56.3%
3	Brandon Jackson	GB	42.0%
4	Darren McFadden	OAK	40.8%
5	Mike Tolbert	SD	37.2%
6	Knowshon Moreno	DEN	35.9%
7	Felix Jones	DAL	35.4%
8	Jamaal Charles	KC	31.3%
9	Maurice Jones-Drew	JAC	29.4%
10	Donald Brown	IND	28.5%

Joseph Addai
Height: 5-11 Weight: 210 College: Louisiana State   Draft: 2006/1 (30) Born: 3-May-1983   Age: 28 Risk: Green

Year	Team	G	Runs	Yds	Yd/R	TD	FUM	DVOA	Rk	DYAR	Rk	YAR	Suc%	Rec	Pass	Yds	C%	Yd/C	TD	DVOA	Rk	DYAR	Rk
2008	IND	12	155	544	3.5	5	1	-1.3%	26	49	27	44	48%	25	39	206	64%	8.2	2	5.3%	22	40	29
2009	IND	15	219	828	3.8	10	1	7.6%	17	151	13	133	53%	51	63	336	81%	6.6	3	9.1%	22	89	10
2010	IND	8	116	495	4.3	4	2	9.6%	8	92	19	102	54%	19	26	124	73%	6.5	0	-2.9%	40	15	42
2011	IND		203	777	3.8	4		-6.5%						47	65	336	72%	7.1	3	18.2%			

Addai has never really delivered on the promise he showed in his rookie year, when it looked like he would be the next great Colts' offensive star. Instead, he has battled injuries and ineffectiveness. The primary problem is the offensive line, which struggles to open up holes for anybody. Still, Addai has now played five years and never gotten more than 261 carries. He is a part-time back who runs behind one of the worst lines in the league. His solid DVOA almost every season, including ranking in the top 10 last year, proves that, when healthy, he is an asset, but Addai is merely a role player and will never be a star.

Lance Ball
Height: 5-9 Weight: 223 College: Maryland   Draft: 2008/ (FA) Born: 19-Jun-1985   Age: 26 Risk: Red

Year	Team	G	Runs	Yds	Yd/R	TD	FUM	DVOA	Rk	DYAR	Rk	YAR	Suc%	Rec	Pass	Yds	C%	Yd/C	TD	DVOA	Rk	DYAR	Rk
2008	IND	1	13	83	6.4	0	1	20.0%	--	17	--	12	77%	1	1	5	100%	5.0	0	-18.6%	--	0	--
2010	DEN	10	41	158	3.9	0	1	-23.2%	--	-23	--	-20	34%	3	6	16	50%	5.3	0	-20.6%	--	-2	--
2011	DEN		54	211	3.9	2		0.5%						9	12	83	75%	9.2	0	7.2%			

Ball rose up the depth chart in 2010, ostensibly as a favorite of Denver running backs coach (and post-McDaniels interim head coach) Eric Studesville. With Studesville still on staff in the new regime, Ball could get a few more looks, since he does have the powerful downhill style preferred by John Fox.

Marion Barber
Height: 5-11 Weight: 221 College: Minnesota   Draft: 2005/4 (109) Born: 10-Jun-1983   Age: 28 Risk: Yellow

Year	Team	G	Runs	Yds	Yd/R	TD	FUM	DVOA	Rk	DYAR	Rk	YAR	Suc%	Rec	Pass	Yds	C%	Yd/C	TD	DVOA	Rk	DYAR	Rk
2008	DAL	15	238	885	3.7	7	7	-4.4%	35	43	30	31	41%	52	61	417	85%	8.0	2	4.3%	26	56	20
2009	DAL	15	214	932	4.4	7	2	8.9%	15	168	10	155	53%	26	37	221	73%	8.5	0	-9.7%	41	9	42
2010	DAL	13	113	374	3.3	4	0	-12.5%	38	-21	36	-20	48%	11	15	49	73%	4.5	0	-48.1%	--	-27	--
2011	CHI		87	342	3.9	1		-12.7%						10	16	74	63%	7.4	1	-12.6%			

The NFC East has three cautionary tales about signing long-term contracts for running backs, and here's the first one. Barber's career has cratered since signing an extension in May of 2008. In his three seasons before the new deal, Barber averaged 4.5 yards per carry and scored a touchdown once every 17 touches. After adding zeroes to his bank account, Barber has produced just 3.9 yards per carry while scoring once every 34 touches. He's also missed time in each of the three seasons since pen hit paper. Throw in a fine for violating Jason Garrett's team dress code immediately after Garrett's ascension to the head coaching job, and it's no surprise that he's out in Big D. (We'll get to our other cautionary tales, Brandon Jacobs and Clinton Portis, in a few pages.) Barber scored only three touchdowns on 16 carries inside the five last year, a league-high 3.6 touchdowns short of what you would expect on average. Normally, that kind of thing regresses to the mean, but Barber signed with the one team that seems to be an exception to the idea of goal-line regression: Chicago.

Jackie Battle Height: 6-2 Weight: 238 College: Houston Draft: 2007/ (FA) Born: 1-Oct-1983 Age: 28 Risk: Red

Year	Team	G	Runs	Yds	Yd/R	TD	FUM	DVOA	Rk	DYAR	Rk	YAR	Suc%	Rec	Pass	Yds	C%	Yd/C	TD	DVOA	Rk	DYAR	Rk
2008	KC	9	0	0	0.0	0	0	0.0%	--	0	--	0	--	1	1	-2	100%	-2.0	0	-177.1%	--	-8	--
2009	KC	5	7	21	3.0	0	0	13.4%	--	6	--	6	43%	2	2	-3	100%	-1.5	0	-159.7%	--	-14	--
2010	KC	16	20	50	2.5	1	0	-4.1%	--	5	--	7	45%	1	3	9	33%	9.0	0	-55.1%	--	-9	--
2011	KC		35	145	4.2	1		-2.5%						8	10	69	80%	8.6	0	1.9%			

The Chiefs tried to give Battle a shot at competing for the short-yardage role when Thomas Jones proved ineffective, but Battle couldn't beat out the veteran. They non-tendered him after the season, then resigned him so somebody could comfortably sit at the bottom of the depth chart.

Mike Bell Height: 6-0 Weight: 215 College: Arizona Draft: 2006/ (FA) Born: 23-Apr-1983 Age: 28 Risk: Red

Year	Team	G	Runs	Yds	Yd/R	TD	FUM	DVOA	Rk	DYAR	Rk	YAR	Suc%	Rec	Pass	Yds	C%	Yd/C	TD	DVOA	Rk	DYAR	Rk
2008	NO	4	13	42	3.2	1	0	-4.5%	--	2	--	9	38%	1	2	14	50%	14.0	0	113.5%	--	10	--
2009	NO	13	172	654	3.8	5	2	-3.1%	34	41	34	50	54%	4	4	12	100%	3.0	0	-31.5%	--	-4	--
2010	2TM	16	47	99	2.1	0	2	-44.0%	--	-68	--	-79	28%	7	10	67	70%	9.6	0	-12.2%	--	1	--
2011	DET		27	102	3.8	1		-2.8%						6	8	43	75%	7.2	0	-3.4%			

The Eagles signed Bell as a free agent last year, then sent him to Cleveland for Jerome Harrison in a player-for-player challenge trade. Philadelphia won that challenge. Bell hasn't averaged four yards per carry since 2006, and he's almost useless as a receiver. We know the Browns prefer to build a stable of power backs rather than finding a shiftier compliment to Peyton Hillis and Montario Hardesty, but still, they can do better than this. Note: Signed with Detroit after Mikel Leshoure's injury.

Cedric Benson Height: 5-11 Weight: 222 College: Texas Draft: 2005/1 (4) Born: 28-Dec-1982 Age: 29 Risk: Yellow

Year	Team	G	Runs	Yds	Yd/R	TD	FUM	DVOA	Rk	DYAR	Rk	YAR	Suc%	Rec	Pass	Yds	C%	Yd/C	TD	DVOA	Rk	DYAR	Rk
2008	CIN	12	214	747	3.5	2	2	-12.6%	44	-35	45	-70	40%	20	26	185	77%	9.3	0	-2.8%	35	15	39
2009	CIN	13	301	1251	4.2	6	1	3.7%	21	151	14	123	44%	17	24	111	71%	6.5	0	-14.7%	47	-1	47
2010	CIN	16	321	1111	3.5	7	7	-13.1%	39	-61	42	-91	45%	28	37	178	76%	6.4	1	-3.2%	41	22	41
2011	CIN		312	1188	3.8	8		-6.3%						27	39	217	69%	8.0	1	-6.9%			

Much has been made of Benson's renaissance in Cincinnati, but the dirty secret is that he's actually been one of the worst starting running backs in the league over the last four seasons. 2009 is the exception, when Benson had a slightly above-average DVOA and a career-high 4.16 yards per carry. Otherwise, he's been below replacement level in 2010, 2008, and his last year in Chicago, 2007. Our offensive line stats also give a hint that maybe Benson's not all he's cracked up to be: the Bengals finished 31st in Open-Field Yards per carry in both 2008 and 2010, and 16th in 2009. Benson will have a lot of fantasy value because the Bengals will feed him the ball in an offense designed to make a rookie quarterback comfortable. But he may not be doing much to actually help the Bengals win games.

Jahvid Best

Height: 5-10 Weight: 199 College: California   Draft: 2010/1 (30) Born: 30-Jan-1989 Age: 22 Risk: Green

Year	Team	G	Runs	Yds	Yd/R	TD	FUM	DVOA	Rk	DYAR	Rk	YAR	Suc%	Rec	Pass	Yds	C%	Yd/C	TD	DVOA	Rk	DYAR	Rk
2010	DET	16	171	555	3.2	4	1	-18.0%	44	-62	43	-73	37%	58	80	487	73%	8.4	2	-2.0%	38	52	27
2011	DET		176	756	4.3	4		-4.3%						50	77	420	65%	8.4	1	-11.1%			

Best led the league with five touchdowns after Week 2, then scored just one more touchdown the rest of the year. Turf toe was part of the problem; but improper usage was also to blame. Best ran 21 draw plays for 103 yards (4.9 yd/att); from two-back sets (mostly I-formations) he rushed 47 times for 117 yards (2.5 yd/att). All indicators, including his 190-pound frame, say that Best is a scat back, and by the second half of the season Scott Linehan stopped handing him the ball 17 times per game and let him concentrate on passing downs and shotgun sets. The open-field creativity and quickness is there; the Lions must just let Best focus on what he is really good at.

Ladell Betts

Height: 5-10 Weight: 222 College: Iowa   Draft: 2002/2 (56) Born: 27-Aug-1979 Age: 32 Risk: N/A

Year	Team	G	Runs	Yds	Yd/R	TD	FUM	DVOA	Rk	DYAR	Rk	YAR	Suc%	Rec	Pass	Yds	C%	Yd/C	TD	DVOA	Rk	DYAR	Rk
2008	WAS	13	61	206	3.4	1	1	-6.1%	--	7	--	-13	48%	22	35	200	63%	9.1	0	-1.4%	33	19	36
2009	WAS	10	56	210	3.8	2	0	-2.1%	--	15	--	12	41%	17	20	179	85%	10.5	0	60.2%	--	78	--
2010	NO	8	45	150	3.3	2	1	-10.6%	--	-5	--	-1	51%	23	31	141	74%	6.1	0	-20.4%	50	-11	50

Saints running back option number 47 in 2010, Betts isn't likely to be playing in New Orleans in 2011, and perhaps not anywhere else, either. At 32 and coming off a serious concussion and neck injury, Betts would do well to call it a career.

LeGarrette Blount

Height: 6-1 Weight: 241 College: Oregon   Draft: 2010/ (FA) Born: 5-Dec-1986 Age: 25 Risk: Yellow

Year	Team	G	Runs	Yds	Yd/R	TD	FUM	DVOA	Rk	DYAR	Rk	YAR	Suc%	Rec	Pass	Yds	C%	Yd/C	TD	DVOA	Rk	DYAR	Rk
2010	TB	13	201	1007	5.0	6	4	4.0%	15	98	18	101	45%	5	7	14	71%	2.8	0	-93.0%	--	-33	--
2011	TB		262	1228	4.7	9		15.7%						17	31	130	55%	7.6	0	-25.0%			

For some people, things need to hit bottom before they can get better. After proving himself to be a malcontent at Oregon. Blount went undrafted, was cut by the Titans, and landed on the Bucs' roster as an afterthought at best. He then shocked just about everyone by becoming the team's catalyst on the ground despite playing little in the first month of the season. By the last month of the season, Blount picked up the Offensive Rookie of the Month award. The 2010 Tampa Bay team was a bounty of opportunity for young players; 2011 will prove to be about learning the finer points of success, and Blount still has issues. The Success Rate is a slight concern for a bigger back, and was even worse in the red zone (36 percent). Many power backs have washed out of the league because they wore out the one-trick act and couldn't handle the refinements — that's Blount's challenge in 2011.

Ahmad Bradshaw

Height: 5-11 Weight: 195 College: Marshall   Draft: 2007/7 (250) Born: 19-Mar-1986 Age: 25 Risk: Yellow

Year	Team	G	Runs	Yds	Yd/R	TD	FUM	DVOA	Rk	DYAR	Rk	YAR	Suc%	Rec	Pass	Yds	C%	Yd/C	TD	DVOA	Rk	DYAR	Rk
2008	NYG	15	67	355	5.3	1	2	-1.4%	--	20	--	-2	49%	5	6	42	83%	8.4	1	93.3%	--	25	--
2009	NYG	15	163	778	4.8	7	3	9.7%	13	129	18	131	52%	21	30	207	70%	9.9	0	5.8%	26	27	32
2010	NYG	16	276	1235	4.5	8	7	2.5%	17	121	12	98	46%	47	59	314	81%	6.7	0	10.6%	27	71	20
2011	NYG		246	1046	4.3	4		-1.2%						44	69	377	64%	8.6	1	26.1%			

Bradshaw's issues with fumbles aren't anything new. Before getting the starting gig in 2010, he had eight fumbles on 281 pro touches; in fact, his fumble rate improved slightly last year. It's not a fatal flaw. Giants fans undoubtedly remember the strides that Tiki Barber made with his fumble woes under Tom Coughlin, while Adrian Peterson managed to quietly cure his fumble issues in 2010. The best recent comp might be Thomas Jones, who had 13 fumbles on 596 touches through his fourth season before becoming a relatively steady back. All good signs. One question, though: If there was some magic elixir that Coughlin knew that would have prevented Bradshaw from fumbling, why didn't he teach it to Bradshaw until now?

Aaron Brown   Height: 6-1   Weight: 196   College: TCU   Draft: 2009/6 (192)   Born: 10-Oct-1985   Age: 26   Risk: Red

Year	Team	G	Runs	Yds	Yd/R	TD	FUM	DVOA	Rk	DYAR	Rk	YAR	Suc%	Rec	Pass	Yds	C%	Yd/C	TD	DVOA	Rk	DYAR	Rk
2009	DET	15	27	131	4.9	0	0	17.8%	--	24	--	18	48%	9	15	84	60%	9.3	1	13.6%	--	26	--
2010	DET	6	17	58	3.4	0	0	-5.6%	--	2	--	4	47%	8	13	45	62%	5.6	0	-28.9%	--	-13	--
2011	DET		47	205	4.4	1		13.7%						17	20	86	85%	5.0	0	-7.2%			

Brown appeared to have the kick returner job sewn up in 2010 training camp, but when the Lions signed Stefan Logan just before the start of the season, Brown became a player without a role. A hand injury erased part of the season, and most of Brown's production came in mop-up duty in the Thanksgiving blowout loss to the Patriots. Brown has the talent to stick somewhere as a third-down back and return man, but he has a reputation for mental lapses, and players of his type are not hard to find in the waiver pool.

Donald Brown   Height: 5-11   Weight: 210   College: Connecticut   Draft: 2009/1 (27)   Born: 11-Apr-1987   Age: 24   Risk: Green

Year	Team	G	Runs	Yds	Yd/R	TD	FUM	DVOA	Rk	DYAR	Rk	YAR	Suc%	Rec	Pass	Yds	C%	Yd/C	TD	DVOA	Rk	DYAR	Rk
2009	IND	11	78	281	3.6	3	1	-12.5%	--	-12	--	-20	46%	11	14	169	79%	15.4	0	76.6%	--	68	--
2010	IND	13	129	497	3.9	2	0	-4.8%	29	22	29	15	44%	20	28	205	71%	10.3	0	28.5%	10	67	21
2011	IND		84	340	4.0	3		1.5%						9	10	81	90%	9.0	0	-29.1%			

The drafting of Brown always seemed bizarre; why get two first-round backs to split carries? Plus, while Brown has some big-play ability, he is not radically different in style from starter Joseph Addai. Brown has struggled in his two years to develop any rhythm running behind the Colts' poor offensive line and has not broken four yards per carry in either of his two seasons. He does provide more big-play ability than Addai, including in the passing game, so the Colts continue to hope he develops the consistency to be more than a backup.

Ronnie Brown   Height: 6-0   Weight: 233   College: Auburn   Draft: 2005/1 (2)   Born: 12-Dec-1981   Age: 30   Risk: Red

Year	Team	G	Runs	Yds	Yd/R	TD	FUM	DVOA	Rk	DYAR	Rk	YAR	Suc%	Rec	Pass	Yds	C%	Yd/C	TD	DVOA	Rk	DYAR	Rk
2008	MIA	16	214	916	4.3	10	1	5.1%	17	127	15	132	49%	33	43	254	77%	7.7	0	11.6%	19	57	19
2009	MIA	9	147	648	4.4	8	1	14.6%	8	144	15	157	51%	14	20	98	70%	7.0	0	-2.7%	--	13	--
2010	MIA	16	200	734	3.7	5	3	-4.2%	27	36	27	11	43%	33	42	242	79%	7.3	0	5.1%	32	45	28
2011	PHI		83	398	4.8	4		7.2%						28	47	207	60%	7.4	1	-14.2%			

Brown is coming off his worst season since 2006, one where his yards per carry average dipped below four for the first time in his career, but it is difficult to know how much of that is Brown declining and how much was decline on the Miami offensive line. Brown left money on the table to come to Philly and back up LeSean McCoy, and he probably left carries on the table as well, judging by how infrequently the Eagles run the ball, particularly with their reserve backs. Brown is versatile enough to work his way in on passing downs or to take a few direct snaps, but this is Philadelphia, and unless Andy Reid dramatically changes his play calling tendencies, Brown's fantasy impact will be negligible barring an injury to McCoy.

Correll Buckhalter   Height: 6-0   Weight: 222   College: Nebraska   Draft: 2001/4 (121)   Born: 6-Oct-1978   Age: 33   Risk: N/A

Year	Team	G	Runs	Yds	Yd/R	TD	FUM	DVOA	Rk	DYAR	Rk	YAR	Suc%	Rec	Pass	Yds	C%	Yd/C	TD	DVOA	Rk	DYAR	Rk
2008	PHI	14	76	369	4.9	2	0	11.0%	--	69	--	55	50%	26	32	324	81%	12.5	2	62.1%	2	153	5
2009	DEN	14	120	642	5.4	1	3	6.3%	18	76	26	96	58%	31	38	240	82%	7.7	0	4.2%	30	36	31
2010	DEN	15	59	147	2.5	2	1	-32.4%	--	-56	--	-65	25%	28	38	240	74%	8.6	2	24.5%	13	71	19

Buckhalter may be just about done; his DVOA splits revealed an especially ineffective runner on third down (15 carries for 27 yards, -38.8% DVOA, 20 percent Success Rate), but he didn't do much on first or second downs, either. Buckhalter was released in late July.

Eldra Buckley

Height: 5-9   Weight: 207   College: Tennessee-Chattanooga   Draft: 2007/ (FA)   Born: 23-Jun-1985   Age: 26   Risk: Red

Year	Team	G	Runs	Yds	Yd/R	TD	FUM	DVOA	Rk	DYAR	Rk	YAR	Suc%	Rec	Pass	Yds	C%	Yd/C	TD	DVOA	Rk	DYAR	Rk
2009	PHI	16	15	44	2.9	1	0	-11.6%	–	-2	–	-6	53%	0	0	0	0%	0.0	0	0.0%	–	0	–
2010	PHI	16	21	67	3.2	0	1	-26.1%	–	-16	–	-18	33%	1	2	10	50%	10.0	0	-151.7%	–	-21	–
2011	PHI		29	142	4.9	1		21.6%						9	13	74	69%	8.2	0	21.5%			

The injury to Leonard Weaver and the trade of Mike Bell forced Buckley into the primary backup role, but Buckley is really a special teamer who is stretched with any sort of carry workload. He was tendered a contract before the lockout, but with the signing of Ronnie Brown and the drafting of Dion Lewis, there would have to be an injury epidemic in the Eagles backfield for Buckley to get carries again.

Michael Bush

Height: 6-1   Weight: 245   College: Louisville   Draft: 2007/4 (100)   Born: 16-Jun-1984   Age: 27   Risk: Green

Year	Team	G	Runs	Yds	Yd/R	TD	FUM	DVOA	Rk	DYAR	Rk	YAR	Suc%	Rec	Pass	Yds	C%	Yd/C	TD	DVOA	Rk	DYAR	Rk
2008	OAK	15	95	421	4.4	3	1	-3.9%	–	17	–	20	41%	19	30	162	63%	8.5	0	7.6%	21	35	31
2009	OAK	16	123	589	4.8	3	2	3.2%	24	57	31	82	47%	17	19	105	89%	6.2	0	-5.8%	–	8	–
2010	OAK	14	158	655	4.1	8	0	6.5%	12	101	17	108	45%	18	25	194	76%	10.8	0	57.9%	1	96	14
2011	OAK		139	576	4.1	4		2.9%						25	36	178	69%	7.1	0	1.8%			

Bush was Oakland's best running back on third down and in the red zone, though Darren McFadden slightly outpaced him in our goal-line efficiency numbers. A restricted free agent in 2011, Bush will come back to a Raiders team that may see more aggressive pass-related playcalling and fewer two-back sets.

Reggie Bush

Height: 6-0   Weight: 200   College: USC   Draft: 2006/1 (2)   Born: 2-Mar-1985   Age: 26   Risk: Yellow

Year	Team	G	Runs	Yds	Yd/R	TD	FUM	DVOA	Rk	DYAR	Rk	YAR	Suc%	Rec	Pass	Yds	C%	Yd/C	TD	DVOA	Rk	DYAR	Rk
2008	NO	10	106	404	3.8	2	3	-9.0%	41	-2	41	8	45%	52	72	440	72%	8.5	4	15.3%	16	118	7
2009	NO	14	70	390	5.6	5	2	30.2%	–	102	–	95	44%	47	68	335	69%	7.1	3	2.4%	32	65	21
2010	NO	8	36	150	4.2	0	0	-11.1%	–	-4	–	0	42%	34	42	208	81%	6.1	1	-1.5%	37	29	37
2011	MIA		108	503	4.7	4		20.4%						53	72	382	74%	7.2	1	-10.0%			

"It's been fun, New Orleans." That was Reggie's tweet when the Saints moved up to get Mark Ingram in the draft. Bush refrained from a tweet touting his "taking his talents to South Beach." Miami's coaches have made noises about using Reggie as an every-down back, which he surely is not. His strength is his hands, and with that catch rate the Dolphins should consider using Bush more at slot receiver than in the backfield.

Delone Carter

Height: 5-9   Weight: 226   College: Syracuse   Draft: 2011/4 (119)   Born: 22-Jun-1987   Age: 24   Risk: Blue

Year	Team	G	Runs	Yds	Yd/R	TD	FUM	DVOA	Rk	DYAR	Rk	YAR	Suc%	Rec	Pass	Yds	C%	Yd/C	TD	DVOA	Rk	DYAR	Rk
2011	IND		30	102	3.4	1		14.7%						5	9	27	56%	5.4	0	27.8%			

A squatty 5-foot-9, 225 pounds, Delone Carter is reasonably fast for his size (Speed Score: 102.7) but did not necessarily separate himself from other backs of similar stature while at Syracuse. He was a durable back who rushed for over 1,000 yards in back-to-back seasons and never fumbled, but his combined Adj. POE in 2009-10 was just minus-10.7. He takes little off the table but brings little to it as well.

Jamaal Charles

Height: 5-11   Weight: 200   College: Texas   Draft: 2008/3 (73)   Born: 27-Dec-1986   Age: 25   Risk: Yellow

Year	Team	G	Runs	Yds	Yd/R	TD	FUM	DVOA	Rk	DYAR	Rk	YAR	Suc%	Rec	Pass	Yds	C%	Yd/C	TD	DVOA	Rk	DYAR	Rk
2008	KC	16	67	357	5.3	0	2	15.3%	–	63	–	66	54%	27	40	272	68%	10.1	1	-6.2%	38	16	37
2009	KC	15	190	1120	5.9	7	3	20.3%	2	233	4	258	53%	40	55	297	73%	7.4	1	-9.5%	40	14	38
2010	KC	16	230	1467	6.4	5	4	33.9%	1	389	1	411	56%	45	64	468	70%	10.4	3	31.3%	8	150	7
2011	KC		255	1290	5.1	7		18.5%						39	55	368	71%	9.4	1	8.1%			

Perception may be reality to some, but the distance between the two concepts in the case of Charles is odd beyond reason. The Chiefs' coaching staff has come up with all sorts of reasons for his sub-feature back workload, and none of them make much sense. He can't block? Well, Kansas City went with two tight ends 38 percent of the time, third-highest in the league. You've got blockers, guys. He's not an every-down back? Charles was actually one of the few backs in the league to put up positive DVOA on every down, while stablemate Thomas Jones racked up negative DVOA on every down. You're afraid of burning him out? From carries 11 through 20 in each game, only Oakland's Darren McFadden (7.3) had a higher yards-per-carry average than Charles' 6.9. Look, we understand the importance of protecting your best assets; we're the people who started the anti-workload arguments for running backs eight years ago. But there are exceptions, and here's one: When you have the next Chris Johnson in your backfield, and you're short on explosive plays overall (take away the 36 plays of 20 yards or more authored by Charles and receiver Dwayne Bowe, and the rest of the team totaled 19 in 2010), it behooves you to throw caution to the wind and ride that very special horse as long as he'll go. Haley has made recent comments to that effect, which should be good news for the Chiefs' faithful — and the Chiefs' offense.

Tashard Choice Height: 5-10 Weight: 215 College: Georgia Tech Draft: 2008/4 (122) Born: 20-Nov-1984 Age: 27 Risk: Yellow

Year	Team	G	Runs	Yds	Yd/R	TD	FUM	DVOA	Rk	DYAR	Rk	YAR	Suc%	Rec	Pass	Yds	C%	Yd/C	TD	DVOA	Rk	DYAR	Rk
2008	DAL	16	92	472	5.1	2	1	32.0%	--	157	--	105	45%	21	30	185	70%	8.8	0	3.9%	27	29	34
2009	DAL	16	64	349	5.5	3	0	24.7%	--	92	--	101	56%	15	22	132	68%	8.8	0	23.0%	--	39	--
2010	DAL	16	66	243	3.7	3	1	-4.9%	--	12	--	15	42%	17	22	109	77%	6.4	0	-19.3%	--	-6	--
2011	DAL		90	390	4.3	1		3.1%						20	26	184	77%	9.2	1	2.3%			

Obviously buoyed by their unbridled success during the first half of the season, the Cowboys kept the promising Choice on the bench until Week 13, at which point he ran for 100 yards and a touchdown against the Colts. With just seven carries against the Eagles a week later, Choice can hardly be blamed for requesting Michael Vick's autograph afterwards. If anything, he should've asked Vick to be LinkedIn colleagues. He would be a useful starter if he ever got a chance, but the Cowboys appear devoted to sucking all the trade value out before they get rid of him.

Kenneth Darby Height: 5-10 Weight: 214 College: Alabama Draft: 2007/7 (246) Born: 26-Dec-1982 Age: 29 Risk: Red

Year	Team	G	Runs	Yds	Yd/R	TD	FUM	DVOA	Rk	DYAR	Rk	YAR	Suc%	Rec	Pass	Yds	C%	Yd/C	TD	DVOA	Rk	DYAR	Rk
2008	STL	10	32	140	4.4	0	1	-1.9%	--	9	--	4	41%	19	21	183	90%	9.6	0	43.6%	--	75	--
2009	STL	16	27	152	5.6	0	0	25.7%	--	33	--	31	42%	18	25	96	76%	5.3	0	-18.3%	49	-5	48
2010	STL	14	34	107	3.1	2	0	-6.6%	--	3	--	10	38%	10	13	61	77%	6.1	1	-4.0%	--	5	--
2011	STL		37	140	3.8	1		-15.9%						20	23	154	87%	7.7	0	-18.0%			

As the No. 2 running back behind a workhorse like Steven Jackson, Darby has received limited opportunities the last two seasons. Darby had 14 carries for 49 yards and a touchdown against the Washington Redskins when Jackson was injured in Week 3, but had just 17 carries (for 54 yards) in the 11 games he was active the rest of the season. On second and third downs, Darby had negative DVOAs rushing *and* receiving, which limits his viability as a legitimate No. 2 back in this league. Darby does possess value as a third-string back and core special teams player (nine tackles on special teams in each of the last two seasons).

Anthony Dixon Height: 6-1 Weight: 233 College: Mississippi State Draft: 2010/6 (173) Born: 24-Sep-1987 Age: 24 Risk: Red

Year	Team	G	Runs	Yds	Yd/R	TD	FUM	DVOA	Rk	DYAR	Rk	YAR	Suc%	Rec	Pass	Yds	C%	Yd/C	TD	DVOA	Rk	DYAR	Rk
2010	SF	16	70	237	3.4	2	0	-14.4%	--	-18	--	-9	46%	5	5	11	100%	2.2	0	-46.6%	--	-11	--
2011	SF		50	170	3.4	1		-14.4%						12	16	67	75%	5.6	0	14.7%			

Dixon was a workhorse in the 2010 preseason, averaging more than 18 carries a game for better than four yards per rush. Then he rotted on the bench, going virtually unused until Frank Gore fractured his hip, once again showing the uselessness of preseason stats. Take away his 34-yard cutback run against Seattle and Dixon averaged fewer than three yards per carry. He'll fight fourth-round rookie Kendall Hunter for carries. Regardless, Dixon's Twitter feed (@Boobie24Dixon) is a keeper, a mix of rap lyrics, free-form poetry, and food updates. A sample: "The Dog go 'Woof',The Cat go 'meow',The Bird go 'Koo Koo',da train go 'Chu Chu,Boobie Dixon Go Boom,Mister I'm the Bomb I'm the Bomb!" Hopefully Boobie Dixon will go boom more often in 2011, because "Mister I'm the Bomb I'm the Bomb" would be a fantastic nickname.

Kevin Faulk

Height: 5-8   Weight: 202   College: Louisiana State   Draft: 1999/2 (46)   Born: 5-Jun-1976   Age: 35   Risk: N/A

Year	Team	G	Runs	Yds	Yd/R	TD	FUM	DVOA	Rk	DYAR	Rk	YAR	Suc%	Rec	Pass	Yds	C%	Yd/C	TD	DVOA	Rk	DYAR	Rk
2008	NE	15	83	507	6.1	3	0	46.5%	–	178	–	193	57%	58	74	486	78%	8.4	3	34.1%	6	192	3
2009	NE	15	62	335	5.4	2	0	36.3%	–	109	–	111	58%	37	53	301	70%	8.1	1	4.4%	28	56	22
2010	NE	2	8	45	5.6	0	0	66.1%	–	19	–	16	50%	6	10	62	60%	10.3	0	22.5%	–	20	

Faulk said in June that he has no plans to retire, even though he is 35 years old, coming off a major injury, was more-than-adequately replaced by Danny Woodhead, may have to battle second-round pick Shane Vereen for a roster spot, and plays for a team that whose 2010 success was based largely on the decision to sweep away the old guard and embrace change. Faulk re-signed with the Patriots but spent the early part of camp on the PUP list. Brace yourself for the storm when Faulk is released in late-August; every Boston columnist will climb on his soapbox and pontificate about "loyalty" simultaneously, causing a cloud of sanctimony to appear over the northeast that changes weather patterns around the globe.

Justin Forsett

Height: 5-8   Weight: 194   College: California   Draft: 2008/7 (233)   Born: 14-Oct-1985   Age: 26   Risk: Yellow

Year	Team	G	Runs	Yds	Yd/R	TD	FUM	DVOA	Rk	DYAR	Rk	YAR	Suc%	Rec	Pass	Yds	C%	Yd/C	TD	DVOA	Rk	DYAR	Rk
2009	SEA	16	114	619	5.4	4	3	18.2%	4	122	19	122	46%	41	57	350	72%	8.5	1	-5.9%	37	23	34
2010	SEA	16	118	523	4.4	2	0	-6.2%	31	12	32	14	38%	33	51	252	65%	7.6	0	-0.2%	35	34	35
2011	SEA		111	497	4.5	0		4.8%						59	82	529	72%	9.0	1	1.5%			

A boom-or-bust runner, Forsett ranked 40th in Success Rate, but 12th in OFY per carry. Once Marshawn Lynch took over as the starter in Week 5, Forsett averaged fewer than six carries per game, despite outperforming Lynch in virtually all per-carry metrics (Success Rate notably excluded). Forsett was also the superior receiver, making his reduced role all the more curious. Forsett deserves at least 10 carries a game, especially for a team like Seattle that needs all the big-play power it can find. Forsett was also the driving force in gathering Seahawks' players for informal workouts during the lockout. Similar players to Forsett include Charlie Garner, Priest Holmes, and Thomas Jones, as well as Jerious Norwood and Onterrio Smith, proving that with proper playing time, Forsett could be one of the league's best all-purpose backs, if he doesn't have his career ruined by a torn ACL and/or a drug testing scandal involving a fake penis.

Matt Forte

Height: 6-1   Weight: 217   College: Tulane   Draft: 2008/2 (44)   Born: 10-Dec-1985   Age: 26   Risk: Green

Year	Team	G	Runs	Yds	Yd/R	TD	FUM	DVOA	Rk	DYAR	Rk	YAR	Suc%	Rec	Pass	Yds	C%	Yd/C	TD	DVOA	Rk	DYAR	Rk
2008	CHI	16	316	1238	3.9	8	1	-7.1%	38	20	38	53	43%	63	76	477	83%	7.6	4	33.1%	8	201	2
2009	CHI	16	258	929	3.6	4	6	-15.5%	44	-75	47	-128	42%	57	72	471	79%	8.3	0	-1.1%	33	45	25
2010	CHI	16	237	1069	4.5	6	3	0.4%	20	87	20	70	41%	51	70	547	73%	10.7	3	14.0%	22	105	12
2011	CHI		225	1048	4.7	7		11.0%						51	68	434	75%	8.5	2	10.6%			

Forte from two-back sets: 99 carries, 571 yards, 5.8 yards per carry, 20 rushes of 10+ yards. He had only nine carries of 10+ yards in 156 attempts (481 yards, 3.6 yards per carry) from single-back sets. Forte is a good Mike Martz back because he can line up in the slot, catch, and block, but he's a build-up runner who is better off with a fullback in front of him. Martz and his staff acknowledged this as the season wore on, but a system can only be adjusted so much, and Forte will probably get most of his carries from an "Ace" formation as long as Martz is around. The good news for fantasy owners is that Forte is so versatile that he can rack up receiving numbers even if Martz goes back to the days when he abandoned the run soon after the kickoff.

Arian Foster

Height: 6-1 Weight: 225 College: Tennessee Draft: 2009/ (FA) Born: 24-Aug-1986 Age: 25 Risk: Yellow

Year	Team	G	Runs	Yds	Yd/R	TD	FUM	DVOA	Rk	DYAR	Rk	YAR	Suc%	Rec	Pass	Yds	C%	Yd/C	TD	DVOA	Rk	DYAR	Rk
2009	HOU	6	54	257	4.8	3	1	24.8%	--	77	--	80	59%	8	9	93	89%	11.6	0	57.1%	--	33	--
2010	HOU	16	327	1616	4.9	16	3	18.0%	4	377	2	372	52%	66	86	604	79%	9.2	2	25.6%	12	197	1
2011	HOU		310	1453	4.7	12		14.3%						53	72	504	74%	9.5	3	11.8%			

Arian Foster was benched last season. It was Week 4, the Texans were playing the Raiders, and Foster sat out the first quarter for missing a team meeting, though his fumble on his final carry the previous week against the Cowboys may have also played a role. That involuntary rest was one of the few setbacks for Foster in 2010, as he took advantage of the opportunity created by Ben Tate's preseason injury and Steve Slaton's injuries and performance to become the first undrafted back to lead the league in rushing since the merger. Foster's vision and decisiveness made him pretty much the ideal fit for Houston's one-cut zone scheme, and leading the league with 45 broken tackles didn't hurt. Unless the fumble and injury issues that plagued his senior year at Tennessee recur, he should again be one of the league's most productive backs. He probably won't be quite as effective in 2011, though, as he was particularly productive in third-down situations (28.0% DVOA, 63% Success Rate) and in the red zone (+1.7 TDs more than we would expect in those situations).

Toby Gerhart

Height: 6-0 Weight: 231 College: Stanford Draft: 2010/2 (51) Born: 18-Mar-1987 Age: 24 Risk: Green

Year	Team	G	Runs	Yds	Yd/R	TD	FUM	DVOA	Rk	DYAR	Rk	YAR	Suc%	Rec	Pass	Yds	C%	Yd/C	TD	DVOA	Rk	DYAR	Rk
2010	MIN	15	81	322	4.0	1	3	-2.8%	--	19	--	17	42%	21	29	167	72%	8.0	0	-26.4%	51	-20	51
2011	MIN		51	229	4.4	3		14.8%						19	24	169	79%	8.9	1	12.2%			

Gerhart stepped up with 22-76-1 and 16-77-0 games when Adrian Peterson was out or limited; also got some attention as an outlet receiver, though he caught a lot of 1-to-3 yard passes. Gerhart lost three fumbles and must prove he can hold onto the football if he wants to inherit the Jason Snelling role in Bill Musgrave's "Falcons of the North" offense.

Mike Goodson

Height: 5-11 Weight: 208 College: Texas A&M Draft: 2009/4 (111) Born: 23-May-1987 Age: 24 Risk: Yellow

Year	Team	G	Runs	Yds	Yd/R	TD	FUM	DVOA	Rk	DYAR	Rk	YAR	Suc%	Rec	Pass	Yds	C%	Yd/C	TD	DVOA	Rk	DYAR	Rk
2009	CAR	8	22	49	2.2	0	1	-77.0%	--	-59	--	-54	23%	2	2	15	100%	7.5	0	55.0%	--	7	--
2010	CAR	16	103	452	4.4	3	4	-14.9%	42	-25	39	-4	38%	40	57	310	70%	7.8	0	-5.6%	42	25	38
2011	CAR		47	223	4.7	1		18.6%						27	34	273	79%	10.1	1	23.0%			

Goodson's most impressive games may have been back-to-back performances against the Browns and Ravens when injuries took DeAngelo Williams and Jonathan Stewart out of the lineup. He's a quick cutback runner with the ability to get linebackers out of place (which he did a lot against Baltimore), and he was helpful to Jimmy Clausen on bailout throw after bailout throw against Cleveland, picking up serious yards after catch. Surprisingly for a faster, smaller back, Goodson was the only regular Panthers back to post a positive red-zone rushing DVOA (12.4%). Though DeAngelo Williams and Jonathan Stewart are still the main men in Carolina's run game, Goodson finally proved that he could add to the equation in a situational role.

Frank Gore

Height: 5-9 Weight: 215 College: Miami Draft: 2005/3 (65) Born: 14-May-1983 Age: 28 Risk: Red

Year	Team	G	Runs	Yds	Yd/R	TD	FUM	DVOA	Rk	DYAR	Rk	YAR	Suc%	Rec	Pass	Yds	C%	Yd/C	TD	DVOA	Rk	DYAR	Rk
2008	SF	14	240	1036	4.3	6	6	-1.7%	29	69	25	72	47%	43	66	373	65%	8.7	2	2.5%	28	62	17
2009	SF	14	229	1120	4.9	10	4	4.7%	20	119	20	106	42%	52	76	406	70%	7.8	3	4.3%	29	77	18
2010	SF	11	203	853	4.2	3	4	-8.9%	34	-2	34	28	48%	46	72	452	64%	9.8	2	0.4%	34	57	23
2011	SF		273	1240	4.5	8		3.7%						46	63	332	73%	7.2	1	7.5%			

A paradox: Gore had the highest Success Rate of his career in 2010, while also producing his lowest DVOA. Since he wasn't fumbling any more than usual, that suggests that Gore's offensive line was opening holes, but Gore struggled to turn good runs into great runs. On a similar note, although he averaged more catches for more yards per game than ever before, his receiving DVOA and DYAR were both the lowest since his rookie season (when he was the target of only 15 passes). Gore was also in the bottom ten running backs in broken tackles per carry. In other words, Gore clearly lost a step in 2010, and that's before he fractured his right hip in Week 12. Though Gore claimed to be at 100 percent as training camp opened, this is a guy who hasn't played 16 games since 2006. If Gore struggles again in 2011, the 49ers may seek out a replacement for 2012.

Earnest Graham

Height: 5-9   Weight: 215   College: Florida   Draft: 2004/ (FA)   Born: 15-Jan-1980   Age: 31   Risk: Red

Year	Team	G	Runs	Yds	Yd/R	TD	FUM	DVOA	Rk	DYAR	Rk	YAR	Suc%	Rec	Pass	Yds	C%	Yd/C	TD	DVOA	Rk	DYAR	Rk
2008	TB	10	132	563	4.3	4	2	-8.5%	39	1	39	25	48%	23	33	174	70%	7.6	0	-1.1%	32	24	35
2009	TB	13	14	66	4.7	0	0	21.1%	--	18	--	19	50%	14	22	109	64%	7.8	0	-12.4%	--	2	--
2010	TB	12	20	99	5.0	1	1	-18.9%	--	-10	--	-9	45%	16	19	130	84%	8.1	1	18.4%	--	36	--
2011	TB		46	224	4.9	1		18.9%						30	43	258	70%	8.6	1	12.3%			

Graham is still trying to regain his status as a marquee name after a one-year wonder season in 2007. Last year, he struggled through injuries and lost traction to Cadillac Williams and LeGarrette Blount. Due a $2 million base salary and a $1.05 million option bonus in 2011, Graham is one of several veterans that may be asked to restructure, but Tampa Bay's enormous room under the new salary cap and the NFL's new cash-to-cap requirements could have those same veterans seeing unusual paydays.

Ryan Grant

Height: 6-1   Weight: 218   College: Notre Dame   Draft: 2005/ (FA)   Born: 9-Dec-1982   Age: 29   Risk: Yellow

Year	Team	G	Runs	Yds	Yd/R	TD	FUM	DVOA	Rk	DYAR	Rk	YAR	Suc%	Rec	Pass	Yds	C%	Yd/C	TD	DVOA	Rk	DYAR	Rk
2008	GB	16	312	1203	3.9	4	4	-10.1%	42	-19	43	-21	46%	18	22	116	82%	6.4	1	1.1%	--	16	--
2009	GB	16	282	1253	4.4	11	1	12.9%	10	252	2	252	49%	25	30	197	83%	7.9	0	11.7%	21	41	28
2010	GB	1	8	45	5.6	0	0	23.5%	--	11	--	8	38%	0	--	0	--	0.0	0	--	--	--	--
2011	GB		194	864	4.5	4		8.8%						32	41	177	78%	5.5	0	0.2%			

Grant is scheduled to make $5.25 million this season. He is coming off an ankle injury, and James Starks proved he can do just about anything Grant can do, for a much lower price. Grant is a poor blocker and so-so receiver, while Starks is a poor receiver and so-so blocker, so establishing a committee could be tricky. The Packers may keep both players just to insulate themselves from injuries. If so, expect them to battle for touches, and be wary of Alex Green eating into the catches and John Kuhn into the goal line opportunities.

Alex Green

Height: 6-2   Weight: 220   College: Hawaii   Draft: 2011/3 (96)   Born: 30-Nov-1989   Age: 22   Risk: Blue

Year	Team	G	Runs	Yds	Yd/R	TD	FUM	DVOA	Rk	DYAR	Rk	YAR	Suc%	Rec	Pass	Yds	C%	Yd/C	TD	DVOA	Rk	DYAR	Rk
2011	GB		27	126	4.6	0		18.1%						13	19	96	68%	7.3	0	32.5%			

Hold onto the ball, Alex! Fumbleitis destroyed Green's draft stock, but his upside is high; Green destroyed the competition in Adj. POE in 2010, producing a plus-55.0 that was more than double the No. 2 rusher in the category. The system helped — with their run-and-shoot, Hawaii is expected to throw on every down — but Green still made the absolute most of his opportunities. He rushed for 1,652 yards (7.1 per carry, 4.7 highlight yards per carry, 20 touchdowns) in his two years in a Hawaii uniform and, perhaps as importantly, caught 38 passes for 461 yards and two touchdowns. His upside is high, like his running style, but if he can't maintain possession of the ball, it doesn't matter.

BenJarvus Green-Ellis
Height: 5-10 Weight: 219 College: Mississippi Draft: 2008/ (FA) Born: 2-Jul-1985 Age: 26 Risk: Red

Year	Team	G	Runs	Yds	Yd/R	TD	FUM	DVOA	Rk	DYAR	Rk	YAR	Suc%	Rec	Pass	Yds	C%	Yd/C	TD	DVOA	Rk	DYAR	Rk
2008	NE	9	74	275	3.7	5	0	6.7%	–	55	–	66	57%	3	6	37	50%	12.3	0	21.4%	–	13	–
2009	NE	12	26	114	4.4	0	0	0.1%	–	9	–	15	58%	2	5	11	40%	5.5	0	-58.7%	–	-13	–
2010	NE	16	229	1008	4.4	13	0	26.4%	2	354	3	303	57%	12	16	85	75%	7.1	0	17.9%	–	31	–
2011	NE		168	766	4.6	10		17.8%						22	30	197	73%	8.9	2	32.0%			

Boston Legal has not fumbled in his NFL career. On goal-to-go carries, he gained 42 yards and scored nine touchdowns on 23 attempts, getting stuffed for a loss just once. Green-Ellis is nearly useless as a receiver, lacks the size most teams would want from their power back, and doesn't have breakaway speed. But the ability to hold onto the football and grind out positive yardage counts for a lot in a committee system. With all of the fresh talent in the Patriots backfield, Green-Ellis won't have another 1,000 yard season, but he is more likely than Danny Woodhead or a rookie to absorb goal-line opportunities.

Shonn Greene
Height: 6-0 Weight: 227 College: Iowa Draft: 2009/3 (65) Born: 21-Aug-1985 Age: 26 Risk: Green

Year	Team	G	Runs	Yds	Yd/R	TD	FUM	DVOA	Rk	DYAR	Rk	YAR	Suc%	Rec	Pass	Yds	C%	Yd/C	TD	DVOA	Rk	DYAR	Rk
2009	NYJ	14	108	540	5.0	2	3	5.7%	19	61	30	74	48%	0	5	0	0%	0.0	0	-107.2%	–	-23	–
2010	NYJ	15	185	766	4.1	2	3	7.8%	11	124	11	129	55%	16	24	120	67%	7.5	0	4.4%	–	27	–
2011	NYJ		287	1185	4.1	8		10.1%						23	35	178	66%	7.8	1	-21.5%			

Fool me once, shame on me. Fool me twice... well, you know. Greene's deceptively impressive 2009 playoff performance convinced many fantasy owners that he was set to emerge as a franchise back, an impression that was reinforced when the Jets released Thomas Jones and replaced him with a decrepit LaDainian Tomlinson. That was a mistake. Tomlinson promptly won the starting job in training camp and opened the season by grabbing the lion's share of the carries. Even though Greene came on late in the year and had another good showing in the playoffs, it wasn't enough to save owners who had plunked down a first- or second-round pick on him. Fast forward one year and Greene is again being touted as the guy who is going to break out of a crowded Jets backfield and emerge as a feature back capable of cracking 1,200 yards and scoring double-digit touchdowns. This time it should happen, especially considering how Tomlinson declined in the second half last year.

Jamie Harper
Height: 5-11 Weight: 235 College: Clemson Draft: 2011/4 (130) Born: 11-Sep-1989 Age: 22 Risk: Blue

Year	Team	G	Runs	Yds	Yd/R	TD	FUM	DVOA	Rk	DYAR	Rk	YAR	Suc%	Rec	Pass	Yds	C%	Yd/C	TD	DVOA	Rk	DYAR	Rk
2011	TEN		37	160	4.3	2		8.8%						10	13	76	77%	7.6	0	-17.5%			

The knock on Harper is that he has trouble keeping his balance, particularly after he makes his first cut. He's a physical specimen and has great timed speed, so he has a chance to make some noise if he can get better at the stop-and-go aspect of running between the tackles. He'll be watching the resolution of Chris Johnson's contract situation in Tennessee with great interest.

Montario Hardesty
Height: 6-0 Weight: 225 College: Tennessee Draft: 2010/2 (59) Born: 1-Feb-1987 Age: 24 Risk: Blue

Year	Team	G	Runs	Yds	Yd/R	TD	FUM	DVOA	Rk	DYAR	Rk	YAR	Suc%	Rec	Pass	Yds	C%	Yd/C	TD	DVOA	Rk	DYAR	Rk
2011	CLE		52	193	3.7	1		-7.6%						16	18	130	89%	8.2	1	-2.5%			

Hardesty is a hard inside runner who can also make plays as a receiver out of the backfield. In fact, he's awfully similar to Peyton Hillis, the player who took what should have been Hardesty's job last year. The problem Hardesty has is that health is a skill, and he doesn't seem to have that skill. Hardesty took a medical redshirt in 2005 after a knee injury against Ole Miss. He missed time in 2007 with undisclosed injuries. Last year, a bone bruise in his right knee cost him all of training camp, and then he tore his left ACL in his first preseason game. If Hardesty can actually stay healthy next year, we have no idea how many carries he'll get as the number-two back, and that makes Hardesty a reasonable fantasy sleeper, especially if you believe in the Madden Curse. Then again, if you believe in the Madden Curse and wasted a pick on Chase Daniel last year, we feel sorry for you.

Jerome Harrison
Height: 5-9   Weight: 195   College: Washington State   Draft: 2006/5 (145)   Born: 26-Feb-1983   Age: 28   Risk: Yellow

Year	Team	G	Runs	Yds	Yd/R	TD	FUM	DVOA	Rk	DYAR	Rk	YAR	Suc%	Rec	Pass	Yds	C%	Yd/C	TD	DVOA	Rk	DYAR	Rk
2008	CLE	15	34	246	7.2	1	0	52.7%	–	79	–	76	53%	12	18	116	67%	9.7	1	14.8%	–	29	
2009	CLE	14	194	862	4.4	5	2	1.1%	30	73	28	92	48%	34	50	220	68%	6.5	2	-14.1%	46	-1	46
2010	2TM	12	71	330	4.6	1	2	-21.1%	–	-35	–	-31	35%	12	13	85	92%	7.1	0	22.9%	–	24	
2011	DET		73	351	4.8	1		22.7%						23	29	176	79%	7.7	1	-26.2%			

Despite a 286-yard game against the Chiefs near the end of 2009, the Browns spent the 2010 offseason hemming and hawing about giving Harrison the starting role. They jerked him all over the depth chart in training camp, then gave him two weeks as the starter before benching him for Peyton Hillis. Having destroyed Harrison's trade value, the Browns took their dollar and turned it into five shiny cents, sending him to the Eagles for Mike Bell. Without any knowledge of the playbook, Harrison was limited to significant action in just two games, in which he had 32 carries for 208 yards. In a world where even smart organizations give Willis McGahee-types big guaranteed contracts, Harrison remains criminally overlooked. He'll have some opportunity in Detroit, but he's not the big back that Detroit was looking for after Mikel Leshoure went down with an Achilles tear.

Mike Hart
Height: 5-8   Weight: 206   College: Michigan   Draft: 2008/6 (202)   Born: 9-Apr-1986   Age: 25   Risk: N/A

Year	Team	G	Runs	Yds	Yd/R	TD	FUM	DVOA	Rk	DYAR	Rk	YAR	Suc%	Rec	Pass	Yds	C%	Yd/C	TD	DVOA	Rk	DYAR	Rk
2008	IND	5	2	9	4.5	0	1	69.7%	–	10	–	8	100%	1	1	18	100%	18.0	0	-216.3%	–	-12	–
2009	IND	9	26	70	2.7	1	0	-18.0%	–	-10	–	-13	46%	5	8	54	63%	10.8	0	29.1%	–	18	–
2010	IND	7	43	185	4.3	1	0	-1.6%	–	14	–	20	47%	6	6	25	100%	4.2	0	1.1%	–	5	–

Maybe it is because Hart is too small or maybe it is the over 1,000 carries he got at Michigan, but he simply cannot stay healthy in the NFL. Hart tore his ACL in 2008 and battled ankle injuries throughout last season. The Colts renounced their rights to him as a restricted free agent, and he has yet to sign elsewhere.

Roy Helu
Height: 5-11   Weight: 216   College: Nebraska   Draft: 2011/4 (105)   Born: 7-Dec-1988   Age: 23   Risk: Yellow

Year	Team	G	Runs	Yds	Yd/R	TD	FUM	DVOA	Rk	DYAR	Rk	YAR	Suc%	Rec	Pass	Yds	C%	Yd/C	TD	DVOA	Rk	DYAR	Rk
2011	WAS		75	362	4.8	1		2.5%						13	19	109	68%	8.4	1	13.4%			

Big, strong and fast, Roy Helu was a favorite of the advanced stats. He rushed for 1,245 yards and a plus-11.2 Adj. POE as a senior at Nebraska, and his 114.8 Speed Score placed him near the top of the rookie class, as did his 3.19-per-carry Highlight Yardage. He fought nagging shoulder and hamstring issues over his last couple of seasons, but the biggest concern with Helu seems to be inconsistency. In 2010, he rushed for 307 yards (11.0 per carry) against Missouri and 59 yards (3.1 per carry) against South Dakota State. In 2009, he rushed for 169 yards (6.0 per carry) against Virginia Tech and 24 (3.4 per carry) against Baylor. Still, Washington was able to wait until the fourth round to get one of this year's most statistically strong prospects.

Tim Hightower
Height: 6-0   Weight: 226   College: Richmond   Draft: 2008/5 (149)   Born: 23-May-1986   Age: 25   Risk: Red

Year	Team	G	Runs	Yds	Yd/R	TD	FUM	DVOA	Rk	DYAR	Rk	YAR	Suc%	Rec	Pass	Yds	C%	Yd/C	TD	DVOA	Rk	DYAR	Rk
2008	ARI	16	143	399	2.8	10	2	-20.5%	48	-79	48	-60	37%	34	50	237	68%	7.0	0	-10.2%	41	10	40
2009	ARI	16	143	598	4.2	8	5	-7.8%	38	6	39	3	44%	63	80	428	79%	6.8	0	6.8%	25	89	9
2010	ARI	16	153	736	4.8	5	5	-1.0%	22	46	25	51	42%	21	42	136	50%	6.5	0	-57.9%	54	-105	54
2011	WAS		203	862	4.2	4		-11.7%						32	47	192	68%	6.0	0	-12.3%			

Hightower's greatest asset is durability; he has now played in 16 games in every season since he's been drafted. Combine that with the fact that's he a decent pass catcher, a willing blocker, and serviceable ball carrier and it's not surprising that he's been able to hold off Beanie Wells the past couple of seasons. The Cardinals decided it was finally time to see what Wells could do, so they sent Hightower off to Washington. He seems to fit the one-cut style of Mike Shanahan, and injuries to Ryan Torain have handed him a shot at the starting job.

Peyton Hillis Height: 6-0 Weight: 240 College: Arkansas   Draft: 2008/7 (227) Born: 21-Jan-1986 Age: 25 Risk: Red

Year	Team	G	Runs	Yds	Yd/R	TD	FUM	DVOA	Rk	DYAR	Rk	YAR	Suc%	Rec	Pass	Yds	C%	Yd/C	TD	DVOA	Rk	DYAR	Rk
2008	DEN	12	68	343	5.0	5	0	41.0%	–	151	–	156	65%	14	19	179	74%	12.8	1	55.7%	–	82	–
2009	DEN	14	13	54	4.2	1	0	-7.8%	–	1	–	8	54%	4	6	19	67%	4.8	0	-47.3%	–	-14	–
2010	CLE	16	270	1177	4.4	11	8	5.0%	13	152	8	152	53%	61	77	477	79%	7.8	2	18.9%	18	138	8
2011	CLE		257	1038	4.0	11		2.0%						53	76	539	70%	10.2	1	34.6%			

Hillis wasn't just impressive because he was good; he was impressive because he was steady. He also tied for eighth in the league with 35 broken tackles by our count. He's got good vision and he's aggressive hitting the hole, although he doesn't really have breakaway speed or elusiveness. He runs a bit upright, which is one of the reasons why he led all running backs with eight fumbles. If you read somewhere that Hillis "faded down the stretch," don't believe it. Hillis' fade came from playing Baltimore and Pittsburgh in the last two weeks of the season.

Kendall Hunter Height: 5-7 Weight: 199 College: Oklahoma St.   Draft: 2011/4 (115) Born: 16-Sep-1988 Age: 23 Risk: Blue

Year	Team	G	Runs	Yds	Yd/R	TD	FUM	DVOA	Rk	DYAR	Rk	YAR	Suc%	Rec	Pass	Yds	C%	Yd/C	TD	DVOA	Rk	DYAR	Rk
2011	SF		24	95	3.9	0		-2.5%						5	6	32	83%	6.4	1	-9.9%			

With a Speed Score of just 94.5, Hunter is not as fast as one probably needs to be at 5-foot-7, 199 pounds, but he is a decisive runner with a low center of gravity, which helps him maximize the speed and strength he possesses. He is also a potentially strong receiver out of the backfield. He fought ankle injuries throughout 2009, but his last two healthy seasons (2008 and 2010) were outstanding: he combined for 3,103 rushing yards (6.1 per carry, 32 touchdowns) and 299 receiving yards on 42 receptions.

Mark Ingram Height: 5-11 Weight: 215 College: Alabama   Draft: 2011/1 (28) Born: 21-Dec-1989 Age: 22 Risk: Yellow

Year	Team	G	Runs	Yds	Yd/R	TD	FUM	DVOA	Rk	DYAR	Rk	YAR	Suc%	Rec	Pass	Yds	C%	Yd/C	TD	DVOA	Rk	DYAR	Rk
2011	NO		192	804	4.2	8		-3.1%						27	31	151	87%	5.6	1	-10.2%			

After winning the Heisman Trophy as a sophomore, Ingram's junior season saw him undergo arthroscopic surgery a week prior to Alabama's opener, While he was a fine back in 2010, he was nothing like the dynamo he was in 2009. His Adj. POE was plus-12.5 in 2008, plus-18.2 in 2009, and just plus-8.3 in 2010. He has marvelous footwork, which helps him out between the tackles, but between his stumbles as a junior (he had just two games where he rushed for more than 100 yards, both before October) and his poor Speed Score (at 94.4, it was the lowest score given to any first-rounder since 1999, the first year we have accurate combine measurables for), his ability to adapt to the NFL game is in question. Only two NFL running backs have become reliable starters with a Speed Score that low: Brian Westbrook and Ahmad Bradshaw. Despite the poor trends, Ingram proved that he had elite NFL potential in 2009 — it's just a question of getting back to that level.

Chris Ivory Height: 6-0 Weight: 222 College: Tiffin   Draft: 2010/ (FA) Born: 22-Mar-1988 Age: 23 Risk: Green

Year	Team	G	Runs	Yds	Yd/R	TD	FUM	DVOA	Rk	DYAR	Rk	YAR	Suc%	Rec	Pass	Yds	C%	Yd/C	TD	DVOA	Rk	DYAR	Rk
2010	NO	12	137	716	5.2	5	4	12.9%	6	133	9	164	59%	1	1	17	100%	17.0	0	146.5%	–	10	–
2011	NO		36	179	5.0	2		1.9%						17	19	96	89%	5.6	1	20.1%			

Ivory was an unknown quantity coming out of college, as injuries ruined his time at Washington State and tiny Tiffin University. (Pop quiz: What conference do the Tiffin Dragons play in? Answer: The Great Lakes Intercollegiate Athletic Conference, or GLIAC, which may or may not star Jane Lynch.) Sure enough, injury derailed Ivory's unlikely journey from undrafted free agent to FedEx Ground Player of the Week, which he won in October after gashing Tampa for 158 yards on 15 carries. Ivory led the team in rushing, broke 27 tackles on only 137 carries, and was a huge factor in getting the Saints to the playoffs, but the NFL isn't much for romance. Ivory's fragility is too much of a handicap for this level. Even after his heroics, he looks to be fourth on the depth chart. A waiver wire pickup, no more.

Brandon Jackson

Height: 5-11   Weight: 210   College: Nebraska   Draft: 2007/2 (63)   Born: 2-Oct-1985   Age: 26   Risk: Yellow

Year	Team	G	Runs	Yds	Yd/R	TD	FUM	DVOA	Rk	DYAR	Rk	YAR	Suc%	Rec	Pass	Yds	C%	Yd/C	TD	DVOA	Rk	DYAR	Rk
2008	GB	13	45	248	5.5	1	1	25.3%	--	62	--	65	51%	30	39	185	77%	6.2	0	-13.2%	44	1	44
2009	GB	12	37	111	3.0	2	1	-15.8%	--	-10	--	-9	38%	21	26	187	81%	8.9	1	40.3%	4	77	17
2010	GB	16	190	703	3.7	3	1	-9.9%	35	-9	35	-35	43%	43	50	342	86%	8.0	1	42.0%	3	156	6
2011	CLE		76	340	4.5	1		14.1%						45	67	300	67%	6.7	1	7.1%			

Jackson told the *Green Bay Post-Gazette* in June that he felt he had "proven himself as an every-down back." That is the very definition of irony: Jackson proved just the opposite last year. His lone 100-yard performance was bolstered by a 71-yard run. He produced a series of 15-carry, 55-yard rushing performances during a long stretch when he was the Packers' only viable running back, provided very rudimentary services as a receiver, and lost his playing time to a waiver wire acquisition and a fullback. Jackson has a similar skill set to Peyton Hillis, so it is hard to perceive him as a change-up back in Cleveland. More likely, he will play when Hillis needs a breather.

Fred Jackson

Height: 6-1   Weight: 215   College: Coe College   Draft: 2007/ (FA)   Born: 20-Feb-1981   Age: 30   Risk: Green

Year	Team	G	Runs	Yds	Yd/R	TD	FUM	DVOA	Rk	DYAR	Rk	YAR	Suc%	Rec	Pass	Yds	C%	Yd/C	TD	DVOA	Rk	DYAR	Rk
2008	BUF	16	130	571	4.4	3	2	7.0%	14	91	19	94	53%	37	45	317	82%	8.6	0	12.4%	18	67	16
2009	BUF	16	237	1062	4.5	2	2	2.7%	25	106	22	132	48%	46	60	371	77%	8.1	2	25.5%	9	123	4
2010	BUF	16	222	927	4.2	5	5	0.2%	21	81	21	74	47%	31	54	215	57%	6.9	2	-32.9%	53	-57	53
2011	BUF		187	652	3.5	3		-12.5%						45	63	349	71%	7.8	1	-0.3%			

Jackson is now entering his fifth year as the running back the Bills really, really want their first-round pick to replace. Jackson remains one of the most determined runners in the league, shedding lots of arm tackles in his quest to get back to the line of scrimmage, and he catches the ball well enough to be an every-down back. He's also 30 years old, lacks breakaway speed, and will fumble while fighting for extra yardage. The tragedy of the Bills and Jackson is not that the team did not get the most out of him — nearly 4,000 scrimmage yards in four years is a good haul from a guy pulled from the minor indoor football leagues — but that the team wasted so many resources on Marshawn Lynch and C.J. Spiller when they could have gotten on just fine with Jackson.

Steven Jackson

Height: 6-3   Weight: 229   College: Oregon State   Draft: 2004/1 (24)   Born: 22-Jul-1983   Age: 28   Risk: Green

Year	Team	G	Runs	Yds	Yd/R	TD	FUM	DVOA	Rk	DYAR	Rk	YAR	Suc%	Rec	Pass	Yds	C%	Yd/C	TD	DVOA	Rk	DYAR	Rk
2008	STL	12	253	1042	4.1	7	5	-2.5%	31	66	26	45	46%	40	62	379	65%	9.5	1	0.2%	31	46	26
2009	STL	15	324	1416	4.4	4	2	8.6%	16	217	6	155	45%	51	75	322	68%	6.3	0	-17.8%	48	-16	50
2010	STL	16	330	1241	3.8	6	1	-12.1%	37	-48	40	-23	40%	46	61	383	75%	8.3	0	-1.2%	36	45	29
2011	STL		289	1155	4.0	6		-7.4%						59	85	560	69%	9.5	1	16.8%			

The lack of a legitimate No. 2 running back behind him on the depth chart led to Jackson once again carrying a heavy workload in the Rams' offense. Jackson fought through an early-season groin injury and a broken left ring finger to play in all 16 games for just the second time in his seven-year career. Jackson topped 1,000 yards for the sixth consecutive season, but the finger injury had him essentially playing one-handed, unable to use his powerful stiff-arm over the final nine weeks of the season. Jackson broke 49 tackles in 2009, which ranked fifth in the NFL that season and would have led the league in 2010. That total dropped to just 28 last season, which may explain why the Rams dropped from fourth to 27th in Second Level Yards. The Rams improved their depth at running back with the signings of Jerious Norwood and Cadillac Williams, but Jackson can still be expected to get the bulk of the team's carries.

Brandon Jacobs Height: 6-4 Weight: 256 College: Southern Illinois Draft: 2005/4 (110) Born: 6-Jul-1982 Age: 29 Risk: Green

Year	Team	G	Runs	Yds	Yd/R	TD	FUM	DVOA	Rk	DYAR	Rk	YAR	Suc%	Rec	Pass	Yds	C%	Yd/C	TD	DVOA	Rk	DYAR	Rk
2008	NYG	13	219	1089	5.0	15	3	22.4%	3	300	2	247	51%	6	12	36	50%	6.0	0	-42.6%	--	-21	--
2009	NYG	15	224	835	3.7	5	2	-7.8%	39	7	38	8	45%	18	31	184	58%	10.2	1	-6.5%	38	12	39
2010	NYG	16	147	823	5.6	9	3	18.1%	3	172	7	184	54%	7	13	59	54%	8.4	0	-15.8%	--	-1	--
2011	NYG		157	657	4.2	11		4.1%						12	19	87	63%	7.2	1	-6.3%			

Jacobs didn't take kindly to his benching, but his demotion had some hidden effects. After missing time in four consecutive seasons due to injury, the diminished workload kept Jacobs fresh and healthy for a full season, producing a dramatic increase in yards per carry and a return to his previously lofty ranks in rushing DVOA and Success Rate. Considering how physical his style can be, this is pretty close to the ideal workload for Jacobs, regardless of who gets the tick in the Games Started box. Since he still can't catch, though, Jacobs remains a luxury item. Once his rushing performance drops, he has no value.

Javarris James Height: 6-0 Weight: 212 College: Miami Draft: 2010/ (FA) Born: 18-Sep-1987 Age: 24 Risk: Red

Year	Team	G	Runs	Yds	Yd/R	TD	FUM	DVOA	Rk	DYAR	Rk	YAR	Suc%	Rec	Pass	Yds	C%	Yd/C	TD	DVOA	Rk	DYAR	Rk
2010	IND	10	46	112	2.4	6	1	4.3%	--	27	--	25	48%	9	11	63	82%	7.0	0	-31.4%	--	-12	--
2011	IND		48	147	3.1	3		-23.1%						13	15	80	87%	6.2	0	16.9%			

With injuries piling up in the Indianapolis backfield, people started speculating that Edgerrin James may come out of retirement. Instead, it was his little, less-heralded cousin Javarris off of the Washington practice squad. James emerged as the team's goal-line back with some success. James could find himself as the Colts' third back moving forward, although a summer marijuana arrest is not the best course of action for a fringe NFL player.

Rashad Jennings Height: 6-1 Weight: 231 College: Liberty Draft: 2009/7 (250) Born: 26-Mar-1985 Age: 26 Risk: Yellow

Year	Team	G	Runs	Yds	Yd/R	TD	FUM	DVOA	Rk	DYAR	Rk	YAR	Suc%	Rec	Pass	Yds	C%	Yd/C	TD	DVOA	Rk	DYAR	Rk
2009	JAC	15	39	202	5.2	1	0	8.8%	--	31	--	35	46%	16	18	101	89%	6.3	0	-7.6%	--	6	--
2010	JAC	13	84	459	5.5	4	0	29.3%	--	137	--	138	52%	26	34	223	76%	8.6	0	9.9%	28	40	32
2011	JAC		75	328	4.4	0		-4.4%						25	32	187	78%	7.5	1	9.0%			

Jennings should enter 2011 as the clear handcuff for Maurice Jones-Drew owners after his explosive 2010 season. While his initial foray into starting (15 carries, 32 yards against the Redskins) didn't turn out too well, with MJD sidelined again in Week 17, Jennings ran for 108 yards on 22 carries against the Texans. He pushed his stock up from last year by working hard on his receiving ability, and he was dominant in the red zone with a 67 percent Success Rate. Jennings will likely grab a bigger share of the offense this year with the Jaguars needing to ease off Jones-Drew's workload, and while he won't put up a DVOA that high again, there is nothing in his statistical record so far to suggest he would be an enormous dropoff from MJD.

Chris Johnson

Height: 5-11 Weight: 197 College: East Carolina   Draft: 2008/1 (24)   Born: 23-Sep-1985   Age: 26 Risk: Yellow

Year	Team	G	Runs	Yds	Yd/R	TD	FUM	DVOA	Rk	DYAR	Rk	YAR	Suc%	Rec	Pass	Yds	C%	Yd/C	TD	DVOA	Rk	DYAR	Rk
2008	TEN	15	251	1228	4.9	9	1	9.2%	10	175	7	165	44%	43	62	260	69%	6.0	1	-19.8%	46	-20	48
2009	TEN	16	358	2006	5.6	14	3	15.2%	7	343	1	322	45%	50	71	503	70%	10.1	2	16.7%	13	113	7
2010	TEN	16	316	1364	4.3	11	3	-7.2%	33	18	31	19	39%	44	57	245	77%	5.6	1	-27.9%	52	-43	52
2011	TEN		332	1398	4.2	10		-1.6%						46	58	387	79%	8.4	1	14.6%			

Matching 2009's production was an unrealistic expectation for Johnson. Opponents concentrated on setting the edge, and his desire for big plays occasionally resulted in spectacular highlights like a touchdown against San Diego where he eluded five potential tacklers but more often resulted in a two-yard loss. Johnson was also below-average in goal-to-go situations, scoring 2.5 fewer touchdowns than expected. (That number should regress to the mean this year.) The decline in his receiver numbers was largely a result of the fall in productivity of the Titans' screen game, which is an area coach Mike Munchak and coordinator Chris Palmer have indicated they want to improve upon for 2011. Rookie Jamie Harper may steal some of the red zone carries, but if the Titans get at least mediocre quarterback play, Johnson should exceed his 2010 production. The biggest wild card is Johnson's contract situation. The Titans delayed the issue with a band-aid solution before 2010, but Johnson and the Titans are currently locked in a standoff that could extend into the regular season if the Titans don't blink.

Maurice Jones-Drew

Height: 5-8 Weight: 205 College: UCLA   Draft: 2006/2 (60)   Born: 23-Mar-1985   Age: 26 Risk: Red

Year	Team	G	Runs	Yds	Yd/R	TD	FUM	DVOA	Rk	DYAR	Rk	YAR	Suc%	Rec	Pass	Yds	C%	Yd/C	TD	DVOA	Rk	DYAR	Rk
2008	JAC	16	197	824	4.2	12	5	4.4%	18	112	18	107	46%	62	75	565	83%	9.1	2	43.8%	4	220	1
2009	JAC	16	312	1391	4.5	15	2	3.5%	22	167	11	204	49%	53	71	374	75%	7.1	1	4.9%	27	77	16
2010	JAC	14	299	1324	4.4	5	3	9.4%	9	238	4	223	51%	34	44	317	77%	9.3	2	29.4%	9	98	13
2011	JAC		302	1413	4.7	12		14.8%						35	46	251	76%	7.2	1	13.2%			

MJD has spent the bulk of this offseason telling everyone that his knee feels great. Of course, he also said at the end of last season, on the Jaguars official website, that he's not supposed to tell people if he's hurting. Which of those quotes do you believe in? The words "bone-on-bone" injury are likely to make you hesitant to snatch him in your fantasy league this year, but aside from that pesky lack of touchdowns, Jones-Drew was every bit as good as he's been the last few years. Add it up and you've got a classic pick that can decide a fantasy league. Flip your coin wisely.

Felix Jones

Height: 5-10 Weight: 207 College: Arkansas   Draft: 2008/1 (22)   Born: 8-May-1987   Age: 24 Risk: Green

Year	Team	G	Runs	Yds	Yd/R	TD	FUM	DVOA	Rk	DYAR	Rk	YAR	Suc%	Rec	Pass	Yds	C%	Yd/C	TD	DVOA	Rk	DYAR	Rk
2008	DAL	6	30	266	8.9	3	0	81.8%	--	118	--	119	73%	2	2	10	100%	5.0	0	6.2%	--	2	--
2009	DAL	14	116	685	5.9	3	2	17.0%	5	115	21	114	46%	19	22	119	86%	6.3	0	-13.1%	--	1	--
2010	DAL	16	185	800	4.3	1	2	8.2%	10	124	10	116	50%	48	53	450	92%	9.4	1	35.4%	7	138	9
2011	DAL		187	782	4.2	6		-2.6%						33	45	315	73%	9.5	1	26.0%			

By staying healthy for 16 games while carving out the lead role in the Cowboys' backfield, Jones calmed fears surrounding his fragility. Those DVOA figures show that Jones was effective when he got the ball, but Jason Garrett has said that he doesn't see Jones as a "feature back," suggesting that his workload might top out around 250 touches. They already took Jones off kick returns, where he had been effective during his first two seasons. He can obviously be valuable getting 15 touches per game, but it's hard to see that as a victory for the player personnel side, who took Jones directly before Rashard Mendenhall and Chris Johnson in the first round of the legendary 2008 running back draft class. Of the seven backs taken in the first two rounds that year, the Cowboys appear to have ended up with the least valuable of the bunch.

Julius Jones   Height: 5-10   Weight: 210 College: Notre Dame   Draft: 2004/2 (43)   Born: 14-Aug-1981   Age: 30 Risk: #N/A

Year	Team	G	Runs	Yds	Yd/R	TD	FUM	DVOA	Rk	DYAR	Rk	YAR	Suc%	Rec	Pass	Yds	C%	Yd/C	TD	DVOA	Rk	DYAR	Rk
2008	SEA	15	158	698	4.4	2	4	-10.1%	43	-9	42	-1	39%	14	25	66	56%	4.7	0	-53.1%	51	-56	50
2009	SEA	14	177	663	3.7	2	0	-3.8%	35	35	36	18	44%	35	43	232	81%	6.6	2	-10.2%	42	9	41
2010	2TM	12	60	223	3.7	0	1	-16.2%	--	-19	--	-26	38%	17	22	59	77%	3.5	0	-51.1%	--	-42	--

Jones found a bonus life in his stint with the Saints, playing an important role in the playoff game against his former team, the Seahawks. He was in black and gold because of the raft of injuries that hammered the Saints backfield. Another plague of strains and pulls is probably the only way Jones sees the field in 2011, regardless of team.

Taiwan Jones   Height: 6-0   Weight: 194 College: Eastern Washington Draft: 2011/4 (125)   Born: 26-Jul-1988   Age: 23 Risk: Green

Year	Team	G	Runs	Yds	Yd/R	TD	FUM	DVOA	Rk	DYAR	Rk	YAR	Suc%	Rec	Pass	Yds	C%	Yd/C	TD	DVOA	Rk	DYAR	Rk
2011	OAK		27	126	4.6	1		19.7%						10	13	75	77%	7.5	0	-12.7%			

Jones was a supreme burner for the EWU Eagles, who still won the FCS Championship game despite Jones being out for the final two playoff contests with a broken bone in his foot. But when Jones was on the field, he amazed with the kind of speed you'd expect the Raiders to go after. Once his foot healed, Jones put on a serious show for several NFL teams at a Northern California pro day by running sub-4.3 times on some clocks. Jones will have to overcome his injury history and a worrisome tendency to fumble (17 in his final two seasons at EWU), but the upside could see him having a Jamaal Charles-style effect on Oakland's offense.

Thomas Jones   Height: 5-10   Weight: 220 College: Virginia   Draft: 2000/1 (7)   Born: 19-Aug-1978   Age: 33 Risk: Green

Year	Team	G	Runs	Yds	Yd/R	TD	FUM	DVOA	Rk	DYAR	Rk	YAR	Suc%	Rec	Pass	Yds	C%	Yd/C	TD	DVOA	Rk	DYAR	Rk
2008	NYJ	16	290	1312	4.5	13	2	11.9%	7	252	5	262	54%	36	42	207	86%	5.8	2	12.7%	17	71	15
2009	NYJ	16	331	1402	4.2	14	2	-1.1%	32	102	23	161	44%	10	18	58	56%	5.8	0	-36.7%	--	-24	--
2010	KC	16	245	896	3.7	6	3	-17.5%	43	-94	45	-86	43%	14	20	122	70%	8.7	0	13.1%	--	29	--
2011	KC		151	543	3.6	7		1.7%						9	12	68	75%	7.6	0	17.4%			

Jones' job is supposedly to bull through in short-yardage situations, but he's found himself lost in enemy defensive lines too often. In 2010, Jones' actual function was to swoop in and poach red zone carries from Jamaal Charles … but even here, Charles left Jones wanting, getting half Jones' carries (42 to 21) but blowing him away in red-zone DVOA, 27.1% to -11.2%, and destroying him in value over average on goal-line carries. The Chiefs have confirmed that Jones will be back in 2011, but the Mr. Inside/Mr. Outside concept Todd Haley had with Jones and Charles last season may be a thing of the past — Jones looks likely to be a short-yardage back, and if he can't get it over more effectively this season, maybe not even that. In 2010, the Chiefs' offensive line ranked fourth in Adjusted Line Yards, but gained almost half a yard more in running back yards, and we know where most of that came from.

Deji Karim   Height: 5-9   Weight: 210 College: Southen Illinois   Draft: 2010/6 (180)   Born: 18-Nov-1986   Age: 25 Risk: Yellow

Year	Team	G	Runs	Yds	Yd/R	TD	FUM	DVOA	Rk	DYAR	Rk	YAR	Suc%	Rec	Pass	Yds	C%	Yd/C	TD	DVOA	Rk	DYAR	Rk
2010	JAC	11	35	160	4.6	0	1	-5.6%	--	4	--	8	51%	3	7	10	43%	3.3	0	-71.0%	--	-25	--
2011	JAC		42	228	5.5	1		15.4%						9	10	86	90%	9.6	1	16.5%			

Abdul-Gafar Olatokumbo Ayodeji Lamar Karim, who goes by "Deji" thanks to a large bribe by computer database creators, was Jacksonville's main kickoff returner last year and reeled off a few big gains in limited time on offense. Rashad Jennings has the first claim on any missed Maurice Jones-Drew carries, but Karim showed enough last year that he could potentially get a few more carries this season

John Kuhn

Height: 6-0   Weight: 255   College: Shippensburg   Draft: 2006/ (FA)   Born: 9-Sep-1982   Age: 29   Risk: Red

Year	Team	G	Runs	Yds	Yd/R	TD	FUM	DVOA	Rk	DYAR	Rk	YAR	Suc%	Rec	Pass	Yds	C%	Yd/C	TD	DVOA	Rk	DYAR	Rk
2008	GB	16	8	10	1.3	1	0	-7.6%	--	1	--	-3	63%	4	7	21	57%	5.3	2	34.5%	--	21	--
2009	GB	14	8	18	2.3	1	0	-13.6%	--	-2	--	-4	38%	7	7	47	100%	6.7	2	112.3%	--	46	--
2010	GB	16	84	281	3.3	4	1	1.3%	--	43	--	33	60%	15	18	97	83%	6.5	2	33.4%	--	50	--
2011	GB		27	105	3.8	2		7.3%						16	18	106	89%	6.6	0	4.6%			

Kuhn in goal-to-go situations: 10 carries, eight yards, three touchdowns, five stuffs for no gain … the Kuhn as Committee Back phenomenon played itself out in the first half of the season. He had just 22 carries from Week 11 until the end of the regular season, most of them as a short-yardage back. As fun as those jumbo formations are to watch, Kuhn fits best as a conventional fullback who catches a pass or two per game and runs the fullback give every two weeks. With James Starks emerging, Ryan Grant healthy, and Alex Green on the roster, Kuhn should spend most of his time blocking.

Mikel Leshoure

Height: 6-0   Weight: 227   College: Illinois   Draft: 2011/2 (57)   Born: 30-Mar-1990   Age: 21   Risk: N/A

Somewhat fast for his size (Speed Score: 105.0) and relatively strong, Mikel Leshoure could create a nice balance with the smaller, faster Jahvid Best in Detroit. In two years as a featured back at Illinois, Leshoure rushed for almost 2,400 yards and a decent plus-7.9 Adj. POE. He provided a lovely combination of speed and power at the collegiate level, but the issue for him will be proving he has enough of one or the other feature. Is he fast enough to make up for average strength? Is he strong enough to make up for average speed? Note: Lost for year with Achilles injury on August 8.

Marshawn Lynch

Height: 5-11   Weight: 215   College: California   Draft: 2007/1 (12)   Born: 22-Apr-1986   Age: 25   Risk: Green

Year	Team	G	Runs	Yds	Yd/R	TD	FUM	DVOA	Rk	DYAR	Rk	YAR	Suc%	Rec	Pass	Yds	C%	Yd/C	TD	DVOA	Rk	DYAR	Rk
2008	BUF	15	250	1036	4.1	8	2	-1.1%	25	77	24	105	46%	47	67	300	70%	6.4	1	-12.5%	43	5	42
2009	BUF	13	120	450	3.8	2	3	-17.3%	46	-40	45	-35	38%	28	37	179	76%	6.4	0	-25.8%	51	-24	51
2010	2TM	16	202	737	3.6	6	4	-14.7%	41	-53	41	-38	44%	22	26	145	85%	6.6	0	-7.6%	44	9	46
2011	SEA		164	611	3.7	3		-17.1%						12	18	90	67%	7.5	0	-9.9%			

So what's your favorite YouTube version of Lynch's 67-yard, tackle-breaking, earthquake-causing touchdown against the Saints in the playoffs? Super Marshawn — er, Mario — getting the star and becoming invulnerable? Marshawn playing Tecmo Bowl? Assorted fan cams shot from dozens of cell phones? That play, maybe the most memorable in team history, showed off the one thing Lynch does very well: break tackles. Lynch's broken tackle rate of 16.1 percent was second among running backs in the regular season. Once you get past that, though, there's not much to like here. In four seasons, Lynch has yet to post a positive rushing DVOA. His receiving DVOA has also been negative for three seasons in a row. Last year, Lynch almost pulled off a reverse triple crown of sorts, finishing next to last in red-zone DVOA, short-yardage DVOA, and Stuff Rate. Obviously, the struggles of Seattle's offensive line had a lot to do with that, but the bottom line is that Lynch has never been a particularly productive runner. He just happens to take a lot of defenders down with him.

Laurence Maroney

Height: 5-11   Weight: 210   College: Minnesota   Draft: 2006/1 (21)   Born: 5-Feb-1985   Age: 26   Risk: N/A

Year	Team	G	Runs	Yds	Yd/R	TD	FUM	DVOA	Rk	DYAR	Rk	YAR	Suc%	Rec	Pass	Yds	C%	Yd/C	TD	DVOA	Rk	DYAR	Rk
2008	NE	3	28	93	3.3	0	0	-10.0%	--	-2	--	-4	54%	0	0	0	0%	0.0	0	0.0%	--	0	--
2009	NE	15	194	757	3.9	9	4	1.2%	29	84	24	102	52%	14	17	99	82%	7.1	0	-3.7%	--	9	--
2010	DEN	4	36	74	2.1	0	1	-62.2%	--	-85	--	-100	28%	4	7	50	57%	12.5	0	24.6%	--	14	--

Unable to make a go of it despite opposing defenses reading pass most of the time, Maroney and his too-high running style may not be long for the NFL; the remaining hope is that another team will want to see if there's anything to a guy Bill Belichick once drafted in the first round.

Ryan Mathews Height: 6-0 Weight: 218 College: Fresno State Draft: 2010/1 (12) Born: 1-May-1987 Age: 24 Risk: Green

Year	Team	G	Runs	Yds	Yd/R	TD	FUM	DVOA	Rk	DYAR	Rk	YAR	Suc%	Rec	Pass	Yds	C%	Yd/C	TD	DVOA	Rk	DYAR	Rk
2010	SD	12	158	678	4.3	7	5	1.9%	18	64	23	70	46%	22	26	145	85%	6.6	0	-19.4%	49	-8	49
2011	SD		217	920	4.2	8		0.1%						38	49	376	78%	9.9	1	24.4%			

It's rough to be your team's most effective back as a rookie and still fall wildly short of expectations, but that's how highly-regarded Mathews was coming out of Fresno State. Expected to be a lead back from day one, Mathews struggled with ball security, pass blocking (leading to some "Goddamit, Donald" moments along the way) and a high ankle sprain that limited the explosiveness which caused A.J. Smith to trade up to get him with the 12th overall pick. It's tough to know what to expect from Mathews in 2011 — we've heard everything from a new commitment to making him the lead back ahead of Mike Tolbert, to more of a committee approach that would give the ball to the guy with the hot hand.

LeSean McCoy Height: 5-11 Weight: 198 College: Pittsburgh Draft: 2009/2 (53) Born: 12-Jul-1988 Age: 23 Risk: Yellow

Year	Team	G	Runs	Yds	Yd/R	TD	FUM	DVOA	Rk	DYAR	Rk	YAR	Suc%	Rec	Pass	Yds	C%	Yd/C	TD	DVOA	Rk	DYAR	Rk
2009	PHI	16	155	637	4.1	4	2	-4.5%	36	25	37	13	46%	40	55	308	73%	7.7	0	-11.2%	44	8	43
2010	PHI	15	207	1080	5.2	7	2	17.8%	5	224	6	206	49%	78	90	592	87%	7.6	2	20.0%	17	179	2
2011	PHI		209	1100	5.3	8		19.9%						75	103	655	73%	8.7	3	19.5%			

McCoy's breakout season came with some help. Not only did he get the boost from Michael Vick that we discussed in the Eagles chapter, but Leonard Weaver's gruesome knee injury in Week 1 just about forced the Eagles to give McCoy as many reps as he could handle. His pass-blocking improved during the season, too, which is a great sign going forward. He should benefit from a full season with Vick in 2011, but his numbers might end up being disappointing. He had a +10.6 Plus-Minus rate, three higher than any other running back. That's unsustainable, even for a running back that catches virtually all dumpoffs. (Consider that Brian Westbrook had just one season with more than 50 targets and a catch rate above 75 percent.)

Darren McFadden Height: 6-1 Weight: 211 College: Arkansas Draft: 2008/1 (4) Born: 27-Aug-1987 Age: 24 Risk: Green

Year	Team	G	Runs	Yds	Yd/R	TD	FUM	DVOA	Rk	DYAR	Rk	YAR	Suc%	Rec	Pass	Yds	C%	Yd/C	TD	DVOA	Rk	DYAR	Rk
2008	OAK	13	113	499	4.4	4	3	-8.9%	40	-2	40	26	38%	29	39	285	77%	9.8	0	33.3%	7	107	10
2009	OAK	12	104	357	3.4	1	5	-30.7%	49	-87	49	-67	38%	21	35	245	60%	11.7	0	-3.9%	35	20	36
2010	OAK	13	223	1157	5.2	7	4	4.6%	14	112	14	121	42%	47	61	507	77%	10.8	3	40.8%	4	172	3
2011	OAK		193	832	4.3	5		-4.9%						54	70	520	77%	9.6	2	24.7%			

The light finally went on for McFadden, aided as it may have been by Tom Cable's blocking concepts. Not only did McFadden show new power between the tackles, but he showed a consistent ability to get his scary speed on the field in a useful fashion. McFadden lost his penchant for negative plays at the same time became one of the better threats to hit seams and make plays outside. He had one 100-yard game in his first two seasons, and six in 2010. Now, the challenge for McFadden is to keep making tracks with a different set of blocking concepts — and several new linemen in front of him.

Willis McGahee Height: 6-0 Weight: 228 College: Miami Draft: 2003/1 (23) Born: 21-Oct-1981 Age: 30 Risk: Yellow

Year	Team	G	Runs	Yds	Yd/R	TD	FUM	DVOA	Rk	DYAR	Rk	YAR	Suc%	Rec	Pass	Yds	C%	Yd/C	TD	DVOA	Rk	DYAR	Rk
2008	BAL	13	170	671	3.9	7	3	3.9%	20	86	21	91	46%	24	32	173	75%	7.2	0	-22.0%	47	-15	46
2009	BAL	16	109	544	5.0	12	1	19.7%	3	131	17	155	55%	15	22	85	68%	5.7	2	-11.4%	--	3	--
2010	BAL	15	100	380	3.8	5	2	-7.1%	32	6	33	-2	49%	14	17	55	82%	3.9	1	-42.5%	--	-27	--
2011	DEN		143	594	4.1	5		-4.8%						22	32	220	69%	10.0	1	-14.4%			

The Broncos plan on using McGahee as their short-yardage and goal-line runner, but of course, there's no indication that he's any better or more consistent at the goal line than any other running back. Last year, McGahee had three touchdowns on nine goal-line carries, 1.1 fewer than what we would expect in the situations where he was given the ball. He also converted only three of nine opportunities on third or fourth down. In McGahee's defense, he was better in both situations in both 2008 and 2009 but again, that just helps point out the year-to-year inconsistency.

Joe McKnight

Height: 6-0   Weight: 198   College: USC   Draft: 2010/4 (112)   Born: 16-Apr-1988   Age: 23   Risk: Green

Year	Team	G	Runs	Yds	Yd/R	TD	FUM	DVOA	Rk	DYAR	Rk	YAR	Suc%	Rec	Pass	Yds	C%	Yd/C	TD	DVOA	Rk	DYAR	Rk
2010	NYJ	9	39	189	4.8	0	0	13.2%	--	34	--	51	59%	3	4	20	75%	6.7	0	48.5%	--	15	--
2011	NYJ		62	294	4.8	1		10.1%						9	12	41	75%	4.6	0	-20.3%			

McKnight was a punching bag for veteran players and coaches alike in several episodes of Hard Knocks, thanks to a combination of sloppy play and apparent inattention to detail, and his struggles carried over into the regular season, where McKnight was a healthy scratch for seven games. In a surprise start for the final game against Buffalo, however, McKnight responded with a 32-carry, 158-yard performance. The coaching staff seems to think that is a taste of things to come, as McKnight is tentatively being penciled in as the third-down back. More likely, LaDainian Tomlinson will hold off McKnight for one more year, leaving nothing but return duties and a few spot carries.

Rashard Mendenhall

Height: 5-10   Weight: 225   College: Illinois   Draft: 2008/1 (23)   Born: 19-Jun-1987   Age: 24   Risk: Yellow

Year	Team	G	Runs	Yds	Yd/R	TD	FUM	DVOA	Rk	DYAR	Rk	YAR	Suc%	Rec	Pass	Yds	C%	Yd/C	TD	DVOA	Rk	DYAR	Rk
2008	PIT	4	19	58	3.1	0	0	-20.8%	--	-8	--	-10	26%	2	3	17	67%	8.5	0	24.7%	--	5	--
2009	PIT	16	242	1108	4.6	7	3	-0.8%	31	80	25	107	46%	25	32	261	78%	10.4	1	55.6%	1	117	5
2010	PIT	16	324	1273	3.9	13	2	-2.8%	26	77	22	81	44%	23	34	167	68%	7.3	0	-2.3%	39	23	39
2011	PIT		327	1374	4.2	12		2.8%						31	38	286	82%	9.2	1	33.5%			

Mendenhall got most of the carries that we projected for him in *FOA 2010*, although he wasn't quite as good as we projected. There were some worries that Isaac Redman would vulture his touchdowns, but the Steelers handed Mendenhall the rock 21 times inside the five-yard line. The controversy about his Twitter comments after Osama bin Laden's death probably teaches us two lessons: First, that it is hard to clearly get your point across in 140 characters, and second, that it would be a good idea for football players to avoid discussing politics on Twitter. That means you too, Jay Feely.

Mewelde Moore

Height: 5-11   Weight: 210   College: Tulane   Draft: 2004/4 (119)   Born: 24-Jul-1982   Age: 29   Risk: Yellow

Year	Team	G	Runs	Yds	Yd/R	TD	FUM	DVOA	Rk	DYAR	Rk	YAR	Suc%	Rec	Pass	Yds	C%	Yd/C	TD	DVOA	Rk	DYAR	Rk
2008	PIT	16	140	588	4.2	5	1	14.3%	6	139	14	105	51%	40	53	320	75%	8.0	1	4.6%	25	56	21
2009	PIT	16	35	118	3.4	0	0	-25.5%	--	-24	--	-21	40%	21	31	153	68%	7.3	2	16.1%	14	49	24
2010	PIT	15	33	99	3.0	0	0	-37.2%	--	-36	--	-35	21%	26	31	205	84%	7.9	0	17.0%	20	53	26
2011	PIT		28	113	4.0	1		-3.5%						36	47	336	77%	9.3	2	23.0%			

Moore is the prototypical third-down back. He's a more efficient pass receiver than he is a runner, and in both of the last two years he had more pass targets on third down than he did on first and second combined. His pass blocking has also improved over the last couple of years.

Knowshon Moreno

Height: 5-11   Weight: 217   College: Georgia   Draft: 2009/1 (12)   Born: 16-Jul-1987   Age: 24   Risk: Green

Year	Team	G	Runs	Yds	Yd/R	TD	FUM	DVOA	Rk	DYAR	Rk	YAR	Suc%	Rec	Pass	Yds	C%	Yd/C	TD	DVOA	Rk	DYAR	Rk
2009	DEN	16	247	947	3.8	7	4	-4.9%	37	40	35	62	50%	28	41	213	68%	7.6	2	-13.8%	45	0	45
2010	DEN	13	182	779	4.3	5	4	-4.4%	28	31	28	45	43%	37	48	372	77%	10.1	3	35.9%	6	131	10
2011	DEN		176	778	4.4	5		8.4%						25	38	198	66%	7.9	0	-12.4%			

After missing his second NFL preseason with a hamstring injury, Moreno tried to play catch-up and seemed out of place far more often than any former first-round pick should be. With a horrible defense forcing the Broncos to go pass-happy last year, Moreno was not often allowed to get into a rushing rhythm, to whatever degree that's applicable. Where Moreno did shine was as a receiver in the Broncos' impressively efficient passing game. Moreno's future is cloudy; there are nebulous questions raised by a speculative press as to his "big time-ness" and the acquisition of Willis McGahee as a touchdown vulture seems to confirm those concerns. But teams with needs along the roster aren't generally well-served by stacking certain positions, and Moreno should get another shot in an offense built to support a cohesive running game.

Maurice Morris   Height: 5-11   Weight: 202   College: Oregon   Draft: 2002/2 (54)   Born: 1-Dec-1979   Age: 32   Risk: Red

Year	Team	G	Runs	Yds	Yd/R	TD	FUM	DVOA	Rk	DYAR	Rk	YAR	Suc%	Rec	Pass	Yds	C%	Yd/C	TD	DVOA	Rk	DYAR	Rk
2008	SEA	13	132	574	4.3	0	1	-1.1%	24	38	32	25	45%	19	27	136	70%	7.2	2	16.8%	13	45	28
2009	DET	14	93	384	4.1	2	1	-5.3%	--	12	--	-5	41%	26	38	210	68%	8.1	0	8.6%	23	44	26
2010	DET	14	90	336	3.7	5	1	4.7%	--	52	--	43	46%	25	31	170	81%	6.8	0	11.2%	26	43	30
2011	DET		44	177	4.0	1		10.2%						27	36	186	75%	6.9	1	-7.0%			

Morris began absorbing carries from Jahvid Best in Week 10 last year, after Scott Linehan realized that a 190-pound rookie with turf toe wasn't a prototypical workhorse runner. Morris performed with his usual bland efficiency for a few weeks, rushed for 109 yards in the Week 15 win over the Buccaneers, then hit the wall, rushing 24 times for 43 yards (and two touchdowns) in the final two games. Mikel Leshoure was expected to provide the thunder to Best's lightning this year, but with Leshoure hurt, Morris may once again be miscast as a big back.

Sammy Morris   Height: 6-0   Weight: 220   College: Texas Tech   Draft: 2000/5 (156)   Born: 23-Mar-1977   Age: 34   Risk: Green

Year	Team	G	Runs	Yds	Yd/R	TD	FUM	DVOA	Rk	DYAR	Rk	YAR	Suc%	Rec	Pass	Yds	C%	Yd/C	TD	DVOA	Rk	DYAR	Rk
2008	NE	13	156	727	4.7	7	1	14.9%	5	166	8	154	49%	17	24	161	71%	9.5	0	18.0%	--	42	--
2009	NE	12	73	319	4.4	2	2	-5.6%	--	10	--	7	51%	19	27	180	70%	9.5	0	30.4%	6	66	20
2010	NE	16	20	56	2.8	0	0	-1.6%	--	7	--	4	50%	7	12	77	58%	11.0	0	-0.6%	--	10	--
2011			15	60	4.0	0		0.0%						6	10	60	60%	10.0	--	0.0%			

Morris has milked every drop of production he could out of his limited skills in the last 11 seasons. He is coming off his worst statistical year since the Bills cast him in a strict special-teams role in 2001-04 (oh, those wacky Bills), and the Patriots just drafted two running backs, one of whom (Steven Ridley) can do many of the things Morris did. Last season really was a transition year, and many old role players like Morris and Kevin Faulk must now be swept aside as the Patriots reinvent themselves.

DeMarco Murray   Height: 6-0   Weight: 213   College: Oklahoma   Draft: 2011/3 (71)   Born: 12-Feb-1988   Age: 23   Risk: Yellow

Year	Team	G	Runs	Yds	Yd/R	TD	FUM	DVOA	Rk	DYAR	Rk	YAR	Suc%	Rec	Pass	Yds	C%	Yd/C	TD	DVOA	Rk	DYAR	Rk
2011	DAL		88	415	4.7	1		7.6%						48	62	462	77%	9.6	0	25.8%			

That DeMarco Murray was drafted in the third round despite being made of paper-mache speaks to his overall skill set, and he has the highest Speed Score of the Class of 2011 at 112.6. Murray missed games due to a dislocated knee suffered his freshman year and a severely torn hamstring suffered his sophomore year. He battled ankle and hamstring issues throughout his final two seasons. Murray never quite regained the explosiveness he showed in 2007 pre-injury, when he gained 764 yards (6.0 per carry) and posted a plus-18.9 Adj. POE. In his final three years in crimson and cream, he rushed for 2,921 yards (4.6 per carry, 37 touchdowns) and a plus-15.2 Adj. POE. There could be an opportunity in Dallas for quite a few carries considering Felix Jones' fragility and how indecisive Tashard Choice looked last year, but Murray was already struggling with hamstring issues again as we went to press.

Dimitri Nance

Height: 5-10 Weight: 219 College: Arizona State   Draft: 2010/ (FA)   Born: 17-Feb-1988   Age: 23   Risk: Red

Year	Team	G	Runs	Yds	Yd/R	TD	FUM	DVOA	Rk	DYAR	Rk	YAR	Suc%	Rec	Pass	Yds	C%	Yd/C	TD	DVOA	Rk	DYAR	Rk
2010	GB	12	36	95	2.6	0	0	-28.6%	–	-31	–	-35	44%	3	4	30	75%	10.0	0	35.6%	–	12	–
2011	GB		29	116	3.9	2		-8.3%						5	6	36	83%	7.2	0	-2.0%			

Yet another undrafted rookie who pitched in for the Packers. Nance rushed for 795 yards in his senior season at Arizona State, spent 2010 training camp with the Falcons, signed with the Packers in September, and got some late-season playing time when Ryan Grant and James Starks were both hurt. He's a compact bowling-ball type who, like Grant and Starks, is a marginal receiver and blocker. No team in the world needs three of these guys.

Jerious Norwood

Height: 6-0   Weight: 205 College: Mississippi State   Draft: 2006/3 (79)   Born: 29-Jul-1983   Age: 28   Risk: Yellow

Year	Team	G	Runs	Yds	Yd/R	TD	FUM	DVOA	Rk	DYAR	Rk	YAR	Suc%	Rec	Pass	Yds	C%	Yd/C	TD	DVOA	Rk	DYAR	Rk
2008	ATL	16	95	489	5.1	4	1	7.1%	–	57	–	72	41%	36	54	338	67%	9.4	2	5.0%	23	55	22
2009	ATL	10	76	252	3.3	0	1	-9.8%	–	-3	–	-5	43%	19	22	186	86%	9.8	1	57.5%	–	86	–
2010	ATL	2	2	8	4.0	0	0	73.0%	–	9	–	6	100%	1	3	9	33%	9.0	0	-40.8%	–	-4	–
2011	STL		48	179	3.7	2		-7.6%						9	13	70	69%	7.7	0	-30.0%			

Repeated injuries have prevented Norwood from living up to our high hopes for his career. He managed to suit up for only a dozen games over the past two seasons. Norwood doesn't rely on cuts, and he has had a long time to rehab (knee injury was in week 2), so if he can stay healthy he can still salvage something of his career in Missouri. But does he have any confidence left?

Adrian Peterson

Height: 6-2   Weight: 217 College: Oklahoma   Draft: 2007/1 (7)   Born: 21-Mar-1985   Age: 26   Risk: Green

Year	Team	G	Runs	Yds	Yd/R	TD	FUM	DVOA	Rk	DYAR	Rk	YAR	Suc%	Rec	Pass	Yds	C%	Yd/C	TD	DVOA	Rk	DYAR	Rk
2008	MIN	16	363	1760	4.8	10	9	-0.3%	22	121	17	172	46%	21	39	125	54%	6.0	0	-46.5%	50	-70	51
2009	MIN	16	314	1383	4.4	18	7	3.2%	23	165	12	131	46%	43	57	436	75%	10.1	0	15.7%	15	90	8
2010	MIN	15	283	1298	4.6	12	2	10.6%	7	229	5	225	45%	36	50	341	72%	9.5	1	20.0%	16	93	15
2011	MIN		340	1601	4.7	12		11.5%						27	37	193	73%	7.1	1	12.8%			

Coordinator Bill Musgrave confirmed in early June that his offense will flow through Peterson. "We'll major in giving the ball to Adrian," Musgrave said, noting that the Vikings will minor in Percy Harvin screens and take a few electives in women's studies. Michael Turner's ankle and groin tried to leap from his body to warn Peterson of what was coming, but to no avail. Peterson has had just three 100-yard games after Week 8 in the last two years, sprinkling in some 13-carry, 19-yard and 14-carry, 31-yard late-season efforts during that same span. But there is no reason to worry about his workload, because he is absolutely, unquestionably 100 percent indestructible and will play forever. Granted, the Vikings have little choice but to force-feed Peterson this season; it's just sad that they got themselves into this mess.

Clinton Portis

Height: 5-11 Weight: 205 College: Miami   Draft: 2002/2 (51)   Born: 1-Sep-1981   Age: 30   Risk: N/A

Year	Team	G	Runs	Yds	Yd/R	TD	FUM	DVOA	Rk	DYAR	Rk	YAR	Suc%	Rec	Pass	Yds	C%	Yd/C	TD	DVOA	Rk	DYAR	Rk
2008	WAS	16	342	1487	4.3	9	3	11.7%	8	285	3	233	48%	28	36	218	78%	7.8	0	15.3%	15	54	23
2009	WAS	8	124	494	4.0	1	1	-16.5%	45	-39	44	-7	40%	9	12	57	75%	6.3	1	19.9%	–	21	–
2010	WAS	5	54	227	4.2	2	0	7.3%	–	35	–	41	48%	5	9	55	56%	11.0	0	40.8%	–	22	–

Portis suffered a separated groin against the Eagles in Week 4. Let that one sink in for a second. An attempted comeback after six weeks produced five carries before Portis hobbled off, done for the year. Two injury-riddled years have caused most folks to write Portis off, but there's still something here. When he's been healthy enough to play over that timeframe, he's been a productive back. Although he's seemingly been in the league for an eternity, that age line above isn't a typo: He turns 30 in September. And while Portis has probably lost a step as a runner, he remains one of the league's best pass blockers at halfback. Spotted as a third-down back,

Portis could very well be a very valuable player. If some team put him and Jerome Harrison together in a platoon, they could have one of the best running back combinations in football for about $4 million.

Isaac Redman
Height: 6-0   Weight: 230   College: Bowie State   Draft: 2009/ (FA)   Born: 10-Nov-1984   Age: 27   Risk: Yellow

Year	Team	G	Runs	Yds	Yd/R	TD	FUM	DVOA	Rk	DYAR	Rk	YAR	Suc%	Rec	Pass	Yds	C%	Yd/C	TD	DVOA	Rk	DYAR	Rk
2010	PIT	16	52	247	4.8	0	2	-1.3%	--	20	--	13	58%	9	10	72	90%	8.0	2	101.4%	--	55	--
2011	PIT		63	277	4.4	2		4.4%						24	28	202	86%	8.4	1	9.5%			

We're all obsessed with speed, speed, speed, but there are other attributes that are useful in a running back. Redman doesn't dance in the backfield, he doesn't go down after first contact, he's a decent pass blocker, and he's surprisingly nimble given that he may be the slowest halfback in the league. The Steelers used him as a short-yardage specialist but not as a goal-line specialist: Rashard Mendenhall got 21 carries inside the five-yard line, and Redman had only three.

Dominic Rhodes
Height: 5-9   Weight: 203   College: Midwestern State   Draft: 2001/ (FA)   Born: 17-Jan-1979   Age: 32   Risk: N/A

Year	Team	G	Runs	Yds	Yd/R	TD	FUM	DVOA	Rk	DYAR	Rk	YAR	Suc%	Rec	Pass	Yds	C%	Yd/C	TD	DVOA	Rk	DYAR	Rk
2008	IND	15	152	538	3.5	6	0	-4.9%	36	25	37	19	49%	45	59	302	76%	6.7	3	2.2%	29	54	24
2010	IND	3	37	172	4.6	0	1	-2.4%	--	10	--	7	51%	1	4	4	25%	4.0	0	-89.2%	--	-18	--

One last hurrah for the former Colt who seemingly was out of football following his former last hurrah with the Colts in 2008. Instead he was playing at a high level in the UFL and earned another return trip to Indianapolis. Rhodes actually played a crucial role in helping the Colts make the playoffs, as the team's leading rusher in must-win games in Week 16 and 17. The magic ran out in the playoffs against the tough Jets defense. If this is an end for Rhodes, eight years, over 3,000 yards, and a Super Bowl are a pretty good career for an undrafted player out of Midwestern State.

Ray Rice
Height: 5-8   Weight: 199   College: Rutgers   Draft: 2008/2 (55)   Born: 22-Jan-1987   Age: 24   Risk: Yellow

Year	Team	G	Runs	Yds	Yd/R	TD	FUM	DVOA	Rk	DYAR	Rk	YAR	Suc%	Rec	Pass	Yds	C%	Yd/C	TD	DVOA	Rk	DYAR	Rk
2008	BAL	13	107	454	4.2	0	1	-2.5%	30	25	36	18	42%	33	43	273	77%	8.3	0	25.8%	9	81	13
2009	BAL	16	254	1339	5.3	7	3	16.8%	6	249	3	268	51%	78	102	702	77%	9.0	1	7.5%	24	117	6
2010	BAL	16	307	1220	4.0	5	0	0.8%	19	115	13	128	46%	63	83	556	76%	8.8	1	14.4%	21	120	11
2011	BAL		313	1409	4.5	10		7.8%						60	83	532	72%	8.9	2	10.3%			

The Ravens improved their offensive line. They brought in Vonta Leach to block. They've got new receivers to stretch the field and move the safeties back. Everything should be set for Ray Rice to rebound from last year's disappointing numbers. The Ravens have also said that they don't plan to pull Rice at the goal line the way they did when Willis McGahee was on the team. That's good for his fantasy value.

Stevan Ridley
Height: 6-0   Weight: 223   College: LSU   Draft: 2011/3 (73)   Born: 27-Jan-1989   Age: 22   Risk: Green

Year	Team	G	Runs	Yds	Yd/R	TD	FUM	DVOA	Rk	DYAR	Rk	YAR	Suc%	Rec	Pass	Yds	C%	Yd/C	TD	DVOA	Rk	DYAR	Rk
2011	NE		57	222	3.9	3		25.2%						11	22	97	50%	8.8	1	-22.0%			

In theory, Stevan Ridley could make for a nice combination of speed, power and durability. Or, he could be neither fast enough nor strong enough to stay in the league. Ridley did not grade out well in the advanced stats: 94.6 Speed Score, plus-0.7 Adj. POE and a terrible 1.52 Highlight Yards per carry. He did not contribute much of anything to the passing game at LSU and looks a bit like a low-ceiling BenJarvus Green-Ellis on paper.

Javon Ringer

Height: 5-9   Weight: 205   College: Michigan State   Draft: 2009/5 (173)   Born: 2-Feb-1987   Age: 24   Risk: Red

Year	Team	G	Runs	Yds	Yd/R	TD	FUM	DVOA	Rk	DYAR	Rk	YAR	Suc%	Rec	Pass	Yds	C%	Yd/C	TD	DVOA	Rk	DYAR	Rk
2009	TEN	7	8	48	6.0	0	0	43.0%	--	16	--	15	50%	0	0	0	0%	0.0	0	0.0%	--	0	--
2010	TEN	16	51	239	4.7	2	0	5.1%	--	25	--	27	37%	7	8	44	88%	6.3	0	20.7%	--	15	--
2011	TEN		51	216	4.2	0		8.5%						12	16	82	75%	6.8	0	-2.2%			

Ringer saw mostly cameo work in 2010 as the Titans' No. 2 rusher, and those carries primarily came only when the Titans wanted to give Chris Johnson a rest. Rookie Jamie Harper likely fills the power back role that Ringer doesn't, so unless Chris Johnson's holdout extends into the regular season, Ringer may have trouble getting into the lineup as the third back without a defined role.

Jacquizz Rodgers

Height: 5-6   Weight: 196   College: Oregon St.   Draft: 2011/5 (145)   Born: 6-Feb-1990   Age: 21   Risk: Blue

Year	Team	G	Runs	Yds	Yd/R	TD	FUM	DVOA	Rk	DYAR	Rk	YAR	Suc%	Rec	Pass	Yds	C%	Yd/C	TD	DVOA	Rk	DYAR	Rk
2011	ATL		33	149	4.5	0		18.9%						15	22	106	68%	7.1	1	31.7%			

With few weapons around him, Pocket Herculizz failed to match an incredible 2009 campaign (1,435 rushing yards, 522 receiving yards, plus-26.9 Adj. POE) in 2010 (just plus-1.7 Adj. POE), and he potentially jumped to the pros simply to avoid the wear and tear of another 25 touches per game in Corvallis. Rodgers doesn't have the top-end speed of the back he was drafted to replace, Jerious Norwood, but is much sturdier, packing a wallop into his 170 pounds. He's also very shifty with a naturally low center of gravity, so he should find a place in the Falcons short passing game.

Bernard Scott

Height: 5-11   Weight: 200   College: Abilene Christian   Draft: 2009/6 (209)   Born: 10-Feb-1984   Age: 27   Risk: Yellow

Year	Team	G	Runs	Yds	Yd/R	TD	FUM	DVOA	Rk	DYAR	Rk	YAR	Suc%	Rec	Pass	Yds	C%	Yd/C	TD	DVOA	Rk	DYAR	Rk
2009	CIN	13	74	321	4.3	0	1	-8.1%	--	1	--	0	43%	5	8	67	63%	13.4	0	62.5%	--	25	--
2010	CIN	16	61	299	4.9	1	0	17.7%	--	70	--	71	54%	11	13	60	85%	5.5	0	-1.9%	--	9	--
2011	CIN		67	286	4.3	0		-0.9%						23	31	172	74%	7.5	0	-11.0%			

Scott has had trouble staying healthy in the NFL, appearing on the injured list with toe, knee, and hamstring problems in various weeks. When he has played, he's been better than Cedric Benson, but its one of those small-sample size performances that you can't quite trust. Still, with Benson not exactly lighting up the world of advanced stats, it would be interesting for the Bengals to give Scott a few more carries and see how he does.

Steve Slaton

Height: 5-9   Weight: 197   College: West Virginia   Draft: 2008/3 (89)   Born: 4-Jan-1986   Age: 26   Risk: Yellow

Year	Team	G	Runs	Yds	Yd/R	TD	FUM	DVOA	Rk	DYAR	Rk	YAR	Suc%	Rec	Pass	Yds	C%	Yd/C	TD	DVOA	Rk	DYAR	Rk
2008	HOU	16	268	1282	4.8	9	3	5.8%	16	166	9	148	44%	50	59	377	85%	7.5	1	-3.8%	37	30	33
2009	HOU	11	131	437	3.3	3	7	-30.8%	50	-115	50	-122	35%	44	55	417	80%	9.5	4	41.8%	3	168	2
2010	HOU	12	19	93	4.9	0	0	10.0%	--	15	--	16	47%	3	4	11	75%	3.7	0	-56.8%	--	-9	--
2011	HOU		33	149	4.5	1		17.2%						15	18	134	83%	8.9	1	-2.9%			

We were cautious last season about the long-term effect of Slaton's January 2010 neck surgery and its effect on his performance. What was clear in 2010 was Slaton had trouble finding and exploiting holes. He didn't have a single carry after Week 5, as Derrick Ward took the carries Arian Foster didn't, and spent the rest of the season as one of the league's worst kick returners. Don't expect him to be more than the Texans' fourth-string running back, if he even makes the team.

Kevin Smith   Height: 6-1   Weight: 217   College: UCF   Draft: 2008/3 (64)   Born: 17-Dec-1986   Age: 25   Risk: N/A

Year	Team	G	Runs	Yds	Yd/R	TD	FUM	DVOA	Rk	DYAR	Rk	YAR	Suc%	Rec	Pass	Yds	C%	Yd/C	TD	DVOA	Rk	DYAR	Rk
2008	DET	16	238	976	4.1	8	2	-0.5%	23	79	23	90	44%	39	54	286	72%	7.3	0	-8.9%	39	15	38
2009	DET	13	217	747	3.4	4	3	-10.7%	43	-18	43	-57	44%	4	57	41	72%	10.3	1	25.7%	7	127	3
2010	DET	6	34	133	3.9	0	1	-25.9%	--	-22	--	-24	29%	11	16	123	69%	11.2	0	39.0%	--	50	--

The Lions made it clear in March that they would not re-sign Smith, then added an exclamation point by drafting Mikel Leshoure. Smith needed ACL surgery in 2009, and his knee was never really healthy last season, though it was a thumb injury that finally shelved him after Week 10. Those 450 carries he absorbed in one season as a 20-year old in Central Florida almost certainly contributed to knee problems that will end his career prematurely and possibly cause lifelong problems, but the NCAA assures us that he should be thankful for having had a scholarship, and if they discover that he managed to earn a few bucks while sacrificing his health to boost his university's image, they promise to only drag his name through the mud a little.

Jason Snelling   Height: 5-11   Weight: 235   College: Virginia   Draft: 2007/7 (244)   Born: 29-Dec-1983   Age: 28   Risk: Yellow

Year	Team	G	Runs	Yds	Yd/R	TD	FUM	DVOA	Rk	DYAR	Rk	YAR	Suc%	Rec	Pass	Yds	C%	Yd/C	TD	DVOA	Rk	DYAR	Rk
2008	ATL	16	15	62	4.1	0	0	9.5%	--	11	--	9	47%	8	11	89	73%	11.1	0	43.9%	--	24	--
2009	ATL	14	142	613	4.3	4	2	1.8%	26	68	29	83	46%	30	39	259	77%	8.6	1	25.6%	8	81	13
2010	ATL	14	87	324	3.7	2	2	-4.5%	--	15	--	25	44%	44	51	303	86%	6.9	3	9.0%	29	60	22
2011	ATL		61	231	3.8	2		-2.6%						41	51	420	80%	10.3	2	17.2%			

Snelling was strong on first-down runs in 2009, which bucked a trend in Atlanta. Last season, Michael Turner's backup struggled mightily on first down (-27.3% DVOA). Snelling is strong but not Turner-strong, and could benefit from a change of scenery and scheme. Snelling became a licensed auto trader during the lockout, so he has the means to pack up and screech out of town with his system up at a moment's notice.

C.J. Spiller   Height: 5-11   Weight: 195   College: Clemson   Draft: 2010/1 (9)   Born: 15-Aug-1987   Age: 24   Risk: Green

Year	Team	G	Runs	Yds	Yd/R	TD	FUM	DVOA	Rk	DYAR	Rk	YAR	Suc%	Rec	Pass	Yds	C%	Yd/C	TD	DVOA	Rk	DYAR	Rk
2010	BUF	14	74	283	3.8	0	2	-10.5%	--	-6	--	-20	43%	24	30	157	80%	6.5	1	12.5%	23	39	33
2011	BUF		97	384	4.0	2		3.5%						35	42	254	83%	7.2	0	-11.2%			

His straight-line speed is apparent whenever Spiller gets a little running room. The trick will be getting Spiller to make his own running room. The Bills targeted Spiller for nine screens or shovel passes, but he produced just 24 yards and one first down on eight receptions. Eight draw plays or shotgun sweeps netted just 27 yards. By the end of the year, even Spiller's kickoff returns were just headlong plunges into the nearest pile. A back like Spiller must be able to generate big plays when coaches are scheming to get him the ball in space. Spiller will remain a role player in 2011, getting a lot of playing time as a slot receiver while spelling Fred Jackson in the backfield. If he doesn't convert his speed into production, he will become the poor man's Reggie Bush, and no one on earth wants that.

Darren Sproles   Height: 5-6   Weight: 181   College: Kansas State   Draft: 2005/4 (130)   Born: 20-Jun-1983   Age: 28   Risk: Yellow

Year	Team	G	Runs	Yds	Yd/R	TD	FUM	DVOA	Rk	DYAR	Rk	YAR	Suc%	Rec	Pass	Yds	C%	Yd/C	TD	DVOA	Rk	DYAR	Rk
2008	SD	16	61	330	5.4	1	1	17.8%	--	64	--	82	49%	29	34	342	85%	11.8	5	73.1%	1	171	4
2009	SD	16	93	343	3.7	3	0	-14.4%	--	-22	--	-2	41%	45	57	497	79%	11.0	4	44.4%	2	181	1
2010	SD	16	50	267	5.3	0	1	-17.4%	--	-16	--	-4	34%	59	75	520	79%	8.8	2	26.9%	11	166	4
2011	NO		40	196	4.9	1		23.6%						62	75	594	83%	9.6	2	23.0%			

The West Coast version of Pocket Hercules will get fairly major money somewhere as a change-of-pace back, but concerns abound regarding his actual effectiveness as anything more. For every game full of "OMG" plays, there's another one in which Sproles gets bottled up behind his defenders and has stats of the "LOL" variety.

This is often the nature of second-level speed backs, but given the Sproles reputation, you'd expect a bit more consistency. Another concern: You want your third-down backs to shoot up in efficiency on those downs, but Sproles generally posts negative DVOA on that down as a runner. However, he's a great third-down receiver, and got a sizeable deal from the New Orleans Saints as Reggie Bush's replacement based on that, on his special teams ability, and the nascent promise of explosiveness that only shows up sometimes. In other words, he's a lot like Bush — both good and bad.

James Starks
Height: 6-2   Weight: 218   College: Buffalo   Draft: 2010/6 (193)   Born: 25-Feb-1986   Age: 25   Risk: Yellow

Year	Team	G	Runs	Yds	Yd/R	TD	FUM	DVOA	Rk	DYAR	Rk	YAR	Suc%	Rec	Pass	Yds	C%	Yd/C	TD	DVOA	Rk	DYAR	Rk
2010	GB	3	29	101	3.5	0	0	6.6%	–	17	–	3	48%	2	4	15	50%	7.5	0	-32.0%	–	-4	–
2011	GB		80	395	4.9	2		29.5%						16	24	127	67%	8.0	0	2.0%			

Starks rushed for 315 yards in four postseason games, averaging 3.9 yards per carry. He was not great, but his 123 yards made a huge difference against the Eagles, and he provided just enough rushing credibility to keep defenses honest. Starks has shown no value as a receiver or big play ability. If he proves that he is a safe, cheap alternative to Ryan Grant in camp, the Packers may dump Grant's salary and name Starks the starter. If not, Starks may be trapped on the bench this season.

LaRod Stephens-Howling
Height: 5-7   Weight: 180   College: Pittsburgh   Draft: 2009/7 (240)   Born: 26-Apr-1987   Age: 24   Risk: Yellow

Year	Team	G	Runs	Yds	Yd/R	TD	FUM	DVOA	Rk	DYAR	Rk	YAR	Suc%	Rec	Pass	Yds	C%	Yd/C	TD	DVOA	Rk	DYAR	Rk
2009	ARI	16	6	15	2.5	0	1	-18.8%	–	-2	–	-3	33%	10	18	83	56%	8.3	1	-25.3%	–	-11	–
2010	ARI	13	23	113	4.9	1	0	9.0%	–	19	–	20	54%	16	22	111	68%	6.9	0	0.2%	–	18	–
2011	ARI		34	139	4.1	0		0.5%						23	30	195	77%	8.5	0	-1.9%			

The return specialist led the league in kickoff return yards last year despite missing three games due to injury. He returned 2 for touchdowns and had another one called back because of holding. Whisenhunt expressed interest in using him more in third down situations on offense, but than Stphens-Howling got injured and missed three games. He does offer an explosiveness the Arizona backfield has lacked, but the Cards have committed serious money in others at the position.

Jonathan Stewart
Height: 5-10   Weight: 235   College: Oregon   Draft: 2008/1 (13)   Born: 21-Mar-1987   Age: 24   Risk: Green

Year	Team	G	Runs	Yds	Yd/R	TD	FUM	DVOA	Rk	DYAR	Rk	YAR	Suc%	Rec	Pass	Yds	C%	Yd/C	TD	DVOA	Rk	DYAR	Rk
2008	CAR	16	184	836	4.5	10	2	7.6%	12	122	16	149	45%	8	17	47	47%	5.9	0	-49.5%	–	-37	–
2009	CAR	16	221	1133	5.1	10	3	14.3%	9	208	7	201	50%	18	26	139	69%	7.7	1	14.5%	16	37	30
2010	CAR	14	178	770	4.3	2	4	-11.7%	36	-21	37	-11	36%	8	14	103	57%	12.9	1	25.0%	–	30	–
2011	CAR		198	961	4.9	3		12.7%						11	14	58	79%	5.3	0	-21.6%			

The world is still waiting for the Stewart that could be; when he ran a 4.46-40 at the 2008 scouting combine with a foot injury at 235 pounds, heads certainly turned. And when he put up 20 total touchdowns in his first two NFL seasons and got over the 1,000-yard barrier in 2009, it was thought that Stewart would hit the proverbial next level and possibly make DeAngelo Williams expendable. That didn't happen,, and the Panthers re-signed Williams. Injuries limited Stewart in 2010, as did the notion given to every defense that eight in the box was the preferred strategy. Stewart has looked very much like a franchise back at times, and with so many other cash commitments on a roster clearly in need of reconstruction, the smart move would be to let him loose as a premium asset in an offense that should have more openings based on Cam Newton's option abilities. Stewart participated in player-only workouts this year and impressed observers who noted that he missed much of previous offseason work with various injuries.

Tyrell Sutton

Height: 5-8   Weight: 213   College: Northwestern   Draft: 2009/ (FA)   Born: 19-Dec-1986   Age: 25   Risk: Green

Year	Team	G	Runs	Yds	Yd/R	TD	FUM	DVOA	Rk	DYAR	Rk	YAR	Suc%	Rec	Pass	Yds	C%	Yd/C	TD	DVOA	Rk	DYAR	Rk
2009	CAR	7	12	68	5.7	0	0	35.3%	--	17	--	17	50%	6	11	62	55%	10.3	0	18.7%	--	17	--
2010	CAR	9	13	71	5.5	0	0	9.3%	--	9	--	13	31%	12	12	70	100%	5.8	0	11.0%	--	17	--
2011	CAR		16	76	4.8	0		18.0%						11	22	95	50%	8.7	0	26.8%			

An undrafted free agent in 2009, Sutton originally slipped ahead of Mike Goodson at the second level of the Panthers' running back depth chart, only to fall back a bit in 2010 when Goodson really turned it around. Like nearly every other Carolina Panthers back, Sutton was waylaid by injuries last season; depending on how the running back rotation plays out, he could get a few more reps as a change-of-pace back.

Ben Tate

Height: 5-11   Weight: 220   College: Auburn   Draft: 2010/2 (58)   Born: 21-Aug-1988   Age: 23   Risk: Green

Year	Team	G	Runs	Yds	Yd/R	TD	FUM	DVOA	Rk	DYAR	Rk	YAR	Suc%	Rec	Pass	Yds	C%	Yd/C	TD	DVOA	Rk	DYAR	Rk
2011	HOU		53	261	4.9	2		23.2%						13	16	112	81%	8.6	1	20.4%			

Last year, Tate was in the mix to be the Texans' starter at running back, but a mid-August season-ending ankle injury killed those chances. He's been medically cleared for the 2011 season and will battle Derrick Ward for the right to be Arian Foster's primary backup.

Chester Taylor

Height: 5-11   Weight: 213   College: Toledo   Draft: 2002/6 (207)   Born: 22-Sep-1979   Age: 32   Risk: Green

Year	Team	G	Runs	Yds	Yd/R	TD	FUM	DVOA	Rk	DYAR	Rk	YAR	Suc%	Rec	Pass	Yds	C%	Yd/C	TD	DVOA	Rk	DYAR	Rk
2008	MIN	16	101	399	4.0	4	2	-1.4%	28	28	35	37	43%	45	55	399	82%	8.9	2	25.4%	10	104	11
2009	MIN	16	94	338	3.6	1	2	-29.3%	--	-73	--	-80	33%	44	59	389	75%	8.8	1	13.5%	17	83	12
2010	CHI	16	112	267	2.4	3	0	-31.2%	46	-107	46	-113	36%	20	26	139	77%	7.0	0	8.1%	30	30	36
2011	CHI		52	195	3.8	0		-5.3%						25	42	162	60%	6.5	0	1.3%			

With 2.38 yards per carry, Taylor is the first running back since the NFL-AFL merger in 1970 to average less than 2.4 yards per carry in over 100 carries. He put up some fascinating stat lines. Ten carries for 13 yards against the Bills. Eleven carries for five yards (!) against the Dolphins. Eleven carries for 10 yards against the Vikings. Six carries for a loss of three (!!) against the Eagles. Was Mike Martz trying to prove some kind of point by feeding him the ball so often and unproductively? Taylor's decade-long run as a Backup to the Stars appears to be over; all the "veteran reliability" in the world cannot offset rushing averages that plunge into 0.45 yards-per-game territory.

Fred Taylor

Height: 6-1   Weight: 234   College: Florida   Draft: 1998/1 (9)   Born: 27-Jan-1976   Age: 35   Risk: N/A

Year	Team	G	Runs	Yds	Yd/R	TD	FUM	DVOA	Rk	DYAR	Rk	YAR	Suc%	Rec	Pass	Yds	C%	Yd/C	TD	DVOA	Rk	DYAR	Rk
2008	JAC	13	143	556	3.9	1	1	-14.3%	46	-32	44	-24	41%	16	22	98	73%	6.1	0	-32.2%	--	-23	--
2009	NE	6	63	269	4.3	4	1	24.4%	--	91	--	65	62%	2	3	17	67%	8.5	0	0.7%	--	3	--
2010	NE	7	43	155	3.6	0	0	-13.1%	--	-8	--	-13	47%	2	3	6	67%	3.0	0	-47.9%	--	-5	--

Taylor led the Patriots in rushing on Opening Day then disappeared, felled by a toe injury and the team's sudden decision to get younger at the skill positions. Taylor said he was "basically retired" in April, which is exactly the same as being retired when you are an injury-prone 35-year-old at a position that can easily be filled in the draft.

Daniel Thomas

Height: 6-2   Weight: 228   College: Kansas St.   Draft: 2011/2 (62)   Born: 29-Oct-1987   Age: 24   Risk: Green

Year	Team	G	Runs	Yds	Yd/R	TD	FUM	DVOA	Rk	DYAR	Rk	YAR	Suc%	Rec	Pass	Yds	C%	Yd/C	TD	DVOA	Rk	DYAR	Rk
2011	MIA		241	922	3.8	6		3.7%						27	36	211	75%	7.8	1	19.1%			

Thomas is a big, physical back in the mold of Ronnie Brown or Ricky Williams, the two players he will be expected to replace. No one ever considered drafting Thomas number two overall, trading an entire draft for him or even outfitting him in a wedding dress, but there are reasons to think Thomas could work out nicely as the centerpiece of a revamped Miami backfield. He is an exceptional inside runner who scored 19 touchdowns in the Big 12 last season, with +19.5 Adj. POE. Despite his stout build, Thomas is also a surprisingly flexible back who can stay on the field on third downs who can catch the ball and make plays in space, even if he was not frequently asked to do so. Just as importantly, Thomas never missed a game in his two seasons at Kansas State, and he proved able to handle a heavy workload, all of which must be music to the ears of Miami fans who have become accustomed to cringing whenever a back ended up at the bottom of a pile. Miami will still try to pair Thomas with a more traditional third-down back, but the need may not be as pressing as people think.

Pierre Thomas   Height: 5-11 Weight: 210 College: Illinois   Draft: 2007/ (FA)   Born: 18-Dec-1984   Age: 27 Risk: Yellow

Year	Team	G	Runs	Yds	Yd/R	TD	FUM	DVOA	Rk	DYAR	Rk	YAR	Suc%	Rec	Pass	Yds	C%	Yd/C	TD	DVOA	Rk	DYAR	Rk
2008	NO	15	129	625	4.8	9	1	16.9%	4	161	11	190	62%	31	41	284	76%	9.2	3	40.2%	5	136	6
2009	NO	14	147	793	5.4	6	2	26.2%	1	222	5	206	56%	39	45	302	87%	7.7	2	20.1%	12	80	15
2010	NO	6	83	269	3.2	2	0	0.7%	--	34	--	23	50%	29	30	201	100%	6.9	0	17.1%	19	56	24
2011	NO		77	334	4.3	0		-7.7%						45	54	446	83%	9.9	2	0.1%			

The ankle injury that cost the Saints their best back last year was pretty severe, leading directly to the drafting of Mark Ingram. If Thomas can regain full use of his ankle, he'll carve out a role in the offense even with the new hotshot around, if only because of his extremely reliable hands.

Mike Tolbert   Height: 5-9 Weight: 243 College: Coastal Carolina   Draft: 2008/ (FA)   Born: 23-Nov-1985   Age: 26 Risk: Yellow

Year	Team	G	Runs	Yds	Yd/R	TD	FUM	DVOA	Rk	DYAR	Rk	YAR	Suc%	Rec	Pass	Yds	C%	Yd/C	TD	DVOA	Rk	DYAR	Rk
2008	SD	13	13	37	2.8	0	0	-28.7%	--	-15	--	-13	54%	13	15	171	87%	13.2	1	72.0%	--	82	--
2009	SD	16	25	148	5.9	1	1	33.2%	--	51	--	58	72%	17	22	192	77%	11.3	3	22.9%	--	52	--
2010	SD	15	182	735	4.0	11	5	-1.9%	24	53	24	66	51%	25	30	216	87%	8.6	0	37.2%	5	84	17
2011	SD		159	716	4.5	6		9.9%						26	29	277	90%	10.7	1	20.6%			

When Ryan Mathews couldn't elevate the running game as expected, it was Tolbert who led the team in carries, rushing yards, and rushing touchdowns. He's your traditional "little bull" running back who gets positive yardage before defenders can see him behind the linemen, and he knows how to fall forward for those extra yards at the end of a play. Tolbert was better in the red zone and at the goal line than in standard situations, which speaks to his limitations in a way — Tolbert doesn't have a lot of explosiveness off the snap, and most of his longer plays came against defenses watching the pass (though he did rank third in the league behind Jamaal Charles and Darren McFadden in ratio of 20-plus-yard runs). Tolbert is a valuable asset and could help comprise one of the NFL's better running back rotations once Mathews gets up to speed.

LaDainian Tomlinson   Height: 5-10 Weight: 221 College: TCU   Draft: 2001/1 (5)   Born: 23-Jun-1979   Age: 32 Risk: Green

Year	Team	G	Runs	Yds	Yd/R	TD	FUM	DVOA	Rk	DYAR	Rk	YAR	Suc%	Rec	Pass	Yds	C%	Yd/C	TD	DVOA	Rk	DYAR	Rk
2008	SD	16	292	1110	3.8	11	1	-1.3%	27	88	20	107	45%	52	77	426	68%	8.2	1	-1.5%	34	52	25
2009	SD	14	223	730	3.3	12	2	-10.1%	41	-15	42	6	43%	20	30	154	67%	7.7	0	-31.2%	52	-28	52
2010	NYJ	15	219	914	4.2	6	4	3.6%	16	110	15	102	44%	52	79	368	66%	7.1	0	-14.2%	48	-2	48
2011	NYJ		126	549	4.4	3		-17.5%						43	62	326	69%	7.6	1	-18.2%			

Tomlinson played well enough in training camp to emerge ahead of Shonn Greene as the opening day starter, and for a few short weeks in September and early October it seemed as if he had discovered the Fountain of Youth. Tomlinson piled up 490 yards rushing in the first six games, averaged 5.33 yards per reception, and posted a superlative DVOA of 23.9%. But Tomlinson hit a wall after the bye--his yards per carry dropped to 3.27

and his DVOA plummeted to -12.6%. Tomlinson continued to receive significant carries in crunch time down the stretch and in the playoffs, but he rarely rewarded that faith. Now he is stuck in a numbers game, competing for carries with Greene, second-year man Joe McKnight, and rookie Bilal Powell. Tomlinson's best asset at this point might be his blocking, which could get him on the field on passing downs ahead of the younger legs.

Ryan Torain Height: 6-0 Weight: 222 College: Arizona State Draft: 2008/5 (139) Born: 10-Aug-1986 Age: 25 Risk: Yellow

Year	Team	G	Runs	Yds	Yd/R	TD	FUM	DVOA	Rk	DYAR	Rk	YAR	Suc%	Rec	Pass	Yds	C%	Yd/C	TD	DVOA	Rk	DYAR	Rk
2008	DEN	2	15	69	4.6	1	0	21.6%	–	21	–	26	60%	0	0	0	0%	0.0	0	0.0%	–	0	–
2010	WAS	10	164	742	4.5	4	2	-5.6%	30	19	30	33	44%	18	27	125	67%	6.9	2	12.3%	25	39	34
2011	WAS		123	533	4.3	2		-1.2%						16	25	96	64%	6.0	0	-19.8%			

Unsurprisingly, Torain continued to flash signs of talent in between injuries. The good news is that his consistently-balky knee was fine, but he had issues with his hamstring that cost him the better part of six weeks. Hamstring woes tend to linger, which is never a good sign for a young back that's already struggling to stay healthy. He would be a serviceable lead back if he could stay healthy for 250 carries, but there's just no guarantees that he will ever stay healthy enough for that to happen. Even if he's pencilled in as the starter on your draft day, he's too fragile to lean on.

Michael Turner Height: 5-10 Weight: 237 College: Northern Illinois Draft: 2004/5 (154) Born: 13-Feb-1982 Age: 29 Risk: Red

Year	Team	G	Runs	Yds	Yd/R	TD	FUM	DVOA	Rk	DYAR	Rk	YAR	Suc%	Rec	Pass	Yds	C%	Yd/C	TD	DVOA	Rk	DYAR	Rk
2008	ATL	16	376	1699	4.5	17	3	4.1%	19	203	6	259	48%	6	9	41	67%	6.8	0	-9.5%	–	2	–
2009	ATL	11	178	871	4.9	10	4	11.0%	12	143	16	152	49%	5	7	35	71%	7.0	0	5.2%	–	9	–
2010	ATL	16	334	1371	4.1	12	2	-1.4%	23	102	16	127	46%	12	20	85	60%	7.1	0	-24.4%	–	-11	–
2011	ATL		316	1413	4.5	12		9.8%						14	19	85	74%	6.1	0	-13.1%			

Like sugar addicts who just can't walk past the candy aisle at the QuickTrip without snagging a couple of peanut butter cups, the Falcons can't seem to implement a game plan that spreads the running load away from Turner's broad shoulders and thick legs. Fortunately, Turner was comfortably shy of 370 carries, but after seeing their bell cow break down in 2009, you'd think Mikes Smith and Mularkey would have erred more on the side of caution. At this point, there's no denying that the Falcons are simply going to ride their big back and put him away wet each week, despite his poor efficiency. Turner was a monster on third-down runs (27.4% DVOA), so give him credit for getting the job done even when defenses knew he was coming. Turner had 38 broken tackles last year by our count, tied for third in the league.

Shane Vereen Height: 5-10 Weight: 205 College: California Draft: 2011/2 (56) Born: 2-Mar-1989 Age: 22 Risk: Green

Year	Team	G	Runs	Yds	Yd/R	TD	FUM	DVOA	Rk	DYAR	Rk	YAR	Suc%	Rec	Pass	Yds	C%	Yd/C	TD	DVOA	Rk	DYAR	Rk
2011	NE		67	314	4.7	4		28.9%						13	26	117	50%	9.0	1	-17.6%			

Shane Vereen combines strength with a low center of gravity and decent speed, but his 1,167 yards with California in 2010 were relatively empty. He averaged just 1.88 Highlight Yards per carry and posted a minus-3.7 Adj. POE. He broke off runs of more than 20 yards in just two of 12 games, and he failed to average five yards per carry in a game even once in the last half of the season. His speed score of 102.4 might have led to decent late-round value, but his going in the second round was a bit of a surprise.

Derrick Ward

Height: 5-11 Weight: 233 College: Fresno State   Draft: 2004/7 (235) Born: 30-Aug-1980 Age: 31 Risk: Yellow

Year	Team	G	Runs	Yds	Yd/R	TD	FUM	DVOA	Rk	DYAR	Rk	YAR	Suc%	Rec	Pass	Yds	C%	Yd/C	TD	DVOA	Rk	DYAR	Rk
2008	NYG	16	182	1025	5.6	2	2	25.8%	2	265	4	214	51%	41	55	384	75%	9.4	0	24.0%	11	107	9
2009	TB	14	114	409	3.6	1	0	-18.6%	47	-46	46	-56	36%	20	24	150	83%	7.5	2	51.5%	—	77	—
2010	HOU	16	50	315	6.3	4	1	39.1%	—	112	—	97	57%	7	11	61	64%	8.7	0	-6.4%	—	4	—
2011	HOU		56	213	3.8	2		12.0%						16	21	125	76%	7.8	1	-1.2%			

After that wilderness year in Tampa Bay, Ward found a better home in Houston. He's a good scheme fit, but will have to fend off a challenge from Ben Tate to hold on to the job as Arian Foster's backup. Even if he manages that, he's about as likely to match his superlative 2010 numbers as he is to bust off a 30-odd yard touchdown every 17 carries.

D.J. Ware

Height: 6-1 Weight: 225 College: Georgia   Draft: 2007/ (FA) Born: 10-Feb-1985 Age: 26 Risk: Red

Year	Team	G	Runs	Yds	Yd/R	TD	FUM	DVOA	Rk	DYAR	Rk	YAR	Suc%	Rec	Pass	Yds	C%	Yd/C	TD	DVOA	Rk	DYAR	Rk
2008	NYG	6	2	15	7.5	0	0	62.0%	—	8	—	8	100%	0	0	0	0%	0.0	0	0.0%	—	0	—
2009	NYG	8	13	73	5.6	1	1	19.3%	—	17	—	15	46%	3	4	15	75%	5.0	0	-11.7%	—	0	—
2010	NYG	14	20	73	3.7	0	0	3.8%	—	11	—	14	65%	7	9	67	78%	9.6	0	34.1%	—	21	—
2011	NYG		28	124	4.4	1		8.7%						9	12	57	75%	6.3	0	-3.9%			

It's the same story every year for the former Danny Ware. The Giants say that they'll give Ware a bigger role to reduce the wear-and-tear on their top two backs, Ware gets a handful of carries in garbage time, and then he disappears for the rest of the year. He looked good on 13 carries against the Seahawks in Week 9, but then he had three carries for -8 yards the rest of the way. The team signed him to a two-year extension for minimal money, but he has no clear path to a steady role.

Leon Washington

Height: 5-8 Weight: 210 College: Florida State   Draft: 2006/4 (117) Born: 29-Aug-1982 Age: 29 Risk: Yellow

Year	Team	G	Runs	Yds	Yd/R	TD	FUM	DVOA	Rk	DYAR	Rk	YAR	Suc%	Rec	Pass	Yds	C%	Yd/C	TD	DVOA	Rk	DYAR	Rk
2008	NYJ	16	76	448	5.9	6	2	23.8%	—	95	—	98	51%	47	61	355	77%	7.6	2	10.2%	20	77	14
2009	NYJ	7	72	331	4.6	0	1	-14.7%	—	-15	—	1	35%	15	26	131	58%	8.7	0	-9.4%	39	5	44
2010	SEA	16	27	100	3.7	1	0	1.0%	—	12	—	4	44%	9	13	79	69%	8.8	0	13.6%	—	20	—
2011	SEA		44	182	4.1	0		-9.6%						19	30	137	63%	7.2	0	1.5%			

Only Josh Cribbs has more touchdowns on kickoff returns in his career than Washington, who nearly single-handedly beat San Diego in Week 3 when he averaged 63 yards a pop (by far the highest average ever for any player with at least four returns in a game) and scored two touchdowns. As such, Washington figures to be one of the biggest casualties to the NFL's new rules that discourage kickoff returns. If his special teams value is neutered, Washington will still have value as a runner. In four years with the Jets, he averaged 4.8 yards per carry with a total DVOA of 8.2%. On the Seahawks, he's somewhat redundant with Justin Forsett, but there are worse things in life than to have too many home run threats in your backfield.

Beanie Wells

Height: 6-1 Weight: 235 College: Ohio State   Draft: 2009/1 (31) Born: 7-Aug-1988 Age: 23 Risk: Red

Year	Team	G	Runs	Yds	Yd/R	TD	FUM	DVOA	Rk	DYAR	Rk	YAR	Suc%	Rec	Pass	Yds	C%	Yd/C	TD	DVOA	Rk	DYAR	Rk
2009	ARI	16	176	793	4.5	7	6	1.3%	28	75	27	51	53%	12	16	143	75%	11.9	0	38.4%	—	53	—
2010	ARI	13	116	397	3.4	2	1	-13.8%	40	-25	38	-20	45%	5	8	74	63%	14.8	0	35.7%	—	25	—
2011	ARI		223	906	4.1	4		-17.8%						20	32	110	63%	5.5	0	-34.6%			

It's time for Beanie Wells to make it rain. The former first rounder from Ohio State was seen as an elite ball carrier coming into the NFL, though possibly suspect in the passing game. Through two seasons he confirmed fears about his blocking and catching, while showing no ability to break tackles through speed or power. The Cardinals' second-round pick of Ryan Williams sends a clear message to Wells.

Brian Westbrook

Height: 5-8   Weight: 200   College: Villanova   Draft: 2002/3 (91)   Born: 2-Sep-1979   Age: 32   Risk: N/A

Year	Team	G	Runs	Yds	Yd/R	TD	FUM	DVOA	Rk	DYAR	Rk	YAR	Suc%	Rec	Pass	Yds	C%	Yd/C	TD	DVOA	Rk	DYAR	Rk
2008	PHI	14	233	936	4.0	9	2	6.9%	15	151	12	130	48%	54	73	402	74%	7.4	5	0.2%	30	59	18
2009	PHI	8	61	274	4.5	1	0	7.9%	--	43	--	55	52%	25	34	181	74%	7.2	1	-3.5%	34	20	35
2010	SF	14	77	340	4.4	4	0	17.3%	--	75	--	95	45%	16	25	150	68%	9.4	1	2.6%	33	22	40

Westbrook against Arizona in Week 12: 23 carries, 5.9 yards per run, 58.6% DVOA. The rest of the year: 54 carries, 3.7 average, -3.6% DVOA. And his receiving numbers were nothing special, which is more common for Westbrook than you might think. He hasn't finished in the top 20 running backs in receiving DVOA since 2005. A free agent, Westbrook probably won't be back with the 49ers. Most likely he will catch on somewhere and have just enough highlights to cause viewers of NFL Gameday to ask each other, "Brian Westbrook's still in the league?"

Cadillac Williams

Height: 5-11   Weight: 217   College: Auburn   Draft: 2005/1 (5)   Born: 21-Apr-1982   Age: 29   Risk: Green

Year	Team	G	Runs	Yds	Yd/R	TD	FUM	DVOA	Rk	DYAR	Rk	YAR	Suc%	Rec	Pass	Yds	C%	Yd/C	TD	DVOA	Rk	DYAR	Rk
2008	TB	6	63	233	3.7	4	1	-6.2%	--	7	--	39	51%	7	7	43	100%	6.1	0	13.3%	--	10	--
2009	TB	16	211	823	3.9	4	1	-2.8%	33	49	32	40	38%	28	40	217	73%	7.8	3	20.2%	11	70	19
2010	TB	16	125	437	3.5	2	1	-22.2%	45	-68	44	-70	36%	46	64	355	72%	7.7	1	6.3%	31	72	18
2011	STL		54	212	3.9	1		-19.9%						26	31	183	84%	7.0	0	-30.0%			

There's still some life in the old Caddy, though Williams' involvement in the Bucs' offense tailed off as LeGarrette Blount became much more of a factor late in the season. In a way, Williams' week 2 performance against the Carolina Panthers, in which he gained 54 yards on 27 carries, spoke to the need for different options in the backfield. Williams got his revenge on the Panthers later in the season with a 45-yard touchdown scamper in a situational role. That's the best place for the guy who's still an effective third-down player (16 carries for 166 yards and a 74.9% DVOA), but will find it tougher and tougher to pound the rock on a regular basis as age and injury history take a further toll. His new role as a co-handcuff with Jerious Norwood behind Steven Jackson in St. Louis, where he signed a one-year, $685,000 contract, should preserve his stats and physical well-being.

DeAngelo Williams

Height: 5-8   Weight: 210   College: Memphis   Draft: 2006/1 (27)   Born: 25-Apr-1983   Age: 28   Risk: Red

Year	Team	G	Runs	Yds	Yd/R	TD	FUM	DVOA	Rk	DYAR	Rk	YAR	Suc%	Rec	Pass	Yds	C%	Yd/C	TD	DVOA	Rk	DYAR	Rk
2008	CAR	16	273	1515	5.5	18	0	28.3%	1	385	1	442	47%	22	30	121	73%	5.5	2	-14.5%	45	-1	45
2009	CAR	13	216	1117	5.2	7	3	12.6%	11	175	9	170	45%	29	41	252	71%	8.7	0	22.7%	10	87	11
2010	CAR	6	87	361	4.1	1	1	-16.2%	--	-24	--	-15	30%	11	13	61	85%	5.5	0	-2.3%	--	9	--
2011	CAR		212	1033	4.9	3		12.5%						24	27	132	89%	5.5	0	6.7%			

His season cut short six games in, Williams had enough currency from previous accomplishments to be considered one of the prime players on the free agent market. The initial rumors had him heading to Denver with John Fox, which would fill a need for a new coaching staff and front office with a long offseason to watch a lot of Knowshown Moreno tape and wonder what Josh McDaniels was thinking. But the running back market proved soft in 2011, and Williams resigned with the Panthers. As is the case with every Carolina back in 2010, one should pay more attention to the film than the stats — the Panthers' anemic passing game gave defenses every opportunity to tee off on the runners. When he was on the field in 2010, Williams was effective, though he's better out of I-formations because he's no longer quick enough in short areas to blow through gaps consistently.

Keiland Williams

Height: 5-11   Weight: 233   College: LSU   Draft: 2010/ (FA)   Born: 14-Aug-1986   Age: 25   Risk: Red

Year	Team	G	Runs	Yds	Yd/R	TD	FUM	DVOA	Rk	DYAR	Rk	YAR	Suc%	Rec	Pass	Yds	C%	Yd/C	TD	DVOA	Rk	DYAR	Rk
2010	WAS	15	65	261	4.0	3	1	14.8%	--	62	--	42	51%	39	58	309	67%	7.9	2	-8.9%	46	15	43
2011	WAS		28	103	3.6	0		-16.8%						18	24	92	75%	5.1	0	-9.4%			

Promoted from the practice squad after virtually every running back on the roster got hurt for the second year in a row, Williams is a serviceable pass blocker who doesn't offer a ton as a running back. His three-touchdown performance in the Monday night blowout by the Eagles will go down in the record books as one of the most legendarily useless performances in fantasy football history.

Ricky Williams Height: 5-10 Weight: 226 College: Texas   Draft: 1999/1 (5)   Born: 21-May-1977   Age: 34 Risk: Red

Year	Team	G	Runs	Yds	Yd/R	TD	FUM	DVOA	Rk	DYAR	Rk	YAR	Rk	Suc%	Rec	Pass	Yds	C%	Yd/C	TD	DVOA	Rk	DYAR	Rk
2008	MIA	16	160	659	4.1	4	5	-3.9%	34	31	33	36		48%	29	39	219	74%	7.6	1	-9.6%	40	8	41
2009	MIA	16	241	1121	4.7	11	5	9.0%	14	178	8	195		55%	35	53	264	66%	7.5	2	-10.4%	43	10	40
2010	MIA	16	159	673	4.2	2	4	-2.8%	25	36	26	31		53%	19	30	141	63%	7.4	1	-7.9%	45	10	45
2011	BAL		72	265	3.7	3		-11.8%							22	34	156	65%	7.1	1	-26.3%			

Williams briefly joined in with the end-of-the-year media venting that took place in Miami, complaining about the commitment of his teammates and about Tony Sparano's tendency to micromanage. It was an unfortunate end to what has been a fascinating tenure in Miami, where Williams put together 1,000-yard seasons six years apart and reinvented himself running jet sweeps in the Wildcat formation. Williams was still effective last year when his blocking held up, and he is going to a good spot in Baltimore, where he will step into the Willis McGahee role. That should be enough to garner him around 100 carries and some goal line work.

Ryan Williams Height: 5-9 Weight: 212 College: Virginia Tech   Draft: 2011/2 (38)   Born: 9-Apr-1990   Age: 21 Risk: Blue

Year	Team	G	Runs	Yds	Yd/R	TD	FUM	DVOA	Rk	DYAR	Rk	YAR	Suc%	Rec	Pass	Yds	C%	Yd/C	TD	DVOA	Rk	DYAR	Rk
2011	ARI		122	451	3.7	1		-10.2%						15	19	149	79%	10.0	1	16.6%			

When healthy, Ryan Williams appears to bring quite a bit to the table: strength, toughness, decent speed. He produced at a high level in 2009 — 1,477 yards, 2.57 Highlight Yards per carry, and a plus-20.5 Adj. POE — and was projected as a future first-rounder. He struggled with hamstring issues to start 2010, however, and lost quite a bit of playing time to Darren Evans. His 2010 season was a lost cause (481 yards, minus-0.4 Adj. POE), but if the hamstring issue doesn't nag him in the future, then the Cardinals potentially got first-round value in the second round.

Danny Woodhead Height: 5-8 Weight: 200 College: Chadron State   Draft: 2008/ (FA)   Born: 25-Jan-1985   Age: 26 Risk: Green

Year	Team	G	Runs	Yds	Yd/R	TD	FUM	DVOA	Rk	DYAR	Rk	YAR	Rk	Suc%	Rec	Pass	Yds	C%	Yd/C	TD	DVOA	Rk	DYAR	Rk
2009	NYJ	10	15	64	4.3	0	0	-4.8%	--	2	--	6		60%	8	14	87	57%	10.9	0	12.5%	--	19	--
2010	2TM	15	97	547	5.6	5	1	41.3%	--	185	--	192		57%	34	44	379	77%	11.1	1	56.3%	2	156	5
2011	NE		54	235	4.3	3		8.5%							38	52	395	73%	10.4	1	10.0%			

If scientists and marketing gurus designed an athlete custom-engineered to make New Englanders swoon, he would look a lot like Woodhead. The Jets castoff (despite some purple mythmaking, they didn't really miss him much) was nearly as good as his notices, putting up Kevin Faulk-ian numbers in the Kevin Faulk role. Woodhead is a fine third-down and change-up back on a team that has always had a lot of use for that type of player, and if you can get through the "fair-haired symbol of all that is wonderful about sports" talk without puking, you discover a very good role player. (Note to our New England readers: ignore the last paragraph. It was written by a New York writer who doesn't understand how gutsy, intelligent, inspirational, and transcendently awesome Woodhead is. We will have the writer flogged with a whip braided from Kevin McHale's hair.)

Going Deep

Anthony Allen, BAL: Think T.J. Duckett. This seventh-round pick from Georgia Tech doesn't bring much to the table in terms of agility, as he was seen by some teams as more of a fullback, but he's got the ability to replace Le'Ron McClain's role in the offense if he gets the chance.

Tiki Barber, FA: Apparently, he forgot the first rule of a comeback, which is that some team has to actually sign you. Miami was the only team to even give him a workout.

Baron Batch, PIT: Take a tip from us, Baron: blogs that use auto-play music (as of this writing, an acoustic cover of "Hey Ya!") are so 2002. He's the heir apparent to Mewelde Moore in Pittsburgh: the pass-catching third-down back who can block well. With the real Moore signed for another year, Batch will have plenty of time to fine-tune his blog on injured reserve, as he tore his ACL during training camp.

Kahlil Bell, CHI: Bell spent all of 2010 on the Bears' inactive list after a promising 40-220-0 season in 2009. (45 DYAR, 12.9% DVOA) In December of last year, Bell fought Chester Taylor during a midweek practice; Taylor was coming off a six-carry, minus-three yard performance against the Eagles, and Bell (who had a 79-yard run against the Eagles in 2009) probably figured that he could provide positive yardage for a fraction of Taylor's salary. Lovie Smith and Mike Martz disagreed, and Bell remained nailed to the bench so Taylor could gain 43 yards on his next 29 carries. Such lunacy can only endure so long, and Bell could beat out Taylor for the spot behind Forte and Marion Barber.

Michael Bennett, OAK: Bennett hasn't done anything of note since 2007, but that didn't stop the Raiders from re-signing him to a one-year, $890,000 deal during Oakland's pre-lockout Contractapalooza. Ostensibly, he's a backup option if Darren McFadden gets hurt or if Michael Bush goes elsewhere. Realistically, his enduring legacy in Oakland will be that he filled JaMarcus Russell's roster spot.

Damien Berry, BAL: Berry's impact will likely be more on special teams than on offense: he's a one-year starter for the Hurricanes who had trouble blocking and ran a bit slow (4.63) in the 40-yard dash at the combine. He's more of a threat to Brendon Ayabandejo than he is to Ray Rice.

Lorenzo Booker, MIN: The bottom of the Vikings depth chart last year read like a catalogue of Brad Childress' bad ideas from Philadelphia: Hank Baskett, Greg Lewis, and Booker, an unreliable third-down back the Vikings turned into an emergency slot receiver. Booker is not as elusive as he thinks he is, so he spends a lot of time catching short passes and making moves that don't fool anyone. At least Childress got canned before he had a chance to sign Reno Mahe. (2010 receiving stats: 5-for-6, 32 yards, 3 DYAR, -5.0% DVOA)

Allen Bradford, TB: Selected in the sixth round as a power option with quick feet and good lead-blocking ability, Bradford might be the short-yardage option to replace Earnest Graham. Perhaps the most graphic boom-and-bust runner in the NCAA last season, Bradford had games for USC in which he gained 131, 212, and 223 yards on the ground ... and others in which he gained 2, 9, and 10.

Curtis Brinkley, SD: Brinkley was called up to the active roster to replace Mike Tolbert when Tolbert went on injured reserve late in the season. Held in reserve on the practice squad as Ryan Mathews' ankle became a problem, Brinkley could find value in that backup role in 2011 ... or he could be waived twice as he was in 2010.

Andre Brown, NYG: Brown tore his Achilles in training camp as a rookie with the 2009 Giants, and when he started to suffer from turf toe at the end of camp this year, the team chose D.J. Ware over him as the third halfback. He bounced around four different practice squads before coming back to New York following his release by Washington. Unless Brown survives cuts, he'll try on practice squad jersey number five this season.

Patrick Cobbs, NO: Cobbs was a longtime favorite of head coach Tony Sparano's because of his versatility and his work ethic, but when your season stat line reads, "four carries for zero yards," it's safe to say that being able to run the Wildcat or return kickoffs isn't going to save your roster spot. Miami declined to tender Cobbs, and he'll end up in some team's training camp competing for one of the bottom roster spots. At the age of 28, his window in the NFL is closing. (2010 receiving stats: 8-for-19, 2 TD, 2.2% DVOA, 16 DYAR)

James Davis, WAS: Davis was a fantasy sleeper back in the 2009 preseason, but that seems like a long, long time ago now. He's struggled with injuries, ineffectiveness as a runner, and difficulties learning how to pass-block. When Cleveland waived him at midseason, he showed up on the Washington practice squad, and only made it onto the active roster because the Redskins were running out of backs. After Washington didn't use him in their preseason opener, he promptly went AWOL and probably took what was left of his NFL career with him. (2010 stats: 19 carries for 60 yards, -6 DYAR, -17.0% DVOA)

Jonathan Dwyer, PIT: Dwyer is a big 230-pound back who does well in Football Outsiders metrics; he had a 103.2 Speed Score and +52.9 Adjusted POE during his career at Georgia Tech. A lot of people thought he was a steal in last year's sixth round, but Ike Redman beat him out for the short-yardage bulldozer job, and he barely saw the field as a rookie. (2010 stats: 9 carries for 28 yards, -12 DYAR, -42.2% DVOA)

Mario Fannin, FA: This year's Speed Score champion (125.5) went undrafted because of a fear of fumblitis. He signed with Denver, then was waived after a knee injury. We still think it can happen for him in 2012: He's a big back who's deceptively fast and good in the passing game, and Auburn products have a pretty good NFL track record.

Jay Finley, CIN: Constant ankle injuries robbed this Baylor product of any chance to be a high-round pick. His only real weakness is a lack of top-end speed, and he does have the decent hands to be a third-down back if he can stay healthy. He'll need a Cedric Benson or Bernard Scott injury to have a chance at real work in Cincinnati.

Quinton Ganther, FA: Journeyman roster fodder. Ganther has played for four teams in three years, arriving in Buffalo after the Seahawks waved him in the wake of the Marshawn Lynch deal. Ganther soaked up a handful of carries when C.J. Spiller was injured, then disappeared from the game plan. He got a long look as a ball carrier during a running back emergency with the Redskins in 2009 but showed little. (2010 stats: 9 carries, 18 yards, -5 DYAR, -22.7% DVOA)

Lynell Hamilton, FA: Hamilton holds the dubious honor of being the first of the Saints backs to get hurt in 2010 — he went down in a preseason practice/scrimmage with the Patriots. The Saints cut him at the start of training camp. (2009 stats: 35 carries for 125 yards, 2 TD, 10 DYAR, -3.2% DVOA)

Jacob Hester, SD: Primarily a lead blocker, Hester was known in college as perhaps the best receiving fullback in the NCAA. He hasn't had much of a chance to show it in the NFL, but was reasonably efficient when he was targeted. (2010 rushing stats: 28 carries for 60 yards, -14 DYAR, -18.7% DVOA; receiving stats: 22-for-26 for 145 yards, 1 TD, 20.2% DVOA, 53 DYAR)

Lex Hilliard, MIA: There was some brief chatter in the offseason that the Dolphins might turn to Hilliard to be the lead back, which tells you more about the dearth of actual football news during the lockout than about Hilliard himself. A big power back, Hilliard has managed to hang around on the active roster for two straight seasons, but his lone contribution to Miami's stat line in 2010 was a single three-yard reception. Hilliard has a similar build to Daniel Thomas, and should stick around as a depth guy who can run similar plays should Thomas get injured.

Kareem Huggins, TB: Like Arrelious Benn, "Lotso" Huggins tore his ACL last season, Unlike Benn, Huggins apparently tore "just about everything else" in his right knee when we went down in October against the Saints. That injury took Huggins out of a potential situational role rotating with Cadillac Williams, and pulled the trigger on the ascent of LeGarrette Blount. Postseason reports indicate that Huggins could really struggle to return from the severity of his injury. (2010 stats: 4 carries for 11 yards, -3 DYAR, -32.7% DVOA)

Gartrell Johnson, ATL: Johnson is a powerful runner, cut from the same mold as Willis McGahee, whose single-season rushing record Johnson broke at Miami Springs High. Unfortunately, Jason Snelling is staying around, depriving Johnson of potential workload.

Dion Lewis, PHI: The speed/size combo (5-foot-7, 193 pounds) brings Darren Sproles to mind, but this Pitt product doesn't return kicks. On a loaded Philadelphia offense where he's behind LeSean McCoy and Ronnie Brown, this will probably be a redshirt year for him.

Derrick Locke, PHI: Locke doesn't lack for confidence, as he compared himself to LaDanian Tomlinson in a pre-draft interview. A shaky medical history highlighted by a chronic spine condition kept him from being selected in the draft and led to him failing a physical with the Vikings. Locke can pass-block, is a willing special teamer, and has speed. It's likely that none of that will be utilized in Philadelphia this season, but he's someone to keep an eye on.

Kregg Lumpkin, TB: After he was waived by the Packers, Lumpkin was picked up as a possible power option, especially as Cadillac Williams and Earnest Graham struggled early in the 2010 season. But he lost that role to LeGarrette Blount and spent most of his time on special teams. The coaching staff is said to be enamored of Lumpkin's potential (or, at the very least, the fact that he has the perfect fullback's name), but his inability to establish himself in a rushing rotation full of holes has to be a matter of concern.

Le'Ron McClain, KC: McClain looked all over free agency for a team that would actually let him tote the rock and found out every team wanted him to block. He would probably be a better short-yardage option than Thomas Jones, but stashing him away on your deep fantasy roster isn't going to do you any good. Todd Haley says McClain is a fullback, period. (2010 stats: 28 carries for 85 yards, 19 DYAR, 1.1% DVOA)

Devin Moore, IND: The Indianapolis native and undrafted Wyoming graduate made his NFL debut when he won the Colts' kickoff return job out of training camp. A neck injury put him on injured reserve after Week 4. The Colts appear to be giving him a real shot to earn a backup running back job, and he has a shot at sticking as a special-teamer/change-of-pace back.

Cedric Peerman, CIN: In his third year and on his fourth NFL team, Peerman finally got his first two regular-season carries and gained a grand total of one yard. The highlight of his career will probably be the 93-yard touchdown he scored against the Colts in the last week of the 2010 preseason.

Bilal Powell, NYJ: Powell was something of a surprise pick, as the Jets are fairly loaded at the running back position, but the team saw the value in bringing in another back with a somewhat different skill set. Powell was a first team All-Big East selection in his senior season at Louisville, after rushing for 1,330 yards and 10 touchdowns. At 5-foot-10, 206 pounds, Powell is a one-cut runner who excels at planting his foot and turning upfield.

Evan Royster, WAS: There isn't much athletic upside here, but on a team where Tim Hightower is seriously being considered as a starter, Royster could have some value this year. He finished as Penn State's all-time leading rusher (take that Ki-Jana!) and while he'll never be considered a big-play threat, he does solid work between the tackles.

Da'Rel Scott, NYG: Running for 200 yards against East Carolina in the Military Bowl gained Scott enough buzz to be taken in the seventh round. He ran a 4.34 40-yard dash at the combine, but wasn't even Maryland's starting running back last year. When the NFL adds a 40-yard dash competition after every touchdown to replace kicking extra points in 2038, players like Scott might have some value.

Jordan Todman, SD: Sixth-rounder Todman projects as a Brian Westbrook type; perhaps he's the replacement for Darren Sproles. The Big East Offensive Player of the Year at UConn, he fell short of 100 yards in just two of the games in which he played in the 2010 season. He could be a real steal if used correctly.

Keith Toston, STL: Signed as an undrafted free agent out of Oklahoma State, Toston led the Rams in rushing last preseason before serving as the Rams' No. 3 running back behind Steven Jackson and Kenneth Darby in the regular season. The arrival of Cadillac Williams and Jerious Norwood probably costs him his roster spot. (2010 stats: 19 carries for 54 yards, -23 DYAR, -35.1% DVOA)

Josh Vaughan, CAR: The undrafted journeyman finally got a bit of a break in mid-November, scoring his first NFL touchdown (and the Panthers' only touchdown of the day) in a loss to the Buccaneers. He got that opportunity after DeAngelo Williams was out for the season, and injuries took Jonathan Stewart and Tyrell Sutton off the depth chart. The Panthers signed him to a reserve/future contract, and he'll probably spend some more time on the practice squad, waiting for the next big break. (2010 stats: 3 carries for 7 yards, 1 TD, 10 DYAR, 73.8% DVOA)

Johnny White, BUF: A track record of solid special teams work as a converted cornerback led the Bills to select White out of North Carolina in the fifth round. He certainly has a diverse enough skill set to be an NFL player, and the Bills' official site thinks he may eventually emerge as the goal-line back for Buffalo. He's also got good hands, so he very well could be a factor in Buffalo this season.

LenDale White, DEN: White tore his Achilles tendon in training camp last year, making him a man ahead of his time. He lost an uphill battle to make the Broncos roster this year, getting released after the first preseason game. (2009 stats: 64 carries for 222 yards, 2 TD, 21 DYAR, -0.3% DVOA)

Garrett Wolfe, FA: Wolfe rushed for eight yards on four carries last season, then got arrested in Florida in May for allegedly refusing to pay a $1,600 bar tab at Cameo nightclub. The club dropped charges after Wolfe agreed to let Carl Hiaasan write him into a novel as a former third-string running back who gets stuffed into a bar's walk-in cooler by Skink. (Other 2010 stats: -13 DYAR, -117.7% DVOA)

Jason Wright, Retired: Wright saw little action on offense and was used primarily on special teams. The Northwestern grad did write an excellent piece on the lockout for ESPN.com in the offseason, far better than the more publicized poem teammate Steve Breaston wrote. Instead of suiting up for a seventh season, Wright will attend the business school at the University of Chicago. (2010 stats: 6 carries for 28 yards, 12 DYAR, 31.9% DVOA)

DeShawn Wynn, NO: Wynn was the last man standing in the Saints backfield last year, although he didn't actually get a carry in the playoff game against Seattle. During the regular season, he played special teams only for both New Orleans and San Francisco. (2009 stats: 6 carries for 19 yards, -6 DYAR, -39.0% DVOA)

Albert Young, FA: Young has been the Vikings' first running back off the practice squad in the last two seasons. Of his 25 career carries, ten came in a 44-7 win over the Giants in 2009 and 10 more came in a 38-14 win over the Bills last year. He also cleans up spilled tomato juice in aisle 11. (2010 stats: 13 carries for 29 yards, -28 DYAR, -67.4% DVOA)

Wide Receivers

How to Read the Receiver Statistics Table

The first line contains biographical data—each player's name, height, weight, college, draft position, birth date, and age. Height and weight are the best data we could find; weight, of course, can fluctuate during the off-season. **Age** is very simple, the number of years between the player's birth year and 2011, but birth date is provided if you want to figure out exact age.

Draft position gives draft year and round, with the overall pick number with which the player was taken in parentheses. In the sample table, it says that Greg Jennings was chosen in the 2006 NFL Draft, during the second round, with the 52nd overall pick. Undrafted free agents are listed as "FA" with the year they came into the league, even if they were only in training camp or on a practice squad.

To the far right of the first line is the player's Risk for fantasy football in 2011. As explained in the quarterback section, the standard is for players to be marked Green. Players with higher than normal risk are marked Yellow, and players with the highest risk are marked Red. Players who are most likely to match or surpass our forecast — primarily second-stringers with low projections — are marked Blue.

Next we give the last three years of player stats. Note that rushing stats are not included for receivers, but that any receiver with at least three carries last year will have his 2010 rushing stats appear in his team's chapter.

On in the receiver table, the first column after the year and team for which that receiver played that year is games played (**G**). This is the official NFL total and may include games in which a player appeared on special teams, but did not play wide receiver. Receptions (**Rec**) counts passes caught, while Passes (**Pass**) counts passes thrown to this player, complete or incomplete. The next five columns list receiving yards (**Yds**), catch rate (**C%**), plus/minus (**+/-**), yards per catch (**Yd/C**), and receiving touchdowns (**TD**).

Catch rate includes all passes listed in the official play-by-play with the given player as the intended receiver, even if those passes were listed by our game charters as "Thrown Away," "Tipped at Line," or "Quarterback Hit in Motion." The average NFL wide receiver has caught 57 percent of passes thrown to them in each of the past three seasons; tight ends have caught 64 percent of the passes thrown to them in each of the past three seasons.

Plus/minus is a new metric that we introduced in *Football Outsiders Almanac 2010*. It estimates how many passes a receiver caught compared to what an average receiver would have caught, given the location of those passes. Unlike simple catch rate, plus/minus does not consider passes listed as "Thrown Away," "Tipped at Line," or "Quarterback Hit in Motion." Player performance is compared to a historical baseline of how often a pass is caught based on the pass distance, the distance required for a first down, and whether it is on the left, middle, or right side of the field. Note that plus/minus is not scaled to a player's target total.

Next comes Yards After Catch (**YAC**), based on information from the game charting project, and rank (**Rk**) in Yards After Catch. That is followed by five columns with our advanced metrics for receiving: **DVOA** (Defense-Adjusted Value Over Average), **DYAR** (Defense-Adjusted Yards Above Replacement), and **YAR** (Yards Above Replacement), along with the player's rank in both DVOA and DYAR. These metrics compare every pass intended for a receiver and the results of that pass to a league-average

Greg Jennings				Height: 5-11		Weight: 195		College: Western Michigan			Draft: 2006/2 (52)			Born: 21-Sep-1983		Age: 28		Risk: Yellow	
Year	Team	G	Rec	Pass	Yds	C%	+/-	Yd/C	TD	FUM	YAC	Rk	DVOA	Rk	DYAR	Rk	YAR	Short	Mid	Deep	Bomb
2008	GB	16	80	140	1292	57%	4.2	16.2	9	1	4.2	27	9.6%	21	243	12	256	22%	43%	23%	12%
2009	GB	16	68	119	1113	57%	5.2	16.4	4	0	6.8	5	10.6%	26	224	17	255	30%	42%	14%	14%
2010	GB	16	76	125	1265	61%	7.9	16.6	12	2	5.3	16	19.6%	7	330	3	329	25%	44%	14%	17%
2011	GB		80	136	1256	59%	--	15.7	9				16.7%								

baseline based on the game situations in which passes were thrown to that receiver. DVOA and DYAR are also adjusted based on the opposing defense and include Defensive Pass Interference yards on passes intended for that receiver. The methods used to compute these numbers are described in detail in the "Statistical Toolbox" introduction in the front of the book. The important distinctions between them are:

• DVOA is a rate statistic, while DYAR is a cumulative statistic. Thus, a higher DVOA means more value per pass play, while a higher DYAR means more aggregate value over the entire season.

• Because DYAR is defense-adjusted and YAR is not, a player whose DYAR is higher than his YAR faced a harder-than-average schedule. A player whose DYAR is lower than his YAR faced an easier-than-average schedule.

To qualify for ranking in YAC, receiving DVOA, or receiving DYAR, a wide receiver must have had 50 passes thrown to him in that season. We ranked 85 wideouts in 2010, 89 wideouts in 2009, and 79 in 2008. Tight ends qualify with 25 targets in a given season; we ranked 45 tight ends in 2010, 49 tight ends in 2009, and 43 in 2008.

The final four columns break down pass length based on the Football Outsiders charting project. The categories are **Short** (5 yards or less), **Mid** (6-15 yards), **Deep** (16-25 yards), and **Bomb** (26 or more yards). These numbers are based on distance in the air only and include both complete and incomplete passes.

The italicized row of statistics for the 2011 season is our 2011 KUBIAK projection based on a complicated regression analysis that takes into account numerous variables including projected role, performance over the past two years, projected team offense and defense, projected quarterback statistics, historical comparables, height, age, and strength of schedule.

It is difficult to accurately project statistics for a 162-game baseball season, but it is exponentially more difficult to accurately project statistics for a 16-game football season. Consider the listed projections not as a prediction of exact numbers, but as the mean of a range of possible performances. What's important is less the exact number of yards we project, and more which players are projected to improve or decline. Actual performance will vary from our projection less for veteran starters and more for rookies and third-stringers, for whom we must base our projections on much smaller career statistical samples. Touchdown numbers will vary more than yardage numbers. Players facing suspension or recovering from injury have those missed games taken into account.

A few low-round rookies, guys listed at seventh on the depth chart, and players who are listed as wide receivers but really only play special teams are briefly discussed at the end of the chapter in a section we call "Going Deep."

Two notes regarding our advanced metrics: We cannot yet fully separate the performance of a receiver from the performance of his quarterback. Be aware that one will affect the other. In addition, these statistics measure only passes thrown to a receiver, not performance on plays when he is not thrown the ball, such as blocking and drawing double teams.

Top 20 WR by DYAR (Total Value), 2010

Rank	Player	Team	DYAR
1	Mike Wallace	PIT	457
2	Brandon Lloyd	DEN	414
3	Greg Jennings	GB	330
4	Roddy White	ATL	294
5	Andre Johnson	HOU	284
6	Hakeem Nicks	NYG	276
7	Calvin Johnson	DET	258
8	Dwayne Bowe	KC	255
9	Kenny Britt	TEN	252
10	Jeremy Maclin	PHI	251
11	Deion Branch	SEA/NE	246
12	Steve Johnson	BUF	236
13	Miles Austin	DAL	236
14	Austin Collie	IND	231
15	Marques Colston	NO	220
16	Derrick Mason	BAL	216
17	Johnny Knox	CHI	207
18	Lance Moore	NO	205
19	Robert Meachem	NO	187
20	Mario Manningham	NYG	187

Top 20 WR by DVOA (Value per Pass), 2010

Rank	Player	Team	DVOA
1	Mike Wallace	PIT	48.8%
2	Kenny Britt	TEN	28.5%
3	Austin Collie	IND	28.4%
4	Robert Meachem	NO	22.7%
5	Deion Branch	SEA/NE	20.5%
6	Brandon Lloyd	DEN	20.0%
7	Greg Jennings	GB	19.6%
8	Jeremy Maclin	PHI	15.5%
9	Johnny Knox	CHI	14.7%
10	Lance Moore	NO	14.6%
11	Hakeem Nicks	NYG	14.6%
12	Jordan Shipley	CIN	14.1%
13	Kevin Walter	HOU	14.0%
14	Derrick Mason	BAL	13.5%
15	Andre Johnson	HOU	13.2%
16	Mario Manningham	NYG	12.4%
17	Miles Austin	DAL	12.2%
18	Dwayne Bowe	KC	11.9%
19	Mike Sims-Walker	JAC	11.5%
20	Calvin Johnson	DET	11.2%

Top 10 TE by DYAR (Total Value), 2010

Rank	Player	Team	DYAR
1	Antonio Gates	SD	371
2	Rob Gronkowski	NE	249
3	Jason Witten	DAL	215
4	Vernon Davis	SF	207
5	Aaron Hernandez	NE	160
6	Anthony Fasano	MIA	144
7	Kellen Winslow	TB	135
8	Todd Heap	BAL	134
9	Benjamin Watson	CLE	125
10	Jacob Tamme	IND	124

Top 10 TE by DVOA (Value per Play), 2010

Rank	Player	Team	DVOA
1	Antonio Gates	SD	79.5%
2	Jermichael Finley	GB	57.8%
3	Rob Gronkowski	NE	53.3%
4	Evan Moore	CLE	41.4%
5	Fred Davis	WAS	40.0%
6	Randy McMichael	SD	31.2%
7	Aaron Hernandez	NE	30.9%
8	Anthony Fasano	MIA	29.1%
9	Joel Dreessen	HOU	28.6%
10	Vernon Davis	SF	27.5%

Seyi Ajirotutu

Height: 6-4　Weight: 204　College: Fresno State　Draft: 2010/ (FA)　Born: 12-Jun-1987　Age: 24　Risk: Yellow

Year	Team	G	Rec	Pass	Yds	C%	+/-	Yd/C	TD	FUM	YAC	Rk	DVOA	Rk	DYAR	Rk	YAR	Short	Mid	Deep	Bomb
2010	SD	10	13	23	262	57%	2.9	20.2	2	0	5.4	--	39.6%	--	91	--	95	25%	40%	20%	15%
2011	SD		10	19	177	53%	--	17.7	1				14.0%								

Ajirotutu came on with some targets at midseason as A.J. Smith and Vincent Jackson continued their contract dance; he was especially impressive in his first career start against the Texans in Week 9, catching four passes for 111 yards and two scores against Houston's vacu-suck pass defense. He's still getting the hang of things, but Ajirotutu is a good straight-line receiver who could get a few more targets in 2011.

Danario Alexander

Height: 6-5   Weight: 215   College: Missouri   Draft: 2010/ (FA)   Born: 7-Aug-1988   Age: 23   Risk: Green

Year	Team	G	Rec	Pass	Yds	C%	+/-	Yd/C	TD	FUM	YAC	Rk	DVOA	Rk	DYAR	Rk	YAR	Short	Mid	Deep	Bomb
2010	STL	8	20	37	306	54%	0.5	15.3	1	0	5.7	--	1.0%	--	43	--	62	44%	25%	9%	22%
2011	STL		25	45	338	56%	--	13.5	1				-9.0%								

Four surgeries on his left knee, including one following the 2010 Senior Bowl, kept the productive (191 receptions, 2,278 yards, 22 touchdowns in college) receiver from the University of Missouri from being selected in the 2010 NFL Draft. Signed in August, the Rams were able to stash Alexander on their practice squad until Mark Clayton landed on injured reserve in Week 5. The Rams think so highly of Alexander, upon being activated from the practice squad, he was signed to a four-year contract with a signing bonus equivalent to that of a late seventh-round pick. Alexander demonstrated his big-play ability in his NFL debut, catching four passes for 72 yards and a 38-yard touchdown against the San Diego Chargers, the team's longest aerial score of the season. Alexander had two of the Rams' four 40+ yard passing plays last season, but also underwent a fifth procedure on his left knee. If healthy, Alexander can be the downfield playmaker the Rams need on the outside. However, that appears to be a very big "if".

Danny Amendola

Height: 5-11   Weight: 183   College: Texas Tech   Draft: 2008/ (FA)   Born: 2-Nov-1985   Age: 26   Risk: Yellow

Year	Team	G	Rec	Pass	Yds	C%	+/-	Yd/C	TD	FUM	YAC	Rk	DVOA	Rk	DYAR	Rk	YAR	Short	Mid	Deep	Bomb
2009	STL	14	43	64	326	69%	0.1	7.6	1	1	4.3	41	-31.2%	87	-97	85	-70	70%	23%	7%	0%
2010	STL	16	85	123	689	69%	3.6	8.1	3	1	4.3	33	-19.8%	76	-70	79	-46	60%	35%	4%	1%
2011	STL		72	103	684	70%	--	9.5	3				2.7%								

Amendola quickly emerged as Sam Bradford's preferred target in the Rams' short-passing game, leading the team in receptions and receiving yards while tying for the lead in receiving touchdowns. However, between injuries to Donnie Avery and Mark Clayton and inconsistent performances from Brandon Gibson and Laurent Robinson, opposing defenses were able to focus on Amendola, who posted negative DVOAs on each down (including a -19.2% on third and fourth down). As a more quick than fast, white slot receiver with punt return ability, Amendola has been compared to Wes Welker since before he (like Welker in 2004) went undrafted out of Texas Tech in 2008. Those comparisons have gone into overload with the Rams' hiring Josh McDaniels as offensive coordinator. Welker's career took off in 2007, becoming a perennial 100-catch player in his first season in a McDaniels-coordinated offense. Welker turned 26 that season, the same age Amendola will turn in November. With Bradford leading McDaniels' spread offense, Amendola could certainly take the next, relatively short step up to the 100-catch mark this season. But without a player to take the top off opposing defenses, the YAC opportunities may not be as available for Amendola as they've been for Welker in New England.

David Anderson

Height: 5-10   Weight: 195   College: Colorado State   Draft: 2006/7 (251)   Born: 28-Jul-1983   Age: 28   Risk: Blue

Year	Team	G	Rec	Pass	Yds	C%	+/-	Yd/C	TD	FUM	YAC	Rk	DVOA	Rk	DYAR	Rk	YAR	Short	Mid	Deep	Bomb
2008	HOU	16	19	29	241	66%	0.5	12.7	2	0	6.3	--	13.1%	--	59	--	52	44%	52%	4%	0%
2009	HOU	16	38	53	370	72%	3.5	9.7	0	0	3.7	58	-3.2%	49	40	56	46	52%	44%	4%	0%
2010	HOU	12	11	18	117	61%	1.1	10.6	0	0	4.8	--	-11.6%	--	2	--	-4	53%	20%	20%	7%
2011	DEN		4	8	44	50%	--	11.1	0				-16.3%								

Another example of the career-enhancing ability of playing college football with the son of an NFL coach (Gary Kubiak's son Klint), Anderson got a token start when the Texans opened in a four-wide receiver set but spent most of the year relegated to the pine, as the emergence of tight end Joel Dreessen left less room for the Texans' fourth receiver. He'll get a shot at playing a similar role in a less pass-happy offense in Denver.

Anthony Armstrong   Height: 5-11   Weight: 183   College: West Texas A&M   Draft: 2005/ (FA)   Born: 29-Mar-1983   Age: 28   Risk: Red

Year	Team	G	Rec	Pass	Yds	C%	+/-	Yd/C	TD	FUM	YAC	Rk	DVOA	Rk	DYAR	Rk	YAR	Short	Mid	Deep	Bomb
2010	WAS	15	44	86	871	51%	1.3	19.8	3	1	3.6	53	7.4%	29	133	31	125	18%	36%	24%	22%
2011	WAS		17	33	226	52%	--	13.3	0				-12.3%								

A former Arena leaguer who spent most of 2009 on the Redskins' practice squad, Armstrong was pushed as the antithesis of Albert Haynesworth and the new regime's sign of what you could accomplish with hard work. Armstrong produced a solid season as a deep threat and second receiver across from Santana Moss, with a 51 percent catch rate on mostly deep routes. In any event, getting decent production for the league minimum is a very rare victory for the Redskins. Jabar Gaffney takes his starting role this year.

Devin Aromashodu   Height: 6-2   Weight: 202   College: Auburn   Draft: 2006/7 (233)   Born: 23-May-1984   Age: 27   Risk: Green

Year	Team	G	Rec	Pass	Yds	C%	+/-	Yd/C	TD	FUM	YAC	Rk	DVOA	Rk	DYAR	Rk	YAR	Short	Mid	Deep	Bomb
2009	CHI	10	24	43	298	56%	-0.5	12.4	4	0	3.5	--	0.8%	--	45	--	61	30%	40%	20%	10%
2010	CHI	14	10	24	149	42%	-2.3	14.9	0	0	5.1	--	-29.2%	--	-31	--	-31	29%	43%	19%	10%
2011	MIN		17	32	239	53%	--	14.1	1				0.2%								

Aromashodu caught five passes in Week 1 last season but also dropped one and ran a few incorrect routes. He quickly dropped out of the Bears game plan, and the team didn't tender him as a restricted free agent in the off-season. Aromashodu has size and wheels, but cannot block and has no special teams value. The Vikings needed fresh bodies at wide receiver, and Aromashodu could fit as a deep threat in the slot, though it's hard to imagine a bad blocker getting a lot of opportunities in Bill Musgrave's run-heavy system.

Miles Austin   Height: 6-3   Weight: 215   College: Monmouth   Draft: 2006/ (FA)   Born: 30-Jun-1984   Age: 27   Risk: Yellow

Year	Team	G	Rec	Pass	Yds	C%	+/-	Yd/C	TD	FUM	YAC	Rk	DVOA	Rk	DYAR	Rk	YAR	Short	Mid	Deep	Bomb
2008	DAL	12	13	23	278	57%	1.7	21.4	3	0	7.7	--	48.7%	--	106	--	99	26%	35%	13%	26%
2009	DAL	16	81	124	1320	65%	6.6	16.3	11	1	7.4	2	28.3%	5	396	4	418	31%	46%	15%	7%
2010	DAL	16	69	119	1041	58%	-1.6	15.1	7	1	6.2	4	12.2%	17	236	13	245	32%	48%	11%	10%
2011	DAL		81	138	1183	59%	--	14.6	9				11.5%								

Austin nearly hit his wildly-pessimistic KUBIAK projection from last year's book (63 catches for 970 yards and seven touchdowns), with a drop in his yards after catch meeting a significant decline in his catch rate. Swapping out ten games of Tony Romo for Jon Kitna didn't help, but Austin had 11 drops, more than all but two players in the league. It's easy to create some murky storyline that involves his summer fling with Kim Kardashian, his contract extension, and a lack of focus during the season, but the skills are still there. In fact, considering Austin's once-wonky hamstring stayed happy for the second consecutive season, maybe we should credit Skechers Shape-Ups. All the ability Austin showed in 2009 is still there, so expect fewer drops as part of a bounce-back season in 2011.

Jason Avant   Height: 6-0   Weight: 210   College: Michigan   Draft: 2006/4 (109)   Born: 20-Apr-1983   Age: 28   Risk: Green

Year	Team	G	Rec	Pass	Yds	C%	+/-	Yd/C	TD	FUM	YAC	Rk	DVOA	Rk	DYAR	Rk	YAR	Short	Mid	Deep	Bomb
2008	PHI	15	32	57	377	56%	-1.2	11.8	2	0	2.4	72	-0.7%	44	51	54	43	31%	39%	24%	6%
2009	PHI	16	41	58	587	71%	6.7	14.3	3	1	4.6	30	20.6%	11	157	29	155	39%	32%	26%	4%
2010	PHI	16	51	75	573	68%	8.5	11.2	1	0	3.1	65	6.6%	32	113	42	113	34%	42%	18%	6%
2011	PHI		41	67	475	61%	--	11.6	2				-0.1%								

With little hope of supplanting the receivers in front of him, Avant had what will probably amount to his career year in 2010. The injury to DeSean Jackson created more targets for Avant, and while his catch rate, DVOA, and yards per attempt all declined, plus-minus shows how good his hands were, even for an underneath slot receiver. Expect his stats to drop in 2011.

Donnie Avery

Height: 5-11 Weight: 192 College: Houston   Draft: 2008/2 (33)   Born: 12-Jun-1984   Age: 27   Risk: Yellow

Year	Team	G	Rec	Pass	Yds	C%	+/-	Yd/C	TD	FUM	YAC	Rk	DVOA	Rk	DYAR	Rk	YAR	Short	Mid	Deep	Bomb
2008	STL	15	53	104	674	52%	-3.8	12.7	3	0	3.8	41	-16.5%	71	-32	75	-7	34%	30%	17%	18%
2009	STL	16	47	98	589	49%	-10.8	12.5	5	1	5.3	16	-22.7%	77	-75	80	-49	38%	34%	15%	14%
2011	STL		31	52	363	60%	--	11.7	1					-14.8%								

Avery's speed was expected to be a valuable asset to the 2010 Rams offense, but a torn right anterior cruciate ligament in the third preseason game ended his season before it began. Perceived as an injury-prone player, Avery had actually appeared in 31 straight games for the Rams prior to the injury. Avery was reportedly running a 4.4 forty in late May, and weighed in the 190-pound range, cutting around ten of the nearly 20 pounds he had put on for the 2010 season. 2011 is a pivotal season for Avery, who is entering the final year of his rookie contract. With increased talent and competition at the receiver position, his future with the Rams hinges not only upon his ability to come back from a serious injury, but to produce at the level expected of a second-round draft pick.

Jonathan Baldwin

Height: 6-5 Weight: 230 College: Pittsburgh   Draft: 2011/1 (26)   Born: 10-Aug-1989   Age: 22   Risk: Red

Year	Team	G	Rec	Pass	Yds	C%	+/-	Yd/C	TD	FUM	YAC	Rk	DVOA	Rk	DYAR	Rk	YAR	Short	Mid	Deep	Bomb
2011	KC		25	52	284	48%	--	11.4	2					-23.7%								

The Chiefs surprised a lot of people by selecting Baldwin in the first round despite needs elsewhere and some questionable college tape on Baldwin's part. While Baldwin gets up to speed pretty well for his size and will make that extra effort to catch the ball out of his area, he tends to struggle with the timing on shorter precision routes. It's as if he has trouble corralling everything in a short space over a short period of time. He isn't especially quick with his feet, and he's not as physical at the line as you'd expect. His numbers show how he was used in a big-play role at Pittsburgh: He averaged over 15 yards per catch in 2010 with a catch rate of just 56 percent, and in 2009, he averaged 19.5 yards per catch with a catch rate of 55 percent. He seems to have too many of the negative traits common to big receivers without enough of the attributes, but the Chiefs seem to believe that he's more than a size/speed guy. The scouting projection seems to say "Dwayne Jarrett," but obviously Kansas City's scouting projection says something else.

Arrelious Benn

Height: 6-1 Weight: 219 College: Illinois   Draft: 2010/2 (39)   Born: 8-Sep-1988   Age: 23   Risk: Yellow

Year	Team	G	Rec	Pass	Yds	C%	+/-	Yd/C	TD	FUM	YAC	Rk	DVOA	Rk	DYAR	Rk	YAR	Short	Mid	Deep	Bomb
2010	TB	15	25	38	395	66%	3.3	15.8	2	1	6.4	--	23.7%	--	113	--	111	42%	33%	8%	17%
2011	TB		45	79	630	57%	--	14.0	5					-2.2%								

The Bucs haven't caught up with the new trend of multi-receiver sets; when guys not named Mike Williams or Kellen Winslow get on the field, they'd better make something happen. Benn got the first targets of his rookie year when Josh Johnson was throwing him passes in garbage time against the Steelers in Week 3, and his role increased through the season as his comfort in the offense increased. Just as he hit his stride, two weeks after a huge game against the Redskins, he tore his left ACL in Week 16 against Seattle. Benn impressed enough to get a larger role alongside Williams if he's healthy enough to make an impact in the preseason.

Earl Bennett

Height: 5-11 Weight: 209 College: Vanderbilt   Draft: 2008/3 (70)   Born: 23-Mar-1987   Age: 24   Risk: Green

Year	Team	G	Rec	Pass	Yds	C%	+/-	Yd/C	TD	FUM	YAC	Rk	DVOA	Rk	DYAR	Rk	YAR	Short	Mid	Deep	Bomb
2008	CHI	10	0	1	0	0%	-0.7	0.0	0	0	0.0	--	-102.7%	--	-7	--	-7	0%	100%	0%	0%
2009	CHI	16	54	88	717	61%	-1.7	13.3	2	1	5.6	13	-4.7%	54	54	50	51	43%	34%	21%	2%
2010	CHI	14	46	70	561	66%	2.5	12.2	3	1	4.5	31	9.2%	23	118	38	124	33%	60%	6%	1%
2011	CHI		56	83	609	67%	--	10.9	3					0.5%								

Either by design or some spooky coincidence, three Bears players were targeted exactly 70 times last season: Bennett, Matt Forte, and Greg Olsen. Devin Hester had 73 targets; when Mike Martz finally abandons offensive coordinating for performance art, it will take us at least three years to notice the difference. Bennett was targeted almost exclusively on short passes, the average throw to him traveling just eight yards through the air. Bennett got a lot of end zone opportunities (he was 7-of-18 in the red zone, with three touchdowns), but he's not a traditional goal-line or third-down receiver, and Roy Williams will probably get a too-long look in that role. He's just a good all-around player who picks up all the roles the other receivers and backs aren't suited for. Bennett should probably absorb some of Hester's targets and get more opportunities than Williams, but Martz moves in mysterious ways.

Bernard Berrian

Height: 6-1 Weight: 190 College: Fresno State   Draft: 2004/3 (78)   Born: 27-Dec-1980   Age: 31   Risk: Red

Year	Team	G	Rec	Pass	Yds	C%	+/-	Yd/C	TD	FUM	YAC	Rk	DVOA	Rk	DYAR	Rk	YAR	Short	Mid	Deep	Bomb
2008	MIN	16	48	95	964	51%	-3.5	20.1	7	0	6.4	3	12.4%	18	197	18	220	16%	45%	14%	24%
2009	MIN	16	55	92	618	60%	-0.4	11.2	4	0	3.4	65	0.0%	42	93	45	92	32%	41%	15%	12%
2010	MIN	14	28	54	252	52%	-4.4	9.0	0	0	2.8	72	-26.8%	81	-65	78	-75	37%	43%	12%	8%
2011	MIN		56	92	762	61%	--	13.6	4				-3.8%								

Berrian's longest catch from a quarterback other than Brett Favre was 14 yards. He doesn't have deep wheels anymore, and the Vikings were at a loss for what to do with a speed receiver who lacked speed. Cutting him was not an option, because the team had too many injuries. Berrian tried to play a screens-and-hitches role, but he lacks the quickness for that role. Berrian skipped the player's workouts in June because he missed a flight; he has either lost a step in airport terminals or was looking for Percy Harvin's phone. This is the kind of fading, somewhat-disgruntled veteran that a rebuilding team should get rid of, but Berrian is still in the Vikings plans, mainly because they are very thin at receiver.

Davone Bess

Height: 5-11 Weight: 193 College: Hawaii   Draft: 2008/ (FA)   Born: 13-Sep-1985   Age: 26   Risk: Green

Year	Team	G	Rec	Pass	Yds	C%	+/-	Yd/C	TD	FUM	YAC	Rk	DVOA	Rk	DYAR	Rk	YAR	Short	Mid	Deep	Bomb
2008	MIA	16	54	75	554	72%	4.0	10.3	1	0	4.5	22	1.3%	38	80	43	91	50%	34%	14%	3%
2009	MIA	16	76	114	758	68%	5.1	10.0	2	3	4.0	54	-0.7%	46	104	41	95	47%	35%	14%	4%
2010	MIA	16	79	126	820	63%	2.2	10.4	5	0	3.9	46	-0.9%	53	111	43	81	38%	50%	10%	2%
2011	MIA		70	111	763	63%	--	10.9	3				2.3%								

Bess is a lot like former Jets standout Wayne Chrebet, another undrafted free agent with marginal speed who nevertheless was able to produce through a combination of skillful route running, excellent hands and a feel for the position. The former Rainbow Warrior's stats ticked up across the board in 2010, as he reached new highs in receptions, yards, yards per reception and touchdowns. He was also easily Miami's most efficient receiver in the red zone with a receiving DVOA of 37.4%, and Bess caught as many touchdowns--three--as the bigger Brandon Marshall, despite having four fewer opportunities. While Bess figures to be used primarily on a combination of crossing patterns and option routes in the new offense, last year he showed he could be effective running intermediate level routes towards the sidelines. He's a good bet to maintain or slightly improve on his numbers.

Anquan Boldin

Height: 6-1 Weight: 218 College: Florida State   Draft: 2003/2 (54)   Born: 3-Oct-1980   Age: 31   Risk: Green

Year	Team	G	Rec	Pass	Yds	C%	+/-	Yd/C	TD	FUM	YAC	Rk	DVOA	Rk	DYAR	Rk	YAR	Short	Mid	Deep	Bomb
2008	ARI	12	89	126	1038	71%	6.9	11.7	11	4	6.1	5	13.9%	14	269	9	248	47%	42%	7%	3%
2009	ARI	15	84	128	1024	66%	9.0	12.2	4	3	4.3	39	-0.6%	45	120	38	170	37%	48%	13%	2%
2010	BAL	16	64	109	837	59%	2.8	13.1	7	1	3.5	55	4.8%	38	152	29	137	25%	47%	17%	11%
2011	BAL		77	124	999	62%	--	13.0	7				11.0%								

Boldin's DVOA stayed constant last year, even while his standard stats looked different. Without a speedy receiver who specialized in getting deep, the Ravens were stuck sending Boldin deep more often than Arizona ever did. However, Boldin did pretty well on those deep passes — probably because his quarterback, Joe Flacco, is better throwing deep passes than short ones. Boldin's DVOA on "bomb" passes was 30 percentage points higher than the average for wide receivers, while his DVOA on "short" passes was 10 percentage points *lower* than the average. With Lee Evans and Torrey Smith in town, Boldin will probably move into a role closer to the one he played in Arizona.

Dwayne Bowe

Height: 6-2   Weight: 221   College: Louisiana State   Draft: 2007/1 (23)   Born: 21-Sep-1984   Age: 27   Risk: Green

Year	Team	G	Rec	Pass	Yds	C%	+/-	Yd/C	TD	FUM	YAC	Rk	DVOA	Rk	DYAR	Rk	YAR	Short	Mid	Deep	Bomb
2008	KC	16	86	157	1022	55%	-9.4	11.9	7	0	4.1	30	-10.3%	66	29	63	53	44%	32%	14%	10%
2009	KC	11	47	87	589	54%	-2.4	12.5	4	1	3.2	67	-4.4%	53	57	49	68	29%	46%	18%	8%
2010	KC	16	72	133	1162	54%	3.4	16.1	15	1	5.1	20	11.9%	18	255	8	294	25%	37%	27%	12%
2011	KC		70	136	1021	51%	--	14.6	8				-0.5%								

Word is that Bowe's targets may drop in 2011 as Todd Haley looks to find ways to spread the ball around, but after the second half of the season that Bowe put in, dropping those targets would be very unwise. Especially against the Broncos in Week 10 and the Seahawks in Week 12, Bowe was targeted constantly and proved to be nearly unstoppable. He was most effective on comebacks and sitting in zones, and while that strategy didn't engineer a lot of breakaway plays, Bowe was one of two engines (Jamaal Charles being the other) who brought some level of consistency to Kansas City's offense.

Deion Branch

Height: 5-9   Weight: 193   College: Louisville   Draft: 2002/2 (65)   Born: 18-Jul-1979   Age: 32   Risk: Yellow

Year	Team	G	Rec	Pass	Yds	C%	+/-	Yd/C	TD	FUM	YAC	Rk	DVOA	Rk	DYAR	Rk	YAR	Short	Mid	Deep	Bomb
2008	SEA	8	30	59	412	51%	-2.7	13.7	4	0	5.0	12	-14.2%	69	-7	69	17	29%	45%	11%	15%
2009	SEA	14	45	79	437	57%	-4.3	9.7	2	0	4.3	40	-22.7%	78	-60	78	-53	47%	28%	13%	12%
2010	2TM	15	61	92	818	66%	6.2	13.4	6	1	4.5	29	20.5%	5	246	11	222	22%	55%	15%	8%
2011	NE		56	88	670	64%	--	12.0	4				7.0%								

After his 9-98-1 homecoming game against the Ravens, Branch settled into a minor role for a few weeks while the Patriots offense found itself. Once receiver roles were sorted out, Branch had back-to-back seven-catch weeks, followed by a three-week, four-touchdown stretch in which Tom Brady started to rediscover ways to connect with Branch on deep passes. Even in his best seasons, Branch was more of a head-of-committee receiver than a true No. 1 guy. At 32, he's a good cog in a great machine, but it's a role he relishes playing in New England. Branch can be limited to a three-catch performance by better cornerbacks, so his fantasy value, like his real value, comes from making him part of a committee and waiting for mismatches. The presence of Chad Ochocinco will create a few of those mismatches.

Steve Breaston

Height: 6-1   Weight: 175   College: Michigan   Draft: 2007/5 (142)   Born: 20-Aug-1983   Age: 28   Risk: Yellow

Year	Team	G	Rec	Pass	Yds	C%	+/-	Yd/C	TD	FUM	YAC	Rk	DVOA	Rk	DYAR	Rk	YAR	Short	Mid	Deep	Bomb
2008	ARI	16	77	113	1006	68%	11.6	13.1	3	0	3.0	60	14.1%	13	239	14	222	31%	42%	15%	12%
2009	ARI	15	55	82	712	67%	7.9	12.9	3	0	2.9	76	12.7%	20	163	27	196	27%	37%	29%	6%
2010	ARI	13	47	87	718	54%	-1.5	15.3	1	0	3.4	57	-0.7%	51	78	51	95	26%	36%	25%	13%
2011	KC		38	69	575	55%	--	15.1	2				-1.7%								

2010 saw Steve Breaston step into the role opposite Larry Fitzgerald as Arizona's number two receiver. Because of the Cardinals QB "situation" it is impossible to tell whether or not he is up to the job after just one season. He has speed to stretch the field, but hasn't shown great ability to beat bump coverage at the line of scrimmage. He signed with his old coordinator Todd Haley in Kansas City, but he will apparently not be starting.

Dezmon Briscoe Height: 6-2 Weight: 207 College: Kansas Draft: 2010/6 (191) Born: 14-Aug-1989 Age: 22 Risk: Red

Year	Team	G	Rec	Pass	Yds	C%	+/-	Yd/C	TD	FUM	YAC	Rk	DVOA	Rk	DYAR	Rk	YAR	Short	Mid	Deep	Bomb
2010	CIN	2	6	7	93	86%	1.7	15.5	1	0	5.5	--	57.0%	--	40	--	38	43%	43%	0%	14%
2011	TB		30	54	456	56%	--	15.2	4				1.4%								

Briscoe was considered a big-time sleeper last year, which makes it odd that Cincinnati thought they could sneak him through waivers and onto the practice squad. They couldn't, and Tampa Bay grabbed him by offering him the rookie minimum ($320,000) rather than the typical practice squad salary ($88,400 in the previous CBA). He's a big, physical receiver with strong hands, and while there were concerns about his speed at the combine last year, he certainly didn't look slow catching a 54-yard bomb from Josh Freeman late in Tampa Bay's last game of the season. He's currently penciled in as the No. 3 receiver.

Kenny Britt Height: 6-3 Weight: 218 College: Rutgers Draft: 2009/1 (30) Born: 19-Sep-1988 Age: 23 Risk: Green

Year	Team	G	Rec	Pass	Yds	C%	+/-	Yd/C	TD	FUM	YAC	Rk	DVOA	Rk	DYAR	Rk	YAR	Short	Mid	Deep	Bomb
2009	TEN	16	42	75	701	56%	1.2	16.7	3	1	4.2	44	10.7%	25	140	36	140	20%	51%	20%	10%
2010	TEN	12	42	73	775	58%	7.7	18.5	9	1	2.9	69	28.5%	2	252	9	253	16%	39%	25%	20%
2011	TEN		59	115	829	51%	--	14.0	6				-5.1%								

Except for the four games he missed with an injury and the week he was manned up against Nnamdi Asomugha where Vince Young never looked his direction, Britt had a phenomenal sophomore campaign. He drew the most highlights for a 7-catch, 225-yard, 3-score game against the Eagles, where he had to make adjustments to several poorly-thrown balls by Kerry Collins, but regularly showcased deep ability, explosiveness, and physicality no Titans receiver had shown in years. The only thing beside health preventing him from being one of the league's top receivers in 2011 is lack of Chris Johnson's "running away from the cops speed," as he was arrested in New Jersey in April and June 2011. His father suggested he might find be better off in Tennessee, but he was questioned and benched in connection with an October bar fight in Nashville and was also wanted by police in connection with lying to the State of Tennessee about his New Jersey driver's license being suspended. Britt may face league discipline for the offseason arrests, so adjust your fantasy expectations accordingly.

Antonio Brown Height: 5-10 Weight: 186 College: Central Michigan Draft: 2010/6 (195) Born: 10-Jul-1988 Age: 23 Risk: Green

Year	Team	G	Rec	Pass	Yds	C%	+/-	Yd/C	TD	FUM	YAC	Rk	DVOA	Rk	DYAR	Rk	YAR	Short	Mid	Deep	Bomb
2010	PIT	9	16	19	167	84%	2.2	10.4	0	0	6.9	--	26.2%	--	57	--	51	63%	21%	11%	5%
2011	PIT		16	26	188	62%	--	11.8	1				10.0%								

Brown gradually surpassed Randle El as Pittsburgh's fourth receiver, then made two huge catches that were integral to the Super Bowl run: a 58-yard bomb in the fourth quarter against Baltimore, and the third-and-6 reception that iced the AFC Championship win over New York. Neither of those catches showed off Brown's best attribute: his ability to turn on the jets and accelerate to make yards after the catch. One knock on him coming out of Central Michigan was that he lacked toughness, avoiding the middle of the field and going out of bounds to avoid contact along the sideline. You would like to think that a couple of Pittsburgh training camps will have worked that out of him.

Vincent Brown Height: 5-11 Weight: 184 College: San Diego St. Draft: 2011/3 (82) Born: 25-Jan-1989 Age: 22 Risk: Green

Year	Team	G	Rec	Pass	Yds	C%	+/-	Yd/C	TD	FUM	YAC	Rk	DVOA	Rk	DYAR	Rk	YAR	Short	Mid	Deep	Bomb
2011	SD		18	31	224	58%	--	12.4	2				4.2%								

Brown made his way in college as the prototypical West Coast-style receiver; all slants, comebacks, and crosses. In 2010, he was one of the best college receivers in the country, averaging 19.6 yards per catch and an incredible 12.9 yards per target. He is reasonably fast but small (5-foot-11), and durability has been an issue (he missed five games in 2009 with an injury to thumb ligaments), but he fits the "competitor" mold to a T. He caught the eye of Chargers receivers coach Charlie Joiner, which was one advantage to being just down the road from his new NFL home. More impressive on field than in timing drills — and much better at the Senior Bowl than at the scouting combine — Brown has a chance to excel in the slot early on.

Dez Bryant

Height: 6-2   Weight: 225   College: Oklahoma State   Draft: 2010/1 (24)   Born: 4-Nov-1988   Age: 23   Risk: Green

Year	Team	G	Rec	Pass	Yds	C%	+/-	Yd/C	TD	FUM	YAC	Rk	DVOA	Rk	DYAR	Rk	YAR	Short	Mid	Deep	Bomb
2010	DAL	12	45	73	561	62%	3.4	12.5	6	0	4.3	34	5.8%	34	105	47	93	39%	33%	14%	13%
2011	DAL		56	96	810	58%	--	14.5	6				7.1%								

While the brouhaha that saw Bryant briefly banned from a Dallas-area mall in March made for a fun story amidst lockout coverage, something more sinister lurked underneath the surface. Bryant was reportedly allowed back in the mall because, well, he was regarded as one of its most fervent customers. Former mentor Deion Sanders decided that Bryant was dishonest and decided to cut ties with him, while Bryant chalked it up to an endorsement dispute. Reports suggested that Bryant hadn't learned the playbook to an acceptable level during his rookie year. Bryant-backers undoubtedly want to compare him to Randy Moss, but Moss caught 17 touchdowns and was top five in DVOA and DYAR from his first year on. His athleticism and raw talent means that Bryant could advance really quickly if the lightbulb ever turns on for him, but there's no reason to think that it's about to. His season-ending fractured fibula should be fine by the time the 2011 campaign starts.

Nate Burleson

Height: 6-0   Weight: 192   College: Nevada   Draft: 2003/3 (71)   Born: 19-Aug-1981   Age: 30   Risk: Green

Year	Team	G	Rec	Pass	Yds	C%	+/-	Yd/C	TD	FUM	YAC	Rk	DVOA	Rk	DYAR	Rk	YAR	Short	Mid	Deep	Bomb
2008	SEA	1	5	9	60	56%	0.2	12.0	1	0	1.4	--	14.4%	--	20	--	21	22%	56%	22%	0%
2009	SEA	13	63	103	812	61%	1.6	12.9	3	2	4.4	33	0.8%	40	110	40	125	31%	40%	22%	7%
2010	DET	14	55	86	625	64%	-1.8	11.4	6	2	5.5	13	-4.3%	62	58	60	61	44%	36%	19%	1%
2011	DET		55	98	670	56%	--	12.2	3				-3.5%								

Freed from the burden of being the go-to receiver Tim Ruskell (and no one else) thought he could be in Seattle, Burleson reinvented himself as a nifty-shifty slot guy, mixing lots of hitches and tunnel screens with the occasional reverse. Burleson could not draw coverage away from Calvin Johnson, but he moved the chains and provided an adequate safety valve for backup quarterbacks Shaun Hill and Drew Stanton. Burleson's targets will decrease with Titus Young around, but his role will be similar, and his per-touch production should increase with defenses focused on two legitimate downfield receivers.

Plaxico Burress

Height: 6-5   Weight: 226   College: Michigan State   Draft: 2000/1 (8)   Born: 12-Aug-1977   Age: 34   Risk: Red

Year	Team	G	Rec	Pass	Yds	C%	+/-	Yd/C	TD	FUM	YAC	Rk	DVOA	Rk	DYAR	Rk	YAR	Short	Mid	Deep	Bomb
2008	NYG	10	35	66	454	53%	-3.1	13.0	4	0	1.8	78	4.9%	30	94	37	98	19%	48%	19%	14%
2011	NYJ		49	93	591	53%	--	12.1	5				-10.4%								

Chase Stuart of pro-football-reference did the best job of explaining why it is hard to expect much from Plaxico Burress' comeback. Even if we look for wide receivers who were similar to Burress before his 2008 decline, we don't find a lot of guys who were hugely successful four years later at the age of 34. The FO similarity scores say the same thing. The most similar receiver to Burress from 2005-2006 was Anthony Carter from 1988-1990. In 1994, Carter had eight catches in four games. Anthony Miller 1993-1995? Wasn't even playing in 1999. Jake Reed 1995-1997? Reed had 309 yards and a touchdown in 2001 at age 34. Johnnie Morton, Bill Schroeder, and Brian Blades didn't last into their mid-30s. Isaac Bruce is the most similar receiver from age 28-30 who was still a top receiver at age 34 (74 catches for 1,098 yards in 2006).

Deon Butler Height: 5-10 Weight: 182 College: Penn State   Draft: 2009/3 (91) Born: 4-Jan-1986 Age: 26 Risk: Green

Year	Team	G	Rec	Pass	Yds	C%	+/-	Yd/C	TD	FUM	YAC	Rk	DVOA	Rk	DYAR	Rk	YAR	Short	Mid	Deep	Bomb
2009	SEA	16	15	42	175	36%	-8.5	11.7	0	0	3.1	--	-40.1%	--	-91	--	-93	20%	60%	3%	18%
2010	SEA	13	36	70	385	51%	-6.4	10.7	4	0	3.2	60	-20.7%	77	-46	76	-34	43%	31%	13%	13%
2011	SEA		23	44	254	52%	--	11.0	1				-22.6%								

You know that cute girl in high school who you talked to every day? But every time you asked her out, she'd mumble something about hanging out with her family, then you'd hear she went out with some other guy? So you'd write her off, but on Monday she'd tell you that you were special and you'd fall for her again, remember her? Uh, neither do we. But if we did, that's who Deon Butler would remind us of, a lost cause who shows just enough brilliant temptations to keep you interested. In a five-game stretch beginning on Halloween, Butler was the target on 32 passes. One of those resulted in a 63-yard touchdown against Arizona. The other 31 balls produced 11 catches for just 40 yards, an average of 3.6 per catch that would be terrible for rushes, let alone receptions. That's particularly galling for a guy who ran a 4.38 forty at the Combine in 2009. A broken leg ended Butler's season in December, and as of mid-June he still wasn't running at full speed. It all adds up to another season in the Friend Zone for Seahawks fans.

Andre Caldwell Height: 6-0 Weight: 204 College: Florida   Draft: 2008/3 (97) Born: 15-Apr-1985 Age: 26 Risk: Green

Year	Team	G	Rec	Pass	Yds	C%	+/-	Yd/C	TD	FUM	YAC	Rk	DVOA	Rk	DYAR	Rk	YAR	Short	Mid	Deep	Bomb
2008	CIN	7	11	19	78	58%	-0.3	7.1	0	0	3.5	--	-30.5%	--	-27	--	-36	50%	44%	6%	0%
2009	CIN	16	51	80	432	64%	-1.7	8.5	3	2	2.6	78	-8.3%	59	27	60	21	41%	50%	5%	4%
2010	CIN	15	25	37	345	68%	2.1	13.8	0	0	4.2	--	16.9%	--	91	--	87	42%	36%	8%	14%
2011	CIN		38	64	415	59%	--	10.9	2				-5.3%								

Jerome Simpson's late-season surge is celebrated by Cincinnati fans, but Caldwell's late-season surge is nearly as impressive. He had just 75 yards through Week 14, then topped that in each of the final three games. Caldwell took Terrell Owens' place once T.O. was out for the year, and proved to fit the outside receiver job better than he had the slot receiver position he mostly played in 2009. He ran longer routes and caught a higher percentage of passes. A.J. Green's arrival means there's one starting spot for Simpson and Caldwell to fight over during training camp.

Greg Camarillo Height: 6-1 Weight: 190 College: Stanford   Draft: 2005/ (FA) Born: 18-Apr-1982 Age: 29 Risk: Green

Year	Team	G	Rec	Pass	Yds	C%	+/-	Yd/C	TD	FUM	YAC	Rk	DVOA	Rk	DYAR	Rk	YAR	Short	Mid	Deep	Bomb
2008	MIA	11	55	83	613	66%	3.8	11.1	2	0	3.0	62	-2.5%	50	64	51	96	37%	43%	16%	4%
2009	MIA	16	50	72	552	69%	8.9	11.0	0	0	2.0	87	9.6%	28	132	37	125	23%	53%	19%	6%
2010	MIN	16	20	33	240	61%	-1.0	12.0	1	0	4.4	--	1.5%	--	35	--	30	31%	50%	16%	3%
2011	MIN		12	21	136	57%	--	11.3	1				-4.8%								

The Vikings acquired Camarillo from the Dolphins at the end of August; he had to move from Miami to Minneapolis so quickly that he left most of his possessions and his dog in Florida. The dog drove the U-Haul up a few weeks later, head out the window the whole way, and said that he relished the chance to get back on the open road. Camarillo fielded punts cleanly, caught what was thrown to him, and didn't get hurt or make waves, making him an MVP-caliber performer compared to other Vikings receivers. Only the Dolphins could look at Camarillo and see a 55-catch starter; a 20-catch role is just right for him.

Chris Chambers Height: 5-11 Weight: 210 College: Wisconsin   Draft: 2001/2 (52) Born: 12-Aug-1978 Age: 33 Risk: N/A

Year	Team	G	Rec	Pass	Yds	C%	+/-	Yd/C	TD	FUM	YAC	Rk	DVOA	Rk	DYAR	Rk	YAR	Short	Mid	Deep	Bomb
2008	SD	14	33	64	462	52%	-1.2	14.0	5	0	1.8	77	0.3%	42	64	52	71	22%	43%	23%	12%
2009	2TM	16	45	92	730	49%	-2.5	16.2	5	0	4.2	46	1.1%	39	99	42	79	25%	38%	17%	20%
2010	KC	13	22	43	213	51%	-2.1	9.7	1	0	1.7	--	-21.4%	--	-30	--	-23	20%	56%	10%	15%

Chambers' biggest play of 2010 was actually a 30-yard pass interference call against Oakland's Chris Johnson in Week 9. It was a ticky-tack call, as were most made that day by Jeff Triplette and his Merry Band of Idiots, but that's a story for another time. The Chiefs took Chambers out of the starting lineup by midseason, and by the playoffs he wasn't even active. They released him after the lockout and his career may be over.

Mark Clayton

Height: 5-10   Weight: 193   College: Oklahoma   Draft: 2005/1 (22)   Born: 2-Jul-1982   Age: 29   Risk: N/A

Year	Team	G	Rec	Pass	Yds	C%	+/-	Yd/C	TD	FUM	YAC	Rk	DVOA	Rk	DYAR	Rk	YAR	Short	Mid	Deep	Bomb
2008	BAL	16	41	82	695	50%	-2.0	17.0	3	0	4.2	28	-7.6%	59	32	61	38	25%	43%	12%	21%
2009	BAL	14	34	74	480	46%	-4.0	14.1	2	1	2.4	80	-18.8%	73	-36	72	-43	19%	44%	18%	19%
2010	STL	5	23	42	306	55%	-1.7	13.3	2	0	4.2	--	-11.9%	--	3	--	19	46%	36%	10%	8%

A $2.3 million salary and no discernable role or special teams value prompted the Baltimore Ravens to trade Clayton to the Rams before last season began. Clayton quickly formed a connection with fellow former Sooner Sam Bradford, catching a career-high ten passes (for 119 yards) in his Rams' debut. Through the first four weeks Clayton had emerged as Bradford's security blanket, ranking among the NFC leaders in receptions (25) and receiving yards (306) before suffering a season-ending patellar tendon in his right knee in Week 5. The Rams say they are interested in re-signing Clayton, but they won't do so until his knee improves.

Randall Cobb

Height: 5-11   Weight: 190   College: Kentucky   Draft: 2011/2 (64)   Born: 22-Aug-1990   Age: 21   Risk: Yellow

Year	Team	G	Rec	Pass	Yds	C%	+/-	Yd/C	TD	FUM	YAC	Rk	DVOA	Rk	DYAR	Rk	YAR	Short	Mid	Deep	Bomb
2011	GB		22	35	207	63%	--	9.4	2				-5.4%								

Cobb started his college career as a quarterback, then became a runner-receiver who threw lots of option passes, then started returning kickoffs, and even held for field goals. He averaged 23.7 yards per kickoff and 7.8 yards per punt return as a senior. The numbers aren't great, but Cobb is sure handed, and he will eliminate the need to use starters like Charles Woodson as return men. Cobb can also fit as a nifty slot receiver, but there are only so many footballs to go around until Donald Driver retires. Crafty Mike McCarthy will probably concoct at least one play in which lefty Cobb throws an option pass to Aaron Rodgers.

Austin Collie

Height: 6-1   Weight: 200   College: BYU   Draft: 2009/4 (127)   Born: 11-Nov-1985   Age: 26   Risk: Yellow

Year	Team	G	Rec	Pass	Yds	C%	+/-	Yd/C	TD	FUM	YAC	Rk	DVOA	Rk	DYAR	Rk	YAR	Short	Mid	Deep	Bomb
2009	IND	16	60	90	676	67%	3.4	11.3	7	0	4.1	49	15.8%	15	209	19	200	44%	28%	24%	3%
2010	IND	9	58	71	649	82%	12.1	11.2	8	1	4.9	23	28.4%	3	231	14	261	59%	20%	10%	10%
2011	IND		64	97	715	66%	--	11.2	3				7.7%								

Whether Collie wants to or not, he now will constantly be defined by the concussions he suffered last year. With the nation finally starting to appreciate the dangers of head trauma to NFL players, Collie got laid-out for his second concussion of the season in Week 15 against Jacksonville. Collie had missed four of the previous five games with concussion-related symptoms. In this uncertain time of brain injuries, nobody can say for certain whether Collie should or should not continue to play. He is undaunted and will return as the Colts' much-needed slot receiver. Collie caught an incredible 82 percent of pass attempts last season and was one of Peyton Manning's favorite red zone targets. Still, for someone who makes his living going over the middle, it will be difficult to watch Collie make plays without worrying about what continuing to play is going to do to his long-term health.

Marques Colston   Height: 6-4   Weight: 225 College: Hofstra   Draft: 2006/7 (252) Born: 5-Jun-1983   Age: 28   Risk: Yellow

Year	Team	G	Rec	Pass	Yds	C%	+/-	Yd/C	TD	FUM	YAC	Rk	DVOA	Rk	DYAR	Rk	YAR	Short	Mid	Deep	Bomb
2008	NO	11	47	88	760	53%	-6.4	16.2	5	1	4.9	14	2.8%	33	111	33	110	29%	44%	20%	7%
2009	NO	16	70	107	1074	65%	6.2	15.3	9	2	5.0	25	25.3%	6	331	7	335	31%	47%	17%	5%
2010	NO	15	84	132	1023	64%	4.3	12.2	7	0	3.2	62	8.6%	27	220	15	247	35%	46%	15%	4%
2011	NO		81	126	1054	64%	--	13.0	8				14.1%								

Robert Meachem was a first-down force; Lance Moore a third-down machine. Colston was the second-down monster. His catch rate was 20-25 percent higher, and he had 137 of his 220 DYAR. Colston declined slightly from his huge 2009, following the team-wide trend, but don't let that affect your fantasy decision. Colston was easily the Saints' top red zone threat, thanks to his size, and figures to be once more.

Terrance Copper   Height: 6-0   Weight: 204 College: East Carolina   Draft: 2004/ (FA)   Born: 12-Mar-1982 Age: 29   Risk: Blue

Year	Team	G	Rec	Pass	Yds	C%	+/-	Yd/C	TD	FUM	YAC	Rk	DVOA	Rk	DYAR	Rk	YAR	Short	Mid	Deep	Bomb
2008	2TM	7	0	2	0	0%	-0.7	0.0	0	0	0.0	--	-101.0%	--	-13	--	-13	0%	100%	0%	0%
2009	KC	15	4	6	68	67%	0.2	17.0	0	0	5.3	--	3.2%	--	8	--	8	33%	50%	0%	17%
2010	KC	16	18	28	157	64%	0.8	8.7	0	0	3.4	--	-19.7%	--	-16	--	-9	48%	40%	12%	0%
2011	KC		4	7	42	57%	--	10.5	0				-8.9%								

Primarily a special-teamer through his career, Copper got more reps than he had in recent years when Dexter McCluster missed time and a hole opened up. The Chiefs re-signed him, but the first-round selection of Jon Baldwin probably puts Copper back on the outs as anything but a special teams guy again.

Jerricho Cotchery   Height: 6-1   Weight: 200 College: North Carolina State Draft: 2004/4 (108) Born: 16-Jun-1982 Age: 29   Risk: Green

Year	Team	G	Rec	Pass	Yds	C%	+/-	Yd/C	TD	FUM	YAC	Rk	DVOA	Rk	DYAR	Rk	YAR	Short	Mid	Deep	Bomb
2008	NYJ	16	71	111	858	64%	5.8	12.1	5	2	4.7	20	-1.6%	48	98	35	124	40%	34%	12%	14%
2009	NYJ	14	57	97	821	60%	0.1	14.4	3	0	5.3	17	11.7%	22	185	22	212	35%	38%	21%	7%
2010	NYJ	14	41	86	433	48%	-8.6	10.6	2	0	2.7	75	-23.1%	78	-70	80	-78	34%	42%	14%	10%
2011	PIT		18	33	223	55%	--	12.4	0				-5.7%								

Cotchery seemed poised to have a big year working the middle of the field while defenses concentrated on Braylon Edwards and Santonio Holmes, but it didn't work out that way. Cotchery played through nagging injuries that robbed him of his short-area burst, and many of the short-to-intermediate opportunities were siphoned off by Dustin Keller and LaDainian Tomlinson. If he's healthy, Cotchery is still a physical receiver who has the ability to consistently produce against the nickel corners, linebackers and safeties he'll match up against out of the slot. He apparently asked to be cut so he could go somewhere he could start. Signed in Pittsburgh in August, where he will not start.

Michael Crabtree   Height: 6-2   Weight: 215 College: Texas Tech   Draft: 2009/1 (10) Born: 14-Sep-1987 Age: 24   Risk: Green

Year	Team	G	Rec	Pass	Yds	C%	+/-	Yd/C	TD	FUM	YAC	Rk	DVOA	Rk	DYAR	Rk	YAR	Short	Mid	Deep	Bomb
2009	SF	11	48	86	625	56%	-2.4	13.0	2	1	4.2	45	-19.8%	75	-47	77	-11	38%	32%	18%	12%
2010	SF	16	55	100	741	55%	-2.6	13.5	6	0	5.3	15	2.8%	42	120	36	115	37%	40%	14%	9%
2011	SF		49	94	683	52%	--	13.9	6				0.5%								

We detailed the Crabtree-Alex Smith soap opera in the 49ers team chapter, so here we'll just discuss Michael Crabtree, football player, what he's good at, and where he needs improvement. For starters, he was poor on third downs (-16.3% DVOA). And that's not just because he was the target on a lot of desperation heaves on third-and-long - he converted less than half his opportunities on third or fourth down with five or fewer yards to go. Perhaps not coincidentally, he was pathetic on all short routes (-29.2% DVOA, compared to a league average of -13.7%). On the flip side of that, he was very productive on passes six or more yards downfield (24.9%

DVOA, league average 15.1%), though he was still unreliable, with a catch rate floating just below 50 percent. The lesson is clear: The 49ers should go to Crabtree early in drives, but get him downfield, and realize that at his best, Crabtree is still something of a gamble. His statistics suggest a young Andre Reed, but the 49ers need to use him more like James Lofton.

Patrick Crayton
Height: 6-0   Weight: 205   College: Northwestern Oklahoma St.   Draft: 2004/7 (216)   Born: 7-Apr-1979   Age: 32   Risk: Green

Year	Team	G	Rec	Pass	Yds	C%	+/-	Yd/C	TD	FUM	YAC	Rk	DVOA	Rk	DYAR	Rk	YAR	Short	Mid	Deep	Bomb
2008	DAL	16	39	69	550	57%	-2.4	14.1	4	1	5.2	9	0.9%	40	70	50	71	28%	55%	11%	6%
2009	DAL	16	37	67	622	55%	-2.1	16.8	5	1	7.2	3	15.2%	16	149	32	150	34%	54%	9%	3%
2010	SD	9	28	42	514	67%	4.5	18.4	1	0	7.6	--	41.1%	--	172	--	181	24%	41%	27%	7%
2011	SD		29	48	371	60%	--	12.8	2				15.9%								

The former FO binky has struggled to find his way recently, proving that some second-tier players are second-tier players for a reason. His targets increased in midseason last year after injuries to Malcom Floyd and Legedu Naanee upset the depth chart, but certain parts of his game preclude him from climbing higher — he tends to struggle in traffic, which makes him a good third or fourth option when the main guys are covered and zone-busting comebacks are the order of the day.

Josh Cribbs
Height: 6-1   Weight: 192   College: Kent State   Draft: 2005/ (FA)   Born: 9-Jun-1983   Age: 28   Risk: Green

Year	Team	G	Rec	Pass	Yds	C%	+/-	Yd/C	TD	FUM	YAC	Rk	DVOA	Rk	DYAR	Rk	YAR	Short	Mid	Deep	Bomb
2008	CLE	15	2	7	18	29%	-2.2	9.0	1	0	6.5	--	-17.4%	--	-3	--	-7	57%	14%	14%	14%
2009	CLE	16	20	37	135	54%	0.4	6.8	1	2	4.4	--	-52.8%	--	-115	--	-132	69%	9%	6%	16%
2010	CLE	15	23	39	292	59%	-0.2	12.7	1	0	6.0	--	-0.3%	--	37	--	21	34%	45%	5%	16%
2011	CLE		29	52	395	56%	--	13.6	1				-10.6%								

Josh Cribbs had his best year as a receiver in 2010, and his worst year as a return specialist. Are the two events connected? Only in that Cribbs' struggled with two injuries, both of which came when he was playing wide receiver. First, James Harrison clocked him with a brutal helmet-to-helmet hit that left Cribbs with a concussion. Then he suffered dislocated toes in Week 10 against the Jets, which cost him three games. Cribbs also had 20 carries for 67 yards, mostly in his occasional role as a Wildcat quarterback. His 2011 projection also includes 16 carries for 70 yards.

Victor Cruz
Height: 6-1   Weight: 200   College: Massachusetts   Draft: 2010/ (FA)   Born: 11-Nov-1986   Age: 25   Risk: Yellow

Year	Team	G	Rec	Pass	Yds	C%	+/-	Yd/C	TD	FUM	YAC	Rk	DVOA	Rk	DYAR	Rk	YAR	Short	Mid	Deep	Bomb
2011	NYG		24	40	305	60%	--	12.7	2				-0.3%								

Cruz made his mark with a three-touchdown game against the Jets in the 2010 preseason; for members of the Giants, merely making it through the Meadowlands Derby without tearing any knee ligaments is considered a success, so Cruz quickly became a fan favorite. Cruz made the active roster, but was inactive for a couple of weeks before being redshirted to IR with a hamstring injury. He's competing with Domenik Hixon for the slot receiver spot vacated by Steve Smith.

Craig Davis
Height: 6-1   Weight: 200   College: Louisiana State   Draft: 2007/1 (30)   Born: 2-Oct-1985   Age: 26   Risk: Green

Year	Team	G	Rec	Pass	Yds	C%	+/-	Yd/C	TD	FUM	YAC	Rk	DVOA	Rk	DYAR	Rk	YAR	Short	Mid	Deep	Bomb
2008	SD	4	4	7	59	57%	-0.8	14.8	0	0	8.8	--	14.2%	--	15	--	17	57%	43%	0%	0%
2009	SD	1	6	7	52	86%	1.7	8.7	0	0	3.8	--	25.4%	--	23	--	23	43%	43%	0%	14%
2010	SD	7	21	39	259	54%	-2.8	12.3	1	0	4.2	--	-13.8%	--	-3	--	2	38%	38%	16%	8%
2011	BUF		14	24	199	58%	--	14.2	1				-4.8%								

Peel away the layers of the "A.J. Smith, Personnel Genus" myth, and things like Davis' first-round selection come to light and cast a more serious pall on the proceedings. It' not Smith's fault that Davis has been plagued by injuries over the past couple of years, but his healthy inactive status at other points throughout his career is cause for larger concern. After his release from San Diego, Davis signed a three-year deal with the Bills — Buffalo GM Buddy Nix was in San Diego's front office when Davis was drafted — and he'll add his name to a group of receivers with solid potential and iffy production.

Eric Decker   Height: 6-3   Weight: 217 College: Minnesota   Draft: 2010/3 (87)   Born: 15-Mar-1987   Age: 24   Risk: Red

Year	Team	G	Rec	Pass	Yds	C%	+/-	Yd/C	TD	FUM	YAC	Rk	DVOA	Rk	DYAR	Rk	YAR	Short	Mid	Deep	Bomb
2010	DEN	14	6	8	106	75%	1.2	17.7	1	1	4.0	–	53.3%	–	33	–	31	13%	50%	25%	13%
2011	DEN		25	40	366	63%	--	14.7	2				5.3%								

In the Obligatory White Guy Receiver Comparison template, Decker matches up best with former Denver favorite Easy Ed McCaffrey — a big guy with deceptive speed (there ya go!) who can succeed in the slot or outside. He struggled with a Lisfranc (foot) injury that carried over from his senior season and hampered his rookie campaign, but he got a few looks late in the year and could be a much bigger part of the plan in 2011. Whoever's playing quarterback for the Broncos this season wouldn't have to worry about Decker dropping the ball. Throughout his Minnesota career, he did so just three times on 354 team-charted targets.

Jarett Dillard   Height: 5-10 Weight: 191 College: Rice   Draft: 2009/5 (144) Born: 21-Dec-1985   Age: 26   Risk: Green

Year	Team	G	Rec	Pass	Yds	C%	+/-	Yd/C	TD	FUM	YAC	Rk	DVOA	Rk	DYAR	Rk	YAR	Short	Mid	Deep	Bomb
2009	JAC	7	6	8	106	75%	1.2	17.7	0	0	3.2	–	52.2%	–	36	–	39	13%	50%	25%	13%
2011	JAC		21	37	260	57%	--	12.4	1				-0.9%								

Despite the lack of competition in Jacksonville, Dillard has failed to capitalize on his opportunities thanks to a stress fracture in his toe suffered in 2010's preseason and a broken ankle suffered late in 2009. He was extremely productive at Rice and looked the part early in his rookie season before the ankle injury ended his year. Of all the non-Mike Thomas Jaguars wideouts, he's probably the one with the greatest upside in fantasy leagues. Since he's battling Cecil Shorts for the slot receiver job in a tight end-heavy Dirk Koetter offense, that doesn't exactly mean he should be a sleeper pick this season, unless you play in a 32-team league.

Early Doucet   Height: 6-0   Weight: 209 College: Louisiana State   Draft: 2008/3 (81)   Born: 28-Oct-1985   Age: 26   Risk: Green

Year	Team	G	Rec	Pass	Yds	C%	+/-	Yd/C	TD	FUM	YAC	Rk	DVOA	Rk	DYAR	Rk	YAR	Short	Mid	Deep	Bomb
2008	ARI	7	14	17	90	82%	1.5	6.4	0	0	3.8	–	-4.4%	–	12	–	12	65%	29%	6%	0%
2009	ARI	9	17	24	214	71%	2.1	12.6	1	0	6.3	–	17.2%	–	58	–	63	39%	43%	9%	9%
2010	ARI	10	26	59	291	44%	-9.8	11.2	1	0	3.1	66	-40.0%	85	-122	83	-106	36%	45%	15%	4%
2011	ARI		22	35	292	63%	--	13.3	1				-3.1%								

At some point the LSU product is going to have to prove he can stay healthy. Doucet had missed 22 games in the past three seasons and seems to have been questionable for the rest. He has shown ability to make catches in traffic, and could replace Steve Breaston as the number two option if he could just stay on the field for an extended period of time. Now seems like a good time to mention that Doucet had offseason surgery for a sports hernia.

Harry Douglas   Height: 5-11   Weight: 176 College: Louisville   Draft: 2008/3 (84)   Born: 16-Sep-1985   Age: 26   Risk: Green

Year	Team	G	Rec	Pass	Yds	C%	+/-	Yd/C	TD	FUM	YAC	Rk	DVOA	Rk	DYAR	Rk	YAR	Short	Mid	Deep	Bomb
2008	ATL	16	23	39	320	59%	-0.3	13.9	1	0	4.6	–	-2.2%	–	31	–	18	45%	29%	18%	8%
2010	ATL	16	22	53	294	42%	-8.1	13.4	1	0	5.6	10	-26.7%	80	-59	77	-59	32%	32%	22%	14%
2011	ATL		22	40	316	55%	--	14.3	0				-8.1%								

Douglas struggled to return to his 2008 rookie form after blowing out a knee in 2009. The best part of his game, open-field swerving, was lost, and his catch rate plummeted along with his confidence, though he remained a willing blocker. Douglas saved his lowest catch rate and DVOA for third down, when he was needed most — but then he wasn't much on third down in 2008, either. Should Douglas regain trust in his repaired knee, he could still be valuable on the Georgia Dome turf.

Donald Driver

Height: 6-0   Weight: 188   College: Alcorn State   Draft: 1999/7 (213)   Born: 2-Feb-1975   Age: 36   Risk: Yellow

Year	Team	G	Rec	Pass	Yds	C%	+/-	Yd/C	TD	FUM	YAC	Rk	DVOA	Rk	DYAR	Rk	YAR	Short	Mid	Deep	Bomb
2008	GB	16	74	116	1012	64%	4.5	13.7	5	0	4.7	18	7.6%	25	185	21	180	44%	33%	14%	9%
2009	GB	16	70	112	1061	63%	3.8	15.2	6	1	5.4	14	12.9%	19	242	14	267	38%	35%	14%	13%
2010	GB	15	51	84	565	61%	-1.9	11.1	4	1	3.5	56	-8.7%	68	27	68	27	38%	41%	16%	5%
2011	GB		49	82	651	60%	--	13.3	4				7.6%								

Driver said in June that he hopes to reach the NFL Hall of Fame. He is currently 37th on the all-time receiving yardage list. Another season like last year will push him past 10,000 yards and up to 33rd or 34th, though Andre Johnson is in position to cruise past him. Driver needs about 1,700 yards to reach Rod Smith, a player with a similar career arc, at 23rd. We don't hear a lot of "Rod Smith for Hall of Fame" chatter, and Driver's goals are probably beyond his reach. He is an often-used third target in a high-powered offense poised to contend for another Super Bowl, which is a pretty sweet late-career consolation prize for not reaching Canton.

Julian Edelman

Height: 6-0   Weight: 198   College: Kent State   Draft: 2009/7 (232)   Born: 22-May-1986   Age: 25   Risk: Green

Year	Team	G	Rec	Pass	Yds	C%	+/-	Yd/C	TD	FUM	YAC	Rk	DVOA	Rk	DYAR	Rk	YAR	Short	Mid	Deep	Bomb
2009	NE	11	37	54	359	69%	-1.3	9.7	1	1	7.1	4	-0.8%	47	49	53	22	73%	25%	0%	2%
2010	NE	15	7	14	86	50%	-3.5	12.3	0	0	14.1	--	-28.3%	--	-16	--	-21	79%	14%	7%	0%
2011	NE		20	35	230	57%	--	11.5	2				4.6%								

The Patriots offense was in danger of lapsing into self-parody early in the year, with Edelman catching four passes for 14 yards in Weeks 2 and 3 on top of Wes Welker's hitch-route-and-fall-forward production. The Patriots then relegated Edelman to punt returns, where he was very good, and gave Edelman's playing time to Danny Woodhead and the tight ends. The arrangement worked well for everyone, even Edelman, who had catch-and-run plays of 22 and 40 yards late in the year in a limited role. Even the Patriots only have room for so many pesky slot guys at one time, but Edelman's return skills will keep him on the roster.

Braylon Edwards

Height: 6-3   Weight: 211   College: Michigan   Draft: 2005/1 (3)   Born: 21-Feb-1983   Age: 28   Risk: Red

Year	Team	G	Rec	Pass	Yds	C%	+/-	Yd/C	TD	FUM	YAC	Rk	DVOA	Rk	DYAR	Rk	YAR	Short	Mid	Deep	Bomb
2008	CLE	16	55	138	873	40%	-19.4	15.9	3	0	3.8	36	-16.8%	73	-45	77	-86	31%	33%	21%	15%
2009	2TM	16	45	95	680	47%	-5.8	15.1	4	1	4.1	49	-3.9%	51	68	48	58	23%	41%	19%	17%
2010	NYJ	16	53	101	904	52%	2.2	17.1	7	1	5.4	14	2.4%	43	125	35	136	27%	37%	13%	23%
2011	SF		49	97	746	51%	--	15.2	5				1.0%								

Edwards had quite a fall from grace in the offseason, where he went from potentially one of the top receivers on the market to signing a one-year show me deal with San Francisco for $1 million. Certainly off-the-field issues were a factor—Edwards was involved in a bar fight in Michigan while still on probation for assault stemming from a similar incident in Cleveland, and there is a good chance that Roger Goodell's office will be sending down a suspension. But Edwards has never developed into a complete receiver. His great speed and size make him an excellent deep threat, as his 17.1 yards per reception attests, and he uses his body to shield defenders on slant patterns, but he is an inconsistent route runner, and his struggles with drops are well-documented. The Edwards signing is good news for Frank Gore owners, as he is a tremendous blocker on the outside.

Lee Evans   Height: 5-10 Weight: 202 College: Wisconsin   Draft: 2004/1 (13)   Born: 11-Mar-1981 Age: 30 Risk: Red

Year	Team	G	Rec	Pass	Yds	C%	+/-	Yd/C	TD	FUM	YAC	Rk	DVOA	Rk	DYAR	Rk	YAR	Short	Mid	Deep	Bomb
2008	BUF	16	63	102	1017	62%	4.9	16.1	3	2	4.0	34	11.2%	20	191	19	213	22%	50%	13%	14%
2009	BUF	16	44	95	612	46%	-5.9	13.9	7	0	2.2	85	-11.1%	64	12	64	-15	20%	46%	18%	16%
2010	BUF	13	37	84	578	44%	-3.1	15.6	4	2	3.2	59	-16.6%	73	-26	73	-34	15%	37%	24%	23%
2011	BAL		52	94	780	55%	--	15.0	5				6.7%								

Despite a three-year decline in numbers, Evans is a good candidate to stick around and possibly add a third act to his career: he's a smart speedster who won't balk at a reduced role and can make an impact with two or three catches per game. He had a three-touchdown game against Baltimore last year, which may have inspired the Ravens to deal a fourth-round pick to acquire him this August. He gives them a veteran deep threat to take advantage of Joe Flacco's arm strength.

Brian Finneran   Height: 6-5 Weight: 210 College: Villanova   Draft: 1999/ (FA)   Born: 31-Jan-1976 Age: 35 Risk: N/A

Year	Team	G	Rec	Pass	Yds	C%	+/-	Yd/C	TD	FUM	YAC	Rk	DVOA	Rk	DYAR	Rk	YAR	Short	Mid	Deep	Bomb
2008	ATL	16	21	36	169	58%	-1.2	8.0	1	1	2.3	--	-22.0%	--	-27	--	-38	29%	57%	14%	0%
2009	ATL	10	11	16	111	69%	0.4	10.1	0	0	4.4	--	-0.7%	--	15	--	12	60%	27%	13%	0%
2010	ATL	16	19	31	166	61%	-0.3	8.7	3	0	2.4	--	-4.3%	--	23	--	33	47%	37%	13%	3%

The Falcons have already held their "thanks for everything!" party for Finneran, but the 35-year-old isn't ready to slip on the gold watch and put his feet up, insisting through the spring that he would try to sign elsewhere. The lockout allowed this fantasy to linger for several months, but Finneran hasn't been "Mr. Third Down" since Mike Vick was still the toast of Atlanta. Popular and bright, Finneran shouldn't have too much trouble adjusting to his post-football life, which will likely begin this fall.

Larry Fitzgerald   Height: 6-3 Weight: 225 College: Pittsburgh   Draft: 2004/1 (3)   Born: 31-Aug-1983 Age: 28 Risk: Green

Year	Team	G	Rec	Pass	Yds	C%	+/-	Yd/C	TD	FUM	YAC	Rk	DVOA	Rk	DYAR	Rk	YAR	Short	Mid	Deep	Bomb
2008	ARI	16	96	154	1431	62%	5.3	14.9	12	1	4.7	19	19.7%	7	402	2	414	34%	41%	16%	9%
2009	ARI	16	97	153	1092	63%	8.9	11.3	13	0	3.2	66	8.8%	30	272	11	324	30%	43%	17%	9%
2010	ARI	16	90	172	1137	52%	-8.5	12.6	6	0	2.4	79	-12.9%	71	-3	71	46	24%	42%	24%	10%
2011	ARI		90	147	1218	61%	--	13.5	10				5.4%								

With the exception of touchdowns, Fitzgerald's conventional stats were about the same as the previous year. The clear decline in his advanced stats was probably caused by the horrible Arizona quarterback carousel, not any decline by Fitzgerald himself. Fitzgerald did set career highs in frustrated looks towards the sideline and throwing his arms up in exasperation after being underthrown by seven yards. So there's that.

Malcom Floyd   Height: 6-5 Weight: 201 College: Wyoming   Draft: 2004/ (FA)   Born: 8-Sep-1981 Age: 30 Risk: Yellow

Year	Team	G	Rec	Pass	Yds	C%	+/-	Yd/C	TD	FUM	YAC	Rk	DVOA	Rk	DYAR	Rk	YAR	Short	Mid	Deep	Bomb
2008	SD	13	27	37	465	73%	8.2	17.2	4	0	1.7	--	58.9%	--	200	--	203	26%	14%	49%	11%
2009	SD	16	45	76	776	59%	5.2	17.2	1	0	2.5	79	23.2%	7	219	18	217	16%	36%	28%	20%
2010	SD	11	37	77	717	48%	-2.2	19.4	6	1	3.0	67	9.1%	24	128	33	147	8%	41%	31%	20%
2011	SD		42	74	708	57%	--	16.8	5				21.2%								

Floyd has been the Chargers' speed receiver for a number of years; not generally consistent but good for a coverage-busting deep cross a few times a season. He re-signed with San Diego after getting a look from the Baltimore Ravens, who could have used his track speed even more then his current team.

Jacoby Ford

Height: 5-9   Weight: 186   College: Clemson   Draft: 2010/4 (108)   Born: 27-Jul-1987   Age: 24   Risk: Red

Year	Team	G	Rec	Pass	Yds	C%	+/-	Yd/C	TD	FUM	YAC	Rk	DVOA	Rk	DYAR	Rk	YAR	Short	Mid	Deep	Bomb
2010	OAK	16	25	54	470	46%	-4.0	18.8	2	0	4.1	39	-2.9%	57	39	66	41	30%	26%	24%	20%
2011	OAK		46	93	764	49%	--	16.6	5				0.7%								

Perhaps the best indicator of how much more value the Raiders got from their 2010 draft after 2009's debacle is the extreme likelihood that Ford, a fourth-round speedster from Clemson, will get more targets than 2009 seventh overall pick Darrius Heyward-Bey. Hue Jackson has already established that he believes Ford will be a household name, and it's easy to see the potential — he's a pure burner with the ability to make serious downfield plays on offense and special teams. Ford returned three kicks for touchdowns in his rookie year, and he gained more yards in the second half of the 2010 season than Heyward-Bey has in his first two NFL years.

Jabar Gaffney

Height: 6-1   Weight: 205   College: Florida   Draft: 2002/2 (33)   Born: 1-Dec-1980   Age: 31   Risk: Yellow

Year	Team	G	Rec	Pass	Yds	C%	+/-	Yd/C	TD	FUM	YAC	Rk	DVOA	Rk	DYAR	Rk	YAR	Short	Mid	Deep	Bomb
2008	NE	16	38	65	468	58%	3.2	12.3	2	0	3.1	54	-4.5%	53	42	56	54	33%	40%	19%	9%
2009	DEN	16	54	87	732	62%	0.1	13.6	2	0	4.9	26	7.8%	32	143	34	138	43%	32%	22%	3%
2010	DEN	16	65	112	875	58%	0.4	13.5	2	1	3.2	61	-0.2%	48	109	44	107	32%	39%	21%	8%
2011	WAS		47	87	505	54%	--	10.7	1				-15.4%								

Gaffney caught a career-high number of passes as part of Josh McDaniels' New England West campaign. Interestingly enough for a player known primarily for one atrocious postseason, Gaffney's catch totals have increased in each of the last five years. That actually may continue in 2011, believe it or not, because Gaffney was traded to the Redskins for former supplemental draft star Jeremy Jarmon and is expected to start alongside Santana Moss.

Justin Gage

Height: 6-4   Weight: 208   College: Missouri   Draft: 2003/5 (143)   Born: 25-Jan-1981   Age: 30   Risk: Green

Year	Team	G	Rec	Pass	Yds	C%	+/-	Yd/C	TD	FUM	YAC	Rk	DVOA	Rk	DYAR	Rk	YAR	Short	Mid	Deep	Bomb
2008	TEN	12	34	74	651	46%	-3.2	19.1	6	0	5.3	8	6.7%	27	116	31	134	16%	36%	26%	22%
2009	TEN	12	28	67	383	42%	-5.6	13.7	3	0	2.4	82	-19.8%	74	-38	74	-45	17%	48%	18%	17%
2010	TEN	11	20	43	266	47%	-2.7	13.3	1	0	2.5	--	-12.5%	--	0	--	5	26%	33%	28%	13%
2011	TEN		18	35	239	51%	--	13.3	2				-5.4%								

Gage's 2011 fate is less in his hands than that of Tennessee's other wide receivers. If Kenny Britt is healthy and not in legal-related hot water, Gage's low catch percentage and mediocre speed will see him on the bench or not on the team. If Britt is suspended or injured, or if Tennessee's young wide receivers show enough development, Gage's scheduled $3.5 million salary may outweigh his veteran reliability, willingness to block, and jumping skills, and he may find himself looking elsewhere for work.

Joey Galloway

Height: 5-11   Weight: 197   College: Ohio State   Draft: 1995/1 (8)   Born: 20-Nov-1971   Age: 40   Risk: N/A

Year	Team	G	Rec	Pass	Yds	C%	+/-	Yd/C	TD	FUM	YAC	Rk	DVOA	Rk	DYAR	Rk	YAR	Short	Mid	Deep	Bomb
2008	TB	9	13	28	138	46%	-3.0	10.6	0	0	3.5	--	-40.2%	--	-55	--	-58	41%	33%	7%	19%
2009	NE	3	7	20	67	35%	-4.5	9.6	0	0	1.6	--	-38.5%	--	-40	--	-64	20%	55%	20%	5%
2010	WAS	10	12	37	173	32%	-6.7	14.4	0	0	1.5	--	-41.9%	--	-83	--	-85	29%	31%	14%	26%

Galloway completely washed out with the 2009 Patriots and couldn't get on the field when he signed with the Steelers at midseason, so it seemed like a joke when he began last season in the Washington starting lineup. Guess what? It was a joke. He can't really get open anymore. We assume his career is over, so instead of remembering him as the guy listed in the lines above, why don't we instead remember him as the guy who stayed lightning fast and valuable all the way to the age of 36 in Tampa Bay.

Pierre Garcon

Height: 6-0 Weight: 210 College: Mount Union Draft: 2008/6 (205) Born: 8-Aug-1986 Age: 25 Risk: Green

Year	Team	G	Rec	Pass	Yds	C%	+/-	Yd/C	TD	FUM	YAC	Rk	DVOA	Rk	DYAR	Rk	YAR	Short	Mid	Deep	Bomb
2008	IND	14	4	4	23	100%	1.1	5.8	0	0	2.5	--	20.2%	--	11	--	5	100%	0%	0%	0%
2009	IND	14	47	91	765	52%	0.2	16.3	4	1	6.0	8	-0.4%	43	92	46	102	32%	29%	17%	22%
2010	IND	14	67	119	784	56%	-2.2	11.7	6	0	3.7	49	-7.0%	67	55	61	71	37%	37%	13%	13%
2011	IND		56	91	712	62%	--	12.7	5				7.5%								

Garcon remains a great story: the late-round draft pick from Mount Union rising to a starter on one of the league's perennial contenders. But, it masks the fact that Garcon simply is not that good. He has good straight-away speed and can burn average cornerbacks. But, in two years as a starter with Peyton Manning as his quarterback, he has below-average DVOAs. He does make his share of big plays, masking the overall mediocre performance. The Colts could upgrade on the position, moving Garcon to be their fourth receiver. Garcon's catch rate did increase radically at midseason, after he began working with Peyton Manning on running the route tree before games.

David Gettis

Height: 6-3 Weight: 217 College: Baylor Draft: 2010/6 (198) Born: 27-Aug-1987 Age: 24 Risk: N/A

Year	Team	G	Rec	Pass	Yds	C%	+/-	Yd/C	TD	FUM	YAC	Rk	DVOA	Rk	DYAR	Rk	YAR	Short	Mid	Deep	Bomb
2010	CAR	15	37	67	508	55%	-1.0	13.7	3	0	4.2	36	-0.8%	52	62	57	66	42%	23%	19%	16%

Amidst the Panthers' comical pass offense, Gettis showed what could be in a two-touchdown performance versus the 49ers in Week 7. Whether in the slot or outside, he was a stone killer, splitting zones, finding perfect placement on passes of different lengths, and scoring two touchdowns. Gettis isn't an elite deep receiver — he needs separation routes by other receivers to take intermediate coverage away, but a quick look at that one game should tell the Panthers' new coaching staff that Gettis can be an asset going forward. Just not this year; he tore his ACL as we were finishing the book and is out for the season.

Brandon Gibson

Height: 6-1 Weight: 210 College: Washington State Draft: 2009/6 (194) Born: 13-Aug-1987 Age: 24 Risk: Red

Year	Team	G	Rec	Pass	Yds	C%	+/-	Yd/C	TD	FUM	YAC	Rk	DVOA	Rk	DYAR	Rk	YAR	Short	Mid	Deep	Bomb
2009	2TM	10	4	69	34	49%	-5.9	8.5	1	2	3.1	71	-29.7%	84	-93	84	-77	34%	45%	12%	9%
2010	STL	10	53	91	620	58%	0.3	11.7	2	0	4.2	35	-9.9%	70	20	70	48	33%	50%	12%	6%
2011	STL		21	34	209	62%	--	10.0	0				-12.9%								

Poor practice habits landed Gibson in Steve Spagnuolo's doghouse to open last season, but the former sixth-round pick out of Washington State would ultimately start 12 of the final 14 games. Gibson's numbers improved across the board, but he struggled with dropped passes and showed a lack of awareness of down-and-distance when the Rams were clinging to a fourth-quarter lead in what turned out to be a costly loss to the San Francisco 49ers in Week 10. Though Spagnuolo would praise Gibson's in-season turnaround in January, the Rams added similarly-sized Austin Pettis in the third round, increasing the level of competition for a roster spot in training camp.

Anthony Gonzalez

Height: 6-0 Weight: 193 College: Ohio State Draft: 2007/1 (32) Born: 18-Sep-1984 Age: 27 Risk: Green

Year	Team	G	Rec	Pass	Yds	C%	+/-	Yd/C	TD	FUM	YAC	Rk	DVOA	Rk	DYAR	Rk	YAR	Short	Mid	Deep	Bomb
2008	IND	16	57	79	664	72%	8.1	11.6	4	0	3.1	58	26.2%	3	242	13	219	36%	47%	13%	4%
2009	IND	1	0	0	0	0%	0.0	0.0	0	0	0.0	--	0.0%	--	0	--	0	0%	0%	0%	0%
2010	IND	2	5	9	67	56%	0.6	13.4	0	0	3.2	--	-28.3%	--	-10	--	-2	43%	29%	0%	29%
2011	IND		11	19	155	58%	--	14.1	1				-9.0%								

The NFL is a physical game, and players get hurt. Many recover and return to their previous levels. Some just simply are unable to gain the explosiveness they once had. Gonzalez, a 2007 first-round pick and as the Colts' third wide-receiver managed to rank first and third in DVOA his first two seasons. After Marvin Harrison retired following the 2008 season, Gonzalez was supposed to step in and become an elite player. Instead, he has battled injuries, fallen behind late-round picks like Pierre Garcon and Austin Collie and is in danger of not making the Colts. The 2009 ACL injury was followed-up by a PCL injury shortly after Gonzalez returned last season. There is still talent there, but whether it is too late remains to be seen.

A.J. Green

Height: 6-4   Weight: 207   College: Georgia   Draft: 2011/1 (4)   Born: 31-Jul-1988   Age: 23   Risk: Red

Year	Team	G	Rec	Pass	Yds	C%	+/-	Yd/C	TD	FUM	YAC	Rk	DVOA	Rk	DYAR	Rk	YAR	Short	Mid	Deep	Bomb
2011	CIN		62	117	955	53%	--	15.4	7				12.3%								

Atlanta may have traded all those picks, but Cincinnati is the team that got the total package. Elite speed? Outstanding acceleration? Great hands? A.J. Green has all that, plus the ability to adjust to an inaccurate pass in the air. He had a 72 percent catch rate in 2009, and a 68 percent catch rate in 2010 despite a freshman quarterback at Georgia. Scouts struggle to find negatives in Green's game. He rounds his cuts sometimes. He may have durability issues; he's thin, and his BMI of 25.2 was the third-lowest of the wide receivers drafted this year. He was suspended for four games in college, but now we're really reaching for criticisms. Green's four-game suspension for selling his own jersey is the kind of nonsense that fuels calls for the NCAA to pay Division I college players, and should in no way suggest character issues that might harm his NFL career. Green's all-around talent and Cincinnati's receiver situation make Green the rare rookie receiver who is likely to have a worthwhile fantasy season.

Derek Hagan

Height: 6-1   Weight: 205   College: Arizona State   Draft: 2006/3 (82)   Born: 21-Sep-1984   Age: 27   Risk: Blue

Year	Team	G	Rec	Pass	Yds	C%	+/-	Yd/C	TD	FUM	YAC	Rk	DVOA	Rk	DYAR	Rk	YAR	Short	Mid	Deep	Bomb
2008	MIA	4	3	6	51	50%	-0.6	17.0	0	0	2.3	--	4.2%	--	7	--	15	17%	50%	33%	0%
2009	NYG	16	8	8	101	100%	3.1	12.6	1	0	0.3	--	74.5%	--	49	--	48	13%	50%	38%	0%
2010	NYG	7	24	43	223	58%	0.2	9.3	1	0	1.3	--	-17.6%	--	-17	--	-19	25%	53%	23%	0%
2011	OAK		5	9	49	56%	--	9.8	0				-20.4%								

Hagan was one of the Giants' many big guys who can't really run or catch that well. He was forced into the line-up by injuries to Steve Smith and Hakeem Nicks, among others, and showed absolutely nothing in the process. His agent found him the right team to sign with, as Oakland might have the worst receiving corps in the league at this point, but Hagan hasn't shown anything in the past that tells us he'll take advantage of the opportunity.

Leonard Hankerson

Height: 6-2   Weight: 209   College: Miami   Draft: 2011/3 (79)   Born: 7-May-1988   Age: 23   Risk: Red

Year	Team	G	Rec	Pass	Yds	C%	+/-	Yd/C	TD	FUM	YAC	Rk	DVOA	Rk	DYAR	Rk	YAR	Short	Mid	Deep	Bomb
2011	WAS		33	61	435	54%	--	13.2	2				-16.8%								

Leonard Hankerson is all arms and legs. The first time you watch him play, you'll swear he's 6-foot-5; he's not (try three inches shorter). Hankerson was the beneficiary of the 2009 Jacory Harris explosion. With strong quarterback play, Hankerson went from an afterthought (17 catches, 50 percent catch rate in his first two years) to an all-conference threat. Despite a leg injury, he caught 45 passes for 801 yards as a junior (61 percent catch rate). He was targeted 60 percent more often in 2010; as the go-to for a struggling Harris, he did his part, catching 72 passes for 1,156 yards (62 percent catch rate) and a whopping 13 touchdowns. Hankerson is not incredibly agile, but his long strides make him a nice vertical threat.

Brian Hartline

Height: 6-2   Weight: 195   College: Ohio State   Draft: 2009/4 (108)   Born: 22-Nov-1986   Age: 25   Risk: Green

Year	Team	G	Rec	Pass	Yds	C%	+/-	Yd/C	TD	FUM	YAC	Rk	DVOA	Rk	DYAR	Rk	YAR	Short	Mid	Deep	Bomb
2009	MIA	16	31	56	506	55%	0.7	16.3	3	0	5.2	18	21.9%	9	156	30	144	21%	46%	20%	13%
2010	MIA	12	43	73	615	59%	2.0	14.3	1	1	4.9	21	6.2%	33	113	41	90	30%	37%	19%	14%
2011	MIA		35	61	505	57%	--	14.4	2				4.2%								

Hartline is developing nicely for a fourth-round pick, having already caught 74 passes for 1,121 yards and four touchdowns in two seasons despite some fairly shaky quarterback play. Last year Miami quarterbacks were much more likely to look for Hartline on short passes, which accounted for 30 percent of his targets, and which also may have contributed to his DVOA dropping even though he was catching more of the balls that were thrown his way. Even so, Hartline is best used as a deep threat, and his closest similarity scores include guys like Andre' Davis, Louis Murphy and Ashlie Lelie, burners who would occasionally have big days but could never be counted on to produce consistently.

Percy Harvin Height: 5-11 Weight: 192 College: Florida Draft: 2009/1 (22) Born: 28-May-1988 Age: 23 Risk: Green

Year	Team	G	Rec	Pass	Yds	C%	+/-	Yd/C	TD	FUM	YAC	Rk	DVOA	Rk	DYAR	Rk	YAR	Short	Mid	Deep	Bomb
2009	MIN	15	60	93	790	67%	4.4	13.2	6	1	5.8	11	11.6%	23	175	26	186	40%	36%	16%	8%
2010	MIN	14	71	109	868	65%	3.1	12.2	5	0	6.0	5	5.2%	36	153	28	145	50%	31%	7%	12%
2011	MIN		79	131	965	60%	--	12.2	5				2.9%								

Harvin missed the Vikings player-organized workouts because he lost his cell phone. Don't feel like jogging around and playing catch with Christian Ponder? There's an app for that ... Harvin led NFL receivers in broken tackles (13) for the second straight year. On screen passes, he was 12-of-13 with 114 yards, one touchdown, and gains of 28, 23, 19, 14, and 15 yards. Harvin risks becoming the birthday present that is too valuable to play with: injuries are going to happen, and the Vikings must find ways to use him without hurting him. A screen per game sounds prudent, mixed with some reverses, hitches, and fly routes. Harvin should definitely get the Brian Westbrook treatment on punt returns — for use in game-changing situations only — and making him run the standard route tree, absorb jams at the line, and catch 10-yard passes does not make a lot of sense from a risk-benefit standpoint. Harvin is going to mix some two-catch, 20-yard games in among his highlights, but he is more useful as a boom-or-bust big play threat than as a guy who catches six passes for 62 yards one week and spends the next two on the sidelines.

Devery Henderson Height: 5-11 Weight: 200 College: Louisiana State Draft: 2004/2 (50) Born: 26-Mar-1982 Age: 29 Risk: Green

Year	Team	G	Rec	Pass	Yds	C%	+/-	Yd/C	TD	FUM	YAC	Rk	DVOA	Rk	DYAR	Rk	YAR	Short	Mid	Deep	Bomb
2008	NO	16	32	56	793	57%	6.0	24.8	3	1	8.3	1	36.5%	1	215	17	207	22%	29%	20%	29%
2009	NO	16	51	83	804	61%	2.7	15.8	2	0	5.8	12	10.8%	24	148	33	156	36%	30%	14%	19%
2010	NO	16	34	59	464	58%	-0.4	13.6	1	0	3.8	48	-5.3%	64	33	67	47	34%	31%	17%	17%
2011	NO		37	68	680	54%	--	18.4	3				22.0%								

Trending downward. The top receiver in DVOA in all of football in 2008, Henderson fell off for the second straight year in just about every metric worth a damn. Henderson is now in the negative in DVOA and +/-. His yards per catch is about half what it was in 2008. Henderson's is due to make $2.25 million in 2011, a sizable number for his production. Adrian Arrington looks ready to fill his spot should Henderson falter any more.

Devin Hester Height: 5-10 Weight: 185 College: Miami Draft: 2007/2 (57) Born: 4-Nov-1982 Age: 29 Risk: Yellow

Year	Team	G	Rec	Pass	Yds	C%	+/-	Yd/C	TD	FUM	YAC	Rk	DVOA	Rk	DYAR	Rk	YAR	Short	Mid	Deep	Bomb
2008	CHI	15	51	92	665	57%	1.9	13.0	3	1	3.8	38	-9.5%	64	23	64	26	33%	28%	24%	15%
2009	CHI	13	57	91	757	64%	2.9	13.3	3	1	5.0	24	-0.6%	44	88	47	99	38%	36%	11%	15%
2010	CHI	16	40	73	475	55%	-3.5	11.9	4	0	5.5	12	-3.2%	60	55	62	46	37%	40%	11%	11%
2011	CHI		36	69	468	52%	--	13.0	2				-18.6%								

Hester on wide receiver screens: 7-of-8 for 48 yards, with 39 of those yards coming on one play. On passes of 20+ yards through the air: 1-of-12, 25 yards, one interception. Hester also dropped five passes, including two of the long ones. As a screens-and-bombs guy, Hester is a washout, and as a regular receiver he doesn't offer much value that the Bears couldn't get from some mid-round pick. The "regular receiver" experiment should really end, with Hester resuming his role as a return specialist who enters the game on offense strictly for surprise value. The Bears do not seem interest in doing that, so look for Hester to get another 70+ pass targets that should probably go to Earl Bennett of Johnnie Knox. The Bears may enter the season with Devin Hester and Roy Williams in the lineup and Bennett and Knox on the bench. Self-deceit is a powerful thing.

Darrius Heyward-Bey

Height: 6-2   Weight: 210   College: Maryland   Draft: 2009/1 (7)   Born: 26-Feb-1987   Age: 24   Risk: Green

Year	Team	G	Rec	Pass	Yds	C%	+/-	Yd/C	TD	FUM	YAC	Rk	DVOA	Rk	DYAR	Rk	YAR	Short	Mid	Deep	Bomb
2009	OAK	11	9	40	124	23%	-10.5	13.8	1	0	1.3	--	-45.5%	--	-107	--	-127	21%	21%	36%	23%
2010	OAK	15	26	64	366	41%	-5.0	14.1	1	0	3.9	45	-28.6%	82	-82	82	-63	19%	44%	19%	19%
2011	OAK		22	45	285	49%	--	13.0	0				-26.1%								

We're still a very long way from Heyward-Bey being anything but a howling bust, but he at least came a few inches closer to matching the seventh-overall pick investment the Raiders made in 2010. As we've pointed out before, it's not Heyward-Bey's fault that he was hideously overdrafted; this was clearly yet another example of Al Davis falling in love with a very quick one-trick pony. But most draft pundits pegged Heyward-Bey with a high second-round grade at the very worst, and he hasn't come close to that projection, either. Plagued by all the common denominators among underdeveloped receivers of his type — consistency, concentration, and hands issues — he's got a bull's-eye on his helmet already by way of new head coach Hue Jackson, who put together the offense in which Heyward-Bey still hasn't succeeded. 2011 is his time to get it done, or to get off the proverbial pot.

Johnnie Lee Higgins

Height: 6-0   Weight: 185   College: Texas-El Paso   Draft: 2007/3 (99)   Born: 8-Sep-1983   Age: 28   Risk: Blue

Year	Team	G	Rec	Pass	Yds	C%	+/-	Yd/C	TD	FUM	YAC	Rk	DVOA	Rk	DYAR	Rk	YAR	Short	Mid	Deep	Bomb
2008	OAK	16	22	42	366	52%	-3.2	16.6	4	0	9.1	--	-3.6%	--	29	--	36	31%	31%	24%	14%
2009	OAK	15	19	45	263	42%	-4.1	13.8	0	0	1.4	--	-27.8%	--	-53	--	-59	24%	37%	32%	7%
2010	OAK	13	10	30	103	33%	-3.1	10.3	0	0	2.2	--	-47.4%	--	-85	--	-88	25%	46%	25%	4%
2011	PHI		8	15	116	53%	--	14.5	0				8.4%								

Talk about a situational receiver — Higgins had a 67 percent catch rate on nine first-down targets, then plummeted to 29 percent on eight second-down passes, and 14 percent on 14 third-down passes. He's a prototypical Raiders speed guy who is no longer on the Raiders; instead, he went to Philadelphia, where he and Nnamdi Asomugha can get together and revel in the joy of playing for a functional football team.

Jason Hill

Height: 6-1   Weight: 204   College: Washington State   Draft: 2007/3 (76)   Born: 20-Feb-1985   Age: 26   Risk: Red

Year	Team	G	Rec	Pass	Yds	C%	+/-	Yd/C	TD	FUM	YAC	Rk	DVOA	Rk	DYAR	Rk	YAR	Short	Mid	Deep	Bomb
2008	SF	16	30	40	317	75%	4.1	10.6	2	1	3.8	--	9.5%	--	72	--	82	50%	38%	8%	5%
2009	SF	11	9	17	90	53%	-0.7	10.0	2	0	6.0	--	-13.6%	--	-1	--	5	60%	27%	7%	7%
2010	JAC	8	11	21	248	52%	0.6	22.5	1	0	3.8	--	-22.2%	--	56	--	55	10%	40%	30%	20%
2011	JAC		51	91	664	56%	--	13.0	3				-20.9%								

Hill joined the Jaguars as a midseason waiver claim from the 49ers. He markedly improved on his career yards per catch ratio in his few games in Jacksonville, but though he was renowned as a deep threat at Washington State, the vast majority of his long completions came against pathetic pass defenses like Houston, Washington, and Indianapolis. Don't expect that to hold up over the long haul. There is still some upside here, but probably not enough to warrant more than a third receiver job. He seems to have tricked the Jaguars into letting him start this year. In conclusion, Jacksonville is a land of contrast. Thank you.

Domenik Hixon   Height: 6-2   Weight: 192   College: Akron   Draft: 2006/4 (130)   Born: 8-Oct-1984   Age: 27   Risk: Yellow

Year	Team	G	Rec	Pass	Yds	C%	+/-	Yd/C	TD	FUM	YAC	Rk	DVOA	Rk	DYAR	Rk	YAR	Short	Mid	Deep	Bomb
2008	NYG	16	43	73	596	59%	2.6	13.9	2	0	3.3	52	11.5%	19	142	28	112	21%	51%	12%	16%
2009	NYG	14	15	28	187	54%	-1.7	12.5	1	0	6.7	--	-8.2%	--	9	--	3	21%	61%	4%	14%
2011	NYG		32	53	456	60%	--	14.3	3				6.9%								

One of the final edits to *FOA 2010* was removing Hixon from the book after a June ACL tear. He's battling Victor Cruz for the main slot receiver job in camp. Should he win the job, KUBIAK likes him to bounce back and be a productive slot receiver ... this season. Jerrel Jernigan and Cruz should continue to push him for snaps as time goes on, so this is probably Hixon's last chance to establish himself as a productive NFL receiver.

Santonio Holmes   Height: 5-10   Weight: 185   College: Ohio State   Draft: 2006/1 (25)   Born: 3-Mar-1984   Age: 27   Risk: Green

Year	Team	G	Rec	Pass	Yds	C%	+/-	Yd/C	TD	FUM	YAC	Rk	DVOA	Rk	DYAR	Rk	YAR	Short	Mid	Deep	Bomb
2008	PIT	15	55	114	821	48%	-5.9	14.9	5	2	3.8	39	-8.2%	60	39	60	25	22%	48%	20%	9%
2009	PIT	16	79	138	1248	57%	0.8	15.8	5	0	6.0	9	12.7%	21	278	10	287	26%	48%	18%	8%
2010	NYJ	12	52	96	746	54%	-1.1	14.3	6	0	4.2	37	4.3%	39	128	32	140	21%	49%	20%	10%
2011	NYJ		72	138	1037	52%	--	14.4	8				-1.9%								

No one doubted that the Jets were getting a steal when they traded a fifth-round pick to Pittsburgh for Holmes, and the former Super Bowl MVP quickly proved his worth, setting up the winning score in overtime against Detroit and then catching game winning touchdown passes against Cleveland and Houston. Strangely, Holmes was much more effective on first downs, where his DVOA was 45.8%. On second and third downs, Holmes was a below-average receiver, posting a negative DVOA and catching fewer than fifty percent of the passes thrown his way. Despite that statistical hiccup, re-signing Holmes was at the top of the Jets' priority list, and they locked him up for $50 million over five years. Holmes will undoubtedly be Mark Sanchez's favorite target, and he should see his numbers go up accordingly.

T.J. Houshmandzadeh   Height: 6-1   Weight: 197   College: Oregon State   Draft: 2001/7 (204)   Born: 26-Sep-1977   Age: 34   Risk: N/A

Year	Team	G	Rec	Pass	Yds	C%	+/-	Yd/C	TD	FUM	YAC	Rk	DVOA	Rk	DYAR	Rk	YAR	Short	Mid	Deep	Bomb
2008	CIN	15	92	137	904	67%	3.5	9.8	4	0	3.8	40	2.5%	34	163	23	118	50%	41%	8%	1%
2009	SEA	16	79	135	911	59%	-1.3	11.5	3	2	3.7	59	-9.1%	60	40	55	67	34%	45%	14%	7%
2010	BAL	16	30	57	398	53%	-1.3	13.3	3	1	2.6	77	6.7%	31	89	49	87	23%	44%	21%	12%

Fate is a fickle beast. According to our game charters, T.J. Houshmandzadeh did not drop a pass during the regular season. Then Joe Flacco threw him the ball on a fourth-and-18 that Baltimore needed to extend its last-gasp drive in the playoff game against Pittsburgh... and the ball went right through his hands and bounced off his chest. Oops. Like Anquan Boldin, Houshmandzadeh was asked to go deep a little too often in 2010 because the Ravens didn't have a faster receiver to stretch the field, and it wasn't the best use of his talents. Still unsigned as of press time, but you've got to figure he'll hook up with a team that loses a possession receiver to injury in the preseason.

Sam Hurd   Height: 6-2   Weight: 187   College: Northern Illinois   Draft: 2006/ (FA)   Born: 24-Apr-1985   Age: 26   Risk: Blue

Year	Team	G	Rec	Pass	Yds	C%	+/-	Yd/C	TD	FUM	YAC	Rk	DVOA	Rk	DYAR	Rk	YAR	Short	Mid	Deep	Bomb
2009	DAL	16	7	12	121	58%	-1.0	17.3	1	0	12.6	--	8.1%	--	23	--	23	67%	25%	0%	8%
2010	DAL	15	14	23	120	61%	-0.4	8.6	0	0	4.8	--	-10.0%	--	5	--	7	50%	36%	9%	5%
2011	CHI		4	7	51	57%	--	12.8	0				-4.1%								

Hurd only made the roster after the team found a place to dump Patrick Crayton, and while he contributed 18 tackles on special teams (tied for fourth in the NFL), he has no place in a healthy offense. He was non-tendered after the season and signed with Bears, where he will play the same role he did in Dallas, if he makes the roster at all.

DeSean Jackson

Height: 5-9   Weight: 169   College: California   Draft: 2008/2 (49)   Born: 1-Dec-1986   Age: 25   Risk: Yellow

Year	Team	G	Rec	Pass	Yds	C%	+/-	Yd/C	TD	FUM	YAC	Rk	DVOA	Rk	DYAR	Rk	YAR	Short	Mid	Deep	Bomb
2008	PHI	16	62	120	912	52%	-5.7	14.7	2	1	4.1	32	-8.3%	61	40	59	43	32%	32%	22%	14%
2009	PHI	15	62	116	1156	53%	-3.1	18.6	9	2	6.4	6	9.0%	29	198	20	188	31%	33%	17%	19%
2010	PHI	14	47	96	1056	49%	-2.0	22.5	6	2	7.2	1	2.3%	44	109	45	114	23%	38%	14%	24%
2011	PHI		57	106	953	54%	--	16.7	6				6.0%								

The catch rate and plus-minus figures aren't pretty, and while that 24 percent bomb rate could be a mitigating factor, Jackson also dropped ten passes in 2010. Only one of those ten passes would qualify as bombs, and the six other players with ten or more drops averaged more than 30 targets beyond Jackson's total. Everyone drops passes, but if Jackson could just cut his drop rate in half going forward, he would be a much more valuable player. It doesn't sound like much, but his catch rate would improve to the 55 percent range, and with his ability after the catch, he could be adding another 100 receiving yards a year to his totals. The current Jackson model, though, is overvalued and likely to receive a contract far beyond his actual level of performance.

Vincent Jackson

Height: 6-5   Weight: 241   College: Northern Colorado   Draft: 2005/2 (61)   Born: 14-Jan-1983   Age: 28   Risk: Red

Year	Team	G	Rec	Pass	Yds	C%	+/-	Yd/C	TD	FUM	YAC	Rk	DVOA	Rk	DYAR	Rk	YAR	Short	Mid	Deep	Bomb
2008	SD	16	59	100	1098	59%	9.0	18.6	7	1	3.3	50	32.9%	2	369	4	387	14%	39%	27%	21%
2009	SD	15	68	109	1167	63%	11.4	17.2	9	0	2.8	77	38.7%	2	448	2	451	15%	44%	18%	23%
2010	SD	5	14	23	248	61%	3.9	17.7	3	0	3.4	--	38.7%	--	96	--	104	16%	47%	26%	11%
2011	SD		64	104	1059	62%	--	16.5	9				28.1%								

We discussed the onerous nature of the negotiations between the Chargers and Jackson's people in the San Diego team chapter, but the on-field effects of Jackson's late start were fairly severe. Jackson didn't really see the field until Week 14, and his bravura performance against the 49ers just a week later — he torched San Francisco's helpless defense for three touchdowns — surely had everyone in San Diego wondering "What if?" Jackson was tagged before the lockout, attached his name to the Brady v. NFL Lawsuit, and eventually signed a one-year tender worth over $11 million. He's a special talent, and he's eventually going to get paid like it, but like the kid in *Almost Famous*, he's just going to have to shine it on for another year. Jackson presents an extremely valuable skill set; there simply aren't too many receivers in the game with his combination of size, physical play, and what we like to call "functional football speed" — the ability to drag through accurate patterns and hit the gas at the right time.

Michael Jenkins

Height: 6-4   Weight: 217   College: Ohio State   Draft: 2004/1 (29)   Born: 18-Jun-1982   Age: 29   Risk: Green

Year	Team	G	Rec	Pass	Yds	C%	+/-	Yd/C	TD	FUM	YAC	Rk	DVOA	Rk	DYAR	Rk	YAR	Short	Mid	Deep	Bomb
2008	ATL	16	50	81	777	62%	6.5	15.5	3	0	3.4	48	16.0%	12	179	22	174	24%	41%	20%	15%
2009	ATL	15	50	90	635	56%	-0.7	12.7	1	0	3.2	69	-11.5%	65	7	65	4	22%	36%	31%	11%
2010	ATL	11	41	73	505	56%	1.9	12.3	2	0	2.0	84	5.8%	35	108	46	86	20%	39%	32%	9%
2011	MIN		21	37	263	57%	--	12.5	2				-2.7%								

Jenkins missed the first five games of the season with a shoulder injury, and didn't help much when he returned, except on third down. Jenkins had a 70 percent catch rate on the money down and a 46.7% DVOA. Those numbers hint at Jenkins' likely role in Minnesota, as Donovan McNabb's security blanket.

Greg Jennings

Height: 5-11   Weight: 195   College: Western Michigan   Draft: 2006/2 (52)   Born: 21-Sep-1983   Age: 28   Risk: Yellow

Year	Team	G	Rec	Pass	Yds	C%	+/-	Yd/C	TD	FUM	YAC	Rk	DVOA	Rk	DYAR	Rk	YAR	Short	Mid	Deep	Bomb
2008	GB	16	80	140	1292	57%	4.2	16.2	9	1	4.2	27	9.6%	21	243	12	256	22%	43%	23%	12%
2009	GB	16	68	119	1113	57%	5.2	16.4	4	0	6.8	5	10.6%	26	224	17	255	30%	42%	14%	14%
2010	GB	16	76	125	1265	61%	7.9	16.6	12	2	5.3	16	19.6%	7	330	3	329	25%	44%	14%	17%
2011	GB		80	136	1256	59%	--	15.7	9				16.7%								

Jennings played a football coach in an episode of *Royal Pains* and had a brief cameo in *Criminal Minds* as a cadaver or laser pointer or something. If Jennings' acting career and Aaron Rodgers' guitar career simultaneously take off, the Packers may enter the kind of Dark Age they have not experienced since the end of the Lombardi years. It will also no longer be fun to watch television or listen to the radio ... Jennings got off to a poor start and refused to talk to the media after a few early-season two-catch games. The Packers coaches met specifically to find ways to increase Jennings' role, and Jennings caught at least four passes per game from Week 6 on. Jennings would catch 90 passes for 1,500 yards on a team that didn't have three other viable receivers and some pretty good tight ends.

Andre Johnson

Height: 6-3 Weight: 219 College: Miami Draft: 2003/1 (3) Born: 11-Jul-1981 Age: 30 Risk: Green

Year	Team	G	Rec	Pass	Yds	C%	+/-	Yd/C	TD	FUM	YAC	Rk	DVOA	Rk	DYAR	Rk	YAR	Short	Mid	Deep	Bomb
2008	HOU	16	115	171	1575	67%	13.5	13.7	8	1	4.1	31	22.1%	6	491	1	461	32%	44%	19%	5%
2009	HOU	16	101	172	1569	59%	4.2	15.5	9	1	5.4	15	6.3%	35	261	13	293	33%	39%	16%	12%
2010	HOU	13	86	139	1216	63%	5.6	14.1	8	1	4.1	38	13.2%	15	284	5	245	39%	30%	20%	12%
2011	HOU		104	167	1473	62%	--	14.2	11				16.7%								

An ankle injury caused him to miss three games, so Johnson failed to match Jerry Rice's feat of leading the league in receiving yards three consecutive seasons and instead settled for leading the league in receiving yards per game for the third time in four seasons. He did much of his damage on second down, where he had a DVOA of 36.6% and a catch rate of 74 percent. The Texans made a concerted effort to get him the ball more on short passes, whether rub routes or quick passes. That was most evident against the Titans, against whom he had 15 catches for 112 yards in the two games. Assuming he stays healthy, he'll again be one of the best and most productive receivers in the league.

Bryant Johnson

Height: 6-2 Weight: 214 College: Penn State Draft: 2003/1 (17) Born: 7-Mar-1981 Age: 30 Risk: N/A

Year	Team	G	Rec	Pass	Yds	C%	+/-	Yd/C	TD	FUM	YAC	Rk	DVOA	Rk	DYAR	Rk	YAR	Short	Mid	Deep	Bomb
2008	SF	16	45	75	546	60%	1.7	12.1	3	0	3.2	53	-3.7%	52	54	53	76	41%	36%	19%	4%
2009	DET	16	35	87	417	40%	-12.8	11.9	3	0	3.0	74	-27.3%	83	-101	87	-98	27%	38%	19%	16%
2010	DET	14	18	49	210	37%	-10.4	11.7	0	0	3.5	--	-41.0%	--	-109	--	-126	25%	44%	23%	8%

Johnson was due to make $3.2 million this season, so his release was one of the foregone conclusions of the start of camp. Johnson has never been able to beat man coverage consistently, has no real special teams value, and turned 30 in March. He is a quiet bust who got more than his share of opportunities to prove that he is a marginal NFL receiver.

Calvin Johnson

Height: 6-5 Weight: 239 College: Georgia Tech Draft: 2007/1 (2) Born: 25-Sep-1985 Age: 26 Risk: Green

Year	Team	G	Rec	Pass	Yds	C%	+/-	Yd/C	TD	FUM	YAC	Rk	DVOA	Rk	DYAR	Rk	YAR	Short	Mid	Deep	Bomb
2008	DET	16	78	150	1331	52%	-8.2	17.1	12	3	6.3	4	9.1%	22	256	10	227	33%	35%	14%	19%
2009	DET	14	67	138	984	49%	-5.9	14.7	5	3	5.1	19	-11.0%	63	19	61	29	24%	41%	17%	18%
2010	DET	15	77	138	1120	57%	2.9	14.5	12	1	3.9	44	11.2%	20	258	7	242	20%	46%	19%	14%
2011	DET		75	134	1097	56%	--	14.6	8				7.6%								

Johnson battled groin and ankle injuries late in the season. He had one remarkable game — a 10-catch, 152-yard effort against the Buccaneers, who were missing cornerback Aqib Talib — but Johnson was not getting his usual separation, and Drew Stanton could not often find him when he did. Johnson is now both healthy and happy: an escalator clause jacked his salary up to $8.875 million, and the Lions' four-game winning streak softened his remarks about wanting to play elsewhere. Best of all, a new rule will allow officials to review every touchdown, so the next time Johnson performs an act in the end zone that any eight-year-old can figure out should be considered a touchdown, the referees can spend ten minutes conferring before misinterpreting the intent of a rule in an utterly asinine way.

Steve Johnson

Height: 6-1   Weight: 210   College: Kentucky   Draft: 2008/7 (224)   Born: 1-Jan-1982   Age: 30   Risk: Yellow

Year	Team	G	Rec	Pass	Yds	C%	+/-	Yd/C	TD	FUM	YAC	Rk	DVOA	Rk	DYAR	Rk	YAR	Short	Mid	Deep	Bomb
2008	BUF	11	10	14	102	71%	1.3	10.2	2	0	2.8	—	24.5%	—	44	—	55	54%	38%	8%	0%
2009	BUF	5	2	3	10	67%	-0.1	5.0	0	0	0.0	--	-40.4%	—	-7	—	-6	100%	0%	0%	0%
2010	BUF	16	82	142	1073	58%	-2.5	13.1	10	1	4.8	24	8.7%	26	236	12	214	30%	49%	14%	7%
2011	BUF		86	146	1156	59%	--	13.4	7				5.6%								

Like Ryan Fitzpatrick, Johnson began to tail off late in the season, once everyone was talking about how great he was. He followed his three-touchdown performance against the Bengals with 30-345-1 on 58 pass attempts in six games. Those are not bad numbers, but they aren't "next big thing" material, either. Lee Evans' injury put additional pressure on Johnson, and a combination of Fitzpatrick's fade and a string of games against good defenses (which compounded Fitzpatrick's fade) cut into Johnson's productivity. Whatever the causes for the decline, Johnson's pending superstardom is based on three great games — the Bengals game, 8-158-1 against the Ravens, and 11-145-0 against the Bears — plus a lot of talk about how Terrell Owens took him under his wing. KUBIAK believes Johnson will see tons of passes and do enough with them to help your fantasy team, but he's still just the third best Johnson in the league at his position, at best.

Donald Jones

Height: 6-0   Weight: 214   College: Youngstown State   Draft: 2010/ (FA)   Born: 17-Dec-1987   Age: 24   Risk: Blue

Year	Team	G	Rec	Pass	Yds	C%	+/-	Yd/C	TD	FUM	YAC	Rk	DVOA	Rk	DYAR	Rk	YAR	Short	Mid	Deep	Bomb
2010	BUF	15	18	41	213	44%	-5.2	11.8	1	0	4.8	—	-35.4%	—	-76	—	-75	53%	19%	14%	14%
2011	BUF		18	30	240	60%	--	13.4	1				0.7%								

Jones, an undrafted rookie from Youngstown State, took over for Roscoe Parrish after Parrish broke his wrist at midseason, catching six receiver screens and two shovel passes among his 18 receptions. He also took over part of Lee Evans' role late in the season, which is where his 40- and 29-yard receptions came from. Factor in some serviceable work as a return man, and Jones is a threat to replace Parrish, though he lacks Parrish's elite quickness. Wide receiver is Buffalo's only position of depth; unfortunately, not even Chan Gailey can find a way to get six receivers on the field at the same time.

Jacoby Jones

Height: 6-3   Weight: 192   College: Lane   Draft: 2007/3 (73)   Born: 11-Jul-1984   Age: 27   Risk: Green

Year	Team	G	Rec	Pass	Yds	C%	+/-	Yd/C	TD	FUM	YAC	Rk	DVOA	Rk	DYAR	Rk	YAR	Short	Mid	Deep	Bomb
2008	HOU	16	3	5	81	60%	0.0	27.0	0	0	10.0	—	54.9%	—	27	—	23	40%	20%	0%	40%
2009	HOU	14	27	40	437	68%	6.0	16.2	6	0	5.1	—	41.9%	—	171	—	175	20%	40%	23%	17%
2010	HOU	15	51	78	562	65%	0.3	11.0	3	1	4.5	28	-4.4%	63	51	63	46	38%	51%	7%	4%
2011	HOU		37	65	510	57%	--	13.8	2				5.2%								

What's not shown in the table is that Jones had 10 drops to go with those 51 receptions. Combining those stone hands with his change from a valuable deep receiver to one who had trouble separating downfield even when he went vertically, Jones changed from an incredibly useful third receiver to one of the weak links in an overall very efficient offense. Nobody signed him away in the offseason to be their disappointing second receiver, so the Texans are hoping he shows his 2010 deep form.

James Jones

Height: 6-1   Weight: 208   College: San Jose State   Draft: 2007/3 (78)   Born: 31-Mar-1984   Age: 27   Risk: Green

Year	Team	G	Rec	Pass	Yds	C%	+/-	Yd/C	TD	FUM	YAC	Rk	DVOA	Rk	DYAR	Rk	YAR	Short	Mid	Deep	Bomb
2008	GB	10	20	30	274	67%	2.0	13.7	1	0	3.1	—	18.2%	—	73	—	92	34%	48%	3%	14%
2009	GB	16	32	61	440	52%	-4.2	13.8	5	0	6.1	7	-5.9%	55	30	58	36	37%	47%	9%	7%
2010	GB	16	50	87	679	57%	3.2	13.6	5	3	5.8	8	-4.0%	61	59	58	73	34%	34%	19%	13%
2011	GB		19	35	249	54%	--	13.1	2				-5.7%								

Jones is strictly a boundary receiver: only 10 of his 87 passes were thrown over the middle. Jones dropped six passes and caught five more out-of-bounds; if he had better hands and tightroped the sideline better, he would be one of the most dangerous deep threats in the league. Instead, he is a useful complementary player who stretches and widens the field but will never graduate to a 10-target per game role. We see him losing targets to Jordy Nelson and/or the return of Jermichael Finley.

Julio Jones

Height: 6-3   Weight: 220   College: Alabama   Draft: 2011/1 (6)   Born: 3-Feb-1989   Age: 22   Risk: Red

Year	Team	G	Rec	Pass	Yds	C%	+/-	Yd/C	TD	FUM	YAC	Rk	DVOA	Rk	DYAR	Rk	YAR	Short	Mid	Deep	Bomb
2011	ATL		57	108	792	53%	--	13.9	6				7.5%								

Like Cincinnati's A.J. Green, Julio Jones was an all-world recruit out of high school. During Alabama's national title run of 2009, Jones was a hit-or-miss option, limping through a bruised knee and posting 596 receiving yards (13.9 per catch, 47 percent catch rate) with limited efficiency. In 2010, however, he bounced back, catching 78 passes for 1,113 yards (14.5 per catch, 72 percent catch rate). Then he kicked everything up a notch by blowing away teams at the Combine. Jones suffered a foot fracture but worked out anyway; all he did was run a 4.39 in the 40-yard dash and broad jump over 11 feet. Our Playmaker Score system, however, doesn't like Jones because he scored only 15 touchdowns in college. Of all the individual elements we use in Playmaker Score, touchdowns are by far the most accurate predictor of NFL success. Yes, the Crimson Tide prefers to run for scores, but they still scored 52 touchdowns in the air over the last three years and rarely targeted Jones in the red zone.

Johnny Knox

Height: 6-1   Weight: 185   College: Abilene Christian   Draft: 2009/5 (140)   Born: 3-Nov-1986   Age: 25   Risk: Green

Year	Team	G	Rec	Pass	Yds	C%	+/-	Yd/C	TD	FUM	YAC	Rk	DVOA	Rk	DYAR	Rk	YAR	Short	Mid	Deep	Bomb
2009	CHI	15	45	80	527	56%	0.9	11.7	5	0	3.9	55	-10.2%	61	15	62	32	32%	40%	17%	11%
2010	CHI	16	51	100	960	51%	-1.9	18.8	5	1	4.7	27	14.7%	9	207	17	201	17%	44%	24%	16%
2011	CHI		49	98	638	50%	--	13.0	4				-0.7%								

Knox led the Bears in targets (100) and yards per pass thrown to him (14.7); in Martz World, the designated deep threat is also the go-to receiver. Knox was 11-of-26 for 424 yards on passes of over 20 yards in air length, fine numbers except for the other-wordly seven interceptions thrown on those balls. Knox has the speed and body control to be a great deep threat, but there isn't much he can do if Jay Cutler decides to throw him the ball blind and off his back foot. It looks like Roy Williams will eat into Knox's opportunities, if not take his starting job outright. No one in Chicago has watched Cowboys game tape or read a Texas newspaper in the last two years.

Max Komar

Height: 5-11   Weight: 202   College: Idaho   Draft: 2010/ (FA)   Born: 30-Nov-1987   Age: 24   Risk: Green

Year	Team	G	Rec	Pass	Yds	C%	+/-	Yd/C	TD	FUM	YAC	Rk	DVOA	Rk	DYAR	Rk	YAR	Short	Mid	Deep	Bomb
2010	ARI	8	12	22	117	55%	-1.1	9.8	0	1	2.8	--	-38.3%	--	-44	--	-35	43%	33%	14%	10%
2011	ARI		16	28	196	57%	--	12.2	1				-5.3%								

Max Komar looks exactly what you would expect an undrafted free agent receiver from Idaho named Max Komar to look like. The Cardinals used him early in the season after he had a big training camp, then left him off the active roster for seven games before bringing him back at the end of the season. Komar was one of the few Arizona wideouts to have a catch rate over 50 percent, but it helps that he was targeted only 22 times. The arrival of Chansi Stuckey may cost him his spot on the roster.

Brandon LaFell

Height: 6-3   Weight: 211   College: LSU   Draft: 2010/3 (78)   Born: 4-Nov-1986   Age: 25   Risk: Green

Year	Team	G	Rec	Pass	Yds	C%	+/-	Yd/C	TD	FUM	YAC	Rk	DVOA	Rk	DYAR	Rk	YAR	Short	Mid	Deep	Bomb
2010	CAR	14	38	77	468	49%	-7.0	12.3	1	0	3.5	54	-19.4%	75	-41	74	-28	33%	46%	11%	10%
2011	CAR		19	40	299	48%	--	15.7	2				-6.1%								

LaFell is a big receiver who takes time to get up to speed; he would seem to be best-placed in route concepts that don't require him to cut and plant to the millisecond. Comebacks and quick outs would have been ideal, but his rookie season started off like a nightmare, even by Panthers standards — 18 of his first 23 targets were incompletions, which puts that catch rate in perspective. The problems seemed to be about equally distributed between LaFell running inaccurate routes he wasn't ready to run, and a series of goatballs and wormburners throws by Carolina's Keystone Cops quarterbacks. More will be asked of LaFell in 2011 — like every Panthers receiver, he just has to hope that his quarterback situation is improved over last season's disaster.

Greg Lewis

Height: 6-0   Weight: 180   College: Illinois   Draft: 2003/ (FA)   Born: 12-Feb-1980   Age: 31   Risk: Green

Year	Team	G	Rec	Pass	Yds	C%	+/-	Yd/C	TD	FUM	YAC	Rk	DVOA	Rk	DYAR	Rk	YAR	Short	Mid	Deep	Bomb
2008	PHI	16	19	35	247	54%	0.8	13.0	1	0	2.7	--	1.8%	--	41	--	45	19%	50%	16%	16%
2009	MIN	13	8	11	96	73%	0.2	12.0	1	0	5.3	--	6.0%	--	15	--	15	64%	27%	0%	9%
2010	MIN	13	17	37	197	46%	-5.3	11.6	0	0	4.2	--	-26.9%	--	-40	--	-51	34%	54%	11%	0%
2011	MIN		4	7	47	57%	--	11.9	1				-1.6%								

Now entering his fifth season as a fringe player, Lewis knows how to hedge his bets. The week before he participated in Vikings player-organized workouts (he was one of the few veteran receivers who bothered), Lewis practiced with the Eagles, running routes with some former teammates and even throwing some passes when Eagles quarterbacks took a break. Can a Joe Webb-like conversion be far behind? Lewis is not the kind of receiver a rebuilding team keeps on the roster, but the Vikings bench is full of veteran journeymen of his ilk, and Lewis has shown surprising staying power in the past.

Greg Little

Height: 6-2   Weight: 220   College: North Carolina   Draft: 2011/2 (59)   Born: 30-May-1989   Age: 22   Risk: Red

Year	Team	G	Rec	Pass	Yds	C%	+/-	Yd/C	TD	FUM	YAC	Rk	DVOA	Rk	DYAR	Rk	YAR	Short	Mid	Deep	Bomb
2011	CLE		36	68	457	53%	--	12.7	3				-20.8%								

By picking Little late in the second round, the Browns brass went with potential over production. Like Marvin Austin and Robert Quinn, Little was suspended for his senior year due to accepting improper agent benefits, so a lot of the hopes about him are based on the idea that he "was poised for a breakout year" that never happened. He was primarily a running back in his first two seasons, and his junior numbers are pedestrian: 724 yards, 11.7 per reception, five touchdowns. Still, he's a great package of size, strength, and fluid movement. He doesn't have the speed to separate on deep routes, but he's fearless catching balls in traffic, and fits the model for the flanker position in a classic West Coast scheme. As an added bonus for the run-heavy Browns, his strength should make him an excellent blocker. Some draftniks compared him to Anquan Boldin, but while Boldin was a similar style of receiver, he was the opposite type of prospect: lots of production in college, disappointing combine numbers.

Brandon Lloyd

Height: 6-0   Weight: 192   College: Illinois   Draft: 2003/4 (124)   Born: 5-Jul-1981   Age: 30   Risk: Red

Year	Team	G	Rec	Pass	Yds	C%	+/-	Yd/C	TD	FUM	YAC	Rk	DVOA	Rk	DYAR	Rk	YAR	Short	Mid	Deep	Bomb
2008	CHI	11	26	49	364	53%	1.2	14.0	2	0	2.3	--	-6.0%	--	26	--	37	13%	49%	24%	13%
2009	DEN	2	8	18	117	44%	-2.1	14.6	0	0	1.8	--	-18.7%	--	-9	--	-9	28%	33%	33%	6%
2010	DEN	16	77	152	1448	51%	2.7	18.8	11	0	2.4	80	20.0%	6	414	2	401	11%	48%	20%	22%
2011	DEN		75	142	1172	53%	--	15.6	8				-2.6%								

Well, who saw this coming? After seven seasons of abject underachievement with four different teams (including the 2009 Broncos), something went off on Lloyd's head, and he became the best deep receiver in the game. Josh McDaniel's offense is designed to open up downfield opportunities, but this was ridiculous — Lloyd averaged 16.5 air yards (from quarterback to receiver before the after-catch run), the best in the game last season. Most impressively, Lloyd wasn't just running go routes past burned cornerbacks — he frequently hit slants and square-ins in zones, giving up his body against defenders primed to attack. Eager to contort his body to catch Kyle Orton's sometimes iffy throws in coverage (the catch rate was far from his primary responsibility), Lloyd was every bit the No. 1 receiver his stats made him appear to be. The question is whether he'll be able to take increased coverage in what's likely to be an offense with fewer multi-receiver sets — in 2010, Lloyd frequently benefitted from formations that took intermediate coverage to slot and flex receivers.

Jeremy Maclin Height: 6-0 Weight: 198 College: Missouri   Draft: 2009/1 (19) Born: 11-May-1988 Age: 23 Risk: Red

Year	Team	G	Rec	Pass	Yds	C%	+/-	Yd/C	TD	FUM	YAC	Rk	DVOA	Rk	DYAR	Rk	YAR	Short	Mid	Deep	Bomb
2009	PHI	15	56	92	773	61%	1.2	13.8	4	0	4.4	34	8.6%	31	153	31	144	31%	44%	12%	12%
2010	PHI	16	70	115	964	61%	8.1	13.8	10	1	3.7	52	15.5%	8	251	10	246	32%	36%	14%	18%
2011	PHI		57	102	783	56%	--	13.7	6				2.9%								

It's pretty nifty to see Maclin retain the same catch rate and yards per catch figures over two consecutive seasons, but it's even cooler that he did that while adding 17 more targets and six more touchdowns to his totals. His biggest game of the year actually came after Vick was injured and Jackson went down with an in-game injury, his 7-159-2 line against the Falcons in Week 6. He won't catch a touchdown pass every seven receptions again, but Maclin is already the best receiver that the Eagles have.

Mario Manningham Height: 5-11 Weight: 181 College: Michigan   Draft: 2008/3 (95) Born: 25-May-1986 Age: 25 Risk: Green

Year	Team	G	Rec	Pass	Yds	C%	+/-	Yd/C	TD	FUM	YAC	Rk	DVOA	Rk	DYAR	Rk	YAR	Short	Mid	Deep	Bomb
2008	NYG	7	4	6	26	67%	-0.6	6.5	0	0	5.5	--	0.3%	--	8	--	4	71%	14%	14%	0%
2009	NYG	14	57	99	822	58%	-0.1	14.4	5	1	4.6	28	7.5%	33	158	28	142	24%	47%	19%	10%
2010	NYG	16	60	92	944	65%	8.8	15.7	9	1	5.8	7	12.4%	16	187	20	213	32%	38%	15%	15%
2011	NYG		63	112	912	56%	--	14.5	6				6.3%								

Alternately infuriating and brilliant, Manningham has sunk the Giants with game-turning fumbles in each of their season-crippling home losses over the past two years. On the other hand, they're also his only two fumbles over that timeframe, and he had 16 catches for 346 yards and four touchdowns as the team's leading receiver during the final three games of 2010. That included long touchdowns against both Tramon Williams and DeAngelo Hall. He'll start next to Hakeem Nicks this year.

Brandon Marshall Height: 6-4 Weight: 229 College: UCF   Draft: 2006/4 (119) Born: 23-Mar-1984 Age: 27 Risk: Green

Year	Team	G	Rec	Pass	Yds	C%	+/-	Yd/C	TD	FUM	YAC	Rk	DVOA	Rk	DYAR	Rk	YAR	Short	Mid	Deep	Bomb
2008	DEN	15	104	181	1265	57%	-3.3	12.2	6	4	3.9	35	-6.8%	58	85	42	105	32%	40%	16%	12%
2009	DEN	15	101	155	1120	66%	5.4	11.1	10	0	5.1	21	2.3%	38	179	24	175	50%	30%	11%	9%
2010	MIA	14	86	146	1014	59%	5.5	11.8	3	2	2.8	73	-1.8%	54	127	34	85	36%	40%	16%	8%
2011	MIA		78	128	908	61%	--	11.6	7				3.9%								

Miami paid good money for the Brandon Marshall Experience, and that is exactly what they got. On the positive side, Marshall came in and provided an immediate focus for the passing attack to flow through. Marshall was one of the busiest receivers in the league, as he was the intended receiver on 146 attempts, a number that would undoubtedly have been higher had he not missed two games with an injured hamstring. Marshall proved his versatility, lining up all over the field and running every route on the passing tree. On the other hand, Marshall publicly insinuated that he preferred playing with backup Tyler Thigpen over Chad Henne, and castigated both Henne and quarterbacks coach David Lee for getting upset when Marshall would change his route based on his pre-snap read. He followed that up in April by checking into a Miami ER with stab wounds he received from his wife, the latest in a long line of domestic disputes that turned violent.

Assuming Marshall can stay healthy and keep his head on straight--a somewhat questionable proposition — he should continue to be a high volume receiver who generates consistent reception and yardage totals, and he's not likely to score only three touchdowns again.

Derrick Mason

Height: 5-10 Weight: 190 College: Michigan State   Draft: 1997/4 (98)   Born: 17-Jan-1974   Age: 37   Risk: Green

Year	Team	G	Rec	Pass	Yds	C%	+/-	Yd/C	TD	FUM	YAC	Rk	DVOA	Rk	DYAR	Rk	YAR	Short	Mid	Deep	Bomb
2008	BAL	16	80	121	1037	67%	7.4	13.0	5	2	3.1	57	13.9%	15	250	11	241	20%	54%	15%	10%
2009	BAL	16	73	134	1028	54%	1.8	14.1	7	0	3.6	60	4.2%	36	180	23	174	13%	54%	20%	13%
2010	BAL	16	61	100	802	61%	8.5	13.1	7	0	2.1	83	13.5%	14	216	16	224	16%	53%	21%	10%
2011	NYJ		43	73	468	59%	--	10.9	3				-12.0%								

According to FO similarity scores, the most similar receiver to Derrick Mason 2008-2010 is Hines Ward 2008-2010. And just like Ward, Mason has entered the "aged wide receiver unknown" where it is difficult to forecast the future. He could be good for another two or three years, or his skills could crumble next week. One item in Mason's favor: He's really consistently good in the red zone, with 36.7% DVOA inside the 20 over the past three seasons.

Mohamed Massaquoi

Height: 6-2   Weight: 210 College: Georgia   Draft: 2009/2 (50)   Born: 24-Nov-1986   Age: 25   Risk: Green

Year	Team	G	Rec	Pass	Yds	C%	+/-	Yd/C	TD	FUM	YAC	Rk	DVOA	Rk	DYAR	Rk	YAR	Short	Mid	Deep	Bomb
2009	CLE	16	34	95	624	36%	-12.2	18.4	3	1	4.6	29	-23.3%	79	-79	83	-86	21%	33%	24%	22%
2010	CLE	15	36	73	483	49%	-1.3	13.4	2	1	3.9	43	-14.0%	72	-8	72	-12	28%	43%	12%	17%
2011	CLE		40	69	470	58%	--	11.8	4				-4.0%								

Massaquoi has been Cleveland's No. 1 receiver by default for two years, and probably will be for a third while Greg Little gets up to speed. He would fit better as a complimentary piece rather than a featured player. At least he's working hard on his game: A report in July said that Massaquoi arranged training sessions with some of the best wide receivers in the league during the lockout, trying to pick up pointers from the likes of Chad Ochocinco, Larry Fitzgerald, and Wes Welker. Oddly, the Browns only threw to Massaquoi three times in the red zone last year, after he was their leading red zone target in 2009.

Dexter McCluster

Height: 5-9   Weight: 172 College: Mississippi   Draft: 2010/2 (36)   Born: 25-Aug-1988   Age: 23   Risk: Blue

Year	Team	G	Rec	Pass	Yds	C%	+/-	Yd/C	TD	FUM	YAC	Rk	DVOA	Rk	DYAR	Rk	YAR	Short	Mid	Deep	Bomb
2010	KC	11	21	39	209	54%	-3.8	10.0	1	0	7.9	--	-19.7%	--	-21	--	-21	67%	28%	6%	0%
2011	KC		6	11	67	55%	--	11.2	1				-27.1%								

McCluster's inability to do anything of value as an offensive weapon in the Chiefs' crushing wild-card loss to Baltimore summarized his rookie campaign. Expected to cut loose after the catch on short passes out of tricky formations, McCluster couldn't quite transcend his size issues with elite explosiveness. Of course, it would help of the Chiefs didn't telegraph him as a target — everyone knows he's the bailout guy when he motions to bunch out of the backfield — but that schematic giveaway indicated the difficulties in getting McCluster to fit. The Chiefs apparently don't plan on using him much on offense this year, and are considering moving him back to running back.

Robert Meachem   Height: 6-2   Weight: 210   College: Tennessee   Draft: 2007/1 (27)   Born: 28-Sep-1984   Age: 27   Risk: Green

Year	Team	G	Rec	Pass	Yds	C%	+/-	Yd/C	TD	FUM	YAC	Rk	DVOA	Rk	DYAR	Rk	YAR	Short	Mid	Deep	Bomb
2008	NO	14	12	20	289	60%	1.4	24.1	3	0	5.1	--	64.0%	--	114	--	110	10%	43%	19%	29%
2009	NO	16	45	64	722	70%	10.6	16.0	9	2	3.8	56	39.2%	1	267	12	249	29%	32%	10%	30%
2010	NO	16	44	66	638	67%	8.6	14.5	5	0	3.0	68	22.7%	4	187	19	190	43%	23%	8%	26%
2011	NO		40	67	572	60%	--	14.3	5				16.3%								

Not much mystery in the way the Saints used Meachem: They either threw him a quick short one or sent him on a fly pattern. No NFL receiver had a higher percentage of bombs thrown his way. It works, apparently. DVOA has loved the former Tennessee Vol since he came into the NFL. Like teammate Lance Moore, Meachem was a third-down weapon (40.5% DVOA). He was even more of a monster on first down, with 49.9% DVOA. Not surprisingly, his effectiveness dwindles as the field shortens to the red zone.

Denarius Moore   Height: 6-0   Weight: 191   College: Tennessee   Draft: 2011/5 (148)   Born: 9-Dec-1988   Age: 23   Risk: Red

Year	Team	G	Rec	Pass	Yds	C%	+/-	Yd/C	TD	FUM	YAC	Rk	DVOA	Rk	DYAR	Rk	YAR	Short	Mid	Deep	Bomb
2011	OAK		30	56	416	54%	--	13.9	2				-9.1%								

Moore had three different head coaches in his college career, and it's arguable as to whether he was ever thrown a pass by a Division I-caliber quarterback. Despite those handicaps, he caught nine touchdowns and gained 912 yards on just 43 catches. The only player in the NCAA to put up two games of 200-plus yards, Moore factors in as a bit of a sleeper pick and a potential big-play guy in certain packages. He certainly impressed in training camp — Steve Corkran of the *Contra Costa Times* raised some eyebrows with his mid-August claim: "It has reached the point where this isn't some one-week wonder, flash in the pan or fluke. The man can flat-out play."

Lance Moore   Height: 5-9   Weight: 177   College: Toledo   Draft: 2005/ (FA)   Born: 31-Aug-1983   Age: 28   Risk: Green

Year	Team	G	Rec	Pass	Yds	C%	+/-	Yd/C	TD	FUM	YAC	Rk	DVOA	Rk	DYAR	Rk	YAR	Short	Mid	Deep	Bomb
2008	NO	16	79	120	928	66%	6.5	11.7	10	0	3.6	45	12.7%	17	232	15	196	39%	40%	15%	6%
2009	NO	7	14	19	153	74%	2.8	10.9	2	0	2.9	--	24.6%	--	58	--	57	53%	29%	18%	0%
2010	NO	16	66	94	763	70%	6.3	11.6	8	1	4.4	32	14.6%	10	205	18	218	46%	40%	5%	9%
2011	NO		56	92	750	61%	--	13.4	4				12.4%								

The system or the player? The Saints decided it was the latter, re-signing Moore to a new deal as soon as free agent signings were kosher. Moore bounced back from an injury-plagued 2009 to essentially recreate his 2008 season. He was a stud on third down, posting the league's highest DVOA (45.3%) and 141 DYAR when the time came to move the chains. Moore was the most-targeted Saint in the red zone despite a slew of competition, so he may be the right Saint to target in your fantasy draft.

Josh Morgan   Height: 6-0   Weight: 219   College: Virginia Tech   Draft: 2008/6 (174)   Born: 20-Jun-1985   Age: 26   Risk: Green

Year	Team	G	Rec	Pass	Yds	C%	+/-	Yd/C	TD	FUM	YAC	Rk	DVOA	Rk	DYAR	Rk	YAR	Short	Mid	Deep	Bomb
2008	SF	12	20	43	319	47%	-3.3	16.0	3	0	4.3	--	-16.3%	--	-12	--	-1	28%	31%	28%	13%
2009	SF	16	52	81	527	64%	3.1	10.1	3	0	4.8	27	-18.4%	72	-36	73	4	53%	32%	9%	5%
2010	SF	16	44	80	698	55%	0.8	15.9	2	1	6.8	2	-3.2%	59	59	59	54	28%	39%	19%	14%
2011	SF		20	34	239	59%	--	11.9	1				-5.6%								

The most similar player to Morgan is Hines Ward, 1998-2000. Is the comparison that ridiculous? Ward's size (6-foot, 205 pounds) made him an effective blocker, like Morgan, and in those years he played for teams that hovered right around .500. Ward's quarterback, Kordell Stewart, bounced in and out of the starting lineup even though there were no other appealing options, just like Alex Smith. And while Morgan is a secondary wideout behind Michael Crabtree, Ward had failed to distinguish himself from the likes of Courtney Hawkins and Bobby Shaw. In 2001, Ward really became Hines Ward, reeling off four straight 1,000-yard seasons. Morgan showed a tantalizing glimpse of potential in Week 15, when he caught seven of nine passes for 106 yards against San Diego. He's one of the more intriguing question marks in the league going into 2011, but the signing of Braylon Edwards takes away his starting job.

Randy Moss

Height: 6-4   Weight: 215 College: Marshall   Draft: 1998/1 (21) Born: 13-Feb-1977 Age: 34 Risk: N/A

Year	Team	G	Rec	Pass	Yds	C%	+/-	Yd/C	TD	FUM	YAC	Rk	DVOA	Rk	DYAR	Rk	YAR	Short	Mid	Deep	Bomb
2008	NE	16	69	125	1008	55%	-0.8	14.6	11	3	5.0	11	0.5%	41	134	29	134	25%	43%	14%	18%
2009	NE	16	83	137	1264	61%	8.0	15.2	13	2	4.1	51	21.9%	10	395	5	347	24%	42%	14%	20%
2010	3TM	16	28	63	391	44%	-3.4	14.0	5	0	2.3	81	2.0%	45	72	54	62	20%	39%	19%	22%

Randy Moss' decision to retire means that we don't have to explore what happened between Moss and Patriots offensive coordinator Bill O'Brien on the plane home from the Week 4 win at Miami. We don't have to revisit last year's incident with the caterer in Minnesota. We don't have to figure out why Tennessee signed him and then refused to play him, and we don't have to figure out whether he has anything left. Instead, we can simply celebrate his great career. He ranked in the top ten in DVOA and DYAR seven times. He led the league in receiving DYAR three times: 2000, 2003, and 2007. That 2007 season is the second-highest DYAR of all-time, just behind Michael Irvin's 1995 but ahead of Jerry Rice's 1994 and 1995. Randy Moss was the greatest vertical threat in NFL history. He had incredible body control to beat double teams. And, most importantly, he introduced us to the phrase "Straight cash, homey." Football won't be quite as fun without him around.

Santana Moss

Height: 5-10 Weight: 185 College: Miami   Draft: 2001/1 (16) Born: 1-Jun-1979   Age: 32 Risk: Green

Year	Team	G	Rec	Pass	Yds	C%	+/-	Yd/C	TD	FUM	YAC	Rk	DVOA	Rk	DYAR	Rk	YAR	Short	Mid	Deep	Bomb
2008	WAS	16	79	138	1044	57%	-3.5	13.2	6	1	5.5	6	-6.0%	57	73	48	96	44%	34%	11%	12%
2009	WAS	16	70	120	902	58%	-0.9	12.9	3	2	5.1	20	-12.6%	67	1	67	10	40%	34%	14%	12%
2010	WAS	16	93	145	1115	64%	2.7	12.0	6	3	5.1	19	-2.1%	55	117	39	132	46%	34%	11%	9%
2011	WAS		71	127	868	56%	--	12.2	5				-4.9%								

After slipping out of a four-game suspension for being linked to a controversial doctor, Moss proceeded to have a reasonably impressive season. Although the jump in his raw numbers had a lot to do with a career-high in targets (which itself had to do with the absence of relevant receivers across from him), Moss also produced a career-high catch rate. Both those figures should drop in 2011, which makes Moss an overvalued property.

Louis Murphy

Height: 6-3   Weight: 203 College: Florida   Draft: 2009/4 (124) Born: 11-May-1987 Age: 24 Risk: Green

Year	Team	G	Rec	Pass	Yds	C%	+/-	Yd/C	TD	FUM	YAC	Rk	DVOA	Rk	DYAR	Rk	YAR	Short	Mid	Deep	Bomb
2009	OAK	16	34	96	521	35%	-15.6	15.3	4	0	3.4	62	-26.3%	81	-106	88	-131	22%	35%	27%	16%
2010	OAK	14	41	78	609	53%	-2.9	14.9	2	2	5.1	18	-8.9%	69	23	69	39	22%	47%	19%	12%
2011	OAK		39	79	484	49%	--	12.4	3				-14.0%								

Like most Raiders receivers, Murphy is still trying to put it all together from a consistently standpoint. With Hue Jackson professing to run a more aggressive passing offense, and the departure of tight end Zach Miller, Murphy's on the hook to provide better production. He's a good possession receiver with decent speed and a good raw skill set, but like every other Raiders receiver now, he's not quite where he needs to be just yet.

Legedu Naanee

Height: 6-2   Weight: 225 College: Boise State   Draft: 2007/5 (172) Born: 16-Sep-1983 Age: 28 Risk: Green

Year	Team	G	Rec	Pass	Yds	C%	+/-	Yd/C	TD	FUM	YAC	Rk	DVOA	Rk	DYAR	Rk	YAR	Short	Mid	Deep	Bomb
2008	SD	16	8	11	64	73%	1.1	8.0	0	0	3.3	--	-3.3%	--	8	--	9	70%	10%	20%	0%
2009	SD	15	24	29	242	83%	4.9	10.1	2	0	5.4	--	32.8%	--	103	--	107	59%	30%	11%	0%
2010	SD	10	23	46	371	50%	-2.4	16.1	1	1	4.6	--	-6.8%	--	21	--	28	29%	40%	21%	10%
2011	CAR		18	32	243	56%	--	13.5	1				-2.7%								

Naanee has had flashes throughout his career, but injuries and his overall "just a guy" status left him expendable by the Chargers after his public intoxication arrest in February. He'll help out in the slot in Carolina as the Panthers try to get Steve Smith out wide … if they have the quarterback to actually throw those passes.

David Nelson   Height: 6-5   Weight: 217   College: Florida   Draft: 2010/ (FA)   Born: 7-Nov-1986   Age: 25   Risk: Red

Year	Team	G	Rec	Pass	Yds	C%	+/-	Yd/C	TD	FUM	YAC	Rk	DVOA	Rk	DYAR	Rk	YAR	Short	Mid	Deep	Bomb
2010	BUF	15	31	47	353	66%	2.6	11.4	3	0	2.5	--	15.2%	--	95	--	92	13%	67%	20%	0%
2011	BUF		65	99	628	66%	--	9.7	3				-8.0%								

Nelson was 11-of-17 for 95 yards, two touchdowns, and five first downs in third down situations. The numbers aren't overwhelming, but all but one of the first downs/ touchdowns came from Week 7 on, when Nelson settled in as the Bills' possession receiver from the slot. Nelson uses his height and size well in the middle of the field, will break the occasional tackle, and has reliable hands. He could take over the No. 2 role in the Bills passing game after Lee Evans was dealt to Baltimore.

Jordy Nelson   Height: 6-2   Weight: 217   College: Kansas State   Draft: 2008/2 (36)   Born: 31-May-1985   Age: 26   Risk: Green

Year	Team	G	Rec	Pass	Yds	C%	+/-	Yd/C	TD	FUM	YAC	Rk	DVOA	Rk	DYAR	Rk	YAR	Short	Mid	Deep	Bomb
2008	GB	16	33	54	366	61%	1.9	11.1	2	0	2.7	66	-2.6%	51	41	58	44	22%	51%	16%	12%
2009	GB	13	22	31	320	71%	4.6	14.5	2	0	4.0	--	39.6%	--	129	--	131	28%	45%	14%	14%
2010	GB	16	45	64	582	70%	6.4	12.9	2	1	5.6	11	9.8%	22	115	40	121	39%	38%	13%	10%
2011	GB		33	56	428	59%	--	13.0	2				4.6%								

Nelson on passes labeled "deep" (15+ yards in the air) in official play-by-play: 6-of-15 for 223 yards, including an 80-yard touchdown. Five of those catches occurred after Week 9, and most of the deep throws came from two-back sets and play action, with safeties focused on Greg Jennings. Nelson has moved beyond the slot receiver stereotype and is being eased into Donald Driver's role. That late-season emergence as a deep threat, which carried into the Super Bowl, is a sign of what's to come.

Hakeem Nicks   Height: 6-3   Weight: 212   College: North Carolina   Draft: 2009/1 (29)   Born: 14-Jan-1988   Age: 23   Risk: Yellow

Year	Team	G	Rec	Pass	Yds	C%	+/-	Yd/C	TD	FUM	YAC	Rk	DVOA	Rk	DYAR	Rk	YAR	Short	Mid	Deep	Bomb
2009	NYG	14	47	74	790	64%	2.9	16.8	6	2	8.8	1	17.5%	14	176	25	155	40%	34%	13%	13%
2010	NYG	13	79	128	1052	62%	5.1	13.3	11	1	3.7	51	14.6%	11	276	6	301	30%	40%	18%	11%
2011	NYG		83	142	1104	58%	--	13.3	9				4.4%								

Nicks was downright uncoverable at times in 2010 before he suffered a series of injuries that slowed him down, including the extremely-painful compartment syndrome that caused him to miss two games. With a player this talented and productive in just his second season, there's every reason to push him up draft boards, right? Well, hold on a second. Although he's not necessarily at risk of suffering from compartment syndrome again, repeated leg and foot injuries at such a young age isn't a good sign. He's probably not going to have three multiple-touchdown games again. And note where his four 100-yard games came from; while one was against the fifth-ranked pass defense of the Bears, the other three came against the Cowboys (28th), Seahawks (29th), and Texans (32nd). Although the Seahawks and Cowboys come back in 2011, their pass defenses are extremely likely to be improved. Nicks is probably a little overvalued heading into 2011.

Ben Obomanu   Height: 6-0   Weight: 203   College: Auburn   Draft: 2006/7 (249)   Born: 30-Oct-1983   Age: 28   Risk: Green

Year	Team	G	Rec	Pass	Yds	C%	+/-	Yd/C	TD	FUM	YAC	Rk	DVOA	Rk	DYAR	Rk	YAR	Short	Mid	Deep	Bomb
2009	SEA	14	4	5	41	80%	0.7	10.3	0	0	3.8	--	30.8%	--	19	--	20	60%	40%	0%	0%
2010	SEA	15	30	49	494	61%	1.4	16.5	4	0	5.6	--	15.8%	--	110	--	111	47%	27%	13%	13%
2011	SEA		19	33	213	58%	--	11.2	0				-13.1%								

After three seasons as a special teams ace and blocking specialist (plus another year on injured reserve with a broken collarbone), Obomanu got the first start of his career in Week 10 against Arizona, and he led the Seahawks in receiving yards in the second half of the season. He was also the best deep threat on the team, leading the squad with six receptions of 25 yards or more even though he caught only six balls in the first half of the season. His best game of the year came with five catches and 159 yards (in only six targets) against Kansas City, including an 87-yard touchdown when he made Brandon Carr look silly on an out-and-up route. Obomanu signed an extension before the lockout that will keep him in grayish-blue until 2014, though the arrival of Sidney Rice and Zach Miller and the development of Golden Tate indicate a likely return to special teams duty.

Chad Ochocinco
Height: 6-1   Weight: 192   College: Oregon State   Draft: 2001/2 (36)   Born: 9-Jan-1978   Age: 33   Risk: Yellow

Year	Team	G	Rec	Pass	Yds	C%	+/-	Yd/C	TD	FUM	YAC	Rk	DVOA	Rk	DYAR	Rk	YAR	Short	Mid	Deep	Bomb
2008	CIN	13	53	97	540	55%	1.8	10.2	4	0	1.7	79	-1.1%	46	91	38	53	13%	64%	15%	8%
2009	CIN	16	72	129	1047	57%	-1.6	14.5	9	2	3.7	57	9.7%	27	234	15	240	20%	52%	19%	8%
2010	CIN	14	67	126	831	53%	-3.2	12.4	4	0	2.8	71	-0.5%	50	120	37	92	21%	55%	16%	8%
2011	NE		63	96	804	66%	--	12.8	6				15.7%								

We'll leave it to others to talk about how playing for Bill Belichick will affect Ochocinco's wacky off-field antics and Twitter-happy lifestyle. Let's talk instead about how Ochocinco can help the Patriots. He is not a replacement for Randy Moss. He's not fast enough at this point to "take the top off the defense," and he's not going to get you a lot of yards after the catch. He is going to help you in the red zone, where he had DVOA over 50% in both 2008 and 2009. He still has the right moves to get himself open against man coverage, where he'll use his great body control to make a spectacular catch. However, according to *NFL Matchup*'s Greg Cosell, he hasn't been very good running routes against zone coverage over the last couple years. The receiver has to pace his route, know where the defenders are, and adjust to the zone properly to be in the right place at the right time to catch the pass. Ochocinco ended up freelancing a bit, and when Carson Palmer put the ball in the right place, Ochocinco wasn't necessarily there. That's not going to fly with Tom Brady.

Kevin Ogletree
Height: 6-2   Weight: 196   College: Virginia   Draft: 2009/ (FA)   Born: 5-Dec-1987   Age: 24   Risk: Red

Year	Team	G	Rec	Pass	Yds	C%	+/-	Yd/C	TD	FUM	YAC	Rk	DVOA	Rk	DYAR	Rk	YAR	Short	Mid	Deep	Bomb
2009	DAL	11	7	8	96	88%	1.2	13.7	0	0	9.9	--	53.5%	--	36	--	39	63%	25%	13%	0%
2010	DAL	6	3	6	34	50%	-1.1	11.3	0	0	2.0	--	-14.3%	--	-1	--	-2	50%	17%	33%	0%
2011	DAL		39	63	534	62%	--	13.7	3				13.5%								

With Roy Williams released, Ogletree suddenly finds himself in possession of the third receiver role in Dallas' offense. Injuries have haunted him in both college and the pros, but he gave Roy Williams a battle last season for a real role in the offense, and his only real challenger for the job is rookie fifth-rounder Dwayne Harris. KUBIAK envisions some decent numbers for him, but it's likely that the Cowboys will look to feature tight end Martellus Bennett rather than Ogletree in non-obvious passing situations, so he isn't really an appealing fantasy football stash at this point.

Terrell Owens
Height: 6-3   Weight: 226   College: Tennessee-Chattanooga   Draft: 1996/3 (89)   Born: 7-Dec-1973   Age: 38   Risk: N/A

Year	Team	G	Rec	Pass	Yds	C%	+/-	Yd/C	TD	FUM	YAC	Rk	DVOA	Rk	DYAR	Rk	YAR	Short	Mid	Deep	Bomb
2008	DAL	16	69	139	1052	50%	-9.2	15.2	10	1	4.2	26	-5.7%	56	75	46	57	24%	45%	15%	16%
2009	BUF	16	55	109	829	50%	-6.8	15.1	5	1	4.2	43	-14.8%	69	-18	70	-9	28%	37%	12%	23%
2010	CIN	14	72	139	983	52%	-5.9	13.7	9	0	4.0	40	-0.2%	49	140	30	117	28%	39%	18%	15%

Three years, three different teams. Three DVOA ratings below zero. Three extremely poor catch rates and plus-minus ratings. It actually gets worse on third downs, where Owens has a 40 percent catch rate over the last three seasons. And in the clubhouse, the surprisingly quiet Owens we saw in Buffalo turned out to be a one-year mirage; Owens criticized coaches and ownership on the national talk show he co-hosted with teammate Chad Ochocinco. The once-great Owens is now simply an average receiver who builds his numbers through quantity, not quality, and it's just not worth dealing with his personal issues.

Roscoe Parrish

Height: 5-10 Weight: 168 College: Miami Draft: 2005/2 (55) Born: 16-Jul-1982 Age: 29 Risk: Red

Year	Team	G	Rec	Pass	Yds	C%	+/-	Yd/C	TD	FUM	YAC	Rk	DVOA	Rk	DYAR	Rk	YAR	Short	Mid	Deep	Bomb
2008	BUF	13	24	45	232	53%	-2.1	9.7	1	0	3.0	--	-30.1%	--	-64	--	-45	40%	40%	14%	5%
2009	BUF	12	3	4	34	75%	0.0	11.3	0	0	4.7	--	-78.5%	--	-17	--	-16	75%	25%	0%	0%
2010	BUF	8	33	52	400	63%	-0.2	12.1	2	1	4.0	41	-2.4%	56	42	65	38	37%	41%	18%	4%
2011	BUF		49	88	636	56%	--	13.0	2				-2.5%								

It was a typical Parrish year. He dropped some passes, mis-ran some routes, called too many fair catches on punts, and made a lot of jukes that resulted in four-yard gains. He also had some solid games before breaking his wrist in Week 9, catching five passes for 83 yards against the Patriots and seven passes for 60 yards with a touchdown against the Bears. Theoretically, the emergence of Steve Johnson and David Nelson should open up lots of opportunities for Parrish on screens, hitches, and short option routes. At the same time, there may be far fewer passes to go around, and Parrish loses focus when he's not heavily involved in the game plan.

Austin Pettis

Height: 6-3 Weight: 209 College: Boise St. Draft: 2011/3 (78) Born: 7-May-1988 Age: 23 Risk: Red

Year	Team	G	Rec	Pass	Yds	C%	+/-	Yd/C	TD	FUM	YAC	Rk	DVOA	Rk	DYAR	Rk	YAR	Short	Mid	Deep	Bomb
2011	STL	14	22	172	62%		--	12.3	1				-6.7%								

Austin Pettis might have the best hands of any rookie in this year's draft class. In his four years at Boise State, Pettis caught 73 percent of the passes thrown at him. His catch rate was an astounding 81 percent his first two years, when he was primarily used as a possession receiver. In 2009-10, his routes opened up a bit more, and as a result his yards per catch went up, from 10.8 in 2007-08 to 13.5 in 2009-10. His catch rate fell to a still respectable 69 percent. While Pettis lacks the speed to be a deep threat, he is a big, versatile, sure-handed receiver who will make the tough catches in traffic and be a factor inside the red zone. With only Brandon Gibson and the oft-injured Danario Alexander blocking his path, Pettis could earn a starting assignment opposite Mike Sims-Walker early in his NFL career.

Antwaan Randle El

Height: 5-10 Weight: 192 College: Indiana Draft: 2002/2 (62) Born: 17-Aug-1979 Age: 32 Risk: N/A

Year	Team	G	Rec	Pass	Yds	C%	+/-	Yd/C	TD	FUM	YAC	Rk	DVOA	Rk	DYAR	Rk	YAR	Short	Mid	Deep	Bomb
2008	WAS	16	53	87	593	61%	-0.1	11.2	4	0	3.7	43	1.4%	37	96	36	78	35%	53%	9%	4%
2009	WAS	16	50	75	530	67%	3.6	10.6	0	1	4.4	36	-3.8%	50	53	51	46	49%	44%	6%	1%
2010	PIT	16	22	39	253	56%	0.0	11.5	0	0	2.3	--	-5.8%	--	21	--	19	24%	58%	8%	11%

The emergence of Emmanuel Sanders and Antonio Brown made Randle El superfluous, so Pittsburgh cut him to save salary cap space. He could probably still help a team as a depth slot receiver, but he doesn't really have special teams value anymore; by our measurements, Randle El's value as a punt returner has been negative each of the last three seasons.

Sidney Rice

Height: 6-4 Weight: 200 College: South Carolina Draft: 2007/2 (44) Born: 1-Sep-1986 Age: 25 Risk: Red

Year	Team	G	Rec	Pass	Yds	C%	+/-	Yd/C	TD	FUM	YAC	Rk	DVOA	Rk	DYAR	Rk	YAR	Short	Mid	Deep	Bomb
2008	MIN	13	15	31	141	48%	-2.7	9.4	4	0	2.2	--	-3.8%	--	23	--	26	26%	55%	13%	6%
2009	MIN	16	83	121	1312	69%	11.8	15.8	8	1	4.4	32	35.4%	3	476	1	487	23%	52%	13%	12%
2010	MIN	6	17	42	280	40%	-3.3	16.5	2	0	2.5	--	-1.5%	--	37	--	18	13%	42%	18%	26%
2011	SEA		56	120	884	47%		--	15.8	6				-4.4%								

The Vikings offered Rice a multi-year contract before the lockout, but Rice decided to roll the dice on free agency. He probably figured that his status as an overvalued Vikings receiver would attract the Seahawks. And he was right. Seahawks fans with Post-Nate Burleson Stress Disorder have reason to be concerned: Rice's status as a top receiver is based on one charmed season. There's a big difference between Brett Favre in 2009 and this year's Seahawks quarterbacks. The Seahawks have such a bad track record with big-name receiving acquisitions that it is easy to be pessimistic, but the real problem in Seattle probably won't be Rice, but the guys fluttering passes to him.

Andre Roberts
Height: 5-11   Weight: 195   College: The Citadel   Draft: 2010/3 (88)   Born: 9-Jan-1988   Age: 23   Risk: Red

Year	Team	G	Rec	Pass	Yds	C%	+/-	Yd/C	TD	FUM	YAC	Rk	DVOA	Rk	DYAR	Rk	YAR	Short	Mid	Deep	Bomb
2010	ARI	15	24	49	307	49%	-6.7	12.8	2	1	5.8	--	-39.7%	--	-102	--	-69	49%	32%	15%	4%
2011	ARI		58	95	847	61%	--	14.6	5				2.7%								

The rookie from the Citadel saw a lot of action in 2010 as both a receiver and punt returner, and could see even more in 2011 with the departure of Steve Breaston. If Doucet is slow to return from injury, Roberts could find himself in the opening day starting lineup opposite Fitzgerald. The offensive staff often praised the big play potential of Roberts throughout the season, but it wasn't until a 74-yard touchdown catch on Christmas Day that he showed it in a game.

Laurent Robinson
Height: 6-2   Weight: 192   College: Illinois State   Draft: 2007/3 (75)   Born: 20-May-1985   Age: 26   Risk: Green

Year	Team	G	Rec	Pass	Yds	C%	+/-	Yd/C	TD	FUM	YAC	Rk	DVOA	Rk	DYAR	Rk	YAR	Short	Mid	Deep	Bomb
2008	ATL	6	5	6	52	83%	0.6	10.4	0	0	5.4	--	36.8%	--	21	--	18	67%	33%	0%	0%
2009	STL	3	13	23	167	57%	-0.7	12.8	1	0	3.3	--	-1.0%	--	21	--	31	27%	55%	5%	14%
2010	STL	14	34	75	344	45%	-6.6	10.1	2	0	3.1	64	-36.6%	84	-141	84	-117	35%	44%	14%	8%
2011	SD		22	38	372	58%	--	16.9	3				15.6%								

Football fans in Atlanta and St. Louis who have been taken in by Robinson's impressive physical tools could start a support group. Robinson had a promising rookie season with the Falcons before missing most of 2008 and, following a trade to St. Louis, 2009 with leg injuries. To put how bad Robinson's 2010 season was into perspective, the 26-year-old ranked 84th in both DYAR and DVOA…out of 85 receivers. Robinson has taken his talents to San Diego, where he'll fight with Seyi Ajirotutu and third-round pick Vincent Brown for playing time.

Brian Robiskie
Height: 6-3   Weight: 209   College: Ohio State   Draft: 2009/2 (36)   Born: 3-Dec-1987   Age: 24   Risk: Green

Year	Team	G	Rec	Pass	Yds	C%	+/-	Yd/C	TD	FUM	YAC	Rk	DVOA	Rk	DYAR	Rk	YAR	Short	Mid	Deep	Bomb
2009	CLE	11	7	20	106	35%	-0.5	15.1	0	0	7.3	--	-36.4%	--	-37	--	-35	36%	29%	21%	14%
2010	CLE	14	29	49	310	59%	-0.7	10.7	3	0	2.0	--	-11.8%	--	3	--	-15	33%	44%	13%	10%
2011	CLE		31	61	400	51%	--	12.9	4				-4.7%								

So far, so meh for the former Ohio State star. He's a high-character, high-motor guy, but you can't expect him to get deep and beat cornerbacks; he simply doesn't have that second gear. Theoretically, he's the kind of smart route runner who should excel as a possession receiver in the West Coast offense, and indeed the Browns did have him running more mid-range routes last year. Nevertheless, the Browns just spent another second-round pick on another receiver (Greg Little) with the same skill set. Note that if Robiskie had enough passes to be ranked — he's one short — he would have been next-to-last in Yards After Catch.

Naaman Roosevelt
Height: 6-0   Weight: 189   College: Buffalo   Draft: 2010/ (FA)   Born: 24-Dec-1987   Age: 24   Risk: Blue

Year	Team	G	Rec	Pass	Yds	C%	+/-	Yd/C	TD	FUM	YAC	Rk	DVOA	Rk	DYAR	Rk	YAR	Short	Mid	Deep	Bomb
2010	BUF	6	9	17	139	53%	1.3	15.4	0	0	3.7	--	0.6%	--	18	--	17	6%	69%	25%	0%
2011	BUF		4	8	56	50%	--	14.0	0				-9.4%								

Roosevelt had a handful of fine late-season games after Lee Evans got hurt, catching four passes for 74 yards against the Patriots in Week 16 and three passes from Brian Brohm in the season finale. (Catching anything thrown by Brohm is an accomplishment for a non-defender.) Roosevelt has the Evans skill set, so he fits best as a deep threat who rarely works the middle. The Bills have a lot of guys vying for roster spots behind Evans, Steve Johnson, and David Nelson; Roosevelt's lack of versatility and special teams value will put him behind Roscoe Parrish, Donald Jones, and others.

Eddie Royal   Height: 5-9   Weight: 184   College: Virginia Tech   Draft: 2008/2 (42)   Born: 21-May-1986   Age: 25   Risk: Yellow

Year	Team	G	Rec	Pass	Yds	C%	+/-	Yd/C	TD	FUM	YAC	Rk	DVOA	Rk	DYAR	Rk	YAR	Short	Mid	Deep	Bomb
2008	DEN	15	91	129	980	71%	9.6	10.8	5	1	3.8	37	-1.4%	47	115	32	120	45%	35%	12%	9%
2009	DEN	14	37	79	345	47%	-6.8	9.3	0	0	3.4	64	-34.9%	89	-139	89	-134	43%	46%	7%	3%
2010	DEN	16	59	106	627	57%	-6.3	10.6	3	1	6.6	3	-17.9%	74	-43	75	-35	49%	35%	11%	4%
2011	DEN		61	104	671	59%	--	11.0	3				-10.0%								

Yes, we went a bit overboard with the Wes Welker comparisons in last year's book, but Royal did play the Welker role in the Denver version of Josh McDaniels' offense — he was the primary third-down receiver, ran infinite slants and curls out of the slot, and frequently made plays after the catch behind solid second-level blocking. The plan in Denver's new administration is to get Royal back to more of a return role while maintaining his value as a receiver.

Emmanuel Sanders   Height: 5-11   Weight: 186   College: SMU   Draft: 2010/3 (82)   Born: 17-Mar-1987   Age: 24   Risk: Yellow

Year	Team	G	Rec	Pass	Yds	C%	+/-	Yd/C	TD	FUM	YAC	Rk	DVOA	Rk	DYAR	Rk	YAR	Short	Mid	Deep	Bomb
2010	PIT	13	28	50	376	56%	0.1	13.4	2	0	2.5	78	5.2%	37	67	55	51	19%	46%	27%	8%
2011	PIT		46	76	673	61%	--	14.6	5				12.2%								

In the first eight games of the year, Sanders had only five targets. In Weeks 10-17, Sanders had 45 targets, only one fewer than Hines Ward. The bone he broke in his left foot during the Super Bowl should be fully healed by the time you read this book. The next step for Sanders will be getting that catch rate up, which he'll need to do if he's going to have the breakout fantasy football season so many people are predicting.

Chaz Schilens   Height: 6-4   Weight: 225   College: San Diego State   Draft: 2008/7 (226)   Born: 7-Nov-1985   Age: 26   Risk: Yellow

Year	Team	G	Rec	Pass	Yds	C%	+/-	Yd/C	TD	FUM	YAC	Rk	DVOA	Rk	DYAR	Rk	YAR	Short	Mid	Deep	Bomb
2008	OAK	16	15	32	226	47%	-1.4	15.1	2	0	2.8	--	-11.8%	--	2	--	2	28%	31%	28%	14%
2009	OAK	8	29	51	365	57%	-1.2	12.6	2	0	3.2	70	-4.1%	52	33	57	27	33%	37%	24%	6%
2010	OAK	5	5	9	40	56%	0.1	8.0	1	0	2.6	--	3.9%	--	12	--	9	56%	22%	11%	11%
2011	OAK		21	45	227	47%	--	10.8	0				-21.7%								

According to CSN Bay Area, Schilens was "put on notice" by the fifth-round selection of Denarius Moore. We're not exactly sure how one can be put on notice by a third-day pick, but what we do know is that Schilens' NFL talent has been waylaid by a series of injuries, and that he's generally looked pretty solid when he can make it on the field.

Jordan Shipley   Height: 5-11   Weight: 193   College: Texas   Draft: 2010/3 (84)   Born: 23-Dec-1985   Age: 26   Risk: Green

Year	Team	G	Rec	Pass	Yds	C%	+/-	Yd/C	TD	FUM	YAC	Rk	DVOA	Rk	DYAR	Rk	YAR	Short	Mid	Deep	Bomb
2010	CIN	15	52	74	600	70%	4.8	11.5	3	0	4.0	42	14.1%	12	156	26	138	49%	43%	6%	3%
2011	CIN		55	92	630	60%	--	11.5	3				-7.8%								

New offensive coordinator Jay Gruden made comments after he was hired, saying that he thought Shipley might have been afraid to go over the middle after his Week 4 concussion, but Shipley still had 35 percent of his targets listed as "middle" after he returned in Week 7. However, there's no doubt that Shipley's play fell off a bit in the second half of the year. Shipley had his best game in his first game back from the concussion, catching six passes for 131 yards and drawing a 26-yard DPI. But from Week 8 onwards, his catch rate dropped from 84 percent to 63 percent, his yards per catch dropped from 15.3 to 9.0, and his DVOA dropped from 56.8% to -10.9%. At least his hands stayed steady all year: Shipley and T.J. Houshmandzadeh were the only two receivers who were targeted at least 50 times without dropping a pass during the regular season.

Jerome Simpson

Height: 6-2   Weight: 199   College: Coastal Carolina   Draft: 2008/2 (46)   Born: 4-Feb-1986   Age: 25   Risk: Green

Year	Team	G	Rec	Pass	Yds	C%	+/-	Yd/C	TD	FUM	YAC	Rk	DVOA	Rk	DYAR	Rk	YAR	Short	Mid	Deep	Bomb
2008	CIN	6	1	3	2	33%	-1.0	2.0	0	0	3.0	--	-46.2%	--	-12	--	-14	25%	75%	0%	0%
2009	CIN	2	0	1	0	0%	-0.6	0.0	0	0	--	--	-66.6%	--	-4	--	-7	0%	100%	0%	0%
2010	CIN	5	20	25	277	80%	4.3	13.9	3	2	3.9	--	44.1%	--	109	--	95	20%	60%	12%	8%
2011	CIN		49	89	600	55%	--	12.2	3				-5.7%								

Simpson had so much trouble learning the Cincinnati playbook that it took him nearly three years to get into the lineup. Once he did, he exploded for 247 yards and three touchdowns in just two games. The good news: He did this against two tough defenses, San Diego and Baltimore. The bad news: Again, this was just two games from a player who previously wore a capital "B" for bust. Remember when Devin Aromashodu was going to be a big fantasy breakout star after 196 yards and three touchdowns in Chicago's last two games of 2009? How did that work out?

We went looking for players with Simpson's history who had big breakouts in their fourth seasons. We looked for players with fewer than 50 yards in their first two years, 200-400 yards in their third seasons, and 750 or more yards in their fourth seasons. We found two of them: Patrick Jeffers in 1999 and Lance Moore in 2008. So it could happen. On the other hand, if Simpson took so long to learn one playbook, does it augur well for him that Jay Gruden brings in an entirely new offense?

Mike Sims-Walker

Height: 6-2   Weight: 208   College: UCF   Draft: 2007/3 (79)   Born: 11-Nov-1984   Age: 27   Risk: Red

Year	Team	G	Rec	Pass	Yds	C%	+/-	Yd/C	TD	FUM	YAC	Rk	DVOA	Rk	DYAR	Rk	YAR	Short	Mid	Deep	Bomb
2008	JAC	9	16	30	217	53%	-0.1	13.6	0	0	1.5	--	3.7%	--	38	--	18	10%	52%	28%	10%
2009	JAC	15	63	111	869	57%	2.6	13.8	7	2	4.0	53	0.4%	41	114	39	102	33%	39%	21%	7%
2010	JAC	14	43	79	562	53%	-1.5	13.1	7	1	2.9	70	11.5%	19	154	27	134	20%	54%	21%	6%
2011	STL		56	100	715	56%	--	12.8	6				-1.7%								

Sims-Walker's injuries and drama earned him a one-way ticket out of Jacksonville despite the fact that he may have been the most talented receiver on the Jaguars roster. Now with the Rams on a one-year trial contract, he'll have to rehabilitate his image and stay healthy to earn some real money. The talent and opportunity are both there, so if Sims-Walker wants to be an upper-echelon receiver, he can be. Fun side note: Sims-Walker caught just seven of 17 balls in the red zone last year, but all seven of them went for touchdowns.

Brad Smith

Height: 6-2   Weight: 210   College: Missouri   Draft: 2006/4 (103)   Born: 12-Dec-1983   Age: 28   Risk: Green

Year	Team	G	Rec	Pass	Yds	C%	+/-	Yd/C	TD	FUM	YAC	Rk	DVOA	Rk	DYAR	Rk	YAR	Short	Mid	Deep	Bomb
2008	NYJ	15	12	19	64	63%	-2.0	5.3	0	1	4.2	--	-53.8%	--	-59	--	-54	63%	32%	5%	0%
2009	NYJ	13	7	12	63	58%	-1.1	9.0	0	0	4.1	--	-46.8%	--	-32	--	-28	58%	33%	8%	0%
2010	NYJ	16	4	7	44	57%	-0.1	11.0	0	0	2.5	--	-37.7%	--	-13	--	-11	83%	0%	17%	0%
2011	BUF		4	8	29	50%	--	7.3	0				-41.4%								

The Bills plan on listing Smith as a quarterback, which makes some sense. As you can see from these numbers, he's never really been able to establish himself as an NFL-quality wide receiver. Not listed above is his true value: playing triggerman in a single-wing package, what everyone now calls "Wildcat" but the Jets called

"Seminole." Last year he had 299 yards and a touchdown on 38 runs (45.5% DVOA). The year before he had 207 yards and a touchdown on 18 runs (115.4% DVOA). If the Bills run him out there for a couple plays a game as a change-up, he'll get some yardage. If they run him out more than that, teams will start figuring out how to stop the package. Smith also has lots of special teams value, both as a gunner and a return man, although it isn't like the Bills really need the latter. Don't they already have C.J. Spiller, Terrence McGee, Leodis McKelvin, and Roscoe Parrish?

Smith's projection also includes 21 carries for 235 yards and a touchdown, plus 4-for-7 passing for 50 yards.

Steve Smith

Height: 5-9   Weight: 185   College: Utah   Draft: 2001/3 (74)   Born: 12-May-1979   Age: 32   Risk: Red

Year	Team	G	Rec	Pass	Yds	C%	+/-	Yd/C	TD	FUM	YAC	Rk	DVOA	Rk	DYAR	Rk	YAR	Short	Mid	Deep	Bomb
2008	CAR	14	78	129	1421	60%	6.8	18.2	6	1	5.5	7	22.7%	4	365	5	391	26%	37%	18%	20%
2009	CAR	15	65	128	982	51%	-7.4	15.1	7	1	5.1	22	-7.6%	57	51	52	37	39%	32%	15%	15%
2010	CAR	9	48	99	529	46%	-8.6	11.0	3	2	4.7	25	-32.7%	83	-153	85	-156	40%	36%	18%	6%
2011	CAR		64	142	914	45%	--	14.3	5				-16.9%								

Smith's numbers have plummeted over the last two seasons, but even a cursory look at Smith's game tape in 2010 tells us that there's still enough left in the tank. Frequently doubled as the focus of opposing defenses (as he has been though most of his career), Smith showed younger defensive backs like Aqib Talib, Brent Grimes, and the Johnathan Joseph/Leon Hall combo that there's still some life in the old dog — that is, when Carolina's atrocious quarterback situation allowed it. Smith is still as good as anyone in the league in getting pesky with slants and quick outs, he has no fear of traffic, and he's got enough escapability to be impressive in the right offense. After Smith insisted on a trade and held that position through the lockout, he reversed field and said that he wanted to be a "Panther for life." He'll be Cam Newton's primary target early on, and most likely a surprising mentor to Carolina's young receivers.

Steve Smith

Height: 6-0   Weight: 195   College: USC   Draft: 2007/2 (51)   Born: 6-May-1985   Age: 26   Risk: Red

Year	Team	G	Rec	Pass	Yds	C%	+/-	Yd/C	TD	FUM	YAC	Rk	DVOA	Rk	DYAR	Rk	YAR	Short	Mid	Deep	Bomb
2008	NYG	16	57	82	574	70%	5.2	10.1	1	1	2.5	71	1.0%	39	88	40	89	38%	46%	10%	6%
2009	NYG	16	107	157	1220	68%	13.8	11.4	7	0	2.3	84	13.2%	18	320	8	306	32%	41%	16%	10%
2010	NYG	9	48	75	529	64%	4.8	11.0	3	0	2.2	82	1.9%	46	88	50	98	26%	49%	14%	11%
2011	PHI		20	40	176	50%	--	8.8	1				-6.3%								

Not all knee injuries are created equal. A torn ACL sucks, but it's not the sort of injury that will end a guy's career in his mid-twenties. Smith required microfracture surgery and mosaicplasty to repair his articular cartilage, an injury rarely seen in NFL players and difficult to treat. The hope is that the microfracture surgery will create enough cushion in Smith's knee to allow him to play, but even if it does, the sharp cuts that make up Smith's game will only aggravate and wear away at whatever small cushion forms there. The Giants were lucky to have held off on giving Smith a long-term deal, as both his short-term and long-term prognoses are not good. Right before we went to press, he signed in Philadelphia, and they claim he'll be back sometime in October.

Torrey Smith

Height: 6-1   Weight: 204   College: Maryland   Draft: 2011/2 (58)   Born: 26-Jan-1989   Age: 22   Risk: Red

Year	Team	G	Rec	Pass	Yds	C%	+/-	Yd/C	TD	FUM	YAC	Rk	DVOA	Rk	DYAR	Rk	YAR	Short	Mid	Deep	Bomb
2011	BAL		31	52	452	60%	--	14.6	2				0.1%								

There were a lot of complaints last year that the Ravens needed a receiver who could stretch the field. Ta da! Here's your guy. Smith is a deep threat with excellent burst at the line and straight line speed. He also shows toughness when he has to go after a ball in traffic, though he sometimes mis-times his launch when he needs to jump to get a pass. You can expect to see Smith on the outside with Boldin kicking inside to the slot when the Ravens go three-wide.

Micheal Spurlock
Height: 5-10 Weight: 214 College: Mississippi   Draft: 2006/ (FA)   Born: 31-Jan-1983 Age: 28 Risk: Green

Year	Team	G	Rec	Pass	Yds	C%	+/-	Yd/C	TD	FUM	YAC	Rk	DVOA	Rk	DYAR	Rk	YAR	Short	Mid	Deep	Bomb
2009	2TM	6	0	0	0	0%	0.0	0.0	0	0	0	--	0.0%	--	0	--	0	0%	0%	0%	0%
2010	TB	16	17	33	250	52%	0.4	14.7	2	0	1.9	--	-2.9%	--	25	--	20	25%	25%	28%	22%
2011	TB		5	10	51	50%	--	10.2	0				-17.6%								

The first player in team history to return a punt or kickoff for a touchdown (he did it in 2007; it took over 30 years for Tampa Bay to get that return score), Spurlock was forced into the lineup by injuries last year but will likely be back to a special teams role in 2011.

Donte' Stallworth
Height: 6-0 Weight: 197 College: Tennessee   Draft: 2002/1 (13)   Born: 10-Nov-1980 Age: 31 Risk: Yellow

Year	Team	G	Rec	Pass	Yds	C%	+/-	Yd/C	TD	FUM	YAC	Rk	DVOA	Rk	DYAR	Rk	YAR	Short	Mid	Deep	Bomb
2008	CLE	11	17	45	170	38%	-7.4	10.0	1	0	5.1	--	-40.0%	--	-91	--	-101	49%	33%	5%	13%
2010	BAL	8	2	5	82	40%	-0.3	41.0	0	0	11.0	--	20.1%	--	13	--	12	20%	20%	20%	40%
2011	WAS		19	34	240	56%	--	12.6	1				-19.1%								

Stallworth's grand dreams of a comeback were dashed when he broke his foot in the preseason. As a result, he didn't play until the second half and even then barely got on the field. One quirk of Stallworth's season: He had as many end-around runs as he did pass targets, with five carries for 45 yards and a fumble. Washington is the land of opportunity, but it is also a place veterans go for a few summer months before drifting out of the league. Stallworth could go either way.

Brandon Stokley
Height: 5-11 Weight: 197 College: Louisiana-Lafayette Draft: 1999/4 (105) Born: 23-Jun-1976 Age: 35 Risk: N/A

Year	Team	G	Rec	Pass	Yds	C%	+/-	Yd/C	TD	FUM	YAC	Rk	DVOA	Rk	DYAR	Rk	YAR	Short	Mid	Deep	Bomb
2008	DEN	15	49	85	528	58%	-2.4	10.8	3	0	3.4	49	-5.6%	55	47	55	66	34%	55%	8%	4%
2009	DEN	16	19	33	327	58%	0.5	17.2	4	0	11.0	--	21.0%	--	93	--	89	52%	38%	10%	0%
2010	SEA	11	31	43	354	72%	4.0	11.4	0	0	2.9	--	16.5%	--	91	--	95	27%	59%	10%	5%

A third-down machine (DVOA: 24.1%), Stokley is tremendous in small doses, but you don't want to rely on him too often. If Stokley was a baseball player, he would be a LOOGY who racked up a lot of holds. (If you're reading this book, you know what those words mean, right?) In 2010, he showed ridiculous consistency. He was thrown at least one pass in 11 games, and posted a positive DYAR nine times. An unrestricted free agent, Stokley will probably once again be a dangerous weapon on third-down crossing routes, in Seattle or somewhere else. We'd compare Stokley to Wes Welker, but that was last year's running gag.

Sammie Stroughter
Height: 5-10 Weight: 189 College: Oregon State   Draft: 2009/7 (233) Born: 3-Jan-1986 Age: 26 Risk: Green

Year	Team	G	Rec	Pass	Yds	C%	+/-	Yd/C	TD	FUM	YAC	Rk	DVOA	Rk	DYAR	Rk	YAR	Short	Mid	Deep	Bomb
2009	TB	13	31	58	334	53%	-6.8	10.8	1	0	4.1	52	-16.0%	71	-16	69	-25	45%	45%	7%	3%
2010	TB	12	24	39	239	64%	-1.0	10.0	0	0	4.0	--	-9.1%	--	11	--	-1	49%	33%	13%	5%
2011	TB		22	39	250	56%	--	11.3	1				-6.4%								

Stroughter got a few looks early in the season before Arrelious Benn established himself as a target to be reckoned with. Overall, he proved prone to route-running issues, and he doesn't have the kind of separation speed required in Tampa Bay's quick-strike passing offense, where the idea is to get open and exploit the fact that other defenders are tied up with complementary route concepts. Week 6 against the Saints was the worst example — a three-catch, nine-target, one-fumble debacle where Stroughter and Josh Freeman never did get on the same page. Stroughter will have to find another level to beat Benn and Dezmon Briscoe out for a big role in the receiver corps.

Chansi Stuckey

Height: 5-10 Weight: 182 College: Clemson   Draft: 2007/7 (235) Born: 4-Oct-1983   Age: 28   Risk: Red

Year	Team	G	Rec	Pass	Yds	C%	+/-	Yd/C	TD	FUM	YAC	Rk	DVOA	Rk	DYAR	Rk	YAR	Short	Mid	Deep	Bomb
2008	NYJ	15	32	45	359	71%	2.6	11.2	3	0	5.6	--	24.0%	--	131	--	137	55%	33%	10%	2%
2009	2TM	15	30	66	318	45%	-11.8	10.6	2	0	4.3	37	-31.2%	88	-100	86	-88	49%	26%	18%	6%
2010	CLE	16	40	64	346	64%	1.4	8.7	0	2	5.2	17	-26.5%	79	-70	81	-78	64%	25%	11%	0%
2011	ARI		47	72	541	65%	--	11.5	2				0.2%								

Stuckey put up basically the same DVOA and DYAR despite a much higher catch rate than he had in 2009, because he was running so much shorter routes. Stuckey actually had more YAC than you would expect given the route lengths he was running, but he just can't get downfield to make big plays. That's why the Browns non-tendered him even though he was the team leader in receptions in 2010.

Brandon Tate

Height: 5-10 Weight: 183 College: North Carolina   Draft: 2009/3 (83) Born: 5-Oct-1987   Age: 24   Risk: Green

Year	Team	G	Rec	Pass	Yds	C%	+/-	Yd/C	TD	FUM	YAC	Rk	DVOA	Rk	DYAR	Rk	YAR	Short	Mid	Deep	Bomb
2009	NE	2	0	2	0	0%	-0.5	0.0	0	0	--	--	-113.9%	--	-17	--	-15	0%	0%	0%	100%
2010	NE	16	24	46	432	52%	-0.2	18.0	3	1	5.8	--	-0.3%	--	41	--	24	34%	37%	5%	24%
2011	NE		18	39	254	46%	--	14.1	2				-14.1%								

The average pass to Tate was thrown 13.7 yards downfield, as opposed to 11.7 yards for Deion Branch and 5.4 yards for Wes Welker. The average pass to Randy Moss by the Patriots was thrown 19.1 yards downfield, which is just silly … Tate ran for 22, 17, 12, 6, and 5 yards on various end-arounds during the season. Factor in fine work on kickoff returns, and he filled the speedster niche in the offense relatively well. Moss just happened to set an unreasonable, and possibly counterproductive, standard for what a speedster receiver is supposed to do in an offense.

Golden Tate

Height: 5-10 Weight: 199 College: Notre Dame   Draft: 2010/2 (60) Born: 2-Aug-1988   Age: 23   Risk: Green

Year	Team	G	Rec	Pass	Yds	C%	+/-	Yd/C	TD	FUM	YAC	Rk	DVOA	Rk	DYAR	Rk	YAR	Short	Mid	Deep	Bomb
2010	SEA	11	21	40	227	55%	-2.8	10.8	0	0	5.3	--	-26.5%	--	-42	--	-36	46%	31%	10%	13%
2011	SEA		29	55	331	53%	--	11.4	1				-23.2%								

Pete Carroll told the *Tacoma News-Tribune* in June that he expected Tate to break out in 2011, and that he would see a lot more playing time in the slot on third downs. In other words, he'll be filling Brandon Stokley's role in the offense. He'll need to take a quantum leap forward, then — he converted just two-of-12 third-down opportunities last year. On the plus side, he admitted on 710 ESPN radio in Seattle that his struggles as a rookie were mostly his own fault. "When I first came in, I was kinda just an athlete, going wherever the ball was going, making plays," he said. "Once the defense figured that out, they kinda knew what to do to stop me from doing that. This year, I learned some things — releases, coming in and out of my breaks — and now I just have to execute that early in camp and show the coaches that I can do this." If Tate's actions back up his words, he'll start to justify the second-round draft pick Seattle spent on him in 2010. With Sidney Rice now atop the depth chart, Tate will likely battle Ben Obomanu for the third receiver spot.

Demaryius Thomas

Height: 6-3 Weight: 224 College: Georgia Tech   Draft: 2010/1 (22) Born: 25-Dec-1987   Age: 24   Risk: Red

Year	Team	G	Rec	Pass	Yds	C%	+/-	Yd/C	TD	FUM	YAC	Rk	DVOA	Rk	DYAR	Rk	YAR	Short	Mid	Deep	Bomb
2010	DEN	10	22	39	283	56%	-2.5	12.9	2	1	6.2	--	-4.9%	--	23	--	7	42%	26%	26%	5%
2011	DEN		10	20	138	50%	--	13.8	1				-11.9%								

Thomas had some comparing him to Dez Bryant and an embryonic Michael Irvin as a draft prospect for his ability to get downfield and make catches with violent coverage-bashing intentions. He flashed a lot of that potential early on with the Broncos, especially when he beat Darrelle Revis for a touchdown out of a single-high safety look in Week 6. Revis tried to get physical near the line, but Thomas just stutter-stepped his way out of it, outran Revis to the end zone in a way most receivers never will, and tiptoed both feet in the end zone for good measure. He's still struggling with consistency — especially in the drive-killing drops area — but there's a lot to like here. Thomas suffered a torn Achilles during a February workout and will be out for at least the first half of the season, maybe longer.

Mike Thomas

Height: 5-8   Weight: 195   College: Arizona   Draft: 2009/4 (107)   Born: 4-Jun-1987   Age: 24   Risk: Green

Year	Team	G	Rec	Pass	Yds	C%	+/-	Yd/C	TD	FUM	YAC	Rk	DVOA	Rk	DYAR	Rk	YAR	Short	Mid	Deep	Bomb
2009	JAC	14	48	62	453	77%	6.6	9.4	1	0	4.3	37	7.4%	34	98	43	101	60%	28%	12%	0%
2010	JAC	16	66	102	820	66%	3.6	12.4	4	0	4.5	30	11.2%	21	185	21	179	41%	30%	18%	10%
2011	JAC		78	127	881	61%	--	11.3	3				-0.6%								

After wasting a pair of first round picks on Matt Jones and Reggie Williams, Jacksonville finally found a solid wideout in the later rounds of the draft. Thomas, perhaps best known for the +5 bonus he grants on Hail Mary throws, actually does a majority of his work in the short game. Per the game charting crew, about a third of his targets came on screens, hitches, and quick slants. In an ideal world, he's a No. 2 receiver at best. Has anything about Jacksonville's passing game been ideal since Jimmy Smith was still kicking it?

Tiquan Underwood

Height: 6-1   Weight: 184   College: Rutgers   Draft: 2009/7 (253)   Born: 17-Feb-1987   Age: 24   Risk: Blue

Year	Team	G	Rec	Pass	Yds	C%	+/-	Yd/C	TD	FUM	YAC	Rk	DVOA	Rk	DYAR	Rk	YAR	Short	Mid	Deep	Bomb
2010	JAC	10	8	22	111	36%	-3.4	13.9	0	0	2.4	--	-23.1%	--	-18	--	-21	10%	52%	14%	24%
2011	JAC		4	9	51	44%	--	12.7	1				-14.4%								

Underwood dropped three of 22 balls thrown at him, and it would have been four of 24 had we counted plays cancelled by penalty. He was completely overmatched as a starter, and the drafting of Cecil Shorts buries him even deeper down on the depth chart. Barring a rash of injuries, it would be a real upset to see him on the opening day roster.

Mike Wallace

Height: 6-1   Weight: 199   College: Mississippi   Draft: 2009/3 (84)   Born: 1-Aug-1986   Age: 25   Risk: Red

Year	Team	G	Rec	Pass	Yds	C%	+/-	Yd/C	TD	FUM	YAC	Rk	DVOA	Rk	DYAR	Rk	YAR	Short	Mid	Deep	Bomb
2009	PIT	16	39	72	756	54%	0.5	19.4	6	1	3.4	63	29.6%	4	232	16	224	18%	35%	21%	25%
2010	PIT	16	60	98	1257	61%	7.2	21.0	10	1	6.0	6	48.8%	1	457	1	444	26%	32%	15%	27%
2011	PIT		68	114	1213	60%	--	17.8	8				26.5%								

Mike Wallace is a great wide receiver with a ridiculous haircut. Seriously, when did we all decide we wanted triangles on our heads? One interesting thing about his great 2010 performance: as the year went on, he ran shorter routes with more YAC, but played at a very high level throughout.

Mike Wallace by Week, 2010

Weeks	Avg Pass Length	YAC	DVOA	Yd/Rec	Catch Rate
1-4	18.8	3.8	28.8%	23.4	47%
6-9	20.3	4.1	43.9%	22.8	65%
10-13	14.5	6.5	60.6%	19.0	66%
14-17	12.4	7.9	52.7%	20.5	63%

Kevin Walter

Height: 6-3 Weight: 221 College: Eastern Michigan Draft: 2003/7 (255) Born: 4-Aug-1981 Age: 30 Risk: Green

Year	Team	G	Rec	Pass	Yds	C%	+/-	Yd/C	TD	FUM	YAC	Rk	DVOA	Rk	DYAR	Rk	YAR	Short	Mid	Deep	Bomb
2008	HOU	16	60	95	899	63%	7.6	15.0	8	0	4.9	16	16.8%	11	225	16	229	33%	44%	17%	6%
2009	HOU	14	53	70	611	76%	9.0	11.5	2	0	2.2	86	22.6%	8	196	21	211	33%	45%	19%	3%
2010	HOU	16	51	80	621	64%	5.9	12.2	5	0	2.6	76	14.0%	13	183	22	178	34%	45%	15%	6%
2011	HOU		40	60	477	67%	--	11.9	2				3.0%								

Walter faced a challenge to his second receiver spot from Jacoby Jones last year, and they ended up with similar target and reception totals, but Walter started all 16 games because he willingly does all the dirty work needed to keep an offense running. As long as he's a willing blocker and effective over the middle, Walter can safely be the number two opposite a strong top receiver like Andre Johnson. Just don't ever expect him to be more than that or have a breakout season of his own.

Hines Ward

Height: 6-0 Weight: 205 College: Georgia Draft: 1998/3 (92) Born: 8-Mar-1976 Age: 35 Risk: Green

Year	Team	G	Rec	Pass	Yds	C%	+/-	Yd/C	TD	FUM	YAC	Rk	DVOA	Rk	DYAR	Rk	YAR	Short	Mid	Deep	Bomb
2008	PIT	16	81	125	1043	66%	2.4	12.9	7	1	5.0	13	16.9%	10	294	7	299	33%	48%	14%	6%
2009	PIT	16	95	137	1167	69%	8.8	12.3	6	2	4.2	42	14.0%	17	281	9	266	35%	41%	19%	5%
2010	PIT	16	59	95	755	64%	1.8	12.8	5	1	3.9	47	9.1%	25	157	25	155	34%	36%	27%	3%
2011	PIT		46	71	614	65%	--	13.4	5				19.0%								

Some wide receivers play well into their mid 30's and then fall off a cliff. Others age gracefully and fade out slowly. Ward seems to have started the "graceful aging" portion of his career. (Does anything represent "graceful aging" more than winning *Dancing with the Stars*?) A list of similar receivers over a three-year span suggests he'll be giving way to Emmanuel Sanders sooner rather than later. Torry Holt (2008), Isaac Bruce (2007), Andre Reed (1998), and Terance Mathis (2000) each had one subpar year left. Art Monk (1990) had one good year left, and Keenan McCardell (2002) had a couple. The Steelers might help him out by reversing the recent trend which has him running more deep patterns; those midrange 10-15 yard patterns were always his strength.

Nate Washington

Height: 6-1 Weight: 185 College: Tiffin Draft: 2005/ (FA) Born: 28-Aug-1983 Age: 28 Risk: Green

Year	Team	G	Rec	Pass	Yds	C%	+/-	Yd/C	TD	FUM	YAC	Rk	DVOA	Rk	DYAR	Rk	YAR	Short	Mid	Deep	Bomb
2008	PIT	16	40	78	631	51%	0.0	15.8	3	0	3.3	51	-0.8%	45	70	49	51	11%	49%	21%	19%
2009	TEN	16	47	95	569	49%	-1.4	12.1	6	1	1.9	88	-10.8%	62	14	63	20	20%	40%	24%	16%
2010	TEN	16	42	94	687	45%	-6.1	16.4	6	0	2.7	74	-3.0%	58	74	53	71	19%	40%	21%	21%
2011	TEN		41	87	605	47%	--	14.8	4				-8.2%								

What you see is what you get with Washington. The Titans targeted him more often downfield in 2010, with up-and-down results. He was more productive with Vince Young in the lineup, as Kerry Collins occasionally struggled to get him the ball downfield. With Kenny Britt in the lineup, he slots comfortably in the pecking order as a second receiver who can be a vertical threat and catch a couple passes every week.

Reggie Wayne

Height: 6-0 Weight: 198 College: Miami Draft: 2001/1 (30) Born: 17-Nov-1978 Age: 33 Risk: Green

Year	Team	G	Rec	Pass	Yds	C%	+/-	Yd/C	TD	FUM	YAC	Rk	DVOA	Rk	DYAR	Rk	YAR	Short	Mid	Deep	Bomb
2008	IND	16	82	130	1145	63%	8.6	14.0	6	0	3.6	44	19.1%	9	332	6	327	33%	38%	13%	17%
2009	IND	16	100	149	1264	67%	16.9	12.6	10	0	4.1	47	18.2%	13	373	6	381	38%	37%	14%	11%
2010	IND	16	111	175	1355	63%	5.8	12.2	6	1	3.7	50	0.3%	47	180	23	218	43%	30%	14%	13%
2011	IND		95	144	1133	66%	--	11.9	8				11.4%								

Wayne set a career high in receptions, and had his second-highest yardage total. However, he had his lowest DVOA since his rookie year and was able to build up his stats by being targeted on 175 passes. Much of Wayne's per-play decline was based on a) Manning forcing him passes in an overly pass-heavy offense and b) injuries to other receivers leaving Wayne few one-on-one opportunities. Still, Wayne has lost half-a-step, and he no longer is the player he was. Wayne can be contained by elite cornerbacks and grew frustrated with the double coverage at times. Over the years, Wayne is increasingly being used underneath. His number of short targets has increased each year since 2006 to the point where last season, more than 40 percent of his targets were under ten yards.

Wes Welker

Height: 5-9 Weight: 190 College: Texas Tech Draft: 2004/ (FA) Born: 1-May-1981 Age: 30 Risk: Green

Year	Team	G	Rec	Pass	Yds	C%	+/-	Yd/C	TD	FUM	YAC	Rk	DVOA	Rk	DYAR	Rk	YAR	Short	Mid	Deep	Bomb
2008	NE	16	111	150	1165	75%	8.5	10.5	3	1	6.6	2	3.5%	31	188	20	195	63%	30%	6%	1%
2009	NE	14	123	162	1348	76%	14.3	11.0	4	1	5.9	10	20.3%	12	424	3	363	58%	35%	6%	2%
2010	NE	15	86	124	848	69%	1.4	9.9	7	1	4.7	26	4.2%	40	166	24	122	58%	38%	3%	1%
2011	NE		88	122	994	72%	--	11.3	7				20.6%								

The Patriots' overreliance on Welker in the opening weeks of the season was almost as big a problem for them as their need to force bombs to Randy Moss. Welker was still on the mend from an ACL injury, and just as importantly, teams were ready for his screens-and-slants game. He went through a three-week 11-85-0 snap before the Patriots discovered their new offensive identity. Once Deion Branch and the tight ends integrated themselves fully into the system, Welker reemerged as a more conventional wide receiver whose eight catches per game came from the route tree, with only a few screens sprinkled in. This new Welker is not a 100-catch record setter, but he is still a solid starter and worthy security blanket for Brady. He should have a few more 80-800-7 type seasons before the wheels give out for good.

Blair White

Height: 6-2 Weight: 209 College: Michigan State Draft: 2010/ (FA) Born: 20-Feb-1987 Age: 24 Risk: Green

Year	Team	G	Rec	Pass	Yds	C%	+/-	Yd/C	TD	FUM	YAC	Rk	DVOA	Rk	DYAR	Rk	YAR	Short	Mid	Deep	Bomb
2010	IND	13	36	57	355	63%	1.2	9.9	5	0	1.8	85	7.0%	30	90	48	96	45%	29%	22%	4%
2011	IND		15	27	177	56%	--	11.8	1				-8.0%								

An undrafted free agent out of Michigan State (where he was a walk-on), injuries to other receivers meant White was starting in the playoffs and leading the team in receptions. White made a number of big catches for the Colts, including two fourth-quarter touchdowns against New England, and posted a very respectable DVOA. White , despite his name and race, is not a shifty inside receiver and shares no attributes with Wes Welker. Instead, he is a prototypical Colts' outside receiver with good hands, decent speed, and a good head. He went undrafted for a reason — the tools are not exceptional — but White is the best fourth receiver the Colts have had during their run of prominence, and while he lacks Pierre Garcon's deep speed, he is more reliable and arguably a better option against teams consistently playing two-deep coverages.

Roddy White

Height: 6-1 Weight: 201 College: Alabama-Birmingham Draft: 2005/1 (27) Born: 2-Nov-1981 Age: 30 Risk: Green

Year	Team	G	Rec	Pass	Yds	C%	+/-	Yd/C	TD	FUM	YAC	Rk	DVOA	Rk	DYAR	Rk	YAR	Short	Mid	Deep	Bomb
2008	ATL	16	88	148	1382	59%	1.5	15.7	7	1	4.1	33	22.1%	5	399	3	361	27%	45%	17%	12%
2009	ATL	16	85	165	1153	52%	-9.1	13.6	11	1	4.5	31	-1.7%	48	141	35	79	30%	43%	20%	7%
2010	ATL	16	115	180	1389	64%	7.4	12.1	10	1	3.2	63	8.3%	28	294	4	291	36%	40%	19%	5%
2011	ATL		96	154	1372	62%	--	14.3	10				16.7%								

White's 180 targets not only led the NFL last season but were the second-highest total since 2004 — only Brandon Marshall (181 in 2008) had more. His nickname for 2010 should have been "Ryan's Hope." The other Atlanta receivers underwhelmed, allowing defenses to roll coverage toward White. His routes were shorter than in previous seasons, and his YAC plummeted as well. All this accounts for the large disparity between White's DYAR and DVOA rankings. That's the bad news. The good news? White remains an elite receiver, capable of winning games both with his talent (Baltimore) and with his hustle (San Francisco, when he stripped Nate Clements after what appeared to be the game-clinching interception). The presence of Julio Jones should release some pressure on White and drop that target number down to where his efficiency rebounds. One dissonant note came in the offseason, when White's cousin (who lived with him) was arrested on armed robbery charges. The Falcons specifically told White to avoid bad actors off the field when he signed his large extension in 2009. The team would much prefer White stick to tutoring Jones instead of at-risk old friends, but then that's not the way life works.

Damian Williams   Height: 6-1   Weight: 197   College: USC   Draft: 2010/3 (77)   Born: 26-May-1988   Age: 23   Risk: Green

Year	Team	G	Rec	Pass	Yds	C%	+/-	Yd/C	TD	FUM	YAC	Rk	DVOA	Rk	DYAR	Rk	YAR	Short	Mid	Deep	Bomb
2010	TEN	16	16	28	219	57%	0.7	13.7	0	0	2.5	–	-4.5%	–	17	–	16	19%	42%	27%	12%
2011	TEN		27	52	338	52%	–	12.5	2				-12.8%								

The Titans took Damian Williams with the idea that he would be their main return man, but Marc Mariani won that job. Instead, Williams spent most of 2010 as the Titans' third or fourth receiver. He's competing with Justin Gage for the No. 3 job in 2011.

Mike Williams   Height: 6-5   Weight: 229   College: USC   Draft: 2005/1 (10)   Born: 4-Jan-1984   Age: 28   Risk: Yellow

Year	Team	G	Rec	Pass	Yds	C%	+/-	Yd/C	TD	FUM	YAC	Rk	DVOA	Rk	DYAR	Rk	YAR	Short	Mid	Deep	Bomb
2010	SEA	14	65	110	751	59%	0.6	11.6	2	0	3.3	58	-6.7%	66	50	64	60	35%	42%	16%	8%
2011	SEA		53	99	697	54%	–	13.2	4				-7.0%								

After eating his way out of the league for several years (Lions fans would argue his hiatus began long before 2008), Williams finally got his diet under control, but retained enough size to be an effective midrange pass catcher. Williams often wasn't even running routes, he'd just get downfield, box out defenders like Dwight Howard, and outfight them for the ball. As such, he didn't do much after the catch, but there are worse weapons to have than giant, reliable possession receivers. For all that size, though, he wasn't much in the red zone, where he caught only eight of 16 passes for both of his touchdowns. So, now what? There's not much precedent for a player busting out, disappearing for years, and finally blossoming into something useful. Williams could have gone back to the maple-syrup-and-gravy diet, but even during the lockout he stayed on the wagon, showing up to informal workouts in tip-top shape. So he's not likely to collapse a second time. On the other hand, he'd have to suddenly develop big-play ability at age 27 to be much more than he was in 2010. To make a long story short, expect another 700 yards and a handful of touchdowns this fall.

Mike Williams   Height: 6-2   Weight: 221   College: Syracuse   Draft: 2010/4 (101)   Born: 18-May-1987   Age: 24   Risk: Yellow

Year	Team	G	Rec	Pass	Yds	C%	+/-	Yd/C	TD	FUM	YAC	Rk	DVOA	Rk	DYAR	Rk	YAR	Short	Mid	Deep	Bomb
2010	TB	16	65	128	964	50%	-5.7	14.8	11	3	4.9	22	-6.3%	65	65	56	62	22%	41%	23%	13%
2011	TB		69	123	996	56%	–	14.4	10				2.0%								

One of two NFL reclamation projects with the Mike Williams name last season, Tampa Bay's Williams may have been the more impressive. A first-round talent who dropped because he essentially quit on his Syracuse team in 2009 after missing the 2008 season for academic reasons, Williams somehow got religion when he put on the pewter. The buzz started early in the season, when he busted zones in Week 3 against the Steelers, pinballing through multiple defenders. He showed an unusual understanding of route-running technique for a player who missed so much college time, and had little trouble separating from defensive backs to make big plays. He became the first rookie receiver to put up double-digit touchdowns since Randy Moss, but the challenge in 2011, as it will be for so many of Tampa Bay's young stars, will be to build on that unexpected early success. Cutting down on the drops will be step one.

Roy Williams

Height: 6-4   Weight: 210 College: Texas   Draft: 2004/1 (7)   Born: 20-Dec-1981   Age: 30   Risk: Red

Year	Team	G	Rec	Pass	Yds	C%	+/-	Yd/C	TD	FUM	YAC	Rk	DVOA	Rk	DYAR	Rk	YAR	Short	Mid	Deep	Bomb
2008	2TM	15	36	82	430	44%	-9.2	11.9	2	0	3.5	47	-17.1%	75	-29	73	-74	20%	49%	17%	13%
2009	DAL	15	38	86	596	44%	-10.3	15.7	7	1	5.1	23	-8.2%	58	30	59	40	20%	54%	18%	8%
2010	DAL	15	37	64	530	58%	0.3	14.3	5	3	5.6	9	3.2%	41	77	52	65	27%	45%	22%	7%
2011	CHI		62	119	887	52%	--	14.3	8				-2.0%								

Although his plus-minus finally bounced back after two seasons in the wilderness, his passable season basically consists of a three-game stretch that saw him catch 14 passes for 232 yards and all five of his touchdowns. And even that was really driven by a 117-yard, two-touchdown game against the dismal Texans pass defense. He developed a reputation as a standup player in the locker room as Rome burned, but he didn't get that huge contract to do PR, and the sudden discovery of the company line may have been an attempt at reputation rehabilitation. Williams will get every chance to start fresh in Chicago, where he is reunited with the coordinator (Mike Martz) who masterminded his best season: 2006, when he had 1,310 yards, seven touchdowns, and a career-best 8.7% DVOA.

Stephen Williams

Height: 6-5   Weight: 208 College: Toledo   Draft: 2010/ (FA)   Born: 29-Jun-1986   Age: 25   Risk: Green

Year	Team	G	Rec	Pass	Yds	C%	+/-	Yd/C	TD	FUM	YAC	Rk	DVOA	Rk	DYAR	Rk	YAR	Short	Mid	Deep	Bomb
2010	ARI	11	9	23	101	39%	-5.3	11.2	0	0	4.2	--	-26.1%	--	-26	--	-32	43%	35%	13%	9%
2011	ARI		13	23	195	57%	--	15.0	1				0.1%								

The 6-foot-5 rookie was overshadowed by teammate Andre Roberts in the "rookie wide receiver that plays a lot but doesn't do much" role. Williams saw more action earlier in the year, but got hurt and saw less time as the season progressed and seems to have fallen out of favor a bit. He's sort of the Max Hall to Andre Roberts' John Skelton.

Titus Young

Height: 5-11 Weight: 174 College: Boise St.   Draft: 2011/2 (44)   Born: 21-Aug-1989   Age: 22   Risk: Red

Year	Team	G	Rec	Pass	Yds	C%	+/-	Yd/C	TD	FUM	YAC	Rk	DVOA	Rk	DYAR	Rk	YAR	Short	Mid	Deep	Bomb
2011	DET		27	51	306	53%	--	11.3	1				-19.4%								

A fiery competitor for both better and worse, Titus Young was dinged with penalties and suspensions in his four seasons at Boise State. But he was also one of only two receivers in the country last year (minimum: 25 catches) to average 17.0 yards per catch with a 70 percent catch rate. His upside is enormous, big enough for Detroit to take a risk on him in the second round. Young is not very big, but he has a rare combination of speed, agility and soft hands. When Boise State quarterback Kellen Moore found out he was a Heisman finalist this past December, he better have sent care packages to both Young and Austin Pettis, who helped to make him look very good.

Dominique Zeigler

Height: 6-3   Weight: 185 College: Baylor   Draft: 2007/ (FA)   Born: 11-Oct-1984   Age: 27   Risk: Green

Year	Team	G	Rec	Pass	Yds	C%	+/-	Yd/C	TD	FUM	YAC	Rk	DVOA	Rk	DYAR	Rk	YAR	Short	Mid	Deep	Bomb
2008	SF	8	5	8	97	63%	0.4	19.4	0	0	8.0	--	4.8%	--	10	--	11	22%	44%	22%	11%
2010	SF	11	9	15	98	60%	0.5	10.9	0	0	1.6	--	-19.4%	--	-7	--	-4	20%	33%	33%	13%
2011	SF		16	30	206	53%	--	12.9	1				-5.1%								

Zeigler's season ended in late November with a torn ACL, and though he was running in mid-June, he still wasn't making cuts. Zeigler was a fringe NFL player anyway - after eight games with the 49ers in 2008, he spent the entire 2009 season healthy but on the practice squad - so an injury this serious likely spells the end of his career. A significant chunk of Zeigler's bio on the team's official website is devoted to post-NFL career options, such as video production or high school coaching. The writing on the wall couldn't be much more clear..

Going Deep

Darvin Adams, CAR: Julio Jones was so in-demand that Atlanta traded a bunch of picks to Cleveland so they could trade up for him. Darvin Adams was so not-in-demand that he went undrafted and signed with Carolina as a free agent so he could be reunited with quarterback Cam Newton. Based on stats only, however, Adams is clearly the better receiver. Over his career, he had better numbers than Jones in yards per game (73 to 66) and yards per catch (17.2 to 14.8) while scoring more touchdowns than Jones (17 to 15) in significantly fewer games (27 to 40). It does make you wonder.

Sam Aiken, FA: When Aiken dies, his tombstone will list his name as "Long-Time Special Teams Ace Sam Aiken." Cleveland waived him in mid-October and no other team picked him up, but he's only 31, so it's hard to imagine that he can't help on special teams somewhere.

Adrian Arrington, NO: He was pinned behind the Saints superb quartet of receivers in 2010, but Arrington got his shot in the meaningless finale against Tampa, and put up a nice seven-catch, 79-yard afternoon. He was also a monster in the preseason, leading the team in yards, receptions, and touchdowns. Injuries have set Arrington back, but if there is any breach in the big four ahead of him, he could slot in without the Saints missing a beat. (2010 stats: 7-for-9, 79 yards, 28.0% DVOA, 28 DYAR)

David Ausberry, OAK: USC product Ausberry is a flex tight end in a fullback's body who may make a few waves as an wide receiver in the right system. He's still a very raw player, but the physical potential is there, and it isn't as if the Raiders make you show your Playbook Excellence card before they let you out on the field.

Terrence Austin, WAS: The Redskins drafted Austin in the seventh round as a potential return man, but after the 'Skins gave up on Devin Thomas, they gave the chance to Brandon Banks. Since Banks established himself as a pretty decent return guy, it's hard to find a path for Austin to get on the active roster. (2010 stats: 3-for-5, 47 yards, 21.7% DVOA, 14 DYAR)

Mikail Baker, STL: A pair of medical redshirts (broken collarbone in 2007, torn ACL in 2009) kept Baker at Baylor for six seasons, the first four spent at wide receiver before converting to cornerback in 2009. As a receiver, the 5-foot-11, 191-pound Baker had 26 receptions for 354 yards and two touchdowns, but the one area where he consistently contributed was as the Bears' kick returner. Baker averaged 23.7 yards on 83 returns at Baylor, with one return for a touchdown, and could receive a shot to inject some life into the Rams' stagnant kick return game.

Brandon Banks, WAS: After being cut in training camp, Banks got a second chance at the return job in September and made it his own. By the end of the year, he had established himself as an effective part of both the kick and punt return teams. Banks should be an asset at the league minimum for the foreseeable future, and with plenty of holes to fill elsewhere on the roster, he should get to keep his job for a couple of years. (2010 stats: 2-for-5, 10 yards, -78.6% DVOA, -26 DYAR)

Gary Banks, SD: Banks has been bouncing around the NFL, most recently on and off the Chargers' practice squad. His primary athletic claim to fame to date is that he was selected as an outfielder ahead of one-time pitching phenom Dontrelle Willis in the Cubs' 2000 draft. (2010 stats: 1-for-3, 2 yards, -105.8% DVOA, -22 DYAR)

Ramses Barden, NYG: A Chargers-esque weapon who the Giants hoped to turn into their own Vincent Jackson, Barden has been quickly usurped on the depth chart by Hakeem Nicks, who actually plays like Vincent Jackson. His first shot at playing time was quickly snuffed out by a fractured ankle that came with messy ligament damage, and he may not get another shot. The Giants may need a slot receiver in 2011, but Barden's a lanky drink of water that doesn't get off the line or out of his cuts very quickly. Barden will likely need an injury to Nicks to get off the bench. Barden was headed to the PUP list as we went to press, so it won't happen this year. (2010 stats: 5-for-7, 64 yards, -6.5% DVOA, 3 DYAR)

Hank Baskett, FA: Baskett is not only a reality television star, but a literary character. He figures heavily in *The Silver Linings Playbook*, Matthew Quick's tale of an Eagles fan, just released from a mental institution, who adopts then-rookie Baskett as his favorite player. Soon, there will be the opera *Baskett!* followed by a board game and some commemorative plates. He may even stick around long enough to see his 12th career start. (2010 stats: 1-for-4, 18 yards, -43.6% DVOA, -9 DYAR)

Arnaz Battle, PIT: The longtime San Francisco 49ers receiver is strictly playing on special teams at this point, and didn't have a catch in his first year with the Steelers.

Stephen Burton, MIN: Burton is a pure measurables prospect (6-foot-2, 224 pounds, and a 4.38 40-yard dash) that the Vikings drafted with an eye on returning kicks. He spent last year in the Lone Star Conference with West Texas A&M, so a year of acclimation against top-level competition will probably be necessary before his receiving abilities can be properly evaluated.

Duke Calhoun, NYG: A special-teamer who isn't all that great on special teams, Calhoun is part of the Giants' commitment to hiring stiffs that would be the best rebounders in your pickup basketball game on height alone.

Brian Clark, FA: Clark has had four different uniform numbers in his pro career: 19, 18, 86, and 87. It's a pretty good sign that you are a fringe player when you have to keep changing numbers. A former kickoff returner who was too fumble-prone to keep the job, Clark is now a professional special teamer, and not a remarkable one. He's the kind of player the Lions are hoping to replace as they move forward.

Michael Clayton, NYG: The days when Clayton was a rookie sensation are more than over now, and what's left is a big dude who can block effectively on the outside. The Giants found a role for him when they were beset by injuries, but he's likely going elsewhere in 2011. (2010 stats: 2-for-4, 19 yards, -34.6% DVOA, -6 DYAR)

David Clowney, CAR: Known primarily as one of the bubble guys on the Jets' version of Hard Knocks, Clowney was picked up by Carolina after he fell off that bubble. He spent 2010 fighting for playing time at the bottom of the depth chart with Armanti Edwards and Brandon LaFell. The Panthers gave him a restricted free agent tag in the offseason. Steve Smith aside, that should give you an idea of the state of Carolina's ones and twos. (2010 stats: 7-for-16, 124 yards, -7.4% DVOA, 6 DYAR)

Riley Cooper, PHI: Famously the target of Michael Vick's season-ending interception in the end zone, Cooper is probably the new Hank Baskett. The two share similar size, but Cooper's a better athlete than Baskett was. Three of Cooper's seven receptions went for more than 20 yards, which is a good sign for his ability to beat nickelbacks downfield. Mid-round athletes like this rarely develop into starters, but Cooper has time to develop. (2010 stats: 7-for-18, 116 yards, 2 TD, -9.4% DVOA, 4 DYAR)

Quan Cosby, CIN: Cosby wasn't quite the punt returner that he was in 2009, dropping from 11.0 estimated points worth of field position to -2.0 points. He's a hands and quickness guy, not a downfield speed guy, so it's hard to see him getting much time at receiver unless fellow Longhorn Jordan Shipley goes down with an injury. (2010 stats: 2-for-2, 16 yards, 30.3% DVOA, 7 DYAR)

Kevin Curtis, FA: Curtis still has a bit of ability; not that you'd know from his targets in Kansas City, which is where he wound up after the Dolphins waived him in December. Most of them came in garbage time, and few were successful. He's still trying to mount a comeback after a horrible litany of medical issues — serious knee injury, cancerous testicle, root canal — and you can't help but hope he succeeds.

Rashied Davis, DET: Davis is now 32 years old and two full seasons removed from his 35-catch season in 2008. Seven of Davis' nine catches occurred in the season finale against the Packers. He remains a valuable special teamer, however, and the Lions signed him after he became a free agent post-lockout. (2010 stats: 9-for-13, 84 yards, 1 TD, -20.3% DVOA, 34 DYAR)

Dorin Dickerson, HOU: An outside linebacker, tight end, and receiver in college, Dickerson spent 2010 buried on the Texans' roster as an intriguing size-speed conversion project. He'll get some looks on offense, and has a good chance to start the season as the Texans' fourth receiver.

Tandon Doss, BAL: A fourth-round rookie out of Indiana, Doss was Joe Flacco's favorite receiver at players-only workouts during the lockout. "With Tandon, I saw a guy who can stay on the move and catch the ball well while staying on the move," Flacco told the *Baltimore Sun*. "He can pluck the ball out of the air." The release of Derrick Mason and the subsequent acquisiton of Lee Evans should give Doss more of a role in the offense, as he's more of an underneath receiver. He'll have to battle fellow rookie Torrey Smith for snaps.

Kris Durham, SEA: A fourth-round pick out of Georgia, the 6-foot-5 Durham has a lot of potential, but not a lot of production so far. He had just 13 receptions as a junior in 2008, missed 2009 with a torn labrum, and then caught just 32 balls last year as a redshirt senior. Nonetheless, scouts like his height, his hands, and his route-running. He may have an advantage if Charlie Whitehurst wins the starting job — he's been practicing with Whitehurst the past few summers because his sister lives down the street from where Whitehurst went to high school.

Armanti Edwards, CAR: Well, this was a weird one. The Panthers gave away their 2011 second-round pick to move up and select Edwards in the third round of the 2010 draft. The ridiculously productive two-time Payton Award winner was to be moved from quarterback to receiver, but never really got on the field and was rumored to be less than a favorite of John Fox's. "I tried to get Armanti on the field," Fox said toward the end of the season. "He's making a big transition at the receiver position. I'm not sure that people in the league evaluated him as an NFL quarterback." However the Panthers evaluated him, it's pretty clear that he'll have to make his bones as a receiver with Cam Newton taking all the option-style snaps behind center. And any Josh Cribbs fantasies may have been negated by the two punt returns he took in the season finale against the Falcons — one was called back on a hold, and the other was a muffed catch for no gain. Edwards may be the most obvious indicator of the disconnect between Carolina's front office and coaching staff in 2010.

Andy Fantuz, CHI: Fantuz won the CFL Most Outstanding Canadian award for 2010 as a slot receiver for the Saskatchewan Roughriders, with 87 receptions for 1,380 yards and six touchdowns. He signed with the Bears over other interested teams, including the Bills and Patriots, and at 6-foot-4, 220 pounds could give Jay Cutler a nice big target to go with all the Bears' smaller speedsters.

Yamon Figurs, TEN: Figurs is a return specialist who occasionally gets thrown a pass. In fact, last year with Oakland, he got thrown two! (2010 stats: 2-for-2, 17 yards, 41.5% DVOA, 9 DYAR)

Edmund Gates, MIA: Gates ran a 4.35 at the combine, cementing his status as one of the draft's better pure vertical threats. Gates does one thing well, and that's run fast. Fortunately, he's landed on a team that will be happy to let him do just that. As a fourth receiver on a running team, Gates will likely put up some paltry numbers, but if he can take the lid off the defense and give Brandon Marshall or Davone Bess room to operate, Gates will have done his job.

Mardy Gilyard, STL: Highly productive his final two seasons in college, the Rams expected much more than the six receptions for 63 yards and 22.3-yard kick return average they got from their fourth-round pick last season. The University of Cincinnati operating on the "quarters" system kept him out of most of the OTAs and mini-camps, and he was slowed in training camp by a wrist injury. Gilyard never really picked up the team's playbook, ultimately leading him being a game day inactive for five of the final 11 games of the season. With the addition of Austin Pettis and Greg Salas, Gilyard will need an impressive training camp and preseason to make the 53-man roster. (2010 stats: 6-for-16, 63 yards, -44.6% DVOA, -38 DYAR)

Ted Ginn, SF: A non-factor as a receiver and just average returning kickoffs, Ginn somewhat justified his roster spot as a punt returner, finishing third in the league in punt return average. Take away his 78-yard touchdown against St. Louis in Week 16, though, and his average drops to 10.6 yards per return, which would have ranked just 14th. Given the new rules that lessen the value of kick returners, it's hard to imagine Ginn playing in the league much longer. (2010 stats: 12-for-35, 163 yards, 1 TD, -35.9% DVOA, -61 DYAR)

Richard Goodman, SD: The Chargers signed Goodman to a reserve/future contract based more on his role as a gunner on the Chargers' special teams — he was a rare bright spot on San Diego's craptastic units — but he has limited potential as a pure receiver.

Chad Hall, PHI: Hall had a nice Week 17 start against the Cowboys, catching six passes for 84 yards and a touchdown. While it's tempting to see an undersized white guy and wishcast Danny Amendola (once an Eagle) or Wes Welker comparisons, Hall was a college running back who profiles primarily as a kick returner for now. (2010 stats: 11-for-18, 115 yards, 1 TD, -24.5% DVOA, -17 DYAR)

James Hardy, BAL: Hardy was a massive disaster in Buffalo after the Bills took him in the second round of the 2008 draft. He's still 6-foot-5, so the Ravens signed him to a futures contract after the season, hoping that he's motivated to grab what is probably his last chance.

Dwayne Harris, DAL: Harris has been a solid kick returner, and finished his career at East Carolina as their all-time leading receiver by yardage. With Dallas losing Roy Williams in the offseason, don't be surprised if he gets some reps in the slot this season. Harris has a reputation for dogging it, but he was a steal on talent in the sixth round.

Lavelle Hawkins, TEN: Passed in the slot receiver pecking order by Marc Mariani and Damian Williams and not a contributor on special teams, Hawkins only has 19 career catches in 3 seasons and may not make it to 20 until he finds a home outside of Tennessee. (2010 stats: 5-for-6, 61 yards, 55.7% DVOA, 35 DYAR)

Jesse Holley, DAL: The "4th and Long" winner isn't the sort of prima donna you might associate with a reality show star. Instead, Holley's a grinder with good size but limited skills that makes his hay on special teams. The Cowboys had one of those in Sam Hurd, but with Hurd gone, Holley should be good enough to make the team as the Cowboys' final wideout. Unfortunately, special teamers have the job security and staying power of, well, a reality show star.

Paul Hubbard, BUF: Hubbard made the Browns roster in 2008 after an injury-prone, not-too-productive career at Wisconsin. He spent a few years as practice squad and camp fodder in Cleveland and Oakland before resurfacing for a late-season appearance in Buffalo, where he caught his first regular season pass: an eight-yarder. He's a hard-working big body who is just good enough to lurk on the bottoms of rosters. The Bills are flooded at wide receiver, and Hubbard picked up a DWI right as the lockout was ending, so he'll likely be in a different uniform again in the near future.

Brandon James, CFL: James got a mid-year promotion from the practice squad to be the Colts' kickoff return man, but he struggled and was let go after three weeks. A running back in college, James showed some flashes as a slot receiver, catching four passes in a Week 10 game against Cincinnati. Now playing with the Edmonton Eskimos. (2010 stats: 6-for-11, 40 yards, -36.0% DVOA, -21 DYAR)

Dwayne Jarrett, FA: Jarrett is only 24, but It seems like he's been underperforming on the field and overperforming for the cops far longer than he actually has. Waived by the Panthers after an October DWI (his second), Jarrett has just one touchdown in four NFL seasons. Regarding his future, consider this: He couldn't stick on a Panthers roster in desperate need of receiver help, and after he was cut, he failed to grab one of Pete Carroll's (surprisingly limited) USC scholarships via tryout with the Seahawks. No matter what happens with his current legal situation, this isn't going to end pretty for Jarrett in a football sense. (2010 stats: 2-for-5, 40 yards, 6.5% DVOA, 6 DYAR)

Jerrel Jernigan, NYG: With Steve Smith's microfracture surgery taking him out of the Giants plans, Jernigan has a chance to see some early playing time if he can beat out Victor Cruz in the slot. Jernigan has the ability to make Domenik Hixon expendable in New York, and he should be returning kicks immediately if he can do that. Keep an eye on him in dynasty leagues.

Manuel Johnson, DAL: The former Oklahoma wideout spent the majority of a second consecutive season on the practice squad. Guys like this are usually tied to a regime that believes in them, so unless Garrett falls for him during the offseason, his time in Dallas is likely up. (2010 stats: 1-for-5, 6 yards, -87.6% DVOA, -30 DYAR)

Ronald Johnson, SF: Blessed with good speed but cursed with bad hands, Johnson played four mediocre seasons at USC, with just one 100-yard game and never topping eight touchdowns in a season. Considering the poor record of Pac-10 receivers in the pros, it's hard to see Johnson sticking around on most NFL rosters. The sixth-round draftee may spend a year or two in a 49ers uniform by default, but it would be surprising if he ever made a significant impact.

Malcolm Kelly, WAS: A fortuitously-timed pulled hamstring got Kelly on injured reserve in August, allowing him to win his roster long bet with fellow second-round bust Devin Thomas. With virtually no production after three years and a regime in place that didn't draft him, Kelly should be renting in that tough DC market, not buying. (2009 stats: 25-for-41, 347 yards, -1.9% DVOA, 35 DYAR)

Jeremy Kerley, NYJ: Kerley wasn't asked to do much downfield running at TCU, where he primarily caught the ball at or near the line of scrimmage, but he impressed scouts at the Senior Bowl with his ability to handle the route tree. Kerley has the classic slot receiver build, and that is ultimately where he'll earn his keep, but for now he's most likely to see the field as a returner or possibly in Wildcat sets.

Stefan Logan, DET: Teams say they are "trying to find ways to get the ball" to players like Logan, but they aren't really trying. Every team does the same thing when it gets the itch to use its 177-pound return man on offense: here come the end arounds, the direct snap plays, and so on. Logan threw a pass on an option play last year (the replay suggests that he may have just panicked on a sweep and threw the ball away), took a Pistol snap on a draw play to nowhere, and ran a few of those end arounds that the defense always sniffs out because they start asking questions like "why is the kick returner lined up in the slot?" Late in the season, the Lions started lining up Logan in the backfield and using him like a normal running back, and the results weren't bad: he had 11, 12, and 13-yard rushes among his 13 "normal" carries. Logan could save the Lions a roster spot elsewhere if they trust him as a No. 3 runner behind Jahvid Best and Jerome Harrison. (2010 running stats: 15 carries for 95 yards, 49 DYAR, 30.4% DVOA)

Jeff Maehl, HOU: Physically comparable to ex-Texan David Anderson, Maehl was primarily a receiver in short routes for Oregon and has the ability to contribute on special teams, but his slight build has some worried about his ability to take punishment over the middle. Houston's depth chart at wide receiver is unsettled after the top three, so Maehl could make the roster with a good preseason.

Marc Mariani, TEN: Mariani made the Pro Bowl for his return ability and will again see most of his action there, but could end up with a few catches as the Titans' fourth or fifth receiver. Jimmy Farris, watch out: Mariani is coming after your record seven NFL catches by a Montana wide receiver.

Ruvell Martin, FA: Martin's DVOA of 68.9% would have led the league last season if only he had been targeted on 41 more passes. He's just over 1,000 yards for his career, but one bubble screen gone awry could push him back in the 900s. Fortunately that won't happen, what with his career likely being over and all. (Other 2010 stats: 7-for-9, 158 yards, 1 TD, 59 DYAR)

Scotty McKnight, NYJ: McKnight is a high school friend of Mark Sanchez, who came out to Colorado to throw for McKnight's Pro Day, and it's easy to see why the Jets might use their seventh-round pick as a way to keep their starting quarterback happy rather than on a fringe player with little hope of making the final roster. McKnight has a similar scouting profile to Jeremy Kerley, who he will compete with for slot duty.

Kerry Meier, ATL: The 2010 fifth-round pick lost his season to a preseason knee injury. Mike Smith is enamored of Meier, and he'll get the first crack at taking over for the (finally) departed Brian Finneran. Meier is from the football-mad town of Pittsburg, Kansas, and has three brothers who all played college ball. Not quite the hockey-playing Sutter Brothers, but pretty respectable nonetheless.

Nick Miller, OAK: Miller didn't get a lot of looks in 2010, but he's doing everything possible to learn from the best — he worked out with Larry Fitzgerald and Greg Jennings in the offseason after Charlie Frye introduced him to Fitzgerald. "You notice all their techniques, things they do like stutters at the top of their routes, what you can do to confuse cornerbacks on certain routes, different ways to catch the ball," Miller told the San Francisco Chronicle. "It's so cool, because they answer all my questions - I am getting the best receiver education in the world free of charge." Perhaps Miller should have considered bringing Darrius Heyward-Bey along for those lessons. (2010 stats: 3-for-4, 40 yards, -6.7% DVOA, 2 DYAR)

Carlton Mitchell, CLE: This raw South Florida project has excellent size (6-foot-3) and speed, and Mike Holmgren and Pat Shurmur are very high on him. A 2010 sixth-rounder, Mitchell basically took a redshirt year, learning route-running technique and honing his comedy routines on Twitter (@C_Mitch18). "I think that limiting the nuggeting of animals to only chicken was a mistake."

Marlon Moore, MIA: Moore's primary claim to fame is that he can run fast in a straight line, which is good enough to keep you on the speed-challenged Miami roster. Tony Sparano mentioned the Fresno State UDFA as a potential playmaker, but aside from a single 57-yard touchdown against Oakland, there wasn't much to see in 2010. Moore doesn't contribute on special teams, and while he is certainly fast, he doesn't get in and out of his breaks cleanly or show particularly good hands. Moore's upside is probably no better than the fourth receiver. (2010 stats: 6-for-19, 128 yards, 1 TD, -22.0% DVOA, -13 DYAR)

Kassim Osgood, JAC: Osgood pleaded with the Chargers for years to let him be a receiver before finally fleeing to Jacksonville for the chance to do it. How did that go? Well, it's never a good sign when your catch rate (38 percent) is roughly equivalent to your negative DVOA (-36.2%). To his credit, he did provide a boost to the Jags special teams. (Other 2010 stats: 6-for-16, 60 yards, -29 DYAR)

Preston Parker, TB: Is Parker the next Troy Brown? Perhaps. Tampa Bay's receiver corps was fairly loaded last season, so Parker took a few reps at safety and actually recorded a quarterback hurry on Detroit's Drew Stanton in a December game after bugging Raheem Morris to give him a shot on the other side of the ball. "I think they just wanted to try something new, and they thought I could get the job done," Parker told the St. Petersburg Times. "They wanted to see what I would do with the opportunity. And I was trying to get to (Stanton). I had two big boys (blocking) me, so I had to try to get through them." The rookie found it difficult to wrest slot duty from Sammie Stroughter and return reps from Michael Spurlock, so any post in a storm… (2010 stats: 5-for-10, 49 yards, -30.8% DVOA, -16 DYAR)

Niles Paul, WAS: College production was hard to come by for Paul as Nebraska hasn't had much in the way of quarterbacking for the last few seasons, but he has the ability to be a solid gunner and good kick returner. His lack of attention to things like blocking and route-running will probably preclude him from making much of an impact in Washington this season.

Kealoha Pilares, CAR: Pilares played running back and slot receiver in Hawaii's turbo spread offense. He was appealing to the Panthers as a possible Davone Bess-style option, and is well-equipped to get some slot targets in an offense dialed back from a complexity perspective.

Taylor Price, NE: Price took a while to learn the offense and barely got on the field as a rookie, but he was impressing observers with his 4.40 speed and overall improvement this year's training camp. The acquisition of Chad Ochocinco seems to block either Price or Brandon Tate out of a role in the offense, but it looks like the Patriots will figure out a way to carry Price's potential on the roster for another year. (2010 stats: 3-for-4, 41 yards, 36.7% DVOA, 16 DYAR)

David Reed, BAL: In their effort to find receivers under 30, it sure seems like the Ravens are throwing everything at the wall to see what sticks. They've got the two rookie receivers they drafted this year (Torrey Smith and Tandon Doss). They've got Reed and the two tight ends (Ed Dickson and Dennis Pitta) from the 2010 draft, and tight end Davon Drew from the 2009 draft. On top of that, they signed James Hardy to a futures contract, and 2008 fourth-rounder Marcus Smith and former Tennessee Titan Brandon Jones are hanging around as well. Reed was tough and highly productive at Utah, and his return ability (7.9 points of punt value on just 21 returns last year) gives him a step up on making the roster.

Darius Reynaud, NYG: Acquired in the Sage Rosenfels trade, Reynaud was abysmal on special teams before losing his job during the bye. The Giants re-signed him, but they must have a half-dozen guys on the roster who profile as better return candidates than him.

Aldrick Robinson, WAS: Think about fellow Redskins draftee Niles Paul, then flip it in reverse. Robinson was an extremely productive college receiver at Southern Methodist with great deep speed, but contributed very little on special teams. He's probably competing with offseason signing Donte' Stallworth for one roster spot, but there is some upside here if he can make it onto the field. Jump balls are a weakness, but other than his physicality, Robinson has all the tools to survive in the NFL.

Courtney Roby, NO: Roby was on both ends of the scary injury spectrum last year. In October, he flattened a member of the Superdome chain gang while covering a kickoff, an incident that left the linesman, Al Nastasi, with a severe concussion and Roby badly shaken. Several weeks later, it was Roby's turn to be backboarded off the field, after getting kneed in the neck in a fumble pileup. Roby should be fine for 2011, but Darren Sproles will complicate Roby's prior command of kick return duties.

Greg Salas, STL: The University of Hawaii's all-time leader in receiving yards (4,345) is coming off a season that saw him break single-season records for receptions (119, previously held by Davone Bess) and receiving yards (1,889, previously held by Ashley Lelie). The 6-foot-1, 210-pound Salas dropped to the fourth round as there were questions about his ability to run routes and beat press coverage at the NFL level after working primarily of the slot in Hawaii's hybrid pistol/run-and-shoot offense. Salas is a sure-handed receiver who is a threat after the catch, and the ability to work out of the slot is a valuable skill in Josh McDaniels' offense.

DeMarco Sampson, ARI: The Cardinals' final draft pick out of San Diego State was very productive in his final two seasons of college. He comes into the league with a reputation of winning jump-ball situations in traffic. At age 25 he is older than most rookies, but does have the physical strength to make a quick transition into the NFL.

Dane Sanzenbacher, CHI: The leading receiver for Ohio State in 2010, Sanzenbacher will probably be called "gritty" at some point in an NFL telecast. You might think of him as just an underneath receiver and special teams guy, but he did average 17.2 yards a catch as a senior. His makeup and headiness could earn him a few roster spots.

Cecil Shorts, JAC: Shorts, another small school special from Jaguars GM Gene Smith, has drawn many comparisons to Pierre Garcon based on the fact that they both attended Mount Union. Only one of them gets to have Peyton Manning as his quarterback, and it isn't Shorts. He will likely spend most of his time on special teams in his first year, and for that we salute him.

Matt Slater, NE: Slater led the Patriots with 15 solo tackles on special teams. He no longer has a role on offense, and he won't get one anytime soon: the Patriots are overloaded with guys who can play the slot-outlet receiver role.

Marcus Smith, BAL: The 2008 fourth-rounder was finally healthy enough to spend the whole year on the active roster, but was special teams only, with no receptions. It will be hard to hold onto the job with Torrey Smith and Tandon Doss coming in.

Maurice Stovall, DET: The best way to explain Stovall's season is to point out that his biggest play of the 2010 campaign came on a play in which he wasn't even the target. In the second half of the season finale against the Saints, Kellen Winslow, who ran a square out about 10 yards downfield., The ball bounced off Winslow's hands, traveled another 10 yards in the air past three Saints defenders, and landed right in the hands of Stovall, who turned his good fortune into a 38-yard gain. He'll have that memory to entertain himself as he's watching younger receivers take his targets again in 2011, this time with the Detroit Lions. (2010 stats: 7-for-9, 81 yards, 1 TD, 12.1% DVOA, 19 DYAR)

Brett Swain, GB: Swain fought his way back from a 2009 ACL injury to play in every game last year and make an impact on special teams. He may need the Packers to keep six receivers if he hopes to stick this year; his special teams value, and the Packers' love of multi-receiver sets, make that a possibility. (2010 stats: 6-for-9, 72 yards, -6.6% DVOA, 4 DYAR)

Limas Sweed, PIT: The former Texas star has spent his pro career battling demons both mental (depression) and physical (an Achilles tear in last year's preseason that forced him out for the year). If anything keeps him on the Steelers roster this year, it will be his 6-foot-4 height; Arnaz Battle is the only other receiver on the roster over six feet tall. (2009 stats: 1-for-5, 6 yards, -87.5% DVOA, -32 DYAR)

Devin Thomas, NYG: Thomas is a data point against drafting one-year wonder receivers; the Redskins used a 2008 second-round pick on him even though he had just six catches in his first two years before he had 79 catches as a junior. Washington finally gave up on him last year, and he bounced to Carolina and then the Giants without getting in on any offensive snaps. He did show a high motor on special teams, which could help him snag the last receiver spot on the Giants this season. (2009 stats: 25-for-47, 325 yards, 3 TD, -3.5% DVOA, -34 DYAR)

Terrence Toliver, HOU: A big, durable receiver who was one of the highest-rated high school recruits in the country, Toliver's college career at LSU was defined more by the poor quarterback play around him than his actual skill set. He could possibly develop into a solid possession receiver down the line, and with the release of David Anderson, the lower end of Houston's wideout depth chart is there for the taking.

Verran Tucker, KC: From junior college to Cal to the pros? Hey, it worked for Aaron Rodgers. Tucker has a slightly steeper climb, but he did get some starting spots toward the end of his rookie season and acquitted himself fairly well as a sideline and slant receiver in open and empty sets. But just as Tucker was able to get more reps after Chris Chambers jumped the shark, Jon Baldwin may take targets away from Tucker in that kind of role. (2010 stats: 6-for-19, 114 yards, 1 TD, -27.6% DVOA, -21 DYAR)

Patrick Turner, NYJ: Turner played with Mark Sanchez at USC, which is a point in his favor. Another point is his 6-foot-5 frame, which helped him become the latest in a long line of Trojans receivers to overwhelm college corners with their size and athleticism. Miami way over-drafted him in the second round, and he spent most of last season on the Jets practice squad.

Roberto Wallace, MIA: Wallace is one of several guys with good speed but raw skills who are fighting at the bottom of the Miami depth chart. Wallace was the starting flanker for the opening drive in Week 8 against Cincinnati, but he didn't record a catch in the game. Wallace is no longer eligible for the practice squad, which means that he could have an uphill climb to make the roster. He does play special teams, which represents his best chance to contribute in 2011. (2010 stats: 6-for-10, 62 yards, -6.3% DVOA, 4 DYAR)

Kelley Washington, SD: Always a great special-teamer, Washington is primarily known for his habit of wildly celebrating the smallest on-field accomplishment ("A five-yard out on second-and-17! WOO-HOO!!!") Where he had legitimate reason to celebrate in 2010 was in his ability to be a third-down monster — he caught all nine passes thrown to him for 125 yards on that down and put up a ridiculous DVOA of 115.8%. The Chargers liked what they saw enough to re-sign him to a one-year deal. (2010 stats: 13-for-14, 173 yards, 1 TD, 80.0% DVOA, 96 DYAR)

Eric Weems, ATL: Weems had four of his six catches on opening Sunday, then disappeared from the field to concentrate on returning kicks, where he was among the league's best in 2010. With Julio Jones and Jacquizz Rodgers in town, don't look for Weems' role to change in 2011. (2010 stats: 6-for-6, 61 yards, 58.7% DVOA, 36 DYAR)

Ryan Whalen, CIN: The Bengals took Whalen out of Stanford in the sixth round. He has the size and hands to be a strong red zone target, but is he fast enough to be useful on the rest of the field? Whelan is similar to Evan Moore, another Stanford receiver who gained 20 pounds and became a useful TE/WR hybrid for Cleveland.

Demetrius Williams, CLE: The Ravens finally gave up on Williams' upside last year. The Browns picked him up and he played two games with no receptions. He should consider a UFL career if they ever solve that whole "having enough money to operate" problem. (2009 stats: 8-for-17, 142 yards, 1 TD, -76.0% DVOA, -11 DYAR)

Derrick Williams, DET: The Lions have a lot of all-purpose players who can line up in the slot (Jahvid Best, Stefan Logan, Tony Scheffler) so the fourth receiver position is largely ceremonial. (2010 stats: 3-for-5, 30 yards, -44.7% DVOA, -14 DYAR)

Jeremy Williams, PHI: An undrafted free agent who ended up in training camp with the Chargers, Williams failed to make the San Diego squad and caught on with the Eagles, spending the year on their practice squad. With just 1,205 followers to his credit, Williams may qualify as the "verified" Twitter account with the fewest fans.

Kyle Williams, SF: This sixth-round rookie out of Arizona was a healthy scratch in seven games in 2010, a remarkable number considering the dire state of the 49ers receiving corps. He tweaked a hamstring during informal player workouts in June, but is expected to make a full return... to being a healthy scratch. (2010 stats: 1-for-1, 8 yards, 36.5% DVOA, 4 DYAR)

Roydell Williams, FA: After serving as the Titans' top receiver in 2007, Williams spent 2008 and 2009 in the wilderness before making it back onto the Redskins' active roster in 2010. There are probably hundreds of guys who could serve as the fifth wideout on an NFL roster for the league minimum, and the only thing that Williams has going for him versus them is his past. (2010 stats: 8-for-18, 109 yards, -29.4% DVOA, -23 DYAR)

Matt Willis, DEN: Generally a special-teamer who will occasionally surprise and excite in preseason and training camp, Willis was lost for the season after hurting his foot. He'll be a bubble guy with the Broncos' stacked receiver corps and fewer opportunities schematically under John Fox.

Tight Ends

Billy Bajema

Height: 6-5　Weight: 261　College: Oklahoma State　Draft: 2005/7 (249)　Born: 31-Oct-1982　Age: 29　Risk: Green

Year	Team	G	Rec	Pass	Yds	C%	+/-	Yd/C	TD	FUM	YAC	Rk	DVOA	Rk	DYAR	Rk	YAR	Short	Mid	Deep	Bomb
2008	SF	16	2	4	34	50%	-0.3	17.0	0	0	7.0	--	-9.7%	--	-1	--	0	25%	25%	50%	0%
2009	STL	16	8	11	94	73%	1.0	11.8	0	0	4.8	--	29.1%	--	25	--	24	60%	40%	0%	0%
2010	STL	13	14	24	145	58%	-0.5	10.4	2	1	5.8	--	-10.0%	--	-4	--	-1	48%	43%	10%	0%
2011	STL		9	14	80	64%	--	8.9	0				-10.7%								

Injuries to athletic rookie tight ends Michael Hoomanawanui and Fendi Onobun opened the door for Bajema, a block-first tight end, to start eight games. The Rams carried four tight ends into the 2010 regular season, a roster strategy that figures to continue as Josh McDaniels intends to frequently employ two-tight end sets. Bajema's blocking and ability to play some fullback all but assures he'll be back in 2011.

Travis Beckum

Height: 6-3　Weight: 243　College: Wisconsin　Draft: 2009/3 (100)　Born: 24-Jan-1987　Age: 24　Risk: Red

Year	Team	G	Rec	Pass	Yds	C%	+/-	Yd/C	TD	FUM	YAC	Rk	DVOA	Rk	DYAR	Rk	YAR	Short	Mid	Deep	Bomb
2009	NYG	15	8	10	55	80%	0.7	6.9	0	0	3.3	--	-9.9%	--	-2	--	-2	70%	30%	0%	0%
2010	NYG	16	13	18	116	72%	0.8	8.9	2	0	3.1	--	9.9%	--	21	--	22	56%	22%	22%	0%
2011	NYG		33	51	366	65%	--	11.1	3				9.2%								

The Giants want Beckum to be versatile enough to catch passes as a slot receiver or serve as an in-line blocker. In other words, they want him to be Jermichael Finley or Jared Cook. What they have is, well, Travis Beckum. He was an effective receiver at the goal line last year while teams focused in on Hakeem Nicks, and that should remain the case in 2011.

Martellus Bennett

Height: 6-6　Weight: 259　College: Texas A&M　Draft: 2008/2 (61)　Born: 10-Mar-1987　Age: 24　Risk: Green

Year	Team	G	Rec	Pass	Yds	C%	+/-	Yd/C	TD	FUM	YAC	Rk	DVOA	Rk	DYAR	Rk	YAR	Short	Mid	Deep	Bomb
2008	DAL	16	20	27	283	74%	2.0	14.2	4	0	6.1	5	59.0%	1	112	13	113	52%	22%	22%	4%
2009	DAL	14	15	30	159	50%	-4.1	10.6	0	0	3.5	39	-26.3%	44	-36	42	-38	41%	52%	3%	3%
2010	DAL	16	33	47	260	70%	1.4	7.9	0	1	5.5	13	-24.8%	42	-53	42	-57	71%	26%	2%	0%
2011	DAL		28	43	281	65%	--	10.0	2				-0.9%								

He hasn't really advanced since a promising rookie season in 2008. Even his famously open, un-PC quotes have become bland in a Twitter era. One of the main problems is that there's a great player ahead of him; as long as Jason Witten's healthy, Bennett's never going to get the reps he needs as the primary tight end in standard offensive sets to improve. The good news is that the Cowboys are using more two-tight end sets than ever before. In 2008, they went with two tight ends on 26.1 percent of their snaps; in 2010, that figure was up to 31.4 percent. Bennett may end up being a starting tight end somewhere, but it's probably not going to be in Big D.

Kevin Boss

Height: 6-7　Weight: 255　College: Western Oregon　Draft: 2007/5 (153)　Born: 11-Jan-1984　Age: 27　Risk: Red

Year	Team	G	Rec	Pass	Yds	C%	+/-	Yd/C	TD	FUM	YAC	Rk	DVOA	Rk	DYAR	Rk	YAR	Short	Mid	Deep	Bomb
2008	NYG	15	33	55	384	60%	-1.1	11.6	6	0	4.8	14	14.8%	15	84	16	68	45%	40%	15%	0%
2009	NYG	15	42	69	567	61%	-0.3	13.5	5	0	5.5	13	12.4%	13	88	17	81	41%	41%	19%	0%
2010	NYG	15	35	70	531	50%	-7.4	15.2	5	1	7.0	3	-5.0%	32	11	32	13	44%	31%	25%	0%
2011	OAK		44	73	536	60%	--	12.2	4				0.3%								

Boss was one of the few Giants to get stronger in the second half of the season, putting up a 21-316-4 line over the final eight games of the year. He battled gamely as a frequent blocker because the offensive line was so bad, but Boss is always going to be a pass-first tight end. The Giants attempted to lock him up because they don't have a serious threat behind him on the roster, but Boss is a second-division starter. That seems to make him a perfect fit with the Raiders, where he'll attempt to fill Zach Miller's shoes.

John Carlson   Height: 6-4   Weight: 255   College: Notre Dame   Draft: 2008/2 (38)   Born: 12-May-1984   Age: 27   Risk: Green

Year	Team	G	Rec	Pass	Yds	C%	+/-	Yd/C	TD	FUM	YAC	Rk	DVOA	Rk	DYAR	Rk	YAR	Short	Mid	Deep	Bomb
2008	SEA	16	55	80	627	69%	5.4	11.4	5	0	4.0	27	19.2%	9	144	8	147	32%	54%	14%	0%
2009	SEA	16	51	83	574	61%	-2.8	11.3	7	0	5.1	21	-0.1%	27	40	22	55	41%	47%	11%	1%
2010	SEA	15	31	58	318	53%	-3.1	10.3	1	0	4.1	32	-31.2%	44	-94	44	-85	50%	31%	15%	4%
2011	SEA		31	52	331	60%	--	10.7	1				-19.1%								

When Michael Robinson was injured, Carlson spent a lot of time in the backfield as a default fullback. That explains why his targets dropped so precipitously, and why he ran more short routes than ever before. It does not explain, however, how or why his catch rate dropped, when it should have been boosted by his proximity to the line of scrimmage. Based on FO's charting data, it doesn't look like much of the blame should go to Carlson. Of Carlson's 23 incompletions, only three were drops. Five times passes thrown his way were defensed, a sign of a receiver who failed to get separation. On the other hand, 11 of Carlson's incompletes were either overthrown or thrown ahead. The offensive line must also take some of the blame. Other reasons listed for Carlson incompletions include "thrown away" (three times), "QB hit in motion" (twice), and "tipped at line" (once). Darrell Bevell's offense in Seattle is expected to use a lot of multiple-tight end formations, which should put Carlson back on the line where he belongs, although he'll be the clear No. 2 option behind the newly signed Zach Miller.

Brent Celek   Height: 6-4   Weight: 261   College: Cincinnati   Draft: 2007/5 (162)   Born: 25-Jan-1985   Age: 26   Risk: Yellow

Year	Team	G	Rec	Pass	Yds	C%	+/-	Yd/C	TD	FUM	YAC	Rk	DVOA	Rk	DYAR	Rk	YAR	Short	Mid	Deep	Bomb
2008	PHI	16	27	38	318	71%	2.9	11.8	1	0	6.1	4	21.9%	7	77	17	68	53%	35%	12%	0%
2009	PHI	16	76	112	971	68%	3.9	12.8	8	0	5.4	15	19.8%	10	201	5	207	43%	39%	16%	2%
2010	PHI	16	42	79	511	53%	-7.7	12.2	4	0	5.7	10	-8.9%	35	-9	35	-13	49%	29%	12%	11%
2011	PHI		51	80	566	64%	--	11.1	4				7.9%								

After tying for the league lead in drops for tight ends in 2009, Celek only dropped five passes in 2010. That's the good news. On the other hand, his target rate, catch rate, and plus-minus all dropped precipitously, and the former DVOA darling and Top 25 Prospect was an absolute non-factor in the Eagles' offense. All the injuries along the offensive line led Celek to block far more frequently than expected, depressing his numbers. However, the offensive line should be better in 2011, and if his catch rate bounces back, he should be able to re-create those 2009 numbers.

Dallas Clark   Height: 6-3   Weight: 257   College: Iowa   Draft: 2003/1 (24)   Born: 12-Jun-1979   Age: 32   Risk: Red

Year	Team	G	Rec	Pass	Yds	C%	+/-	Yd/C	TD	FUM	YAC	Rk	DVOA	Rk	DYAR	Rk	YAR	Short	Mid	Deep	Bomb
2008	IND	15	77	107	848	72%	6.8	11.0	6	2	4.7	16	18.3%	11	187	4	192	58%	25%	16%	1%
2009	IND	16	100	133	1106	75%	12.9	11.1	10	1	4.8	23	22.2%	8	260	2	281	52%	32%	13%	2%
2010	IND	6	37	53	347	70%	1.5	9.4	3	0	3.7	38	6.0%	23	48	24	54	52%	40%	6%	2%
2011	IND		65	100	835	65%	--	12.9	8				26.9%								

A Week 6 wrist injury against Washington led to season-ending surgery and cost the Colts their most versatile weapon. The Colts had three of their four best offensive performances in the six games Clark played. Clark remains a dynamic receiver who can play as a true tight end, a slot receiver, or even on the outside. Clark is getting on in years, at age 32, and if athletic linebackers can start covering him underneath, the Colts lose much of the match-up advantage he provides. Still, there is no reason to suspect he will not be productive this season, although it is much more likely to resemble 2008 than his career-year in 2009.

Jared Cook

Height: 6-6   Weight: 246   College: South Carolina   Draft: 2009/3 (89)   Born: 7-Apr-1987   Age: 24   Risk: Red

Year	Team	G	Rec	Pass	Yds	C%	+/-	Yd/C	TD	FUM	YAC	Rk	DVOA	Rk	DYAR	Rk	YAR	Short	Mid	Deep	Bomb
2009	TEN	14	9	15	74	60%	-0.7	8.2	0	0	4.0	--	-16.6%	--	-10	--	-8	46%	38%	15%	0%
2010	TEN	16	29	45	361	64%	1.8	12.4	1	0	4.7	21	23.6%	13	82	18	88	37%	44%	15%	5%
2011	TEN		54	87	680	62%	--	12.6	5				15.5%								

While Cook improved from a disappointing rookie season, he still struggled to see playing time until late in the year. When he did get on the field, he combined outstanding physical ability with woeful blocking and at least one major mental error a game. Cook will be given every opportunity early in the season to show he's improved in those areas. If he has, he'll likely get thrown the ball a lot in 2011. If he hasn't, well, he may get thrown the ball a lot anyway.

Chris Cooley

Height: 6-3   Weight: 252   College: Utah State   Draft: 2004/3 (81)   Born: 11-Jul-1982   Age: 29   Risk: Red

Year	Team	G	Rec	Pass	Yds	C%	+/-	Yd/C	TD	FUM	YAC	Rk	DVOA	Rk	DYAR	Rk	YAR	Short	Mid	Deep	Bomb
2008	WAS	16	83	111	849	75%	8.0	10.2	1	3	5.7	8	7.6%	18	105	14	114	59%	30%	10%	1%
2009	WAS	7	29	45	332	64%	0.0	11.4	2	1	7.1	3	2.0%	24	25	25	35	53%	40%	8%	0%
2010	WAS	16	77	126	849	61%	-1.4	11.0	3	3	4.8	20	-7.2%	34	0	34	3	48%	42%	10%	0%
2011	WAS		68	106	775	64%	--	11.4	4				3.5%								

The erstwhile Redskins tight end hit a career-high in targets, thanks to a Redskins offense that threw the ball more frequently than all but three other NFL teams. The absence of established receivers at running back and behind Santana Moss at wide receiver helped, too. Unless the Redskins suddenly become New Orleans North, though, that sort of target rate is unlikely to recur again. Cooley will have a huge role in the offense again this year; the Redskins plan a lot of two-TE sets, and the team is once again trying to cobble together a receiving corps from Santana Moss, some Indoor Football League alums, and guys the Patriots soured on four years ago.

Owen Daniels

Height: 6-3   Weight: 245   College: Wisconsin   Draft: 2006/4 (98)   Born: 9-Nov-1982   Age: 29   Risk: Yellow

Year	Team	G	Rec	Pass	Yds	C%	+/-	Yd/C	TD	FUM	YAC	Rk	DVOA	Rk	DYAR	Rk	YAR	Short	Mid	Deep	Bomb
2008	HOU	16	70	99	862	71%	8.3	12.3	2	2	5.8	7	18.2%	12	173	5	168	52%	42%	6%	0%
2009	HOU	8	40	58	519	69%	3.0	13.0	5	1	5.6	9	27.3%	5	134	13	123	41%	43%	13%	4%
2010	HOU	11	38	68	471	56%	-1.8	12.4	2	0	6.6	5	1.2%	26	39	26	36	45%	37%	18%	0%
2011	HOU		61	91	755	67%	--	12.4	5				23.2%								

After a mid-season 2009 ACL injury (his third), Daniels struggled badly at the start of 2010 but by the end of the year seemed to recover the speed and explosiveness that made him one of the league's best vertical tight ends. The Texans hope so, as they rewarded the would-be free agent with a 4 year, $22 million deal. If he truly is at full strength, it's a good deal and he'll again be one of the league's top fantasy tight ends. If not, Joel Dreessen is also available and a better blocker, though Daniels isn't that bad.

Fred Davis

Height: 6-4   Weight: 248   College: USC   Draft: 2008/2 (48)   Born: 15-Jan-1986   Age: 25   Risk: Green

Year	Team	G	Rec	Pass	Yds	C%	+/-	Yd/C	TD	FUM	YAC	Rk	DVOA	Rk	DYAR	Rk	YAR	Short	Mid	Deep	Bomb
2008	WAS	11	3	10	27	30%	-2.5	9.0	0	0	4.7	--	-53.1%	--	-31	--	-33	75%	0%	25%	0%
2009	WAS	16	48	76	509	63%	0.3	10.6	6	0	5.2	19	11.3%	15	92	15	91	46%	46%	9%	0%
2010	WAS	16	21	30	316	70%	3.0	15.0	3	0	8.0	1	40.0%	5	97	16	99	56%	30%	11%	4%
2011	WAS		20	31	214	65%	--	10.7	2				6.1%								

The Redskins only went with two tight ends on 30 percent of their snaps, and even when they did, Mike Sellers was used as a tight end a fair amount of the time. As you can see, the Redskins were wildly effective when they actually threw Davis the ball. Still, a full 42 percent of his receiving yardage came on two plays, and it's always sweet when a tight end has the James Jett gamelog. He deserves a bigger role in the offense.

Vernon Davis

Height: 6-3   Weight: 250   College: Maryland   Draft: 2006/1 (6)   Born: 31-Jan-1984   Age: 27   Risk: Green

Year	Team	G	Rec	Pass	Yds	C%	+/-	Yd/C	TD	FUM	YAC	Rk	DVOA	Rk	DYAR	Rk	YAR	Short	Mid	Deep	Bomb
2008	SF	16	31	49	358	63%	-0.1	11.5	0	2	7.8	1	-24.6%	37	-54	37	-49	63%	7%	15%	15%
2009	SF	16	78	129	965	60%	5.4	12.4	13	0	4.2	27	8.7%	19	131	14	149	47%	29%	15%	10%
2010	SF	16	56	93	914	60%	0.7	16.3	7	0	7.5	2	27.5%	10	207	4	209	37%	34%	20%	9%
2011	SF		69	105	855	66%	--	12.4	6				21.0%								

What Michael Vick is to running quarterbacks, Vernon Davis is to long-ball tight ends. Davis was targeted on Deep or Bomb patterns 26 times last season, six more than any other tight end, and tied Antonio Gates for the league lead with 14 catches (including one defensive pass interference call) on those throws. Davis finished with five 40-yard plays, the most by a tight end since at least 1991, and the fourth time in his career he has led all tight ends in this category. He was also the first player at his position to catch at least 50 passes and average more than 16 yards per reception since 1978. Add in his devastating blocking (the 49ers were 13th in overall ALY, but second to left tackle and third to right tackle) and you have one of the league's best players. Did we mention that he's only 27 years old and signed through 2015? An 85 jersey in scarlet is one of the wisest investments a 49ers fan can make.

Ed Dickson

Height: 6-4   Weight: 249   College: Oregon   Draft: 2010/3 (70)   Born: 25-Jul-1987   Age: 24   Risk: Yellow

Year	Team	G	Rec	Pass	Yds	C%	+/-	Yd/C	TD	FUM	YAC	Rk	DVOA	Rk	DYAR	Rk	YAR	Short	Mid	Deep	Bomb
2010	BAL	15	11	23	152	48%	-2.4	13.8	1	0	6.5	--	-24.5%	--	-24	--	-22	45%	35%	10%	10%
2011	BAL		30	44	319	68%	--	10.6	3				14.2%								

Dickson is another entry in the modern line of receiver-first, blocker-second tight ends. Scouts loved his speed and hands coming out of Oregon a year ago, and he's the heir apparent to Todd Heap. Dickson's potential is best exemplified by a play early in Week 5 against the Broncos. He completely blew past Brian Dawkins up the seam, and when an underthrown Joe Flacco pass let Dawkins catch up with him, he used his body to outmanuever Dawkins, catch the ball — and then drag Dawkins an extra 14 yards after the catch.

Joel Dreessen

Height: 6-4   Weight: 260   College: Colorado State   Draft: 2005/6 (198)   Born: 26-Jul-1982   Age: 29   Risk: Green

Year	Team	G	Rec	Pass	Yds	C%	+/-	Yd/C	TD	FUM	YAC	Rk	DVOA	Rk	DYAR	Rk	YAR	Short	Mid	Deep	Bomb
2008	HOU	16	11	17	77	65%	1.4	7.0	0	1	3.5	--	-35.2%	--	-31	--	-34	69%	23%	8%	0%
2009	HOU	16	26	39	320	67%	2.7	12.3	1	0	5.3	17	8.9%	18	45	20	51	53%	38%	9%	0%
2010	HOU	16	36	54	518	67%	3.8	14.4	4	1	5.1	17	28.6%	9	120	12	121	32%	54%	12%	2%
2011	HOU		29	43	361	67%	--	12.4	2				17.8%								

Dreessen was the beneficiary of Owen Daniels' injury struggles last year, and was a productive and complete tight end for the Texans. His excellent DVOA numbers are more a product of his reliability and the parts around him, as he lacks Daniels' ability to separate from defenders and must be schemed open. Even with Daniels around, he's an excellent blocker who should see work in the Texans' multiple-tight end sets and catch some passes.

Anthony Fasano

Height: 6-4   Weight: 255   College: Notre Dame   Draft: 2006/2 (53)   Born: 20-Apr-1984   Age: 27   Risk: Green

Year	Team	G	Rec	Pass	Yds	C%	+/-	Yd/C	TD	FUM	YAC	Rk	DVOA	Rk	DYAR	Rk	YAR	Short	Mid	Deep	Bomb
2008	MIA	16	34	53	454	64%	1.5	13.4	7	0	4.1	26	34.8%	4	156	6	164	28%	56%	16%	0%
2009	MIA	14	31	53	339	58%	-0.5	10.9	2	2	3.8	33	-15.8%	37	-31	41	-31	37%	45%	14%	4%
2010	MIA	15	39	60	528	65%	2.8	13.5	4	0	5.1	16	29.1%	8	144	6	140	40%	45%	13%	2%
2011	MIA		40	58	419	69%	--	10.5	4				21.8%								

At this point in his career, Fasano has established himself as a do-everything tight end who isn't going to wow you with his receiving but who can block pretty well and can provide a safety outlet on third downs. Fasano is actually at his best on first down, when defenses have their base personnel on the field and are cued to the run;

his 59% DVOA was easily tops among all Dolphins receivers. Brian Daboll likes to throw to the tight ends, as evidenced by Ben Watson's 68 receptions last year, so it's possible that Fasano's numbers will inch up a bit more, but not to the point where you'd want him starting on your fantasy team every week.

Daniel Fells

Height: 6-4   Weight: 252   College: California-Davis   Draft: 2006/ (FA)   Born: 23-Sep-1983   Age: 28   Risk: Red

Year	Team	G	Rec	Pass	Yds	C%	+/-	Yd/C	TD	FUM	YAC	Rk	DVOA	Rk	DYAR	Rk	YAR	Short	Mid	Deep	Bomb
2008	STL	12	7	11	81	64%	0.2	11.6	0	0	5.6	--	6.2%	--	10	--	9	36%	27%	36%	0%
2009	STL	14	21	35	273	60%	-1.4	13.0	3	1	6.2	7	5.4%	22	31	24	34	41%	41%	19%	0%
2010	STL	16	41	65	391	63%	1.8	9.5	2	0	6.5	6	-2.5%	31	19	30	20	67%	30%	4%	0%
2011	DEN		32	51	361	63%	--	11.3	2				7.1%								

After pinballing around three NFL teams (Atlanta, Oakland, Tampa Bay) in his first three years in the league, Fells found a home in St. Louis in 2008. Fells was a part-time starter last season, but ranked fourth among Rams skill-position players in targets, and was at his best on third and fourth downs, posting a 22.0% DVOA. The emergence of Michael Hoomanawanui and the selection of Lance Kendricks in the second round of the 2011 NFL Draft allowed the Rams to let Fells test free agency. Fells was signed by the Denver Broncos, where he quickly assumed the No. 1 spot on a very unimpressive depth chart.

Jermichael Finley

Height: 6-4   Weight: 243   College: Texas   Draft: 2008/3 (91)   Born: 26-Mar-1987   Age: 24   Risk: Red

Year	Team	G	Rec	Pass	Yds	C%	+/-	Yd/C	TD	FUM	YAC	Rk	DVOA	Rk	DYAR	Rk	YAR	Short	Mid	Deep	Bomb
2008	GB	14	6	12	74	50%	-1.2	12.3	1	0	2.5	--	-21.8%	--	-13	--	-12	58%	17%	17%	8%
2009	GB	13	55	72	676	76%	8.0	12.3	5	1	5.3	18	27.2%	6	172	6	165	48%	38%	11%	3%
2010	GB	5	21	26	301	81%	4.7	14.3	1	0	4.6	22	57.8%	2	109	13	110	32%	40%	24%	4%
2011	GB		60	91	782	66%	--	13.0	7				27.1%								

Finley attended the Packers' charity softball game in June but did not play. He said his knee was 100 percent, but there was no sense in taking risks. The Packers also held him out of early preseason action, though Finley said he could play if he had to. Finley had two 100-yard games before the knee injury and was the second option in the Packers' passing game. He enters camp as the first among a bunch of guys clamoring for passes after Greg Jennings gets his share: Jordy Nelson emerged in the second half, Donald Driver wants to reach the Hall of Fame, and so on. Assuming Mike McCarthy and Aaron Rodgers can keep everyone busy, Finley will be a backbreaker for defenses.

Antonio Gates

Height: 6-4   Weight: 260   College: Kent State   Draft: 2003/ (FA)   Born: 18-Jun-1980   Age: 31   Risk: Yellow

Year	Team	G	Rec	Pass	Yds	C%	+/-	Yd/C	TD	FUM	YAC	Rk	DVOA	Rk	DYAR	Rk	YAR	Short	Mid	Deep	Bomb
2008	SD	16	60	92	704	65%	7.0	11.7	8	1	3.7	31	15.5%	14	140	9	142	32%	50%	14%	4%
2009	SD	16	79	114	1157	69%	9.7	14.6	8	1	6.1	8	38.4%	2	358	1	356	43%	35%	16%	6%
2010	SD	10	50	65	782	77%	11.1	15.6	10	0	6.2	8	79.5%	1	371	1	370	43%	31%	25%	2%
2011	SD		77	109	1004	71%	--	13.0	10				33.6%								

The only way Gates could have been better in 2010 would have been to actually play the entire season; he blew opposing defenses away despite a foot injury (plantar fasciitis) that dogged him through the second half of the season and finally put him in injured reserve in mid-December. When he was healthy in the first half of the season ... forget about it. Gates was as uncoverable as any tight end in recent years, and this was especially impressive given the fact that he was Philip Rivers' only elite target during that time. Any pretense of his playing a traditional tight end role was gone; Gates used his size and intermediate speed to tower over cornerbacks as LeBron James would over so many high-school shlubs. When his targets were especially high in games against the Seahawks and Jaguars, Rivers didn't even look Gates off before throwing. No point in the exercise; everyone knew where the ball was going. In just ten games, Gates set the all-time DYAR record for tight ends, surpassing his own record which he set the year before. KUBIAK gives him the best projection for a tight end, yet again, and it still might be too low.

John Gilmore

Height: 6-4   Weight: 260   College: Penn State   Draft: 2002/6 (196)   Born: 21-Sep-1979   Age: 32   Risk: Green

Year	Team	G	Rec	Pass	Yds	C%	+/-	Yd/C	TD	FUM	YAC	Rk	DVOA	Rk	DYAR	Rk	YAR	Short	Mid	Deep	Bomb
2008	TB	16	15	21	147	71%	0.5	9.8	1	0	5.8	--	9.2%	--	24	--	22	75%	15%	10%	0%
2009	TB	13	3	7	23	43%	-0.5	7.7	0	0	5.0	--	-50.6%	--	-19	--	-19	40%	60%	0%	0%
2010	TB	16	13	18	160	72%	2.2	12.3	1	0	7.5	--	30.9%	--	47	--	47	67%	33%	0%	0%
2011	PIT		8	13	90	62%	--	11.2	1				-1.8%								

Primarily a blocker when the Bucs run two-tight end sets (which isn't very often), Gilmore has tried to get more targets through his career with the same kind of ardent fervor and lack of success that shadowed Lucy Ricardo through her acting/singing efforts. Whether he'll find his own Copa Club as Heath Miller's backup in Pittsburgh, or continue to be as misfit to his desires as Fred Mertz's English accent, remains to be seen.

Tony Gonzalez

Height: 6-5   Weight: 251   College: California   Draft: 1997/1 (13)   Born: 27-Feb-1976   Age: 35   Risk: Green

Year	Team	G	Rec	Pass	Yds	C%	+/-	Yd/C	TD	FUM	YAC	Rk	DVOA	Rk	DYAR	Rk	YAR	Short	Mid	Deep	Bomb
2008	KC	16	96	155	1058	62%	-0.4	11.0	10	0	2.6	40	16.5%	13	243	1	232	30%	57%	10%	3%
2009	ATL	16	83	134	867	62%	0.9	10.4	6	0	2.8	45	10.6%	16	161	9	142	29%	61%	9%	1%
2010	ATL	16	70	109	656	64%	0.3	9.4	6	0	2.7	43	2.2%	25	72	21	68	41%	49%	10%	1%
2011	ATL		67	95	665	71%	--	9.9	5				22.6%								

Just when you thought history's greatest tight end would keep churning out great seasons into the 2020s, last year came along to prove that even Gonzalez, despite his patented nutrition shakes and healthy diet, is vulnerable to age. It wasn't like Gonzalez fell off dramatically, like the drops in the seafloor at his beloved Manhattan Beach, but the slippage was noticeable pretty much across the board. The 2009 trade that brought Gonzalez to a city five hours from any decent beach was supposed to be about getting the Hall-of-Famer a shot at a Super Bowl, or at least a playoff win to his name. It still hasn't happened (Gonzalez caught all of one pass for seven yards in the playoff blowout against Green Bay). If the regular-season erosion and postseason futility continue in 2011, Gonzalez may decide that 15 seasons are enough and head back to Cali.

Daniel Graham

Height: 6-3   Weight: 257   College: Colorado   Draft: 2002/1 (21)   Born: 16-Nov-1978   Age: 33   Risk: Green

Year	Team	G	Rec	Pass	Yds	C%	+/-	Yd/C	TD	FUM	YAC	Rk	DVOA	Rk	DYAR	Rk	YAR	Short	Mid	Deep	Bomb
2008	DEN	16	32	50	389	64%	0.0	12.2	4	0	6.2	3	6.7%	19	48	20	60	48%	37%	11%	4%
2009	DEN	16	28	43	289	65%	0.1	10.3	1	0	7.1	2	-2.2%	29	13	30	11	65%	27%	8%	0%
2010	DEN	16	18	37	148	49%	-4.3	8.2	0	1	2.7	44	-60.7%	45	-133	45	-136	63%	25%	9%	3%
2011	TEN		12	20	113	60%	--	9.4	1				-18.9%								

Graham led the Broncos in tight end targets, which didn't mean much in Josh McDaniels' offense. The Broncos released Graham for salary reasons, and though Graham believes he can make an impact as a receiving tight end, his new role with the Tennessee Titans will be more as a pure blocker.

Jimmy Graham

Height: 6-6   Weight: 260   College: Miami   Draft: 2010/3 (95)   Born: 24-Nov-1986   Age: 25   Risk: Green

Year	Team	G	Rec	Pass	Yds	C%	+/-	Yd/C	TD	FUM	YAC	Rk	DVOA	Rk	DYAR	Rk	YAR	Short	Mid	Deep	Bomb
2010	NO	15	31	43	356	72%	3.9	11.5	5	1	4.5	26	24.8%	12	98	15	93	43%	38%	12%	7%
2011	NO		42	58	522	72%	--	12.4	6				27.2%								

Scouts have been drooling over Graham's potential since he decided to forego hoops and play football at Miami. Those "next Gates, next Gonzalez" whispers are heard whenever a basketball player manages to put his helmet on correctly, but in Graham's case they were legit. His rookie year was strong enough to bounce Jeremy Shockey — who actually was an All-American tight end in Coral Gables, unlike Graham — right out of New Orleans. Gates certainly prospered from playing with Drew Brees. Graham seems ready to do likewise.

Jermaine Gresham

Height: 6-5   Weight: 261   College: Oklahoma   Draft: 2010/1 (21)   Born: 16-Jun-1988   Age: 23   Risk: Yellow

Year	Team	G	Rec	Pass	Yds	C%	+/-	Yd/C	TD	FUM	YAC	Rk	DVOA	Rk	DYAR	Rk	YAR	Short	Mid	Deep	Bomb
2010	CIN	15	52	83	471	63%	-3.2	9.1	4	2	7.0	4	-13.0%	37	-33	38	-26	67%	28%	5%	0%
2011	CIN		51	79	544	65%	--	10.7	3				5.8%								

Gresham had about the usual rookie season you would expect from a first-round tight end. He led all rookie tight ends in catches, although he didn't run the downfield routes quite as often as some fans expected. Among tight ends with at least 25 passes, only Martellus Bennett ran a higher percentage of short routes than Gresham's 67 percent. The West Coast offense is big on medium-length routes and two-tight end sets, which would seem to suggest a nice big role for Gresham. They'll have to explain to Andy Dalton what a "tight end" is, though, since he didn't have one who caught more than six passes at TCU.

Rob Gronkowski

Height: 6-6   Weight: 264   College: Arizona   Draft: 2010/2 (42)   Born: 14-May-1989   Age: 22   Risk: Yellow

Year	Team	G	Rec	Pass	Yds	C%	+/-	Yd/C	TD	FUM	YAC	Rk	DVOA	Rk	DYAR	Rk	YAR	Short	Mid	Deep	Bomb
2010	NE	16	42	59	546	71%	5.4	13.0	10	1	4.4	28	53.3%	3	249	2	243	42%	33%	19%	5%
2011	NE		42	64	550	66%	--	13.1	6				26.9%								

Gronkowski on passes listed as "deep" in the official play-by-play: 16 targets, 12 catches, 263 yards (21.9 ypc), two touchdowns. These passes traveled an average of 20.7 yards in the air, so they truly were deep passes. Almost all of this production came from a two-tight end set, with both Gronkowski and Aaron Hernandez (or occasionally Alge Crumpler) on the same side of the formation. Gronkowski does not have outstanding deep speed, but the twin-tight end alignments forced most opponents to cover him with a linebacker or a safety in less-than-ideal position to chase him. Gronkowski is a very solid blocker with good hands and body control, but he is not the kind of player who should be open deep regularly, and defenses will find a way to limit the matchup problems the Hernandez-Gronkowski pairing provides. When that happens, the bombs may disappear, but Gronkowski will still be solid over the middle and in the red zone.

Todd Heap

Height: 6-5   Weight: 252   College: Arizona State   Draft: 2001/1 (31)   Born: 16-Mar-1980   Age: 31   Risk: Red

Year	Team	G	Rec	Pass	Yds	C%	+/-	Yd/C	TD	FUM	YAC	Rk	DVOA	Rk	DYAR	Rk	YAR	Short	Mid	Deep	Bomb
2008	BAL	16	35	64	403	55%	-2.6	11.5	3	1	5.1	10	4.2%	20	49	19	36	38%	40%	15%	7%
2009	BAL	16	53	75	593	71%	7.3	11.2	6	1	3.4	41	27.4%	4	170	7	172	43%	35%	18%	4%
2010	BAL	13	40	64	599	63%	1.5	15.0	5	1	5.6	12	25.9%	11	134	8	134	43%	30%	17%	10%
2011	ARI		44	67	500	66%	--	11.4	4				14.6%								

Todd Heap is an old-school tight end. Don't believe us? Compare the most similar three-year stretches to Heap's last three seasons, and you get a bunch of guys from the eighties: Rodney Holman, Steve Jordan, Pete Holohan, Riley Odoms, and Jay Novacek. Heap's yards-per-catch number for 2010 is somewhat skewed by a single 65-yard touchdown against Tampa Bay, more yards than Heap had in 41 of his 45 games over the last three seasons.

Aaron Hernandez

Height: 6-3   Weight: 245   College: Florida   Draft: 2010/4 (113)   Born: 6-Nov-1989   Age: 22   Risk: Green

Year	Team	G	Rec	Pass	Yds	C%	+/-	Yd/C	TD	FUM	YAC	Rk	DVOA	Rk	DYAR	Rk	YAR	Short	Mid	Deep	Bomb
2010	NE	14	45	64	563	70%	1.3	12.5	6	0	6.5	7	30.9%	7	160	5	162	50%	39%	11%	0%
2011	NE		31	47	414	66%	--	13.4	3				23.5%								

Hernandez was targeted eight times in empty backfield formations in the first six weeks of the season, catching six passes for 66 yards. He was targeted just four times in an empty backfield formation for the rest of the year, as his role diminished somewhat and the Patriots moved away from such tactics … Hernandez was on his way to Rookie of the Year consideration before he got a case of the dropsies. He dropped two passes against the Ravens, a short pass against the Browns, and finally a screen against the Steelers before Bill Belichick said "enough's enough" and gave Hernandez fewer snaps for about a month. Hernandez rebounded for 9-101-3 in his final three games, so the crisis has passed. But like so many other Patriots weapons, Hernandez can disappear for weeks at a time, based on the vagaries of the game plan or weaknesses of the opponent.

Michael Hoomanawanui

Height: 6-4   Weight: 264   College: Illinois   Draft: 2010/5 (132)   Born: 4-Jul-1988   Age: 23   Risk: Red

Year	Team	G	Rec	Pass	Yds	C%	+/-	Yd/C	TD	FUM	YAC	Rk	DVOA	Rk	DYAR	Rk	YAR	Short	Mid	Deep	Bomb
2010	STL	8	13	22	146	59%	-1.2	11.2	3	0	7.9	--	1.1%	--	13	--	20	85%	0%	15%	0%
2011	STL		40	64	427	63%	--	10.7	3				1.0%								

A pair of high ankle sprains limited the fifth-round pick out of Illinois to just eight games in his rookie season. An ankle injury also bothered him throughout his senior season in college, which should raise some flags about his durability. When healthy, Hoomanawanui is a solid blocker with deceptive speed, above average hands, and the power and agility to gain yards after the catch. First-year Rams offensive coordinator Josh McDaniels should be familiar with what Hoomanawanui is capable of. In McDaniels' final home game as the Denver Broncos head coach, Hoomanawanui took a tight end screen pass 36 yards for a touchdown. During the player-run lockout workouts, Hoomanawanui likened the tight end usage in the Rams' new offense to how the New England Patriots used their tight ends. If that's the case, and he's able to stay healthy, Hoomanawanui's size and skill-set project him to the "Rob Gronkowski" role as the team's No. 1 tight end.

Rob Housler

Height: 6-6   Weight: 249   College: Florida Atlantic   Draft: 2011/3 (69)   Born: 17-Mar-1988   Age: 23   Risk: Green

Year	Team	G	Rec	Pass	Yds	C%	+/-	Yd/C	TD	FUM	YAC	Rk	DVOA	Rk	DYAR	Rk	YAR	Short	Mid	Deep	Bomb
2011	ARI		18	26	166	69%	--	9.2	0				8.5%								

A great athlete for his position, Housler broke off a 68-yard touchdown run for Florida Atlantic against arch-rival Florida International in 2007, and he ran a sub-4.6 40 at the combine. He slowly turned himself from a 210-pound receiver into an actual tight end through the years, redshirting in 2009 to bulk up. After two seasons of nothingness (seven receptions and 80 yards in 23 targets in 2006-07), he exploded in the seasons surrounding the redshirt. He caught 32 passes for 519 yards in 2008, then 38 passes for 626 yards as a senior. The problem is that if he isn't an elite receiver, he has little chance of contributing on offense. At best he is an inexperienced blocker; at worst he is ineffective with no interest in engaging anyone. That will have to change.

Dustin Keller

Height: 6-2   Weight: 242   College: Purdue   Draft: 2008/1 (30)   Born: 25-Sep-1984   Age: 27   Risk: Green

Year	Team	G	Rec	Pass	Yds	C%	+/-	Yd/C	TD	FUM	YAC	Rk	DVOA	Rk	DYAR	Rk	YAR	Short	Mid	Deep	Bomb
2008	NYJ	16	48	78	535	62%	-1.1	11.1	3	0	3.5	33	2.3%	21	55	18	68	50%	31%	13%	6%
2009	NYJ	16	45	81	522	56%	-6.1	11.6	2	1	3.9	32	-4.2%	30	16	29	14	38%	41%	19%	2%
2010	NYJ	16	55	100	687	55%	-4.1	12.5	5	0	3.9	35	-1.6%	29	38	27	35	41%	40%	15%	3%
2011	NYJ		54	88	669	61%	--	12.4	5				12.0%								

Keller has the athleticism to be one of the top receiving tight ends in the NFL, and there are games where he rips up every coverage scheme a defense throws against him. He torched the Patriots in Week 2 with a seven-catch, 115-yard performance, including one touchdown reception, and then followed it up the next week in Miami with six catches for 98 yards and two touchdowns. But Keller did not catch more than four balls again until Week 15, and he too frequently failed to make much impact when he did see the ball. Moreover, while Keller would seem to be the perfect security blanket for a young quarterback, he has struggled in the role, catching only 44 percent of the passes directed at him on third down and posting a -16.2% DVOA. The talent is certainly there, and if Brian Schottenheimer made a conscious effort to have the passing offense go through Keller, he might put up Dallas Clark-type numbers. As it is, Keller has to share the ball with too many other receiving options on a team that doesn't throw the ball all that much, which means he's a risky play as an every-week start.

Lance Kendricks

Height: 6-3   Weight: 243   College: Wisconsin   Draft: 2011/2 (47)   Born: 30-Jan-1988   Age: 23   Risk: Yellow

Year	Team	G	Rec	Pass	Yds	C%	+/-	Yd/C	TD	FUM	YAC	Rk	DVOA	Rk	DYAR	Rk	YAR	Short	Mid	Deep	Bomb
2011	STL		30	50	319	60%	--	10.6	2				1.0%								

With Michael Hoomanawanui drawing comparisons to Rob Gronkowski, the selection of Kendricks in the second round invited the "And now Josh McDaniels has his Aaron Hernandez" comments from draft analysts. When Travis Beckum got hurt in 2009, Kendricks distinguished himself with 29 catches for 356 yards and, despite some drops, a 73 percent catch rate. As the main man in 2010, he was even better. He caught 43 of 54 passes thrown his way (an 80 percent catch rate) for 663 yards. He is an eager, strong blocker, though he truly is small for the position (he's a converted wideout). McDaniels will use the versatile Kendricks in a variety of ways to create mismatches with linebackers and safeties, and, like the Patriots did with Hernandez, will use him on the occasional reverse.

Jeff King

Height: 6-5   Weight: 250   College: Virginia Tech   Draft: 2006/5 (155)   Born: 19-Feb-1983   Age: 28   Risk: Green

Year	Team	G	Rec	Pass	Yds	C%	+/-	Yd/C	TD	FUM	YAC	Rk	DVOA	Rk	DYAR	Rk	YAR	Short	Mid	Deep	Bomb
2008	CAR	16	21	34	195	62%	0.3	9.3	1	0	3.8	28	-10.7%	31	-7	30	-12	60%	23%	17%	0%
2009	CAR	16	25	33	200	76%	2.1	8.0	3	1	2.5	47	1.8%	25	21	27	22	61%	30%	3%	6%
2010	CAR	16	19	31	121	61%	-0.4	6.4	2	0	1.8	45	-17.6%	40	-23	37	-26	59%	41%	0%	0%
2011	ARI		9	12	60	75%	--	6.7	1				-19.7%								

King was primarily used as a blocker in Carolina and that doesn't figure to change in Arizona. With his targets decreasing in each of the last four seasons, it's best to consider King's value as an ancillary lineman who will shoot off blocks into the seam at times. How much we see of him depends on how much Ken Whisenhunt wants to change his offensive strategies with King, Todd Heap, and Rob Housler around; the last couple years, the Cardinals have rarely gone with two-tight end sets outside of short-yardage situations.

Jim Kleinsasser

Height: 6-3   Weight: 272   College: North Dakota   Draft: 1999/2 (44)   Born: 31-Jan-1977   Age: 34   Risk: Green

Year	Team	G	Rec	Pass	Yds	C%	+/-	Yd/C	TD	FUM	YAC	Rk	DVOA	Rk	DYAR	Rk	YAR	Short	Mid	Deep	Bomb
2008	MIN	16	6	13	92	46%	-0.4	15.3	0	0	7.0	--	-2.0%	--	4	--	3	36%	27%	36%	0%
2009	MIN	16	10	16	70	63%	-0.7	7.0	0	0	2.8	--	-42.0%	--	-37	--	-37	73%	13%	13%	0%
2010	MIN	16	17	20	148	85%	3.7	8.7	0	0	4.6	--	8.1%	--	19	--	22	67%	28%	6%	0%
2011	MIN		5	9	39	56%	--	7.9	0				-22.6%								

Kleinsasser is now 34 and will earn $3 million this season. Kleinsasser's ability to handle outside linebackers in pass protection extended his career, but rookie Kyle Rudolph will take away many of his snaps.

Marcedes Lewis

Height: 6-6   Weight: 255   College: UCLA   Draft: 2006/1 (28)   Born: 19-May-1984   Age: 27   Risk: Green

Year	Team	G	Rec	Pass	Yds	C%	+/-	Yd/C	TD	FUM	YAC	Rk	DVOA	Rk	DYAR	Rk	YAR	Short	Mid	Deep	Bomb
2008	JAC	16	41	73	489	56%	-1.6	11.9	2	0	3.7	30	-4.6%	27	13	27	3	36%	44%	17%	3%
2009	JAC	15	32	59	518	54%	-1.9	16.2	2	1	5.2	19	4.3%	23	44	21	44	35%	22%	39%	4%
2010	JAC	16	58	88	700	66%	1.2	12.1	10	2	4.5	25	13.0%	18	124	11	132	58%	26%	14%	1%
2011	JAC		52	78	620	67%	--	11.9	4				8.8%								

With the release of Torry Holt and the majority of their NFL Draft efforts going towards fixing the defense, the Jaguars were forced to incorporate Lewis into the short passing game more last season. He responded by having his best season to date, becoming a respectable goal-line threat, and even blocking at a higher level. As long as the Jaguars continue to stall on solutions at wide receiver, Lewis can add "credible fantasy option" to a resume that probably sees him as one of the top ten all-around tight ends in the NFL.

Randy McMichael Height: 6-3 Weight: 250 College: Georgia Draft: 2002/4 (114) Born: 28-Jun-1979 Age: 32 Risk: Green

Year	Team	G	Rec	Pass	Yds	C%	+/-	Yd/C	TD	FUM	YAC	Rk	DVOA	Rk	DYAR	Rk	YAR	Short	Mid	Deep	Bomb
2008	STL	4	11	21	139	52%	-1.3	12.6	0	0	6.0	--	-2.2%	--	6	--	3	32%	42%	21%	5%
2009	STL	16	34	62	332	55%	-7.2	9.8	1	0	4.1	30	-18.4%	38	-46	43	-50	45%	43%	12%	0%
2010	SD	16	20	27	221	74%	2.2	11.1	2	0	4.2	31	31.2%	6	69	22	72	38%	50%	12%	0%
2011	SD		26	44	293	59%	--	11.3	1				5.4%								

In 2010, McMichael's primary role was to suck up targets after Antonio Gates got hurt. He's primarily a stationary target at this point in his career, but he's still a smart player with good hands who was especially effective on third down. He re-signed with San Diego after the lockout.

Heath Miller Height: 6-5 Weight: 256 College: Virginia Draft: 2005/1 (30) Born: 22-Oct-1982 Age: 29 Risk: Green

Year	Team	G	Rec	Pass	Yds	C%	+/-	Yd/C	TD	FUM	YAC	Rk	DVOA	Rk	DYAR	Rk	YAR	Short	Mid	Deep	Bomb
2008	PIT	14	48	66	514	73%	2.5	10.7	3	1	4.8	13	20.8%	8	116	12	115	58%	33%	9%	0%
2009	PIT	16	76	98	789	78%	11.4	10.4	6	2	5.6	11	18.1%	12	163	8	165	61%	30%	9%	0%
2010	PIT	14	42	67	512	63%	0.0	12.2	2	1	5.4	14	1.0%	27	36	28	42	38%	43%	16%	3%
2011	PIT		43	66	561	65%	--	13.1	6				23.5%								

Miller's higher fantasy numbers in 2009 were a bit of an aberration, and in 2010 he had a season much closer to his career averages. His lower advanced stats in 2010 are also a bit of an aberration, the worst DYAR and DVOA of his career. His lower catch rate was caused in large part by the decision to use him less often on short routes of five yards or less. The drop has nothing to do with Ben Roethlisberger's suspension, as Miller had roughly the same DVOA and catch rate both before and after Roethlisberger's return.

Zach Miller Height: 6-5 Weight: 256 College: Arizona State Draft: 2007/2 (38) Born: 11-Dec-1985 Age: 26 Risk: Yellow

Year	Team	G	Rec	Pass	Yds	C%	+/-	Yd/C	TD	FUM	YAC	Rk	DVOA	Rk	DYAR	Rk	YAR	Short	Mid	Deep	Bomb
2008	OAK	16	56	86	778	65%	2.2	13.9	1	0	4.3	21	9.2%	16	92	15	103	40%	35%	21%	4%
2009	OAK	15	66	99	805	67%	5.8	12.2	3	0	5.6	10	5.8%	21	82	18	96	41%	36%	20%	3%
2010	OAK	15	20	92	216	65%	-0.2	10.8	1	1	4.6	24	6.2%	22	81	19	99	55%	31%	13%	0%
2011	SEA		59	90	724	66%	--	12.3	4				9.3%								

Oakland's 2010 offense didn't fit the usual Raider clichés. They ran more often than you'd ever expect, and a tight end was Jason Campbell's primary target. While Oakland's receivers generally struggled with consistency, Miller kept the passing offense together on a game-to-game basis. Slants and flat patters were generally the order of the day, with Miller frequently getting yards after the catch in the fashion of the West Coast offense Jon Gruden ran with the Raiders a decade ago. Though the Raiders tried to bring Miller back, the free agent followed Tom Cable to Seattle and signed a huge five-year deal. Oakland's offense will struggle without its former centerpiece.

Zach Miller Height: 6-4 Weight: 233 College: Nebraska-Omaha Draft: 2009/6 (180) Born: 4-Oct-1984 Age: 27 Risk: Green

Year	Team	G	Rec	Pass	Yds	C%	+/-	Yd/C	TD	FUM	YAC	Rk	DVOA	Rk	DYAR	Rk	YAR	Short	Mid	Deep	Bomb
2009	JAC	14	21	27	212	78%	1.6	10.1	2	0	6.9	4	11.9%	14	36	23	45	59%	37%	4%	0%
2010	JAC	15	20	26	216	77%	3.8	10.8	1	0	4.9	19	19.1%	14	44	25	49	42%	42%	17%	0%
2011	JAC		25	39	269	64%	--	10.7	1				0.3%								

75 percent of Miller's DYAR came on first downs, a good number of which involved him as a play-action underneath receiver. He's a sure-handed cog that has a place in a productive offense, and the Jaguars utilized many motion sets that shuffled him in and out of the backfield. He'll always be known as The Other Zach Miller, but he's got the skills to hang in this niche for awhile.

Tony Moeaki

Height: 6-3   Weight: 245   College: Iowa   Draft: 2010/3 (93)   Born: 8-Jun-1987   Age: 24   Risk: Yellow

Year	Team	G	Rec	Pass	Yds	C%	+/-	Yd/C	TD	FUM	YAC	Rk	DVOA	Rk	DYAR	Rk	YAR	Short	Mid	Deep	Bomb
2010	KC	15	47	72	556	65%	3.9	11.8	3	0	4.0	33	13.9%	17	98	14	97	36%	48%	14%	2%
2011	KC		58	92	708	63%	--	12.2	3				15.2%								

Dwayne Bowe's best complementary receiver turned out to be a rookie tight end. Injuries kept Moeaki under the radar at Iowa, but there were no such issues when he hit the field for the Chiefs, because he became one of Matt Cassel's targets very early on. Through the season, Moeaki was Cassel's main escape hatch on all kinds of routes — quick slants out of tight end stacks, quick release stuff out of bunch, and zone-busters out of the flex position. And unless Kansas City's offense suddenly becomes a great deal more explosive in the passing game (hint: don't bet on it), Moeaki should get many more opportunities as Cassel's security blanket.

Evan Moore

Height: 6-6   Weight: 247   College: Stanford   Draft: 2008/ (FA)   Born: 3-Jan-1985   Age: 27   Risk: Green

Year	Team	G	Rec	Pass	Yds	C%	+/-	Yd/C	TD	FUM	YAC	Rk	DVOA	Rk	DYAR	Rk	YAR	Short	Mid	Deep	Bomb
2009	CLE	5	12	23	158	52%	-1.3	13.2	0	0	5.4	--	-2.0%	--	7	--	9	23%	50%	27%	0%
2010	CLE	12	16	26	322	62%	1.9	20.1	1	1	5.6	11	41.4%	4	83	17	80	32%	24%	24%	20%
2011	CLE		23	31	245	74%	--	10.7	3				21.2%								

Finally, we have a tight end who is even less of a tight end than Dallas Clark is. Of course, that makes sense, since he was a wide receiver at Stanford. (He was teammates with our very own Ben Muth, and Trent Edwards' BFF.) Moore rarely lines up tight, and he runs deep routes far more often than other players who are nominally tight ends. Moore ran Deep or Bomb routes 44 percent of the time — no other tight end with at least ten passes was over 33 percent. When you run deeper routes than everyone else at your "position," and you catch a couple more balls than usual with a small sample size, you're going to end up with sweet numbers like Moore had last year. Don't get too hung up on him, he's not the next Antonio Gates. But he is a useful piece of the puzzle.

Brandon Myers

Height: 6-4   Weight: 250   College: Iowa   Draft: 2009/6 (202)   Born: 4-Sep-1985   Age: 26   Risk: Red

Year	Team	G	Rec	Pass	Yds	C%	+/-	Yd/C	TD	FUM	YAC	Rk	DVOA	Rk	DYAR	Rk	YAR	Short	Mid	Deep	Bomb
2009	OAK	11	4	6	19	67%	-0.3	4.8	0	0	3.8	--	-60.0%	--	-18	--	-18	67%	17%	17%	0%
2010	OAK	15	12	16	80	75%	0.8	6.7	0	0	3.2	--	-19.5%	--	-13	--	-16	75%	25%	0%	0%
2011	OAK		18	30	168	60%	--	9.3	1				-28.8%								

Brought on as a blocking tight end, Myers impressed in his first training camp and has disappeared to a large degree ever since. Like every other tight end on the roster, he'll get more targets with Zach Miller gone.

Greg Olsen

Height: 6-6   Weight: 254   College: Miami   Draft: 2007/1 (31)   Born: 11-Mar-1985   Age: 26   Risk: Green

Year	Team	G	Rec	Pass	Yds	C%	+/-	Yd/C	TD	FUM	YAC	Rk	DVOA	Rk	DYAR	Rk	YAR	Short	Mid	Deep	Bomb
2008	CHI	16	54	82	574	66%	2.3	10.6	5	2	4.6	17	0.0%	24	41	22	48	62%	24%	11%	4%
2009	CHI	16	60	108	612	56%	-5.1	10.2	8	0	2.9	44	-9.0%	32	-13	33	-10	47%	28%	19%	6%
2010	CHI	16	41	70	404	59%	0.3	9.9	5	2	3.8	36	-15.0%	39	-36	41	-27	44%	32%	21%	3%
2011	CAR		40	72	518	56%	--	13.0	4				-0.2%								

Olsen lined up at fullback 101 times and at wide receiver 41 times according to our game charters; we don't consider a tight end a "wide receiver" when he is flexed or in the slot, where Olsen lined up at least 50 other times. That versatility will be a boon to the Panthers, who don't have a lot of talent anywhere but at running back and need an all-purpose blocker-receiver. If the Panthers incorporate a lot of Cam Newton shotgun creativity into their offense, Olsen could prove invaluable as a point-of-attack blocker on quarterback draws or "choice" plays. That won't help his fantasy value much, but you probably gave up on Olsen as a fantasy threat the moment Mike Martz materialized on the Bears sideline.

Brandon Pettigrew

Height: 6-6   Weight: 263 College: Oklahoma State Draft: 2009/1 (20) Born: 23-Feb-1985 Age: 26 Risk: Green

Year	Team	G	Rec	Pass	Yds	C%	+/-	Yd/C	TD	FUM	YAC	Rk	DVOA	Rk	DYAR	Rk	YAR	Short	Mid	Deep	Bomb
2009	DET	11	30	54	346	56%	-4.8	11.5	2	1	6.3	6	-11.6%	33	-15	35	-7	45%	43%	10%	2%
2010	DET	16	71	111	722	64%	-2.9	10.2	4	0	4.9	18	3.2%	24	74	20	72	61%	31%	8%	1%
2011	DET		54	93	673	58%	--	12.5	3				9.0%								

The Lions threw 11 tight end screens to Pettigrew. He caught nine of them for 72 yards, although the last four netted a total of just one yard, suggesting that opponents had caught on to the play. Shaun Hill threw most of the screens, which makes sense because it takes experience to not telegraph the play. Pettigrew is a matchup nightmare against linebackers and did a fine job as the de-facto possession receiver last season. He will be more effective with Titus Young around to help Calvin Johnson occupy the safeties, but he probably will not see 111 targets again in his career.

Dennis Pitta

Height: 6-5   Weight: 245 College: BYU   Draft: 2010/4 (114) Born: 29-Jun-1985 Age: 26 Risk: Green

Year	Team	G	Rec	Pass	Yds	C%	+/-	Yd/C	TD	FUM	YAC	Rk	DVOA	Rk	DYAR	Rk	YAR	Short	Mid	Deep	Bomb
2010	BAL	11	1	5	1	20%	-1.9	1.0	0	0	0.0	--	-65.8%	--	-23	--	-23	20%	20%	60%	0%
2011	BAL		19	29	240	66%	--	12.6	1				-2.9%								

This 2010 fourth-round pick out of BYU is an athletic, receiving-first tight end, a slightly thinner version of Dallas Clark with excellent hands and acceleration. If the Ravens go with two-tight end sets, he's more likely to go out on a route with Dickson blocking. It's not hard to imagine Pitta leap-frogging Dickson as one of Joe Flacco's favored targets, even if Dickson is the nominal starter.

Andrew Quarless

Height: 6-5   Weight: 254 College: Penn State   Draft: 2010/5 (154) Born: 6-Oct-1988 Age: 23 Risk: Green

Year	Team	G	Rec	Pass	Yds	C%	+/-	Yd/C	TD	FUM	YAC	Rk	DVOA	Rk	DYAR	Rk	YAR	Short	Mid	Deep	Bomb
2010	GB	13	21	33	238	64%	0.3	11.3	1	1	5.3	15	-2.1%	30	12	31	13	45%	42%	6%	6%
2011	GB		18	24	215	75%	--	11.9	2				20.8%								

Quarless caught four passes for 51 yards after Jermichael Finley got hurt against the Redskins, then settled into a two-target per game role once Mike McCarthy had time to scale back the tight end's role in the offense. Quarless is a pass-catching tight end on a team overflowing with receiving options, so it's hard to project him with a large role.

Dante Rosario

Height: 6-3   Weight: 244 College: Oregon   Draft: 2007/5 (155) Born: 25-Oct-1984 Age: 27 Risk: Green

Year	Team	G	Rec	Pass	Yds	C%	+/-	Yd/C	TD	FUM	YAC	Rk	DVOA	Rk	DYAR	Rk	YAR	Short	Mid	Deep	Bomb
2008	CAR	16	18	31	209	58%	-1.6	11.6	1	0	3.3	35	-0.9%	26	13	26	21	27%	57%	13%	3%
2009	CAR	14	26	48	313	54%	-2.9	12.0	2	0	5.0	22	-0.3%	28	21	26	25	42%	42%	13%	2%
2010	CAR	16	32	58	264	55%	-5.8	8.3	0	0	4.3	29	-28.6%	43	-79	43	-91	62%	27%	7%	4%
2011	DEN		21	34	229	62%	--	10.9	1				0.2%								

You can thank the Panthers quarterbacks for that huge drop in DVOA last year. Rosario comes to Denver and is reunited with his old coach John Fox, which is somewhat interesting because Rosario is a receiving-first tight end in a distinctly run-oriented offense. He'll play a lot as an H-back, or "move" tight end.

Kyle Rudolph

Height: 6-6   Weight: 265 College: Notre Dame   Draft: 2011/2 (43) Born: 9-Nov-1989 Age: 22 Risk: Yellow

Year	Team	G	Rec	Pass	Yds	C%	+/-	Yd/C	TD	FUM	YAC	Rk	DVOA	Rk	DYAR	Rk	YAR	Short	Mid	Deep	Bomb
2011	MIN		32	51	328	63%	--	10.2	2				10.6%								

A hard-working injury case at a position of less-than-immediate need, Rudolph was an odd second-round choice for the Vikings. He is a fine all-purpose tight end when healthy, but shoulder and hamstring injuries plagued him at Notre Dame and sapped him of his speed in his final season. Rudolph's blocking and usefulness as a safety valve receiver will help the Vikings run the football and develop Christian Ponder in 2011, but the team left a lot of needs unfilled while stacking themselves at tight end. But then, once you risk your first-round pick on an injury-prone "effort" guy at quarterback, you might as well complete the set.

Bo Scaife

Height: 6-3   Weight: 249   College: Texas   Draft: 2005/6 (179)   Born: 6-Jan-1981   Age: 31   Risk: Blue

Year	Team	G	Rec	Pass	Yds	C%	+/-	Yd/C	TD	FUM	YAC	Rk	DVOA	Rk	DYAR	Rk	YAR	Short	Mid	Deep	Bomb
2008	TEN	16	58	84	561	69%	4.5	9.7	2	1	5.9	6	-0.4%	25	39	23	40	67%	24%	6%	3%
2009	TEN	14	45	70	440	64%	2.0	9.8	1	1	4.3	26	-13.3%	35	-28	39	-28	53%	34%	11%	2%
2010	TEN	14	36	52	318	69%	1.6	8.8	4	2	2.9	42	-11.0%	36	-13	36	-16	58%	28%	14%	0%
2011	CIN		9	14	81	64%	--	9.0	0					-2.0%								

For the first time in his career, Bo Scaife was a good target in the red zone in 2010, ranking second among all Titans pass-catchers with a 37.5% DVOA. He also caught 15 of the 17 passes thrown his way on third down. Unfortunately, Scaife was also a reason for Chris Johnson's lack of success in 2010. Opponents set the edge successfully against Scaife, and after Robert Ayers abused him in Week 4, Scaife tended to play largely in multiple-tight end sets and obvious passing situations. After paying him over $9 million the last two seasons, the Titans will let Scaife find his way in free agency. He signed with Cincinnati for just $1 million, and you won't see much of him unless Jermaine Gresham or Chase Coffman gets hurt.

Tony Scheffler

Height: 6-5   Weight: 255   College: Western Michigan   Draft: 2006/2 (61)   Born: 15-Feb-1983   Age: 28   Risk: Red

Year	Team	G	Rec	Pass	Yds	C%	+/-	Yd/C	TD	FUM	YAC	Rk	DVOA	Rk	DYAR	Rk	YAR	Short	Mid	Deep	Bomb
2008	DEN	13	40	62	645	66%	4.9	16.1	3	1	5.0	12	22.1%	6	123	11	133	32%	30%	32%	7%
2009	DEN	15	31	50	416	62%	1.2	13.4	2	0	5.6	12	18.7%	11	90	16	84	34%	47%	13%	6%
2010	DET	15	45	72	378	63%	0.1	8.4	1	1	3.3	40	-14.9%	38	-35	40	-35	55%	38%	5%	3%
2011	DET		40	68	496	59%	--	12.4	1					7.3%								

The Lions spent a lot last season trying to hide the fact that they lacked a true No. 2 receiver or No. 1 running back. That required Scheffler to work overtime. The Lions used two-tight end personnel groupings often, with Scheffler as a flex receiver, and he caught a lot of five-yard passes that did not amount to much. Brandon Pettigrew is a better overall tight end, and the Lions have far more weapons this year, so Scheffler's role may decrease.

Visanthe Shiancoe

Height: 6-4   Weight: 250   College: Morgan State   Draft: 2003/3 (91)   Born: 18-Jun-1980   Age: 31   Risk: Red

Year	Team	G	Rec	Pass	Yds	C%	+/-	Yd/C	TD	FUM	YAC	Rk	DVOA	Rk	DYAR	Rk	YAR	Short	Mid	Deep	Bomb
2008	MIN	16	42	59	596	71%	6.4	14.2	7	0	4.3	20	50.3%	2	221	2	215	26%	46%	25%	4%
2009	MIN	16	56	79	566	71%	4.3	10.1	11	0	3.6	37	33.7%	3	226	3	228	53%	29%	17%	1%
2010	MIN	16	47	79	530	59%	-2.4	11.3	2	0	3.7	37	-6.1%	33	6	33	1	39%	41%	16%	4%
2011	MIN		54	82	607	66%	--	11.2	4					17.0%								

Shiancoe tied for the NFL lead with 15 penalties, the first skill player in our penalties database (going back to 1997) to top the league. He drew seven False Starts, three Offensive Holds, two Offensive Pass Interference, an Illegal Shift, an Illegal Formation, and one of those ridiculous Delay of Game penalties for not handing the ball right back to an official after a catch ... Shiancoe was 6-of-12 for 151 yards on passes labeled "deep middle" in the play-by-play. Brett Favre always threw a heck of a seam pass, and he hit Shiancoe for two 33 yarders last year, plus a 25-yarder and three 20-yarders. Shiancoe did not catch any deep middle passes from Tweedle Dee or Dum ... Shiancoe spent a lot of lockout time playing video games. He Tweeted for Call of Duty opponents a few times, and he talked about gaming with Complex magazine, expressing his love for games like SOCOM and the Metroid series. Some players date models or American Idol singers; with Shiancoe and Chris Kluwe in the fold, the Vikings may be the only team with more than one player willing to troll E3 looking to pick up Zero Suit Samus.

Jeremy Shockey Height: 6-5 Weight: 253 College: Miami Draft: 2002/1 (14) Born: 18-Aug-1980 Age: 31 Risk: Yellow

Year	Team	G	Rec	Pass	Yds	C%	+/-	Yd/C	TD	FUM	YAC	Rk	DVOA	Rk	DYAR	Rk	YAR	Short	Mid	Deep	Bomb
2008	NO	12	50	72	486	69%	1.6	9.7	0	2	4.2	23	-5.0%	28	11	28	14	50%	34%	16%	0%
2009	NO	13	48	67	569	72%	5.8	11.9	3	0	2.7	46	23.4%	7	136	12	144	31%	52%	17%	0%
2010	NO	13	41	59	408	69%	4.2	10.0	3	0	3.0	41	8.7%	21	65	23	71	38%	48%	13%	2%
2011	CAR		36	62	428	58%	--	11.9	1				8.5%								

Despite a laundry list of injuries, Shockey remains a quality tight end. His catch rate and YAC were stable and stellar, and while his targets were down with wunderkind Jimmy Graham around, Shockey made most of the plays asked of him. It seems like yesterday when Shockey was the young turk calling Bill Parcells off-color names and creating athletic mismatches with linebackers and safeties. Now it is Shockey who was expendable in New Orleans thanks to the new young thing. Shock signed with division rival Carolina before the lockout hit, choosing the Cats over the Fish (Miami). The reason appears to be a reunion with new offensive coordinator Rob Chudzinski, who was Shockey's position coach at The U. Ever honest, Shockey noted in the spring, "That was ten years and several collisions ago." Cam Newton was effective throwing to his tight ends at Auburn, but it remains to be seen how much Shockey will miss Drew Brees.

Luke Stocker Height: 6-5 Weight: 258 College: Tennessee Draft: 2011/4 (104) Born: 17-Jul-1988 Age: 23 Risk: Yellow

Year	Team	G	Rec	Pass	Yds	C%	+/-	Yd/C	TD	FUM	YAC	Rk	DVOA	Rk	DYAR	Rk	YAR	Short	Mid	Deep	Bomb
2011	TB		24	40	242	60%	--	10.1	2				-1.5%								

A big, tough target who resembles an embryonic Jason Witten, Stocker proved his mettle during Senior Bowl practice week, when Alabama quarterback Greg McElroy threw him into a gruesome sandwich hit by two flying defensive backs. Stocker stood up, brushed himself off, and ran back to the huddle as if nothing had happened. Surprisingly for his size, he's more a pure pass-catcher than a prototype blocker, and he'll certainly have to brush up on that skill before he sees a lot of action. Preseason reps could bring out his considerable potential.

Jonathan Stupar Height: 6-3 Weight: 254 College: Virginia Draft: 2008/ (FA) Born: 24-Jul-1984 Age: 27 Risk: Blue

Year	Team	G	Rec	Pass	Yds	C%	+/-	Yd/C	TD	FUM	YAC	Rk	DVOA	Rk	DYAR	Rk	YAR	Short	Mid	Deep	Bomb
2009	BUF	14	6	11	40	55%	-2.6	6.7	0	0	7.2	--	-36.7%	--	-20	--	-21	91%	0%	9%	0%
2010	BUF	16	12	13	111	92%	2.7	9.3	0	1	7.1	--	-0.9%	--	5	--	4	83%	17%	0%	0%
2011	BAL		6	10	62	60%	--	10.3	1				-7.9%								

The final nine of the 13 passes thrown to Stupar last year were marked as "short left" in the official play-by-play. Nearly all of them occurred on second-and-long, with some third-and-15 sprinkled in. One catch-and-run netted 35 unlikely yards, as a Browns safety tried to tackle the ball instead of Stupar and failed, but most receptions were of the three-to-eight yard variety, with Brian Brohm managing to throw an interception on what should be an incredibly simple pass (to be fair, Jason Taylor brushed Brohm's arm as he threw). As specialized roles go, this is as specialized as they come: if you need a tight end to catch one pass in the left flat per game for seven yards on second-and-12, Stupar is your man.

Jacob Tamme

Height: 6-3   Weight: 236   College: Kentucky   Draft: 2008/4 (127)   Born: 15-Mar-1985   Age: 26   Risk: Green

Year	Team	G	Rec	Pass	Yds	C%	+/-	Yd/C	TD	FUM	YAC	Rk	DVOA	Rk	DYAR	Rk	YAR	Short	Mid	Deep	Bomb
2008	IND	12	3	5	12	60%	0.1	4.0	0	0	1.7	--	-54.1%	--	-17	--	-20	100%	0%	0%	0%
2009	IND	16	3	10	35	30%	-2.7	11.7	0	0	4.0	--	-37.5%	--	-19	--	-23	22%	56%	22%	0%
2010	IND	16	67	93	631	72%	5.2	9.4	4	0	4.6	23	12.6%	19	124	10	130	56%	30%	11%	3%
2011	IND		35	50	437	70%	--	12.5	3				25.1%								

The Colts were not sure they had a serviceable second tight end before the season started. After Dallas Clark got injured, Tamme became the primary tight end. Before he took over in Week 7, he had zero catches on the season and only six for his career. Over the last ten weeks of the season, Tamme had a remarkable 67 catches. For his efforts, Tamme ranked tenth in the league in DYAR. Still, while Tamme has good hands, he lacks downfield speed and does not present the match-up problems that Clark does. Also, Tamme never forced teams to move to nickel and dime packages, which hurt the running backs. Tamme's emergence, however, gives the Colts an additional weapon. When he's the fifth option on the field, he should be the beneficiary of easy match-ups and gain crucial first downs for the Colts.

David Thomas

Height: 6-3   Weight: 240   College: Texas   Draft: 2006/3 (86)   Born: 5-Jul-1983   Age: 28   Risk: Green

Year	Team	G	Rec	Pass	Yds	C%	+/-	Yd/C	TD	FUM	YAC	Rk	DVOA	Rk	DYAR	Rk	YAR	Short	Mid	Deep	Bomb
2008	NE	15	9	17	93	53%	-1.9	10.3	0	0	4.9	--	-22.6%	--	-18	--	-16	38%	50%	13%	0%
2009	NO	15	35	48	356	73%	4.3	10.2	1	0	5.3	16	6.9%	20	48	19	53	65%	26%	7%	2%
2010	NO	13	9	46	93	65%	-0.4	10.3	0	0	4.4	27	-18.3%	41	-35	39	-35	67%	26%	7%	2%
2011	NO		23	33	246	70%	--	10.7	1				12.3%								

With Jeremy Shockey gone, Thomas will have an expanded role, especially as a blocker. He emerged as a decent enough option for Drew Brees during the Super Bowl run, but declined along with his quarterback last year. KUBIAK likes his numbers to rebound, although not enough to have any real fantasy impact.

Delanie Walker

Height: 6-1   Weight: 241   College: Central Missouri   Draft: 2006/6 (175)   Born: 12-Aug-1984   Age: 27   Risk: Yellow

Year	Team	G	Rec	Pass	Yds	C%	+/-	Yd/C	TD	FUM	YAC	Rk	DVOA	Rk	DYAR	Rk	YAR	Short	Mid	Deep	Bomb
2008	SF	15	10	16	155	63%	-0.6	15.5	1	1	10.8	--	-1.1%	--	7	--	15	38%	31%	25%	6%
2009	SF	16	21	33	233	64%	-0.2	11.1	0	1	7.6	1	-20.0%	41	-29	40	-35	59%	19%	19%	3%
2010	SF	14	29	46	331	65%	-0.3	11.4	0	1	5.8	9	0.3%	28	24	29	24	65%	21%	7%	7%
2011	SF		36	58	347	62%	--	9.6	2				-2.7%								

Nobody was happier than Walker to see the 49ers hire Jim Harbaugh, who used his tight ends in the passing game perhaps more than any other coach in college football. Walker has long been an athletic marvel who was not a particularly good NFL player, and in his first four seasons the 49ers tried him at tight end, wide receiver, fullback and even kickoff returner with minimal success. He had his best season by far in 2010, peaking with a career-high 85 yards in Week 8 against Denver and nearly matching it with 80 yards in the next game against St. Louis. Unlike his tag team partner Vernon Davis, who excels on deep routes, Walker is a YAC specialist, one of the few tight ends to gain more yards after the catch than he did through the air. Between Harbaugh's affection for tight ends and the 49ers' thin depth chart at wide receiver, expect to see Walker spend a lot of time in the slot on third downs. If Davis misses any chunk of time, Walker becomes an immediate must-start in all fantasy leagues.

Benjamin Watson

Height: 6-3   Weight: 255   College: Georgia   Draft: 2004/1 (32)   Born: 18-Dec-1980   Age: 31   Risk: Green

Year	Team	G	Rec	Pass	Yds	C%	+/-	Yd/C	TD	FUM	YAC	Rk	DVOA	Rk	DYAR	Rk	YAR	Short	Mid	Deep	Bomb
2008	NE	14	22	47	209	47%	-5.2	9.5	2	1	2.4	42	-29.5%	40	-73	41	-71	33%	45%	19%	2%
2009	NE	16	29	41	404	71%	5.4	13.9	5	0	3.2	42	49.3%	1	161	10	160	33%	28%	30%	10%
2010	CLE	16	68	103	763	67%	3.4	11.2	3	0	3.9	34	11.3%	20	125	9	113	37%	44%	15%	3%
2011	CLE		50	76	515	66%	--	10.3	4				7.3%								

Benjamin Watson is a talented player, but when Benjamin Watson is your leading receiver, your offense has problems. We often hear that tight ends are an important part of the West Coast offense, but Pat Shurmur probably doesn't want his quarterbacks throwing to Watson 100 times again. Then again, with Evan Moore and Jordan Cameron behind him on the depth chart, last year's leading Browns receiver is also now clearly the Browns' best blocking tight end — so he's going to spend plenty of time on the field this year.

Kellen Winslow

Height: 6-4   Weight: 254   College: Miami   Draft: 2004/1 (6)   Born: 21-Jul-1983   Age: 28   Risk: Green

Year	Team	G	Rec	Pass	Yds	C%	+/-	Yd/C	TD	FUM	YAC	Rk	DVOA	Rk	DYAR	Rk	YAR	Short	Mid	Deep	Bomb
2008	CLE	10	43	83	428	52%	-4.1	10.0	3	1	2.8	38	-11.6%	32	-23	35	-31	34%	52%	14%	0%
2009	TB	16	77	127	884	61%	3.5	11.5	5	0	3.2	43	10.5%	17	143	11	134	37%	40%	19%	4%
2010	TB	16	66	97	730	68%	7.0	11.1	5	1	3.5	39	14.8%	16	135	7	137	40%	41%	16%	3%
2011	TB		47	73	561	64%	--	11.9	4				13.7%								

Winslow's targets went down a bit in 2010 as Mike Williams became the favorite weapon in Tampa Bay's aerial game, but Winslow was no less important to the team's surprising success. Battling through injuries most of the season, he lived up to a bit of the legendary "F'in Soldier" talk by springing some truly spectacular blocks for his running backs, including the one that allowed LeGarrette Blount to run roughshod through Seattle's alleged zone-defense for a season-high 53-yard scamper in Week 16. Schematically, Winslow was responsible for a lot of zone-busters — quick slants and comebacks over the middle from an inline position. He also occupied middle-distance coverage in ways that created opportunities for other receivers. Winslow was the unsung weapon in an offense where the kids got most of the credit, but that doesn't mean his contributions were negligible in any way.

Jason Witten

Height: 6-5   Weight: 257   College: Tennessee   Draft: 2003/3 (69)   Born: 6-May-1982   Age: 29   Risk: Yellow

Year	Team	G	Rec	Pass	Yds	C%	+/-	Yd/C	TD	FUM	YAC	Rk	DVOA	Rk	DYAR	Rk	YAR	Short	Mid	Deep	Bomb
2008	DAL	16	81	120	952	68%	4.1	11.8	4	0	4.1	25	19.0%	10	203	3	194	41%	41%	15%	3%
2009	DAL	16	94	124	1030	76%	11.1	11.0	2	0	4.5	25	20.1%	9	216	4	213	49%	38%	11%	2%
2010	DAL	16	94	128	1002	73%	10.7	10.7	9	1	4.2	30	18.9%	15	215	3	220	47%	43%	9%	1%
2011	DAL		87	115	959	76%	--	11.0	5				25.3%								

Those 2009 and 2010 lines underscore just how volatile a player's touchdown total can be. Witten's raw numbers are virtually identical outside of that touchdown figure, but that upward swing propelled him from eighth to first in fantasy points at tight end. After four years of elite performance, the question has to start coming up: Is Witten in the middle of a Hall of Fame-caliber career? Nobody has more receptions (617) or receiving yards (6967) by age 28 than Witten does, and the only player close to him is Tony Gonzalez, who at age 28 was 47 receptions short of Witten's total. There's always the possibility that his nagging injuries finally start turning "Questionable" weeks into "Out" ones, but if he continues on this career path, Witten should end up in Canton one day.

Going Deep

Chris Baker, FA: Technically, Baker was a first-string player for Seattle last year, though he caught only nine passes in 13 starts. Seattle cut him in March. (2010 stats; 9-for-19, 116 yards, -12.9% DVOA, -8 DYAR)

Jake Ballard, NYG: A good run blocker at Ohio State, Ballard swears that he would be a great receiver if someone just gave him the chance. Nobody's given him the chance yet.

Gary Barnidge, CAR: Barnidge was on last year's Top 25 Prospects list. We noted that Barnidge has the speed to hit the seam and the hands to hang on to the ball in traffic. So, what happened? The Panthers were more creative and diverse with their tight ends in 2009 than in 2010, and Barnidge struggled with injuries. We also must point at the horrid quarterback situation once again. Barnidge was thrown nine passes and caught none of them (-85.3% DVOA, -48 DYAR). It will be hard for him to break out now that he's behind Greg Olsen and Jeremy Shockey on the depth chart.

Nate Byham, SF: A blocking specialist buried on the depth chart behind Vernon Davis and Delanie Walker, Byham tore his ACL in camp and will be out for the season. (2010 stats; 5-for-6, 27 yards, -28.7% DVOA, -9 DYAR)

Jordan Cameron, CLE: Cameron started out as a BYU basketball player before transferring to USC to play tight end. He blew people away at the combine with a 4.59-second 40-yard dash and a 37.5-inch vertical leap. But before you get too excited, understand that Cameron wasn't even the starting tight end at USC; junior Rhett Ellison was. Our friend Russ Lande put it best in his GM Jr. draft guide: "most players who were primarily backups as seniors in college struggle to become anything more than backups in the NFL." Cameron also has a thin frame and needs to add strength if he wants to become an all-around starting tight end instead of just an overgrown wide receiver.

Scott Chandler, BUF: Chandler has great size (6-foot-7, 265 pounds) but it hasn't helped him get many snaps on offense since he was drafted in the fourth round back in 2007. He's primarily been a special teamer for San Diego, Dallas, and now Buffalo. The Bills were talking him up as their starting tight end for 2011, which would be swell for Chandler if they weren't planning on going four- and five-wide all the time. (2010 stats; 1-for-3, 8 yards, -46.6% DVOA, -8 DYAR)

Desmond Clark, CHI: The Bears had little use for a backup pass-catching tight end last year, so Clark was a healthy or not-really-that-injured scratch for most of the year. He's now 34 and coming off two unproductive years, but with Greg Olson traded and Brandon Manumaleuna released, the Bears re-signed him anyway. (2010 stats; 1-for-2, 12 yards, -41.9% DVOA, -6 DYAR)

Chase Coffman, CIN: The all-time receiving leader at Missouri was supposed to be Jermaine Gresham before Jermaine Gresham was, but he couldn't even get on the field for his first two seasons. Last year he spent time on the practice squad, but finally got called up and saw his first-ever NFL game action. (2010 stats; 3-for-5, 30 yards, 3.3% DVOA, 3 DYAR)

Tom Crabtree, GB: Crabtree caught 35- and 21-yard passes as the Packers' backup tight end last year. He is similar to Jermichael Finley and Andrew Quarless: a big seam runner who can block a little bit. The Packers released Donald Lee because they are high on Crabtree; it's hard to imagine what they need with three versions of the same type of player, but the Packers are masters at using redundancy to cover for injuries. (2010 stats: 4-for-7, 61 yards, -14.5% DVOA, -4 DYAR)

Alge Crumpler, FA: Crumpler is coming off shoulder surgery, was released in July, and has yet to find work. The Patriots drafted Lee Smith to fill the block-only role behind Aaron Hernandez and Rob Gronkowski. If Boston columnists decide to play the tired "leadership is missing!" angle after a Pats loss, look for Crumpler to be one of the first players they point to. (2010 stats; 6-for-10, 60 yards, 2 TD, 5.9% DVOA, 10 DYAR)

Kellen Davis, CHI: A 6-foot-7 thumper who played some defensive end in college, Davis is now Chicago's starting tight end by default. He is primarily a blocker but could be a real weapon in red zone packages. Davis was married in the offseason, and he spent more time in the Chicago society pages than your typical third tight end should: the *Sun-Times* mentioned him twice in July at the end of articles that namedropped everyone from Rosie O'Donnell to William and Kate. Maybe the columnist is Davis' cousin, or something. (2010 stats; 1-for-2, 19 yards, 1 TD, 66.1% DVOA, 21 DYAR)

Jim Dray, ARI: The Stanford graduate and punishing run blocker started three games as a rookie in 2010. That shows that the staff was high on Dray as a player. The fact that the Cardinals took a receiving tight end in the third round shows that they probably weren't that high on Dray as a pass catcher. (2010 stats; 3-for-9, 47 yards, -27.9% DVOA, -12 DYAR)

Davon Drew, BAL: The Ravens drafted Drew in the fifth round of the 2009 draft, but within a year they had drafted two more tight ends (Ed Dickson and Dennis Pitta) to render him irrelevant. He's practice squad fodder.

Jeff Dugan, MIN: Dugan wears number 83 but is as much a fullback as a tight end; the Vikings gave him 2-to-4 short yardage carries per year for reasons that only make sense to Brad Childress. Minnesota plans to use fullbacks and tight ends a lot this year, but there is only room for three or four of this type of player on the roster, and the Vikings have about eight of them.

Brody Eldridge, IND: Last year's fifth-round pick out of Oklahoma does not have the downfield speed to be a real asset in the passing game but should stick as the team's best run-blocking tight end. (2010 stats; 5-for-9, 39 yards, -30.9% DVOA, -14 DYAR)

Dedrick Epps, MIA: Epps was Jimmy Graham's backup at Miami, so of course he hoped that his NFL situation would provide him with more of an opportunity. Unfortunately, he landed on the Chargers' roster by virtue of a seventh-round pick, and languished early in the season while Antonio Gates was having perhaps the best half-season any tight end has ever enjoyed. Released by the Chargers, Epps will give it another shot with the Dolphins.

Richard Gordon, OAK: This sixth-rounder was supposed to get more reps for the Hurricanes after Jimmy Graham left to become a star with the Saints, but injuries got in the way. He's very athletic for his size, and he impressed coaches with a penchant for film study when he was hurt.

Garrett Graham, HOU: Like Owen Daniels, Graham was a fourth-round pick out of Wisconsin. In Daniels' rookie year, he started 12 games and caught 34 passes for 352 yards. He went into his second season as the starter. In Graham's rookie year, he appeared in six games, starting none, and was not thrown the ball once. He goes into his second season fourth on the depth chart.

Virgil Green, DEN: Green is one of the new wave of athletically freakish tight ends — he ran a 4.5 40 and put up a 42.5-inch vertical leap at the scouting combine. Not a blocker per se, he's a good slot and flex target in hybrid multi-receiver sets.

Dan Gronkowski, DEN: Possibly the least impressive of the three current NFL Gronkowskis, Dan replaced Spencer Larsen at fullback and saw some time as a blocking tight end in his second season before going down with an ankle injury in December. The difference between Dan and Rob is that while both players can block, Rob can also break away and make like a young Tony Gonzalez. The media tends to fixate on try-hard guys who look like Tim Riggins (avoid any hype, please), but Dan was rated as a limited offensive player coming out of college, and that's what we've seen from him in the NFL. (2010 stats; 8-for-13, 65 yards, -23.7% DVOA, -14 DYAR)

Clay Harbor, PHI: After Cornelius Ingram went down with another injury, Harbor filled his spot on the roster as the speedy tight end that presents matchup problems for linebackers. About half of his seasonal totals came during the Week 17 mop-up game against the Cowboys, so don't read a lot into even those limited reception totals. He's a project with great athleticism, but he'll have to beat out Cornelius Ingram for a roster spot. (2010 stats; 9-for-15, 72 yards, 1 TD, -19.9% DVOA, -13 DYAR)

Daniel Hardy, TB: This underrated Mackey Award semifinalist lost some visibility when a broken arm cost him the last five games of the 2010 season, but he recovered to play in the NFLPA game. He's a major work in progress as a blocker, but may provide initial value as an H-back.

Ben Hartsock, CAR: Hartsock was released by the Jets after he refused to take a pay cut on the $1.6 million he was due. You can sympathize with Hartsock, who just signed a two-year contract in 2010, but that's the way the NFL works these days. If you are looking for a tight end who can split the seam and make a team pay for playing Cover-2, look elsewhere, but if you need a second or third tight end for your goal-line sets, Hartsock might well be your guy. This year, he'll be Ron Rivera's guy.

Will Heller, DET: Heller has caught at least one touchdown in seven of his eight NFL seasons. He has also caught four passes or less in five of those seasons. It's fun to be a third-string tight end. (2010 stats; 4-for-5, 37 yards, 1 TD, 42.7% DVOA, 16 DYAR)

Tory Humphrey, NO: Humphrey has been around since 2005, and has exactly one season with more than one catch: 2008, when he had 11 receptions for the Packers. He's been with the Saints the last two years, mostly on the practice squad, but will probably serve as the third tight end with Jeremy Shockey gone.

Cornelius Ingram, PHI: After back-to-back ACL tears, you would have been forgiven if you wished for Ingram to get a break. Instead, a cyst in his knee had to be removed during the preseason, and Ingram was one of the final cuts from the roster. He made it onto the practice squad and stayed healthy the rest of the way, but he hasn't played a meaningful game since the Bush administration. Even if he stays healthy, who knows what athleticism he has left?

Darcy Johnson, FA: Injuries derailed two of Johnson's final three seasons with the New York Giants, who opted not to extend a qualifying offer to the restricted free agent in the 2010 offseason. Signed to a one-year contract by the Rams last March, Johnson was not among the quartet of tight ends brought into the regular season, but was re-signed in mid-September and made two starts in the four games he was active before a concussion ended his season.

David Johnson, PIT: Pittsburgh's third tight end is essentially their first fullback; according to game charters, only three tight ends lined up in the backfield more often than Johnson did in 2010. (2010 stats; 4-for-6, 46 yards, -6.3% DVOA, 0 DYAR)

Reggie Kelly, ATL: Kelly is a long-time Bengals stalwart, a blocking H-back who doesn't spend a lot of time going out on passing routes. It's somewhat surprising that the Bengals didn't bring him back once the lockout ended. Boxers have had more sincere retirements than Kelly, who put the pads away on August 10th, then signed with the Falcons on the 16th. (2010 stats; 10-for-13, 42 yards, -50.2% DVOA, -36 DYAR)

Donald Lee, PHI: The Packers released Lee in March. He was scheduled to make $2 million in 2011, which is a lot of money for a 31-year-old tight end expected to battle for the No. 3 job. Lee has averaged 7.3 yards per catch over the last three years, and it's hard to see him doing much better than that in the limited playing time he'll have in Philadelphia. (2010 stats; 11-for-12, 73 yards, 3 touchdowns, 11.7% DVOA, 17 DYAR)

Brandon Manumaleuna, FA: It's not clear how much value Manumaleuna even has in his familiar role as Mike Martz's Extra Blocker. He blew too many blocks for someone who was supposed to be a steadying influence on the edge of the line, and he's gone from catching about a pass per game to catching a little more than one per month. He was released by Chicago after failing a physical. Martz is reportedly looking into starting a nightclub and signing Manumaleuna to be the bouncer. (2010 stats: 5-for-7, 43 yards, 1 TD, 16.7% DVOA, 13 DYAR)

David Martin, BUF: Three of Martin's seven receptions gained zero yards last season. Martin is now 32 and on the back end of a career marked by unfulfilled potential but surprising longevity. (2010 stats: 7-for-8, 43 yards, 1 TD, -7.3% DVOA, 0 DYAR)

Anthony McCoy, SEA: In Week 10, Seattle had a first-and-goal at the Arizona 1 and lined up with John Carlson at fullback and Cam Morrah, Chris Baker, and Anthony McCoy on the line of scrimmage. It made McCoy a part of history, as the fourth part of what might have been the league's first (and probably last) four-tight end formation. It resulted in an incomplete pass, and McCoy played just one more game after that. But he'll always have that magic moment in Phoenix.

Garrett Mills, FA: Mills is a "move" H-back who spent three years as Minnesota's third-string tight end. Last year he was with the Eagles for most of the year, then hooked up with the Bengals for the last two weeks but didn't play.

Cameron Morrah, SEA: Morrah started three games in December and January, and in those three games he caught four passes. With Zach Miller joining John Carlson atop the depth chart, Morrah will probably never start again. (2010 stats: 9-for-18, 117 yards, -16.6% DVOA, -11 DYAR)

Matthew Mulligan, NYJ: Both Mulligan and fellow Maine alumnus Mike DeVito were voted "Iron Jets" by their teammates in August, and Mulligan got an even more meaningful award from his coaches this offseason — a promotion. With Ben Hartsock gone, Mulligan will get a shot at the second tight end job, which in the New York offense means a lot of in-line blocking and a handful of reception opportunities down in the red zone.

Shawn Nelson, BUF: Nelson looked like a player on the rise after catching 17 passes in limited action as a rookie. He then earned a four-game substance abuse suspension, missed another game while recovering from surgery, and fumbled in overtime to lose the Ravens game. Not surprisingly, Chan Gailey didn't have much use for him after that. Nelson is a great size-speed prospect who can make leaping catches and block a little, so he could resurface. (2010 stats: 3-for-4, 25 yards, -63.4% DVOA, -15 DYAR)

Jake O'Connell, KC: O'Connell was a developmental pick who struggled early on — having a pass bounce off your facemask while the coach yells at you is not an auspicious start to your career. Primarily, O'Connell's been a special-teamer. (2010 stats: 3-for-4, 31 yards, 15.5% DVOA, 7 DYAR)

Fendi Onobun, STL: At 6-foot-6 and 252 pounds, Onobun possesses excellent size and, as a former college basketball player, is a gifted athlete. Onobun is coming off an abbreviated rookie season as a bulging disc in his back limited him to just three games in 2010. With the lockout preventing the talented but raw Onobun from receiving a desperately need offseason of NFL-caliber coaching, he enters 2011 as a longshot to make the 53-man roster. (2010 stats: 2-for-4, 15 yards, -21.1% DVOA, -4 DYAR)

Michael Palmer, ATL: The pride of local Parkview High (not counting Jeff Francoeur, of course), Palmer cracked the 53-man roster as an undrafted free agent, then spent the season covering kicks and apprenticing under his Jedi Master, Tony Gonzalez. That doesn't make Palmer Anakin Skywalker; he's more like one of those background Knights the Emperor had killed. Palmer has the size (6-foot-5, 260) and physicality to stick around the league for a while. (2010 stats: 5-for-8, 29 yards, 1 TD, -9.8% DVOA, -1 DYAR)

Bear Pascoe, NYG: He moved to fullback after Madison Hedgecock went down with an injury, but Pascoe's a work in progress as a move blocker. The Giants would be better off bringing in a real fullback for that. Pascoe should see time as the Giants tight end in run formations this season. (2010 stats: 9-for-13, 72 yards, 6.5% DVOA, 11 DYAR)

Ben Patrick, Retired: Patrick led all Arizona tight ends in receiving last year — with a grand total of 123 yards. He signed with the Giants in the offseason, then suddenly retired. (2010 stats: 15-for-18, 123 yards, -13.6% DVOA, -7 DYAR)

Logan Paulsen, WAS: Paulsen was an undrafted free agent out of UCLA who backed up Chris Cooley and Fred Davis. According to his Wikipedia page, Paulsen is currently engaged to Kelly Cochran, who is "the bestest teacher in the world." Does Cochran teach Wikipedia Editing 101?

Justin Peelle, ATL: Peelle missed three games with a sports hernia, then returned to catch his lone touchdown of the season against the Rams, a beautifully executed play fake from the goal line. In his nine-year career, Peelle has scored at least once in every season save his rookie campaign in San Diego. Nice to see that Peelle's excellent blocking gets rewarded on occasion. (2010 stats: 10-for-15, 96 yards, 1 TD, 10.5% DVOA, 20 DYAR)

John Phillips, DAL: The Cowboys' third tight end tore his ACL in the Hall of Fame game and missed the entire season. He had actually been rather impressive before the injury, so if he returns at 100 percent and Martellus Bennett continues to struggle, he could end up eating away at Bennett's snaps. (2009 stats: 7-for-9, 62 yards, -0.8% DVOA, 4 DYAR)

Leonard Pope, KC: Pope's stardom has come in fits and starts, but when he hits the big time, he does it with authority. In June of 2010, he saved the life of a six-year old boy at a pool party near his Georgia home — apparently, he was the only adult at the party who knew how to swim. Pope has not proven to be as indispensable on the football field, mostly because he never learned to block. At least we know that he holds a high grade in "protective instincts" when it really counts. (2010 stats:10-for-19, 76 yards, 2 TD, -21.4% DVOA, -20 DYAR)

Zach Potter, JAC: Potter, who converted from defensive end in college to tight end in the pros, figured prominently in the Jags power formations and appeared in 13 games as a blocker. For his role to grow any further, Hogwart's would have to introduce Catching a Football as part of their third-year curriculum. (2010 stats: 3-for-8, 24 yards, -35.1% DVOA, -15 DYAR)

Ryan Purvis, TB: One of Matt Ryan's primary targets at Boston College, Purvis was signed from the Tampa Bay practice squad last year after the Bucs finally tired of Jerramy Stevens' ever-expanding rap sheet. He's not a threat to expand his role, especially with the selection of Luke Stocker in the draft. (2010 stats: 5-for-6, 38 yards, 3.9% DVOA, 4 DYAR)

Richard Quinn, DEN: Yet another questionable personnel move from a Josh McDaniels era that gave us so many. The Broncos actually traded up to select Quinn in the second round, despite the fact that he's primarily a blocking tight end, he caught just 12 passes in his college career, and Denver didn't do much with two-tight end sets. However, John Fox loves him some two-tight sets, especially for blocking purposes, so Quinn could provide value in that way.

Gijon Robinson, FA: A solid, if unspectacular blocker, Robinson's production (and opportunities) declined for the second straight year. Waived mid-year, he re-signed and finished the season with the Colts. He remains unsigned at this point. (2010 stats: 3-for-7, 12 yards, 1 TD, -36.3% DVOA, -16 DYAR)

Robert Royal, FA: Despite his subpar hands, Robert Royal is like some kind of non-giving-up ... tight end guy. He scored a touchdown on Cleveland's wacky "Emory and Henry" play, the one with two offensive tackles lined up wide next to the wide receivers. He's unsigned as we go to press. (2010 stats: 5-for-12, 56 yards, 1 TD, -30.7% DVOA, -21 DYAR)

Martin Rucker, DAL: A former Top 25 Prospect thanks to his soft hands and athleticism, Rucker remains tantalizing enough for teams to continue stashing him away on their practice squads. He's still just 26, but he doesn't have much longer to establish himself in the league. A team with a blocking tight end as the starter could do a lot worse than giving him a shot.

Derek Schouman, WAS: A second knee injury in as many years submarined a prime opportunity for Schouman to solidify himself as the Buffalo Bills' No. 1 tight end during the 2010 preseason. Waived with an injury settlement by the Bills, Schouman rehabilitated the knee injury until joining the Rams in mid-November, playing sparingly in four games. Oddly enough, the oft-injured Schouman was signed by the Redskins as injury insurance for Chris Cooley, who suffered a knee injury early in training camp. (2009 stats: 9-for-11, 103 yards, 14.8% DVOA, 16 DYAR)

Mickey Shuler, MIA: Mickey Shuler Sr. was a Pro Bowl-caliber receiving tight end for many years with the Jets and had many signature games against the Dolphins, which may have factored ever so slightly into their decision to put in a waiver claim for Mickey Jr. when the Vikings were attempting to sneak him onto their practice squad. Shuler was beaten out for the second tight end spot by Jeron Mastrud, and will need to rely on his blocking prowess if he wants to stick on the roster. (2010 stats: 2-for-5, 44 yards, 14.4% DVOA, 6 DYAR)

Alex Smith, CLE: The veteran receiving tight end was active for just three games last year, catching one pass for six yards, but the Browns signed him to a 2011 contract after the season anyway. There doesn't seem to be much room for him on the team behind Ben Watson, Evan Moore, and Cameron Jordan.

Lee Smith, NE: Smith is a 265-pound blocking specialist with decent hands and almost no speed. He can also long snap in a pinch. Smith should see a lot of playing time - the Patriots use two-tight end sets so often that the third-string guy sees the field a lot — but his production will be limited to a few dump-offs and one or two goal-line touchdowns.

Stephen Spach, ARI: The veteran was the primary tight end for the Cardinals last year, but that only meant 70 yards. Spach is still a very effective blocker and is valuable in that role, but there may not be space for him with the three tight ends the Cardinals added this offseason. (2010 stats: 7-for-17, 70 yards, -57.0% DVOA, -55 DYAR)

Matt Spaeth, CHI: Fantasy football players got excited when Spaeth caught two touchdown passes in his first two games back in 2007. He's only caught three touchdown passes in the 50 games since. He may have started 13 games last year as part of a two-tight end set, but he will never be useful for fantasy purposes. Now with the Bears, Spaeth will be the designated sixth blocker in the Mike Martz offense. (2010 stats: 9-for-18, 80 yards, 1 TD, -21.5% DVOA, -17 DYAR)

Kory Sperry, SD: Sperry had cups of coffee with the Dolphins and Broncos before landing on the Chargers' roster, and he caught Norv Turner's eye when he got some looks last season following Antonio Gates' abbreviated campaign. Norv Turner said in August of this year that Sperry may be the team's most improved player, so he could get a lot of targets this preseason. (2010 stats: 4-for-4, 73 yards, 117.9% DVOA, 33 DYAR)

Craig Stevens, TEN: Stevens started 13 games in 2011 and caught 11 passes on 23 targets. The catch percentage is partly a product of the small sample size, but Stevens is clearly in the lineup for his blocking skills. If Jared Cook fails to improve, Stevens' catch total could go up by default, but he'll never be more than an average receiver. (2010 stats: 11-for-23, 122 yards, 2 TD, -16.0% DVOA, -14 DYAR)

Jerramy Stevens, FA: In truth, Stevens was in the NFL far too long ... and according to criminal reports of his time at Washington, he probably didn't deserve to be in the league at all. There are good guys who do bad things, but Stevens isn't one of those types. He's a scary character with real social issues that have never been addressed because he was a big, fast guy who could (occasionally) catch a football. Drug and assault charges have dogged him through the last year, and he's probably out of the NFL for good. The NFL is better for it. (2010 stats: 3-for-5, 43 yards, 22.4% DVOA, 9 DYAR)

Ryan Taylor, GB: Taylor caught 36 passes for North Carolina last season, but more importantly, he served as the team's special teams captain. Taylor played linebacker early in his college career and should inherit Spencer Havner's old role as the all-purpose guy everyone loves but no one can find a way to keep on the roster. The Packers have lots and lots of guys looking to stick as kick gunners and specialists, including fellow rookie tight end D.J. Williams.

Julius Thomas, DEN: The Broncos drafted two tight ends on 2011, and while Nevada's Virgil Green is expected to be the new slot/flex target, Thomas is more a raw prospect. That's not a bad thing, though — Thomas has a great deal of basketball experience and hopes to follow everyone from Tony Gonzalez to Jimmy Graham down that road to NFL success. Thomas' stock rose with a great performance in the East-West Shrine Game, and he has the potential to become a consistent deep seam target.

Ernest Wilford, FA: It's a tight end! It's a wide receiver! The positionally androgynous Wilford was pushed out of the Jacksonville offense by Zach Miller and will likely find himself playing the role of Guy Sitting By The Phone this year. At least he'll always have that time the Dolphins made him their premier free-agent acquisition.

D.J. Williams, GB: Williams was a very productive receiver at Arkansas, with 147 receptions as a tight end/H-back in three years. He also grades out well as a blocker. He's not a burner and lacks the height and reach of a true NFL tight end, but he fits as a blocking back or H-back. Williams must battle fellow rookie Ryan Taylor and others for what amounts to a highly specialized role in the offense.

Kris Wilson, BAL: Wilson signed a two-year contract to stay with the Chargers before the 2010 season, ensuring his role as a primary backup for Antonio Gates. Given his time behind Tony Gonzalez in Kansas City, Wilson's used to being an understudy for the best. The Chargers released him, and he caught on with Baltimore. Another good sign for FO top prospect Ed Dickson! (2010 stats: 6-for-9, 75 yards, -33.1% DVOA, -9 DYAR)

Kicker and Defense Projections

2011 Kicker Projections

Listed below are the 2011 KUBIAK projections for kickers. Because of the inconsistency of field-goal percentage from year to year, kickers are projected almost entirely based on team forecasts, although a handful of individual factors do come into play:

• More experience leads to a slightly higher field-goal percentage in general, with the biggest jump be-tween a kicker's rookie and sophomore seasons.

• Kickers with a better career field-goal percentage tend to get more attempts, although they are not nec-essarily more accurate.

• Field-goal percentage on kicks over 40 yards tends to regress to the mean.

Kickers are also listed with a Risk of Green, Yellow, Red, or Blue, as explained in the introduction to the section on quarterbacks.

Fantasy Kicker Projections, 2011

Kicker	Team	FG	Pct	XP	Pts	Risk	Kicker	Team	FG	Pct	XP	Pts	Risk
Matt Bryant	ATL	30-34	88%	43	133	Yellow	Ryan Succop	KC	26-32	81%	37	115	Red
Bill Cundiff	BAL	28-32	88%	41	125	Green	Dan Carpenter	MIA	26-34	76%	37	115	Yellow
Robbie Gould	CHI	29-34	85%	35	122	Yellow	David Akers	SF	28-35	80%	31	115	Yellow
Mason Crosby	GB	26-30	87%	44	122	Yellow	Jay Feely	ARI	28-33	85%	29	113	Green
Stephen Gostkowski	NE	23-28	82%	53	122	Green	Josh Scobee	JAC	25-30	83%	38	113	Red
Lawrence Tynes	NYG	28-33	85%	38	122	Red	Rian Lindell	BUF	27-35	77%	31	112	Green
Shaun Suisham	PIT	23-29	79%	53	122	Green	Mike Nugent	CIN	27-34	79%	30	111	Red
Neil Rackers	HOU	25-29	86%	46	121	Yellow	Josh Brown	STL	27-35	77%	30	111	Yellow
Garrett Hartley	NO	24-32	75%	49	121	Green	David Buehler	DAL	24-30	80%	38	110	Green
Nick Folk	NYJ	27-35	77%	39	120	Red	Rob Bironas	TEN	27-31	87%	27	108	Green
Ryan Longwell	MIN	27-33	82%	37	118	Green	Sebastian Janikowski	OAK	26-32	81%	28	106	Blue
Jason Hanson	DET	27-35	77%	36	117	Yellow	Matt Prater	DEN	23-29	79%	36	105	Green
Adam Vinatieri	IND	25-29	86%	42	117	Green	Olindo Mare	CAR	24-29	83%	30	102	Blue
Phil Dawson	CLE	26-33	79%	38	116	Yellow	Jeff Reed	SEA	25-31	81%	25	100	Green
Alex Henery	PHI	22-28	79%	50	116	Green	Connor Barth	TB	22-28	79%	33	99	Red
Nate Kaeding	SD	22-27	81%	50	116	Yellow	Graham Gano	WAS	23-33	70%	21	90	Green

2011 Fantasy Team Defense Projections

Listed below are the 2011 KUBIAK projections for fantasy team defense. The projection method is discussed in an essay in *Pro Football Prospectus 2006*, the key conclusions of which were:

• Schedule strength is very important for projecting fantasy defense.

• Categories used for scoring in fantasy defense have no consistency from year-to-year whatsoever, with the exception of sacks and interceptions.

Fumble recoveries and defensive touchdowns are forecast solely based on the projected sacks and in-terceptions, rather than the team's totals in these categories from a year ago. This is why the 2011 projections will look very different from the fantasy defense values from the 2010 season. Safeties and shutouts are not common enough to have a significant effect on the projections. Team defenses are also projected with Risk factor of Green, Yellow, Red, or Blue; this is based on the team's projection compared to performance in recent seasons.

In addition to projection of separate categories, we also give an overall total based on our generic fantasy scoring formula: one point for a sack, two points for a fumble recovery or interception, and six points for a touchdown. Special teams touchdowns are listed separately and are not included in the fantasy scoring total listed.

Fantasy Team Defense Projections, 2011

Team	Fant Pts	Sack	Int	Fum Rec	Def TD	Risk	ST TD	Team	Fant Pts	Sack	Int	Fum Rec	Def TD	Risk	ST TD
PHI	122	48.2	16.0	11.4	3.2	Yellow	0.7	NE	108	35.2	19.4	8.0	3.1	Yellow	0.7
BAL	121	39.7	17.1	9.6	4.7	Red	0.9	SF	107	35.2	18.9	7.2	3.3	Yellow	0.4
CHI	121	39.9	17.7	12.6	3.4	Red	2.5	STL	106	32.2	17.4	11.0	2.8	Red	0.6
PIT	119	46.2	18.3	10.7	2.5	Yellow	0.8	DET	103	31.9	17.5	9.3	2.9	Yellow	0.9
SD	118	40.1	18.4	9.0	3.9	Red	0.9	NO	102	38.8	12.3	11.4	2.7	Yellow	1.0
GB	117	40.7	18.5	8.2	3.8	Green	0.7	BUF	99	34.0	15.3	10.8	2.1	Yellow	0.7
NYJ	116	40.1	19.4	8.6	3.3	Yellow	1.0	DAL	97	33.2	15.7	9.0	2.4	Yellow	1.0
CLE	116	33.3	20.0	10.5	3.5	Red	1.4	CAR	96	29.8	15.2	9.5	2.8	Yellow	0.7
NYG	114	39.4	15.8	11.3	3.4	Yellow	0.4	IND	94	32.5	12.9	10.2	2.6	Yellow	0.8
MIA	114	41.1	18.4	9.2	2.9	Red	0.8	OAK	94	27.8	16.8	8.4	2.5	Yellow	0.7
HOU	112	41.5	15.7	10.2	3.1	Red	0.9	KC	93	33.7	14.8	8.1	2.2	Yellow	0.7
SEA	111	37.3	18.1	11.2	2.6	Red	1.0	TEN	91	27.6	15.0	8.5	2.7	Green	0.9
MIN	111	35.3	20.3	9.0	2.9	Red	1.0	JAC	91	32.7	15.9	9.0	1.3	Red	0.8
ARI	111	35.4	16.2	11.9	3.3	Yellow	0.8	TB	90	29.7	14.1	7.9	2.7	Yellow	1.0
CIN	111	31.6	21.6	6.8	3.7	Red	0.6	WAS	85	27.3	16.9	6.9	1.7	Yellow	0.7
ATL	111	37.3	17.5	10.7	2.8	Yellow	1.0	DEN	77	28.5	11.7	9.0	1.1	Green	0.7

College Football Introduction and Statistical Toolbox

Whether you are a fan of college football or one of its largest detractors, you saw plenty in 2010 to back up your line of thinking. Fans got everything they could possibly want out of a given season: explosive offenses (Oregon, Boise State and Oklahoma State all averaged over 44 points per game), wild upsets (the nation's No. 1 team lost in three consecutive weekends: Alabama to South Carolina, Ohio State to Wisconsin and Oklahoma to Missouri), incredible rivalry games (Auburn overcame a 24-0 deficit in Tuscaloosa to win the Iron Bowl), entertaining bowls (three of five BCS matchups were decided by a touchdown or less, as were 11 other bowls), and a fun national title game (Auburn used a late run by Michael Dyer to set up the game winning touchdown and beat Oregon, 22-19). The passion, pageantry, drama and every-game-counts meme were all on display throughout 2010.

Detractors, however, had their say as well. Even before Auburn qualified for the BCS championship game, allegations arose that Auburn quarterback Cam Newton had his services offered to the highest bidder, leading to an overflow of "How long until Auburn has to vacate the 2010 season?" snark from both media and fans. Agents continued to run amok, finding new (and old) ways to get access to players. The age-old debates about football playoffs and player compensation not only persisted, but thrived, as college football generated more revenue and more of the media spotlight. There was plenty of negativity if you were looking for it.

The drama has continued this offseason. Ohio State coach Jim Tressel resigned in light of allegations of both illegal benefits and a cover-up in Columbus. USC's appeal of their sanctions was denied, meaning the significant penalties assigned to the Trojans in the wake of the Reggie Bush scandal will officially begin to take effect (with a substantial cut in scholarships, their depth will slowly begin to disappear in coming seasons). Auburn saw an abnormal amount of arrests as well.

Plus, there has been tragedy. An Alabama walk-on was injured, and his girlfriend was killed, during a strong Tuscaloosa tornado this spring; then, offensive lineman Aaron Douglas passed away after a party. Oklahoma linebacker Austin Box died at a friend's house (former Sooner All-American Brandon Everage passed away at a young age as well).

In football-crazy towns like Tuscaloosa and Norman, this fall will aide in the grieving and recovery process. The season begins on Thursday, September 1, and wraps up with the BCS championship in New Orleans on January 9. Transition will be the name of the game. Auburn must replace a significant portion of its championship lineup, and three of last year's ten BCS bowl participants will be breaking in new coaches. Oklahoma and Alabama will begin the season as the favorites of both pundits and Football Outsiders projections, but neither the pundits nor projections saw an Auburn-Oregon title game taking shape last year. Expect the unexpected in college football.

For eight years, Brian Fremeau has been developing and tweaking the drive-based Fremeau Efficiency Index (FEI) and its companion statistics; for the last four years, Bill Connelly's research has explored play-by-play data, developing measures of efficiency and explosiveness and creating his system, the S&P+ ratings. Both systems are schedule-adjusted and effective in both evaluating teams and uncovering strengths and weaknesses. The combination of the two ratings, the F/+, provides the best of both worlds.

The College Statistical Toolbox section that follows this introduction explains the methodology of FEI, S&P+, F/+ and other stats you will encounter in the college chapters of this book. There are similarities to Football Outsiders' NFL-based DVOA ratings in the combined approach, but college football presents a unique set of challenges different from the NFL. All football stats must be adjusted according to context, but how? If Team A and Team B do not play one another and don't share any common opponents, how can their stats be effectively compared? Should a team from the SEC or Big 12 be measured against an average team in its own conference, or an average FBS team? With six years of full data, we are still only scratching the surface with these measures, but the recent progress has been both swift and exciting.

This book devotes a chapter to each of the six BCS conferences, with a seventh chapter covering the best of the non-AQ teams. The chapters provide a snapshot of each team's statistical profile in 2010 and projections for 2011, along with a summary of the keys to its upcoming season. Player and coaching personnel changes, offensive and defensive advantages and deficiencies, and schedule highlights and pitfalls are all discussed by our team of college football writers. The top prospects for the 2012 NFL draft are listed at the end of each team segment. An asterisk denotes a player who may or may not enter the draft as a junior eligible.

As we introduced last season, each chapter concludes with a Win Probability table. For each of the 120 FBS teams, we project the likelihood of every possible regular season record, conference and non-conference alike. We hope the Win Probability tables provide a broader understanding of our projections and the impact of strength of schedule on team records.

Though the landscape of college football might be changing drastically, the arguments about which conferences and team should claim superiority are not. By taking two different statistical approaches to reach one exciting series of answers to college football's most important questions, we feel we are at the forefront of the ongoing debates. Enjoy the college football section of *Football Outsiders Almanac 2011*, and join us at www.FootballOutsiders.com/college throughout the season.

College Statistics Toolbox

Regular readers of FootballOutsiders.com may be familiar with the FEI and Varsity Numbers columns and their respective stats published throughout the year. Others may be learning about our advanced approach to college football stats analysis for the first time by reading this book. In either case, this College Statistics Toolbox section is highly recommended reading before getting into the conference chapters. The stats that form the building blocks for F/+, FEI, and S&P+ are constantly being updated and refined.

Each team profile in the conference chapters begins with a statistical snapshot (defending BCS champion and Auburn is presented here as a sample). Within each chapter, teams are organized by division (or conference in the final chapter) and Projected F/+ rank. The projected overall and conference records — rounded from the team's projected Mean Wins — are listed alongside the team name in the header. Estimates of offensive and defensive starters returning in 2011 were collected from team websites, spring media guides, and other reliable sources. All other stats and rankings provided in the team snapshot are explained below.

Drive-by-Drive Data

FREMEAU EFFICIENCY INDEX: Fremeau Efficiency Index (FEI) analysis begins with drive data instead of play-by-play data and is processed according to key principles. A team is rewarded for playing well against a strong opponent, win or lose, and is punished more severely for playing poorly against bad teams than it is rewarded for playing well against bad teams.

To calculate FEI, the nearly 20,000 possessions in every season of major college football are filtered to eliminate first-half clock-kills and end-of-game

No. 4 Auburn Tigers (9-3, 5-3)

2010: 14-0 (8-0) / F/+ #1 / FEI #1 / S&P+ #4

Program F/+	+14.6%	13	Returning Starters: 3 OFF, 4 DEF			5-Yr Recruiting Rank		11
2010 Offense			**2010 Defense**			**2010 Field Position**		
Offensive F/+	+25.0%	1	Defensive F/+	+7.2%	31	Field Position Advantage	0.517	39
Offensive FEI:	0.805	1	Defensive FEI	-0.478	6	**2011 Projections**		
Offensive S&P+	153.6	1	Defensive S&P+	111.7	36	**Mean Wins**	8.8	
Rushing S&P+	150.1	1	Rushing S&P+	118.6	21	Proj. F/+	+18.3%	4
Passing S&P+	166.7	1	Passing S&P+	109.4	42	Offensive F/+	+13.9%	2
Standard Downs S&P+	144.3	1	Standard Downs S&P+	109.6	37	Defensive F/+	+4.3%	39
Passing Downs S&P+	178.0	1	Passing Downs S&P+	120.8	22	Strength of Schedule	0.043	1

garbage drives and scores. A scoring rate analysis of the remaining possessions then determines the baseline possession efficiency expectations against which each team is measured. Game Efficiency is the composite possession-by-possession efficiency of a team over the course of a game, a measurement of the success of its offensive, defensive, and special teams units' essential goals: to maximize the team's own scoring opportunities and to minimize those of its opponent. Finally, each team's FEI rating synthesizes its season-long Game Efficiency data, adjusted for the strength of its opposition; special emphasis is placed on quality performance against good teams, win or lose.

OFFENSIVE AND DEFENSIVE FEI: Game Efficiency is a composite assessment of the possession-by-possession performance of team over the course of a game. In order to isolate the relative performance of the offense and defense, more factors are evaluated.

First, we ran a regression on the national scoring rates of tens of thousands of college football drives according to starting field position. The result represents the value of field position in terms of points expected to be scored by an average offense against an average defense — 1.4 points per possession from its own 15-yard line, 2.3 points per possession from its own 40-yard line, and so on. These expected points are called Field Position Value (FPV).

Next, we ran a regression on the value of drive-ending field position according to national special teams scoring expectations. To determine the true national baseline for field-goal range, we took into account not only the 2200 field goals attempted annually, but also the 1400 punts kicked from opponent territory each year. In other words, if a team has an average field goal unit and a coach with an average penchant for risk-taking, the offensive value of reaching the opponent's 35-yard line is equal to the number of made field goals from that distance divided by the number of attempts plus the number of punts from that distance.

Touchdowns credit the offense with 6.96 points of drive-ending value, the value of a touchdown adjusted according to national point-after rates. Safeties have a drive-ending value of negative two points. All other offensive results are credited with a drive-ending value of zero.

Offensive efficiency is then calculated as the total drive-ending value earned by the offense divided by the sum of its offensive FPV over the course of the game. Defensive efficiency is calculated the same way using the opponent's offensive drive-ending value and FPV. Offensive and defensive efficiency are calibrated as a rating above or below zero — a good offense has a positive rating and a good defense has a negative one. These numbers are represented in the college chapters as Unadjusted Offense and Unadjusted Defense.

Offensive FEI and Defensive FEI are the opponent-adjusted values of offensive and defensive efficiency. As with FEI, the adjustments are weighted according to both the strength of the opponent and the relative significance of the result. Efficiency against a team's best competition is given more weight in the formula.

FIELD POSITION ADVANTAGE (FPA): FPA was developed in order to more accurately describe the management of field position over the course of a game. For each team, we calculate the sum of the FPV for each of its offensive series. Then, we add in a full touchdown value (6.96 points) for each non-offensive score earned by the team. (This accounts for the field position value of special teams and defensive returns reaching the end zone versus tripping up at the 1-yard line.) Special teams turnovers and onside kicks surrendered have an FPV of zero. The sum of the FPV of every possession in the game for both teams represents the total field position at stake in the contest. FPA represents each given team's share of that total field position.

FPA is a description of which team controlled field position in the game and by how much. Two teams that face equal field position over the course of a game will each have an FPA of .500. Winning the field position battle is quite valuable. College football teams that play with an FPA over .500 win two-thirds of the time. Teams that play with an FPA over .600 win 90 percent of the time.

Play-by-Play Data

SUCCESS RATES: Our play-by-play analysis was introduced throughout the 2008 season in Bill Connelly's Varsity Numbers columns. More than 600,000 plays over five seasons in college football have been collected and evaluated to determine baselines for success for every situational down in a game. Similarly to DVOA, basic success rates are determined by national standards. The distinction for college football is in defining the standards of success. We use the following determination of a "successful" play:

• First-down success is 50 percent of necessary yardage;

• Second-down successis 70 percent of necessary yardage;

• Third- or fourth-down success is 100 percent of necessary yardage

On a per play basis, these form the standards of efficiency for every offense in college football. Defensive success rates are based on preventing the same standards of achievement.

EQUIVALENT POINTS AND POINTS PER PLAY: All yards are not created equal. A 10-yard gain from a team's own 15-yard line does not have the same value as a 10-yard gain that goes from the opponent's 10-yard line into the end zone. Based on expected scoring rates similar to FPV described above, we can calculate a point value for each play in a drive. Equivalent Points (EqPts) are calculated by subtracting the value of the resulting yard line from the initial yard line of a given play. This assigns credit to the yards that are most associated with scoring points, the end goal in any possession.

With EqPts, the game can be broken down and built back up again in a number of ways. With the addition of penalties, turnovers and special teams play, EqPts provides an accurate assessment of how a game was played on a play-by-play basis. We also use it to create a measure called Points per Play (PPP), representative of a team's or an individual player's explosiveness.

S&P: Like OPS (on-base percentage plus slugging average) in baseball, we created a measure that combines consistency with power. S&P represents a combination of efficiency (Success Rates) and explosiveness (Points per Play) to most accurately represent the effectiveness of a team or individual player.

A boom-or-bust running back may have a strong yards per carry average and PPP, but his low Success Rate will lower his S&P. A consistent running back that gains between four and six yards every play, on the other hand, will have a strong Success Rate but possibly low PPP. The best offenses in the country can maximize both efficiency and explosiveness on a down-by-down basis. Reciprocally, the best defenses can limit both.

S&P+: As with the FEI stats discussed above, context matters in college football. Adjustments are made to the S&P unadjusted data with a formula that takes into account a team's production, the quality of the opponent, and the quality of the opponent's opponent. To eliminate the noise of less-informative blowout stats, we filtered the play-by-play data to include only those that took place when the game was "close." This excludes plays where the score margin is larger than 24 points in the first quarter, 21 points in the second quarter, or 16 points in the second half.

The result is S&P+, representing a team's efficiency and explosiveness as compared to all other teams in college football. S&P+ values are calibrated around an average rating of 100. An above-average team, offensively or defensively, will have an S&P+ rating greater than 100. A below-average team will have an S&P+ rating lower than 100.

In the team capsules in each conference chapter, the S&P+ ratings are broken down further as follows:

• Rushing S&P+ includes only running plays, and unlike standard college statistics, does not include sacks.

• Passing S&P+ includes sacks and passing plays.

• Passing Downs S&P+ includes second-and-8 or more, third-and-5 or more, and fourth-and-5 or more. These divisions were determined based on raw S&P data showing a clear distinction in Success Rates as compared with Standard Downs.

• Standard Downs S&P+ includes all close-game plays not defined as Passing Downs.

POE AND ADJ. POE: The collegiate stepchild of DYAR, POE stands for Points Over Expected. It is a running back-specific measure that compares a runner's EqPts output to what an average back would have done with carries in the same situations against the same opponents. The Adj. POE figure, used most in these chapters, adjusts POE to account for the relative strength (or weakness) of the offensive line.

Combination Data

F/+: Introduced with a passing mention in Football Outsiders Almanac 2009, the F/+ measure combines FEI and S&P+. There is a clear distinction between the two individual approaches, and merging the two diminishes certain outliers caused by the quirks of each method. The resulting metric is both powerfully predictive and sensibly evaluative.

PROGRAM AND PROJECTED F/+: Relative to the pros, college football teams are much more consistent in year-to-year performance. Breakout seasons and catastrophic collapses certainly occur, but generally speaking, teams can be expected to play within a reasonable range of their baseline program expectations. The idea of a Football Outsiders program rating began with the introduction of Program FEI in *Pro Football Prospectus 2008* as a way to represent those individual baseline expectations.

As the strength of the F/+ system has been fortified with more seasons of full drive-by-drive and play-by-play data, the Program F/+ measure has emerged. Program F/+ is calculated from five years of FEI and S&P+ data. The result not only represents the status of each team's program power, but provides the first step in projecting future success.

The Projected F/+ found in the following chapters starts by combining Program F/+ (weighted more toward recent seasons) with measures of five-year recruiting success (using Rivals.com ratings for signees who actually ended up enrolling at each school) and offensive and defensive performance. We adjust that baseline with transition factors like returning offensive and defensive starters, talent lost to the NFL Draft, and disproportional success on passing downs. The result, Projected F/+, is a more accurate predictor of next-year success than any other data we have tested or used to date (Table 1), a remarkable 0.85 correlation between projected and actual output:

Table 1: Correlation of Stats, Year to Year+1 (2005-10)

Statistic	Correl.	Statistic	Correl.
Conf. Win Pct.	0.52	S&P+	0.76
Win Pct.	0.60	Program F/+ (to F/+)	0.76
Pyth. Win Pct.	0.65	Projected F/+ (to F/+)	0.85
FEI	0.74		

STRENGTH OF SCHEDULE: Unlike other rating systems, our Strength of Schedule (SOS) calculation is not a simple average of the Projected F/+ data of each team's opponents. Instead, it is calculated from a "privileged" perspective, representing the likelihood that an elite team (typical top-five team) would win every game on the given schedule. The distinction is valid. For any elite team, playing No. 1 Alabama and No. 120 New Mexico State in a two-game stretch is certainly more difficult than playing No. 60 California and No. 61 Rutgers. An average rating might judge these schedules to be equal.

The likelihood of an undefeated season is calculated as the product of Projected Win Expectations (PWE) for each game on the schedule. PWEs are based on an assessment of five years of F/+ data and the records of teams of varying strengths against one another. Roughly speaking, an elite team may have a 65 percent chance of defeating a team ranked No. 10, a 75 percent chance of defeating a team ranked No. 20, and a 90 percent chance of defeating a team ranked No. 40. Combined, the elite team has a 44 percent likelihood of defeating all three (0.65 x 0.75 x 0.90 = 0.439).

A lower SOS rating represents a lower likelihood of an elite team running the table — a stronger schedule. For our calculations of FBS versus FCS games, with all due apologies to James Madison et al, the likelihood of victory is considered to be 100 percent.

MEAN WINS AND WIN PROBABILITIES: To project records for each team, we use Projected F/+ and PWE formulas to estimate the likelihood of victory for a given team in its individual games. The probabilities for winning each game are added together to represent the average number of wins the team is expected to tally over the course of its scheduled games. Potential conference championship games and bowl games are not included.

The projected records listed next to each team name in the conference chapters are rounded from the mean wins data listed in the team capsule. Mean Wins are not intended to represent projected outcomes of specific matchups, rather they are our most accurate forecast for the team's season as a whole. The correlation of mean wins to actual wins is 0.69 for all games, 0.61 for conference games.

The Win Probability tables that appear in each conference chapter are also based on the game-by-game PWE data for each team. The likelihood for each record is rounded to the nearest whole percent.

Brian Fremeau and Bill Connelly

Atlantic Coast Conference

Last year at this time, the ACC looked ripe for plucking as the power conferences jockeyed for expansion. When the dust settled, however, the conference was unchanged, and it seems set for the immediate future. ESPN outbid Fox Sports for the TV rights, doubling revenue for the athletic departments. There will be a second Game of the Week production, giving more exposure to the ACC schools not in Florida or Blacksburg, Virginia.

Most importantly, a group of young promising quarterbacks seems ready to step in right away and have success, rather than going through the traditional growing pains. Some, like E.J. Manuel at Florida State and Logan Thomas at Virginia Tech, are once-heavily recruited prep stars now taking over for longtime stalwarts. Others, like Bryn Renner at North Carolina and Mike Glennon at N.C. State, replace solid but ultimately disappointing signal callers. And if other passers with potential – like Stephen Morris at Miami, Chase Rettig at Boston College, and Sean Renfree at Duke – step up and produce, the ACC could see some wide-open excitement during those two weekly featured games, not to mention all the others.

Of course, all that firepower could well translate to another season of conference parity, which has been a problem for the ACC – few teams stand out on the national scene. With Virginia Tech after yet another ten-win season, the onus falls on Florida State to live up to its advance billing; on Clemson, Miami, and North Carolina to stop disappointing fans by playing below their talent levels; and for an X-factor team to emerge – perhaps North Carolina State. ACC football will never have the cachet of the SEC, or even that of ACC basketball, but at least it still exists as a recognizable, and viable, entity.

ATLANTIC

No. 10 Florida State Seminoles (10-2, 7-1)

2010: 10-4 (6-2) / F/+ #15 / FEI #18 / S&P+ #13

Program F/+	+11.0%	24	Returning Starters: 8 OFF, 8 DEF			5-Yr Recruiting Rank		8
2010 Offense			**2010 Defense**			**2010 Field Position**		
Offensive F/+	+13.9%	7	Defensive F/+	+4.0%	41	Field Position Advantage	0.531	20
Offensive FEI:	0.434	8	Defensive FEI	-0.115	38	**2011 Projections**		
Offensive S&P+	127.9	8	Defensive S&P+	113.2	32	**Mean Wins**	9.6	
Rushing S&P+	132.5	5	Rushing S&P+	108.7	40	Proj. F/+	+15.3%	10
Passing S&P+	127.5	11	Passing S&P+	117.1	27	Offensive F/+	+12.5%	3
Standard Downs S&P+	119.0	16	Standard Downs S&P+	118.4	19	Defensive F/+	+2.8%	47
Passing Downs S&P+	150.3	3	Passing Downs S&P+	104.9	51	Strength of Schedule	0.233	32

In his second season at the helm, Jimbo Fisher has the Seminoles poised to return to the school's once-assumed place among the Top Five. The most important element will be new quarterback E.J. Manuel, who replaces Christian Ponder, the oft-injured nice guy who couldn't quite get the 'Noles over the hump, especially in big games. Manuel is from the Virginia Tidewater region, but unlike earlier area stars like Michael Vick and Tyrod Taylor, he spurned Virginia Tech for FSU.

He played well in 2010 in Ponder's stead, going 4-2 as a starter, and led the team to victory in the Chick-Fil-A Bowl after Ponder was lost to a concussion. Manuel, whose deep, sibilant voice recalls a young James Earl Jones and heralds a future in broadcasting, showed complete command during the spring. Good as Ponder was, Manuel could easily surpass his exploits assuming he stays healthy for the next two seasons.

Florida State is loaded in the backfield, with three capable backs returning, plus top recruit Devonta Freeman. Pressure is on returning veteran Bert Reed (614 yards, 10.6 per catch) to up his level of play, especially with Taiwan Easterling's decision to give up football and pursue professional baseball opportunities. The offensive line was banged up throughout the spring, and must cohere despite the loss of leaders Rodney Hudson and Ryan McMahon. Left tackle Andrew Datko, the unit's best player, needs to fully recover from a shoulder injury.

Last year, Landry Jones and Oklahoma's fleet of wideouts shattered any illusions FSU had about its defensive progress, wiping the floor with the 'Noles 47-17. This year's rematch in Tallahassee needs to look markedly different, and the key is FSU's secondary, the presumed strength of a young defense. Corners Greg Reid and Mike Harris return to cover enemy receivers. Other than senior and top NFL prospect Nigel Bradham, the linebackers are young but extremely athletic and promising. The front four features top pass rusher Brandon Jenkins, who had 13.5 sacks as a

sophomore in 2010. Talent wasn't an issue last season, but mastering new coordinator Mark Stoops' schemes was. The defense started to improve near the end of the season, and evinced impressive physicality in the bowl game, a characteristic that has been missing from recent Seminole defenses.

FSU was 20th in Field Position Advantage a year ago, and that figures to get even better. Punter Shaun Powell is a candidate for the Ray Guy Award, and kicker Dustin Hopkins doesn't figure to go Wide Right at crunch time – he hit a 60-yard field goal during spring game. Much will be revealed about Florida State's 2011 before October – after two warmups, FSU has the Sooners and top Atlantic Division rival Clemson in back-to-back weeks.

Top 2012 NFL Prospects: CB Greg Reid* (1), DE Brandon Jenkins* (1-2), LB Nigel Bradham (1-2), T/G Andre Datko (2-3), S Nick Moody* (3-4), CB Mike Harris (5-6), K Dustin Hopkins* (6-7).

No. 23 Clemson Tigers (7-5, 5-3)

2010: 6-7 (4-4) / F/+ #25 / FEI #24 / S&P+ #34

Program F/+	+13.7%	16	Returning Starters: 8 OFF, 7 DEF			5-Yr Recruiting Rank		15
2010 Offense			**2010 Defense**			**2010 Field Position**		
						Field Position Advantage	0.500	60
Offensive F/+	-1.0%	68	**Defensive F/+**	+12.2%	10	**2011 Projections**		
Offensive FEI:	0.054	50	Defensive FEI	-0.471	7	**Mean Wins**	7.5	
Offensive S&P+	102.0	63	Defensive S&P+	122.3	14	Proj. F/+	+11.0%	23
Rushing S&P+	107.8	46	Rushing S&P+	134.4	6	Offensive F/+	+0.1%	57
Passing S&P+	98.8	72	Passing S&P+	108.8	43	Defensive F/+	+10.8%	5
Standard Downs S&P+	100.0	64	Standard Downs S&P+	125.5	10	Strength of Schedule	0.130	10
Passing Downs S&P+	98.3	67	Passing Downs S&P+	111.3	33			

Clemson's 2010 season took a wrong turn when the Tigers choked away a big lead at Auburn on September 18. A talented team went on to lose seven games, five of them by less than a touchdown, a record coach Dabo Swinney called "unacceptable." Clemson has gotten into a bad habit of slow starts, and the 2011 schedule has a rough stretch after a pair of opening cupcakes – Auburn, Florida State, Virginia Tech, and Boston College in a brutal month. The Tigers season will rise or fall depending on how they handle it.

Clemson will try to replicate Auburn's spread success, and hired Chad Morris, a Gus Malzahn disciple, away from Tulsa to replace Billy Napier as offensive coordinator. The man pulling the strings will be new quarterback Tahj Boyd, a superb athlete who should flourish in Malzahn's system of simple reads (albeit perhaps not to the level of Cam Newton). If Boyd can improve his

accuracy, the offense should improve from last season's mediocre showing. Andre Ellington (684 yards and a stellar plus-21.1 Adj. POE) returns to lead the rushing attack, with prep sensation Mike Bellamy (110 high school touchdowns!) looking to play the role Marcus Lattimore did for cross-state rival South Carolina a year ago.

The defense will have to replace Da'Quan Bowers and his 15.5 sacks. Andre Branch steps up – he had six sacks in 2010 and is a potential first-round draft choice. Fellow end Malliciah Goodman is a freakish athlete who, if reaches his potential, could make the memory of Bowers fade rapidly in Death Valley.

Top 2012 NFL Prospects: DE Andre Branch (1-2), DE Malliciah Goodman* (1-2), RB Andre Ellington* (2-4), TE Dwayne Allen* (2-4), DT Brandon Thompson (3-4), S Rashard Hall* (3-4), DT Dawson Zimmerman (7).

No. 27 North Carolina State Wolfpack (9-3, 5-3)

2010: 9-4 (5-3) / F/+ #23 / FEI #13 / S&P+ #38

Program F/+	+1.7%	53	Returning Starters: 7 OFF, 8 DEF			5-Yr Recruiting Rank		46
2010 Offense			**2010 Defense**			**2010 Field Position**		
Offensive F/+	+5.3%	33	**Defensive F/+**	+8.4%	24	Field Position Advantage	0.521	35
Offensive FEI:	0.238	25	Defensive FEI	-0.407	13	**2011 Projections**		
Offensive S&P+	108.8	39	Defensive S&P+	109.6	40	**Mean Wins**	8.7	
Rushing S&P+	106.8	48	Rushing S&P+	115.0	23	Proj. F/+	+8.8%	27
Passing S&P+	108.9	45	Passing S&P+	106.2	47	Offensive F/+	+2.4%	43
Standard Downs S&P+	109.1	40	Standard Downs S&P+	102.3	51	Defensive F/+	+6.4%	28
Passing Downs S&P+	112.9	38	Passing Downs S&P+	112.4	31	Strength of Schedule	0.370	66

In the movie *Almost Famous*, the band Stillwater is overshadowed by – and almost implodes due to – a talented egomaniac named Russell. Seeking to avoid a similar fate for his N.C. State Wolfpack, head coach Tom O'Brien told his starting quarterback named Russell (Wilson) that his solo forays into professional baseball were hurting the team, and relieved him as starter. Wilson, an outfielder in the Colorado Rockies chain and an All-ACC choice as a freshman in 2009, chose to transfer to Wisconsin instead of getting the band back together with him in a reduced role.

The new Golden God in Raleigh is Mike Glennon, who takes over at quarterback. At 6-foot-6 and 225 pounds, Glennon has the size and arm strength to exceed Wilson, who threw for more than 3,500 yards last season. O'Brien, whose immediate coaching future is admittedly hogtied to Glennon's success, lavished praise upon his new starter all spring, even comparing him to another quarterback O'Brien coached, Matt Ryan. If Wilson excels at Wisconsin this season, Glennon had better be Ryan 2.0 or the outcries will be loud on Tobacco Road.

Elsewhere, State's receiving depth was lacerated by graduation, so Glennon will have to rely on running back Mustafa Greene (597 yards, minus-8.5 Adj. POE), who seized the starting role in 2010. Defensive star Nate Irving is gone, but the secondary should be much improved, with all four starters returning. Injuries have played an outsized role in limiting the Wolfpack over the past few seasons, with several more walk-ons forced onto the depth chart than the coaching staff would have liked. If players can remain healthy, and Glennon lives up the hype, N.C. State could rocket up the charts in the Atlantic Division.

Top 2012 NFL Prospects: TE George Bryan (3).

No. 37 Maryland Terrapins (7-5, 4-4)

2010: 9-4 (5-3) / F/+ #31 / FEI #24 / S&P+ #37

Program F/+	+2.8%	51	Returning Starters: 7 OFF, 7 DEF			5-Yr Recruiting Rank		35
2010 Offense			**2010 Defense**			**2010 Field Position**		
Offensive F/+	+1.0%	52	**Defensive F/+**	+9.1%	22	Field Position Advantage	0.531	20
Offensive FEI:	0.028	56	Defensive FEI	-0.339	20	**2011 Projections**		
Offensive S&P+	105.5	44	Defensive S&P+	114.1	31	**Mean Wins**	6.5	
Rushing S&P+	98.3	77	Rushing S&P+	111.2	28	Proj. F/+	+5.8%	37
Passing S&P+	112.3	39	Passing S&P+	116.5	29	Offensive F/+	-1.6%	70
Standard Downs S&P+	106.2	48	Standard Downs S&P+	117.0	23	Defensive F/+	+7.4%	18
Passing Downs S&P+	111.6	41	Passing Downs S&P+	111.2	34	Strength of Schedule	0.230	31

The Terps essentially came in third place in the ACC last season, the best team not to make the conference title game. The school then pulled a *Glengarry Glen Ross* on coach Ralph Friedgen: "Third place means you're fired." The corpulent Fridge, who really wanted the set of steak knives, has been replaced by Randy Edsall, who built the UConn program from a scattered bunch of sticks on the ground into a roaring BCS-level bonfire. Edsall has taken a Coughlin/Belichick approach in College Park; earrings and do-rags are banned, and the media are being treated like lepers. So while little has slipped out about Edsall's evaluation of the team's talent, we're pretty sure the players have been early for every meeting.

Certainly Edsall should be happy with quarterback Danny O'Brien, who came from nowhere to win the ACC Rookie of the Year award in 2010. With a more up-tempo spread attack likely to be installed by new coordinator Gary Crowton, O'Brien will be slinging it even more than he did a year ago, when he threw 22 touchdowns with more than 2,200 yards despite not taking over as starter until the fourth game of the season. Maryland returns 14 of 22 starters, but loses the best player on each side of the ball, wide receiver Torrey Smith and linebacker Alex Wujciak. A flotilla of wideouts will catch balls from O'Brien, including Kerry Boykins (12.4 yards per catch in limited opportunities) and Kevin Dorsey (12.5). On defense, top athlete Kenny Tate is moving from safety to linebacker to help fill the tackling void left in Wujciak's wake. Maryland's defense was Top 30 almost across the board in our stats, and Tate's ability to handle the "Star" linebacker position (Terps lingo for roverback) will decide if the unit can repeat that performance.

If opponents are to truly Fear the Turtle, the offensive line must stay healthy, which it has been unable to do for the last couple of seasons. Left tackle Justin Gilbert reinjured his torn-up knee during spring practice and will be out until midseason at the earliest. That puts pressure on projected starters R.J. Dill and Justin Lewis to overcome injuries of their own and get on the field. At least the schedule is favorable; the Terps don't play a road game until October 8.

Top 2012 NFL Prospects: S Kenny Tate (2), DB Cameron Chism (4-6), WR Tony Logan (6-7).

No. 41 Boston College Eagles (6-6, 3-5)

2010: 7-6 (4-4) / F/+ #48 / FEI #50 / S&P+ #47

Program F/+	+10.6%	26	Returning Starters: 8 OFF, 7 DEF		5-Yr Recruiting Rank		47
2010 Offense			**2010 Defense**		**2010 Field Position**		
Offensive F/+	-10.4%	104	**Defensive F/+**	+13.5%	6	Field Position Advantage	0.501	56
Offensive FEI:	-0.289	100	Defensive FEI	-0.405	15	**2011 Projections**		
Offensive S&P+	86.1	100	Defensive S&P+	123.3	12	**Mean Wins**	5.7	
Rushing S&P+	88.9	95	Rushing S&P+	146.0	2	Proj. F/+	+4.9%	41
Passing S&P+	83.7	97	Passing S&P+	110.7	36	Offensive F/+	-7.5%	106
Standard Downs S&P+	90.9	94	Standard Downs S&P+	124.3	11	Defensive F/+	+12.4%	1
Passing Downs S&P+	78.4	108	Passing Downs S&P+	121.1	21	Strength of Schedule	0.149	13

Eagles linebacker Mark Herzlich was the feel-good story of 2010. He came back from life-threatening bone cancer to play, and play well. The deserved praise tossed in Herzlich's direction obscured the play of fellow linebacker Luke Kuechly, who turned in one of the best seasons of any defensive player in the country. Kuechly led the nation in tackles with 183 (110 individual). He combines exceptional instincts with speed and smarts, and is the frontrunner for the Butkus Award.

Chase Rettig came from deep down the depth chart to solidify the quarterback position a year ago. For his troubles, Rettig (1,238 yards, 105.5 passer rating) now gets to learn a new system under first-year coordinator Kevin Rogers, who is perhaps best known for combining pro sets with highly efficient option looks while at Syracuse in the 1990s. Rettig looked good for most of the spring, adapting quickly to the change in scheme, but he will need to show it with a middling group of receivers as targets. The expected return of Colin Larmond from a torn ACL should help. Running back Montel Harris could be one of the better senior running backs in the nation with help – BC's horrid Rushing S&P+ in 2010 was largely a reflection of the instability at quarterback as teams loaded up to stop Harris, who nonetheless ran for 1,243 yards. One of Rogers' primary tasks will be to make things happen on offense without relying too heavily on his feature back.

The Eagles routinely turn out pro-ready offensive linemen, with 2011 first-round pick Anthony Castonzo merely the latest. This year's unit lost three starters but looked typically sound in spring ball, keyed by center Mark Spinney. Kaleb Ramsey leads a front four that is overshadowed by the linebackers, and Donnie Fletcher is among the nation's top corners. It stands to reason that BC will stop opponents – how much the offense improves will determine whether the Eagles can make a run at the division title.

Top 2012 NFL Prospects: LB Luke Kuechly (1), RB Montel Harris (2-3), CB Donnie Fletcher (4-5).*

No. 77 Wake Forest Demon Deacons (3-9, 1-7)

2010: 3-9 (1-7) / F/+ #97 / FEI #105 / S&P+ #91

Program F/+	+2.9%	50	Returning Starters: 8 OFF, 8 DEF		5-Yr Recruiting Rank		69

2010 Offense			2010 Defense			2010 Field Position		
Offensive F/+	-6.3%	92	Defensive F/+	-7.0%	93	Field Position Advantage	0.459	108
Offensive FEI:	-0.273	99	Defensive FEI	0.225	93	2011 Projections		
Offensive S&P+	94.3	85	Defensive S&P+	89.0	94	Mean Wins	3.0	
Rushing S&P+	108.1	43	Rushing S&P+	88.6	96	Proj. F/+	-4.7%	77
Passing S&P+	80.7	103	Passing S&P+	88.3	91	Offensive F/+	-2.5%	77
Standard Downs S&P+	105.6	50	Standard Downs S&P+	81.9	113	Defensive F/+	-2.2%	69
Passing Downs S&P+	73.4	114	Passing Downs S&P+	99.8	68	Strength of Schedule	0.271	44

The Deacons were horrid in 2010, especially defensively, but there are hopeful signs of a rebound season, at least to .500. Last year graduation, personnel, and injury forced an uneasy transition to a 3-4 scheme, with two freshman corners starting behind it. Unsurprisingly, Wake plummeted to the bottom third of the nation in our defensive stats. Coordinator Brad Lambert is gone, and the remaining staff is hoping that with all four starters back and the bitter taste of an 11th-in-conference pass defense ranking spurring them on, the secondary is ready to improve.

That's the optimistic line from head coach Jim Grobe, anyway. The unit was a shambolic miasma of missed assignments, penalties, and blown tackles in 2010. Turning that ship around in a single offseason is a lot to ask, even from Grobe. Top flight end Kyle Wilbur is a piece to build around up front.

Wake's signal callers were young last year too. Freshman Tanner Price bested Ted Stachitas to grab the starting job, but injuries and poor decisions marked his debut campaign. Both quarterbacks return, and showed signs of maturity in spring practice, especially the junior Stachitas. Up front, four starters return on the offensive line – unfortunately, solid center Russell Nenon (now graduated) isn't one of them.

Top 2012 NFL Prospects: DE Kyle Wilbur (2-3).

COASTAL

No. 6 Virginia Tech Hokies (11-1, 7-1)

2010: 11-3 (8-0) / F/+ #10 / FEI #5 / S&P+ #14

Program F/+	+19.5%	8	Returning Starters: 6 OFF, 7 DEF		5-Yr Recruiting Rank		21

2010 Offense			2010 Defense			2010 Field Position		
Offensive F/+	+12.7%	10	Defensive F/+	+8.5%	23	Field Position Advantage	0.564	3
Offensive FEI:	0.406	11	Defensive FEI	-0.293	27	2011 Projections		
Offensive S&P+	124.0	12	Defensive S&P+	116.8	28	Mean Wins	11.2	
Rushing S&P+	124.3	12	Rushing S&P+	104.1	48	Proj. F/+	+16.7%	6
Passing S&P+	127.9	10	Passing S&P+	128.2	13	Offensive F/+	+9.3%	10
Standard Downs S&P+	113.2	30	Standard Downs S&P+	116.7	24	Defensive F/+	+7.4%	19
Passing Downs S&P+	132.9	11	Passing Downs S&P+	116.2	28	Strength of Schedule	0.626	99

Few programs could lose their all-time leading passer and top two running backs, yet fully expect to win double-digit games and contend for the BCS title. The Hokies are one of those programs. 2010 marked one of coach Frank Beamer's best coaching jobs. Virginia Tech was 0-2 after a tough late loss to Boise State on national TV, followed by a Galifianakis-level hangover loss to FCS school James Madison. With a national record seventh straight ten-win season in serious jeopardy, Beamer rallied the troops and ripped off ten straight victories before falling to powerful Stanford in the Orange Bowl.

Can Beamer's Boys make it eight straight? Signs point to yes, even with the graduation of quarterback Tyrod Taylor, reigning ACC Player of the Year. Into his large shoes steps Logan Thomas, who at 6-foot-6 wears size 18 cleats, so let's find another metaphor. The redshirt sophomore was outstanding in the spring, leaving no doubt that he is ready to take over. Thomas was a top-rated recruit coming into Blacksburg – at tight end! He lined up at wideout last year and caught a touchdown pass, so there should be no doubts about his athleticism, though Thomas is much more of a classic dropback thrower than Taylor, who excelled on the move.

Thomas will ease into the job behind a potent offensive line that returns four senior starters, and running back David Wilson (619 rushing yards, plus-2.5 Adj. POE) will smooth the loss of Ryan Williams and Darren Evans. Wilson, who caught 15 passes for 234 yards last fall, is a better receiver out of the backfield than either Williams or Evans, which will be a nice safety valve for a developing quarterback.

Tech made its bones last season on offense, while the defense struggled to stop teams, an unusual circumstance under defensive coordinator Bud Foster. Look for the unit to improve in 2011, keyed by a potent front four led by tackle Antoine Hopkins. Depth is a concern, but the starting eleven should return the Hokie defense to its expected level of savagery. At the very least, Tech's talent, coaching, and easy schedule (Miami and Clemson at home, albeit in consecutive weeks, and games with Appalachian State, Arkansas State, and Marshall) should return the Hokies to the conference title game.

Top 2012 NFL Prospects: RB David Wilson* (2-3), CB Jayron Hosely (2-3), OT Blake DeChristopher (2-3), S Eddie Whitley (3-4), G/T Jaymes Brooks (4-6), LB Barquell Rivers (7).

No. 24 Miami Hurricanes (8-4, 5-3)

2010: 7-6 (5-3) / F/+ #19 / FEI #22 / S&P+ #15

Program F/+	+8.7%	34	Returning Starters: 6 OFF, 7 DEF			5-Yr Recruiting Rank		16
2010 Offense			**2010 Defense**			**2010 Field Position**		
Offensive F/+	+3.3%	40	Defensive F/+	+12.2%	12	Field Position Advantage	0.486	76
Offensive FEI:	0.137	40	Defensive FEI	-0.441	9	**2011 Projections**		
Offensive S&P+	113.3	28	Defensive S&P+	125.7	9	**Mean Wins**	8.2	
Rushing S&P+	114.6	27	Rushing S&P+	119.4	19	Proj. F/+	+10.6%	24
Passing S&P+	112.8	38	Passing S&P+	131.1	8	Offensive F/+	+0.1%	58
Standard Downs S&P+	125.8	8	Standard Downs S&P+	127.5	9	Defensive F/+	+10.5%	7
Passing Downs S&P+	95.6	78	Passing Downs S&P+	118.5	25	Strength of Schedule	0.195	22

While it feels like Jacory Harris has been in Coral Gables for decades, he's only been teasing Hurricane Nation with perfectly arced bombs and endearingly crazy hairstyles for three seasons (while simultaneously frustrating with interceptions thrown at critical times). But will Miami's own Jekyll-and-Hyde continue to torture Hurricane fans as a senior? A nasty concussion suffered in the Virginia game last season opened the door for Stephen Morris to take charge, and the position battle between Harris, Morris and Spencer Whipple was still tight through the spring.

The Randy Shannon Era is over at The U, but the talent he assembled remains (a lot of it, anyway – quite a few transfers punctuated Miami's spring). It falls to Al Golden, who rebuilt the Temple program into something Bill Cosby could crow about, to coach up thoroughbreds like defensive tackle Marcus Forston, linebacker Sean Spence, and safeties Ray Ray Armstrong and Vaughn Telemaque. The Canes were strong across the board in our defensive stats from 2010, but in the three biggest games of the season, the unit surrendered 36 to Ohio State, 45 to Florida State, and 31 to Virginia Tech before getting strafed by Notre Dame in the Sun Bowl. The U has lost its rep as a big-game monster – getting the D to step up in the rivalry games would be a good place for Golden to start.

While the quarterback position is mired in mediocrity, the running back corps is stacked with studs. Mike James (398 yards, plus-3.0 Adj. POE) and Lamar Miller (646, plus-5.7) should take pressure off whoever emerges from the passing derby. Miami will know right away if the supposed "new attitude" under Golden has taken hold, with a road game at Maryland to open the season and Ohio State coming to South Florida two weeks later.

Top 2012 NFL Prospects: DT Marcus Forston* (1), S Ray Ray Armstrong* (1), LB Sean Spence (3-4), S Vaughn Telemaque* (3-4), G Brandon Washington* (3-4), C Tyler Horn (4-6), DT Micanor Regis (5-6).

No. 40 North Carolina Tar Heels (7-5, 4-4)

2010: 7-6 (4-4) / F/+ #39 / FEI #31 / S&P+ #46

Program F/+	+4.2%	44	Returning Starters: 5 OFF, 7 DEF		5-Yr Recruiting Rank		19
2010 Offense			**2010 Defense**			**2010 Field Position**	
Offensive F/+	+1.4%	48	**Defensive F/+**	+5.3%	37	Field Position Advantage	0.454	113
Offensive FEI:	0.146	37	Defensive FEI	-0.318	24	**2011 Projections**	
Offensive S&P+	104.3	50	Defensive S&P+	107.3	44	**Mean Wins**	7.2
Rushing S&P+	98.4	76	Rushing S&P+	111.6	27	Proj. F/+	+5.4%	40
Passing S&P+	109.1	44	Passing S&P+	103.2	54	Offensive F/+	-1.2%	66
Standard Downs S&P+	109.3	38	Standard Downs S&P+	109.4	38	Defensive F/+	+6.6%	26
Passing Downs S&P+	98.2	68	Passing Downs S&P+	111.1	35	Strength of Schedule	0.279	47

The Heels found out the hard way that when you hire Butch Davis as your head coach, you get the entire package, for good and ill. The scandals that follow Butch's recruitment of NFL-ready prospects are as sure as buzzards following dying game. UNC was primed for a big year in 2010, with a core of top defenders including high draft picks Robert Quinn, Marvin Austin, and Bruce Carter, along with wideout Greg Little. Only Carter managed to avoid suspension for accepting illegal benefits from an agent. In all, 13 players lost all or part of their seasons, a disgrace that would have had most coaches dropping off their card key with the security guard and being ushered out of the complex.

Not Butch, though. Davis sacrificed his toxic main recruiting assistant, John Blake, and held on to his job for 2011, mainly because the suddenly undermanned Heels played well for most of the season, culminating in a thrilling double-overtime win over Tennessee in the Music City Bowl. Now the team, despite seeing nine players drafted, remains a dark horse candidate for the division title, ironically because of the valuable experience many young players received subbing for the suspended ones.

Those include another passel of defenders causing NFL scouts to drool uncontrollably. End Quinton Coples is a potential top-five pick coming off a 10-sack, 15.5-TFL season during which he was forced to play tackle. Restored to his natural end spot, there is no limit on the damage Coples may do in enemy backfields now that the NCAA has ruled him eligible for the fall. Tackle Tydreke Powell is a 305-pound, blocker-occupying beast in the middle. Hybrid pass rusher Donte Paige-Moss had seven sacks in 2010, while linebacker Zack Brown should make Heels fans forget Carter. The secondary is young, but should get a boost from the pass rush.

Despite the defensive talent, Carolina fans are most excited about the quarterback position, where highly touted sophomore Bryn Renner takes over for the capable but inconsistent T.J. Yates. Renner had an exceptional spring game and looks ready to become an upper-echelon passer. Explosive Dwight Jones (946 receiving yards and a stellar 15.3 yards per catch) returns as the primary wide receiver, and he is joined by a younger but even more electric talent, Erik Highsmith (348, 8.9). The running game should flourish behind a huge and experienced line anchored by guard Jonathan Cooper. A ten-win season is certainly within reach in Chapel Hill, with one big assumption – that all the players remain eligible and on the field.

Top 2012 NFL Prospects: DE Quinton Coples (1), DE/LB Donte Paige-Moss* (1), LB Zack Brown (1), DT Tydreke Powell (1-2), WR Dwight Jones (1-3), WR Erik Highsmith* (2-3), LB Kevin Reddick* (2-4), G/T Jonathan Cooper* (3-5).

No. 50 Georgia Tech Yellow Jackets (6-6, 3-5)

2010: 6-7 (4-4) / F/+ #64 / FEI #51 / S&P+ #70

Program F/+	+8.4%	35	Returning Starters: 6 OFF, 5 DEF		5-Yr Recruiting Rank		38
2010 Offense			**2010 Defense**		**2010 Field Position**		
Offensive F/+	+2.9%	44	**Defensive F/+**	-4.3%	77	Field Position Advantage	0.486	76
Offensive FEI:	0.094	45	Defensive FEI	0.071	70	**2011 Projections**		
Offensive S&P+	104.6	48	Defensive S&P+	91.0	85	**Mean Wins**	6.2	
Rushing S&P+	111.6	34	Rushing S&P+	94.7	76	Proj. F/+	+3.3%	50
Passing S&P+	80.7	104	Passing S&P+	87.4	95	Offensive F/+	+4.9%	31
Standard Downs S&P+	107.1	46	Standard Downs S&P+	92.7	82	Defensive F/+	-1.6%	66
Passing Downs S&P+	95.1	80	Passing Downs S&P+	95.8	75	Strength of Schedule	0.317	55

2010 was the season the doubters of Paul Johnson's spread option system got to shout their "toldyasos!" from rooftops across Atlanta. The running attack wasn't nearly as indomitable as it had been in recent years, and worsened when triggerman Joshua Nesbitt went down to injury in November. The defense struggled under first-year coordinator Al Groh and his switch to a 3-4 scheme. And the special teams were brutal – 114th in the country in net punting, for example.

Can Johnson turn it around, and do so without the prime athletes recruited by predecessor Chan Gailey? Tech got a glimpse of life without Nesbitt when he broke his arm trying to make a tackle after throwing a pick against Virginia Tech last season. Tevin Washington was a suitable replacement carrying the ball, but he lacked Nesbitt's bulldog ability to get tough yards. Washington was overmatched as a passer (of course, so was Nesbitt), though he was forced to play some snarling defenses in his four and a half games at the helm. Any complacency Washington may have had entering the spring as presumed starter was erased in the spring game. Washington threw three picks, fumbled twice, and looked lost against a Tech D that has issues of its own. Backup Synjyn Days and top recruit Vad Lee might be talented enough to push Washington, and a midseason course correction at quarterback could be in the offing.

The running backs are a strength, especially senior sprinter Roddy Jones (353 rushing yards, plus-1.5 Adj. POE), and the defense has talent and can only improve after spending most of 2010 out of position and a step slow. Linebacker Steven Sylvester and end Jason Peters are standouts. But the offensive line, an unheralded strength when Tech won the ACC championship in 2009, is wanting. The unit lacked cohesion and looked tentative this spring, and there isn't much depth behind the starters. The schedule is workable, with an easy start and Virginia Tech and Clemson coming to Bobby Dodd Stadium. Whether the home fans will have checked out by the time those two powers visit around Halloween is an open question.

Top 2012 NFL Prospects: RB Roddy Jones (6-7), LB Steven Sylvester (7).

No. 66 Virginia Cavaliers (5-7, 2-6)

2010: 4-8 (1-7) / F/+ #83 / FEI #80 / S&P+ #82

Program F/+	+0.2%	60	Returning Starters: 8 OFF, 7 DEF		5-Yr Recruiting Rank		43
2010 Offense			**2010 Defense**		**2010 Field Position**		
Offensive F/+	+0.1%	58	**Defensive F/+**	-7.8%	99	Field Position Advantage	0.476	88
Offensive FEI:	-0.002	64	Defensive FEI	0.186	85	**2011 Projections**		
Offensive S&P+	102.1	61	Defensive S&P+	87.2	103	**Mean Wins**	5.0	
Rushing S&P+	109.0	39	Rushing S&P+	83.1	109	Proj. F/+	-1.3%	66
Passing S&P+	96.0	80	Passing S&P+	92.4	81	Offensive F/+	+3.4%	37
Standard Downs S&P+	104.6	54	Standard Downs S&P+	95.1	76	Defensive F/+	-4.6%	84
Passing Downs S&P+	97.5	72	Passing Downs S&P+	83.5	106	Strength of Schedule	0.252	41

The Cavaliers exited the spring with four quarterbacks in the mix for the starting gig. Virginia also loses leading rusher Keith Payne (749 rushing yards, plus-8.9 Adj. POE), with no clear-cut replacement in sight. Meanwhile, cornerback Ras-I Dowling was the first pick of the second round in the NFL draft. Despite the return of 15 starters, Virginia seems poised for a difficult season of transition under second-year coach Mike London.

There are some good pieces left in Charlottesville, mainly along the lines. Defensive end Cam Johnson had 6.5 sacks, and the defensive tackle combo of Matt Conrath and Nick Jenkins is potent. Cornerback Chase Minnifield actually outshone Dowling in 2010, with six picks and a penchant for physical play, and is an All-Conference level performer. The defense will have to step up and carry the team until the offense finds an identity under whoever wins the quarterback job.

Top 2012 NFL Prospects: CB Chase Minnifield (1), DE Cam Johnson (4-6), DT Matt Conrath (6-7).

No. 79 Duke Blue Devils (4-8, 1-7)

2010: 3-9 (1-7) / F/+ #80 / FEI #77 / S&P+ #74

Program F/+		-8.8%	85	Returning Starters: 7 OFF, 6 DEF				5-Yr Recruiting Rank			66
2010 Offense				**2010 Defense**				**2010 Field Position**			
Offensive F/+		-0.8%	65	**Defensive F/+**		-5.1%	85	Field Position Advantage		0.490	70
Offensive FEI:		-0.148	82	Defensive FEI		0.217	92	**2011 Projections**			
Offensive S&P+		101.7	64	Defensive S&P+		91.9	78	**Mean Wins**		3.6	
Rushing S&P+		100.4	67	Rushing S&P+		99.5	65	Proj. F/+		-5.2%	79
Passing S&P+		102.7	57	Passing S&P+		82.3	107	Offensive F/+		-0.4%	64
Standard Downs S&P+		99.8	65	Standard Downs S&P+		97.4	66	Defensive F/+		-4.7%	87
Passing Downs S&P+		109.2	51	Passing Downs S&P+		84.2	104	Strength of Schedule		0.286	48

The Blue Devils have flirted with decency since David Cutcliffe took over as coach. Cutcliffe enters his fourth season in charge, and this year's team could get to a bowl for the first time since 1995. Eight starters return on offense, including quarterback Sean Renfree, who passed for 3,131 yards, 14 touchdowns and 17 interceptions last fall as a sophomore. He doesn't have the pedigree of other conference QBs, but Renfree improved in his decision-making (only two picks in his last 188 attempts) and is a very good athlete. Renfree will throw to a strong pair of wideouts, Conner Vernon (973 yards, 13.3 per catch) and Donovan Varner (736, 12.3).

Any chance Duke has of getting to six wins depends on showing some defensive improvement. Their passing defense finished near the bottom of the country, and managed exactly one sack per game. In the hopes of improving their horrific play, Duke hired "pass rush whisperer" Rick Petri as defensive line coach. Petri has developed some renowned front-four types, including Warren Sapp, John Abraham, and Kenard Lang. Petri won't have that sort of raw material to work with in Durham, of course, but if he can improve the Devils up front from an F to a C-, Duke will at least be competitive on passing downs. The back four has talent, in particular corner Johnny Williams.

Top 2012 NFL Prospects: WR Donovan Varner (5-7), DB Johnny Williams (6-7), S Matt Daniels (6-7).

Robert Weintraub

Projected Win Probabilities For ACC Teams

ACC Atlantic	Overall Wins												Conference Wins								
	12-0	11-1	10-2	9-3	8-4	7-5	6-6	5-7	4-8	3-9	2-10	1-11	0-12	8-0	7-1	6-2	5-3	4-4	3-5	2-6	1-7	0-8
Boston College	-	-	-	2	7	18	29	26	14	4	-	-	-	-	-	2	10	26	35	22	5	-
Clemson	-	1	6	16	27	27	16	6	1	-	-	-	-	1	9	24	32	23	9	2	-	-
Florida State	4	18	32	28	13	4	1	-	-	-	-	-	-	23	40	27	9	1	-	-	-	-
Maryland	-	-	2	6	16	26	26	17	6	1	-	-	-	-	2	9	24	31	23	9	2	-
N.C. State	1	7	20	29	25	13	4	1	-	-	-	-	-	2	12	28	31	19	7	1	-	-
Wake Forest	-	-	-	-	-	-	2	8	22	34	26	8	-	-	-	-	1	5	21	42	31

ACC Coastal	12-0	11-1	10-2	9-3	8-4	7-5	6-6	5-7	4-8	3-9	2-10	1-11	0-12	8-0	7-1	6-2	5-3	4-4	3-5	2-6	1-7	0-8
Duke	-	-	-	-	-	1	5	17	32	31	13	1	-	-	-	-	-	2	11	32	40	15
Georgia Tech	-	-	1	4	13	24	28	20	8	2	-	-	-	-	-	2	11	25	31	22	8	1
Miami	-	3	13	26	29	19	8	2	-	-	-	-	-	1	9	27	35	21	6	1	-	-
North Carolina	-	-	4	13	25	29	19	8	2	-	-	-	-	-	1	8	23	35	25	7	1	-
Virginia	-	-	-	2	9	23	31	24	9	2	-	-	-	-	-	-	1	6	21	37	29	6
Virginia Tech	40	40	16	4	-	-	-	-	-	-	-	-	-	43	40	14	3	-	-	-	-	-

Big East Conference

If nothing else, the Big East conference got more exciting this past winter. In a region known for fullbacks and snow, two of the conference's relative powers brought in up-tempo, high-potential offensive minds in attempt to breathe a bit of life into a stagnant group of squads.

To be sure, there were interesting developments before Tulsa's Todd Graham came to Pittsburgh and Oklahoma State's Dana Holgorsen packed up his permanent hotel room for Morgantown. Charlie Strong led Louisville to an impressive first-year turnaround in 2010, while Doug Marrone made Syracuse relevant for the first time since Paul Pasqualoni (Connecticut's new coach) left a few years ago. The Big East has been the source of interesting intra-conference battles and tight title races, but the upside was questionable. Cincinnati went undefeated two years ago but ranked only 15th in overall F/+ when all was said and done. ESPN's Brian Bennett has referred to the conference as a "torso conference," with no head (elite teams) and no bottom (dregs) … just a bunch of torsos.

This was never more evident than in 2010, when Connecticut – a disciplined, likable team with little discernible upside – managed to snatch a conference title and Fiesta Bowl bid despite ranking just a middling 55th in F/+, its worst ranking of the last four years. With "The Mountain West is stronger than the Big East" sentiment growing and the conference narrowly avoiding serious damage during last summer's conference realignment developments, new life was needed. And in the offenses of Graham and Holgorsen, the conference may have found just that.

The 2011 Big East race could be yet another interesting one, with Pittsburgh and West Virginia breaking in new offensive philosophies; a high-upside, depressing-downside Cincinnati squad looking to bounce back; South Florida and Louisville looking to make leaps in their respective coaches' second seasons on the job; and Connecticut looking to defend its crown with a new head coach. There is probably not an elite team in the bunch again, but this season's developments prove, if nothing else, that the effort is there. And with quite a few young teams still getting their footing, the conference as a whole could see at least a slight rise in profile in the coming seasons.

No. 16 Pittsburgh Panthers (10-2, 6-1)

2010: 8-5 (5-2) / F/+ #22 / FEI #20 / S&P+ #24

Program F/+	+11.1%	23	Returning Starters: 8 OFF, 8 DEF			5-Yr Recruiting Rank		33
2010 Offense			**2010 Defense**			**2010 Field Position**		
Offensive F/+	+8.6%	20	**Defensive F/+**	+6.0%	35	Field Position Advantage	0.519	37
Offensive FEI:	0.211	29	Defensive FEI	-0.278	29	**2011 Projections**		
Offensive S&P+	121.4	16	Defensive S&P+	108.9	41	**Mean Wins**	9.6	
Rushing S&P+	129.5	6	Rushing S&P+	100.3	62	Proj. F/+	+12.5%	16
Passing S&P+	117.4	25	Passing S&P+	118.3	25	Offensive F/+	+6.3%	24
Standard Downs S&P+	118.7	17	Standard Downs S&P+	115.0	29	Defensive F/+	+6.1%	29
Passing Downs S&P+	121.6	24	Passing Downs S&P+	96.3	74	Strength of Schedule	0.403	67

What's more important: producing a team capable of playing at an extremely high level, or purely winning football games? Because Dave Wannstedt managed to do one without necessarily doing the other in his time as Pittsburgh head coach. The Panthers rank 22nd in Four-Year F/+ and ranked 22nd or better in each of the last three seasons, and yet they won double-digit games only once. The Panthers went just 1-3 in games decided by one possession in 2010, and disappointing blowout losses at home to Miami and West Virginia spelled doom for The Wannstache.

Now, Todd Graham inherits the job and is tasked with instituting a rather significant identity change. Graham was the head man for Tulsa's high-octane, high-paced attack in recent years. Tulsa's situational run-pass ratios were quite similar to Pittsburgh's last year – there is a lot more rushing in Graham's spread, though not an Oregon level, by any means – but they moved at nearly twice the pace, and their variability was high depending on the situation and opponent. Sometimes Tulsa produced crazy rushing numbers, sometimes crazy passing numbers. At Pittsburgh, Graham will utilize an experienced quarterback (Tino Sunseri), a quality running back (Ray Graham, who rushed for 922 yards and produced a plus-5.3 Adj. POE in support of Dion Lewis, who is now a Philadelphia Eagle), a pair of interesting receivers (big Mike Shanahan and sophomore Devin Street), and three senior starters on the offensive line. The Panthers are not guaranteed to thrive immediately by any means, but the potential here is high for Graham's first offense in the Eastern time zone.

Graham also brings with him his Tulsa defensive coordinator, Keith Patterson. Patterson's Golden Hurricane defenses attacked and often got to the quarterback, but they gave up a lot of big plays in the process. Pittsburgh was strong at avoiding big plays last year, but a primary cause of that – star safety Dom DeCicco (six tackles for loss, five interceptions, a name that legally required him to play football in Pennsylvania) – is now gone. Patterson should have a lot of fun with end Brandon Lindsey (17.5 tackles for loss, three forced fumbles), but there will be pressure on the secondary to cover for a dice-rolling front seven.

Pittsburgh's 2011 projection is surprisingly high, but the Panthers' peripherals really have been stellar in recent seasons. If the high-octane identity sticks – and honestly, it is odd thinking about the school of Tony Dorsett and Ironhead Heyward playing at a breakneck pace – then the talent is in place for an interesting, surprising squad. Road games at Iowa, Louisville and West Virginia are tricky, but Pitt still projects as the conference favorite in Graham's first season.

Top 2012 NFL Prospects: DE Brandon Lindsey (2-3), C Chris Jacobson (4-5), OG Lucas Nix (6-7).

No. 20 West Virginia Mountaineers (10-2, 6-1)

2010: 9-4 (5-2) / F/+ #18 / FEI #14 / S&P+ #20

Program F/+	+17.4%	11	Returning Starters: 8 OFF, 4 DEF			5-Yr Recruiting Rank		27
2010 Offense			**2010 Defense**			**2010 Field Position**		
Offensive F/+	-1.1%	69	**Defensive F/+**	+17.5%	2	Field Position Advantage	0.507	52
Offensive FEI:	0.046	52	Defensive FEI	-0.636	1	**2011 Projections**		
Offensive S&P+	102.5	60	Defensive S&P+	130.6	5	**Mean Wins**	9.6	
Rushing S&P+	95.4	84	Rushing S&P+	137.6	5	Proj. F/+	+12.3%	20
Passing S&P+	109.9	42	Passing S&P+	125.3	15	Offensive F/+	+0.0%	59
Standard Downs S&P+	104.5	55	Standard Downs S&P+	131.5	3	Defensive F/+	+12.2%	3
Passing Downs S&P+	109.8	47	Passing Downs S&P+	118.4	26	Strength of Schedule	0.439	79

If football players were stocks, West Virginia quarterback Geno Smith would have been a high-volume gainer this offseason. As a sophomore, Smith threw for 2,763 yards in 2010, completing 65 percent of his passes at 7.4 yards per toss and compiling a strong 25-to-7 touchdown-to-interception ratio. He was a rising star in the Big East ... and that was *before* new head coach Dana Holgorsen came to town. Holgorsen is a Mike Leach and Hal Mumme disciple who bears a striking resemblance to *Dazed and Confused's* Wooderson at 40. At Oklahoma State last fall, he engineered a devastating, high-paced attack that he will look to duplicate in Morgantown, and Smith's stat line should benefit significantly.

Of course, *how* Holgorsen came to town was the story of the offseason. New West Virginia athletic director Oliver Luck attempted to name Holgorsen as Bill Stewart's "head coach in waiting" with the goal of Holgorsen taking over once the 2011 season had ended. Predictably, Stewart was not high on this idea and asked a couple of local reporters to dig up dirt on his new offensive assistant. When this effort was discovered in early June, Stewart resigned, and the job was Holgorsen's a year earlier than intended.

Despite Holgorsen's lack of head coaching experience, it is difficult not to get excited about the potential of the Mountaineers' offense with him in charge. They suffered through some droughts and brain cramps last year, and they didn't bother showing up in a 23-7 pasting by North Carolina State in the Champs Sports Bowl, but their potential was already quite high. Four of Smith's top five targets return, including

Tavon Austin, who mixed solid explosiveness (13.6 yards per catch, eight touchdowns) with reliability (a 71-percent catch rate that resulted in an extremely healthy 9.6 yards per target). He is no Justin Blackmon (Oklahoma State's star receiver and last year's Biletnikoff winner), but he is very good, and his stock will also rise this fall. Replacing Noel Devine (a strong running back who struggled with injuries in 2010) is a concern, but you could do worse than Shawne Alston (248 yards, minus-0.8 Adj. POE). Holgorsen should have more than enough toys with which to play.

If the offense is clicking, a defense that was significantly underrated in 2010 should be able to stay out of the way. The Mountaineers run a high-risk, high-reward, 3-3-5 system high on unpredictability and play-making potential. When it clicks, as it did in 2010, it is exciting and vicious. WVU ranked fifth in Def. S&P+: fifth against the run, 15th against the pass. Their only discernible weakness was that they gave up a few big plays on passing downs while going for big sacks (of which they also had plenty).

With the departure of safeties Sidney Glover and Robert Sands, it is possible that the Mountaineers will give up a few more big plays in 2011. However, WVU still returns some serious playmakers in ends Julian Miller (14 tackles for loss in 2010) and Bruce Irvin (14) and weakside linebacker Najee Goode (8.5). All-conference cornerback Keith Tandy (six interceptions, 11 passes broken up) is also an aggressive weapon.

Top 2012 NFL Prospects: DE Julian Miller (3-4), QB Geno Smith* (4-5), OT Don Barclay (5-6).

No. 36 Cincinnati Bearcats (8-4, 4-3)
2010: 4-8 (2-5) / F/+ #54 / FEI #54 / S&P+ #57

Program F/+	+10.5%	27	Returning Starters: 5 OFF, 11 DEF			5-Yr Recruiting Rank		62
2010 Offense			**2010 Defense**			**2010 Field Position**		
Offensive F/+	+7.0%	28	**Defensive F/+**	-6.4%	88	Field Position Advantage	0.458	109
Offensive FEI:	0.144	38	Defensive FEI	0.067	68	**2011 Projections**		
Offensive S&P+	118.5	22	Defensive S&P+	87.4	100	**Mean Wins**	7.8	
Rushing S&P+	120.1	19	Rushing S&P+	100.9	58	Proj. F/+	+5.9%	36
Passing S&P+	117.0	27	Passing S&P+	77.5	113	Offensive F/+	+3.3%	39
Standard Downs S&P+	122.6	11	Standard Downs S&P+	90.4	97	Defensive F/+	+2.6%	48
Passing Downs S&P+	110.6	44	Passing Downs S&P+	92.9	81	Strength of Schedule	0.444	80

In a season that featured some absolutely stunning collapses – Texas, Florida and Kansas, to name three – it is somewhat easy to overlook just how far Cincinnati fell from 2009 to 2010. The Bearcats went from a 12-0 regular season and Top 15 F/+ ranking to 4-8 and 54th. Butch Jones succeeded Brian Kelly (just like he had done at Central Michigan), but between the coaching change, lost personnel and injuries, the 2010 Cincinnati squad just never could get rolling. The highs were still high, but there were not nearly enough of them. Either everything clicked (only one of their four wins was by less than 31 points) or everything very much did not (only two losses were by single digits, and each of their last four losses came by at least 18 points). Can the Bearcats make things click a few more times in 2011?

The answer to that depends quite a bit on quarterback Zach Collaros' ability to stay healthy, and on the emergence of a new No. 2 passing target. Cincy passes to set up the run, and the departure of receiver Armon Binns, the target of 31 percent of Collaros' passes a year ago, creates a void. D.J. Woods (898 receiving yards, 15.8 per catch) was a great No. 2 man, but as he steps up to No. 1, who fills Woods' void? Possession receiver Anthony McClung? Junior college transfer Kenbrell Thompkins?

The issue for a defense returning all 11 starters is much simpler: Stop the pass. The run defense was actually solid, anchored by a deep line (end Brandon Mills and tackles Derek Wolfe and John "Sixteen Candles" Hughes are the stars) and play-making linebackers. But if the play got beyond the front seven, it was probably going all the way. The Bearcats were bludgeoned by big plays all year, and the pressure will be on returning safeties Drew Frey and Wesley Richardson (or anybody who can overtake them) to tighten things up.

Top 2012 NFL Prospects: DT Derek Wolfe (4-5), WR D.J. Woods (6-7), QB Zach Collaros (6-7).

No. 47 South Florida Bulls (7-5, 3-4)

2010: 8-5 (3-4) / F/+ #41 / FEI #29 / S&P+ #55

Program F/+	+9.2%	33	Returning Starters: 4 OFF, 6 DEF			5-Yr Recruiting Rank		50
2010 Offense			**2010 Defense**			**2010 Field Position**		
Offensive F/+	-2.2%	74	**Defensive F/+**	+7.8%	27	Field Position Advantage	0.508	50
Offensive FEI:	-0.055	70	Defensive FEI	-0.368	18	**2011 Projections**		
Offensive S&P+	99.0	70	Defensive S&P+	107.2	45	**Mean Wins**	6.7	
Rushing S&P+	103.9	57	Rushing S&P+	109.5	36	Proj. F/+	+3.6%	47
Passing S&P+	96.0	81	Passing S&P+	104.2	51	Offensive F/+	-5.9%	99
Standard Downs S&P+	99.2	66	Standard Downs S&P+	118.3	20	Defensive F/+	+9.5%	14
Passing Downs S&P+	102.5	55	Passing Downs S&P+	83.9	105	Strength of Schedule	0.334	57

It should be clear by now that South Florida head coach Skip Holtz is indeed a Holtz. Like his father Lou, Holtz has crafted a rather clear identity at USF and, before that, East Carolina: Run the ball, play killer defense, and take calculated risks in the passing game. With the talent on hand, that translated into a pretty decent first season in St. Pete. The Bulls went 8-5 and finished rather strong, winning at Louisville and Miami and taking out Clemson in the Meineke Car Care Bowl.

USF was not particularly proficient at any one thing in 2010, but they were decent at almost everything. The run-heavy attack was supplemented by a couple of all-conference linemen (Sampson Genus and Jacob Sims) and a decent back in Mo Plancher (793 yards, minus-6.4 Adj. POE). All three of these players are gone, but in run-pass quarterback B.J. Daniels (1,685 passing yards, 396 pre-sack rushing yards), running back Demetri Murray (542 yards, minus-6.5 Adj. POE), and Colorado transfer Darrell Scott, there are at least some interesting pieces in place. Receiver Dontavia Bogan (685 yards, 14.6 per catch) is also gone,

so No. 2 man Evan Landi (390 yards, 13.9 per catch) will have to raise his game a bit.

Defense was never much of a problem for former head coach Jim Leavitt, at least until 2009, when the Bulls regressed to a below-average unit. Holtz was able to implement minor improvements, but despite the presence of all-conference cornerback Mistral Raymond, any gains the Bulls made on standard downs, they tended to give up on passing downs. Now, Raymond is gone, meaning the pressure shifts both to the front seven to get into quarterbacks' faces and new in-the-spotlight cornerbacks Quenton Washington and Kayvon Webster to break up a few more passes.

South Florida is likely not ready for a run at a Big East title (though if UConn's 2010 squad could do it, anything is possible), but they should be able to maintain their mid-conference showing before raising expectations for Daniels' senior season in 2012.

Top 2012 NFL Prospects: CB Quenton Washington (6-7), G Jeremiah Warren (6-7), G Chaz Hine (6-7).

No. 52 Connecticut Huskies (8-4, 3-4)

2010: 8-5 (5-2) / F/+ #55 / FEI #49 / S&P+ #68

Program F/+	+3.3%	48	Returning Starters: 6 OFF, 9 DEF			5-Yr Recruiting Rank		80
2010 Offense			**2010 Defense**			**2010 Field Position**		
Offensive F/+	-2.9%	80	**Defensive F/+**	+3.2%	45	Field Position Advantage	0.539	14
Offensive FEI:	-0.189	93	Defensive FEI	-0.093	40	**2011 Projections**		
Offensive S&P+	97.4	75	Defensive S&P+	99.7	60	**Mean Wins**	7.6	
Rushing S&P+	108.4	41	Rushing S&P+	99.5	64	Proj. F/+	+2.0%	52
Passing S&P+	86.8	96	Passing S&P+	100.2	60	Offensive F/+	-5.1%	93
Standard Downs S&P+	100.8	61	Standard Downs S&P+	102.8	48	Defensive F/+	+7.1%	22
Passing Downs S&P+	92.8	84	Passing Downs S&P+	109.5	37	Strength of Schedule	0.430	76

Since Connecticut made the move to the FBS level in the late-1990s, only one man had served as the Huskies' head coach: Randy Edsall. He led UConn to a surprise conference title and Fiesta Bowl bid in 2010

… and a couple of days later, he accepted an offer to take the Maryland job. Like Jim Leavitt at South Florida, Edsall more or less built the program as we know it from scratch, and he did an outstanding job overall, even if the Huskies were really nowhere near good enough to justifiably claim an elite bowl slot. (UConn's presence in a BCS bowl, and their inability to avoid losing major dollars due to lack of ticket sales and long travel, was used as Exhibit D by critics in the growing case against the BCS system.)

Now Edsall turns the reins over to Paul Pasqualoni, the former head man at Syracuse. Pasqualoni is somehow only 61 (it seems as if he's been around forever), and the defense-minded coach inherits an interesting defensive unit. The Huskies must replace three of their top four linebackers, including all-conference star Lawrence Wilson, but a line anchored by three strong tackles – Kendall Reyes, Twyon Martin and Shamar Stephen – returns intact, as does a secondary that struggled with efficiency but did a strong job of preventing big plays. Safeties Jerome Junior and Harris Agbor were turnover machines; Junior intercepted four passes and Agbor forced three fumbles.

The face of the UConn offense – running back Jordan Todman (1,695 yards, plus-4.1 Adj. POE) – is now a San Diego Charger, and top receiver Michael Smith is academically ineligible. Pasqualoni and offensive coordinator George DeLeone (his O.C. at Syracuse) will have to craft a new identity around receiver Kashif Moore (449 receiving yards, 12.5 per catch), and possibly running back Robbie Frey (389 yards, plus-5.1 Adj. POE). Having two all-conference linemen (tackle Mike Ryan and center Moe Petrus) up front is not a bad thing.

Top 2012 NFL Prospects: OT Mike Ryan (3-4), DT Kendall Reyes (3-4), C Moe Petrus (6-7).

No. 53 Louisville Cardinals (6-6, 3-4)
2010: 7-6 (3-4) / F/+ #40 / FEI #31 / S&P+ #48

Program F/+	+4.6%	43	Returning Starters: 3 OFF, 6 DEF			5-Yr Recruiting Rank		54
2010 Offense			**2010 Defense**			**2010 Field Position**		
Offensive F/+	+3.3%	41	**Defensive F/+**	+2.9%	46	Field Position Advantage	0.528	25
Offensive FEI:	0.023	60	Defensive FEI	-0.083	41	**2011 Projections**		
Offensive S&P+	107.1	42	Defensive S&P+	102.3	51	**Mean Wins**	5.9	
Rushing S&P+	112.9	30	Rushing S&P+	98.1	68	Proj. F/+	+1.7%	53
Passing S&P+	102.9	56	Passing S&P+	106.9	46	Offensive F/+	-2.7%	78
Standard Downs S&P+	105.3	53	Standard Downs S&P+	98.3	61	Defensive F/+	+4.4%	38
Passing Downs S&P+	110.5	45	Passing Downs S&P+	123.5	18	Strength of Schedule	0.407	69

Charlie Strong inherited a positive situation in Louisville last fall. His first squad was laden with talented seniors, and he pushed the right buttons, leading the Cardinals to their first bowl since 2006, Bobby Petrino's final season in the home of horse racing and bourbon. Running back Bilal Powell rushed for 1,405 yards (plus-11.6 Adj. POE), and quarterbacks Adam Froman and Justin Burke combined for 2,423 yards passing, 21 touchdowns and seven interceptions. Now, all three are gone, along with the two top receiving targets, both starting cornerbacks, and both starting defensive ends. Strong has made some recruiting waves since he came to town, but it takes a while for recruiting to have a significant impact. Signs point to a season of potential stagnation before the Cardinals pick up more steam.

To avoid regression, the Cardinals are going to need help from new names, and a couple of old ones. It appears the offensive backfield will be manned by former walk-on quarterback Will Stein, (who saw playing time under the last head coach, Steve Kragthorpe) and running back Victor Anderson (who was a freshman star before getting sidetracked by injuries). Stein will have interesting targets in tight end Josh Chichester (317 yards, five touchdowns in 2010) and receivers Josh Bellamy (401 yards, five TDs) and Andrell Smith (377 yards, three TDs), but it is unclear who will step up on the line – four starters are gone, and injuries were such a problem this spring that for a while the team only had seven healthy linemen.

On defense, it is pretty clear who some of the primary replacements will be: end B.J. Butler looked strong for a freshman last year, and cornerback Darius Ashley was solid before he got hurt. Add to this a couple of nice safeties – Hakeem Smith (all-conference as a redshirt freshman) and Shenard Holton – and an intriguing tackle in Greg Scruggs, and it's clear that the cupboard isn't entirely bare. Depth, however, will be a problem for this young squad.

Top 2012 NFL Prospects: TE Josh Chichester (5-6), RB Victor Anderson (6-7), WR Josh Bellamy (6-7).

No. 61 Rutgers Scarlet Knights (5-7, 2-5)

2010: 4-8 (1-6) / F/+ #84 / FEI #69 / S&P+ #98

Program F/+		+5.6%	40	Returning Starters: 10 OFF, 5 DEF			5-Yr Recruiting Rank		49
2010 Offense				**2010 Defense**			**2010 Field Position**		
Offensive F/+		-7.4%	95	**Defensive F/+**	-0.7%	59	Field Position Advantage	0.514	43
Offensive FEI:		-0.238	95	Defensive FEI	-0.019	54	**2011 Projections**		
Offensive S&P+		86.0	101	Defensive S&P+	91.8	80	**Mean Wins**	5.4	
Rushing S&P+		84.2	107	Rushing S&P+	103.0	54	Proj. F/+	-0.5%	61
Passing S&P+		89.2	92	Passing S&P+	81.8	108	Offensive F/+	-0.1%	62
Standard Downs S&P+		95.2	84	Standard Downs S&P+	91.2	91	Defensive F/+	-0.4%	57
Passing Downs S&P+		90.7	87	Passing Downs S&P+	106.0	45	Strength of Schedule	0.519	92

It's been a steady, incremental slide for Rutgers in recent seasons. After their fantastic 11-2 campaign in 2006, the Scarlet Knights won eight, eight and nine games the next three years, then fell apart with a 4-8 season in 2010. To shake things up, head coach Greg Schiano brought in a new offensive coordinator: Frank Cignetti, Dave Wannstedt's former coordinator at Pittsburgh.

Cignetti's Pitt offenses played a very balanced offense, but they were best when running a couple of good, small backs behind a huge fullback and huger line. That should fit into the Schiano mentality just fine, though Cignetti inherits a couple of interesting all-purpose athletes. Mohamed Sanu finished last season with 418 receiving yards, 309 rushing yards and 160 passing yards while splitting time between wideout and Wildcat quarterback. Meanwhile, Jeremy Deering rushed for 352 yards and caught 16 passes for 338 yards as a freshman. The Scarlet Knights were incredibly young overall last season: Quarterback Chas Dodd, Deering and leading returning rusher Jordan Thomas were all true freshmen, Sanu a sophomore.

This year, everybody but center Howard Barbieri returns; improvement from a line that couldn't have been any worse last year (107th in Adj. Line Yards, 120th in Adj. Sack Rate) could go a long way with experience at the skill positions.

Though it was not as much of a liability as the offense, last year's Rutgers defense was the worst Schiano has fielded in a while. RU could not generate any sort of pass rush, and as a result the Scarlet Knights ranked a paltry 108th in Def. Passing S&P+. Plus, their best pass rusher, end Alex Silvestro, was a senior. Rutgers racked up the tackles for loss and should do so again, but if they weren't making a big play, they were giving one up, especially on standard downs. There is talent here – tackle Scott Vallone, linebacker Steve Beauharnais, safety Khaseem Greene – but a rebound here will be necessary to avoid neutralizing likely offensive gains.

Top 2012 NFL Prospects: WR Mohamed Sanu (2-3), LB Manny Abreu (6-7).

No. 74 Syracuse Orange (5-7, 2-5)

2010: 8-5 (4-3) / F/+ #57 / FEI #43 / S&P+ #78

Program F/+		-7.0%	79	Returning Starters: 7 OFF, 5 DEF			5-Yr Recruiting Rank		65
2010 Offense				**2010 Defense**			**2010 Field Position**		
Offensive F/+		-3.8%	83	**Defensive F/+**	+3.6%	43	Field Position Advantage	0.476	88
Offensive FEI:		-0.111	76	Defensive FEI	-0.147	37	**2011 Projections**		
Offensive S&P+		91.6	89	Defensive S&P+	99.9	58	**Mean Wins**	4.8	
Rushing S&P+		104.4	53	Rushing S&P+	100.5	60	Proj. F/+	-3.4%	74
Passing S&P+		82.9	100	Passing S&P+	99.3	61	Offensive F/+	-4.5%	87
Standard Downs S&P+		100.4	63	Standard Downs S&P+	102.5	50	Defensive F/+	+1.1%	53
Passing Downs S&P+		85.1	100	Passing Downs S&P+	103.3	57	Strength of Schedule	0.363	64

The expectations will rise soon enough – they probably already have – but in 2010, achieving an average level of play was a reason for celebration. The program that produced everybody from Jim Brown and

Ernie Davis, to Larry Csonka and Moose Johnston, to Don McPherson and Donovan McNabb, had forgotten how to win, failing to finish above .500 since 2001. But a 6-2 start led to a bid in the inaugural Pinstripe

Bowl, where the Orange topped Kansas State in one of the more exciting games of the 2010 bowl season.

For the first time in a long time, Syracuse has positive momentum. Can they capitalize with another nice performance in 2011? Depends on how they start. Home games against Wake Forest, Rhode Island, Toledo and Rutgers punctuate the early schedule; pile up the wins there, and things could fall into place. With the loss of stalwarts like running back Delone Carter and linebacker Derrell Smith, however, Syracuse will have to find some new playmakers and could be vulnerable early on.

Last year, the Syracuse defense got away with playing the bend-don't-break game because of stellar red zone play and a healthy number of tackles for loss. With ends Chandler Jones and Mikhail Marinovich returning, along with safeties Phillip Thomas and Shamarko Thomas, these aspects could remain strong. However, the holes in the middle created by the departures of Smith and two good tackles could prove costly against opposing ground games.

Meanwhile, the offense could be leaning on quarterback Ryan Nassib to connect with receivers Van Chew and Marcus Sales early on while determining the best ways to use running backs Antwon Bailey and Prince-Tyson Gulley.

Top 2012 NFL Prospects: DE Chandler Jones (6-7), QB Ryan Nassib (6-7), DE Mikhail Marinovich (6-7).

Bill Connelly

Projected Win Probabilities For Big East Teams

Big East	Overall Wins													Conference Wins							
	12-0	11-1	10-2	9-3	8-4	7-5	6-6	5-7	4-8	3-9	2-10	1-11	0-12	7-0	6-1	5-2	4-3	3-4	2-5	1-6	0-7
Cincinnati	-	2	8	20	28	24	13	4	1	-	-	-	-	1	8	24	33	23	9	2	-
Connecticut	-	1	5	18	29	27	14	5	1	-	-	-	-	-	1	10	28	35	20	5	1
Louisville	-	-	-	3	9	20	29	24	12	3	-	-	-	-	1	4	17	33	31	12	2
Pittsburgh	4	19	31	27	14	4	1	-	-	-	-	-	-	15	41	31	11	2	-	-	-
Rutgers	-	-	-	2	6	15	25	26	18	7	1	-	-	-	-	2	10	24	33	24	7
South Florida	-	-	2	7	18	27	26	14	5	1	-	-	-	-	3	13	27	31	19	6	1
Syracuse	-	-	-	-	2	8	20	30	25	12	3	-	-	-	-	-	4	15	32	35	14
West Virginia	5	20	31	26	13	4	1	-	-	-	-	-	-	19	37	29	12	3	-	-	-

Big Ten Conference

Through the second weekend in October last season, Big Ten football fans were salivating over the future of the soon-to-be 12-team league. Ohio State was the number-one team in the country and appeared capable of winning every game for as long as quarterback Terrelle Pryor was in uniform. Michigan's Denard Robinson and Nebraska's Taylor Martinez were the most lethal fleet-footed quarterbacks in the nation through the early part of last season and would have two more years each to contend head-to-head for Big Ten division championships. Michigan State, Wisconsin and Iowa were positioned to be consistent threats to expand the league's first tier. It appeared the Big Ten was on its way to challenging the SEC as the college football world's best collection of superstar programs.

But by season's end, the excitement had worn off and the familiar doubts about Big Ten national expectations had set in. From that group of future Leaders and Legends, only Iowa and Ohio State had managed to win bowl games. By December, the Buckeyes were under scrutiny for potential NCAA violations that would ultimately result in an offseason full of unflattering headlines and the unceremonious departures of Pryor and head coach Jim Tressel. Robinson and Martinez each suffered injuries and their respective teams struggled down the stretch. Michigan's head coach Rich Rodriguez was canned as a result of the Wolverines' slide.

Instead of a conference ready to step up as a whole, the Big Ten is a conference in transition heading into the 2011 season. Is Ohio State's dominant run over the last decade about to come to an abrupt halt? If so, are there any programs truly ready to fill those elite shoes?

Nebraska joins the league this fall and may be an immediate contender for the conference championship. But the Cornhuskers might also still be a year or two away from being a national contender. Wisconsin, Penn State, Michigan State, and Iowa should all be decent this fall as well, but our metrics don't indicate that any of those teams will be BCS bound. We project six Big Ten teams ranked between No. 22 and No. 33 this year, so the conference title race may be totally up for grabs. And with new head coaches at the helm at Ohio State and Michigan, it is oddly discomforting to find our F/+ projections favoring the two most distinguished programs in Big Ten history in position to come out on top.

We don't have numbers that can identify what will happen with all the turmoil in Columbus, and the installation of a new offense in Ann Arbor may not be a smooth one. But five-year performance and recruiting success favor the Buckeyes and Wolverines to meet in Indianapolis for the first ever Big Ten Championship game. Strangely enough, that title game is scheduled to be played exactly one week after Ohio State travels to the Big House to play Michigan in their traditional regular season-ending clash. It seems like the peculiarity of back-to-back games might be the only appropriate conclusion to what we expect will be a wild year in the Big Ten.

BIG TEN LEADERS

No. 15 Ohio State Buckeyes (10-2, 6-2)

2010: 12-1 (7-1) / F/+ #5 / FEI #8 / S&P+ #3

Program F/+	+24.6%	2	Returning Starters: 7 OFF, 4 DEF		5-Yr Recruiting Rank		10
2010 Offense			**2010 Defense**		**2010 Field Position**		
					Field Position Advantage	0.543	10
Offensive F/+	+9.1%	17	**Defensive F/+**	+17.3%	3		
Offensive FEI:	0.333	16	Defensive FEI	-0.534	2	**2011 Projections**	
Offensive S&P+	124.6	11	Defensive S&P+	140.7	2	**Mean Wins**	9.5	
Rushing S&P+	126.7	9	Rushing S&P+	132.7	7	Proj. F/+	+13.2%	15
Passing S&P+	123.1	16	Passing S&P+	148.9	3	Offensive F/+	+4.9%	32
Standard Downs S&P+	117.8	21	Standard Downs S&P+	138.4	2	Defensive F/+	+8.3%	17
Passing Downs S&P+	120.1	27	Passing Downs S&P+	157.9	2	Strength of Schedule	0.351	60

Despite everything that has transpired this offseason, our projections have identified Ohio State as a division favorite and given them a strong chance at a seventh straight Big Ten championship. A cloud of uncertainty hovers over the short- and long-term future of the program following Jim Tressel's resignation and Terrelle Pryor's exit to the NFL supplemental draft. There are still five-game suspensions to be served by other key contributors on both sides of the ball, and at some point in the coming months, more sanctions could be levied against the program. Nevertheless, Ohio State has assembled more talent than any other team in the Big Ten and interim head coach Luke Fickell should be capable of making the post-Tressel transition as smooth as possible. Even if the Buckeyes don't exhibit national championship form, there are enough weapons to claim the Leaders division title and a conference championship game berth.

Despite Pryor's departure, there are strong contributors on the offensive side of the ball. Ohio State ranked seventh nationally last year in points scored per offensive drive with a balanced attack as good as it has ever been in Columbus. Running back Daniel "Boom" Herron racked up 1,155 yards (plus-9.0 Adj. POE) and scored a touchdown in each of the Buckeyes' last 12 games in 2010. Herron and top returning receiver Devier Posey (848 yards, 7 TDs) won't see the field until after serving five-game suspensions in the wake of the tattoos-for-memorabilia scandal. Lightly tested but talented sophomore wide receiver Corey Brown will be the top target early on. Senior Joe Bauserman and incoming freshman Braxton Miller are expected to share quarterback responsibilities to start the year.

Of course, the defense truly steers the ship in Columbus, and with former defensive coordinator Fickell in charge, that isn't likely to change. Ohio State ranked fifth nationally in limiting opponent third-down conversions (30.2 percent) and were second-best in the country on third-and-short (44.8 percent on opponent third-down attempts with one to three yards to go). The Buckeyes are reloading at several key positions, losing six of the top ten tacklers from 2010 to graduation. But linebacker Andrew Sweat and defensive linemen Nathan Williams and John Simon will anchor the front seven, a group that helped Ohio State force three-and-outs on 47 percent of opponent possessions last year, the second-best defensive rate in the nation.

The Buckeyes were once again a leader in field position advantage in 2010, bolstered not only by a strong defense but one of the top kickoff return units in the country. Ohio State had a field position disadvantage in its four closest games last year, wins over Arkansas, Iowa, Illinois, and the loss to Wisconsin. When they controlled field position, they comfortably beat everyone else.

The schedule isn't particularly daunting overall, but a road trip to Miami and the Big Ten home opener against Michigan State won't be a picnic without Herron and Posey. Ultimately, though, the Leaders division will likely be settled on October 29th when Wisconsin visits Columbus.

2012 NFL Prospects: C Michael Brewster (1-2), OT Mike Adams (1-2), RB Daniel Herron (3-4), WR Devier Posey (3-4).

No. 22 Wisconsin Badgers (10-2, 6-2)

2010: 11-2 (7-1) / F/+ #12 / FEI #12 / S&P+ #10

Program F/+	+12.2%	19	Returning Starters: 4 OFF, 6 DEF			5-Yr Recruiting Rank		44
2010 Offense			**2010 Defense**			**2010 Field Position**		
Offensive F/+	+14.7%	6	Defensive F/+	+5.7%	36	Field Position Advantage	0.545	7
Offensive FEI:	0.551	5	Defensive FEI	-0.188	34	**2011 Projections**		
Offensive S&P+	127.4	9	Defensive S&P+	117.6	26	**Mean Wins**	9.6	
Rushing S&P+	132.9	4	Rushing S&P+	110.1	35	Proj. F/+	+11.9%	22
Passing S&P+	124.5	14	Passing S&P+	124.5	16	Offensive F/+	+9.0%	13
Standard Downs S&P+	127.5	7	Standard Downs S&P+	105.5	42	Defensive F/+	+2.9%	46
Passing Downs S&P+	143.8	4	Passing Downs S&P+	116.5	27	Strength of Schedule	0.431	77

There were moments last season when Wisconsin appeared to be as invincible as any team in the country. Down the stretch of the regular season, the Badgers won seven straight Big Ten games by an average score of 48-22. A trip to the Rose Bowl was spoiled by TCU's heroics, but the foundation is solid for perennial Big Ten championship contention. All coach Bret Bielema needs is a quarterback, and a few others to step into key roles vacated by graduated Badgers.

The passing game hasn't been the focal point of Wisconsin's attack, but that's largely because departed two-year starter Scott Tolzien was so consistently efficient and reliable. Wisconsin ranked fourth nationally in quarterback passer rating last season and 14th in passing S&P+, but preferred to keep the ball on the ground on 68 percent of its plays, the ninth highest rate in the country. Running backs Montee Ball (996 yards, plus-13.4 Adj. POE, 18 TDs) and James White (1012 yards, plus-16.1 Adj. POE, 14 TDs) return to the backfield, and each will be featured frequently throughout the season. In late June, Wisconsin lured former North Carolina State quarterback Russell Wilson to play his final season of college football in Madison. Wilson threw for 3,500 yards last year and has the size and speed to make plays with his feet. However, there are questions about his accuracy (59 percent completions, 14 interceptions) and limiting mistakes will be critical.

Wisconsin turned the ball over only nine times last year, fewest in the nation.

Defensively, Wisconsin will be pressed to find another menacing defensive end to replace all-conference standout J.J. Watt (20.5 tackles for loss, eighth most in the nation). Junior linebacker Mike Taylor is the team's leading returning tackler and seniors Antonio Fenelus (four interceptions) and Aaron Henry (two interceptions, each returned for a touchdown) anchor the secondary. A particular area of focus on defense will be getting off the field. The Badgers only forced three-and-outs on 30 percent of opponent possessions last year. Wisconsin allowed a 65 percent conversion rate on third-and-short, 99th nationally and worst in the Big Ten. TCU converted 60 percent of its third down attempts in the Rose Bowl against the Badgers, allowing the Horned Frogs to extend possessions and control the game.

Wisconsin hosts Nebraska and Penn State and should be favored to win every game at Camp Randall this season. Road trips to Michigan State and Ohio State are the toughest road tests, and the Badgers won't have to face either Michigan or Iowa from the Legends division.

2012 NFL Draft Prospects: G Kevin Zeitler (2-3), S Aaron Henry (3-4), OT Josh Oglesby (4-5), WR Nick Toon (5-6).

No. 30 Penn State Nittany Lions (8-4, 5-3)

2010: 7-6 (4-4) / F/+ #50 / FEI #56 / S&P+ #42

2010 Offense			2010 Defense			2010 Field Position		
Program F/+	+14.2%	14	Returning Starters: 7 OFF, 8 DEF			5-Yr Recruiting Rank		24
2010 Offense			**2010 Defense**			**2010 Field Position**		
						Field Position Advantage	0.506	54
Offensive F/+	-1.9%	73	**Defensive F/+**	+4.2%	40	**2011 Projections**		
Offensive FEI:	-0.118	77	Defensive FEI	-0.051	49	**Mean Wins**	7.8	
Offensive S&P+	102.1	62	Defensive S&P+	111.4	38	Proj. F/+	+7.6%	30
Rushing S&P+	100.3	68	Rushing S&P+	110.1	34	Offensive F/+	+0.4%	54
Passing S&P+	104.2	54	Passing S&P+	111.5	34	Defensive F/+	+7.1%	21
Standard Downs S&P+	109.3	37	Standard Downs S&P+	103.3	45	Strength of Schedule	0.192	21
Passing Downs S&P+	102.4	56	Passing Downs S&P+	121.7	20			

It wasn't a devastating year in Happy Valley last season, but there wasn't too much to be happy about either. The Nittany Lions had only one victory over an F/+ top-40 opponent (Michigan) and only two wins versus teams that earned bowl eligibility (Michigan and Northwestern). The when-will-Joe-Paterno-retire drum has been beating for a while now, but he's ramping up for his 46th straight season at the helm. And there are reasons to believe Penn State will improve.

There remains an unresolved quarterback competition, but unlike a year ago, both sophomore Rob Bolden and junior Matt McGloin bring significant game experience to the position this fall. They may both see the field again, though McGloin has the momentum after taking over midseason in 2010 and posting breakout 300-yard passing games against Indiana and Michigan State down the stretch. Running backs Silas Redd and Stephon Green will share the load vacated by Evan Royster, who led the Nittany Lions in all-purpose yards each of the last two seasons. Four offensive linemen, led by senior left tackle Quinn Barham, have logged significant starting experience for a unit that surrendered only 12 sacks last year.

The Nittany Lions return their entire starting secondary, and they'll have an opportunity to build off of late-season success from a year ago. Penn State held each of its last six opponents below their passing yards per game average. The Nittany Lions need to step up in quarterback pressure, having recorded only 1.3 sacks per game, one for every 20.6 opponent pass attempts (91st nationally). Defensive tackle Devon Still anchors an experienced line that will be responsible for boosting those stats. Despite the departures of Chris Colasanti and Bani Gbadyu, the linebacker position is stocked with playing experience.

Penn State welcomes Alabama to Happy Valley on September 10th, a thrill for fans of big-time interconference play, but Penn State won't have much of a shot to topple the Tide. The Nittany Lions can show improvement in 2011 by having success against the league's middle tier. Road trips to Ohio State and Wisconsin will be very difficult, but with Nebraska and Iowa making the trip to State College, a 5-3 conference season is manageable.

2012 NFL Draft Prospects: DT Devon Still (3-4), CB D'Anton Lynn (3-4), LB Nathan Stupar (4-5), DE Jack Crawford (5-6), WR Derek Moye (6-7).

No. 45 Illinois Fighting Illini (7-5, 4-4)

2010: 7-6 (4-4) / F/+ #33 / FEI #35 / S&P+ #31

2010 Offense			2010 Defense			2010 Field Position		
Program F/+	+3.3%	47	Returning Starters: 6 OFF, 6 DEF			5-Yr Recruiting Rank		37
2010 Offense			**2010 Defense**			**2010 Field Position**		
						Field Position Advantage	0.520	36
Offensive F/+	-0.8%	66	**Defensive F/+**	+10.2%	17	**2011 Projections**		
Offensive FEI:	0.032	55	Defensive FEI	-0.311	26	**Mean Wins**	7.3	
Offensive S&P+	102.6	58	Defensive S&P+	122.6	13	Proj. F/+	+3.9%	45
Rushing S&P+	106.1	49	Rushing S&P+	129.6	9	Offensive F/+	-3.0%	80
Passing S&P+	98.0	73	Passing S&P+	117.4	26	Defensive F/+	+7.0%	23
Standard Downs S&P+	101.8	58	Standard Downs S&P+	117.3	22	Strength of Schedule	0.493	89
Passing Downs S&P+	103.5	53	Passing Downs S&P+	120.4	24			

Ron Zook is now the third longest-tenured coach in the Big Ten behind only Joe Paterno and Kirk Ferentz. It seems he has entered almost every year in Champaign on the proverbial hot seat, and he has amassed a 28-45 record in six seasons. But the Illini produced big scoring outbursts down the stretch last year and whipped Baylor in the Texas Bowl to finish 7-6. As long as expectations aren't too great at Illinois, Zook should be able to maintain such modest successes for as long as they'll let him.

The offensive firepower late in the year was helped by the fact that Illinois faced six bottom-30 FEI defenses in its last seven games. The Illini led the conference in rushing yards per game (246) but when adjusted for opposition, they were merely a bit above average (49th in rushing S&P+). Mikel Leshoure took his team-leading 1,700 yards to the NFL, so dual-threat sophomore quarterback Nathan Scheelhaase

is the key on offense in 2011. He built confidence against weaker defenses in the second half of the year and will look to carry that experience forward against the meat of the schedule this fall.

The Illinois defense was a strength last year, but with only six starters returning, there should be some regression. Three leading tacklers are gone, and the departures of juniors Martez Wilson and Corey Liuget will be toughest to replace. Linebacker Ian Thomas had his career-best game in the season opener last year and could be the anchor for a strong start again this season.

In order to get to bowl eligibility, Illinois will need a fast start. A tough stretch from mid-October to mid-November features Ohio State, Penn State, Michigan and Wisconsin in a five-week span.

2012 NFL Prospects: S Tavon Wilson (4-5), RB Jason Ford (6-7), K Derek Dimke (6-7).

No. 76 Purdue Boilermakers (4-8, 2-6)

2010: 4-8 (2-6) / F/+ #87 / FEI #87 / S&P+ #80

Program F/+		-1.2%	66	Returning Starters: 7 OFF, 9 DEF			5-Yr Recruiting Rank		64
2010 Offense				**2010 Defense**			**2010 Field Position**		
Offensive F/+		-13.1%	112	Defensive F/+	+4.4%	38	Field Position Advantage	0.483	81
Offensive FEI:		-0.417	110	Defensive FEI	-0.074	44	**2011 Projections**		
Offensive S&P+		81.8	110	Defensive S&P+	108.2	43	**Mean Wins**	4.4	
Rushing S&P+		87.8	102	Rushing S&P+	106.5	43	Proj. F/+	-3.8%	76
Passing S&P+		76.2	109	Passing S&P+	109.9	40	Offensive F/+	-11.2%	115
Standard Downs S&P+		81.1	110	Standard Downs S&P+	101.7	52	Defensive F/+	+7.3%	20
Passing Downs S&P+		75.1	113	Passing Downs S&P+	106.2	44	Strength of Schedule	0.314	54

It has been a very rough start in West Lafayette for head coach Danny Hope, who would love to have a healthy team as much as anything else this fall. Knee injuries took out two Purdue quarterbacks and the starting wide receiver and running back all by midseason a year ago. If a six-game losing streak to finish the year isn't totally excused, it certainly can be explained by debilitating injuries.

Running back Ralph Bolden looked very good in 2009 (935 yards, plus-1.4 Adj. POE, nine touchdowns) before missing all of last season, and he should factor into the game plan significantly this fall. At quarterback, three men with varying skill sets saw action last year and perhaps all three might have a shot again in 2011. Rob Henry earned the most experience passing last year, but Robert Marve had the edge in efficiency. Efficiency would be a nice change – Purdue avoided three-and-out only 52.4 percent of its drives last year,

the fifth-worst mark in college football.

On defense, Purdue will have to find production from someone other than defensive end Ryan Kerrigan, a one-man wrecking crew who seemed to single-handedly keep Purdue competitive. Combined, the linebackers and secondary return six of seven starters, and that group led by safety Logan Link was successful a year ago in limiting big-play drives. Up front, defensive tackle Kawann Short (six sacks, 12.5 tackles for loss) will be more of a focal point for opposing offensive linemen in Kerrigan's absence.

Purdue has the toughest conference schedule in the Big Ten according to our data, with games against Michigan, Wisconsin, Ohio State and Iowa in consecutive weeks. Hope will be happy if the Boilermakers just have enough healthy bodies to compete.

2012 NFL Draft Prospects: K Carson Wiggs (6-7).

No. 86 Indiana Hoosiers (4-8, 1-7)

2010: 5-7 (1-7) / F/+ #88 / FEI #89 / S&P+ #86

Program F/+	-7.8%	80	Returning Starters: 6 OFF, 7 DEF			5-Yr Recruiting Rank		72
2010 Offense			**2010 Defense**			**2010 Field Position**		
Offensive F/+	+0.9%	54	**Defensive F/+**	-10.2%	107	Field Position Advantage	0.438	117
Offensive FEI:	0.083	47	Defensive FEI	0.233	94	**2011 Projections**		
Offensive S&P+	103.3	55	Defensive S&P+	84.8	111	**Mean Wins**	4.0	
Rushing S&P+	87.8	101	Rushing S&P+	95.3	72	Proj. F/+	-6.9%	86
Passing S&P+	110.6	41	Passing S&P+	76.7	115	Offensive F/+	+0.7%	51
Standard Downs S&P+	91.9	91	Standard Downs S&P+	87.7	106	Defensive F/+	-7.6%	106
Passing Downs S&P+	120.2	26	Passing Downs S&P+	71.8	118	Strength of Schedule	0.333	56

There are low points at programs around the country, and then there are days like November 13, 2010, when a conference opponent buries you with 83 points on the scoreboard. Wisconsin made that epic drubbing look easy against Indiana, and it *was* easy considering the field position the Hoosiers spotted the Badgers. On average, Wisconsin started its non-garbage time possessions of that game at *midfield*. It was the same song throughout the season for Indiana. Poor special teams play and minus-7 turnover margin put the Hoosiers in a field position hole in seven conference games last year.

This year, newly minted head coach Kevin Wilson takes the reins and would love to not have to play catch-up on field position all day. The former offensive coordinator at Oklahoma has experience coaching a prolific offense, but is still seeking a new starting quarterback. Injury-prone running back Darius Willis (plus-6.5 Adj. POE in 2009) carried only 64 times last year and will take on more of the load behind a veteran offensive line returning four starters. Defensively, the line is the most experienced unit while almost the entire secondary will be overhauled. That's probably a good thing since the Hoosiers were 115th in the nation in passing S&P+ and allowed at least 250 yards passing in six Big Ten games last year. Linebackers Jeff Thomas and Leon Beckum were the most productive run-stoppers last season, but everything's relative. If Indiana can improve from dreadful to merely bad, Wilson might be able to eke out a couple of conference victories. Realistically, the Hoosiers are at least a few years away from making any noise.

2012 NFL Draft Prospects: None.

BIG TEN LEGENDS

No. 25 Michigan Wolverines (9-3, 5-3)

2010: 7-6 (3-5) / F/+ #42 / FEI #55 / S&P+ #30

Program F/+	+8.2%	37	Returning Starters: 9 OFF, 9 DEF			5-Yr Recruiting Rank		13
2010 Offense			**2010 Defense**			**2010 Field Position**		
Offensive F/+	+17.2%	3	**Defensive F/+**	-12.0%	115	Field Position Advantage	0.476	88
Offensive FEI:	0.603	2	Defensive FEI	0.375	108	**2011 Projections**		
Offensive S&P+	134.2	5	Defensive S&P+	91.0	86	**Mean Wins**	8.6	
Rushing S&P+	137.3	2	Rushing S&P+	92.1	86	Proj. F/+	+9.4%	25
Passing S&P+	137.8	5	Passing S&P+	88.4	90	Offensive F/+	+18.9%	1
Standard Downs S&P+	132.0	3	Standard Downs S&P+	96.3	70	Defensive F/+	-9.5%	111
Passing Downs S&P+	130.3	13	Passing Downs S&P+	80.4	110	Strength of Schedule	0.430	74

The Rich Rodriguez experiment is over in Ann Arbor, and former San Diego State coach Brady Hoke is now in charge. The fan base was fractured over the decision initially, but Hoke's "Michigan Man" promise to restore the program's hard-nosed identity is playing well so far. There are reasons to believe an immediate impact can be made this fall, with returning starters all over the field and a defense that has nowhere to go but up. The biggest question facing the Wolverines, and one that our metrics aren't well suited to predict, is whether Hoke will take full advantage of the team's best asset, junior quarterback Denard Robinson.

Robinson was born to run from a spread attack as evidenced by his spectacular performances a year ago – 502 total yards against Notre Dame (258 rushing, 244 passing), 494 yards against Indiana, nine games with 100-plus yards rushing, seven games with 200-plus passing. On every play from a shotgun formation, he was a threat to distribute the ball quickly or scamper down the field on his own. This season, he'll be under center and may not be as comfortable passing from the pocket. He was an efficient passer last season (20th nationally in pass rating) but his biggest pass plays came from tossing the ball while running along the line in an option set. If he transitions well and is still able to pick up first downs with his legs when under duress, Michigan's offense won't be an issue. The Wolverines return every skill position contributor from last season and three starting linemen, so at least they're all in this transition together.

It was the defense that held Michigan back last year and needs the most attention under Hoke. The Wolverines gave up 54.3 percent of opponent available yards last year (total yardage measured from starting field position to end zone), 106th worst nationally and worst in the conference. Michigan scored 2.6 points per possession on offense but gave up 2.9 points per possession on defense. Almost everyone is back on defense this year except Michigan's leading tackler Jonas Mouton. Defensive coordinator Greg Mattison is back in Ann Arbor to install a new 4-3 defense and focus on limiting the opponent's run game. They'll have time to adjust to the new system since Michigan won't face a top-30 offense according to our projections until the regular season finale against Ohio State.

The other area of focus for Michigan is special teams. The field goal kicking duties split between Seth Broekhuizen and Brendan Gibbons were an epic failure (4-of-14, zero successful field goal attempts outside the 20-yard line). Michigan was also dreadful in managing field position. In the eight games the Wolverines played with a field position deficit last year, Michigan lost six times and barely escaped upsets by Illinois and Indiana.

2012 NFL Draft Prospects: C David Molk (3-4), DE Ryan Van Bergen (3-4), DT Mike Martin (4-5), TE Kevin Koger (6-7).

No. 26 Nebraska Cornhuskers (8-4, 5-3)

2010: 11-3 (6-2) / F/+ #20 / FEI #19 / S&P+ #26

Program F/+	+9.4%	30	Returning Starters: 5 OFF, 7 DEF			5-Yr Recruiting Rank		18
2010 Offense			**2010 Defense**			**2010 Field Position**		
Offensive F/+	+1.2%	50	Defensive F/+	+13.8%	5	Field Position Advantage	0.535	18
Offensive FEI:	0.097	44	Defensive FEI	-0.481	5	**2011 Projections**		
Offensive S&P+	105.0	47	Defensive S&P+	124.6	11	**Mean Wins**	8.4	
Rushing S&P+	108.3	42	Rushing S&P+	112.6	25	Proj. F/+	+9.2%	26
Passing S&P+	100.5	63	Passing S&P+	142.5	4	Offensive F/+	-3.1%	81
Standard Downs S&P+	109.2	39	Standard Downs S&P+	115.9	27	Defensive F/+	+12.3%	2
Passing Downs S&P+	99.4	63	Passing Downs S&P+	138.5	9	Strength of Schedule	0.357	63

The Cornhuskers had a pretty good thing going for the first two months of 2010. Then they proceeded to lose three of six games down the stretch, including a half-hearted bowl loss to Washington. Those losses and key personnel losses on both sides of the ball make us cautious about Nebraska's chances to immediately contend for a Big Ten championship.

The main culprits in the skid were a series of injuries suffered by quarterback Taylor Martinez. The redshirt freshman ran wild in September and October, ringing up 250-plus yards of total offense and more than 100 yards per game on the ground. His 241-yard, four-touchdown ground assault on Kansas State will remain a lasting memory of the college football season. Un-

fortunately, so will Martinez's public clash with head coach Bo Pelini in a loss to Texas A&M that left many fans wondering if their relationship would survive.

It did and Martinez is back. But he won't have many familiar faces in the huddle. Three offensive line starters are gone, and Nebraska graduated its top rusher (Roy Helu) and receiver (Niles Paul) who combined for nearly 2,500 yards of all-purpose yards last season. As much of a big-play threat as Martinez proved to be, Nebraska will need to focus more on grinding out drives. The Cornhuskers earned at least one first down on only 61.8 percent of offensive possessions. Only the 3-9 Kansas Jayhawks were worse in Big 12 conference play a year ago.

On defense, Nebraska was outstanding and seven starters are back, mostly in the front seven. That group was able to be particularly aggressive and frequently trust shutdown corner Prince Amukamara to take on receivers one-on-one. It helped Nebraska achieve top-10 defensive ratings in passing S&P+ and on passing downs. The Cornhuskers surrendered only 30 percent of conversions on third down, the fourth-best rate nationally. Defensive tackle Jared Crick (70 tackles, 14.5 for loss) and linebacker Lavonte David (152 tackles, third most in college football) are the leading contributors back on defense.

Nebraska's inaugural season in the Big Ten starts with back-to-back battles in early October against Ohio State and Wisconsin. The Cornhuskers do have the league's easiest non-conference schedule and should be 4-0 heading into that one-two punch. Even if Nebraska struggles against the Buckeyes and Badgers, they'll still have all five of their division games down the stretch to earn a trip to Indianapolis.

2012 NFL Draft Prospects: DT Jared Crick (1-2), CB Alfonzo Dennard (1-2), DE Baker Steinkuhler (2-3), LB David Lavonte (5-6).

No. 29 Iowa Hawkeyes (9-3, 5-3)

2010: 8-5 (4-4) / F/+ #21 / FEI #21 / S&P+ #21

Program F/+	+10.4%	28	Returning Starters: 5 OFF, 4 DEF			5-Yr Recruiting Rank		42
2010 Offense			**2010 Defense**			**2010 Field Position**		
Offensive F/+	+5.2%	34	Defensive F/+	+9.5%	20	Field Position Advantage	0.527	27
Offensive FEI:	0.255	23	Defensive FEI	-0.336	22	**2011 Projections**		
Offensive S&P+	111.5	34	Defensive S&P+	120.9	16	**Mean Wins**	8.8	
Rushing S&P+	104.4	54	Rushing S&P+	119.6	18	Proj. F/+	+8.4%	29
Passing S&P+	118.2	23	Passing S&P+	123.2	18	Offensive F/+	+2.8%	42
Standard Downs S&P+	116.2	24	Standard Downs S&P+	112.7	34	Defensive F/+	+5.6%	30
Passing Downs S&P+	88.1	96	Passing Downs S&P+	144.5	4	Strength of Schedule	0.487	87

Close games mostly went Iowa's way in 2009 but that magic vanished in 2010. The Hawkeyes' five losses last season came by a combined 18 points, and Iowa was either tied or had a lead late in the second half of each game. Those disappointments were only aggravated by a tumultuous offseason in Iowa City headlined by player arrests and a workout incident that hospitalized 13 players. To get off on the right foot this fall, coach Kirk Ferentz will be seeking leadership from a relatively inexperienced team.

The biggest loss offensively is quarterback Ricky Stanzi, who led the Hawkeyes for the past three seasons and was among the nation's most efficient signal callers (25 touchdowns, six interceptions) in 2010. Junior James Vanderberg will take over under center with limited experience, though he did sub in for Stanzi in 2009 as a freshman. The offensive line is experienced and running back Marcus Coker played well after being pressed into action in the second half of his freshman season. He exploded for 219 yards and two touchdowns in a bowl win over Missouri. Leading wide receiver senior Marvin McNutt (861 yards, eight touchdowns) is also back to help Vanderberg settle in.

There are big holes to fill defensively with the departures of three defensive linemen and Iowa's leading tackler from last year. Seniors were responsible for more than half of Iowa's sacks and tackles for loss a year ago and were instrumental in the Hawkeyes 20th ranked F/+ defense. Iowa led the Big Ten in interceptions last season (19) but 40 percent of those takeaways are gone as well. Cornerbacks Shaun Prater and Micah Hyde, linebacker James Morris, and defensive tackle Mike Daniels will be the focal points this fall. Iowa was very successful last season in preventing explosive drives (10-plus yards per play), but several offenses were able to wear down the Hawkeyes with long, methodical drives, a style of attack that might be exploited against Iowa this fall due to limited experience in the front seven.

Working in Iowa's favor is a schedule that does not include cross-divisional games against Wisconsin or Ohio State. They'll face Michigan, Michigan State and Nebraska in a four-week span in November.

2012 NFL Draft Prospects: OT Riley Reiff (1-2), CB Shaun Prater (3-4), DT Mike Daniels (4-5), WR Marvin McNutt (5-6), LB Tyler Nielsen (5-6).*

No. 33 Michigan State Spartans (7-5, 4-4)

2010: 11-2 (7-1) / F/+ #30 / FEI #39 / S&P+ #25

Program F/+	+5.5%	41	Returning Starters: 6 OFF, 6 DEF			5-Yr Recruiting Rank		32
2010 Offense			**2010 Defense**			**2010 Field Position**		
Offensive F/+	+6.2%	31	**Defensive F/+**	+4.0%	42	Field Position Advantage	0.481	86
Offensive FEI:	0.207	30	Defensive FEI	-0.205	32	**2011 Projections**		
Offensive S&P+	118.5	21	Defensive S&P+	111.3	39	**Mean Wins**	7.2	
Rushing S&P+	115.5	26	Rushing S&P+	110.5	31	Proj. F/+	+6.3%	33
Passing S&P+	122.4	20	Passing S&P+	112.8	33	Offensive F/+	+3.4%	38
Standard Downs S&P+	110.2	35	Standard Downs S&P+	112.8	33	Defensive F/+	+3.0%	45
Passing Downs S&P+	120.8	25	Passing Downs S&P+	95.0	77	Strength of Schedule	0.263	42

It wasn't all fake punts and field goals that led the Spartans to 11 victories last season, but our metrics weren't terribly impressed by most of their victories either. Michigan State needed three-touchdown fourth-quarter rallies to win against both Purdue and Northwestern. The blowout losses at the hands of Iowa and Alabama were additional indicators that this was an eight-win team masquerading with an elite record. Is the program elevating under coach Mark Dantonio or is Michigan State poised to slide back into the Big Ten's second tier?

Working in the Spartans' favor is quarterback Kirk Cousins, back for his senior season as one of the most experienced and efficient quarterbacks in the nation. His favorite wide receiver and tight end are gone, but seven other receivers caught at least ten passes last year for Michigan State. Cousins will also be joined in the backfield by Edwin Baker (1,201 yards, plus-14.1 Adj. POE, 13 touchdowns) plus every other Spartans running back that carried the ball in 2010. Both starting tackles and the center need to be replaced, however.

Though the loss of linebacker Greg Jones and defensive tackle Colin Neely (10 tackles for loss apiece) will be tough to overcome, Michigan State's three leading sack generators are back. Defensive linemen Jerel Worthy, Tyler Hoover and Johnathan Strayhorn will anchor the Spartans up front, and this group was very strong in stopping opponent third-and-short attempts last season (49 percent conversions, 15th best in the nation). MSU also brings back Trenton Robinson at cornerback; he led the secondary in tackles (76) and interceptions (four) last year.

Michigan State special teams were very good, particularly place kicker Dan Conroy (14-of-15) who returns for his junior season. Keshawn Martin sprung a few punt returns for big gains. It will take big strides on offense and defense, however, to match last season's success in the win column.

2012 NFL Draft Prospects: DT Jerel Worthy* (1-2), QB Kirk Cousins (1-2), TE Brian Linthicum (5-6), G Joel Foreman (6-7).

No. 63 Northwestern Wildcats (5-7, 3-5)

2010: 7-6 (3-5) / F/+ #75 / FEI #71 / S&P+ #81

Program F/+	-3.1%	70	Returning Starters: 9 OFF, 7 DEF			5-Yr Recruiting Rank		63
2010 Offense			**2010 Defense**			**2010 Field Position**		
Offensive F/+	+2.1%	46	**Defensive F/+**	-7.5%	97	Field Position Advantage	0.524	31
Offensive FEI:	0.084	46	Defensive FEI	0.265	99	**2011 Projections**		
Offensive S&P+	100.2	67	Defensive S&P+	89.6	92	**Mean Wins**	5.4	
Rushing S&P+	106.1	50	Rushing S&P+	82.6	111	Proj. F/+	-0.9%	63
Passing S&P+	96.8	77	Passing S&P+	97.4	66	Offensive F/+	+6.2%	25
Standard Downs S&P+	97.7	76	Standard Downs S&P+	90.7	93	Defensive F/+	-7.2%	102
Passing Downs S&P+	97.0	75	Passing Downs S&P+	91.9	85	Strength of Schedule	0.446	81

In March, Northwestern signed head coach Pat Fitzgerald to a 10-year contract extension, so it's clear that the modest expectations of the Wildcats program are being met. Northwestern isn't a program des-

tined to be a regular conference contender, but under Fitzgerald, they have been consistently plucky and capable of knocking off a big boy program in any given week. And under the leadership of senior quarterback

Dan Persa, Northwestern will once again expect to finish in the middle of the Big Ten standings and earn a fourth-straight bowl berth. They'll have to win one eventually, right?

Persa was one of the most efficient quarterbacks in the nation last season before suffering an Achilles injury in November that ended his junior season. He'll be happy to see nearly everyone back in the huddle, including four starting offensive linemen, running back Mike Trumpy, and wide receiver Jeremy Ebert (953 yards, eight touchdowns). The Wildcats dink and dunk down the field out of a spread attack, ranking first in the na-tion in producing methodical drives (10 or more plays).

They can only keep the ball out of the other team's hands for so long, however, and Northwestern's de-fense has been a liability. Opponents averaged more than five yards per carry against the Wildcats last year, but improvement is expected with more experi-ence along the line anchored by defensive end Vince Browne. Safety Brian Peters was the team's leading tackler a year ago.

2012 NFL Draft Prospects: DE Vince Browne (3-4), OT Al Netter (5-6), FB Drake Dunsmore (6-7).

No. 71 Minnesota Golden Gophers (5-7, 2-6)

2010: 3-9 (2-6) / F/+ #77 / FEI #76 / S&P+ #75

Program F/+	-2.6%	69	Returning Starters: 4 OFF, 9 DEF			5-Yr Recruiting Rank		39
2010 Offense			**2010 Defense**			**2010 Field Position**		
			Defensive F/+	-8.0%	101	Field Position Advantage	0.458	109
Offensive F/+	+2.5%	45	Defensive F/+	-8.0%	101			
Offensive FEI:	0.127	41	Defensive FEI	0.237	95	**2011 Projections**		
Offensive S&P+	103.4	54	Defensive S&P+	89.9	90	**Mean Wins**	4.8	
Rushing S&P+	101.6	61	Rushing S&P+	98.3	67	Proj. F/+	-1.9%	71
Passing S&P+	105.8	51	Passing S&P+	80.2	110	Offensive F/+	+1.4%	47
Standard Downs S&P+	98.9	68	Standard Downs S&P+	97.3	67	Defensive F/+	-3.3%	74
Passing Downs S&P+	117.1	33	Passing Downs S&P+	75.4	115	Strength of Schedule	0.345	58

Golden Gophers fans got a sneak preview of their new head coach Jerry Kill when his Northern Illinois team beat Minnesota 34-23 in Minneapolis last September. Kill's Huskies went 2-3 against Big Ten teams over the last three seasons and scored as many points as they gave up. Minnesota certainly wants to be a win-ner, but for now they would gladly prefer that modest level of success over some of the ugly blowouts and embarrassments in the past few years.

Minnesota's defense and special teams were terrible a year ago. They gave up 2.8 points per possession de-fensively and the kickoff and punt units consistently cost the Gophers points on field position value. They were very young, however, and almost everyone is back on defense with another year under his belt. A trio of linebackers – Gary Tinsley, Keanon Cooper,

and Mike Rallis (195 combined tackles, 20 for loss) – are the unit to keep an eye on.

Kill's NIU teams were productive offensively and took advantage of a dual-threat quarterback. He in-herits another in Marqueis Gray, who has seen the field as both a wide receiver and a backup to departed four-year starter Adam Weber. Senior running back Duane Bennett shared the backfield load last season (529 yards, three touchdowns) but will be the primary threat this fall after DeLeon Eskridge left the team to be closer to home. Wide receiver Da'Jon McKnight and tight end Eric Lair will be Gray's top targets.

2012 NFL Draft Prospects: LB Gary Tinsley (6-7).

Brian Fremeau

Projected Win Probabilities For Big Ten Teams

Big Ten Leaders	Overall Wins													Conference Wins								
	12-0	11-1	10-2	9-3	8-4	7-5	6-6	5-7	4-8	3-9	2-10	1-11	0-12	8-0	7-1	6-2	5-3	4-4	3-5	2-6	1-7	0-8
Illinois	-	1	5	14	25	27	18	8	2	-	-	-	-	-	2	10	24	31	22	9	2	-
Indiana	-	-	-	-	2	9	22	31	24	10	2	-	-	-	-	-	-	1	9	29	41	20
Ohio State	4	18	30	27	15	5	1	-	-	-	-	-	-	10	28	33	20	7	2	-	-	-
Penn State	-	1	7	22	32	24	11	3	-	-	-	-	-	-	7	23	33	25	10	2	-	-
Purdue	-	-	-	-	1	4	14	28	31	17	5	-	-	-	-	-	1	5	18	35	31	10
Wisconsin	4	20	32	26	13	4	1	-	-	-	-	-	-	7	26	35	23	8	1	-	-	-

Big Ten Legends	Overall Wins													Conference Wins								
	12-0	11-1	10-2	9-3	8-4	7-5	6-6	5-7	4-8	3-9	2-10	1-11	0-12	8-0	7-1	6-2	5-3	4-4	3-5	2-6	1-7	0-8
Iowa	1	8	21	30	24	12	4	-	-	-	-	-	-	3	16	31	30	15	4	1	-	-
Michigan	1	7	18	27	25	15	6	1	-	-	-	-	-	3	13	28	30	19	6	1	-	-
Michigan State	-	-	3	11	24	30	21	9	2	-	-	-	-	-	2	9	24	33	23	8	1	-
Minnesota	-	-	-	-	2	7	18	30	28	13	2	-	-	-	-	-	2	7	20	33	28	10
Nebraska	1	5	15	27	28	17	6	1	-	-	-	-	-	1	5	18	30	28	14	4	-	-
Northwestern	-	-	-	1	5	14	26	28	18	7	1	-	-	-	-	1	5	15	30	31	15	3

Big 12 Conference

Can a conference get stronger and weaker at the same time? In losing Nebraska to the Big Ten, the Big 12 is minus one marquee program, but the addition of a ninth conference game for each team will add to the overall number of big-time games that will take place in the conference in a given year. Now, not only do teams in what was once the Big 12 South have to play each other, but they also have to face a strong Missouri program on an annual basis. Meanwhile, Missouri (and the other former North programs) must face Oklahoma *and* Texas, Oklahoma State *and* Texas A&M, every year. There are no shortcuts to a Big 12 title.

Then again, the new route to a conference title might not mean a lot if the same team continues to win. Oklahoma has won four of the last five Big 12 Championship games, and is the clear favorite to win the first championship of the new Big 12 era as well.

The Sooners are not beyond vulnerability – they were pushed around in the trenches a bit more than viewers were accustomed to seeing last year, and the teams that pushed them around (Missouri and Texas A&M, to name two) will be just as strong in that regard this coming season.

But the Sooners still face the fewest question marks of any conference team. Oklahoma State must prove it can thrive without masterful offensive coordinator Dana Holgorsen, who left for West Virginia. Missouri returns a lot of experience but must replace top-ten draft pick Blaine Gabbert. Texas A&M has to overcome both significant expectations and the departure of Von Miller. And Texas is looking at an almost entirely new coaching staff under Mack Brown.

The Big 12 is dynamic and exciting, but for now, the new boss is the old boss.

No. 2 Oklahoma Sooners (11-1, 8-1)

2010: 11-3 (6-2) / F/+ #8 / FEI #9 / S&P+ #8

Program F/+	+22.7%	3	Returning Starters: 8 OFF, 6 DEF			5-Yr Recruiting Rank		7
2010 Offense			**2010 Defense**			**2010 Field Position**		
Offensive F/+	+9.8%	14	**Defensive F/+**	+12.9%	8	Field Position Advantage	0.515	42
Offensive FEI:	0.398	13	Defensive FEI	-0.484	4	**2011 Projections**		
Offensive S&P+	122.4	15	Defensive S&P+	128.2	8	**Mean Wins**	10.7	
Rushing S&P+	105.2	52	Rushing S&P+	126.1	12	Proj. F/+	+19.7%	2
Passing S&P+	136.1	7	Passing S&P+	130.0	10	Offensive F/+	+9.2%	11
Standard Downs S&P+	117.3	22	Standard Downs S&P+	124.0	12	Defensive F/+	+10.5%	8
Passing Downs S&P+	125.0	20	Passing Downs S&P+	144.4	5	Strength of Schedule	0.277	46

Ho hum, another Big 12 championship. They must get old after a while. When they knocked off Nebraska in the conference's final championship game, the Sooners locked down their fourth title in five years; they even won their first BCS bowl in six attempts as well. But to some degree, the entire 2010 season felt like a starting point for 2011. Most of the Sooners' stars return and a host of extremely young players thrust into key positions last fall are now a year older. It is easy to see why pundits are counting Oklahoma as a de facto national title favorite.

For the Sooners, the key to living up to preseason expectations will be their work in the trenches. The of-

fensive line, which ranked 90th in Adjusted Line Yards, struggled to open up holes. The defensive line got pushed around a lot more than fans were accustomed to seeing, and at inopportune moments – the second halves against Missouri and Texas A&M, for instance. The 2011 offensive line will be more experienced than it has been in recent memory, but the defensive line suffered a key offseason loss in end Jeremy Beal.

Longtime Oklahoma offensive coordinator Kevin Wilson took the Indiana head coaching job this offseason, and it will be interesting to see how new coordinator (and former title-winning Oklahoma quarterback) Josh Heupel handles the pace issue. Under Wilson,

Oklahoma was constantly the most fast-paced team in the country. Wilson was an aggressive play-caller, running very little on passing downs and trusting his quarterback to make a play.   Quarterback Landry Jones made the most of that trust in 2010, throwing for 4,718 yards and 38 touchdowns with just 12 interceptions. If a running attack featuring Roy Finch and others can improve a bit, Oklahoma might avoid facing as many passing downs, and Jones' passing line could improve. It also might help if targets emerge to take of the pressure off of Ryan Broyles (1,622 receiving yards, 14 touchdowns), by far the most targeted receiver in the country last season. Jones targeted him 179 times in 2010, 19 more than the second-most highly targeted receiver, Hawaii's Greg Salas. Further emergence of Kenny Stills (786 receiving yards, five touchdowns as a true freshman) could be a godsend.

Linebacker Travis Lewis surprised many by deciding to stay in Norman for his senior season instead of jumping to the pros. He is a likely All-American, and he will direct traffic for the Sooners' other stars. End Frank Alexander is dynamic but will need a play-making partner to replace Beal. Meanwhile, the secondary is potentially star-studded. Safety Tony Jefferson racked up seven tackles for loss and two picks as a freshman and is poised for a breakout, and the return of outstanding cornerback Jamell Fleming (8.5 tackles for loss, five interceptions, 19 passes defensed) after some spring academic issues is a huge boost.

It should also be noted that the Sooner family faced tragedy in May, when linebacker Austin Box died unexpectedly. There is an emotional component in sports that statistics cannot measure, and how Oklahoma responds to such an awful occurrence will be every bit as impactful in 2011 as development and play-calling.

Top 2012 NFL Prospects: LB Travis Lewis (1-2), QB Landry Jones (1-2), WR Ryan Broyles (3-5).*

No. 14 Oklahoma State Cowboys (9-3, 7-2)

2010: 11-2 (6-2) / F/+ #14 / FEI #17 / S&P+ #12

Program F/+	+11.1%	22	Returning Starters: 9 OFF, 5 DEF		5-Yr Recruiting Rank		26
2010 Offense			**2010 Defense**		**2010 Field Position**		
Offensive F/+	+11.2%	11	**Defensive F/+**	+7.2%	29	Field Position Advantage	0.527	27
Offensive FEI:	0.316	19	Defensive FEI	-0.33	23	**2011 Projections**		
Offensive S&P+	128.4	7	Defensive S&P+	114.3	30	**Mean Wins**	9.3	
Rushing S&P+	122.3	16	Rushing S&P+	121.8	16	Proj. F/+	+13.3%	14
Passing S&P+	134.9	8	Passing S&P+	108.5	44	Offensive F/+	+10.1%	7
Standard Downs S&P+	127.8	6	Standard Downs S&P+	119.6	18	Defensive F/+	+3.2%	44
Passing Downs S&P+	127.7	16	Passing Downs S&P+	98.4	70	Strength of Schedule	0.305	50

Missouri is not the only Big 12 program that has recently over-achieved according to historic expectations; Mike Gundy's Oklahoma State Cowboys have won 29 games in three years (the most ever) and have finished with a winning record for five consecutive seasons (one away from the most ever).

OSU's recent offensive exploits are like what one might produce in a video game; they have scored 450 points and an Offensive F/+ ranking of 16th or better in four of five seasons (they scored 575 and ranked 11th in 2010). With ageless quarterback Brandon Weeden (4,277 yards, a 67-percent completion rate, 34 touchdowns, and 13 interceptions) and Biletnikoff winner Justin Blackmon (1,782 receiving yards, 16.1 per catch, 20 touchdowns) returning, along with eight other receivers who caught at least 100 yards of passes last year, it is not unfair to expect much of the same in 2011.

Really, the losses on offense are mostly limited to two individuals: running back Kendall Hunter and offensive coordinator Dana Holgorsen. Hunter rushed for 1,548 yards (plus-6.5 Adj. POE) last year, but the loss of Holgorsen could be a bigger deal. Despite a host of newcomers, the 'Pokes improved significantly from an injury-plagued 2009 campaign, and while there's no questioning the talent Holgorsen had to work with, he was clearly pressing a lot of correct buttons. New coordinator Todd Monken faces high expectations in his first year.

Even if the OSU offense does suffer a slight regression following the losses of Hunter and Holgorsen, they will still score a lot of points. What held the Cowboys back in 2010 – in those rare times when they *were* held back – was the defense. Taking schedule into account, defensive coordinator Bill Young's Cowboys still ranked a respectable 29th in Def. F/+ last season, but they gave up 98 combined points in their two losses – 51 to Nebraska, 47 to Oklahoma, both at home.

The slate of offenses they face in 2011 will not be any easier, and OSU will need to up its level of play-making. The Cowboys were excellent against the run, but they were shaky against solid aerial attacks, of which there is no shortage in the Big 12. The experience is there – safeties Johnny Thomas and Markelle Martin combined for six interceptions and broke up 15 passes a year ago, and cornerback Brodrick Brown was tested quite a bit. But with a pass rush that likely will not improve this fall (at end, Richetti Jones returns, but Ugo Chinasa does not), the secondary will still face quite

a bit of pressure. The loss of Chinasa is not the only worrisome departure in the front seven – tackles Chris Donaldson and Shane Jarka are also gone, as is tackling machine and weakside linebacker Orie Lemon. Linebacker Shaun Lewis showed extreme potential for a freshman, but there are certainly question marks regarding overall depth. Lack of quality depth could rear its ugly head during a four-game stretch from September 24 to October 22, in which the 'Pokes visit College Station, Austin and Columbia.

Top 2012 NFL Prospects: WR Justin Blackmon* (1), OT Levy Adcock (2-4), QB Brandon Weeden (4-5)

No. 17 Missouri Tigers (9-3, 7-2)

2010: 10-3 (6-2) / F/+ #16 / FEI #14 / S&P+ #17

Program F/+	+11.9%	20	Returning Starters: 9 OFF, 6 DEF			5-Yr Recruiting Rank		28
2010 Offense			**2010 Defense**			**2010 Field Position**		
Offensive F/+	+7.1%	26	**Defensive F/+**	+10.5%	16	Field Position Advantage	0.511	46
Offensive FEI:	0.262	21	Defensive FEI	-0.494	3	**2011 Projections**		
Offensive S&P+	119.9	18	Defensive S&P+	118.2	24	**Mean Wins**	9.3	
Rushing S&P+	128.5	7	Rushing S&P+	102.0	56	Proj. F/+	+12.5%	17
Passing S&P+	113.7	34	Passing S&P+	135.7	6	Offensive F/+	+5.7%	27
Standard Downs S&P+	114.3	28	Standard Downs S&P+	123.9	13	Defensive F/+	+6.7%	25
Passing Downs S&P+	128.0	15	Passing Downs S&P+	105.0	49	Strength of Schedule	0.212	24

Missouri coach Gary Pinkel has made a habit of exceeding expectations for most of the last half-decade. His program was expected to fall apart after the departure of quarterback Brad Smith; instead, it thrived. It was supposed to fall apart again after Chase Daniel and Jeremy Maclin departed for the pros; instead, after a step backwards in 2009, the Tigers won ten games again in 2010. They knocked off Oklahoma for the first time in 12 years and produced two more first-round draft picks, their fourth and fifth of the last three years. In winning 40 games in four seasons, the Missouri football program has not only achieved, but *sustained* heights it had not seen since the 1960s. The 2011 Tigers could be Pinkel's most experienced, athletic team yet … but will inexperience at the quarterback position hold Mizzou back?

A funny thing happened in Missouri in 2010: a program known for a wide-open passing attack and defensive deficiencies ran the ball more (and more effectively) and fielded one of the country's best pass defenses. The Tigers ranked sixth overall in Def. Passing S&P+ last year, utilizing a deep set of defensive ends and an experienced secondary. End Aldon Smith is now a San Francisco 49er, but the more im-

portant losses may have taken place in the secondary, where both starting cornerbacks and steady safety Jarrell Harrison have all departed. Filling the void left by Harrison will be a particular key for a defense that made its living by avoiding big pass plays. If a safety like Matt White or Tavon Bolden is ready for prime time, everything else is in place for another stout defense. Ends Brad Madison (11.0 tackles for loss last season) and Jacquies Smith (10.0) were as productive as Aldon Smith in 2010, linebacker Zaviar Gooden (7.5 tackles for loss, two interceptions) is underrated, and a unit that was forced to overcome injury after injury last season (starters were lost for 28 games) is, at least for now, healthy.

On offense, the losses from last season are easy to list: quarterback Blaine Gabbert and center Tim Barnes. Everybody else returns from a unit that lacked in explosiveness but maintained extreme efficiency most of the season. All of Gabbert's primary targets – T.J. Moe (1,045 yards, six touchdowns), All-American tight end Michael Egnew (762 yards, five touchdowns), Jerrell Jackson and Wes Kemp – return for new quarterback James Franklin, but the key to success for the Tigers might be an underrated by-committee rushing attack.

There is nothing better for breaking in a new quarter-back than a steady run game and an experienced line. Well, backs De'Vion Moore, Henry Josey, Kendial Lawrence and Marcus Murphy combined for 1,557 yards (5.8 per carry), 19 touchdowns and a plus-23.9 Adj. POE last year, and the line returns 105 career starts. There is no guarantee Franklin will succeed immediately, especially with a brutal early schedule, but he's got quite a few friendly pieces around him.

Top 2012 NFL Prospects: TE Michael Egnew (1-2), OT Elvis Fisher (3-4), OT Dan Hoch (6-7).

No. 28 Texas A&M Aggies (8-4, 6-3)

2010: 9-4 (6-2) / F/+ #24 / FEI #28 / S&P+ #18

Program F/+	+2.2%	52	Returning Starters: 9 OFF, 8 DEF			5-Yr Recruiting Rank		19
2010 Offense			**2010 Defense**			**2010 Field Position**		
Offensive F/+	+3.4%	39	Defensive F/+	+9.8%	19	Field Position Advantage	0.460	105
Offensive FEI:	0.196	31	Defensive FEI	-0.406	14	**2011 Projections**		
Offensive S&P+	112.5	32	Defensive S&P+	122.0	15	**Mean Wins**	7.9	
Rushing S&P+	114.2	28	Rushing S&P+	123.3	14	Proj. F/+	+8.8%	28
Passing S&P+	113.0	36	Passing S&P+	119.0	23	Offensive F/+	+2.3%	45
Standard Downs S&P+	114.6	26	Standard Downs S&P+	122.6	14	Defensive F/+	+6.6%	27
Passing Downs S&P+	111.1	43	Passing Downs S&P+	126.7	13	Strength of Schedule	0.145	12

Compare Football Outsiders' projections to most pre-season Top 25 polls, and you'll typically see one or two significant outliers. It happens every summer – a team that got hot late in the season is given a ranking much higher than it probably deserves, raising expectations to an unfair level. It happened with Clemson in 2008, Ole Miss in 2009, and Nebraska in 2010; the Huskers won ten games as predicted in *Football Outsiders Almanac 2010*, but the season was a disappointment in part because of unfair expectations.

This year, Texas A&M gets the honor. The Aggies won six in a row after installing quarterback Ryan Tannehill into the starting lineup, beating Oklahoma and Nebraska at home in the process, but the F/+ projections suggest that we tap the brakes on this bandwagon a little bit.

To be sure, there is a lot to like about A&M. The Aggies' offense took a huge step forward over the last half of the season because Tannehill (1,638 yards, 13 touchdowns, six interceptions) was able to avoid the mistakes and turnovers that plagued incumbent Jerrod Johnson, and the resulting offense was extremely efficient. Receiver Jeff Fuller (1,066 yards, 14.8 per catch) is a big, strong downfield threat, while Ryan Swope (825 yards) is a solid underneath option; the running backs are often frequent targets as well, which hints at attempted efficiency. The Aggies move at a fast pace and pass to set up the run, and the improved passing game – combined with a super-young offensive line growing more experienced by the snap – opened lanes up for running back Cyrus Gray (1,133

yards, plus-17.8 Adj. POE). Gray was a revelation once he took over full-time duties from an injured Christine Michael (631 yards, minus-0.7 Adj. POE).

Of course, what made the Aggies impressive over the last half of the season wasn't the offense, as they've been a good offensive team for a couple of years now. Instead, it was the significant improvement on the defensive side of the ball. The Aggies moved to a 3-4 alignment in Tim DeRuyter's first season as defensive coordinator, and the returns were quite encouraging. Eight players racked up at least five tackles for loss, and A&M ranked in the Top 15 in both Standard Downs and Passing Downs S&P+.

DeRuyter must replace three stellar players this fall: stud end/OLB hybrid Von Miller (17.5 tackles for loss), inside linebacker Michael Hodges, and end Lucas Patterson. But returnees like outside linebacker Sean Porter should benefit from a second year in the new system, and a rotation of two underrated defensive tackles – Jonathan Mathis and Eddie Brown – should anchor another solid unit. Damontre Moore could be a keeper as well; a potential favorite to replace Miller, Moore had 6.5 tackles for loss and forced three fumbles as a freshman.

The Aggies might be ranked too high by conventional wisdom, but this is a very good team, and getting Oklahoma State, Missouri and Texas at home could help them exceed our conservative projections.

Top 2012 NFL Prospects: WR Jeff Fuller (1-2), RB Cyrus Gray (2-3), QB Ryan Tannehill (3-4).

No. 39 Texas Longhorns (7-5, 5-4)

2010: 5-7 (2-6) / F/+ #65 / FEI #72 / S&P+ #56

Program F/+	+16.4%	12	Returning Starters: 8 OFF, 6 DEF			5-Yr Recruiting Rank		3
2010 Offense			**2010 Defense**			**2010 Field Position**		
						Field Position Advantage	0.497	62
Offensive F/+	-10.9%	106	**Defensive F/+**	+9.3%	21	**2011 Projections**		
Offensive FEI:	-0.331	104	Defensive FEI	-0.237	31	**Mean Wins**	7.1	
Offensive S&P+	87.0	98	Defensive S&P+	119.1	23	Proj. F/+	+5.5%	39
Rushing S&P+	99.2	73	Rushing S&P+	109.1	38	Offensive F/+	-4.7%	89
Passing S&P+	78.1	107	Passing S&P+	129.9	11	Defensive F/+	+10.2%	9
Standard Downs S&P+	94.8	86	Standard Downs S&P+	115.6	28	Strength of Schedule	0.238	34
Passing Downs S&P+	88.8	93	Passing Downs S&P+	140.4	8			

Elite programs have off-years. Oklahoma went 8-4 in 2005, 8-5 in 2009. Florida went 9-4 in 2007, 8-5 in 2010. USC has gone 9-4 and 8-5 over the last two years. It happens, and you can recover from it. But ... 5-7? Texas did more than just have a customary off-year in 2010, the Longhorns damn near fell off a cliff.

The fall from 2009 national runner-up to a losing season was so steep that assuming an immediate recovery is difficult. Perhaps sensing this, head coach Mack Brown didn't try to temporarily patch holes — he gutted the house. Offensive coordinator Greg Davis "resigned," replaced by co-coordinators, former Texas quarterback Major Applewhite and Boise State import Bryan Harsin. Defensive coordinator Will Muschamp, whose unit was clearly less to blame for last year's struggles than the offense, took the head coaching job at Florida and was replaced by former Mississippi State coordinator Manny Diaz.

It is easy to assume that coaching was a good portion of Texas' problem last year. Brown basically did just that, both with the moves he engineered and the admission that he was in a bit of a funk last year after losing the 2009 national title game. But the superior talent Texas is supposed to have should have been able to overcome bad coaching to a degree. The scale of Texas' collapse raises question marks about the talent as well, particularly at offensive skill positions. Former blue-chip quarterback Garrett Gilbert (2,744 yards, 59 percent completion rate, 10 touchdowns, 17 interceptions) rarely played up to his recruiting profile, and he got little help from his supporting cast. Cody Johnson is a decent short-yardage running back, but the Longhorns got little explosiveness from speedy backs like Fozzy Whittaker and Tre' Newton. At receiver, Gilbert had decent possession options in James Kirkendoll and then-freshman Mike Davis, but there was no consistency. Expect incoming freshmen from the most recent highly-touted recruiting class to get a lengthy look, especially five-star running back Malcolm Brown.

A defense that was far less problematic then the offense in 2010 should be solid once again, but there's a difference between "solid" and "outstanding." The Texas defensive line was not quite as good last year as in recent seasons, and improvement is not guaranteed; Kheeston Randall and Calvin Howell are interesting options at tackle, but they were inconsistent in 2010, and the 'Horns will have a new set of defensive ends (not that they don't have plenty of one-time blue-chippers from which to choose). Middle linebacker Emmanuel Acho (brother of the Arizona Cardinals' Sam Acho) is outstanding, and the safety position features a lot of experience. The primary area of concern beyond the line is at cornerback, where cornerbacks Curtis Brown and Aaron Williams have both departed.

Top 2012 NFL Prospects: DT Kheeston Randall (2-4), LB Emmanuel Acho (2-4), LB Keenan Robinson (5-7).

No. 46 Texas Tech Red Raiders (7-5, 4-5)

2010: 8-5 (3-5) / F/+ #61 / FEI #65 / S&P+ #54

Program F/+		+9.3%	32	Returning Starters: 5 OFF, 8 DEF			5-Yr Recruiting Rank			34
2010 Offense				**2010 Defense**			**2010 Field Position**			
Offensive F/+		+1.1%	51	**Defensive F/+**	-1.7%	60	Field Position Advantage		0.487	73
Offensive FEI:		0.077	48	Defensive FEI	-0.033	52	**2011 Projections**			
Offensive S&P+		106.8	43	Defensive S&P+	99.8	59	**Mean Wins**		7.0	
Rushing S&P+		95.1	86	Rushing S&P+	106.4	44	Proj. F/+		+3.9%	46
Passing S&P+		114.5	30	Passing S&P+	95.5	74	Offensive F/+		+0.6%	53
Standard Downs S&P+		105.8	49	Standard Downs S&P+	95.5	74	Defensive F/+		+3.2%	43
Passing Downs S&P+		114.7	35	Passing Downs S&P+	108.4	40	Strength of Schedule		0.185	18

For a decade, things were comfortably familiar in Lubbock. Mike Leach's teams were going to put up video game yardage and point totals, his defenses were going to occasionally give most of it back, he was going to say some funny things, and Texas Tech was going to win football games. When Leach was shown the door after an alleged player abuse episode in 2009, Tech brought in former Ole Miss and Auburn head coach Tommy Tuberville, and it's been change, change, change ever since. The offense maintained its pace and pass-heavy tendencies, but the results and personnel changed, and the defense heads into the fall under its third coordinator and alignment in three years.

Recruiting is on the upswing – that's never really been a problem for Tuberville – but with a mostly new batch of skill position players on offense, it will be interesting to see what change might be underway. Gone are quarterbacks Taylor Potts (3,726 yards, 35 touchdowns, 10 interceptions in 2010) and Steven Sheffield, gone is running back Baron Batch (816 yards and minus-9.6 Adj. POE in an injury-plagued senior season), and gone are go-to receivers Detron Lewis and Lyle Leong, who combined for 1,778 receiving yards, 25 touchdowns and almost 40 percent of Tech's targets last fall. Quarterback Seth Doege, receiver Darrin Moore, and running back Ronnie Daniels are among the new names you might hear this fall.

On defense, new coordinator Chad Glasgow will attempt to make waves with a TCU-style 4-2-5 alignment. In Tuberville's first season, he and then-coordinator James Willis implemented a 3-4 with mixed results. Despite a solid line, youth in the secondary led to far too many big plays, and Tech ranked 74th in Defensive Passing S&P+. An abundance of youth can eventually pay off, however, and with players like corners Tre' Porter and Jarvis Phillips entering their sophomore seasons, the hope is that a deeper secondary can provide the speed necessary to swarm and leverage offenses into more passing downs than Tech faced last year. How quickly can this unit adapt to more change?

Top 2012 NFL Prospects: OT Mickey Okafor (6-7), G Lonnie Edwards (6-7).

No. 62 Kansas State Wildcats (5-7, 3-6)

2010: 7-6 (3-5) / F/+ #52 / FEI #48 / S&P+ #66

Program F/+		-3.7%	72	Returning Starters: 5 OFF, 6 DEF			5-Yr Recruiting Rank			57
2010 Offense				**2010 Defense**			**2010 Field Position**			
Offensive F/+		+8.7%	19	**Defensive F/+**	-7.5%	98	Field Position Advantage		0.517	39
Offensive FEI:		0.274	20	Defensive FEI	0.31	102	**2011 Projections**			
Offensive S&P+		109.0	38	Defensive S&P+	91.2	82	**Mean Wins**		5.0	
Rushing S&P+		112.6	33	Rushing S&P+	92.8	84	Proj. F/+		-0.8%	62
Passing S&P+		107.7	48	Passing S&P+	88.3	92	Offensive F/+		+7.4%	22
Standard Downs S&P+		114.4	27	Standard Downs S&P+	100.3	59	Defensive F/+		-8.2%	109
Passing Downs S&P+		106.5	52	Passing Downs S&P+	66.5	120	Strength of Schedule		0.233	33

Year Two of Bill Snyder's second tenure as Kansas State head coach saw the Wildcats go to just their second bowl since their 2003 Big 12 title, but defensive breakdowns pre-empted a more solid overall run. Aggrieved defensive coordinator Chris Cosh was in charge of the worst passing-downs defense in the country, and that defense loses three of its top four defensive ends (not a huge loss, as the Wildcats did not have much of a pass rush) and its top two cornerbacks. Without improvement in this regard, KSU's overall ceiling is somewhat limited.

You don't finish 120th out of 120 in a major rankings category without a combination of poor talent and coaching, and it appears that neither talent nor coaching will change much in 2011, at least as it pertains to passing downs. David Garrett moves from safety to cornerback; he was KSU's most statistically impressive player last year, racking up 15.0 tackles for loss and breaking up nine passes. With experience remaining at the safety position, Garrett's presence could help the secondary improve overall, but who rushes the passer? Garrett's not exactly going to get 15 more tackles for loss playing cornerback. Though the pass defense is still iffy, at least the run defense should be in decent hands with Miami transfer and former blue-chip recruit Arthur Brown lining up at linebacker be-hind solid tackles Raphael Guidry and Ray Kibble.

The KSU offense will have to cope with the loss of all-star running back Daniel Thomas (1,585 yards, 19 TD, plus-19.5 Adj. POE) and quarterback Carson Coffman. Converted tight end Collin Klein takes over behind center full-time; he got quite a bit of playing time last year and looked fantastic running the option, but the staff didn't trust him to throw a pass and usually brought in Coffman on passing downs. Between receivers Brodrick Smith, Chris Harper and Tramaine Thompson and incoming Tennessee transfer Bryce Brown (a running back who, yes, is Arthur's brother and a fellow former blue-chipper), Klein will have some interesting weapons around him. The defense is a much bigger concern than the offense.

Top 2012 NFL Prospects: CB David Garrett (5-7).

No. 68 Baylor Bears (5-7, 3-6)

2010: 7-6 (4-4) / F/+ #62 / FEI #73 / S&P+ #44

Program F/+	-5.9%	77	Returning Starters: 8 OFF, 5 DEF			5-Yr Recruiting Rank		56
2010 Offense			**2010 Defense**			**2010 Field Position**		
Offensive F/+	+8.5%	22	Defensive F/+	-9.2%	105	Field Position Advantage	0.485	80
Offensive FEI:	0.15	36	Defensive FEI	0.313	103	**2011 Projections**		
Offensive S&P+	121.3	17	Defensive S&P+	90.5	89	**Mean Wins**	4.7	
Rushing S&P+	120.1	20	Rushing S&P+	90.0	93	Proj. F/+	-1.6%	68
Passing S&P+	124.7	13	Passing S&P+	91.0	83	Offensive F/+	+9.4%	9
Standard Downs S&P+	121.4	13	Standard Downs S&P+	94.1	78	Defensive F/+	-11.0%	116
Passing Downs S&P+	119.3	31	Passing Downs S&P+	88.1	94	Strength of Schedule	0.229	29

Can your first bowl bid since 1994 end up a little disappointing? If so, Baylor's was just that. The Bears jumped out to a 7-2 start and found themselves ranked for the first time since Mariah Carey's "Dreamlover" was atop the charts. But as the schedule got tougher in November, Baylor did not; they lost to Oklahoma State, Texas A&M and Oklahoma (giving up 150 points in the process) to finish the regular season, then got rocked by Illinois in the Texas Bowl to wrap up a 7-6 season. Offer that to Baylor fans at the beginning of the season, and they would have taken it in a heartbeat. But it still had to feel disappointing the way it played out.

Baylor's 2011 squad is likely going to feature the same strengths and weaknesses as last season: a well-rounded, explosive offense capable of keeping up in any contest, and a defense vulnerable to big running plays and all-day, eight-yard passes. The key to the Baylor offense is, yet again, exciting quarterback Robert Griffin III. A former Big 12 track champion, Griffin has developed the "running quarterback" repu-tation over the years, and to be sure, he can run a little bit. But he was also one of the most efficient, accurate quarterbacks in the country in 2010, throwing 35 times a game and completing 67 percent of his passes. All of his primary targets return in the receiving corps as well, led by speedy Kendall Wright (952 receiving yards, 12.2 per catch). Overall, the losses are minimal but potentially impactful; both left tackle Danny Watkins and running back Jay Finley were drafted last April, Watkins in the first round.

There is less to say about the defense. They had a bad run defense despite the presence of first-round defensive tackle Phil Taylor, and they had a bad pass defense despite an abundance of seniors in the secondary. Coach Art Briles has done a solid job of improving Baylor's overall athleticism, but it has not translated into tangible defensive improvement yet. If only Robert Griffin could play a little cornerback as well.

Top 2012 NFL Prospects: QB Robert Griffin III* (3-5), WR Kendall Wright (5-7).

No. 89 Iowa State Cyclones (3-9, 1-8)

2010: 5-7 (3-5) / F/+ #81 / FEI #82 / S&P+ #73

Program F/+	-10.2%	88	Returning Starters: 5 OFF, 7 DEF			5-Yr Recruiting Rank		61
2010 Offense			**2010 Defense**			**2010 Field Position**		
Offensive F/+	-2.5%	77	**Defensive F/+**	-4.5%	80	Field Position Advantage	0.501	56
Offensive FEI:	-0.162	87	Defensive FEI	0.208	89	**2011 Projections**		
Offensive S&P+	98.9	71	Defensive S&P+	95.0	73	**Mean Wins**	2.7	
Rushing S&P+	103.0	59	Rushing S&P+	98.3	66	Proj. F/+	-7.1%	89
Passing S&P+	97.1	75	Passing S&P+	90.7	85	Offensive F/+	-4.6%	88
Standard Downs S&P+	98.4	72	Standard Downs S&P+	97.9	62	Defensive F/+	-2.4%	70
Passing Downs S&P+	90.5	89	Passing Downs S&P+	104.0	53	Strength of Schedule	0.165	15

Iowa State head coach Paul Rhoads has accomplished something almost impossible: He has become almost universally liked. He has proven the ability to win with less than just about anybody else, he is incredibly entertaining on the sideline, he is capable of engineering huge upsets, and ... he has not shown that his teams will be serious threats in terms of conference titles and postseason honors. Iowa State is a salty, interesting team that is simply not talented enough to achieve at significant levels.

After receiving quite a bit of fumble-recovery luck in 2009 and winning seven games and the Insight Bowl, the Cyclones took a step or two backwards last year. In two years in Ames, Rhoads is 12-13 with both blowout losses and huge upsets at Nebraska and Texas. (OK, beating Texas wasn't *that* significant last year; it was symbolic, however.) This team can win any single game, but winning a lot of games has proven difficult.

The Cyclones have interesting individual talent. Running back Shontrelle Johnson is small but potentially explosive (and explosiveness is something the offense has severely lacked recently), linebackers Jake Knott and A.J. Klein combined for 14 tackles for loss and seven interceptions last year, and cornerback Leonard Johnson is feisty and fast. But there just isn't enough depth to contend for anything beyond a sneaky six wins and minor bowl bid in 2011.

Top 2012 NFL Prospects: OT/G Kelechi Osmele (2-4), CB Leonard Johnson (6-7), DT Stephen Ruempolhamer (6-7).

No. 93 Kansas Jayhawks (2-10, 1-8)

2010: 3-9 (1-7) / F/+ #113 / FEI #110 / S&P+ #116

Program F/+	-0.3%	64	Returning Starters: 8 OFF, 6 DEF			5-Yr Recruiting Rank		41
2010 Offense			**2010 Defense**			**2010 Field Position**		
Offensive F/+	-13.6%	114	**Defensive F/+**	-7.4%	96	Field Position Advantage	0.472	96
Offensive FEI:	-0.342	105	Defensive FEI	0.265	99	**2011 Projections**		
Offensive S&P+	72.8	117	Defensive S&P+	86.5	107	**Mean Wins**	2.3	
Rushing S&P+	81.6	111	Rushing S&P+	87.4	99	Proj. F/+	-9.3%	93
Passing S&P+	64.6	120	Passing S&P+	84.7	102	Offensive F/+	-5.2%	94
Standard Downs S&P+	83.0	109	Standard Downs S&P+	89.1	103	Defensive F/+	-4.1%	78
Passing Downs S&P+	67.1	120	Passing Downs S&P+	79.7	113	Strength of Schedule	0.243	35

When he was head coach of the Buffalo Bulls, Turner Gill was known for getting the most out of the talent on hand. His teams played conservative, fundamental, mistake-free ball, and won a surprise Mid-American Conference title in 2008. Conservatism can work if you have just enough talent on hand to take advantage of opponents' mistakes. In his first season at Kansas last year, either there wasn't enough talent on hand, or Gill's team did not play Gill-style ball. According to F/+ rankings, Kansas was the worst BCS conference team in the country in 2010, combining tentative defense with hopeless offense. They were able to squeeze out three wins, which was impressive, but the seeming lack of talent on hand was disturbing.

At first glance, nothing is guaranteed to improve in 2011. Gill landed a potential star in running back Darrian Miller, but relying on a true freshman is not typically a winning strategy. If Kansas is to make their way up the totem pole this fall, it will likely happen because of their returning core. Players like sophomore quarterback Jordan Webb, running back James Sims (742 yards, minus-1.4 Adj. POE), receiver Daymond Patterson (487 receiving yards), running-back-turned-defensive-end Toben Opurum, linebacker Steven Johnson, cornerback Isiah Barfield, and receiver-turned-safety Bradley McDougald will have to raise their games to as-yet unseen levels. Anything can happen, but the prospects are not particularly great. Kansas' projections are propped up by the use of four-year history and their great 2007 season. In watching the 2010 team, it was quite easy to conclude that 2007 was a long, long time ago.

Top 2012 NFL Prospects: LB Steven Johnson (6-7), CB Isiah Barfield (6-7).

Bill Connelly

Projected Win Probabilities For Big 12 Teams

Big 12	Overall Wins													Conference Wins									
	12-0	11-1	10-2	9-3	8-4	7-5	6-6	5-7	4-8	3-9	2-10	1-11	0-12	9-0	8-1	7-2	6-3	5-4	4-5	3-6	2-7	1-8	0-9
Baylor	-	-	-	-	1	6	17	31	29	13	3	-	-	-	-	-	1	5	18	33	30	11	2
Iowa State	-	-	-	-	-	-	1	4	15	33	35	11	1	-	-	-	-	2	11	33	42	12	
Kansas	-	-	-	-	-	-	2	11	27	37	22	1		-	-	-	-	1	6	23	42	28	
Kansas State	-	-	-	2	9	23	33	24	8	1	-	-		-	-	-	2	8	24	36	23	6	1
Missouri	2	14	30	31	17	5	1	-	-	-	-	-	-	3	21	37	27	10	2	-	-	-	-
Oklahoma	23	41	27	8	1	-	-	-	-	-	-	-	-	40	42	15	3	-	-	-	-	-	-
Oklahoma State	3	14	29	30	17	6	1	-	-	-	-	-	-	4	18	34	29	12	3	-	-	-	-
Texas	-	-	3	12	24	29	21	9	2	-	-	-	-	-	1	6	20	33	27	11	2	-	-
Texas A&M	-	1	9	23	31	23	10	3	-	-	-	-	-	1	7	23	33	24	10	2	-	-	-
Texas Tech	-	-	2	10	23	31	23	9	2	-	-	-	-	-	-	3	13	29	32	17	5	1	-

Pac-12 Conference

No conference has made more waves in the last 12 months than what is now known as the Pacific-12 Conference. Last summer, the Pac-10 teams set the conference realignment alarms to DEFCON 1 with their attempt to convince most of the Big 12 South to move to a new Pac-16 alignment, and it almost worked. In the end, the conference had to settle for stealing Colorado from the Big 12 and Utah from the Mountain West, then sealing the deal on an incredible new television deal that threatens to make more money per team than the SEC. The conference has raised its profile about as much as it possibly can without winning a national title, although Oregon came pretty close to doing that this past January as well.

With USC facing some serious sanctions and once again ineligible for postseason action (including a spot in the inaugural Pac-12 championship game), the conference enters 2011 with only two legitimate powers: Oregon and Stanford, both from the newly-formed North Division. But there are plenty of subplots among the high volume of teams either putting the pieces together or putting the pieces *back* together. And there is star power. Oh, is there star power.

Stanford's Andrew Luck is the likely first overall selection in the 2012 NFL Draft, but he'll still have to fight for first- or second-team all-conference against Oregon's Darron Thomas, USC's Matt Barkley, Washington State's Jeff Tuel, Oregon State's Ryan Katz,

Arizona State's Brock Osweiler, and Arizona's Nick Foles. At running back, Oregon's LaMichael James is the standard-bearer, but USC's Marc Tyler, Arizona State's Cameron Marshall, Stanford's Stepfan Taylor, Washington's Chris Polk, UCLA's Johnathan Franklin and Colorado's Rodney Stewart are going to put up serious yardage. At receiver, you've got Washington's Jermaine Kearse, USC's Robert Woods, Oregon State's Markus Weaton and James Rodgers, Arizona's Juron Criner, and others.

Though the skill positions are loaded, it doesn't stop there. Colorado guard Ryan Miller is a top draft prospect, every team has an interesting defensive tackle, and Arizona State's Junior Onyeali is a potentially devastating end (as are USC's Nick Perry, Colorado's Josh Hartigan, and others). Plus, you might not find a better linebacker than Arizona State's Vontaze Burfict or a better cornerback than Oregon's Cliff Harris.

For quite a while, USC dominated the Pac-10 to the point that it almost wasn't worth paying attention. Now the conference is a little more complicated, and that's a good thing. There are still national title contenders, Oregon and perhaps Stanford, but there are stars and landmines every stop along the way. There is even potential in Pullman, where at the very least, Washington State is no longer the slam-dunk worst BCS conference team in the country.

NORTH

No. 7 Stanford Cardinal (10-2, 8-1)

2010: 12-1 (8-1) / F/+ #4 / FEI #2 / S&P+ #6

Program F/+		+4.9%	42	Returning Starters: 5 OFF, 6 DEF			5-Yr Recruiting Rank		30
2010 Offense				**2010 Defense**			**2010 Field Position**		
Offensive F/+		+17.4%	2	Defensive F/+	+10.5%	15	Field Position Advantage	0.529	23
Offensive FEI:		0.517	6	Defensive FEI	-0.434	11	**2011 Projections**		
Offensive S&P+		137.7	2	Defensive S&P+	119.6	21	**Mean Wins**	10.3	
Rushing S&P+		119.2	22	Rushing S&P+	118.9	20	Proj. F/+	+15.7%	7
Passing S&P+		157.4	2	Passing S&P+	118.5	24	Offensive F/+	+8.8%	15
Standard Downs S&P+		122.5	12	Standard Downs S&P+	112.1	36	Defensive F/+	+6.9%	24
Passing Downs S&P+		163.5	2	Passing Downs S&P+	103.0	58	Strength of Schedule	0.369	65

Stanford has been on a nearly unprecedented positive trajectory in recent years. Jim Harbaugh took over the Cardinal program in 2007, immediately built an average team out of below-average parts, then put together incredible gains in 2009 and 2010. Both the Stanford offense and defense played at an elite or nearly elite level in 2010, and stars return on both sides of the ball. But how much of a hit did the program take when Harbaugh left to take over the San Francisco 49ers this offseason? Can new head coach David Shaw, Harbaugh's former offensive coordinator, maintain momentum?

In the short term, signs point to yes. Not much should change with an offense that was explosive, efficient and well-rounded in 2010. And besides, what is there to fear when Andrew Luck is your quarterback? Stanford was a run-first offense, plowing forward with Stepfan Taylor (1,137 yards, plus-5.7 Adj. POE) and Anthony Wilkerson (408 yards, minus-4.5 Adj. POE) on standard downs; on passing downs, they told Luck to make a play, and he always did. Stanford ranked second in Passing Downs S&P+, second in Passing S&P+, and first in Adjusted Sack Rate. Opponents couldn't get to Luck and couldn't cover a wide variety of weapons. Luck loses his top two targets, Doug Baldwin and Ryan Whalen (combined receiving yards: 1,296), but in Chris Owusu, Griff Whalen and tight end Coby Fleener, he will still see familiar options all over the field.

Perhaps the most impressive part of Stanford's recent charge was their downright drastic defensive improvement. The Cardinal were 92nd in Def. F/+ in 2008 and 105th in 2009, then steeply rose to 15th in 2010. Few defenses prevented big plays better than Stanford. The two safeties most responsible for this (Michael Thomas and Delano Howell, who combined for 7.5 tackles for loss, six interceptions, four forced fumbles, and 14 passes defensed) both return, as do two playmaking linebackers (Shayne Skov and Chase Thomas). Three Cardinal defenders are now in the NFL, and five starters were lost in all, but stellar depth should account for most of the loss. The toughest job will be replacing Sione Fua, the only tackle to make any major impact last season.

Stanford has taken significant leaps toward elite status, and while there is really barely any room to improve in 2011, maintenance is the name of the game. Can an offensive line that loses three stellar starters protect Luck as well? Will Owusu and Whalen thrive as much in larger roles? If there is a drop-off on the defensive line, how much will that impact the swarming secondary? Stanford hosts Oregon, which could give them a key edge in the battle for the North Division title, but the battle to maintain their edge without Harbaugh could be just as important.

Top 2012 NFL Prospects: QB Andrew Luck (1), S Delano Howell (2-3), WR Chris Owusu (4-5).

No. 8 Oregon Ducks (10-2, 7-2)

2010: 12-1 (9-0) / F/+ #9 / FEI #4 / S&P+ #16

2010 Offense			2010 Defense			2010 Field Position		
Program F/+	+18.0%	10				5-Yr Recruiting Rank		17
						Field Position Advantage	0.544	9
Offensive F/+	+9.4%	16	Defensive F/+	+12.1%	13	2011 Projections		
Offensive FEI:	0.338	15	Defensive FEI	-0.458	8	Mean Wins	9.6	
Offensive S&P+	118.0	24	Defensive S&P+	120.2	19	Proj. F/+	+15.6%	8
Rushing S&P+	116.0	24	Rushing S&P+	116.3	22	Offensive F/+	+6.6%	23
Passing S&P+	121.9	21	Passing S&P+	124.1	17	Defensive F/+	+9.1%	16
Standard Downs S&P+	118.2	20	Standard Downs S&P+	114.1	32	Strength of Schedule	0.192	20
Passing Downs S&P+	120.0	28	Passing Downs S&P+	142.7	7			

Returning Starters: 6 OFF, 5 DEF

There is power in simple perseverance. In 2010, Oregon fielded yet another great team – their third in four seasons, really – and, with the perfect combination of scheduling and well-timed ball-hawking, broke through with an undefeated regular season and a BCS championship game appearance. The Ducks were explosive and entertaining, and though there are new question marks in the receiving corps and on defense,

they should be equally entertaining in 2011.

No offense in the country was put under the microscope in 2010 more than Chip Kelly's at Oregon. The Ducks went all-in with their no-huddle attack, running the second-fastest offense in the country but doing so on the ground instead of through the air like most other full-throttle attacks. They were only good on a play-by-play basis, not spectacular, but they ran so many plays and moved the chains so many times that eventually defenses broke down.

Most of the key operators on offense return. Quarterback Darron Thomas (2,881 passing yards, 540 pre-sack rushing yards) proved masterful in running the zone read, and Heisman finalist LaMichael James (1,731 rushing yards, 208 receiving yards, 24 combined touchdowns, plus-26.4 Adj. POE) was masterful, period. They are joined by Kenjon Barner (551 rushing yards) and redshirt freshman Lache Seastrunk in the backfield. The major loss on offense comes at receiver, where the Ducks must replace the frequently-targeted Jeff Maehl. Expect sophomore Josh Huff (303 receiving yards, 214 rushing yards) to become more of a factor in this Maehl-less world.

As impressive as the offense was, Oregon's defense made the difference between 2010 being a very good season and Oregon's best ever. The Ducks had one of the best passing defenses in the country (seventh in Passing Downs S&P+); if you stayed on schedule and in standard downs, you could move the ball, but with so many ballhawks, falling into second- or third-and-long was deadly. Quite a few of the Ducks' best playmakers are gone, including linebacker Casey Matthews (nine tackles for loss, three interceptions),

end Kenny Rowe (16.5 tackles for loss, five forced fumbles) and tackle Brandon Bair (16 tackles for loss, eight passes defensed). As a result, there are question marks amid the front seven. The secondary, however, should remain fantastic. Cornerback Cliff Harris intercepted six passes, broke up a ridiculous 17 more, and returned four punts for touchdowns as well. If or when he returns from an "indefinite" suspension (he committed several impressive traffic violations this offseason), he and ball-hawking safety John Boyett (five interceptions, 14 passes defensed) will lead the way for the Ducks in 2011.

Oregon's path to a second straight national title game really features two major bumps. First, they open the season with a neutral-site game (in Dallas) against another surefire top-ten team, LSU. Then, they must travel to face Stanford on November 12. There are plenty of other landmines along the way (a trip to Arizona on September 24, plus potentially tricky home games against California, Arizona State, USC, and Oregon State), but it is hard to look past those two specific marquee games.

Top 2012 NFL Prospects: RB LaMichael James (1-2), TE David Paulson (2-3), S Eddie Pleasant (6-7).

No. 38 Oregon State Beavers (7-5, 5-4)

2010: 5-7 (4-5) / F/+ #35 / FEI #45 / S&P+ #23

Program F/+	+10.9%	25	Returning Starters: 7 OFF, 4 DEF			5-Yr Recruiting Rank		55
2010 Offense			**2010 Defense**			**2010 Field Position**		
Offensive F/+	+7.5%	25	**Defensive F/+**	+1.8%	48	Field Position Advantage	0.540	13
Offensive FEI:	0.038	54	Defensive FEI	0.154	82	**2011 Projections**		
Offensive S&P+	119.8	19	Defensive S&P+	112.1	34	**Mean Wins**	6.7	
Rushing S&P+	117.8	23	Rushing S&P+	111.0	29	Proj. F/+	+5.7%	38
Passing S&P+	124.0	15	Passing S&P+	110.4	37	Offensive F/+	+7.8%	19
Standard Downs S&P+	114.1	29	Standard Downs S&P+	112.6	35	Defensive F/+	-2.0%	68
Passing Downs S&P+	129.1	14	Passing Downs S&P+	106.7	42	Strength of Schedule	0.230	30

In an era where great non-conference matchups are becoming rarer and rarer, Oregon State earned a great deal of respect by loading up the non-Pac-10 portion of its schedule in 2010. They agreed to take on TCU and Boise State away from home, something almost no team would have done, and they ended up playing four of the top nine teams in the country according to F/+.

Just think how much respect they'd have earned if they had actually *beaten* one of those teams. The Beavers were respectable most of the season despite losing star receiver James Rodgers early on. They whipped USC and California and knocked off Ari-

zona on the road, but they could still only manage five wins. This year's schedule still includes non-conference games against BYU and Wisconsin, but the presence of even one gimme (Sacramento State) is a step in the right direction.

Against a brutal stretch of defenses and missing his number one target, quarterback Ryan Katz put together a solid profile: 2,401 yards, 60 percent completion rate, 18 touchdowns, 11 interceptions. With the return of Rodgers and the emergence of receiver Markus Wheaton (675 yards, 12.3 per catch; 220 rushing yards), the Beavers' passing game could improve enough to account for the loss of three-time all-conference running back Jacquizz Rodgers.

The Beavers love to attack on defense, but they were only decent at it last season. They ranked ninth in Adjusted Sack Rate, but they were vulnerable to draw plays and overpursuit. It will be interesting to see if they become more conservative in 2011, having to replace one of the nation's best pairs of playmaking tackles (Stephen Paea and Brennan Olander) and perhaps their best cornerback (James Dockery). The linebacker and safety positions were a bit ho-hum a year ago, but they are the most experienced units the Beavers' defense will have in 2011.

Top 2012 NFL Prospects: S Lance Mitchell (2-3), FB/ TE Joe Halahuni (3-4), OT Mike Remmers (6-7).

No. 59 Washington Huskies (5-7, 3-6)

2010: 7-6 (5-4) / F/+ #51 / FEI #58 / S&P+ #41

Program F/+	-2.3%	68	Returning Starters: 6 OFF, 7 DEF			5-Yr Recruiting Rank		31
2010 Offense			**2010 Defense**			**2010 Field Position**		
Offensive F/+	+4.9%	35	**Defensive F/+**	-2.7%	67	Field Position Advantage	0.482	83
Offensive FEI:	-0.048	68	Defensive FEI	0.108	77	**2011 Projections**		
Offensive S&P+	117.8	25	Defensive S&P+	97.0	67	**Mean Wins**	5.2	
Rushing S&P+	113.3	29	Rushing S&P+	93.4	82	Proj. F/+	+0.3%	59
Passing S&P+	122.9	18	Passing S&P+	100.8	58	Offensive F/+	+1.3%	48
Standard Downs S&P+	111.5	32	Standard Downs S&P+	100.4	58	Defensive F/+	-1.0%	61
Passing Downs S&P+	109.6	49	Passing Downs S&P+	102.3	60	Strength of Schedule	0.205	23

For 25 years, Washington was one of the steadiest winners in college football. Beginning with Don James' third season in 1977, the Huskies went 27 seasons without a losing record. But in the wake of minor sanctions and Rick Neuheisel's awkward departure after the 2002 season, things took a severe turn. Keith Gilbertson's Huskies went 1-10 in 2004, and successor Tyrone Willingham won just 11 games in four seasons.

Now, under third-year coach Steve Sarkisian, the rebound has begun. The Huskies went 7-6 last season with their first bowl win since 2000, and their five-year recruiting average suggests a decent amount of talent percolating under the surface.

With Jake Locker gone and youth abound, this season will be about the Huskies maintaining their current stature instead of taking another step forward. Quarterback Keith Price beat out Nick "Joe's Son" Montana for the starting job, and his progress will obviously be watched closely. He'll have running back Chris Polk (1,415 rushing yards, minus-0.8 Adj. POE) and experienced receivers Jermaine Kearse (1,005 yards, 16.0 per catch) and Devin Aguilar (352 yards, 12.6 per catch) at his disposal. A line that was only average last year returns three starters, including senior tackle Senior Kelemete. With Price running the offense, expect a more conservative, efficiency-over-explosiveness attack this fall.

On defense, Washington's strengths might get stronger, and their weaknesses might get weaker. Playmaking linebackers Victor Aiyewa and Mason Foster are gone, and a defense that finished just 82nd in Def. Rushing S&P+ might struggle to maintain even that poor ranking unless players like tackle Alameda Ta'amu and linebacker Cort Dennison can raise their respective games. Meanwhile, the pass rush and overall pass defense were a bit stronger, ranking 58th in Def. Passing S&P+; three of four starters return in the secondary, including a pair of solid cornerbacks in Desmond Trufant and Quinton Richardson. The duo combined for 3.5 tackles for loss, three interceptions, and 15 passes defensed last fall.

Top 2012 NFL Prospects: DT Alameda Ta'amu (2-3), WR Jermaine Kearse (3-4), LB Cort Dennison (6-7).

No. 60 California Golden Bears (5-7, 3-6)

2010: 5-7 (3-6) / F/+ #68 / FEI #83 / S&P+ #45

Program F/+		+8.4%	36	Returning Starters: 7 OFF, 5 DEF			5-Yr Recruiting Rank			25
2010 Offense				**2010 Defense**			**2010 Field Position**			
Offensive F/+		-8.9%	101	**Defensive F/+**	+6.1%	34	Field Position Advantage		0.507	52
Offensive FEI:		-0.388	108	Defensive FEI	0.062	66	**2011 Projections**			
Offensive S&P+		92.2	88	Defensive S&P+	119.4	22	**Mean Wins**		5.1	
Rushing S&P+		103.9	56	Rushing S&P+	110.4	32	Proj. F/+		+0.1%	60
Passing S&P+		78.5	106	Passing S&P+	127.1	14	Offensive F/+		-4.9%	92
Standard Downs S&P+		98.0	74	Standard Downs S&P+	116.5	26	Defensive F/+		+5.0%	35
Passing Downs S&P+		86.2	99	Passing Downs S&P+	132.5	11	Strength of Schedule		0.223	28

California's Memorial Stadium is undergoing an extensive, $300 million renovation this season, with Cal playing home games at Candlestick Park and AT&T Park instead. Memorial Stadium is being retrofitted and modernized, reducing the risk of earthquake damage, improving sight lines, and just making the Cal game day experience better. Now Cal just needs a well-renovated team as well, preferably one with a little more structural (mental) stability of its own. The Golden Bears were one of the best teams in the country when playing at Memorial Stadium last fall, and one of the worst away from Berkeley.

Few offenses utilize athleticism in a more diverse way than California. Last fall, the Bears' top two running backs caught 27 passes, and their top three receivers were given 35 carries. The problem last fall was that they needed to be a little better at the basics. A run game led by Shane Vereen (1,167 rushing yards, plus-5.6 Adj. POE) was decent enough, but the passing game went from decent to miserable when quarterback Kevin Riley got hurt in the eighth game. Now both Vereen and Riley are gone, and a bounce-back season for Cal will be driven by quarterback transfer Zach Maynard (2,694 passing yards, 300 rushing yards for University of Buffalo in 2009) and running back Isi Sofele. Receivers Marvin Jones and Keenan Allen give Maynard a couple of interesting targets, but there is a long way to go for this aerial attack.

On defense, the Bears' 3-4 attack needs to avoid the breakdowns that plagued the team away from home last fall. The defense wasn't the only reason the Bears went a lackluster 5-7 last year, but they did get lit up by Nevada, USC, Oregon and Stanford. Cal fielded one of the country's better passing and passing downs defenses last year and, on a play-by-play basis, did a stellar job. Their primary problem was that letdowns came with particularly bad timing. With end Trevor Guyton and outside linebacker Mychal Kendricks roaming around, they should be as effective in terms of swarming and making plays; they just need to be a bit more consistent about it.

Top 2012 NFL Prospects: S Sean Cattouse (3-4), OT Mitchell Schwartz (3-4), LB D.J. Holt (5-6).

No. 99 Washington State Cougars (2-10, 1-8)

2010: 2-10 (1-8) / F/+ #94 / FEI #96 / S&P+ #93

Program F/+		-12.9%	97	Returning Starters: 7 OFF, 7 DEF			5-Yr Recruiting Rank			81
2010 Offense				**2010 Defense**			**2010 Field Position**			
Offensive F/+		-0.9%	67	**Defensive F/+**	-11.2%	112	Field Position Advantage		0.487	73
Offensive FEI:		-0.143	79	Defensive FEI	0.575	119	**2011 Projections**			
Offensive S&P+		94.0	86	Defensive S&P+	87.6	98	**Mean Wins**		2.5	
Rushing S&P+		88.7	96	Rushing S&P+	82.7	110	Proj. F/+		-11.2%	99
Passing S&P+		99.6	67	Passing S&P+	92.6	79	Offensive F/+		+1.0%	49
Standard Downs S&P+		92.5	90	Standard Downs S&P+	92.6	84	Defensive F/+		-12.2%	119
Passing Downs S&P+		98.9	64	Passing Downs S&P+	90.0	90	Strength of Schedule		0.357	62

Washington State went 2-10 in 2010, scored fewer than 20 points per game (only four other BCS conference teams did that) and allowed over 35 points per game (only four other BCS teams did *that* too). This depressing record actually represented significant improvement over the incredible depths to which the Cougars sank in 2008-09. It even earned Paul Wulff a fourth year in charge in Pullman despite a rather incredible 3-32 record versus FBS teams in three seasons.

If Wulff wants a fifth year in charge, however, "improving" from 2-10 to 3-9 probably will not cut it. Wazzu will need to make serious strides, and if they do so it will be driven by the passing game. Junior quarterback Jeff Tuel (2,780 yards, 18 touchdowns, 12 interceptions in 2010) found two interesting targets last year in playmaker Marquess Wilson (1,006 yards, 18.3 per catch as a true freshman) and possession man Jared Karstetter (658 yards, 10.6 per catch); all three return, and Tuel will have more time to find his receiv-

ers because it is impossible for the offensive line to get any worse than it was last year.

The offense should improve, but the defense must as well if bowl eligibility is to remain a possibility, and it is a little less clear how that will happen. The linebackers, a relative weakness last year, should be improved with Mike Ledgerwood returning to full strength (he lost half of last season to injury) and athletic-but-moody C.J. Mizell maturing. But with losses on the line and in the secondary, overall improvement is iffy.

Top 2012 NFL Prospects: LB Alex Hoffman-Ellis (6-7), LB Mike Ledgerwood (6-7).

SOUTH

No. 18 USC Trojans (9-3, 7-2)

2010: 8-5 (5-4) / F/+ #27 / FEI #26 / S&P+ #35

2010 Offense			2010 Defense					
Program F/+	+22.4%	4	Returning Starters: 6 OFF, 7 DEF			5-Yr Recruiting Rank		2
2010 Offense			**2010 Defense**			**2010 Field Position**		
Offensive F/+	+8.6%	21	**Defensive F/+**	+2.1%	47	Field Position Advantage	0.551	5
Offensive FEI:	0.194	32	Defensive FEI	0.001	59	**2011 Projections**		
Offensive S&P+	116.5	26	Defensive S&P+	106.9	46	**Mean Wins**	8.8	
Rushing S&P+	121.7	18	Rushing S&P+	103.8	49	Proj. F/+	+12.4%	18
Passing S&P+	112.9	37	Passing S&P+	107.4	45	Offensive F/+	+8.3%	16
Standard Downs S&P+	120.0	15	Standard Downs S&P+	102.6	49	Defensive F/+	+4.1%	40
Passing Downs S&P+	109.8	48	Passing Downs S&P+	102.2	61	Strength of Schedule	0.246	37

Thirty scholarships over three seasons, postseason bans over two. Recruiting classes of 15 players, max. Now that the NCAA has officially rejected their appeal, USC can move on to Life Under Probation. It is harsh terrain, and the damage it might do to depth in a couple of years could be devastating, but USC has no choice but to pay for the charmed life it led for the last decade.

Scholarship limitations are a slow killer, and they will not do much damage to Lane Kiffin's 2011 squad. What might, however, is a totally rebuilt run game. Make no mistake: USC's offense was most dependent on quarterback Matt Barkley (2,791 yards, 63 percent completion rate, 26 touchdowns, 12 interceptions) and the pass, but the Trojans were much better on the ground. The Trojans ranked 18th in Rushing S&P+, powered by a line that ranked fourth in Adjusted Line Yards. In 2011, they will be without star center Kris O'Dowd, tackle (and early NFL entry) Tyron Smith, running backs Allen Bradford and C.J. Gable, and

fullback-slash-lifer Stanley Havili. We're pretty sure Havili was in uniform when USC won their titles in 2003-04, but he will not be in 2011, nor will receiver Ronald Johnson.

USC passes a lot on standard downs, but with a less effective run game, they could find themselves in quite a few more passing downs – unless, of course, some blue-chip youngsters take less-than-surprising star turns. Running back Dillon Baxter (252 yards, minus-8.0 Adj. POE) turned heads in practice but was a bit overwhelmed as a true freshman; he could take a step forward while splitting time with fifth-year senior Marc Tyler (913 yards, minus-0.8 Adj. POE). Meanwhile, receiver Robert Woods (792 yards, 12.2 per catch, six touchdowns) was absolutely outstanding for a first-year guy and will likely be again this fall. With three starting linemen returning as well, there is plenty to like on the offense as long as certain skill position players continue to develop.

The defense, however, remains questionable. Despite blue-chip talent, and despite the presence of one of the most successful defensive coordinators of all-time, Monte Kiffin, things just didn't click for the Trojans' defense in 2010. They ranked 49th in Rushing S&P+ and 45th in Passing S&P+. They were basically mediocre across the board, which is baffling with the perceived talent on hand. If they are to improve in 2011, it will likely be because playmakers like end-turned-tackle Armond Armstead and a deep

unit of stellar linebackers broke through as they have been expected to do.

The defense could potentially also use some extra conditioning. USC ranked 36th and 12th in the First- and Third-Quarter S&P+, respectively; they ranked 81st and 103rd in the second and fourth quarters.

Top 2012 NFL Prospects: LB Chris Galippo (1-2), DT Armond Armstead (3-4), RB Marc Tyler (4-5).

No. 31 Arizona State Sun Devils (8-4, 6-3)
2010: 6-6 (4-5) / F/+ #38 / FEI #37 / S&P+ #40

Program F/+		+4.2%	45	Returning Starters: 10 OFF, 9 DEF			5-Yr Recruiting Rank			39
2010 Offense				**2010 Defense**			**2010 Field Position**			
Offensive F/+		+0.5%	55	**Defensive F/+**	+6.4%	33	Field Position Advantage		0.503	55
Offensive FEI:		-0.005	65	Defensive FEI	-0.174	36	**2011 Projections**			
Offensive S&P+		103.7	51	Defensive S&P+	111.9	35	**Mean Wins**		7.6	
Rushing S&P+		98.0	78	Rushing S&P+	131.6	8	Proj. F/+		+7.3%	31
Passing S&P+		108.0	47	Passing S&P+	95.8	71	Offensive F/+		+2.1%	46
Standard Downs S&P+		98.9	69	Standard Downs S&P+	114.5	31	Defensive F/+		+5.2%	34
Passing Downs S&P+		109.3	50	Passing Downs S&P+	106.5	43	Strength of Schedule		0.308	51

This is a particularly impressive example of damning with faint praise, since bowl bids are given out like Oprah once gave out cars ("YOU get a bowl! YOU get a bowl!"), but aside from USC, Arizona State was perhaps the best team in the country that did not finish bowl-eligible last season. They lost four games by four points or less – including games against outstanding Wisconsin and Arizona State squads – and they hung around with Oregon as well as anybody in the conference before falling because of turnovers. The Sun Devils return a boatload of starters on both sides of the ball, so it isn't hard to see why they are generating a bit of a buzz heading into the season. With USC ineligible for the Pac-12 title game and other South programs rebuilding a bit, ASU might be the division favorite among postseason-eligible teams.

Dennis Erickson's defense only started one senior last fall, but they suffered a bit more attrition when tackle Lawrence Guy declared early for the draft and all-conference cornerback Omar Bolden was lost with an ACL tear this spring. Still, there's a lot to like about a unit that ranked eighth in Rushing S&P+ last fall, starting

with Vontaze Burfict. The junior linebacker is one of the wildest, biggest hitters in the country. He and ends Jamaar Jarrett and Junior Onyeali were big-play threats a year ago, though the gap at tackle might be tough to overcome. The front seven needs to be as impressive as it was last year, as there are question marks in a pass defense that ranked 71st in Passing S&P+.

A pass-heavy offense will lean heavily on the gigantic shoulders of quarterback Brock Osweiler. The 6-foot-8, 235-pound junior from Montana took over when starter Steven Threet's career was cut short by concussions. Osweiler was more conservative with the ball than Threet, averaging slightly fewer yards per pass but throwing zero interceptions in 109 passes (Threet threw 16 in 336). He will have a solid pair of running backs taking the heat off of him. Cameron Marshall and Deantre Lewis combined for 1,326 rushing yards (plus-11.6 Adj. POE) and 597 receiving yards a year ago.

Top 2012 NFL Prospects: LB Vontaze Burfict (1-2), CB Omar Bolden (3-4), DE James Brooks (5-6).*

No. 34 Arizona Wildcats (6-6, 4-5)

2010: 7-6 (4-5) / F/+ #36 / FEI #44 / S&P+ #27

Program F/+	+7.5%	38	Returning Starters: 6 OFF, 6 DEF			5-Yr Recruiting Rank		45
2010 Offense			**2010 Defense**			**2010 Field Position**		
						Field Position Advantage	0.486	76
Offensive F/+	+4.4%	36	**Defensive F/+**	+4.3%	39	**2011 Projections**		
Offensive FEI:	0.224	28	Defensive FEI	-0.02	53	**Mean Wins**	6.3	
Offensive S&P+	109.4	37	Defensive S&P+	119.7	20	Proj. F/+	+6.0%	34
Rushing S&P+	101.4	63	Rushing S&P+	123.1	15	Offensive F/+	+4.5%	34
Passing S&P+	114.5	31	Passing S&P+	116.5	28	Defensive F/+	+1.5%	51
Standard Downs S&P+	108.4	44	Standard Downs S&P+	120.6	16	Strength of Schedule	0.217	25
Passing Downs S&P+	124.2	21	Passing Downs S&P+	107.7	41			

Slowly but surely, eighth-year Arizona head coach Mike Stoops has built a steady winner in Tucson. He has basically fielded the exact same level of team over the last four years, and they've settled into a seven- to eight-win niche. This year could be more of the same, but only if the Wildcats can overcome some serious attrition in the trenches.

Arizona had one of the deeper, more underrated defensive lines in the country last year, powering a defense that ranked 15th in Rushing S&P+. Five players registered at least six tackles for loss, but four of them have now departed, including strong ends Ricky Elmore and Brooks Reed. It will be up to sophomore tackles Justin Washington and Sione Tuihalamaka to hold the fort; with 11.5 tackles for loss as a redshirt freshman last year, Washington could be a star in the making. The line could also get assistance from a more experienced back seven. Paul Vassallo leads a decent linebacker corps, and the Wildcats have three solid corners, led by Robert Golden.

The Arizona offense, meanwhile, will be a study in the importance of the offensive line. The Wildcats return all six starters at skill positions ... and return just one career start on the offensive line. In the last five seasons, only four teams have lost all five offensive line starters, and their production decreased by an average of 7.8 percent in Offensive S&P+ and 8.2 percent in OFEI. If Arizona can overcome this turnover, however, the offense has plenty of interesting pieces. Though they don't necessarily get mentioned as such, Arizona is almost as pass-heavy as any team in the country; despite having to throw a high percentage of the time on passing downs, Nick Foles threw for 3,191 yards last year, completing 67 percent of his passes. He will have some weapons, assuming Juron Criner (1,233 receiving yards) returns. Criner, a downfield threat who manages to combine explosiveness (15.0 yards per catch) with efficiency (69 percent catch rate), is uncertain for the fall because of some unspecified medical issues.

Top 2012 NFL Prospects: QB Nick Foles (1-2), WR Juron Criner (2-3), CB Robert Golden (6-7).

No. 35 Utah Utes (7-5, 6-3)

2010: 10-3 (7-1) / F/+ #32 / FEI #47 / S&P+ #19

Program F/+	+9.4%	31	Returning Starters: 7 OFF, 5 DEF			5-Yr Recruiting Rank		52
2010 Offense			**2010 Defense**			**2010 Field Position**		
						Field Position Advantage	0.523	32
Offensive F/+	+1.3%	49	**Defensive F/+**	+8.3%	25	**2011 Projections**		
Offensive FEI:	-0.076	72	Defensive FEI	-0.182	35	**Mean Wins**	7.4	
Offensive S&P+	113.1	31	Defensive S&P+	120.8	17	Proj. F/+	+5.9%	35
Rushing S&P+	103.3	58	Rushing S&P+	154.3	1	Offensive F/+	+0.4%	55
Passing S&P+	122.4	19	Passing S&P+	104.8	49	Defensive F/+	+5.5%	31
Standard Downs S&P+	120.3	14	Standard Downs S&P+	118.3	21	Strength of Schedule	0.356	61
Passing Downs S&P+	100.5	61	Passing Downs S&P+	105.4	47			

Last summer's conference realignment drama did not result in as much change as once feared/desired, but that didn't stop the Utes from watching their lot in life change considerably. They make their BCS conference debut in the Pac-12 this season, and well, the timing could be a lot better. Coach Kyle Whittingham faces this fall with a brand new running game and huge holes both in the secondary and on the defensive line. That they are projected to win seven games is a sign of the job Whittington has done in building both depth and consistency in Salt Lake.

Utah's defensive line was incredibly underrated a year ago. They fielded the best run defense in the country according to Rushing S&P+ and ranked third overall in Adjusted Line Yards, yet they placed only one lineman (end Christian Cox) on the Mountain West all-conference team. Cox is gone, as is tackle Sealver Siliga, who left early for the pros. Their departures put a dent in what was some stellar depth up front. It also puts pressure on a pass defense that wasn't very good to begin with. Utah ranked just 49th in Passing S&P+, and they must make do with only one returning starter in the secondary. Strong safety Brian Blechen (3.5 tackles for loss, four interceptions) earned honorable mention all-conference honors as a freshman, but now he is, by default, the steely-eyed veteran leader.

Utah fans have to hope that quarterback Jordan Wynn is 100 percent healthy this fall. With him, the Utes' offense was aggressive and explosive. Wynn completed 62 percent of his passes at 7.8 yards per toss, but he missed two games with a sprained thumb, then missed the Poinsettia Bowl battle versus Boise State because of shoulder surgery that also kept him out this spring. In his absence, Utah's effectiveness was limited; none of the other quarterback candidates did much to earn confidence this spring either. That the top three running backs and two all-conference linemen are gone puts more pressure on the quarterback position in an already quarterback-friendly offense.

Utah is projected with a lower F/+ ranking than its new conference rival Arizona, but a better record because of an easier schedule. Somehow, the Utes managed to avoid both Stanford and Oregon in the first year of cross-division scheduling.

Top 2012 NFL Prospects: QB Jordan Wynn* (2-3), FB Shawn Asiata (6-7), LB Chaz Walker (6-7).

No. 64 UCLA Bruins (5-7, 3-6)

2010: 4-8 (2-7) / F/+ #72 / FEI #80 / S&P+ #65

Program F/+		+1.6%	54	Returning Starters: 7 OFF, 8 DEF			5-Yr Recruiting Rank		23
2010 Offense				**2010 Defense**			**2010 Field Position**		
Offensive F/+		-5.9%	89	**Defensive F/+**	+0.9%	51	Field Position Advantage	0.495	66
Offensive FEI:		-0.324	102	Defensive FEI	0.081	72	**2011 Projections**		
Offensive S&P+		96.7	78	Defensive S&P+	103.6	48	**Mean Wins**	4.7	
Rushing S&P+		110.1	38	Rushing S&P+	96.9	70	Proj. F/+	-1.0%	64
Passing S&P+		75.0	111	Passing S&P+	110.7	35	Offensive F/+	-4.8%	91
Standard Downs S&P+		105.5	51	Standard Downs S&P+	101.4	54	Defensive F/+	+3.9%	41
Passing Downs S&P+		69.1	118	Passing Downs S&P+	111.6	32	Strength of Schedule	0.264	43

It doesn't make sense, does it? A program that lives in prime football real estate and puts together solid recruiting classes every year has put together just two seasons of eight or more wins in the last 12 years and has gone 28-35 since its 10-win campaign of 2005. Former UCLA quarterback Rick Neuheisel enters his fourth season as the Bruins' head coach, and, strangely enough, it's been the quarterback position that has held him back as much as anything. Due to some combination of injury and ineffectiveness, Neuheisel has continued the trend that began under previous coach (and frequent mid-1980s Neuheisel target) Karl Dorrell; in four of the past five seasons, UCLA has seen at least two quarterbacks throw 90 or more passes. In 2010, Richard Brehaut took over when Kevin Prince was lost for the season after five games, but Neuheisel's lack of faith led to him giving snaps to Darius Bell and Clayton Tunney as well. This spring, things became no clearer. Brehaut and a still-injured Prince were listed as co-starters, while Bell, Tunney and blue-chip true freshman Brett Hundley are all still close enough to make up ground. Hundley is seen as The Future, but gambling on a true freshman is tough to consider for a coach on the hot seat.

There is a bit more offensive uncertainty beyond the quarterback position: A line that ranked 45th in Adjusted Line Yards must replace four starters. If the hosses are decent, then Neuheisel's Pistol offense could still be interesting with the return of backs Johnathan Franklin, Derrick Coleman and Malcolm Jones.

New defensive coordinator Joe Tresey inherits what was one of the younger defenses in the country last year. The Bruins must replace stars Akeem Ayers (linebacker) and Rahim Moore (free safety), but an upgrade in overall experience among the front seven could offset that loss. Freshmen like tackle Cassius Marsh, ends Keenan Graham and Owamagbe Odighizuwa, and linebacker Jordan Zumwalt played integral roles last season even though they weren't necessarily ready; this should eventually pay off. Linebackers Sean Westgate and Pat Larimore should add solid "veteranosity" in the middle as well.

Top 2012 NFL Prospects: S Tony Dye (2-3), C Kai Maiava (6-7), LB Steve Sloan (6-7).

No. 70 Colorado Buffaloes (4-9, 3-6)

2010: 5-7 (2-6) / F/+ #71 / FEI #79 / S&P+ #64

Program F/+	-4.3%	74	Returning Starters: 9 OFF, 7 DEF			5-Yr Recruiting Rank		48
2010 Offense			**2010 Defense**			**2010 Field Position**		
			Defensive F/+	-4.2%	75	Field Position Advantage	0.476	88
Offensive F/+	-0.6%	64	Defensive FEI	0.129	79	**2011 Projections**		
Offensive FEI:	0.047	51	Defensive S&P+	99.3	61	**Mean Wins**	4.2	
Offensive S&P+	101.5	65	Rushing S&P+	111.0	30	Proj. F/+	-1.9%	70
Rushing S&P+	93.8	88	Passing S&P+	89.8	87	Offensive F/+	+2.8%	40
Passing S&P+	111.6	40	Standard Downs S&P+	101.2	55	Defensive F/+	-4.7%	86
Standard Downs S&P+	96.8	81	Passing Downs S&P+	90.6	88	Strength of Schedule	0.191	19
Passing Downs S&P+	112.5	39						

What do you do when your program has become rather far removed from its glory days? Bring back constant reminders of said glory days in the form of a good portion of the coaching staff. Former Colorado star tight end Jon Embree takes over for the embattled Dan Hawkins in Boulder, while former All-American running back Eric Bieniemy is the new offensive coordinator and former All-American defensive tackle Kanavis McGee is, naturally, defensive line coach.

Of course, while former stars can restore pride, they cannot necessarily restore a team's standing. Embree, Bieniemy and company inherit a team that hasn't recruited particularly well and isn't winning a lot of ballgames. The Buffaloes haven't finished with a winning record since 2005 (the year before Hawkins arrived), and staring down a brutal 2011 slate, they probably will not win a ton of games this fall either.

Establishing the run will be key to a surprise season for the Buffs. Senior running back Rodney Stewart is more durable than his size (5-foot-6, 175 pounds) suggests, and he was able to shoulder a large load in 2010 (1,318 yards) despite little help from his offensive line. The offensive line starters return (except for first-round draft pick Nate Solder) as do a couple of senior fullbacks. If Colorado can improve on its dreadful first-down performance (102nd in First-Down S&P+), it will take the pressure off of wheeler-dealer quarterback Tyler Hansen to improvise too much on third-and-long.

Offensive struggle punctuated much of Dan Hawkins' tenure in Boulder, but the defense regressed in 2010. New coordinator Greg Brown inherits a defense that was decent against the run but horribly inefficient in the passing game. (Odd, considering corners Jimmy Smith and Jalil Brown were both drafted this past April; Smith was picked in the first round, no less.) There are intriguing options on the defensive line, including end Josh Hartigan and tackle Will Pericak, but if the pass defense was bad *with* two NFL cornerbacks, then it's hard to be too excited about how the secondary will fare without them.

Top 2012 NFL Prospects: G Ryan Miller (1-2), TE Ryan Deehan (6-7), S Anthony Perkins (6-7).

Bill Connelly

Projected Win Probabilities For Pac-12 Teams

Pac 12 North	Overall Wins													Conference Wins									
	12-0	11-1	10-2	9-3	8-4	7-5	6-6	5-7	4-8	3-9	2-10	1-11	0-12	9-0	8-1	7-2	6-3	5-4	4-5	3-6	2-7	1-8	0-9
California	-	-	-	1	3	10	22	29	23	10	2	-	-	-	-	-	1	7	19	32	28	12	1
Oregon	3	18	34	28	13	3	1	-	-	-	-	-	-	12	37	33	14	4	-	-	-	-	-
Oregon State	-	-	2	7	18	28	25	14	5	1	-	-	-	-	1	7	21	31	26	11	3	-	-
Stanford	12	32	33	17	5	1	-	-	-	-	-	-	-	17	38	31	12	2	-	-	-	-	-
Washington	-	-	-	-	3	11	25	31	21	8	1	-	-	-	-	-	2	11	28	34	20	5	-
Washington State	-	-	-	-	-	-	2	11	31	43	12	1		-	-	-	-	-	2	11	36	51	
Pac 12 South	12-0	11-1	10-2	9-3	8-4	7-5	6-6	5-7	4-8	3-9	2-10	1-11	0-12	9-0	8-1	7-2	6-3	5-4	4-5	3-6	2-7	1-8	0-9
Arizona	-	-	1	5	14	25	28	19	7	1	-	-	-	-	-	3	12	24	30	21	8	2	-
Arizona State	-	2	7	19	27	25	14	5	1	-	-	-	-	1	6	20	32	26	12	3	-	-	-
Colorado*	-	-	-	-	1	4	12	23	29	22	8	1	-	-	-	-	-	2	10	26	36	23	3
UCLA	-	-	-	-	2	8	18	28	26	14	4	-	-	-	-	-	1	8	24	35	24	7	1
USC	1	7	21	30	24	12	4	1	-	-	-	-	-	3	17	32	29	14	4	1	-	-	-
Utah	-	1	5	15	26	27	17	7	2	-	-	-	-	1	7	22	31	25	11	3	-	-	-

*Colorado will play 13 regular season games; for projected overall records, 12-0 means 12-1, 11-1 means 11-2, etc.

Southeastern Conference

There is no question that the SEC has been the best conference of the BCS era. The Big Ten has had more BCS bowl berths, but the SEC has more BCS bowl wins (15) and national championships (seven) than any other conference – and it's not even close. The SEC wins 79 percent of its games against non-conference opponents and 61 percent of its bowl games. The conference has also had the most players drafted into the NFL in each of the past five seasons.

However, there is a question about which division within the SEC is the best. There is a perception that the East has dominated the West because of Florida's and Tennessee's run of championships in the 1990s. The East does boast more conference titles than the West (11-8), but it has been less successful this decade.

Historically, the West also has a slight regular-season edge over the East, with a 172-157-3 record. But last season, the SEC West commanded the conference, finishing with a 15-3 record against its SEC East opponents.

And the West looks likely to continue its run this season. By our metrics, the division has four teams in the Top 10 – No. 1 Alabama, No. 4 Auburn, No. 5 LSU, and No. 9 Arkansas. The East's highest team is Florida at No. 12, although South Carolina and Georgia are right behind at Nos. 13 and 14, respectively.

The battle between the divisions isn't just important because it determines which side is better in the conference, but because it almost always determines which team is the best in the country.

SEC EAST

No. 12 Florida Gators (8-4, 4-4)

2010: 8-5 (4-4) / F/+ #34 / FEI #36 / S&P+ #32

Program F/+	+27.4%	1	Returning Starters: 7 OFF, 6 DEF			5-Yr Recruiting Rank		4
2010 Offense			2010 Defense			2010 Field Position		
Offensive F/+	+0.9%	53	Defensive F/+	+8.3%	26	Field Position Advantage	0.537	17
Offensive FEI:	0.026	57	Defensive FEI	-0.273	30	2011 Projections		
Offensive S&P+	107.5	41	Defensive S&P+	117.5	27	Mean Wins	7.8	
Rushing S&P+	112.7	32	Rushing S&P+	113.7	24	Proj. F/+	+14.0%	12
Passing S&P+	101.0	61	Passing S&P+	121.1	22	Offensive F/+	+4.0%	36
Standard Downs S&P+	110.4	34	Standard Downs S&P+	122.4	15	Defensive F/+	+10.0%	11
Passing Downs S&P+	114.2	36	Passing Downs S&P+	122.2	19	Strength of Schedule	0.045	2

The Gators may be the toughest team to predict in college football this season. For the first time in six years, the Gators won't have head coach Urban Meyer running the show from the sidelines. Florida athletic director Jeremy Foley hired Texas defensive coordinator and Gainesville native Will Muschamp as his new head coach.

In turn, Muschamp hired highly regarded offensive coordinator (but lowly regarded head coach) Charlie Weis to run his offense. Most of Weis' work will be devoted to developing John Brantley into the quarterback that most fans expected him to be. After breaking Tim Tebow's high school touchdown record and being

named a Gatorade National Player of the Year, Brantley waited three years behind the chosen one before finally getting his chance behind center last season. Unfortunately, he was awful. He averaged just 6.26 yards per attempt and threw nine touchdowns against 10 interceptions. The offensive line was porous and partially to blame, but Brantley seems to struggle in big-game situations. His worst games came against Alabama, South Carolina (with the SEC East title on the line) and Florida State. It's understandable that he would feel pressure in replacing one of the best college quarterbacks of all time, but even under the low-

469

expectation situation of the spring game, Brantley still struggled. When the lights go on, his seem to turn off.

As the spring game showed, the Gators also need to develop the talent around Brantley. The combination of speedy senior running backs Chris Rainey and Jeff Demps (combined totals: 917 yards, plus-9.8 Adj. POE) will be solid (and will have more opportunities than the continual dive play under Steve Addazio), but the Gators will need either Mike Gillislee or Mack Brown to recover from his spring injuries and become an every-down back in the fall. At wide receiver, the Gators need Quinton Dunbar to be a consistent threat. Muschamp praised him this spring as the best of the young (and shallow, due to the transfers of Chris Dunkley and Javares McRoy) crop of receivers. Tight end will be the strongest position, with the versatile and dynamic Jordan Reed moving back from quarterback and A.C. Leonard emerging as a threat.

On defense, new coordinator Dan Quinn told the *Florida Times-Union* he wants to be "a 4-3 team with 3-4 principles," which likely means sometimes bringing the linebackers and dropping linemen into coverage.

The switch should suit the strengths of a dynamic and dangerous defensive line that returns known playmakers Omar Hunter, Jaye Howard and Leon Orr and offers second-year soon-to-be stars in Sharrif Floyd, Dominique Easley and Ronald Powell. The pass rush will have to keep the pressure off the secondary, which lost interception-leader Ahmad Black to the NFL and top-rated corner Janoris Jenkins to a marijuana-related expulsion. Their replacements are in place but unproven.

Muschamp, who is nicknamed "Coach Boom," has been heavy on talk but short on show so far. For the first time in years, he closed Florida's spring practices to the public and the media. As a result, any information about Florida this year has come directly from the athletic department, making it slightly less revealing than a steel door. Yet even as diehard fans have become skeptics, the numbers have remained faithful to Florida.

Top 2012 NFL Prospects: DT Jaye Howard (1-2), RB Chris Rainey (3), RB Jeff Demps (3), QB John Brantley (3-5), G James Wilson (3-5), WR Deonte Thompson (6).

No. 13 South Carolina Gamecocks (9-3, 5-3)

2010: 9-5 (5-3) / F/+ #11 / FEI #16 / S&P+ #7

Program F/+	+12.4%	18	Returning Starters: 7 OFF, 6 DEF		5-Yr Recruiting Rank		14
2010 Offense			**2010 Defense**		**2010 Field Position**		
Offensive F/+	+10.9%	13	**Defensive F/+**	+10.2%	18	Field Position Advantage	0.530	22
Offensive FEI:	0.455	7	Defensive FEI	-0.283	28	**2011 Projections**		
Offensive S&P+	123.1	13	Defensive S&P+	130.0	6	**Mean Wins**	8.7	
Rushing S&P+	119.2	21	Rushing S&P+	141.2	3	Proj. F/+	+13.9%	13
Passing S&P+	128.0	9	Passing S&P+	122.9	20	Offensive F/+	+9.1%	12
Standard Downs S&P+	118.6	18	Standard Downs S&P+	127.5	8	Defensive F/+	+4.9%	37
Passing Downs S&P+	131.9	12	Passing Downs S&P+	125.6	15	Strength of Schedule	0.168	16

Last season, Steve Spurrier returned to the SEC Championship Game for the first time in 10 years. Although the Ol' Ball Coach won six SEC championships at Florida during the '90s and in 2000, South Carolina had never reached Atlanta.

Now that they have, the expectations in Columbia are approaching a fever pitch. The excitement starts with the best running back and wide receiver combination in the SEC: Marcus Lattimore and Alshon Jeffery. Lattimore rammed his way to 1,197 yards (plus-11.7 Adj. POE), 17 touchdowns and SEC Freshman of the Year honors last season. This offseason, he has reportedly put on 15 pounds and quickened his 40-yard dash time to 4.5 seconds. On the outside, Jeffery is coming off a season in which he broke school

records with 88 catches and 1,517 yards receiving. The 6-foot-4, 233-pound burner is a terror to opposing defenses. The offensive line also seems to be settling into shape, with Kyle Nunn snagging the starting left tackle spot and A.J. Cann grabbing left guard. T.J. Johnson is on the preseason watch list for the Rimington Award, given to the nation's best center.

But none of that matters if the quarterback situation isn't settled soon. On the depth chart, fifth-year senior Stephen Garcia and sophomore Connor Shaw are listed as co-starters. Garcia would be the unquestioned starter if not for his multiple suspensions this spring. (He has been suspended five times during his tenure at South Carolina.) Garcia has had a rocky relationship with Spurrier, but he is third on the school's all-time passing list with 6,753 yards. Shaw has played too sparingly to predict how successful he would be as the full-time starter, but he pushed Garcia as a freshman last season and could steal the starting spot from Garcia this year even if Garcia is fully eligible for the fall.

Against the pass, the Gamecocks' defense allowed opponents to rack up the yards. They ranked 10th in the SEC in passing yards allowed and allowed 23 touchdown passes, though their Passing S&P+ rank of 20th suggests they faced quite a few elite attacks. This season, the defensive line should help them finish even higher in S&P+ while improving their conventional stats. Although he finished second in the SEC with 7.5 sacks last season, Devin Taylor is relatively unknown among college football fans. He'll partner with Melvin Ingram, who had six sacks, and the best high school player in America, Jadeveon Clowney, to intimidate opposing passers. When they do get the chance to throw, opponents will have to get it past one of the nation's best corners, Stephon Gilmore. Strong safety is set with D.J. Swearinger, but free safety is still a concern, with DeVonte Holloman being moved around the field to find his best position.

The Gamecocks have one of the most talented teams in the nation, and they give Steve Spurrier his best shot so far at another SEC Championship.

Top 2012 NFL Prospects: WR Alshon Jeffery* (1), CB Stephon Gilmore* (1), DE Devin Taylor* (1), S DeVonte Holloman* (2-3), DT Melvin Ingram (3), DT Travian Robertson (5), G Kevious Watkins (5).

No. 21 Georgia Bulldogs (8-4, 5-3)
2010: 6-7 (3-5) / F/+ #29 / FEI #34 / S&P+ #28

Program F/+	+13.0%	17	Returning Starters: 8 OFF, 7 DEF			5-Yr Recruiting Rank		6
2010 Offense			**2010 Defense**			**2010 Field Position**		
Offensive F/+	+7.0%	27	**Defensive F/+**	+3.5%	44	Field Position Advantage	0.538	15
Offensive FEI:	0.164	33	Defensive FEI	-0.016	55	**2011 Projections**		
Offensive S&P+	115.7	27	Defensive S&P+	112.4	33	**Mean Wins**	8.5	
Rushing S&P+	111.2	36	Rushing S&P+	108.9	39	Proj. F/+	+12.2%	21
Passing S&P+	121.2	22	Passing S&P+	113.8	32	Offensive F/+	+8.8%	14
Standard Downs S&P+	112.7	31	Standard Downs S&P+	115.0	30	Defensive F/+	+3.4%	42
Passing Downs S&P+	122.4	23	Passing Downs S&P+	110.5	36	Strength of Schedule	0.222	27

The Bulldogs head into the fall as they have for the past two seasons: high in talent and tumult.

The talent starts at the most important position, where Aaron Murray emerged as a star in his debut last season, passing for 3,049 yards and tossing 24 touchdowns against eight interceptions. The word around the program is that the SEC's best quarterback has spent more time this offseason watching tape. But an improved Murray will still have to survive and succeed without A.J. Green, who was selected fourth overall in the NFL Draft by the Bengals.

Most of the concerns coming out of Athens this offseason have centered on Green's departure, but Murray still has his high school teammate, the talented Orson Charles, at tight end. Junior Tavarres King and freshman Chris Conley should emerge as above-average receivers and help open up the field for Murray. Marion Brown and Rantavious Wooten have also shown great talent and athleticism at times and either could break out during the season. The real concerns for Georgia are along the offensive line and at running back.

The offensive line is a full-body game of Twister right now. This spring, potential right tackle A.J. Harmon left the team for personal reasons and potential left tackle Trinton Sturdivant suffered a season-ending knee injury. As a result, senior Cordy Glenn (who had been battling for the spot) will start at left tackle, and Justin Anderson – who played defense last year – will start on the right. If they struggle, left guard Kenarious Gates may move to tackle, forcing redshirt freshman Kolton Houston to start at guard. The interior should remain tough, though, thanks to center Ben Jones and right guard Chris Burnette.

The line won't be blocking for either running back Washaun Ealey or Caleb King. Ealey elected to transfer earlier this year, and King was deemed academically ineligible in July. With damaged depth, freshman Isaiah Crowell faces both unreasonably high expectations and pressure to produce immediately.

Defensively, the Bulldogs boast a tremendous linebacker corps. The coaching staff has praised USC transfer Jarvis Jones all spring for his play at strong-side linebacker and converted safety Alec Ogletree will man the middle. Christian Robinson returns as the leader of the unit.

Georgia faithful are hoping that the talent will finally translate to success on the field again. Mark Richt is hoping for the same thing, as he looks to retain his job and start a cycle of steadier offseasons.

Top 2012 NFL Prospects: CB Brandon Boykin (2-3), C Ben Jones (2-3), TE Orson Charles* (3), K Blair Walsh (7), G Cordy Glenn (7), P Drew Butler (7).

No. 43 Kentucky Wildcats (7-5, 3-5)

2010: 6-7 (2-6) / F/+ #47 / FEI #45 / S&P+ #51

Program F/+	+3.4%	46	Returning Starters: 6 OFF, 9 DEF			5-Yr Recruiting Rank		52
2010 Offense			**2010 Defense**			**2010 Field Position**		
Offensive F/+	+7.9%	23	**Defensive F/+**	-4.4%	78	Field Position Advantage	0.509	48
Offensive FEI:	0.237	27	Defensive FEI	0.143	81	**2011 Projections**		
Offensive S&P+	113.3	30	Defensive S&P+	95.3	72	**Mean Wins**	6.9	
Rushing S&P+	112.9	31	Rushing S&P+	89.6	94	Proj. F/+	+4.6%	43
Passing S&P+	114.0	33	Passing S&P+	103.3	53	Offensive F/+	+6.0%	26
Standard Downs S&P+	115.3	25	Standard Downs S&P+	90.2	98	Defensive F/+	-1.4%	64
Passing Downs S&P+	119.4	30	Passing Downs S&P+	103.3	56	Strength of Schedule	0.175	17

Kentucky relied almost entirely on four offensive players last season – quarterback Mike Hartline, running back Derrick Locke and receivers Chris Matthews and Randall Cobb – as they headed to their fifth-straight bowl game.

Now they're all gone. The loss of Cobb is the biggest blow to the Wildcats – he broke the SEC single-season record for all-purpose yards and scored touchdowns running, receiving, returning, and throwing last season. He and Chris Matthews were the only vertical threats last year, and no candidates have emerged to replace them this spring.

Kentucky has confidence in new quarterback Morgan Newton, and a strong offensive line that features four returning starters and boasts an average weight of 310 pounds. They'll also be blocking for sophomore running back Raymond Sanders, who should be able to replace Hartline's production.

First-year coordinator Rick Minter's new multi-look approach will create hybrid roles for linebacker/defensive end Ridge Wilson and linebacker/safety Winston Guy. It will have to exceed expectations to keep Kentucky in games while the offense grows up. If it can't, the streak of bowl appearances could come to a close.

Top 2012 NFL Prospects: LB Danny Trevathan (4-5), S Winston Guy (5-6).

No. 44 Tennessee Volunteers (6-6, 2-6)

2010: 7-6 (3-5) / F/+ #58 / FEI #59 / S&P+ #59

Program F/+	+9.8%	29	Returning Starters: 7 OFF, 6 DEF			5-Yr Recruiting Rank		12
2010 Offense			**2010 Defense**			**2010 Field Position**		
Offensive F/+	-0.5%	62	**Defensive F/+**	+0.0%	56	Field Position Advantage	0.482	83
Offensive FEI:	0.02	62	Defensive FEI	-0.044	50	**2011 Projections**		
Offensive S&P+	102.8	57	Defensive S&P+	102.8	49	**Mean Wins**	5.6	
Rushing S&P+	93.7	89	Rushing S&P+	95.3	73	Proj. F/+	+4.3%	44
Passing S&P+	109.3	43	Passing S&P+	110.1	39	Offensive F/+	+2.4%	44
Standard Downs S&P+	107.3	45	Standard Downs S&P+	107.6	39	Defensive F/+	+1.9%	50
Passing Downs S&P+	94.9	81	Passing Downs S&P+	101.5	64	Strength of Schedule	0.047	3

It's hard to remember the last time Tennessee was a threat in the SEC.

It's been more than a decade since the Volunteers played in a BCS bowl game. They've had three losing seasons in the past six years, and three coaches in the past three, during which time they've gone 18-20. But for the first time since 2008, the Volunteers have retained a coach for his second year, and Derek Dooley is set on staying in Tennessee until the program returns to its former glory. His two Top 15 recruiting classes should help him take the Vols back over .500 this season, but how much higher is unknown.

Defensive depth is the primary area of concern for Tennessee heading into the summer. USC transfer Malik Jackson was forced to move from end to tackle last season and excelled, but he'll need help from end Jacques Smith and junior college transfer Maurice Couch to pressure the passer and clog the running game. Two other junior college transfers, defensive backs Byron Moore and Izauea Lanier, could also start right away. The emergence of Brent Brewer at strong safety should help heal some of the growing pains, but the Vols are only set in the secondary if Janzen Jackson returns to school as expected. Jackson had been suspended a total of four games for off-the-field issues, but this spring he temporarily withdrew from the program in good academic standing to deal with "personal issues."

Fortunately, they should have the firepower to keep up with most other SEC offenses. Although defense typically has ruled the SEC, Auburn showed just how far offense could take a team last season. Quarterback Tyler Bray had a poor performance in the spring game, but he has the full faith of the coaching staff. He also has complete protection from what should be a stellar offensive line. The line returns starters in tackle Ja'Wuan James, guard Zach Fulton and center James Stone. Freshman Marcus Jackson has already claimed the open guard spot, and Notre Dame transfer Alex Bullard will be able to play immediately in the fall. With time to throw, Bray should be able to find sophomore stars Justin Hunter and Da'Rick Rogers at receiver.

The talent is finally back in Tennessee, and the results could be better than anyone outside Knoxville expects.

Top 2012 NFL Prospects: S Janzen Jackson* (2-3), RB Tauren Poole (5), DT Malik Jackson (5).

No. 82 Vanderbilt Commodores (3-9, 1-7)

2010: 2-10 (1-7) / F/+ #96 / FEI #98 / S&P+ #95

Program F/+		-4.6%	76	Returning Starters: 11 OFF, 8 DEF			5-Yr Recruiting Rank			71
2010 Offense				**2010 Defense**			**2010 Field Position**			
Offensive F/+		-14.1%	115	**Defensive F/+**	+0.9%	52	Field Position Advantage		0.474	93
Offensive FEI:		-0.461	112	Defensive FEI	0.02	62	**2011 Projections**			
Offensive S&P+		79.7	112	Defensive S&P+	100.7	54	**Mean Wins**		3.0	
Rushing S&P+		89.8	93	Rushing S&P+	104.4	47	Proj. F/+		-5.7%	82
Passing S&P+		70.0	117	Passing S&P+	95.9	70	Offensive F/+		-7.1%	100
Standard Downs S&P+		84.4	105	Standard Downs S&P+	100.6	57	Defensive F/+		+1.3%	52
Passing Downs S&P+		71.2	115	Passing Downs S&P+	108.8	38	Strength of Schedule		0.064	7

In May, Vanderbilt football finally won something: The Commodores were the only SEC football team to receive a Public Recognition award for classroom performance and graduation success from the Academic Progress Rate released by the NCAA.

... Yawn.

New coach James Franklin is going to have to do a little bit better than that if he wants to keep his job longer than the last coach did. Fortunately, the former Maryland offensive coordinator will have a lot of talent to work with. Wesley Tate emerged in a crowded backfield this spring to be the thunder to the lightning of Warren Norman or Zac Stacy. If senior quarterback Larry Smith can take the next step, so can the Commodores offense.

If the offense emerges, a solid secondary should keep games within reach and give Vandy fans a victory they actually want.

Top 2012 NFL Prospects: LB Chris Marve (3-4), CB Casey Hayward (4-5).

SEC WEST

No. 1 Alabama Crimson Tide (11-1, 7-1)

2010: 10-3 (5-3) / F/+ #3 / FEI #3 / S&P+ #2

Program F/+	+20.3%	6	Returning Starters: 6 OFF, 9 DEF			5-Yr Recruiting Rank		1
2010 Offense			**2010 Defense**			**2010 Field Position**		
Offensive F/+	+17.0%	4	Defensive F/+	+12.2%	11	Field Position Advantage	0.548	6
Offensive FEI:	0.56	4	Defensive FEI	-0.403	16	**2011 Projections**		
Offensive S&P+	137.2	3	Defensive S&P+	129.8	7	**Mean Wins**	10.9	
Rushing S&P+	136.4	3	Rushing S&P+	127.2	11	Proj. F/+	+23.7%	1
Passing S&P+	137.8	4	Passing S&P+	132.6	7	Offensive F/+	+12.0%	4
Standard Downs S&P+	130.7	4	Standard Downs S&P+	131.5	4	Defensive F/+	+11.6%	4
Passing Downs S&P+	140.2	6	Passing Downs S&P+	149.1	3	Strength of Schedule	0.125	9

For once and for the worse, Alabama football wasn't the biggest news in the state this spring. A tornado ravaged through Tuscaloosa and left the Crimson Tide more motivated than ever to compete for an SEC title. "We can't wait until this season" Trent Richardson told ESPN.com. "We know how much this season means to a lot of people in Alabama, and we also know those folks need us. If we can bring a little bit of joy to their lives, that's what we plan on doing."

Richardson will be the focal point of the offense and a Heisman frontrunner. The junior running back is a physical marvel, weighing in at 225 pounds and clocking in at 4.37 seconds in the 40-yard dash. The coaching staff capped him at 465 pounds on the bench press and 600 pounds on squats. On the field, he averaged 6.3 yards per carry (plus-6.7 Adj. POE) and scored six times while spelling Heisman Trophy winner Mark Ingram last season. This season, he'll lead the rushing attack, and Eddie Lacy will get the spare carries.

A new quarterback, either sophomore A.J. McCarron or redshirt freshman Phillip Sims, will lead them all. After an intense battle in spring practices, the two have emerged as equals in the competition. Sims is more athletic than McCarron and can make more plays on the run, but both quarterbacks look to throw first, and the coaches are confident that either can lead the Tide back to Atlanta and beyond. Coach Nick Sa-

ban has even considered rotating the quarterbacks in games this fall.

Even if the offense decided to kneel for three downs and punt, the Tide would still have a chance in a few games because of how good the defense will be. Linebackers Courtney Upshaw and Dont'a Hightower are healthy and ready to bookend one of the best pass rushes in the nation. They both have first-round potential in the NFL Draft, as do safeties Mark Barron and Robert Lester. Corner Dre Kirkpatrick may emerge as the best in the country, and his counterpart, DeQuan Menzie, is tremendous, too. The Tide's defense cost them a couple games last season – which is rare to say about a Saban-coached team – but the maturation should make them almost impenetrable.

They'll need to be at their best this fall because, despite last year's disappointing record, Alabama is still the class of the SEC and will get every team's best shot. With a schedule that takes them to Florida, Mississippi State and Auburn, the road back to the SEC title won't be easy, but the Tide won't just be playing for themselves.

Top 2012 NFL Prospects: CB Dre Kirkpatrick* (1), S Mark Barron (1), S Robert Lester* (1), RB Trent Richardson* (1-2), LB Dont'a Hightower* (2), LB Courtney Upshaw (2), DeQuan Menzie* (2), LB Nico Johnson* (2-3), C William Vlachos (3-5).

No. 4 Auburn Tigers (9-3, 5-3)

2010: 14-0 (8-0) / F/+ #1 / FEI #1 / S&P+ #4

Program F/+	+14.6%	13	Returning Starters: 3 OFF, 4 DEF		5-Yr Recruiting Rank		11
2010 Offense			**2010 Defense**		**2010 Field Position**		
					Field Position Advantage	0.517	39
Offensive F/+	+25.0%	1	**Defensive F/+**	+7.2%	31		
Offensive FEI:	0.805	1	Defensive FEI	-0.478	6	**2011 Projections**	
Offensive S&P+	153.6	1	Defensive S&P+	111.7	36	**Mean Wins**	8.8
Rushing S&P+	150.1	1	Rushing S&P+	118.6	21	Proj. F/+	+18.3%	4
Passing S&P+	166.7	1	Passing S&P+	109.4	42	Offensive F/+	+13.9%	2
Standard Downs S&P+	144.3	1	Standard Downs S&P+	109.6	37	Defensive F/+	+4.3%	39
Passing Downs S&P+	178.0	1	Passing Downs S&P+	120.8	22	Strength of Schedule	0.043	1

Auburn's season was picture perfect last season. The Tigers took down all their rivals and outlasted Oregon to finish the season as BCS champions and the unanimous best team in the country. But quarterback Cam Newton and defensive tackle Nick Fairley, by far the Tigers' best players on either side of the ball, were both plucked in the first round of the NFL Draft. In all, the Tigers lost 18 starters from that championship team.

Auburn still has tons of talent, but most of it is in an unproven sophomore class. The offense should stay dangerous on the ground thanks to backs Onterio Mc-Calebb and Michael Dyer, who combined for 1,903 yards, a plus-10.6 Adj. POE and 14 touchdowns last year. The only advantage to Newton's departure is that Dyer will get a larger share of carries. But the question of who will hand the ball off to the backs remains unanswered. Barrett Trotter was the backup last season, but Clint Mosley was fierce competition in the spring. Freshman Kiehl Frazier, who enrolled in the spring, isn't to be counted out either. Whoever wins the quarterback job will get back Trovon Reed, who missed most of last season with knee issues. Reed adds an extra dimension in the backfield and can even throw the ball on some trick plays.

On the other side of the ball, the Tigers need a tackle who can take up space and penetrate the pocket like Fairley did. Sophomores Jeffrey Whitaker and Ken Carter are the starting tackles, but they combined for just over a dozen tackles last season. Fellow sophomore defensive ends Corey Lemonier and Craig Sanders should help to provide some pressure off the edge.

A year removed from a national championship, Gene Chizik could be facing his toughest challenge as a coach. The Tigers have a deep roster, but the talent at the top isn't nearly the same level as it was last year. If the young players emerge quickly, particularly at quarterback, then the Tigers have a chance to make a run at another SEC Title. If not, then this will be a rebuilding year.

Top 2012 NFL Prospects: RB Onterio McCalebb (4-5), WR Emory Blake (5), OT A.J. Greene (4-6).

No. 5 LSU Tigers (9-3, 6-2)

2010: 11-2 (6-2) / F/+ #13 / FEI #6 / S&P+ #22

Program F/+	+20.4%	5	Returning Starters: 8 OFF, 7 DEF		5-Yr Recruiting Rank		4
2010 Offense			**2010 Defense**		**2010 Field Position**		
					Field Position Advantage	0.587	2
Offensive F/+	+7.5%	24	**Defensive F/+**	+11.5%	14		
Offensive FEI:	0.258	22	Defensive FEI	-0.339	20	**2011 Projections**	
Offensive S&P+	112.1	33	Defensive S&P+	120.2	18	**Mean Wins**	9.0
Rushing S&P+	123.2	14	Rushing S&P+	109.5	37	Proj. F/+	+17.2%	5
Passing S&P+	101.5	59	Passing S&P+	130.8	9	Offensive F/+	+7.8%	18
Standard Downs S&P+	123.2	10	Standard Downs S&P+	120.4	17	Defensive F/+	+9.3%	15
Passing Downs S&P+	97.1	74	Passing Downs S&P+	131.6	12	Strength of Schedule	0.050	4

The Sporting News ranked LSU its top team for the start of the fall. The Tigers are a consensus top five pick among preseason polls, and No. 1 isn't a stretch considering this team's defense.

LSU lost one of the best players in the country, defensive back Patrick Peterson. They also said goodbye to linebacker Kelvin Sheppard and defensive tackles Drake Nevis and Pep Levingston. Yet despite those losses, the Tigers are teeming with young talent. Third-year sophomore edge rushers Sam Montgomery and Barkevious Mingo should be menaces for opposing offensive coordinators. Defensive coordinator John Chavis also likes what he has in the secondary. Morris Claiborne will return as one of the best cornerbacks in the conference, and senior safety Brandon Taylor will lead the young unit. Tyrann Mathieu is a rangy and athletic nickel corner who will roam around the field.

Outside of replacing Peterson, finding the next Kelvin Sheppard will be Chavis' biggest challenge. Kevin Minter is the likely replacement, but safety Karnell Hatcher could switch into the middle (as he did during much of the spring) to provide more athleticism. Chavis has shown that he chooses speed over size every time, so don't be surprised if Hatcher plays significant minutes at the position, or even ends up as the starter. Ryan Baker and Stefoin Francois, who have already proven their worth, will flank whoever ends up in the middle.

An overlooked area of concern for the Tigers is special teams. Josh Jasper, who was a reliable field goal kicker and a fiend on trick plays, is gone, as is punter Derek Hilton, who was the second-best punter in the SEC last season. Peterson, of course, was the best return man in the league last year. LSU prides itself on – and has won several games with – its special teams.

On offense, the Tigers hope that quarterback Jordan Jefferson's improvements during spring will translate into a better season. Last year, he threw just seven touchdowns against 10 interceptions and amassed only 1,411 yards through the air. Word around the bayou is that his footwork is better now, and he is more comfortable in the pocket. The Tigers weren't expecting for running back Stevan Ridley to go pro, but sophomore Spencer Ware seems ready to take his place.

Whether the Tigers are worthy of their top ranking be revealed quickly – their opener is against last year's No. 2 team, Oregon.

Top 2012 NFL Prospects: CB Morris Claiborne (2), S Kamell Hatcher (5), QB Jordan Jefferson (5-6).

No. 9 Arkansas Razorbacks (9-3, 5-3)
2010: 10-3 (6-2) / F/+ #7 / FEI #7 / S&P+ #9

Program F/+	+13.8%	15	Returning Starters: 6 OFF, 7 DEF			5-Yr Recruiting Rank		29
2010 Offense			**2010 Defense**			**2010 Field Position**		
Offensive F/+	+15.7%	5	**Defensive F/+**	+7.6%	28	Field Position Advantage	0.508	50
Offensive FEI:	0.561	3	Defensive FEI	-0.365	19	**2011 Projections**		
Offensive S&P+	133.1	6	Defensive S&P+	116.8	29	**Mean Wins**	9.1	
Rushing S&P+	124.6	11	Rushing S&P+	111.6	26	Proj. F/+	+15.6%	9
Passing S&P+	136.9	6	Passing S&P+	122.9	19	Offensive F/+	+10.2%	6
Standard Downs S&P+	135.2	2	Standard Downs S&P+	116.6	25	Defensive F/+	+5.4%	32
Passing Downs S&P+	136.2	8	Passing Downs S&P+	120.8	23	Strength of Schedule	0.061	6

Arkansas got a brief glimpse of the future last season when they faced Auburn on the road. Star gunslinger Ryan Mallett went down with a concussion and in came backup Tyler Wilson. The Hogs lost the game, 65-43, but Wilson played well, throwing for more than 300 yards and four touchdowns and giving the Hogs hope until the fourth quarter.

This spring, Wilson has emerged as the frontrunner in a surprising quarterback battle against sophomore Brandon Mitchell, who has some serious wheels. Wilson should be the starter in the fall, though, and he will have a full toolbox. The Hogs return last year's leading receiver, Joe Adams, as well as playmaker Greg Childs and burner (he runs a 4.27 in the 40) Jarius Wright. And on the ground, the Hogs have running back Knile Davis, who rushed for 1,322 yards (plus-

16.5 Adj. POE) and 13 touchdowns last year. The only concerns on offense come along the line. Freshman Brey Cook is the probable starter at one tackle spot, and sophomore Anthony Oden (who didn't play because of mono last year) is the starter on the other side. The interior features two sophomore starters in Travis Swanson and Alvin Bailey, but they each have a year of starting experience.

Arkansas' offense has the potential to be just as potent as last year. But the better news for the Razorbacks? The defense could be better. The defensive line, which will return DeQuinta Jones and Byran Jones and add juco-transfer Robert Thomas, should be deep and dangerous. Behind them, senior linebackers and team-leading tacklers from last year Jerry Franklin and Jerico Nelson return ready to show they can take the next step to the NFL.

The Razorbacks have to show that they are ready for the next step as well. Last year, they talked about competing for an SEC title but fell short thanks to Rammin' Cam Newton and the Tigers. They made it to their first BCS bowl under coach Bobby Petrino, but fell short to Ohio State in a 31-26 loss. Now the Razorbacks hope that BCS bowl berth was just a brief glimpse of the future.

Top 2012 NFL Prospects: LB Jerry Franklin (1), RB Knile Davis* (2), WR Greg Childs (2-3), LB Jerry Franklin (3-4), S Tramain Thomas (5), CB Isaac Madison (5-6).

No. 32 Mississippi State Bulldogs (6-6, 2-6)

2010: 8-5 (4-4) / F/+ #26 / FEI #27 / S&P+ #33

Program F/+	+1.3%	55	Returning Starters: 8 OFF, 7 DEF			5-Yr Recruiting Rank		36
2010 Offense			**2010 Defense**			**2010 Field Position**		
						Field Position Advantage	0.522	34
Offensive F/+	-2.5%	76	Defensive F/+	+13.5%	7	**2011 Projections**		
Offensive FEI:	-0.034	66	Defensive FEI	-0.435	10	**Mean Wins**	6.0	
Offensive S&P+	99.8	68	Defensive S&P+	125.0	10	Proj. F/+	+6.5%	32
Rushing S&P+	99.1	74	Rushing S&P+	127.9	10	Offensive F/+	-3.3%	83
Passing S&P+	103.4	55	Passing S&P+	122.9	21	Defensive F/+	+9.8%	12
Standard Downs S&P+	108.8	41	Standard Downs S&P+	128.2	7	Strength of Schedule	0.054	5
Passing Downs S&P+	95.9	77	Passing Downs S&P+	125.7	14			

As with their state counterparts Ole Miss a couple seasons ago, Mississippi State has become the popular pick as a dark horse SEC contender.

The Bulldogs finished 9-4 and put a huge exclamation point on the season by beating Michigan 52-14 in the Gator Bowl. But as Football Outsiders' readers know well by now, momentum from bowl victories has almost no bearing on success the following season. "We have expectations this year," Mullen told boosters in May. "Last year we went out to prove people wrong -- we wanted to prove we could be better than what they expected of us. Now we have high expectations. Now we have to prove people right this year."

Because of Mullen's background as an offensive coordinator, expectations are particularly high for quarterback Chris Relf. He showed great arm strength toward the end of the season, finishing with more than 200 yards passing in each of his last three games. He will have a deep stable of wide receivers at his service this season.

But the defense was the heart of the Bulldogs' improbable run a year ago. The unit, which finished third in the SEC in points allowed, lost its best player in defensive end Pernell McPhee and must find three new starters at linebacker. The secondary is solid with returning starters (and ballhawks) Corey Broomfield, Johnthan Banks, and Nickoe Whitley.

The biggest challenge for the Bulldogs, though, will be he increased expectations. Two years ago, they contributed to the collapse of the Rebels. The Bulldogs must learn from Ole Miss' mistakes.

Top 2012 NFL Prospects: RB Vick Ballard (4-5), CB Charles Mitchell (7).

No. 49 Mississippi Rebels (5-7, 2-6)

2010: 5-7 (1-7) / F/+ #63 / FEI #61 / S&P+ #61

Program F/+	+3.1%	49	Returning Starters: 9 OFF, 5 DEF			5-Yr Recruiting Rank		22
2010 Offense			**2010 Defense**			**2010 Field Position**		
						Field Position Advantage	0.488	72
Offensive F/+	-0.3%	61	Defensive F/+	-0.6%	58	**2011 Projections**		
Offensive FEI:	0.007	63	Defensive FEI	-0.038	51	**Mean Wins**	5.2	
Offensive S&P+	103.5	53	Defensive S&P+	100.6	55	Proj. F/+	+3.4%	49
Rushing S&P+	100.9	64	Rushing S&P+	102.3	55	Offensive F/+	+4.3%	35
Passing S&P+	106.8	49	Passing S&P+	100.6	59	Defensive F/+	-0.9%	60
Standard Downs S&P+	97.2	79	Standard Downs S&P+	101.5	53	Strength of Schedule	0.088	8
Passing Downs S&P+	125.6	19	Passing Downs S&P+	91.7	86			

Houston Nutt's seat is almost certainly the hottest among SEC coaches, and he has his hands full in trying to turn Mississippi's program around this year.

The big issue facing Ole Miss is the same one affecting much of the SEC – inexperience and uncertainty at quarterback. Redshirt junior Randall Mackey supposedly has the edge after spring practices, but West Virginia transfer Barry Brunetti was granted eligibility for the fall. The more athletic Brunetti could be a better fit in an Ole Miss offense that will rely heavily on the ground game.

Senior Brandon Bolden (976 yards and a league-leading plus-24.5 Adj. POE) leads the way for the Rebs on the ground, and backups Jeff Scott and Enrique Davis should provide a nice change of pace to Bolden's power running style.

Ole Miss' ability to control the ball will be crucial for their success. Last season, the Rebels finished last in the SEC in points allowed per game and second to last in yards allowed. The loss of linebacker D.T. Shackelford (a defensive leader) for his senior season was a huge blow for the team, but it's balanced by the return of defensive end Kentrell Lockett, who was granted a hardship waiver by the NCAA.

But that's not the best news for Nutt. This is: If Ole Miss fires him this season, he'll get $6 million in severance. Maybe the hot seat isn't so bad after all.

Top 2012 NFL Prospects: DT Bobby Massie (2-3), RB Brandon Bolden (4-5).

David Gardner

Projected Win Probabilities For SEC Teams

SEC East	Overall Wins													Conference Wins								
	12-0	11-1	10-2	9-3	8-4	7-5	6-6	5-7	4-8	3-9	2-10	1-11	0-12	8-0	7-1	6-2	5-3	4-4	3-5	2-6	1-7	0-8
Florida	-	1	7	21	31	26	11	3	-	-	-	-	-	-	2	11	28	34	20	5	-	-
Georgia	1	5	17	27	27	16	6	1	-	-	-	-	-	3	15	30	30	16	5	1	-	-
Kentucky	-	-	2	8	22	30	24	11	3	-	-	-	-	-	-	2	12	28	33	19	5	1
South Carolina	1	8	20	29	25	13	4	-	-	-	-	-	-	2	11	26	32	21	7	1	-	-
Tennessee	-	-	-	1	5	16	31	31	14	2	-	-	-	-	-	-	1	8	24	38	26	3
Vanderbilt	-	-	-	-	-	-	1	7	22	36	27	7	-	-	-	-	-	-	2	11	39	48
SEC West	12-0	11-1	10-2	9-3	8-4	7-5	6-6	5-7	4-8	3-9	2-10	1-11	0-12	8-0	7-1	6-2	5-3	4-4	3-5	2-6	1-7	0-8
Alabama	27	41	24	7	1	-	-	-	-	-	-	-	-	30	42	22	5	1	-	-	-	-
Arkansas	1	9	26	34	22	7	1	-	-	-	-	-	-	1	11	31	35	18	4	-	-	-
Auburn	1	8	21	30	24	12	4	-	-	-	-	-	-	2	11	26	31	21	8	1	-	-
LSU	1	10	24	30	22	10	3	-	-	-	-	-	-	3	20	35	27	12	3	-	-	-
Mississippi	-	-	-	-	3	11	24	31	22	8	1	-	-	-	-	-	1	6	21	37	29	6
Mississippi State	-	-	-	2	8	22	34	25	8	1	-	-	-	-	-	-	2	10	25	35	23	5

Non-AQs and Independents

In each of the last three seasons, at least one non-automatic qualifying team (non-AQ) achieved unprecedented success. In 2008, Utah finished the year as the only undefeated FBS team in the nation. In 2009, Boise State and TCU clashed in a BCS bowl game. Last year, TCU knocked off Wisconsin in the Rose Bowl. Those success stories helped those teams court interest from stronger conferences. Utah made the leap to join the Pac-12 this fall, TCU will bolt for the Big East in 2012, and Boise State is the new top dog in the Mountain West.

The dust has settled from last year's round of conference musical chairs, and several of the non-AQ upper class will soon be major conference players. It remains to be seen if any other programs will step in and fill the gap. More than a few teams are capable of posting gaudy records, but it may take several years for the next generation of non-AQ powers to break through to a BCS bowl appearance. Boise State paid its dues for a decade to earn privileged preseason poll status, but the Broncos still have trouble leaping major conference teams due to schedule strength concerns.

Nine different non-AQ teams won at least ten games apiece last year, but only TCU, Boise State, and Utah spent any time ranked among the top 10 in the polls. Multiple years of success convinced pollsters to give those teams the benefit of the doubt, while teams like Nevada (13-1) never threatened to contend for a BCS bowl. Our metrics, of course, were also unconvinced about the Wolf Pack, along with a slew of other non-AQ teams that feasted on weak opposition. Other than TCU and Boise State, no other non-AQ teams finished in the F/+ top 25, and four non-AQ teams with 10 or more wins ranked outside of the top 40.

Last year, nearly all of the non-AQ power programs played schedules ranked 90th or worse according to F/+. It will be the same story again in 2011. Boise State is our projected No. 3 team this fall but will play the 93rd toughest schedule. It would be easier for a top team to play the Broncos' schedule three times and win every time (36-0) than for the same team to run the table once (12-0) against Alabama's schedule.

There is little that can be done about that stark reality, so Boise State can only lace 'em up and do its best to dominate week in and week out. TCU will take a small step back due to heavy personnel losses, but we expect the Horned Frogs to be solid again as well. If any other non-AQ contenders emerge, it will be because they pulled off upsets in one or more of their limited opportunities against the big boys. Such success may be incrementally more likely today than five or ten years ago, but most of the have-nots in college football still have a long way to go.

MOUNTAIN WEST CONFERENCE

No. 3 Boise State Broncos (11-1, 7-0)

2010: 12-1 (7-1) / F/+ #2 / FEI #11 / S&P+ #1

Program F/+	+19.1%	9	Returning Starters: 7 OFF, 7 DEF			5-Yr Recruiting Rank		81
2010 Offense			**2010 Defense**			**2010 Field Position**		
						Field Position Advantage	0.541	12
Offensive F/+	+12.8%	9	**Defensive F/+**	+17.7%	1	**2011 Projections**		
Offensive FEI:	0.317	18	Defensive FEI	-0.369	17	**Mean Wins**	11.2	
Offensive S&P+	136.8	4	Defensive S&P+	149.4	1	Proj. F/+	+18.5%	3
Rushing S&P+	122.0	17	Rushing S&P+	140.7	4	Offensive F/+	+7.7%	20
Passing S&P+	149.7	3	Passing S&P+	158.6	2	Defensive F/+	+10.8%	6
Standard Downs S&P+	130.5	5	Standard Downs S&P+	138.9	1	Strength of Schedule	0.521	93
Passing Downs S&P+	119.4	29	Passing Downs S&P+	144.2	6			

The Boise State program has played the part of the plucky underdog fighting for respect for most of the last decade. Its success has paved the way to a move to the Mountain West Conference and a second straight consensus preseason top-10 ranking. This fall includes a date with the Georgia Bulldogs, an opportunity for coach Chris Petersen to ascend another rung up the respect ladder by knocking off an SEC team in its own backyard. Might there be enough success in 2011 to reach the promised land of a BCS championship game berth? If so, it will come down to many circumstances outside of the Broncos' control. But they'll have an opportunity to get into position with a veteran team on offense and defense.

The Broncos boasted one of the most prolific offenses in college football a year ago: 45 points and 521 yards per game, with a top- five rating in passing S&P+ and raw drive efficiency. Boise State had very little trouble moving the ball and was a constant big play threat, ranking first nationally in fewest three-and-outs (13.1 percent of drives) and first in "explosive" drives (31.1 percent of possessions averaged at least 10 yards per play). Senior quarterback Kellen Moore will be a Heisman contender again in 2011 after leading the nation in passer efficiency a year ago (35 touchdowns, six interceptions, 295 yards per game) and finishing fourth in the Heisman ballot. He didn't face many top defenses, but against Virginia Tech and Utah (top-25 F/+ defenses), he threw for 554 yards and five touchdowns.

Moore will be joined in the backfield by senior running back Doug Martin (1,260 yards, 12 touchdowns) and the Broncos return several experienced linemen.

The big hole to fill for Boise State on offense is at wide receiver. Moore's favorite targets from each of the last two seasons, Austin Pettis and Titus Young, are gone. Pettis and Young hauled in roughly 50 percent of Broncos receptions in 2009 and 2010. Senior wide receiver Tyler Shoemaker will see more action, as will senior tight end Kyle Efaw.

Boise State has been known for its offense, but it was every bit as good defensively last season. The Broncos ranked first in both points per drive (3.8) and points per drive surrendered (1.0). Most of the defensive front seven are experienced seniors, including defensive ends Billy Winn and Shea McClellin plus a trio of linebackers, Aaron Tevis, Hunter White and Byron Hout. Boise State ranked first in defensive F/+ in 2010 and was balanced in limiting both opponent rushing and passing attacks according to S&P+.

In many ways, it feels like a now-or-never season at Boise State, at least in terms of the potential for a national championship. A senior-laden roster and an opportunity to win in SEC territory don't come along every year, and the Mountain West did the Broncos a favor by scheduling a blue turf home game against TCU in November. Outside of the Georgia and TCU games, our metrics predict 94-plus percent win likelihoods in every other Boise State game. A BCS bowl is once again within reach and the Broncos may be part of the national championship discussion all season.

2012 NFL Draft Prospects: G Nate Potter (2-3), DE Billy Winn (2-3), QB Kellen Moore (3-4), RB Doug Martin (3-4), S George Iloka (4-5), DE Shea McClellin (5-6).

No. 11 TCU Horned Frogs (11-1, 6-1)

2010: 13-0 (8-0) / F/+ #6 / FEI #10 / S&P+ #5

Program F/+	+19.8%	7	Returning Starters: 4 OFF, 4 DEF		5-Yr Recruiting Rank		60
2010 Offense			2010 Defense		2010 Field Position		
Offensive F/+	+9.6%	15	Defensive F/+	+15.6%	4	Field Position Advantage	0.559	4
Offensive FEI:	0.367	14	Defensive FEI	-0.43	12	2011 Projections		
Offensive S&P+	122.6	14	Defensive S&P+	138.6	3	Mean Wins	10.8	
Rushing S&P+	125.7	10	Rushing S&P+	119.9	17	Proj. F/+	+15.1%	11
Passing S&P+	123.0	17	Passing S&P+	165.9	1	Offensive F/+	+5.1%	29
Standard Downs S&P+	118.6	19	Standard Downs S&P+	128.5	6	Defensive F/+	+10.0%	10
Passing Downs S&P+	133.6	9	Passing Downs S&P+	164.6	1	Strength of Schedule	0.411	70

After watching Utah and Boise State carry the torch for non-AQ teams for multiple seasons, TCU finally had its one shining moment in last year's Rose Bowl. Facing a formidable Wisconsin offense, the Horned

Frogs won the battle at the line of scrimmage and denied a two-point conversion in the waning minutes of the game to cap an undefeated campaign. Head coach Gary Patterson's teams have been consistently strong on defense, and his offenses have been underrated. But both sides of the ball have big holes to fill – how quickly will the new starters find their footing?

Quarterback Andy Dalton was a four-year starter for TCU, amassing a 42-7 record and posting a top-10 passer rating in both his junior and senior seasons. Now the Horned Frogs will turn to sophomore Casey Pachall, who has nine career pass attempts. He won't have the luxury of trusted protection or pass targets either. TCU will break in new starters at three positions on the offensive line, and three of the Horned Frogs' top four receivers are also gone. Pachall can trust junior running back Ed Wesley, who carried the load on the ground last year. TCU had the 10th best rushing attack in the nation according to S&P+. Sophomore wide receiver Josh Boyce was a big play threat, averaging 19 yards per reception in 2010.

The defense in Fort Worth has been nothing short of spectacular under Patterson. TCU has finished with a top-five S&P+ defensive ranking in each of the last three seasons and they've dealt with new starters stepping into big shoes before. The experience heading into this fall is at the linebacker position. Seniors Tank Carder and Tanner Brock are the heart of TCU's 4-2-5 spread and were primary playmakers in the Rose Bowl. The defensive line and secondary will be almost entirely rebuilt, however, and it will be difficult to match the production from a year ago. TCU ranked first in the nation in forcing three-and-outs (49 percent of opponent drives) and first in available yards allowed (giving up only 26 percent of possible yardage measured from starting field position to end zone).

The toughest challenge on TCU's schedule is a November 12th trip to Mountain West newcomer Boise State. The conference championship is likely to be determined on that date, though TCU does have a pair of road trips against the third and fourth best teams in the conference, Air Force and San Diego State. Our numbers like the potential for another great record, but TCU isn't likely to be as dominant as it was a year ago.

2012 NFL Draft Prospects: LB Tank Carder (2-3), CB Greg McCoy (4-5).

Other Mountain West

Boise State and TCU stand head and shoulders above the rest of the league, and part of the reason they've been dinged by pollsters and computers is due to the dreck that populates the bottom of the conference. Colorado State, New Mexico, Wyoming and UNLV combined to win only nine games a year ago, and we project those four teams to improve by only about a game apiece this fall. Two other Mountain West programs aren't going to threaten to win a conference title, but have the potential to put a scare or two into the top dogs.

All the major skill position players are back for Air Force, led by senior quarterback Tim Jefferson and senior running back Asher Clark. Those two combined for 1,800 yards on the ground and the Falcons ranked second nationally in rushing yards per game. Unlike its fellow service academies that employ a patient attack, Air Force prefers to work quickly in its triple option. On a per-play basis, Air Force was only moderately successful (No. 45 rushing S&P+). Jefferson will throw the ball about 13 times per game and his top target, senior wide receiver Jonathan Warzeka (22.6 yards per reception), is back as well. Most of last year's Falcons starting defense will be back in the fold, a unit that held top offenses like Oklahoma and Navy well below their average production.

After a string of six straight losing seasons, San Diego State had a breakout year in 2010, losing only four games by a total of only 15 points. Head coach Brady Hoke left for Michigan, but the Aztecs return talent at key positions and should be able keep progressing under new head coach Rocky Long. Senior quarterback Ryan Lindley was the Mountain West conference leader in total offense (292 yards passing per game). San Diego State was especially effective on passing downs, ranking fifth nationally. Sophomore running back Ronnie Hillman rushed for 1,532 yards last year, the best freshman debut at the school since Marshall Faulk in 1991.

2012 NFL Draft Prospects: QB Ryan Lindley, San Diego St. (2-3); DE Johnathan Rainey, New Mexico (4-5); LB Carmen Messina, New Mexico (4-5); CB Tashaun Gipson, Wyoming (4-5); LB Adrien Cole, Louisiana Tech (5-6).

INDEPENDENTS

No. 19 Notre Dame Fighting Irish (9-3)

2010: 8-5 (-) / F/+ #17 / FEI #23 / S&P+ #11

Program F/+	+6.7%	39	Returning Starters: 8 OFF, 8 DEF			5-Yr Recruiting Rank		9
2010 Offense			**2010 Defense**			**2010 Field Position**		
Offensive F/+	+3.9%	37	**Defensive F/+**	+12.8%	9	Field Position Advantage	0.501	56
Offensive FEI:	0.122	42	Defensive FEI	-0.316	25	**2011 Projections**		
Offensive S&P+	113.3	29	Defensive S&P+	131.4	4	**Mean Wins**	8.6	
Rushing S&P+	111.3	35	Rushing S&P+	125.9	13	Proj. F/+	+12.4%	19
Passing S&P+	113.2	35	Passing S&P+	138.0	5	Offensive F/+	+2.8%	41
Standard Downs S&P+	111.2	33	Standard Downs S&P+	130.6	5	Defensive F/+	+9.6%	13
Passing Downs S&P+	100.6	60	Passing Downs S&P+	123.8	17	Strength of Schedule	0.221	26

For the first time in recent memory, the good vibe felt by Notre Dame fans heading into a football season comes from actual results in the previous season rather than blind optimism generated by the spring game. It is especially refreshing that the defensive side of the ball is Notre Dame's strong suit. The Irish gave up only one non-garbage time touchdown in their final four games of last season, a four-play, two-yard drive by USC. No other defense played as well down the stretch. Will that momentum carry forward into this year?

On defense, the Irish will field experienced contributors at most positions, though depth will be an issue. As a whole, Notre Dame returns 80 percent of its tackles, sacks, and tackles for loss from last season, almost all of them produced by starters. Safety Harrison Smith locked in on opposing quarterbacks in the late-season surge, recording five interceptions against Utah, USC and Miami. Senior cornerbacks Robert Blanton and Gary Gray are reliable, but their backups are complete unknowns. Junior inside linebacker Manti Te'o is the team's leading tackler, run stopper, and crowd pleaser. Most starters in the Irish 3-4 will be upperclassmen, but 340-pound sophomore nose tackle Louis Nix will see his first action this fall and freshman defensive end Aaron Lynch is expected to be an immediate playmaker.

On offense, the quarterback position remains a bit of a question mark coming out of spring practice. Senior Dayne Crist started most games in 2010 before a knee injury sidelined him, while sophomore Tommy Rees led the Irish through the late-season win streak. Kelly had success at Cincinnati interchanging quarterbacks so it's possible Crist, Rees, plus fleet-footed freshmen Everett Golson and Andrew Hendrix will all see situational action this fall. Junior running back Cierre Wood will pick up most of the carries, though the Irish rushed on only 46 percent of their plays last year, the 17th lowest rate in the nation. Senior wide receiver Michael Floyd (1,025 yards, 12 touchdowns) will get the vast majority of targets, so long as he stays out of trouble. Floyd was suspended in March following a DWI arrest but was reinstated shortly before team practice began in early August.

Against what may be a schedule devoid of juggernauts, Notre Dame has the potential to contend for an at-large BCS bowl berth. There are tough road trips, including a visit to the Big House for the first-ever night game in Michigan Stadium history and a season-ending clash with Stanford. Regardless of the final record, however, coach Brian Kelly appears to have the Irish pointed in the right direction.

2012 NFL Draft Prospects: LB Manti Te'o* (1-2), WR Michael Floyd (1-2), DE Darius Fleming (5-6), DE Ethan Johnson (5-6), S Harrison Smith (5-6), G Trevor Robinson (6-7).

No. 42 BYU Cougars (8-4)

2010: 7-6 (5-3) / F/+ #53 / FEI #66 / S&P+ #43

Program F/+	+11.3%	21	Returning Starters: 10 OFF, 6 DEF			5-Yr Recruiting Rank		59
2010 Offense			**2010 Defense**			**2010 Field Position**		
						Field Position Advantage	0.526	29
Offensive F/+	-6.2%	91	**Defensive F/+**	+7.2%	30	**2011 Projections**		
Offensive FEI:	-0.249	96	Defensive FEI	-0.076	43	**Mean Wins**	8.2	
Offensive S&P+	94.9	84	Defensive S&P+	118.2	25	Proj. F/+	+4.7%	42
Rushing S&P+	99.8	70	Rushing S&P+	110.2	33	Offensive F/+	-0.2%	63
Passing S&P+	92.6	86	Passing S&P+	129.8	12	Defensive F/+	+4.9%	36
Standard Downs S&P+	96.2	83	Standard Downs S&P+	105.0	43	Strength of Schedule	0.430	75
Passing Downs S&P+	96.7	76	Passing Downs S&P+	135.6	10			

After flirting with the Pac-12 during the conference shuffle last summer, the Cougars ultimately elected to leave the Mountain West and declare their independence for 2011 and beyond. With ten starters back on offense and riding the momentum of an eight-game winning streak to close last year, BYU hopes it can reclaim its potential for consistent nine and ten-win seasons – if the schedule allows. Their first four weeks as an independent – trips to Mississippi and Texas, and home dates against Utah and Central Florida – will be no picnic.

Sophomore quarterback Jake Heaps lit up the BYU freshman quarterback record book a year ago, but is still seeking a breakout performance against a top opponent. He threw 14 touchdown passes against only three interceptions in the Cougars' final six games of 2010, but five of those opponents ranked among the ten worst defenses in the nation according to F/+. Ad-justed for opponent, BYU has a long way to go. Heaps is joined by senior running back J.J. Di Luigi (917 yards rushing, 443 yards receiving), more than 85 percent of the team's receiving production from last year, and an experienced offensive line led by senior tackle Matt Reynolds.

Head coach Bronco Mendenhall took over the reins of the defense during BYU's final eight games and will continue to lead that unit this fall. The front seven is experienced and welcomes back senior defensive tackle Romney Fuga, who was injured for most of last season but is expected to be a primary run stopper for the Cougars. BYU was very strong against the pass last year (top-15 in passing S&P+) but will be replacing the entire starting secondary except for senior free safety Travis Uale.

2012 NFL Draft Prospects: OT Matt Reynolds (2-3).

Other Independents

Navy and Army are the only other college football independents, and the academies share a few commonalities. Both like to run the triple option, patiently move the ball down the field, limit game possessions, and hope their team discipline will help overcome the talent disadvantages they face in every game. The Midshipmen and Black Knights both effectively produce methodical drives, ranking in the top ten in percentage of possessions with ten or more plays (22 percent for Navy, 20 percent for Army).

For Navy, the key this fall will be filling the void left by quarterback Ricky Dobbs. The offense clicked seamlessly with Dobbs' experienced decision-making for much of the last two seasons, and he connected for 10 yards per pass attempt on the rare occasions Navy went to the air. Senior Kriss Proctor takes over under center and has seen limited action, though he did lead Navy to victory over Central Michigan in a relief start last season. On defense, Navy needs to replace its top four tacklers from last year. Senior defensive end Jabaree Tuani led the Midshipmen with 15.5 tackles for loss and will anchor an otherwise inexperienced front seven. Navy hasn't had an S&P+ top-50 defense in any year for which we have data, and we project a bit of regression this fall.

Army earned its first bowl bid in 15 years in 2010, but the Black Knights didn't beat a top-50 F/+ team last year. They won't even face a single top-50 team this year according to our projections, but personnel losses on offense and defense will probably keep Army out of bowl contention in 2011.

2012 NFL Draft Prospects: None

CONFERENCE USA

Since Conference USA expanded to 12 teams in 2005 and began hosting a championship game, three teams from each of its East and West Divisions have appeared in the title game. In 2011, the F/+ ratings foresee a down-to-the-wire championship battle between all six of those programs. Central Florida, Tulsa, Southern Miss, East Carolina, SMU, and Houston are all projected to be ranked between No. 54 and No. 72 overall, and all six teams have a mean conference projection between 5.1 and 6.2 wins. This year's title may come down to a loose ball here or there, or simply the quirks of unbalanced schedules.

In the East Division, Central Florida has the slight edge in national projected rank but Southern Mississippi and East Carolina are hot on its heels. Those three teams will clash in consecutive weekends in November, and none of those games are UCF home games. All three teams were solid last season offensively, averaging 2.7 points per drive, though only the Knights had a defense to match. But Central Florida has more defensive personnel losses to deal with, returning only three of their top ten tacklers from a year ago. The secret to UCF's success last year was also the No 1 field position advantage in college football, spurred by strong kick and punt return units. UCF junior Quincy McDuffie ranked second nationally in yards per kickoff return and took two to the house.

East Carolina and Southern Mississippi each return senior quarterbacks (Dominique Davis and Austin Davis, respectively) that can light up the scoreboard with their arms and legs. Neither team has a reliable defense, though the Pirates were particularly horrific, surrendering 40 or more points in ten games.

Tulsa is the F/+ favorite in the West Division and has a favorable conference schedule, including home games against SMU and Houston and only one game against the big three from the east. They'll be in good shape if their confidence isn't totally rocked out of the gate with the nation's toughest non-conference schedule (at Oklahoma, home vs. Oklahoma State, at Boise State). Tulsa returns eight starters on each side of the ball, including senior quarterback G.J. Kinne and senior wide receiver Damaris Johnson, who led the nation in all-purpose yards in 2010 (202 per game). SMU has 18 starters back in the fold and was keyed in 2010 by its defense, led by junior linebacker Taylor Reed (145 tackles). Houston's Case Keenum was injured early in the year and returns for a sixth-year medical redshirt season at quarterback. He threw for 44 touchdowns and 5,600 yards as a junior and will need to post that level of production again to cover for Houston's abysmal defense (104th in defensive F/+, 117th defending passing downs).

2012 NFL Draft Prospects: DE Vinny Curry, Marshall (2-3); DE Cordarro Law, Southern Mississippi (3-4); LB Korey Williams, Southern Mississippi (3-4); CB Emanuel Davis, East Carolina (3-4); QB G.J. Kinne, Tulsa (4-5); QB Case Keenum, Houston (4-5); OT Matt McCants, UAB (4-5), WR Lance Lewis, East Carolina (5-6); DT D'Angelo McCray, Memphis (5-7).

WESTERN ATHLETIC CONFERENCE

If you can't beat 'em, do you join 'em? Once Boise State decided to jump to the Mountain West, the leftovers in the WAC were faced with the decision to stick together or follow the Broncos and move on up. The second-tier WAC teams (Nevada, Fresno State, Hawaii) will ultimately bolt for the Mountain West next year, leaving behind a decimated football conference starting in 2012. For this fall, the Wolf Pack, Bulldogs, and Warriors are the favorites for one last WAC title chase.

Nevada may be our F/+ pick to claim the championship, but they face the biggest identity crisis with the graduation of four-year starting quarterback Colin Kaepernick and three-year starting running back Vai Taua. Senior quarterback Tyler Lantrip won't be nearly as productive as Kaepernick, but his primary job will be to effectively feed a stable of new running backs, including sophomore Stefphon Jefferson and senior Mark Lampford. Nevada ranked eighth in offensive F/+ and rushing S&P+ last year, and should still boast a top-25 ground game out of the pistol offense.

Fresno State will be breaking in a new starting

quarterback as well, but sophomore Derek Carr has the pedigree (he's the brother of former Fresno State standout David Carr) to step in and be effective. He'll be joined by junior running back Robbie Rouse (1,129 yards) and a handful of talented receivers in an offense poised to improve upon its 82nd-ranked offensive F/+ rating from last year. On defense, the Bulldogs will have difficulty replacing defensive end Chris Carter and middle linebacker Ben Jacobs, and will likely regress. Senior placekicker Kevin Goessling was one of the best in the nation and will be an asset in close games when the young offense sputters.

Hawaii was extremely prolific on offense a year ago and has to feel good about the leadership of senior quarterback Bryant Moniz (5,040 yards passing, 39 touchdowns) this fall. Unfortunately, the rest of the offense has only one returning offensive lineman, virtually no experience at running back, and just 20 percent of the receiving production from last year. The outlook is a little brighter on defense, anchored by senior defensive tackles Vaughn Meatoga and Kaniela Tuipulotu and senior linebacker Corey Paredes, whose 151 tackles were fourth most nationally.

2012 NFL Draft Prospects: DT Logan Harrell, Fresno State (3-4); LB James-Michael Johnson, Nevada (3-4); WR Risard Matthews, Nevada (5-6); LB Bobby Wagner, Utah State (5-6);

MID-AMERICAN CONFERENCE

It might be due to coaches being poached by big conferences, but top MAC programs are having a difficult time staying on top. Three different teams from both the East and West Divisions have appeared in the MAC title game in the last three seasons. Northern Illinois and Miami (Ohio) were last year's championship participants, and each lost its coach a few weeks later. Our numbers like Northern Illinois to pick right up where it left off, but we won't be completely shocked if the baton is handed off yet again.

Northern Illinois' senior quarterback Chandler Harnish was one of the nation's most efficient quarterbacks in 2010, throwing for 21 touchdowns and only five interceptions while fighting through a knee injury all season. All but one of his favorite receivers are back for the Huskies, and senior running back Jasmin Hopkins (9.6 yards per carry) should fill in nicely in the hole left by Chad Spann. NIU was a top-30 offense according to F/+ last year and returns the entire starting offensive line for 2011. There will probably be some regression defensively with NIU losing seven starters to graduation. Junior defensive end Sean Progar was an all-MAC first team selection and will anchor an otherwise very inexperienced front seven. The Huskies ranked fifth nationally in punt return efficiency, helping give NIU a field position advantage in 11 of 14 games last year.

We project a handful of other MAC teams to dance along the threshold of bowl eligibility, including a race for second place in the West between Western Michigan, Central Michigan, and Toledo. The race for the east division championship should be very competitive as Temple, Ohio, Miami (Ohio), and Kent State are all projected within ten ranking spots of one another. The Redhawks were conference champs a year ago but we expect they'll crash back to earth after going 6-0 in games decided by a single score last year, including four victories against bottom-30 opponents.

2012 NFL Draft Prospects: OT Trevor Olson, Northern Illinois (3-4); C Scott Wedige, Northern Illinois (4-5); QB Chandler Harnish, Northern Illinois (5-6); C Ben Bojicic, Bowling Green (5-6); CB Josh Pleasant, Kent State (5-6).

SUN BELT CONFERENCE

The Sun Belt projects once again to be the nation's worst conference, narrowly edging out the MAC for the lowest projected average F/+ team rating. Outside of Troy, Sun Belt teams are rarely competitive in non-conference battles and the league as a whole is the SEC's personal chew toy. The Trojans have won at least a share of the conference title in five straight seasons and look to be the frontrunners again in 2011.

Troy's defense was a liability last season (84th in defensive F/+) but figures to improve with eight returning starters. Junior defensive end Jonathan Massaquoi ranked fourth nationally in sacks last season

(12.5) and had a career day in the bowl game victory over Ohio (2.5 sacks, 3 tackles for loss). On offense, sophomore quarterback Corey Robinson is expected to build on his solid debut (64 percent completion rate, 3,700 yards), though his top returning receiving target, senior Chip Reeves, only caught 30 passes a year ago. Troy is an annual threat to push at least one AQ conference big boy to the brink of an upset, almost knocking off Oklahoma State in 2010 and LSU in 2008. Arkansas and Clemson are in the Trojans' crosshairs this fall.

Florida International and Arkansas State have the best opportunity to challenge Troy for the conference crown. FIU has reliable weapons at running back (senior Darriet Parry, 839 yards rushing) and wide receiver (senior T.Y. Hilton, 848 yards receiving), but senior quarterback Wesley Carroll needs to improve

his decision making for the offense to progress (16 touchdowns, 14 interceptions). Arkansas State's junior quarterback Ryan Alpin was responsible for 32 of the Red Wolves' 47 touchdowns last year (21 passing, 11 rushing) and is expected to continue to develop under new head coach and offensive guru Hugh Freeze.

2012 NFL Draft Prospects: WR T.Y. Hilton, Florida International (3-4); TE Ladarius Green, Louisiana-Lafayette (4-5); RB Lance Dunbar, North Texas (5-6).

Top FCS 2012 NFL Draft Prospects: CB Janoris Jenkins, North Alabama (2-3); DT Renard Williams, Eastern Washington (3-4); S Trumaine Johnson, Montana (3-4); OT David Pickard, Southern Illinois (4-5).

Brian Fremeau

NCAA Teams, No. 1 to No. 120

Rk	Team	Conf	Proj F/+	MW	Rec	Conf	SOS	Rk	Rk	Team	Conf	Proj F/+	MW	Rec	Conf	SOS	Rk
1	Alabama	SEC	23.7	10.9	11-1	7-1	0.125	9	29	Iowa	Big Ten	8.4	8.8	9-3	5-3	0.487	87
2	Oklahoma	Big 12	19.7	10.7	11-1	8-1	0.277	46	30	Penn State	Big Ten	7.6	7.8	8-4	5-3	0.192	21
3	Boise State	MWC	18.5	11.2	11-1	7-0	0.521	93	31	Arizona State	Pac-12	7.3	7.6	8-4	6-3	0.308	51
4	Auburn	SEC	18.3	8.8	9-3	5-3	0.043	1	32	Mississippi St.	SEC	6.5	6.0	6-6	2-6	0.054	5
5	LSU	SEC	17.2	9.0	9-3	6-2	0.050	4	33	Michigan State	Big Ten	6.3	7.2	7-5	4-4	0.263	42
6	Virginia Tech	ACC	16.7	11.2	11-1	7-1	0.626	99	34	Arizona	Pac-12	6.0	6.3	6-6	4-5	0.217	25
7	Stanford	Pac-12	15.7	10.3	10-2	8-1	0.369	65	35	Utah	Pac-12	5.9	7.4	7-5	6-3	0.356	61
8	Oregon	Pac-12	15.6	9.6	10-2	7-2	0.192	20	36	Cincinnati	Big East	5.9	7.8	8-4	4-3	0.444	80
9	Arkansas	SEC	15.6	9.1	9-3	5-3	0.061	6	37	Maryland	ACC	5.8	6.5	7-5	4-4	0.230	31
10	Florida State	ACC	15.3	9.6	10-2	7-1	0.233	32	38	Oregon State	Pac-12	5.7	6.7	7-5	5-4	0.230	30
11	TCU	MWC	15.1	10.8	11-1	6-1	0.411	70	39	Texas	Big 12	5.5	7.1	7-5	5-4	0.238	34
12	Florida	SEC	14.0	7.8	8-4	4-4	0.045	2	40	North Carolina	ACC	5.4	7.2	7-5	4-4	0.279	47
13	South Carolina	SEC	13.9	8.7	9-3	5-3	0.168	16	41	Boston College	ACC	4.9	5.7	6-6	3-5	0.149	13
14	Oklahoma St.	Big 12	13.3	9.3	9-3	7-2	0.305	50	42	BYU	Ind.	4.7	8.2	8-4	-	0.430	75
15	Ohio State	Big Ten	13.2	9.5	10-2	6-2	0.351	60	43	Kentucky	SEC	4.6	6.9	7-5	3-5	0.175	17
16	Pittsburgh	Big East	12.5	9.6	10-2	6-1	0.403	67	44	Tennessee	SEC	4.3	5.6	6-6	2-6	0.047	3
17	Missouri	Big 12	12.5	9.3	9-3	7-2	0.212	24	45	Illinois	Big Ten	3.9	7.3	7-5	4-4	0.493	89
18	USC	Pac-12	12.4	8.8	9-3	7-2	0.246	37	46	Texas Tech	Big 12	3.9	7.0	7-5	4-5	0.185	18
19	Notre Dame	Ind.	12.4	8.6	9-3	-	0.221	26	47	South Florida	Big East	3.6	6.7	7-5	3-4	0.334	57
20	West Virginia	Big East	12.3	9.6	10-2	6-1	0.439	79	48	Nevada	WAC	3.6	8.9	9-3	6-1	0.248	40
21	Georgia	SEC	12.2	8.5	8-4	5-3	0.222	27	49	Ole Miss	SEC	3.4	5.2	5-7	2-6	0.088	8
22	Wisconsin	Big Ten	11.9	9.6	10-2	6-2	0.431	77	50	Georgia Tech	ACC	3.3	6.2	6-6	3-5	0.317	55
23	Clemson	ACC	11.0	7.5	7-5	5-3	0.130	10	51	Navy	Ind.	2.3	7.9	8-4	-	0.451	82
24	Miami-FL	ACC	10.6	8.2	8-4	5-3	0.195	22	52	Connecticut	Big East	2.0	7.6	8-4	3-4	0.430	76
25	Michigan	Big Ten	9.4	8.6	9-3	5-3	0.430	74	53	Louisville	Big East	1.7	5.9	6-6	3-4	0.407	69
26	Nebraska	Big Ten	9.2	8.4	8-4	5-3	0.357	63	54	Central Florida	C-USA	1.0	7.9	8-4	6-2	0.808	109
27	NC State	ACC	8.8	8.7	9-3	5-3	0.370	66	55	Tulsa	C-USA	0.9	7.3	7-5	6-2	0.144	11
28	Texas A&M	Big 12	8.8	7.9	8-4	6-3	0.145	12	56	Air Force	MWC	0.9	7.9	8-4	5-2	0.248	39

Rk	Team	Conf	Proj F/+	MW	Rec	Conf	SOS	Rk	Rk	Team	Conf	Proj F/+	MW	Rec	Conf	SOS	Rk
57	N. Illinois	MAC	0.6	9.5	10-2	7-1	0.759	107	89	Iowa State	Big 12	-7.1	2.7	3-9	1-8	0.165	15
58	Southern Miss	C-USA	0.4	8.6	9-3	6-2	0.896	116	90	Louisiana Tech	WAC	-8.6	5.2	5-7	4-3	0.736	106
59	Washington	Pac-12	0.3	5.2	5-7	3-6	0.205	23	91	Ohio	MAC	-9.1	7.4	7-5	5-3	0.937	120
60	California	Pac-12	0.1	5.1	5-7	3-6	0.223	28	92	Miami-OH	MAC	-9.2	5.1	5-7	4-4	0.645	100
61	Rutgers	Big East	-0.5	5.4	5-7	2-5	0.519	92	93	Kansas	Big 12	-9.3	2.3	2-10	1-8	0.243	35
62	Kansas State	Big 12	-0.8	5.0	5-7	3-6	0.233	33	94	Marshall	C-USA	-9.3	3.4	3-9	3-5	0.480	86
63	Northwestern	Big Ten	-0.9	5.4	5-7	3-5	0.446	81	95	UL-Monroe	Sun Belt	-9.9	5.1	5-7	4-4	0.311	52
64	UCLA	Pac-12	-1.0	4.7	5-7	3-6	0.264	43	96	Kent State	MAC	-10.1	5.8	6-6	4-4	0.247	38
65	East Carolina	C-USA	-1.2	6.4	6-6	6-2	0.429	73	97	Army	Ind.	-10.1	4.0	4-8	-	0.876	115
66	Virginia	ACC	-1.3	5.0	5-7	2-6	0.252	41	98	Wyoming	MWC	-10.5	5.3	5-7	2-5	0.312	53
67	San Diego St.	MWC	-1.3	7.5	7-5	4-3	0.431	78	99	Washington St.	Pac-12	-11.2	2.5	2-10	1-8	0.357	62
68	Baylor	Big 12	-1.6	4.7	5-7	3-6	0.229	29	100	M. Tennessee	Sun Belt	-11.9	4.5	5-7	3-5	0.848	113
69	SMU	C-USA	-1.7	6.6	7-5	5-3	0.459	84	101	Ball State	MAC	-12.2	3.9	4-8	3-5	0.351	59
70	Colorado	Pac-12	-1.9	4.2	4-9	3-6	0.191	19	102	San Jose State	WAC	-12.3	3.5	4-8	3-4	0.492	88
71	Minnesota	Big Ten	-1.9	4.8	5-7	2-6	0.345	58	103	W. Kentucky	Sun Belt	-12.7	4.0	4-8	3-5	0.456	83
72	Houston	C-USA	-2.4	8.4	8-4	5-3	0.924	118	104	North Texas	Sun Belt	-12.8	4.0	4-8	3-5	0.245	36
73	Troy	Sun Belt	-3.1	7.1	7-5	6-2	0.424	72	105	Rice	C-USA	-12.9	3.2	3-9	3-5	0.831	110
74	Syracuse	Big East	-3.4	4.8	5-7	2-5	0.363	64	106	Bowling Green	MAC	-12.9	4.3	4-8	3-5	0.687	104
75	Hawaii	WAC	-3.6	8.7	9-4	5-2	0.832	111	107	UTEP	C-USA	-13.1	3.9	4-8	2-6	0.852	114
76	Purdue	Big Ten	-3.8	4.4	4-8	2-6	0.314	54	108	Utah State	WAC	-13.5	4.6	5-7	2-5	0.405	68
77	Wake Forest	ACC	-4.7	3.0	3-9	1-7	0.271	44	109	Tulane	C-USA	-13.7	4.0	4-9	2-6	0.930	119
78	W. Michigan	MAC	-5.1	6.6	7-5	5-3	0.686	103	110	Florida Atlantic	Sun Belt	-13.8	3.2	3-9	3-5	0.271	45
79	Duke	ACC	-5.2	3.6	4-8	1-7	0.286	48	111	Idaho	WAC	-14.2	4.1	4-8	2-5	0.688	105
80	Fresno State	WAC	-5.4	6.2	6-7	5-2	0.497	91	112	UL-Lafayette	Sun Belt	-14.9	3.7	4-8	3-5	0.594	95
81	Florida Int'l	Sun Belt	-5.6	7.3	7-5	5-3	0.899	117	113	Colorado State	MWC	-15.3	3.6	4-8	2-5	0.418	71
82	Vanderbilt	SEC	-5.7	3.0	3-9	1-7	0.064	7	114	E. Michigan	MAC	-16.4	4.2	4-8	2-6	0.663	102
83	C. Michigan	MAC	-6.1	6.1	6-6	5-3	0.647	101	115	Akron	MAC	-16.6	3.1	3-9	2-6	0.599	96
84	Toledo	MAC	-6.7	5.7	6-6	4-4	0.468	85	116	Buffalo	MAC	-16.6	3.3	3-9	2-6	0.620	98
85	Arkansas St.	Sun Belt	-6.8	7.1	7-5	5-3	0.494	90	117	Memphis	C-USA	-17.0	2.5	2-10	1-7	0.848	112
86	Indiana	Big Ten	-6.9	4.0	4-8	1-7	0.333	56	118	New Mexico	MWC	-17.1	3.2	3-9	2-5	0.150	14
87	Temple	MAC	-6.9	7.3	7-5	5-3	0.790	108	119	UNLV	MWC	-17.3	2.4	2-10	1-6	0.290	49
88	UAB	C-USA	-7.0	4.5	5-7	3-5	0.566	94	120	New Mexico St.	WAC	-21.9	1.5	2-11	1-6	0.615	97

Projected Win Probabilities For Mountain West Teams

Mountain West	Overall Wins													Conference Wins							
	12-0	11-1	10-2	9-3	8-4	7-5	6-6	5-7	4-8	3-9	2-10	1-11	0-12	7-0	6-1	5-2	4-3	3-4	2-5	1-6	0-7
Air Force	-	-	4	21	41	26	7	1	-	-	-	-	-	69	29	2	-	-	-	-	-
Boise State	40	43	15	2	-	-	-	-	-	-	-	-	-	-	-	-	2	13	34	37	14
Colorado State	-	-	-	-	-	1	6	17	27	28	16	5	-	-	-	-	1	10	39	39	11
New Mexico	-	-	-	-	-	-	1	8	29	38	20	4	-	-	2	23	52	20	3	-	-
San Diego State	-	-	2	14	34	31	14	4	1	-	-	-	-	20	65	14	1	-	-	-	-
TCU	16	56	24	4	-	-	-	-	-	-	-	-	-	-	-	-	-	6	27	45	22
UNLV	-	-	-	-	-	-	-	2	12	30	36	18	2	-	-	1	9	41	37	11	1
Wyoming	-	-	-	3	14	29	31	17	5	1	-	-	-	-	-	-	-	-	-	-	-

Projected Win Probabilities For Independent Teams

Independents	12-0	11-1	10-2	9-3	8-4	7-5	6-6	5-7	4-8	3-9	2-10	1-11	0-12
Army	-	-	-	-	1	3	10	21	28	24	11	2	-
BYU	-	2	11	26	32	21	7	1	-	-	-	-	-
Navy	-	1	9	22	30	23	11	3	1	-	-	-	-
Notre Dame	1	7	19	29	25	13	5	1	-	-	-	-	-

Projected Win Probabilities For Conference USA Teams

C-USA East	Overall Wins													Conference Wins								
	12-0	11-1	10-2	9-3	8-4	7-5	6-6	5-7	4-8	3-9	2-10	1-11	0-12	8-0	7-1	6-2	5-3	4-4	3-5	2-6	1-7	0-8
Central Florida	-	2	10	21	27	23	12	4	1	-	-	-	-	3	17	31	30	15	4	-	-	-
East Carolina	-	-	1	5	15	26	27	17	7	2	-	-	-	5	20	33	27	12	3	-	-	-
Marshall	-	-	-	-	-	1	4	13	26	30	19	6	1	-	-	1	7	21	33	27	10	1
Memphis	-	-	-	-	-	-	1	4	13	28	33	19	2	-	-	-	-	2	9	26	39	24
Southern Miss.	1	6	18	28	26	15	5	1	-	-	-	-	-	8	26	34	22	8	2	-	-	-
UAB	-	-	-	-	1	6	16	26	27	17	6	1	-	-	1	4	14	28	31	17	5	-
C-USA West	12-0	11-1	10-2	9-3	8-4	7-5	6-6	5-7	4-8	3-9	2-10	1-11	0-12	8-0	7-1	6-2	5-3	4-4	3-5	2-6	1-7	0-8
Houston	1	6	16	26	25	17	7	2	-	-	-	-	-	3	15	30	30	16	5	1	-	-
Rice	-	-	-	-	-	3	11	25	32	21	7	1	-	-	-	1	5	18	36	29	10	1
SMU	-	-	1	6	18	29	27	14	4	1	-	-	-	1	9	25	35	23	6	1	-	-
Tulane*	-	-	-	-	1	3	9	20	29	25	11	2	-	-	-	-	3	11	28	36	19	3
Tulsa	-	-	2	13	31	31	17	5	1	-	-	-	-	10	32	34	18	5	1	-	-	-
UTEP	-	-	-	-	2	8	20	31	26	11	2	-	-	-	-	-	1	3	13	30	36	17

*Tulane will play 13 regular season games; for projected overall records, 12-0 means 12-1, 11-1 means 11-2, etc.

Projected Win Probabilities For Western Athletic Conference Teams

WAC	Overall Wins													Conference Wins							
	12-0	11-1	10-2	9-3	8-4	7-5	6-6	5-7	4-8	3-9	2-10	1-11	0-12	7-0	6-1	5-2	4-3	3-4	2-5	1-6	0-7
Fresno State*	-	-	-	3	12	26	30	20	7	2	-	-	-	2	14	37	32	13	2	-	-
Hawaii*	1	7	19	28	25	14	5	1	-	-	-	-	-	4	24	38	25	8	1	-	-
Idaho	-	-	-	-	-	3	10	23	30	23	9	2	-	-	-	3	14	30	33	17	3
Louisiana Tech	-	-	-	1	4	12	25	29	20	8	1	-	-	-	-	4	18	34	30	12	2
Nevada	-	3	22	44	24	6	1	-	-	-	-	-	-	54	36	9	1	-	-	-	-
New Mexico State*	-	-	-	-	-	-	1	4	13	29	35	18		-	-	-	-	3	17	42	38
San Jose State	-	-	-	-	1	5	15	28	29	17	4	1		-	-	5	18	35	31	10	1
Utah State	-	-	-	-	1	6	17	28	27	15	5	1	-	-	-	3	13	30	34	17	3

*Fresno St., Hawaii, and New Mexico St. will play 13 regular season games; for projected overall records, 12-0 means 12-1, 11-1 means 11-2, etc..

Projected Win Probabilities For Mid-American Conference Teams

MAC East	12-0	11-1	10-2	9-3	8-4	7-5	6-6	5-7	4-8	3-9	2-10	1-11	0-12	8-0	7-1	6-2	5-3	4-4	3-5	2-6	1-7	0-8
Akron	-	-	-	-	-	1	3	10	22	30	24	9	1	-	-	-	2	9	22	32	26	9
Bowling Green	-	-	-	-	1	6	14	24	26	19	7	3	-	-	-	1	5	15	27	30	18	4
Buffalo	-	-	-	-	-	1	3	12	25	31	21	7	-	-	-	-	3	12	27	33	20	5
Kent State	-	-	-	2	8	20	28	24	13	4	1	-	-	-	-	2	9	22	31	24	10	2
Miami (OH)	-	-	-	1	4	12	22	28	21	10	2	-	-	-	-	3	11	25	31	21	8	1
Ohio	-	1	7	16	25	25	17	7	2	-	-	-	-	1	8	22	29	24	12	3	1	-
Temple	-	1	5	16	26	26	17	7	2	-	-	-	-	4	17	29	28	16	5	1	-	-
MAC West	12-0	11-1	10-2	9-3	8-4	7-5	6-6	5-7	4-8	3-9	2-10	1-11	0-12	8-0	7-1	6-2	5-3	4-4	3-5	2-6	1-7	0-8
Ball State	-	-	-	-	1	3	9	19	27	24	13	4	-	-	-	2	9	22	31	25	10	1
Central Michigan	-	-	-	3	12	24	29	21	9	2	-	-	-	1	9	23	31	23	10	3	-	-
Eastern Michigan	-	-	-	-	2	10	26	33	21	7	1	-	-	-	-	-	3	13	29	34	18	3
Northern Illinois	2	19	33	28	13	4	1	-	-	-	-	-	-	24	39	26	9	2	-	-	-	-
Toledo	-	-	-	2	7	18	28	25	14	5	1	-	-	1	4	15	28	28	17	6	1	-
Western Michigan	-	-	1	6	18	29	27	14	4	1	-	-	-	2	12	29	32	18	6	1	-	-

Projected Win Probabilities For Sun Belt Conference Teams

Sun Belt	12-0	11-1	10-2	9-3	8-4	7-5	6-6	5-7	4-8	3-9	2-10	1-11	0-12	8-0	7-1	6-2	5-3	4-4	3-5	2-6	1-7	0-8
Arkansas State	-	-	3	12	24	28	20	9	3	1	-	-	-	3	12	26	29	20	8	2	-	-
Florida Atlantic	-	-	-	-	1	4	12	24	28	21	7	3	-	-	-	2	8	21	30	25	12	2
Florida Int'l	-	1	6	15	24	25	17	8	3	1	-	-	-	3	16	29	29	16	6	1	-	-
La. Lafayette	-	-	-	-	-	2	7	17	28	27	15	4	-	-	-	1	5	15	28	30	17	4
Louisiana Monroe	-	-	-	-	4	13	24	28	20	9	2	-	-	-	3	13	25	29	20	8	2	-
Middle Tennessee	-	-	-	2	7	16	25	26	17	6	1	-	-	-	1	5	15	27	29	17	5	1
North Texas	-	-	-	1	3	11	22	27	22	10	4	-	-	-	-	4	14	28	30	18	5	1
Troy	-	-	2	12	26	30	20	8	2	-	-	-	-	9	28	34	20	7	2	-	-	-
Western Kentucky	-	-	-	1	3	10	21	28	24	10	3	-	-	-	-	2	9	21	30	25	11	2

Introducing the Blind Side Project

Mark Rypien, over the first 46 starts of his career, played behind one of the greatest offensive lines in history with the Washington Redskins. He was sacked only 43 times, including a whopping *seven* sacks for the entire 1991 season in which he was Super Bowl MVP. After the 1991 season, the Redskins line went downhill due to age and injuries, and Rypien was sacked 54 times in his final 32 starts (not all with the Redskins). During those first 46 starts, he averaged a healthy 7.9 yards per pass attempt. During the final 32 starts, he averaged only 6.1 yards per attempt. Clearly the line had an impact on his career and Super Bowl performance; we just do not know exactly (or even roughly) how much. With the proper statistics, perhaps linemen such as Jim Lachey and Russ Grimm would have received a little more credit for what they accomplished during the 1991 season. This is what led me to spend a good portion of the 2010-11 NFL season charting NFL games, with the irreplaceable help of my then-intern Keith Goldner, for the pilot season of the Blind Side Project.

The Blind Side Project worked differently than the general Football Outsiders game charting project, with a much more specific goal: to track pass blocking. Throughout the 2010 NFL season, Keith and I collected data on individual offensive linemen and other relevant play-by-play data from a large set of passing plays. We charted games for 22 teams, with more than 1,200 plays. Our goal was to chart many of the relevant variables needed to begin measuring the contribution of offensive linemen. For every play, we recorded down, distance, and whether the offense was using the Shotgun formation. We also recorded whether or not each individual offensive lineman successfully maintained his block. A lineman was judged to be successful on a play if, through the best judgment of the observer, the lineman kept the defensive player he was blocking from getting past them and interfering with the quarterback's throw.

This standard of success is admittedly subjective and is the single area of greatest push back that this research project receives. The argument goes something like this: Blocking schemes are very complicated (we entirely agree), you don't know what the blocking scheme was on any play (again, we completely agree), therefore you cannot properly judge whether a lineman was successful or not (not so fast). If that were true, then no one would be able to evaluate any lineman that was not on their own team, as no team shares its line calls on a play-by-play basis. When this data is collected, each play is looked at four or more times. With this kind of repetition, we are able, generally speaking, to get a good idea of what the lineman is supposed to do — and then we use our judgment based upon hours and hours of watching film to give the lineman a pass or fail on each play. On the sample of plays that Keith and I both charted, we agreed on more than 95 percent of plays. This is not an argument that our data is the gospel on every play, but that most coaches would not likely disagree with our judgments any more than they would disagree with each other's[1], and that we are regularly measuring the same thing whether or not that meets any particular coach's definition of success.

We measured time in the pocket (TIP) twice on each play to the hundredth of a second. The stop watch started at the snap of the ball and stopped when the quarterback released the ball, rolled, or was forced out of the pocket,;at the time the pocket collapsed; or at initial contact for a sack. The correlation between the two timing trials was 0.98 throughout the sample. For the best estimate of TIP, the average of the two trials was used. On the plays that both Keith and I charted, the correlation between the TIP variables was calculated to be 0.94. Again, coaches may argue the definition of TIP, but we were consistently applying

---

[1]In vetting this work with several NFL front offices, one executive told me that every coach believes that he is the only person in the league who can properly evaluate linemen.

the definition described.

We also collected some other bits of data from each play including: completion, sack, interception, designed screen play, designed rollout, and whether the quarterback was forced out of the pocket. Distance and direction of the pass were recorded for all plays, as well as yards after the catch for completions. Distance was recorded from the line of scrimmage and the field was divided into five segments to measure pass direction. We also counted the number of defenders rushing the quarterback on each pass play. Our data show that positions along the line have different success rates, with centers having the highest success rate (0.93) and right tackles the lowest (0.88). This is why players are only compared within position below. We also found that the average pass travels 8.6 yards in the air and the average time in the pocket for a quarterback is 2.38 seconds.

Using success rates and the other control variables, we estimated the probability an individual lineman can hold a block relative to an average lineman, given time in the pocket. Put another way: If the time in the pocket for a play is known, how much more/less likely is it for an offensive lineman to hold his block compared to an average player of the same position[2].

The functions are estimated with the following significant control variables: TIP, down, yards to go, Shotgun, Rushers, Dropback, and Rollout. Figure 1 displays the baseline survival curve for left tackles.

The probability above/below average for each lineman was then **correlated** with length of throw and out of pocket as to estimate the probability that a given pass would be completed[3]. The effect on probability was then used to estimate the total number of yards a player contributed to his team's passing game compared to an average lineman at his position (positive yards added suggest better than average and negative yards suggest below average performance), assuming he had played all 16 games of the season. We called this stat "Passing Line Yards." Finally, we summed the yards contributed by team to rank the relative strengths of all of the offensive lines in our data set (the 2010 NFL Playoff teams).

Of the teams that made the 2010 playoffs, the Jets and Colts were found to have the best lines during the regular season, and the Falcons and Packers had the worst. (That Colts result obviously goes contrary to conventional wisdom, although we note that the Colts

Table 1: 2010 Playoff Team Rankings

Team	Passing Line Yards	Variation Score
Jets	897.1	-0.74
Colts	512.3	-0.34
Ravens	422.9	-0.94
Saints	352.3	-0.41
Patriots	292.3	-0.20
Eagles	93.8	1.02
Steelers	71.3	0.26
Chiefs	56.8	-1.52
Bears	-283.4	0.90
Seahawks	-323.1	0.76
Falcons	-513.6	-0.48
Packers	-761.8	2.07

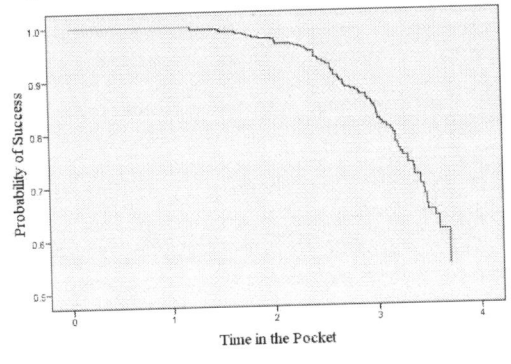

Figure 1. Probability of Success for Left Tackles

[2]As the ball is typically thrown before all linemen have failed, the data is right-censored — meaning we can't know on any given play how long a successful player could have held his block. Not accounting for this in the estimation would create biased estimates of the survival function. The estimation for each position along the line (left tackle, left guard, center, right guard, and right tackle) was done with what is known as a shared frailty, random effects model. This technique accounts for the fact that each player within a position is on a different team and that there is censoring in the data.

[3]While the estimated effect of each position on the probability a pass would be complete was found to be significant, as there is uncertainty in the probability above average values, some care in the interpretation of the results may be warranted.

and Seahawks were tied for the average lowest time in the pocket on passes.) We also calculated a variation score for each team which indicates how evenly distributed the skill level of the offensive linemen are for each team. The score was calculated as the standard deviation of the five linemen's passing line yards created, normalized for the sample. This means that higher scores are teams with higher variation of strength along the offensive line. So the Jets are high in passing line yards and low in variation, which means that they have good linemen across the line (D'Brickashaw Ferguson was the second-highest ranked left tackle and Nick Mangold the highest ranked center, with all players ranking above average), while the Packers, who have low passing line yards, have very high variation, indicating that they have some good and some very poor offensive linemen (Bryan Bulaga was one of the highest ranking right tackles while Scott Wells was the worst center in the sample).

In an attempt to demonstrate that the data and analysis is actually meaningful, and not just a way for a statistician to show off, we looked at the relation-

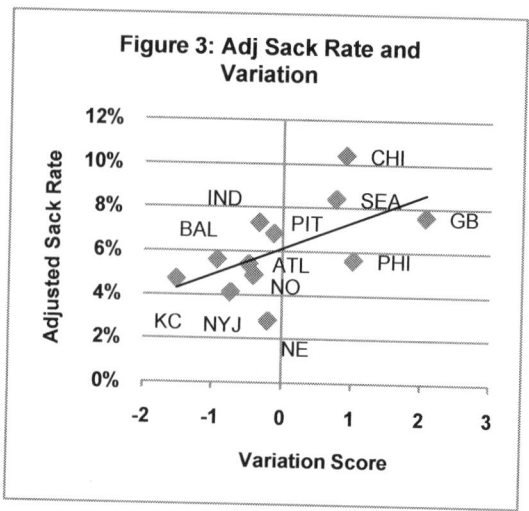

Figure 3: Adj Sack Rate and Variation

ship on a team and player level between the analysis above and standard metrics for offensive lines. On pass plays, the best we can do currently at looking at the offensive line is adjusted sack rate. This is not a perfect measure of line quality as quarterbacks have some control over sacks and different teams face different types of defensive pressure. It does, however, give us a starting point.

Figure 2 plots Adjusted Sack Rate for each of the 2010 playoff teams with their total Passing Line Yards. There is a strong negative correlation between ASR and Passing Line Yards, which indicates that teams with better linemen as measured by the Blind Side Project analysis give up fewer sacks. While this seems to be a obvious result, it lends some credence to the analysis — good offensive linemen who do their jobs well give up fewer sacks.

Interestingly, we also graphed adjusted sack rate with the variation score (Figure 3), and again found a very strong correlation. This shows that lines that are highly variable in quality can be attacked more effectively by defensive schemes than those with more even quality, as teams with higher variation scores tend to give up more sacks.

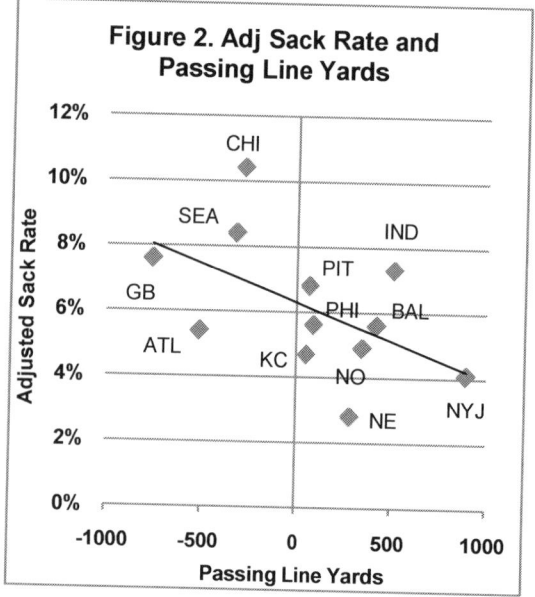

Figure 2. Adj Sack Rate and Passing Line Yards

We also took a look at the correlation between adjusted sack rate and line yards by position. Left tackles (Figure 4) had the strongest correlation between sack rate and line yards. This suggests that the highest paid position on the line may in fact deserve to be so. The two results for left tackles and variation of line talent sets up an interesting future question: Should the marginal dollar spent on the offensive line be spent on upgrading the left tackle, or upgrading the weakest position on a team's line?

The Blind Side Project is still in its infancy and these results are certainly not conclusive of anything yet. What they do suggest though is a way forward. One that requires significant data collection, but one that has the potential to more properly gauge the impact that an offensive lineman has on his team as well as the optimal way to spend salary cap dollars on those offensive linemen.

Ben Alamar

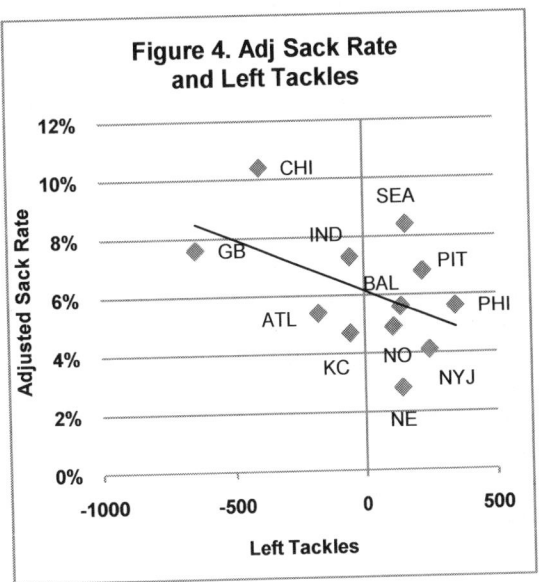

Figure 4. Adj Sack Rate and Left Tackles

Quarterbacks Will Make You Jump, Jump

Quarterbacks get the credit for just about everything. When a defensive player goes offside and gifts the offense five yards (and/or a free play), it's not because the defender was thinking about his shopping list or distracted by the trash-talker across from him. Instead, you're likely to hear a string of comments about how the quarterback really works on his hard count in practice and how his hard count is one of the best in the league. (No mention is made of that hard count potentially causing a false start.)

As a result, ask 100 fans who has the best hard count in the league, and you're likely to get 20 answers, depending on which quarterback those fans see most often. Fans will likely refer to one particularly egregious defensive penalty to defend their choice; the neutral zone infraction Drew Brees drew against the Bengals on a key fourth-and-3 inside their 10-yard line comes to mind. What we really need to do is answer two questions: Do quarterbacks actually exhibit a consistent skill at picking up penalties like defensive offsides from the opposition? And if so, which quarterbacks are consistently good or bad at it?

Figuring out the answers is a little tricky. As ESPN.com NFL West blogger Mike Sando noted in his December piece on this topic, the NFL has three penalties that could reasonably qualify as ones the quarterback might draw with a hard count: defensive offsides, encroachment, and the neutral zone infraction. The quarterback doesn't inherently draw all these penalties. A player can just line up offsides because he's blithely unaware, with no real prodding from the quarterback. Without any data on whether the penalty was drawn by a player that jumped early or one that just lined up in the wrong place, we'll treat all of these penalties as "drawn" by the quarterback. (This isn't a huge deal; it would be hard to argue that there's any rhyme or reason to a quarterback causing a defender to line up in the wrong spot.)

In addition, we don't have data that confirms which quarterback was on the field for each particular penalty, just the offense and defense in question. While we can remove penalties on special teams plays from the equation, this can still be dicey for games in which two quarterbacks saw action for one team. For these games, we'll credit the penalties to the quarterback that threw more passes. Finally, since a penalty should still count if the resulting free play produces a full play, we'll be considering both accepted and declined penalties.

In 2010, the grizzled veteran that drew the most opposing defensive offsides, encroachment, and neutral zone infraction penalties was ... Sam Bradford. The rookie Rams quarterback picked up a league-high 27 penalties across those three categories, six more than any other quarterback. We often think of the timing that comes with experience being required to induce these sort of penalties, but that doesn't appear to be the case. Bradford's total is the second-highest figure since 2002, tied with another young quarterback, albeit one that Bradford might not want to be linked to: Tim Couch. The record is 29, which Eli Manning achieved during the 2007 season.

The player who ranked second in 2010 represents the first sign that drawing these sorts of penalties can be a skill. Matt Ryan drew 21 such penalties in 2010, which was nothing new for him. In his rookie year of 2008, he picked up a league-high 25 calls, and in 2009, his 19 penalties were second in the league. That came despite missing about three full games due to injury. Perpetual comparison Joe Flacco also has ranked highly by this metric, finishing second to Ryan as a rookie, third in 2009, and seventh in 2010. The aforementioned Eli Manning had a four-year stretch from 2006-09 where he never ranked lower than seventh, but he was 13th in the league in both 2005 and 2010.

On the opposite side of the coin is the oft-belittled Mark Sanchez. During his two years in the league, Sanchez has finished 21st out of 23 quarterbacks (2009, with a minimum of 12 games as the primary passer) and 20th out of 22 quarterbacks (2010). He has been a part of just nine such penalties in 30 games, producing a 0.30 penalties-per-game figure that's the worst in the league since 2002 (minimum: 30 games).

He ranks just ahead of backup Mark Brunell (0.33 pen/gm) and another frequently-insulted quarterback, Jay Cutler (0.34 pen/gm). In 2010, the league low belonged to Dolphins quarterback Chad Henne, who could muster just two induced penalties in 14 games. Matt Hasselbeck finished with the second-lowest figure among qualifying quarterbacks in both 2009 and 2010, although he finished in the top six in both 2005 and 2007.

So, we have a few players that appear to make a habit of showing up at the top or bottom of our lists. If there's a strong year-to-year relationship for most players, we can infer that drawing penalties the way that Ryan does (or avoiding them the way Sanchez does) is a skill and not just the vagaries of luck and chance. To measure how consistent of a stat this is, we'll look at the penalties per game drawn in consecutive seasons since 2002 by players who had 12 or more qualifying games in each of those seasons.

The correlation coefficient in penalties per game from one season to the next for these players is 0.42. (Correlation coefficient is a statistical tool that measures how two variables are related by using a number between 1 and -1. The closer to -1 or 1, the stronger the relationship, but the closer to 0, the weaker the relationship.) About 18 percent of a player's penalties per game drawn are explained by his penalties per game from the previous year. That's a decent percentage for football without any other variables, but it's far from a perfect indicator.

Although we're basing that on 106 season pairs, those pairs only consist of 40 unique players, so we'll certainly learn more as our sample size of quarterbacks increases. At the moment, though, it appears that quarterbacks have a limited amount of control over the defense's propensity for jumping early.

Bill Barnwell

Table 1: Penalties Drawn, 2002-10

Name	Penalties	Games	Pens/Gm	Name	Penalties	Games	Pens/Gm
Matt Ryan	65	45	1.44	Tom Brady	93	127	0.73
Alex Smith	60	50	1.20	Brett Favre	85	117	0.73
Joe Flacco	57	48	1.19	David Garrard	55	76	0.72
Marc Bulger	105	89	1.18	Josh McCown	23	32	0.72
Kerry Collins	108	92	1.17	Matt Hasselbeck	81	115	0.70
Byron Leftwich	54	48	1.13	Matt Cassel	33	47	0.70
Rex Grossman	37	34	1.09	Aaron Brooks	47	67	0.70
Brian Griese	50	46	1.09	Jon Kitna	52	78	0.67
Eli Manning	109	102	1.07	Matt Schaub	37	55	0.67
Drew Bledsoe	70	69	1.01	Kurt Warner	45	71	0.63
Aaron Rodgers	47	47	1.00	Vince Young	28	45	0.62
J.P. Losman	34	34	1.00	Tommy Maddox	19	31	0.61
Brad Johnson	55	57	0.96	Derek Anderson	29	48	0.60
Chad Pennington	75	82	0.91	Kyle Orton	36	60	0.60
Gus Frerotte	31	34	0.91	Ben Roethlisberger	59	99	0.60
Vinny Testaverde	29	32	0.91	Jason Campbell	35	62	0.56
Michael Vick	61	72	0.85	Steve McNair	36	69	0.52
Daunte Culpepper	60	71	0.85	David Carr	38	77	0.49
Joey Harrington	60	71	0.85	Jake Delhomme	47	96	0.49
Trent Green	63	77	0.82	Tony Romo	29	61	0.48
Carson Palmer	77	96	0.80	Donovan McNabb	49	113	0.43
Drew Brees	108	135	0.80	Jeff Garcia	31	72	0.43
Peyton Manning	109	139	0.78	Kyle Boller	17	48	0.35
Philip Rivers	62	80	0.78	Jay Cutler	23	67	0.34
Ryan Fitzpatrick	31	40	0.78	Mark Brunell	17	52	0.33
Jake Plummer	51	69	0.74	Mark Sanchez	9	30	0.30

Minimum: 30 games

The Value of Pass Pressure

We've always known there was more to pass pressure than just the sack. Sacks are great, but you can also affect the quarterback by hitting him as he throws, or just plain getting in his face.

The NFL started tracking quarterback hits a few years ago, defined as any play where the quarterback was knocked to the ground after the pass. We started counting quarterback hurries on our own as part of the Football Outsiders game charting project in 2006. Since *Pro Football Prospectus 2007*, we've listed sacks, hurries, and hits for every player in the front seven, in the tables in our team chapters. But we haven't yet answered the question: Just how important is a hit or a hurry compared to a sack?

To answer that question, we put together all our data from 2008 through 2010. We looked at every play with some sort of pass pressure to see how much it changed the offense's chances of getting a new set of downs,

as well as how it changed the expected next score of the game. Complicating things somewhat is that a defensive lineman can have both a hit and a hurry on the same play. Therefore we looked at five distinct situations: no pressure, hit, hurry, hit with hurry, and sack.

In Tables 1 and 2, each of these events is compared to the difference between a sack and no pressure at all. In other words, if a sack is a "100 percent" successful pass rush, how successful is a hurry or a hit?

In one of our tables, a hit is slightly more valuable than a hurry. In the other table, a hurry is slightly more valuable than a hit. If we average the values, we get 24.4 percent for a hit, 23.6 percent for a hurry, and 41.2 percent for both. If we want to round that in a way that makes it easier to explain to the people sitting next to you at the local sports bar, it means that a hit or a hurry is worth about 25 percent of a sack, while a hit *with* a hurry is worth about 40 percent of a sack.

Table 1. Next Score by Offense, Based on Pass Pressure

Event	Next Score by Offense	Next Score vs. Average	Value vs. Sack
No Pressure	2.03	0.24	0%
Hit	1.37	-0.41	31%
Hurry	1.53	-0.25	24%
Hurry and Hit	1.12	-0.67	44%
Sack	-0.06	-1.84	100%
Average	**1.79**		

Table 2. Odds of First Down, Based on Pass Pressure

Event	Leads to First Down	Leads to FD vs. Average	Value vs. Sack
No Pressure	63%	4.9%	0%
Hit	55%	-3.0%	18%
Hurry	53%	-5.7%	24%
Hurry and Hit	46%	-12.5%	39%
Sack	19%	-39.8%	100%
Average	**58%**		

That allows us to put together a total "pressure" rating of how much defenders harassed quarterbacks in 2010. It's not quite as simple as adding together sacks, hits, and hurries with some coefficients. Sometimes a play got a hit and a hurry from two different players. Sometimes two or more players were in on a hurry, but only one got a hit. We broke down each pass pressure situation in 2010 to get our table of the top 30 pass rushers of the year. (Table 3) One big difference between this and the tables in the team chapters: Those tables include all hits, including hits on plays cancelled by penalty. In order to compare players on equal ground, this pressure rating does not include hits on plays cancelled by penalty.

The next question we have to ask is whether hits and hurries help us to forecast which players might have more sacks in the future. Baseball analysts know that a player who hits a lot of doubles often develops into a player who hits a lot of home runs. Does the same effect exist with pass pressure? Can we expect a player with more hits and hurries but not too many sacks to have more sacks the following season?

Based on the numbers from the five years we've been tracking such things, the answer is yes. We took all players with at least eight games in two consecutive years, from 2006 through 2010, and looked at

Table 4. Correlation of Pass Rush Stats to Next Year Sacks, 2006-2010

	Sacks/G	Hits/G	Hur/G	Events/G	Pressure/G
Correlation to Same Stat, Y+1	0.648	0.640	0.706	0.775	0.763
Correlation to Sacks/G, Y+1	0.648	0.557	0.619	0.675	0.691

the correlation of these different statistics both to the same statistic the following year and to sacks per game the following year. In Table 4, "Events" is the total of hits, hurries, and sacks; "Pressure" is the adjusted total pressure rating introduced earlier.

For the last part of this look at pass pressure, I want to look at hitting the quarterback. What is the purpose of knocking the quarterback to the ground after the pass? Sure, sometimes you will hit him in motion, affecting the path of the ball. But often, the pass is already off, and the hit does nothing on that particular play.

It's generally accepted that quarterback hits build up. Quarterbacks don't want to hit the ground over and over again. They get happy feet trying to avoid another knockdown, right?

Maybe not.

Table 3. Top 30 Players in "Total Pressure," 2010

Player	Team	Sacks	Hits	Hurries	Pressure	Player	Team	Sacks	Hits	Hurries	Pressure
D.Ware	DAL	15.5	9	39	27.0	M.Williams	HOU	9	10	34	19.3
T.Hali	KC	14.5	12	36.5	26.1	C.Clemons	SEA	11	8	27	19.2
C.Wake	MIA	14	14	38	25.9	T.Cole	PHI	10	10	26.5	18.8
T.Suggs	BAL	11	10	38	22.3	J.Peppers	CHI	8	13	30.5	18.6
J.Babin	TEN	12.5	15	25.5	21.8	R.Mathis	IND	11	7	23.5	18.4
C.Long	STL	8	14	42.5	21.5	C.Avril	DET	8.5	2	33.5	17.4
C.Johnson	CAR	11.5	11	30.5	21.4	A.Smith	HOU	4	19	36.5	16.9
J.Allen	MIN	11	15	28.5	21.4	R.Edwards	MIN	8	9	27.5	16.6
C.Matthews	GB	13.5	11	20.5	20.6	B.Orakpo	WAS	8	9	24.5	16.1
D.Freeney	IND	10	10	33.5	20.2	J.Hall	STL	10.5	5	18	16.0
J.Harrison	PIT	10.5	12	31	20.2	N.Suh	DET	10	7	18	15.9
J.Abraham	ATL	13	5	23.5	20.0	J.Smith	SF	8.5	9	20	15.3
O.Umenyiora	NYG	11.5	17	18.5	19.7	S.Phillips	SD	11	1	13	14.5
J.Tuck	NYG	11.5	12	21	19.4	R.Brock	SEA	8	10	18.5	14.4
L.Woodley	PIT	9.5	8	33	19.4	I.Idonije	CHI	8	9	16	14.0

We went over every play of the last three seasons to look at how teams played based on the number of times the quarterback had been knocked down prior to the play in question: both sacks and quarterback hits. Overall, quarterback performance barely changes as the knockdowns add up, until you get about 12 knockdowns in the game. (Table 5) And that level of knockdowns is pretty rare. Only 34 times in the last three years did a defense get at least 12 knockdowns in a game. As you might imagine, by the time your quarterback has been knocked down a dozen times, the game is pretty much lost anyway. On the average pass play after 12 knockdowns, the offense is behind by two touchdowns. So it's not surprising that these quarterbacks don't play well. They probably weren't playing very well the rest of the game, either.

Aaron Schatz

Table 5. Pass Performance based on Number of Previous QB Knockdowns, 2008-2010

Knockdowns	Pass Plays	Avg Yds	Play Leads to First Down	Average Score on Drive	Knockdowns	Pass Plays	Avg Yds	Play Leads to First Down	Average Score on Drive
0	13286	6.2	60%	2.3	8	954	5.7	60%	2.0
1	10990	6.2	58%	2.4	9	667	6.4	56%	1.6
2	9866	6.0	57%	2.1	10	438	5.7	58%	2.0
3	7483	6.0	57%	2.2	11	199	5.2	62%	1.8
4	5795	5.7	58%	2.2	12	123	3.7	53%	1.0
5	3958	5.8	58%	2.1	13	41	2.4	34%	0.5
6	2700	6.1	60%	2.2	14	16	4.1	75%	0.0
7	1901	5.8	60%	2.1	15	10	3.0	20%	0.0

Home-Field Advantage

We all know that home-field advantage is an important issue in the NFL. Last year, to give a simple example, home teams finished the regular season 143-113.

To determine which team has enjoyed the best home field advantage when it comes to winning football games, we looked at their point differential in games at home and on the road from 2002 through 2010. (The study starts with 2002 for two reasons: It's the year that the Houston Texans became the NFL's 32nd team, and it allows for every team to have played each of the other divisions in their conference three times.) We know that point differential is a stronger predictor of wins than wins themselves, which is why we don't just use winning percentage.

In order to get the best representation of what it's like to play in a certain location, we've removed home games that really took place on neutral fields, like the games that have taken place in London or Mexico City over the past few years. And the 2005 Saints "home" game against the Giants in the Meadowlands is considered a road game.

The team with the biggest difference between its average point differential at home and on the road was the Seattle Seahawks (Table 1). The Seahawks won their average game at home by 6.1 points, but they lost their average road game by nearly the same amount, 5.6 points. As a result, without accounting for any other factors, the Seahawks were nearly 12 points better in Qwest Field (coincidentally opened in 2002) than they were on the road. Incredible.

This methodology, naturally, does a much better job of evaluating teams within context than merely looking at their performance at home. Take the New England Patriots, for example. With a league-best point differential of 11.2 at home, merely looking at their home point differential, winning percentage, or even their home DVOA would suggest that they were enjoying some incredible home field advantage in Foxboro. By comparing it to their road performance — where they have also been the best team in the league — we can find that they're not all that much better at home than they are outside of Massachusetts. The same is true for the Oakland Raiders on the other side of the coin; bad at home, worse on the road, but not by a particularly large amount.

Look at the teams who finished second through fourth behind the Seahawks. That's right: It's the rest of the NFC West. Of course, the NFC West also has had something in common for most of the past eight seasons. It's been terrible. Are these teams just benefiting from getting six games a year against awful opposition that can't do anything of consequence on the road?

That doesn't appear to be the case. If we remove the divisional games from the study and run the numbers again, the Seahawks remain No. 1. In fact, their differential rises to 13.8 points of difference. The Cardinals are just behind them at 13.3 points, while the 49ers rank fifth and the Rams are sixth (See Table 1, next page).

Table 1: Point Differential, Home and Away, 2002-2010

Team	Home Score Differential	Away Score Differential	Absolute Differential	Team	Home Score Differential	Away Score Differential	Absolute Differential
SEA	6.1	-5.6	11.7	DEN	2.6	-2.5	5.0
SF	0.3	-9.2	9.5	BUF	-0.1	-5.0	4.9
ARI	0.2	-9.3	9.5	ATL	2.4	-2.3	4.7
STL	-1.1	-10.4	9.3	GB	6.9	2.3	4.7
BAL	8.1	-1.1	9.2	NE	11.2	7.2	4.0
KC	4.0	-4.3	8.3	PIT	7.3	3.6	3.7
MIN	4.9	-2.9	7.9	CLE	-2.7	-6.2	3.5
JAC	3.3	-3.6	6.9	OAK	-3.1	-6.5	3.4
DET	-4.1	-10.9	6.9	PHI	6.4	3.4	3.0
HOU	-0.9	-7.2	6.2	WAS	-1.0	-3.8	2.8
NYJ	3.9	-2.2	6.0	TB	1.6	-0.4	2.0
CHI	3.0	-2.9	5.9	CIN	-1.6	-3.2	1.6
DAL	3.4	-2.6	5.9	NO	2.4	0.8	1.6
SD	8.1	2.2	5.9	MIA	-0.8	-2.3	1.6
TEN	2.3	-3.1	5.4	NYG	1.3	0.1	1.2
IND	9.9	4.5	5.3	CAR	-0.2	-1.0	0.8

It does appear to be true, though, that playing an easy schedule contributes to home field advantage. The average Seahawks opponent over the nine-year stretch has had a winning percentage of .454 (Table 2); that's the easiest schedule of any NFL team. On the whole, 17 percent of the variance in a team's home field advantage over the timeframe can be explained by the quality of the opposing teams they played, a not-insignificant amount.

It's been theorized that domes and/or cold weather can play a large part in affecting home field advantage, but our research doesn't show that to be the case. While Arizona (third) and Minnesota (seventh) play in domes, so do teams like Atlanta (19th) and New Orleans (29th). The bottom half of the rankings, meanwhile, are littered with cold-weather teams.

Table 2: Home Point Differential vs. Strength of Schedule

Team	Avg Point Differential	Opposition Avg Win %	Avg PD Rank	Ease of Schedule	Team	Avg Point Differential	Opposition Avg Win %	Avg PD Rank	Ease of Schedule
SEA	11.7	0.454	1	1	DEN	5.0	0.508	17	17
SF	9.5	0.471	2	3	BUF	4.9	0.523	18	27
ARI	9.5	0.511	3	20	ATL	4.7	0.462	19	2
STL	9.3	0.508	4	16	GB	4.7	0.499	20	9
BAL	9.2	0.492	5	7	NE	4.0	0.513	21	21
KC	8.3	0.510	6	19	PIT	3.7	0.523	22	28
MIN	7.9	0.491	7	6	CLE	3.5	0.546	23	32
JAC	6.9	0.515	8	22	OAK	3.4	0.528	24	31
DET	6.9	0.521	9	26	PHI	3.0	0.496	25	8
HOU	6.2	0.516	10	24	WAS	2.8	0.506	26	13
NYJ	6.0	0.501	11	11	TB	2.0	0.516	27	23
CHI	5.9	0.483	12	4	CIN	1.6	0.507	28	14
DAL	5.9	0.508	13	17	NO	1.6	0.507	29	15
SD	5.9	0.505	14	12	MIA	1.6	0.524	30	29
TEN	5.4	0.518	15	25	NYG	1.2	0.527	31	30
IND	5.3	0.500	16	10	CAR	0.8	0.484	32	5

While we're here, let's check on one more theory that gets tossed around a lot when particularly old stadiums get replaced by new ones. Do teams lose a home field advantage edge when they move into a new stadium? We can make an educated guess by looking at how teams performed in this home field advantage metric during their final three years at their old stadium, and then comparing it to how they did during their first three years at their new stadium.

Table 3 does just that for the last ten stadiums built with three years of "old stadium" and "new stadium" results to go off of (therefore excluding the new stadiums built in Dallas and New York, as well as the expansion Houston stadium), and it certainly doesn't look like those teams lost anything by moving to their new stadiums. The only team that exhibited a noticeable decline was Arizona. Although the book on Philadelphia has long been that the move away from Veterans Stadium cost them home field advantage, they actually enjoyed a far greater home field advantage during their first three years at Lincoln Financial Field than they did during the dying days of the Vet.

It's true that the Eagles fielded a better overall team at the Linc, which could artificially make their home numbers look better, but take a look at how the move by the Patriots played out. The 2002-04 Patriots were superior to the 1999-2001 teams, but that improved team played better than the old unit on the road, too. As a result, their home field advantage stayed just about identical.

In the near future, we hope to duplicate this study using DVOA, but we expect to get similar results.

Bill Barnwell

Table 3: New Stadium Effects, 2000-2008

Team	Year Into New Stadium	H/A Pt Difference, 3Yrs Before	H/A Pt Difference, 3Yrs After	Difference
IND	2008	3.6	3.5	-0.1
ARI	2006	13.6	9.6	-3.9
PHI	2003	-1.8	2.6	4.4
DET	2002	3.3	6.3	3.0
SEA	2002	4.3	6.3	2.0
NE	2002	3.3	3.2	-0.1
DET	2002	3.3	6.3	3.0
PIT	2001	-1.2	5.8	7.0
DEN	2001	4.2	7.4	3.2
CIN	2000	4.2	3.3	-1.0

Rookie Projections

Over the years, Football Outsiders has developed four different methods for forecasting the NFL success of highly-drafted players at various positions. Here is a rundown of those four methods and what they say about the NFL's Class of 2011.

Quarterbacks: Lewin Career Forecast

The Lewin Career Forecast, named after original designer David Lewin, was first introduced in *Pro Football Prospectus 2006*. Originally, the basic idea behind the LCF was that we could accurately project the NFL success of quarterbacks chosen in the first two rounds of the draft using just two stats from their college careers: a) completion percentage and b) games started.

There have been some questions about the Lewin Career Forecast in recent years because it hasn't had a good track record since 2006. A number of quarterbacks with strong college completion percentages and lots of experience have been drafted high and then flopped in the NFL, including Matt Leinart, Brady Quinn, Brian Brohm, and John Beck. Nonetheless, even if we go all the way back to 1990, college games started are still the most important factor in projecting the NFL performance of a high draft pick at the quarterback position. It will take another couple years of similar busts before we can say for sure that this is no longer the case.

However, recent quarterback performances have suggested that the importance of career completion percentage was overstated in the original LCF. Therefore, in April on our website we introduced Lewin Career Forecast 2.0[1]. The new version of LCF makes the variable for completion rate into a logarithmic variable. Now there is very little difference between a quarterback who completes 62 percent of passes and one who completes 66 percent of passes, but as completion percentage goes down, the penalty for inaccuracy gets larger.

The new LCF also adds a few new variables. Most important is a variable that tracks when quarterbacks decline in their senior year. There is also a variable that penalizes quarterbacks from non-BCS conferences (FBS only), and variables that look at how often a quarterback scrambles or gets sacked.

The independent variable projected by LCF v2.0 is the quarterback's total DYAR in his third, fourth, and fifth NFL seasons. Here are the projections for quarterbacks chosen in the first three rounds of the 2011 draft:

Table 1: LCF QB Projections

Name	Team	Rnd	Pick	Projection
Andy Dalton	CIN	2	35	1,616 DYAR
Colin Kaepernick	SF	2	36	1,187 DYAR
Blaine Gabbert	JAC	1	10	656 DYAR
Jake Locker	TEN	1	8	569 DYAR
Ryan Mallett	NE	3	74	471 DYAR
Christian Ponder	MIN	1	12	413 DYAR
Cam Newton	CAR	1	1	175 DYAR

Some of the specific reasons for these forecasts are discussed in their respective player comments elsewhere in the book.

Running Backs: Speed Score

Speed Score was created by Bill Barnwell and introduced in *Pro Football Prospectus 2008*. The basic theory is simple: Not all 40-yard dash times are created equal. A fast time means more from a bigger running back, and the range of 40 times for backs is so small that even a miniscule difference can be meaningful. The formula for Speed Score is:

$$(Weight \times 200) / 40 \text{ time } ^4$$

This year saw a surprisingly large disconnect between Speed Score and the actual draft order of running backs. Mark Ingram has the lowest Speed Score of

---

[1]For more on the new version of LCF, see http://www.footballoutsiders.com/stat-analysis/2011/introducing-lewin-career-forecast-v20.

any running back chosen in the first round since 1999, while the player with this year's highest Speed Score wasn't even drafted. Auburn's Mario Fannin ran a 4.38 40-yard dash at 231 pounds for an all-time Speed Score record of 125.5. (The previous Speed Score record belonged to Brandon Jacobs at 123.5.) Fannin wasn't drafted, but did sign as a free agent with Denver after the lockout ended.

Here are the Speed Scores for all backs chosen in the first three rounds, as well as the top five Speed Scores for backs chosen in the final four rounds:

Table 2: Speed Score RB Projections

Name	Team	Rnd	Pick	40	Weight	Speed Score
DeMarco Murray	DAL	3	71	4.41	213	112.6
Alex Green	GB	3	96	4.53	225	106.9
Shane Vereen	NE	2	56	4.50	210	102.4
Mikel Leshoure	DET	2	57	4.59	227	102.3
Stevan Ridley	NE	3	73	4.66	225	95.4
Mark Ingram	NO	1	30	4.62	215	94.4
Ryan Williams	ARI	2	38	4.61	212	93.9
Da'Rel Scott	NYG	7	221	4.34	211	118.9
Roy Helu	WAS	4	105	4.42	219	114.8
Allen Bradford	TB	6	187	4.58	242	110.0
Jordan Todman	SD	6	183	4.40	203	108.3
Jamie Harper	TEN	4	130	4.59	233	105.0

Daniel Thomas, chosen in the second round by Miami, did not run the 40 at the combine and therefore does not have a Speed Score.

Wide Receivers: Playmaker Score

Playmaker Score was created by Vince Verhei and introduced in *Football Outsiders Almanac 2009*. The original Playmaker Score simply multiplied career yards per reception by career touchdown total. It was moderately successful at pointing out players to avoid, but didn't do a particularly good job of pointing out future stars.

This summer, an article on ESPN.com Insider introduced an updated version of Playmaker Score. This new formula is more complex and does more to account for the different offensive environments that different players perform in.

The formula begins by multiplying four factors together:
- Career receiving yards per game
- Career yards per catch
- Career touchdowns
- Team yards per attempt over career

Divide this product by team passes per game. Then divide that product by 20. Finally, multiply the result by a conference factor which adjusts for the quality of teammates, opposition, and weather:
- ACC: 2.087
- Big Ten/Notre Dame: 1.463
- SEC: 1.331
- Non-AQ: 1.088
- Big 12: .853
- Pac-12: .807
- Big East: .736

The resulting score gives the average number of yards the player is expected to average per season during his NFL career. More than any other of our formulas for projecting college prospects, the new Playmaker Score works for players from the first round all the way to the seventh.

Table 3: Playmaker Score Results, 2004-08

Playmaker Score	WRs qualifying	Avg Yds/Season
600+	5	745
500-599	8	634
400-499	9	368
300-399	7	162
200-299	30	247
100-199	37	161
<100	36	82

Here are projections for wide receivers chosen in the first four rounds of the 2011 draft, along with one undrafted player who distinguishes himself with a high Playmaker Score (Table 4).

Cleveland's Greg Little and Green Bay's Randall Cobb are not listed because they played running back for much of their college careers. Miami's Edmond Gates and Jacksonville's Cecil Shorts are not included because they played below the Division I level.

No player chosen between the fifth and seventh rounds has a Playmaker Score higher than 250.

Edge Rushers: SackSEER

Created by Nathan Forster, SackSEER is a method introduced in *Football Outsiders Almanac 2010* which projects the NFL performance of edge rushers. That includes both 3-4 outside linebackers and 4-3 defensive ends. SackSEER applies only to those

Table 4: Playmaker WR Projections

Name	Team	Round	Pick	College	Yd/G	Yd/Rec	TD	Team Yd/At	Playmaker
A.J. Green	CIN	1	4	Georgia	82	15.8	23	8.5	592
Leonard Hankerson	WAS	3	79	Miami	60	16.1	22	7.1	509
Darvin Adams	CAR	FA	--	Auburn	73	17.2	17	7.8	435
Gregory Salas	STL	4	112	Hawaii	101	15.2	26	8.2	411
Austin Pettis	STL	3	78	Boise State	58	12.4	39	8.6	390
Titus Young	DET	2	44	Boise State	71	15.0	25	8.6	372
Torrey Smith	BAL	2	58	Maryland	58	14.6	19	6.8	368
Julio Jones	ATL	1	6	Alabama	66	14.8	15	8.1	312
Vincent Brown	SD	3	82	San Diego St.	72	14.9	23	7.2	262
Jonathan Baldwin	KC	1	26	Pittsburgh	67	18.3	16	7.4	193
Tandon Doss	BAL	4	123	Indiana	69	12.0	13	6.6	142
Jerrel Jernigan	NYG	3	83	Troy	64	11.9	18	7.0	127
Kris Durham	SEA	4	107	Georgia	35	17.3	4	8.0	45

players chosen in the first two rounds of the draft. It combines four metrics: the prospect's vertical leap, short shuttle time, per-game sack productivity in college (with certain adjustments), and missed games of NCAA eligibility[2].

Here are SackSEER projections for players drafted in the first two rounds of the 2011 draft, which SackSEER suggests was a very strong draft for edge rushers. Defensive ends drafted by 3-4 teams are not included. SRAM stands for "Sack Rate as Modified," an adjusted measure of sacks per game. Projections represent number of sacks projected through the fifth year of the player's NFL career.

Justin Houston, listed on our website as the second-highest projected edge rusher before the draft, ended up going to Kansas City in the third round. If we do use SackSEER on him, he's projected with 26.0 sacks in his first five seasons.

Table 5: SackSEER Pass Rusher Projections

Name	Team	Rnd	Pick	Vertical	Shuttle	SRAM	Missed Games	Projection
Von Miller	DEN	1	2	37.0	4.06	0.76	4	36.4 sacks
Adrian Clayborn	TB	1	20	33.0	4.13	0.37	1	24.8 sacks
Ryan Kerrigan	WAS	1	16	33.5	4.39	0.70	1	24.7 sacks
Da'Quan Bowers	TB	2	19	34.5	4.45	0.60	2	22.0 sacks
Aldon Smith	SF	1	7	34.0	4.50	0.62	3	20.0 sacks
Cameron Jordan	NO	1	24	31.0	4.37	0.37	1	16.5 sacks
Robert Quinn	STL	1	14	34.0	4.40	0.56	13	15.5 sacks
Brooks Reed	HOU	2	10	30.5	4.28	0.34	5	15.1 sacks
Jabaal Sheard	CLE	2	5	31.5	4.65	0.39	5	10.6 sacks

[1]For more on SackSEER, see http://www.footballoutsiders.com/nfl-draft/2010/introducing-sackseer or http://www.footballoutsiders.com/ramblings/2011/sackseer-lets-try-again

Top 25 Prospects

Want to be a great NFL organization? Find talent in places where other teams don't. It's one thing to find a great player in the first round of the draft, where talent is unquestioned and success is more a question of scheme and fit than anything else. When teams supplement success in the first round with great work on the final day of the draft and in rookie free agency, they create advantages up and down the roster that other teams simply can't compete with.

Take last year's Green Bay Packers. Thanks to a bevy of injuries, the Packers were forced to plug players with little or no experience into key roles during their title run. Guys like Aaron Rodgers and Charles Woodson did a lot of the heavy lifting, but the Packers got significant contributions in 2011 from a group of late-round picks, undrafted free agents, and practice squad favorites. Thanks to guys like James Starks, Andrew Quarless, Frank Zombo, and Erik Walden, the Packers didn't skip many beats when they lost prominent talent on either side of the ball.

Across from them in the Super Bowl were the Pittsburgh Steelers, who got their own set of contributions from players on the bottom of the roster. In addition to former Defensive Player of the Year James Harrison (an undrafted free agent), an almost-comical amount of injuries to their offensive line left the Steelers starting players like undrafted free agent Doug Legursky. And, of course, arguably the best Steelers player in the Super Bowl was the player who ranked number one on our Top 25 Prospects list last year: Wide receiver Mike Wallace.

Wallace's breakout 1,257-yard season wasn't the only hit on our list from last year. Running back Arian Foster (19th) led the league in rushing yards and rushing touchdowns, while Giants running back Ahmad Bradshaw (14th) took over as a starter and exceeded 1,200 yards. On the other side of the ball, Panthers defensive end Charles Johnson (23rd) quietly produced 11.5 sacks in a year where he beat the guy whose job he inherited — Julius Peppers — by 3.5 sacks. Elsewhere, guys like Jonathan Goff (seventh) and Matt Shaughnessy (12th) emerged as valuable contributors to impressive defenses.

Of course, nobody's perfect. The long-awaited breakout season from Jacob Ford (second) never came, with Jason Babin taking his job and picking up 12.5 sacks. At least Ford made his team; cornerback Justin Tryon (fifth) was traded away for a seventh-round pick, and tight end Marquez Branson (24th) was cut by the lowly Broncos.

For the uninitiated, this list is not like the prospect lists you read about in the world of baseball. Because the top prospects in college football are stars on national television before they get taken in the first round of the NFL, there's not much utility in listing them here. Instead, we use a combination of statistics, measurables, context, and expected role to compile a list of under-the-radar players whom we expect to make an impact in the NFL, both in 2011 and beyond. To focus on these players, we limit the pool to guys who fit the following criteria:

• Drafted in the third round or later, or signed as a college free agent
• Entered the NFL between 2008 and 2010
• Fewer than five career games started
• Still on their initial contract

This year's top prospect is a player who made it onto our list last year and did just about nothing during the first half of the season. In the second half, though, an injury and a poorly-timed comment to the press by the starter ahead of him opened up his opportunity, and our number-one prospect emerged as a potentially devastating talent for his team. After what we've seen over the past two years from both Wallace and 2009 number-one prospect Miles Austin, he has a lot to live up to.

1. Jared Cook, TE, Titans

Cook is, as we noted last year, a Jermichael Finley clone in terms of size and pedigree, with one pound and two slots in the draft separating them as far as measurables. The scary thing is that Cook is a significantly better athlete than Finley, putting up a 4.49 40-yard dash and 41-inch vertical leap at the Scouting Combine, one year after Finley put up a 4.82 and had a 27.5-inch vertical. Like Finley, Cook was basically a shiny bauble with little use until his second pro season, although Finley broke out in training camp, while Cook was barely on the field before Week 11. Once Cook got his chance, though, he delivered. Over the final seven games of the year, Cook produced 26 catches for 303 yards and his first NFL touchdown, including a 96-yard game against the Chiefs in Week 16. And this was with Kerry Collins and Rusty Smith at quarterback. With a full year as the starter ahead of him in 2011, Cook should be a occasionally-dominant receiver as the number-two option in Tennessee's passing offense, running past safeties worried about Chris Johnson. He could become a regular Pro Bowler as early as this season.

2. Morgan Burnett, S, Packers

The Packers traded up to grab Burnett in the third round of last year's draft, and when starter Atari Bigby was placed on the Physically Unable to Perform list to start the season, Burnett went straight into the starting lineup. He impressed before tearing his ACL in Week 4, which ended his season. He'll be healthy for the beginning of the 2011 season, and as a solid all-around player with great athleticism, he's going to get better with experience. With Bigby not tendered a contract and the best secondary in the league around him, Burnett should end up maturing into the next great Packers defensive back.

3. Wallace Gilberry, DE, Chiefs

If you're looking for a good rule of thumb when it comes to evaluating the potential impact of young defensive linemen, there's one simple rule: Sacks trump everything. If you can get to the passer as a young player, you will have a job in the NFL. It's that easy. And although Gilberry was an undrafted free agent who the Giants signed and quickly released, he's exhibited an ability to make plays as a pass rusher since the Chiefs signed him. After a 4.5-sack season in 2009, Gilberry contributed seven sacks, eight quarterback hits, and 10 hurries for the Kansas City defense in 2010. In each category, that was behind only Tamba Hali for the team lead, despite the fact that Gilberry started just two games. The only issue for Gilberry is opportunity: At defensive end, he's playing behind two top-five picks in Glenn Dorsey and Tyson Jackson, and he's probably too big to play outside linebacker in the 3-4. He could be a double-digit sack guy if he moves to a team that plays a 4-3, which could happen in 2012.

4. Jamar Chaney, LB, Eagles

Since Andy Reid took over as the main man in Philadelphia before the 1999 season, the Eagles have struggled to find useful, consistent linebackers to play in their famously aggressive defense. High draft picks like Matt McCoy and veteran acquisitions like Ernie Sims seem to fail with equal aplomb. Their new hope is Chaney, a seventh-round pick in the 2010 draft who took over at middle linebacker after Stewart Bradley dislocated his elbow. By the end of the season, the Eagles were talking about moving Bradley to the strong side and leaving Chaney in as an every-down linebacker; Bradley ended up signing elsewhere in the offseason. Truthfully, it's a mystery how Chaney fell to the seventh round at all. An undersized, speedy linebacker who's conversant with pass defense is something every team needs in a shotgun-friendly league. Although Philly will continue to rotate their other linebackers, expect Chaney to be a mainstay for the Eagles going forward.

5. Danny Woodhead, RB, Patriots

Although he was bound to receive umpteen amounts of hype upon succeeding as a member of the league's best offense, Woodhead deserves to be noted as a wildly efficient player in an incredibly cheap backfield. Woodhead was second amongst running backs in receiving DVOA, and with three additional carries, he would have led qualifying backs in rushing DVOA. The easy comp is Kevin Faulk, but Faulk was never this effective. A better statistical comp is Charlie Garner, whose career wouldn't be a bad return for a guy the Patriots picked up for nothing.

6. Geno Atkins, DT, Bengals

At first glance, Atkins doesn't look like a great prospect; he had three sacks in a full season while playing for a mediocre defense. With Atkins, though, it's the more subtle stuff that suggests he has serious potential. For one, Atkins is a defensive tackle. Getting even three sacks as a rookie is a positive sign. There's also a lot bubbling under the surface suggesting that his sack rate could rise, too. While pre-season stats aren't consistently meaningful, he produced 4.5 sacks in five games. And during the regular season, Atkins led the team in our advanced pass rush metrics by a good amount. He had nine quarterback hits, four more than any other Bengals defender, while his 17.5 hurries paced the rest of the lineup by five. A great pass-rusher with the size to play inside in the 4-3 is rare indeed, but it looks like the Bengals have just that in Atkins.

7. Shonn Greene, RB, Jets

Poised to take over as the lead back on a run-happy team after a great 2009 playoff run, Greene struggled to hold onto the ball in Week 1 (admittedly against the Ravens) and spent the rest of the year in a timeshare with LaDainian Tomlinson. Nobody doubts Greene's ability to run effectively with the ball in his hands, but with a quarterback as limited as Mark Sanchez, the running back's role as a pass blocker and dumpoff receiver is essential. Young backs often struggle with those dark arts before improving with time, so don't fret: Greene's still on pace to be a very good running back.

8. Tashard Choice, RB, Cowboys

On the other hand, Choice is already fully-formed as a receiver and pass blocker. Unfortunately, he got lost in the shuffle in 2010 behind Marion Barber and Felix Jones, virtually disappearing from the lineup before returning in Week 13 with a 100-yard game against the Colts. You may have noticed his absence when fullback Chris Gronkowski missed the block that led to Tony Romo's season-ending collarbone fracture. With Romo's return, expect Jason Garrett to place a premium on keeping his quarterback healthy, which could mean more time for Choice in the lineup. Last year's 3.7 yards per carry average is really the product of small sample size; Choice's abilities are better represented by his 4.8 yards per carry career average.

9. Lardarius Webb, CB, Ravens

While Webb was expected to miss time recovering from a torn ACL, he made it back to the lineup in Week 2 and played the rest of the way as a nickel cornerback. Unfortunately, he was far from 100 percent, and it showed. Teams picked on him as the weak link in an already-limited Ravens secondary, and while he responded with ten passes defensed, he was also in coverage on eight plays that produced 20 yards or more. Another year removed from surgery, he should blossom into a starting-caliber cornerback on one of the league's best defenses.

10. Jordan Shipley, WR, Bengals

85 players qualified for the leaderboard in our receiver statistics by being targeted on 50 passes. Of those 85 players, only one — Austin Collie — had a catch rate greater than the 70 percent figure put up by Jordan Shipley last year. His catch rate was actually slightly ahead of the other (white) slot receivers he's often compared to, Wes Welker and Danny Amendola. He even posted the best DVOA of the three, along with the only positive receiving DVOA by any qualifying Bengals receiver. Shipley isn't going to be a star, but he's going to be a contributor on the next effective Bengals offense.

11. Matt Flynn, QB, Packers

Sure, he got to play with some of the best offensive talent in football during that narrow loss to the Patriots, but remember: He was replacing Aaron Rodgers. A guy who could do a reasonable impression of Aaron Rodgers in most weeks would be worth a lot of money, and while he struggled in relief of Rodgers against the Lions, Flynn showed more poise than anyone could have expected against the Patriots before that ugly final drive. Even if he doesn't take another snap for the Packers, he'll end up competing for a starting job somewhere down the line.

12. Derek Hardman, OL, Buccaneers

It's hard enough to be a rookie in the NFL. For Derek Hardman, it was harder than most. After being cut in training camp and falling to the practice squad, he was added to the active roster during the season once injuries started to beset the Bucs. After guard Davin Joseph went down with a foot injury, Hardman was placed into the lineup to replace him. One problem: As a college tackle, he had never played guard before. Hardman ended up doing a fine job in Joseph's stead, and he'll be in the mix for a starting job somewhere along the line next season.

13. Andre Roberts, WR, Cardinals

The Cardinals coaching staff became more and more enamored with this third-round pick as the season went on; by the final two weeks, he was basically playing ahead of starter Steve Breaston. With Breaston gone, Roberts' hands, athleticism, and health should give him the No. 2 receiver job ahead of Early Doucet. His poor rookie DVOA of -39.7% can be blamed in large part on last year's awful quarterback situation. Ten of the 25 incomplete passes to Roberts were marked by our game charters as "overthrown," including a quick hitch pass behind the line of scrimmage.

14. Emmanuel Sanders, WR, Steelers

Sanders inherited the slot receiver role vacated by Mike Wallace before the season, impressed coaches with his blocking ability during camp, and then emerged as a valuable part of the team's three-wide-out sets during the second half of the season. 45 of his 50 targets came after Week 9, and he had just one target all year in a two-wideout set. He didn't show the promise Wallace did as a rookie, but Sanders is on pace to become the number-two wideout behind him once Hines Ward bows out.

15. James Starks, RB, Packers

A Speed Score favorite (106.3) taken in the sixth round of the 2010 draft, Starks spent most of the year as a rumor tossed around by Packers fans desirous of an effective replacement to the injured Ryan Grant. And while his eventual run as the starter during Week 17 and the playoffs was a success owing partly to huge carry totals and middling run defenses, he did show the potential to be an eventual starter at the pro level. In 2011, he should be part of a one-two combi-nation with Ryan Grant.

16. Erik Walden, LB, Packers

Finishing up our Super Bowl run is a player who was injured and didn't actually appear in the big game. Walden wasn't even the first afterthought to show up at linebacker for the Packers; Frank Zombo won a roster spot in training camp and then became a starter, only to go down with a knee injury in Week 14 that kept him out until the Super Bowl. That gave Walden, a veteran of four NFL teams in two years, a spot in the starting lineup. All Walden did was win Defensive Player of the Week in the season-ending win over the Bears, thanks to a three-sack perfor-mance. He served as an effective spy in the Packers' nickel package, and if he doesn't make the team this year, he'll bounce back somewhere as a linebacker specializing in pass defense.

17. Chris Ivory, RB, Saints

After injuries to Pierre Thomas and Reggie Bush, the Saints were forced to hand over the reins of their running game to Ivory, an undrafted free agent out of Tiffin. Ivory promptly produced a 59 percent Suc-cess Rate, the best of any back in football, on his 137 carries. Although he offered nothing as a receiver and wasn't a great blocker, his contributions as a runner for the league minimum were nothing short of extraordinary. He needs to improve on the small stuff and work on holding onto the ball (35 touches per fumble just won't cut it), but he should be part of an above-average rotation at halfback starting now. And the upside is that he turns into Arian Foster.

18. Desmond Bryant, DT, Raiders

A Harvard graduate playing for the Raiders is, on its face, comical. Getting past the fish-out-of-water jokes might be tough, but Bryant has emerged as a valuable rotation player on one of the league's best defensive lines. 21 tackles don't seem all that impressive, but Bryant showed an impressive ability to penetrate and make plays in the backfield, including six Defeats and 2.5 sacks.

19. Ed Dickson, TE, Ravens

With Todd Heap's career as a starter winding down, the Ravens drafted Dickson and Dennis Pitta in 2010, hoping that one of them would develop into Heap's replacement. So far, Dickson looks like the better of the two, having stepped into the starting role while Heap missed time with an ankle injury at the end of the season. As a former Oregon tight end, he's natu-rally a speedy tight end with good hands who remains a project as a blocker. Expect his role in the passing game to increase in 2011, with the hopes that he'll take over as the starter in 2012.

20. Doug Legursky, OL, Steelers

One of the many Steelers reserves to step in on the offensive line during the regular season, Legursky was thrust into the national spotlight as the replace-ment for the injured Maurkice Pouncey in Super Bowl XLV. Despite expectations that he would struggle mightily against a frequently-dominant Packers front three, Legursky had a solid day in the biggest game of his career. At the very least, he's a versatile reserve with steel nerves. He could compete for a starting spot at guard in training camp this season.

21. Blair White, WR, Colts

Let's make this clear: White isn't a great player. He's a decent wide receiver with good size that happens to be in the best offense for a player with his skill set. And while he's currently fifth on the depth chart at wideout, he's behind two players (Austin Collie and Anthony Gonzalez) with severe injury issues, and a third guy (Pierre Garcon) who can be wildly inconsistent from play-to-play. In other words, if everything goes right, he could carve out a very meaningful role in one of the league's best passing attacks. And the odds of things going right are higher than they are for any other fifth wideout in football.

22. Donald Butler, LB, Chargers

Butler is the only player on this list yet to take an NFL snap, owing to a torn Achilles tendon that ended his rookie year before it started. Heading into the year, the Chargers' third-round pick was talked about as a potential starter at inside linebacker, which has been a troublesome position for the Chargers to fill over the past few seasons. The team could use his David Harris-style play against the run, and while the Achilles tear might slow him down at the beginning of the season, don't be surprised if he's starting by the end of the year.

23. Daniel Te'o-Nesheim, DE, Eagles

A SackSEER favorite, Te'o-Nesheim spent most of his rookie year on special teams. In their meaningless Week 17 game, though, the Eagles gave him a start at defensive end and let him just rush Stephen McGee to his heart's content. He finished the game with a sack and a quarterback hurry while holding up effectively against the run. He'll be in the rotation at defensive end this year for legendary defensive line coach Jim Washburn. The hope is that Washburn can do for Te'o-Nesheim what he did for another high-motor defensive end: Kyle Vanden Bosch.

24. Stevenson Sylvester, LB, Steelers

The Pittsburgh Steelers don't generally put rookies right into the lineup, at least on defense. They give players one or two years on special teams or in part-time roles while they can learn how the system works. Despite playing mostly special teams last year, this 2010 fifth-round pick from Utah has been set up as the heir apparent to 36-year-old inside linebacker James Farrior. He's an aggressive, high-motor player, although he dropped in the draft because scouts felt he was somewhat undersized (6-foot-2, 231 pounds is not much different from Lawrence Timmons). Pittsburgh linebackers coach Keith Butler has praised Sylvester's feel for blitzes, an important part of playing inside linebacker in Dick LeBeau's defense.

25. David Nelson, WR, Bills

Our last cut in turning the Top 26 into a Top 25 last year was Stevie Johnson of the Bills; while Johnson was best known for his drop against the Steelers, he had quite the breakout season. We're not going to make the same mistake twice. While the Bills aren't exactly known for having an explosive passing game, the trade of Lee Evans makes Nelson a likely starter. He finished the year with touchdowns in three straight games before suffering a season-ending rib injury against the Patriots.

Honorable Mention

Danario Alexander, WR, Rams
Kevin Barnes, CB, Redskins
Kam Chancellor, S, Seahawks
Keenan Clayton, LB, Eagles
Kaluka Maiava, LB, Browns
Evan Moore, TE, Browns
Ropati Pitoitua, DE, Jets
Myron Pryor, DT, Patriots
Andrew Quarless, TE, Packers
Andy Studebaker, LB, Chiefs

by Bill Barnwell and Aaron Schatz

Fantasy Appendix

Here are the top 240 players according to the KU-BIAK projection system, ranked by projected fantasy value (FANT) in 2011. We've used the following generic scoring system:

- 1 point for each 10 yards rushing, 10 yards receiving, or 20 yards passing
- 6 points for each rushing or receiving TD, 4 points for each passing TD
- -2 points for each interception or fumble lost
- 1 point for each extra point, 3 points for each field goal
- Team defense: 2 points for a fumble recovery, interception, or safety, 1 point for a sack, and 6 points for a touchdown.

These totals are then adjusted based on each player's listed Risk for 2011:

- Green: Standard risk, no change
- Yellow: Higher than normal risk, value dropped by 5 percent
- Red: Highest risk, value dropped by 10 percent
- Blue: Significantly lower than normal risk, value increased by 5 percent

Note that fantasy totals may not exactly equal these calculations, because each touchdown projection is not necessarily a round number. (For example, a quarterback listed with 2 rushing touchdowns may actually be projected with 2.4 rushing touchdowns, which will add 14 fantasy points to the player's total rather than 12.) Fantasy value does not include adjustments for week-to-week consistency.

Players are ranked in order based on marginal value of each player, the idea that you draft based on how many more points a player will score compared to the worst starting player at that position, not how many points a player scores overall. The ranks in this table are based on a 12-team league that starts 1 QB, 2 RB, 2 WR, 1 FLEX (RB/WR), 1 TE, 1 K, and 1 DEF. The rankings reduce the value of kickers and defenses to reflect the general drafting habits of fantasy football players. We urge you to draft using common sense, not a strict reading of these rankings.

A customizable spreadsheet featuring these projections is also available at FootballOutsiders.com for a $20 fee. This spreadsheet is updated based on injuries and changing forecasts of playing time during the preseason, and also has a version which includes individual defensive players.

Rk	Player	Team	Bye	Pos	PaYd	PaTD	INT	Ru	RuYd	RuTD	Rec	RcYd	RcTD	FL	XP	FG	Fant	Risk
1	Arian Foster	HOU	11	RB	0	0	0	310	1453	12	53	504	3	4	0	0	266	Yellow
2	Adrian Peterson	MIN	9	RB	0	0	0	340	1601	12	27	193	1	6	0	0	248	Green
3	Ray Rice	BAL	5	RB	0	0	0	313	1409	10	60	532	2	4	0	0	247	Yellow
4	LeSean McCoy	PHI	7	RB	0	0	0	209	1100	8	75	655	3	1	0	0	227	Yellow
5	Rashard Mendenhall	PIT	11	RB	0	0	0	327	1374	12	31	286	1	3	0	0	224	Yellow
6	Chris Johnson	TEN	6	RB	0	0	0	332	1398	10	46	387	1	5	0	0	220	Yellow
7	Maurice Jones-Drew	JAC	9	RB	0	0	0	302	1413	12	35	251	1	3	0	0	217	Red
8	Andre Johnson	HOU	11	WR	0	0	0	0	0	0	104	1473	11	1	0	0	214	Green
9	Steven Jackson	STL	5	RB	0	0	0	289	1155	6	59	560	1	2	0	0	211	Green
10	Peyton Hillis	CLE	5	RB	0	0	0	257	1038	11	53	539	1	4	0	0	204	Red
11	Jamaal Charles	KC	6	RB	0	0	0	255	1290	7	39	368	1	4	0	0	199	Yellow
12	Michael Turner	ATL	8	RB	0	0	0	316	1413	12	14	85	0	3	0	0	198	Red
13	Matt Forte	CHI	8	RB	0	0	0	225	1048	7	51	434	2	2	0	0	196	Green
14	Roddy White	ATL	8	WR	0	0	0	2	8	0	96	1372	10	1	0	0	194	Green

Rk	Player	Team	Bye	Pos	PaYd	PaTD	INT	Ru	RuYd	RuTD	Rec	RcYd	RcTD	FL	XP	FG	Fant	Risk
15	Michael Vick	PHI	7	QB	3763	26	11	125	519	8	0	0	0	14	0	0	337	Yellow
16	Aaron Rodgers	GB	8	QB	4207	31	14	75	331	4	0	0	0	11	0	0	334	Yellow
17	Cedric Benson	CIN	7	RB	0	0	0	312	1188	8	27	217	1	4	0	0	186	Green
18	Shonn Greene	NYJ	8	RB	0	0	0	287	1185	8	23	178	1	3	0	0	186	Green
19	Philip Rivers	SD	6	QB	4430	34	12	23	9	1	0	0	0	4	0	0	333	Green
20	Ryan Mathews	SD	6	RB	0	0	0	217	920	8	38	376	1	5	0	0	182	Green
21	Frank Gore	SF	7	RB	0	0	0	273	1240	8	46	332	1	3	0	0	181	Red
22	Larry Fitzgerald	ARI	6	WR	0	0	0	0	0	0	90	1218	10	1	0	0	180	Green
23	LeGarrette Blount	TB	8	RB	0	0	0	262	1228	9	17	130	0	4	0	0	176	Yellow
24	Darren McFadden	OAK	8	RB	0	0	0	193	832	5	54	520	2	4	0	0	175	Green
25	Greg Jennings	GB	8	WR	0	0	0	2	11	0	80	1256	9	1	0	0	170	Yellow
26	Ahmad Bradshaw	NYG	7	RB	0	0	0	246	1046	4	46	424	2	4	0	0	167	Yellow
27	Drew Brees	NO	11	QB	4390	34	13	26	22	1	0	0	0	4	0	0	314	Yellow
28	Miles Austin	DAL	5	WR	0	0	0	5	28	0	81	1183	9	1	0	0	162	Yellow
29	Reggie Wayne	IND	11	WR	0	0	0	0	0	0	95	1133	8	1	0	0	160	Green
30	Calvin Johnson	DET	9	WR	0	0	0	3	15	0	75	1097	8	1	0	0	156	Green
31	Ben Roethlisberger	PIT	11	QB	3865	28	12	42	121	3	0	0	0	8	0	0	303	Green
32	Daniel Thomas	MIA	5	RB	0	0	0	241	922	6	27	211	1	3	0	0	155	Yellow
33	Hakeem Nicks	NYG	7	WR	0	0	0	2	10	0	83	1104	9	1	0	0	154	Yellow
34	Mike Wallace	PIT	11	WR	0	0	0	4	17	0	68	1213	8	1	0	0	153	Red
35	Tom Brady	NE	7	QB	4033	31	10	16	20	1	0	0	0	9	0	0	300	Red
36	Brandon Lloyd	DEN	6	WR	0	0	0	2	12	0	75	1172	8	1	0	0	149	Green
37	Santonio Holmes	NYJ	8	WR	0	0	0	3	13	0	72	1037	8	1	0	0	149	Green
38	Dwayne Bowe	KC	6	WR	0	0	0	2	14	0	70	1021	8	1	0	0	149	Green
39	Joseph Addai	IND	11	RB	0	0	0	203	777	4	47	336	3	2	0	0	149	Green
40	Felix Jones	DAL	5	RB	0	0	0	187	782	6	33	315	1	2	0	0	149	Yellow
41	Steve Johnson	BUF	7	WR	0	0	0	3	16	0	86	1156	7	1	0	0	148	Yellow
42	Mike Williams	TB	8	WR	0	0	0	0	0	0	81	1054	8	1	0	0	147	Yellow
43	Marques Colston	NO	11	WR	0	0	0	0	0	0	81	1054	8	1	0	0	147	Green
44	Matt Ryan	ATL	8	QB	4084	26	15	62	61	2	0	0	0	5	0	0	293	Red
45	BenJarvus Green-Ellis	NE	7	RB	0	0	0	168	766	10	22	197	2	1	0	0	150	Yellow
46	Antonio Gates	SD	6	TE	0	0	0	0	0	0	77	1004	10	1	0	0	150	Red
47	Vincent Jackson	SD	6	WR	0	0	0	2	15	0	64	1059	9	0	0	0	143	Red
48	Jahvid Best	DET	9	RB	0	0	0	176	756	4	50	420	1	2	0	0	143	Green
49	Anquan Boldin	BAL	5	WR	0	0	0	0	0	0	77	999	7	1	0	0	141	Green
50	Tony Romo	DAL	5	QB	4194	26	13	28	29	1	0	0	0	7	0	0	287	Green
51	Wes Welker	NE	7	WR	0	0	0	0	0	0	88	994	7	1	0	0	139	Green
52	Brandon Jacobs	NYG	7	RB	0	0	0	157	657	11	12	87	1	2	0	0	137	Green
53	Mark Ingram	NO	11	RB	0	0	0	192	804	8	27	151	1	3	0	0	136	Yellow
54	Percy Harvin	MIN	9	WR	0	0	0	9	41	0	79	965	5	1	0	0	132	Green
55	Peyton Manning	IND	11	QB	4354	31	14	27	14	0	0	0	0	6	0	0	279	Red
56	Josh Freeman	TB	8	QB	3566	22	10	84	346	1	0	0	0	9	0	0	278	Green
57	Brandon Marshall	MIA	5	WR	0	0	0	2	18	0	78	908	7	1	0	0	130	Green
58	Mario Manningham	NYG	7	WR	0	0	0	2	11	0	63	912	6	0	0	0	127	Green
59	Knowshon Moreno	DEN	6	RB	0	0	0	176	778	5	25	198	0	3	0	0	126	Green
60	Mike Tolbert	SD	6	RB	0	0	0	159	716	6	26	277	1	5	0	0	125	Yellow
61	A.J. Green	CIN	7	WR	0	0	0	2	11	0	62	955	7	0	0	0	123	Red
62	DeSean Jackson	PHI	7	WR	0	0	0	7	46	0	57	953	6	0	0	0	123	Red

Rk	Player	Team	Bye	Pos	PaYd	PaTD	INT	Ru	RuYd	RuTD	Rec	RcYd	RcTD	FL	XP	FG	Fant	Risk
63	Matt Schaub	HOU	11	QB	3977	27	12	38	11	1	0	0	0	6	0	0	269	Yellow
64	Fred Jackson	BUF	7	RB	0	0	0	187	652	3	45	349	1	4	0	0	121	Green
65	Roy Williams	CHI	8	WR	0	0	0	0	0	0	62	887	8	0	0	0	120	Red
66	Jonathan Stewart	CAR	9	RB	0	0	0	198	961	3	11	58	0	2	0	0	120	Green
67	Dez Bryant	DAL	5	WR	0	0	0	2	10	0	56	810	6	0	0	0	117	Green
68	Ryan Grant	GB	8	RB	0	0	0	194	864	4	32	177	0	3	0	0	117	Yellow
69	Vernon Davis	SF	7	TE	0	0	0	0	0	0	69	855	6	1	0	0	123	Green
70	Santana Moss	WAS	5	WR	0	0	0	0	0	0	71	868	5	1	0	0	115	Green
71	Kenny Britt	TEN	6	WR	0	0	0	2	9	0	59	829	6	0	0	0	115	Green
72	Eli Manning	NYG	7	QB	3797	27	14	26	30	0	0	0	0	11	0	0	262	Green
73	Sidney Rice	SEA	6	WR	0	0	0	2	11	0	56	884	6	0	0	0	114	Red
74	DeAngelo Williams	CAR	9	RB	0	0	0	212	1033	3	24	132	0	7	0	0	114	Red
75	Chad Ochocinco	NE	7	WR	0	0	0	0	0	0	63	804	6	0	0	0	111	Yellow
76	Dallas Clark	IND	11	TE	0	0	0	0	0	0	65	835	8	1	0	0	117	Red
77	Reggie Bush	MIA	5	RB	0	0	0	108	503	4	53	382	1	4	0	0	110	Yellow
78	Tim Hightower	WAS	5	RB	0	0	0	203	862	4	32	192	0	6	0	0	110	Red
79	Jason Witten	DAL	5	TE	0	0	0	0	0	0	87	959	5	1	0	0	116	Yellow
80	Mike Thomas	JAC	9	WR	0	0	0	8	40	0	78	881	3	1	0	0	109	Green
81	LaDainian Tomlinson	NYJ	8	RB	0	0	0	126	549	3	43	326	1	1	0	0	109	Green
82	Steve Smith	CAR	9	WR	0	0	0	0	0	0	64	914	5	0	0	0	108	Red
83	Beanie Wells	ARI	6	RB	0	0	0	223	906	4	20	110	0	4	0	0	108	Red
84	Willis McGahee	DEN	6	RB	0	0	0	143	594	5	22	220	1	6	0	0	106	Yellow
85	Julio Jones	ATL	8	WR	0	0	0	5	23	0	57	792	6	0	0	0	105	Red
86	Justin Forsett	SEA	6	RB	0	0	0	111	497	0	59	529	1	2	0	0	103	Yellow
87	Joe Flacco	BAL	5	QB	3749	22	14	43	44	2	0	0	0	10	0	0	250	Green
88	Pierre Garcon	IND	11	WR	0	0	0	3	12	0	56	712	5	0	0	0	102	Green
89	Jeremy Maclin	PHI	7	WR	0	0	0	3	17	0	57	783	6	0	0	0	102	Green
90	Michael Crabtree	SF	7	WR	0	0	0	0	0	0	49	683	6	0	0	0	102	Red
91	Jermichael Finley	GB	8	TE	0	0	0	0	0	0	60	782	7	0	0	0	102	Green
92	Andre Roberts	ARI	6	WR	0	0	0	2	7	0	58	847	5	0	0	0	100	Red
93	Lance Moore	NO	11	WR	0	0	0	2	12	0	56	750	4	0	0	0	100	Green
94	Thomas Jones	KC	6	RB	0	0	0	151	543	7	9	68	0	2	0	0	100	Green
95	Jacoby Ford	OAK	8	WR	0	0	0	9	45	0	46	764	5	0	0	0	97	Red
96	Emmanuel Sanders	PIT	11	WR	0	0	0	0	0	0	46	673	5	0	0	0	96	Green
97	Davone Bess	MIA	5	WR	0	0	0	2	16	0	70	763	3	1	0	0	96	Green
98	Michael Bush	OAK	8	RB	0	0	0	139	576	4	25	178	0	4	0	0	96	Green
99	Matt Bryant	ATL	8	K	0	0	0	0	0	0	0	0	0	0	43	30	123	Yellow
100	Bill Cundiff	BAL	5	K	0	0	0	0	0	0	0	0	0	0	41	28	123	Green
101	Bears D	CHI	8	D	0	0	0	0	0	0	0	0	0	0	0	0	110	Red
102	Malcom Floyd	SD	6	WR	0	0	0	0	0	0	42	708	5	0	0	0	95	Yellow
103	Mike Sims-Walker	STL	5	WR	0	0	0	2	8	0	56	715	6	0	0	0	95	Red
104	Darren Sproles	NO	11	RB	0	0	0	40	196	1	62	594	2	2	0	0	95	Yellow
105	Colt McCoy	CLE	5	QB	3510	22	16	60	265	2	0	0	0	14	0	0	242	Yellow
106	Packers D	GB	8	D	0	0	0	0	0	0	0	0	0	0	0	0	109	Green
107	Lee Evans	BAL	5	WR	0	0	0	0	0	0	52	780	5	0	0	0	94	Red
108	Eagles D	PHI	7	D	0	0	0	0	0	0	0	0	0	0	0	0	108	Yellow
109	Owen Daniels	HOU	11	TE	0	0	0	0	0	0	61	755	5	0	0	0	99	Yellow
110	Hines Ward	PIT	11	WR	0	0	0	0	0	0	46	614	5	0	0	0	92	Green

Rk	Player	Team	Bye	Pos	PaYd	PaTD	INT	Ru	RuYd	RuTD	Rec	RcYd	RcTD	FL	XP	FG	Fant	Risk
111	Steelers D	PIT	11	D	0	0	0	0	0	0	0	0	0	0	0	0	106	Yellow
112	Braylon Edwards	SF	7	WR	0	0	0	0	0	0	49	746	5	0	0	0	91	Red
113	Cam Newton	CAR	9	QB	2945	14	16	115	575	5	0	0	0	8	0	0	238	Yellow
114	Johnny Knox	CHI	8	WR	0	0	0	2	9	0	49	638	4	1	0	0	90	Green
115	Shaun Suisham	PIT	11	K	0	0	0	0	0	0	0	0	0	0	53	23	117	Green
116	Jets D	NYJ	8	D	0	0	0	0	0	0	0	0	0	0	0	0	104	Yellow
117	Tony Gonzalez	ATL	8	TE	0	0	0	0	0	0	67	665	5	1	0	0	96	Green
118	Eddie Royal	DEN	6	WR	0	0	0	4	16	0	61	671	4	0	0	0	89	Yellow
119	Bernard Berrian	MIN	9	WR	0	0	0	0	0	0	56	762	4	0	0	0	89	Red
120	Stephen Gostkowski	NE	7	K	0	0	0	0	0	0	0	0	0	0	53	23	115	Green
121	Ryan Longwell	MIN	9	K	0	0	0	0	0	0	0	0	0	0	37	27	115	Green
122	Adam Vinatieri	IND	11	K	0	0	0	0	0	0	0	0	0	0	42	25	115	Green
123	Garrett Hartley	NO	11	K	0	0	0	0	0	0	0	0	0	0	49	24	115	Green
124	Ravens D	BAL	5	D	0	0	0	0	0	0	0	0	0	0	0	0	102	Red
125	Dustin Keller	NYJ	8	TE	0	0	0	0	0	0	54	669	5	0	0	0	94	Green
126	Sam Bradford	STL	5	QB	3877	21	17	37	69	1	0	0	0	11	0	0	234	Yellow
127	Browns D	CLE	5	D	0	0	0	0	0	0	0	0	0	0	0	0	101	Red
128	Austin Collie	IND	11	WR	0	0	0	2	8	0	64	715	3	0	0	0	86	Yellow
129	Robert Meachem	NO	11	WR	0	0	0	3	16	0	40	572	5	0	0	0	86	Green
130	DeMarco Murray	DAL	5	RB	0	0	0	88	415	1	48	462	0	1	0	0	86	Yellow
131	Matthew Stafford	DET	9	QB	3639	17	15	60	141	3	0	0	0	6	0	0	233	Yellow
132	Chargers D	SD	6	D	0	0	0	0	0	0	0	0	0	0	0	0	100	Red
133	Chris Cooley	WAS	5	TE	0	0	0	0	0	0	68	775	4	1	0	0	92	Red
134	Arrelious Benn	TB	8	WR	0	0	0	4	19	0	45	630	5	0	0	0	85	Yellow
135	Deion Branch	NE	7	WR	0	0	0	0	0	0	56	670	4	0	0	0	85	Yellow
136	Mike Williams	SEA	6	WR	0	0	0	0	0	0	53	697	4	0	0	0	85	Yellow
137	Pierre Thomas	NO	11	RB	0	0	0	77	334	0	45	446	2	3	0	0	85	Yellow
138	Mason Crosby	GB	8	K	0	0	0	0	0	0	0	0	0	0	44	26	112	Yellow
139	Falcons D	ATL	8	D	0	0	0	0	0	0	0	0	0	0	0	0	99	Yellow
140	Giants D	NYG	7	D	0	0	0	0	0	0	0	0	0	0	0	0	99	Yellow
141	Donald Driver	GB	8	WR	0	0	0	0	0	0	49	651	4	0	0	0	84	Yellow
142	Devery Henderson	NO	11	WR	0	0	0	2	10	0	37	680	3	0	0	0	84	Green
143	David Garrard	JAC	9	QB	3104	19	14	70	253	4	0	0	0	9	0	0	231	Yellow
144	Robbie Gould	CHI	8	K	0	0	0	0	0	0	0	0	0	0	35	29	111	Yellow
145	Neil Rackers	HOU	11	K	0	0	0	0	0	0	0	0	0	0	46	25	111	Yellow
146	Cardinals D	ARI	6	D	0	0	0	0	0	0	0	0	0	0	0	0	98	Yellow
147	Zach Miller	SEA	6	TE	0	0	0	0	0	0	59	724	4	0	0	0	90	Yellow
148	Heath Miller	PIT	11	TE	0	0	0	0	0	0	43	561	6	0	0	0	90	Green
149	Marshawn Lynch	SEA	6	RB	0	0	0	164	611	3	12	90	0	2	0	0	83	Green
150	Nate Burleson	DET	9	WR	0	0	0	4	18	0	55	670	3	0	0	0	82	Green
151	Danny Woodhead	NE	7	RB	0	0	0	54	235	3	38	395	1	1	0	0	82	Green
152	Jay Feely	ARI	6	K	0	0	0	0	0	0	0	0	0	0	29	28	109	Green
153	Alex Henery	PHI	7	K	0	0	0	0	0	0	0	0	0	0	50	22	109	Green
154	Patriots D	NE	7	D	0	0	0	0	0	0	0	0	0	0	0	0	96	Yellow
155	Jimmy Graham	NO	11	TE	0	0	0	0	0	0	42	522	6	0	0	0	88	Green
156	Nate Washington	TEN	6	WR	0	0	0	2	9	0	41	605	4	0	0	0	81	Green
157	Kevin Kolb	ARI	6	QB	3786	21	17	35	22	1	0	0	0	7	0	0	228	Yellow
158	Rob Gronkowski	NE	7	TE	0	0	0	0	0	0	42	550	6	0	0	0	87	Yellow

Rk	Player	Team	Bye	Pos	PaYd	PaTD	INT	Ru	RuYd	RuTD	Rec	RcYd	RcTD	FL	XP	FG	Fant	Risk
159	Mark Sanchez	NYJ	8	QB	3281	21	16	43	108	3	0	0	0	13	0	0	227	Green
160	Ryan Fitzpatrick	BUF	7	QB	3467	18	17	46	158	2	0	0	0	11	0	0	227	Green
161	Jerome Simpson	CIN	7	WR	0	0	0	2	9	0	49	600	3	0	0	0	79	Green
162	Jordan Shipley	CIN	7	WR	0	0	0	2	8	0	55	630	3	0	0	0	79	Green
163	Jason Snelling	ATL	8	RB	0	0	0	61	231	2	41	420	2	2	0	0	79	Yellow
164	Jared Cook	TEN	6	TE	0	0	0	0	0	0	54	680	5	0	0	0	85	Red
165	Jason Hill	JAC	9	WR	0	0	0	2	12	0	51	664	3	0	0	0	78	Red
166	Earl Bennett	CHI	8	WR	0	0	0	2	7	0	56	609	3	0	0	0	78	Green
167	Jay Cutler	CHI	8	QB	3555	22	18	49	218	1	0	0	0	6	0	0	225	Red
168	Tony Moeaki	KC	6	TE	0	0	0	0	0	0	58	708	3	0	0	0	84	Yellow
169	Marcedes Lewis	JAC	9	TE	0	0	0	0	0	0	52	620	4	0	0	0	84	Green
170	Danny Amendola	STL	5	WR	0	0	0	5	17	0	72	684	2	0	0	0	77	Yellow
171	Plaxico Burress	NYJ	8	WR	0	0	0	0	0	0	49	591	5	0	0	0	77	Red
172	Brandon Pettigrew	DET	9	TE	0	0	0	0	0	0	54	673	3	0	0	0	83	Green
173	C.J. Spiller	BUF	7	RB	0	0	0	97	384	2	35	254	0	4	0	0	75	Green
174	Ronnie Brown	PHI	7	RB	0	0	0	83	398	4	28	207	1	3	0	0	75	Red
175	Donovan McNabb	MIN	9	QB	3599	18	16	45	27	1	0	0	0	5	0	0	220	Green
176	Mohamed Massaquoi	CLE	5	WR	0	0	0	0	0	0	40	470	4	0	0	0	71	Green
177	Ryan Williams	ARI	6	RB	0	0	0	122	451	1	15	149	1	3	0	0	71	Blue
178	Kellen Winslow	TB	8	TE	0	0	0	0	0	0	47	561	4	0	0	0	77	Green
179	David Nelson	BUF	7	WR	0	0	0	0	0	0	65	628	3	0	0	0	70	Red
180	Visanthe Shiancoe	MIN	9	TE	0	0	0	0	0	0	54	607	4	0	0	0	76	Red
181	Chad Henne	MIA	5	QB	3623	21	15	52	75	1	0	0	0	8	0	0	216	Red
182	Matt Cassel	KC	6	QB	3247	20	15	39	78	1	0	0	0	10	0	0	216	Green
183	Brent Celek	PHI	7	TE	0	0	0	0	0	0	51	566	4	0	0	0	75	Yellow
184	Greg Olsen	CAR	9	TE	0	0	0	0	0	0	40	518	4	0	0	0	75	Green
185	Benjamin Watson	CLE	5	TE	0	0	0	0	0	0	50	515	4	0	0	0	75	Green
186	Roscoe Parrish	BUF	7	WR	0	0	0	2	5	0	49	636	2	0	0	0	68	Red
187	Jacoby Jones	HOU	11	WR	0	0	0	2	11	0	37	510	2	0	0	0	67	Green
188	Steve Breaston	KC	6	WR	0	0	0	2	11	0	38	575	2	0	0	0	67	Yellow
189	Ryan Torain	WAS	5	RB	0	0	0	123	533	2	16	96	0	3	0	0	67	Yellow
190	Brandon Jackson	CLE	5	RB	0	0	0	76	340	1	45	300	1	3	0	0	66	Yellow
191	Devin Hester	CHI	8	WR	0	0	0	3	11	0	36	468	2	0	0	0	65	Yellow
192	Louis Murphy	OAK	8	WR	0	0	0	3	11	0	39	484	3	0	0	0	65	Green
193	Kevin Boss	OAK	8	TE	0	0	0	0	0	0	44	536	4	0	0	0	71	Red
194	Brian Hartline	MIA	5	WR	0	0	0	2	17	0	35	505	2	0	0	0	64	Green
195	Kevin Ogletree	DAL	5	WR	0	0	0	0	0	0	39	534	3	0	0	0	63	Red
196	Jason Campbell	OAK	8	QB	3402	17	15	58	236	2	0	0	0	9	0	0	209	Red
197	Andy Dalton	CIN	7	QB	3138	16	17	68	169	2	0	0	0	8	0	0	209	Green
198	Todd Heap	ARI	6	TE	0	0	0	0	0	0	44	500	4	0	0	0	68	Red
199	Kevin Walter	HOU	11	WR	0	0	0	0	0	0	40	477	2	0	0	0	61	Green
200	Derrick Mason	NYJ	8	WR	0	0	0	0	0	0	43	468	3	0	0	0	61	Green
201	Shane Vereen	NE	7	RB	0	0	0	67	314	3	13	117	1	1	0	0	61	Green
202	Tashard Choice	DAL	5	RB	0	0	0	90	390	1	20	184	1	3	0	0	61	Yellow
203	James Starks	GB	8	RB	0	0	0	80	395	2	16	127	0	1	0	0	61	Yellow
204	Alex Smith	SF	7	QB	3363	18	14	22	27	0	0	0	0	8	0	0	208	Green
205	Jermaine Gresham	CIN	7	TE	0	0	0	0	0	0	51	544	3	0	0	0	67	Yellow
206	Josh Cribbs	CLE	5	WR	21	0	0	16	70	0	29	395	1	0	0	0	60	Green

Rk	Player	Team	Bye	Pos	PaYd	PaTD	INT	Ru	RuYd	RuTD	Rec	RcYd	RcTD	FL	XP	FG	Fant	Risk
207	Chansi Stuckey	ARI	6	WR	0	0	0	2	7	0	47	541	2	0	0	0	60	Red
208	Brian Robiskie	CLE	5	WR	0	0	0	0	0	0	31	400	4	0	0	0	60	Green
209	Greg Little	CLE	5	WR	0	0	0	4	19	0	36	457	3	0	0	0	59	Red
210	Jason Avant	PHI	7	WR	0	0	0	0	0	0	41	475	2	0	0	0	59	Green
211	Kyle Orton	DEN	6	QB	3565	19	13	49	86	1	0	0	0	10	0	0	206	Red
212	Jerome Harrison	DET	9	RB	0	0	0	73	351	1	23	176	1	3	0	0	58	Yellow
213	Tarvaris Jackson	SEA	6	QB	3680	21	19	48	91	1	0	0	0	14	0	0	205	Red
214	Jordy Nelson	GB	8	WR	0	0	0	0	0	0	33	428	2	0	0	0	57	Green
215	Domenik Hixon	NYG	7	WR	0	0	0	0	0	0	32	456	3	0	0	0	57	Yellow
216	Isaac Redman	PIT	11	RB	0	0	0	63	277	2	24	202	1	2	0	0	57	Yellow
217	Mewelde Moore	PIT	11	RB	0	0	0	28	113	1	36	336	2	1	0	0	57	Green
218	Toby Gerhart	MIN	9	RB	0	0	0	51	229	3	19	169	1	2	0	0	57	Green
219	Stevan Ridley	NE	7	RB	0	0	0	57	222	4	11	97	1	1	0	0	57	Green
220	Donald Brown	IND	11	RB	0	0	0	84	340	3	9	81	0	1	0	0	56	Green
221	Anthony Fasano	MIA	5	TE	0	0	0	0	0	0	40	419	4	0	0	0	62	Green
222	Jabar Gaffney	WAS	5	WR	0	0	0	0	0	0	47	505	1	0	0	0	55	Yellow
223	Torrey Smith	BAL	5	WR	0	0	0	4	25	0	31	452	2	0	0	0	54	Red
224	Ricky Williams	BAL	5	RB	0	0	0	72	265	3	22	156	1	3	0	0	54	Red
225	Andre Caldwell	CIN	7	WR	0	0	0	0	0	0	38	415	2	0	0	0	53	Green
226	Mike Goodson	CAR	9	RB	0	0	0	47	223	1	27	273	1	1	0	0	53	Yellow
227	Laurent Robinson	SD	6	WR	0	0	0	0	0	0	22	372	3	0	0	0	52	Green
228	Roy Helu	WAS	5	RB	0	0	0	75	362	1	13	109	1	2	0	0	52	Yellow
229	Rashad Jennings	JAC	9	RB	0	0	0	75	328	0	25	187	1	3	0	0	52	Yellow
230	Jacob Tamme	IND	11	TE	0	0	0	0	0	0	35	437	3	0	0	0	58	Green
231	Patrick Crayton	SD	6	WR	0	0	0	0	0	0	29	371	2	0	0	0	51	Green
232	Earnest Graham	TB	8	RB	0	0	0	46	224	1	30	258	1	2	0	0	50	Red
233	Aaron Hernandez	NE	7	TE	0	0	0	0	0	0	31	414	3	0	0	0	56	Green
234	Denarius Moore	OAK	8	WR	0	0	0	2	10	0	30	416	2	0	0	0	49	Red
235	Ben Tate	HOU	11	RB	0	0	0	53	261	2	13	112	1	1	0	0	49	Green
236	Derrick Ward	HOU	11	RB	0	0	0	56	213	2	16	125	1	2	0	0	48	Yellow
237	Michael Hoomanawanui	STL	5	TE	0	0	0	0	0	0	40	427	3	0	0	0	54	Red
238	Leonard Hankerson	WAS	5	WR	0	0	0	3	18	0	33	435	2	0	0	0	47	Red
239	Eric Decker	DEN	6	WR	0	0	0	2	7	0	25	366	2	0	0	0	46	Red
240	Bernard Scott	CIN	7	RB	0	0	0	67	286	0	23	172	0	3	0	0	43	Yellow

Statistical Appendix

Broken Tackles by Team, Offense

Rk	Team	Plays	Plays w/ BTkl	Pct	Total BTkl
1	TB	951	77	8.1%	94
2	PHI	1022	77	7.5%	92
3	JAC	1014	72	7.1%	80
4	BUF	950	67	7.1%	73
5	NYG	1022	71	6.9%	80
6	CLE	914	61	6.7%	68
7	CAR	962	63	6.5%	76
8	OAK	1024	67	6.5%	75
9	SEA	947	61	6.4%	71
10	ATL	1090	68	6.2%	78
11	DAL	1026	63	6.1%	73
12	NO	1053	64	6.1%	75
13	MIN	983	59	6.0%	65
14	NE	970	57	5.9%	69
15	TEN	902	53	5.9%	61
16	CIN	1039	61	5.9%	71
17	DEN	1017	58	5.7%	67
18	PIT	975	55	5.6%	68
19	HOU	1023	57	5.6%	66
20	KC	1052	58	5.5%	62
21	STL	1046	57	5.4%	65
22	WAS	993	54	5.4%	62
23	MIA	1031	55	5.3%	57
24	SD	1020	54	5.3%	61
25	DET	1057	53	5.0%	56
26	SF	937	46	4.9%	58
27	IND	1081	52	4.8%	60
28	CHI	924	41	4.4%	47
29	ARI	933	40	4.3%	45
30	BAL	1009	43	4.3%	48
31	GB	988	42	4.3%	46
32	NYJ	1078	43	4.0%	44

Broken Tackles by Team, Defense

Rk	Team	Plays	Plays w/ BTkl	Pct	Total BTkl
1	HOU	998	81	8.1%	91
2	DET	996	77	7.7%	89
3	ARI	1084	80	7.4%	95
4	TB	980	70	7.1%	75
5	IND	996	71	7.1%	80
6	ATL	954	66	6.9%	76
7	TEN	1135	77	6.8%	90
8	NO	944	63	6.7%	75
9	PHI	992	63	6.4%	77
10	BUF	1062	67	6.3%	70
11	CAR	1049	65	6.2%	75
12	SEA	1058	65	6.1%	79
13	STL	1003	59	5.9%	66
14	JAC	941	55	5.8%	62
15	WAS	1039	60	5.8%	69
16	CIN	947	53	5.6%	63
17	BAL	1001	56	5.6%	63
18	MIA	969	53	5.5%	60
19	SD	927	50	5.4%	59
20	OAK	985	53	5.4%	61
21	CHI	987	52	5.3%	57
22	KC	1017	52	5.1%	63
23	SF	1024	52	5.1%	59
24	DAL	965	49	5.1%	54
25	NYG	966	49	5.1%	54
26	CLE	1028	50	4.9%	59
27	PIT	975	46	4.7%	53
28	NYJ	976	45	4.6%	50
29	GB	971	42	4.3%	49
30	DEN	1042	45	4.3%	50
31	MIN	964	41	4.3%	47
32	NE	1058	42	4.0%	44

Top 20 Defenders in Broken Tackles

Rk	Player	Team	BTkl
1	M.Griffin	TEN	17
2	A.Wilson	ARI	16
3	W.Witherspoon	TEN	15
4	P.Lenon	ARI	14
4	R.Barber	TB	14
6	B.Pollard	HOU	13
6	S.Tulloch	TEN	13
8	K.Rivers	CIN	12
8	Q.Mikell	PHI	12
8	L.Tatupu	SEA	12
11	K.Rhodes	ARI	11
11	W.Moore	ATL	11
11	R.Marshall	CAR	11
11	L.Briggs	CHI	11
11	G.Quin	HOU	11
11	S.Shanle	NO	11
11	D.Hawthorne	SEA	11
11	S.Spencer	SF	11
11	R.McIntosh	WAS	11
20	9 tied with		10

Top 20 Defenders, Broken Tackle Rate

Rk	Player	Team	BTkl	Tkl	Rate
1	J.Smith	SF	0	62	0.0%
1	C.Matthews	GB	0	53	0.0%
1	V.Wilfork	NE	0	46	0.0%
1	J.Allen	MIN	0	46	0.0%
1	S.Pouha	NYJ	0	43	0.0%
1	A.Garay	SD	0	40	0.0%
7	J.Mayo	NE	1	118	0.8%
8	B.Fletcher	STL	1	64	1.5%
9	M.Boley	NYG	1	61	1.6%
10	B.Flowers	KC	1	57	1.7%
11	R.Mathis	JAC	1	48	2.0%
11	J.Hall	STL	1	48	2.0%
13	T.Spikes	SF	2	92	2.1%
13	J.Allen	HOU	1	46	2.1%
15	J.Babin	TEN	1	45	2.2%
16	S.Johnson	BUF	1	43	2.3%
16	C.Pace	NYJ	1	43	2.3%
18	K.Brooking	DAL	2	79	2.5%
19	P.Posluszny	BUF	3	114	2.6%
20	J.Harrison	PIT	2	75	2.6%

Broken Tackles divided by Broken Tackles + Solo Tackles.

Special teams not included; min. 40 Solo Tackles

Bottom 20 Defenders, Broken Tackle Rate

Rk	Player	Team	BTkl	Tkl	Rate
1	W.Witherspoon	TEN	15	62	19.5%
2	D.Rodgers-Cromartie	ARI	10	43	18.9%
3	A.Francisco	IND	9	42	17.6%
4	R.Barber	TB	14	66	17.5%
5	K.Rivers	CIN	12	58	17.1%
6	V.Davis	MIA	9	44	17.0%
7	S.Shanle	NO	11	54	16.9%
8	A.Wilson	ARI	16	79	16.8%
9	E.Wilson	HOU	8	41	16.3%
10	M.Griffin	TEN	17	88	16.2%
11	D.Grant	NYG	9	47	16.1%
12	L.Tatupu	SEA	12	64	15.8%
13	W.Moore	ATL	11	61	15.3%
14	M.Jenkins	NO	10	56	15.2%
15	G.Brackett	IND	9	51	15.0%
16	S.Martin	CAR	10	57	14.9%
17	L.McKelvin	BUF	9	52	14.8%
18	R.Williams	CIN	7	41	14.6%
18	J.Sanders	NE	7	41	14.6%
18	K.Moore	WAS	7	41	14.6%

Broken Tackles divided by Broken Tackles + Solo Tackles.

Special teams not included; min. 40 Solo Tackles

Most Broken Tackles, Running Backs

Rk	Player	Team	BTkl
1	A.Foster	HOU	45
2	C.Johnson	TEN	41
3	L.McCoy	PHI	38
3	M.Turner	ATL	38
3	A.Bradshaw	NYG	38
6	D.McFadden	OAK	37
7	M.Lynch	BUF/SEA	36
8	A.Peterson	MIN	35
8	P.Hillis	CLE	35
10	F.Jackson	BUF	34
11	L.Blount	TB	33
11	R.Mendenhall	PIT	33
13	F.Jones	DAL	30
13	C.Benson	CIN	30
13	Drew	JAC	30
16	S.Jackson	STL	28
17	J.Charles	KC	27
17	C.Ivory	NO	27
19	K.Moreno	DEN	25
19	J.Stewart	CAR	25

Most Broken Tackles, WR/TE

Rk	Player	Team	BTkl
1	P.Harvin	MIN	13
2	P.Garcon	IND	12
2	N.Burleson	DET	12
4	J.Morgan	SF	11
4	B.Gibson	STL	11
6	T.Owens	CIN	10
6	J.Gresham	CIN	10
8	E.Bennett	CHI	9
8	K.Winslow	TB	9
8	M.Manningham	NYG	9
8	B.Marshall	MIA	9
12	D.Bowe	KC	8
12	J.Witten	DAL	8
12	C.Stuckey	CLE	8
12	D.Branch	SEA/NE	8
12	A.Hernandez	NE	8
12	V.Davis	SF	8
12	R.Wayne	IND	8
12	M.Lewis	JAC	8
12	S.Smith	CAR	8
12	St.Johnson	BUF	8
12	M.Crabtree	SF	8
12	B.Smith	NYJ	8

Best Broken Tackle Rate, Offensive Players (min. 100 touches)

Rk	Player	Team	BTkl	Touch	Rate
1	C.Ivory	NO	27	138	19.6%
2	M.Lynch	BUF/SEA	36	223	16.1%
3	L.Blount	TB	33	206	16.0%
4	D.Woodhead	NYJ/NE	20	131	15.3%
5	P.Thomas	NO	17	112	15.2%
6	J.Forsett	SEA	21	151	13.9%
7	D.McFadden	OAK	37	270	13.7%
8	J.Stewart	CAR	25	186	13.4%
9	F.Jackson	BUF	34	253	13.4%
10	L.McCoy	PHI	38	285	13.3%
11	F.Jones	DAL	30	233	12.9%
12	C.Williams	TB	21	171	12.3%
13	W.McGahee	BAL	14	114	12.3%
14	R.Torain	WAS	22	182	12.1%
15	M.Goodson	CAR	17	143	11.9%
16	R.Jennings	JAC	13	110	11.8%
17	A.Bradshaw	NYG	38	323	11.8%
18	B.Jacobs	NYG	18	155	11.6%
19	A.Foster	HOU	45	393	11.5%
20	C.Johnson	TEN	41	360	11.4%

Top 20 Defenders in Defeats

Rk	Player	Team	Dfts
1	D.Smith	JAC	35
2	J.Tuck	NYG	33
3	C.Wake	MIA	32
4	J.Harrison	PIT	31
4	D.Ware	DAL	31
6	J.Anderson	CAR	30
7	L.Timmons	PIT	29
7	G.Hayes	TB	29
7	N.Suh	DET	29
10	C.Greenway	MIN	28
10	D.Williams	DEN	28
10	L.Briggs	CHI	28
10	D.Hall	WAS	28
14	L.Fletcher	WAS	27
14	B.Urlacher	CHI	27
14	K.Burnett	SD	27
14	C.Matthews	GB	27
18	W.Witherspoon	TEN	26
18	T.Cole	PHI	26
18	T.Thomas	NYG	26

Top 20 Defenders in Passes Defensed

Rk	Player	Team	PD
1	B.Carr	KC	24
2	T.Williams	GB	20
3	B.Grimes	ATL	17
3	D.Rodgers-Cromartie	ARI	17
5	P.Buchanon	WAS	16
5	D.Florence	BUF	16
5	J.Haden	CLE	16
5	E.Reed	BAL	16
9	A.Cromartie	NYJ	15
9	J.Wilson	BAL	15
11	P.Cox	DEN	14
11	A.Samuel	PHI	14
13	A.Cason	SD	13
13	D.McCourty	NE	13
13	T.Thomas	NYG	13
13	K.Jennings	SEA	13
13	B.Flowers	KC	13
13	C.Bailey	DEN	13
13	S.Routt	OAK	13
20	8 tied with		12

Based on the definition given in the Statistical Toolbox, not NFL totals.

Top 20 Defenders in Broken Tackles

Rk	Player	Team	Hits
1	M.Griffin	TEN	17
2	A.Wilson	ARI	16
3	W.Witherspoon	TEN	15
4	P.Lenon	ARI	14
4	R.Barber	TB	14
6	B.Pollard	HOU	13
6	S.Tulloch	TEN	13
8	K.Rivers	CIN	12
8	Q.Mikell	PHI	12
8	L.Tatupu	SEA	12
11	K.Rhodes	ARI	11
11	W.Moore	ATL	11
11	R.Marshall	CAR	11
11	L.Briggs	CHI	11
11	G.Quin	HOU	11
11	S.Shanle	NO	11
11	D.Hawthorne	SEA	11
11	S.Spencer	SF	11
11	R.McIntosh	WAS	11
20	9 tied with		10

Top 20 Defenders in Quarterback Hits

Rk	Player	Team	Hits
1	A.Smith	HOU	20
2	O.Umenyiora	NYG	18
3	C.Long	STL	16
3	J.Harrison	PIT	16
5	J.Allen	MIN	15
5	J.Babin	TEN	15
5	J.Peppers	CHI	15
5	C.Wake	MIA	15
9	J.Tuck	NYG	14
10	C.Johnson	CAR	13
11	T.Hali	KC	12
11	C.Matthews	GB	12
11	T.Suggs	BAL	12
11	T.Cole	PHI	12
11	A.Kampman	JAC	12
16	K.Vanden Bosch	DET	11
17	11 with		10

Adjusted based on official scorer tendencies.

Top 20 Defenders in QB Knockdowns (Sacks + Hits)

Rk	Defender	Team	KD
1	O.Umenyiora	NYG	30
1	C.Wake	MIA	30
3	J.Harrison	PIT	28
3	J.Babin	TEN	28
3	T.Hali	KC	28
6	J.Tuck	NYG	27
6	C.Matthews	GB	27
8	J.Allen	MIN	26
9	A.Smith	HOU	25
9	C.Long	STL	25
9	C.Johnson	CAR	25
9	D.Ware	DAL	25
13	T.Suggs	BAL	24
14	J.Peppers	CHI	22
14	T.Cole	PHI	22
16	L.Woodley	PIT	21
17	D.Freeney	IND	20
17	R.Brock	SEA	20
17	M.Williams	HOU	20
17	C.Clemons	SEA	20

Full credit for whole and half sacks

Top 20 Defenders in Hurries

Rk	Defender	Team	Hur
1	C.Long	STL	42.5
2	D.Ware	DAL	39
3	T.Suggs	BAL	38
3	C.Wake	MIA	38
5	A.Smith	HOU	36.5
5	T.Hali	KC	36.5
7	M.Williams	HOU	34
8	D.Freeney	IND	33.5
8	C.Avril	DET	33.5
10	L.Woodley	PIT	33
11	J.Harrison	PIT	31
12	C.Johnson	CAR	30.5
12	J.Peppers	CHI	30.5
14	J.Allen	MIN	28.5
15	R.Edwards	MIN	27.5
16	C.Clemons	SEA	27
17	T.Cole	PHI	26.5
18	J.Babin	TEN	25.5
19	M.Roth	CLE	24.5
19	Cain	NE	24.5
19	B.Orakpo	WAS	24.5

Adjusted based on game charter tendencies

Top 20 Defenders in Drawing Offensive Holding Flags

Rk	Player	Team	Total	Pass	Run
1	B.Orakpo	WAS	9	7	2
1	C.Wake	MIA	9	7	2
3	J.Harrison	PIT	8	7	1
4	J.Ratliff	DAL	5	5	0
4	T.Hali	KC	5	4	1
4	R.Starks	MIA	5	4	1
4	K.Williams	MIN	5	2	3
4	C.Williams	DET	5	1	4
9	J.Hunter	DEN	4	3	1
9	J.Peppers	CHI	4	3	1
9	F.Robbins	STL	4	3	1
9	J.Anderson	CAR	4	2	2
9	C.Matthews	GB	4	2	2
9	J.Porter	ARI	4	2	2
9	R.Edwards	MIN	4	2	2
9	D.Freeney	IND	4	2	2
9	P.Williams	MIN	4	2	2
9	J.Hall	STL	4	2	2
9	R.Ayers	DEN	4	1	3
9	C.Kelsay	BUF	4	1	3
9	C.Campbell	ARI	4	1	3
9	K.Wimbley	OAK	4	1	3

Top 20 Quarterbacks in QB Hits

Rk	Player	Team	Adj Hits
1	D.Garrard	JAC	55
1	D.McNabb	WAS	55
1	M.Vick	PHI	55
4	S.Bradford	STL	51
4	M.Schaub	HOU	51
6	C.Palmer	CIN	49
7	M.Ryan	ATL	48
7	J.Freeman	TB	48
9	D.Brees	NO	47
9	J.Flacco	BAL	47
11	R.Fitzpatrick	BUF	45
12	B.Favre	MIN	43
12	M.Cassel	KC	43
14	J.Cutler	CHI	40
15	E.Manning	NYG	37
16	P.Rivers	SD	36
17	A.Smith	SF	35
17	C.Henne	MIA	35
19	B.Roethlisberger	PIT	33
20	P.Manning	IND	32

Adjusted based on official scorer tendencies

Top 20 Quarterbacks in QB Knockdowns (Sacks + Hits)

Rk	Player	Team	Adj KD	Rk	Player	Team	Adj KD
1	D.McNabb	WAS	89	12	D.Brees	NO	68
2	J.Cutler	CHI	87	12	M.Cassel	KC	68
3	D.Garrard	JAC	85	14	R.Fitzpatrick	BUF	66
3	M.Vick	PHI	85	14	C.Henne	MIA	66
5	S.Bradford	STL	83	16	B.Favre	MIN	64
6	J.Flacco	BAL	82	17	B.Roethlisberger	PIT	61
7	M.Schaub	HOU	79	17	J.Campbell	OAK	61
8	C.Palmer	CIN	74	19	K.Orton	DEN	60
8	J.Freeman	TB	74	20	A.Smith	SF	58
10	M.Ryan	ATL	72	20	A.Rodgers	GB	58
11	P.Rivers	SD	71				

Includes sacks cancelled by penalties

Does not include "self sacks" with no defender

Top 10 Quarterbacks in Knockdowns per Pass

Rk	Player	Team	KD	Pct
1	T.Edwards	BUF/JAC	34	28.3%
2	T.Smith	SF	37	21.3%
3	D.Garrard	JAC	85	20.4%
4	M.Vick	PHI	85	20.2%
5	M.Moore	CAR	29	18.1%
6	J.Cutler	CHI	87	16.9%
7	D.McNabb	WAS	89	16.8%
8	B.Favre	MIN	64	15.6%
9	J.Clausen	CAR	54	15.6%
10	C.McCoy	CLE	40	15.6%

Min. 100 passes

Bottom 10 QBs in Knockdowns per Pass

Rk	Player	Team	KD	Pct
1	P.Manning	IND	47	6.5%
2	K.Collins	TEN	24	7.8%
2	E.Manning	NYG	50	8.4%
4	M.Sanchez	NYJ	47	8.5%
5	D.Stanton	DET	11	8.6%
6	J.Webb	MIN	9	8.9%
7	V.Young	TEN	16	8.9%
8	S.Wallace	CLE	10	9.0%
9	T.Brady	NE	50	9.1%
10	S.Hill	DET	42	9.4%

Min. 100 passes

Best Quarterbacks, Passing DVOA When Hurried

Rk	Player	Team	Plays	Yds	DVOA
1	B.Roethlisberger	PIT	113	8.2	74.6%
2	A.Rodgers	GB	89	8.5	60.3%
3	J.Freeman	TB	165	7.2	54.8%
4	P.Rivers	SD	104	7.1	53.4%
5	J.Cutler	CHI	110	8.2	40.0%
6	C.McCoy	CLE	57	6.0	33.2%
7	C.Palmer	CIN	100	6.4	25.3%
8	J.Campbell	OAK	74	7.0	22.2%
9	S.Hill	DET	108	5.5	21.2%
10	M.Vick	PHI	100	5.9	13.9%

Min. 30 hurries; sacks not included.

Worst Quarterbacks, Passing DVOA When Hurried

Rk	Player	Team	Plays	Yds	DVOA
1	J.Delhomme	CLE	30	1.9	-147.2%
2	B.Favre	MIN	62	3.4	-129.2%
3	R.Grossman	WAS	30	3.9	-69.2%
4	T.Edwards	BUF/JAC	34	4.1	-63.7%
5	A.Smith	SF	75	4.0	-40.8%
6	B.Gradkowski	OAK	38	2.4	-38.8%
7	J.Kitna	DAL	53	4.1	-38.5%
8	D.Garrard	JAC	80	3.6	-37.3%
9	S.Bradford	STL	119	4.4	-31.5%
10	D.McNabb	WAS	106	5.3	-30.3%

Min. 30 hurries; sacks not included.

Most Passes Tipped at line, Quarterbacks

Rk	Player	Team	Total
1	S.Bradford	STL	21
2	D.McNabb	WAS	18
2	C.Henne	MIA	18
4	J.Clausen	CAR	14
4	M.Sanchez	NYJ	14
4	C.Palmer	CIN	14
4	R.Fitzpatrick	BUF	14
4	M.Cassel	KC	14
9	J.Kitna	DAL	13
10	J.Cutler	CHI	12
10	D.Brees	NO	12
10	J.Campbell	OAK	12
10	M.Vick	PHI	12

Most Passes Tipped at line, Defenders

Rk	Player	Team	Total
1	K.Williams	MIN	8
2	D.Johnson	KC	6
2	J.Peppers	CHI	6
2	Paul	NYG	6
5	B.Keisel	PIT	5
5	F.Robbins	STL	5
7	M.Johnson	CIN	4
7	S.Phillips	SD	4
7	J.Bannan	DEN	4
7	T.McDaniel	MIA	4
7	R.Brock	SEA	4
7	W.Smith	NO	4
7	J.Taylor	NYJ	4
7	G.McCoy	TB	4
7	D.Tapp	PHI	4

Top 20 Players, Passes Dropped

Rk	Player	Team	Total
1	W.Welker	NE	13
2	P.Garcon	IND	12
3	B.Marshall	MIA	11
3	M.Austin	DAL	11
5	D.Jackson	PHI	10
5	J.Jones	HOU	10
5	R.Wayne	IND	10
8	C.Cooley	WAS	9
8	T.Owens	CIN	9
10	D.Keller	NYJ	8
10	B.Pettigrew	DET	8
10	M.Colston	NO	8
10	C.Ochocinco	CIN	8
10	D.Butler	SEA	8
15	H.Nicks	NYG	7
15	B.Gibson	STL	7
15	D.Bowe	KC	7
15	S.Johnson	BUF	7
15	J.Maclin	PHI	7
15	M.Crabtree	SF	7
15	D.Amendola	STL	7
15	F.Jackson	BUF	7
15	J.Charles	KC	7
15	T.Gonzalez	ATL	7

Top 20 Players, Pct. Passes Dropped

Rk	Player	Team	Drops	Passes	Pct
1	C.Buckhalter	DEN	6	38	15.8%
2	M.Sellers	WAS	6	40	15.0%
3	T.Hightower	ARI	6	42	14.3%
4	T.Ginn	MIA	5	35	14.3%
5	D.Graham	DEN	5	37	13.5%
6	F.Jackson	BUF	7	54	13.0%
7	J.Jones	HOU	10	78	12.8%
8	D.Butler	SEA	8	70	11.4%
9	J.Dreessen	HOU	6	54	11.1%
10	J.Charles	KC	7	64	10.9%
11	D.Walker	SF	5	46	10.9%
12	W.Welker	NE	13	124	10.5%
13	D.Jackson	PHI	10	96	10.4%
14	B.Johnson	DET	5	49	10.2%
15	E.Doucet	ARI	6	59	10.2%
16	A.Bradshaw	NYG	6	59	10.2%
17	P.Garcon	IND	12	119	10.1%
18	Bey	OAK	6	64	9.4%
19	R.Williams	DAL	6	64	9.4%
20	M.Austin	DAL	11	119	9.2%

Min. five drops

Top 20 Intended Receivers on Interceptions

Rk	Player	Team	Total	Rk	Player	Team	Total
1	T.Owens	CIN	12	10	M.Austin	DAL	6
2	J.Knox	CHI	11	10	C.Johnson	DET	6
3	S.Johnson	BUF	10	10	S.Smith	CAR	6
4	L.Fitzgerald	ARI	8	15	J.Galloway	WAS	5
4	M.Crabtree	SF	8	15	M.Manningham	NYG	5
6	B.Marshall	MIA	7	15	L.Murphy	OAK	5
6	H.Nicks	NYG	7	15	P.Harvin	MIN	5
6	M.Massaquoi	CLE	7	15	A.Johnson	HOU	5
6	N.Washington	TEN	7	15	R.Wayne	IND	5
10	G.Jennings	GB	6	15	B.Watson	CLE	5
10	S.Moss	WAS	6	15	R.Williams	DAL	5

Top 10 Plus/Minus for Running Backs

Rk	Player	Team	Pass	+/-
1	L.McCoy	PHI	83	+10.6
2	P.Hillis	CLE	68	+7.6
3	J.Snelling	ATL	48	+7.0
4	F.Jones	DAL	53	+5.7
5	D.McFadden	OAK	52	+5.5
6	P.Thomas	NO	30	+5.4
7	R.Brown	MIA	36	+4.8
8	D.Sproles	SD	70	+4.2
9	C.Spiller	BUF	27	+3.7
10	C.Johnson	TEN	51	+3.6

Min. 25 passes; totals adjusted for passes tipped/thrown away.

Bottom 10 Plus/Minus for Running Backs

Rk	Player	Team	Pass	+/-
1	T.Hightower	ARI	38	-8.6
2	F.Jackson	BUF	47	-6.1
3	L.Tomlinson	NYJ	73	-4.9
4	M.Sellers	WAS	34	-4.7
5	K.Williams	WAS	54	-4.0
6	J.Forsett	SEA	47	-2.9
7	F.Gore	SF	62	-2.9
8	J.Best	DET	75	-2.6
9	R.Mendenhall	PIT	30	-1.2
10	C.Buckhalter	DEN	37	-1.2

Min. 25 passes; totals adjusted for passes tipped/thrown away.

Top 10 Plus/Minus for Wide Receivers

Rk	Player	Team	Pass	+/-
1	A.Collie	IND	69	+12.1
2	M.Manningham	NYG	85	+8.8
3	R.Meachem	NO	61	+8.6
4	J.Avant	PHI	65	+8.5
5	D.Mason	BAL	91	+8.5
6	J.Maclin	PHI	103	+8.1
7	G.Jennings	GB	118	+7.9
8	K.Britt	TEN	64	+7.7
9	R.White	ATL	171	+7.4
10	M.Wallace	PIT	93	+7.2

Min. 25 passes; totals adjusted for passes tipped/thrown away.

Bottom 10 Plus/Minus for Wide Receivers

Rk	Player	Team	Pass	+/-
1	E.Doucet	ARI	54	-9.8
2	J.Cotchery	NYJ	79	-8.6
3	S.Smith	CAR	84	-8.6
4	L.Fitzgerald	ARI	165	-8.5
5	H.Douglas	ATL	50	-8.1
6	B.LaFell	CAR	71	-7.0
7	L.Robinson	STL	64	-6.6
8	D.Butler	SEA	68	-6.4
9	E.Royal	DEN	97	-6.3
10	N.Washington	TEN	90	-6.1

Min. 25 passes; totals adjusted for passes tipped/thrown away.

Top 10 Plus/Minus for Tight Ends

Rk	Player	Team	Pass	+/-
1	A.Gates	SD	61	+11.1
2	J.Witten	DAL	120	+10.7
3	K.Winslow	TB	89	+7.0
4	R.Gronkowski	NE	57	+5.4
5	J.Tamme	IND	88	+5.2
6	J.Finley	GB	25	+4.7
7	J.Shockey	NO	55	+4.2
8	T.Moeaki	KC	66	+3.9
9	J.Graham	NO	42	+3.9
10	J.Dreessen	HOU	49	+3.8

Min. 25 passes; totals adjusted for passes tipped/thrown away.

Bottom 10 Plus/Minus for Tight Ends

Rk	Player	Team	Pass	+/-
1	B.Celek	PHI	76	-7.7
2	K.Boss	NYG	64	-7.4
3	D.Rosario	CAR	55	-5.8
4	D.Graham	DEN	32	-4.3
5	D.Keller	NYJ	91	-4.1
6	J.Gresham	CIN	76	-3.2
7	J.Carlson	SEA	52	-3.1
8	B.Pettigrew	DET	104	-2.9
9	V.Shiancoe	MIN	74	-2.4
10	O.Daniels	HOU	59	-1.8

Min. 25 passes; totals adjusted for passes tipped/thrown away.

Fewest YAC Allowed in Coverage

Rk	Player	Team	YAC
1	J.Hanson	PHI	1.4
2	C.Bailey	DEN	1.7
3	C.Munnerlyn	CAR	1.8
4	A.Samuel	PHI	1.9
5	B.Flowers	KC	2.0
6	J.Tryon	IND	2.0
7	B.Grimes	ATL	2.0
8	B.Fletcher	STL	2.2
9	L.Webb	BAL	2.3
10	J.Joseph	CIN	2.3
11	C.Carr	BAL	2.3
12	C.Johnson	OAK	2.4
13	A.Verner	TEN	2.4
14	W.Gay	PIT	2.5
15	L.McKelvin	BUF	2.5
16	B.McFadden	PIT	2.5
17	C.Houston	DET	2.5
18	J.Arenas	KC	2.7
19	N.Jones	DEN	2.7
20	P.Buchanon	WAS	2.7

Min. 40 passes or 8 games started.

Most YAC Allowed in Coverage

Rk	Player	Team	YAC
1	A.Goodman	DEN	8.4
2	F.Washington	BAL	5.9
3	K.Jackson	HOU	5.9
4	M.Adams	ARI	5.7
5	D.Hall	WAS	5.6
6	J.Wilson	BAL	5.4
7	S.Routt	OAK	5.1
8	V.Davis	MIA	4.9
9	L.Hall	CIN	4.9
10	A.Smith	DET	4.8
11	R.Mathis	JAC	4.8
12	T.Porter	NO	4.7
13	D.Revis	NYJ	4.6
14	A.Allen	MIN	4.6
15	D.Coleman	NYJ	4.5
16	E.Wright	CLE	4.5
17	J.Lacey	IND	4.4
18	C.Gamble	CAR	4.4
19	M.Jenkins	DAL	4.4
20	B.Sapp	MIA	4.3

Min. 40 passes or 8 games started.

Top 20 Passing Yards Allowed in Coverage

Rk	Player	Team	Yards
1	D.Hall	WAS	933
2	M.Jenkins	DAL	931
3	K.Jackson	HOU	883
4	B.McFadden	PIT	839
5	C.Finnegan	TEN	821
6	B.Carr	KC	817
7	M.Trufant	SEA	816
8	P.Cox	DEN	804
9	T.Thomas	NYG	803
9	D.Rodgers-Cromartie	ARI	788
11	T.Newman	DAL	756
12	G.Toler	ARI	719
13	C.Tillman	CHI	704
14	R.Marshall	CAR	695
15	D.McCourty	NE	694
16	S.Brown	CLE	693
17	R.Mathis	JAC	688
18	A.Cromartie	NYJ	682
19	I.Taylor	PIT	677
20	G.Quin	HOU	648

Includes Defensive Pass Interference.

Most First Downs/Touchdowns Allowed

Rk	Player	Team	Total
1	D.Hall	WAS	43
2	B.McFadden	PIT	40
2	M.Trufant	SEA	40
4	D.McCourty	NE	39
5	M.Jenkins	DAL	38
5	T.Thomas	NYG	38
5	C.Finnegan	TEN	38
8	D.Rodgers-Cromartie	ARI	37
8	R.Marshall	CAR	37
10	B.Carr	KC	36
10	C.Tillman	CHI	36
12	P.Cox	DEN	34
12	T.Newman	DAL	34
14	B.Fletcher	STL	33
14	K.Jackson	HOU	33
16	B.Flowers	KC	32
16	G.Quin	HOU	32
16	A.Cromartie	NYJ	32
19	D.Florence	BUF	31
19	G.Toler	ARI	31
19	R.Mathis	JAC	31
19	K.Arrington	NE	31

Most Dropped Interceptions, 2010

Rk	Player	Team	Drops
1	D.Johnson	KC	5
1	S.Smith	MIA	5
1	A.Talib	TB	5
4	C.Rogers	WAS	4
5	C.Clemons	MIA	3
5	N.Collins	GB	3
5	D.Hall	WAS	3
5	M.Huff	OAK	3
5	J.McGraw	KC	3
5	W.Moore	ATL	3
5	E.Thomas	SEA	3
5	T.Thomas	NYG	3
5	T.Ward	CLE	3

Most Dropped Interceptions, 2009-10

Rk	Player	Team	Drops
1	N.Collins	GB	6
1	S.Smith	MIA	6
1	A.Talib	TB	6
4	A.Bethea	IND	5
4	D.Florence	BUF	5
4	M.Huff	OAK	5
4	T.Jennings	IND/CHI	5
4	C.Johnson	OAK	5
4	D.Johnson	KC	5
4	Q.Mikell	PHI	5
4	C.Rogers	WAS	5
5	T.Thomas	NYG	3
5	T.Ward	CLE	3

Fewest Avg Yards on Run Tackle, DL

Rk	Player	Team	Tkl	Avg
1	J.Jones	TEN	27	0.4
2	T.Knighton	JAC	25	0.9
3	P.Williams	MIN	27	1.0
4	A.Dixon	PHI	27	1.1
5	P.Soliai	MIA	36	1.1
6	L.Houston	OAK	33	1.3
7	W.Smith	NO	29	1.4
8	A.Smith	HOU	30	1.4
9	D.Landri	CAR	40	1.5
10	C.Williams	DET	28	1.5
11	J.Cesaire	SD	26	1.5
12	K.Williams	MIN	33	1.5
13	J.Mincey	JAC	25	1.6
14	J.Babin	TEN	36	1.6
15	E.Foster	IND	25	1.6
16	B.Mebane	SEA	28	1.6
17	A.Garay	SD	41	1.7
18	A.Branch	ARI	30	1.7
19	I.Idonije	CHI	32	1.8
20	R.Seymour	OAK	41	1.8

Min. 25 run tackles

Fewest Avg Yards on Run Tackle, LB

Rk	Player	Team	Tkl	Avg
1	T.Suggs	BAL	48	1.6
2	B.Thomas	NYJ	27	1.7
3	J.Taylor	NYJ	29	1.9
4	Q.Groves	OAK	32	1.9
5	D.Ware	DAL	35	1.9
6	J.Harrison	PIT	59	2.0
7	L.Briggs	CHI	39	2.0
8	J.Goff	NYG	53	2.0
9	J.Farrior	PIT	64	2.1
10	P.Wheeler	IND	32	2.1
11	L.Woodley	PIT	28	2.1
12	D.Connor	CAR	39	2.1
13	G.Hayes	TB	44	2.1
14	C.Pace	NYJ	36	2.1
15	J.Cunningham	NE	31	2.2
16	J.Durant	JAC	27	2.2
17	D.Clark	NO	41	2.3
18	B.Orakpo	WAS	36	2.3
19	P.Haralson	SF	29	2.3
20	C.Wake	MIA	34	2.4

Min. 25 run tackles

Fewest Avg Yards on Run Tackle, DB

Rk	Player	Team	Tkl	Avg
1	S.Brown	CLE	22	3.4
2	A.Winfield	MIN	21	3.5
3	C.Woodson	GB	43	4.0
4	T.Polamalu	PIT	24	4.1
5	A.Wilson	ARI	52	4.2
6	M.Mitchell	OAK	21	4.2
7	R.Harper	NO	57	4.4
8	R.Barber	TB	42	4.7
9	B.Flowers	KC	21	4.7
10	K.Hayden	IND	26	4.7
11	B.Pollard	HOU	65	4.7
12	N.Clements	SF	30	4.8
13	G.Quin	HOU	27	5.0
14	T.Ward	CLE	60	5.1
15	S.Gregory	SD	20	5.1
16	P.Oliver	SD	30	5.1
17	R.Clark	PIT	44	5.1
18	A.Rolle	NYG	50	5.1
19	Y.Bell	MIA	58	5.4
20	Q.Mikell	PHI	51	5.4

Min. 20 run tackles

Top 20 Players in Blown Blocks

Rk	Player	Team	BB
1	A.Davis	SF	13
2	L.Brown	ARI	12.5
3	S.Baker	ATL	9
4	J.Webb	CHI	8.5
5	D.Diehl	NYG	8
5	T.Williams	WAS	8
7	E.Winston	HOU	7
7	M.Light	NE	7
7	J.Veldheer	OAK	7
10	R.Diem	IND	6
10	E.Monroe	JAC	6
10	F.Omiyale	CHI	6
10	Z.Beadles	DEN	6
10	G.Schwartz	CAR	6
10	J.Scott	PIT	6
10	K.Cook	CIN	6
10	J.Smith	STL	6
10	P.Loadholt	MIN	6
19	R.Clady	DEN	5.5
20	17 tied with		5

Only includes blown blocks which lead to sacks or offensive holding calls

Most False Starts

Rk	Player	Team	Pen
1	R.Diem	IND	8
1	M.Oher	BAL	8
3	V.Shiancoe	MIN	7
3	J.Scott	TEN	7
3	A.Davis	SF	7
3	J.Veldheer	OAK	7
7	D.Free	DAL	6
7	A.Hicks	WAS	6
7	F.Omiyale	CHI	6
7	S.Peterman	DET	6
7	B.Bulaga	GB	6
7	S.Andrews	SEA	6
7	R.Saffold	STL	6
7	K.Barnes	OAK	6
7	P.Loadholt	MIN	6
7	J.Bushrod	NO	6
17	B.Richardson	KC	5
17	M.Colombo	DAL	5
17	J.Smith	STL	5
17	B.Williams	CIN	5
17	C.Kuper	DEN	5

Includes declined and offsetting

Most Penalties, Offense

Rk	Player	Team	Pen	Yds
1	V.Shiancoe	MIN	15	99
2	J.Veldheer	OAK	14	105
3	P.Rivers	SD	13	86
4	M.Oher	BAL	13	88
5	P.Loadholt	MIN	13	79
6	J.Evans	NO	12	82
7	S.Peterman	DET	12	88
8	A.Davis	SF	11	70
9	J.Scott	TEN	11	64
10	J.Scott	PIT	10	70
11	F.Omiyale	CHI	10	40
12	D.Free	DAL	10	50
13	A.Smith	SF	10	72
14	B.Pettigrew	DET	10	83
15	B.Richardson	KC	10	63
16	B.Bulaga	GB	10	60
17	C.Kemoeatu	PIT	10	47
18	R.Diem	IND	10	65
19	7 with		9	

Includes declined and offsetting, but not special teams

Most Penalties, Defense

Rk	Player	Team	Pen	Yds	Rk	Player	Team	Pen	Yds
1	C.Williams	DET	14	65	9	N.Suh	DET	9	72
2	J.Babin	TEN	12	90	9	M.Jenkins	DAL	9	104
2	C.Woodson	GB	12	91	9	D.Patterson	PHI	9	48
4	S.Routt	OAK	11	154	9	D.Cox	JAC	9	47
5	J.Harrison	PIT	10	70	15	I.Taylor	PIT	8	84
5	T.Kelly	OAK	10	50	15	C.Johnson	OAK	8	105
5	D.Florence	BUF	10	91	15	R.Bartell	STL	8	74
5	R.Marshall	CAR	10	105	15	D.Rodgers-Cromartie	ARI	8	88
9	T.Cole	PHI	9	55	15	C.Johnson	CAR	8	55
9	A.Smith	HOU	9	50	20	10 with		7	

Includes declined and offsetting, but not special teams

Top 10 Kickers, Gross Kickoff Value over Average

Rk	Player	Team	Kick Pts+	Net Pts+	Kicks
1	B.Cundiff	BAL	14.2	13.5	79
2	O.Mare	SEA	7.9	11.8	66
3	R.Lloyd	CAR	6.7	6.3	50
4	P.McAfee	IND	6.0	-1.3	79
5	M.Koenen	ATL	5.9	13.6	85
6	D.Buehler	DAL	5.3	0.6	79
7	D.Akers	PHI	4.1	8.2	91
8	J.Feely	ARI	3.9	7.3	64
9	S.Janikowski	OAK	3.5	0.8	89
10	T.Morstead	NO	2.9	-0.5	47

Min. 20 kickoffs; squibs and onside not included

Bottom 10 Kickers, Gross Kickoff Value over Average

Rk	Player	Team	Kick Pts+	Net Pts+	Kicks
1	M.Crosby	GB	-8.3	-7.0	81
2	N.Kaeding	SD	-7.6	-15.9	70
3	J.Reed	PIT/SF	-6.4	-11.1	68
4	R.Longwell	MIN	-6.3	-15.7	63
5	C.Barth	TB	-5.9	-3.1	73
6	N.Folk	NYJ	-4.8	-0.1	76
7	J.Hanson	DET	-4.5	-4.0	37
8	S.Graham	NYG/NE	-3.4	-2.5	59
9	S.Suisham	PIT	-3.4	-4.8	37
10	C.Stitser	CIN	-3.3	-0.7	23

Min. 20 kickoffs; squibs and onside not included

Top 10 Punters, Gross Punt Value over Average

Rk	Player	Team	Punt Pts+	Net Pts+	Punts
1	S.Weatherford	NYJ	14.0	14.8	84
2	S.Koch	BAL	12.5	17.4	81
3	S.Lechler	OAK	8.3	9.1	77
4	D.Jones	STL	6.2	5.6	94
5	A.Lee	SF	5.5	4.9	91
6	T.Morstead	NO	5.4	4.1	57
7	C.Kluwe	MIN	5.1	6.2	83
8	D.Sepulveda	PIT	4.8	9.6	56
9	B.Graham	ARI	4.2	0.7	94
10	S.Rocca	PHI	4.0	8.6	73

Min. 20 punts

Bottom 10 Punters, Gross Punt Value over Average

Rk	Player	Team	Punt Pts+	Net Pts+	Punts
1	M.Scifres	SD	-11.2	-34.3	56
2	B.Maynard	CHI	-7.6	-0.2	83
3	H.Smith	WAS	-7.1	-14.5	57
4	M.Turk	HOU	-6.9	-4.5	63
5	P.McAfee	IND	-6.7	-8.1	65
6	J.Baker	CAR	-5.9	-6.4	95
7	B.Colquitt	DEN	-5.5	-13.0	86
8	M.Dodge	NYG	-4.9	-15.6	74
9	B.Kern	TEN	-4.4	4.5	77
10	M.Koenen	ATL	-4.1	0.0	75

Min. 20 punts

Top 10 Kick Returners, Value over Average

Rk	Player	Team	Pts+	Returns
1	B.Smith	NYJ	20.4	49
2	L.Washington	SEA	17.3	56
3	L.Stephens-Howling	ARI	15.8	55
4	M.Mariani	TEN	12.0	58
5	S.Logan	DET	9.4	54
6	D.Hester	CHI	9.2	12
7	E.Weems	ATL	8.9	39
8	B.Tate	NE	8.4	41
8	D.Reed	BAL	7.9	21
10	M.Spurlock	TB	7.1	44

Min. eight returns

Bottom 10 Kick Returners, Value over Average

Rk	Player	Team	Pts+	Returns
1	S.Slaton	HOU	-8.8	39
2	B.McCann	DAL	-8.2	23
2	M.Goodson	CAR	-7.3	47
4	J.Cribbs	CLE	-5.5	40
5	J.Calvin	PHI	-5.4	32
6	B.James	IND	-5.2	14
7	D.Amendola	STL	-4.5	50
8	J.Arenas	KC	-4.3	23
9	D.Gettis	CAR	-4.2	9
10	T.Ginn	SF	-4.2	47

Min. eight returns

Top 10 Punt Returners, Value over Average

Rk	Player	Team	Pts+	Returns
1	D.Hester	CHI	26.0	33
2	D.Bryant	DAL	10.9	15
3	J.Edelman	NE	8.3	21
4	M.Mariani	TEN	7.3	27
5	T.Ginn	SF	7.1	24
6	D.McCluster	KC	7.0	13
7	E.Weems	ATL	6.3	18
8	D.Amendola	STL	6.0	40
9	A.Cason	SD	6.0	14
10	B.Banks	WAS	4.9	38

Min. eight returns

Bottom 10 Punt Returners, Value over Average

Rk	Player	Team	Pts+	Returns
1	N.Miller	OAK	-6.1	35
2	A.Randle El	PIT	-5.4	14
3	A.Roberts	ARI	-4.5	35
4	W.Blackmon	NYG	-4.2	14
5	R.Bush	NO	-4.2	14
6	J.Jones	HOU	-4.0	29
7	K.Wilson	NYJ	-3.9	15
8	D.Reynaud	NYG	-3.8	23
9	M.Spurlock	TB	-3.4	28
9	L.McKelvin	BUF	-3.2	6

Min. eight returns

Top 20 Special Teams Plays

Rk	Player	Team	Plays	Rk	Player	Team	Plays
1	C.Graham	CHI	23	12	H.Eugene	OAK	16
2	J.Wendling	DET	22	12	A.Madison	PIT	16
3	N.Bowman	SF	20	12	K.Fox	PIT	16
4	T.Shaw	TEN	19	12	P.Bailey	TEN	16
5	S.Hurd	DAL	18	12	T.White	NE	16
5	G.Wilson	BUF	18	17	E.Weems	ATL	15
5	D.McCray	DAL	18	17	M.Slater	NE	15
5	T.Ward	CLE	18	17	D.Skuta	CIN	15
5	M.McCoy	SEA	18	17	M.Fokou	PHI	15
10	S.Brown	OAK	17	17	C.Chamberlain	STL	15
10	J.Casey	HOU	17				

Plays = tackles + assists

Top 10 Offenses, 3-and-out per drive

Rk	Team	Pct
1	JAC	10.5%
2	HOU	18.5%
3	SD	18.6%
4	NO	18.8%
5	IND	19.3%
6	ATL	19.7%
7	PHI	20.2%
8	NYG	20.4%
8	CIN	20.4%
10	MIA	20.9%

Top 10 Defenses, 3-and-out per drive

Rk	Team	Pct
1	NYJ	32.3%
2	SD	30.9%
3	CHI	29.8%
4	GB	28.0%
5	OAK	27.2%
6	NYG	26.3%
7	SF	26.1%
8	WAS	25.3%
9	MIA	25.1%
9	SEA	25.1%
9	STL	25.1%

Top 10 Offenses, Yards per drive

Rk	Team	Yds/Dr
1	HOU	36.16
2	NE	36.11
3	IND	36.04
4	SD	35.53
5	NO	34.67
6	ATL	32.93
7	GB	32.90
8	TB	32.54
9	PHI	32.30
10	JAC	31.76

Top 10 Defenses, Yards per drive

Rk	Team	Yds/Dr
1	NYG	24.03
2	NYJ	24.29
3	SD	24.67
4	PIT	25.22
5	CHI	25.25
6	OAK	26.45
7	GB	26.49
8	MIN	26.90
9	MIA	27.01
10	KC	27.20

Bottom 10 Offenses, 3-and-out per drive

Rk	Team	Pct
23	GB	25.7%
24	DEN	26.6%
25	TEN	27.4%
26	DET	27.6%
27	SEA	28.8%
28	SF	29.0%
29	CHI	29.6%
30	STL	29.9%
31	ARI	30.2%
32	CAR	31.1%

Bottom 10 Defenses, 3-and-out per drive

Rk	Team	Pct
23	ATL	21.7%
24	BUF	21.5%
25	DEN	20.6%
26	DAL	18.9%
27	ARI	18.7%
28	NE	18.3%
29	TEN	17.7%
30	CLE	16.9%
31	TB	16.8%
32	HOU	16.7%

Bottom 10 Offenses, Yards per drive

Rk	Team	Yds/Dr
23	TEN	26.86
24	MIN	26.45
25	WAS	26.44
26	SF	26.39
27	BUF	26.28
28	STL	25.05
29	SEA	24.97
30	CHI	24.32
31	ARI	22.60
32	CAR	20.62

Bottom 10 Defenses, Yards per drive

Rk	Team	Yds/Dr
23	ATL	30.70
24	DAL	30.98
25	IND	31.05
26	SEA	31.16
27	CLE	32.38
28	DEN	32.93
29	TEN	33.20
30	NE	33.79
31	JAC	35.06
32	HOU	35.81

Top 10 Offenses, avg LOS to start drive

Rk	Team	LOS
1	CHI	33.4
2	NYJ	32.7
3	NE	32.7
4	PHI	31.6
5	TEN	31.4
6	CIN	31.4
7	PIT	31.3
8	SEA	31.1
9	KC	30.7
10	ATL	30.6

Top 10 Defenses, avg LOS to start drive

Rk	Team	LOS
1	ATL	24.6
2	KC	26.7
3	BAL	27.3
4	PHI	27.5
5	NYJ	27.6
6	NE	28.3
7	STL	28.4
8	JAC	28.6
9	IND	28.9
10	DAL	28.9

Top 10 Offenses, Points per drive

Rk	Team	Pts/Dr
1	NE	2.90
2	SD	2.36
3	IND	2.34
4	HOU	2.25
5	PHI	2.22
6	ATL	2.18
7	NO	2.17
8	GB	2.06
9	JAC	2.01
10	PIT	1.98

Top 10 Defenses, Points per drive

Rk	Team	Pts/Dr
1	GB	1.24
2	PIT	1.25
3	CHI	1.36
4	BAL	1.49
5	NYJ	1.53
6	ATL	1.54
7	SD	1.55
8	NYG	1.59
9	KC	1.60
10	STL	1.61

Bottom 10 Offenses, avg LOS to start drive

Rk	Team	LOS
23	DAL	28.7
24	SD	28.7
25	SF	28.7
26	NO	28.6
27	OAK	28.6
28	CAR	28.5
29	MIA	28.3
30	IND	27.5
31	DEN	27.4
32	HOU	25.6

Bottom 10 Defenses, avg LOS to start drive

Rk	Team	LOS
23	SEA	30.9
24	CHI	30.9
25	MIA	30.9
26	OAK	31.4
27	DEN	31.8
28	ARI	32.4
29	SD	32.6
30	NYG	32.9
31	CAR	33.2
32	BUF	33.6

Bottom 10 Offenses, Points per drive

Rk	Team	Pts/Dr
23	STL	1.48
24	CLE	1.46
25	MIA	1.46
26	SF	1.45
27	SEA	1.43
28	BUF	1.43
29	MIN	1.41
30	WAS	1.41
31	ARI	1.16
32	CAR	0.95

Bottom 10 Defenses, Points per drive

Rk	Team	Pts/Dr
23	CIN	1.90
24	CAR	1.95
25	IND	1.99
26	SEA	2.05
27	ARI	2.06
28	DAL	2.13
29	BUF	2.20
30	JAC	2.37
31	DEN	2.39
32	HOU	2.42

Top 10 Offenses, Better DVOA with Shotgun

Rk	Team	% Plays Shotgun	DVOA Shot	DVOA Not	Yd/Play Shot	Yd/Play Not	DVOA Dif
1	DEN	51%	28.8%	-13.0%	6.1	5.3	41.8%
2	CAR	34%	-9.1%	-41.1%	5.0	4.0	32.1%
3	PIT	37%	40.2%	8.3%	6.2	5.5	31.9%
4	SD	39%	40.3%	8.8%	7.0	5.7	31.4%
5	SEA	38%	4.9%	-23.9%	5.2	5.0	28.8%
6	DET	64%	14.0%	-13.9%	5.7	4.2	27.8%
7	DAL	45%	15.3%	-11.6%	6.6	4.9	27.0%
8	TB	40%	28.4%	1.8%	6.4	5.3	26.6%
9	NO	39%	26.2%	0.6%	6.8	5.0	25.5%
10	NE	40%	62.6%	37.4%	6.5	5.9	25.2%

Top 10 Defenses, Better DVOA vs. Shotgun

Rk	Team	% Plays Shotgun	DVOA Shot	DVOA Not	Yd/Play Shot	Yd/Play Not	DVOA Dif
1	BUF	27%	-5.5%	14.8%	5.7	5.5	-20.3%
2	PIT	39%	-29.3%	-12.7%	4.6	4.7	-16.5%
3	GB	40%	-17.4%	-7.1%	5.3	5.0	-10.4%
4	ARI	32%	4.5%	9.7%	6.0	5.5	-5.2%
5	CLE	29%	0.7%	5.3%	6.8	5.0	-4.5%
6	CAR	32%	0.5%	2.3%	6.3	4.8	-1.8%
7	CHI	46%	-7.3%	-8.0%	5.3	5.1	0.7%
8	DAL	40%	10.4%	9.6%	6.2	5.7	0.8%
9	STL	40%	6.7%	5.7%	5.5	5.4	1.0%
10	MIA	35%	-1.0%	-2.2%	5.3	5.1	1.2%

Bottom 10 Offenses, Better DVOA with Shotgun

Rk	Team	% Plays Shotgun	DVOA Shot	DVOA Not	Yd/Play Shot	Yd/Play Not	DVOA Dif
23	SF	40%	-9.4%	-6.2%	5.6	5.3	-3.3%
24	OAK	33%	-9.5%	-2.2%	5.7	5.6	-7.3%
25	CLE	37%	-7.3%	1.3%	5.5	4.9	-8.6%
26	HOU	31%	19.1%	28.6%	6.0	6.3	-9.5%
27	NYG	39%	4.0%	15.3%	6.4	5.9	-11.2%
28	KC	31%	-5.8%	12.8%	5.4	5.3	-18.6%
29	TEN	35%	-15.7%	5.5%	5.6	5.5	-21.2%
30	CHI	10%	-39.8%	-9.4%	5.6	5.1	-30.4%
31	ARI	48%	-51.4%	-16.3%	4.4	4.9	-35.1%
32	MIN	34%	-39.3%	-1.2%	5.1	5.3	-38.0%

Bottom 10 Defenses, Better DVOA vs. Shotgun

Rk	Team	% Plays Shotgun	DVOA Shot	DVOA Not	Yd/Play Shot	Yd/Play Not	DVOA Dif
23	NO	36%	7.9%	-7.4%	5.7	5.2	15.4%
24	IND	35%	19.7%	3.1%	6.1	5.3	16.6%
25	KC	43%	16.8%	-0.5%	5.7	4.9	17.3%
26	ATL	40%	12.6%	-5.1%	6.2	5.3	17.7%
27	TEN	43%	6.9%	-11.3%	6.0	4.8	18.3%
28	SF	37%	14.5%	-5.5%	5.6	5.0	20.0%
29	NE	43%	16.9%	-3.2%	6.3	5.3	20.1%
30	NYG	39%	7.2%	-16.0%	5.8	4.8	23.2%
31	DET	37%	27.3%	-3.8%	6.5	5.0	31.1%
32	NYJ	41%	19.1%	-22.9%	6.5	4.0	42.0%

Top 10 Offenses, Better DVOA with Play Action

Rk	Team	% PA	DVOA PA	DVOA No PA	Yd/Play PA	Yd/Play No PA	DVOA Dif
1	MIN	19%	41.4%	-21.9%	7.7	5.5	63.3%
2	CIN	13%	80.0%	18.4%	7.8	6.0	61.6%
3	NYG	16%	73.9%	15.8%	9.0	6.8	58.1%
4	OAK	22%	41.4%	-7.4%	8.3	5.7	48.7%
5	STL	24%	26.1%	-17.1%	7.0	4.9	43.2%
6	IND	17%	69.9%	26.7%	9.0	6.3	43.2%
7	TEN	15%	53.1%	10.4%	9.6	5.9	42.6%
8	HOU	25%	63.7%	25.0%	8.9	6.4	38.7%
9	TB	19%	66.1%	30.9%	7.9	6.5	35.2%
10	DEN	25%	59.5%	24.5%	9.8	5.9	35.1%

Top 10 Defenses, Better DVOA vs. Play Action

Rk	Team	% PA	DVOA PA	DVOA No PA	Yd/Play PA	Yd/Play No PA	DVOA Dif
1	NYJ	14%	-31.6%	10.9%	4.8	6.1	-42.5%
2	NO	16%	-25.2%	13.0%	5.4	6.1	-38.2%
3	GB	13%	-38.3%	-8.1%	4.3	6.0	-30.2%
4	NE	15%	-14.1%	13.3%	8.0	6.3	-27.4%
5	DET	18%	-6.5%	18.3%	6.6	6.5	-24.9%
6	OAK	25%	6.6%	12.2%	7.2	5.8	-5.6%
7	KC	16%	8.3%	10.2%	6.2	5.8	-1.9%
8	ATL	17%	7.6%	7.3%	6.4	6.2	0.3%
9	CAR	19%	7.2%	3.0%	5.9	6.4	4.2%
10	BAL	15%	1.5%	-3.5%	6.9	5.7	5.0%

Bottom 10 Offenses, Better DVOA with Play Action

Rk	Team	% PA	DVOA PA	DVOA No PA	Yd/Play PA	Yd/Play No PA	DVOA Dif
23	NO	20%	20.6%	25.4%	6.1	6.6	-4.8%
24	WAS	21%	-2.1%	8.3%	7.8	5.8	-10.4%
25	SEA	15%	-13.0%	-2.2%	5.8	5.9	-10.7%
26	PHI	20%	22.3%	36.8%	8.1	6.6	-14.4%
27	BAL	31%	16.8%	40.8%	6.5	6.5	-24.0%
28	DAL	16%	-6.2%	21.8%	5.9	6.9	-27.9%
29	BUF	10%	-27.1%	0.9%	7.6	5.6	-28.0%
30	MIA	20%	-7.3%	28.6%	6.9	5.7	-35.9%
31	SD	17%	20.1%	57.0%	8.7	7.4	-36.9%
32	CAR	21%	-74.1%	-18.0%	2.8	4.7	-56.1%

Bottom 10 Defenses, Better DVOA vs. Play Action

Rk	Team	% PA	DVOA PA	DVOA No PA	Yd/Play PA	Yd/Play No PA	DVOA Dif
23	SF	21%	35.3%	9.2%	7.7	6.0	26.1%
24	PHI	17%	30.9%	4.6%	7.5	6.0	26.3%
25	HOU	20%	58.2%	31.6%	9.6	6.9	26.6%
26	MIA	15%	38.8%	8.1%	8.8	5.8	30.7%
27	CHI	24%	23.8%	-11.6%	7.2	5.5	35.4%
28	STL	19%	41.1%	4.9%	7.4	5.7	36.2%
29	BUF	20%	49.4%	10.6%	7.6	6.0	38.8%
30	TB	15%	41.3%	1.4%	6.9	5.8	39.8%
31	TEN	17%	49.7%	-1.6%	9.2	5.7	51.3%
32	MIN	17%	57.8%	1.3%	8.2	5.7	56.6%

Author Bios

Editor-in-Chief and Statistician

Aaron Schatz is the creator of FootballOutsiders.com and the proprietary NFL statistics within *Football Outsiders Almanac*, including DVOA, DYAR, Adjusted Line Yards, and the KUBIAK fantasy football projections. He writes regularly for ESPN.com and *ESPN the Magazine*, and he has done custom research for a number of NFL teams. *The New York Times Magazine* has referred to him as "the Bill James of football." Before creating Football Outsiders, he was a radio disc jockey and spent three years tracking search trends online as the writer and producer of the Internet column "The Lycos 50." He has a B.A. in Economics from Brown University and lives in Framingham, Massachusetts with his wife Kathryn and daughter Mirinae.

Layout and Design

Vince Verhei is a freelance writer and editor, and has been a writer and editor for Football Outsiders since 2007. In addition to writing for *Football Outsiders Almanac 2011*, he did all layout and copy editing on the book. A regular contributor to the pro and college football sections of Rumor Central at ESPN.com, he also writes the "Any Given Sunday" column covering the week's top upset using Football Outsiders metrics. His writings have also appeared in *ESPN the Magazine* and in Maple Street Press publications, and he has done layout for a number of other books for Football Outsiders and for Prospectus Entertainment Ventures. A graduate of Western Washington University, he is also a writer and podcast host for pro wrestling/MMA website Figurefouronline.com.

Contributors

Dr. Benjamin Alamar is the founding editor of the *Journal of Quantitative Analysis in Sports* and has consulted for various NFL and NBA franchises. He holds a doctorate in Economics from the University of California at Santa Barbara.

Bill Barnwell served as the Managing Editor of Football Outsiders for the 2008-10 seasons. He is currently a staff writer for Grantland and resides in Las Vegas.

Bill Connelly analyzes the ins and outs of college football play-by-play data in the weekly Football Outsiders column, "Varsity Numbers." He lives in Missouri with his wife and pets, working for his alma mater, and writing for the Missouri blog, Rock M Nation. He's also the writer of the college football blog FootballStudyHall.com.

A Seattleite since 1985, **Doug Farrar** now holds true allegiance to the Emerald City and all she possesses. Doug has written for FO since 2006, and his current responsibilities include the weekly X-and-O column "Cover-2," and adding snarky comments about Tim Ruskell to "Audibles at the Line." When he's not going over as much All-22 film as he can get from NFL Game Rewind, Doug is also an NFL feature writer and blogger for Yahoo! Sports, a stringer for the Associated Press, and a contributor to the *Washington Post*.

Brian Fremeau contributes the Fremeau Efficiency Index (FEI) and other college football stats, analysis, and data visualization design to FootballOutsiders. com, ESPN Insider, and Maple Street Press college football publications. He recently launched bcftoys. com, a personal archive of his stat analysis and graphics work. He lives in South Bend, Indiana, with his wife and daughter.

David Gardner served as assistant editor of Football Outsiders until July 2011. He is a University of Florida graduate and a former correspondent for the St. Petersburg Times and editorial intern for Yahoo! Sports. He now serves as an overseas missionary with The World Race.

Tom Gower joined the writing staff in 2009 after being a game charter for three seasons. He co-wrote "Scramble for the Ball" this past season, and his work also appeared on ESPN.com. He has degrees from Georgetown University and the University of Chicago, whose football programs have combined for an Orange Bowl appearance and seven Big Ten titles but are still trying to find success after Pearl Harbor. When not practicing law in the Chicago area or writing for FO, he keeps a keen eye on Tennessee for the blog Total Titans.

Ned Macey has been writing for Football Outsiders since 2005, and his work has appeared on ESPN.com, FoxSports.com, AOLSports.com and various other outlets. When not frittering away time trying to develop statistical models to explain the Colts' repeated playoff failures, Ned works as an attorney in Detroit and teams with his wife Melanie to insure that their two young daughters, Kathryn and Elizabeth, understand that Michigan football used to be great.

Sean McCormick is a graduate of the University of Pennsylvania and holds an MFA in Creative Writing from Arizona State University. In addition to being a regular contributor at FootballOutsiders.com, his draft coverage has appeared at FOXSports.com. He also indulges his inner masochist as a contributing writer for TheJetsBlog.com and is the proud owner of the lone Richard Todd jersey still in existence. He lives in Brooklyn, New York.

Rivers McCown started charting games for Football Outsiders in 2007 on a lark and soon found himself engrossed in football writing, statistics, and the idea that Phil Simms was often wrong about things. A lifelong Houstonian by choice, he has built up a tolerance to humidity and bad football teams. Prior to joining Football Outsiders this summer as an assistant editor, Rivers was Managing Editor for SB Nation Houston; he still contributes sparingly to Battle Red Blog and his personal blog, From Mom's Basement.

Brian McIntyre is from central Massachusetts, but grew up a fan of the Seattle Seahawks. Brian caught the football bug early, passionately following the sport even after having his six-year-old heart broken when the NFL went on strike six days before he was to attend his first NFL game (Seahawks-Patriots at Schaefer Stadium) in 1982. He was recently added to the Football Outsiders writing team, but has written about the NFL since 2005 at his own site (Mac's Football Blog), on Scout.com, and for the *Tacoma News Tribune.*

Ben Muth was born and raised in Arizona, but educated in California, where he played offensive line at Stanford from 2004-08. He was named first-team all-Pac-10 in his final season and went to camp with the San Diego Chargers in 2009, although he was released due to a combination of injury and giving up too many sacks in practice. He currently lives in Nashville and writes a weekly column on offensive line play for Football Outsiders called "Word of Muth."

Mike Tanier has been part of the Football Outsiders team since 2005. In addition to his "Walkthrough" column at FO, Mike writes the weekly NFL matchups for the *New York Times*, contributes to *ESPN the Magazine*, and has provided content for everyone from *Sports Illustrated Kids* to *Maxim*. He recently finished his first solo book, *The Phanatic Code*, which covers the history of Philadelphia sports and should arrive in autumn 2011.

Football Outsiders assistant editor **Danny Tuccitto** holds a Masters in Sport Psychology from the University of Florida. Before coming to Football Outsiders, he was the resident statistics nerd at SB Nation's 49ers blog, Niners Nation. He lives in Miami.

Robert Weintraub bleeds orange, both because of his inexplicable passion for the Cincinnati Bengals (he grew up in suburban New York, not Ohio) and because of his alma mater, Syracuse University. He now lives in Atlanta, the epicenter of college football hyper-allegiance, so that Syracuse degree comes in handy (maintaining plausible deniability when writing about Georgia and Florida and Alabama is crucial). Robert also works as a freelance television producer and writes for Slate and *The Guardian*. His first book, *The House That Ruth Built: A New Yankee Stadium, the First Championship, and the Redemption of 1923*, was published in the spring of 2011.

Acknowledgements

We want to thank all the Football Outsiders readers, all the people in the media who have helped to spread the word about our website and books, and all the people in the NFL who have shown interest in our work. This year, instead of the never-ending long list naming everyone who's ever acknowledged our existence, we wanted to give a few specific acknowledgements:

• FO techmaster Elias Holman.

• Jason Beattie for cover design.

• Rory Hickey for compiling the Year in Quotes

• Mike Kurtz, co-author of our "Scramble for the Ball" column

• Programmers Pat Laverty and Sean McCall, Excel stat report guru John Argentiero, and drive stats guru Jim Armstrong.

• David Lewin, creator of the Lewin Career Forecast; Jason McKinley, creator of O-Line Continuity Score; and Nathan Forster, creator of SackSEER.

• Chris Povirk, the greatest Internet data-scraper in the history of Internet data-scraping.

• Roland Beech of TwoMinuteWarning.com and 82games.com, who came up with the original ideas behind our individual defensive stats.

• Our editors at ESPN.com and *ESPN the Magazine*, particularly Daniel Kaufman, Scott Burton, and Ben Fawkes.

• Bill Simmons, for constantly promoting us on his podcast, and Peter King, for lots of promotion in his SI.com column.

• Ron Jaworski, Greg Cosell, and the entire *NFL Matchup* production team, for the annual film-study lessons.

• Chris Hoeltge at the NFL, for responding to our endless questions about specific items in the official play-by-play, and for collecting old gamebooks and making them available to us.

• All the media relations people at various NFL teams who have helped with our search for old play-by-play, plus Jon Kendle at the Hall of Fame for filling the gaps.

• All the friends we've made on coaching staffs and in front offices across the National Football League, who generally don't want to be mentioned by name. You know who you are.

• Russ Lande, whose draft guide was extremely helpful in researching this year's rookies.

• Our comrades in the revolution: Doug Drinen (creator of the indispensible pro-football-reference.com), Jason Lisk, Chase Stuart, Neil Paine, and K.C. Joyner, plus our friends at Prospectus Entertainment Ventures.

• Interns who helped prepare data over the past year or for this book specifically, including Ryan Guillory, Jeremy Spangler, and Cody Wiewandt.

• All those who have volunteered their time and effort for the Football Outsiders game charting project, particularly those people who have been consistently charting for multiple seasons. Our regular charters last year included: Chris Berney, Chris Bojar, Michael Bonner, Dave DuPlantis, Nathan Eagan, Robert Finley, Kwame Flaherty, Ryan French, Dan Haverkamp, Peter Koski, Justin Kramer, Shawn Krest, Bin Lee, Ryan Marsh, Braden Moore, Sander Philipse, Matthew Raymond, Nate Richards, Matt Scribbins, Navin Sharma, Derek Snyder, Rob Stewart, Ken Swanson, and Abe vanderBent.

• Everyone who has participated in the old play-by-play transcription project, particularly the absurdly prolific Jeremy Snyder.

Infinite gratitude goes to our wives, girlfriends, and children, for putting up with this silliness.

Follow Football Outsiders on Twitter

Follow the official account announcing new Football Outsiders articles at **@fboutsiders** and the official account of Football Outsiders College at **@ FO_College**.

You can follow other FO writers at these Twitter addresses:

Bill Connelly: **@BillConnelly1**
Doug Farrar: **@FO_DougFarrar**
Brian Fremeau: **@bcfremeau**
Tom Gower: **@ThomasGower**
Rivers McCown: **@FO_RiversMcCown**
Brian McIntyre: **@brian_mcintyre**
Ben Muth: **@FO_WordofMuth**
Aaron Schatz: **@FO_ASchatz**
Mike Tanier: **@FO_MTanier**
Danny Tuccitto: **@FO_DTuccitto**
Vince Verhei: **@FO_VVerhei**
Rob Weintraub: **@robwein**.

Made in the USA
Lexington, KY
28 August 2011